Date Due

PUBLIC PAPERS OF THE PRESIDENTS

OF THE UNITED STATES

PUBLIC PAPERS OF THE PRESIDENTS

OF THE UNITED STATES

Jimmy Carter

1979

(IN TWO BOOKS)

BOOK II—JUNE 23 TO DECEMBER 31, 1979

UNITED STATES GOVERNMENT PRINTING OFFICE

WASHINGTON : 1980

Published by the
Office of the Federal Register
National Archives and Records Service
General Services Administration

For sale by the Superintendent of Documents, U.S. Government Printing Office
Washington, D.C. 20402

Foreword

To function effectively, and to keep faith with our founding principles, the government and the citizens of this country must work together in partnership.

One of the purposes of these Presidential papers is to record that partnership—to set down the requests and responses, concerns and hopes of a President and a people.

The partnership is vividly demonstrated by the fact that between the accounts of Presidential words and action during the latter half of 1979 are transcribed the voices of dozens of Americans—teachers and farmers, shopowners and factory workers—who have spoken with me in town halls, schools, churches, and synagogues across the country.

The 6-month period covered by this volume saw a number of significant developments for our country—the submission to the Senate of the SALT II treaty, the Tokyo economic summit, the domestic discussions at Camp David, our steady progress towards national energy security, the establishment of a new Department of Education, and the uniting of the American people behind our responses to crises in Iran and Afghanistan.

Throughout these months, the American people and their government have met the tests of change in keeping with our commitment to the ideals that have guided this Nation since its creation.

The record of that partnership in these papers represents the achievement of many. It is open to all, and I encourage all to read it. For democracy, more than other systems of government, depends upon an open and honest interchange of facts and feelings between leaders and citizens.

Jimmy Carter

Preface

This book contains the papers and speeches of the 39th President of the United States which were issued by the White House Press Office during the period June 23–December 31, 1979. The material has been compiled and published by the Office of the Federal Register, National Archives and Records Service, General Services Administration.

The material is presented in chronological order within each week, and the dates shown in the headings are the dates of the documents or events. In instances when the release date differs from the date of the document itself, that fact is shown in the textnote. Every effort has been made to ensure accuracy. Tape recordings are used to protect against errors in transcription of Presidential remarks, and signed documents are checked against the original to verify the correct printing. Textnotes, footnotes, and cross references have been provided by the editors for purposes of identification or clarity. Speeches were delivered in Washington, D.C., and other documents released there, unless indicated. All times noted are local times.

The index covers both Books I and II of the 1979 volume. In addition to the usual subject-matter entries in the index, the material has been classified in categories reflecting the type of Presidential activity or document. For example, a reader interested in the President's speeches will find them listed in the index under "Addresses and Remarks."

The Public Papers series was begun in 1957 in response to a recommendation of the National Historical Publications Commission. An extensive compilation of messages and papers of the Presidents covering the period 1789 to 1897 was assembled by James D. Richardson and published under congressional authority between 1896 and 1899. Since then, various private compilations have been issued, but there was no uniform publication comparable to the Congressional Record or the United States Supreme Court Reports. Many Presidential papers could be found only in the form of mimeographed White House releases or as reported in the press. The Commission therefore recommended the establishment of an official series in which Presidential writings, addresses, and remarks of a public nature could be made available.

The Commission's recommendation was incorporated in regulations of the Administrative Committee of the Federal Register, issued under section 6 of the Federal Register Act (44 U.S.C. 1506), which may be found in Title 1, Part 10, of the Code of Federal Regulations.

Preface

A companion publication to the Public Papers series, the Weekly Compilation of Presidential Documents, was begun in 1965 to provide a broader range of Presidential materials on a more timely basis to meet the needs of the contemporary reader. Beginning with the administration of Jimmy Carter, the Public Papers series expanded its coverage to include all material as printed in the Weekly Compilation. That coverage provides a listing of the President's daily schedule and meetings, when announced, and other items of general interest issued by the White House Press Office. Also included are lists of the President's nominations submitted to the Senate, materials released by the Press Office which are not printed full-text in the book, and acts approved by the President. This information is compiled on a weekly basis and appears at the end of each week's coverage.

Volumes covering the administrations of Presidents Hoover, Truman, Eisenhower, Kennedy, Johnson, Nixon, and Ford are also available.

This series is under the direction of John E. Byrne, Director, Office of the Federal Register, and is produced by the Presidential Documents Division, Robert E. Lewis, Director. Editors of this book were Katherine A. Mellody, Kenneth R. Payne, Wilma P. Greene, and Brenda A. Robeson. The index was prepared by Brian L. Hermes and D. Michael Smith.

White House liaison was provided by Patricia Y. Bario, Deputy Press Secretary. The frontispiece and photographs used in the portfolio were supplied by the White House Photo Office.

The typography and design of the volume were developed by the United States Government Printing Office under the direction of Samuel L. Saylor, Acting Public Printer.

ROBERT M. WARNER
Archivist of the United States

R. G. FREEMAN III
Administrator of General Services
November 1980

Contents

Administration of Jimmy Carter

1979

Interview With the President

Question-and-Answer Session With Members of the Japanese Press.   June 20, 1979

TOKYO SUMMIT MEETING

Q. Mr. President, it has been widely assumed that energy will be one of the key issues in the Tokyo summit. I wonder if you would delineate for us what is it you would like to accomplish in the coming Tokyo summit? What is it you think is significant in this particular summit as compared to the past four previous summits?

THE PRESIDENT. This will be the first opportunity that the major Western nations' leaders will have to address the energy question as a top item on the agenda. In the past, we have dealt primarily with macroeconomic matters. Obviously, some of them still prevail. Inflation, unemployment, enhanced trade are of importance to our country and will be discussed. But energy will be the major topic.

We have done a great deal of preparatory work among the nations who will be represented in Tokyo. I will spend a day or two with Prime Minister Ohira before the other leaders arrive in Japan. We will be sharing our ideas in preparation for the summit.

Obviously, some of the considerations will be a continuation of our past discussions. We have committed ourselves, a major consuming nation, to reduce our imports of oil by 2 million barrels per day by the end of 1979, compared to projected use. We will discuss means to implement this commitment and also to extend the conservation effort through 1980 and subsequent years.

Additionally, we will explore new ways to increase the production and use of nonfossil fuel supplies of energy. Coal, nuclear power, solar power will all be discussed quite thoroughly. We are, obviously, interested in safety and the preservation of the quality of our environment.

A special consideration which I would like to explore with Prime Minister Ohira and others is the international sharing of responsibility for technological developments, liquefaction, gasification of coal, the use of renewable energy sources, and direct use of sunlight, and how to assure that nuclear power is both safe and efficient.

These are the kind of issues we will be exploring in energy among ourselves. The last point is we will try to provide a common approach to the OPEC nations and others who export energy, oil, so that there will be an assured, stable supply of oil and natural gas on the international market, and so that there will be a stable and predictable price for energy.

These are some of the considerations we will explore, both bilaterally and among the entire group at the summit.

MEETINGS WITH PRIME MINISTER OHIRA

Q. Mr. President, you are going to meet Mr. Ohira twice within a month or so. What do you expect to accomplish by this meeting vis-a-vis your Japanese relationship?

THE PRESIDENT. The most important thought in my mind is a tremendous amount of commonality between Japan and the United States. We have the same basic goals: to preserve peace in the Asian region, to enhance exchange of goods and people and ideas, to provide a greater security for the people in our country, Japan, and in other Asian nations.

We share a common interest in commerce, scientific development, technological advances, international trade, the reduction of protections—barriers to trade, stable and a sound international monetary system, tourism. We explore common ideas of education and culture. So, the overriding consideration is how much we share, both now and in the future.

The second point is that we have a few problems between us, because we are highly developed, technological nations. We have very aggressive outlooks on life, great confidence about the future, hardworking people, innovative. We, therefore, on occasion, compete with one another. We have developed a very beneficial habit of discussing our problems quickly—without timidity or restraint—and openly, so that the people of both countries can know what the difficulties are and what progress is being made.

Quite often, the focus of publicity is on these few differences and how we struggle to resolve them without delay and without embarrassment. What we forget is how relatively insignificant these differences are, compared to the great area of cooperation and mutual advantage.

I was pleased at the result of my discussions in this room with Prime Minister Ohira in May. I found him to be a sound and experienced and enlightened leader, and a warm and forthcoming, friendly leader. And I felt the progress that we made to alleviate some of our trade differences was very beneficial and encouraging. We will continue with that progress.

I have no doubt that we will both have a more fruitful experience with the economic summit because of our meetings on a bilateral basis before the economic summit begins.

U.S.-JAPANESE TRADE

Q. In his recent speech in Washington, former Governor John Connally accused Japan of still closing its market to certain American products, particularly citrus, beef, and grain. Specifically, he stated, and I quote, "If I were President of the United States, I would say to the Prime Minister, 'Unless you are prepared to take American goods and services, you better tell your people they better be ready to sit on the docks of Yokohama in their own Toyotas watching their own televisions.'" My question, first, is how do you respond to Mr. Connally's statement, and also, thus far, to what extent do you feel the issue of trade imbalance between the U.S. and Japan have been alleviated or resolved?

THE PRESIDENT. In the first place, I would not respond to Mr. Connally's statement. [*Laughter*] This is a free country, and we have freedom of speech, as is the case in Japan. I would like to point out Mr. Connally holds no public office, and perhaps when you analyze his statement, you will see why he holds no public office. [*Laughter*] But he has a right to speak.

We would point out with gratification the progress that has been made in the so-called Tokyo Round of economic discussions. Just this week, I have submitted to the Congress legislation to implement the Multilateral Trade Negotiation results, and my prediction is the Congress will approve these legislative proposals without delay. This will help to lower protectionist trends that were of concern to us, and I think the downward trend in protectionism will extend several years in the future.

We do import a great quantity of Japanese goods, more than we export to Japan. There have been several voluntary agreements reached to look to lessen this disparity. We are pleased with the progress that has been made. We would like to see more opportunity for us to sell American goods in Japan, not only finished goods, where we are highly competitive with the Japanese producers, but also coal, timber, citrus, grapes, other things that we have to export.

I might point out the proposal that involves American citrus, since you raise that issue, only amounts to 2 or 3 percent as much as Japan produces in citrus. And the months that we would like to have a chance to sell more citrus are during June, July, and August, for instance, when Japan citrus production is at its lowest point.

So, when we can have an open market for our goods without damaging the farm economy or the economic economy of Japan, we would certainly like to increase our sales to Japan. But we have explored those possibilities with a common respect, and we have made good progress.

ASIAN SECURITY ISSUES

Q. Mr. President, partly because of the growing threat from the North, the Japanese attitude toward security matters has changed so much that Japan can now cooperate with the U.S. even in the security field. Can you tell us your views on the role Japan should play in the security field? Is it more desirable for the United States that Japan's role be confined to the defense of Japan herself, or should Japan, along with the United States, play a regional security role to maintain peace and stability in Asia?

THE PRESIDENT. It is obvious that both the United States and Japan want to see peace and stability in Asia. Our own military involvement in Asia will not be decreased. We want to do our share in assuring the security of our own people and the people of Japan and our other allies and also enhancing peace for all who live in the Western Pacific area.

We are very proud of our alliance with Japan, carefully formed voluntarily by the leaders of both nations. We have been pleased at the commitment of Japan to provide for its own defense. The level of defense expenditures by Japan is a decision for the Japanese people to make, not for us to try to influence. We respect this independent decisionmaking process, and we have complete confidence that Japan and its Government will make wise decisions.

So, we share common goals, we work together in harmony, we respect the independent decision rights of one another, and we are very pleased with the present arrangement and the future prospect.

1147

KOREA

Q. Mr. President, let me ask two questions about our neighboring country Korea. First of all, the CIA has just completed the reevaluation of North Korean military forces, and, based on the result of the reevaluation, I wonder what you are going to do with the South Korean troop withdrawal plan? The second question is, while you are in Korea, are you going to see some opposition party leaders in Korea, including Kim Dae-jung?

THE PRESIDENT. We have been concerned about the new estimates of North Korean military strength, which are higher than we had previously supposed. I will be discussing this matter with President Park and also with our own military commanders in South Korea. Whatever decision I make about the level of American forces, I will keep the commitment that I originally made, that is, not to do anything to disturb the military balance or to create instability on the Korean peninsula.

My custom has been on all my foreign visits to meet with opposition leaders. And while I am in South Korea, my intention is to meet with the opposition leaders there, both those that are actually involved directly in politics and those that might be outside the political realm, both religious leaders and others. So, I do plan to continue this process while I am in South Korea.

My own hope is there might be fruitful meetings directly between the leaders of South Korea and North Korea in the near future, either with or without an American presence during those meetings. I think this is the ultimate solution to the present divisions of the people of Korea. But in any case, we will do our part to maintain stability there, the security of our allies, and to let the world know we resolutely will maintain our responsibilities.

SOVIET MILITARY BUILDUP IN THE FAR EAST

Q. Mr. President, as my colleague mentioned earlier, there is growing concern in Japan about the Soviet major buildup in the Far East, the possible deployment of the Soviet military carrier *Minsk,* and Soviet military activity in Vietnam. How do you assess this Soviet military buildup in this region, and how do you react to this situation?

THE PRESIDENT. We have no fear of Soviet military presence there. We are concerned about a buildup whenever we consider it to be excessive beyond what is required for Soviet security. I discussed the South Vietnamese question with President Brezhnev this week, and particularly the Soviet presence there, both ships and airplanes. He assured me personally that there would be no establishment of Soviet bases in South Vietnam and that the present ship and plane use of the ports and airports is of a routine nature.

We will maintain American military presence in the Western Pacific, adequate to protect American interests and to protect the interest of our allies. I think in our alliances—with South Korea, with Japan, with New Zealand, with Australia, new leases on Philippine bases, our growing friendship with the ASEAN group, the honoring of their independence, the normalization of relations with the People's Republic of China, plus the new SALT agreement with the Soviet Union and the prospect for better relations between ourselves and the Soviet Union brought about by the summit conference this past weekend—all of those factors combined lead me to expect increased stability in the Far East.

I think we have made great progress since the Vietnam war. And our whole thrust has been to ensure peace, to respect the individual rights of people in the Far East, to do what we can to decrease tension, to eliminate combat with respect to the national borders, and to ensure that those people who live there have the right to self-determination.

We have been concerned about the invasion of Kampuchea by the South Vietnamese; they have continued presence there with large military forces. And we are especially concerned about the plight of the refugees who are now being forced out of Vietnam in increasing numbers. These are issues that we will be discussing with the Japanese leaders and with the other leaders on my visit to Japan.

JAPANESE DEFENSE EXPENDITURES

Q. You said earlier that the level of the Japanese defense expenditures should be decided upon by the Japanese themselves, but I would like to pursue this question by putting it into a more American prospective. In your view, Mr. President, will Japan be able to fulfill the defense goals, as expected by the United States, to have a more equitable and more effective security bilateral relationship, by adhering to the policy of maintaining defensive expending to 1 percent per GNP?

THE PRESIDENT. As you know, because of the dynamic growth of Japan's national product, the actual level of expenditures within the 1-percent guideline has been increasing substantially. Japan, in my opinion, has spent its defense funds very wisely. And we have confidence that the Japanese military strength is adequate to provide for the defense of Japan.

ENERGY

Q. Mr. President, you mentioned some kind of a collective or concerted effort being made which would be discussed at the Tokyo summit meeting. Could you outline more specific approaches or specific products to cope with the energy shortage situation, corrective measures?

THE PRESIDENT. We will be sharing with Japan ideas on building design, the efficiency of automobiles, new types of machinery and the use of such machinery, other measures that can let the consumption of energy be much more efficient.

Secondly, we will explore with Japan the increased technological ability of the consumption of energy to be more efficient, safer, and more compatible with clean air and water.

Third, we will be exploring with Japan the financing and the sharing of basic research data in nuclear power; the conversion of coal to liquids and gaseous fuels; more efficient burning of combustible materials; increased use of solar energy in all its forms, including hydroelectric; the production of methanol and other materials from replenishable growing plants, animal waste; the conversion of solar energy directly into electricity, for instance; new forms of the use of geothermal power; the sharing of basic research on metals, friction. These kinds of ideas can be explored jointly by Japan and the United States and, of course, with other nations.

In some instances, these experimental efforts are quite expensive, and there is no reason, if Japan is taking the leadership role in a certain area of experimental work, for the United States to duplicate what Japan is already accomplishing. The exchange of basic research data and the sharing of the financing of pilot projects is a very fruitful opportunity for the future.

Recently, for instance, Japan and Germany have agreed to join in with the United States in a project concerning the liquefaction and gasification of coal. We would obviously like to see Japan increase its purchase of American coal in the future, with the knowledge the coal can be burned cleanly and efficiently.

So, these are the kinds of areas where we can cooperate fully in the future.

TRADE WITH CHINA

Q. Mr. President, both the United States and Japan have expressed the willingness and intention, desire, possibly, of cooperating with the modernization program by the People's Republic of China. In so doing, however, isn't there a possibility that your country and Japan might end up competing over the Chinese market?

THE PRESIDENT. I might say that we favor the modernization program of the People's Republic of China, an attitude shared by the leaders of Japan. We see nothing threatening about this, and the turning toward Japan and toward the United States by China, we believe, is a very good recent development for stability and peace in Asia.

Obviously, there will be some competition for markets, but this is a benefit to both countries. We have the same competition with each other for markets in Canada, in Europe, in Asia. This is nothing new for us.

We are able to compete successfully in the technological field. There are some areas of science and industry where the United States is preeminent; there are

other areas where Japan is preeminent; and there is a third category of areas where we are roughly equivalent to one another in our progress and we can compete successfully. We believe there is enough market throughout the world to meet the expanding production of both Japan and the United States.

I might point out there are a few realms of economic development in China where Japan and the United States will be cooperating. But this is of benefit also to both countries, but we have no fear of this. We believe that, overall, a friendly competition for the increasing markets with China will be of benefit to both our countries. And it is obvious that the openness of China's attitude and its economic developments is better for the entire world.

INDOCHINESE REFUGEES

Q. Going back to the Indochinese refugee issue that you briefly referred to earlier, specifically, what would be your expectations concerning an increased Japanese role in this international problem?

THE PRESIDENT. All countries must play a larger role. The United States is accepting a very large number of refugees, tens of thousands of refugees. Japan has accepted very few. [*Laughter*] I think when Prime Minister Ohira was over here, the total number of refugees accepted in Japan was only three. [*Laughter*] This, however, has been combined in Japan with very generous contributions to the U.N.'s effort to alleviate the refugee problem.

We recognize Japan has a very homogeneous society; ours is quite heterogeneous. We are a nation that is comprised of refugees or immigrants. It is easier for us to accept refugees, perhaps, than Japan. But there is no doubt in my mind Japan can do more, and there is no doubt in my mind the United States can do more.

We would like to turn this critical problem into a much more wide ranging area of responsibility among numerous nations. Malaysia, Hong Kong, Thailand have been heavily burdened with an excessive number of refugees. And I would hope the People's Republic of China and Japan, the United States, European areas, and others can do more in the future. This is one of the items that will be on the agenda for the next summit conference.

PRESIDENT'S JOGGING

Q. Mr. President, are you going to jog while you are in Japan?

THE PRESIDENT. I have a habit of jogging every day.

Q. With your wife?

THE PRESIDENT. With my wife, yes.

Q. In Tokyo?

THE PRESIDENT. Yes, that is our present plan. There are a lot of excellent runners in Japan.

PRESIDENT'S MEETINGS IN KOREA

Q. Mr. President, if in fact you might be seeing Mr. Kim Dae-jung in Korea, would you?

THE PRESIDENT. My intention is to meet with opposition leaders. I have not established a definite agenda yet, but that has been my custom.

REPORTER. Thank you.

NOTE: The interview began at 2:45 p.m. in the Cabinet Room at the White House.

As printed above, the item follows the transcript of the interview, which was released on June 23.

Korean and East Asian Issues

Questions and Answers for Publication in the Orient Press. June 21, 1979

REPUBLIC OF KOREA SECURITY

Q. Many Asians are still concerned over "gradual United States retreat from Asia," complaining that the United States is leaning more heavily toward West European defense. There are also criticisms in Korea that the United States is too restrictive in its security cooperation policy toward Korea to approve sales of coproduction of sophisticated weapons such as F–16, A–10 aircraft, submarines, and so on, while taking every measure to prevent even a possibility of South Korean production of nuclear weapons.

Mr. President, what are your guidelines for U.S. security commitments to the Republic of Korea? Furthermore, would you recommit American ground combat troops to South Korea after completion of your troop withdrawal plan, in case of another North Korean attack, as President Harry Truman did?

A. Anyone with a knowledge of U.S. history, geography, politics, and economics knows that the United States will not "retreat" from Asia. We are there. We are a major partner in the Pacific community. We are a Pacific nation. We firmly intend to remain one. Recent policy developments—normalization of relations with China, strengthening of ties with Japan, renegotiation of the Philippine base agreement, and our burgeoning economic ties with the region—all strengthen our relationship. Any discussion of our Korean security commitment occurs in the context of our strong interest as a Pacific power.

For many years, in support of our Korean commitment, we have made available weapons and other military materiel essential to Korea's defense. Within the constraints of our worldwide arms transfer policy, we intend to continue to make such equipment available. With respect to the possibility of reintroducing ground combat forces into Korea in the event of renewed conflict, the United States Government is prepared to take whatever action may be necessary to fulfill its security commitment.

U.S. POLICY TOWARDS EAST ASIA

Q. Northeast Asia appears to be in a period of change or adjustment in the balance of power, even though a delicate strategic equilibrium still exists there. The normalized relations between the United States and the People's Republic of China, Sino-Japanese friendship treaty, the Soviet naval buildup in the area, rivalry or even conflicts among the Communist nations (including Southeast Asia), and North Korea's obstinate intransigence in peace efforts are some noticeable recent events.

Mr. President, how do you assess the situation there, and what is your policy toward this critical area? Do you plan to announce any comprehensive policy statement like a "Carter Doctrine" or "Tokyo Doctrine" during your trip to Tokyo and Seoul late June?

A. Our policy toward East Asia is based on several consistent principles designed to maintain stability, further prosperity, and take account of changes occurring in the region. The basic ingredients of that policy are well known to you: American determination to remain actively involved as a Pacific power; the cornerstone alliance with Japan; our firm security commitment to the Republic of Korea; improvement of relations with the People's Republic of China; strong support for ASEAN and ANZUS; encour-

agement of trade and economic development throughout the region.

We have been responsive to change. We have normalized our relations with China, while Japan has concluded the peace and friendship treaty with Peking. We would like to see a reduction of tensions on the Korean peninsula, provided that this can be accomplished with officials of the South Korean Government as full and equal participants in the process. We are improving the quality of the 7th Fleet. At the same time, we have moved to strengthen key relationships with allies of the region. Our partnership with Japan has never been more productive. Our security commitment to Korea remains unshakable. We have concluded an agreement with the Philippines, enabling us to maintain stable access to our bases through the next decade. We have increased support for ASEAN.

Our Asian policy serves the interests of the United States and its Asian allies well. I have no plan to change it.

U.S.-R.O.K. RELATIONS

Q. Senior administration officials in their congressional testimony or public speeches stated that your trip to South Korea will mark the end of a difficult phase in the U.S.-R.O.K. relationship and "begin a new period of better mutual understanding and confidence." Mr. President, what is your perspective for the U.S.-R.O.K. relations in 1980's—political, economic, security, and so forth?

A. The outlook for the relationship between the United States and the Republic of Korea in the 1980's is excellent. The dramatic pace of Korea's economic development of the past few years shows every sign of continuing, and in the 1980's we expect Korea to be one of our most important trading partners and a major market for U.S. exports. The South will have far outdistanced North Korea in economic growth. Similarly, we can look forward with confidence to an enhanced defense capability in South Korea. As I have said before, our security commitment will remain firm. We are hopeful that the decade ahead will bring comparable development in the political area. Specifically, we hope to see greater emphasis on the protection of political rights and more rapid development of political institutions.

GROUND TROOP WITHDRAWALS

Q. Mr. President, your Korean troop withdrawal policy has been controversial in this country up to now—illustrated by the Senate Armed Services Committee's approval of Senator Sam Nunn's subcommittee recommendation on Army active duty ceiling following its House counterpart committee's adoption of an amendment on it in mid-May.

You said in an interview on February 9 that you are holding in abeyance further troop withdrawals from South Korea until reassessment of new intelligence study of increased North Korean military strength, impact of Sino-U.S. normalization, and perspective of the North-South dialog. Mr. President, have you made your determination on this issue? If not, when do you think you would announce your decision—before, during, or after your Far East trip?

A. I have made no decision on ground troop withdrawals yet. I want to take a firsthand look at the situation, talk to President Park, and consult with Congress before making up my mind. Whatever decision is made, one thing is clear: Our commitment to the security of the Republic of Korea is unshakable. Our policy will be based on this commitment

and the maintenance of stability and peace on the Korean peninsula.

RELATIONS WITH NORTH KOREA

Q. When the U.S. table tennis team traveled to North Korea to participate in the international championship there in late April, it was widely speculated that the United States might try another "Ping-pong diplomacy." I understand that North Korean leaders have sent feelers to Washington through various ways for bilateral talks on trade and cultural relations with the United States, and you have stated many times that the United States wants to open relations with all the countries with which she does not have now.

Mr. President, may I ask you to specify your policy toward the North Koreans? Do you have any proposal or plan for solving the perennial Korean question, other than four-power conference among the United States, China, North and South Korea, and cross-recognition of Seoul and Pyongyang by major powers?

A. Let me state our policy toward North Korea quite simply. We are prepared to participate in discussions with North Korean officials aimed at reducing tensions on the Korean peninsula, but only if officials of the South Korean Government are full and equal participants. We have also said that to promote an atmosphere conducive to the reduction of tensions, the United States Government is prepared to improve our relations officially and unofficially with North Korea, provided that there are parallel improvements by the Soviet Union or China in relations with South Korea. We are not hostile toward North Korea. However, we are not going to take unilateral steps which are unreciprocated by North Korea's major allies, nor allow ourselves to become manipulated in a manner which ignores the rights and sovereignty of our ally, the Republic of Korea. We recognize that solution of the problems on the Korean peninsula can only be resolved through the direct involvement of the Governments of both North and South Korea.

U.S.-SOVIET TALKS

Q. Mr. President, you have met with your Soviet counterpart, Leonid Brezhnev, June 15–18 in Vienna. Arms control is one of your foreign policy objectives. Will you discuss with the Soviet leader on the Korean question in the context of "control of transfer of conventional weapons" and of "better communications" with the Soviets for regional stability?

A. There are no discussions of Korean arms transfers with Soviet representatives in Vienna.

HUMAN RIGHTS

Q. Another major foreign policy objective of your administration is enhancement of human rights at home and abroad. Mr. President, do you plan or expect to see some Korean political dissidents during your trip to Seoul—either at a church service or at a reception?

A. The schedule for my visit to Korea is not yet fully fixed. However, in addition to the important consultations between our two Governments, I look forward to meeting with other elements of Korean society. This will include opportunities for discussion with elected political leaders, including the opposition, and with leading churchmen. However, my worship at church is a personal matter and will not be an occasion for political meetings.

NOTE: The written questions were submitted to the President by So-Whan Hyon of the Orient Press. The answers were given to him by the President on June 21. The texts of the questions and answers were released on June 23.

The President's Trip to Japan and the Republic of Korea

Remarks on Departure From the White House. June 23, 1979

I leave in a few minutes for an economic summit meeting that can affect the daily life of every American citizen. Oil shortages and oil prices threaten the very strength of our own economy and also the fabric of our society. This will be the major economic item on our agenda when I arrive in Japan. Concerted action by all the industrialized nations—there will be seven of us leaders there—is absolutely crucial to solve the energy problems facing the American people today. This is a primary reason for my trip. We must act now to bring these global energy problems under control.

This is not just an American challenge. The long gas lines, the shortages of diesel fuel, the concern about heating homes, the mounting frustration over fuel supplies that we see here in America are symptoms of a global energy shortage. Our planet is simply not producing enough oil to meet rising demands.

We now are consuming about 2 million barrels of oil per day more than is being produced. And as I know many of you realize, since last December the price of OPEC oil has increased more than 35 percent. The challenge to the industrialized democracies is very clear. We must not be set one against another in a desperate competition to buy every barrel of scarce oil regardless of its price. Together, we must import less. Together, we must produce more. Together, we must reduce our dependence on a handful of oil producing and exporting countries.

At Tokyo I will call on our allies to join with the United States to meet our targets for reducing oil imports in 1979 and to reduce our imports even more in 1980. Also, we will work together to stop the unnecessary and unacceptable competitive bidding against one another over the oil prices that we pay. And we will marshal the vast resources, engineering, technological, scientific resources of our industrialized nations to produce more domestic energy, such as coal, solar energy, and synthetic fuels.

To meet these goals, of course, here at home, the Congress must act now to pass the windfall profits tax and to establish the national energy security fund to help us have the means to develop alternatives to foreign oil.

While I work with our allies on these energy problems on a global basis, Vice President Mondale will monitor the situation here at home, will keep me informed about what is happening, and will act, as necessary, to minimize adverse effects of shortages in the United States.

Whatever our successes might be in Japan, there should be no illusions, no false expectations, by the people of our country or other nations. Gas lines and fuel shortages will not disappear any time soon.

This is a difficult time for our Nation. All of us must make some painful adjustments in our daily lives. What we cannot afford is to give in to a mood of panic or desperation or, worse, to the idea that each of us is somehow pitted against our neighbor in a desperate scramble for scarce energy supplies.

Three times in this century we've overcome challenges far more serious than this one, with two long World Wars and with a massive depression that actually rocked the world's economy.

Now, as in the past, we can overcome the challenge of the energy crisis if we in this country are united as a people, if each of us will do our part as a citizen and as a neighbor, and with full confidence in the greatness of the United States. Now, as in the past, after this time of testing and trial, we can emerge an even stronger, an even more prosperous nation for having met this test together. That is the spirit which I will take to Tokyo.

Thank you very much for coming out to see me off.

NOTE: The President spoke at 12:47 p.m. on the South Lawn of the White House.

On the same day, the White House made available a list of the principal members of the official parties accompanying the President. Mrs. Carter and Amy, Secretary of State and Mrs. Cyrus R. Vance, Secretary of the Treasury W. Michael Blumenthal, Assistant to the President for National Security Affairs Zbigniew Brzezinski, and Senator and Mrs. Spark M. Matsunaga accompanied the President to Japan and the Republic of Korea. Additional members of the party to Japan were Ambassador and Mrs. Mike Mansfield and Secretary of Energy James R. Schlesinger. Ambassador and Mrs. William Gleysteen and Secretary of Defense and Mrs. Harold Brown accompanied the President to the Republic of Korea.

Treaty on the Limitation of Strategic Offensive Arms

Message to the Senate Transmitting the Treaty and Related Documents. June 22, 1979

To the Senate of the United States:

I transmit herewith, for the advice and consent of the Senate to ratification, the Treaty on the Limitation of Strategic Offensive Arms, known as SALT II, including the Protocol thereto, both signed in Vienna, Austria, on June 18, 1979.

I transmit also, for the information of the Senate, the Report of the Secretary of State with respect to the Treaty, together with the following related documents:

1. a series of Agreed Statements and Common Understandings concerning the

obligations of the Parties under particular articles of the Treaty;

2. a Memorandum of Understanding that will establish an agreed data base by categories of strategic offensive arms along with associated statements of current data;

3. a Joint Statement of Principles and Basic Guidelines on the Limitation of Strategic Arms concerning the next phase of negotiation on this subject; and

4. a Soviet statement on the Backfire bomber, together with a U.S. response.

For thirty years the United States has pursued a fundamentally bi-partisan foreign policy towards the Soviet Union, with the objectives of deterring aggression by maintaining strategic forces second to none, creating a pattern and tradition of negotiation to settle differences, building a strong framework of allies, and stabilizing the globe by halting the uncontrolled growth and spread of nuclear weapons.

SALT II strengthens each of these objectives. The seven years of negotiations, under three administrations representing both political parties, were carried out in closer consultation with Congress and under greater public scrutiny than any other arms limitation treaty. SALT II is truly a national accomplishment.

It is my best judgment and firm belief that these patiently negotiated agreements further the long-standing goals for our nation's security. They improve our strategic situation and allow for further improvements in the future. They reaffirm our leadership of the world in the cause of nuclear arms control. They allow us to negotiate for peace from strength in SALT III.

Like SALT I, the Test Ban Treaty, and the Non-Proliferation Treaty, SALT II is another important step forward toward our basic goal of a secure America at peace in a stable world.

I pledge the full cooperation of my Administration in helping to explain the principles and details of the agreements.

Therefore, I request with a sense of special urgency the advice and consent of the U.S. Senate to ratification of the SALT II Treaty.

JIMMY CARTER

The White House,
June 22, 1979.

NOTE: The message of transmittal was announced by the White House Press Office on June 25.

The texts of the treaty and the related documents are printed on page 1051 of this volume.

United States Ambassador to Trinidad and Tobago

Nomination of Irving G. Cheslaw.
June 25, 1979

The President today announced that he will nominate Irving G. Cheslaw, of Los Angeles, Calif., to be Ambassador Extraordinary and Plenipotentiary of the United States to the Republic of Trinidad and Tobago. He would replace Richard Fox, resigned. Cheslaw is Chief of the Senior Officer Division at the State Department's Bureau of Personnel.

He was born December 5, 1921, in Los Angeles. He received an A.B. from the University of California at Los Angeles in 1942 and an M.A. (1947) and Ph. D. (1952) from Columbia University. He served in the U.S. Army from 1942 to 1946.

Cheslaw was a lecturer in history and political science at Columbia University from 1949 to 1951. From 1951 to 1954, he was a historian at the Defense Department. From 1953 to 1959, he was a lecturer in political science at George Washington University, and from 1954 to 1956, he was also senior research analyst at the University of Pittsburgh.

Cheslaw joined the State Department as an intelligence research specialist in 1956, and was then posted in Port of Spain, Kingston, and Dublin. From 1966 to 1970, he served as supervisory foreign affairs officer, then supervisory international relations officer, at the State Department.

In 1970–71 Cheslaw attended the senior seminar in foreign policy at the Foreign Service Institute. From 1971 to 1974, he was Deputy Chief of Mission in Kuala Lumpur, and from 1972 to 1976, he was Deputy Chief of Mission in Dacca. He has been Chief of the Senior Officer Division since 1977.

Equal Employment Opportunity Commission

Nomination of Leroy D. Clark To Be General Counsel. June 25, 1979

The President today announced that he will nominate Leroy D. Clark, of New York City, to be General Counsel of the Equal Employment Opportunity Commission for a 4-year term. He would replace Abner Sibal, who has resigned.

Clark is a professor of law at New York University School of Law, and an arbitrator with the American Arbitration Association and the Federal Mediation and Conciliation Service.

He was born April 27, 1934, in New York City. He received a B.A. from City College of New York in 1956 and an LL.B. from Columbia University School of Law in 1961.

From 1961 to 1962, Clark was staff counsel with the State of New York Attorney General's Office. From 1962 to 1968, he was assistant counsel with the NAACP Legal Defense and Education Fund. He has been a professor at N.Y.U.

since 1968 and has been an arbitrator since 1974.

Clark is a member of the National Conference of Black Lawyers and the advisory council of the Association for Union Democracy. He was on the commission on juvenile justice standards of the Institute for Judicial Administration and the American Bar Association.

National Museum Services Board

Nomination of Emily Rauh Pulitzer To Be a Member. June 25, 1979

The President today announced that he will nominate Emily Rauh Pulitzer, of St. Louis, Mo., to be a member of the National Museum Services Board for a 5-year term.

Pulitzer, 45, was curator of the St. Louis Art Museum from 1964 to 1973. She has also been associated with the Fogg Art Museum at Harvard University and with the Cincinnati Art Museum. She is active in professional activities in art and is the author of numerous articles and exhibition catalogs.

Department of Health, Education, and Welfare

Nomination of Susanna B. McBee To Be an Assistant Secretary. June 25, 1979

The President today announced that he will nominate Susanna B. McBee, of Los Angeles, Calif., to be an Assistant Secretary of Health, Education, and Welfare. She would replace Eileen Shanahan, who has resigned, and her area of responsibility would be public affairs. McBee is currently a consultant at HEW and was previously a national staff writer for the Washington Post.

She was born March 28, 1935, in Santa Fe, N. Mex. She received an A.B. in journalism from the University of Southern California in 1956 and an M.A. in political science from the University of Chicago in 1962.

McBee was with the Washington Post from 1957 to 1965, as a copy aide for a year, then as a staff reporter covering general news, education, and civil rights. From 1965 to 1969, she was a Washington correspondent for Life magazine.

From 1970 to 1972, McBee was Washington editor for McCall's magazine. She returned to the Washington Post in 1973 as a national staff writer on urban affairs and Justice Department coverage. From 1974 to 1977, she was assistant national editor at the Post. She was a national staff writer covering urban affairs and Federal-State-local relations from 1977 until she joined HEW earlier this year.

Negotiations on Combatting Terrorism

Nomination of Anthony C. E. Quainton for the Rank of Ambassador While Representing the United States.   June 25, 1979

The President today announced that he will nominate Anthony C. E. Quainton, of Seattle, Wash., for the rank of Ambassador, which would pertain when he is representing the United States at negotiations dealing with combatting terrorism.

Quainton, 45, has been Director of the State Department's Office for Combatting Terrorism since 1978. He has been a Foreign Service officer since 1959.

Bill Stewart

Telegram to the American Broadcasting Company for Use at a Memorial Service for the News Correspondent.   June 28, 1979

The murder of ABC correspondent Bill Stewart in Nicaragua is a tragedy for his family, his friends, and for freedom-loving people everywhere.

Bill Stewart was a dedicated and courageous journalist. At the time of his death, he was attempting to perform the highest duty of the American press: to inform the public on the important issues of the day.

As nations become increasingly interdependent, our ability to solve our common problems, our very ability to survive and our hope of peace depends to a large degree upon our knowledge of conditions and events around the world. It is important that our journalists, as well as those of other countries, be allowed to cover world events without undue restraint.

When journalists are intimidated, the search for truth is intimidated.

On behalf of all Americans, Rosalynn and I extend our heartfelt condolences to Bill Stewart's wife, his family and friends.

JIMMY CARTER

NOTE: The text of the telegram was made available by the White House on June 29, the date of the memorial service, which was held in New York City.

Digest of Other White House Announcements

The following listing includes the President's public schedule and other items of general interest announced by the White

House Press Office and not included elsewhere in this issue.

June 23

The President met at the White House with Zbigniew Brzezinski, Assistant to the President for National Security Affairs, before departing for Japan and the Republic of Korea.

The President declared a major disaster for the State of New Mexico as a result of severe storms, snowmelt runoff, and flooding, beginning on or about May 2, which caused extensive public and private property damage.

June 28

The White House announced that the President has decided to cancel a planned vacation in Hawaii following his visit to the Republic of Korea and will return to Washington for congressional and staff meetings on the increasingly serious domestic and international energy situation.

NOMINATIONS SUBMITTED
TO THE SENATE

The following list does not include promotions of members of the Uniformed Services, nominations to the Service Academies, or nominations of Foreign Service officers.

Submitted June 25, 1979

IRVING G. CHESLAW, of California, a Foreign Service officer of Class one, to be Ambassador Extraordinary and Plenipotentiary of the United States of America to the Republic of Trinidad and Tobago.

ANTHONY C. E. QUAINTON, of Washington, Director of the Department of State's Office for Combatting Terrorism, for the rank of Ambassador.

SUSANNA B. McBEE, of California, to be an Assistant Secretary of Health, Education, and Welfare, vice Eileen Shanahan, resigned.

NOMINATIONS—Continued
Submitted June 25—Continued

LEROY D. CLARK, of New York, to be General Counsel of the Equal Employment Opportunity Commission for a term of 4 years, vice Abner Woodruff Sibal, resigned.

EMILY RAUH PULITZER, of Missouri, to be a member of the National Museum Services Board for a term expiring December 6, 1983, vice Joan Mondale, term expired.

CHECKLIST OF WHITE HOUSE
PRESS RELEASES

The following listing contains releases of the White House Press Office which are not included in this issue.

Released June 23, 1979

Advance text: remarks on departure for the trip to Japan and the Republic of Korea

Released June 27, 1979

News conference: on the *Weber* case decision—by Eleanor Holmes Norton, Chair of the Equal Employment Opportunity Commission, Robert J. Lipshutz, Counsel to the President, Assistant Attorney General Drew S. Days III, and Assistant Secretary of Labor for Employment Standards Donald E. Elisburg

Released June 29, 1979

Text: mailgram to State Governors on the independent truckers' strikes—by Jack H. Watson, Jr., Chairman of the White House Management Task Force on Energy Shortages

Announcement: 6-point program negotiated by members of the White House Management Task Force on Energy Shortages and trucking representatives—by Mr. Watson

News conference: on the 6-point program negotiated by members of the White House Management Task Force on Energy Shortages and trucking representatives—by Mr. Watson

ACTS APPROVED BY
THE PRESIDENT

Approved June 27, 1979

S. 429_____ Public Law 96–29 Department of Defense Supplemental Appropriation Authorization Act, 1979.

Editor's Note

The President's Trip to Japan and the Republic of Korea

On Friday, June 29, the President was in Japan. Releases and announcements issued during his visit to Japan and the Republic of Korea will be printed next week.

PRESIDENTIAL DOCUMENTS

Week Ending Friday, July 6, 1979

Elmendorf Air Force Base, Alaska

Remarks at a Reception. **June 23, 1979**

I really thank you for coming out this afternoon to meet me. I told Bob Strauss that I was going to stop, the first stop on the way to Tokyo, in Alaska to see my friends, and he said, "Well, that won't take long." [*Laughter*]

I think if anybody in the last 2½ years has thought about Alaska and studied about Alaska, it has been your President. There are two maps in the world with which I have become thoroughly familiar. One is in the Sinai, and I think you know which one the other is. [*Laughter*]

This is a State of unbelievable beauty, as you know, and it's a State where the conflicts of the world peculiarly are focused.

I go from Washington to Tokyo to meet with the leaders of France, Germany, Italy, Great Britain, Japan, Canada to talk about the most burning issue of our time, and that is energy, development of the quality of life, rapid change, whether or not people can govern themselves in a time of crisis and change that sometimes escapes us, a time of division, a time of argument, a time of debate, a time of soul-searching, a time of patriotism, and in our country, a time of greatness.

I've just come back from concluding an agreement with the Soviet Union. It's not the first wonderful agreement we've worked out with Russia, as you well know. [*Laughter*] But the times press on us. And I think Alaska, our most beautiful State, is also a State where the youth and the vigor and the dynamism and the strength of our Nation is most vividly demonstrated.

I recognize acutely, being a politician who hungers after the friendship and the approbation of Americans, how deeply disturbed you all have been on one side or the other about the Alaska lands legislation and the frustration that you feel in this relatively remote State from Washington that the decisions are made by those who don't know you well enough and who are too far away to hear your voice clearly.

You're not the first people in this Nation who've felt that way. I come from the South, as you know, and there have been decisions made in Washington with which we had violent disagreement. Once

1161

the basic decisions are made, modifications can then be accomplished. We can accommodate one another. The tensions tend to alleviate, and I think the harmony of our Nation can be restored again.

I look forward to coming back to Alaska. The first time I came here was exactly 4 years ago in June of 1975. I'm grateful to have a chance to meet you all personally, and I hope and I pray that when I go to Tokyo to represent our country, that I can make you proud of me and again proud of our country.

Last weekend in Vienna, in our negotiations with the Soviet Union, I negotiated from a position of political strength and military strength. We are the strongest nation on Earth.

This weekend I will be negotiating with the other leaders from a position of economic strength and cohesion, brought about by an allegiance to a nation which is, again, the greatest and the strongest on Earth.

I'm very proud to be President of this country, and I'm very proud to be in a State that inspires us all with your beauty and your dynamism, your confidence and your youth. You're typical of the pioneer spirit of our Nation, and it's an honor for me to be here with you.

And now, if you don't mind, Rosalynn and I would like to meet every one of you personally, if you would come by and let us shake your hand.

God bless you all. Thank you very much.

NOTE: The President spoke at 1:50 p.m. at the Officers' Club. Following the reception, the President left for Japan.

On his arrival in Tokyo, the President went to the residence of the U.S. Ambassador to Japan, where he stayed during his visit to Japan.

Tokyo, Japan

*Toasts at a Luncheon Hosted by Prime Minister Masayoshi Ohira.
June 25, 1979*

THE PRIME MINISTER. *Mr. President, Mr. Secretary of State, Mr. Secretary of the Treasury, Mr. Secretary of Energy, Your Excellencies, and distinguished guests:*

It is indeed a very great pleasure for us all to have with us today President Carter and the members of the President's party. On behalf of the Government and people of Japan, I would like to extend our sincere welcome.

Mr. President, the warm welcome and courtesies which you have extended to me and my wife when we visited the United States last month will forever remain in our memory. I wish to take this opportunity to express again our heartfelt thanks to you.

I wish to take this opportunity to express my deep respect and gratitude to President Carter, who is discharging his responsibilities in leading his great country, the United States of America, in this difficult age, which is full with problems.

There is a strong bond that ties our two countries together. In fact, there is no other example of a relationship between any two countries in world history which are so different in culture and tradition and are so far apart geographically but are enjoying an interchange of such a great scope and substance. I believe, as Ambassador Mansfield aptly described it, this is precisely because the relationship is based on the essential similarity of the way we see the world, of the political goals we pursue, and of the basic values they reflect.

The ties between Japan and the United States serve to enhance the honor of Japan and the United States respectively, and at the same time serve the benefits of both our countries. At the same time, this close tie between our two countries enable our two countries to discharge their responsibilities and roles respectively for the benefit of peace and stability of the international community. It is in this sense that I feel that our two countries are today called upon to make further efforts to deepen and strengthen the relationship of mutual trust and understanding between our two countries.

Mr. President, I am convinced that your visit to Japan this time will serve to strengthen this valuable tie of trust and understanding between our two countries, and will thus contribute greatly to peace and stability of the Asian region.

On the 28th and 29th of this month, Mr. President, you will be representing the United States at the economic summit which will take place here in Tokyo. In this economic summit, all the participating countries share the common goal of working together to stand up to the new challenges to the world economy. I am hopeful that thanks to the wisdom and leadership of President Carter, this economic summit will prove to be a very successful meeting.

Ladies and gentlemen, let us join in a toast to the great contribution President Carter has made in world affairs since his assumption of office, to further development and prosperity of the United States of America under his wise and able leadership, and to the continued health and happiness of President and Mrs. Carter.

THE PRESIDENT. *Mr. Prime Minister, distinguished Japanese guests and friends:*

I'm delighted to be in your country and to enjoy the special hospitality and friendship for which the Japanese people are known throughout the world.

During our discussions in Washington in May, Prime Minister Ohira and I became not only partners, but also we became friends and mutual students. In addition to reading the voluminous briefing books prepared for us by our staffs we also were required to read each other's autobiography. His was much better than mine. [*Laughter*]

I learned that we were both farmers and that we both came from the southern part of our country. I have developed a special theory that being from the southern part of one's country is not incompatible with great statesmanship. [*Laughter*]

I come here for our bilateral discussions in a spirit of good will and friendship, bringing to the people of Japan the best wishes of the people of my country.

I agree with Prime Minister Ohira that in the history of the relationship among nations, I doubt that there has ever been two countries so different in history, in culture, in traditions, in geography and language, but still bound so closely together in a spirit of productivity with a far-reaching commitment to common goals, common ideals, and personal friendships.

Yours is one of the most ancient of nations, ours is relatively new. Yours is one of the most homogeneous people, so closely bound together that you can almost communicate with one another without even speaking. Ours is a nation of immigrants, of refugees extremely different one from another, coming from all nations on Earth with different languages, different heritage, different backgrounds, different interests, but still bound together in one nation, deriving strength because we have a common goal and a common purpose.

Yet, our two countries, so different, are bound together with a common belief in freedom, a common belief in democracy, respect for the individuality of human beings, a reverence for freedom of speech, open debate, for truth, for the exercise of exploration of ideas without constraint, for freedom of the press, and for an open political process. We both believe that the greatest source of energy and creativity is the initiative in individuality derived from this personal freedom. We both believe in world peace. We both believe in the control of nuclear and other weapons.

Our relationship today is more than just one between two governments. It's a relationship almost like members of one extended family. More than 1 million American and Japanese citizens visit back and forth each year between countries. We meet in corporate boardrooms, in government councils, in factories, in concert halls, in scientific laboratories, in universities, on farmlands, on the sports fields, and many other ways. More Members of your Diet and our Congress visit each other to learn and to share ideas than between any other two congressional bodies on Earth.

We have much to learn from you. We admire your vigor, your thirst for knowledge, your sense of self-discipline, your commitment to hard work. We respect the stability of your family bonds, the worth of your community unity, the Japanese grace and delicacy, the sense of harmony and beauty that you've preserved down through the ages, and your own special achievement in balancing this reverence for the past with the utilization in an effective way of the opportunities of the present and the future.

These personal characteristics have permitted you to build Japan, your nation, into a great world power. Our relationship permits both our people to derive great benefits, one from another. Annual trade between our countries is more than $40 billion, more than the gross national product of 134 other nations in the world.

In closing, let me point out that we cannot rest on our achievements. Your great Admiral Togo, in 1904, said, "After victory, tighten the straps of your helmet."

With success comes differences. We both want equal advantages from this great mutual trade. It's a great tribute to Japan that you will be the host of what might very well be the most important economic summit conference ever held.

In addition, as a regional leader, you recognize, along with us, that Asia is the fastest growing economic region in the world, a region of rapid change, and we are certainly moving into a new era in the life of our shared Pacific community.

The United States is a Pacific nation in history, geography, and interest, and the partnership between the United States and Japan is the cornerstone of our own foreign policy in this region of the world. Together I am sure that you and we can be a force for hope, stability, prosperity, and peace in which all the world's people can share.

I would like to propose a toast to the health of Prime Minister Ohira and Mrs. Ohira, to the deep friendship and mutual respect and affection which exists between the people of Japan and the United States, and to the bright future which we share together.

NOTE: The exchange began at 1:55 p.m. at the Prime Minister's residence.

Prior to the luncheon, the President and Prime Minister Ohira and members of their delegations met at the residence.

Earlier in the day, the President was officially welcomed to Japan by Emperor Hirohito at Akasaka Palace. Following the ceremonies, the President and the Emperor went to the Imperial Palace to meet with members of the imperial family.

The Prime Minister spoke in Japanese, and his remarks were translated by an interpreter.

Tokyo, Japan

White House Statement on the Consultative Group on US-Japan Economic Relations. June 25, 1979

President Carter and Prime Minister Ohira agreed today to create a Consultative Group on US-Japan Economic Relations, announcing selection of Robert S. Ingersoll and Nobuhiko Ushiba as Co-Chairmen.

The decision follows agreement at the May 2 summit in Washington to establish a small group of distinguished persons drawn from private life who will submit recommendations to the President and the Prime Minister concerning actions that will help maintain a healthy bilateral economic relationship between the United States and Japan.

Mr. Ingersoll and Mr. Ushiba will recommend to the President and the Prime Minister the names of other people to serve in the Group.

Mr. Ingersoll, a 1937 graduate of Yale University, was formerly Ambassador to Japan (1972–73), Assistant Secretary of State for East Asian and Pacific Affairs (1974), and Deputy Secretary of State (1974–76). At the time of his Ambassadorial appointment he was chairman of the board and chief executive officer of the Borg-Warner Corp. in Chicago, where he had spent the previous 33 of his total of 35 years in industry. Chairman of the Japan Society since September 1978, Mr. Ingersoll has been a member of many international business committees and councils, including the Advisory Council on US-Japan Economic Relations and the Emergency Committee for American Trade. He is also deputy chairman of the board of trustees of the University of Chicago.

Mr. Ushiba, a graduate of the Faculty of Law of Tokyo Imperial University, entered the Foreign Service in 1932. He has served in various capacities abroad and in Tokyo, including Ambassador to Canada (1961–64), Vice Minister of Foreign Affairs (1967–70), and Ambassador to the United States (1970–73). Mr. Ushiba was named State Minister for External Economic Relations in November 1977. He has served as Ambassador for the Multilateral Trade Negotiations since December 1978.

NOTE: The statement was released in Tokyo, Japan.

Tokyo, Japan

Toast at the State Dinner. June 25, 1979

Your Majesty, you do my country and the American people great honor by receiving me, my wife, and my party to this beautiful room. There is a strong sense of history here: the history of your ancestors as Emperors of Japan stretching back to the very beginning of the nation; the history of Japan's development as a nation with great world influence, that began with the reign of your grandfather; and, the history of relations between Japan and the United States, reaching back to the visit of Commodore Perry in 1853.

We are proud to be part of this great flow of history, to build on the exchange of visits begun in 1974 by President Ford and continued during Your Majesty's memorable trip to the United States in 1975.

The American people still remember fondly the warmth and the friendship of your visit with us. The past century and a quarter has seen the relationship between our two countries and between the peoples grow to be as busy and as close as between any two nations on Earth. Together we have developed a combination of unmatched productivity and economic strength and a strong, shared devotion to the ideals of freedom, democracy, and the betterment of mankind.

Our relationship has seen times of great trouble and tragedy. But the close partnership we have forged in the last generation, in the Pacific region and around the world, amply justifies the common vision of the Japanese and Americans who saw in the 19th century that the future of our two nations would inevitably be linked.

Our achievements together over the years—in trade, in education, in science, in culture, in sports, in the cause of peace and friendship among nations—are a triumph of determination and hard work.

Your grandfather expressed that spirit eloquently in one of his poems. He said: "Even up a mountain peak which seems to reach the skies, we dare to say for him whose will is set on climbing it, there is a way."

We have much to learn from you. You've succeeded in preserving the best of your own traditions while harnessing the opportunities offered by change. You've maintained a sense of community bonds, the closeness of families, a special grace and civility and gentleness in your relations with each other despite the noise and the pressures of an industrial society. You've preserved the special Japanese ability to create and discover delicate beauty and harmony in every aspect of life, from the simplest, most natural things, to great architectural structures.

At the same time, you've grown to be an economic super power. You've harnessed the ingenuity and the creativity and energy of your people to gain the fruits of industry, technology, productivity, vigorous trade, prosperity, and growth.

Most important to Americans, you've achieved all of this in one of the most open, democratic, free societies on Earth. You've found a harmony between the dignity and worth of each individual human being and the responsibilities of shared effort and common purposes that a democracy demands.

We live in a world of rapid, sometimes bewildering change. People in many nations are struggling to preserve the values of their cultures and their traditions while they meet the complex challenges of development and growth. Japan offers a model of hope from which all nations can learn.

Your Majesty, I understand that at the beginning of each year you plant a tiny rice seedling as a symbol of your hope that your people will enjoy a bountiful future. I am a farmer. I know about the hard work, the attention, the care that successful crops require. I share your faith that working together, both our peoples can enjoy a more hopeful, more prosperous future, and that together with our allies and our friends who meet with us this week, we can do much to spread the blessings of prosperity and peace to disadvantaged peoples around the world.

During the next few days, leaders of great nations will represent the industrial democracies at the economic summit. It would be easy to focus only on the magnitude of the challenges we face in energy, in our own economies, in helping to meet the needs of the developing nations, in working together to build a more secure and a peaceful world. But I also think about the tremendous resources of our seven nations; the resources of our economies, the strongest, most vital, most dynamic in the world; the resources of our farmland and agricultural systems, the most productive on this Earth; our achievements in technology and science, in which we are unequaled; and the resources of our centers of learning and education and research, which attract students from almost every land. Most of all, I think of the resources of the spirit of the more than one-half billion free people in the major industrial democracies. I think of the strength of the ideals of freedom and individual dignity that our nations embody, ideals that still exert an almost magnetic attraction to disadvantaged people all over the Earth.

I have no doubt that together we have the resources, the skill, and the dedication to assure that people everywhere can be adequately fed; that our factories and farms and homes can draw on abundant, secure sources of energy; that the prosperity so many of us have enjoyed can be shared by others for whom life is little more than the struggle to survive from day to day. I'm confident that together we can build a world in which all peoples can live in peace.

Drawing upon the strength and the flow of history uniting our two nations, we shall together reach the goal that Your Majesty set in a poem you wrote for the new year nearly 40 years ago, and you said then:

"We pray for the time to come
When East, West and all
Making friends with one another
Will share in a prosperous future."

Your Majesty, with this goal in mind, I offer a toast to the health and well-being of Your Imperial Majesty, your family, the great people of Japan, and the harmony and friendship which binds us all together.

NOTE: The President spoke at 9:02 p.m. in the Bright Abundance Hall at the Imperial Palace in response to a toast by Emperor Hirohito.

Earlier in the afternoon, the President visited the Meiji Shrine and the nearby Iris Gardens.

Tokyo, Japan

Informal Exchange With Reporters.
June 26, 1979

Q. While we are waiting, can you tell us anything about how the talks are going?

THE PRESIDENT. They couldn't be better. Most of our serious difficulties were discussed and basically resolved back in May, when Prime Minister Ohira came to the United States, and then when Ambassador Strauss came here. So, we have been planning for the summit, talking about energy, refugees, and discussing international matters that are of mutual interest to us.

Q. Mr. President, do you feel you have made any progress on the refugee issue?

THE PRESIDENT. Yes, I think so. What we want to do, obviously, is to get the entire world to participate in the acceptance of the refugees and the financing of the very expensive programs, and also to get the world to induce the Vietnamese to change their policy, to cut down on the large numbers who are having to leave Vietnam. But the more nations who become interested and who join in the effort makes it possible to solve both these problems—to stop the problem at the source, and also to accommodate those who have already left.

Q. Mr. President, did Prime Minister Ohira give any indication what Japan can do?

THE PRESIDENT. I think it is better to let him speak for Japan.

Q. Did you have any discussions on U.S.-Soviet relations?

THE PRESIDENT. Yes. I gave the Japanese leaders a report on the Vienna conference, on the elements of SALT II, some of the prospects for the future. This was part of the discussion today.

Q. Did they indicate to you any concern over U.S. presence in North Asia or in Asian countries?

THE PRESIDENT. Not concern. I think our intentions and their desires are compatible.

Q. They are not concerned about our maintaining our presence here?

THE PRESIDENT. As I say, I think our intentions and desires are compatible.

Q. Mr. President, is there anything more that the United States can do about the refugees?

THE PRESIDENT. Well, of all the refugees who leave Southeast Asia now, we are taking about 70 percent of them. We have already committed to take 7,000 per year. We have already accepted—I mean, a month. And we have already taken about 200,000. What we want now is to increase what we are doing, but to get many other nations to join in with us.

Q. Do you think you will discuss this at the summit meeting?

THE PRESIDENT. Yes.

Q. Do you think there will be some specific proposal to come out of the summit meeting?

THE PRESIDENT. Yes.

Q. Can you give us any indication what that might be?

THE PRESIDENT. No, I can't speak for anybody except ourselves.

Q. But you will have specific proposals to put forward at the summit?

THE PRESIDENT. Yes.

Q. Mr. President, will you make any direct approach to Hanoi on this?

THE PRESIDENT. That is a continuing effort.

NOTE: The exchange began at approximately 1:30 p.m. outside the U.S. Ambassador's residence. As printed above, the item follows the press release.

Following his remarks, the President went inside to meet with former Japanese Prime Minister Takeo Fukuda.

Earlier in the day, the President and Prime Minister Ohira and members of their delegations met at Yoshida Villa in the town of Oiso.

Tokyo, Japan

Remarks at a Reception With Members of the Japanese Diet. June 26, 1979

Speaker Nadao, President Yasui, distinguished Members of the Japanese Diet, other guests:

It's a great honor for me and my wife to be here with you.

First of all, let me thank those among you who were here 4 years ago when I visited in May of 1975, who welcomed me when I was beginning my own campaign for President of the United States. At that time you gave me a much better welcome than I was getting in my own country. [*Laughter*]

As I stated yesterday, no other two legislative bodies in the world exchange more visits than do the Members of the Diet of Japan and the Members of the Congress of the United States. It is very reassuring and gratifying to me as President of our country to know that two great democracies are bound together through our people, through the heads of state, and through the great democratically elected congresses.

This strength, derived from friendship and close consultation, permits our countries to bear the burdens of responsibility and the great, wonderful opportunities of a better life in the future. My conversations with your Prime Minister and other officials today in Oiso, at what can be known in our country as a shrine of peace, were very productive and typical of the frank discussions which have bound our nations together through years of trial and years of achievement.

The economic achievements of Japan and the beneficent political influence of Japan throughout the world are a legitimate source of admiration for all other people. This great achievement of yours, which has aroused admiration, is closely bound with the friendship and the quiet gentleness which makes visiting here in your beautiful country such a pleasure for us.

Tomorrow I will go to Shimoda, where the interrelationship between our countries began, and my wife will then visit Kyoto, the more ancient capital of your beautiful country. This will give us an additional opportunity to let the people of Japan know how dearly we cherish the friendship which binds us together, providing a sense of strength as we deal with bilateral questions, as we improve the quality of life and the peace and stability of the Pacific region, as we favorably impress upon other nations the influence of our two countries throughout the world.

On behalf of 220 million Americans, I want to say to you Members of the great Diet of Japan, thank you for this partnership, thank you from the bottom of our heart for your friendship.

To the great people of Japan, to the friendship that binds us together, to peace throughout the world.

NOTE: The President spoke at 5:40 p.m. at the residence of Hirokichi Nadao, Speaker of the House of Representatives. In his opening remarks, he also referred to Ken Yasui, Speaker of the House of Councillors.

Following the reception, the President went to the National Theater for a Kabuki performance.

Shimoda, Japan

Remarks and a Question-and-Answer Session at a Town Meeting. June 27, 1979

THE PRESIDENT. Thank you very much, Mr. Mayor and distinguished citizens of Shimoda. My wife and I and my daughter, Amy, have been touched by the warmth of your welcome.

I have already had the honor of an audience with your Emperor, and I have had very productive meetings with your Prime Minister Ohira, but I especially wanted to come to this historic city.

Shimoda is where our friendship first took root and flowered. A century and a quarter ago when our relationship began, Japan was a feudal society on the verge of social revolution. The United States was edging toward a war between the States over the issue of slavery. Neither of us has devised a perfect political system since then, but we share a fundamental belief in freedom and in democracy.

As free people, we share common challenges as well. None is more important today than the energy crisis. Our planet is not producing enough oil to meet all our demands. The industrialized nations like the United States and Japan must face this challenge together, rather than competing with one another for every available barrel of oil regardless of price.

Energy is the principal subject of the summit meeting your country is hosting this week for the leaders of the major industrialized nations. Together we must restrain and reduce our imports. Together we must reduce waste and conserve our precious energy supplies. Together we must find ways to explore and to develop alternate energy supplies and new technologies of solar power and synthetic fuels.

This is a great opportunity as well as a challenge. Each of us must make painful adjustments in our society and some sacrifices in our daily lives. No one ever promised us that freedom would be easy or that democracy can be preserved without effort or without sacrifice.

All nations can learn from the example of the Japanese people in grappling with the complex challenges of development and of change. You've built your nation into an economic super power, but you've preserved the grace and the humanity and the beauty of Japanese society.

Your Emperor made a wise statement to leaders in a poem he wrote in 1966. He said, "Would that the wise voice of the man in the street spoke daily to guide us in the performance of our duties."

I have learned a great deal from the citizens of my country attending town meetings such as this one. In the same way, I would like to learn from your own wisdom and your own experience. I will take your questions now, with great pleasure.

VISIT TO SHIMODA

Q. I am sorry, I don't think I'm a good questioner. Mr. President, I understand you went to a *yakitori* restaurant last night.

THE PRESIDENT. Yes.

Q. I watched that on TV, and I felt you very close to us. We speak of the good intentions—at the *yakitori* restaurant, that sort of place I believe you can always get an impression of the true feelings of the people. What I would like to ask is the following: Why did you choose Shimoda for your town meeting? The friendship treaty between Japan and the United States was first concluded here in Shimoda, and there is the exchange of the instruments of ratification was conducted. Gyokusen-Ji, the place you will be visiting today; there you'll find five tombs of Americans, and I believe I can get your true thoughts here.

So, I would like to have your views on why you chose Shimoda for a town meeting.

THE PRESIDENT. Thank you very much for this excellent question.

I was here in Japan 4 years ago, before I was a famous man and when I had an opportunity to meet many people in Japan in a free and friendly way. Last night, without notice to the Japanese

security, we went to a private restaurant, the same restaurant that I visited 4 years ago, and there we found a friendship and warmth and exchange of ideas so valuable to me as one of the leaders of a great country in the world.

We wanted to have an opportunity to hear questions directly and to meet with other members of the Japanese community outside of Tokyo, and the obvious place to me was Shimoda, where the good relationship between your country and ours first began more than 100 years ago.

We felt that in Shimoda there was a good historical base for interest in the United States, and that perhaps more than the average Japanese community, you've studied about our own Nation and you would have questions to ask, and you would not be fearful to ask frank and freely what questions actually concerned you.

So, because of the historical relationship many years between us and because we hope that you'll ask very frank and free questions was the reason that I decided to come to Shimoda. The friendship between our two countries is very important to me, and I look forward to having questions now from a group who are very interested in our country and who, I think, would be representative of interested Japanese throughout your great country.

ATHLETICS

Q. What sorts of games did you play when you were small? And looking at the games children nowadays play in the United States, how would you compare the games; and what are your thoughts?

THE PRESIDENT. When I was a child, I played baseball, which Japanese play extremely well, as demonstrated by your great Mr. Oh, whom I met day before yesterday. I also played basketball. I lived on a farm. I liked to fish and to wander in the woods and streams.

I think the Americans have still maintained this great interest in sports. This morning, quite early, my wife and Amy and I were in swimming about 6 o'clock, and we run every day to stay in good physical condition.

My own belief is that the modern-day American young person is a better athlete than they were when I was a child. The standard of sports is higher, the competition is greater. And I think one of the new sports that has come to our country is soccer or international football. This is a very popular sport now in our country. It was hardly known when I was a child.

I think one of the greatest things that people can do in Japan or the United States is to stay in good physical condition by participating in competitive sports. And I'm glad even at the ancient age of almost 55, I'm still able to participate in athletics and sports.

FAMILY LIFE

Q. I'm a housewife and therefore don't really know much about difficult problems. I would like to ask a question about households.

I have three daughters. When they were small, my husband didn't look after them too well. Now that they have grown up—and the one in the middle is 11 years old, the same as Amy—and these daughters, after supper, they would add to the very warm atmosphere at home. We have very good rapport. And my husband seems to be very happy being surrounded by three daughters all the time.

I read in some article, I understand President Carter said that one of the most important women for you is Amy. I'm sure Amy will be getting married some years from now. Then I wonder if you'll feel you want to keep Amy close to you—[*laughter*]—will not want her to go away to someone else. How do you feel?

THE PRESIDENT. You were much more fortunate than I much earlier. My first three children were boys, and my wife and I were married 21 years before Amy came along. She's very close to us and we would like to keep her at home, of course. However, I think in a few more years, I hope at least 7 or 8 more years, I hope that Amy will find a good young man and get married and move away. We would obviously like for her to visit us often after she does so.

We have a very close family. We now have three grandchildren, two grandsons and a baby granddaughter who was born just a few months ago. So, I think the closeness of families is very important in the lives of every person.

One of the great things that Americans admire about Japanese is the very close-knit family and community relationships you enjoy in spite of a very great technological change that you've accommodated in your own lives. We have many things to learn from you, and I think that's one of the most admirable characteristics that we admire about the Japanese society, your strong families.

ROLE OF JAPANESE YOUTH

Q. Mr. President, I'm a student at—[*inaudible*]—Senior High School. I'm very happy to see you. I've been looking forward to talking with you today. This is a marvelous opportunity. I want to ask you many questions, but as time is limited, I will ask you only one. However, before the question: I read your book, "Why Not the Best?", and I was very much impressed by it. Here I have your books. I brought them through very tight guard at the entrance, so please give me your signature later.

I know you, like us, try to do your best, and so do I. I think we, the young people, must always try to do our best, like you. So, the question, Mr. President: What do you most expect young Japanese people to do for world peace? Please give me your frank opinion.

THE PRESIDENT. Thank you very much.

I might say, first of all, that your English is perfect, and I want to congratulate you already on doing such a superb job. You've obviously done your best in your study of our language. One of the things that you could do in the future is to be a professional interpreter at the United Nations. [*Laughter*]

It's very important for young people of this age to learn about other people and learn about other nations on Earth. There is a genuine worldwide hunger, in my opinion, for friendship, for understanding, and for peace.

One of the responsibilities of the leaders of nations like my own and like yours is to search for better degrees of understanding. Not much more than a week ago, I was in Vienna, Austria, meeting with President Brezhnev and other leaders of the Soviet Union to search for ways to control nuclear weapons and to have peace and friendship between the Soviet Union and the United States.

Beginning tomorrow, I will be meeting with leaders from Japan, from Canada, Great Britain, from Germany, France, Italy, and from the European Community, searching for ways for us to have better understanding. It's a mistake, however, for young people like you or for average citizens like those who live in Shimoda to leave this responsibility only to elected leaders. It's very important for you to study and to learn about others and to encourage your own lead-

ers to explore not for war, but for peace, not for subjugation of citizens, but for freedom. And the very wonderful democracy that you enjoy gives us a chance to learn about others in an unrestricted way. A free press is also very important.

I hope sometimes you can come to the United States to visit us. If you come while I'm still President, we would love to have you come to the White House to see my family personally.

Also, I would like to—[*applause*]——

Q. Thank you very much, Mr. President.

THE PRESIDENT. If you will bring your books up here, I will be glad to sign them when I get through, okay?

PRESIDENT'S CHILDHOOD

Q. President Carter, when you were a child, what sort of strongest reminiscence do you have? What do you recall the most of your childhood?

THE PRESIDENT. I think the strongest memory I have is the closeness of my family. I lived on a farm, and we had a lifestyle much more similar to what it was 2,000 years ago than what it is today. We worked in the fields together, and we traveled very little. I always knew that my mother and father were near, and we were very closely bound together. We had very little contact with the outside world. Later, of course, with the modern technological age, with television, telephones, with travel by all people, the family structure became much less close together. And I would say that's the most vivid memory of my youth.

Also, I lived in the fields and on the farm, in the woods, along the streams. And when I'm now in the White House in Washington, my greatest hunger is to be alone, away from security, away from the press, and to be in the fields and the woods again. Maybe after I am no longer

President, I'll have this chance, but we want to keep a strong family in any circumstances.

SOUTHEAST ASIAN REFUGEES

Q. Let me ask you a rather serious question. With the slogan of rectifying the united society after Vietnam war and the Watergate, you came to the White House as the first President from the South after the Civil War. What I was most interested was that you have advocated human rights on the diplomatic front and also zero [base] budget for domestic budget. You've also sent letters to Sakharov in the Soviet Union, and you have also seriously worked for the Agreement of Helsinki. At the same time, you have with unfailing belief of democracy been working vis-a-vis Nicaragua and Zimbabwe-Rhodesia, and I would like to express my full respect to you.

Now, today we are faced with energy and other important problems. As the leader of the democratic world on questions of assistance to less developed countries, on questions of Vietnamese refugees, I hope you will play an even greater role. And I wonder if I could have some of your views on these questions.

THE PRESIDENT. The people of Japan and the people of the United States enjoy great privileges of freedom and democracy which others do not enjoy. My own belief is that we should take a bold stand in encouraging the basic human rights of freedom and liberty and proper attention to the worth of each individual human being no matter how powerful or weak, no matter how rich or poor, no matter how influential or well recognized they might be. I have tried to let the United States be one of the leading lights of the enhancement of human rights throughout the world.

I have already met twice with Prime Minister Ohira and other leaders of Japan to explore ways to alleviate the present intense problem of the tens of thousands of refugees who are coming out of Vietnam because of oppressive policies of the Vietnam Government.

Of all the refugees who now leave Asia, the United States receives about 70 percent of them, and we also provide very heavily financial resources for the United Nations and for others who attempt to deal with this increasing problem. Japan has been very generous in financial contributions, but because of the homogeneous nature of your own society, Japan has not yet decided to receive very many of the Vietnam refugees.

With the other Western democratic leaders, this will be the number two item on the agenda, along with energy the most important thing we will discuss. I hope that the United Nations will very quickly arouse interest among all 150 nations on Earth to receive a large number or a small number of the refugees and that all of us might focus our criticism or influence on Vietnam to relieve this growing problem at its source.

I think the humane treatment of these refugees is a major responsibility for me as President. We have been taking about 7,000 per month. We have already received 220,000 of the refugees from Vietnam and Southeast Asia. We are prepared to take even more, and I will be joining in with Prime Minister Ohira and others to make this a worldwide effort to alleviate this very serious human problem.

Thank you for your very good question.

PRESIDENT'S EDUCATION

Q. My name is Matsaki Imati. I'm a ninth grader. When you were in junior high school, I wonder if you've ever been scolded by your teacher, and what sort of memory do you have and what sort of dream did you have in those days?

THE PRESIDENT. I have not only been scolded by my teacher, I have been severely punished by my teacher with a paddle, which did not hurt me permanently. Perhaps one of the reasons that I ultimately became President was because my teachers were very strict and encouraged me to abide by the rules of the school and also inspired me to study harder.

I think the primary goal that I had in mind when I was a ninth grader was to be a student at the United States Naval Academy and to be a naval officer. My own family has been in the United States for more than 300 years, and neither my father nor his father nor any of his ancestors had ever finished high school and gone to college. And I felt that because of the Government opportunity at the military school, the Naval Academy, that I would have a chance for the first time to get a college education and also to serve in the U.S. Navy.

I did finally go to the Naval Academy, was in the Navy for 11 years, was a submarine officer, then resigned to go into public service, eventually, and became President. So, I think the ambition to get a better education was my major one as a ninth grader.

I received scolding and punishment when I was not a good young boy. I don't think the scolding and the punishment and the discipline hurt me at all.

U.S.-JAPANESE RELATIONS

Q. Mr. President, in this city where Commodore Perry and Harris, who opened up the friendly relations between the two countries, you visited this town on account of that historic background. At the same time in this city of Shimoda,

at that time those two distinguished American citizens, Perry and Harris, we learned what was happening in the world from these two distinguished Americans. And as a result, we decided to open our country and conclude relations, friendship with the United States, even during the ban put on by the then Bakufu Shogunate.

Do you know of this particular incident?

THE PRESIDENT. Yes, I've studied this when I was a student, and in preparation for coming to Shimoda, I have studied even more.

Q. So, today you are visiting Gyokusen-Ji Temple at the entrance of that. We always think about those two distinguished American citizens, as well as Shoin Yoshida, who also made a great contribution to the opening of our country at that particular time.

If circumstances permit, I hope you will slow down your car and pay respects to the great Shoin Yoshida. If you are kind enough to do that, Dr. Yoshida and other distinguished ancestors of ours will feel very happy thinking about the even closer relations we enjoy with the Americans, I think they will enjoy beneath their graveyard.

I sincerely hope that you do that and pay respect to those great ancestors as well.

THE PRESIDENT. Thank you. The point you've made is very good. It would be a mistake for Americans to forget about the reception given to the American officials, Perry and Harris, by the people of Japan. We recognize how difficult this was 120 years or more ago, and I want to express my thanks on behalf of the American people for the friendship and hospitality and openness that was offered to the world by Japan at that time, under the most difficult circumstances. And you're absolutely right, it's not equitable to honor Perry and Harris and to forget about Mr. Yoshida and other Japanese leaders who made the great progress between our two nations possible.

Thank you for this reminder. It's very well that you have done so.

EDUCATION

Q. Welcome, Mr. President. My uncle of my husband visited the U.S. when he was 17, and he still lives in Chicago. He's now 84. Three years ago, that particular uncle visited Japan, and at that time he mentioned that the new President is Mr. Carter, and I am very, very happy that I personally am able to see you like we do now.

At this moment, we have two children, one kindergarten pupil, the other going to primary school. In your household, President Carter, what kind of practices and hope do you express for educating and training your children, including Amy?

THE PRESIDENT. My children and Amy have always attended the public schools, both when I was in Plains, Georgia, the little town where we grew up; when I was Governor of Georgia, living in Atlanta, the capital city of that State; and now in Washington, D.C., while I'm being President.

In addition to the regular classroom opportunities, Amy goes to a class at the local university for specialized training, and she also studies violin under the great leadership of a Japanese master. We have enjoyed yesterday, for instance, a violin class that Amy attended with several other Japanese children.

I think in addition to that, we provide Amy with an opportunity to travel. She's here with us this morning, and she learns about other countries and other people because of my own experiences. I might point out very quickly that a father or mother does not have to be President of the United States to provide young children with an opportunity to learn more about the world.

She also learns, of course, from television, and from the reading which she does every day. Most of the time when you see Amy, except when she's very active, she'll have a book in her hand and reading on her own initiative. And I think this combination of schoolwork, family travel, in the home reading, and broadening one's life through violin or piano lessons is all a very good combination for education.

Thank you very much for letting me tell about my favorite daughter.

RACE RELATIONS

Q. One year from last, we received a student from the State of New York and had him stay in my house. So, I feel very intimate with the Americans.

A few days ago, a well-known actor, John Wayne, passed away. According to what I've heard, he is one of the representatives of great Americans. What he didn't like, according to the newspaper, was the colored people. You have well-developed democracy in your society. Still, currently, many people, including the educated people, may have some misunderstanding about the color of the people. In some regions of your country, even the overt form of segregation is practiced, as I was told. What do you think about such practices?

If, Mr. President, if you are not married—suppose you are not married and suppose you fall in love with a colored girl, what would you do? Would you marry her without any resistance?

THE PRESIDENT. Thank you very much.

There has been a time in our country when there was a great official and unofficial discrimination against black people and others, other people of color. Even 25 years ago, this was prevalent in the southern part of the United States, where I lived. This was something inherited from the early years of our Nation, when slavery was part of our societal structure and was approved by the laws of our Nation.

It was very difficult for us to make this change. But it was one of the most wonderful changes that has taken place in our own Nation, and I hope that what we have accomplished in the United States in the last 25 years will be an inspiration to others where racial discrimination is still practiced. I can't say that this attitude has been completely removed from the hearts of our people, but we have made great progress.

As far as intermarriages are concerned, I've never been in love with any other woman except my wife. But I would hope that in the true spirit of equality and in an absence of racial prejudice, that I would not let the color of a woman's skin interfere with my love for her if I felt that way—and marriage, of course, would be part of that relationship if the circumstances should permit.

I hope my wife will forgive my answering the question this way. It is a hypothetical question, Rosalynn, and I have no intention to leave you for another woman.

Q. Thank you very much, Mr. President. I like the U.S. more because of your answer.

THE PRESIDENT. I might add that we still have our problems, and we don't claim to be a perfect society. You have a very homogeneous society in Japan with very little differences among races. Our country is a nation of people who come from every country on Earth. Ours is a nation of immigrants. Ours is a nation of refugees. We have hundreds and hundreds of different languages spoken in our country, but we are bound together with a common purpose under a democratic structure of government based on human freedom. And it makes it difficult for us in some ways, but I think it gives strength to our Nation, because this diversity of background and heritage and language and interest and history can be melded together in such a good way as it presently is in our Nation.

We are not perfect. But we are making progress.

U.S. AGRICULTURE

Q. I am 78 years old. Mr. President, it is indeed a great honor beyond any expectation to have this opportunity of meeting you and exchange views with you. I will carry that to my posterity, and I certainly welcome Mrs. Carter, as well as your daughter. It is a great honor for citizens of Shimoda to receive you. This will clearly tell us the great benefit of the free and democratic society.

I would like to ask, Mr. President, as one—I'm talking about you—who was brought up in the farms, what do you produce in your farm at the present time?

THE PRESIDENT. My State produces more peanuts than any other two States in the Nation, and on my own farm, this is the number one crop. We also produce on our farms, cotton, corn, swine, cattle. In the past, we've produced poultry— chickens—and we produce all kinds of feed grains, some oats, wheat, barley, and rye.

We have pine forests. We produce timber on our land. It's fairly typical of a farm for my own State of Georgia. We have about 60 inches of rain each year, almost two meters of rain each year. We do some irrigating, and near my farm, but not on my farm, are produced other crops like vegetables and tobacco, but most of the crops produced on my farm are very large fields and the crops that I have enumerated to you.

I might point out that we are very proud of the sale of American farm products to Japan. I forgot to mention that we also produce soybeans on our farm. As a matter of fact, there are more acres of land in the United States which produce food for the Japanese than there is land in Japan which produces food for Japanese. So, we are very proud of an opportunity to sell you our farm products, and it gives a great opportunity for trade back and forth between our nations.

Thank you very much for letting me talk about my favorite subject of farming.

FAMILY LIFE

Q. Welcome, Mr. President, to the city of Shimoda. I am the mother of a first grader, as well as a year-and-a-half girl. This is a very friendly atmosphere. I really enjoy talking to you, Mr. President.

I would like to ask you, sir, for a young mother like me, who has responsibility for the next generation, as a mother—you are a father, of course, Mr. President—but for a mother, what do you expect us mothers to do for the next generation? That is my question, Mr. President.

THE PRESIDENT. In a day of women's liberation, it's getting more difficult to distinguish between the responsibilities of women and men. My wife gives me advice on matters of a broad range. She shares the responsibilities with me, both for my business affairs and also political affairs, and so she and I have an equal partnership which I think is very typical of American life.

My own impression in being here in Shimoda and listening to the questions thus far is of the intense interest of this community and Japanese people in general in the family and the growth of children and the cohesion of the family structure. I think to provide support for a husband, to share his burdens and responsibilities and achievements, to keep a stable family group, to accommodate the varied interests and characteristics of children, to give them a better life and a better opportunity than we ourselves had when we were growing up, to try to acquaint them with the outside world and the principles of a good life—those are things which are obvious to me as a father. I'm sure they're obvious to you as a mother.

But ultimately, a nation's strength rests very heavily on the strength of individual families and individual communities. That's the root of our progress and the root of the stability of life which lets us accommodate and overcome serious problems and obstacles. That's one of the reasons Japan has made such great progress; that's one of the reasons that you are one of the greatest nations on Earth, the strong family.

U.S. TRADE WITH JAPAN

Q. It is indeed a great honor to be able to see you, Mr. President.

I am with a farming family; I'm 25 years old, producing the Japanese tangerine, oranges.

In Japan, at this moment, we have the import agriculture products such as oranges. As a result of the development of the agricultural products import, we tangerine producers are having hard times because of the import of oranges and other agricultural products from the U.S. So, in this connection, I would like to have your thinking about this.

And on top of that, if I get unemployed, can I be employed on your farm in the U.S.? What would be the wages? Will that be enough to support myself, my wife, and my children? I will be happy to be employed by you with that wage, Mr. President.

THE PRESIDENT. First of all, let me say that we are very careful in our export policies toward Japan to have a minimum disruption of the market for your own products.

We actually sell to Japan very little citrus products, including oranges and tangerines, grapefruit, lemons. You have a total production of 3½ million tons of citrus products within Japan itself.

The present target which has been negotiated between Japan and the United States says that by 1983 the American citrus sales to Japan would be not much more than 2 percent of the total that you produce here in your own country. And we are trying to focus the sale of American citrus to Japan during the months when your own production is least, I believe, in June, July, and August.

So, we have to have some markets for our products in Japan in order to purchase the tremendous amount of products that we buy from your factories. But in negotiating these agreements, we try to keep the disruption of your products very minimally. I think the amount of citrus that is being sold or will be sold in Japan from the United States has been greatly exaggerated.

I don't operate my farm now. When I became President, I wanted to break away from any direct relationship with business. So, I rent my farm to others for a fixed amount per year. My own belief is that you will be much more prosperous in Japan growing superb tangerines than you would to come to my very poor farm in Georgia and to produce peanuts.

LIONS CLUBS

Q. Mr. President, I'm a charter member of the Shimoda Lions Club. I overheard that you are one of the members of the Lions Club. Since you have assumed your office, have you been there regularly, attending the club meetings, or are there other activities that you engage in?

In Japan, there is a saying, namely, that if you do it once, you will do it twice. So, I hope that you will win your election next year and come back to Shimoda very much.

THE PRESIDENT. Thank you very much. I'll remember your good wishes very carefully and with gratitude.

My father was a charter member of the Plains Lions Club. When I resigned from the Navy, I became a member the first week I was home. I later became Tail Twister, president of our club, zone chairman, deputy district governor, ultimately a district governor of the Lions Clubs in District 18–C, and chairman of all the Lions Clubs in Georgia, about 200 of them. But the Lions Club meant a great deal to me, and it gave me a chance to learn about public service without holding public office.

I do not attend the Lions Club now because of the duties of President and because I represent also Kiwanians and Rotarians and others as well as Lions. But when I return to Plains after serving as President, I intend to be again an active member of the Plains Lions Club.

PRESIDENT'S CHILDHOOD

Q. Mr. President, I am a pupil, a sixth grader, and I am 11 years old, as is Miss Amy.

Mr. President, you are a great man today, but what kind of a child were you when you were growing up?

THE PRESIDENT. It's hard for me to answer that question.

I was mischievous. My parents had to exert very good discipline on me, particularly my father. I had to work very hard, but not any harder than the other members of my family. I played with neighbors, although living on an isolated farm, we didn't have very many neighbors then. Most of my neighbors were black children, who were my only friends when I was a little child. I went to school about 2½ miles away in a tiny town called Plains, which has a total population of about 650 people then and now. Plains has not grown in the last 50 years.

I had a good life as a child and was very close to my mother, father, and my brothers and sisters. I might say I had great opportunities to improve myself, as do you, and I was, I would say, a typical child with problems and achievements— some good, some bad. And I turned out to be President, because in our country, as in yours, there is no limit on what an individual human being can be, because our Government gives us freedom and because in our society, each person has equal opportunity, and we look upon every person as a very valuable part of the Nation.

So, that's one of the great things about being in a democracy, in a free nation like you enjoy and that I enjoy, that no matter what your background or how poor you might be at the beginning of your life, you can still have a chance to be a very influential person, either in politics or out of it. And no matter what your life might amount to at the end, it can still be a full and gratifying life.

Thank you for letting me describe in a fumbling way my life as a child. It's been a long time ago. It's hard for me to remember all about it.

Q. President Carter, I am sure you respected your father. What sort of man was he? When you were a small child, what sort of thing did your father use to tell you?

THE PRESIDENT. Until I was 13 years old, I was the only son in the family, and my father and I were very close. We worked in the same field, we hunted together, fished together, walked in the woods together, went on short trips together.

My father was a very stern father in that when he spoke, I jumped. I didn't disobey him. When I was an unruly child or when I hurt my sisters or did something improper, my father would punish me for it.

My father was a hard-working man, very honest. He died in 1953. My mother, who is 81 years old this year, is still living, and she was also a great influence in my family. My mother was a registered nurse, and my father was a farmer. But both my parents were very important factors in my life and guided me, I think, in a proper way.

I might say, I won't have time to take another question, I don't believe, but I would like to close by making these comments.

This has been an exciting experience for me. I feel a warmth of friendship and good will from you that's typical of the attitude of Japanese people toward Americans. And it's very exciting for me as President of a great country to have that sense of our partnership and our common views toward the basic elements of human life.

We occupy positions of leadership in the world, and we have a great responsibility on us—not only Presidents but fathers and mothers, those who grow tangerines, those who go to school to learn about how we can be a credit to our country in our own individual lives and our own individual achievements.

Although many things change in a modern world with jet airplanes and television, the most important things do not change—love in a family, honesty, friendship among people, a desire for peace, a respect for one another, the beauty of nature, the reaching for a better life for children than parents had—those kinds of things never change. And I'm very glad to be part of Shimoda today and to have your questions covering such a wide range of interest.

I hope that through television, the people of Japan will see that what started here 125 years ago as the first little tiny seed of friendship between our two countries has now grown into an enormous tree of very wonderful friendship that can be an inspiration to our own people and an inspiration to peace-loving and freedom-loving people around the world.

I'm very proud and thankful to be with you, and I thank you for a chance to let me hear from you and to let you hear my voice as a leader of a great nation visiting the people of another great nation.

And now I would like to make a presentation to your community, and I'd like for the mayor and other officials to come to the stage, if they will.

While I'm here at the microphone, I would like to say that this is a plaque—I wrote some words very carefully on the plane coming over to Japan, and they've now been inscribed on this plaque—and I hope it will remind you of my visit with you. And now I'd like to go over and unveil the plaque, which you might keep in your own community.

I might read it. It says, "Here in Shimoda, friendship between the Japanese and the American people first took root and flowered. We have built together a lasting friendship based on trust and un-

derstanding. Our partnership offers hope that all peoples will one day learn to live together in brotherhood, prosperity and peace." And it's signed Jimmy Carter.

Thank you very much.

MAYOR AOKI. We have just received this message commemorating the President's visit to Shimoda, and also this is a replica that shall be kept in our minds forever. And I would like to thank you from the bottom of my heart, Mr. President.

I would also like to take this opportunity to say a few words of thanks.

Commodore Perry led the flagship fleet and surprised the citizens of Shimoda. Thanks to that, the doors to Japan were opened and the foundation for modern Japan was established.

President Jimmy Carter of the United States of America has led the fleet of Mrs. Carter and Amy, your most loved child, to come to Shimoda. On the 27th of June 1979, a new bridge of friendship starts in this small town of Shimoda, and in front of us, President Carter stands with us, sharing the same feeling and breathing the same air with us.

The United States of America and Japan have come so close together, so friendly, and we have established such great mutual understanding, and I would like to thank you for this wonderful town meeting. The great honor bestowed on us today will be handed down for posterity forever.

Mr. President, Mrs. Carter, and Amy, let us meet each other again once more in Shimoda.

NOTE: The President spoke at 11 a.m. in the Shimoda Middle School gymnasium, following an introduction by Mayor Yoshio Aoki. The participants in the town meeting spoke in Japanese, and their remarks were translated by an interpreter.

Following his tour of Gyokusen-Ji Temple, the President returned to Tokyo.

Tokyo, Japan

White House Statement on Meetings With Prime Minister Joe Clark of Canada and Prime Minister Margaret Thatcher of the United Kingdom. June 27, 1979

The President met with Prime Minister Joe Clark of Canada from 5:45 p.m. until about 6:15 p.m. Also in the meeting were Secretary of State Vance and Foreign Minister Flora MacDonald.

At 6:15 p.m., British Prime Minister Margaret Thatcher and Foreign Minister Lord Carrington joined the meeting.

Prime Minister Clark and Foreign Minister MacDonald departed at 7:15 p.m. and the President and Secretary Vance continued to meet with Prime Minister Thatcher and Lord Carrington until 7:30 p.m.

The bilateral discussions focused on bilateral matters. In the three-way meeting the focus was on the summit agenda—energy, refugees, and economic issues.

NOTE: The statement was released in Tokyo, Japan.

Tokyo, Japan

Remarks and a Question-and-Answer Session With Reporters on the OPEC Oil Price Increase. June 29, 1979

THE PRESIDENT. The OPEC nations have just increased their price again by an extraordinary amount. The cumulative effect of these increases has been a 60-percent increase in the price of oil since last December. This causes an economic watershed for the United States and also for the rest of the world. There is no one on Earth who will fail to suffer from these extraordinary increases in oil prices.

So far, we in the United States have failed to prepare ourselves for these actions by OPEC. Between 1973 and 1977, the United States took no action to deal with the inevitable increases in oil prices and the inevitable decreases in the supply of oil.

In 1977 I proposed to the Congress a comprehensive energy plan. Until this moment, the Congress has passed no legislation concerning oil. It is absolutely imperative that Congress act without delay to pass the windfall profits tax and to establish the energy security fund.

I have decided to cut short my own visit to foreign countries to go back home, arriving late Sunday, to encourage the Congress to act more expeditiously on the legislation I've already described and also to pass legislation authorizing the production of synthetic fuels and other energy supplies to make our country more self-sufficient, more immune from the damaging effect of outside decisions from OPEC and others.

In addition, I'll be meeting with my own advisers to see what other action can be taken within the next few months to protect our country from future actions such as these I've just described.

Domestic energy supplies must be increased. Oil, gas, coal, synthetic fuels, liquefied and gasified coal supplies, solar energy—these actions must be taken, and without further delay. We must invest literally billions of dollars in these technological advancements, and the money is available to us with the windfall profits tax and the establishment of the energy security fund.

It's been estimated that by the end of 1980, the OPEC price increases in the last 6 months will cost our Nation at least 2 percent in increased inflation and at least a 2-percent decrease in the rate of growth of the economy of the United States.

Our country is able to be self-sufficient. We have the technological ability, we have the finances, we have the natural resources. It's imperative that we act expeditiously. It's imperative that we cooperate with one another. It's necessary for us to be determined, bold, aggressive, and also that we are creative and that the Americans harness the tremendous resources of our country in the most effective and efficient and cooperative fashion.

There is no other threat to our life in America so important as these economic threats that not only weaken our Nation's structure but also endanger our own security in the future. My belief is that now the American people are aroused and the Congress is aroused enough to act without delay. This will be my major purpose when I return to the United States in just a few days.

Thank you very much.

Q. Mr. President, is there any economic or other type of retaliatory action we and our partners could take directly against OPEC?

THE PRESIDENT. The most important single thing that can be done on a multinational basis is what has been under consideration here in Tokyo for the last 2 days. My prediction is that the major Western allies, those who are assembled here for the economic summit, will act aggressively and without precedent to cut down on our imports and our dependence on OPEC oil. This will have a major stabilizing effect. So, with multilateral approach here in eliminating waste, cutting down on imports, investing jointly to produce new supplies of energy based on new technologies—that will be a major step on a multinational basis. But I think the major responsibility is on us to act within the United States.

Q. Mr. President, have you been in touch with other leaders since the price increase has been announced to see what their reaction is?

THE PRESIDENT. Yes. I discussed this announcement with the other leaders last night. We had a good indication of what it would be, and I think that I can say that they all share my deep concern about the economic consequences of it. But there are two phases that must be addressed: One is the multinational phase, where we work together on technology and to cut down demand for OPEC oil; and the second and obviously the most direct responsibility is for the United States to act on its own. We must do both.

Q. Mr. President, do you think there will be any effect on the dollar—immediate effect on the dollar or any kind of shifting away by the oil companies to other countries?

THE PRESIDENT. My belief is that the prospective OPEC price increase has already been assimilated by the international monetary markets. If we act boldly and aggressively here in Tokyo, which I believe we will do today, that should help to stabilize the dollar.

Q. What will the consequences be of continued congressional inaction on energy?

THE PRESIDENT. The same consequences that we've already suffered. The Congress has not acted for the last 2 years on any legislation that affects oil. I've just gotten a report from the Vice President a few minutes ago that the House finally passed the windfall profits tax. It must now go to the Senate. But for the last 2 years, the Congress has passed no legislation concerning oil. The windfall profits tax, when passed, the establishment of the energy security fund will give us a substantial reservoir of financing for the creation of synthetic fuels, the movement on solar energy, the liquefaction and gasification of coal, and other actions that can make us more energy self-sufficient.

Q. Is there anything immediate you can do to reduce the gas lines in the United States?

THE PRESIDENT. My information is that in the next few weeks—hopefully sooner—there will be an increase in supply of gasoline to the affected areas. The oil companies and the Department of Energy—and I talked to the Vice President this morning—all agree that the percentage of gasoline being allotted in the affected areas will be increased to about 97 percent [1] of what it was last year, a much better supply than we have experienced the last couple of weeks.

Thank you very much.

NOTE: The President spoke at 7:27 a.m. outside the U.S. Ambassador's residence.

Following his remarks, the President left for the French Embassy for breakfast with French President Valéry Giscard d'Estaing, British Prime Minister Margaret Thatcher, and German Chancellor Helmut Schmidt.

Earlier at a meeting in Geneva, Switzerland, members of the Organization of Petroleum Exporting Countries set a price ceiling for petroleum of $23.50 per barrel.

---

[1] On the same day, the White House Press Secretary issued the following notice to the press.

For your information on the President's statement and questions and answers this morning—

After reviewing the briefing material provided to the President, it appears that it is more accurate to speak of an increase to a range of 95 percent to 97 percent of last year's supply of gasoline, rather than the 97 percent figure which the President used.

You should note, however, that the President is committed as a primary goal to take the necessary steps to prevent a shortage of home heating oil. It could become necessary to reduce the amount of gasoline being produced this summer to avoid running out of oil to heat our homes this winter.

To make sure there is no misunderstanding, the President also asks that I relay to you this comment:

Tokyo Economic Summit Conference

Remarks and a Question-and-Answer Session With Reporters. June 29, 1979

THE PRESIDENT. Well, first of all, let me make an opening comment, and then you can ask questions. I'll be brief.

First of all, the Japanese did a superb job, under very difficult circumstances, in putting together arrangements for my state visit and also for a very important conference. Secondly, I thought the results of the economic summit conference were superb. They equaled our highest expectations, and we accomplished several important goals.

First of all—and this was the most controversial all the way through—specific, tangible, individual nations' quotas or goals or imports for 1979, 1980, and extending through 1985. The individual European quotas will be assigned to those countries at the next European Community meeting in Dublin this fall, and then

---

"Even if we reach the 97 percent figure, there is no guarantee that gasoline lines will end without significant conservation efforts. We will still have a substantial shortfall compared to projected demand, and the amount of gasoline available to the average motorist will be reduced by the necessity of providing priorities to such essential users as ambulances and fire-fighting vehicles."

For your additional information, to reach the 95 percent to 97 percent figure, it will be necessary for oil companies to draw down their crude stocks by about 20 million barrels, as we have asked them to do. It will also be necessary for crude oil imports to continue to average 6.2 million barrels per day or better, which is consistent with import levels over the past 3 weeks and with our IEA pledge to reduce consumption by 5 percent compared to projected demand.

the European Community will be responsible for monitoring those goals. The cumulative total will not exceed their 1978 import levels.

We, the Canadians, and the Japanese also adopted goals. Our 1985 goal for imports will not exceed the lower of either 1977 or 1979, no more than 8.5 million barrels per day.

The second thing that we did was to commit ourselves individually and jointly to pursue, with the full resources of our nations, the development of alternative forms of energy.

The third thing we did about energy was to issue, for the first time, a very significant comment about the OPEC nations' recent actions. I won't go into that now. My guess is that that will be the most newsworthy item. It's the first time that the other nations of the world have expressed ourselves clearly and forcefully about the unwarranted increases in oil prices levied against the rest of the world by the OPEC countries. The fact that seven industrialized nations have agreed on the text jointly, I think, is significant.

We also aroused, I think, a great deal of interest in the refugee question. We called upon Vietnam to restrain the outflow of refugees and to minimize its impact on the people concerned, particularly the refugees themselves. We have agreed to double our own monthly quota of refugees coming from Vietnam. The Japanese have agreed to double the percentage of financing for the United Nations High Commissioner's fund on refugees.

There were other elements in the communique that will be issued when we get back to the New Otani Hotel, but those were the most significant items. Perhaps you would have a followup question.

Q. It sounds like you won your point——

THE PRESIDENT. Yes.

Q. ——in terms of the ceilings and the

freeze, that they took the American plan. Is that basically it?

THE PRESIDENT. They did, and we were gratified at this.

Q. Was there a fight about it?

THE PRESIDENT. Well, there was a constant debate. I think the problem was that the European Community had decided collectively at Strasbourg not to deviate from the collective target. This was a much less restrictive target, because they could absorb the increased production from the North Sea and not be limited to individual countries' goals. They had a difficulty in departing from the Strasbourg agreement.

Q. How did you convince them?

THE PRESIDENT. Well, we felt very deeply about it. And I think that the longer we discussed these issues, the more they saw that the outcome of the conference would be disappointing if it was expressed in generalities and if the particular nation-by-nation quotas were not very specific and stringent. There was a general feeling, the longer we were here— I think sharpened by the very high increase in OPEC prices—that we have a serious worldwide problem. And we were ready for the first time to take action that we have never been willing to take before.

Q. When were you able to turn the corner on that, Mr. President, in terms of getting the agreement and clearing that item?

THE PRESIDENT. Well, there was an amendment offered a half an hour before we left to go back to a collective European quota—*[laughter]*—between 1980 and 1985. But this amendment, supported by three other people there, was finally——

Q. So it went down to the last half hour.

THE PRESIDENT. Yes, to the last half hour.

Q. Who offered the amendment?

Q. Margaret Thatcher?

THE PRESIDENT. I think I would rather not comment on who offered which amendment.

Q. Do you have a few choice words for Giscard?

THE PRESIDENT. No. We got along well.

Q. Got along well? [*Laughter*]

Q. Did you discuss the remarks that he made in the interview in Newsweek? [1]

THE PRESIDENT. I pointed out the great amount of attention that I have paid to the energy conservation effort in the United States since I've been in office, yes.

Q. What do you think that this will do to the American gas lines?

THE PRESIDENT. I don't think we can expect any immediate alleviation of the energy problem in the United States on a collective basis. We have not addressed the energy problem adequately in the past. The Congress has not been willing to pass a single line of legislation about oil, in spite of 2 years of importunities and requests. And this lack of action over a number of years has caught up with us. We have a limited amount of oil to distribute. And we can try to have an equitable allocation of oil between tractor fuel and diesel fuel for trucks and home heating oil and gasoline for motorists, but there is no easy answer to it. It's just going to take time.

But in my opinion, the deep commitment to restrain imports, the deep commitment to go to new forms of energy—synthetic fuels, the liquefaction and gas-

---

[1] In the interview, printed in the Newsweek issue of July 2, 1979, President Giscard d'Estaing criticized U.S. energy conservation efforts, as well as several aspects of U.S. foreign policy.

ification of oil [coal], oil derived from oil shale, tar sands in Canada, an increased use of coal, a commitment to solar energy—we'll do this in an accelerating way because of the newly aroused concern and commitment on the part of American people and the Congress. And this will be enhanced because it will be a multinational effort as well.

Q. Mr. President, do you have any plans to go back and discuss this on television in the United States or try to summarize this in any way?

THE PRESIDENT. I haven't discussed with Jody and Jerry yet exactly what and when. I think it would be better to let me reserve the answer to that question for a little bit later.

Q. Mr. President, can you tell us in any more detail how you persuaded, in particular, the Germans, because we know they came into the summit with a different attitude?

THE PRESIDENT. I think Henry Owen can give you that information at the general briefing this afternoon.

Q. But you've said that 8.5 will be the limit through 1985 from this point on?

THE PRESIDENT. That's correct.

Q. And the OPEC statement, which you think will be striking in its effect——

THE PRESIDENT. I think you'll see it is. In the past, it's been a difficult thing for an individual nation, highly vulnerable to the interruption of oil supplies, to make any sort of critical comment about OPEC action. You've observed that yourself. But the fact that Japan and Italy, for instance, who have practically no energy sources of their own, combined with France and Germany, Great Britain, Canada, and us—to make this strong statement, I think, is a very significant move. What the OPEC nations have done with their 60-percent increase in prices in the last 6 months has obviously had a disconcerting effect on the very strong industrialized nations. In some cases, it's had an almost devastating effect on the developing nations of the world.

One of the things that we considered in our private sessions, for instance, was that some countries now spend 100 percent of all their external earned income just to buy oil. And other countries, reasonably strong, like Brazil, that in 1973 were spending 10 percent of its earned income on oil, now spend 40 percent of its earned income on oil.

This is a potential catastrophe for the developing nations of the world, in spite of the fact that all of the industrialized countries are increasing our aid to the most severely impacted countries.

Q. Mr. President, before we came to the summit, we were told that any sort of a public confrontation with the OPEC countries would drive the moderate producers straight into the camp of the price hawks, if you will. Is it a situation now that they're going to do it anyway? They're going to have these price increases so the industrial countries have to get on the record with a strong response?

THE PRESIDENT. All of us recognize that Saudi Arabia, the Emirates, and maybe one or two others have been a moderating factor, but the final action of OPEC is what we have to address. And obviously, some of the more demanding members of OPEC would have had much higher prices than they have imposed. But I think that looking at the statement on OPEC from an historical point of view, it's a very significant and unprecedented action.

Q. Was there a lot of debate about the wisdom of doing it——

THE PRESIDENT. No.

Q. ——or did the sentiment for it grow sharply with the decision taken in Geneva?

THE PRESIDENT. The decision started out with a great deal of reluctance and timidity on the part of some, but after the actions were taken by OPEC and announced, and after reading their communique, there was a unanimous belief that we should have a strong statement.

Q. Which is to say, today?

THE PRESIDENT. Which is to say, today. And we instructed the Foreign Ministers, during the lunch hour, to prepare the statement. It was strengthened somewhat in the afternoon session, not weakened by anyone.

Q. Is it a statement, or does it call for any action?

THE PRESIDENT. It's a part of the communique, expressing our concern, deep concern about the unwarranted and damaging action of the OPEC countries in raising their prices.

Q. Mr. President, is there any room in all this for a dialog in the future with OPEC, with a meeting of some sort?

THE PRESIDENT. Well, the OPEC communique pretty well prohibits a dialog on the basis that we had contemplated. That was one of the attitudes of theirs which caused us some concern. But we're all obviously willing to have a dialog with the OPEC countries to see how the quantity of oil, the price of oil, and the consumption of oil can be stabilized. And this is something that we hope will develop in the future.

I think I need to go.

REPORTER. Thank you.

NOTE: The President spoke at 4:55 p.m. at the U.S. Ambassador's residence.

Tokyo Economic Summit Conference

Remarks to Reporters at the Conclusion of the Conference. June 29, 1979

PRIME MINISTER OHIRA. Now, then, I would like to open the joint press conference.

To this summit there have gathered a great number of members of the press from Japan and from outside Japan, and for showing your interest in what goes on in the summit, I would like to express our appreciation. Because of security considerations, we may have caused you many inconveniences, but I hope you understand this.

Our conference during the past 2 days has been extremely useful, but in order for the fruit of our discussions to be appreciated in various parts of the world, much depends on you members of the press. I would be grateful for your cooperation.

I am going to shortly ask various heads of state and government to speak, but as the host, I would first like to give my overall evaluation.

In this summit we have welcomed three new members, of whom one is the first woman Prime Minister to the summit and the other is the youngest Prime Minister. The two new Prime Ministers have contributed much to the success of the conference with their charm and wisdom. The third new member is somewhat older, me, and I would refrain from making any comment.

Although nearly half of the members in this summit are new, I believe our summit has been able to create an extremely close human relation on the basis of the spirit of mutual support of the summit, which I believe is an important product of our endeavor.

This summit has been held as it was at the time when the attention of the world is focused on the oil problem. In order to respond to the situation, it has been said that our summit will be a failure unless bold and concrete measures are agreed upon.

Shortly the communique will be distributed to you, but from the viewpoint of both immediate measures and medium- and long-term points of view, I believe we have been able to reach concrete consensus that can respond to meet the expectations of the world.

As the Prime Minister of Japan, to give the specific goal of our effort to the year 1985 has taken considerable amount of courage, but recognizing the fact that we all live in a global community faced with the oil anxiety, and recognizing the need for placing our economy on a stable basis well into the future, I felt it was necessary for us to agree to that statement.

In areas other than oil, we have discussed questions such as inflation and employment, showing strong interest in protecting industrial democracies, from long-term and fundamental points of view. Although industrialized economies find ourselves in respective economic difficulties, the summit leaders have shown strong interest in the relationship with the developing nations. I have found this very encouraging. The old economies of the world are in the same boat. By sharing the new sense of responsibility and new sense of partnership, I would like to see the constructive relationship and cooperation be developed further.

Further, in the present summit, following up on what was taken up in the last summit in Bonn, we adopted a statement on air hijacking, which I will now read.

"All the heads of state and government"—excuse me, I take it back; I have the wrong text in front of me. [*Laughter*]

This is concerning the statement. At the request of heads of state and government who participated in the summit, I, in my capacity of chairman of the meeting, am pleased to make the following statement which concerns the declaration of air hijacking issued in Bonn in July 1978. I now read the statement.

"The heads of state and government express their pleasure with the broad support expressed by other states for the declaration on hijacking made at the Bonn Summit in July 1978.

"They noted that procedures for the prompt implementation of the declaration have been agreed upon and that to date enforcement measures under the declaration have not been necessary.

"They also noted with satisfaction the widespread adherence to the conventions dealing with unlawful interference with international civil aviation. Extensive support for these conventions and the Bonn declaration on hijacking reflects the acceptance by the international community as a whole of the principles expressed therein."

That is the statement.

Also, in the present summit, we have adopted a special statement on the question of refugees from Indochina,[1] which is

another major fruit. Japan itself feels we must make our utmost contribution to the solution of this problem, and I would like to see that the statement be transmitted to other various countries and various international organizations and invite their further participation in international efforts on this question.

This has been an unprecedentedly important international event, but this Tokyo summit has now come to its safe and successful conclusion, and next year we have unanimously agreed to meet again in Italy. We look forward to our reunion in Italy.

And I would like to take this opportunity to express our heartfelt appreciation to all the people, both within and without Japan, who have supported this meeting. Because we have taken unexpected, unprecedentedly elaborate security measures in connection with the convening of this summit—and I know we have dealt inconveniences with many people, but because of their cooperation we have been able to successfully carry this conference. I thank all of these people concerned.

Thank you very much.

---

[1] [Issued on June 28 by the seven nations meeting at the Tokyo Economic Summit.]

STATEMENT ON INDOCHINESE REFUGEE CRISIS

The plight of refugees from Vietnam, Laos and Cambodia poses a humanitarian problem of historic proportions and constitutes a threat to the peace and stability of Southeast Asia. Given the tragedy and suffering which are taking place, the problem calls for an immediate and major response.

The Heads of State and Government call on Vietnam and other countries of Indochina to take urgent and effective measures so that the present human hardship and suffering are eliminated. They confirm the great importance they attach to the immediate cessation of the disorderly outflow of refugees without prejudice

to the principles of free emigration and family reunification.

The governments represented will, as part of an international effort, significantly increase their contribution to Indochinese refugee relief and resettlement by making more funds available and by admitting more people, while taking into account the existing social and economic circumstances in each of their countries.

The Heads of State and Government request the Secretary-General of the United Nations to convene a conference as soon as possible with a view to attaining concrete and positive results. They extend full support to this objective and are ready to participate constructively in such a conference.

The Heads of State and Government call on all nations to join in addressing this pressing problem.

PRESIDENT GISCARD D'ESTAING. Ladies and gentlemen, I think that we can say that the Tokyo summit has indeed achieved the aims that had been set. The leaders of the major industrialized nations, also the major consumers of oil, have done what might have been expected of them.

Faced by difficult situations, they have demonstrated their sense of responsibility and their courage—and I am speaking, of course, of my partners—by agreeing to enter into specific commitments after discussions that at times were difficult. But it must be recognized the subject and the situation are both difficult, too.

For the first time since the onset of the energy crisis 6 years ago, we agreed to adopt a joint attitude, a common attitude on three essential points. And indeed, what was expected of us? A commitment on limits of imported oil, a massive effort to develop alternative energy sources, and, lastly, an effort to eliminate practices conducive to excessively high prices on the oil markets.

Now we have agreed to limit quantities of oil that are imported, in the short term, in 1979 and in 1980, and also in the medium term, 1985. We jointly agreed on quantified targets, country by country. As far as the European Community is concerned, these targets, of course, comply with the targets and aims defined in Strasbourg.

Secondly, efforts to develop alternative energy sources. First of all, those that are available—coal and nuclear generated electricity, and a very substantial program for the technological development of new energy sources. Lastly, eliminating practices that have led to speculative increases in prices on some markets.

So, I think that it can be said that our countries have taken the decisions that they were able to take. But we know that this is only one part of the problem, because we do not hold the key to the energy problem among ourselves alone. And I hope that our sense of responsibility will be met by an equal sense of responsibility by those who also hold part of the key to the problem. And as Acting President of the Council of the European Economic Community, I would like to emphasize the role that has been played by the Community.

First of all, by arriving at an agreement in Strasbourg last week among the nine members of the Community, which was part of our preparations for the Tokyo meeting, and then by arriving at an agreement among the seven of us here, that this, of course, presupposed that our partners were prepared, ready, and willing to collaborate, that is to say, Japan, the United States, and Canada.

Now, there remains a great deal for us to do, it cannot be denied, in order to define the paths to be followed by the world economy. Growth that at the same time is energy saving, growth that is perhaps more steady, less spectacular. We are going to have to work a lot; we are going to have to invent a lot; we are going to have to improvise; we are going to have to change a number of the habits that grew up when times were easier. But we have tackled the problems in an orderly fashion and standing together. And this is what our Tokyo agreement means to us.

And I would like to add, with your permission, Mr. Chairman, three comments. Firstly, I would like to express our concern with regard to the situation of non-oil-producing, developing countries. Their situation is very much more difficult, very much more painful, very often, than ours. And this is why in discussions over the past 2 days, we have sought to bear their situation in mind, and we must ensure that the approaches that are adopted do take account of their particular difficulties.

I would like to emphasize the importance we attach to the statement adopted, the declaration we have adopted on refugees from Indochina, and certainly France will maintain its efforts to support and welcome in the refugees of Indochina.

And then, Mr. Chairman, we would like to thank you for your hospitality in Tokyo, worthy of the reputation of the Japanese for hospitality, and we would like to thank you for the important contribution you made to the success of our conference.

I would also like to ask you to express our thanks to his Majesty the Emperor of Japan for the welcome he extended to us yesterday evening.

Thank you, Mr. Chairman.

PRESIDENT CARTER. First of all, I would like to add my word of thanks to Prime Minister Ohira, to the officials of Japan, to His Majesty the Emperor, to the people of Japan who have made this conference possible, and who have also welcomed us for an official state visit.

In my own opinion, this economic summit conference might be proven in history to have a historic meaning for most of the people on Earth. We are in trouble as we approach increasing shortages of energy and rapidly increasing prices for energy. But we have decided individually and collectively not to despair, but to take action which will be meaningful and which might very well encourage others to emulate the decisions that we ourselves have made.

We recognize the seriousness of the energy question. And we have decided to act as individual nations and also as a group of nations to try to resolve this difficulty with minimum adverse effect on the people whom we represent.

One of the most difficult decisions for us, which we finally did make, was to adopt individual national goals for limiting imports of oil for 1979, 1980, and all the way through until 1985. These goals are not expressed in generalities. They will be expressed in specific terms. They are quite substantive commitments, tangible and restrictive.

In addition, we committed ourselves individually and collectively to the rapid development of alternate supplies of energy, to increase our own production of oil and gas when we have it available, to increase the production and use of coal, taking care to protect the quality of the environment, to emphasize synthetic fuel development, oil to be derived from shale, tar sands, solar power, nuclear power with a special emphasis on safety—these types of commitments have been thoroughly discussed and will be binding upon us in the future.

We also address a difficult problem of marketing procedures, so that after the price of oil is established at the source, there will be a minimum unnecessary increase in the price of oil during the marketing and delivery process.

I think for the first time publicly a group of responsible leaders representing industrial countries have spoken out forcefully and expressed our concern about the recent action of the OPEC nations. Just quoting a few words from the communique which I think are significant—"We deplore the decisions taken by the recent OPEC Conference"—we refer to the unwarranted rises in oil prices and point out the serious economic and social consequences of these decisions. We emphasize that this will result in a worldwide inflation, less growth, more unemployment, will endanger the stability of the economic system of the world, and particularly emphasized, as the President of France has already said, the adverse impact on the developing nations of the world, who don't share the wealth that some of us have.

The refugee question was discussed with attention and concern and compassion for those who are suffering. We have collectively called on Vietnam and others who create the source of the refugee problem to try to help in dealing with it in a humane and effective way. And we have all discussed what we might do as individual nations to alleviate this problem.

Our country has accepted 220,000 refugees from Southeast Asia. We are taking in now about 7,000 per month. I have committed my Nation yesterday to double this rate and to accept 14,000 refugees per month.

We have also, I think in almost every debate—quite different from my own previous experience in conferences—moved toward the boldest position, the most constructive position, the most specific position, and the most tangible position. We've not yielded to compromise by going into generalities.

I think when you read the communique, you'll discover that what I have said is accurate. In my opinion, because of these reasons and others, I consider this summit conference to have been very successful.

PRIME MINISTER OHIRA. Thank you, President Carter.

CHANCELLOR SCHMIDT. Mr. Chairman, I would first of all like to thank you for your hospitality, the hospitality that has been extended to us, and for your chairmanship of this fifth economic summit. I would like to say that our chairman, Prime Minister Ohira, has contributed significantly to the success of our conference.

I would also, like the speakers before me, like to express my warm thanks for the hospitality of the Japanese people as a whole and particularly for the hospitality of His Majesty the Emperor. And to that, I might add that I would like to thank you for the effective and very courteous work of the security forces.

As far as the substance of our work is concerned, we have arrived at compromises among ourselves. We have found common denominators, and the basis of the energy policy of our countries for the years ahead has been laid down jointly. However, I would also like to say that it is very pleasing, very satisfying to me to find in our communique a number of the positions that the Government of the Federal Republic of Germany has been advancing both within Germany and abroad for some years.

The readiness to compromise is essential to a successful economic summit, and this is demonstrated by the fact that we Europeans—this is true also for my country, the Federal Republic of Germany—that we have successfully sought to arrive at common positions. This has not always been easy for the four member countries of the European Community represented here. President Giscard d'Estaing has already made this point for the Federal Republic of Germany, for France, for Italy, and for the United Kingdom. We have to follow up the decisions that were taken by the European Council a week ago in Strasbourg.

And we have jointly agreed to limit our oil imports through to 1985. Here we have ensured that we have not prejudiced the interest of those partners of the European Community who were not with us yesterday and today. But we have based ourselves on the decisions taken at the Strasbourg meeting.

These limitations upon our oil imports, which have been decided through to 1985, will, as President Carter has just said, mean that our economies, indeed, our societies as a whole, will have to undergo far-reaching changes, and that means far-reaching efforts.

It is quite clear to us, and we hope that it will be quite clear to all our citizens, that after the Tokyo agreement, we are then going to have to proceed more rapidly to achieving our oil targets than we had imagined even quite recently. We are compelled to do this by the new unjustified price increases adopted by OPEC. The communique that we publish today clearly indicates the joint general approach to energy problems and the economy generally.

And the Federal Republic of Germany has, since 1973, been following a clear energy policy, and today's decisions do not require us in any way to change that. But we are going to have to substantially step up our efforts in the Federal Republic, and there fine words are going to be of little use to us. And in my country, we are going to continue to stick to the basic outlines of our energy policy, the one we have been following for some years. That is a policy which aims at oil substitution in various ways, stepping up the domestic production of coal. Thirdly, a policy aimed at extending the necessary extension of the generation of electricity from nuclear sources. Fourth, a greatly strengthened research and technological policy aimed at making energy savings and at opening up new energy sources.

These goals have been ours for many years, but now we are going to have to tackle them with increased energy, and we are going to have to step up our efforts at achieving them. But the most important impetus can't come from the state; it must come from the citizens, from industry to save energy, to be economical in the use of energy, not just because energy is increasingly expensive but also because energy is going to be increasingly rare, there is going to be an increasing shortage of energy throughout the world.

I would also clearly like to say to President Giscard d'Estaing, nobody must be misled if we, the industrial countries, manage to limit our use of energy, our consumption of energy, into thinking that the several countries who are aiming at development, development to which we contribute, who have increasing energy requirements, and for which we feel a certain political and moral responsibility, that must not be thought that if we save energy, if we can substitute for oil other energy sources—we must not be misled into thinking that we are thinking only of ourselves and our needs, but also the very difficult circumstances in which the developing countries find themselves.

And, indeed, in this connection, I would like to warn everybody against thinking that increased energy costs, increased energy difficulties can be avoided, and that one can indeed genuinely derive benefits from these enhanced, increased energy costs.

I think that we must all jointly tackle the problems posed. I think that we must approach the situation in sober fashion, that it would be unwise to be carried away. We must, in our industrial life, in our economic life, in our political life, and indeed in our private activities, maintain a sober, clear attitude, for our nations, for our people, for our economies, for governments, and for parliaments.

All of this means that we are going to have to work very much harder, and we are going to have to make very considerable efforts to embody in practice the outcome of the Tokyo agreement.

As far as my own country, the Federal

Republic of Germany, is concerned, I shall, at the beginning of next week, make a statement before the German parliament, before the Bundestag, in which I will explain the conclusions that we must draw in order to embody in practice what has been recognized and decided in Tokyo. This is an aim we set ourselves, and I am fully convinced that we are going to be able to overcome the problem.

Thank you very much.

PRIME MINISTER ANDREOTTI. I wish to associate myself with the words of thanks which have been spoken to the Japanese Government and the Imperial Court, and to the Government.

I was here 15 years ago for the Olympic Games, and I was able to see that more problems are produced for the police by the heads of states rather than so many thousands of athletes.

President Giscard and the others who have spoken before me have told you of the results achieved in these 2 days. I would confine myself to two comments of a political nature.

Every year we meet to study our problems of growth, of the struggle against unemployment, the fight against inflation, but every year increasingly I see that all our discussions develop not within the limited interests of the seven countries which come together, but within a framework of a far more general character. And it is most important that the energy policy should have been the subject of concrete agreements between we European countries, between the United States and Canada, and also with Japan.

We had some doubts as to whether we should succeed in this, and these doubts have been dissipated. But as Chancellor Schmidt has said, we have always borne in mind all the time throughout these 2 days the need for a consensus policy. And in embarking in a discussion with the oil-producing countries—but here this is not only a question of the countries where oil is produced but with enormous international interests which often regulate the market, and in the communique, you will find a clear expression of our intention better to appreciate and assess this complicated oil market. But our concern is for those countries who are the poorest and who feel more than us the consequences of decisions to raise the price both of oil and other essential commodities.

This year, too, in the communique, emphasis was placed on a policy in favor of developing countries, expressing a wish which I think has political value that all the countries, even those which are differently governed than ours, should cooperate in this broad design for development for humanity as a whole.

Our peoples must be accustomed, become accustomed not only to look at those who are better off than us but those who are worse off than us, and I know that this is not something which is easy to do. It isn't the popular thing to do, but it is the spirit which I think moves and animates our annual meetings. And I think that this should be brought out, and recognition should be made of those who are cooperating in this annual opportunity to study together problems which are old problems and problems which are arising.

Finally, may I thank all of the heads of state and the heads of government who have agreed to accept the invitation to travel in May 1980 to Venice for the new meeting of the summit.

Let us express the hope that there will not be moments of crisis that we shall have to face and that, on the other hand, we can resume in a spirit of greater tranquility a discussion of the global developments. And I hope that you journalists, that to you journalists, we should be able in Venice to give you the help and the hospitality which I think is extremely important, because if that is lacking, even the positive results of the conference are not made known adequately.

Thank you.

PRIME MINISTER OHIRA. Thank you very much, Prime Minister Andreotti.

PRIME MINISTER THATCHER. Prime Minister, friends of the press, my colleagues have already given you the bare bones of the communique and some of the details as well and have set out the course which this historic summit took. I, of course, endorse everything they've said, and I thought therefore it would be best if I tried just to step back and look at this summit meeting in slightly wider perspective.

I think first if we look at this summit meeting as one of the fourth quarter of this century, we see how very different the problems are from those which we encountered in the third quarter of this century. Then we were trying to restore the economy of the free world to try to harness everything that it can do to give a higher standard of living to our people and to try to see that we got as much growth as it was possible to get. Perhaps the country where we're meeting is an excellent example of how successful the free economy could be and of how much growth could be obtained and how much growth the free world had during those years of the third quarter of this century.

Because of its very success, we now come into new problems. Part of its very success gives us a problem over the consumption of oil. It will also give us a problem over the shortage of some other commodities. And so, in this quarter of the century—and this summit is an example of it—we really are facing very different problems. No longer can we assume automatically that growth will go on if

we order our economies properly. All of a sudden we've been brought face to face with these shortages and the problems that they will mean for all of us for the standard of living for our own peoples and for the possibility of rising standard of living for those in countries less fortunate than ourselves. And really this summit was an example of how to tackle the problems of the moment, and today the problem is energy, but it won't only be today. It'll be the same problem for a number of years.

And so, we tackled it in two ways. First, to try to deal with the immediate problem, very ironic in a way that we were meeting the very day that OPEC announced its price increases. So, we had an immediate problem to tackle, and we did tackle it in the way that my colleagues have announced, by trying to set specific targets, not only for this year but for future years, to demonstrate to those suppliers that we are determined to cut down demand and limit it as far as we can and make the best, most economical use of energy.

But secondly, we're determined not to be so reliant on that source of energy, because we know that twice in this very decade, the free world has shown how vulnerable it is to the increase in the price of oil, and we know how damaging that can be to our countries.

So, my first point is, looking at it in historical perspective, we recognize that the problems we face now are very different from those we faced in the third quarter of the century, and we have demonstrated our will to meet the problems of the day and to tackle them in the way my colleagues have described.

And my second point is this: Among us, there are three producer oil countries, and there are four who are consumer countries. You might think that our interests are different. They're not. What this particular conference has demonstrated is that our interests are very similar indeed. I represent Great Britain, a comparatively new producer country. But my interests as a citizen of Great Britain are just exactly the same as those of our colleagues represented here, because if oil takes too large a slice of the world's income, it will affect us all.

It will affect us in many ways. We, like Japan, have to export to live. If other countries have to pay so much for their oil, they haven't enough left to import the goods which we wish to export, and the same problem affects the developing countries. So, we're affected in that way.

We're affected in another way, that any action taken by a group of nations which severely cuts the possibility of a rising standard of living introduces an element of political instability into the world, and that, too, affects us all.

And then, perhaps in a different way we all recognize that though we are facing economic problems from shortage of energy and the rising price of oil, twice in this decade those economic problems have been caused by political problems. And we must also, if we're to solve our economic problems, look to solving them by way of a solution to the political problems of the world as well.

But the second point is that although we were three producer countries, our interests were just the same as those of all of the seven countries represented here and the rest of the Community, equally represented for the President of the Community and the President of the Commission.

The third point, the third general theme I wish to make is this: We met here under those very, very difficult circumstances. And the reason for seven countries meeting under these circumstances is this: that we believe we can give a clear lead; that if we make the right decisions, we can have some effect on the future course of the world and some effect on the destiny of our peoples.

That meant that we really had to get down to business in a very certain way. We had to reach, as President Carter and President Giscard have said, specific targets, give clear general directions of what governments can do and what governments can't. I believe that that has been achieved.

We also made one further point: The last time we had an oil crisis, we tried somehow to accommodate, some of us, the increase in oil price by printing money. If we do that again, we shall have much, much worse inflation, and we shall finish up with even worse problems than we encountered before. So, in that community you will find resolution that we accept for the time being that if we have to pay a lot more for oil, this means that we have, in fact, a reduction in our genuine income in terms of what it will buy for the future.

Nevertheless, perhaps because we're leaders, it didn't depress us. It means that we have to tackle the problems of growth in another way. And the only way you can ever tackle the problems of growth is to face the situation realistically, and that we have done at this summit.

So, Mr. Chairman, my contribution is those three points. In historical perspective and facing our new problems, first; secondly, that our interests are as one—no country is an island, and I think I'm the right country to say that—no country is an island in its interests, and we are not any more than Japan is. Our interests are together. And our future prosperity and happiness and success of our people will only be achieved together and in concert with other nations, including those not represented here. And thirdly, that we did try to give a lead in these very difficult world problems.

Finally, Mr. Chairman, may I join my colleagues in thanking the Emperor for his wonderful hospitality, in thanking you, Mr. Prime Minister, for steering us through sometimes very difficult debates to a successful and succinct communique—and I'm particularly pleased about the "succinct," as well as the "successful"—to thank also the security forces, who've made a tremendous effort, and to thank all of the administrative staff, who've attended to every meticulous detail.

We thank you for your generosity, for your kindness, and we wish you well in the future.

Thank you.

PRIME MINISTER OHIRA. Thank you.

Prime Minister Clark?

PRIME MINISTER CLARK. Thank you very much, Mr. Prime Minister. And as the Prime Minister of a nation that is a good neighbor to Japan, separated only by a little bit of ocean, I wanted to begin by expressing on behalf of the government and the people of Canada my very real congratulations to you personally and to your colleagues in government, and our very real appreciation to the people of Japan for the excellent way in which arrangements have been made for a summit that I think the world will see is an historic summit.

[*In French*] For Canada this summit was of the greatest importance, since the main issue to be discussed was energy. Canada, in fact, is privileged, since it has abundant energy resources, and it is incumbent upon us to develop them as fast as possible for our own use as well as for other countries.[1]

----

[1] Translation provided by the Canadian Embassy in the United States.

[*In English*] My Government consequently is going to take all necessary action to achieve our own domestic goals of energy self-sufficiency for 1990. The work of this summit meeting provides a solid foundation from which we can launch this major Canadian effort.

In the immediate future, we in Canada are faced with the problem of declining oil production in our major producing province of Alberta. Until the mid-1980's, our oil production from conventional sources in that Province will decline and decline dramatically. Consequently, imports into Canada must rise.

[*At this point, the Prime Minister again spoke in French. He then translated his remarks as follows.*]

Faced with the world oil shortage and in our own economic interests, I am firmly decided to keep imports as low as possible. We shall achieve this target by accelerating our energy conservation program, replacing oil by other energy sources, and by developing as quickly as possible energy sources of nonconventional character.

In keeping with that commitment, I have pledged Canada at this summit to reduce our net oil imports in 1985 to 600,000 barrels per day, from the projected need of 650,000 barrels per day.

Now, I'm convinced, Mr. Chairman, and colleagues, that working together, the countries represented at this summit will deal effectively with the energy problems now facing us. I'm convinced that, working together, all of the people of my country in Canada will be able to achieve the goals which we have established here of moving towards energy self-sufficiency.

Now, while we have all, throughout the summit, been very concerned about the impact of the energy situation on industrialized countries of the world, I am very pleased that attention has also been paid to the special energy problems of the

Third World, and that we have also called the attention of the world to the appalling refugee situation in Southeast Asia and requested immediate action both as to the cause and to the consequences of that tragedy.

Thank you, Mr. Chairman.

PRIME MINISTER OHIRA. Thank you very much.

Lastly, but not the least, Mr. Jenkins.

PRESIDENT JENKINS. Mr. Prime Minister, ladies and gentlemen, at this stage there is little to add, and I believe that brevity will be more valued than any other quality.

Like the heads of state and government who have spoken before me, I am glad that we have been able to concentrate on the challenge of the energy crisis and agree on medium-term goals for oil imports, as well as for conservation and new development measures in the energy field.

I take satisfaction in the fact that the work done by the European Council at Strasbourg provided such a good foundation for and contribution to the results of this summit. Here in Tokyo, the industrialized nations have, I believe, put themselves in a better position to deal with the inevitable damage caused to us by scarce and expensive oil. We have done so without forgetting the still worse, indeed potentially crushing impact upon the developing countries, and we have done so in the knowledge that we must follow our words with action if they are to succeed.

I add my thanks to the Emperor, to the Prime Minister, the Government and people of Japan for the welcome they have given us.

PRIME MINISTER OHIRA. Thank you very much, President Jenkins.

Ladies and gentlemen, this closes the joint press conference.

Thank you very much for your attention.

NOTE: Prime Minister Masayoshi Ohira of Japan, chairman of the Conference, spoke at 5:35 p.m. in the Banquet Room at the New Otani Hotel. He spoke in Japanese. President Valéry Giscard d'Estaing of France, Chancellor Helmut Schmidt of the Federal Republic of Germany, and Prime Minister Giulio Andreotti of Italy also spoke in their native languages. The translations of their remarks follow the press release.

President Carter, Prime Minister Margaret Thatcher of the United Kingdom, Prime Minister Joe Clark of Canada, and Roy Jenkins, President of the Commission of the European Communities, spoke in English.

The remarks of the participants concluded 2 days of meetings, consisting of four sessions, at the Akasaka Palace. On the evening of the first day's meetings, the conference participants attended a state dinner, hosted by Emperor Hirohito, at the Imperial Palace.

Tokyo Economic Summit Conference

Declaration Issued at the Conclusion of the Conference. June 29, 1979

The Heads of State and Government of Canada, the Federal Republic of Germany, France, Italy, Japan, the United Kingdom of Great Britain and Northern Ireland, and the United States of America met in Tokyo on the 28th and 29th of June, 1979. The European Community was represented by the President of the European Council and by the President of the European Commission for discussion of matters within the Community's competence.

1. The agreements reached at the Bonn Summit helped to improve the world economy. There was higher growth in some countries, a reduction of payments imbalances, and greater currency stability.

2. But new challenges have arisen. Inflation, which was subsiding in most countries, is now regaining its momentum. Higher oil prices and oil shortage have reduced the room for maneuver in economic policy in all our countries. They will make inflation worse and curtail growth, in both the industrial and developing countries. The non-oil developing countries are among the biggest sufferers.

We are agreed on a common strategy to attack these problems. The most urgent tasks are to reduce oil consumption and to hasten the development of other energy sources.

Our countries have already taken significant actions to reduce oil consumption. We will intensify these efforts.

The European Community has decided to restrict 1979 oil consumption to 500 million tons (10 million barrels a day) and to maintain Community oil imports between 1980 and 1985 at an annual level not higher than in 1978. The Community is monitoring this commitment and France, Germany, Italy and the United Kingdom have agreed to recommend to their Community partners that each member country's contribution to these annual levels will be specified. Canada, Japan, and the US will each achieve the adjusted import levels to which they are pledged in IEA for 1979, will maintain their imports in 1980 at a level not higher than these 1979 levels, and will be monitoring this.

The seven countries express their will to take as goals for a ceiling on oil imports in 1985, the following figures:

—For France, Germany, Italy*, and the United Kingdom: the 1978 figure.

—Canada whose oil production will be

---

*Footnote: Italy's commitment with reference to the 1978 level is accepted in the context of the overall commitment of the European Community.

declining dramatically over the period between now and 1985, will reduce its annual average rate of growth of oil consumption to 1%, with the consequent reduction of oil imports by 50,000 barrels per day by 1985. Canada's targets for imports will therefore be 0.6 million barrels per day.

—Japan adopts as a 1985 target a level not to exceed the range between 6.3 and 6.9 million barrels a day. Japan will review this target periodically and make it more precise in the light of current developments and growth projections, and do their utmost to reduce oil imports through conservation, rationalization of use and intensive development of alternative energy sources in order to move toward lower figures.

—The United States adopts as a goal for 1985 import levels not to exceed the levels either of 1977 or the adjusted target for 1979, i.e. 8.5 million barrels per day.

These 1985 goals will serve as reference to monitor both energy conservation and the development of alternative energy sources.

A high level group of representatives of our countries and of the EEC Commission, within the OECD, will review periodically the results achieved. Slight adjustments will be allowed to take account of special needs generated by growth.

In fulfilling these commitments, our guiding principle will be to obtain fair supplies of oil products for all countries, taking into account the differing patterns of supply, the efforts made to limit oil imports, the economic situation of each country, the quantities of oil available, and the potential of each country for energy conservation.

We urge other industrialized countries to set similar objectives for themselves.

We agree to take steps to bring into

the open the working of oil markets by setting up a register of international oil transactions. We will urge oil companies and oil-exporting countries to moderate spot market transactions. We will consider the feasibility of requiring that at the time of unloading crude oil cargoes, documents be presented indicating the purchase price as certified by the producer country. We will likewise seek to achieve better information on the profit situation of oil companies and on the use of the funds available to these companies.

We agree on the importance of keeping domestic oil prices at world market prices or raising them to this level as soon as possible. We will seek to minimize and finally eliminate administrative action that might put upward pressure on oil prices that result from domestic underpricing of oil and to avoid new subsidies which would have the same effect.

Our countries will not buy oil for governmental stockpiles when this would place undue pressure on prices; we will consult about the decisions that we make to this end.

3. We pledge our countries to increase as far as possible coal use, production, and trade, without damage to the environment. We will endeavor to substitute coal for oil in the industrial and electrical sectors, encourage the improvement of coal transport, maintain positive attitudes toward investment for coal projects, pledge not to interrupt coal trade under long-term contracts unless required to do so by a national emergency, and maintain, by measures which do not obstruct coal imports, those levels of domestic coal production which are desirable for reasons of energy, regional and social policy.

We need to expand alternative sources of energy, especially those which will help to prevent further pollution, particularly increases of carbon dioxide and sulphur oxides in the atmosphere.

Without the expansion of nuclear power generating capacity in the coming decades, economic growth and higher employment will be hard to achieve. This must be done under conditions guaranteeing our people's safety. We will cooperate to this end. The International Atomic Energy Agency can play a key role in this regard.

We reaffirm the understanding reached at the Bonn Summit with respect to the reliable supply of nuclear fuel and minimizing the risk of nuclear proliferation.

New technologies in the field of energy are the key to the world's longer-term freedom from fuel crises. Large public and private resources will be required for the development and commercial application of those technologies. We will ensure that these resources are made available. An International Energy Technology Group linked to the OECD, IEA and other appropriate international organizations will be created to review the actions being taken or planned domestically by each of our countries, and to report on the need and potential for international collaboration, including financing.

We deplore the decisions taken by the recent OPEC Conference. We recognise that relative moderation was displayed by certain of the participants. But the unwarranted rises in oil prices nevertheless agreed are bound to have very serious economic and social consequences. They mean more world-wide inflation and less growth. That will lead to more unemployment, more balance of payments difficulty and will endanger stability in developing and developed countries of the world alike. We remain ready to examine with oil exporting countries how to define supply and demand prospects on the world oil market.

4. We agree that we should continue with the policies for our economies agreed at Bonn, adjusted to reflect current circumstances. Energy shortages and high oil prices have caused a real transfer of incomes. We will try, by our domestic economic policies, to minimize the damage to our economies. But our options are limited. Attempts to compensate for the damage by matching income increases would simply add to inflation.

5. We agree that we must do more to improve the long-term productive efficiency and flexibility of our economies. The measures needed may include more stimulus for investment and for research and development; steps to make it easier for capital and labor to move from declining to new industries; regulatory policies which avoid unnecessary impediments to investment and productivity; reduced growth in some public sector current expenditures; and removal of impediments to the international flow of trade and capital.

6. The agreements reached in the Tokyo Round are an important achievement. We are committed to their early and faithful implementation. We renew our determination to fight protectionism. We want to strengthen the GATT, both to monitor the agreements reached in the MTNs and as an instrument for future policy in maintaining the open world trading system. We will welcome the full participation of as many countries as possible in these agreements and in the system as a whole.

7. We will intensify our efforts to pursue the economic policies appropriate in each of our countries to achieve durable external equilibrium. Stability in the foreign exchange market is essential for the sound development of world trade and the global economy. This has been furthered since the Bonn Summit by two important developments—the November 1st 1978 program of the United States in conjunction with other monetary authorities, and the successful emergence of the European Monetary System. We will continue close cooperation in exchange market policies and in support of the effective discharge by the IMF of its responsibilities, particularly its surveillance role and its role in strengthening further the international monetary system.

8. Constructive North-South relations are essential to the health of the world economy. We for our part have consistently worked to bring developing countries more fully into the open world trading system and to adjust our economies to changing international circumstances. The problems we face are global. They can only be resolved through shared responsibility and partnership. But this partnership cannot depend solely on the efforts of the industrialized countries. The OPEC countries have just as important a role to play. The latest decision substantially to increase oil prices will also severely increase the problems facing developing countries without oil resources as well as the difficulties for developed countries in helping them. The decision could even have a crippling effect on some of the developing countries. In this situation, we recognize, in particular, the need for the flow of financial resources to the developing countries to increase, including private and public, bilateral and multilateral resources. A good investment climate in developing countries will help the flow of foreign investment.

We are deeply concerned about the millions of people still living in conditions of absolute poverty. We will take particular account of the poorest countries in our aid programs.

Once more we urge COMECON countries to play their part.

We will place more emphasis on co-operation with developing countries in overcoming hunger and malnutrition. We will urge multilateral organizations to help these countries to develop effective food sector strategies and to build up the storage capacity needed for strong national food reserves. Increased bilateral and multilateral aid for agricultural research will be particularly important. In these and other ways we will step up our efforts to help these countries develop their human resources, through technical cooperation adapted to local conditions.

We will also place special emphasis on helping developing countries to exploit their energy potential. We strongly support the World Bank's program for hydrocarbon exploitation and urge its expansion. We will do more to help developing countries increase the use of renewable energy; we welcome the World Bank's coordination of these efforts.

Camp Casey, Republic of Korea

Remarks at the Welcoming Ceremony.
June 30, 1979

This is an exciting time in the life of me as President of our country.

I've come here for two reasons. Basically, one is to express my deep thanks to all of you for your tremendous, courageous service to our country, and the second, in the hopes that if the Commander in Chief could come here, your messhall might eventually be completed. [*Laughter*]

I want particularly to express my thanks to those who ran with me this morning. I'm much better at competing with you in running than I would be in boxing. [*Laughter*] I've heard from your very unbiased commanding officer that when you compete in boxing, the match never lasts more than one round, and I want to congratulate you for that as well.

The next time I come back, I'll run in combat boots and let you run in running shoes. Maybe it'll be more even. But I'll only run against those who are 55 years old. [*Laughter*]

I am very proud to stand before you as Commander in Chief, proud of our country, and proud of you, the historic combat record that you exemplify in your present service, and proud of your superb commander, General Kingston, who in my opinion represents the finest in military service.

As you know, the Signal Corps plays the closest possible role to a President. Wherever I go, either at the White House, in remote areas of the world, I must have instant communication throughout the entire world with others. I've seen the special accomplishment that you yourselves have realized under the most difficult simulated combat conditions in recent maneuvers. More battles have been won or lost because of the quality of communications than perhaps because of any other single factor. And so you represent the key to victory or defeat, and with your superb record, this would enhance our chance for victory.

I know that all of you serving so far from home miss your families. I served for 11 years in the Navy, and that was perhaps the worst part of my life—being away from home, being away from those I love. But I can assure you that those of you who serve here are never forgotten by those in our own home, in your homes, or throughout our country.

Thirty years ago, on this remote peninsula, 50,000 young Americans gave their lives for principles in which we still believe, the principle that people should be permitted to live in peace, free of the threat of successful aggression, and the right to live in freedom.

We have since that time maintained peace, a fragile peace, not ever completely free of challenge or danger. But America is a nation that is strong. We maintain our strength, not because we love war or because we desire war, but because we are committed to peace. And we know that peace can only be maintained with strength.

As I shook hands with the fine young men this morning, they all gave a slogan that is typical, I think, not only of you but of our country as well—"Fit to Fight." I have no doubt that you are fit to fight. And I can assure you, as President, that our Nation is also fit to fight, and we will avoid combat by maintaining our strength.

We believe in certain very precious principles—equality, justice, freedom, the preservation of basic human rights, and we also believe in standing by our allies.

You represent the finest of America, and I am deeply proud to be the President and to be Commander in Chief of men and women like you.

Thank you for honoring me by this ceremony this morning. God bless every one of you. Thanks from the bottom of my heart.

Thank you.

NOTE: The President spoke at 7:10 a.m. at Robertson Memorial Field after reviewing the troops. Following his remarks, the President had breakfast in the messhall with members of the 122d Signal Battalion, and then returned to Seoul.

The President had arrived in Seoul on the evening of June 29. He was met at Kimpo International Airport by President Park Chung Hee and then went to Camp Casey, where he stayed overnight at the residence of Gen. Robert C. Kingston, Commanding General, 2d Infantry Division.

Seoul, Republic of Korea
Toasts at the State Dinner.   June 30, 1979

PRESIDENT PARK. *Mr. President, Mrs. Carter, distinguished guests, ladies and gentlemen:*

This evening, we are honored to have as our guests the leader of our closest ally and the champion of world peace, President Jimmy Carter of the United States, and Mrs. Carter. It gives me a great pleasure to extend to them a heartfelt welcome on behalf of all my fellow countrymen.

I am very happy that this afternoon I had a sincere and fruitful exchange of views with President Carter on many matters of mutual interest and concern in a very friendly atmosphere.

President Carter's state visit to the Republic of Korea at this time, I believe, will provide a momentum for further strengthening the traditional bonds of friendship between our two countries and will offer encouragement to all peace-loving nations whose interests are linked to the United States policy toward Asia.

I also believe that President Carter's visit to Korea, one of the most conspicuous conflict areas of the world today, will give him a valuable opportunity to deepen his understanding of the heart of the problem in this area.

It is noteworthy that recently a series of important changes have been taking place in Asia and the Pacific. The developments include the improvement in the Sino-American relations, the Sino-Japanese relations, conflicts in Indochina, with their repercussions, and the fluid Sino-Soviet relations.

In the vortex of these changes, many Asian nations are striving harder for their national security and economic development by fortifying their spirits of self-reliance.

I note, in this connection, that the firm determination and the power of the United States to preserve peace have been playing a significant role in the developments of situation in Asia and the Pacific.

We have been following closely the subtle changes and the developments in this area. We will continue to endeavor to overcome many challenges with wisdom and steadfastness in shaping our destiny courageously.

Mr. President, it is really regrettable that the clouds of war still hang over the Korean peninsula despite our sincere efforts to deter a recurrence of war and to establish peace on the peninsula.

The North Korean Communists are implacably pursuing their military build-up in defiance of the international trend toward rapprochement and of the stark reality of the Korean situation, as well as of the long-cherished aspiration of the 50 million Koreans. The North Koreans have already constructed a number of underground invasion tunnels across the Demilitarized Zone.

In contrast, the Republic of Korea has opened wide its doors on the basis of principle of reciprocity to all nations of the world, including those who have ideologies and institutions different from ours. Furthermore, we have repeatedly proposed to North Korea to conclude a non-aggression agreement aimed at establishing peace—a most urgent task in the Korean peninsula—and to start social and economic exchanges between the South and North of Korea.

At the beginning of this year also, I called upon the North Korean side to open dialog between the responsible authorities of the South and the North at any place, at any time, and at any level, in order to prevent a recurrence of war and to cooperate to speed up the peaceful unification of our fatherland. However,

no sincere response has yet been made by North Korea.

But we shall not despair. We shall keep our doors open for dialog in our firm belief that the day of our national reunion will eventually come.

We want peace. We are making every effort to bring about peace. We will continue our peace efforts.

Over the last generation, the Republic of Korea and the United States have continued to develop a close and effective, cooperative relationship to promote our common interests with the firm conviction that the peace and stability on the Korean peninsula are essential to the maintenance of peace in Northeast Asia and are also closely related to world peace.

Mr. President, it is a common aspiration of the developing countries today that their living standards should be enhanced in order to live in peace without fear of war, to expel poverty, and to restore human dignity.

Even in the face of the threats and provocations from the North, the Republic of Korea has established a remarkable record of continued economic development and made long strides in building our national strength for self-defense and for the safeguard of peace.

I firmly believe that the achievements we have made in such a short period of time without sufficient national resources, particularly after the total destruction from the Korea war, are the fruits of the sweat and toil of all our people. This record of achievements is not only an actual proof that demonstrates the superiority of a free, open society we have defended together but also constitutes a valuable national asset.

Furthermore, as a nation with a 5,000-year history of culture and tradition, we are marching forward to build a welfare

1203

society where social justice, humanity, and morality prevail.

We have found a democratic system which best suits our actual circumstances and which is the most effective in solving our own problems. This system upholds freedom based on law and order and assures the full creativity of the individual.

Mr. President, the relations between the Republic of Korea and the United States date back to 100 years ago. During the last three decades in particular, our two countries have developed a very close relationship. The alliance relationship between the Republic of Korea and the United States will remain the bedrock of our foreign policy.

Our friendship, which was further strengthened through the Korean war and and the Vietnam war, has today grown through the promoting of trade, as well as through the expansion of exchanges and cooperation in social, scientific, cultural, and other fields.

We are well aware that the growth of our national strength which we have achieved owes to the friendly support of the Government and people of the United States.

I have a firm conviction that the growth of our national strengths will not only serve the interests of the Republic of Korea but also make constructive contributions to the peace and prosperity of Northeast Asia and the Pacific.

Our two countries, reaffirming the necessity for productive cooperation in various fields, are now entering a new era of mature partnership based on mutual respect and deepened mutual understanding.

I sincerely hope the ties of friendship and cooperation between our two countries would be steadily consolidated as a result of President Carter's state visit to the Republic of Korea and further hope that this auspicious occasion will serve as a powerful propelling force in opening for us a glorious Pacific era in the 1980's.

Ladies and gentlemen, may I now ask you to rise and join me in a toast to the everlasting friendship and prosperity of our two countries and to the continued good health and success of our state guests, President of the United States of America and Mrs. Jimmy Carter.

Thank you.

PRESIDENT CARTER. *Mr. President, distinguished officials of the Governments of our two great nations, and distinguished guests:*

The Korean people have been famous throughout history for the kindness and graciousness with which you receive visitors and guests. This has been proven again by the warmth and the affection of your welcome for Rosalynn, for Amy, for me, and for all the American party.

I have come to Asia to demonstrate the deep interest of the United States in this vital and dynamic part of the world. The United States has been, is, and will remain a Pacific nation and a Pacific power.

I've come to Korea to seek a new and even more constructive stage in one of our Nation's oldest and most valuable strategic, political, and economic relationships.

What has impressed me most about my visit to your country is the existence side by side of a deep sense of the continuity of history with dramatic signs of rapid growth and rapid change.

The respect and reverence of the people of Korea for your history is visible in the lovely shrines, temples, and monuments throughout Seoul. Ancient Korea had a profound cultural impact on the rest of the world, as was clearly shown by the magnificient exhibition which you recently sent to the United States.

As a former naval officer, I was particularly intrigued by the statue of Admiral Yi in the center of Seoul. I'm told that the "turtle boats" of the Admiral commanded in the 16th century were the world's first ironclad naval vessels. I suspect that in his time these Korean ships were as new and revolutionary as the nuclear submarines which I helped to develop.

My visit with our combat troops last night and this morning, Mr. President, was a reminder that in our more recent history, tens of thousands of your countrymen and mine fought and died side by side to defend this country against aggression. Everyone must know that Koreans and Americans will continue to stand shoulder to shoulder to prevent aggression on this peninsula and to preserve the peace. Our military commitment to Korea's security is strong, unshakable, and enduring.

The security interests of the United States are directly involved in that commitment. The vital interests of four great powers intersect in this very region today. That is why the maintenance of peace on the Korean peninsula is so vital to the international community.

Evidence of change in Korea is all around us. You can see among the Korean people the dynamism, the creative energy and dedication that have produced Korea's economic miracle out of a nation once so badly scarred by war.

I am impressed that the benefits of prosperity are widely shared by the Korean people. I understand that the income, for instance, of the average rural family in Korea now exceeds that of its urban counterpart. That accomplishment is almost unique among developing nations and should be a source of special pride to you.

Compare your progress with that of the economy in the North. The Republic of Korea is proof that a free economy is the clearest road to shared prosperity and a better life for all.

We also believe strongly in the United States that a free society is the key to realizing the full potential for development and growth.

There is a growing consensus among the international community about the fundamental value of human rights, individual dignity, political freedom, freedom of the press, and the rule of law. The free expression of ideas stimulates innovation and creativity. The right to participate in the political process helps to unite a country in the pursuit of common goals.

There is abundant evidence in Korea of the dramatic economic progress a capable and energetic people can achieve by working together. I believe that this achievement can be matched by similar progress through the realization of basic human aspirations in political and human rights.

Accelerating change is also the central fact of life throughout the international community in recent years—nowhere more so than in Asia, the home of one-third of the world's people today. China has turned outwards toward the United States, Japan, and the Western world in search of modern techniques and new relationships. Japan has assumed a position of new global influence. Korea, always strategically vital, has become a world economic force. The unity of the ASEAN nations is becoming a stabilizing factor throughout Southeast Asia.

Today we are entering a more mature stage in the U.S.-Korean relations. Our success will depend on whether we can take advantage of both historical continuity and dynamic change to foster progress in the areas which concern us both. Cooperation is the key.

We will cooperate to keep the Republic of Korea safe and secure. There need be no concern about this. As Korea grows stronger, the United States will do its part to preserve the military balance and to deter aggression.

We must take advantage of changes in the international environment to lower tensions between South and North and, ultimately, to bring permanent peace and reunification to the Korean peninsula.

We must work together to build a world in which the rule of law and the freedom and dignity of the individual govern all the affairs of mankind.

Finally, Mr. President, you have a saying in Korea, "Even something as light as a piece of paper can be lifted more easily together." None of the goals I've mentioned are light or easy. But I'm convinced that we can achieve them by working together in the spirit of cooperation and friendship that has united us down through the years.

Ladies and gentlemen, I ask you to rise and join me in a toast to President Park, to the great people of the Republic of Korea, and to our common efforts for cooperation, for friendship, and for peace.

This is an extraordinary occasion, and I would like to make an extraordinary request, that we jointly honor a man who has served both our countries so well. With your permission, Mr. President, I would like to ask General Vessey to join us before this group.

This is a citation to accompany the award of the Defense Distinguished Service Medal to John W. Vessey, Jr.

"General John W. Vessey, Jr., United States Army, distinguished himself by exceptionally distinguished service as a Commander-in-Chief, United Nations Command, and R.O.K.-U.S. Combined Forces Command, and as Commander, United States Forces, Korea, Eighth

United States Army, during the period November 1976 to June 1979.

"General Vessey's superb performance has been clearly evidenced by outstanding leadership and managerial skills. With a keen perception of complex and sensitive military and political relationships, he solidified elements of the Armed Forces of the Republic of Korea, United States, and representative armed forces of other allied nations into a cohesive and formidable military force.

"In doing so, he conceived and refined new objectives and operational concepts which he persuasively articulated to the highest government officials of both nations. A significant historical milestone was reached during his tenure with the birth of the R.O.K.-U.S. Combined Forces Command.

"With General Vessey as its first Commander this organization of diverse national and military backgrounds has progressed into a most effective command, which has greatly enhanced participation by Republic of Korea armed forces in directing defense operations.

"General Vessey's professionalism and concerned leadership have been important factors in guiding the development of the military forces of both nations. His performance in a position of vital national interest and sensitivity has been clearly in keeping with the highest traditions of the military profession and reflects great credit upon himself, the United States Army, and the Department of Defense."

I would like to ask General Vessey to join us on the platform.

It's with great pleasure and an honor for my country, General Vessey, that I pin this medal on your breast as a token of your superb performance for the United States of America and for the Republic of Korea.

GENERAL VESSEY. [*In Korean*] Tonight is my wife's birthday. [*In English*] What I said, Mr. President, was today is my wife's birthday, and thank you very much for the very special party. I don't know what I'll do next year.

I want to say it's been a singular honor for me to serve with the brave, fine Korean and American soldiers that serve to defend this country. It's been a great experience.

See, they don't trust my Korean. [*Laughter*] I could have said that myself.

Thank you.

NOTE: The exchange began at 9 p.m. in the Dining Hall of the Blue House, the official residence of the Korean President. President Park spoke in Korean, and his remarks were translated by an interpreter.

Earlier in the day, the President was greeted by President Park at the welcoming ceremony at Yoido Plaza. The two Presidents then motorcaded to the Blue House for bilateral discussions with their advisers in the Summit Room.

In the afternoon, President Carter went to the National Cemetery, where he placed wreaths at the Tomb of the Unknown Soldier and at the gravesite of Madame Park, the late wife of President Park. He then toured the gardens of the Chang Duk Palace.

Following the dinner, the President went to the residence of the U.S. Ambassador to Korea, where he stayed overnight.

Seoul, Republic of Korea

Joint Communique Issued at the Conclusion of Meetings With President Park.   July 1, 1979

1. At the invitation of President Park Chung Hee, President of the United States of America and Mrs. Jimmy Carter made a state visit to the Republic of Korea from June 29 to July 1, 1979. In addition to consultations with President Park and other senior officials, and meetings with other prominent Korean leaders in Seoul, President Carter visited field in-

stallations of both the United States and Korean armed forces.

2. The two Presidents met at the Blue House on June 30 and July 1, 1979 to review United States-Korea relations and a variety of subjects of vital mutual interest in an atmosphere of cordial respect and confidence. Among those present at these meetings were Prime Minister Choi Kyu Hah, Minister of Foreign Affairs Park Tong Jin, Minister of National Defense Ro Jay Hyun, Presidential Secretary-General Kim Kae Won, and Ambassador Kim Yong Shik from the Korean side, and Secretary of State Cyrus R. Vance, Secretary of Defense Harold Brown, National Security Advisor Zbigniew Brzezinski, Assistant Secretary of State Richard Holbrooke and Ambassador William H. Gleysteen from the United States side.

3. President Carter outlined the policies of his Government to seek peace and the reduction of tensions around the world, including his efforts to promote a lasting peace in the Middle East and to reach agreement with the Soviet Union on limitation of strategic weapons. President Park endorsed these peace efforts and emphasized his view that the United States should continue to demonstrate its firm leadership wherever challenges to peace occurred.

4. The two Presidents reviewed the events which have significantly altered the recent political face of Asia. Among these were the normalization of Sino-American relations and the signing of the Peace and Friendship Treaty between Tokyo and Beijing. They noted that armed conflicts in Southeast Asia and the Indochina refugee problem are creating major difficulties affecting the entire region, and agreed that there is a need to prevent the extension of these conflicts to other countries. President Carter reaffirmed that the United States as a

Pacific power is vitally engaged in Asia and the Pacific and will continue its best efforts to ensure the peace and security of the region.

5. On the Indochina refugee problem, President Carter outlined the discussions at the Tokyo Summit and steps being taken by the United States and other countries to deal with the situation. He stressed the need for all nations to make the maximum effort possible, whether by resettlement, financial contributions, or temporary shelter. President Park, noting the serious situation both in terms of individual human suffering and destabilizing impact on the directly affected nations in Southeast Asia, stated that the Government of the Republic of Korea would make an additional grant of a considerable sum to the United Nations High Commission for Refugees.

6. President Carter, referring to the basic relations between the United States and the Republic of Korea, noted the existence of strong bonds of friendship and cooperation and assured President Park that the United States will continue to support the efforts of the Government of the Republic of Korea to maintain peace and stability in Korea and sustain economic and social development. President Carter stressed the solidarity that exists between the United States and the Republic of Korea as traditional allies.

SECURITY COOPERATION

7. The two Presidents reaffirmed the importance which the United States and Korea attach to the reciprocal commitments contained in the United States-Republic of Korea Mutual Defense Treaty of 1954. They also agreed that the continued security of the Republic of Korea is pivotal to the preservation of peace and stability in the northeast Asian region.

President Park reviewed the security situation on the peninsula and the continuing threat to peace posed by the North Korean military build-up. The two Presidents agreed that US–ROK cooperation in maintaining a high degree of strength and combat readiness to deter and defend against possible aggression was an important contribution to peace and stability. They noted that the activation last November of the ROK–US Combined Forces Command had enhanced the effectiveness of the joint defense cooperation between military authorities of the two countries. President Carter reiterated the firm commitment of the United States to render prompt and effective assistance to repel armed attack against the Republic of Korea in accordance with the Mutual Defense Treaty, and affirmed that the United States nuclear umbrella provided additional security for the area.

8. President Carter expressed his appreciation for the full consultations between the two Presidents and their Defense Ministers on security issues and said that he would be consulting with U.S. congressional leaders on his return in the light of these detailed discussions. President Carter reaffirmed the deep interest of the United States in preventing any destabilization of the peninsula or region and assured President Park in connection with the question of further withdrawal of American ground combat forces from Korea that the United States will continue to maintain an American military presence in the Republic of Korea to ensure peace and security.

9. President Park reviewed the extensive and continuing efforts of the Republic of Korea to modernize and enhance its self-reliant defense capabilities and the progress achieved in the first five-year Force Improvement Plan which is nearing completion. President Carter expressed

United States agreement with the objectives of the force improvement program and reaffirmed the readiness of the United States to continue to support the successful implementation of the program. President Carter assured President Park that the United States will continue to make available for sale to Korea appropriate weapons systems and defense industry technology necessary for enhancing Korea's ability to deter or defeat aggression and for the development of appropriate defense industries in the Republic of Korea.

REDUCTION OF TENSIONS ON THE KOREAN
PENINSULA

10. The two Presidents agreed on the priority need to continue the search for means to reduce tensions on the Korean peninsula. President Park explained the recent efforts of the Republic of Korea government, beginning with his initiative of January 19, 1979, to resume productive dialogue with North Korean authorities. President Carter assured President Park of United States support for these efforts and expressed the hope that meetings between the responsible authorities of the South and the North of Korea would become possible.

11. In view of the importance of this issue for peace and stability on the Korean peninsula and in the region, and as a testament to the personal commitment of the two Presidents to seek honorable means to promote dialogue and reduce tensions, President Park and President Carter have decided jointly to propose the convening of a meeting of senior official representatives of the South and the North of Korea and the United States to seek means to promote dialogue and reduce tensions in the area. In order to promote this effort and to prepare for the

meeting which it is hoped can be arranged, the two Presidents have directed the Foreign Minister and the Secretary of State to communicate jointly with the Foreign Minister of North Korea in this regard in an appropriate manner.

12. The two Presidents agreed that any arrangements that would reduce tension and establish lasting peace leading ultimately to the peaceful unification of the Korean people should result from dialogue between the two responsible authorities of both the South and the North of Korea. President Park noted the consistency with which the Republic of Korea has pursued efforts at dialogue and the reduction of tensions, as exemplified in the policies which he announced on June 23, 1973.

13. President Carter stated that, if and when North Korea's principal allies are prepared to expand relationships with the Republic of Korea, the United States is prepared to take similar steps with North Korea. President Carter also noted that unilateral steps toward North Korea which are not reciprocated toward the Republic of Korea by North Korea's principal allies do not improve stability or promote peace in the area.

14. The two Presidents shared the view that the admission of both the South and the North of Korea to the United Nations as an interim measure pending their eventual unification would provide authorities of both Korean parties with broader opportunities for dialogue aimed at the resolution of their differences.

RESPECT FOR INTERNATIONALLY
RECOGNIZED HUMAN RIGHTS

15. The two Presidents noted the importance to all nations of respect for internationally recognized human rights. President Carter expressed the hope that the

process of political growth in the Republic of Korea would continue commensurate with the economic and social growth of the Korean nation. In this connection, President Park explained his view on this matter together with the current unique circumstances confronting the Republic of Korea.

ECONOMIC COOPERATION

16. President Carter expressed to President Park his great admiration for Korea's remarkable record of achievement in sustained economic development over the past fifteen years under his leadership in the face of various obstacles and adverse conditions, thus offering a model and an inspiration for other countries as an example of economic growth and equity. President Park acknowledged with appreciation the United States' contribution to Korea's development in the economic, scientific, and technological areas, and affirmed his intention to continue to give high priority to economic and social goals. The two Presidents shared the view that possible cooperative efforts between the two Governments should be explored to enhance assistance to third countries.

17. President Park and President Carter also reviewed the current international economic situation, and President Carter reported on the discussions at the Seven-Nation Economic Summit just completed in Tokyo. President Park expressed concern about the world energy problem in particular, and the two Presidents shared the view that there is an urgent need for concerted international efforts to arrive at a reasonable solution to the problem.

18. The two Presidents expressed satisfaction at the rapid expansion in scope of the economic relations between the Republic of Korea and the United States, and confidence that this mutually benefi-

cial trend will continue. They noted the advantages which accrue to the people of both nations when the freest possible system of trade exists, and they pledged their mutual efforts to promote and preserve an open world trading system. President Carter noted the commendably progressive import-liberalization and other measures that the Government of the Republic of Korea had recently taken with a view to developing a more balanced trade with the United States. These actions and the recent buying mission to the United States will help promote export of American products to Korea. President Park expressed his hope that the United States would continue its efforts to promote, in the MTN and elsewhere, a freer trading system, and to preserve fair access to the United States market for Korean goods. The two Presidents agreed that further efforts to expand trade and economic cooperation between their two countries will be highly beneficial to their respective peoples.

CULTURAL AND EDUCATIONAL EXCHANGES

19. Noting that their meeting had deepened understanding and cooperation on many matters of mutual interest, the two Presidents recognized that, at a time when the Republic of Korea and the United States have entered into a new era of mature partnership based on mutual respect and confidence, there remains need for further promotion of mutual understanding and exchanges between the two peoples. As evidence of their joint desire to deepen the contact and understanding between the two nations, the two Presidents agreed that cultural and educational exchanges should be expanded. The two Governments agreed to enhance these exchanges by supporting the activities of organizations such as the Korean-American Educa-

tional Commission and to establish a Korean-American Cultural Exchange Committee to be funded jointly by the two Governments. The Committee would be designed to stimulate activities in both countries aimed at further mutual understanding and to endorse mutually agreed programs of this nature. Details will be worked out through diplomatic channels.

20. President and Mrs. Carter, on behalf of themselves and all the members of their party, expressed their deepest thanks to President Park and the people of the Republic of Korea for the warmth of their reception and the courtesies extended to them during the visit.

21. President Carter cordially invited President Park to visit the United States of America, and President Park accepted the invitation with pleasure. They agreed that the visit would take place at a time of mutual convenience. Both Presidents expressed their desire to maintain close personal contact in order to preserve and further cultivate the close partnership existing between their two countries.

The President's Trip to Japan and the Republic of Korea

Remarks During a Background Briefing Given by Administration Officials for Reporters on Board Air Force One. July 1, 1979

BILATERAL RELATIONS WITH JAPAN;
TOKYO ECONOMIC SUMMIT

THE PRESIDENT. The bilateral discussions with Japan were no great challenge, because they are so sound and so harmonious now that there was really no deep concern before we arrived.

I think the intense dispute that existed between us and Japan earlier in the year was basically resolved after Prime Min-

ister Ohira's visit in May, followed up by the Strauss visit to Japan. So, in my opinion, the relationships between us and Japan are very good.

The challenge at the economic summit was to try to be substantive and specific on commitments about energy, on conservation in the future, and to try to get a proper balance between individual nations' actions on alternative energy supplies, research, development, production; combined with a mechanism by which we could cooperate on very large projects. For instance, the liquefaction and gasification of coal in the United States—that'll take place in West Virginia—it's already been joined now by Japan and West Germany. So, we'll have, I think, a growing common basis there.

One of the most serious problems as far as the negotiations was concerned was the previous agreement in Strasbourg that the European nations would act in concert and not individually. And this was a very nonsubstantive commitment, because they could pool the increase in production from the North Sea and not be bound by individual commitments. And this was a subject of a very intense discussion.

Q. Can you identify for us the—you made the remark after, I think, the final session, that there were three who supported the amendment. You wouldn't identify them at that time. I don't know what kind of basis we're on, background or what, but can you identify them now? [*Laughter*]

ADMINISTRATION OFFICIAL.[1] I tell you what, we'll look at this after we get through, and then I'll decide whether I want to put the remarks on the record or keep it on background.

---

[1] White House Press Office transcripts of background briefings customarily do not identify the speakers by name.

THE PRESIDENT. A half hour before we adjourned, three of the European leaders put forward a very strong amendment proposal that the European Community go back into a pool.

Q. You still can't identify those three?

THE PRESDIENT. Well, I can tell you that Giscard d'Estaing helped me defeat that amendment.

Q. That was my next question. We heard that he stuck with you on this, so that doesn't leave anybody but Mr. Erhardt [Schmidt],[2] Mr. Andreotti, and Mrs. Thatcher. So, we assume that by process of elimination we've got them. [*Laughter*]

ADMINISTRATION OFFICIAL. There have been press reports on this matter which are, for the large part, accurate. [*Laughter*]

THE PRESIDENT. I'll only give you one other comment. The Federal Republic of Germany did not participate in that debate.

FOLLOWUP ACTIONS ON ENERGY

Q. Mr. President, how will all this translate in terms of what you're going to do when you go back home?

THE PRESIDENT. Well, I was going to take a few days off—[*laughter*]—but I'm pleased with what we've accomplished, and I would like to initiate, immediately, actions to follow up on the energy question. I'll be getting a briefing from my own staff, who have been preparing it now at my direction for the last week. I'll be getting it, as a matter of fact, tomorrow, Monday, in Washington. And then as soon as the congressional leaders come back to Washington, I'll be prepared to meet with a group of Senate and House Members who've already been designated

---

[2] Printed in the transcript.

as a special energy task force, and a second group who have been designated as a special inflation task force.

I think it's high time that the Congress proceeded to a final legislative package with the windfall profits tax, the energy security fund, the alternate supplies of energy, as supported by Jim Wright and Moorhead, and also some expeditious way to complete major projects in our country, as proposed by the Energy Committee in the Senate under Senator Jackson.

I think this combination of actions will be very beneficial, and I want to do it without delay.

Q. Do these actions include the multinational facility, Mr. President? Will you make that announcement of a specific proposal in the next few weeks?

THE PRESIDENT. Yes, I would say within the next few weeks. We've done some background work on that already, but it's hard for me to say unilaterally what we will do collectively. That's why I'm hesitant about it.

POSSIBILITY OF RECESSION

Q. Sir, you said at the summit that the OPEC price increases are going to make it more difficult for us to realize our economic goals.

THE PRESIDENT. Yes.

Q. What is your latest assessment about the likelihood of a recession?

THE PRESIDENT. I think the OPEC decision will make a recession much more likely than it was before. We figure that by the end of 1980, this might cost us 2 or 2½ percent in our gross national product increase, and maybe 2 to 2½ percent in the inflation rate. It might cost us as many as 800,000 jobs—just the increase in OPEC prices that have taken place since last December.

STANDBY GASOLINE RATIONING
AUTHORITY

Q. Will you go forward with a new gas rationing——

THE PRESIDENT. Yes, that will be part of the result of the joint study by my people, the House and Senate small ad hoc committee.

Q. On a standby basis?

THE PRESIDENT. On a standby basis.

Q. In other words, you anticipate, despite what you said earlier, going back to Congress now and trying to get standby rationing authority again?

THE PRESIDENT. The Wednesday before I left home, I think it was—the morning we had the leadership breakfast, I think it was Wednesday—Bob Byrd and Tip O'Neill and I had a private meeting before the breakfast. And we agreed to go ahead and move on these two special groups, one purpose of which would be to devise an acceptable rationing plan on a standby basis.

OPEC DECISION ON OIL PRICES

Q. It's very early; of course the summit has just ended. But have you any indication as to what might be OPEC's reaction to the collective criticism that was in the communique?

THE PRESIDENT. No. It's obvious that there has been an excessive amount of timidity on the part of the consuming nations. Both the industrialized nations, up until this week, and especially the developing nations of the world—for instance, the Republic of Korea imports almost all of its energy; it has only a tiny amount of coal and oil.

And Helmut Schmidt made a very interesting report. I won't call the name of the countries, but one major European country, one of our NATO Allies, according to Chancellor Schmidt, spends a hundred percent of all its external earnings now on oil.

Another major ally of ours in South America, in 1973, was only spending 10 percent of their external earnings on oil; now they spend 40 percent.

Q. That's Brazil.

THE PRESIDENT. That's Brazil.

Q. The external earnings, what they earn from——

THE PRESIDENT. Their net earnings from what they export.

So, the devastating blow to the world is really most acutely felt in the developing nations, the very poor nations, who have very little cash reserves and are deeply in debt and who've seen their energy prices go up so extraordinarily high. It's obviously serious to us; it's much more than an inconvenience. But it can be devastating to a country that's so vulnerable as they.

Q. One of the things that we heard, Mr. President, about the collective criticism that the summit issued, was that in addition to the price increase the previous Thursday, the leaders of the summit were also affronted and indignant about what OPEC had had to say about the LDC's [less developed countries], or lack of what they say was our lack of aid to the LDC's. Was that correct? Was that a factor in the decision to criticize the increase?

THE PRESIDENT. Yes, I think so, because the OPEC communique was highly inaccurate and was designed, obviously, to mislead the developing countries.

Q. Was it you who brought the statement to the summit and read it to them? Someone on our side actually brought this to their attention? Or was it one of the Europeans who brought it up?

THE PRESIDENT. All of us were familiar with the communique. As a matter of fact, we discussed the communique of the OPEC nations that morning at the private breakfast with the so-called Berlin group: ourselves, the Germans, the French, and the British. And I think we four then took it to the others.

Q. Sir, what do we hope to gain by talking tougher at OPEC?

THE PRESIDENT. Well, I don't see how the rest of the world can continue to sit back in a quiescent state and accept unrestrained and unwarranted increases in OPEC oil prices. I think there's no doubt that all seven of our nations agree very strongly with this deep concern. We also all agreed that the 60-percent increase in 6 months is unnecessarily high and completely unwarranted.

Q. But given all of that, given the fact that all of this is unrestrained and unwarranted, what can we do besides making strong statements?

THE PRESIDENT. I'd rather not go into that. [*Laughter*]

Q. You mean there are things we can do?

THE PRESIDENT. Well, I'd just rather not go into that.

Q. Besides going in with just—taking the oil——

THE PRESIDENT. I'll let the press speculate on what can be done. The first thing, I think, is to let all the consuming nations on Earth, both advanced, industrialized nations and those who are semideveloped, and those who are very poor and poverty stricken, realize the serious threat that already has been mounted to the world economy and what more serious threats can be mounted in the future unless there's some public, concerted statement of concern toward the OPEC nations. It's very difficult for a single nation like Japan, or like Germany, or like France, maybe like the United States, to let a lonely voice be mounted against the OPEC countries, because they can single that country out with punitive withholding of oil or some other action.

And I think we've all recognized that so far, and we've been timid. And I think the statement in Tokyo, collectively, might have some special significance in the future. We'll just have to wait and see.

ENERGY SUPPLIES AND ECONOMIC
GROWTH RATE

Q. What does the 8.5 million barrels a day for U.S. mean to the Americans?

ADMINISTRATION OFFICIAL. It means that the level of imports that we experienced in 1977 and the level of imports that we're experiencing this year will be maintained as a goal. We'll have to assess our progress each year. All of us agreed to that. It'll be our goal that we will not exceed that amount of imports in 1985.

This could be accomplished by three basic means: One is to maximize production of oil in our own country; secondly, to conserve energy in all its forms; and, third, what might be considered a rational basis to develop alternative sources of energy—solar; coal; nuclear, with special attention paid to safety and environmental considerations; oil derived from tar sand, shale. These kinds of energy sources must be aggressively developed.

And I think that all of the countries assembled in Tokyo recognized that we have a special advantage in our country in having some reserves. Germany has no oil. France has no appreciable oil or coal. Germany has pretty good coal supplies. Great Britain has both coal and oil. We have coal, oil; obviously, we have tremendous resources in shale. Canada has diminishing, rapidly diminishing supplies of oil, tremendous potential in tar sands. So, each country is so different, one from another—Japan, almost completely dependent on imported energy. So, we had a very serious problem to address.

Also, our country this year ought to

have roughly a zero growth rate. Germany's will be in the neighborhood of 4 percent; Japan's even higher. And we, in the past few years, have had a very high growth rate compared to the other nations.

We had a need to accommodate that wide disparity in the characteristics of nations. I think we successfully did it. But all the nations took a very difficult stand in setting a restrictive target.

ADMINISTRATION OFFICIAL. May I interject one thing here? With regard to what we said earlier on what we will need to do to reach our goal by 1985, it seems to me that it's worth noting that had the 1977 national energy plan been passed as it was submitted, that we would now have in place programs that would guarantee that we would not only meet that goal in 1985 but that we would be significantly below it.

You can get different arguments about how many hundreds of thousands of barrels below it it would be, but there's no doubt that if that had been done in 1977, 8.5 million barrels in 1985 would be no problem.

ADMINISTRATION OFFICIAL. And I might say that we cannot meet the 1985 goal if we don't have the windfall profits tax and the energy security fund, because we won't have the capability of developing the alternative energy supplies.

POSSIBILITY OF TAX CUTS

Q. Could I go back to something that you said at the outset? You said that the OPEC price increase, the cumulative increase made the possibility of a recession a good deal stronger.

ADMINISTRATION OFFICIAL. Yes, not only for us but for all nations.

Q. In the light of that, have you begun to do any rethinking or do you plan to do

any restudying on the question of a tax cut?

ADMINISTRATION OFFICIAL. No, not anytime soon. I can't say that we'll never do that, but that's not in my immediate——

POSSIBILITY OF RECESSION

Q. You mentioned a moment ago that there would be a zero growth rate for the United States this year. That means there will be a recession?

ADMINISTRATION OFFICIAL. We don't know yet.

ADMINISTRATION OFFICIAL. We're just recalculating now, but it will certainly for the rest of the year—and in fact, the new estimates will come out in about 10 days. And we'll have the definite numbers then. But for the rest of the year, the growth rate is, I think it's going to be around zero, I can't imagine below that.

Q. That's the first time I've heard you say that.

Q. It's not recession until we have actual negatives for two quarters.

ADMINISTRATION OFFICIAL. Yes, but that's the average for the year. We will have to see how—it may well go into negative numbers. We just don't know.

ADMINISTRATION OFFICIAL. Well, I don't want to be that specific. I've got to get back and go over this with OMB and Charlie Schultze to get an exact figure. But I would say that we'll have just about a level growth rate this year, plus or minus——

Q. Is that all brought around by the OPEC increases?

ADMINISTRATION OFFICIAL. I can't say all, no. But it's obviously a very major factor.

Q. Mr. President, if I'm correct, that's the first time I've heard you use that phrase "zero growth rate." You've been talking 2½ percent, something like that.

Are you less optimistic now as a result of the——

THE PRESIDENT. [The President nods affirmatively.] [3]

ADMINISTRATION OFFICIAL. Mr. President, I would just interject, without the 60-percent increase from OPEC, we would not face this problem. Clearly, that problem, Mr. President, is in fact due to the 60-percent increase in oil.

ADMINISTRATION OFFICIAL. With regard for inflation, also.

U.S. BALANCE OF TRADE

THE PRESIDENT. What will the OPEC price increase cost us in balance of trade?

ADMINISTRATION OFFICIAL. We estimate now that next year the cost may be around $70 billion; this year, $58 billion, which compares to $42 billion last year. So, it's a substantial increase in the bill we have to pay for imported oil.

ADMINISTRATION OFFICIAL. It's a very serious economic problem. The only thing I would hesitate to—the only thing I'd like for you not to do is to pin me down specifically to a zero growth rate. Until we see the final figures run through the computer, I won't know.

ADMINISTRATION OFFICIAL. It'll be about 10 days.

THE PRESIDENT. We'll issue that new estimate on the 15th, I think.

ENERGY AND INFLATION TASK FORCES

Q. You mentioned the inflation task force a little while ago. Is that something new?

THE PRESIDENT. Yes.

Q. And are they studying controls as one of the options at this point?

THE PRESIDENT. The inflation task force is something new.

---

[3] Printed in the transcript.

Q. Would you like to talk a little bit about it?

THE PRESIDENT. No, I don't want to presuppose anything. I think the Congress Members would resent my saying what we collectively are going to do. The essence of it is that Bob Byrd and Tip and all recognize that we have some special problems economically, and instead of the executive branch developing a program or the Congress developing programs and just having proper consultations, that we'll work much more closely on a continuing basis with a few key people.

Before I left Washington, Bob Byrd called me on the phone and gave me the list of the Members of the Senate that he had recommended. And I understand that after I left, Tip O'Neill has submitted his list of the House Members—two lists, one for energy and one for inflation. Both Democrats and Republicans could be designated by the leaders.

Q. Do you anticipate that they will suggest mandatory controls at all?

THE PRESIDENT. I don't want to presuppose that.

Q. How would you feel if they did?

THE PRESIDENT. I would say no.

Q. Are controls one of the options that the task force will consider?

THE PRESIDENT. I'm opposed to mandatory controls.

Q. When do you expect to have a report or a recommendation?

THE PRESIDENT. This is in the embryonic stage. We've set up the mechanism, and I can't——

Q. Is it an all-congressional group—the task force?

THE PRESIDENT. If I remember right, Bob Byrd gave me about seven or eight names from the Senate. I presume Tip will do about the same on the House, and then I'll appoint members representing my own administration. Mike [4] will undoubtedly serve, along with Schlesinger, maybe Stu Eizenstat, Charlie Schultze, and others—Juanita Kreps—depending on—I haven't decided on specific names, but those would be, obviously.

PRESIDENT'S SUMMARY OF TRIP

I might say, in summary, that I think the trip has been a very good one. I'm pleased with the results. We accomplished all the goals that we established for ourselves. Many of the commitments that were made still have to be carried out—in Japan, at the economic summit, and also in my visit with President Park and Korean leaders.

I think that the alleviation of tension between South Korea and North Korea, if we can accomplish this, will be of great benefit. I would like to see trade open up between South Korea and the People's Republic of China; between ourselves and North Korea on the same time basis.

I think that our genuine concern about human rights has been imparted very clearly to President Park and all the members of the Government of the Republic of Korea. My belief is that the military relationship has been much more actively clarified. We will accommodate the recent development of the buildup in North Korea adequately. We will not abandon our commitments to the Republic of Korea.

So, I think all those issues that we studied and worked on so long have been successfully concluded.

Q. Have you pretty well formed a decision in your mind on troop withdrawals?

THE PRESIDENT. A general framework, yes.

Thank you all very much.

---

[4] Secretary of the Treasury Blumenthal.

REPORTER. Thank you.

NOTE: The briefing was held during the flight from the Republic of Korea to Hawaii. The President joined the group approximately midway through the briefing, and only that portion attended by the President is printed above.

Earlier in the day, the President met at the U.S. Ambassador's residence in Seoul with a group of Korean religious leaders and attended a reception with members of the National Assembly at the National Assembly building.

Prior to departure ceremonies at Kimpo International Airport, the President went to the Blue House, where he met with President Park. President Park then accompanied the President to the airport.

Hickam Air Force Base, Hawaii

Remarks at a Reception.   *July 1, 1979*

Aloha!

You don't know how nice it is to be home.

This is our second Sunday, July 1st. We spent the first one in Seoul, Korea, and worshiped there in a new church and then had meetings with the President and the leaders of that country, close allies of ours. And if I had to pick one place on Earth that I would rather spend my second Sunday, it would be Hawaii with you.

It was a pleasure to be welcomed by Governor Ariyoshi and his wife. I've asked him, by the way, later on this month, to go out and represent me at the new Republic of Kiribati, formerly the Gilbert Islands, on their first independence day. And, Governor, I hope you can do that for me. Thank you very much. He'll be a great representative for our country.

And Senator and Mrs. Matsunaga, Sparky Matsunaga, has been with me on this entire trip. He's been a special good will ambassador. And when I've been closed up in those rooms trying to negotiate about energy and defense and human rights and other questions, he's been a special representative for the State of Hawaii and for the United States of America. And, Sparky, I want to thank you for doing such a superb job, you and your wife both.

Congressman Akaka, Congressman Heftel, thank you very much for being with me this morning. And I particularly want to say to Mr. and Mrs. Hirabara, thank you for helping me become President.

We are really coming back home. As you know, my wife and I and my first son came to live in Hawaii in December of 1948. Rosalynn got here, I think, in March or April of 1949, and we spent two of the best years of our lives here, and it's one of the places on Earth closest to our hearts.

My former pastor in Plains, Bruce Edwards, and his wife, Sandra, are here to meet us this morning, and there are many things that cause my heart to fill with gratitude to God for being so good to us and so good to our country.

I'm particularly eager to shake hands with each one of you individually and to thank you for your friendship and for your coming out to welcome us today. But I particularly wanted to say that this trip has been a good one for me personally, for me as President, and for our Nation.

We went first to Japan, a great nation, one of our closest allies, which has had literally a rebirth since the Second World War. We share many things in common. And I would guess that except for two nations that join one another physically, there is no nation, no two nations on Earth who are any closer now than we and the people of Japan.

I went to strengthen our partnership. I'm only the second United States President in history who's ever visited Japan. We had a wonderful visit with the Em-

peror, with the people there, a kind of person-to-person effort which I thought was highly successful.

We also went from Japan to Korea. I spent the first night with our troops near Seoul. This is a nation that we joined in the early 1950's when I was still in submarines in the Pacific Fleet. Fifty thousand of our American young men gave their lives in Korea for freedom, for a chance for the people of that country to live in peace and to meet the constant threat of aggression.

The troops there have a very high morale. The 2d Infantry Division has the highest reenlistment rate of any military force in the United States, anywhere in the world. And I was privileged to see them, their dedication, their courage, their heroism, their commitment to the same principles that have always made our Nation great. And I know the military means so much here in the State of Hawaii as well, where I served as a young naval officer. It reminded me again of what patriotism really means and what a great debt we owe to our military forces throughout the world, who stand for peace and who stand for freedom still.

I talked to President Park frankly about our military alliance, which is strong and which will stay strong, about our firm and permanent commitment to continue to join with them in the defense of freedom on the peninsula of Korea. I talked to him very deeply about human rights, some of my own concerns about the need for improvement in the administration of the rule of law, of personal freedom, freedom of the press, and I thought those meetings, those frank discussions, were very, very fruitful.

I would guess that the most significant part of the trip, however, was meeting with the leaders of other industrialized nations at the economic summit in Tokyo.

I won't go into detail, because this was a very difficult and very complicated negotiation. But I thought we made some historic decisions there. It may be that this meeting will go down in history as one that has affected the lives of almost every person on Earth.

We have very serious problems with energy. We decided first of all to set rigid targets on imports, to cut down on the unwarranted control of our lives by the OPEC nations. Since December, the OPEC countries have increased the price of oil an average of more than 60 percent, from $12.50 per barrel back in December to as high as $22 a barrel now.

We have got to take action. We can take action. Our country is strong enough to take action to make us energy independent in the future. And all of our nations bound ourselves together to cut down on imports, to remove the unwarranted increases in price resulting from the distribution system, and to commit ourselves individually and collectively to develop new sources of energy and to develop our own existing sources of energy so that we can rest with assurance that we will take care of our own energy needs in the future.

There is no other place in our country which has best exemplified this than the State of Hawaii. On the big island, Hawaii, on Kauai as well, now almost 50 percent of all the energy used comes from biomass, primarily from sugarcane. There'll be a new ocean temperature energy project that will begin in just 2 or 3 days, the first of any size anywhere, and this is another very great credit to this island.

I talked to Sparky Matsunaga the last few minutes before we landed. I would like to see the State of Hawaii become completely energy independent by the year 1990. And if all of us continue to work together with the same spirit and dedication which we've shown so far, we have an excellent chance to do that.

You have geothermal energy, and obviously from the sugarcane wastes there can be ethanol, methanol made to take care of gasoline replacement.

So, I'm very excited about what has gone on here and what will go on. Photovoltaic cells from solar power directly are another tremendous potential source of power for Hawaii. So, you are really in the forefront of what can be done on a nationwide basis.

I'd like to just add one other thing and then I'll close.

I had planned to stay 2 or 3 days here to get some rest and to be with you, my friends. I believe, however, that the economic problems of our Nation and the energy problems of my Nation require me to go on back to Washington.

Between 1973 and 1977, we did absolutely nothing as a nation to meet the rapidly changing energy shortages and the rapidly changing energy price increases. In 1977, as you know, I presented to the Congress a comprehensive energy policy. Had it been passed expeditiously, many of our energy problems now would not exist.

The Congress has not yet passed a single piece of legislation, a single line of legislation, dealing with oil. Now with apparent energy shortages, with gas lines the Congress is beginning to move. We are moving as partners.

The windfall profits tax will establish a multibillion dollar fund, an energy security fund that will let us develop alternative sources of energy and existing sources of energy to be expanded in the years ahead, to give us a better rapid transit system, and to meet the special needs of the poor.

We also are moving toward higher technology in energy and a means by which we can expedite the construction of projects that will give us energy more quickly. I have no doubt now that the public has been so aroused about the direct threat that we will act without delay.

I'll be meeting immediately with my staff when I return to Washington and then with groups of House and Senate leaders in the field of energy and also in the field of inflation control as soon as I return to Washington.

Our country has been blessed, as you know, by God with tremendous human resources and tremendous natural resources. There's no way for me to look at a welcoming crowd at the airfield or to look on your faces without realizing that Hawaii not only has a great natural beauty but also a great human and political beauty.

Ours is a country of immigrants. It's a country of refugees. My parents and all of yours, except the native Hawaiians, came here from other countries seeking a better life. It's the kind of spirit that has bound our Nation together in the past, and it's the kind of spirit that's given us strength.

This is the first time in history when our Nation has been substantially inconvenienced without a direct threat to our security, like during a time of war or massive depression. I think Americans can stand it. I think we can weather difficulty. I think we can meet challenges. I think we can answer questions if we live and work together as we have in the past.

It is not easy being President these days. But I feel renewed in my own commitment and strength when I know from history how great a nation we have and, looking on your faces, see what a great nation we have in the future.

Working together, we can meet any difficulty and any challenge. And with your help and with God's help, we will do it again.

Thank you for coming out to meet me this morning. I love you all. God bless you.

NOTE: The President spoke at 7:33 a.m. at the Officer's Club.

Following his remarks, the President left for Washington, D.C.

National Consumer Cooperative Bank

Nomination of 11 Members of the Board of Directors. July 2, 1979

The President today announced that he will nominate six public members and five Government members of the Board of Directors of the National Consumer Cooperative Bank. They are:

Public members

RONALD GRZYWINSKI, of Chicago, president of the Illinois Neighborhood Development Corp., the bank holding company that owns the South Shore Bank, which operates a strong neighborhood reinvestment program that has been responsible for lending over $17 million to minority-owned businesses, voluntary community organizations, social service agencies, and single and multifamily residences;

JOSEPH L. HANSKNECHT, JR., of Detroit, Mich., director of public affairs of the League Insurance Companies and of the Michigan Credit Union League, active in community development organizations;

FRANCES LEVENSON, of New York City, director of urban housing and vice president of the New York Bank for Savings; for the past 7 years, in charge of the bank's program of sponsoring, financing, and promoting low- and moderate-income housing;

REV. ALBERT JOSEPH MCKNIGHT, of Lafayette, La., president of the Southern Cooperative Development Fund, a developmental financial institution with assets over $11 million, making loans to emerging cooperatives and community-controlled organizations in the South;

Juan J. Patlan, of San Antonio, Tex., executive director of the Mexican American Unity Council, active in civic groups concerned with housing, downtown redevelopment, and immigration and naturalization;

Derek N. Shearer, of Santa Monica, Calif., a lecturer at the UCLA Graduate School of Architecture and Urban Planning, an economist and consultant, and an expert in cooperative and community economic development.

Government members

Roger C. Altman, Assistant Secretary of the Treasury for Domestic Finance;

Geno C. Baroni, Assistant Secretary of Housing and Urban Development for Neighborhoods, Voluntary Associations, and Consumer Protection;

Sam W. Brown, Jr., Director of ACTION;

Lawrence Connell, Jr., Administrator of the National Credit Union Administration;

Carol Tucker Foreman, Assistant Secretary of Agriculture for Food and Consumer Services.

The President will announce nominations for the two remaining Government members of the Board of Directors in the future.

Department of Housing and Urban Development

Nomination of Jane McGrew To Be General Counsel. July 3, 1979

The President today announced that he will nominate Jane McGrew, of Chevy Chase, Md., to be General Counsel of the Department of Housing and Urban Development. She would replace Ruth Prokop, who has been appointed Chairman of the Merit Systems Protection Board.

McGrew is a partner in the Washington law firm of Steptoe & Johnson. She was born March 16, 1947, in New York City. She received a B.A. from Swarthmore

College in 1967 and a J.D. from the University of Pennsylvania Law School in 1970.

McGrew has been with Steptoe & Johnson since 1970, and has been a partner since 1977. She is primarily involved in Federal administrative practice, legislation, and litigation in the Federal courts in such areas as employment discrimination, antitrust litigation, contract compliance, and consulting on drug control programs.

She is a member of the hearing committee of the Disciplinary Board of the District of Columbia Bar and of the Women's Legal Defense Fund. She has been a consultant to the Drug Abuse Council and has served as vice president of the Washington Council of Lawyers, Inc.

Camp David Meetings on Domestic Issues

Statements by the White House Press Secretary on the President's Activities.
July 5, 1979

The President has authorized me to state that, pursuant to the agreements reached at the Tokyo summit, he intends to propose at an early date a series of strong measures to restrain United States demand for imported oil.

———

The President is in the process of assessing major domestic issues which he believes are important to the country and which include, but go beyond, the question of energy.

He will be consulting with a number of individuals whose judgment he respects, both in and outside of government.

Digest of Other White House Announcements

The following listing includes the President's public schedule and other items of general interest announced by the White House Press Office and not included elsewhere in this issue.

July 1

The President declared a major disaster for the State of Iowa as a result of high winds and tornadoes, beginning on or about June 28, which caused extensive public and private property damage.

July 2

The President met at the White House with:

—members of the White House Management Task Force on Energy Shortages;

—Secretary of Energy James R. Schlesinger, Secretary of the Treasury W. Michael Blumenthal, Deputy Attorney General Benjamin R. Civiletti, George C. Eads, member of the Council of Economic Advisers, James T. McIntyre, Jr., Director of the Office of Management and Budget, Ambassador at Large Henry D. Owen, Special Representative of the President for International Economic Summits, Stuart E. Eizenstat, Assistant to the President for Domestic Affairs and Policy, Alfred E. Kahn, Advisor to the President on Inflation, and other administration officials, to discuss energy issues.

July 3

The President met at the White House with:

—Zbigniew Brzezinski, Assistant to the President for National Security Affairs;

—members of the Economic Policy Group Steering Committee;

—Secretary Schlesinger, Secretary Blumenthal, Charles L. Schultze, Chairman of the Council of Economic Advisers, Mr. McIntyre, Ambassador Owen, Mr. Eizenstat, Mr. Kahn, Barbara Blum, Deputy Administrator, Environmental Protection Agency, James Gustave Speth, member, Council on Environmental Quality, and other administration officials, to discuss energy issues.

The President announced the appointment of Gov. George Ariyoshi of Hawaii as the President's Personal Representative to the Gilbert Islands independence celebrations, to be held July 12 in Tarawa. Mrs. Ariyoshi will accompany the Governor. Other Representatives of the President, also with the rank of Special Ambassador, are: John P. Condon, U.S. Ambassador to Fiji; Gen. Louis Wilson, former Commandant of the U.S. Marine Corps; Evelyn Colbert, Deputy Assistant Secretary of State for East Asian and Pacific Affairs; Frank M. Tejeda, member of the Texas State House of Representatives; James Alexander Hodges, president of Paragon Agency, Macon, Ga.; Allan Schaefer, a Hartford, Conn. attorney; and Lee M. Sessions, Jr., vice president of the Citizens and Southern National Bank, Atlanta, Ga.

The President left the White House for a stay at Camp David, Md.

July 6

The White House announced that the President has cancelled his trip to Louisville, Ky., scheduled for July 7 and 8. He will remain at Camp David for meetings on major domestic issues with individuals both in and outside of government. The President has asked Gov. Julian Carroll of Kentucky, chairman of the National Governors' Association, to bring a representative group of Governors to Camp David this evening for discussions prior to the convening of the National Governors' Association meeting. The Vice President and the First Lady will substitute for the President at the Kentucky Democratic Party fundraiser on Saturday evening. The Vice President will attend a breakfast meeting of the Democratic Governors' Caucus on Sunday morning and address the full association in the afternoon.

NOMINATIONS SUBMITTED TO THE SENATE

The following list does not include promotions of members of the Uniformed Services, nominations to the Service Academies, or nominations of Foreign Service officers.

Submitted July 2, 1979

The following-named persons to be members of the Board of Directors of the National Consumer Cooperative Bank for terms of 3 years (new positions):

RONALD GRZYWINSKI, of Illinois
JOSEPH L. HANSKNECHT, JR., of Michigan
FRANCES LEVENSON, of New York
ALBERT JOSEPH McKNIGHT, of Louisiana
JUAN J. PATLAN, of Texas
DEREK N. SHEARER, of California
ROGER C. ALTMAN, Assistant Secretary of the Treasury
CAROL TUCKER FOREMAN, Assistant Secretary of Agriculture
GENO CHARLES BARONI, Assistant Secretary of Housing and Urban Development
SAM W. BROWN, JR., Director of the ACTION Agency
LAWRENCE CONNELL, JR., Chairman, National Credit Union Administration Board

Submitted July 5, 1979

JANE McGREW, of Maryland, to be General Counsel of the Department of Housing and Urban Development, vice Ruth Prokop, resigned.
JAMES M. SPROUSE, of West Virginia, to be United States Circuit Judge for the Fourth Circuit, vice a new position created by P.L. 95–486, approved October 20, 1978.

NOMINATIONS—Continued
Submitted July 5—Continued

MATTHEW J. PERRY, JR., of South Carolina, to be United States District Judge for the District of South Carolina, vice a new position created by P.L. 95–486, approved October 20, 1978.

CHECKLIST OF WHITE HOUSE PRESS RELEASES

The following listing contains releases of the White House Press Office which are not included in this issue.

Released June 25, 1979

Advance text: toast at the state dinner in Tokyo, Japan

Released June 30, 1979

Advance text: toast at the state dinner in Seoul, Republic of Korea

Released July 1, 1979

News conference: on the President's trip to Japan and the Republic of Korea—by Secretary of State Cyrus R. Vance

Released July 3, 1979

Announcement: creation of two special working groups under the White House Management Task Force on Energy Shortages to deal with problems of independent truckers

Announcement: nomination of James M. Sprouse to be United States Circuit Judge for the Fourth Circuit

Announcement: nomination of Matthew J. Perry, Jr., to be United States District Judge for the District of South Carolina

Announcement: appointment of Gov. George Ariyoshi of Hawaii as the President's Personal Representative to the Gilbert Islands independence celebrations

ACTS APPROVED BY THE PRESIDENT

Approved June 30, 1979

S. 1317_____ Public Law 96–30
An act to extend the existing antitrust exemption for oil companies that participate in the Agreement on an International Energy Program.

Energy Emergency in Florida

Memorandum From the President.
July 6, 1979

Memorandum for the Administrator of the Environmental Protection Agency

Based on a request submitted to me by the Governor of the State of Florida to extend my June 12, 1979 determination that a regional energy emergency continues to exist in the State of Florida of such severity that a temporary suspension of certain air pollution control regulations which apply to fossil-fuel fired electric generating plants under the Florida Air Quality Implementation Plan may be necessary, and that other means of responding to the energy emergency may be inadequate, I hereby extend that determination from July 5, 1979, to and including October 15, 1979. This extension is limited by the same conditions as my original determination and is expanded to include any necessary temporary suspension of sulfur dioxide as well as opacity and particulate requirements.

If, during the extension, I find that a regional energy emergency no longer exists in Florida, I will direct that this extension be rescinded, and that all suspension orders issued by the Governor be terminated on the day of that rescission. Please continue to work with State officials to monitor carefully the residual oil supply in Florida and to inform me if the emergency should cease to exist. You will continue to retain full authority to disapprove temporary suspension of regulations in Florida and to exercise your emergency powers authority under Section 303 of the Clean Air Act, when and if necessary. It is important to keep suspensions to an absolute minimum since Section 110(f) of the Clean Air Act limits each suspension to a maximum duration of 120 days.

While my determination permits the temporary suspension of certain emission limiting requirements, it in no way permits the suspension of any national ambient primary or secondary air quality standard. Protection of these national health and welfare protective standards is consistent with Governor Graham's petition, and I commend him for his past restraint in using the authority to suspend some air pollution requirements. (This determination shall be published in the FEDERAL REGISTER.)

JIMMY CARTER

[Filed with the Office of the Federal Register, 2:39 p.m., July 10, 1979]

NOTE: The text of the memorandum was released on July 9.

Saudi Arabian Crude Oil Production

White House Statement.   July 9, 1979

The President told Members of the Senate and House at Camp David this morning that he has received a personal commitment from Crown Prince Fahd of Saudi Arabia to increase substantially crude oil production for a significant and specific period of time. Details of production plans will be announced by the Saudi Government in the near future.

The personal message to the President made clear that the Saudi decision is based on their historic friendly relationship with the United States and their commitment to be a dependable supplier of oil to the world.

The President has expressed the appreciation of the American people for this decision. He wishes to emphasize, however, that while the increased production will be helpful in the short term, it does not relieve the United States or other oil-consuming nations of the necessity for firm action to reduce significantly their dependence on imported oil.

NOTE: Deputy Press Secretary Rex Granum read the statement at 11:39 a.m. at the regular news briefing for reporters, held in the Briefing Room at the White House.

President's Council on Physical Fitness and Sports

Appointment of Abbi Fisher as a Member.
July 10, 1979

The President today announced the appointment of Abbi Fisher, of South Conway, N.H., as a member of the President's Council on Physical Fitness and Sports.

Fisher, 21, is a member of the U.S. Olympic Ski Team and won the slalom event in the 1978 World Cup. She has been skiing since the age of 3 and racing since 16. She placed second and third in the giant slalom in the 1977 World Cup season and won the slalom event in the 1977 Europa Cup.

Death of Arthur Fiedler

Statement by the President.   July 10, 1979

Music lovers everywhere were saddened to learn of the death of Arthur Fiedler, who had a special place in our hearts as the courtly man who introduced millions to the infinite variety and pleasures of music.

The Fourth of July concerts he originated on the banks of the Charles River became a part of our national tradition. He gave us the best loved classics with a joyous mixture of country, jazz, and popular works. He knew how to take music seriously without taking the fun out of it, and he shared that gift with us all.

Rosalynn and I join a nation filled with the grateful recipients of that gift in sending our deepest sympathy to his wife, Ellen Bottomly Fiedler, and the rest of his family.

National Energy Supply Shortage

Proclamation 4667.   July 10, 1979

By the President of the United States of America

A Proclamation

The Secretary of Energy has advised me that the continued reduction in world crude oil production has resulted in a national energy supply shortage constituting a severe energy supply interruption as defined in Section 3(8) of the Energy Policy and Conservation Act (42 U.S.C. 6202 (8)). The Secretary based his conclusion on the fact that current and projected imports of crude oil and petroleum products, plus available stocks, are not adequate to meet normal demand and that shortages of essential fuels have begun to have a major adverse impact on the economy with the possibility of more severe impacts occurring in the future. Recent shortages of gasoline in some areas of the Nation and the current inadequate levels of heating oil stocks have underscored the seriousness of the situation and demonstrate that action must be taken now to conserve available supplies of petroleum.

On the basis of the Secretary's report, and other information available to me, I hereby find and determine, in accordance with Sections 201(b) and 3(8) of the Energy Policy and Conservation Act (42 U.S.C. 6261(b), 6202(8)), the existence of a national energy supply shortage constituting a severe energy supply interruption, which:

(A) is of significant scope and duration and of an emergency nature;

(B) may cause major adverse impact on national safety or the national economy; and

(C) has resulted from an interruption in the supply of imported petroleum products.

I further find that implementation of the Emergency Building Temperature Restrictions, Energy Conservation Contingency Plan No. 2, is required by the severe energy supply interruption. This Plan was transmitted by me to the Congress on March 1, 1979, and approved by a resolution of each House (S. Res. 122, 125 Cong. Rec. S 5135 (May 2, 1979); H. Res. 209, 125 Cong. Rec. H 3018 May 10, 1979)), which resolutions have been transmitted to me by the Secretary of the Senate and the Clerk of the House. Those resolutions were received by me on May 4 and May 15, 1979, respectively.

Now, THEREFORE, I, JIMMY CARTER, President of the United States of America, by the authority vested in me by the Constitution and laws of the United States, including Section 201(b) of the Energy Policy and Conservation Act (42 U.S.C. 6261(b)), do hereby proclaim that:

SECTION 1. A severe energy supply interruption, as defined in Section 3(8) of the Energy Policy and Conservation Act (42 U.S.C. 6202(8)) currently exists with respect to the supply of imported crude oil and petroleum products.

SEC. 2. This finding shall be immediately transmitted to the Congress.

SEC. 3. The provisions of the Emergency Building Temperature Restrictions, Energy Conservation Contingency Plan No. 2 (44 FR 12911 of March 8, 1979), shall become effective as of July 16, 1979.

SEC. 4. In accordance with the provisions of the Plan, the Secretary of Energy is hereby authorized to issue regulations for the purpose of implementing the Energy Conservation Contingency Plan No. 2 and to administer the program in all respects.

IN WITNESS WHEREOF, I have hereunto set my hand this tenth day of July, in the year of our Lord nineteen hundred seventy-nine, and of the Independence of the United States of America the two hundred and fourth.

JIMMY CARTER

[Filed with the Office of the Federal Register, 4:40 p.m., July 10, 1979]

National Energy Supply Shortage

Message to the Congress on the Implementation of Energy Conservation Contingency Plan No. 2.   July 10, 1979

To the Congress of the United States:

Pursuant to the authority vested in me by the Energy Policy and Conservation Act, I have found and proclaimed (copy of the Proclamation is enclosed) that a severe energy supply interruption currently exists with respect to the supply of imported crude oil and petroleum products and have implemented the authority vested in me to impose emergency building temperature restrictions as set forth in Standby Energy Conservation Contingency Plan No. 2.

The Plan will become effective as of July 16, 1979. A copy of the final Department of Energy regulations which more fully explain the manner for the exercise of the Plan is enclosed.

JIMMY CARTER

The White House,
   July 10, 1979.

NOTE: The Department of Energy regulations are printed in the FEDERAL REGISTER of July 5, 1979.

United States Ambassador to Papua New Guinea and the Solomon Islands

Nomination of Harvey J. Feldman. July 11, 1979

The President today announced that he will nominate Harvey J. Feldman, of Miami, Fla., to be Ambassador Extraordinary and Plenipotentiary of the United States to Papua New Guinea and to the Solomon Islands. He would replace Mary S. Olmsted, who is resigning.

Feldman has been Coordinator for Taiwan Affairs at the State Department since 1977.

He was born June 25, 1931, in Brooklyn, N.Y. He received a B.A. (1951) and M.A. (1954) from the University of Chicago.

Feldman joined the Foreign Service in 1954, and served in Hong Kong, Tokyo, Nagoya, and at the State Department. He took language training at the Foreign Service Institute in 1962–63 and then in Taipei, where he also served as a political-military officer. From 1965 to 1970, he was detailed to the U.S. Information Agency in Hong Kong as publication officer, assistant information officer, then cultural affairs officer.

From 1970 to 1973, Feldman was at the State Department as a political officer, then a member of the Planning and Coordinating Staff. From 1973 to 1975, he was Counselor for Political Affairs in Taipei, and from 1975 to 1977, he was Deputy Chief of Mission in Sofia.

Steel Imports

Proclamation 4668.   July 11, 1979

MODIFICATION OF TEMPORARY QUANTITATIVE LIMITATIONS ON THE IMPORTATION OF CERTAIN ARTICLES OF STAINLESS STEEL OR ALLOY TOOL STEEL

By the President of the United States of America

A Proclamation

On June 12, 1979, by Proclamation 4665, I proclaimed, pursuant to the Constitution and the statutes of the United States (including section 203 of the Trade Act of 1974 (19 U.S.C. 2253) (the Trade

Act)), an extension for the period of June 14, 1979 through February 13, 1980, of the temporary quantitative limitations imposed by Proclamation 4445, as amended, on the importation into the United States of certain articles of stainless or alloy tool steel provided for in items 923.20 through 923.26, inclusive, of the Tariff Schedules of the United States (TSUS) (19 U.S.C. 1202).

Now, THEREFORE, I, JIMMY CARTER, President of the United States of America, in order to assure equitable treatment under Proclamation 4445, as amended, and acting under the authority vested in me by the Constitution and the statutes of the United States, including section 203 of the Trade Act (19 U.S.C. 2253), and in accordance with Article XIX of the General Agreement on Tariffs and Trade (GATT) (61 Stat. (pt. 5) A58; 8 UST (pt. 2) 1786) do proclaim that Subpart A, part 2 of the Appendix to the TSUS is modified as set forth in the Annex to this proclamation.

IN WITNESS WHEREOF, I have hereunto set my hand this eleventh day of July, in the year of our Lord nineteen hundred seventy-nine, and of the Independence of the United States of America the two hundred and fourth.

JIMMY CARTER

ANNEX

Subpart A, part 2 of the Appendix to the Tariff Schedules of the United States (19 U.S.C. 1202) is modified—

(a) by redesignating headnote 2(d) as headnote 2(e);
and

(b) by inserting the following new headnote 2(d):

"(d) Adjustments.—If the Special Representative determines that it is necessary or appropriate to assure equitable treatment in a manner consistent with the objective of phasing-out import relief he may:

(1) Allocate or reallocate specific quota quantities to any country or instrumentality subject to restriction (either individually or by inclusion in the "other" country grouping), either on an item by item basis, or for all items; or

(2) Adjust the quota quantities between countries or instrumentalities, among or within items 923.20 through 923.26, inclusive, or among or within restraint periods, provided that any such adjustment does not affect the sum of all quota quantities for all items 923.20 through 923.26, inclusive, for the period June 14, 1979, through February 13, 1980.

Such modifications are to be effective on or after the date of their publication in the FEDERAL REGISTER;".

[Filed with the Office of the Federal Register, 4:27 p.m., July 11, 1979]

Department of Education

Statement on House of Representatives Action Approving the Legislation.
July 11, 1979

The department of education legislation approved by the House today will streamline administration of more than 150 Federal education programs, saving tax dollars and cutting redtape. It will also permit better management of the Government's health and human service programs.

The department of education legislation is an important administration priority. It will make a single agency and a single Cabinet official responsible fulltime for Federal education programs. It will ensure that programs costing $14 billion annually receive the high-level management attention and broad public scrutiny they deserve.

I would like to thank Speaker O'Neill and others in the House leadership, Chairman Brooks, and Congressmen Fascell and Horton for their efforts on behalf of this historic legislation. I look forward to early action by the House-Senate conference committee.

United States International Development Cooperation Agency

White House Statement on Congressional Approval of Reorganization Proposals. July 11, 1979

President Carter today expressed his appreciation for the approval given by the Congress of his proposals for reorganizing and strengthening the management of U.S. foreign economic development activities.

Noting that these proposals largely adopted suggestions of the late Senator Hubert Humphrey, the President said he wished to especially thank Chairmen Zablocki and Brooks of the responsible House committees and Chairmen Church and Ribicoff of the Senate committees for their leadership in achieving congressional support for the reorganization.

The President said the administration can now move ahead to establish the International Development Cooperation Agency (IDCA), the centerpiece of his plan to improve the programs and policies affecting the developing nations.

The principal components of the IDCA will be the Agency for International Development, the Overseas Private Investment Corporation, and the pro-posed Institute for Scientific and Technological Cooperation. The President hopes the Congress soon will complete action to establish this Institute, which will help developing countries create and adapt technologies capable of reducing their enormous problems in such fields as health, food, and energy.

Meeting With Prime Minister Abel Tendekai Muzorewa of Rhodesia

White House Statement.   July 11, 1979

President Carter met with Bishop Muzorewa this afternoon because of the President's deep personal commitment to help find a solution for the peaceful transfer of responsible political authority from the white minority to the black majority in Zimbabwe-Rhodesia.

In a frank exchange of views, the President emphasized his sincere desire to see an end to the bitterness and bloodshed in Zimbabwe-Rhodesia. He believes this can be accomplished by the establishment of a broadly based consensus on constitutional procedures and administrative processes which are responsive to the legitimate political aspirations of all the peoples of Zimbabwe-Rhodesia.

The President restated his intention to work closely with the Government of the United Kingdom, which has the primary legal and historic responsibility to bring Zimbabwe-Rhodesia to independence based on full political participation and human rights guarantees for all its citizens. He expressed the hope that the Muzorewa administration would work closely with the United Kingdom in seeking nonmilitary, political means to further this goal.

Skylab

Message to Australian Prime Minister J. Malcolm Fraser. July 11, 1979

I was concerned to learn that fragments of Skylab may have landed in Australia. I am relieved to hear your Government's preliminary assessment that no injuries have resulted. Nevertheless, I have instructed the Department of State to be in touch with your Government immediately and to offer any assistance you may need.

NOTE: Skylab was launched by the National Aeronautics and Space Administration on May 14, 1973. The orbiting spacecraft, weighing approximately 77 tons, was used as a research observatory workshop.

On reentering the Earth's atmosphere, Skylab disintegrated, and about two-thirds of the debris burned up during its descent. The remaining pieces were scattered over the Indian Ocean and Australia in an estimated 100-mile-wide, 4,000-mile-long path.

Combined Federal Campaign

Memorandum From the President. July 12, 1979

Memorandum for Heads of Departments and Agencies

It is a pleasure to announce The Honorable Bob Bergland, Secretary of Agriculture, has agreed to serve as Chairman of the Combined Federal Campaign for the National Capital Area this fall.

The solicitation efforts of the United Way of the National Capital Area, the National Health Agencies, and the International Service Agencies are combined into a single drive to meet the needs of more than 150 local, national, and international health, welfare, and social service agencies in this one drive.

These organizations deserve our wholehearted support, to enable them to provide assistance to our neighbors and friends who have special needs. By working through the Combined Federal Campaign we can provide the voluntary agencies a beacon of hope for providing the needed assistance.

The Combined Federal Campaign offers a unique opportunity through a once a year gift—a pledge made easier through the use of voluntary payroll deductions—for Federal personnel to help persons in our community, in our Nation, and in overseas lands. I am confident Mr. Bergland will have your wholehearted support in this endeavor. Additionally, I hope you will commend the campaign with its payroll deduction feature to Federal employees and military personnel in your organization.

I request that you serve personally as Chairman of the Combined Federal Campaign in your organization and appoint one of your top assistants as your Vice Chairman. Please advise Mr. Bergland of the person you designate as your Vice Chairman.

JIMMY CARTER

Combined Federal Campaign

Memorandum From the President. July 12, 1979

Memorandum for Federal Employees and Military Personnel

Federal government employees traditionally have responded generously in aiding those less fortunate than ourselves. Particularly noteworthy have been the tremendous compassion and support we have demonstrated through our contributions to the Combined Federal Campaign.

Once again, this yearly opportunity to support the services of voluntary health and welfare agencies, including the

United Way, The American Red Cross, National Health Agencies and International Service Agencies, by participating in the Combined Federal Campaign is upon us. These agencies help make our community a better place in which to live; they alleviate pain and suffering, and seek cures from dreaded diseases; they bring hope to those in overseas lands, and reinforce a sense of security in the aged, infirm, and handicapped.

In the spirit of neighborliness, we will continue our tradition of generosity and concern for others through contributions to the Combined Federal Campaign. I am confident of your support.

JIMMY CARTER

Digest of Other White House Announcements

The following listing includes the President's public schedule and other items of general interest announced by the White House Press Office and not included elsewhere in this issue.

July 7–July 13

The President remained at Camp David, Md., during the week for a series of discussions and meetings on a broad range of domestic issues, particularly energy and the economy. Participants in the discussions included, at various times, Members of Congress, current and former Federal, State, and local government officials, members of the White House staff, representatives of civic, religious, and labor organizations, businessmen, civil rights leaders, and university officials.

July 12

In the evening, the President went by helicopter to Carnegie, Pa., and the home of Mr. and Mrs. William Fisher to discuss a broad range of issues with about a dozen private citizens. He then returned to Camp David.

July 13

In the morning, the President went by helicopter to Martinsburg, W. Va., and the home of Mr. and Mrs. Marvin Porterfield to discuss a broad range of issues with a group of 17 private citizens. He then returned to Camp David.

NOMINATIONS SUBMITTED TO THE SENATE

The following list does not include promotions of members of the Uniformed Services, nominations to the Service Academies, or nominations of Foreign Service officers.

Submitted July 12, 1979

HARVEY J. FELDMAN, of Florida, a Foreign Service officer of Class two, to be Ambassador Extraordinary and Plenipotentiary of the United States of America to Papua New Guinea and to serve concurrently and without additional compensation as Ambassador Extraordinary and Plenipotentiary of the United States of America to Solomon Islands.

J. JEROME FARRIS, of Washington, to be United States Circuit Judge for the Ninth Circuit, vice a new position created by P.L. 95–486, approved October 20, 1978.

BETTY BINNS FLETCHER, of Washington, to be United States Circuit Judge for the Ninth Circuit, vice a new position created by P.L. 95–486, approved October 20, 1978.

JAMES C. PAINE, of Florida, to be United States District Judge for the Southern District of Florida, vice a new position created by P.L. 95–486, approved October 20, 1978.

BENJAMIN F. GIBSON, of Michigan, to be United States District Judge for the Western District of Michigan, vice a new position created by P.L. 95–486, approved October 20, 1978.

DOUGLAS W. HILLMAN, of Michigan, to be United States District Judge for the Western District of Michigan, vice a new position created by P.L. 95–486, approved October 20, 1978.

CHECKLIST OF WHITE HOUSE PRESS RELEASES

The following listing contains releases of the White House Press Office which are not included in this issue.

Released July 11, 1979

Announcement: nomination of Benjamin F. Gibson to be United States District Judge for the Western District of Michigan

Announcement: nomination of J. Jerome Farris to be United States Circuit Judge for the Ninth Circuit

Announcement: nomination of Betty Binns Fletcher to be United States Circuit Judge for the Ninth Circuit

Announcement: nomination of Douglas W. Hillman to be United States District Judge for the Western District of Michigan

Announcement: nomination of James C. Paine to be United States District Judge for the Southern District of Florida

Fact sheet: reorganization of U.S. foreign assistance activities

CHECKLIST—Continued

Released July 12, 1979

News conference: on the administration's mid-session review for the fiscal year 1980 budget, and other economic and budgetary issues— by James T. McIntyre, Jr., Director of the Office of Management and Budget, Lyle E. Gramley, member of the Council of Economic Advisers, and Daniel H. Brill, Assistant Secretary of the Treasury

ACTS APPROVED BY THE PRESIDENT

Approved July 7, 1979

S. 984_____ Public Law 96–31
An act to provide the Secretary of Agriculture with authority to reduce marketing penalties for peanuts.

Approved July 10, 1979

S.J. Res. 14_____ Public Law 96–32
A joint resolution to amend the Public Health Service Act and related health laws to correct printing and other technical errors.

Energy and National Goals

Address to the Nation.   July 15, 1979

Good evening.

This is a special night for me. Exactly 3 years ago, on July 15, 1976, I accepted the nomination of my party to run for President of the United States. I promised you a President who is not isolated from the people, who feels your pain, and who shares your dreams and who draws his strength and his wisdom from you.

During the past 3 years I've spoken to you on many occasions about national concerns, the energy crisis, reorganizing the Government, our Nation's economy, and issues of war and especially peace. But over those years the subjects of the speeches, the talks, and the press conferences have become increasingly narrow, focused more and more on what the isolated world of Washington thinks is important. Gradually, you've heard more and more about what the Government thinks or what the Government should be doing and less and less about our Nation's hopes, our dreams, and our vision of the future.

Ten days ago I had planned to speak to you again about a very important subject—energy. For the fifth time I would have described the urgency of the problem and laid out a series of legislative recommendations to the Congress. But as I was preparing to speak, I began to ask myself the same question that I now know has been troubling many of you. Why have we not been able to get together as a nation to resolve our serious energy problem?

It's clear that the true problems of our Nation are much deeper—deeper than gasoline lines or energy shortages, deeper even than inflation or recession. And I realize more than ever that as President I need your help. So, I decided to reach out and listen to the voices of America.

I invited to Camp David people from almost every segment of our society—business and labor, teachers and preachers, Governors, mayors, and private citizens. And then I left Camp David to listen to other Americans, men and women like you. It has been an extraordinary 10 days, and I want to share with you what I've heard.

First of all, I got a lot of personal advice. Let me quote a few of the typical comments that I wrote down.

This from a southern Governor: "Mr. President, you are not leading this Nation—you're just managing the Government."

"You don't see the people enough any more."

"Some of your Cabinet members don't seem loyal. There is not enough discipline among your disciples."

"Don't talk to us about politics or the mechanics of government, but about an understanding of our common good."

"Mr. President, we're in trouble. Talk to us about blood and sweat and tears."

"If you lead, Mr. President, we will follow."

Many people talked about themselves and about the condition of our Nation. This from a young woman in Pennsylvania: "I feel so far from government. I feel like ordinary people are excluded from political power."

And this from a young Chicano: "Some of us have suffered from recession all our lives."

"Some people have wasted energy, but others haven't had anything to waste."

And this from a religious leader: "No material shortage can touch the important things like God's love for us or our love for one another."

And I like this one particularly from a black woman who happens to be the mayor of a small Mississippi town: "The big-shots are not the only ones who are important. Remember, you can't sell anything on Wall Street unless someone digs it up somewhere else first."

This kind of summarized a lot of other statements: "Mr. President, we are confronted with a moral and a spiritual crisis."

Several of our discussions were on energy, and I have a notebook full of comments and advice. I'll read just a few.

"We can't go on consuming 40 percent more energy than we produce. When we import oil we are also importing inflation plus unemployment."

"We've got to use what we have. The Middle East has only 5 percent of the world's energy, but the United States has 24 percent."

And this is one of the most vivid statements: "Our neck is stretched over the fence and OPEC has a knife."

"There will be other cartels and other shortages. American wisdom and courage right now can set a path to follow in the future."

This was a good one: "Be bold, Mr. President. We may make mistakes, but we are ready to experiment."

And this one from a labor leader got to the heart of it: "The real issue is freedom. We must deal with the energy problem on a war footing."

And the last that I'll read: "When we enter the moral equivalent of war, Mr. President, don't issue us BB guns."

These 10 days confirmed my belief in the decency and the strength and the wisdom of the American people, but it also bore out some of my longstanding concerns about our Nation's underlying problems.

I know, of course, being President, that government actions and legislation can be very important. That's why I've worked hard to put my campaign promises into law—and I have to admit, with just mixed success. But after listening to the American people I have been reminded again that all the legislation in the world can't fix what's wrong with America. So, I want to speak to you first tonight about a subject even more serious than energy or inflation. I want to talk to you right now about a fundamental threat to American democracy.

I do not mean our political and civil liberties. They will endure. And I do not refer to the outward strength of America, a nation that is at peace tonight everywhere in the world, with unmatched economic power and military might.

The threat is nearly invisible in ordinary ways. It is a crisis of confidence. It is a crisis that strikes at the very heart and soul and spirit of our national will. We can see this crisis in the growing doubt about the meaning of our own lives and in the loss of a unity of purpose for our Nation.

The erosion of our confidence in the future is threatening to destroy the social and the political fabric of America.

The confidence that we have always had as a people is not simply some romantic dream or a proverb in a dusty book that we read just on the Fourth of July. It is the idea which founded our Nation and has guided our development as a people. Confidence in the future has supported everything else—public institutions and private enterprise, our own families, and the very Constitution of the United States. Confidence has defined our course and has served as a link between generations. We've always believed in something called progress. We've always had a faith that the days of our children would be better than our own.

Our people are losing that faith, not only in government itself but in the ability as citizens to serve as the ultimate rulers and shapers of our democracy. As a people we know our past and we are proud of it. Our progress has been part of the living history of America, even the world. We always believed that we were part of a great movement of humanity itself called democracy, involved in the search for freedom, and that belief has always strengthened us in our purpose. But just as we are losing our confidence in the future, we are also beginning to close the door on our past.

In a nation that was proud of hard work, strong families, close-knit communities, and our faith in God, too many of us now tend to worship self-indulgence and consumption. Human identity is no longer defined by what one does, but by what one owns. But we've discovered that owning things and consuming things does not satisfy our longing for meaning. We've learned that piling up material goods cannot fill the emptiness of lives which have no confidence or purpose.

The symptoms of this crisis of the American spirit are all around us. For the first time in the history of our country a majority of our people believe that the next 5 years will be worse than the past 5 years. Two-thirds of our people do not even vote. The productivity of American workers is actually dropping, and the willingness of Americans to save for the future has fallen below that of all other people in the Western world.

As you know, there is a growing disrespect for government and for churches and for schools, the news media, and other institutions. This is not a message of happiness or reassurance, but it is the truth and it is a warning.

These changes did not happen overnight. They've come upon us gradually over the last generation, years that were filled with shocks and tragedy.

We were sure that ours was a nation of the ballot, not the bullet, until the murders of John Kennedy and Robert Kennedy and Martin Luther King, Jr. We were taught that our armies were always invincible and our causes were always just, only to suffer the agony of Vietnam. We respected the Presidency as a place of honor until the shock of Watergate.

We remember when the phrase "sound as a dollar" was an expression of absolute dependability, until 10 years of inflation began to shrink our dollar and our savings. We believed that our Nation's resources were limitless until 1973, when we had to face a growing dependence on foreign oil.

These wounds are still very deep. They have never been healed.

Looking for a way out of this crisis, our people have turned to the Federal Government and found it isolated from the mainstream of our Nation's life. Washington, D.C., has become an island. The gap between our citizens and our Government has never been so wide. The people are looking for honest answers, not easy answers; clear leadership, not false claims and evasiveness and politics as usual.

What you see too often in Washington and elsewhere around the country is a system of government that seems incapable of action. You see a Congress twisted and pulled in every direction by hundreds of well-financed and powerful special interests. You see every extreme position defended to the last vote, almost to the last breath by one unyielding group or another. You often see a balanced and a fair approach that demands sacrifice, a little sacrifice from everyone, abandoned like an orphan without support and without friends.

Often you see paralysis and stagnation and drift. You don't like it, and neither do I. What can we do?

First of all, we must face the truth, and then we can change our course. We simply must have faith in each other, faith in our ability to govern ourselves, and faith in the future of this Nation. Restoring that faith and that confidence to America is now the most important task we face. It is a true challenge of this generation of Americans.

One of the visitors to Camp David last week put it this way: "We've got to stop crying and start sweating, stop talking and start walking, stop cursing and start praying. The strength we need will not come from the White House, but from every house in America."

We know the strength of America. We are strong. We can regain our unity. We can regain our confidence. We are the heirs of generations who survived threats much more powerful and awesome than those that challenge us now. Our fathers and mothers were strong men and women who shaped a new society during the Great Depression, who fought world wars, and who carved out a new charter of peace for the world.

We ourselves are the same Americans who just 10 years ago put a man on the Moon. We are the generation that dedicated our society to the pursuit of human rights and equality. And we are the generation that will win the war on the energy problem and in that process rebuild the unity and confidence of America.

We are at a turning point in our history. There are two paths to choose. One is a path I've warned about tonight, the path that leads to fragmentation and self-interest. Down that road lies a mistaken idea of freedom, the right to grasp for ourselves some advantage over others. That path would be one of constant conflict between narrow interests ending in chaos and immobility. It is a certain route to failure.

All the traditions of our past, all the lessons of our heritage, all the promises of our future point to another path, the path of common purpose and the restoration of American values. That path leads to true freedom for our Nation and ourselves. We can take the first steps down that path as we begin to solve our energy problem.

Energy will be the immediate test of our ability to unite this Nation, and it can also be the standard around which we rally.

On the battlefield of energy we can win for our Nation a new confidence, and we can seize control again of our common destiny.

In little more than two decades we've gone from a position of energy independence to one in which almost half the oil we use comes from foreign countries, at prices that are going through the roof. Our excessive dependence on OPEC has already taken a tremendous toll on our economy and our people. This is the direct cause of the long lines which have made millions of you spend aggravating hours waiting for gasoline. It's a cause of the increased inflation and unemployment that we now face. This intolerable dependence on foreign oil threatens our economic independence and the very security of our Nation.

The energy crisis is real. It is worldwide. It is a clear and present danger to our Nation. These are facts and we simply must face them.

What I have to say to you now about energy is simple and vitally important.

Point one: I am tonight setting a clear goal for the energy policy of the United States. Beginning this moment, this Nation will never use more foreign oil than we did in 1977—never. From now on, every new addition to our demand for energy will be met from our own production and our own conservation. The generation-long growth in our dependence on foreign oil will be stopped dead in its tracks right now and then reversed as we move through the 1980's, for I am tonight setting the further goal of cutting our dependence on foreign oil by one-half by the end of the next decade—a saving of over 4½ million barrels of imported oil per day.

Point two: To ensure that we meet these targets, I will use my Presidential authority to set import quotas. I'm an-

nouncing tonight that for 1979 and 1980, I will forbid the entry into this country of one drop of foreign oil more than these goals allow. These quotas will ensure a reduction in imports even below the ambitious levels we set at the recent Tokyo summit.

Point three: To give us energy security, I am asking for the most massive peacetime commitment of funds and resources in our Nation's history to develop America's own alternative sources of fuel—from coal, from oil shale, from plant products for gasohol, from unconventional gas, from the Sun.

I propose the creation of an energy security corporation to lead this effort to replace 2½ million barrels of imported oil per day by 1990. The corporation will issue up to $5 billion in energy bonds, and I especially want them to be in small denominations so that average Americans can invest directly in America's energy security.

Just as a similar synthetic rubber corporation helped us win World War II, so will we mobilize American determination and ability to win the energy war. Moreover, I will soon submit legislation to Congress calling for the creation of this Nation's first solar bank, which will help us achieve the crucial goal of 20 percent of our energy coming from solar power by the year 2000.

These efforts will cost money, a lot of money, and that is why Congress must enact the windfall profits tax without delay. It will be money well spent. Unlike the billions of dollars that we ship to foreign countries to pay for foreign oil, these funds will be paid by Americans to Americans. These funds will go to fight, not to increase, inflation and unemployment.

Point four: I'm asking Congress to mandate, to require as a matter of law, that our Nation's utility companies cut their massive use of oil by 50 percent within the next decade and switch to other fuels, especially coal, our most abundant energy source.

Point five: To make absolutely certain that nothing stands in the way of achieving these goals, I will urge Congress to create an energy mobilization board which, like the War Production Board in World War II, will have the responsibility and authority to cut through the redtape, the delays, and the endless roadblocks to completing key energy projects.

We will protect our environment. But when this Nation critically needs a refinery or a pipeline, we will build it.

Point six: I'm proposing a bold conservation program to involve every State, county, and city and every average American in our energy battle. This effort will permit you to build conservation into your homes and your lives at a cost you can afford.

I ask Congress to give me authority for mandatory conservation and for standby gasoline rationing. To further conserve energy, I'm proposing tonight an extra $10 billion over the next decade to strengthen our public transportation systems. And I'm asking you for your good and for your Nation's security to take no unnecessary trips, to use carpools or public transportation whenever you can, to park your car one extra day per week, to obey the speed limit, and to set your thermostats to save fuel. Every act of energy conservation like this is more than just common sense—I tell you it is an act of patriotism.

Our Nation must be fair to the poorest among us, so we will increase aid to needy Americans to cope with rising energy prices. We often think of conservation only in terms of sacrifice. In fact, it is the most painless and immediate way of rebuilding our Nation's strength. Every gallon of oil each one of us saves is a new form of production. It gives us more freedom, more confidence, that much more control over our own lives.

So, the solution of our energy crisis can also help us to conquer the crisis of the spirit in our country. It can rekindle our sense of unity, our confidence in the future, and give our Nation and all of us individually a new sense of purpose.

You know we can do it. We have the natural resources. We have more oil in our shale alone than several Saudi Arabias. We have more coal than any nation on Earth. We have the world's highest level of technology. We have the most skilled work force, with innovative genius, and I firmly believe that we have the national will to win this war.

I do not promise you that this struggle for freedom will be easy. I do not promise a quick way out of our Nation's problems, when the truth is that the only way out is an all-out effort. What I do promise you is that I will lead our fight, and I will enforce fairness in our struggle, and I will ensure honesty. And above all, I will act.

We can manage the short-term shortages more effectively and we will, but there are no short-term solutions to our long-range problems. There is simply no way to avoid sacrifice.

Twelve hours from now I will speak again in Kansas City, to expand and to explain further our energy program. Just as the search for solutions to our energy shortages has now led us to a new awareness of our Nation's deeper problems, so our willingness to work for those solutions in energy can strengthen us to attack those deeper problems.

I will continue to travel this country, to hear the people of America. You can help me to develop a national agenda for the 1980's. I will listen and I will act. We will act together. These were the promises I made 3 years ago, and I intend to keep them.

Little by little we can and we must rebuild our confidence. We can spend until we empty our treasuries, and we may summon all the wonders of science. But we can succeed only if we tap our greatest resources—America's people, America's values, and America's confidence.

I have seen the strength of America in the inexhaustible resources of our people. In the days to come, let us renew that strength in the struggle for an energy-secure nation.

In closing, let me say this: I will do my best, but I will not do it alone. Let your voice be heard. Whenever you have a chance, say something good about our country. With God's help and for the sake of our Nation, it is time for us to join hands in America. Let us commit ourselves together to a rebirth of the American spirit. Working together with our common faith we cannot fail.

Thank you and good night.

NOTE: The President spoke at 10 p.m. from the Oval Office at the White House. His remarks were broadcast live on radio and television.

Kansas City, Missouri

Remarks at the Annual Convention of the National Association of Counties.
July 16, 1979

Senator Tom Eagleton, Senator Jack Danforth, Congressmen Ike Skelton and Harold Volkmer, President Charlotte Williams, distinguished guests, ladies and gentlemen:

You may have heard that I spoke to the Nation last night on television. [*Laughter*] That speech encompassed the ideas, the concerns, the dreams, the hopes, the determination of many Americans. Your own president, Charlotte Williams, came to Camp David to help me write that speech.

Last night I spoke to you about the deep wounds our society has suffered and about my absolute conviction that we have the power and the will to heal these wounds and to restore the unity and confidence of America. I promised last night to keep on discussing our Nation's most serious problems with Americans. And I also promised to keep on acting with the people to tackle these problems.

And today, I've come to Kansas City to meet with you to do both—to discuss the energy problem and to get you to help me succeed. I want to know, will you help me succeed? [*Applause*]

My belief is that almost all Americans feel the same way. Just as the energy shortage has forced us to face our deepest fears and divisions, so our goal of an energy secure America will help us to rebuild our strength and our confidence as a people. We are coming to understand that the reasons for our energy crisis go beyond gas lines and wasteful habits to a loss of confidence that divides us and threatens us and which, for years, too many years, has prevented Presidents and the Congress and a great nation from acting courageously to meet this energy challenge. That is why we must decide here and now that we can and will regroup, we can and will unite, we can and will restore our confidence, we can and will win the battle to solve our energy problems and restore our Nation's security and keep us strong.

There are no easy answers. That is why I will continue to explore new ideas and I will open new fronts and I will develop new points of attack. That is why I will seek more and more Americans, allies to join me in this fight for our energy security, because on the battlefield of energy, this democracy which we love is going to make its stand. And on that battlefield you and I, fighing side by side, will win the energy war.

The underlying cause of the energy crisis, the energy problem, the energy challenge, the energy opportunity, is the same as it has been for many years—a massive, dangerous, growing dependence on oil, and particularly our dependence, excessive dependence on imported oil. A generation ago, we sent more oil out of the country than we brought in. Now we import almost half the oil we use, and after the latest price increase, the price we pay OPEC for our oil has almost doubled in the last 7 months.

With a government shakeup in distant Iran last winter, we lost in imports about 100 million barrels of oil. The gasoline lines are directly related to this particular vulnerability; so are the diesel fuel shortages among our farmers and among our truckers; and so are the present low home heating oil stocks as we face next winter. We simply must remove this threat to our people. I must act, the Congress must act, all of you must act now without delay, with determination, unity, courage, and confidence. With your recent expression of support for me, I have no doubt that we in this great country will succeed.

The first thing we've got to do is to face facts. There is simply not enough oil available in the world to meet all the demands of all the people in all the nations on Earth.

Americans are just now beginning to realize with simple common sense that there are only two ways to guarantee supply—one is obviously to control our demand, to cut back on the waste of energy; and the other is to develop our own sources of energy to replace foreign

imports so that we can have control over our own destiny. And with your help, I promise to do exactly that.

I believe Americans will join together if there is good leadership at every level of government, not only from the White House but from the courthouse as well. There must be clear, fair goals and programs, and we must implement courageously, sometimes without regard to political consequences, the programs that we know are best for the people who've chosen us to lead.

Let me start by making clear what our priorities for using the present oil supplies are right now. My first priority as President is to protect the lives and the wellbeing of all Americans. Therefore, our emergency services, such as police, fire, and health, must be maintained. So must the essentials of food and shelter.

We must have fuel to produce and to distribute food. We must have heating fuel to prevent suffering next winter in almost every part of this country, and particularly, of course, in the northern States.

We've drawn down our winter fuel stocks because of the earlier supply cutoff from Iran, which I've already mentioned. We simply must build them back. We are doing so now, and we will meet the goal that I've established for our Nation.

We will distribute limited supplies of gasoline fairly and equitably among the motorists of this country. There are things we can do to manage the current shortage of energy. We can do it better, and we will get this done.

We are pressing the refineries, for instance, to increase their production of fuel and heating oil. As a byproduct this will also produce more gasoline, as well.

We are requiring the oil industry to cooperate. If they do not cooperate voluntarily, we will not hesitate to use the authority that I have to require the oil companies to meet the basic energy needs of our Nation. The oil companies must cooperate.

I have ordered almost 200 auditors into the field to ensure that the Nation's refiners comply with the law, and another 400 will be sent to monitor fuel jobbers and dealers. At my direction, the Department of Justice and the Department of Energy are jointly investigating the oil companies to see if the current shortage involves any improper or illegal activity. We will bring the full force of the law to bear on those who profiteer from our national shortage or who try to cheat the American public.

We now have an independent accounting firm checking on the effectiveness of the new Department of Energy in verifying oil industry data. It's very difficult to get accurate information, but I want to make sure that the information that is achieved by us and is distributed to the American people is absolutely accurate.

I'm ordering the Energy Information Administration, which is an independent group, to send its weekly report to our news media throughout the country, telling what are our present energy supplies that week. I would like the interested American public, individual citizens like you, to be just as familiar with the energy situation as you are with local weather reports.

But again, let me be totally honest with you and very direct. All of this that I have described to you does not save oil and it does not create oil. In the short term, we will simply have to stretch out a limited supply. We will have to play a kind of shuffling game, allocating limited supplies of oil among our farmers, our truckers, our homeowners, industry, and also, of course, among motorists.

This will have to go on until our long-term efforts start paying off. Therefore, I urge the Congress to give me power to set mandatory State-by-State conservation goals and to impose mandatory conservation. If a State fails to meet its target, I want to give local and State officials authority first and hope that all of you and all Governors will carry out this responsibility. If you do not, then I will act from Washington as President.

Congress must also act finally to give me authority to develop a standby gasoline rationing plan. It is absolutely crucial for us to arm ourselves against the possibility of further serious interruptions in our energy supplies. We never know when we might lose a major portion of our oil imports. If this happens, a gasoline rationing plan will help us distribute those limited supplies fairly.

But I want to now mention the most important thing of all. Every single American must stop wasting energy. These are some of the things that we can do to defend ourselves in the immediate crisis.

More than 2 years ago, you may remember, I called the energy crisis the moral equivalent of war. There were a lot of jokes about it from the oil industry and from the news media. Now the battle has been joined. This time there can be no delay, this time there can be no retreat.

Last night I set forth a general strategy for winning the energy war, one which will enable us to meet all America's new energy needs from America's own energy resources. We will have to succeed both by conservation and production, because from this time forth we will never import one drop of oil more than we did 2 years ago in 1977. I am drawing our line of defense here and now.

Now I'm going to mention one of the biggest figures you ever heard. Overall we're going to take the unparalleled peacetime commitment, an investment of $140 billion, for American energy security, so that never again will our Nation's independence be hostage to foreign oil.

Where is the money coming from? All of this investment of Federal funds must come from the windfall profits tax on the oil industry, which I have proposed to the Congress. It's now more critical than it ever was that Congress swiftly pass a strong, permanent windfall profits tax. And I want each of you as county leaders and all Americans who hear my voice to bring your full power to bear to make sure that Congress acts to give the American people the financial weapons to win the energy war.

Let me brief you now on some of the new points of attack.

Each year I will set targets for the amount of foreign oil we import. I'm today announcing a quota for this year, 1979, which will hold U.S. imports to 8.2 million barrels per day—300,000 below the ceilings we set at the Tokyo summit and 400,000 barrels per day below what we used in 1977. And we will meet this goal.

The energy security corporation that I proposed last night to produce American energy from new sources will not be—will not be—just another Federal agency. It will be outside the Federal Government, outside the Federal bureaucracy, free to use its independent business judgment in order to produce enough alternate energy sources to meet its 10-year target of reducing our imports by 2½ million barrels of oil per day.

I'm announcing new incentives for the production of heavy oil, oil shale, and hard-to-get-at natural gas—all of which this country has in great abundance.

To make certain that energy projects such as critical pipelines, port facilities, production plants are built, a new energy mobilization board will slash through redtape and bureaucratic obstacles and will set absolute deadlines for action at the Federal, State, and local level. We are leaving with State and local authorities the first line of responsibility to remove roadblocks to these critical projects, but our energy crisis is so severe that if any level of government fails to act within a reasonable time, this board will see to it that action is taken, just as similar boards made sure that action was taken to protect our Nation's existence in World War II. It's time for us to take this bold action, and we will.

I want to make energy goals as compelling to every homeowner and every renter as for business and industry. Utilities must shift from oil to coal. But I'm also proposing to Congress a unique new program to require gas and electric utility companies to provide low-cost loans to their customers, the homeowners of America, to finance conservation improvements, repayable only at the time of sale of the home.

I'm proposing another program that will offer incentives to convert homes that are now oil-heated to natural gas and to help oil-heated homes which cannot convert with conservation.

I've earmarked $16.5 billion in new funds for the next 10 years to improve buses, subways, and other mass transit, and to build more fuel-efficient automobiles.

Recognizing that low-income families have been hardest hit by the OPEC price increases and rising energy costs in general, I'm proposing to triple the size of the assistance program which I recommended to Congress on April 5. This will also be paid for out of the windfall profits tax, which Congress is already considering.

In addition, we'll be expanding the weatherization program to improve homes and to make them more efficient in conserving energy.

I want to explain one thing very clearly, because misinformation is being spread among the American people. And I want you to listen to this.

We are working very closely with Mexico and Canada. The total quantity of production and export of oil and gas from Mexico is obviously a decision to be made by the people and the Government of Mexico. But we now purchase more than 80 percent of all the oil exported by Mexico—more than 80 percent. We are now negotiating a new agreement to purchase the natural gas which Mexico will be willing to export.

Although Canada's oil production will be steadily dropping during the next few years, we will continue to share hydroelectric power and other energy sources with our neighbor to the north. One major project will be the new pipeline to be built from Alaska through Canada to bring natural gas to the lower 48 States.

By 1985 Alaskan and Canadian natural gas can displace almost 700,000 barrels of imported oil per day. The North Slope producers have dragged their feet in helping to finance a pipeline needed to bring that gas to market. I've instructed the Secretary of Energy to call them in and get them going, and I will insist personally that this gas pipeline be built without further delay.

We are and we will continue to be a good customer, a good neighbor, and a good trading partner with both Mexico and with Canada.

This Nation will need to rely on a broad range of energy sources. The hard fact is that we depend on nuclear power now for 13 percent of all the electricity consumed in the United States.

A few communities—for instance, Chicago—derive more than 50 percent of all their electricity from nuclear power-plants. The recommendations of Kemeny Commission investigating the Three Mile Island incident will help us to ensure safety, but nuclear power must play an important role in the United States to ensure our energy future.

In June I set an ambitious but important goal for meeting 20 percent of the Nation's energy needs from the Sun by the year 2000. With steeply rising OPEC prices and greater supply uncertainties, attainment of this goal is more important than it ever was. No cartel can control the price of solar power. No country can embargo solar power.

We've already tripled our Federal investment in solar energy, and the new solar bank that I have proposed will permit all Americans to join in making widespread solar power use a reality.

The actions that I've already taken with Congress the last 2 years will reduce our projected imports of foreign oil by 4 million barrels per day. The new actions I've described for you last night and today will save us an additional 4½ million barrels of oil, foreign oil, a day below what we are presently consuming, by the year 1990. I'm going to keep these initiatives moving, and every one of us, public official and private citizen, must keep up this pressure for progress.

Our basic strategy is as clear as it can be. Together you and I and every American are simply going to change the way this society creates and uses its energy. And as we do, we're going to find ourselves growing stronger, more free, and more confident at home and around the world.

As the recent positive decision made by Saudi Arabia to increase production has shown, forceful action by this country proving that we are going to save energy can encourage moderation on the part of some of the OPEC nations and make us better able to deal with all the others. The important thing I want to get across today is that each action every one of us takes will not only improve our own lives but affect the future of the world.

The heartbreaks and the triumphs of each county, each city, each neighborhood, the successes or the failures are also the successes and failures, the triumphs and the heartbreaks of our Nation. The tragedy of an elderly family who are not able to pay for heat in the winter is a national tragedy, just as the success of a local weatherization program or carpool program is a triumph of or success for the whole Nation.

I ask you to work with me throughout the counties of America to plan conservation efforts that go beyond attempts to convince people that an energy crisis is real. Together we must challenge people to make specific actions possible, as workers, employers, commuters, customers, homeowners, renters, all put together, can really comprise a genuine, workable national effort.

It's easy for us to try to leave the job for others, to the Federal Government, to the oil companies, to OPEC. We must not do that. We will not do that. That's what I want you to do for our country. I want you to make it possible for every citizen who lives in your county to join in setting local conservation standards and targets.

I'm not asking now that the leaders of every county in the country work to create another government agency. I want you to have a group of your best private citizens to look at the needs and resources that you have in your own com-munities, to evaluate your strengths and your weaknesses, and agree with your own tactics in your own way to meet local conservation targets.

As you work with local citizens and community leaders in taking up this call to action, you can count on the support and you can count on the help of Federal officials, including myself, to live and to work with you to make this dream, this challenge a reality. I will put all Federal employees—agriculture, forestry, HUD, HEW, welfare, whatever—on notice that they must cooperate with county officials to cut out the waste of energy in your county.

In your county you are vital local leaders. I know you can get the job done, and you certainly deserve the help of the officials from the President on down in our Federal Government. You can enforce the law on speed limits. You can enforce the new regulations on building thermostat settings. There is a $10,000 fine for setting the thermostat on a public building lower than 78 degrees in the summer and higher than 65 degrees in the winter. I intend to enforce it, and I intend to have your help in making sure that it is enforced.

You can make sure that gasoline consumption is reduced by improving public transit, by dealing with county vehicles. You can help business and industry and government employers develop ride-sharing carpools, to stagger working hours, and to reduce employee workday travel.

Some communities have done so. My wife was recently in Davis, California, for instance, which has done a tremendous job and slashed total energy use more than 35 percent below what it used to be. In so doing we're better able to understand ourselves, and we are better able to understand other tough choices that America must meet in facing the challenges of the future.

1246

For example, last January, I set forth an austere budgetary policy for fiscal 1980, working toward a balanced Federal budget in the future to meet our serious inflation problem. I intend to hold that course steady and to enforce the program I've put forward to deal with successfully the inflation problem of our Nation. If we fail to do so, American workers, businesses, consumers will lose faith in the Government's willingness to cope with inflation. The value of the dollar would weaken and further aggravate our inflation rate.

I will also not hesitate to take action to avoid a serious recession. Now more than ever, Congress must enact our existing proposals, which you helped to develop, for targeted fiscal assistance and counter-cyclical aid to hard-pressed local governments when the unemployment rate goes up very much. These are proposals which are important, but inflation is still our Nation's most serious economic problem, and I'm determined to stick with my policies to fight inflation. And also here I need and expect your help.

In closing, let me say this: You are fellow public servants along with me. These are the kinds of choices that I have to make, because finally I only have one constituency—all the people of this Nation. These are people that you represent. Every one of your constituents is a constituent of mine. For 203 years, our Nation has stood proud and free. We have met challenge after challenge. We've overcome them all for one fundamental reason. In a crisis, we Americans have always stood together.

On the way here from Washington this morning on the airplane, Congressman Ike Skelton gave me a letter, and I'd like to read it to you.

"Mr. President: You will recall that I was a polio patient at Warm Springs, Georgia, in the late 1940's. While I was there, I copied Franklin D. Roosevelt's undelivered address where the original is located. From that speech, may I suggest that you use his words that ended the speech as follows, and I quote from Roosevelt, 'The only limit to our realization of tomorrow will be our doubts of today. Let us move forward with strong and active faith.' "

And Ike Skelton continues, "I memorized those words as a teenager, and they summarized what you said last night in your address to the Nation. Most respectfully, your friend, Ike Skelton."

We have had some serious doubts in our Nation about our Nation. Today, not only our Nation's economy but our very independence is threatened. Our freedom is beyond price. We must not let it be endangered by the energy problem. As a people, as a nation, let us join together in our struggle to secure our Nation's energy independence with all the fullness that we have in our great Nation and our will to live in freedom. We must fight together for our Nation, and, together with our renewed dedication and our renewed faith in America, we will again, as Americans, join together, lead our Nation to victory.

Thank you very much.

NOTE: The President spoke at 10:06 a.m. in the H. Roe Bartle Convention Center ballroom. His remarks were broadcast live on radio and television.

Detroit, Michigan

Remarks and a Question-and-Answer Session at the Annual Convention of the Communications Workers of America.   ·
July 16, 1979

THE PRESIDENT. *President Glenn Watts, Communications Workers of America, my fellow Americans:*

I'd like to say a few words before I begin to take your questions.

National Goals

Last night I spoke to you about a nation in a time of crisis. I sounded a warning in harsh terms, terms not often used by a President speaking to the people of our country.

I did not speak this way from a sense of hopelessness or despair. I described this crisis of confidence and sounded the warning to our Nation, because our future will equal the promise of the past only if we face the truth, heed the warning, and change our course.

I spoke this way because it is the truth.

In a time of shadowy dread and fear, of growing anger and frustration, the only firm ground on which we can regroup and rebuild our own confidence is to be honest about ourselves.

The energy proposals which I presented last night and this morning in Detroit [Kansas City] will complete the list of campaign promises that I made in 1976 for legislation to be passed. But today I want to talk to you about a larger promise, the promise I made in my acceptance speech and the promise I made hundreds of times during my campaign throughout this Nation—the promise that I would describe for you and to carry forward the vision of this Nation that I hold in my heart. That's the promise that I pledged to redeem last night.

It is our common task to commit ourselves to a renaissance of America—to a rebirth of the American spirit. First of all, we must restore our confidence and our sense of the future. Somehow we've lost it, and all else pales in comparison to the importance of the need for return of confidence of Americans in the future of our Nation.

The second thing we must do is to revitalize our basic human values. What is it that we individually in our own lives value most? We must believe and we must belong to something bigger than just ourselves, whether it be religion or community or family or our national service.

The third thing we must do is to regenerate our sense of unity, joining hands with each other in a sense of commitment to a national purpose of which we can be proud and which we can serve with commitment and determination—our belief that we are building a better nation for the years to come.

And we must define, finally, new goals for our Nation and encourage all Americans—the President and all of you—to join in determining these goals. What will our Nation be? What do we want to achieve in the years ahead for ourselves and for our children? We must bring together the different elements in America—producers, consumers, labor, business—bring all of us together from the battlefield of selfishness to a table of common purpose.

This is a vision of America towards which I will lead this Nation. In the months ahead, I will come to you throughout America with fresh proposals. Some will involve the traditional government, some will not. Above all, I will defend our common national purpose against those narrow special interests who often forget the overriding needs of America. I will persuade, I will speak against, I will fight any selfish interest that undermines our national purpose, and I will demand that the Government reflect those commitments which I make to you today.

Obviously I can't do this by myself. As I promised last night, I will continue to travel across this country to hear the people of America. I will listen, and I will act. I intend to open the government process as wide as possible so the fresh air of America can blow across Washington, D.C.

These are the promises that I made to you 3 years ago, and I intend to keep them.

I will start right here and now by hearing your views, answering your questions about America's future. Before I do, I would like to say one final thing.

I can point the way, Congress can enact laws, government can execute programs, but true success can only come from the commitment of the people of the United States. Your concerns, your sacrifices, your values, your participation will determine the future life of the nation which we all love.

A great labor union such as yours was not built by Americans who said, "Me first, me last, me always." Your organization, one of the greatest on Earth, was built the way great causes in America's past were always built—by decent, caring citizens working together with confidence for a common purpose, a common goal, a common good.

I ask each of you today for a renewed commitment to a greater America. Do I have your commitment for a greater America? [*Applause*]

Thank you very much.

You've got a partner here. You've answered my question, and now I'll answer yours. I'll be glad to answer the first question.

QUESTIONS

TAX RATES

Q. Mr. President, I'm A. D. Boutwell, vice president of Local 10509, in Hattiesburg, Mississippi.

I understand that there may be some type tax proposal in the future if the inflation rate continues at its present level, and certainly we hope and pray that it will not continue in the future as it has in the past. And I was wondering if you might tell us what type of tax break you had in mind and when this action may be taken.

THE PRESIDENT. I do not plan on any tax increases. My primary concern at this time is to control inflation as far as the economy goes. We will monitor very carefully the economic situation in America.

In the last 2½ years, since I have been in office, we've been fortunate in cutting the unemployment rate from more than 8 percent down to 5.6 percent—more than a 25-percent reduction. We've cut unemployment compensation payments down 55 percent. In the coming months, because of a very high OPEC price increase—they've almost doubled the price of oil in the last 7 months—we do face some increase in inflation, perhaps some increase in unemployment.

If we see a real need to do something about the economy, if the unemployment rate starts getting too high, then I will take action. But that action will not be to raise taxes. It would be to lower taxes. And if we lower them, my first preference would be to lower the payroll tax.

So, I think you need not fear of tax increases while I'm in office.

OIL INDUSTRY

Q. Mr. President, Jewell White, Lockport, Illinois, Local 5011.

Mr. John Swearingen, chairman of the board of Standard Oil of Indiana, stated in the New York Times on June 4 that the oil companies won't increase production until gasoline reaches $1.50 a gallon.

My question, Mr. President: Do you agree that to resolve the energy crisis we must reorganize by abolishing the secrecy of the oil industry and let workers learn all the facts about costs, profits, imports, refining capacity, and alternate energy sources?

THE PRESIDENT. I feel a great responsibility on my shoulders as President of this country. I have a lot of authority to deal with the oil industry, not yet enough, but I will guarantee you that we will not permit the oil companies to hold back on production, waiting for the gasoline prices to go up.

We now have the authority to require accurate information from the oil companies about imports, the amount of oil they have on hand, and the amount that they sell. This is new authority that we've just gotten recently.

I have hired one of the finest accounting firms in the Nation to look at the Department of Energy and its new responsibility, to be sure that it is getting the most accurate information now about the oil companies, what they are producing, what they can produce.

Six weeks ago they were only producing at a rate of about 82 percent of capacity. Now, because of proddings from us, the production rate of the oil refineries is about 91 percent. This is almost all they can do under the present circumstances.

In addition, there's an independent agency, not associated with government, that gets data, information about oil. And I have encouraged them—I announced this this morning in Kansas City—to distribute this information every week to all the news media throughout the country—newspapers, the weekly newspapers, the magazines, radio, television—so that you might become familiar with oil supplies on hand and production from our wells and refinery output, just like Americans do now about checking on the weather reports. So, I think you'll see a definite increase in the future, both in the volume of information that we get and distribute to you on the oil industry, and also you'll see a great increase or improvement in the accuracy of those reports.

Finally, I've asked the Department of Energy and the Department of Justice to check the oil industry to make sure there are no improper or illegal acts. If there are, they will be prosecuted to the ultimate length of the law. I'm not going to permit the oil companies or anyone else to profiteer on the shortage of oil in this country nor to cheat the American people, and you can depend on it.

U.S. SPACE PROGRAM

Q. Mr. President, Odus Rigdon, vice president, CWA Local 3112, West Palm Beach, Florida—born in Waycross, Georgia, and proud of it. [*Laughter*]

I personally feel that the energy crisis can be solved in space exploration. I would like to know if you could tell us today why you feel that the space program is so important to us as Americans? Where do you think we are today in space exploration, and where do we go from here?

THE PRESIDENT. Fine. Almost exactly 10 years ago, as you know, the first American put his foot on the Moon. No other country has been able to match this achievement, and I would predict that in our lifetime, no other country will be able to do it.

Since then, we've had tremendous space exploration flights past the other satellites; the satellites have gone past the other parts of our solar system—recently, Jupiter, Saturn, and even Uranus. Now we're shifting toward a more routine way to deal with space with the space shuttle.

Before another year goes past, we'll be seeing space shuttle flights. We'll put them up into space, manned with a crew, carrying a cargo. They'll cruise around the Earth as many times they desire and then come down, not in parachutes in the ocean, but down-gliding, landing on airstrips just like airplanes. That same space shuttle then can unload its valuable cargo with all the data they've collected, or instruments that have been tested. It can reload and take off again into space. This means that we now have a way at a reasonable price to have routine trips into space and back, for the first time, as you know.

So, I think we've approached the time when we can continue very advanced, very exciting research programs, trips to the planets, and even beyond, and have equipment tested in the space shuttle on a routine basis.

The first priority will be defense and our Nation's intelligence. The next will be the leasing of space, just like you rent part of a freight car or part of a truck body going across the country to transport material. We'll lease that space, that cargo space to private companies. When those needs are met, we'll lease additional space to some of our allies and friends around the world, and it'll be done to keep the space shuttles going.

I've already approved four space shuttles. The first ones will be fired from the east coast. Later, the space shuttles will be fired from the west coast. Because of various reasons, if you want to go east and west, parallel pretty much with the Equator, you fire the shuttles from the east coast. If you want to go over the poles, north and south, you fire from Vandenburg Air Base in California. Soon we'll be doing it both ways.

So, I think we're making great progress to make routine achievements out of what was formerly just an experimental effort in space. I think the prospects are right for our country. We're ahead of anybody else in this program, and I'm determined to stay ahead of everybody else.

WHEAT EXPORTS

Q. Mr. President, I'm Mike Agnew. I am from Local 2336 in Washington, D.C. And I'd like to have you share with us this afternoon your views on the ever-popular slogan, "A bushel of wheat for a barrel of oil."

THE PRESIDENT. I was hoping that all my answers could be popular. [*Laughter*] But this answer is not going to be popular.

Our Nation produces 14 percent of all the world's wheat. Of all the wheat sold among countries in foreign trade, about 40 percent of it is produced in the United States. Every time our Nation's farmers produce 100 bushels of wheat, 60 bushels are exported to foreign countries.

As you know now, the price of wheat varies up and down, around $4 a bushel. The price of oil is up as high as $22, sometimes $35 a bushel [barrel]. It would be impossible to find anyone in Mexico or in the Persian Gulf area or in Venezuela or in Nigeria that would swap us a $22 barrel of oil for a $4 bushel of wheat.

A lot of people have said, "Well, why don't we cut off wheat shipments to the OPEC countries and force them to bring their prices down?" Let me remind you of this: First of all, the OPEC countries, in general, particularly those in the Middle East, have a very tiny population. Saudi Arabia, for instance, produces about 8½, 9 million barrels of oil a day. They only have five or six million people. A little tiny country in Europe could provide all the wheat that Saudi Arabia needs out of their surplus. If we cut off all wheat shipments to any country that produced oil, they could very easily get their wheat anywhere else. We could not punish them accordingly.

Another thing is that if I put an embargo on the shipment of American farmers' wheat to any oil-producing country, there would be more farmers in Washington trying to run over me with tractors than you've ever seen before. [*Laughter*]

So, it's a good song and a good slogan, and we are doing tremendous amount of trade, but that equal swap is just not possible.

Let me close by saying this: Last year we set a record on agricultural exports. The year before that we set a record on agricultural exports. This year we're going to set another record on agricultural exports. Our exports of wheat are going up, and I predict to you that in the generations ahead, maybe just the decades ahead, maybe just the years ahead, we're going to find that wheat is a much more valuable export item for the world than oil is going to be, coming from the OPEC nations. So, we're in a good position in the United States of America. We're going to stay that way.

WAGE GUIDELINES

Q. Mr. President, Norman Henschel, president, Local 1108, Suffolk County, Long Island, New York.

Mr. President, with the inflation rate nearing 14 percent, and with the Communications Workers of America going into major negotiations in 1980, is it fair or realistic to stay with 7-percent wage guidelines?

THE PRESIDENT. Did Glenn Watts ask you to ask me that question? [*Laughter*]

First of all, in 1980, I do not expect the inflation rate to be 14 percent. Secondly, we have been consulting very closely with Glenn Watts and with Doug Fraser of the UAW and with other labor leaders, and also with leaders in management, to try to set wage and price guidelines that will be fair and equitable. And I don't want to punish any working people, obviously. But it must be remem-bered that everybody has to take the best interests of our Nation at heart.

I have been very pleased at the response of the workers of our country, in very strong, well-organized unions, in trying to accommodate the needs of other Americans in the wage settlements. Most, I think, have been satisfied, and I would predict that the CWA, one of the best organized unions in America, can very carefully, on their own, negotiate a contract that will be fair to the workers that Glenn Watts represents, and also fair to our country.

That's the best answer I can give you at this point.

TRADE UNIONISM

Q. My name is Ann Kelly. I'm from Local 7102, Des Moines, Iowa, and I represent directory assistance operators.

As a trade unionist, my question is, why does the U.S. Government continue to buy products from the J. P. Stevens Company, with their long history of anti-union activities?

THE PRESIDENT. I don't know. [*Laughter*]

Q. Back into it for us.

THE PRESIDENT. It would be very difficult, I think, for the United States Government to pass a law or to enforce a law that all products bought by the Government had to be made by union workers. There would be a lot of products that were in the borderline between what was manufactured and what was not. And I think that ordinarily we work very closely with the trade unions in assuring that their products are adequately assessed.

I don't think we've punished those who do organize. Some industries, as you know, are almost 100-percent organized. Some, like the textile industry, are not very highly organized. But I think it's very important that you ask a question like this, and I think we are treating the trade unions fairly.

I don't think we can completely freeze out, though, the purchase of any goods that might be produced by nonunion workers, even though you might prefer it.

Q. The nonunion—it's their total disregard for the law.

THE PRESIDENT. I know. As you know, our administration—I personally have strongly favored labor law reform. And with your help, if we can keep this line of enthusiasm up in CWA, UAW, and others, I believe that next year we can go back to Congress and get labor law reform passed. That's what we need to do.

ENERGY CORPORATION BONDS

Q. Mr. President, I'm Larry Vandeventer from Corpus Christi, Texas, Local 12137. I support your proposals to win our energy fight, and I would like to know when you think we will be able to buy the energy bonds that you spoke of.

THE PRESIDENT. By the way, we keep the thermostat set on 78 degrees in the Oval Office. Some of the news people send me word here that it's 80 degrees where they are and it's 86 degrees where I am. [*Laughter*]

First of all, the Congress will have to pass a law authorizing the establishment of this private corporation. It will be given special authority and a special status. I'm sure that all of you are familiar with the COMSAT arrangement, where the special Communications Satellite Corporation was set up and stock was sold in that corporation to get the original communications satellites in space. A similar arrangement will be followed in getting established the special corporation to produce energy from shale, coal, and other means in our country.

As soon as the Congress passes the law authorizing this special corporation, it will be set up. It will not be a Government agency. It will be an independent, private corporation. And at that time, hopefully sometime this year, you'll be able to buy energy bonds and own a part of our Nation's energy security future. I don't know the exact date, but if you'll help me, we'll cut out the delays that have held up Congress too long.

That's a good question.

ARMED FORCES OFFICERS

Q. Mr. President, Bob Armacher, vice president, Local 11503, Panorama City, California, representing the great San Fernando Valley. This is in a little lighter vein.

The last time we had the pleasure of your presence at one of our conventions, you were a candidate for the nomination as President of the United States for the Democratic Party. Obviously, you impressed many others as favorably as you impressed me, particularly on your talk about waste in government. I remember two items you brought up. One of them was the fact that we had more admirals sitting in Washington than we have ships in the ocean; we have more colonels in the Air Force than we have airplanes.

My question is, what is the status of this situation at the present time? [*Laughter*]

THE PRESIDENT. I'll have to check on it and let you know. [*Laughter*]

I remember very well the convention in San Diego and the fact that I pointed out we did have more admirals than we do ships, more colonels than we do airplanes in the Air Force. I'll have to find out the exact number now and let you know.

We have been cutting down, by the way, on the number of flag officers in the

Armed Forces, compared to the number of enlisted men and noncommissioned officers. But I've got your—no, the only thing I've got is Panorama City, California. If I could get your exact address, I'll get you the numbers and I'll mail them to you personally.

Q. The exact address is 8155 Van Nuys Boulevard.

THE PRESIDENT. 81—what?

Q. 55 Van Nuys Boulevard, Panorama City.

THE PRESIDENT. How do you spell the boulevard. [*Laughter*]

Q. B-l-v-d. Boulevard.

THE PRESIDENT. Van Nuys—Van Nuys Boulevard. I got you.

Q. Suite 902.

THE PRESIDENT. All right. A-r-m-a-c-h-e-r?

Q. That's correct, sir.

THE PRESIDENT. Thank you. You'll hear from me within a week.

WAGE GUIDELINES

Q. Mr. President, my name is Gerry Hefferan. I am the president of Local 1172, CWA. I represent the employees of ITT World Communications.

The last 25-year dinner I attended at ITT World Communications, the president of that company, Mr. George Knapp, announced the profits of the company at some $220 million. Now, we were the first company out of the box after your speech on October 24. That morning, the negotiating team for the company came in and told us that they sent you a telegram that morning saying that they were going to stand behind your guidelines and, thus, make it mandatory on the union to accept them. We did because we felt what you had put down was effective or hoped to be effective.

Now with the rate of inflation—by the way, we would have been justified asking for, with those profits, 20 percent, 20 percent, and 20 percent over a 3-year period of time. But we didn't. We stuck by the guidelines. We sold the contract.

Now with the rate of inflation coming up at the end of the year at 10 percent, we had 7 percent, of which we had to use 2 percent for pensions and another percent for a 10-year progression. So, that meant 5 percent across the board. At the end of the year, it looks like a 10-percent inflation. We're now 5 percent down the tubes.

How is the working man going to recuperate these moneys? We took a 2-year contract, because that's all we could buy to satisfy our members. Now we have another 5 percent coming up November of this year.

Is there something that can be done in respect to catching up the way we did when President Nixon made restrictions and we got put under that one? Is there something that can be done? That's my question.

THE PRESIDENT. I don't know enough about the contract to know whether or not it can be renegotiated. Most of the settlements recently have had a cost-of-living clause in them that substantially compensated the workers when the inflation rate was increased more than we anticipated because of OPEC's action.

One of the things that we will be considering when we come out with new wage and price guidelines which, as you know, are voluntary—but it depends a lot on the patriotism of people, which you've already demonstrated. But we'll try to accommodate in those guidelines the kind of situation that you describe.

I think the way to get around it easiest is to have the cost-of-living clause included. But I don't know enough about the details of your contract to be able to answer any better.

Q. Mr. President, ITT had four contracts that they did have COLA clauses. They took strikes on all four and did away with them. ITT conglomerate does not have a contract now that has a COLA clause in it. I wish that the Government would make it mandatory. I would settle for simply a COLA, cost-of-living.

THE PRESIDENT. I understand. I want to make sure that you understand. I'm not trying to get involved in the contract negotiations. I've got enough to handle on my own. [*Laughter*] But we will try to make the guidelines fair, and we will talk very carefully to Glenn Watts and to other labor leaders before we come out with what we recommend as voluntary wage guidelines this fall. I am sure Glenn is listening very carefully to your voice, as have I. Thank you very much.

Q. Whatever you decide, we are behind you.

THE PRESIDENT. Thank you very much.

FUEL PRICES

Q. Mr. President, Tom Scanlan, sales bargaining unit, president, Local 1395, Watertown, Massachusetts.

I live in the Northeast, where people are paying almost 90 cents a gallon for home heating oil. This really frightens the old and the poor and people on fixed incomes. How do you justify wage guidelines for workers who already pay a fourth or a large portion of their income just to keep warm? What do you plan to help us up in that area?

THE PRESIDENT. I take responsibility for a lot of things, but I can't take the responsibility for the increase in energy prices. And I cannot tell you that the prices are not going to increase further in the future. Prices are going up on a worldwide basis, and I know that Americans are very upset and very disappointed and sometimes very angry because we have reached a 90-cent to a dollar price for gasoline and also a very high cost for home heating oil.

The price of gasoline in Italy is $2.75 a gallon; in France, $2.50; in England, $2.25; in Germany, about the same. We've been very fortunate to be not only the world's greatest consumers of oil, but we are also one of the world's greatest producers of oil. But no matter what I do, no matter what the Congress does, no matter what anybody does in the years ahead, the price of energy is going to go up. That is a fact. It's a worldwide fact, and I cannot mislead you.

Now, the second point is this: It's particularly hard on the poor people of our country. I'm trying to get the Congress to pass a permanent windfall profits tax on the oil companies. I hope you'll help me get it passed, because this money, which is a lot of money, will be used for three basic purposes.

First of all, to finance the development of our own energy resources which we have not yet used—shale oil, oil from coal, other sources. The second reason that we want this windfall profits tax is to improve the quality of our public mass transit systems—buses, subways, trains, and so forth. The third reason is to give special allocations of financial help to the very poor in our country who must depend on energy to heat their homes in particular.

We proposed originally $800 million a year to this fund to meet the kind of problem that you describe—when a poor family has the price of fuel oil go up through no fault of their own and it takes a major part of their income to pay for it. We're going to at least double this amount, maybe even triple it, when the Congress

1255

passes the windfall profits tax, to make sure that we do not have anybody in America, particularly New England, the north, where it's so cold and where the houses are heated with oil, who have to go cold because of the price of energy increases.

We're now building up to 240 million barrels of home heating oil by the end of October. That's one thing we'll do. And the other one is to compensate those very poor families who have a large increase in the price of heating oil through no fault of their own—and, I might add, through no fault of mine.

But if the Congress will pass the windfall profits tax, we'll have enough money without increasing the taxes on you by taxing the oil companies to make sure that that suffering that you are concerned about does not happen.

VIEWS ON THE PRESIDENCY

Q. Mr. President, I'm Clint Boling from Jonesboro, Arkansas, president of Local 6505.

In your speech last night, you talked about many problems that affect all of us today. One of those problems was the lack of trust and faith that we as Americans have in the Government. Do you have a specific plan, other than some that you may have outlined today, to provide the leadership to help restore this trust and faith that is required to improve these problems?

THE PRESIDENT. The only part of your question that bothers me is something I haven't mentioned so far. I worked for 10 days on that speech, including the background for it. I had about 150 people to come to Camp David in the quietness of that mountaintop area, just to talk to me. I listened 95 percent of the time to Americans saying, "Mr. President, this is what concerns me about my Nation, this is what concerns me about my life, this is why I'm doubtful about the future, this is why I can't work with my neighbor, this is what I don't like about the Government, this is what I don't like about you, and this is what I want you to do to change."

And I thought about it and I prayed about it, and I wrote that speech and gave it last night to tell you from the bottom of my heart that we do have some serious problems in our great Nation.

One thing is we've started dividing from one another. This country is a country of immigrants. We are a country of refugees. I bet you there are a hundred different foreign nations represented in this 4,000 people in this hall. In the past, in times of trouble, like a depression, like the First World War, like the Second World War, American people came together to meet the challenge with courage and bravery and commitment and sacrifice and unselfishness. Now we are faced with some serious problems that divide us.

When you have to sit in a gas line or when your home heating bill goes up, it doesn't pull people together. It separates people one from another, because you're mad at your neighbors, you're mad at the Government, you're mad at OPEC, you're mad at the oil companies. It's tended to divide us apart.

So, my point that I would like to make again is this: There's only one clear voice in this country on a sustained basis. That's the voice of the President of the United States. If I can't speak to you so you can understand me about the problems of our Nation, then nobody can. If I don't tell you the truth, then my voice will not be meaningful. If I don't go out among the people and listen, then I don't know what you are thinking. And if you don't believe I've got confidence in you, then you are not going to have confidence in me.

I've made some mistakes since I've been President. As I said last night, many of the people said, "Mr. President, you're not out among the people enough, you don't listen to us enough. You've been so bogged down in managing the Government that you haven't been leading our Nation." Well, I listened to that, and I've learned my lesson.

So, for the rest of the time that I'm in office, I'm going to spend more time among you, I'm going to listen to your voice, I'm going to work closer to you. During the campaign, I had to do that, because otherwise I would never have been elected. If I hadn't come to San Diego to listen to you and to talk to you then and to bare my heart to you, I would not have been elected.

So, the best thing I can do is to put my faith in the American people, and God willing, I will act to the best of my human ability so that you can always have confidence in me. I'll do the best I can. If you will join me, I guarantee you we'll have the greatest nation on Earth, like we always have.

WAGE AND PRICE GUIDELINES

Q. That's a tough question to follow, Mr. President. Ray Cordova, Local 11571, Long Beach, California. And I am experienced in the controlled 78 degrees right now, as you notice.

Mr. President, I have a brief statement as well as a question that addresses itself to the 7-percent wage guideline. When I have a member of my local who is being paid $4 or less an hour, caring for three children, whose spouse has abandoned her, is eligible for food stamps, eligible to draw welfare payments, no child care facilities that are affordable to her,

but because of pride and dignity, attempts to work and be a productive citizen, but then, Mr. President, she is told that 7 percent is the guideline.

We are experiencing double-digit inflation, and we cannot justify to our members 7 percent. So how, Mr. President, when labor is hamstrung with 7 percent, do you intend to have business live within 7 percent?

THE PRESIDENT. Well, this kind of question really concerns me, as you've already noticed. It's not the first one I've had today.

I've tried the best I could to stay away from mandatory wage standards. My own belief is that the system of free enterprise, the great union organizations can best handle their affairs through equal authority at the bargaining table.

As President, I evolved what I thought was the best standard I could devise. In the past, our inflation rate has been running 7, 7½, 8 percent—for about 10 years. In '74 it did get up to about 13 percent, as you remember, when OPEC clamped down on the price of oil. When we set the voluntary wage and price guidelines, that was a reasonable figure, and as the inflation rate built up, different labor organizations negotiated different kinds of contracts. We've tried to be reasonably flexible in giving our approval to the contract. I don't have any authority to tear up a contract. I don't have any authority to reverse what has been negotiated. And as I've said before, I'm deeply concerned about excessive restrictions that hurt the working people of our country.

In the fall, with this new rise in inflation that's been brought about by a doubling, almost, of the price of oil, we'll have to accommodate the new circumstances, and I think the cost-of-living clause in some of the contracts have helped.

I don't know how to answer your question. I'm not trying to justify that somebody ought to suffer. I do not believe that the working people of this country ought to suffer.

One additional problem that we face is, as I said last night, that the productivity of the American workers, not through your fault, but because of different things, has been going down—in most countries it's still going up. We still have, however, the highest worker productivity in the world.

The American worker is still the most productive in the world. And I would say that with a flexible attitude, which I do have, working with great labor leaders who represent you, I believe we can come out with a wage and price guideline that will do the maximum amount to hold down inflation and at the same time accommodate local problems and also regional problems and also the problems of certain kinds of workers who, like the woman you described already, has too low an income.

I can just promise you I'll do the best I can. I'll work with Glenn Watts and others to make sure that future wage and price guidelines are fair. I think the one we set up as a target was fair at the time we did it. And now we're ready to revise it when it's been in effect for 1 year.

Let me say this in closing—I've been here now for 55 minutes—I think you've seen an outstanding cross-section of the expression of interest and a few congratulations, a few concerns, a few criticisms that come from the American people. I've learned in the process, and I'll continue to learn. In fact, we'll have to learn together.

There's one thing I want all of us to do. I asked you to do it at the end of my speech last night. Do you remember what it was? I asked all of you, whenever you've got a chance, to—what? To say something good about our Nation.

Look, we live in the greatest nation on Earth, but quite often we get so bogged down, so concerned about a transient problem. Now, inflation's bad, gas lines are bad, home heating oil shortages are bad, sometimes unemployment is bad; but we still live in the greatest nation on Earth. And quite often we don't remember it, and we don't express our appreciation for it.

I believe one of the things that can pull our Nation back together to give us confidence, to give us unity, to restore American values, to improve the quality of our families, to strengthen our communities, to strengthen our churches, to strengthen our schools, to strengthen our government, to make sure that you can govern your own selves better, to make sure that all government officials—mayors and county commissioners and Governors and Congressmen and Presidents—will listen to your voice better, is to remember what we've got.

We've got a democracy, strong, firm, made up of free people, the best free enterprise system on Earth. Research, development—God's given us 24 percent of all the energy supplies in the world; the Middle East all put together only has 5 percent. And I think we've got reason to be confident. And one thing that can bring back confidence is for your neighbor to hear you saying, "There might be some things I don't like about it, but the United States of America is still the greatest place on Earth to live, and our country's going to be even greater in the future."

NOTE: The President spoke at 4:34 p.m. in Convention Hall "C" at the Cobo Hall Convention Center.

Department of Labor

Nomination of William P. Hobgood To Be an Assistant Secretary.   July 17, 1979

The President today announced that he will nominate William P. Hobgood, of Springfield, Va., to be Assistant Secretary of Labor for labor-management relations.

Hobgood was born February 19, 1939, in Atlanta, Ga. He received a B.S. from Florida State University in 1961, an M.A. from George Washington University in 1965, and a J.D. from the University of Louisville in 1972. He served in the U.S. Navy from 1961 to 1965.

He has been active in labor relations since 1965. He has served as a mediator in Louisville, Ky.; Charlotte, N.C.; and Washington, D.C. Hobgood has worked with the Federal Mediation and Conciliation Service since 1965 and has been Director of Mediation Services since 1977.

He is also Coordinator of Labor Relations for the President's Commission on the Coal Industry and has been adjunct professor at Georgetown University Law Center since 1974.

Apollo 11 Anniversary

Message of the President.   July 17, 1979

On July 20, 1969, man first reached out and touched an extraterrestrial body in the solar system. That touch, those first footsteps on the moon, greatly enlarged our thinking about our future on earth and beyond. The moon was no longer simply our visitor, to recall Shakespeare's phrase, for we had visited the moon.

The touchdown of the Apollo 11 *Eagle* in the Sea of Tranquility is an unforget-

table milestone in the history of exploration. Whatever else historians of the future may say about this century, they will surely describe our nation as dynamic and resourceful. Not only did we fulfill mankind's age-old dream of human flight, but we also successfully ventured into space.

At this moment, automated extensions of human intelligence—Viking, Pioneer and Voyager spacecraft—are exploring the solar system. While orbital observatories search the distant universe, satellites are providing data which may someday help us better to preserve and manage our earth. We look forward, as early as next year, to even greater knowledge when the Space Shuttle brings us easier, more economical and more regular access to space.

Today, as we observe the tenth anniversary of the lunar landings, our determination must be to ensure that the possibilities we have glimpsed from our Apollo missions will be developed for the benefit of all mankind.

JIMMY CARTER

Equal Employment Opportunity Commission

Nomination of Daniel E. Leach To Be a Member, and Redesignation as Vice Chairman. July 17, 1979

The President today announced that he has nominated Daniel E. Leach for reappointment as a member of the Equal Employment Opportunity Commission (EEOC) for a 5-year term. Leach would be redesignated Vice Chairman of the Commission on confirmation.

Leach has been a member of the EEOC since 1976 and has served as Vice Chairman since 1977.

He was born April 2, 1937, in Detroit, Mich. He received an A.B. from Colgate University in 1958, an LL.B. from Detroit College of Law in 1961, and an LL.M. from Georgetown University Law Center in 1963.

From 1962 to 1965, Leach was a trial attorney in the Civil Division at the Justice Department, where he handled the prosecution and defense of actions relating to the Government's water transportation and shipping interests. From 1965 to 1966, he practiced law with the Detroit firm of Sullivan, Eaimes, Moody and Petrillo.

From 1966 to 1976, Leach was general counsel to the Democratic Policy Committee of the United States Senate.

As Vice Chairman of the EEOC, Leach also serves as a member of the President's Regulatory Council, the Task Force on Youth Unemployment, and the Administrative Conference of the United States. He is the author of a number of articles on affirmative action and employment discrimination.

United States Space Observance, 1979

Proclamation 4669. July 17, 1979

By the President of the United States of America

A Proclamation

Ten years ago this week, the Apollo astronauts changed forever, for all humanity, our concept of the universe and our relation to it. Their electrifying landing on the Moon—that "giant leap" to the surface of another world—was an unparalleled triumph of determination and technological genius. It epitomized the strength and the potential of the American people.

During ten years since, space has become part of our daily lives. We use it for essential communications and for monitoring our environment. Nationally and internationally, the exploration and use of space hold even greater promise in the future for the wiser management of our planetary resources, for the expansion of knowledge, and for the development of civilization.

In recognition of this triumph, the Congress, by joint resolution (H.J. Res. 353), has requested that the period of July 16 through 24, 1979, be designated as "United States Space Observance."

As we face new challenges as a nation—notably the challenge of achieving energy security—let us reflect upon the courage of the Apollo astronauts, and their predecessors in the Mercury and Gemini programs. And let us take courage and inspiration from the success of America's effort to land the first men on the Earth's Moon and return them safely.

Now, THEREFORE, I, JIMMY CARTER, President of the United States of America, do hereby proclaim the period of July 16 through July 24, 1979, as "United States Space Observance." In accord with the congressional resolution, I call upon the people of the United States to observe this period with appropriate ceremonies and activities.

IN WITNESS WHEREOF, I have hereunto set my hand this seventeenth day of July, in the year of our Lord nineteen hundred seventy-nine, and of the Independence of the United States of America the two hundred and fourth.

JIMMY CARTER

[Filed with the Office of the Federal Register, 10:56 a.m., July 18, 1979]

Foreign Service Retirement and Disability System

Executive Order 12145. July 18, 1979

By the authority vested in me as President by the Constitution and statutes of the United States of America, including Section 805 of the Foreign Service Act of 1946, as added by Section 503 of Public Law 94–350 (90 Stat. 835; 22 U.S.C. 1065), in order to conform the Foreign Service Retirement and Disability System to certain amendments to the Civil Service Retirement and Disability System, it is hereby ordered as follows:

1–101. (a) The enactment (after January 1, 1974) of certain laws has affected a number of provisions of general applicability in the Civil Service Retirement and Disability System (subchapter III, Chapter 83 of Title 5 of the United States Code) or otherwise affected current or former participants, annuitants, or survivors under that System which, immediately prior to the enactment of such laws, had been substantially identical to corresponding provisions of law affecting participants, former participants, annuitants or survivors under the Foreign Service Retirement and Disability System. Those laws are set forth at Annex I, attached hereto and made a part hereof.

(b) The provisions of the laws referred to in subsection (a) above are extended, as provided by Section 805 of the Foreign Service Act of 1946, as amended (22 U.S.C. 1065), to the Foreign Service Retirement and Disability System in accordance with the provisions of this Order, which provisions shall modify, supersede, or render inapplicable all inconsistent prior provisions of law.

1–102. In accord with Section 1 of Public Law 93–260, Section 804(2) of the Foreign Service Act of 1946, as amended (22 U.S.C. 1064(2)), is deemed to be amended by striking out "two years" wherever it appears and inserting in lieu thereof "one year". This amendment shall apply only in the cases of participants, former participants, or annuitants who died on or after April 9, 1974 but no annuity shall be paid or recomputed, by virtue of this amendment, for any period prior to May 1, 1974.

1–103. In accord with Section 1(b) of Public Law 95–382, Section 811 of the Foreign Service Act of 1946, as amended (22 U.S.C. 1071), shall be deemed to be amended to provide that, "No contribution shall be required for any period for which credit is allowed to persons of Japanese ancestry for being interned or otherwise detained during World War II, as described in Section 1(a) of Public Law 95–382.".

1–104. In accord with Section 1 of Public Law 93–273, and notwithstanding any other provision of Section 821 of the Foreign Service Act of 1946, as amended (22 U.S.C. 1076), said Section 821 shall be deemed to be amended to provide for the payment of a minimum annuity as set forth at Section 821–1 of Annex II attached hereto and made a part hereof.

1–105. In accord with Section 2 of Public Law 93–273, Section 821 of the Foreign Service Act of 1946, as amended (22 U.S.C. 1076), shall be deemed to be amended to provide an increase in annuities, which have been computed on the highest five consecutive years of service, as set forth at Section 821–2 of Annex II, attached hereto and made a part hereof.

1–106. In accord with Sections 1(a) and 4 of Public Law 95–317, Section 821 of the Foreign Service Act of 1946, as amended (2 U.S.C. 1076), shall be deemed to be amended to provide for the recomputation of annuities for nonmarried annuitants as set forth at Section 821–3 of Annex II, attached hereto and made a part hereof.

1–107. (a) In accord with Section 1 (c) of Public Law 95–317, the last sentence of Section 821(g) of the Foreign Service Act of 1946, as amended (22 U.S.C. 1076(g)), shall be deemed to be amended to read as follows: "The annuity reduction or recomputation shall be effective the first day of the first month beginning one year after the date of marriage."

(b) The amendment made by paragraph (a) above shall apply with respect to survivor elections received by the Secretary on or after October 1, 1978.

1–108. (a) In accord with Section 2 of Public Law 95–317, Section 821(f) of the Foreign Service Act of 1946, as amended (22 U.S.C. 1076(f)), shall be deemed to be amended by adding at the end thereof the following: "An annuity which is reduced under this subsection or any similar prior provisions of law shall, effective the first day of the month following the death of the beneficiary named under this subsection, be recomputed and paid as if the annuity had not been so reduced.".

(b) The amendment made by paragraph (a) above shall apply with respect to annuities which commence before, on, or after October 1, 1978, but no monetary benefit by reason of such amendment shall accrue for any period before October 1, 1978.

1–109. In accord with Section 3 of Public Law 95–317, Section 821 of the Foreign Service Act, as amended (22 U.S.C. 1076), shall be deemed to be amended to provide a requirement for annual notice to participants, as set forth at Section 821–4 of Annex II, attached hereto and made a part hereof.

1–110. In accord with subsections (c) and (d) of Section 2 of Public Law 95–382, Section 821 of the Foreign Service Act of 1946, as amended (22 U.S.C. 1076), shall be deemed to be amended to provide World War II Internment annuity credit as set forth at Section 821–5 of Annex II, attached hereto and made a part hereof.

1–111. In accord with Sections 1(a) and 2 (a) and (b) of Public Law 95–382, Section 851 of the Foreign Service Act of 1946, as amended (22 U.S.C. 1091), shall be deemed to be amended to provide additional creditable service as set forth at Section 851–1 at Annex III attached hereto and made a part hereof.

1–112. In accord with Public Law 94–166 and Public Law 95–366, Section 864 of the Foreign Service Act of 1946, as amended (22 U.S.C. 1104), shall be deemed to be amended to read as set forth at Annex IV, attached hereto and made a part hereof.

1–113. Because the provisions of Executive Order No. 11952 of January 7, 1977, have been incorporated into this Order or its Annexes, Executive Order No. 11952 is revoked.

JIMMY CARTER

The White House,
    July 18, 1979

[Filed with the Office of the Federal Register, 4:29 p.m., July 18, 1979]

NOTE: The annexes are printed in the FEDERAL REGISTER of July 20, 1979.

United States Ambassador to Bulgaria

Nomination of Jack Richard Perry.
July 18, 1979

The President today announced that he will nominate Jack Richard Perry, of Georgia, to be Ambassador Extraordinary and Plenipotentiary of the United States to Bulgaria.

Perry was born March 21, 1930, in Atlanta. He received his A.B. (1951) and LL.D. (honorary, 1971) from Mercer University and his M.A. (1958) from Columbia University. He served in the U.S. Army from 1951 to 1954.

From 1954 to 1957, Perry was with the Associated Press. He was director of Mercer University News Bureau from 1955 to 1956 and a reporter for the Macon Telegraph in 1957.

Perry joined the Foreign Service in 1959, and served in Moscow from 1962 to 1964 and in Paris as political officer with NATO from 1964 to 1966. From 1966 to 1969, he was political officer in Paris. From 1970 to 1972, he was International Relations Officer at the State Department. Perry was Deputy Chief of Mission in Prague from 1972 to 1976 and in Stockholm from 1976 to 1978. Since 1978 he has been Deputy Executive Secretary at the State Department.

United States Ambassador to Zambia

Nomination of Frank George Wisner II. July 18, 1979

The President today announced that he will nominate Frank George Wisner II, of the District of Columbia, to be Ambassador Extraordinary and Plenipotentiary of the United States to the Republic of Zambia. He would replace Stephen Low, who is being appointed to another post.

Wisner has been Deputy Executive Secretary at the State Department since 1977.

He was born July 2, 1938, in New York City. He received a B.A. from Princeton University in 1961.

Wisner joined the Foreign Service in 1962, and served in Algiers, Saigon, Tunis, Dacca, and at the State Department. He took Arabic language training in Tangier. From 1974 to 1975, he was Director of the Office of Plans Management of the State Department's Bureau of Public Affairs. He was Special Assistant to the Under Secretary for Political Affairs from 1975 to 1976. Wisner was director of the Office of Southern African Affairs from 1976 to 1977.

President's Commission for the Study of Ethical Problems in Medicine and Biomedical and Behavioral Research

Appointment of the Membership and Nomination of the Chairman. July 18, 1979

The President today announced that he will appoint the 11 members of the President's Commission for the Study of Ethical Problems in Medicine and Biomedical and Behavioral Research.

This Commission was created in November 1978 by Public Law 95–622 to study issues such as the definition of death, genetic testing and counseling, and the differences in the availability of health services depending on income or residence.

The members announced today are:

Morris Abram, a New York attorney and former president of Brandeis University. Abram was U.S. Representative to the United Nations Commission on Human Rights for 4 years and has served as a member of the Mt. Sinai Hospital Human Subjects Review Panel. He will be nominated as Chairman of this Commission.

Renee Claire Fox, professor of sociology at the University of Pennsylvania, a medical sociologist who has written extensively on allocation of health resources. She is a member of the ethics committee of the Institute of Medicine, and of the Institute of Social Ethics and Life Sciences.

Mario Garcia-Palmieri, professor and head of the department of medicine of the University of Puerto Rico. He was formerly secretary of health for Puerto Rico and is chairman of the Latino Caucus of the American Congress of Cardiology.

Albert Rupert Jonsen, professor of ethics in medicine at the University of California School of Medicine at San Francisco, and chairman of the bioethics group for the five University of California schools of medicine. He served as a member of HEW's National Commission for the Protection of Human Subjects of Biomedical and Behavioral Research for 4 years.

Patricia A. King, associate professor of law at Georgetown University. She is a member of the National Commission for the Protection of Human Subjects of Biomedical and Behavioral Research, the Institute of Society, Ethics and the Life Sciences, and the Washington Area Seminar on Science, Technology and Ethics.

Mathilde Krim, an associate member of the Sloan-Kettering Institute for Cancer Research and coordinator of its International Laboratories for the Molecular Biology of Interferon Systems. She is on the board of directors of the National Biomedical Research Foundation, and is a member of the National Endowment for the Humanities' advisory committee on science, technology, and human values.

Donald N. Medearis, chief of children's service at Massachusetts General Hospital and Charles Wilder professor of pediatrics at Harvard University. He is a specialist in infectious diseases of children.

Arno G. Motulsky, professor of medi-

cine and genetics and director of the Center for Inherited Diseases at the University of Washington. He is an expert in genetics who has been responsible for many advances in genetic screening, testing, counseling, and education programs.

Fritz C. Redlich, professor of psychiatry at the University of California at Los Angeles, and former director of the Behavioral Sciences Center at Yale University.

Anne A. Scitovsky, chief of the health economics division of the Palo Alto Medical Research Foundation and an expert on the economics of medical care. She is a consultant to the National Center for Health Services Research.

Charles J. Walker, a Nashville, Tenn., doctor in private medical practice. He is on the board of governors of the Matthew Walker Community Health Center, and the board of trustees of Fisk University.

Management of Federal Legal Resources

Executive Order 12146. July 18, 1979

By the authority vested in me as President by the Constitution and statutes of the United States of America, it is hereby ordered as follows:

1.1 *Establishment of the Federal Legal Council.*

1–101. There is hereby established the Federal Legal Council, which shall be composed of the Attorney General and the representatives of not more than 15 other agencies. The agency representative shall be designated by the head of the agency.

1–102. The initial membership of the Council, in addition to the Attorney General, shall consist of representatives designated by the heads of the following agencies:

(a) The Department of Commerce.
(b) The Department of Defense.
(c) The Department of Energy.
(d) The Environmental Protection Agency.
(e) The Equal Employment Opportunity Commission.
(f) The Federal Trade Commission.
(g) The Department of Health, Education, and Welfare.
(h) The Interstate Commerce Commission.
(i) The Department of Labor.
(j) The National Labor Relations Board.
(k) The Securities and Exchange Commission.
(l) The Department of State.
(m) The Department of the Treasury.
(n) The United States Postal Service. and
(o) The Veterans Administration.

1–103. The initial members of the Council shall serve for a term of two years. Thereafter, the agencies which compose the membership shall be designated annually by the Council and at least five positions on the Council, other than that held by the Attorney General, shall rotate annually.

1–104. In addition to the above members, the Directors of the Office of Management and Budget and the Office of Personnel Management, or their designees, shall be advisory members of the Council.

1–105. The Attorney General shall chair the Council and provide staff for its operation. Representatives of agencies that are not members of the Council may serve on or chair subcommittees of the Council.

1–2. *Functions of the Council.*

1–201. The Council shall promote:

(a) coordination and communication among Federal legal offices;
(b) improved management of Federal lawyers, associated support personnel, and information systems;
(c) improvements in the training provided to Federal lawyers;
(d) the facilitation of the personal donation of *pro bono* legal services by Federal attorneys;
(e) the use of joint or shared legal facilities in field offices; and
(f) the delegation of legal work to field offices.

1–202. The Council shall study and seek to resolve problems in the efficient and effective management of Federal legal resources that are beyond the capacity or authority of individual agencies to resolve.

1–203. The Council shall develop recommendations for legislation and other actions: (a) to increase the efficient and effective operation and management of Federal legal resources, including those matters specified in Section 1–201, and (b) to avoid inconsistent or unnecessary litigation by agencies.

1–3. *Litigation Notice System.*

1–301. The Attorney General shall establish and maintain a litigation notice system that provides timely information about all civil litigation pending in the courts in which the Federal Government is a party or has a significant interest.

1–302. The Attorney General shall issue rules to govern operation of the notice system. The rules shall include the following requirements:

(a) All agencies with authority to litigate cases in court shall promptly notify the Attorney General about those cases that fall in classes or categories designated from time to time by the Attorney General.

(b) The Attorney General shall provide all agencies reasonable access to the information collected in the litigation notice system.

1-4. *Resolution of Interagency Legal Disputes.*

1-401. Whenever two or more Executive agencies are unable to resolve a legal dispute between them, including the question of which has jurisdiction to administer a particular program or to regulate a particular activity, each agency is encouraged to submit the dispute to the Attorney General.

1-402. Whenever two or more Executive agencies whose heads serve at the pleasure of the President are unable to resolve such a legal dispute, the agencies shall submit the dispute to the Attorney General prior to proceeding in any court, except where there is specific statutory vesting of responsibility for a resolution elsewhere.

1-5. *Access to Legal Opinions.*

1-501. In addition to the disclosure now required by law, all agencies are encouraged to make available for public inspection and copying other opinions of their legal officers that are statements of policy or interpretation that have been adopted by the agency, unless the agency determines that disclosure would result in demonstrable harm.

1-502. All agencies are encouraged to make available on request other legal opinions, when the agency determines that disclosure would not be harmful.

1-6. *Automated Legal Research and Information Systems.*

1-601. The Attorney General, in coordination with the Secretary of Defense and other agency heads, shall provide for a computerized legal research system that will be available to all Federal law offices on a reimbursable basis. The system may include in its data base such Federal regulations, case briefs, and legal opinions, as the Attorney General deems appropriate.

1-602. The Federal Legal Council shall provide leadership for all Federal legal offices in establishing appropriate word processing and management information systems.

1-7. *Responsibilities of the Agencies.*

1-701. Each agency shall (a) review the management and operation of its legal activities and report in one year to the Federal Legal Council all steps being taken to improve those operations, and (b) cooperate with the Federal Legal Council and the Attorney General in the performance of the functions provided by this Order.

1-702. To the extent permitted by law, each agency shall furnish the Federal Legal Council and the Attorney General with reports, information and assistance as requested to carry out the provisions of this Order.

JIMMY CARTER

The White House,
July 18, 1979

[Filed with the Office of the Federal Register,
10:40 a.m., July 19, 1979]

Management of Federal Legal Resources

Memorandum From the President.
July 18, 1979

Memorandum for the Heads of Executive Departments and Agencies

Subject: Management of Federal Legal Resources

I have today signed an Executive Order entitled Federal Legal Resources concerning the management of Federal legal resources.

In addition to the matters specified in that Executive Order, and subject to the statutory responsibilities of the Director of the Office of Personnel Management, the Attorney General shall plan, coordinate, and operate programs to provide suitable training for Federal legal personnel. The functions now performed by the Legal Education Institute of the Office of Personnel Management shall hereafter be performed by the Department of Justice.

JIMMY CARTER

Future Farmers of America

Remarks to the Organization's State Presidents. July 19, 1979

MARK SANDBORN.[1] Mr. President, this morning we have gathered at your beautiful home as members of the Future Farmers of America; as farmers and agriculturalists and as friends, but above all, today we come as Americans.

We are so appreciative of your generous hospitality in the face of the many challenges and responsibilities that you have facing you to take time to meet with those people that you mean so much to.

All Americans feel a strong tie to you, but we feel a special tie because of your association with our organization. It is for that reason that we would like to present you with a plaque that we wanted to make special by putting on it and including in it something of your past that is a big part of our present and a part of all Americans' futures. You see, Mr. President, you are admired, respected, and loved wherever corn is grown and future farmers

---

[1] National president, Future Farmers of America.

meet. And so, today, on behalf of the Future Farmers of America, I present you with this plaque with the secretary's station marker, a part from the opening ceremony, and the words from our organization, which read, "Congratulations, Jimmy Carter, from secretary of Plains, Georgia FFA Chapter, to the President of the United States. On behalf of the national FFA organization, we thank you for your outstanding leadership, States Presidents Conference, July 19, 1979." And we say in the simplest and most sincere way that we can, Mr. President, thank you.

THE PRESIDENT. The first public words that I ever said in a position of responsibility was the secretary stationed by the ear of corn, your duties there, "I keep an accurate record of all meetings and correspond with other secretaries wherever corn is grown and future farmers meet."

Mark, I want to thank you and the FFA leaders here and FFA members, more than half million, all across the country for this recognition and this honor. I hope that there are other lowly secretaries around the Nation who will ultimately be President of the United States. I can vouch for the fact that it's good preparation for the highest elective office in our Nation.

FFA members mean a lot to me personally, and your organization means a lot to our country now, in the past, and in the future. The first organization that I belonged to was a Baptist church; the second organization was the FFA. And both have and do mean a lot to me.

It's no secret around the Nation that the FFA organization, the Future Farmers of America, is one of my favorite organizations. I have spoken to local chapters; I've spoken to State groups; I've spoken to the national convention, as you well know. It's been an integral part of my life.

I look forward each year to having the time to meet with the State officers who are assembled here at the White House to show the national importance of FFA, and to show your close ties with the incumbent President, no matter what background that particular President might have.

You adopted a bold theme for this year: "FFA Preparing For Progress." Progress does not just happen. Real progress comes only as a result of discipline, planning, and a lot of hard work. Our Nation faces difficult challenges in the years ahead. I described some of those challenges, some of those problems, some of those opportunities in my address to the Nation last Sunday evening. Your Government, which is distrusted by some, which is supported by almost all, is an important element in your lives, in the lives of all Americans, obviously in the lives of farmers.

I'm now involved in an intense effort to review my own role as President and the makeup, the constitution of my Government, our relationship to the Congress, to the Governors, local officials, to officials who are not in government, and to the individual citizens of our Nation, to strengthen these crucial ties between government and people. I'll make the tough decisions that are necessary for improvements, and I know that you as leaders understand that quite often the decisions of a leader are not easy.

I want you to listen to me very closely. I want to talk directly to you.

Two of the most important questions in the future of this Nation, in the future of people throughout the world, are fuel and food, for the remainder of this century, and into the next century as well.

Our Nation has been generously en-

dowed by God with tremendous reserve supplies of these precious natural resources; fuel, perhaps more than any other country on Earth, and the most bountiful gift of productive land for the production of food on which our own Nation and many nations throughout the world now depend, and will depend even more heavily in the future.

How to provide more food for a growing world population while we use less energy is a very difficult task. Our Nation must be well fed, and we must have an increasing quantity of food to export to others. How we do both these things while consuming less energy is the challenge. You, the present and future leaders of the agricultural community, must assess this basic, inherent conflict and resolve it, study agricultural practices, make changes, create new techniques and new concepts when necessary. This is what is meant by progress, and, in short, you will be called upon to transform American agriculture in the years ahead.

I have every confidence that you young men and women, the leaders of the Future Farmers of America, can take up this gauntlet and can meet this new day both with imagination, with strength, with confidence, and with vigor.

Now I would like to ask you all together for a unique call from the President to you, one tailored especially for FFA. Since everyone knows that FFA is important to me, I today ask you to link your hands and your hearts with me as President in the energy battle that we now face. I ask you to take the lead among all other youth groups in the United States, in our war for energy security. To that end, in consultation with your own leaders, I set before you this extraordinary challenge.

I'm asking every FFA chapter in this country to get involved in this basic question of energy conservation and production tied intimately with that of food, in conserving energy and in finding new ways to use it more efficiently. It has to come from you. I cannot do it for you. I can't go into every FFA chapter in the Nation and create the leadership and the inspiration and the drive and the determination and the planning and the commitment and, sometimes, the courage that will be required to make this leadership felt, not only in your own organization but among others which involve young leaders of our country. But I will give recognition as a kind of constant symbol of my participation to the one FFA chapter in the Nation chosen by you and your leaders who does the most outstanding job in carrying out this response to the energy crisis.

Are you willing to accept the challenge? [*Applause*] Very good.

I'm going to depend upon the FFA to take the lead in energy conservation, and I'm going to depend upon you to pay the personal prices in your own lives necessary to guarantee the freedom of this Nation through restoring our energy security. I know you will do this, and it's a solemn commitment between me and you.

A quality future of our lives is built on a strong today. We've got some weaknesses in our country that I tried to outline as best I could Sunday evening. Many things change rapidly in our world, and these changes upset people. New energy facts are hard to accept.

For the first time, Americans have had to recognize the fact that there are limits, that we don't have the right anymore to squander the precious fuel reserves which our Nation possesses. We've got to husband those and to conserve those and to be good stewards over what we have been given. This is what comprises the proper attitude of an American citizen, to assess problems, to face them frankly, to let the truth be known, to search our own lives, our own hearts, our own influence, and say, "What can I do to make my life purer, better, stronger, more admirable, and to let my life be felt meaningfully in the future of a nation which has been so good to me?"

So many changes take place; many things don't change. The fundamentals don't change—love within a family, honesty, friendship among people, a desire for peace, a respect for one another, the beauty of nature, and the genuine patriotism based on confidence in our country. As these unchangeable values become deeply engrained in our lives today, the future obviously grows even brighter.

On my recent trip to Japan, I met the Emperor of Japan and all his family. I learned that at the beginning of each year, as a symbol, the Emperor of Japan plants a tiny rice seedling—the nation watches this simple act—as a symbol of abundance and hope and confidence for the year ahead. You young people who live so close to the earth or whose families or friends live so close to the earth are a similar symbol of abundance and hope for me.

Plant your lives carefully in a foundation based on principles which do not change. Work hard. Love deeply. Commit your lives faithfully, let your lives bloom and constantly grow, no matter how many years you might spend on Earth. With these kinds of personal traits and beliefs in your lives, you become a precious possession.

Our Nation desperately needs you, and I'm sure that our Nation will not be disappointed in you.

Thank you very much.

MR. SANDBORN. Mr. President, before you stands a group that eagerly accepts constructive challenge. You asked us to join our hands and our hearts in addressing the problem of the energy that you mentioned. We want you to know that we have already joined our hands and hearts in accepting your guidance and direction in doing whatever we can as future farmers.

We will directly accept your challenge in two ways: first, by addressing the challenge you presented and encouraging chapters across the United States to participate actively in energy conservation; but secondly, we pledge to you that we will continue to train and develop the kind of young people with leadership, citizenship, skills, and abilities that have made you great as President of the United States and have produced such a great leader like yourself.

Mr. President, we gladly accept your challenge.

Thank you very much.

NOTE: The President spoke at 10:20 a.m. in the Rose Garden at the White House.

Department of Health, Education, and Welfare

Resignation of Joseph A. Califano, Jr., and Nomination of Patricia Roberts Harris To Be Secretary.   July 19, 1979

The President has accepted the resignation of Secretary of Health, Education, and Welfare Joseph Califano. The President will nominate Patricia Harris, Secretary of Housing and Urban Development, to be Secretary of Health, Education, and Welfare.

The President said, "Secretary Harris has established an admirable record of efficient and compassionate leadership at the Department of Housing and Urban Development. She has my full confidence and support as she begins to assume the responsibility for leading the department which more than any other directly touches the lives of those who must depend most upon government."

Secretary Harris and Secretary Califano have already discussed plans for an orderly transition. A successor to Secretary Harris at the Department of Housing and Urban Development will be named in the near future to ensure no interruption in the operations of that department.

NOTE: Press Secretary Jody Powell read the announcement at 12:04 p.m. to reporters assembled in the Briefing Room at the White House.

Department of Health, Education, and Welfare

Exchange of Letters on the Resignation of Joseph A. Califano, Jr., as Secretary. July 19, 1979

To Secretary Joe Califano

I accept your resignation with a genuine feeling of appreciation and of recognition for your notable accomplishments as Secretary of Health, Education and Welfare.

You have, indeed, demonstrated that major public service can exemplify both competence and compassion.

My desire is that you continue to serve with my confidence and support until your successor assumes the office. Your pledge of a smooth, harmonious and orderly transition is typical of your attitude and performance.

You have my personal best wishes and friendship.

Sincerely,

JIMMY CARTER

Dear Mr. President:

In accord with our conversation yesterday afternoon, I hereby formally tender my resignation as Secretary of Health, Education, and Welfare.

For me, it has been a deeply enjoyable and satisfying experience to administer so many of the programs enacted into law under President Lyndon Johnson.

I have called HEW the Department of the people because its programs touch the lives of so many Americans each day. The Department reflects the compassion of the American people. It tends to the needs of the old and the young, of the poor, the ill, and the handicapped. It exists to protect the health of all Americans, to assure equal educational opportunity for all citizens, and to guarantee the individual rights of victims of discrimination of all kinds. It administers Social Security and the other basic income maintenance programs of our nation.

My goal as Secretary has been to demonstrate that Government can do all these things, not only with compassion, but with competence. Achieving that goal is urgently necessary because there are still in this nation millions of people whose needs can be met only by Government—and they are the most vulnerable among us.

To do this job effectively, I needed the authority to run this Department and the freedom to decide and speak out on controversial public issues. You have given me that authority and freedom, and I appreciate it.

Whenever the laws that the Congress charges the Secretary of HEW to execute are administered with vigor, there will be controversy. I have tried to execute these laws vigorously.

I appreciate the opportunity you have given me to serve our nation and you.

I wish you well as you continue striving to fulfill the enormous responsibilities of your office, and to build upon your achievements, of which you can be justly proud.

Sincerely,

JOSEPH A. CALIFANO, JR.

[The President, The White House, Washington, D.C.]

Agency for International Development

Nomination of Douglas J. Bennet, Jr., To Be Administrator.   July 19, 1979

The President today announced that he will nominate Douglas J. Bennet, Jr., of Connecticut, to be Administrator of the Agency for International Development. He will replace John J. Gilligan who has resigned.

Bennet was born June 23, 1938, in Orange, N.J. He received a B.A. (1959) from Wesleyan University, an M.A. (1960) from the University of California, and a Ph. D. (1968) from Harvard University.

From 1963 to 1964, he was assistant to the Economic Advisor of AID. Bennet was special assistant to the Ambassador to India from 1964 to 1966. From 1967 to 1969, he was an assistant to Vice President Hubert Humphrey. He was administrative assistant to Senator Thomas Eagleton 1969 to 1973 and also held the same position on Senator Abraham Ribicoff's staff from 1973 to 1974. From 1974 to 1977, he was staff director for the Senate Budget Committee. Since 1977 he has been Assistant Secretary of State for Congressional Relations.

United States International Development Cooperation Agency

Nomination of Thomas Ehrlich to Be Director. July 19, 1979

The President today announced that he will nominate Thomas Ehrlich, of California, to be Director of the United States International Development Cooperation Agency. This is a new position created by Reorganization Plan No. 2.

Ehrlich was born March 4, 1934, in Cambridge, Mass. He received an A.B. (1956) from Harvard College and an LL.B. (1959) from Harvard Law School.

From 1962 to 1964, he was special assistant to the Legal Advisor at the State Department and then special assistant to the Under Secretary at State from 1964 to 1965. Ehrlich was professor (1965–1971) and dean (1971–1975) at Stanford University Law School. From 1976 to 1979, he was President of the Legal Services Corporation. Since April of this year he has been a consultant at the State Department.

Department of Justice

Resignation of Griffin B. Bell and Nomination of Benjamin R. Civiletti To Be Attorney General. July 19, 1979

As you know, Attorney General Bell has previously stated on several occasions his intention to leave the Department of Justice prior to the 1980 election year.

The President will nominate Deputy Attorney General Benjamin Civiletti to succeed Attorney General Bell. To ensure an orderly transition in this important department, Attorney General Bell's resignation will become effective when Mr. Civiletti is confirmed by the Senate and sworn into office.

NOTE: Press Secretary Jody Powell read the announcement at 3:35 p.m. to reporters assembled in the Briefing Room at the White House.

United States International Development Cooperation Agency

Executive Order 12147. July 19, 1979

By the authority vested in me as President of the United States of America by Section 9 of Reorganization Plan No. 2 of 1979, both Houses of Congress having defeated a resolution of disapproval (S. Res. 140, 125 Cong. Rec. S 8829 (July 9, 1979); H. Res. 231, 125 Cong. Rec. H. 5729 (July 11, 1979)), it is hereby ordered that Sections 2, 3, and 4 of that Plan, providing for the offices of Director, Deputy Director, and Associate Directors, are effective immediately.

JIMMY CARTER

The White House,
  July 19, 1979.

[Filed with the Office of the Federal Register, 10:48 a.m., July 20, 1979]

National Science Foundation

Message to the Congress Transmitting a Report. July 19, 1979

To the Congress of the United States:

I am pleased to transmit to the Congress the 28th Annual Report of the National Science Foundation.

The Foundation supports a large part of the nation's basic research in science and engineering and has national significance in its science education and training programs.

Throughout my Administration, I have frequently called to your attention that much of our social and economic progress depends upon a firm base of science and technology. In March 1979, I addressed this theme in a special message to you, highlighting the science and technology initiatives taken in my Administration in domestic, national security, and international arenas. I also pointed out that our national investment in scientific research, especially basic research, is returned to us many times over in the advances it generates in health care, energy, food production, and the protection and proper use of our resources and environment.

We live in an increasingly demanding world, in which we are called on to make judgments that affect our progress and well-being as human beings and nations. Our planning and decision-making require better understanding of the laws of nature, the effects of technological development, and the complexities of human relationships. The search for such understanding demands the aggressive development of new knowledge, an adequate supply of trained, responsible scientists, and a well-informed citizenry.

The National Science Foundation plays an important role in developing these scientific and human resources. It is my hope that this Annual Report of the Foundation will encourage your continued strong support.

JIMMY CARTER

The White House,
   July 19, 1979.

NOTE: The report is entitled "National Science Foundation—Twenty-Eighth Annual Report for Fiscal Year 1978" (Government Printing Office, 143 pages).

Department of the Treasury

Resignation of W. Michael Blumenthal and Nomination of G. William Miller To Be Secretary.   July 19, 1979

The President has accepted the resignation of Secretary of the Treasury Michael Blumenthal. The President will nominate William Miller, Chairman of the Federal Reserve Board, as Secretary of the Treasury. The President said, "Chairman Miller has, in his tenure at the Federal Reserve Board, established a reputation at home and abroad that will enable him to provide strong, effective leadership for economic policy. He has demonstrated a firm commitment to the defense of the dollar, sound economic policy, the fight against inflation, and strong measures to deal with our energy problem. He has my confidence and support."

The President, Secretary Blumenthal, and Chairman Miller have agreed that the transition will be handled in a manner that will ensure maximum continuity and no interruption of the effective performance at both the Treasury Department and the Federal Reserve Board.

NOTE: Press Secretary Jody Powell read the announcement at 4:38 p.m. to reporters assembled in the Briefing Room at the White House.

The press release also includes a transcript of the question-and-answer session which followed the announcement.

Department of the Treasury

Exchange of Letters on the Resignation of W. Michael Blumenthal as Secretary. July 19, 1979

To Secretary Mike Blumenthal

I accept your resignation with great appreciation for the excellent service you have rendered at the Treasury, both for me and for the country.

The policies you have helped me mold and implement, to orient our efforts toward the fight against inflation, to maintain the strength and stability of the dollar, to assure the economic strength of our nation, to protect the integrity of the budget—have all been right and necessary for the wellbeing of the United States and our place in the world economy. These policies will be pursued with consistency and vigor.

You have served the nation well during a difficult period. I admire the strength and steadfastness with which you have presented your views, and I look forward to your continuing help and counsel. Your willingness to serve until your successor takes office will help to assure the smooth continuity in the making of economic decisions.

Mike, you have been a leading example of the readiness of prominent Americans from the private sector to render service in the public interest. As you return to private life, you have my personal best wishes for the future and my thanks for your distinguished service.

Sincerely,

JIMMY CARTER

———

Dear Mr. President:

This is to confirm to you that I have decided to resign as Secretary of the Treasury. I would like this resignation to be effective as early as possible and, in any case, as soon as my successor is available. I hope that this can be accomplished by the time Congress leaves for the August recess, thus ensuring a smooth transition.

As we discussed, I feel strongly that the time has come for me to return to private life and that someone else should carry on as Secretary of the Treasury in my place. I appreciate your agreeing with this assessment and am delighted to learn that you intend to nominate Bill Miller,

Chairman of the Federal Reserve Board, to succeed me. You have made an excellent choice and I am fully confident that Bill Miller will serve you and the country well.

Most importantly, I am certain that he will give you maximum and effective support in your continuing fight for sound economic policies in general and in the pursuit of your anti-inflationary policies in particular. I am convinced that Bill is as dedicated as you and I have been in our efforts to maintain a strong dollar and responsible fiscal and monetary policies.

It has been a privilege to serve as your Secretary of the Treasury for the last 2½ years. I am proud to have had that opportunity and appreciate your offering me the chance to serve.

The assignment has not always been easy. The national and international economic scene has been beset by difficulties for which there is no quick solution. As you know, I think it is vital that you continue to pursue economic policies designed to deal with these problems over the longer run. First and foremost is the issue of inflation, which I hope will remain the major preoccupation of your economic policy. A tight fiscal policy, strict controls on Government spending, efforts to bring the Federal budget under better control, and to reduce Government regulations wherever possible will be the key to success—as will continuing policies to expand the enormous productive potential of the American free enterprise system. At the same time, we must continue to defend the integrity and strength of the dollar and to play a constructive leadership role for a free and open international economic system.

I have every confidence that, with the help of your new Secretary of the Treasury, you will continue to pursue these policies. They are the best guarantees that we will win the fight against inflation while expanding rapidly our domestic energy resources, so as to reduce the intolerable dependence of the U.S. economy on imported oil.

You have my best wishes as you continue to lead our nation and to deal with the many difficult problems we face. I am sure you will have a strong ally in Bill Miller in the future shaping of your economic policy.

As I return to private life, you can count on my wholehearted support in your efforts to achieve these goals.

With best wishes.

Sincerely,

MIKE BLUMENTHAL

W. Michael Blumenthal

[The President, The White House, Washington, D.C.]

United States Troop Withdrawals From the Republic of Korea

Statement by the President. July 20, 1979

Last February it was announced that withdrawals of U.S. ground combat forces from Korea would be held in abeyance pending the completion of a reassessment of North Korea's military strength and the implications of recent political developments in the region. That reassessment has been completed, and these policy issues have been discussed with our key allies in Asia, with principal defense and foreign policy advisers, and leaders of the Congress. Circumstances require these further adjustments in the troop withdrawal plan:

—Withdrawals of combat elements of the 2d Division will remain in abeyance. The structure and function of the Combined Forces Command will continue as established last year.

—Between now and the end of 1980 some reductions of personnel in U.S. support units will continue. This will include one I–Hawk air defense battalion whose transfer to the ROK had been planned since 1976.

—The timing and pace of withdrawals beyond these will be reexamined in 1981. In that review the United States will pay special attention to the restoration of a satisfactory North-South military balance, and evidence of tangible progress toward a reduction of tensions on the peninsula.

These decisions have been shaped by the following considerations:

—First, recent studies by the intelligence community have confirmed that the size of North Korea's ground forces, armor, firepower, and mobility are larger than previously estimated. Given the inherent economic strength of the Republic of Korea and with U.S. support, the existing imbalance in North-South military strength can be remedied. Holding further withdrawals of U.S. ground combat units in abeyance will help reinforce deterrence, avoid conveying misleading signals to the North, and provide additional time for the ROK to put its ground defenses in order. For its part the Republic of Korea recognizes the need to augment its self-defense efforts, and President Park has stated that his government would expand defense spending significantly beyond previously planned levels and accord special urgency to improving its ground defenses.

—Second, during the recent visit to Seoul, President Park and President Carter jointly announced their desire to explore possibilities for reducing tensions in Korea with representatives of North Korea. Only through authoritative discussions between representatives of the

North and South Korean Governments can a framework for peaceful coexistence between the North and South be established and progress toward eventual reunification of Korea be achieved. The United States is prepared to assist in that diplomatic effort. It is the judgment of the United States that further reductions of our combat elements in Korea should await credible indications that a satisfactory military balance has been restored and a reduction in tension is underway.

—Third, in recent months we have normalized relations with China and deepened defense cooperation with Japan. Concurrently we have witnessed the steady growth of Soviet military power in East Asia and the eruption of renewed conflict and new uncertainties in Southeast Asia. Under these circumstances, it is believed that these adjustments in our Korean withdrawal plan—together with the recent stabilization of our base agreement with the Philippines, initiation of defense planning discussions with Japan, and increased support for the security of ASEAN countries—will serve wider U.S. strategic security interests by reassuring our principal allies of our steadiness and our resolve.

Over time we will continue to adjust the detailed features of our contribution to the security of the Republic of Korea to reflect growing ROK economic and military strength and changes in the international situation. At present, however, these modifications in our withdrawal plans will best assure the maintenance of our security commitment, preserve an adequate deterrent, nurture the resumption of a serious North-South dialog, and stabilize a favorable U.S. strategic position in East Asia.

NOTE: Zbigniew Brzezinski, Assistant to the President for National Security Affairs, read the statement to reporters assembled in the Briefing Room at the White House.

Apollo 11 Anniversary

Remarks at a Ceremony in Observance of the 10th Anniversary of the Moon Landing. July 20, 1979

MR. ARMSTRONG. Mr. President, we're delighted that you would take the opportunity to note this occasion that is very meaningful to those of us who were charged with the responsibility of meeting a national goal. And nothing matches success like more success, and the 10th anniversary of that occasion is very pleasant for all of us today.

We would like to present to you a flag that was carried on our flight 10 years ago and a replica of the one that was planted there 10 years ago today, presented to you with our very good wishes and hopes for the future.

THE PRESIDENT. Thank you very much.

MR. FROSCH. We'd like to add to this the first copy of a piece of the history of Apollo inscribed to you from the crew.

THE PRESIDENT. Well, this is a great honor.

This 10th anniversary, even, is a great moment for our Nation and for the world. Ten years ago, all humanity watched with wonder as two brave men—Neil Armstrong and Buzz Aldrin, on my right—stepped boldly onto the Moon while a third brave astronaut, Mike Collins, was in lunar orbit. The touchdown of Apollo II *Eagle* in the Sea of Tranquility was a stunning achievement, without precedent in human experience. These three astronauts, representing the spirit of our entire Nation, fulfilled the age-old dream of mankind of venturing beyond Earth to the surface of another world.

As we honor these three bold adventurers today, we take pride in our Nation and in the unequaled technological ability that made this great endeavor possible and which still exists. The pioneer spirit that built our great country is symbolized by the footprints of American astronauts on the bleak landscape of the Moon.

The first lunar landing and those which followed it were due to the unique and the specialized contributions of tens of thousands of Americans—scientists, engineers, astronauts, skilled craftsmen, and many others. We must continue to use these skills and build upon the success and the inspiration of the Apollo program.

The 10th anniversary of the lunar landing is a time to reflect on what we as a nation can accomplish with unity, daring, and determination. We landed on the Moon because our Nation set a firm goal, and we united behind that effort. Today, we face an equally challenging goal in fighting for energy security. Like the Apollo mission, it is a test of our Nation's resources and our spirit as a people.

We will win energy security for our Nation in the same way we won the race to the Moon. We will marshal the unequaled technological and scientific capacity of the American people. We will draw upon our vast and abundant natural resources, and we will unite as a people in our determination to preserve our freedom and our independence as a nation.

I know that the spirit to unite, to prevail, to overcome this energy crisis is strong among the American people today. I've seen it on the faces of those with whom I have met and talked in the last few weeks. I have no doubt that as a nation we will succeed.

Our Nation will also face a number of other difficult challenges in the years ahead. But this Nation and this Government must be prepared with confidence to meet these challenges. I'm now involved in an intense and serious period of review and evaluation. I will make the decisions necessary to ensure that my administra-

tion, representing the American people, can provide the leadership this country needs.

As President, I am also determined to maintain America's leadership in space. The first great era of space exploration is about over; as an initiative, unprecedented. But the second—the era of the space shuttle, when we harvest the great benefits that have been made possible by that exploration—is about to begin.

As the poet Robert Browning wrote over a century ago, "Man's reach should exceed his grasp, or what's a heaven for?" As a nation, we always must have the boldness to reach for the heavens and to set a brave example for all peoples of this Earth.

On behalf of the United States of America, I want to repeat the gratitude of our country to these three brave men, those who followed them and preceded them in space, and the many scientists, workers, average Americans, technicians who helped to make this enormous achievement possible. Thank you very much.

NOTE: The President spoke at 12:17 p.m. in the Rose Garden at the White House. Robert A. Frosch is Administrator of the National Aeronautics and Space Administration.

Federal Emergency Management
Executive Order 12148.   July 20, 1979

By the authority vested in me as President by the Constitution and laws of the United States of America, including the Federal Civil Defense Act of 1950, as amended (50 U.S.C. App. 2251 *et seq.*), the Disaster Relief Act of 1970, as amended (42 U.S.C. Chapter 58 note), the Disaster Relief Act of 1974 (88 Stat. 143; 42 U.S.C. 5121 *et seq.*), the Earthquake Hazards Reduction Act of 1977 (42 U.S.C. 7701 *et seq.*), Section 4 of Public Law 92–385 (86 Stat. 556), Section 43 of the Act of August 10, 1956, as amended (50 U.S.C. App. 2285), the National Security Act of 1947, as amended, the Defense Production Act of 1950, as amended (50 U.S.C. App. 2061 *et seq.*), Reorganization Plan No. 1 of 1958, Reorganization Plan No. 1 of 1973, the Strategic and Critical Materials Stock Piling Act, as amended (50 U.S.C. 98 *et seq.*), Section 202 of the Budget and Accounting Procedures Act of 1950 (31 U.S.C. 581c), and Section 301 of Title 3 of the United States Code, and in order to transfer emergency functions to the Federal Emergency Management Agency, it is hereby ordered as follows:

SECTION 1. TRANSFERS OR REASSIGNMENTS

1–1. *Transfer or Reassignment of Existing Functions.*

1–101. All functions vested in the President that have been delegated or assigned to the Defense Civil Preparedness Agency, Department of Defense, are transferred or reassigned to the Director of the Federal Emergency Management Agency.

1–102. All functions vested in the President that have been delegated or assigned to the Federal Disaster Assistance Administration, Department of Housing and Urban Development, are transferred or reassigned to the Director of the Federal Emergency Management Agency, including any of those functions redelegated or reassigned to the Department of Commerce with respect to assistance to communities in the development of readiness plans for severe weather-related emergencies.

1–103. All functions vested in the President that have been delegated or as-

signed to the Federal Preparedness Agency, General Services Administration, are transferred or reassigned to the Director of the Federal Emergency Management Agency.

1–104. All functions vested in the President by the Earthquake Hazards Reduction Act of 1977 (42 U.S.C. 7701 *et seq.*), including those functions performed by the Office of Science and Technology Policy, are delegated, transferred, or reassigned to the Director of the Federal Emergency Management Agency.

1–2. *Transfer or Reassignment of Resources.*

1–201. The records, property, personnel and positions, and unexpended balances of appropriations, available or to be made available, which relate to the functions transferred, reassigned, or redelegated by this Order are hereby transferred to the Director of the Federal Emergency Management Agency.

1–202. The Director of the Office of Management and Budget shall make such determinations, issue such orders, and take all actions necessary or appropriate to effectuate the transfers or reassignments provided by this Order, including the transfer of funds, records, property, and personnel.

SECTION 2. MANAGEMENT OF EMERGENCY PLANNING AND ASSISTANCE

2–1. *General.*

2–101. The Director of the Federal Emergency Management Agency shall establish Federal policies for, and coordinate, all civil defense and civil emergency planning, management, mitigation, and assistance functions of Executive agencies.

2–102. The Director shall periodically review and evaluate the civil defense and civil emergency functions of the Executive agencies. In order to improve the efficiency and effectiveness of those functions, the Director shall recommend to the President alternative methods of providing Federal planning, management, mitigation, and assistance.

2–103. The Director shall be responsible for the coordination of efforts to promote dam safety, for the coordination of natural and nuclear disaster warning systems, and for the coordination of preparedness and planning to reduce the consequences of major terrorist incidents.

2–104. The Director shall represent the President in working with State and local governments and private sector to stimulate vigorous participation in civil emergency preparedness, mitigation, response, and recovery programs.

2–105. The Director shall provide an annual report to the President for subsequent transmittal to the Congress on the functions of the Federal Emergency Management Agency. The report shall assess the current overall state of effectiveness of Federal civil defense and civil emergency functions, organizations, resources, and systems and recommend measures to be taken to improve planning, management, assistance, and relief by all levels of government, the private sector, and volunteer organizations.

2–2. *Implementation.*

2–201. In executing the functions under this Order, the Director shall develop policies which provide that all civil defense and civil emergency functions, resources, and systems of Executive agencies are:

(a) founded on the use of existing organizations, resources, and systems to the maximum extent practicable;

(b) integrated effectively with organizations, resources, and programs of State and local governments, the private sector and volunteer organizations; and

(c) developed, tested and utilized to prepare for, mitigate, respond to and recover from the effects on the population of all forms of emergencies.

2–202. Assignments of civil emergency functions shall, whenever possible, be based on extensions (under emergency conditions) of the regular missions of the Executive agencies.

2–203. For purposes of this Order, "civil emergency" means any accidental, natural, man-caused, or wartime emergency or threat thereof, which causes or may cause substantial injury or harm to the population or substantial damage to or loss of property.

2–204. In order that civil defense planning continues to be fully compatible with the Nation's overall strategic policy, and in order to maintain an effective link between strategic nuclear planning and nuclear attack preparedness planning, the development of civil defense policies and programs by the Director of the Federal Emergency Management Agency shall be subject to oversight by the Secretary of Defense and the National Security Council.

2–205. To the extent authorized by law and within available resources, the Secretary of Defense shall provide the Director of the Federal Emergency Management Agency with support for civil defense programs in the areas of program development and administration, technical support, research, communications, transportation, intelligence, and emergency operations.

2–206. All Executive agencies shall cooperate with and assist the Director in the performance of his functions.

2–3. *Transition Provisions.*

2–301. The functions which have been transferred, reassigned, or redelegated by

Section 1 of this Order are recodified and revised as set forth in this Order at Section 4, and as provided by the amendments made at Section 5 to the provisions of other Orders.

2-302. Notwithstanding the revocations, revisions, codifications, and amendments made by this Order, the Director may continue to perform the functions transferred to him by Section 1 of this Order, except where they may otherwise be inconsistent with the provisions of this Order.

SECTION 3. FEDERAL EMERGENCY MANAGEMENT COUNCIL

3-1. *Establishment of the Council.*

3-101. There is hereby established the Emergency Management Council.

3-102. The Council shall be composed of the Director of the Federal Emergency Management Agency, who shall be the Chairman, the Director of the Office of Management and Budget and such others as the President may designate.

3.2. *Functions of the Council*

3-201. The Council shall advise and assist the President in the oversight and direction of Federal emergency programs and policies.

3-202. The Council shall provide guidance to the Director of the Federal Emergency Management Agency in the performance of functions vested in him.

3-3. *Administrative and General Provisions.*

3-301. The heads of Executive agencies shall cooperate with and assist the Council in the performance of its functions.

3-302. The Director of the Federal Emergency Management Agency shall provide the Council with such administrative services and support as may be necessary or appropriate.

SECTION 4. DELEGATIONS

4-1. *Delegation of Functions Transferred to the President.*

4-101. The following functions were transferred to the Director of the Office of Defense Mobilization by Section 2 of Reorganization Plan No. 3 of 1953 (50 U.S.C. 404 note); they were subsequently transferred to the President by Section 1 (a) of Reorganization Plan No. 1 of 1958, as amended (50 U.S.C. App. 2271 note), and they are hereby delegated to the Director of the Federal Emergency Management Agency:

(a) The functions vested in the Secretaries of the Army, Navy, Air Force, and Interior by the Strategic and Critical Materials Stock Piling Act, as amended (50 U.S.C. 98 *et seq.*), including the functions vested in the Army and Navy Munitions Board by item (2) of Section 6(a) of that Act (50 U.S.C. 98e(a)(2)), but excluding the functions vested in the Secretary of the Interior by Section 7 of that Act (50 U.S.C. 98f).

(b) The functions vested in the Munitions Board of the Department of Defense by Section 4(h) of the Commodity Credit Corporation Charter Act, as amended (15 U.S.C. 714b(h)).

(c) The function vested in the Munitions Board of the Department of Defense by Section 204(f) [originally 204(e)] of the Federal Property and Administrative Services Act of 1949, as amended (40 U.S.C. 485(f)).

4-102. The functions vested in the Director of the Office of Defense Mobilization by Sections 103 and 303 of the National Security Act of 1947, as amended by Sections 8 and 50 of the Act of September 3, 1954 (Public Law 779; 68 Stat. 1228 and 1244) (50 U.S.C. 404 and 405), were transferred to the President by Section 1(a) of Reorganization Plan No. 1

of 1958, as amended (50 U.S.C. App. 2271 note), and they are hereby delegated to the Director of the Federal Emergency Management Agency.

4–103. (a) The functions vested in the Federal Civil Defense Administration or its Administrator by the Federal Civil Defense Act of 1950, as amended (50 U.S.C. App. 2251 *et seq.*), were transferred to the President by Reorganization Plan No. 1 of 1958, and they are hereby delegated to the Director of the Federal Emergency Management Agency.

(b) Excluded from the delegation in subsection (a) is the function under Section 205(a)(4) of the Federal Civil Defense Act of 1950, as amended (50 U.S.C. App. 2286(a)(4)), relating to the establishment and maintenance of personnel standards on the merit basis that was delegated to the Director of the Office of Personnel Management by Section 1(b) of Executive Order No. 11589, as amended (Section 2–101(b) of Executive Order No. 12107).

4–104. The Director of the Federal Emergency Management Agency is authorized to redelegate, in accord with the provisions of Section 1(b) of Reorganization Plan No. 1 of 1958 (50 U.S.C. App. 2271 note), any of the functions delegated by Sections 4–101, 4–102, and 4–103 of this Order.

4–105. The functions vested in the Administrator of the Federal Civil Defense Administration by Section 43 of the Act of August 10, 1956 (70A Stat. 636) were transferred to the President by Reorganization Plan No. 1 of 1958, as amended (50 U.S.C. App. 2271 note), were subsequently revested in the Director of the Office of Civil and Defense Mobilization by Section 512 of Public Law 86–500 (50 U.S.C. App. 2285) [the office was changed to Office of Emergency Planning by Public Law 87–296 (75 Stat. 630) and then

to the Office of Emergency Preparedness by Section 402 of Public Law 90–608 (82 Stat. 1194)], were again transferred to the President by Section 1 of Reorganization Plan No. 1 of 1973 (50 U.S.C. App. 2271 note), and they are hereby delegated to the Director of the Federal Emergency Management Agency.

4–106. The functions vested in the Director of the Office of Emergency Preparedness by Section 16 of the Act of September 23, 1950, as amended (20 U.S.C. 646), and by Section 7 of the Act of September 30, 1950, as amended (20 U.S.C. 241–1), were transferred to the President by Section 1 of Reorganization Plan No. 1 of 1973 (50 U.S.C. App. 2271 note), and they are hereby delegated to the Director of the Federal Emergency Management Agency.

4–107. That function vested in the Director of the Office of Emergency Preparedness by Section 762(a) of the Higher Education Act of 1965, as added by Section 161(a) of the Education Amendments of 1972, and as further amended (20 U.S.C. 1132d–1(a)), to the extent transferred to the President by Reorganization Plan No. 1 of 1973 (50 U.S.C. App. 2271 note), is hereby delegated to the Director of the Federal Emergency Management Agency.

4–2. *Delegation of Functions Vested in the President.*

4–201. The functions vested in the President by the Disaster Relief Act of 1970, as amended (42 U.S.C. Chapter 58 note), are hereby delegated to the Director of the Federal Emergency Management Agency.

4–202. The functions (related to grants for damages resulting from hurricane and tropical storm Agnes) vested in the President by Section 4 of Public Law 92–385 (86 Stat. 556) are hereby delegated to the

Director of the Federal Emergency Management Agency.

4–203. The functions vested in the President by the Disaster Relief Act of 1974 (88 Stat. 143; 42 U.S.C. 5121 *et seq.*), except those functions vested in the President by Sections 301 (relating to the declaration of emergencies and major disasters), 401 (relating to the repair, reconstruction, restoration, or replacement of Federal facilities), and 409 (relating to food coupons and surplus commodities), are hereby delegated to the Director of the Federal Emergency Management Agency.

4–204. The functions vested in the President by the Earthquake Hazards Reduction Act of 1977 (91 Stat. 1098; 42 U.S.C. 7701 *et seq.*) are hereby delegated to the Director of the Federal Emergency Management Agency.

SECTION 5. OTHER EXECUTIVE ORDERS

5–1. *Revocations.*

5–101. Executive Order No. 10242, as amended, entitled "Prescribing Regulations Governing the Exercise by the Federal Civil Defense Administrator of Certain Administrative Authority Granted by the Federal Civil Defense Act of 1950", is revoked.

5–102. Sections 1 and 2 of Executive Order No. 10296, as amended, entitled "Providing for the Performance of Certain Defense Housing and Community Facilities and Service Functions", are revoked.

5–103. Executive Order No. 10494, as amended, relating to the disposition of remaining functions, is revoked.

5–104. Executive Order No. 10529, as amended, relating to federal employee participation in State and local civil defense programs, is revoked.

5–105. Section 3 of Executive Order No. 10601, as amended, which concerns the Commodity Set Aside, is revoked.

5–106. Executive Order No. 10634, as amended, relating to loans for facilities destroyed or damaged by a major disaster, is revoked.

5–107. Section 4(d)(2) of Executive Order No. 10900, as amended, which concerns foreign currencies made available to make purchases for the supplemental stockpile, is revoked.

5–108. Executive Order No. 10952, as amended, entitled "Assigning Civil Defense Responsibilities to the Secretary of Defense and Others", is revoked.

5–109. Executive Order No. 11051, as amended, relating to responsibilities of the Office of Emergency Preparedness, is revoked.

5–110. Executive Order No. 11415, as amended, relating to the Health Resources Advisory Committee, is revoked.

5–111. Executive Order No. 11795, as amended, entitled "Delegating Disaster Relief Functions Pursuant to the Disaster Relief Act of 1974", is revoked, except for Section 3 thereof.

5–112. Executive Order No. 11725, as amended, entitled "Transfer of Certain Functions of the Office of Emergency Preparedness", is revoked.

5–113. Executive Order No. 11749, as amended, entitled "Consolidating Disaster Relief Functions Assigned to the Secretary of Housing and Urban Development", is revoked.

5–2. *Amendments.*

5–201. Executive Order No. 10421, as amended, relating to physical security of defense facilities is further amended by (a) substituting the "Director of the Federal Emergency Management Agency" for "Director of the Office of Emergency Planning" in Sections 1(a), 1(c), and 6(b); and, (b) substituting "Federal

Emergency Management Agency" for "Office of Emergency Planning" in Sections 6(b) and 7(b).

5–202. Executive Order No. 10480, as amended, is further amended by (a) substituting "Director of the Federal Emergency Management Agency" for "Director of the Office of Emergency Planning" in Sections 101(a), 101(b), 201(a), 201 (b), 301, 304, 307, 308, 310(b), 311(b), 312, 313, 401(b), 401(e), and 605; and, (b) substituting "Director of the Federal Emergency Management Agency" for "Administrator of General Services" in Section 610.

5–203. Section 3(d) of Executive Order No. 10582, as amended, which relates to determinations under the Buy American Act is amended by deleting "Director of the Office of Emergency Planning" and substituting therefor "Director of the Federal Emergency Management Agency".

5–204. Paragraph 21 of Executive Order No. 10789, as amended, is further amended by adding "The Federal Emergency Management Agency" after "Government Printing Office".

5–205. Executive Order No. 11179, as amended, concerning the National Defense Executive Reserve, is further amended by deleting "Director of the Office of Emergency Planning" in Section 2 and substituting therefor "Director of the Federal Emergency Management Agency".

5–206. Section 7 of Executive Order No. 11912, as amended, concerning energy policy and conservation, is further amended by deleting "Administrator of General Services" and substituting therefor "Director of the Federal Emergency Management Agency".

5–207. Section 2(d) of Executive Order No. 11988 entitled "Floodplain Management" is amended by deleting "Federal Insurance Administration" and substituting therefor "Director of the Federal Emergency Management Agency".

5–208. Section 5–3 of Executive Order No. 12046 of March 29, 1978, is amended by deleting *"General Services Administration"* and substituting therefor *"Federal Emergency Management Agency"* and by deleting "Administrator of General Services" and substituting therefor "Director of the Federal Emergency Management Agency".

5–209. Section 1–201 of Executive Order No. 12065 is amended by adding "The Director of the Federal Emergency Management Agency" after "The Administrator, National Aeronautics and Space Administration" and by deleting "Director, Federal Preparedness Agency and to the" from the parentheses after "The Administrator of General Services".

5–210. Section 1–102 of Executive Order No. 12075 of August 16, 1978, is amended by adding in alphabetical order "(p) Federal Emergency Management Agency".

5–211. Section 1–102 of Executive Order No. 12083 of September 27, 1978 is amended by adding in alphabetical order "(x) the Director of the Federal Emergency Management Agency".

5–212. Section 9.11(b) of Civil Service Rule IX (5 CFR Part 9) is amended by deleting "the Defense Civil Preparedness Agency and".

5–213. Section 3(2) of each of the following described Executive orders is amended by adding "Federal Emergency Management Agency" immediately after "Department of Transportation".

(a) Executive Order No. 11331 establishing the Pacific Northwest River Basins Commission.

(b) Executive Order No. 11345, as amended, establishing the Great Lakes Basin Commission.

(c) Executive Order No. 11371, as amended, establishing the New England River Basins Commission.

(d) Executive Order No. 11578, as amended, establishing the Ohio River Basin Commission.

(e) Executive Order No. 11658, as amended, establishing the Missouri River Basin Commission.

(f) Executive Order No. 11659, as amended, establishing the Upper Mississippi River Basin Commission.

5–214. Executive Order No. 11490, as amended, is further amended as follows:

(a) Delete the last sentence of Section 102(a) and substitute therefor the following: "The activities undertaken by the departments and agencies pursuant to this Order, except as provided in Section 3003, shall be in accordance with guidance provided by, and subject to, evaluation by the Director of the Federal Emergency Management Agency.".

(b) Delete Section 103 entitled "Presidential Assistance" and substitute the following new Section 103: *"Sec. 103 General Coordination.* The Director of the Federal Emergency Management Agency (FEMA) shall determine national preparedness goals and policies for the performance of functions under this Order and coordinate the performance of such functions with the total national preparedness programs.".

(c) Delete the portion of the first sentence of Section 401 prior to the colon and insert the following: "The Secretary of Defense shall perform the following emergency preparedness functions".

(d) Delete "Director of the Federal Preparedness Agency (GSA)" or "the Federal Preparedness Agency (GSA)" and substitute therefor "Director, FEMA", in Sections 401(3), 401(4), 401

(5), 401(9), 401(10), 401(14), 401(15), 401(16), 401(19), 401(21), 401(22), 501(8), 601(2), 904(2), 1102(2), 1204 (2), 1401(a), 1701, 1702, 2003, 2004, 2801(5), 3001, 3002(2), 3004, 3005, 3006, 3008, 3010, and 3013.

(e) The number assigned to this Order shall be substituted for "11051 of September 27, 1962" in Section 3001, and for "11051" in Sections 1802, 2002(3), 3002 and 3008(1).

(f) The number assigned to this Order shall be substituted for "10952" in Sections 1103, 1104, 1205, and 3002.

(g) Delete "Department of Defense" in Sections 502, 601(1), 804, 905, 1103, 1104, 1106(4), 1205, 2002(8), the first sentence of Section 3002, and Sections 3008(1) and 3010 and substitute therefor "Director of the Federal Emergency Management Agency.".

SECTION 6. This Order is effective July 15, 1979.

JIMMY CARTER

The White House,
  July 20, 1979.

[Filed with the Office of the Federal Register, 2:18 p.m., July 20, 1979]

United States Ambassador to the Soviet Union

Nomination of Thomas J. Watson, Jr.
July 20, 1979

The President today announced that he will nominate Thomas J. Watson, Jr., of Connecticut, to be Ambassador Extraordinary and Plenipotentiary of the United States to the Union of Soviet Socialist Republics. He will replace Malcolm Toon who is resigning.

Watson was born January 8, 1914, in Dayton, Ohio. He received his B.A. in 1937 from Brown University. He served in the U.S. Army Air Corps as lieutenant colonel from 1940 to 1945.

He has been with International Business Machines Corp. since 1937, successively as vice president, executive vice president, president, chairman of the board, and presently as chairman of the executive committee.

Since 1978 he has been Chairman of the General Advisory Committee of the Arms Control and Disarmament Agency. He has served on the President's Advisory Committee on Labor-Management Policy; as director of Bankers Trust Co., Pan American World Airways, Time, Inc.; and as trustee of the American Museum of Natural History, Brown University, and Rockefeller Foundation.

Department of Transportation

Resignation of Brock Adams and Appointment of W. Graham Claytor, Jr., as Acting Secretary. July 20, 1979

The President has accepted the resignation of Secretary of Transportation Brock Adams. Secretary Adams has expressed a desire for an early transition.

Secretary of the Navy Graham Claytor will serve as Acting Secretary of the Department of Transportation for a period up to 30 days until a permanent successor has been confirmed and sworn into office.

NOTE: Press Secretary Jody Powell read the announcement at 1:37 p.m. to reporters assembled in the Briefing Room at the White House.

The press release also includes a transcript of the question-and-answer session which followed the announcement.

Department of Transportation

Exchange of Letters on the Resignation of Brock Adams as Secretary. July 20, 1979

To Secretary Brock Adams

I accept your resignation with friendship, respect and appreciation for the accomplishments of our nation during your service as Secretary of Transportation. I share your belief that our country's system of transportation can and must be greatly improved in the future. Your continuing advice and support as we make this progress will be very valuable.

You and Betty have my best wishes, and my thanks on behalf of a nation which has benefited from your service.

Sincerely,

JIMMY CARTER

My dear Mr. President:

I hereby tender my resignation as United States Secretary of Transportation.

I have appreciated your courtesy and the personal kindness you and your wife have extended to Betty and me during the period I have served as a member of your Cabinet.

I particularly appreciated the position you stated in your Sunday night speech regarding public transportation and the need for a more fuel-efficient automobile. I hope these programs will be fully implemented soon. As you know, during the last two years I have repeatedly urged that more attention be focused on these areas because maintaining American mobility through alternatives to and more efficient use of the motor vehicle are essential to maintaining the American economy and a quality standard of living as we go through the difficult period of the future. I believe the American public shares this view and will support using the resources and technological development necessary to achieve it. The many fine people serving in the Department of Transportation stand ready to help you in this effort.

I hope you find happiness in your job, and I join with the whole Nation in hoping that the remainder of your administration will be successful.

Respectfully submitted,

BROCK ADAMS

[The President, The White House, Washington, D.C.]

White House Conference on Families

Remarks at a White House Reception. July 20, 1979

First of all, I want to thank Jim Guy Tucker [1] and all of you for being willing to serve in this most important and responsible effort.

As you know, the American family is under unprecedented pressure, and it's good to meet with people who will think and study and consider and learn before we act.

The purpose of the family conference to be held here at the White House will be not to set up some big new expensive Federal program; it's to see what we can do, not simply as a government, but as a nation, to strengthen American families. In some instances, this may mean just getting government out of the way. You'll be looking at what many public and private institutions of all kinds are doing now at all levels to see how these activities affect families.

I hope that you will not look just at the programs that were originally designed to

---

[1] Chairperson, White House Conference on Families.

affect families, but also look at other programs that were designed for other purposes that might have an adverse effect on the cohesion and the strength of American families today. You must reach out, not only to scholars and to experts but to many thousands of American citizens around this country who know from their own experience what makes a family strong.

Our generation has been through a time of great social and technological change, affecting the way we live, the way we think, the way we act, the way we work, the way we assess our own status as individuals. Our institutions do not seem to offer the same degree of support for a cohesive family arrangement as they did in years past. And the signs of strain within families, those signs are all around us.

I talked last Sunday night about a crisis of confidence in our country. And the family is very much part of that crisis—part of the problem, yes, but much more importantly, it is a major part of the solution. For couples who married in the early years of this century, 1 marriage in 10 ended in divorce; for couples who have married since World War II, 1 marriage in 3 ends in divorce.

I was talking to Jody Powell the other day—who's a little bit older than my oldest son, who lived in a small Georgia town not very far from Plains—and neither he nor I could recall any divorced person who lived in Vienna, Georgia, or Plains, Georgia, in the years we were growing up. There are a lot of them there now. The rate of teenage suicide has doubled in the last 10 years. Half a million youngsters each year run away from home. Too many of our older people are lonely and sometimes even afraid. Without question, the American family is in trouble.

The family has survived, though, many social and technological revolutions in the past, and our families can survive the current changes and stresses. They are too precious—the families are too basic, too essential not to survive. Ultimately, the family may emerge from this test even stronger if we are successful and the American people are successful in facing facts and acting together.

This will obviously not be automatic, and it will obviously not be easy. We all know that change is nothing new. The people who created this country were engaged in changes that shook old institutions and old ways of living profoundly; the pioneers who pushed west, the immigrants who added to the rich diversity of our people were cut off from old certainties and faced with troubling change just as we are today. They, too, had to live with dramatic, often wrenching change in their lives, and they had to adapt to new patterns of living.

They quickly learned—and this is important—to rely on each other, to build new families and new communities. They saw a change not as something to be feared, but as an opportunity. They learned to hold onto their real values and not let them change, values that bound together families. They learned to work for the family as individuals. They learned to let the families strengthen communities, and they learned to let those communities, based on the families, strengthen and develop a nation.

There's a difference. In those times—revolution, moving west, the assimilation of broad and diverse types of people—those fearsome changes had a strong tendency to bring families together for mutual support, mutual reassurance, mutual love. These days, the changes that affect us have a tendency to fragment families, to drive one part of a family in one direction, a different part of a family, maybe a different generation, in an opposite direction. That tendency, which is the new

thing, will be a major subject for you to address.

We often feel nostalgic about a past that seems to be simpler and sometimes seems to be better, and we can learn from the past. But we must not limit our vision of what a good family is just to what a family was in the past. Instead, we must find meaning in today's challenges and today's realities, which we cannot change, honestly, creatively, with courage and with compassion.

Our people are searching not for an artificially constructed family unit that we might try to impose on them, but they're searching for freedom to make their own decisions and for opportunity, as they always have. And this search is having profound effects on the modern family. For many it's already proven to be liberating and rewarding, but it also leaves many who are unsure, who are lonely and afraid. Lily Tomlin jokes that we are all in this alone. [*Laughter*] But for many of our people, these words seem not funny, but tragically true. Too many feel that they have no one to whom they can turn in a moment of crisis or a moment of need.

These problems that I've described to you so briefly are real, but they are also the kinds of problems that families have always specialized in solving. Many of our toughest problems, from energy to the decay of our cities, from inflation to coping with old age, even the strengthening of a nation's spirit can be resolved if every family does its share and takes seriously its responsibilities to its own members and to the community.

Families, as you well know, are more than just households. They are a network of relationships rooted not only in kinship based on blood but a kinship based on shared experiences, shared joys and sorrows, and I think, most of all, in shared love that crosses vast distances and also crosses very easily the barrier of generations. Families are groups of people, some small, some large, who do not necessarily live together in one place, but who do take responsibility for each other.

There is an old Yiddish proverb, "God gave burdens, but also shoulders." Not only our own shoulders but shoulders to help us bear the burdens that are too heavy for us alone, shoulders to cry on, shoulders to be patted in a gesture of encouragement, shoulders to help others bear their loads and their burdens. That's what a family is—kind of a collection of shoulders.

We're not in this alone. With strong families, I'm convinced, as I know you are, that our Nation's strength now and in the future will be assured. That's a task that I give to you to open your hearts, to study the family structure, the structure of communities and our Nation, and building upon strong families assure the strength of the United States.

Thank you very much.

NOTE: The President spoke at 2:36 p.m. in the East Room at the White House.

Federal Regional Councils

Executive Order 12149.   July 20, 1979

By the authority vested in me as President by the Constitution and statutes of the United States of America, and in order to provide a structure for interagency and intergovernmental cooperation, it is hereby ordered as follows:

1-1. *Establishment of Federal Regional Councils.*

1-101. There is hereby continued a Federal Regional Council for each of the ten standard Federal regions (Office of Management and Budget Circular No. A-105).

1-102. Each Council shall be composed of a representative designated by the head of each of the following agencies:

  (a) The Department of the Interior.
  (b) The Department of Agriculture.
  (c) The Department of Commerce.
  (d) The Department of Labor.
  (e) The Department of Health, Education, and Welfare.
  (f) The Department of Housing and Urban Development.
  (g) The Department of Transportation.
  (h) The Department of Energy.
  (i) The Environmental Protection Agency.
  (j) The Community Services Administration.
  (k) The Office of Personnel Management.
  (l) The General Services Administration.
  (m) ACTION.
  (n) The Small Business Administration.
  (o) The Federal Emergency Management Agency.
  (p) The U.S. Army Corps of Engineers.
  (q) The Regional Action Planning Commissions.

1-103. The President shall designate one member of each Council to be Chairman. The Chairman may convene an Executive Committee to carry out specific initiatives of the Council.

1-104. Each member of each Council shall be a principal official in the region at the Administrator, Director, Secretarial Representative, or equivalent level. For the Regional Action Planning Commissions (established pursuant to Title V of the Public Works and Economic Development Act of 1965, as amended (42

U.S.C. 3181 *et seq.*)) the Federal co-chairman shall serve as the Council member. Representatives of the Office of Management and Budget shall participate in the deliberations of each Council.

1–105. Each member of each Council shall designate an alternate to serve whenever the regular member is unable to attend any meeting of the Council. The alternate shall be a principal official in the Region at the deputy or equivalent level, or the head of an operating unit of the agency.

1–106. When a Chairman determines that matters which significantly affect the interests of agencies which are not represented on the Council are to be considered by that Council, the Chairman shall request the regional director or other appropriate representative of the affected agency to participate in the deliberations of the Council.

1–2. **Federal Regional Council Functions.**

1–201. The Federal Regional Council, as the major interagency mechanism in the field, shall ensure that Federal programs are implemented in a manner which is consistent with overall Government policy, and shall be responsive to State, tribal, regional, and local government concerns.

1–202. Each Council shall develop a mechanism for sharing information about major agency decisions or actions among agencies in the field, and shall ensure a timely and consistent Federal response to State, tribal, regional, and local concerns or inquiries about such actions.

1–203. Each Council shall establish practical and appropriate liaison functions with State, tribal, regional, and local officials, and shall implement regular procedures to inform elected officials about Government policies and initiatives.

1–204. Each Council shall attempt to identify significant problems with Federal policies and actions and, if such problems cannot be resolved in the Region, refer such problems to the appropriate agencies and the Interagency Coordinating Council.

1–3. *General Provisions.*

1–301. The Interagency Coordinating Council, in conjunction with the Office of Management and Budget shall, consistent with the objectives and priorities established by the President, establish policy with respect to Federal Regional Council matters, provide guidance to the Councils, respond to their initiatives and seek to resolve policy issues referred to it by the Councils. The Interagency Coordinating Council shall also provide policy guidance to the Federal Cochairmen of the Regional Action Planning Commissions on intergovernmental matters pertaining to activities undertaken by the Federal Regional Councils.

1–302. The Office of Management and Budget shall provide direction for and oversight of the implementation by the Councils of Federal management improvement actions and of Federal aid reforms.

1–303. Each Agency represented on a Council shall provide, to the extent permitted by law, appropriate staff for common or joint interagency task forces as requested by the Federal Regional Council Chairman or by the Interagency Coordinating Council.

1–304. Each Council member shall be provided administrative support by the member's agency.

1–305. Administrative support required by the Council shall be provided by the Chairman's agency.

1–306. The Federal Regional Councils are encouraged to work with Federal Executive Boards, Federal Executive Associations, River Basin Commissions, Regional Councils of Government, and other similar organizations in the Region.

1–307. Executive Order No. 11647, as amended, is revoked.

JIMMY CARTER

The White House,
    July 20, 1979.

[Filed with the Office of the Federal Register,
    4:26 p.m., July 20, 1979]

Departments of Energy and Defense

Resignation of James R. Schlesinger and Nominations of Charles W. Duncan, Jr., To Be Secretary of Energy and W. Graham Claytor, Jr., To Be Deputy Secretary of Defense. July 20, 1979

As you know, Secretary of Energy Schlesinger has twice asked the President to accept his resignation. As you also know, Secretary Schlesinger has previously stated his intention to leave the Department of Energy by the fall of this year. The President will nominate Deputy Secretary of Defense Charles William Duncan, Jr., to succeed Secretary Schlesinger. Additionally, the President will nominate W. Graham Claytor, Jr., Secretary of the Navy, to succeed Mr. Duncan as Deputy Secretary of Defense.

The exact date of Secretary Schlesinger's departure will be determined by the President and Secretary Schlesinger, consistent with the mutual desire for a smooth transition. Until that time the Secretary will continue to have the President's full confidence and support.

Mr. Duncan, who has served as Deputy Secretary of Defense since the beginning of this administration, has proven to be a manager of exceptional skill at the Department of Defense. Prior to entering Government service, he had extensive experience in managing some of the largest public and private enterprises in the world. The President feels that Mr. Duncan will provide the sort of leadership that is needed in our continuing efforts to deal with our energy problems.

NOTE: Press Secretary Jody Powell read the announcement at 3:45 p.m. to reporters assembled in the Briefing Room at the White House.

The press release also includes a transcript of the question-and-answer session which followed the announcement.

Department of Energy

Exchange of Letters on the Resignation of James R. Schlesinger as Secretary. July 20, 1979

To Secretary James Schlesinger

With regret but with great appreciation I accept your resignation as Secretary of Energy. Under the most difficult of circumstances you have performed your many duties superbly.

The progress you have described in your letter of resignation has been the product of a team effort, and you have headed the team. It may be many years before the people of our nation can realize the benefits which have already been brought to them by your accomplishments.

During the months ahead, with your advice and support, we will implement the program we have evolved together. An aroused and united country can then guarantee our vital energy security.

You have my best wishes and thanks.
    Sincerely,

JIMMY CARTER

———

Dear Mr. President:

It is now two and one-half years since you assigned to me the onerous and miscelleneous responsibilities falling to the lot of the "energy czar." My tenure in that anomalous position has by far exceeded that of any of my predecessors. It has covered the establishment of this Department, the long battle over passage of the National Energy Act of 1978, the severe short-term difficulties posed by the fall of the Shah, the Iranian shutdown and its aftermath—as well as such lesser matters as the coal strike of 1978 and the natural gas crisis of 1977.

As we discussed prior to the Tokyo Summit, it would be far better for you to have in place one who is less scarred by earlier battles. On August 4 I shall have completed two years in this office. I trust that you will accept the resignation that I have previously offered. I would thus hope to be out of office by October 1— the second anniversary of the establishment of this Department. In the interim I shall provide steady and continuing support for the new programs you have initiated and ready assistance to Charles Duncan during this period of transition.

Mr. President, under your leadership, the energy problems, so easy to ignore, have come to be better understood. Conservation, so widely dismissed a few years ago, has now become a simple reality. The thirty year war over natural gas pricing has been ended. The controls on oil prices—with their crippling effects— are being phased out. The nuclear option has been preserved—and the age of renewables has been initiated. We have made a start on a synthetics program which promises within a decade to become massive. Despite all the difficulties, impressive achievements have occurred during these last two years.

Yet, despite all the efforts, Mr. President, I fear that the depth of our national problem has not as yet been accepted by the American people. The severe impacts on our economy—and potentially on our political and social institutions—posed by the prospective oil stringencies of the 1980's have not been fully recognized. Even more important, the geopolitical implications of the dependence of the United States and her allies on the most volatile and vulnerable region in the world should cause the deepest apprehensions. The geostrategic risks are stark— as is the attendant precariousness of supply. The revolution in Iran, as the embargo before it, should have swept away all illusions regarding these geostrategic risks.

The task remaining is therefore, Mr. President, an imposing one. You shall have whatever assistance I can provide— as well as my best wishes—as you continue to grapple with these intractable problems.

> Sincerely yours,
> JAMES R. SCHLESINGER

[The President, The White House, Washington, D.C. 20500]

Changes in the Cabinet
Remarks to Reporters. July 20, 1979

I have a brief statement to make, consisting of five parts.

First, after a long and very careful assessment, I have made some major changes in my Cabinet.

Secondly, these changes are all constructive, and the transition from one leader to another in each case will be orderly and properly conducted.

Third, I do not expect any further resignations from the Cabinet, other than those that have already been made. There are a few vacancies which I will fill without delay.

Fourth, I want to express my thanks to those who have served and who will now be leaving.

And fifth, I need the full support of the American people in the future.

I am well pleased with all the changes that have been made. Every single change has been a positive change. There is absolutely no doubt in my mind that I and my administration will now be better able to serve this country and to resolve those problems and to meet those challenges which I described to the American people in my television address Sunday evening.

Thank you very much.

NOTE: The President spoke at 4:17 p.m. in the Briefing Room at the White House.

Department of State

Nomination of J. Brian Atwood To Be an Assistant Secretary.   July 20, 1979

The President today announced that he will nominate J. Brian Atwood, of Maryland, to be an Assistant Secretary of State for congressional relations. He will replace Douglas J. Bennet, Jr., who has resigned.

Atwood was born July 25, 1942, in Wareham, Mass. He received his B.A. in 1964 from Boston University and attended graduate studies at American University in 1970.

He was research analyst at the National Security Agency from 1964 to 1966. From 1966 to 1971, he worked for the Department of State, first as regional administrative specialist at Abidjan and then as personnel officer at Madrid. From 1971 to 1977, he was legislative assistant to Senator Thomas F. Eagleton. Since 1977 he has held the position of Deputy Assistant Secretary of State for Congressional Relations.

Digest of Other White House Announcements

The following listing includes the President's public schedule and other items of general interest announced by the White House Press Office and not included elsewhere in this issue.

July 14

The President returned to the White House from Camp David, Md.

July 17

The President met at the White House with:

—Zbigniew Brzezinski, Assistant to the President for National Security Affairs;

—the bipartisan congressional leadership;

—the senior White House staff;

—the Cabinet.

The White House announced that the members of the Cabinet and the senior White House staff have offered their resignations to the President.

July 18

The President met at the White House with:

—Dr. Brzezinski;

—Frank B. Moore, Assistant to the President for Congressional Liaison;

—Secretary of Housing and Urban Development Patricia R. Harris.

The White House announced that the President has appointed Hamilton Jordan, Assistant to the President, as White House chief of staff.

July 19

The President met at the White House with:

—Secretary of Health, Education, and Welfare Joseph A. Califano, Jr.;

—Dr. Brzezinski;

—Mr. Moore;

—Secretary of the Treasury W. Michael Blumenthal;

—Deputy Attorney General Benjamin R. Civiletti.

The President hosted a reception for Americans for SALT in the State Dining Room at the White House.

The President declared a major disaster for the State of Kentucky as a result of severe storms and flash flooding on July 15, which caused extensive public and private property damage.

The President declared a major disaster for the State of Wyoming as a result of severe storms and tornadoes on July 16, which caused extensive public and private property damage.

The President transmitted to the Congress the 1978 annual report of the National Advisory Council on Extension and Continuing Education.

July 20

The President met at the White House with:

—Secretary of State Cyrus R. Vance, Secretary of Defense Harold Brown, Dr. Brzezinski, and Mr. Jordan;

—Mr. Moore;

—Jaime Roldós, President-elect of Ecuador;

—Secretary of Transportation Brock Adams;

—Gov. Hugh Gallen of New Hampshire.

The President declared a major disaster for the Commonwealth of Virginia as a result of severe storms and flash flooding on July 15–16, which caused extensive public and private property damage.

NOMINATIONS SUBMITTED TO THE SENATE

The following list does not include promotions of members of the Uniformed Services, nominations to the Service Academies, or nominations of Foreign Service officers.

NOMINATIONS—Continued

Submitted July 16, 1979

DANIEL EDWARD LEACH, of Virginia, to be a member of the Equal Employment Opportunity Commission for the term expiring July 1, 1984 (reappointment).

Submitted July 18, 1978

WILLIAM P. HOBGOOD, of Virginia, to be an Assistant Secretary of Labor, vice Francis X. Burkhardt, resigned.

JAMES W. KEHOE, of Florida, to be United States District Judge for the Southern District of Florida, vice a new position created by P.L. 95–486, approved October 20, 1978.

Submitted July 19, 1979

JACK RICHARD PERRY, of Georgia, a Foreign Service officer of Class one, to be Ambassador Extraordinary and Plenipotentiary of the United States of America to Bulgaria.

FRANK GEORGE WISNER II, of the District of Columbia, a Foreign Service officer of Class two, to be Ambassador Extraordinary and Plenipotentiary of the United States of America to the Republic of Zambia.

DOUGLAS J. BENNET, JR., of Connecticut, to be Administrator of the Agency for International Development, vice John J. Gilligan, resigned.

DUDLEY H. BOWEN, JR., of Georgia, to be United States District Judge for the Southern District of Georgia, vice a new position created by P.L. 95–486, approved October 20, 1978.

JUAN GUERRERO BURCIAGA, of New Mexico, to be United States District Judge for the District of New Mexico, vice a new position created by P.L. 95–486, approved October 20, 1978.

IRVIN B. SMITH, JR., of Delaware, to be United States Marshal for the District of Delaware for the term of 4 years, vice Peter J. McLaughlin, resigned.

THOMAS EHRLICH, of California, to be Director of the United States International Development Cooperation Agency (new position).

Submitted July 20, 1979

BENJAMIN R. CIVILETTI, of Maryland, to be Attorney General, vice Griffin B. Bell, resigning.

PATRICIA ROBERTS HARRIS, of the District of Columbia, to be Secretary of Health, Education, and Welfare.

NOMINATIONS—Continued

Submitted July 20—Continued

THOMAS J. WATSON, JR., of Connecticut, to be Ambassador Extraordinary and Plenipotentiary of the United States of America to the Union of Soviet Socialist Republics.

MORRIS ABRAM, of New York, to be Chairman of the President's Commission for the Study of Ethical Problems in Medicine and Biomedical and Behavioral Research (new position).

G. WILLIAM MILLER, of California, to be Secretary of the Treasury.

J. BRIAN ATWOOD, of Maryland, to be an Assistant Secretary of State, vice Douglas J. Bennet, Jr.

CHECKLIST OF WHITE HOUSE PRESS RELEASES

The following listing contains releases of the White House Press Office which are not included in this issue.

Released July 16, 1979

Advance text: remarks at the annual convention of the National Association of Counties in Kansas City, Mo.

Fact sheet: oil import reduction program

News conference: on the oil import reduction program—by James R. Schlesinger, Secretary, and Alvin L. Alm, Assistant Secretary for Policy and Evaluation, Department of Energy; Eliot R. Cutler, Associate Director for Natural Resources, Energy and Science, Office of Management and Budget; and Bertram W. Carp, Deputy Assistant for Domestic Affairs and Policy

Advance text: remarks at the annual convention of the Communications Workers of America in Detroit, Mich.

Announcement: settlement of Pennsylvania and Delaware Gasoline Dealers' Association strike

Released July 17, 1979

Announcement: nomination of James W. Kehoe to be United States District Judge for the Southern District of Florida

CHECKLIST—Continued

Released July 18, 1979

Announcement: nomination of Dudley H. Bowen, Jr., to be United States District Judge for the Southern District of Georgia

Announcement: nomination of Juan Guerrero Burciaga to be United States District Judge for the District of New Mexico

Announcement: nomination of Irvin B. Smith, Jr., to be United States Marshal for the District of Delaware

Released July 19, 1979

News conference: on the proposed reorganization of the Federal Government's international trade activities—by Ambassador Robert S. Strauss, Special Representative for Trade Negotiations, and James T. McIntyre, Jr., Director of the Office of Management and Budget

Fact sheet: proposed reorganization of the Federal Government's international trade activities

News conference: on White House activities in the energy field pursuant to the President's proposals contained in his address to the Nation—by Anne Wexler, Assistant to the President, Mr. Carp, and Mr. Cutler

Statements: support for the President's energy program—by leaders of business and labor organizations and civic associations

Biographical data: G. William Miller, nominated to be Secretary of the Treasury

Released July 20, 1979

Transcript: statement by the President on U.S. troop withdrawals from the Republic of Korea (as read by Zbigniew Brzezinski, Assistant to the President for National Security Affairs, in the Briefing Room at the White House)

Statements: support for the President's energy program—by civic and religious leaders (two releases)

Announcement: nomination of Barbara B. Crabb to be United States District Judge for the Western District of Wisconsin

Announcement: nomination of Terence T. Evans to be United States District Judge for the Eastern District of Wisconsin

Announcement: nomination of Eugene P. Spellman to be United States District Judge for the Southern District of Florida

ACTS APPROVED BY THE PRESIDENT

Approved July 16, 1979

H.R. 4556_____ Public Law 96–33
An act to amend section 1521 of the Public Health Service Act to authorize the Secretary of Health, Education, and Welfare to extend conditional designations of State health planning and development agencies.

Approved July 17, 1979

H.J. Res. 353_____ Public Law 96–34
A joint resolution congratulating the men and women of the Apollo program upon the tenth anniversary of the first manned landing on the Moon and requesting the President to

ACTS APPROVED—Continued

Approved July 17—Continued

proclaim the period of July 16 through 24, 1979, as "United States Space Observance".

Approved July 20, 1979

S. 1007_____ Public Law 96–35
Special International Security Assistance Act of 1979.

S. 927_____ Public Law 96–36
An act to authorize the Smithsonian Institution to plan for the development of the area south of the original Smithsonian Institution Building adjacent to Independence Avenue at Tenth Street, Southwest, in the city of Washington.

Citizenship Day and Constitution Week, 1979

Proclamation 4670. July 23, 1979

By the President of the United States of America

A Proclamation

On September 17, 1787, in Independence Hall, Philadelphia, our Founding Fathers adopted the Constitution of the United States. With this great document as its cornerstone, our country has become the finest example in all history of the principle of government by law, in which every individual is guaranteed certain inalienable rights. The strong beliefs of its authors in the worth of the individual and the rights to be enjoyed by all citizens have made the Constitution not only an enduring document but one which finds new life with the passing of years and continues to inspire freedom-seeking people all over the world.

On February 29, 1952, by joint resolution (36 U.S.C. 153), the Congress designated September 17 as Citizenship Day, in commemoration of the formation and signing of the Constitution as a reminder of the privileges and responsibilities of citizenship. By a joint resolution of August 2, 1956 (36 U.S.C. 159), Congress authorized the President to designate the period beginning September 17 and ending September 23 of each year as Constitution Week and to issue a proclamation calling for the observance of that week.

Now, THEREFORE, I, JIMMY CARTER, President of the United States of America, call upon appropriate Government officials to display the flag of the United States on all Government buildings on Citizenship Day, September 17, 1979. I urge Federal, State and local officials, as well as leaders of civic, educational and religious organizations to conduct meaningful ceremonies and programs on that day.

I also designate as Constitution Week the period beginning September 17 and ending September 23, 1979, and urge all Americans to observe that week with appropriate ceremonies and activities in their schools, churches and in other suitable places in order to foster a better understanding of the Constitution, and of the rights and duties of United States citizens.

IN WITNESS WHEREOF, I have hereunto set my hand this twenty-third day of July, in the year of our Lord nineteen hundred seventy-nine, and of the Independence of the United States of America the two hundred and fourth.

JIMMY CARTER

[Filed with the Office of the Federal Register, 10:18 a.m., July 24, 1979]

United States Sinai Support Mission

Executive Order 12150.   July 23, 1979

By the authority vested in me as President of the United States of America, including Chapter 6 of Part II of the Foreign Assistance Act of 1961, as amended (22 U.S.C. 2348, 2348a.–2348c.), Section 1(b) of Executive Order No. 11896 of January 13, 1976, is hereby amended to read:

"(b) The Mission shall, in accordance with the Foreign Assistance Act of 1961, as amended, including Part II, Chapter 6 thereof, the Joint Resolution of October 13, 1975 (Public Law 94–110, 89 Stat. 572, 22 U.S.C. 2441 note), and the provisions of this Order, carry out the duties and responsibilities of the United States Government to implement the "United States Proposal for the Early Warning System in Sinai" in connection with the Basic Agreement between Egypt and Israel, signed on September 4, 1975, and the Annex to the Basic Agreement, as superseded by the Treaty of Peace between the Arab Republic of Egypt and the State of Israel, signed on March 26, 1979, and Article VII of the Appendix to Annex I of the Treaty of Peace, subject to broad policy guidance received through the Assistant to the President for National Security Affairs, and the continuous supervision and general direction of the Secretary of State pursuant to Section 622(c) of the Foreign Assistance Act of 1961, as amended (22 U.S.C. 2382(c)).".

JIMMY CARTER

The White House,
July 23, 1979.

[Filed with the Office of the Federal Register, 10:19 a.m., July 24, 1979]

United Nations

Nomination of James W. Spain To Be Deputy U.S. Representative.   July 23, 1979

The President today announced that he will nominate James W. Spain, of California, to be Deputy Representative of the United States to the United Nations. He would replace James F. Leonard, who has been transferred to the position of deputy to Ambassador Robert Strauss.

Spain has been U.S. Ambassador to the United Republic of Tanzania since 1975.

He was born July 22, 1926, in Chicago, Ill. He received an M.A. from the University of Chicago in 1949 and a Ph. D. from Columbia University in 1959. He served in the U.S. Army from 1946 to 1947.

Spain was a consultant to the Secretary of the Army in Tokyo from 1949 to 1950, and cultural officer in Karachi from 1951 to 1953. From 1953 to 1955, he was a research fellow with the Ford Foundation, and from 1955 to 1963, he was a researcher and lecturer at Columbia University.

From 1963 to 1964, Spain was on the Policy Planning Staff at the State Department, and from 1964 to 1966, he was Director of the Office of Research and Analysis for Near East-South Asian Affairs. He was Country Director for Pakistan and Afghanistan from 1966 to 1969, and chargé d'affaires in Islamabad in 1969.

From 1970 to 1972, Spain was Consul General in Istanbul, and from 1972 to 1974, he was Deputy Chief of Mission in Ankara. In 1974–75 he was diplomat in residence at Florida State University, and in 1975 he served as a Foreign Service Inspector at the State Department.

National Credit Union Administration Board

Nomination of Harold Alonza Black To Be a Member.   July 23, 1979

The President today announced that he will nominate Harold Alonza Black, of Carrboro, N.C., to be a member of the National Credit Union Administration Board for a 2-year term.

Black is an associate professor of finance at the University of North Carolina's School of Business Administration.

He was born July 3, 1945, in Macon, Ga. He received a B.B.A. from the University of Georgia in 1966 and an M.A. (1968) and Ph. D. (1972) from Ohio State University. His major fields of interest are financial markets and institutions, monetary and macroeconomics.

Black was an assistant professor of economics at the University of Florida in Gainesville from 1971 to 1975. From 1976 to 1978, he was Deputy Director of the Department of Economic Research and Analysis in the Office of the Comptroller of the Currency, and also served as a lecturer in economics at Howard University.

Black is the author of numerous articles on economics and banking. He was a visiting professor in the National Urban League's Black Executive Exchange Program in 1977, and he received the Treasury Department's Special Achievement Award in 1977.

Budget Deferral

Message to the Congress.   July 24, 1979

To the Congress of the United States:

In accordance with the Impoundment Control Act of 1974, I herewith report a new deferral of $6.2 million in budget authority for the Bureau of Prisons in the Department of Justice.

The details of this deferral are contained in the attached report.

JIMMY CARTER

The White House,
July 24, 1979.

NOTE: The attachment detailing the deferral is printed in the FEDERAL REGISTER of July 30, 1979.

National Mediation Board

Nomination of Robert Joseph Brown To Be a Member.   July 24, 1979

The President today announced that he will nominate Robert Joseph Brown, of Bethesda, Md., to be a member of the National Mediation Board for a term expiring July 1, 1982. He would replace David Stowe, whose term has expired.

Brown has been Under Secretary of Labor since 1977.

He was born September 10, 1929, in Seattle, Wash. He received an A.A. from the University of Minnesota in 1951.

From 1948 to 1954, Brown was a spinner with the Donaldson Co. in St. Paul, Minn., and served as president of United Auto Workers Local 41 in St. Paul. In 1952 and 1954, he was education representative of the Minnesota State CIO.

From 1955 to 1957, Brown worked for the State of Minnesota, writing manuals and reports. From 1957 to 1963, he was a personnel officer for the State, and from 1963 to 1965, he served as deputy commissioner of conservation for Minnesota. From 1965 to 1966, he was commissioner of employment security for the State of Minnesota.

Brown was Associate Manpower Administrator for the U.S. Department of

Labor from 1966 to 1974. From 1974 to 1977, he was Regional Administrator for the Labor Department in Denver, Colo.

United States Ambassador to the United Arab Emirates

Nomination of William D. Wolle.
July 25, 1979

The President today announced that he will nominate William D. Wolle, of Sioux City, Iowa, to be Ambassador Extraordinary and Plenipotentiary of the United States to the United Arab Emirates. He would replace Francois M. Dickman, who is being transferred to another post.

Wolle has been director of the Office of Research and Analysis for Near East and South Asia at the State Department since 1978.

He was born March 11, 1928, in Sioux City, Iowa. He received a B.A. from Morningside College in 1949 and an M.I.A. from Columbia University in 1951. He served in the U.S. Army from 1946 to 1947.

Wolle joined the Foreign Service in 1951 and was posted in Baghdad, Manchester, Beirut, Aden, and Jidda. From 1962 to 1965, he was at the State Department as an international economist, then an international relations officer. From 1965 to 1967, he was officer in charge of of Arab-Israel affairs.

In 1967–68 Wolle attended the National War College, and from 1968 to 1970, he was counselor for political affairs in Kuwait. He was economic-commercial officer in Amman from 1970 to 1972 and commercial officer in Nairobi from 1972 to 1974. From 1974 to 1978, he was Ambassador to the Sultanate of Oman.

Federal Reserve System

Nomination of Paul A. Volcker To Be Chairman of the Board of Governors.
July 25, 1979

The President will nominate Paul A. Volcker as Chairman of the Federal Reserve Board. Mr. Volcker has been President of the Federal Reserve Bank of New York since 1975.

The President said, in making the announcement, "Mr. Volcker has broad economic and financial experience and enjoys an outstanding international reputation. He shares my determination to vigorously pursue the battle against inflation at home and to ensure the strength and stability of the dollar abroad."

Mr. Volcker served as Deputy Under Secretary of Treasury for Monetary Affairs, 1963 to 1965, and Under Secretary of Treasury for Monetary Affairs, 1969 to 1974. Mr. Volcker is a 1949 graduate of Princeton University. He received master's degree in political economics from Harvard and did postgraduate work at the London School of Economics. He was vice president and director of planning for the Chase Manhattan Bank from 1965 to 1969.

NOTE: Press Secretary Jody Powell read the announcement at 10:30 a.m. to reporters assembled in the Briefing Room at the White House.

Senior Adviser to the President

Appointment of Hedley W. Donovan.
July 25, 1979

The President has asked Mr. Hedley Donovan to serve as a Senior Adviser to the President. Mr. Donovan has accepted the position. He will provide substantive advice on the full range of matters before the President and will undertake special assignments which the President may request from time to time.

Mr. Donovan will work in the White House and report only to the President. He will assume his responsibilities in mid-August. The details and duration of these responsibilities will be determined by the President and Mr. Donovan.

Mr. Donovan retired on June 1 as editor-in-chief of Time, Incorporated, a position he had held since 1964. From 1959 until 1964, he was editorial director of Time, Incorporated. He joined Fortune magazine in 1945 as a writer and in 1953 moved up to managing editor, a position he held until 1959.

Mr. Donovan graduated from the University of Minnesota in 1934 and was a Rhodes Scholar at Oxford. He was a reporter with the Washington Post from 1937 to 1942. He then served in the United States Navy during most of the Second World War.

He was born May 24, 1914.

NOTE: Press Secretary Jody Powell read the announcement at 3 p.m. to reporters assembled in the Briefing Room at the White House.

The press release also includes a transcript of the question-and-answer session which followed the announcement.

The Cyprus Conflict

Letter to the Speaker of the House and the Chairman of the Senate Foreign Relations Committee. July 25, 1979

To Speaker Tip O'Neill (To Chairman Frank Church)

In accordance with the provisions of Public Law 95–384, I am submitting the following report on progress made during the past sixty days toward the conclusion of a negotiated solution of the Cyprus problem.

In my last report to the Congress on Cyprus, dated June 4, I took note of the decision reached by President Kyprianou and Turkish Cypriot leader Denktash during their May 18–19 meetings to resume intercommunal negotiations on June 15. These negotiations resumed as scheduled under the chairmanship of United Nations Under Secretary General Perez de Cuellar. A number of procedural issues were settled in the course of the first session. Unfortunately, however, differences soon arose over the interpretation of the ten-point communique agreed upon in Nicosia on May 18–19, which serves as a broad agenda for the talks. The Greek Cypriots took the position that the Varosha issue should be discussed first in accordance with point five of the communique which states that "priority will be given to reaching agreement on the resettlement of Varosha." The Turkish Cypriots, on the other hand, maintained that point two of the communique, dealing with the overall basis for the talks, should be discussed first.

When it became clear that these differences of approach could not easily be overcome, Under Secretary General Perez de Cuellar decided to recess the negotiations on June 22 and to pursue a compromise resolution through informal consultations with the parties. These consultations have now been in progress in Nicosia for some four weeks. As of this writing, no firm date has been set for reconvening the talks, although there have been indications of greater flexibility and the elements of a solution are beginning to emerge. Our assessment is that given sufficient determination on the part of all concerned a practical way can be found out of these current difficulties that will permit the negotiators to return to the table within a short time. I assure you that this Administration will continue to work closely with the United Nations, the Cypriot parties and our allies both to overcome the present, hopefully temporary, difficulties and to help ensure ultimate success in the negotiations.

The Turkish Cypriot side has not yet given final endorsement to the procedures worked out in Nicosia on May 18–19 concerning the formation of a joint committee to trace and account for missing persons in Cyprus. With the assistance of expert organizations such as the International Red Cross, the proposed joint committee should be in a position to resolve this long-standing humanitarian problem.

I enclose with this report a copy of Secretary-General Waldheim's comprehensive report on May 31 to the United Nations Security Council on the United Nations operation in Cyprus.

Sincerely,

JIMMY CARTER

NOTE: This is the text of identical letters addressed to Thomas P. O'Neill, Jr., Speaker of the House of Representatives, and Frank Church, chairman of the Senate Foreign Relations Committee.

Wharton School of Finance and Commerce and the University of Pennsylvania Law School. He also received the diploma of The Hague Academy of International Law in 1962.

He served as assistant public defender in Philadelphia from 1959 to 1961, and earlier practiced law there. He was an associate professor of law at the University of Virginia from 1961 to 1964.

From 1964 to 1968, Wertheim was with the Peace Corps, serving as Deputy General Counsel and then as associate director of the Peace Corps in Brazil. He has been with Ginsburg, Feldman and Bress since 1969. In 1977 he served as Alternate U.S. Representative to the United Nations Conference on Law of the Sea.

Wertheim is a trustee of Arena Stage. He is also a director of the nonprofit Associates for Renewal in Education, Inc., a member of the American Civil Liberties Union, and was a founding trustee of the Capitol Children's Museum.

Merit Systems Protection Board

Nomination of Ronald P. Wertheim To Be a Member.   July 25, 1979

The President today announced that he will nominate Ronald P. Wertheim, of Washington, D.C., to be a member of the Merit Systems Protection Board for a term expiring March 1, 1981.

Wertheim is a partner in the Washington law firm of Ginsburg, Feldman and Bress, specializing in Federal litigation and practice before Federal regulatory agencies.

He was born September 7, 1933, in Philadelphia, Pa. He is a graduate of the

President's Commission on the Coal Industry

Statement on Receiving the Commission's Report.   July 25, 1979

Increased coal production is a crucial element of the energy program I outlined to the Nation on July 16. The bold and constructive recommendations of the Coal Commission played an important part in the design of that program, and I deeply appreciate the work that the Commission has done. Today's discussion with the Commission and with representatives of the Congressional Coal Caucus was helpful in underlining the importance of a more active immediate effort to convert our Nation to reliance on our bountiful supplies of coal.

I agree with the Commission's view that we can convert to coal without sacrificing our environment or the health and safety of coal workers.

At a time when thousands of coal miners have been thrown out of work, we must redouble our efforts to insist that the energy needs of our Nation are supplied as much as possible by coal.

THE PRESIDENT'S NEWS CONFERENCE OF JULY 25, 1979

NATIONAL GOALS

THE PRESIDENT. *My fellow citizens and men and women of the press:*

Ten days ago, I spoke to you about my deep concern for the future of our country—about a crisis of the American spirit, which I know to be just as real as the problems that face us on energy or inflation or any other problem of a material nature. But I also know that we can overcome these crises by uniting in a common purpose as we have done so often in the past when our Nation faces a serious challenge. The opportunity which we now have is to seize control of our energy future—to work together to overcome our dangerous overdependence on foreign oil.

Millions of Americans have responded positively to what I said—because they know that I'm telling the truth.

We have lost confidence in our government, and we have lost confidence in many other institutions—all of us know that. But we also know that we can overcome the pessimism, and with

patriotism and with hard work, we can move forward together as Americans.

In these 10 days since I addressed the Nation, I have moved swiftly—I do not believe too swiftly—to create a better administration team to work with me, a team that will be unified, a team that will be filled with confidence, a team that will be in good fighting shape to face the problems together.

And during this same period, I have proposed to the Congress a bold program to harness American ingenuity and to harness American strength to lay a groundwork for American energy security. This massive effort will cost a great deal of money, funds that can only come from a windfall profits tax on the oil companies, a tax on profits which the oil companies have not earned.

The American people overwhelmingly support such a tax, a message clearly demonstrated by the action already taken by the House of Representatives of our U.S. Congress, which has passed a bill which will finance the energy proposal that I have made and still leave plenty of new funds, additional funds, for the oil companies to proceed with exploration and production of new oil and new gas within our own country.

Now it is the turn of the United States Senate to act, and there will be a massive struggle to gut the windfall profits tax bill. If this happens, then we cannot reach our energy goals.

I want to serve notice tonight that I will do everything in my power as President to see that the windfall profits tax is passed, because I consider it to be crucial to our Nation's future.

I need your help. I need the help of the people of America. This is a democracy. Your voice can be heard. Your voice must be heard. Those of you who believe in the future of our country, those of you who believe that our energy program must be passed, please speak to the Congress of the United States and especially to the United States Senate, which still has the responsibility to act.

Based on this windfall profits tax on the oil companies, we will have the resources to meet the energy challenge which we must face together in the future. And we will have taken a major step toward uniting our country in the effort to restore our spirit, the spirit of America, and our confidence, our confidence as people in the future of our great country.

Thank you very much. And now I'd like to answer questions.

Mr. Cormier [Frank Cormier, Associated Press].

QUESTIONS

FEDERAL BUDGET

Q. Mr. President, Republicans in the House are talking about introducing what they call a budget of hope, as contrasted to what they call your budget of despair. And their budget of hope, so-called, they say is going to be roomy enough to accommodate a very large election year tax cut for all of us. Now, that might be pretty hard to vote against in an election year. I wonder what you think about it.

THE PRESIDENT. I believe the Congress and the American people have enough judgment to know that you can't get something for nothing, that there is no free lunch involved. This is not a time for wastefulness. It's not a time to destroy our budget. It's not a time to avoid the responsibilities that we all have to make some sacrifice based on a belief and a confidence in the future of our Nation.

I think we will be restoring hope if we pass a program which, by the way, the

House has already passed, with the support of some Republicans, with the opposition of others. But I think that the bold proposals that we have made do have the confidence of the American people, do have the support of the American people, and my prediction is that before the Congress adjourns in 1979, we will have this program passed with or without the support of the Republicans in the House.

CABINET CHANGES; 1980 PRESIDENTIAL CAMPAIGN

Q. Mr. President, was it worth it to you to cause some destabilization of the dollar and demoralization of the Federal Government, spreading doubt through the land, in order to repudiate much of your Cabinet? And do you agree with Senator Jackson that your problems will force you to forgo any reelection plans and hand the Democratic nomination to Senator Kennedy?

THE PRESIDENT. Well, let me answer the first question first.

I felt, and still feel, that I had to make some changes in my Cabinet, as I said earlier, to create a new team to work with me, a team that will be united, that will be forceful and aggressive and confident in facing the problems that we must meet in the months ahead. I have no apology to make for it. Some people thought it was made too rapidly. I had the choice of either dragging it out week after week after week, with speculation and doubt and confusion, or getting it over, in effect, in 48 hours. And I felt that the abrupt action, based on a long and careful consideration, was the best approach.

Senator Jackson. Three or four years ago I was running for President against Senator Jackson. At that time he predicted that he would be the next President, beginning in 1977. His judgment was not very good then.

And now I'm ready for the next question. [*Laughter*]

PRESIDENT'S HEALTH; SECRETARY OF
ENERGY

Q. Sir, could you please tell me about your pick of Mr. Duncan as the new Energy Secretary?

THE PRESIDENT. Yes.

Q. That's the second in a line of Energy Secretaries from the Defense Department. Is this a signal to the American people that the White House is going to be taking control of energy decisions, sir, and that in fact the Energy Department is going to be taking a second place? And also, sir, there has been some concern on your health in the recent months? Could you please comment on that, please?

THE PRESIDENT. I feel perfectly healthy.

The President is the one who makes the basic decisions on policy of the administration, whether it be in health, education, welfare, transportation, housing, energy, defense, foreign affairs. The President, I and all my predecessors seek—all of us seek the widest possible area of consultation and advice, because we desperately want to make the right decisions for our country. That's my motivation.

Jim Schlesinger, the present Secretary of Energy, has done an excellent job in putting together a new department under the most difficult circumstances and putting through Congress the major parts of an energy program that he and I shaped along with the help of many others early in 1977, more than 2 years ago. About 65 percent of that package was passed in November of 1978. At that time, Secretary Schlesinger asked that he be permitted to

step down. I asked him to stay on, to help me during this session of the Congress. In February he asked again that he be permitted to step down. Since we had not passed any legislation at that time, because of the efforts of the oil lobby concerning oil, I wanted Jim Schlesinger to stay and help me evolve and present to the Congress the program that I have just outlined to the American people.

Now I've decided to let Jim Schlesinger step down as Secretary of Energy. The change will be made in an orderly fashion. The transition will be done methodically and properly, as soon as Charles Duncan is confirmed.

Charles Duncan is an outstanding manager. He has done an absolutely superb job as [Deputy] [1] Secretary of Defense. I consider him to be qualified to be Secretary of any department in the Government, including that of Defense. I asked him to take the Energy Department, because I think at this point it does need to begin to implement the programs that Congress has already passed and will be passing this year. He's a tough, competent manager. In addition to doing a good job in Defense, he's also had a superb career, educational background, and experience in the management of some of the largest responsibilities in the free enterprise system of our country. I have no doubt that he will do an equally good job as Secretary of Energy.

HAMILTON JORDAN

Q. Mr. President, sir, what qualifications does Hamilton Jordan have, aside from the loyalty to you, to be chief of staff in the White House, and to what extent will he be making decisions at a level below your level?

---

[1] Printed in the transcript.

THE PRESIDENT. This event, my designation of Hamilton Jordan as chief of staff, has been one of the most grossly distorted of my career in politics. Hamilton Jordan will be chief of staff—chief of the White House staff. Because of Hamilton's knowledge of me, his closeness to me, his superb leadership capabilities, the trust that other people in the White House have in him repeatedly since I've been President, the other top members of my staff have asked me to let Hamilton be chief of staff. Had he been willing earlier, he would have already been chief of staff, like a year or a year and a half ago.

Recently I asked Hamilton again to take over the job of chief of staff. He's agreed to do it. He has my full support, he has the full support of all others who work in the White House with us. He will not be the chief of the Cabinet; I will be chief of the Cabinet. He will not be the chief of the Congress; the Congress is an independent body. We'll have the same relationship with the Congress, with the same people that we have all the time.

Hamilton Jordan will be chief of the White House staff. That's his responsibility, assigned by me. That's the job he will fulfill, and I have absolutely no doubt, based on his past experience and my knowledge of him, that he will do a superb job.

RELATIONS WITH THE NEWS MEDIA

Q. Mr. President, you were reported to have told some of those whom you saw at Camp David about reservations that you had about the Washington press corps. It was reported that you have expressed those reservations, to use a mild word, even more strongly to the Cabinet last Tuesday. Tonight you appear, tonight, before the Washington press corps and others. You are reported to have said you wanted to speak more to the press outside Washington.

To put the question simply: What bugs you about the Washington press corps? [*Laughter*]

THE PRESIDENT. I'm sure that if I said that the Washington press corps was a group of superbly qualified, highly objective, extremely intelligent analysts of the American news scene, that all of you would agree completely—[*laughter*]—if I said it.

I have nothing against the White House press corps nor the Washington press. My own judgment is that for the first 2½ years, when I felt it was extremely important for me in effect to get acquainted with the American people, to get acquainted with the Washington scene, that I have had, I think, between 50 and 60 press conferences exclusively with the White House press corps. Now I will continue to have interviews with the White House press corps, as we are doing tonight, but not twice a month.

In lieu of that, and I don't think with any reflection on the White House press corps, my decision is now to go to different places around the country. I'll be going to Louisville, Kentucky, area next week. And then sometimes to Miami and Bangor, Maine, and San Francisco, and perhaps Des Moines, Iowa, to have press conferences there and to answer questions both from professional members of the press and also from American people in a townhall meeting format. The Washington press corps will accompany me, the White House press corps, and I will answer questions from you, too.

But I think it's better for me not to have all the questions focused on me by a group that's almost exclusively oriented within Washington as a prime place of their residence and interest, and I would like to let my voice be heard and felt and the questions be heard by me and felt from various places in the country.

1980 PRESIDENTIAL CAMPAIGN

Q. Mr. President, if I may follow through on part of the thrust of Helen's [Helen Thomas, United Press International] earlier question; as you know, there have been suggestions that in order to restore the confidence that you have talked about in the country, and in order to restore confidence in the Presidency, that perhaps you might consider withdrawing yourself from politics next year, turning your attention primarily to governing the Nation. Now, although recent suggestions come from a Republican Member of the Senate—you have in recent months advocated the concept of a one-term, 6-year Presidency. I wonder if you might have considered not entering the 1980 campaign.

THE PRESIDENT. I think it's a compliment to me that Republican leaders are advocating that I not run again. I have considered all the options, and my decision will be announced later on this year.

VALUE OF THE DOLLAR

Q. Mr. President, are you planning to install any foreign exchange controls or capital controls in order to protect the decline of the dollar, and are you planning any further appointments from the corporate section?

THE PRESIDENT. I do not contemplate taking action of that kind. I think the dollar is sound. In the long run, the principles which will decide the value of the dollar are determined by how effective we are in dealing with the energy question, how effective we are in dealing with the inflation question, how much we act to resolve the adverse balance of payments, how we deal with the Federal budget deficit, and so forth. The basic underlying economic factors will be what causes the value of the dollar, not some contrived action that I might take to interfere with the normal operation of the international monetary scene.

I have just announced today that I'm appointing Paul Volcker, a highly qualified person, internationally respected as a knowledgeable man on monetary systems, on whom I can depend. There's no doubt that he will work harmoniously with me, with Bill Miller, who will be the new Secretary of the Treasury. And I believe that this new team will be very effective.

I would like to reserve the right to make future appointments from the corporate world or the academic world or the journalistic world or from among mayors and Governors or Members of the Congress. But I can't exclude the corporate sector. But I can't say now where I'll make future appointments from.

Yes, sir. In the back row.

NICARAGUA

Q. Mr. President, I wonder, in looking at Nicaragua, if we are in danger of another Cuba there, and what the White House plans to do in terms of taking some positive steps to assure their safety?

THE PRESIDENT. It's a mistake for Americans to assume or to claim that every time an evolutionary change takes place, or even an abrupt change takes place in this hemisphere, that somehow it's the result of secret, massive Cuban intervention. The fact in Nicaragua is that the incumbent government, the Somoza regime, lost the confidence of the Nicaraguan people. There was a broad range of forces assembled to replace Somoza and his regime as the head of the Nicaraguan Government.

We worked as closely as we could without intervening in the internal affairs of Nicaragua with the neighboring countries and with the so-called Andean Group in the northern part of South America to bring about an orderly transition. Our effort was to let the people of Nicaragua ultimately make a decision on who should be their leader, what form of government they should have. We also wanted to minimize bloodshed and to restore stability. That is presently being done. We have a good relationship with the new government. We hope to improve it. We are providing some minimum humanitarian aid for the people of Nicaragua, who've suffered so much.

I think that our posture in Nicaragua is a proper one. I do not attribute at all the change in Nicaragua to Cuba. I think the people of Nicaragua have got enough judgment to make their own decisions, and we will use our efforts in a proper fashion without interventionism, to let the Nicaraguans let their voice be heard in shaping their own affairs.

CHANGES IN THE CABINET

Q. Mr. President, I would like to follow up on the earlier question about Hamilton Jordan.

THE PRESIDENT. Good.

Q. Some of your fellow Democrats on Capitol Hill feel you've misdiagnosed your biggest problem—leading effectively. They claim it lies largely in the senior White House staff, and that the Cabinet shakeup won't cure it. Have any congressional Democrats made that criticism to you directly, and how would you respond to it?

THE PRESIDENT. No, they have not. A few have said that in the heat of the publicity focused on the changes that took place over a 2- or 3-day period— and that is expectable—to be expected.

I did not make the rapid changes in my Cabinet without, obviously, some sense that there would be a disturbance in Washington, in the Congress, and otherwise. But I have no doubt that the changes I made are in the best interests of me as President, in the best interests of my administration, which is trying to serve the American people in the finest fashion, and also in the best interests of our country, whom we all serve.

I have had many congratulations given to me by Members of the Congress, and I might say that some of those changes that I did make were long advocated by Members of the Congress.

So, I don't have any hesitancy at all to say that the changes I made were the best, and I don't have any hesitancy to say that I think it was better to go ahead and get it done in about 2 days, rather than to drag it out over a period of weeks or months.

THE NATION'S ECONOMY

Q. Mr. President, with the country apparently headed into a recession, and with unemployment expected to go up, what new ideas do you have, sir, to deal with the worsening economy?

THE PRESIDENT. I think this is a time for stability. I think it's a time for the continuation of our present economic monetary and budgetary policies. While I was at Camp David, I invited a fairly large group of Members of the Congress— Democrats, Republicans, from the House and the Senate—to consult with me. And there was almost unanimity there, surprisingly so, that we ought to maintain our commitment, that inflation is the biggest single threat to the American people, both rich and poor, and to the future of our Nation's economy in the months ahead.

There will be a period of slow growth in our country. I believe that next year we'll see this growth restored to a moderate rate. We will watch this situation very closely. Obviously inflation is not the only factor. I am deeply concerned about the chronic unemployment in some of the types of people in our country. We've done the best we could to reduce unemployment. We've had remarkable success in creating 8 million new jobs. I saw some figures the other day that said the unemployment compensation had been slashed 55 percent. But we're going to watch unemployment.

But my judgment now is to maintain our steady course and to dwell as best I can on a balanced growth in the economy as best we can manage, but let us remember that inflation is the biggest threat to all Americans at this time.

WINDFALL PROFITS TAX

Q. Mr. President, related to your earlier statement about energy, there's talk in the Senate about exemptions of the first 3,000 barrels of oil produced daily by independent oilmen from the windfall profits tax. How would this or a plowback provision or other exemptions affect your energy security corporation, the other parts of your bill, and how much room does the Senate have to tamper with the House-passed bill?

THE PRESIDENT. We need the revenues that would have been derived from my original windfall profits tax proposal to the House. The net income from the House-passed bill is roughly the same as I proposed. My proposal was a permanent tax; the House passed a tax that will be terminated in 1990.

There's a threat now that the oil lobby will focus its attention on the Senate. I think it's almost a sure thing. And unless the American people speak out, because of one reason or another claimed by some of the Members of the Senate, we'll see the windfall profits tax robbed under the proposals that you described of about $54 billion, which will make it impossible for us to have an adequate synthetic fuels program, to have an adequate mass transit program, to have an adequate care for the poor people who are severely impacted by rapidly rising energy costs. It would in effect make it impossible for us to meet our crucial energy goals.

And I think that I cannot prevail alone here in Washington with an oil lobby working quietly unless the American people let their voice be heard. But if these exemptions are made, it'll be a grant of $54 billion to the oil companies on top of greatly increased income to the oil companies by the phased decontrol, and they'll be able to spend these new revenues, which they have not earned, in order to increase production of oil and gas in our own country.

So, what you describe is a great threat to the very program that is so important to me and to the country.

PATRICIA ROBERTS HARRIS

Q. Mr. President, does Mrs. Harris have your full approval and encouragement to continue such HEW programs as the desegregation of the North Carolina college system, the desegregation of public schools in Chicago and other cities, and the antismoking campaign? And if the answer to that question is yes, why did you fire Secretary Califano?

THE PRESIDENT. The answer is yes.

I think the reasons for my replacement of the Cabinet are something that I don't care to discuss publicly. I have nothing but gratitude and admiration for the people that have served in my administration and left.

I expect Mrs. Harris to carry out the provisions of the laws of this country, to represent our Nation in the courts when suits are brought concerning equal opportunity in all its phases, and to be responsible for the health of Americans. And she will have my support just as the previous Secretary had.

I have no doubt that she will do an excellent job both in the administration of that very complicated bureaucracy—Health, Education, and Welfare—and I have no doubt that she has a basic commitment to the service of the constituent groups that are uniquely dependent upon government, particularly HEW. And I have no doubt that she will be a superb teamplayer, able to work with me, to work with the White House staff, to work with the Congress, and to work with other Cabinet members to carry out the policies of my administration, once those policies have been established by me.

VALUE OF THE DOLLAR

Q. Sir, you said earlier that you think that the U.S. dollar is sound. The dollar seems to be taking a pounding on the foreign exchange markets, and it's approaching the low levels that once before you had to launch a dramatic rescue program last November.

In addition to that, you've just named Paul Volcker, a conservative Republican, to head the Federal Reserve Board. How do the poundings that the dollar is undergoing on the exchange markets and your naming of Mr. Volcker square with your earlier description?

THE PRESIDENT. I see no incompatibility at all. Mr. Volcker, by the way, happens to be a Democrat. But he, I think, is a conservative in that he believes in controlling inflation and he believes in maintaining a sound dollar.

I can't guarantee what the exact value of the dollar might be in months ahead. We don't freeze the value of the dollar. That's determined by international monetary considerations. What I said was that the basic value of the dollar will be determined not by the identity of a President or even the identity of the Chairman of the Federal Reserve; it will be shaped by how effectively our Nation moves to meet the energy challenge. There is some present doubt that the Congress will pass the proposals that I have put forward. I have no doubt that the dollar will increase in value when the Congress has passed the programs that I proposed. And, obviously, the dollar will be adversely affected if inflation should increase.

My prediction is that inflation will decrease in the months ahead. And I'm sure that the dollar would be adversely affected if I abandoned my commitment to a responsible Federal budget and start on wild spending programs when they are not needed.

So, basic decisions made of fiscal soundness in our Government is a much more important factor in shaping the value of the dollar than is the identity of officials who might serve in a transient time.

STANDBY GASOLINE RATIONING PLAN

Q. Mr. President, the House of Representatives today amended a standby rationing plan bill to give either House the authority to veto any rationing plan that you would come up with. Now, is that acceptable to you, or if that survives in both Houses, would you veto the legislation?

THE PRESIDENT. This action today by the House illustrates once again the timidity of the Congress in dealing with a sensitive political issue. I criticized the House when they failed to pass the rationing plan a few months ago. The House leadership has now promised me that an adequate rationing standby plan would be passed.

I don't object to the one-House veto if it's done expeditiously. I think only 15 days would elapse. What I do object to are the other restraints that have been placed on the evolution of a standby gasoline rationing plan. Under the proposed plan, even before it got to the floor of the House today, for instance, we could have a 50-percent shortage of gasoline, which would almost devastate our Nation's economy, and unless that shortage lasted for 20 days, I could not implement a rationing plan.

So, I hope that the House and the Senate will rapidly pass an adequate standby rationing plan so that I can develop one, have it on the shelf, if we have a severe and sustained shortage of gasoline, assure that we have equitable distribution. And I have no objection to the House, within 2 weeks, either approving the plan that I have tried to put into being, or if either House wants to veto it, they can do that. But I need the authority to go ahead with a good plan and make sure that it can be implemented rapidly when and if it's needed.

MR. CORMIER. Thank you, Mr. President.

THE PRESIDENT. Thank you.

NOTE: President Carter's fifty-first news conference began at 9 p.m. in the East Room at the White House. It was broadcast live on radio and television.

Trade Agreements Act of 1979
Remarks on Signing H.R. 4537 Into Law.
July 26, 1979

THE PRESIDENT. I think the number of people who are assembled here and the kind of people who are assembled here in the Rose Garden is indicative of the importance of the legislation that I am about to sign.

I will sign into law in a few minutes perhaps the most important and far-reaching piece of trade legislation in the history of the United States.

The Trade Agreements Act of 1979 received an overwhelming, bipartisan mandate from both Houses of the United States Congress. And this is an achievement of cooperation that's almost unprecedented between the executive branch of Government, the Congress, business, labor, farmers, consumers, others interested in the economic strength of our country. This degree of unity and cooperation sets a prime example, a demonstration of what we can do during these troubled times when divisiveness is so often a part of the American scene.

I'd like to pause here and make a very important observation. I know that everyone will agree with what I am about to say. Special Trade Ambassador Robert Strauss did a masterful job throughout the Tokyo negotiations and throughout the equally important negotiations with the United States Congress, and I want to congratulate him. As modest as he is— [*laughter*]—I knew that if I didn't make that comment, it might go unmade. [*Laughter*]

I would like to say as President, though, that the first time I went to an economic summit meeting in London, there was a general knowledge—not belief—that the Tokyo Round that might

1311

lead to this momentous achievement had reached a dead end and that it was very unlikely that it would ever be revived. I don't know of anyone else who could have done it except Bob Strauss. And the other leaders of the Western industrial nations have all expressed to me the same sentiments, that without Bob Strauss, from the United States, it would not have been possible.

I particularly want to praise the efforts of Chairman Russell Long and Abraham Ribicoff, of Bill Roth and Bob Dole in the Senate and of Chairman Al Ullman and Charlie Vanik, Barber Conable, Bill Frenzel in the House, and many others, both Democrats and Republicans, who put aside partisanship in order to work harmoniously for the best interests of our Nation.

We truly live in an interdependent world. Our dependence on foreign oil is one example of this. But this is just part of the picture. Today, one-third of all the agricultural acreage in our country is used to produce food and fiber for people who live outside the United States. One out of seven of our manufacturing jobs in this country go to produce goods which are sold overseas. The strength of the dollar is determined to a major degree by how successful we are in developing new markets for American goods. This legislation, which I will sign in a few minutes, will open up vast new opportunities for American exports.

The Trade Agreements Act of 1979 builds upon the foundation of one of the most highly publicized and well-known achievements of the Kennedy administration, the passage of similar legislation in 1962. This new legislation strengthens and solidifies America's position in the international trade community. It will revise the rules of international trade to create a fairer and more equitable and more open environment for world trade.

This legislation will remove the barriers for fair trade and will reduce unfair trade practices which sometimes cheat those and hamper those who are interested in improving the quality of the world economy.

The trade reorganization proposal, which I have now presented to the Congress to change the mechanism within the Federal Government of dealing with trade, will strengthen the ability. of our own Government to take advantage of these new opportunities described in the legislation on my left and will let us administer the provisions of this act more effectively.

Our Nation has the most productive economy which the world has ever known. Our agricultural abundance and our technological leadership are important sources of America's innate, unshakable strength. This legislation will help our manufactured goods and our agricultural products to become more fully competitive on the world market.

This legislation will also help us to preserve peace and prosperity. Expanded international trade brings strength and growth to economies throughout the world. It enhances understanding, it opens up thousands of unpublicized avenues of consultation and cooperation and the sharing of responsibility which quite often can help to alleviate political tensions and eliminated divisions that sometimes make international borders an obstacle rather than an avenue for cooperation.

Peace and expansion of human rights are natural byproducts of this lessening of tension and this increase of an acknowledged and productive interdependence. Increased American exports will mean new jobs for American workers, new markets for American business, more secure income for American farmers, a strengthened American dollar, and lower costs for American consumers.

We all share the goal of a prosperous and secure America at peace with the world. This legislation provides us with an important milestone in preserving and promoting the economic strength and the political strength of the Nation we all love so much.

On behalf of the people of our country, I would like to thank those assembled here for the roles that you have played in making this momentous achievement possible.

Thank you very much.

[At this point, the President signed the bill.]

We've got a new law.

AMBASSADOR STRAUSS. *Mr. President, distinguished guests in the Congress, other dear friends in the Government:*

First, Mr. President, for myself and for my two primary colleagues, Ambassadors Wolff and McDonald, for all of our staffs out there and our other colleagues throughout the Government, for the country itself, I want to say to you what I have said on many occasions, that this truly has been a classic example of how the system can work. And at the forefront of that was your willingness to do the courageous, the tough, and take the tenacious positions that sometimes were less than popular. You took them in London, you took them in Bonn, and, more importantly, you took them all across America. You never choked, and the people who were representing you in the Congress, in the executive branch, Republicans or Democrats alike, never choked. And it's for that reason we have this bill.

And may I now say very quickly one additional thing. I know it's wrong, but to try to single out a few—I mentioned Ambassador McDonald, who was in Geneva, Ambassador Wolff who was here. I see

Julius Katz in the State Department, Dale Hathaway from the Agriculture Department; I see so many others. And for all of your staffs, I always seem to have a habit of getting a good deal more credit than most people think I deserve—not always more than I think I deserve. *[Laughter]*

But I do know who made all of this possible for the President and for our country, and, indeed, for the world, and it's all of you. And on a very personal basis, even though it's in this rather large group, I say to you, thank you, each, very much, and God bless us all and the country.

Thank you.

SENATOR LONG. Mr. President, I feel that this occasion vindicates my judgment that occurred before you took the oath of office as President. I fought to see that the Special Trade Representative would be a Cabinet-level job. And without that I don't think you could have gotten Bob Strauss for the job, and without that this effort might have failed.

THE PRESIDENT. Bob has always considered himself to be above the Cabinet. *[Laughter]* I hope he won't be offended by what you said. *[Laughter]*

SENATOR LONG. Well, we worked on this for a long time, and I think that after 4 years, all those of us on the Finance Committee and the Ways and Means Committee are extremely proud. We have to commend every Member. But in particular, I want to commend my dear friend and a great statesman, Abe Ribicoff, the chairman of our trade subcommittee, for the fine work he did on the Senate side, and the same goes for all the members of the committee—but Senator Ribicoff worked especially hard on that, and a great deal of this success is due to him.

Thank you.

REPRESENTATIVE ULLMAN. Mr. President, I want to echo the commendation that you have made for the Ambassador and all those that assisted him; also for Charlie Vanik, chairman of our trade subcommittee, Russell Long, Abe Ribicoff, Guy Vander Jagt, Bill Frenzel, all of the people who—and, of course, Barber Conable—who participated in a major bipartisan effort. This, indeed, should set an example and should set the pace for other things we're doing in areas that are vital to the future security of America.

I well remember back in the summer of '73, when the Ways and Means Committee met long hours, hard decisions, drafting a creative new piece of legislation that took a totally new approach to the whole problem of trade. And we set up a procedure during those hard months that laid out for the Congress a timetable without which we would not be here today. And so, I think this whole effort from the very beginning to the end should be studied as an example for other decisions that we can make in this Government, at a very critical time when we're going to all have to begin working together better than we have sometimes in the past.

Thank you.

THE PRESIDENT. I want to thank all of you again and particularly the Members of Congress. It would be nice if I could call on many others, because there were so many who played leadership roles. But because of the press of time and because there are so many who had a role in this, I think I'll thank the rest of them from the bottom of my heart for the great role they played and all of you played in making this momentous achievement possible.

Thank you very much, everyone.

NOTE: The President spoke at 11:30 a.m. at the ceremony in the Rose Garden at the White House.

As enacted, H.R. 4537 is Public Law 96–39, approved July 26.

United States-Australia Agreement on Nuclear Energy

Message to the Congress Transmitting the Agreement.   July 27, 1979

To the Congress of the United States:

I am pleased to transmit to the Congress, pursuant to Section 123 d of the Atomic Energy Act of 1954, as amended (42 U.S.C. 2153(d)), the text of the proposed Agreement Between the United States and Australia Concerning Peaceful Uses of Nuclear Energy and accompanying annex and agreed minute; my written approval, authorization and determination concerning the agreement; and the Memorandum of the Director of the United States Arms Control and Disarmament Agency with the Nuclear Proliferation Assessment Statement concerning the agreement. The joint memorandum submitted to me by the Secretaries of State and Energy, which includes a summary analysis of the provisions of the agreement, and the views of the Members of the Nuclear Regulatory Commission are also enclosed.

The proposed agreement with Australia is the first such agreement submitted to the Congress since enactment of the Nuclear Non-Proliferation Act of 1978, which I signed into law on March 10, 1978 and which, among other things, calls upon me to renegotiate existing peaceful nuclear cooperation agreements to obtain the new provisions set forth in that Act. In my judgment, the proposed agreement for cooperation between the United States and Australia, together with its agreed minute, meets all statutory requirements.

I am particularly pleased that this first agreement is with Australia, a strong supporter of the Non-Proliferation Treaty and of international non-proliferation efforts generally. The proposed agreement reflects the desire of the Government of the United States and the Government of Australia to update the framework for peaceful nuclear cooperation between our two countries in a manner which recognizes both the shared non-proliferation objectives and the close relationship between the United States and Australia in the peaceful applications of nuclear energy. The proposed agreement will, in my view, further the non-proliferation and other foreign policy interests of the United States.

I have considered the views and recommendations of the interested agencies in reviewing the proposed agreement and have determined that its performance will promote, and will not constitute an unreasonable risk to, the common defense and security. Accordingly, I have approved the agreement and authorized its execution, and urge that the Congress give it favorable consideration.

JIMMY CARTER

The White House,
    July 27, 1979.

Department of Housing and Urban Development

Nomination of Moon Landrieu To Be Secretary.   July 27, 1979

The President will nominate Moon Landrieu, former mayor of New Orleans, as Secretary of Housing and Urban Development.

The President said, "Mayor Landrieu enjoys a national reputation as a progressive mayor and strong administrator, as well as a respected and effective spokesman for local government. His service at the Department of Housing and Urban Development will be a contribution to this

administration and to the country. He enjoys my full confidence and support, and I am confident that he will build upon the outstanding record of Secretary Harris."

Mayor Landrieu and Secretary Harris have already discussed transition plans. The details of the transition will be worked out in a manner that will ensure continuity and efficiency of service at HUD.

NOTE: Press Secretary Jody Powell read the announcement at 12:03 p.m. to reporters assembled in the Briefing Room at the White House.

The press release also includes a transcript of the question-and-answer session which followed the announcement.

Solar Energy Development Bank

Letter to the Speaker of the House and the President of the Senate Transmitting Proposed Legislation.   July 27, 1979

Dear Mr. Speaker: (Dear Mr. President:)

I am transmitting proposed legislation which would establish, within the Department of Housing and Urban Development, a Solar Energy Development Bank. This proposal is an essential element of my recently announced national strategy for accelerating the use of solar and other renewable resources. It provides for incentives which can, in conjunction with other governmental actions to be undertaken as part of the Administration's program, stimulate the installation of solar energy systems in residential and commercial properties on a significant scale.

The Solar Bank would be governed by a Board of Directors chaired by the Secretary of Housing and Urban Development. The Board would also include the

Secretary of Energy and the Secretary of the Treasury. The Board would establish all major Solar Bank policies, particularly the depth of the subsidies to be provided.

The proposed Bank would pay subsidies to private lenders for the purchase and installation of solar energy systems. These lenders would, in turn, provide below-market financing to builders or owners of residential and commercial properties. The subsidized portion of a loan allocable to the purchase and installation of solar energy systems would be limited to $10,000 per unit for a one- to four-family structure, $5,000 per unit (up to a maximum of $500,000) for structures containing more than four units, and $200,000 for commercial properties.

Funds for operation of the Solar Bank would be derived from the proposed Energy Security Trust Fund. For this purpose, authorized expenditures would be up to (a) $35 million for fiscal year 1980 and (b) $150 million annually for fiscal years 1981 through 1985. Personnel within the Department of Housing and Urban Development, including personnel of the Government National Mortgage Association, would be used to administer Solar Bank programs.

I view the Solar Bank as a key component in my program to accelerate the development and use of solar technologies. Together with my Administration's other solar energy initiatives, the Solar Bank will ensure a sound national solar strategy. These measures will provide critical assistance in overcoming our Nation's energy problems. I urge its early enactment.

Sincerely,

JIMMY CARTER

NOTE: This is the text of identical letters addressed to Thomas P. O'Neill, Jr., Speaker of the House of Representatives, and Walter F. Mondale, President of the Senate.

Oil Import Reduction Program

Letter to the Speaker of the House and the President of the Senate Transmitting Tax Initiative Proposals. July 27, 1979

Dear Mr. Speaker: (Dear Mr. President:)

I am pleased to transmit to you the energy tax initiatives of my Oil Import Reduction Program.

On May 7, 1979, I transmitted to the Congress the second National Energy Plan, as required by section 801 of the Department of Energy Organization Act (Public Law 95–91). The initial step in that plan was to direct the phasing out of price controls on domestic crude oil. This was begun on June 1 of this year. By October 1, 1981, all domestic oil will be decontrolled.

The next step was to recommend the imposition of a windfall profits tax on domestic crude oil production and the creation of an Energy Security Trust Fund to utilize the tax revenues generated by the windfall profits tax and increased income tax collection attributable to decontrol. This proposal is presently pending before the Congress.

I now propose several tax incentives to help achieve the goals of the Oil Import Reduction Program.

First, to help achieve the goal of generating 20 percent of the Nation's energy requirements by the use of solar energy by the year 2000, I propose tax credits to encourage the use of solar energy devices in residential and commercial construction. In addition, I propose investment tax credits for solar equipment used for process heat in industrial and agricultural applications.

Second, to further reduce our reliance on imported oil, I propose production incentive tax credits for the production of shale oil and natural gas from unconventional sources in addition to financial assistance which will be provided by the Energy Security Corporation. In addition, I propose to make woodburning stoves eligible for the residential energy credit, and make permanent the excise tax exemption for gasohol.

Finally, as I indicated on July 16, the Administration is moving to decontrol heavy oil and I propose to exempt it from the windfall profits tax.

These tax credits will encourage the development and use of new energy technologies and add significantly to our independence from foreign sources of petroleum.

Sincerely,

JIMMY CARTER

NOTE: This is the text of identical letters addressed to Thomas P. O'Neill, Jr., Speaker of the House of Representatives, and Walter F. Mondale, President of the Senate.

Department of Transportation

Nomination of Neil Goldschmidt To Be Secretary.   July 27, 1979

The President will nominate Neil Goldschmidt of Portland, Oregon, as Secretary of Transportation.

The President said, "Mayor Goldschmidt is known as an aggressive and innovative mayor with outstanding administrative abilities. He understands from personal experience the transportation needs of local governments. He will have my full support and confidence, and I have no doubt that he will be an outstanding Secretary of Transportation."

Mayor Goldschmidt and Acting Secretary of Transportation Graham Claytor have already discussed plans for a smooth transition.

Mayor Goldschmidt served as chairman of the transportation committee of the U.S. Conference of Mayors, and has established a transportation system in Portland that is nationally recognized.

NOTE: Press Secretary Jody Powell read the announcement at 4:32 p.m. to reporters assembled in the Briefing Room at the White House.

The press release also includes a transcript of the question-and-answer session which followed the announcement.

National Consumer Cooperative Bank

Nomination of Two Government Members of the Board of Directors.   July 27, 1979

The President today announced that he will nominate the remaining two Government members of the Board of Directors of the National Consumer Cooperative Bank. They are:

WILLIAM A. CLEMENT, JR., Associate Administrator of SBA for Minority Small Business and Capital Ownership Development. Clement, 36, is a former vice president of the Citizens Trust Bank of Atlanta, Ga., one of the oldest and largest minority-owned banks in the country;

GRACIELA OLIVAREZ, Director of the Community Services Administration.

The other five Government members and the six public members of the Board of Directors were nominated on July 2.

Nicaragua

Announcement of Emergency Assistance and Trip of U.S. Ambassador.   July 27, 1979

President Carter is sending a special flight to Nicaragua on Saturday, July 28, to deliver emergency food and medical supplies. The U.S. Ambassador to Nicaragua, Lawrence A. Pezzullo, will return to Managua on Saturday's flight. He will present his credentials to the new Government of Nicaragua early next week. The President is sending this special plane as an expression of his personal good will to the people of Nicaragua and to the new Government and to symbolize the concern of Americans for the hunger and distress of the Nicaraguan people after many months of devastating conflict.

The United States has already provided 732 metric tons of emergency food supplies to Nicaragua. Another 1,000 tons of food from the United States is on its way to Nicaragua by ship. In addition, the United States is providing supplies and financial assistance for airlifts being carried out by the international committee of the Red Cross. Of 9,600 pounds of medical supplies purchased by the U.S. Government for shipment to Nicaragua, 75 percent has already been delivered, and the remaining 2,500 pounds of U.S.-purchased medicines, together with 3,300 pounds of Red Cross medical supplies and 5,200 pounds of baby formula, are arriving in Nicaragua this weekend on a special flight chartered by the Agency for International Development.

Digest of Other White House Announcements

The following listing includes the President's public schedule and other items of general interest announced by the White House Press Office and not included elsewhere in this issue.

July 21

The President met at the White House with Zbigniew Brzezinski, Assistant to the President for National Security Affairs.

July 23

The President met at the White House with:

—Dr. Brzezinski;
—Frank B. Moore, Assistant to the President for Congressional Liaison;
—Vice President Walter F. Mondale;
—Hedley Donovan;
—James T. McIntyre, Jr., Director of the Office of Management and Budget.

July 24

The President met at the White House with:

—Dr. Brzezinski;
—the Democratic congressional leadership;
—Mr. Moore.

In a ceremony in the Oval Office, the President received diplomatic credentials from Ambassadors Marcial Perez-Chiriboga of Venezuela, Antonio Francisco Azeredo da Silveira of the Federative Republic of Brazil, Faisal Alhegelan of the Kingdom of Saudi Arabia, Andreas J. Jacovides of the Republic of Cyprus, and Sir Nicholas Henderson of the United Kingdom.

July 25

The President met at the White House with:

—Dr. Brzezinski;
—Mr. Moore.

July 26

The President met at the White House with:

—Dr. Brzezinski;
—Mr. Moore;
—the executive committee of the American Farm Bureau Federation;
—former Mayor Moon Landrieu of New Orleans, La.

The President transmitted to the Congress the 1978 annual report of the Saint

Lawrence Seaway Development Corporation.

July 27

The President met at the White House with:

—Vice President Mondale, Secretary of State Cyrus R. Vance, Secretary of Defense Harold Brown, Hamilton Jordan, Assistant to the President, and Dr. Brzezinski;

—Dr. Brzezinski;

—Mr. Moore;

—a group of editors and news directors (transcript will be printed next week);

—Mayor Neil Goldschmidt of Portland, Oreg.

The President declared a major disaster for the State of California as a result of heavy rains, flash flooding, and mudflows on July 19–20, which caused extensive property damage.

The President left the White House for a weekend stay at Camp David, Md.

NOMINATIONS SUBMITTED TO THE SENATE

The following list does not include promotions of members of the Uniformed Services, nominations to the Service Academies, or nominations of Foreign Service officers.

Submitted July 21, 1979

BARBARA B. CRABB, of Wisconsin, to be United States District Judge for the Western District of Wisconsin, vice a new position created by P.L. 95–486, approved October 20, 1978.

TERENCE T. EVANS, of Wisconsin, to be United States District Judge for the Eastern District of Wisconsin, vice a new position created by P.L. 95–486, approved October 20, 1978.

EUGENE P. SPELLMAN, of Florida, to be United States District Judge for the Southern District of Florida, vice a new position created by P.L. 95–486, approved October 20, 1978.

CHARLES WILLIAM DUNCAN, JR., of Texas, to be Secretary of Energy.

NOMINATIONS—Continued

Submitted July 21—Continued

W. GRAHAM CLAYTOR, of the District of Columbia, to be Deputy Secretary of Defense, vice Charles William Duncan, Jr.

Submitted July 24, 1979

JAMES W. SPAIN, of California, a Foreign Service officer of Class one to be the Deputy Representative of the United States of America to the United Nations, with the rank and status of Ambassador Extraordinary and Plenipotentiary.

HAROLD ALONZA BLACK, of North Carolina, to be a member of the National Credit Union Administration Board for the term of 2 years (new position).

ROBERT JOSEPH BROWN, of Maryland, to be a member of the National Mediation Board for the term expiring July 1, 1982, vice David H. Stowe, term expired.

Withdrawn July 24, 1979

SUSANNA B. McBEE, of California, to be an Assistant Secretary of Health, Education, and Welfare, vice Eileen Shanahan, resigned, which was sent to the Senate on June 25, 1979.

Submitted July 25, 1979

WILLIAM D. WOLLE, of Iowa, a Foreign Service officer of Class two, to be Ambassador Extraordinary and Plenipotentiary of the United States of America to the United Arab Emirates.

RONALD P. WERTHEIM, of the District of Columbia, to be a member of the Merit Systems Protection Board for the remainder of the term expiring March 1, 1981, vice Ruth T. Prokop.

Submitted July 27, 1979

GENE E. BROOKS, of Indiana, to be United States District Judge for the Southern District of Indiana, vice a new position created by P.L. 95–486, approved October 20, 1978.

The following-named persons to be members of the Board of Directors of the National Consumer Cooperative Bank for terms of 3 years (new positions):

WILLIAM A. CLEMENT, JR., Associate Administrator for Minority Small Business and Capital Ownership Development, Small Business Administration.

GRACIELA (GRACE) OLIVAREZ, Director, Community Services Administration.

NOMINATIONS—Continued

Submitted July 27—Continued

PAUL A. VOLCKER, of New Jersey, to be a member of the Board of Governors of the Federal Reserve System for the unexpired term of 14 years from February 1, 1978, vice G. William Miller.

PAUL A. VOLCKER, of New Jersey, to be Chairman of the Board of Governors of the Federal Reserve System for a term of 4 years (new position).

CHECKLIST OF WHITE HOUSE PRESS RELEASES

The following listing contains releases of the White House Press Office which are not included in this issue.

Released July 25, 1979

Advance text: opening statement at the President's news conference

Released July 27, 1979

Announcement: nomination of Gene E. Brooks to be United States District Judge for the Southern District of Indiana

Biographical data: Moon Landrieu, nominated to be Secretary of Housing and Urban Development

CHECKLIST—Continued

Released July 27—Continued

News conference: on proposed legislation to establish a solar energy development bank and proposed energy tax incentives—by Stuart E. Eizenstat, Assistant to the President for Domestic Affairs and Policy

Biographical data: Neil Goldschmidt, nominated to be Secretary of Transportation

ACTS APPROVED BY THE PRESIDENT

Approved July 23, 1979

H.R. 3978_____ Public Law 96–37 An act to amend the Federal Trade Commission Act to exempt savings and loan institutions from the application of certain provisions contained in such Act.

Approved July 25, 1979

H.R. 4289_____ Public Law 96–38 Supplemental Appropriations Act, 1979.

Approved July 26, 1979

H.R. 4537_____ Public Law 96–39 Trade Agreements Act of 1979.

PRESIDENTIAL DOCUMENTS

Week Ending Friday, August 3, 1979

Interview With the President

Remarks and a Question-and-Answer Session With Editors and News Directors. July 27, 1979

ADMINISTRATION POLICIES

THE PRESIDENT. Ordinarily we don't have this large a group. In general, when we invite editors from around the country, about half of them prefer to come at a later time. But this time almost everyone decided to come. And I can understand why, because there's such a tremendous interest focused now on what is going on here in the Nation's Capital because of the rapidly changing series of events concerning me, personally, and the Presidency and the Cabinet, and also because of the crucial importance of decisions that will be made in the next few weeks: a series of legislative proposals—concerning energy, standby rationing, production board to expedite decisions on refineries and pipelines, power company installations, a production corporation that will meet our goal of cutting down energy imports, and, as you know, windfall profits tax to finance over the next 10 years— I think what will be a successful effort to restore our Nation's energy security. In addition, the Congress is considering many

other items, the most important of which, in foreign affairs, is obviously the SALT treaty.

I think this is a time, too, when Americans are particularly and deeply involved in a reassessment of themselves, perhaps, or of our country—who we are, what our Nation is, what we can be, how we can work more closely with one another, how natural divisiveness can be assuaged, how we can set clear goals for ourselves and achieve those goals with both competence and confidence.

I think every now and then, in every person's life there comes a time of reassessment. I think we are going through a time of national reassessment, not initiated by me; it's a self-examination process that was initiated long ago. I think we more narrowly focus now our interest on this question, but it's something that has been of concern for a long time to me as President.

There is really only one person in this country that has a constant and sustained voice in politics, and that is the President. Others, on a transient basis, because of a focus of an event, have a loud and clear voice, and during the campaigns for office, these voices are dispersed. But ordinarily, the President must be the one to speak for our country and indeed to our country.

I think there's been a much more sharpened interest lately in what I had to say, which is gratifying to some degree. It puts a responsibility on me to soberly consider what I impart to the American people and how I perform my own duties here in the White House.

I think the changes that have been made in the Cabinet recently have been all for the good. Some of them were overdue. I had a judgment to make about whether to have this done rapidly and get it concluded, recognizing that there would be some sharp shock waves going through Washington and perhaps the rest of the country, or to let it drag out, with columns and editorials and public speculation about who would go next or who would stay, and so forth. My judgment was to go ahead and do it and get it over with. And all of the departures have been harmonious as far as my relationship with the former Cabinet members is concerned. I think the appointments that I have made and will very quickly make to conclude the filling of the vacancies demonstrate that these are very fine and competent people who will be taking office. And I have no doubt there will be a more adequate teamwork in the future than there has been in the past.

I think it's best for me to answer your questions.

QUESTIONS

VISIT OF POPE JOHN PAUL II

Q. Mr. President, Father Shmaruk from Boston, from the Planet. It's been reported that Pope John Paul II will meet with you at the White House in the fall. This has to do with world politics. What subjects generally do you hope to discuss with him, and how do you evaluate his unique position in terms of world politics, human rights, and peace?

THE PRESIDENT. I think the visit of the Pope to our country is one that will be welcomed by American people of all religious faiths. There's no doubt in my mind that he will get an overwhelmingly friendly welcome and an enthusiastic welcome. I expect to meet with him in the White House in a private fashion. My belief is that his desires to come to our country, not on a political mission, but on one involving religion, morals, and ethics. I look forward to meeting with him.

I don't have any way yet to know what subjects we will discuss. I have exchanged several letters with him since he's been in his present office, and he and I have had a good and friendly relationship. Several members of my family have been there, both political family and immediate family. We do share a common desire for peace, for the broadening of the beneficial effects of religion throughout the world, and also on such major matters as human rights. But I don't know now this early how to describe the agenda any more definitely than that.

I wrote him a letter this morning, by the way, and sent it to him.

RELATIONS WITH THE CONGRESS

Q. Mr. President, I've been here for 24 hours, talking with Democrats, both in the Senate and also in the Congress itself. And the Democrats there from west Texas, where I'm from, and Oklahoma and New Mexico right now want to be disassociated with you because of the windfall profits situation, also the fact that we've had a 65-percent cutback in energy, in diesel fuel in our area.

What about these good representatives the people have confidence in, saying right now that they don't back your policies and you need the confidence of the American people?

THE PRESIDENT. I don't agree with your premise. I think your information is incorrect. Recently, as you know, there were two polls conducted among the Members of the House, one by the Washington Post; one by the New York Times. I didn't participate in them, but I saw the results. I think in the South, which did include Texas, 88 percent of the Democrats said they prefer to have me on the ballot with them next year. I think 3 percent said Kennedy, and the rest were divided among a numerous number of people.

I have already seen the effectiveness with which the House has dealt with the windfall profits tax. I think they did a good job. Their bill is roughly equivalent to my own. The only problem with it is it only lasts until 1990. I prefer a permanent windfall profits tax.

This is a very difficult political season, and for someone from Texas and from the other oil-producing States, I realize that there is a duality of responsibility to the consumers, on the one hand—and there are many consumers in Texas—and to all those who depend upon the oil industry and the natural gas industry for their livelihood or who have a natural affinity for it because Texas is an oil-producing State.

My belief is that the Congress will act courageously and will implement the windfall profits tax, the security fund derived from it, the proper expenditure of those funds through the corporation to produce new kinds of energy, and the production board to expedite those decisions. My guess is that the House will, next Tuesday, vote for the standby rationing authority in an acceptable fashion. So, I don't really recruit people now to say, "I want to run with or without President Carter, if the 1980 election should throw us together."

But I think the polls that were conducted by those two news media, respectable news media, are a better indication than the results that you apparently got from your interviews.

MAYOR NEIL GOLDSCHMIDT

Q. Mr. Carter, I'm from Portland, Oregon, and I understand the mayor's in town. I'd like to know, sir, if you intend to appoint him—or have you—as head of the Department of Transportation or some other Federal job?

THE PRESIDENT. I haven't met with him and don't know what I will do yet. I will discuss this matter with him and some others as well. I have a great respect for Neil Goldschmidt and so do all the members of my staff. I will make a decision on this matter soon. He's not the only one being considered, and I don't want to predict what the outcome might be.

Q. Will it be today, sir?

THE PRESIDENT. I can't say. Do you—does anyone know when Neil's coming? We'll find out. I don't know when he's going to see me.

HOME HEATING OIL SUPPLIES

Q. Mr. President, I'm from Hillsboro, New Hampshire. As I'm sure you're aware, we have a primary election there in February. February's a cold month up there; between now and then there's a lot of cold nights. According to Senator John Durkin we are 20 million barrels behind last year in stockpiling oil. What I would like to know is, do you, as a candidate, seriously believe that you'll have a chance without taking further direct action to ensure a more adequate supply of heating oil? And if you do intend to take that sort of action, what effect might that have on the price of the oil?

THE PRESIDENT. Let me answer your question as President instead of as a candidate, okay?

Q. I was hoping you would answer as both. [*Laughter*]

THE PRESIDENT. [*Referring to Mayor Goldschmidt*] He'll be here this afternoon.

I have promised the people of New England that they will have adequate home heating oil this fall and have set as a target goal 240 million barrels of oil to be in storage and ready in October. This can be compared with last year's inventory at that time, I think, of 133 [233] [1] million barrels.

We have had a depletion of our oil stocks, not only crude oil stocks but also the number two, number six distillates, as well as gasoline. None of those stocks have yet come up to their normal range, because we lost 100 million barrels of crude oil, ordinarily which would have been bought from Iran early this year. We're rebuilding those stocks, and this is the top priority for me now among the variables that I have to deal with.

The refineries are now operating above 90 percent capacity, which is almost 100 percent for them as far as their capability is concerned. At the beginning of last month, they were only operating at like 82 percent capacity. Part of this is because of our urging to them to produce more home heating oil. Part of it is because we've had increased supplies of crude oil coming into our country.

So, I think that I would be perfectly willing to be judged in February on the performance of my administration. Jack Watson, who works with local officials and with my agencies and also with Governors, is monitoring this on a daily basis,

and he feels quite sure that we are on schedule.

ENERGY PRODUCTION

Q. Mr. President, John Still, WWEE Radio, Memphis. With the push towards renewable energy supplies, how will future energy projects be protected against some small technicality that could stop it in its tracks, such as the $100 million Tellico Dam project that was stopped by a 3-inch fish.

And the second part of my question, with additional appropriations from Congress to the Clinch breeder reactor project last week, will you continue your opposition to it?

THE PRESIDENT. Yes, my opposition to the Clinch River breeder reactor is unshakable. And I think it's a waste of money, and I intend to continue to oppose it, I believe successfully.

We have about a half billion dollars, which I have proposed on an annual basis, to proceed with research and development in breeder reactor technology. At the time we need a breeder reactor, at that moment, we will freeze the design and build an advanced design breeder reactor. I don't think this will come during my own administration. It'll come later than that. But I see no reason to waste hundreds of millions of dollars in building a breeder reactor plant which we do not need, which is already obsolete before it's completed.

That answers the second part of your question.

The first part is: The energy production board [Energy Mobilization Board],[2] when passed by the Congress—and it's making good progress—will be responsible for the expeditious decision of whether

---

[1] Printed in the transcript.

[2] Printed in the transcript.

a project should be built or not built. I mentioned earlier power production plants of all kinds, pipelines, refineries, and so forth. I don't believe there is any need for us to reduce the standards that we presently have of protecting endangered species or of protecting the quality of air or water in our Nation.

This week I received a report from the President's commission on coal use. We anticipate a doubling in the use of coal by 1985 if all the recommendations are carried out. The basic premise for this recommendation was that we would not lower air quality standards.

So, I can't see us changing the basic laws that protect the quality of life of American people. Our technological capability is good enough already to make these changes to more plentiful supplies of energy without basic changes in the laws that I've described.

ADDRESSES TO THE NATION; LILLIAN CARTER'S HEALTH

Q. Mr. President, my name is Sam Oates with KRIG Radio in Odessa, Texas. And I think without a doubt the people of west Texas thought that your recent speech was probably the best of your administration. However, they seem to be—the feedback that I've gotten— they seem to be somewhat unsure of your recent earnestness with your speeches and what not. Also, they're not quite sure about your ideas of establishing another agency to help the oil situation.

Are you being helped along with Mr. Rafshoon or anyone else in your administration as far as communication over the television or in any other media at this point?

And secondly, how's your mother?

THE PRESIDENT. Mother's fine. I talked to Billy and Sybil just a few minutes ago,

who were right outside Mother's room. I think the diagnosis is that she has either arthritis or bursitis in her left shoulder and arm, and there's no problem with a cardiac problem or vascular problem, and I'm very pleased with that.

You know, I get help from every place I can. The Sunday evening speech was made literally from the bottom of my heart. I think a contrivance or posturing or an artificial attitude toward the American people on television would instantly be revealed, and I don't think the speech would have had as good a response as it has received if I had been trying to do something false or had been trying to mislead the American people.

As a matter of fact, I only practiced that speech twice, because I wrote it— my wife and several other people helped me with the basic structure of the speech—but I did it myself. I think Saturday afternoon at Camp David, I came in, gave the speech once, all the ones in the room said, "You don't need to practice it any more." Sunday afternoon I came to the Oval Office to get into the exact place, and I gave the speech once more before the cameras just to make sure that the timing was proper, and so forth. And again I didn't have to practice it any more. I didn't have any voice teaching; I didn't have any speech coaches and things of that kind.

It's a serious mistake for anyone in public office to try to mislead the American people about basic issues concerning the future of our Nation or concerning the psychological attitude of American people or concerning confidence or unity or trust or truth. Certainly it's a mistake to mislead the American people about their own security, either energy, on domestic economic security, or things like SALT. That would be a travesty. I would not be capable of it, and if I should ever try it, I hope that I would be caught and that the American people would demonstrate their lack of confidence by their actions on election day.

AMTRAK

Q. Mr. President, Saul Kohler, Harrisburg Patriot News. With your admonition to the American people to conserve every drop of oil and with your request that we do without unnecessary automobile trips, why does the White House persist in cutting Amtrak service, both on the commuter and on the long lines basis? By commuter basis, I mean by cutting out tickets at commuter rates.

THE PRESIDENT. What we proposed on Amtrak several months ago was to eliminate those Amtrak services where the cost per passenger mile exceeded those by automobile or other means. These were routes and scheduled trips where people had almost abandoned them. It doesn't help to run a full-sized train at 10 percent capacity day after day and maintain a schedule whether you have the passengers or not.

With the advent of the gasoline lines, first in California and then later on the east coast, there's been a substantial increase in the use of Amtrak services, both commuter and longer distance travel. Now the Congress has passed—not exactly what I proposed, but a modification of that. Our proposal was that there be $65 million set up in extra funds, and that those funds would be oriented to support additional Amtrak services above what we originally proposed if the passenger use level warranted continuation of that service.

So, I think the additional use of Amtrak brought about by an awareness of gasoline shortages has been accommodated with a change in administration

position. But it doesn't save fuel to have an empty train running, if a full train is more economical.

Q. Should the need arise, will you loosen the Amtrak schedules further?

THE PRESIDENT. Well, we already have. Yes, if the need arises, we will, but it's got to be measured on an individual route basis. There's no reason to run an empty train just because it's a train.

ENERGY POLICIES

Q. Mr. President, in north Missouri, we're somewhat isolated from the direct impact of inflation because of good crops this year. However, the people there want some good news, if they can get it, from Washington as far as short-term solutions to the energy problem.

Do they have to wait to 1984 or to 1990 to see the solutions of the impact?

THE PRESIDENT. No, I don't think so at all. I met with some distinguished oil executives, for instance, at Camp David during the 10 days I was there, with consultation and with other people like the head of the Audubon Society, representing environmentalists and consumers, the president of MIT, who's done most of the work, more work than any other institution, I believe, on alternate sources of energy—I had a broad range of people.

One major oil executive said that just the decision that I made to decontrol the price of oil over a phased period from now until the end of September 1981 had been enough of an incentive in his own company to make this change. They had never before expended more than a billion dollars a year on exploration for new oil and gas. As soon as I decided to decontrol, on a phased basis, oil prices, they had a board of directors meeting and decided to spend $2 billion a year for 5 years, more than they would ever have done otherwise.

So, just the certainty of the future prices of oil and natural gas, that in itself is a major incentive for increased domestic production.

As I just outlined, the coal commission has now advocated that the shifting of presently oil-burning power company installations, electric power company installations, to coal will save a tremendous amount of oil and make this oil available for other uses.

We anticipate that over a period of time that many of the New England homes that are presently almost exclusively dependent on coal [oil] [3] will be shifting toward natural gas as a heat source, and we hope to get some hydropower and other sources of energy from Canada across the border. We're pursuing that as well.

I am going to expedite the completion now of the gas pipeline coming down from Alaska to our country. We are already buying about 80 or 90 percent of all the oil that Mexico exports. We'll continue to do that, and we're trying to trade now on the basis of buying a limited amount of natural gas which Mexico will have available to sell to us in the future.

So, the shift toward coal; the enhancement of solar power; the development over a longer period of time of alternative sources of energy, like oil from shale; the bringing in of our own natural gas from Alaska—all these things put together will have immediate impact.

Overriding all this, though, is the benefits to be derived from conservation. We're now getting along fairly well in our Nation with 80 to 85 percent of the gasoline being delivered to motorists as before. In the Los Angeles area, there's been an enormous increase in the use of public transportation facilities. The number of cars on the highway has dropped. The

---

[3] Printed in the transcript.

number of passengers per car has increased. The American people are much more careful in not wasting fuel than they have been in the past.

We expect substantial benefits to be derived from the mandatory setting of thermostats in buildings like this one, and we have little recording monitors set around at appropriate places throughout the Government buildings to make sure that we do stay at 78 degrees, and this will result in a large savings in fuel.

So, all these things put together, I believe, will have an immediate impact. The long-range impact will be quite expensive, but it's something that we need to accomplish.

STRATEGIC ARMS LIMITATION

Q. Mr. President, why should minorities, specifically black and Spanish-speaking people on the south and northwest side of Chicago, where I'm from—my name is Steen King—why should they be concerned about SALT II or the fact that General Alexander Haig wants the measure held for ransom until there's more money for defense spending?

THE PRESIDENT. I would guess minorities would be concerned about life or death or war or peace; increased trade with other countries, instead of a separation of one people from another. These kinds of factors are involved, either directly or indirectly, in the SALT II decision.

There is also a competition for limited Federal funds. Without a SALT agreement to limit immediately the level of strategic nuclear weapons, we would have to have a very large increase in expenditures for military defense, above and beyond what we would have to have with SALT II. And if we have to spend—I think Les Aspin, one of the Members of the Congress, estimated that $21 billion would be required extra if we don't pass SALT. That $21 billion in a given level of budget would have to be taken from, maybe some of the social programs—housing and so forth—in which you are deeply interested.

So, I'd say an increase above what we need in defense expenditures and a general preservation of peace, increased trade that provides jobs, would be an additional tangible benefit.

We've got superb black leaders who have been briefed thoroughly on SALT and who are now speaking around the country on behalf of SALT just because a SALT treaty would help the people who look to them for leadership. One from your own region has been especially helpful, Jesse Jackson. Jesse's making speeches now to colleges and high schools and other fora around the Nation, telling them why as a black leader he knows that SALT is best for minority groups.

So, I think if you would be interested, when Jesse gets back from South Africa, he would be prepared, after thorough briefings here in the White House from me and others, to explain this even more thoroughly than I can at this moment.

Q. Mr. President, to follow up your answer to that question, you said, for example, that without the treaty, Les Aspin estimates that we have to spend another $21 billion on arms. And yet, what seems to be building up, movement that seems to be building up among the critics of SALT, is that as a condition of agreeing to SALT that there has to be a very substantial increase in weapons involving particularly the strategic side, and apparently a good deal more than you committed yourself to in your original presentation of the SALT II arguments.

Do you feel now that in the light of this kind of building argument that you're going to have to make a very hard com-

mitment to a substantially larger increase in defense spending and particularly on the strategic weapons involvement in order to meet that kind of criticism and get this thing sold?

THE PRESIDENT. Let me respond by giving you three points.

First of all, my ultimate responsibility as President, above everything else, is to guarantee the security of my Nation, and the defense budgets that I have proposed and will propose will be adequate for that purpose.

Second, no matter what level of defense expenditure we might have—$140 billion, $160 billion, $180 billion, it doesn't matter—under any level of expenditure for defense purposes within reason, we are better off with the SALT treaty than without it. I could give you the reasons, but I won't go into that, because it'll take too much time.

And the third thing is that, habitually, Presidents have—including myself—have been more inclined toward a strong defense budget than has the Congress in the ultimate analysis. The Congress is the one that makes the final judgment about budget levels.

I've had two budgets that have been made effective since I've been President—one, fiscal year 1978 and then this fiscal year 1979. The Congress has reduced the defense expenditures or authorizations that I have requested, I think roughly $5 billion during just those 2 years alone.

So, because of those three factors, I think that the answer is that SALT is needed regardless of defense expenditures. I will provide adequate defense recommendations to the Congress. The likelihood is that if I tried to escalate defense requests substantially above what they are needed just to get Senate votes, which I would not do, the Congress would not approve them.

Ms. BARIO. Thank you, Mr. President.

THE PRESIDENT. Thank you all very much.

We've got a larger crowd than we ordinarily have. If you don't have any objection, I'd like to get an individual photograph with you before I leave. I'll stay a few extra minutes, if you can. It is a little warm.

I thank you very much for being here.

NOTE: The interview began at 1:18 p.m. in Room 450 of the Old Executive Office Building. Patricia Y. Bario is a Deputy Press Secretary.

The transcript of the interview was released on July 28.

United States-Panama Treaty on Penal Sentences

Message to the Senate Transmitting the Treaty.   July 30, 1979

To the Senate of the United States:

With a view to receiving the advice and consent of the Senate to ratification, I transmit herewith the Treaty between the United States of America and the Republic of Panama on the Execution of Penal Sentences which was signed at Panama on January 11, 1979.

I transmit also, for the information of the Senate, the report of the Department of State with respect to the Treaty.

The Treaty would permit citizens of either nation who had been convicted in the courts of the other country to serve their sentences in their home country; in each case, the consent of the offender would be required.

This Treaty represents the fulfillment of a commitment undertaken by both nations in the Panama Canal Treaty of 1977. It would complement the wide range of protections and benefits afforded United States Government personnel under the Panama Canal Treaty and related agreements during the life of that Treaty, and would establish a mechanism for other nationals of both countries to serve their sentences in their home countries. Its ratification would provide our personnel stationed in the Republic of Panama further assurance that their interests will be fully protected upon the entry into force of the Panama Canal Treaty.

I recommend that the Senate give prompt and favorable consideration to this Treaty.

JIMMY CARTER

The White House,
   July 30, 1979.

Camp David Meetings on Domestic Issues

Remarks at a White House Luncheon for Participants in the Meetings.   July 30, 1979

As I stand up here and look at this group of faces, all of whom joined me at Camp David in a time of absolute frankness, with no rules on what we should discuss, no limits on the depth of analysis, I am a little bit timid, a little bit nervous.

At Camp David yesterday morning we had a new chaplain, who serves Fort Ritchie—the first time he's ever preached to the President—and he told a story that illustrated the way I feel in some ways, about this itinerant barber who had drifted all over the country out west, cutting hair and giving shaves. He finally settled in this one town and he opened his own shop. And he was extremely nervous that the people wouldn't like him and he'd have to get back on the road.

His first customer was a one-armed man who was really a rugged-looking guy, so the barber cut his hair without much problem, and he stropped his razor, and when he got started shaving, the barber got more and more nervous. He cut the guy three or four times and was wiping off blood visibly, and he couldn't think of anything to say. And finally he desperately tried to start a conversation. He said, "Have I ever served you before?" And the guy said, "No, I lost my arm in a sawmill accident." [*Laughter*]

Well, I feel somewhat the same way with you. You're people who came to Camp David in a time of deep thought and reassessment, a time of frankness, and to some degree a time of courage. We met in an atmosphere of privacy, and we discussed in the bluntest possible terms what is our Nation, what are our problems, what can be done to resolve them. And I think the product was very beneficial for our Nation.

I benefited from your judgment, from your experience, and from your wisdom, and in the process my own determination and self-assurance and confidence and will was restored. I prepared a speech and delivered a speech on Sunday evening that encapsulated as best I could the sense of our Nation, pointing out that we do have a severe crisis of the spirit, a severe crisis of confidence in one another, in our institutions, including government, and an absence of confidence about the future of our Nation.

The facing of that fact on the part of the American people, I think, has already begun. Up through last Friday we had received 39,000 telegrams and letters, personal ones, the biggest outpouring of mail that I've ever gotten from any single event. Seventy-seven percent of the people said they agreed with what I said and wanted to do something about it. Fourteen percent of the people just had suggestions about how we could save energy, just constructive suggestions. And a very small portion, only 9 percent, had unfavorable or critical remarks to make.

Four percent said that I shouldn't use transportation to go to Camp David, to go to Kansas City, or to go to Detroit, that I could save energy by staying in Washington. Two percent said that if I would eliminate forced busing, I could eliminate the energy problem. Two percent said we should decontrol oil immediately. And one percent said they were inconvenienced enough already with high thermostat settings and less use of their own automobiles. But an unbelievable 77 percent of the people, that were either pro or con, were pro; only 9 percent negative. So, I think there has been a favorable response to what we evolved at Camp David as an analysis of our Nation.

So, we've got the wisdom; I think we've got the will. Now we've got to succeed and to take the necessary action. It's important for our people to pull together. In a time of stress or inconvenience or trial, without an overriding national emergency that unifies people, we tend to become isolated. And with isolation there's a sense of potential helplessness, and with potential helplessness comes a desire to grasp for an advantage and to cling to it, for a special advantage, for a special interest. And this causes those who are divided into small groups to fail to marshal to a spirit of unity, to seek for a national purpose or a broader purpose, or to move toward unselfishness and generosity and concern and compassion and love for one another.

Instead of being pulled apart, it's obvious that it's time for us to put our Nation together and to move toward a common goal. I pointed out that we are at a crossroads, deciding between increased diversity and division on the one hand, or toward increased unity and a common purpose on the other.

It became obvious to me over a long period of months, accentuated at Camp David, that we do have a severe energy problem, but that our basic problem in this country goes much deeper than energy. But in the resolution of the energy question, in the solution of it, in the meeting of it, courageously, in unifying ourselves to achieve our energy goals, in that process, we have a chance to show again the strength of America, the ability of our people to work together, and the ability of us demonstrably to be successful. And I think that process will have far-reaching effects, far beyond that of energy.

There is no easy answer. There is no free lunch. There is no quick solution to problems that have been evolving in our Nation for many years, decades, even generations. But I am convinced that this is a time to meet those challenges, persistently and courageously. The people have responded well. Hundreds of organizations have already sent me word, "We are supporting you, Mr. President."

When I went to Kansas City to speak to the county officials—Democrats and Republicans—the outpouring was almost unanimous in pledging their support to go back home and organize community effort to conserve energy, to seek for new ways to strengthen our Nation and its purposes, and to bind people together again in a spirit of harmony and cooperation.

In closing my remarks, let me say that you were carefully chosen. There were a limited number of people from throughout our Nation who could come to Camp David. And I deeply appreciate every one of you being willing to do it. It was a

time of criticism of me and some doubt about what was going on there. And you came partially on faith, perhaps partially out of curiosity. But it was a very constructive thing for me and for my administration and, I think, for the Nation. And I thank you for it.

There was a wide diversity of opinion expressed, and as all of you know, I listened about 90 percent of the time and talked about 10 percent of the time. And I took careful notes, not only on a scratchpad but in my mind and in my heart, and I'll never forget some of the advice that you gave me. I'm not the kind of person who responds easily to criticism. I hate to admit that I have defects and that I have made errors. But over a period of a few days, I began to see how constructive and how helpful this could be to me as President. Because you are natural leaders, chosen to come to Camp David because of that, and because you represent a broad and diverse spectrum of America, and also because you and I in many ways, I hope in every instance, have broken the ice between us, I think your advice to me in the future will be extremely valuable.

I hope that you will retain the sense of friendship and the sense of ease in communicating with me in the future that you had at Camp David. You need not be embarrassed about giving me tough advice and very personal criticisms and suggestions in the future. We've already crossed that bridge. And I would hope that I've got a special group of people now throughout the Nation who can deal with me as a human being and without restraint and with a maximum degree of frankness. In that way, you can be an extra benefit to me and to our country.

And I would like to ask you, in addition, to add your influence and your support and your dedication to the goal that I have described for our Nation in the energy field and the repairing of the consciousness and the attitudes of our Nation.

I hope that you will feel not only a sense of gratification that you came to Camp David and that you're having lunch at the White House, but also that you will consider yourself, Democrats or Republicans, no matter whom you might support politically in the future or have supported in the past, that you will consider yourself kind of a member of a team of people who are dedicated to assuring that our Nation will be stronger in the future, will be more united in the future, that confidence which has been lost will be restored, and that there be a searching on the part of every one of you among those who listen to your voice—your peer group, those who look to you for leadership—to make sure that our Nation is stronger in the future.

I've made some, I think, good decisions since we left Camp David. Some have been controversial, but I think they've been sound. There is no doubt in my mind that I now have a stronger and more cohesive and perhaps even a more competent Cabinet. But at least we'll be stronger and more cohesive.

I think the analysis of those who will serve in the future will soon replace in the Washington press the analysis of what did occur when I made the changes. And I think as people are assessed, who will be serving in HEW and HUD and Transportation and the Federal Reserve and Treasury and in Energy, there will be an assurance that we have replaced excellent people with excellent people. This I think you can help me with as well.

I'll be glad to answer, for about 10 minutes, any questions that you might

have. I have nothing to conceal from you. And I would appreciate not only the questions but perhaps suggestions as well.

Does anybody have a comment or question to ask?

NOTE: The President spoke at 12:55 p.m. in the East Room at the White House.

The press release does not include a transcript of the question-and-answer session which followed the President's remarks.

Meeting With United Nations Secretary-General Kurt Waldheim

White House Statement.   July 30, 1979

President Carter met this afternoon with United Nations Secretary-General Kurt Waldheim for 50 minutes in the Cabinet Room. The President congratulated Secretary-General Waldheim on the results of the Geneva meeting on Indochina refugees. The President felt the Secretary-General's efforts were a key factor in the progress made on substantially increasing funding pledges and commitments from a variety of countries to resettle refugees.

On the Middle East, the President discussed U.S. policies for advancing the peace process. The two leaders discussed the question of a continued U.N. presence in the Sinai. The President told the Secretary-General that we will be consulting closely with Israel and Egypt on this question. The United States will remain in close touch with the Secretary-General and his staff.

The President urged the Secretary-General to continue to give top priority to his efforts to resolve the problem of Cyprus. He also discussed the Secretary-

General's continuing efforts to find a solution to the Namibian situation.

Those attending, along with the President, were the Vice President, Deputy Secretary of State Warren Christopher, Assistant to the President for National Security Affairs Zbigniew Brzezinski, Ambassador to the United Nations Andrew Young, Assistant Secretary of State for International Organization Affairs Charles William Maynes, and NSC staff member Lincoln P. Bloomfield.

Accompanying the Secretary-General were Under Secretary-General for Political and General Assembly Affairs William Buffum and Director, Executive Office of the Secretary-General, Albert Rohan.

Council on Wage and Price Stability

Nomination of R. Robert Russell To Be Director.   July 31, 1979

The President today announced his intention to nominate R. Robert Russell to be Director of the Council on Wage and Price Stability (COWPS). He would replace Barry Bosworth, who has resigned as Director effective August 3. The President said he will designate Russell as Acting Director effective August 4.

Russell, of Escondido, Calif., has been Deputy Director of COWPS since 1978.

He was born February 17, 1938, in Rock Springs, Wyo. He received a B.A. from the University of California at Santa Barbara in 1961 and a Ph. D. from Harvard University in 1965.

From 1965 to 1966, he was on the professional staff of the Council of Economic Advisers. He was associate professor of economics at the University of California

at Santa Barbara from 1966 to 1973. He was on the faculty of the University of California at San Diego from 1973 to 1978, as associate professor, then professor.

Russell was a Woodrow Wilson graduate fellow and a Harvard graduate fellow and received a National Science Foundation Doctoral Dissertation Fellowship. He is the author of a book and numerous articles and papers on economic matters.

Panama Canal Commission

Nomination of Lt. Gen. Dennis P. McAuliffe, USA, To Be Administrator.   July 31, 1979

The President today announced his intention to nominate Lt. Gen. Dennis P. McAuliffe to be the Administrator of the Panama Canal Commission. This position was created by the Panama Canal treaties and would be established by the legislation now pending in Congress to implement the treaties.

McAuliffe has been Commander in Chief of the United States Southern Command in Quarry Heights, Canal Zone, since 1975 and has over 35 years of active service in the Army.

He was born April 8, 1922, in New York City and holds a B.S. in military science from the U.S. Military Academy and an M.S. in electrical engineering from the University of Pennsylvania.

McAuliffe was the Army member of the Joint Chiefs of Staff Chairman's Staff Group from 1966 to 1967, and served as Executive Officer to the Chairman of the Joint Chiefs of Staff from 1967 to 1969. He served in Vietnam from 1969 to 1970, as Assistant Division Commander of the 1st Infantry Division, then Deputy Senior Adviser to III Corps and Military Region 3 (concurrently Commanding General of the U.S. Army Advisory Group, III Corps and Military Region 3).

From 1971 to 1973, he was Chief of the Policy Branch in the Plans and Policy Division, Supreme Headquarters, Allied Powers, Europe. From 1973 to 1974, he was Deputy Commanding General, Combined Arms Combat Developments Activity, at Fort Leavenworth. He was director of the European region for the Office of the Assistant Secretary of Defense for International Security Affairs from 1974 until 1975, when he began serving in the Canal Zone.

As Commander in Chief of the Southern Command, McAuliffe has been a member of the Canal Zone Civilian Personnel Coordinating Board and the Panama Review Committee.

1979 World Administrative Radio Conference

Accordance of Personal Rank of Ambassador to Glen O. Robinson, Chairman of the U.S. Delegation.   July 31, 1979

The President today announced that he has accorded Glen O. Robinson the personal rank of Ambassador while he serves as Chairman of the United States Delegation to the 1979 World Administrative Radio Conference. The Conference is scheduled to be held in Geneva, Switzerland, from September 24 through November 30, 1979.

Robinson was a professor of law at the University of Virginia and the Aspen Institute in New York City before becoming Chairman of the U.S. Delegation to this Conference. He was a Commissioner of the Federal Communications Commission from 1974 to 1976.

Inter-American Council for Education, Science and Culture and Inter-American Economic and Social Council

Accordance of Personal Rank of Ambassador to Irving G. Tragen, Head of the U.S. Delegation.   July 31, 1979

The President today announced that he has accorded Irving G. Tragen the personal rank of Ambassador while he serves as head of the United States Delegation to the meeting of the Inter-American Council for Education, Science and Culture, and the meeting of the Inter-American Economic and Social Council.

These meetings are scheduled to be held in Barbados from September 5 to 13 and September 18 to 22, respectively.

Tragen is the Deputy Permanent Representative of the United States to the Organization of American States.

Federal Bureau of Investigation

Message to the Congress Transmitting Proposed Legislation.   July 31, 1979

To the Congress of the United States:

I am transmitting today the FBI Charter Act of 1979, which will provide the first comprehensive Charter for the functioning of the Federal Bureau of Investigation. This legislative proposal will govern all the investigative and law enforcement functions of the Federal Bureau of Investigation.

The foreign intelligence and counterintelligence functions of the Bureau will be governed by a separate charter for the entire foreign intelligence community.

This proposal was developed by the FBI and the Justice Department and has received close scrutiny and personal approval from Attorney General Griffin Bell, Deputy Attorney General Benjamin Civiletti, and Director William Webster.

The law enforcement Charter would bring together in one statute the authorities and responsibilities that the FBI now exercises as a matter of custom and practice.

Although most departments and agencies operate under detailed statutory schemes, the FBI has lacked a statutory framework, although it is one of the most important and sensitive of all Executive Branch agencies. A one-paragraph 1908 law creating the Bureau is all that presently exists. The controversies in past years regarding particular actions of the Bureau, such as those directed at Dr. Martin Luther King, Jr., and various other persons and organizations, are to some degree attributable to this lack of statutory direction. It was these controversies which led me to call for a clear and binding charter for the FBI when I ran for President. Statutory safeguards would insure that the Bureau exercises its responsibilities in a manner sensitive to the fundamental rights of all Americans. The public must be assured that the FBI is acting properly under the law.

We need to recognize that the FBI serves a vital national function and that it has rendered distinguished service to the Nation. It has set a standard for competence, dedication and professionalism of which we should all be proud. We must be careful to maintain the fundamental capability of an institution which has served us so well. This Charter maintains that capability. Under Director William Webster the conduct of the Bureau has been exemplary and I applaud his leadership.

A clear definition of the authorities and responsibilities of the FBI is essential to its proper functioning and is in the best interest of national law enforcement and the proper administration of justice. Enactment of this Charter will enable FBI agents to carry out their duties with greater certainty, confidence, and effectiveness.

The bill I submit today reflects three fundamental objectives:

• The Charter should be a document of broad principles, not a long detailing of procedures. It should enumerate the FBI's jurisdiction, functions and powers and set forth the limits on its activities, but should leave to the Attorney General the power to issue specific detailed procedures and guidelines.

• With few exceptions, coupled with procedural safeguards, the investigative power of the FBI should be limited to the detection, prevention and prosecution of federal crimes. This will prevent the unrestricted accumulation of information concerning individuals not suspected of criminal conduct.

• The Charter should strike a proper balance between the true needs of law enforcement and the civil liberties guaranteed by our Constitution. The greater the potential for impairment of rights, the stronger the authorization and accountability systems required.

The Charter authorizes the FBI to employ traditional and lawful investigative techniques in carrying out its responsibilities. These include confidential informants, undercover agents, and undercover operations.

Two primary types of criminal investigations are authorized: investigation of criminal acts that violate federal law and investigations into criminal enterprises that involve racketeering or terrorism. No investigation may be commenced unless based on "facts and circumstances that reasonably indicate" a criminal violation.

For the most part, this bill simply codifies current practices. However, FBI authority would be significantly expanded in two areas:

1. The FBI could issue "investigative demands" for financial records. This is a compulsory process enforceable in the courts comparable to the administrative subpoenas issued by agencies such as the Securities and Exchange Commission and the new Inspectors General in each Federal agency. This is essential if the FBI is to be effective in combatting white collar crime, fraud, corruption, and organized crime.

2. The FBI could investigate patterns of terrorist acts that involve violations of state criminal laws even without federal violations, following the model of current racketeering statutes.

The bill continues existing restrictions, procedural controls, and requirements for accountability on FBI activities. It adds, however, several new restrictions providing tighter controls over the use of informants. For example, infiltration of groups under investigation for terrorist activities and participation by an informant in criminal activity must now be approved by a supervisory FBI official.

The Charter requires that the Attorney General promulgate, and periodically review, operational guidelines for each of the Bureau's major activities. These guidelines will be filed with the Congress and made available to the public unless, in a specific case, their release would jeopardize the investigative process. The FBI is also required to report on important and sensitive activities to the Attorney General and the Congress.

This Charter strikes the proper balance between assuring both that the civil rights and liberties guaranteed to Americans by our Constitution are protected and that the FBI can fully pursue its appropriate functions.

I urge the Congress to give this bill the careful and urgent attention it deserves and to pass the first Charter for the FBI.

JIMMY CARTER

The White House,
July 31, 1979.

Federal Home Loan Bank Board

Nomination of Jay Janis To Be a Member, and Designation as Chairman. July 31, 1979

The President today announced his intention to nominate Jay Janis, of Coral Gables, Fla., to be a member of the Federal Home Loan Bank Board. The President said that on confirmation, Janis would be designated Chairman of the Board. He would replace Robert H. McKinney, who has resigned.

Janis is currently Under Secretary of the Department of Housing and Urban Development, a post he has held since 1977.

He was born December 22, 1932, in Los Angeles, Calif., and received a B.A. degree from Yale University in 1954.

Janis was a builder for the Janis Construction Co. from 1956 to 1964. From 1964 to 1966, he was a special assistant to the Under Secretary of Commerce.

Janis was executive assistant to the Secretary of Housing and Urban Development from 1966 to 1969. From 1969 to 1975, he was a coprincipal in MGIC-Janis Properties, Inc., a building and community development company in Florida. In 1976 he became a vice president at the University of Massachusetts.

Janis was chairman of Florida Gov. Reubin Askew's Housing Goals Council from 1973 to 1975. In 1972-73 he was chairman of the NAHB Land Use Policy Committee. In 1974–75 Janis served as president of the board of trustees of the Florida International University Foundation. He was chairman of the Dade County Community Relations Board in 1972.

Louisville, Kentucky

Remarks Following a Tour of the Cane Run Generating Station of the Louisville Gas & Electric Company.   July 31, 1979

President Royer, Governor Carroll, Senator Huddleston, Senator Ford, Congressman Mazzoli, and my fellow workers:

It's good to be with you.

One of the interesting and exciting things about being President is to have a chance to travel throughout our great country and to see the challenges which confront us all being met successfully by dedicated men and women like you.

This powerplant, burning American fuel, American coal, both safely and cleanly, is kind of a testimony to the technological genius of America and to the dedication of American working men and women. It's a signpost toward a future of energy security, prosperity for our people, and national strength.

As a people, we are now embroiled in a struggle to meet the challenge of the energy crisis. Most Americans don't even know that we import foreign oil. We actually import about half all the oil we use, which takes more than $50 billion of American money and sends it to foreign nations.

We also know that the oil supplies from foreign countries are not dependable. Back in 1973, 1974, primarily because of political considerations, the oil-supplying nations, the OPEC nations, had an embargo against our country, and some of those countries refused to sell us oil. We still face that possible challenge to our country. This is a struggle not just for the forms of energy we use but for our Nation's very independence, for our economic freedom as Americans.

As President, I will not permit our country to fall further and further each passing year into a dark and dangerous dependence on undependable foreign oil. I have pledged to you that our Nation will never import one drop more foreign oil than we did in 1977. With your help, America will keep that pledge, and I know you'll help me.

It's absolute folly for the United States to ship billions of dollars overseas each year to bring tankers of foreign oil to our shores, while beneath our feet, in your great State of Kentucky and others, lie more than 300 years of coal reserves just waiting to be mined and waiting to be used. It's folly that here in Kentucky, and in other States, we have idle mine capacity, mines not being used, because our Nation has failed so far to develop creative ideas to use our vast coal potential.

The United States is the Saudi Arabia of coal. In all the world, the United States owns 31 percent of all the coal reserves. We are blessed with the largest reserves in the whole world. And I'm determined to see our coal supplies light the way of our country toward a future of energy security. I want to see America's coal mines producing—not only new energy supplies for our country but new revenues for our economy, new jobs for the American people, and new security for our Nation.

I have proposed and the Congress is now acting on the most massive peacetime investment in the history of our country— a program to cut our oil imports in half and to change forever the way we use our coal reserves.

First, I want Congress to give me the authority to require utility companies to cut in half their use of oil and to switch to other fuels, especially coal. I want legislation to permit the early retirement of oil-burning power companies [plants] [1] that cannot convert to coal. And I want Congress to provide grants and loans to utilities to make these changes at a reasonable cost to consumers. You have already led the way here in this plant. I want other power companies to follow your leadership.

First of all, we need to conserve energy, to stop wasting energy; and, secondly, to have more direct use of coal. These are the two fastest ways to move toward energy independence, and we must take these steps immediately.

We will also protect our environment. I will not permit America to be forced to choose between breathing foul air and having our waters filthy on the one hand or mortgaging our future to the OPEC oil cartel. We don't need to do either one.

This plant, burning high sulfur coal cleanly and safely, proves that our country can chart a different course for the future. With commitment, with imagination, with national unity, with courage, with America's technological genius and with our vast resources given to us by God, we can meet our energy goals while we preserve the quality of our precious land, air, and water. And we will do it. You have proven here that it can be done.

Secondly, we will launch a massive effort to produce more domestic energy supplies and synthetic fuels—oil and gas from coal.

What I want to do with Congress help is to set up an energy security corporation, a corporation where Americans can own

_____
[1] Printed in the transcript.

stock and let the private enterprise system of our country, not hamstrung or tied down by government redtape, but funded from a windfall profits tax on the oil companies on their unearned profits to convert coal into oil, to extract new supplies of natural gas, and to process oil from shale. America has talked about starting a synthetic fuels industry for years, even generations. The time has now come to stop talking and start producing oil from coal through a good synthetic fuels program.

One of the most important things with energy security is that it will provide new jobs for America, not jobs exported overseas. We can increase coal production by hundreds of millions of tons in the next 10 years and create as many as 80,000 new jobs in the coal mines alone. As you well know, being from Kentucky, the Nation's number one coal-producing State, a lot of those jobs are going to be in Kentucky, and they'll make your lives and my life both better.

This is going to cost a lot of money. I don't think it ought to be paid for by taxing the American people and going through the Federal budget. Oil prices are going to go up. And what we have proposed to the Congress and what the House of Representatives has already passed is what we call a windfall profits tax. It taxes the oil companies on profits that they do not earn. It leaves with them enough new money to increase production of American oil and gas, but it takes the rest of that money and spends it on the synthetic fuels program, develop better transportation systems, and to increase conservation both in homes and also in the production of power.

If the windfall profits tax is stopped or defeated by the oil lobby, then we will not be able to reach the goals that I've just described to you. And there is a real danger unless your voices are heard that this may happen.

I've talked about the gap between the Government in Washington and the people in our country, about the gap between Washington and the rest of the Nation. Now, here's a perfect and an unfortunate example: The American people overwhelmingly support a tough and a fair tax on the oil companies to give us the financial basis for energy security, new jobs, new production of synthetic fuels, new conservation, a better life for us all. Yet, despite this support, this tax on the unearned profits—and with it, our hopes for energy security—is in danger of being killed or crippled.

I'm very proud that Congressman Mazzoli has already helped us and that Senator Wendell Ford, who's the chairman of the Senate Coal Caucus, and Senator Dee Huddleston, who's one of the leaders in the Senate, are both with me in this fight. I hope you'll stick with them while they stick with me to give us this tax money, to give us energy security. Will you help do that? [*Applause*] Right on!

When the Senate passes this bill, we will have the ability to meet our responsibility as a nation and to have the financial weapons to win this energy battle. But this will not happen unless the voices of working Americans like you are heard loud and clear in Washington. You can rest assured that the oil lobbyists' voices are going to be heard loud and clear in Washington. And we need for your voice also to be heard.

With the revenues from a good, tough windfall profits tax and the oil companies, America will be uniquely equipped to win this energy war. We have unsurpassed technology. We have the enormous strength of a free economy. We've got a free enterprise system that's the best

on Earth. We've got a democratic Government that the people can run, and we've got dedicated men and women who are not afraid to work if they know what they're working for and they have confidence in the Government and confidence in our own Nation.

The skills of the American people and the dedication and courage of the American people is our single greatest resource. We need all of this to see our battle through. We need to unite with one another. We need to have confidence in our Government, confidence in ourselves, confidence in one another, confidence in the future. We need to set aside our narrow, regional interests and work together to join in a common purpose to strengthen and to serve the country that we love, the United States of America, the greatest nation on Earth.

You do your part, I'll do my part, and we'll win.

Thank you very much.

NOTE: The President spoke at 2:50 p.m. outside the Cane Run facility. In his opening remarks, he referred to Robert L. Royer, president of Louisville Gas & Electric Company.

Following his remarks, the President met at the facility with a group of coal industry executives.

The White House later issued the following information on the meeting.

At his meeting with coal industry leaders, the President responded to concerns about Government regulations by announcing that he has directed the Regulatory Council to begin an effort to eliminate overlapping and inconsistent Federal and State regulations affecting coal production and coal use.

The Regulatory Council, chaired by Doug Costle of the Environmental Protection Agency and comprised of the Federal Government's major regulatory agencies, was established by the President to improve and simplify the regulatory process. Following the President's directive, the Council will establish a Coal Regulation Project and will immediately begin a comprehensive assessment of regulatory problems affecting the coal industry. The Project will seek information from the industry as well as the public. In today's meeting, the President invited the participants to submit to the Council their specific concerns about particular coal regulations.

In inviting those submissions, however, the President indicated his focus, as well as that of the Council, would be on improving the regulatory process, not on changing the substance of environmental laws. The President stated that those laws could not realistically be changed, and the industry's efforts would be best directed to working within existing laws and to helping pass a strong windfall profits tax, an energy security corporation, and a meaningful energy mobilization board. The President indicated that the tax, the corporation, and the board would provide the funds and the means to meet our energy goals without adversely affecting our health and safety.

Bardstown, Kentucky

Remark sand a Question-and-Answer Session at a Town Meeting. July 31, 1979

THE PRESIDENT. Well, I finally made it to Bardstown. I'm glad to be here. My wife said that she never has had a better welcome nor made more friends in such a short time than when she came to Bardstown. And she wanted me to tell you thank you and she loves every one of you.

Two and a half weeks ago, I was planning to come to Bardstown myself, but I couldn't get away from Camp David. Every time I started to leave, I had another mess of company come— [*laughter*]—and I had to stay there and entertain them. But Rosalynn came to represent me.

And I thought a lot about our Nation and what I should do as President. And Sunday night before last, I made a speech about two problems of our country—energy and malaise. Senator Wendell Ford, on the helicopter, said that Bardstown could take care of both of them. He said

Kentucky could provide coal for the energy, and Bardstown could provide bourbon for the malaise. As a Baptist, I did not comment. [*Laughter*]

I am glad to be here.

ADMINISTRATION POLICIES

About 2 weeks ago, I did speak to you about the problems facing our country—a crisis of confidence, the fact that American people in recent years have begun to lose confidence in ourselves, in our neighbors, in our communities, in our churches, in our homes, in our schools, in our government, in our institutions; and also to talk to you about our energy problems. We have become overly dependent on foreign countries for our oil. We get more than 50 percent of all our oil from overseas, and we have to take American dollars, billions of them, every year and export those dollars and jobs overseas and import inflation. And I think it's better for us as Americans to face the facts, and as long as I'm President, I intend to tell you the facts, to tell you the truth, and to ask for your help.

Now, the energy problem is more than just statistics or figures or charts or graphs or speeches. This energy problem threatens the very security of our Nation. It threatens our economic independence. You know what happened in 1973, 1974, when a few OPEC oil-producing countries embargoed the shipment of oil to our Nation. And we've become, since then, even more dependent on foreign oil.

What we must do is to approach this threat to American security just as we have approached threats in the past to our Nation's security, like the Great Depression, the First World War, the Second World War. We are actually in a battle to win our energy independence. It's a battle that all Americans must fight together.

It's a battle that I do not intend to lose, did not intend to lose, and I believe with your help, we can win. Will you help me? [*Applause*]

Now, I don't want to mislead you. There are no easy answers. And some of the things that I propose are going to take a long time, like the synthetic production of fuels. But there are two things that we can do right away. One of them is to quit wasting energy—conservation. It doesn't cost anything. It saves money. It doesn't damage the quality of our lives. Save energy every way you can. And the second thing depends on Kentucky. Kentucky is the Nation's number one producer of coal, and we're going to use a lot of coal in the next few years.

We must see America provide basic energy from America. I would rather burn a ton of Kentucky coal than to see our Nation become dependent by buying another barrel of OPEC oil.

In the last 2 or 3 weeks, I've done a lot of thinking about my job as President—working for world peace, being certain that our Nation was secure, providing jobs for Americans. We've added 175,000 new jobs with the help of your Governor, industry, labor, and all of you in Kentucky in the last 2 years, making the Federal Government more open, more confident, more efficient. All this is part of my job as President.

But a President has an even larger responsibility, and that is to draw on the spirit of America, to call out the best that's in our people, to inspire Americans, and to work with Americans to unite, to combine ourselves together in a common purpose so that we can solve our Nation's problems, no matter what they are.

We do have some problems with energy, with confidence, with inflation, with some remaining unemployment, lot of other things, but we must never forget that America is the strongest and the brightest and the best nation on Earth, and we've got more to be thankful for than we have to complain about.

In that speech 2 weeks ago, I talked about the separation of American people from our Government, particularly in Washington, and, again, those were not just empty words. Now, I can tell you that the Members of the Congress and the Federal employees and the Cabinet members, who work with me, are all filled with dedicated people trying sincerely to do a good job for you. But the more you live in Washington, and the more you talk to each other in Washington, you tend to become insulated from the rest of the Nation, you tend to become isolated from the people of our country. We start getting our ideas from each other, and we start getting our thoughts from each other. We spend too much time reading Federal Government forms and regulations instead of listening to people like you. And we've got to change that and listen to the people like you.

It affects me, too, but I'm determined that I'm not going to let anything erect barriers between your President and you, and I need for you to help me keep those barriers torn down.

I'll just give you one example, and then I want to answer your questions.

There is no way that we can meet our goals on energy and preserve our Nation's energy independence or our Nation's security without moving toward conservation—and that costs money—moving toward solar energy—that costs money—increase production and use of coal to make sure that consumers of electricity don't have to pay too much money; making sure that we have good air and water and land quality so that our children will have a delightful place to live as well; developing synthetic fuels in the future from coal, gas and oil from coal.

These kinds of things cost a lot of money. I don't want to be responsible for putting another tax on the American people to pay for it. What I want to do is to see the Congress pass a windfall profits tax on the oil companies to make sure that all we take from them are taxes, through taxes of profits that they have not earned. In the process, we're going to leave the oil companies with additional income which they can use to produce more oil and more gas within our country. That's a real fair proposition for the oil companies.

As I say, this bill's already passed through the House of Representatives, and now it's in the Senate. And the oil lobby is letting its voice be heard very quietly, very effectively in the halls of the U.S. Congress. There's only one way to meet that competition. Does anybody know what it is? Right with you—right? If you will let your voices be heard, we can prevail.

Now, I would hasten to add that your United States Senators, Dee Huddleston and Wendell Ford, are on my side and they're on your side. But I hope that you will write the other leaders in the Senate, the members of the Finance Committee, and let them know that you believe in the future of our Nation, that you're willing to do your share, and that the passage of the windfall profits tax is an integral part of reaching our energy security that we all want. And if you'll join in with me and with Wendell Ford and with Dee Huddleston, we will prevail, we'll pass the windfall profits tax, we'll have a secure nation and a better life for all Americans in the future.

Now I want to answer your questions. I'm ready for the first question.

QUESTIONS

WELFARE REFORM

Q. Good evening, Mr. President.

THE PRESIDENT. Good evening.

Q. My name is Catherine Roberts of Shepherdsville, Kentucky. Yesterday morning I heard on the news there were over 6,000 illegitimate children born last year alone. As a taxpayer, I would like to know if there would be job openings for mothers after the first child whereas the taxpayer would not have to support them, buy them homes—I mean, you know, help give them homes and steaks and cars to ride around in.

THE PRESIDENT. I think one of the most important things that we can do in our Nation is to strengthen American families; to cut down on the birth of unwanted children, particularly those who are illegitimate. But once they are born, I don't want to see the child branded for life and deprived of an opportunity to be a healthy and a strong and a prosperous and a happy American.

Now, one thing that we have proposed to the Congress is to reform the welfare laws, to take what money we do collect for welfare payments and not just perpetuate people who are able to work on the welfare rolls. Many people now, because of the confused welfare laws, are better off not working than they are to work, even if they're able to work.

So, I think your question's a very good one, and this is what we're trying to do, to give people who really need welfare payments and who cannot work an opportunity to live a decent life, to provide mothers who want to work a chance to keep their children in a good day care center and get jobs. And people who are able-bodied and don't have children, I don't believe in any welfare payments for them. I think they ought to go to work.

STANDBY GASOLINE RATIONING PLAN

Q. [*Inaudible*]

THE PRESIDENT. I don't think the mike's working. Come up here and use this one. [*Laughter*]

Q. Mr. President, my name is Sean Cantrell, and I live right here in Bardstown. And what would the circumstances have to be before you ration gas, should Congress give you their permission to do so?

THE PRESIDENT. Very good. Thank you. Good question.

I've asked the Congress to give me authority to develop a standby gasoline rationing plan. The House of Representatives is voting on that authority this afternoon.

I just talked to Washington before I came in here, and the predictions are—I can't guarantee it, you don't ever know what Congress is going to do—but the prediction is that this afternoon or tonight the House of Representatives will give me that standby authority. What it means is that I will prepare for gasoline rationing. It will not be implemented. We'll put the rationing plan on the shelf as a standby, but we'll be ready. And if we do have a severe and sustained loss of gasoline, then it will be put into effect.

I hope that it will never have to be implemented. And if I do a good job as President, and if we get a good energy program through the Congress, that I've described to you in my opening remarks, then we won't have to have gasoline rationing. But I would rather have a standby gasoline rationing plan than to see gasoline rationed by price so that only the rich people can afford it. You've only got those two alternatives.

So, I will have a standby rationing plan. It will only be implemented if we have a severe shortage that lasts a long time. We need it. I believe we'll have it.

Dan, how about checking all three of the mikes?

TELEPHONE SERVICE IN BULLITT COUNTY

Q. Mr. President, I am Juanita Smith of Bullitt County. We have a terrific problem in our county, where our telephone company provides direct service—[*microphone feedback*]——

THE PRESIDENT. You shouldn't have said anything about the telephone company. [*Laughter*]

Q. ——where our telephone systems provide direct service for over half of Bullitt County. The other half, which I am in, do not have the direct service. We have to pay toll charges for every call we make. We have tried to go through the Public Service Commission of Kentucky, but we have failed.

I have personally written to Senator Walter D. Huddleston. I think you might remember me writing to you. I have written to Senator Wendell Ford. We are referred back to the Public Service Commission. We get nowhere from the Public Service Commission.

My question to you, Mr. President: Could you appoint someone that could talk to us and see what they can do to help us secure this service?

THE PRESIDENT. As soon as this program is over, I will not only talk to Julian Carroll, but tomorrow morning I'll get on the telephone, and I will call the chairman of the Public Service Commission and see if I can't help Bullitt County get better telephone service. I'm not guaranteeing you any results, but I guarantee you I'll call them.

VOLUNTEER ARMED FORCES

Q. Mr. President, my name is McKay Chauvin, and my question concerns the volunteer draft. Each year the Armed Forces are losing valuable manpower, and so my question is, what can you do as President to make the services more attractive to the average American?

THE PRESIDENT. I think so far the volunteer program has worked well. Lately, however, as the unemployment rate has gone down, other jobs in some parts of the country have become much more available. So, we've lost one incentive for young men who couldn't get a job other places, who formerly came into the Armed Forces. Now they can get a job easier than they could in the past, and we are having problems getting enough young people, men and women, to volunteer for the Armed Forces to fill out our quotas.

We're now reassessing the status of whether or not people ought to be registered. I don't see any prospect anytime soon of actually calling people up to a draft, but we might have to have as a precautionary measure registration for the draft just as a standby measure.

As far as making the Armed Forces attractive, we have increased substantially the pay for young people going into the Armed Forces. As you know, there is a superb opportunity for a career training, and I think the living conditions, the food, the rapidity of transfer from one site to another, and the degree of choice you have is much better than it was when I was in the Navy for 11 years as a young person.

So, we might have a standby registration, if I decided it's needed. I don't think we'll have a mandatory draft. We'll do everything we can to make sure that the service in the Armed Forces is satis-

factory from a pay and career and living status is concerned.

The most important thing, though, is patriotism. And I think when we can restore to the United States the unity and the confidence and the true sense of love for our Nation, that will be an additional and perhaps the most important incentive for young people to volunteer to serve their country for a couple of years. I hope that happens here in Bardstown and all over the country.

DEPARTMENT OF EDUCATION

Q. [*Inaudible*]

THE PRESIDENT. Could you all hear it? The question was, since it appears that the campaign promise that I made to have a separate department of education might soon be fulfilled, would I consider appointing a classroom teacher as the secretary of education.

I will certainly consider it. I don't want to make a promise now, because I really want to wait until the bill does pass. It's already passed the House and Senate in different forms. It's to go through the conference committee, and I don't want to be presumptuous about what kind of person or who I would appoint.

But I will certainly consider a classroom teacher along with others. I can't make a promise that it would be a classroom teacher. Is that fair enough?

OIL INDUSTRY PROFITS

Q. I'm Tom Howell, from Hodgenville, Larue County. And my question is, Mr. President, why don't you try to do something about the big oil companies making so much profit?

THE PRESIDENT. I don't want to mislead you all just to get a round of applause. I believe in the free enterprise system of our country, and I believe that the profit motive is the best incentive to provide the services that we need, the goods we need, as long as it's based on tough competition in the marketplace.

Now, we have seen in our own Nation in the last 10 or 12 years an annual decrease in the amount of oil we are producing. The only break in that downward trend was in 1977, 1978, when the Alaskan oil started coming in. We now get about 1.2 million barrels of oil a day from Alaska. But we've also seen the oil companies misuse the profits they have made. If the oil companies take the profits and invest them back into exploration and the production of additional oil and gas in our country, then I have no objection to their profits being made. But what they've done in the past is buy restaurants and motel chains; they've tried to buy circuses. They've bought department stores. They've taken profits off of oil and gasoline and not put it back in the ground to develop more energy for you and me.

We have introduced now and I support a bill that would prevent any of the 18 largest oil companies from purchasing companies like I've just described, which would force them within all practical bounds to take what profits they do make and produce more oil and gas.

We are also investigating, through the Justice Department and the Energy Department, complaints against the oil companies to make sure that they don't violate the antitrust laws, that is, that they maintain a high degree of competition and that they don't violate regulations or rules or proprieties in the adequate provision of gasoline and oil products for you.

So, to summarize, the profits are okay if the oil companies use them the right way. And it's my responsibility and yours to monitor them to make sure that the oil companies act legally and properly to serve the American people under the free enterprise, which is so dear to us all.

ADMINISTRATION GOALS

Q. Good afternoon. My name is Buzz Turner, and I'm from Magnolia, in Larue County. Mr. President, as a graduate student of American history at Western Kentucky University, I'd like to know what do you think the history books will remember your administration for, or at least what you hope it will be remembered for?

THE PRESIDENT. I hope that when the record of my administration is written that the historians say that under the Carter administration, our Nation was secure, that our Nation was at peace, that no young American ever shed blood in a foreign war. I hope that our Nation will report—that history will report that under my administration, we've moved to restore the confidence of the American people in their own government. I hope that the history books will show that I helped to put American people back to work, and I hope that the history books will show that the threats to our security—both from foreign sources and also domestically, like energy shortages—were reduced or removed under my administration. And I hope that the history books will also show that while I served as President that I was honest with the American people when the times were difficult and that I joined in with the American people as partners in searching out the best that's in the hearts and minds of every individual American and that it be expressed in a true sense of patriotism, based on respect for one another, compassion for one another, stronger families, and love for one another. That's what I hope.

Now, you've got to help me make all those wishes come true. I believe they will.

COAL AND THE ENVIRONMENT

Q. I'm Christina Bradford, and I attend Bardstown Junior High School. Mr. President, in your energy message, you indicated an increase in the use of coal. My question is this: Are you going to allow the coal companies to take advantage of this situation to weaken the Federal strip-mining law? And what steps will you take to assure the protection of the environment for future generations?

THE PRESIDENT. Recently I had a report—as a matter of fact, this past week—from what's known as the President's commission on coal. The Chairman of that commission was Governor Jay Rockefeller, from West Virginia, and he and a group of distinguished American leaders, coal operators, environmentalists, representatives of the miners, and others, made a report to me—which is available to all of you, by the way, if you want it—on what we could do to increase the use and the production of coal.

The basic premise on which they based their study was that the environmental laws of our Nation would be carried out completely, that there would be no lowering of standards that would affect the quality of our land, our air, or our water. If we meet those standards of quality of life for Americans and carry out the laws, environmental laws of our Nation, there's an opportunity for us to double the amount of coal that we produce and use, burned cleanly and used cleanly, in the next 6 years to 10 years.

This afternoon I met at a nearby powerplant with about 50 or 60 of the leaders in the Kentucky coal industry—operators, railroad managers, coal miners, and power producers, electric power producers. I told them that the worst mistake that the coal industry could make was to insist upon a lowering of the environmental standards of our Nation. If there's one thing the people of our country fear about coal, is that it is dirty and it will lower the quality of our life. That is not true. We can burn twice as much coal in this nation and not lower our environmental standards at all. That's what I believe our Nation wants to do, and that's what I'm determined to do with the help of people in Kentucky and every other State that produces coal in our country.

REGULATORY REFORM

Q. Mr. President, Gary Hutchins from Bardstown, Kentucky. I would like to inquire as to what your administration is doing at present to reduce Government regulations which businesses are operating on daily—and it's costing each consumer, and I mean each man, woman, and child, a hidden tax, actually, of $450 a year. The businesses in total are spending now in excess of what our national defense budget. So, what is being done to cut it down?

THE PRESIDENT. This has been one of the most difficult things I've tried to do as President. I am a small businessman myself, as you know, and went to the White House with a determination to cut down on regulations and forms, reports that are required by the Federal Government by private citizens. I think we've made a lot of progress already.

I remember one day, year before last, when we eliminated a thousand OSHA regulations in one day, and we've cut down the number of forms and regulations, for instance, in HEW, by more than 20 percent already. But we've still got a long way to go.

This was one of the questions raised this afternoon by the coal industry leaders. And I had the Chairman of our regulatory commission with me, Doug Costle—we've got a group of Federal agencies that meet regularly now to make sure that there's no duplication or extra requirements of reports from the business community of our country that's affected by environmental laws. In the past we've had Energy, Interior, Labor, EPA, and all the rest of them requiring separate reports. Now at least they are meeting together.

Another thing that we are going to do that might be interesting to you is to have a small business convention or White House conference this winter. And in preparation for that conference, we have taken 200 sample small businesses around our Nation, and we've sent staff members in to work with that small business leader to say, "What are you required to do by the Federal Government in reports and forms and regulations compliance that might be eliminated?" And those 200 small businesses will be feeding in to me and the other members of the conference their ideas on how we can change weekly reports to semiannual reports; how we can have 5 questions instead of 50 questions; how many forms can be eliminated or how many forms can be combined between the Department of Labor, Commerce, HEW, HUD, and so forth.

So, I think that by the end of this year, when we have that White House conference, we'll make another step forward to eliminating this burden on the American people.

I don't think the American people are ever going to be satisfied, no matter how much progress we make, but we are plugging away at it and we need your help. If you are interested, you might do this: If you have Federal regulations and forms and reports in your own life that you consider to be too frequent or too complicated or not necessary, if you'll let me know directly, I'll do what I can to modify that burden on you. And since I get so

many letters, and so forth, if you will send your report to Senator Wendell Ford, he can bring your letter to me, and I'll try to use your case as an example and help other people like you who want to get this burden of regulation and paperwork and redtape off your back. Would you do that?

Okay, Wendell?

SENATOR FORD. Anything you say, Mr. President.

THE PRESIDENT. Good. Wendell said he'd be glad to do it—slightly different words.

INDOCHINA REFUGEES

Q. Mr. President, continued great courage to you. My name is Susan McDonald from Nerinx, Kentucky, and my question concerns the Vietnamese refugees. I nursed in Vietnam from 1973 through 1975. I became aware that Vietnam, during the many years of U.S. involvement, depended heavily on the U.S. Food for Peace program. We left Vietnam in '75, and at that time, severed all food aid. Now there's a scarcity of food in Vietnam, and this scarcity is part of the reason for refugees.

My question is: What is preventing us, the United States, from normalizing relations with Vietnam, giving food aid, and instead of severing that aid abruptly, tapering it off in a humane manner, thereby enabling more people of Vietnam to remain in their homeland?

THE PRESIDENT. We believe that the reason for the refugees is not because of a lack of aid from us to Vietnam. Vietnam is a nation which has not turned to us or to the rest of the world for either friendship or economic aid on any sort of reasonable terms. The Vietnamese have been forcing refugees—primarily of Chinese descent—to leave their own country and quite often have been making them pay what money they have saved up to the Vietnamese Government for the right to leave their country under pressure. They've been pushed out from the shores of Vietnam in ships, and literally thousands of them have died.

In the meantime, the Vietnamese Government has invaded Cambodia, now known as Kampuchea, with 15 divisions of armed forces and violated those international borders.

So, under those circumstances, the pushing out under duress and pressure of thousands of refugees—in May, 50,000 alone—without any care about what happens to those refugees once they leave Vietnam, and attacking their neighbor Kampuchea with 15 divisions of armed forces, I don't think it's time for us to normalize relationships with that country.

What we are trying to do, however, is to recognize the need to take care of those refugees. I met during the weekend, the last weekend I was at Camp David before I made my energy and confidence speech, with a group of young people in Pennsylvania—Carnegie, Pennsylvania. And one of the young married women there said she didn't think we ought to take in any refugees because it was too much of a burden on the American people. And I responded to her, I know a lot of American people feel that way, perhaps, that we've already got enough burdens on the Federal Government, we don't want to pay taxes to take care of other folks. But let me repeat very briefly what I told her.

There is a total of about 220,000 Vietnam refugees that we're going to take into our country. These were our allies and friends during the war. They fought alongside of us; their lives were in danger. That's one refugee for every thousand Americans. It's not too heavy a burden for Americans to bear.

In addition to that, this is a nation of refugees. I doubt if there are any native Indians here. If so, they would be the only exceptions to the fact that all of our ancestors were immigrants and that many of them came here as refugees—as religious refugees, sometimes as prisoners who were let out of prison just if they would come to the New World. And I believe that our country is big enough and strong enough and rich enough and generous enough to take care of a few refugees from Vietnam that were our allies and friends during the last war. And that's the way I feel, and I thank you for your question.

I might add one other thing. We have had superb results with those Vietnamese who come to our country. They don't know how to speak English, most of them. They immediately begin to learn how to speak English. They are eager to get a job. They get off welfare faster than anybody I have ever seen. They become self-supporting citizens, and we have tried to place them in communities where the employment rate is very high so they do not contribute to the unemployment rate.

So, we are handling it well, and they are doing their share. I think in a few years, they'll be extremely good American citizens that will make us proud of them and proud of ourselves.

U.S. FOREIGN POLICY

Q. Mike Carney, Mr. President, from Cox's Creek. This is the same line of questioning. You've taken a tough stand on the energy situation. I'd like to know when you're going to take a tough stand on foreign policy in regards to taking up for our allies. For an example, South Korea, Nicaragua, Turkey, and in the past, Iran. And maybe we wouldn't have the energy situation we have today or, for an example, the Panama Canal—if the Government would do what the American people wanted, then we wouldn't have the problem that we've got now.

So, how far does the Government do what we don't want done? And also on the Panama Canal, how far does human rights go, that we don't step in and help our allies and we take over and help the human rights situation?

THE PRESIDENT. I'll try to answer that.

The United States keeps its commitment to our allies. I just came from South Korea just 2 or 3 weeks ago. I have never had such an outpouring of a welcome in my life. There were literally millions of people on the street expressing their thanks to America for guaranteeing the independence and freedom of the people of South Korea.

Since I've been in office, we have substantially strengthened our own Nation's military commitment to our Allies in NATO, in Western Europe. We've got new friends that were formerly intimate allies with the Soviet Union. Egypt is a typical example. You can look at the whole coast of Asia now, from South Korea all the way down around to India; in almost every instance, we have a stronger allegiance and a closer friendship with them than we had 2 years ago, 5 years ago, or 10 years ago.

We've got strong, new allies in Africa. I remember, I think, 3½ years ago, Secretary Kissinger wanted to go to Nigeria as the Secretary of State of our country. He was not permitted to come into the nation of Nigeria, a hundred million people, the largest and the strongest nation in Africa. Now they are very good friends of ours.

So, we stand by our commitments without apology and without deviation.

Now, about Panama. I don't have any apology to make at all about the Panama Canal treaties, which, as you know, were ratified by two-thirds of the people in the Senate. This was not a popular thing to do, but, in my opinion, it was the right thing to do. Our Nation's security is much better off having strong and friendly allies in Panama sharing with us the operation and the maintenance and the defense of the Panama Canal instead of having bitter enemies in Panama, knowing that we had broken our faith, violated our word, and mistreated those people in Panama.

Now, the canal is operated from now until the year 2000 jointly by us and Panama. They're our friends; they trust us; we cooperate. After the year 2000, the Panamanians will be responsible for the operation and maintenance of the canal. The United States will still have the right and the responsibility and the duty to defend the canal. That's what I believe is in the best interests of our own country.

It would not help us to violate our commitment to Panama, to have the Soviet Union and Cuba come in and try to change that government into a Communist government. Since we ratified the Panama Canal treaties, the Panamanians have had a free election; they have chosen 500-and-something members of their Congress. The Congress members have chosen a brand new President, and Panama is on the road now toward a true democracy.

So, I think that our human rights stand, our treating our allies with good faith, and our keeping our word of honor and making sure that we prepare for our Nation's security in the future all are wrapped up in the record that we've carved out for this administration and for the American people.

I have no apology to make, although the Panama Canal treaties was a misunderstood move that our Government made. It was not politically popular. I don't have any doubt that I lost a lot of political support on account of it, but it was right. And I would rather be right in a case like that, when I'm sure it's for the best interests of our country, even if it does cost me something politically.

HEALTH PROGRAMS

Q. How do you do, Mr. President? My name is Tom Bruner, and I'm the director of a drug and alcohol drug treatment unit with North Central Comprehensive Care Center in Elizabethtown. And I would like to lend praise to your administration and to Mrs. Carter in particular for effecting improved mental health services. However, as Secretary Califano exits, do you intend to continue his step-up in alcohol and drug dependency programing and research, as he advocated, or is his absence indicative of a policy modification?

THE PRESIDENT. I have absolute confidence that the new Secretary of HEW, Pat Harris, has the same motivations and the same commitment to health in all its aspects, and also particularly mental health, as did Secretary Califano, who did a very good job.

I know my wife, as you've mentioned, has mental health and the problems of the elderly as her top priorities in her role as First Lady. And I can guarantee you that my wife, Pat Harris, the new Secretary of HEW, myself will be good partners with you in giving our people with mental health problems a better life in the future, including drug addiction as well. You can depend on that.

STRATEGIC ARMS LIMITATION

Q. Good afternoon, Mr. President. I'm Lloyd Bussage from Louisville, Kentucky. Concerning the ratification of SALT II, you as President have called upon the support of the American people to get this SALT II ratified. And yet other domestic leaders are telling the American people differently. For example, General Rowny, the leader of your negotiation team, has resigned—had resigned—and he felt that it was no good, that the Russians were getting the upper hand on negotiations. And just this morning Henry Kissinger stated that he could not support the treaty until American arms and Russian arms were made equal. He felt the Americans were not quite as strong as Russia, and he would not support it until they were brought up to equal. And this sort of puts the American people in a position of being in the middle and not knowing who to believe.

Mr. President, who should we believe, and why?

THE PRESIDENT. Believe me. Also believe the Secretary of State, and also believe the Secretary of Defense. And also believe all the Joint Chiefs of Staff. The top military officer in the Army, the Navy, the Marines, the Air Force, plus the Chairman of that group, had General Rowny as their subordinate. He was their representative in the negotiations. And they all have testified since he did that the SALT treaty, in balance, is good for our country. They agree basically with what Secretary Kissinger said.

Along with a SALT II treaty—which is good for our Nation—there is a requirement that we meet the defense needs of our Nation. And I'm absolutely determined that our defense needs will be met.

We had a long downward trend in defense expenditures before I became President. We have now reversed that trend, not only in NATO but in overall expenditures as well.

I think one of the problems is that the American people need to support a strong defense. In the last 2 years alone, for instance, when I've made my defense recommendations to the Congress, the Congress has reduced those recommendations by a total of $5 billion.

The Soviets are tough negotiators, but so are we. And there is no doubt in my mind that no matter what level of defense spending we have, whether it's exactly right, $5 billion too low, $5 billion too high, we need the SALT II agreement, the treaty ratified. But what I'm going to do as President is work with the United States Senate and the Congress to have the SALT II agreement, which will give us peace; cut down on the nuclear arms race; let us monitor what the Soviets are doing, control the proliferation of nuclear weapons throughout all the rest of the world; stop the Soviets' buildup, which has been faster than ours in the past—all that will come with SALT II. And in addition to that, have a strong defense to make sure our Nation is always as strong as or stronger than the Soviet Union no matter what happens.

That's what I promise you.

One more, one more question.

HAZARDOUS WASTE DISPOSAL

Q. Good afternoon, Mr. President. My name is Frank Smith, State representative from Shepherdsville, Kentucky. I'd like to request that on your return flight to Louisville, that you make a pass over the Valley of the Drums.

My question is, what are your feelings on a super fund for dealing with hazardous waste materials?

THE PRESIDENT. For dealing with atomic waste materials?

Q. Hazardous wastes.

THE PRESIDENT. Hazardous wastes.

We've had nuclear wastes, as you know, for 35 years, and we are now approaching the first recommendation to the Congress on how to deal with nuclear wastes. In addition, we have proposed to the Congress within the last few weeks, after a couple of years of preparation and hard work, a kind of an insurance program for dealing with chemical wastes and poisonous wastes of all kinds.

When a certain quantity of those chemical wastes are sold, there will be an insurance fund built up with a small premium. And then when there comes a time later on that those chemical wastes become a problem, the people who are threatened either with past uncontrolled dumping of wastes or with later deposits of wastes, they will be prevented from suffering, out of that insurance fund—with additional fill, the moving of the leaking barrels, and so forth.

I believe the Congress will act favorably on this, and I think your voice can be a very influential one and get them to do so.

So, in the control of nuclear wastes, which will be proposed to the Congress very shortly, and the chemical and poisonous wastes, which has already been presented to the Congress, I think, for the first time, our Government is moving to deal with the problem that is very serious and which you've pointed out so well.

Let me say this in closing to all of you: I'm very grateful for a chance to be with you. My listening to your questions, my receiving your comments, my shaking hands and having brief conversations with many of you, my coming to Kentucky, my visiting a coal-burning powerplant, my meeting with the coal industry people, my riding with your Congressmen, your Senators, your Governor, candidates for the future—all have given me a much clearer sense of what our Nation is, what its problems are, how to overcome those problems, what our opportunities are, and how we can take advantage of those opportunities.

The last thing I want to say is this: I'll repeat myself—we've got a lot of problems—so has everyone else on Earth—but we still live in the greatest nation in the world. And I want to make sure that all of you kind of take an inventory, count your blessings as an American: food, job opportunities, beauty, natural resources. We've got 24 percent of all the energy on Earth in the United States—the OPEC countries all put together have got less than 5 percent—freedom, the right of an individual American citizen to stand on one's own feet, to make one's own decision, to say one's own speech, to criticize when you think it is advisable; a free enterprise system that encourages innovation and initiative and competition in serving people better; a government based on democratic principles, where you can let your own voice be felt and heard and your own vote be influential, if you cast it. But the responsibility for the future cannot be resting on the shoulders of a Governor or a mayor or a U.S. Senator or a President. The responsibility for the future rests on your shoulders collectively, yours and mine alone, together.

And I believe that if we do count our blessings, analyze our problems, join ourselves together, have confidence in our Nation, fight the good fight together as Americans, there is no doubt in my mind that with God's blessing, we will prevail and we'll make our great Nation even greater in the future.

That's what I'd like to leave with you. God bless you all. He has certainly blessed us.

Thank you very much.

NOTE: The President spoke at 5:30 p.m. in the Bardstown High School gymnasium.

Following the town meeting, the President left Bardstown and went to English, Ind., to inspect the flood damage caused by severe storms on July 25. He then returned to Washington, D.C.

Conference on Security and Cooperation in Europe

Statement on the Fourth Anniversary of the Signing of the Final Act in Helsinki.
August 1, 1979

On this day in 1975, the leaders of 35 states met in Helsinki to sign the Final Act of the Conference on Security and Cooperation in Europe (CSCE). They pledged to build a future of peace and stability in Europe on the strong foundation of mutual understanding and respect for fundamental human rights.

In the years since Helsinki, we have witnessed conscientious efforts on the part of many signatory states to fulfill, fully and completely, their obligations under the Final Act. We have made progress in ensuring the freer flow of people and ideas. Flagrant abuses of human rights no longer go unnoticed and unchallenged. The Final Act provision which calls for notification of large military maneuvers has worked well. The spirit of Helsinki is alive. But there have also been important setbacks. For example, in the German Democratic Republic, harsh new laws designed to restrict contact with foreigners will take effect today, on the anniversary of Helsinki. In Czechoslovakia, members of the Charter 77 movement remain in prison, facing trial for their dedication to basic human freedoms. In the Soviet Union, organizations established to monitor compliance with the Helsinki agreement have been harassed and their members jailed. Acts like these are totally inconsistent with pledges made at Helsinki.

On the anniversary of the Helsinki accords, I rededicate this administration and this Nation to strive tirelessly for full implementation of the Final Act. We will continue to review our own record in preparation for the meeting of CSCE states at Madrid in 1980. And we call upon other signatory states to work with us so that we may mutually fulfill the obligations undertaken at Helsinki to peace, security, and human rights.

National Commission on Air Quality

Appointment of Leonard A. Schine as a Member. August 2, 1979

The President today announced the appointment of Leonard A. Schine, of Westport, Conn., as a member of the National Commission on Air Quality.

Schine, 62, is an attorney who has represented both industry and environmental groups. He is a trustee of the Natural Science for Youth Foundation.

Council on Environmental Quality

Designation of Gustave Speth as Chairman. August 2, 1979

The President today announced that he has designated Gustave Speth, of Washington, D.C., to be Chairman of the Council on Environmental Quality. He replaces Charles Warren, who has resigned.

Speth has been a member of CEQ since March 1977 and has served as Acting Chairman since June 30 of this year.

Among his principal responsibilities at the Council are energy policy, water resources policy and wetlands protection, toxic chemicals and pollution control, and economics and regulatory issues. He has served as Chairman of the admin-

istration's Toxic Substances Strategy Committee and has been a member of the interagency groups which developed the administration's policies on solar energy, nuclear waste management, and water resources.

Before his appointment to CEQ, Speth was with the Natural Resources Defense Council, a national environmental organization which he helped found in 1970.

He was born in Orangeburg, S.C., on March 4, 1942. He received a B.A. from Yale University in 1964 and attended Balliol College, Oxford, England, on a Rhodes Scholarship, where he received an advanced degree in economics. In 1969 he received an LL.B. from Yale Law School.

In 1969 and 1970, Speth was a law clerk to Justice Hugo L. Black of the U.S. Supreme Court. He has served on a number of committees of the District of Columbia Bar Association and the D.C. Bar and was a trustee of the Institute of Ecology from 1972 to 1974.

Environmental Priorities and Programs

Message to the Congress. August 2, 1979

To the Congress of the United States:

Four months after I took office, I presented to the Congress a comprehensive Message on the Environment, a charter for the first years of my Administration. Building on the record of the Congress in the 1970's, I sought both to protect our national heritage and to meet the competing demands on our natural resources.

Certain basic ideas remain the foundation of American environmental policy. Our great natural heritage should be protected for the use and enjoyment of all citizens. The bounty of nature—our farmlands and forests, our water, wildlife and fisheries, our renewable energy sources—are the basis of our present and future material well-being. They must be carefully managed and conserved. The quality of our environment must be nurtured by wise decisions and protected from hasty or unplanned actions. Clean air and water remain essential goals, and we intend to achieve them in the most efficient and effective ways possible. And we have a serious responsibility to help protect the long-term health of the global environment we share with all humanity.

I am proud of the achievements of this period. The program I offer today emphasizes continuity, but it also reflects a keener awareness of certain serious emerging problems—such as disposition of the toxic wastes our highly technological society produces.

ACCOMPLISHMENTS SINCE 1977

We have made great strides together since I took office. With my strong support, the Congress enacted and I signed into law:

- the 1977 Amendments to our two fundamental laws for cleaning up pollution, the Clean Air and Clean Water Acts, including strict but enforceable standards and a strong wetlands protection program;
- the 1977 Surface Mining Reclamation Act, which established the first federal environmental standards for coal mining, and under which regulations were developed with strong public involvement;
- the 1977 Federal Mine Safety and Health Act, which established the Mine Safety and Health Administration in the Department of Labor to promulgate and enforce health and safety standards in all mines;
- the 1977 Nuclear Non-Proliferation Act, which sets conditions on U.S. nuclear exports to deter the spread of nuclear weapons, and offers other countries incentives to cooperate with our safeguards against proliferation;
- indefinite deferral of other activities which might lead to weapons proliferation, particularly nuclear fuel reprocessing and commercialization of the breeder reactor;
- the 1978 National Energy Act, with specific policies and programs emphasizing energy conservation;
- the 1978 Federal Environmental Pesticide Control Act, which provided for generic registration and control of pesticides;
- reauthorization, in 1978, of the Endangered Species Act, including new procedures for resolving conflicts under the Act;
- enactment of the National Parks and Recreation Act of 1978 and other legislation to preserve nationally significant areas, adding 45 million acres to the National Park System, 13 new Wild and Scenic Rivers and National Trails, and protecting more than 4.5 million additional acres of wilderness.

In addition, I issued Executive Orders in 1977 and 1978 directing federal agencies to improve their implementation of the National Environmental Policy Act under new regulations, which were issued in 1978; examine the environmental effects of federal actions abroad; preserve and restore natural values of wetlands and floodplains; protect our public lands from damage caused by off-road vehicles; and analyze the impacts of new federal policies on urban areas. These directives are being implemented.

ENVIRONMENTAL PROGRAM

With these accomplishments behind us, we can turn our attention to new issues and to other key issues that are still unresolved.

In the decade ahead, we will face difficult decisions as we confront the necessity of reducing dangerous dependence on foreign oil. The leaders of the major industrial democracies met in Tokyo last month to chart a course that would help cut the use of imported oil from uncertain foreign suppliers. Each nation committed itself to a specific reduction in imports, to be accomplished in a way appropriate to its particular needs and resources.

For the past two and one-half years, conservation and energy from the sun have been major thrusts of my energy program. Solar energy funding has been tripled during that period and the Congress in 1978 enacted the National Energy Act which will save 2.5 million barrels of imported oil per day. Much of these savings will be accomplished with conservation initiatives. In addition, another 1.5 million barrels of imported oil will be saved as a result of my April energy message and June solar energy package.

To build on these major savings, I have proposed an expanded effort to put this nation on a sound energy footing, with clear goals for the next decade. That effort is based on a bold program to increase domestic energy production and on additional energy conservation initiatives. Overall, this program will reduce our dependence on foreign oil by 4.5 million barrels per day by 1990.

Some of the measures I have proposed will simultaneously serve the goals of reducing oil imports and enhancing our environment. I proposed establishing a major new residential and commercial conservation program designed to save at least 500,000 barrels of oil a day by 1990. I further proposed a total of $16.5 billion over the coming decade for improvements in the nation's public transportation system and in transportation fuel efficiency. A major solar energy program will help us to meet our goal of 20 percent solar energy by the year 2000.

We must also embark on a major energy production effort through a new Energy Security Corporation that will have broad responsibility for developing 2.5 million barrels a day of replacement fuels by 1990. That Corporation will be specifically authorized to develop not only synthetic fuels but also sources of energy which could have significant environmental benefits, such as natural gas and biomass. I do not pretend that all new replacement sources of energy will be environmentally innocuous. Some of the new technologies we will need to develop pose environmental risks, not all of which are yet fully understood. I will work to ensure that environmental protections are built into the process of developing these technologies, and that when tradeoffs must be made, they will be made fairly, equitably, and in the light of informed public scrutiny. We will examine not only the impact of new energy technologies on land and water and the effects of toxic chemicals, but also the longer term implications of increasing carbon dioxide concentration in the atmosphere.

I am pledged to be sensitive both to energy needs and to environmental considerations. There is no excuse for unnecessary red tape, which has plagued construction of some needed energy projects. I have proposed the creation of an Energy Mobilization Board to accelerate decision-making on critical energy facilities. This will cut out excessive delay, but I will not allow it to undermine protection of our nation's environment. I intend, for instance, to make the environmental impact statement process fit the decision schedule set by the Energy Mobilization Board so that waivers of these statements will be rare. Only in exceptional cases will alternative procedures be necessary for the orderly completion of a critical energy facility. With the exception of new requirements imposed when construction of a critical facility is underway, the Board could not waive substantive environmental standards. The President will retain the right to override decisions of the Board on any waiver issue, and Board waiver decisions would be subject to judicial review.

Solving the nation's energy problem is essential to our economy and our security. We will not lose sight of our other goals but we must not fail in ending the energy crisis. This Administration's basic commitment to clean air, clean water and the overall protection of the environment remains strong.

ALASKA LANDS

The highest environmental priority of my Administration is the passage of adequate legislation designating National Parks, Wildlife Refuges, Wilderness Areas, National Forests, and Wild and Scenic Rivers in Alaska.

To protect these magnificent Alaskan lands, I took several actions after the 95th Congress failed to provide protection against exploitation of certain areas in Alaska. By executive action, I designated 17 areas as National Monuments, covering 56 million acres. Additional areas were set aside by the Secretaries of Interior and Agriculture. These areas should be promptly and permanently protected by legislation.

The legislation I support not only protects Alaska's natural and cultural heritage but also accommodates the need for balanced development of Alaska's natural resources. Under the Alaska Statehood Act and Native Claims Settlement Act, federal land comprising an area nearly as large as Texas will soon be in state, native and private ownership. My proposals leave most of Alaska's mineral and timber wealth available for development, both on federal and nonfederal lands. In particular, all of the off-shore and 95 percent of the on-shore areas in Alaska with favorable potential for oil and gas would be open to exploration and development.

The only area with significant potential for oil and gas reserves that would be foreclosed from exploration and development is the Arctic Wildlife Refuge, the calving grounds of the largest remaining caribou herd in the world and an important part of the herd's migratory route. Because of our responsibility to protect this extraordinary remnant of our continent's original wildlife, and because oil and gas are plentifully available elsewhere in Alaska, I firmly believe that the Arctic Wildlife Refuge deserves the full protection the House bill would provide.

There are other Alaskan areas where disagreements and conflicts exist over proper management. The Administration's proposals strike a balance that offers future generations of all Americans—especially Alaskans—broad opportunities for prosperity and enjoyment without the mistakes in land management we have seen elsewhere in the country.

I applaud the recent passage by the House of Representatives, by a margin of 300 votes, of a strong and fair bill which will protect Alaska's wildlife and wild areas, while providing for America's future economic needs. I urge the Senate to act with equal foresight this session.

HAZARDOUS WASTES

In August 1978, I declared Love Canal in Niagara Falls, New York, a national disaster, thus authorizing the use of federal disaster relief aid. The tragedy of Love Canal exemplifies the legacy of past improper hazardous waste disposal.

Last month I submitted to Congress a legislative proposal designed to prevent future disasters like the one at Love Canal. My proposed legislation—the Oil, Hazardous Substances and Hazardous Waste Response, Liability and Compensation Act—will provide the first comprehensive program to address releases of oil and hazardous substances from spills and from inactive and abandoned sites into navigable waters, ground waters, land and air. The legislation builds on present authority and fills gaps where present authority is inadequate to protect the human environment.

We do not yet know all of the problems associated with the disposal of hazardous wastes, but we must take further steps immediately. A report done for the Environmental Protection Agency estimates that there are 33,000–50,000 dumpsites which may contain some hazardous wastes. Of these, EPA estimates that 1,200 to 2,000 may present potentially significant problems, and 500 to 800 of them may have to be abandoned. Other accounts of improper disposal describe shallow burial in steel drums which leak after years in the ground, dumping in open lagoons, and clandestine dumping in sewers and along our highways. These abuses have caused serious damage to human health and economic welfare, pollution of ground and drinking water, and degradation of residential and recreation areas. The cost of cleaning up these sites runs into the billions of dollars. But the costs of ignoring the problem would be far higher.

Timely action by the Congress on my program will enable the Federal government, in cooperation with State and local governments and industry, to:

- identify abandoned hazardous dump sites across the nation;
- establish a uniform system of reporting spills and releases;
- provide emergency government response and containment to clean up and mitigate pollution without delay in cases where those responsible do not respond adequately or cannot be quickly identified;
- provide vigorous investigation of releases of oil, hazardous substances or hazardous waste from spills or abandoned and inactive sites;
- provide stronger authority to compel the responsible parties to clean up dangerous sites wherever possible;
- provide compensation for damages to property and for some other economic losses resulting from spills; and
- provide financing for these actions through a national fund of appropriations and a fee on the oil and chemical industries, and State cost-sharing over certain limits.

SOLAR ENERY

My Solar Energy Message, submitted to the Congress on June 20, 1979, calls for a national commitment to the use of solar energy. That message and the program it lays out came from a 13-month effort by my Administration and the public, begun on Sun Day—May 3, 1978.

Solar energy is renewable and secure. It is clean and safe. In the long run, solar and other renewable sources of energy provide a hedge against inflation. Unlike the costs of depletable resources, which rise at increasing rates as reserves are consumed, the cost of energy from the sun will go *down* as we develop better and cheaper ways of applying it to everyday needs. For everyone in our society—especially our low-income or fixed-income families—solar energy will provide an important way to avoid rising fuel costs in the future. No foreign cartel can embargo the sun or set the price of the energy we harness from it.

I have set a national goal of achieving 20 percent of the Nation's energy from the sun and other renewable resources by the year 2000. To do this we must commit ourselves to several major new initiatives which will hasten the introduction of solar technologies. I am proposing a variety of solar programs to be funded from my proposed Energy Security Trust Fund, including a Solar Bank to help finance solar installations in homes and commercial buildings; tax credits for new buildings that use solar energy and for using the sun's heat for industrial and agricultural processes; and stronger efforts to remove institutional, financial, and information barriers that currently inhibit the use of solar energy by citizens. These proposals are in addition to the expanded research, development and demonstration program I included in my budget for fiscal year 1980.

NUCLEAR   WASTE   MANAGEMENT   AND
SAFETY

I will soon announce a national nuclear waste management policy that will be designed to deal effectively with nuclear wastes from all sources, including commercial, defense, medical, and research activities. This nuclear waste management policy will be based pri-

marily on recommendations presented to me by the Interagency Review Group on Nuclear Waste Management. Some of the important findings of that Report include the following:

• Existing and future nuclear waste from military and civilian activities, including discarded spent fuel from the once-through nuclear fuel cycle, should be isolated from the biosphere so that it does not pose a significant threat to public health and safety.

• The responsibility for establishing a waste program should not be deferred to future generations.

• A broader research and development program for waste disposal, particularly geologic isolation, should begin promptly.

• Public participation should be developed and strengthened for all aspects of nuclear waste management programs.

I also look forward to receiving the recommendations on reactor safety from the Kemeny Commission in the aftermath of the Three Mile Island accident so that we can assure that nuclear reactors are as safe as the public expects them to be.

WATER RESOURCES POLICY

I remain firmly committed to the water resources policy reforms I announced in my Message to Congress one year ago. The revised criteria used by the Administration in reviewing proposed water projects have already shown their worth. They are producing environmental benefits and reducing wasteful government spending. In 1979, for the first time in four years, the Executive branch proposed funding new water projects, using the more systematic and objective evaluation procedures I have instituted. With the help of Congress and State and local governments, the Administration has prepared legislation to make further reforms in water resources management, including cost-sharing and assistance to states for comprehensive water resources planning. I look forward to cooperation with the 96th Congress in this area.

NATIONAL HERITAGE POLICY ACT

I strongly support the establishment of a comprehensive Federal program to identify and protect significant natural areas and historic places. I will soon propose a National Heritage Policy Act which would help Federal agencies, State and local governments, Indian tribes and citizens identify potential heritage areas; establish a new National Register of Natural Areas to supplement the existing National Register of Historic Places; and protect areas listed on either Register, or eligible for listing, from adverse federal actions. This important legislation would support the Heritage Conservation program already established by the Secretary of the Interior in 1977.

SAVING THE WHALES

With U.S. leadership, the nations of the world are making encouraging progress toward protecting the great whales. At the July 1979 meeting of the International Whaling Commission (IWC), proposals by the United States and other countries for a moratorium on commercial whaling led to dramatic improvements. By the necessary three-fourths majority, IWC members voted to:

- End whaling from factory ships on the high seas (except for hunting of the relatively numerous minkes) and allow whaling only from coastal stations;
- Reduce killing of the commercially valuable but jeopardized sperm whales by more than three-quarters,

with world quotas down from 9360 sperm whales to 2203;
- Establish a whale sanctuary in most of the Indian Ocean where no hunting of any of the great whales will be allowed for 10 years.

I am wholeheartedly committed to strong action to guarantee the survival of the great whales. The progress made in this year's IWC meeting shows that many other nations share the American commitment. I will continue to press for better scientific understanding of these magnificent and highly intelligent creatures and will maintain the effort to halt commercial whaling.

IMPLEMENTATION OF 1978 NATIONAL PARKS AND RECREATION ACT

Following passage of the National Parks and Recreation Act of 1978, the Administration has sought to speed the acquisition of new park land before it is spoiled or priced out of reach. We shall continue to do that.

Among the most significant and imaginative actions included in the 1978 legislation is the program to establish a million-acre Pinelands National Reserve in New Jersey. The Department of the Interior will support local and State efforts to protect the Pinelands and its unique scenic and natural resources while maintaining private ownership ond a sound local tax base. The Administration strongly supports this new Federal, State and local partnership in the Pinelands, and will work hard to see that federal agencies cooperate with State and local governments to ensure its success.

POLLUTION CONTROL

Making the Clean Air and Clean Water Acts work is an important commitment of my Administration. We will continue the progress we have made in the past two years in promulgating fair standards and regulations, and we will continue to encourage new approaches to control of pollution, such as alternative and innovative waste water treatment projects. The Environmental Protection Agency has taken a number of steps in the right direction. For example, the "bubble concept," "offset" policy, and permit consolidation are intended to simplify pollution controls.

I will seek the reauthorization of the Safe Drinking Water Act, which expires next year. This law protects our citizens from newly-discovered toxic pollutants within drinking water, as well as imposing standards for conventional contaminants. For toxic substances which may enter the environment in a multitude of ways, my Administration is committed to the reauthorization and vigorous enforcement of the comprehensive Toxic Substances Control Act.

OIL POLLUTION OF THE OCEANS

The recent collision in the Caribbean of two supertanker behemoths, each carrying more than 1.4 million barrels of oil, underscores the importance of effective national and international programs to reduce oil spills. At the outset of my Presidency, I proposed a comprehensive program to reduce the threat of oil pollution from tankers in United States waters, and to win international agreement to higher standards of tanker safety and pollution prevention.

Responding to the U.S. initiative, maritime nations of the world agreed in 1978 to tighten inspection requirements and significantly raise world standards for tanker construction and equipment. The Department of Transportation is completing new rules, based on the international agreement, to require improved

features on both U.S. ships and foreign tankers entering our ports, including: segregated ballast, protective location of ballast space, crude oil washing, inert gas systems, and improved emergency steering systems. Dual radars and other aids to navigation are already required.

In addition, for the past two and one-half years, the Coast Guard has boarded and examined at least once a year every foreign-flag tanker entering our ports, recorded any deficiencies, and required repairs if necessary.

The Secretary of Transportation will promptly add to this program requirements for:

- improved construction of tank barges;
- safe conduct of lightering (ship to ship transfer of oil) ;
- improved U.S. standards for tanker crews and pilots; and
- pollution prevention features for older, smaller tankers not covered by the international standards.

Requirements for collision avoidance aids will also be added; international agreement is near on standards for these important tanker safety devices.

The United States will continue to urge other nations to put into effect promptly the requirements of the 1978 international agreements on tanker safety and pollution prevention. I also urge the prompt adoption by all nations of the new international standards for training and certification of seafarers, agreed upon in 1978.

The proposed Oil, Hazardous Substances and Hazardous Waste Response, Liability and Compensation Act, submitted to the Congress by the Administration, provides for swift cleanup of oil spills, strict liability of spillers, and compensation for victims of oil spill damage.

I expect the Coast Guard to report to me promptly on the results of its study of devices to improve tanker maneuverability and stopping. In addition, the Coast Guard is undertaking a study of past accidents to evaluate further the usefulness of double bottoms and side protection in reducing oil spills. The Department of Transportation will continue to evaluate promising ideas to preserve the oceans and its resources from pollution by oil.

REGULATORY REFORM

Improving government regulations is important to my effort to make government more efficient and private-sector responses more cost-effective. Environmental protection can and should benefit. I intend to improve the regulatory process in a way that does not weaken our commitment to environmental quality.

If there are better methods to achieve our environmental goals, we should use them. Agencies should seek and adopt innovative alternatives to government regulations which reduce burdens on private citizens or businesses. The Environmental Protection Agency has become a leader among federal agencies in examining new approaches and has made several moves to streamline its regulatory process. In addition to the permit consolidation, bubble concept, and offset policy mentioned above, EPA is doing an effective job of implementing my Executive order on regulatory reform and published the first agenda of regulations issued by any federal agency. A regulatory calendar is now prepared and published on a government-wide basis by the Regulatory Council I recently established.

Since 1977 the Occupational Health and Safety Administration has gotten rid of hundreds of unnecessary standards, and has reorganized its program to devote 95 percent of its resources to the most serious workplace hazards. In addition, regulatory agencies have begun to work together to coordinate their activities and use their resources more efficiently. I expect such progress to continue and I intend that it reinforce—not diminish—our environmental improvement efforts.

PENDING LEGISLATION AND REAUTHORIZATIONS

I have proposed and will continue to support reauthorization of important environmental statutes, including the Endangered Species Act, the Toxic Substances Control Act, the Safe Drinking Water Act, and the Resource Conservation and Recovery Act. I also continue to support a nongame wildlife program, and a wide range of wilderness proposals.

The Environmental Program I am outlining today expands upon the efforts we have already begun with a series of new initiatives in land and resource management, agricultural conservation, urban quality, and improving the global environment.

NEW INITIATIVES

I. LAND AND RESOURCE MANAGEMENT

America's land and natural resources have nourished our civilization. Because our original heritage was so abundant, we sometimes take these resources for granted. We can no longer do so. Our land and natural resources do have limits, and our demands upon them are growing at increasing rates. Renewable resources—farmlands, fisheries, and forests—can be depleted through overuse and misuse. We must build into our decisions the understanding that unwise actions affecting our lands and resources are difficult and costly, if not impossible, to correct.

Conservation of resources takes care and planning, and requires a partnership between various levels of government, and public and private actions. The following initiatives for protection and wise management of our coastal resources, public lands, wildlife and rivers and trails reflect this understanding.

National Coastal Protection

America's coast lines are extraordinarily varied, productive and beautiful. Congress recognized the need for special protection in the Coastal Zone Management Act of 1972, which established a voluntary Federal-State partnership for the conservation and management of coastal resources. Under this partnership, many states have already made notable progress. They have passed comprehensive coastal management laws; adopted new measures to protect wetlands, barrier islands, mineral resources, historic sites and other important coastal resources; worked out better management of hazardous areas; and streamlined Federal, State and local actions affecting the coast. By the end of 1979, 75 percent of the U.S. shoreline will be covered by Federally-approved state coastal zone management programs.

The coastal zone is subject to unusual pressures, both from natural causes and human activities. The land and water resources which support the environments and economies of coastal communities are in danger of depletion. The opportunity for our citizens to enjoy beaches, bays, and marshes is often threatened. I support efforts to improve our understanding of these coastal issues, and I heartily endorse the designation by conservation organizations of the year 1980 as the "Year of the Coast."

To help achieve the balanced, comprehensive and wise management intended by the Coastal Zone Management Act, I am announcing three initiatives to continue and improve our resource protection policy.

First, I will submit to Congress legislation to reauthorize Federal assistance to state coastal zone management programs under the Coastal Zone Management Act. Under this extension, each state would be guaranteed a total of five years of federal assistance at current levels after a state management program is approved and before federal support is gradually phased down. This will help ensure that recently developed state and local coastal zone management efforts become fully established and accepted functions of government.

Second, I will recommend enactment of new amendments to the Coastal Zone Management Act that will establish a national coastal protection policy. Working through the states, the goals of this policy will be:

- to protect significant natural resources such as wetlands, estuaries, beaches, dunes, barrier islands, coral reefs, and fish and wildlife;
- to manage coastal development to minimize loss of life and property from floods, erosion, saltwater intrusion and subsidence;
- to provide predictable siting processes for major defense, energy, recreation and transportation facilities;
- to increase public access to the coast for recreation purposes;
- to preserve and restore historic, cultural and aesthetic coastal resources; and
- to coordinate and simplify government decisionmaking to ensure proper and expedited management of the coastal zone.

Third, I am directing the Secretary of Commerce to conduct a systematic review of federal programs that significantly affect coastal resources. This review, to be conducted by the National Oceanic and Atmospheric Administration, will provide the basis for specific recommendations to improve federal actions affecting the coastal zone and to develop any additional legislation needed to achieve our national coastal management goals.

Public Land Resources

Among the many natural resource issues facing the Nation, few are more important than the management, protection and use of the 417 million acres of public lands owned by all Americans and administered by the Secretary of the Interior through the Bureau of Land Management.

The public lands include vast tracts of the arid rangelands of the West which were once lands that no one wanted. Now, some of these lands are highly valued for their energy and other valuable resources, and they have come to be appreciated for their scenic and natural values. My Administration is committed to purposeful management of the public lands and resources administered by the Bureau of Land Management in an environmentally sound and cost-effective manner.

Therefore, I am directing the Secretary of the Interior to manage the public lands administered by BLM in accordance with these principles:

• The Federal Government will be a good steward of the land, seeking to find the best balance of uses to assure that resources are available to meet the Nation's needs and that environmental values are carefully protected.

• The Federal Government will be a good neighbor, providing full opportunities for those affected by our management decisions to be involved in making them, with a special concern for the people and institutions of the Western States that are most directly affected.

• The Federal Government will make cost-effective investments in protecting and enhancing these lands within the constraints of fiscal responsibility.

• The Federal Government will seek to resolve conflicts among competing uses in a spirit of cooperation and trust, and will make—not avoid—tough decisions on the allocation of the valued resources of public lands.

We have already made significant progress in bringing these lands under effective management. A concerted federal effort is now underway to reverse the declining productivity of the 174 million acres of rangeland ecosystems managed by the Bureau of Land Management for livestock, wildlife, soil and moisture conservation, and other beneficial purposes. We have developed a comprehensive on-the-ground planning process for each unit of BLM-managed land which involves the public and assesses the environmental impacts of alternative actions. On June 4, 1979, the Secretary of the Interior announced our new federal coal management program, which establishes a balanced and efficient process for determining coal leasing and management on federal lands.

Much more remains to be done. I am therefore directing that the following actions be taken:

• The Secretary of the Interior will establish a comprehensive "program development process" for managing all the lands under BLM stewardship, which will, for the first time, set long range goals to ensure balanced protection and use of the resources and develop and analyze alternative programs and investment strategies to meet the goals. Each alternative program will be designed to achieve environmentally sound, fiscally responsible, and economically efficient investment, development, protection, and resource use. This new program planning process will supplement BLM's current unit-by-unit planning. It will invite State and local governments and interested citizens to participate in making better informed choices among the alternative programs.

• The Secretary will give special attention to protecting areas of BLM-administered lands with nationally significant wildlife, natural, scientific, cultural, or scenic resources. An example is the Birds of Prey area, located along the Snake River in the Idaho desert, that has North America's richest concentration of birds of prey, including dense nesting populations of falcons, eagles, and other raptors.

• Finally, I am directing the Secretary of the Interior and the Secretary of Agriculture to work together to coordinate their Departments' natural resource policies and programs, particularly those of the Bureau of Land Management and the Forest Service. I am requesting the two Secretaries to develop within six months a detailed statement of coordination objectives and a process and timetable for achieving them.

Wildlife Law Enforcement

A massive illegal trade in wild animals, wild animal parts and products, and wild plants has been uncovered in the last year through investigations by the Department of Justice, the Fish and Wildlife Service, the Customs Service and the Departments of Agriculture and Commerce.

This illegal trade in wildlife and plants has several very serious consequences. It can introduce exotic diseases, threatening agriculture. It creates a market for thousands of species of wildlife and plants taken in violation of the laws of foreign nations, ultimately threatening the survival of these species. It is a danger to the survival of hundreds of species listed on the Convention on International Trade in Endangered Species, to which the U.S. is a signatory nation.

I am therefore submitting to Congress a bill to overcome obstacles inhibiting enforcement efforts.

In addition, I am directing the Departments of Agriculture, Commerce, Interior, Justice, and Treasury to investigate this trade aggressively and to prosecute violators of the law. I am directing the Department of the Interior to coordinate this effort, through an interagency Wildlife Law Enforcement Coordinating Committee which will review enforcement experiences, priorities and problems. I am also directing the Department of Agriculture to chair a task force to investigate the illegal trade in plants and to prosecute where appropriate.

I am further directing that the following specific steps be taken: The Treasury and Commerce Departments will raise the priority of wildlife enforcement cases; the Agriculture Department will place greater emphasis on coordinating its wildlife enforcement program with its disease quarantine program, and will begin hiring special agents to investigate the illegal plant trade; and the Department of Justice will establish a Wildlife Section which will be staffed principally by attorneys trained as wildlife law enforcement specialists.

Wild and Scenic Rivers

Our Nation's river corridors are a rich concentration of natural ecosystems, scenic beauty, and historic and recreational values. Since my Environmental Message of May 1977, eight rivers totalling 695 miles have been added to the National Wild and Scenic Rivers System, and nine new rivers have been recommended for study. As part of the Administration's Alaska proposals, 33 additional rivers have been proposed for National Wild and Scenic Rivers designation.

Development along the banks of our rivers continues to outpace our ability to protect those rivers that might qualify for designation. This problem is particularly acute near urban areas, where there are greater demands for recreational opportunities which can partly be met by river protection.

We need to speed up the process for studying Wild and Scenic Rivers for designation and to consider the protection of rivers or parts of rivers which can protect important natural ecosystems. Moreover, the Federal government should set an example of sound management for state, local, and private landowners by taking an aggressive role in protecting possible Wild and Scenic Rivers which flow through our public lands. Accordingly, I am directing the following actions be taken:

- federal land management agencies shall assess whether rivers located on their lands and identified in the National Inventory prepared by the Heritage Conservation and Recreation Service are suitable for inclusion in the Wild and Scenic Rivers System; if so, these agencies shall take prompt action to protect the rivers—either by preparing recommendations for their designation or by taking immediate action to protect them;
- all federal agencies shall avoid or mitigate adverse effects on rivers identified in the National Inventory; and
- the Secretary of Agriculture and the Secretary of the Interior shall jointly revise their Guidelines for evaluating wild, scenic, and recreational

rivers to ensure consideration of river ecosystems and to shorten the time currently used to study rivers for designation.

In addition to the new policy initiatives, I am reaffirming my support for four river segments proposed in my last Environmental Message and recommending four new river segments which will add a total of 930 miles to the Wild and Scenic Rivers System:

- Gunnison River, Colorado (new)
- Encampment River, Colorado (new)
- Priest River, Idaho (new)
- Illinois River, Oregon (new)
- Bruneau River, Idaho (1977 Message)
- Dolores River, Colorado (1977 Message)
- Upper Mississippi River, Minnesota (1977 Message)
- Salmon River, Idaho (1977 Message)

I am also directing the Secretary of the Interior to develop, through the National Park Service and with full public participation, a conceptual master plan for the Upper Mississippi River in Minnesota. I expect this planning process to determine the specific requirements for protecting the river corridor and providing public access, campgrounds and other recreational facilities on the lands now in private ownership. The conceptual master plan for this important national resource will be developed in cooperation with the Minnesota Department of Natural Resources, affected Indian tribes, and the public. It will be completed by April 1980.

In my last Environmental Message, I proposed 20 river segments for study as potential additions to the National Wild and Scenic Rivers System. Several of those rivers have already been designated. Except for rivers where subsequent development has affected the river's qualifications for designation, I will continue to seek study authorizations for these rivers. In addition, I am submitting legislation to add the North Umpqua River in Oregon to the list of those rivers to be studied.

I am also forwarding to Congress reports on several rivers which, after thorough study, were found to qualify for inclusion in the National System. However, because of the interest of the states or local governments in protecting their natural values, the reports recommend that the rivers be protected and managed by state and/or local action. I am greatly encouraged by the efforts which all levels of government are taking to protect valued natural resources. I am particularly pleased to note that in the case of the Housatonic and Shepaug Rivers in Connecticut, local governmental agencies are taking the lead in developing management plans to protect these significant river resources. I am transmitting reports on:

• Pine Creek, Pennsylvania
• Buffalo River, Tennessee
• Youghiogheny River, Pennsylvania-Maryland
• Shepaug River, Connecticut
• Kettle River, Minnesota
• Lower Wisconsin River, Wisconsin
• Housatonic River, Connecticut
• Illinois River, Oklahoma

National Trails

More than 61 million of the Nation's people go nature walking and more than 28 million people hike or backpack at least five times a year. To meet the growing needs of these and other trail users, Congress enacted the 1968 National Trails System Act and directed that a National Trails System be established. Since the establishment of the National

Trails System, 257 National Recreation Trails have been designated, including 21 trails for those using wheelchairs and 13 trails designed for the use of blind people, with interpretive signs in braille.

The National Trails System is still in its fledgling stage and should grow to meet widespread public interest. National trails near urban areas can serve an energy-conscious nation by providing recreation close to home for the majority of our citizens and, in some cases, by providing commuter routes for bicyclists, walkers, and joggers.

To meet these objectives, under my direction, the U.S. Forest Service will establish 145 additional National Recreation Trails by January 1980, achieving a goal of two National Recreation Trails in each National Forest System unit. I am directing each Federal land management agency to follow the example set by the Forest Service and by January 1980 announce a goal for the number of National Recreation Trails each agency will establish during 1980 on the public lands administered by the agency. I am also directing that, by the end of 1980, a minimum of 75 new National Recreation Trails shall be designated on public land other than National Forests by the Federal land management agencies.

I am directing the Secretary of the Interior, through the Interagency Trails Council, to assist other Federal agencies in surveying existing trails on federal lands to determine which of those can be made part of our National Trails System and to initiate a grass-roots effort in every region of the country to assess our nationwide trails needs. In addition, I am directing the Secretary of the Interior, the Secretary of Agriculture, the Secretary of Defense and the Chairman of the Tennessee Valley Authority to encourage states, localities, Indian tribes, and private landholders to designate trails on their lands.

Finally, I will submit legislation to the Congress which will designate the 513-mile Natchez Trace National Trail through Tennessee, Alabama and Mississippi. I will resubmit legislation to establish the Potomac Heritage Trail through Pennsylvania, Maryland, West Virginia, Virginia and Washington, D.C. And I am reaffirming my support for the 3,200-mile North Country Trail, extending from the State of New York to North Dakota, which has already passed the House of Representatives.

I am also reaffirming the Administration's commitment to assuring the protection of the Appalachian Trail, one of America's best known and most popular recreation trails. The 2,000-mile Appalachian Trail winds through 14 states and is readily accessible to nearly half of the population of the U.S. It has been created by a volunteer movement without parallel in the history of outdoor recreation in America. In 1978 this Administration supported and I signed into law a bill to protect threatened portions of the right-of-way which are located on private lands. I expect this goal to be substantially achieved by September 30, 1981. This is a prompt but realistic timetable for the acquisition program.

II. AGRICULTURAL CONSERVATION

From our beginnings as a nation we have sustained ourselves and others on abundant yields from our farmlands. In this century, scientific and technological advances have increased our agricultural production to unsurpassed levels.

But in emphasizing ever-increasing production we have sometimes neglected to maintain the soil, water, and biological re-

sources upon which the long-term stability and productivity of our agriculture depends. These resources are being degraded in many areas of the country. Our farm and land management practices have led to excessive soil erosion, we have over-used chemical fertilizers and pesticides, and some of our most productive farmlands are being converted to nonagricultural uses. The agricultural conservation initiatives that I am announcing today address these issues.

Soil Conservation Incentives

Over the past half century we have invested more than $20 billion of federal funds in efforts to conserve soil. These funds have been used for cost sharing, technical assistance, resource management, loans, research, and education. Yet in that same half century wind and water erosion have removed half the fertile topsoil from nearly one-third of the Nation's potentially usable croplands. The cost of replacing just the plant nutrients lost to erosion has been estimated at $18 billion a year. Moreover, agricultural runoff adversely affects two-thirds of the Nation's streams.

Our soil protection programs have undoubtedly prevented even worse soil loss, but we must do better to maintain the long-term productivity of the soil.

The Department of Agriculture is now making an important appraisal of soil and water conservation policies under the Soil and Water Resources Conservation Act of 1977. The first Appraisal, Program and Policy reports required by the Resources Conservation Act (RCA) are due in January 1980. These documents will analyze conservation problems nation-wide, set conservation targets and propose ways to solve the problems. They will provide an essential first step in the wise management of agricultural lands, and will guide my Administration's overall soil and water conservation recommendations to the Congress. Reports will be updated every 5 years and I will receive annual reports of progress and program effectiveness.

I am directing the Secretary of Agriculture, in consultation with the Chairman of the Council on Environmental Quality, to build on the RCA process and to undertake a further detailed and systematic study of possible conservation incentives. The study will search for ways to modify or coordinate agricultural assistance programs already in existence in order to reduce soil erosion. Moreover, it will also look for conflicts or inconsistencies between farm income programs and soil conservation programs and will recommend measures to eliminate these conflicts where possible.

The results of this study will be submitted to me in January 1981. This report will provide me with specific administrative and legislative recommendations to reduce soil erosion and to improve soil stewardship in order to maintain the Nation's long-term agricultural productivity, building on the policy recommendations contained in the RCA 1980 program.

A second critical land issue for America's farmers and consumers is the availability of agricultural lands—particularly prime farmlands—and their conversion to other uses. In June, the Administration initiated an important new effort to address this issue. The Secretary of Agriculture and the Chairman of the Council on Environmental Quality are co-chairing an interagency study of factors affecting the availability of land for agricultural uses. The study will evaluate the economic, environmental, and social effects of the conversion or retention of agricultural lands and will make recommendations for consideration by federal, state, and local governments by January 1981.

Many members of Congress are particularly interested in these two critical issues affecting the stewardship of our nation's agricultural lands. I hope that the Administration and the Congress will work together to develop and implement appropriate actions, based on the results of these studies.

Integrated Pest Management

For all their benefits, chemical pesticides can cause unintended damage to human health and the environment. Many pests have developed resistance to chemical pesticides, escalating the cost of pest control by conventional methods. This resistence to pesticides has also decreased our ability to control some pests, which has reduced agricultural yields from what they would otherwise be.

Integrated pest management (IPM) has evolved in recent years as a comprehensive pest control strategy which has important health, economic, and environmental benefits. IPM uses a systems approach to reduce pest damage to tolerable levels through a variety of techniques, including natural predators and parasites, genetically resistant hosts, environmental modifications and, when necessary and appropriate, chemical pesticides. IPM strategies generally rely first upon biological defenses against pests before chemically altering the environment.

The Federal government—which spends more than $200 million a year on pest control research and implementation programs—should encourage the development and use of integrated pest management in agriculture, forestry, public health, and urban pest control. As a result of a governmentwide review initiated by my 1977 Environmental Message, I am now directing the appropriate federal agencies to modify as soon as possible their existing pest management research, control, education, and assistance programs and to support and adopt IPM strategies wherever practicable. I am also directing federal agencies to report on actions taken or underway to implement IPM programs, and to coordinate their efforts through an interagency group.

III. URBAN QUALITY

Our cities give us diversity and enjoyment, occupations and avocations, shopping and services, recreation and culture. By strengthening the health of our urban environment, we broaden the range of opportunities open to all of our citizens, as I emphasized in my National Urban Policy Message last year. The investments we make in maintaining and improving urban quality—particularly those involving federal taxpayer dollars—can be designed to meet environmental objectives, such as safe, convenient, well-planned public transportation, quieter communities, and assistance in mediating potential conflicts between healthy urban economies and environments. The initiatives I am proposing today will help to achieve these goals.

Transportation Policy

Our transportation systems can greatly affect the Nation's environment, for better or worse, especially in our cities. For many years, our energy and other resources were so plentiful that the Federal government encouraged the rapid expansion of a transportation system based on the private automobile without fully considering the profound effects on our resources, our urban environments, and our way of life. Although we have developed an extraordinary transportation system, we have missed opportunities in the past to improve transportation and at the same time to achieve these other national objectives.

The United States has built the most extensive and complex transportation system in the world. Federal transportation expenditures exceed $17 billion annually, including $12 billion in grants to state and local agencies. Transportation consumes approximately 53 percent of all petroleum used in the U.S. The energy and cost advantages of using this system more efficiently—for example, by greater use of carpools, vanpools and mass transit—are now obvious. Better design and use of transportation systems will also help to save and strengthen our cities and their amenities and to reduce air and noise pollution. Thus transportation decisions can help to conserve limited resources, and to further our energy, fiscal, and urban environmental goals.

Federal transportation decisions cannot escape difficult choices among competing objectives, but they must be guided by new transportation policies which I am establishing for my Administration. Urban transportation programs and projects should be reoriented to meet environmental, energy and urban revitalization goals. I am therefore directing the Department to take immediate actions to assure that:

- federal transportation funds are used to promote energy conservation, for example through special lanes for carpools, vanpools and transit vehicles;
- encouragement is given to using federal funds for public transportation projects;

- a careful review is made of any transportation proposals which would encourage urban sprawl (a major cause of high energy consumption) or which would tend to draw jobs away from urban centers;
- consideration is given to improving and rehabilitating existing facilities, or using non-construction methods—such as better traffic management—to improve transportation systems, as alternatives to constructing new facilities;
- major transportation projects are used to help improve the urban economy and to attract jobs to the urban cores; and
- firm actions are taken to mitigate adverse effects of transportation projects on the natural and urban environment and to carry out the environmental commitments that are made in planning and approving transportation projects.

We have done a great deal to make our transportation policies and actions more sensitive to our national environmental and energy goals. We can do a great deal more with cooperation of state and local governments as our partners in the national transportation system. The steps I have outlined will move us in that direction.

Economic Assistance Program

Most Americans benefit directly from the healthier and more agreeable environment that results from our air, water and other pollution control programs. Although economic data indicate that environmental programs are a strong positive factor in providing employment, there is continued concern about their possible adverse impact on individual firms, communities, or groups of workers.

The fact that there have not been a large number of such economic dislocations does not suggest that those that do occur are unimportant. Furthermore, in some instances they can be avoided, or at least significantly mitigated, by appropriate government action.

In 1977 I established an Economic Assistance Task Force, chaired by the Council on Environmental Quality, to investigate whether we needed to improve federal assistance for those cases when jobs are lost partly as a result of actions taken to reduce pollution, and to recommend initiatives we might take. The Task Force concluded that existing federal assistance programs should be adequate, but that we need to take practical steps to let people know about the programs and to make sure help is delivered swiftly when it is needed.

I am therefore directing the Administrator of the Environmental Protection Agency to create an Economic Assistance Program in his agency and to designate Economic Assistance Officers both in headquarters and in the field, who will help the public understand and use the programs, and to make sure that eligible people receive assistance promptly. I am also directing all federal agencies with programs in this area to publicize and coordinate closely their programs. A booklet describing and locating available federal assistance programs will be released soon by the Council on Environmental Quality and the Environmental Protection Agency.

Urban Noise Program

A certain level of urban noise is tolerable or even agreeable, reflecting the multitude of activities that make a city thrive. However, most of our cities suffer from too much noise. Excessive noise is a serious disturbance in city dwellers' lives, and degrades the urban environment.

Most noise abatement actions are taken by state and local governments, but there is an important role for the Federal government. I am initiating today a program to reduce urban noise by directing the Departments of Commerce, Defense, Energy, Housing and Urban Development, Transportation, and the Environmental Protection Agency and General Services Administration, in consultation with other federal agencies, to take a number of actions to improve existing noise abatement programs, including:

- programs to achieve soundproofing and weatherization of noise sensitive buildings, such as schools and hospitals;
- use of quiet-design features in transportation projects affecting urban areas;
- measures to encourage the location of housing developments away from major noise sources;
- purchase of quiet equipment and products—such as typewriters and lawnmowers which have been designed to reduce noise—and assistance to state and local agencies to do likewise; and
- support for neighborhood efforts to deal with noise problems.

IV. GLOBAL ENVIRONMENT

Efforts to improve the environment cannot be confined to our national boundaries. Ten years ago, at the dawn of the environmental decade, we landed on the moon. For the first time people could stand on the surface of another world and look at the whole earth. The sight of earthrise was awesome. It was also sobering. From that moment we could no longer avoid understanding that all life must share this one small planet and its limited resources. The interdependence of nations is plain, and so is the responsibility of each to avoid actions which harm other nations or the world's environment. I am announcing today two initiatives which address global environmental problems of the greatest importance.

World Forests

The world's forests and woodlands are disappearing at alarming rates. Some estimates suggest that world forests could decline by about 20 percent by 2000. More than 40 percent of the closed forests of South Asia, Southeast Asia, Pacific, and Latin America could be lost.

Nearly all the world's forest loss is occurring in or near the tropics. In these areas, environmental damage from deforestation can be severe—even irreversible—and the human costs extremely high. For example, denudation of Himalayan slopes has led to severe soil erosion, silting of rivers, loss of groundwater, and intensified, catastrophic flooding downstream. Many tropical forests, once cut, will not regrow because soils, rainfall, temperature, or terrain are too unfavorable; nor will the land support crops or pasture for more than a few years. Another serious possible consequence of tropical forest loss is accelerating extinction of species. Tropical forests provide habitat for literally millions of plant and animal species—a genetic reservoir unmatched anywhere else in the world. Equally serious is the possibility that forest loss may adversely alter the global climate through production of carbon dioxide. These changes and their effects are not well understood and are being studied by scientists, but the possibilities are disturbing and warrant caution.

The United States and other nations are just beginning to appreciate fully the scope and seriousness of the problem and to assess the effects of development projects on world forests. There is much more to be done. I am therefore directing all relevant federal agencies to place greater emphasis on world forest issues in their budget and program planning. An interagency task force established last fall and chaired by the State Department will report to me in November 1979 on specific goals, strategies, and programs that the United States should undertake. On the basis of these recommendations, I will direct federal agencies to carry out an integrated set of actions to help toward protection and wise management of world forests.

In the international arena, the Governing Council of the United Nations Environment Programme has just adopted a resolution—introduced by the United States—calling for a meeting of experts to develop proposals for an integrated international program for conservation and wise utilization of tropical forests, and to report to the next Governing Council meeting in April 1980. I am asking the Departments of State and Agriculture, the Council on Environmental Quality, and other federal agencies to give this program full support and assistance and to encourage and support high-level multinational conferences on forest problems in regions where forest losses are severe.

To help protect the earth's natural resource base, I issued an Executive Order earlier this year, which directs federal agencies to review carefully in advance the effects of many federal activities abroad. I am directing the Council on Environmental Quality and the Department of State to report to me within six months on the best ways to designate the globally important resources to which the order applies.

Acid Rain

Acid rain has caused serious environmental damage in many parts of the world including Scandinavia, Northern Europe, Japan, Canada and the Northeastern part of the United States. Over the past 25 years the acidity of rainfall has increased as much as fifty-fold in parts of the Eastern half of the United States. In the Adirondacks in New York, many mountain lakes have become devoid of fish partly because of increasing acidification. Adverse effects on crops and forests are suspected; steel and stone buildings and art works may suffer as well.

Acid rain is produced when rain removes sulfur dioxide and nitrogen dioxide from the air, forming sulfuric and nitric acid. Sulfur and nitrogen oxides are emitted in all forms of fossil fuel combustion. Power plants, smelters, steel mills, home furnaces, automobiles—all may contribute to acid rain.

To improve our understanding of acid rain, I am establishing a ten year comprehensive Federal Acid Rain Assessment Program to be planned and managed by a standing Acid Rain Coordination Committee. The assessment program will include applied and basic research on acid rain effects, trends monitoring, transport and fate of pollutants, and control measures. The Committee will establish links with industry to promote cooperative research wherever appropriate. The Committee will also play a role in future research cooperation with Canada, Mexico, and other nations and international organizations. The Committee will prepare a comprehensive 10-year plan for review by the end of the year. In its first full year of operation, the program will have $10 million in reprogrammed research funds available, double the current amount for acid rain research.

It is important to emphasize that such a long-time acid rain research program will not delay application of necessary pollution control measures to meet the mandate of the Clean Air Act. In addition, interim results from the acid rain research program will be made available to the public, to states, to industry and to the federal government agencies responsible for developing measures to reduce air pollution.

CONTINUED AND COOPERATIVE EFFORTS

The preservation of our environment has needed to become a special concern to our country at least since the ending of the Western frontier. A former President put it clearly:

"The conservation of our natural resources and their proper use constitute the fundamental problem which underlies almost every other problem of our National life. We must maintain for our civilization the adequate material basis without which that civilization cannot exist. We must show foresight, we must look ahead. The reward of foresight of this nation is great and easily foretold. But there must be the look ahead, there must be a realization of the fact that to waste, to destroy, our natural resources, to skin and exhaust the land instead of using it so as to increase its usefulness, will result in undermining in the days of our children the very prosperity which we ought by right to hand down to them amplified and developed."

That was President Theodore Roosevelt speaking in a State of the Union Message more than 70 years ago.

That message needs to be repeated and heard just as clearly today. Above all— it needs to be delivered.

My Administration will continue to lead in conserving our resources and reducing risks to the environment through sound and efficient management. But all our citizens must join the effort by contributing energies and ideas.

Only with your cooperation can we maintain our advance towards protecting our environment. Only together can we hope to secure our world for the life to come.

JIMMY CARTER

The White House,
    August 2, 1979.

National Coastal Protection

Memorandum From the President.
August 2, 1979

Memorandum for the Secretary of Commerce

In my Environmental Message of August 2, 1979, I recognized the special protection that we accord coastal resources such as wetlands and barrier islands through the federal/state partnership established by the Coastal Zone Management Act. It is important to develop effective management organizations for dealing with coastal zone issues so that responsible planning and sound decisions can be made on resource protection and development proposals. I also recognized the fact that our experience in implementing the Coastal Zone Management Act has revealed areas where improvements can be made in identified aspects of federal programs which at times conflict with those of the Coastal Zone Management Act. I stressed the need for a systematic review of all federal programs significantly affecting coastal resources to help assure consistency among federal efforts in achieving the objectives of the Coastal Zone Management Act.

Therefore, I am directing you to conduct a systematic review of all federal programs significantly affecting coastal resources and to evaluate and identify: (1) any conflicts in the policies and objectives of existing programs, particularly conflicts with CZMA goals; (2) whether these programs are being implemented in a consistent and coordinated fashion; and (3) if any program contributes to uneconomical or environmentally unsound development activities affecting critical natural systems. The federal agencies, coastal states, local governments, the private sector, scientists and citizen groups should be asked to participate in the review process.

The review shall be completed within one year, in order to provide the basis for specific recommendations to improve implementation of the Coastal Zone Management Act, to improve federal agency administration of programs and procedures affecting the coastal zone, and to develop any additional legislation to achieve our national coastal management goals.

Please give this assignment your immediate attention.

                                    JIMMY CARTER

Public Land Resources

*Memorandums From the President.
August 2, 1979*

Memorandum for the Secretary of the Interior

In my Environmental Message of August 2, 1979, I recognized the importance of the 417 million acres of public lands administered by the Bureau of Land Management for their energy and natural resources and their natural, scenic, and cultural values. I emphasized my Administration's commitment to purposeful management of these lands and resources in an environmentally sound and cost-effective manner. I am therefore directing you to manage the public lands administered by BLM in accordance with the following principles:

• The Federal Government will be a good steward of the land, seeking to find the best balance of uses to assure that resources are available to meet the Nation's needs and that environmental values are promptly and carefully protected.

• The Federal government will be a good neighbor, providing full opportunities for those affected by our management decisions to be involved in making them, with a special concern for the people and institutions of the Western States that are most directly affected.

• The Federal Government will make cost-effective investments in protecting and enhancing these lands within the constraints of fiscal responsibility.

• The Federal Government will seek to resolve conflicts among competing uses in a spirit of cooperation and trust, and will make—not avoid—tough decisions on the allocation of the valued resources of public lands.

Building on the progress we have made in the past two years, I am directing you to improve BLM's overall planning process by establishing a "program development process" for BLM which shall:

• present alternative programs for public investment on federal lands to achieve national objectives in an economically and environmentally sound manner;

- evaluate local, regional, and national demands and needs and assess and compare the value of public land goods and services with the public and private costs of providing such benefits;
- reflect evaluation and comment by the people of neighboring communities and other members of the public, and appropriate local, state, and federal officials;
- be accomplished by using ongoing assessment and planning programs and resources, to the extent possible, within the Bureau, the U.S. Forest Service and other agencies and departments; and
- be coordinated with plans and programs called for by the Resources Planning Act and developed by the Forest Service and other federal agencies.

Furthermore, I am directing that each of the alternative programs developed by BLM shall:

- be designed to reflect environmentally sound, fiscally responsible, and economically efficient resource use, development and investment strategies.
- be based on the capability and suitability of the public land resource as determined by you based on BLM's resource management planning process.
- clearly identify the assumptions used and describe environmental impacts, personnel requirements and program costs, and national, regional, and local benefits, and relate those benefits and costs through the use of cost/benefit, cost effective, or other appropriate analytic techniques.
- clearly state the inventory, planning, protection, rehabilitation, operation and maintenance work that would be

achieved under that program alternative.

In addition, I noted in my Message that lands administered by BLM contain areas of great cultural and ecological value. I am therefore directing you to give special attention to protecting areas of BLM-administered lands with nationally significant wildlife, natural, scientific, cultural, or scenic resources. As part of this effort, the Department shall develop by June 1980 a process and criteria for : (i) identifying those nationally significant resources, and (ii) proposing protective measures to provide special protective management for these resources on a continuing basis, commensurate with their national significance.

Please give these assignments your immediate attention.

JIMMY CARTER

———

Memorandum for the Secretary of Agriculture, the Secretary of the Interior

In my Environmental Message of August 2, 1979, I discussed the public interest to be served by improved coordination of the natural resources programs of your Departments. In particular, there is an urgent need for genuine cooperation between the Bureau of Land Management and the Forest Service—the two multiple-use management agencies that administer most of our public lands.

I recognize that much has been accomplished already by the two agencies, working in a spirit of cooperation—including cooperative fire protection efforts which have resulted in significant cost savings, an agreement for more efficient gathering and exchange of renewable resource information, and development of similar procedures for site-specific land use and resource management planning.

To give further impetus to the cooperation and progress achieved thus far, I am directing you to develop within six months a detailed statement of coordination objectives and a process and timetable for achieving them. Among the objectives you should consider are:

- Better coordination of the overall natural resource inventory and assessment process, and related program development and planning processes used by the Forest Service and Bureau of Land Management and other natural resources agencies, including compatible planning assumptions and management policies and consistent levels of decisionmaking responsibilities, for analogous lands and uses;
- Better coordination of field-level operations, including procedures for granting permits for use of Federal lands and the provision of technical assistance to users of Federal lands and to adjacent landholders;
- Boundary adjustments to permit more effective management;
- Pooling of facilities, equipment, personnel, training, and supplies, particularly where demonstrable cost savings can be achieved;
- Joint research and study of both policy issues and resource management problems, techniques and other matters of mutual concern; and
- Coordinated procedures and schedules for involvement of citizens, neighboring landholders, State and local government and other regional and national interests in planning, program development and management processes.

Furthermore, in my Environmental Message, I directed the Secretary of the Interior to establish a program development process for renewable and nonrenewable natural resources managed by the Bureau of Land Management. In that endeavor, both of your Departments should cooperate fully in the preparation of the National Assessment of Renewable Resources called for by the Resources Planning Act, so that the Assessment meets the needs of the Bureau's renewable resources program preparation as well as that of the Forest Service. You should also cooperate to ensure that the processes and programs developed by both agencies are compatible.

Please give me your recommendations within six months on the desirability of legislation to establish the same 5-year program development cycle for both agencies.

Please give these assignments your immediate attention.

JIMMY CARTER

Wildlife Law Enforcement

*Memorandums From the President.
August 2, 1979*

Memorandum for the Secretary of Agriculture

In my Environmental Message of August 2, 1979, illegal trade in fish and wildlife was identified as a significant environmental problem. Recent criminal and civil investigations have indicated that this trade runs to tens of millions of dollars a year and can introduce serious disease. It is important that we strengthen the individual and collective abilities of agencies to deal with this problem.

We must establish a coordinated federal wildlife enforcement program. To improve the effectiveness of this program, I am submitting legislation that strengthens wildlife enforcement laws. I am also directing agencies to take certain individual actions and to form two task forces to coordinate their activities.

I therefore direct that your Department:

• Assign a representative to a wildlife law enforcement committee chaired by the Department of the Interior which will include representatives from the Departments of Treasury, Justice, Agriculture and Commerce. The committee will review agency enforcement experiences, priorities and problems, expedite review of agency trade regulations, help coordinate federal trade enforcement policies generally and keep agency heads informed.

• Establish and chair a plant enforcement task force which will include representatives from your Department and the Departments of Justice, Interior and Treasury. The task force will investigate the illegal trade in plants and will bring appropriate prosecutions.

• Assign representatives as appropriate to interagency teams, chaired by the Department of the Interior, which will audit wildlife import documents to discover fraudulent documentation.

• Place greater emphasis on coordinating your review of quarantine-related import documents with other documents relating to wildlife imports to protect the quarantine program from the filing of fraudulent documents and to improve enforcement.

• Use special agents to investigate the illegal trade in plants.

Please give these assignments your immediate attention.

JIMMY CARTER

———

Memorandum for the Secretary of Commerce

In my Environmental Message of August 2, 1979, illegal trade in fish and

wildlife was identified as a significant environmental problem. Recent criminal and civil investigations have indicated that this trade runs to tens of millions of dollars a year and can introduce serious diseases. It is important that we strengthen the individual and collective abilities of agencies to deal with this problem.

We must establish a coordinated federal wildlife enforcement program. To improve the effectiveness of this program, I am submitting legislation that strengthens wildlife enforcement laws. I am also directing agencies to take certain individual actions and to form two task forces to coordinate their activities.

I therefore direct that your Department:

• Assign a representative to a wildlife law enforcement committee chaired by the Department of the Interior which will include representatives from the Departments of Treasury, Justice, Agriculture and Commerce. The committee will review agency enforcement experiences, priorities and problems, expedite review of agency trade regulations, help coordinate federal trade enforcement policies generally and keep agency heads informed.

• Assign representatives as appropriate to interagency teams, chaired by the Department of the Interior, which will audit wildlife import documents to discover fradulent documentation.

• Give higher priority to investigating illegal trade in fish and wildlife.

Please give these assignments your immediate attention.

JIMMY CARTER

———

Memorandum for the Secretary of the Interior

In my Environmental Message of August 2, 1979, illegal trade in fish and wildlife was identified as a significant environmental problem. Recent criminal and civil investigations have indicated that this trade runs to tens of millions of dollars a year and can introduce serious diseases. It is important that we strengthen the individual and collective abilities of agencies to deal with this problem.

We must establish a coordinated federal wildlife enforcement program. To improve the effectiveness of this program, I am submitting legislation that strengthens wildlife enforcement laws. I am also directing agencies to take certain individual actions and to form two task forces to coordinate their activities.

I therefore direct that your Department:

• Establish and chair a wildlife law enforcement committee which will include representatives from your Department and the Departments of Treasury, Justice, Agriculture and Commerce. The committee will review agency enforcement experiences, priorities and problems, expedite review of agency trade regulations, help coordinate federal trade enforcement policies generally and keep agency heads informed.

• Assign a representative to a plant enforcement task force, chaired by the Department of Agriculture, which will include representatives from the Departments of Agriculture, Justice, Interior and Treasury. The task force will investigate the illegal trade in plants and will bring appropriate prosecutions.

• Chair and assign representatives as appropriate to interagency teams which will audit wildlife import documents to discover fraudulent documentation.

Please give these assignments your immediate attention.

JIMMY CARTER

Memorandum for the Attorney General

In my Environmental Message of Au-

gust 2, 1979, illegal trade in fish and wildlife was identified as a significant environmental problem. Recent criminal and civil investigations have indicated that this trade runs to tens of millions of dollars a year and can introduce serious diseases. It is important that we strengthen the individual and collective abilities of agencies to deal with this problem.

We must establish a coordinated federal wildlife enforcement program. To improve the effectiveness of this program, I am submitting legislation that strengthens wildlife enforcement laws. I am also directing agencies to take certain individual actions and to form two task forces to coordinate their activities.

I therefore direct that your Department:

• Assign a representative to a wildlife law enforcement committee chaired by the Department of the Interior which will include representatives from the Departments of Treasury, Justice, Agriculture and Commerce. The committee will review agency enforcement experiences, priorities and problems, expedite review of agency trade regulations, help coordinate federal trade enforcement policies generally and keep agency heads informed.

• Assign a representative to a plant enforcement task force, chaired by the Department of Agriculture, which will include representatives from the Departments of Agriculture, Justice, Interior and Treasury. The task force will investigate the illegal trade in plants and will bring appropriate prosecutions.

• Assign representatives as appropriate to interagency teams, chaired by the Department of the Interior, which will audit wildlife import documents to discover fraudulent documentation.

• Seek stiff penalties for persons who engage in illegal wildlife or plant trade including jail sentences for the principal violators.

• Establish a Wildlife Section in the Land and Natural Resources Division which will be staffed principally by attorneys who will be trained to be wildlife law enforcement specialists with responsibilities similar to those of the Justice Department's white-collar crime "economic crime enforcement specialists".

Please give these assignments your immediate attention.

JIMMY CARTER

Memorandum for the Secretary of the Treasury

In my Environmental Message of August 2, 1979, illegal trade in fish and wildlife was identified as a significant environmental problem. Recent criminal and civil investigations have indicated that this trade runs to tens of millions of dollars a year and can introduce serious diseases. It is important that we strengthen the individual and collective abilities of agencies to deal with this problem.

We must establish a coordinated federal wildlife enforcement program. To improve the effectiveness of this program, I am submitting legislation that strengthens wildlife enforcement laws. I am also directing agencies to take certain individual actions and to form two task forces to coordinate their activities.

I therefore direct that your Department:

• Assign a representative to a wildlife law enforcement committee chaired by the Department of the Interior which will include representatives from the Departments of Treasury, Justice, Agriculture and Commerce. The committee will review agency enforcement experiences, priorities and problems, expedite review of agency trade regulations, help coordinate federal trade enforcement policies generally and keep agency heads informed.

• Assign a representative to a plant enforcement task force, chaired by the Department of Agriculture, which will include representatives from the Departments of Agriculture, Justice, Interior and Treasury. The task force will investigate the illegal trade in plants and will bring appropriate prosecutions.

• Assign representatives as appropriate to interagency teams, chaired by the Department of the Interior, which will audit wildlife import documents to discover fraudulent documentation.

• Recognize that violations involving commerical quantities of wildlife, plants or their derivatives are so significant as to be considered white-collar crime and consequently the Department of Treasury will assign a high priority to pursuing investigations of this nature.

Please give these assignments your immediate attention.

JIMMY CARTER

Wild and Scenic Rivers and National Trails

Memorandums From the President. August 2, 1979

Memorandum for the Heads of Departments and Agencies

In my Environmental Message of August 2, 1979, I recognized the important natural, historic, and recreational values of our Nation's river corridors. It is important for the federal agencies to set an example of sound management for state, local, and private landowners by taking an aggressive role in protecting Wild and Scenic Rivers which flow through public lands.

In addition, I recognized that the 1968 National Trails System Act is designed to promote the development of recreational, scenic, and historic trails for persons of diverse interests and abilities—including the young, the handicapped, and the aged—and that the National Trails System is in its fledgling stage. The Act provides for designating trails on state, local and private lands, but only 130 trails have been established since enactment of the Act. In my Environmental Message I stressed the importance of expanding the National Trails System.

Therefore, I am directing that each of you take the following actions:

• Each federal agency shall encourage states, localities and private land holders to designate trails on their lands and to participate with federal agencies and trail users in designing and creating an overall National Trails System which will provide more fully for the trail needs of America.

• Each federal agency shall, as part of its normal planning and environmental review processes, take care to avoid or mitigate adverse effects on rivers identified in the Nationwide Inventory, prepared by the Heritage Conservation and Recreation Service in the Department of the Interior. Agencies shall, as part of their normal environmental review process, consult with the Heritage Conservation and Recreation Service prior to taking actions which could effectively foreclose wild, scenic, or recreational river status on rivers in the Inventory.

• Each Federal agency with responsibility for administering public lands shall, as part of its ongoing land use planning and management activities and environmental review processes, make an assessment of whether the rivers identified in the Nationwide Inventory and which are on their lands are suitable for inclusion in

the Wild and Scenic Rivers System. If an agency determines that a river would be suitable for inclusion in the System, the agency shall, to the extent of the agency's authority, promptly take such steps as are needed to protect and manage the river and the surrounding area in a fashion comparable to rivers already included in the Wild and Scenic Rivers System. In addition, the agency is encouraged, pursuant to the revised Guidelines, to work with the Agriculture and Interior Departments to prepare legislation to designate the river as part of the Wild and Scenic Rivers System if appropriate.

Please give these assignments your immediate attention.

JIMMY CARTER

Memorandum for the Secretary of Agriculture

In my Environmental Message of August 2, 1979, I recognized the important natural, historic, and recreational values of our Nation's river corridors. Unfortunately, development along the banks of our rivers continues to outpace our ability to identify and study those rivers which might qualify for protection under the National Wild and Scenic Rivers System. Thus, we need to improve our techniques for identifying, and designating wild and scenic rivers.

In addition, I recognized in my Environmental Message that the 1968 National Trails System Act is designed to promote the development of recreational, scenic, and historic trails for persons of diverse interests and abilities—including the young, the handicapped and the aged—and that the National Trails System is in its fledgling stage. I stressed the importance of expanding the National Trails System to provide increased recreation opportunities for the millions of

Americans who enjoy hiking, backpacking, bicycling, and similar activities.

Therefore, I am directing you to take the following actions:

• Within 120 days, together with the Secretary of the Interior, revise the Guidelines for studying Wild and Scenic Rivers. The revised Guidelines shall establish procedures to ensure consideration of river ecosystems to shorten the length of time currently used to study rivers for designation.

• Ensure that the Forest Service meets its goal of establishing 145 additional National Recreation Trails by January 1980, thereby achieving the objective of two National Recreation Trails in each National Forest System unit.

Please give these assignments your immediate attention.

Jimmy Carter

Memorandum for the Secretary of the Interior

In my Environmental Message of August 2, 1979, I recognized the important natural, historic, and recreational values of our Nation's river corridors. Unfortunately, development along the banks of our rivers continues to outpace our ability to identify and study those rivers which might qualify for protection under the National Wild and Scenic Rivers System. This problem is particularly acute near urban areas, where there are greater demands for recreational opportunities. Thus, we need to improve our techniques for identifying, and designating wild and scenic rivers.

In addition, I recognized in my Environmental Message that the 1968 National Trails System Act is designed to promote the development of recreational, scenic, and historic trails for persons of

diverse interests and abilities—including the young, the handicapped and the aged—and that the National Trails System is in its fledgling stage. I stressed the importance of expanding the National Trails System to provide increased recreation opportunities for the millions of Americans who enjoy hiking, backpacking, and similar activities.

Therefore, I am directing you to take the following actions:

• Within 120 days, together with the Secretary of Agriculture, revise the Guidelines for studying Wild and Scenic Rivers. The revised Guidelines shall establish procedures to ensure consideration of river ecosystems and to shorten the length of time currently used to study rivers for designation.

• Furnish federal agencies, through the Heritage Conservation and Recreation Service, with the names of the rivers in its Nationwide Inventory—which is a list of rivers having the potential to be designated under the Wild and Scenic Rivers Act—and with any background analysis conducted by the Service.

• Assist other federal agencies, through the Interagency Trails Council, in surveying existing trails on federal lands to determine which of those can be made part of our National Trails System.

• Initiate a grassroots effort in every region of the country to assess our nationwide trail needs. This nationwide assessment shall examine the types of trails now in use and their proximity to trail users: estimate current and anticipated trail needs; and recommend cost-effective programs and energy-conserving actions which could produce the types and number of trails that are needed.

Please give these assignments your immediate attention.

Jimmy Carter

Memorandum for the Secretary of the Interior, the Secretary of Defense, the Chairman of the Board of the Tennessee Valley Authority

In my Environmental Message of August 2, 1979, I recognized that the 1968 National Trails System Act is designed to promote the development of recreational, scenic, and historic trails for persons of diverse interests and abilities—including the young, the handicapped, and the aged—and that National Trails System is in its fledgling stage. I stressed the importance of expanding the National Trails System to provide increased recreation opportunities for the millions of Americans who enjoy hiking, backpacking, and similar activities.

Therefore, I am directing each of you to announce by January 1980 a goal for the number of National Recreation Trails each agency will establish during 1980 on the public lands administered by your agencies. By the end of 1980, I am directing that, at a minimum, 75 new National Recreation Trails shall be designated on these lands.

Please report your progress in meeting your goal to the Chairman of the Council on Environmental Quality and the Director of the Office of Management and Budget on June 30, 1980 and on December 31, 1980.

JIMMY CARTER

Soil Conservation Incentives

Memorandum From the President.
August 2, 1979

Memorandum for the Secretary of Agriculture

In my Environmental Message of August 2, 1979, I underscored my serious concern that since 1935 wind and water erosion have reduced by half the top soil on nearly one-third of the Nation's potentially usable croplands. Although more than $20 billion in federal funds has been invested in soil and water conservation programs of the Department of Agriculture, erosion continues to occur at very high rates. There are 28 existing soil conservation and water quality-related Department of Agriculture programs which are designed to help remedy this problem. The Resources Conservation Act (RCA) and Resources Planning Act (RPA) processes will review these and other programs and provide me in January 1980 with recommended improvements in program design and administration.

Due to the importance of the soil erosion problem I direct you, in consultation with the Chairman of the Council on Environmental Quality, to undertake a comprehensive study of possible conservation incentives, building on the analysis of the RCA process, and to provide me with a report in January 1981.

A major goal of your effort should be to analyze the implications of modifying or interrelating existing agricultural assistance programs to bring about a greater reduction in soil erosion and related nonpoint pollution. The study shall also identify conflicts between farm income programs and soil conservation programs and develop recommendations for eliminating these conflicts where possible. The report shall set forth specific administrative and legislative recommendations to reduce soil erosion and to improve soil stewardship in order to maintain the Nation's long-term agricultural productivity, building on policy recommendations contained in the RCA 1980 Program report.

Please give this assignment your immediate attention.

JIMMY CARTER

Integrated Pest Management

Memorandum From the President.
August 2, 1979

Memorandum for the Secretary of Agriculture, the Secretary of Commerce, the Secretary of Defense, the Secretary of Health, Education & Welfare, the Secretary of Housing and Urban Development, the Secretary of the Interior, the Secretary of Labor, the Secretary of Transportation, the Administrator of the Environmental Protection Agency, the Administrator of the General Services Administration, the Chairman of the Council on Environmental Quality

In my Environmental Message of August 2, 1979, I recognized that integrated pest management (IPM) has both economic and environmental benefits and should be encouraged in both research and operational programs of federal agencies. Therefore, I am directing that each of your agencies:

• Modify as soon as possible your existing pest management, research, control, education, and assistance programs to support and adopt IPM strategies wherever practicable within the limits of existing resources.

• Review your pest management research, control, education, and assistance programs to assess the potential for increased emphasis on integrated pest management.

• Report actions taken to implement IPM strategies and the results of this review and assessment to the IPM coordinating committee in six months.

I am establishing an interagency IPM Coordinating Committee to assure implementation of this directive and to oversee further development and implementation of integrated pest management practices. The Committee shall be chaired by the Council on Environmental Quality. Your agency should appoint one representative to serve on this Committee who is an Assistant Secretary, Assistant Administrator, or the equivalent. The Committee is to report to me by June 30, 1980 on progress made by federal agencies in the advancement of IPM and on any institutional barriers thereto.

The Committee may request any Executive agency to furnish such information, advice, and service as may be useful for the fulfillment of the Committee's functions. Each of your agencies shall cooperate with and furnish support to the Committee as needed to carry out its functions.

Please give these assignments your immediate attention.

JIMMY CARTER

Transportation Policy

Memorandum From the President.
August 2, 1979

Memorandum for the Secretary of Transportation

In my Environmental Message of August 2, 1979, I recognized that our transportation systems can greatly affect, for better or worse, our nation's environment, our utilization of energy, and our urban areas. I also recognized that it is my Administration's policy to enhance environmental protection, energy conservation, and urban revitalization and that the nation's transportation system must provide greater support for these national goals.

I fully support the reorientation of urban transportation programs and projects to meet energy and urban goals and to improve overall environmental quality. I am directing you to act immediately to assure that:

- transportation funds are used to promote energy conservation through such energy saving features as special lanes for carpools, vanpools, and transit vehicles, and that encouragement be given to applying funds to public transportation projects;

- careful review is given to any transportation proposals which would encourage urban sprawl—one of the major causes of our high energy consumption—or which would tend to attract jobs out of our urban centers;

- consideration is given to the improvement and rehabilitation of existing facilities and the use of non-construction methods as alternatives to constructing new facilities;

- major transportation projects are utilized as a positive factor for improving the urban economy and attracting jobs to the nation's urban cores; and

- firm actions are taken to mitigate adverse effects of transportation projects on the environment—both the natural environment and the urban environment—and that the environmental commitments that we make in approving transportation projects are carried out when the projects are built.

Please report on your progress in implementing this directive to the Chairman of the Council on Environmental Quality and the Director of the Office of Management and Budget on February 1, 1980 and August 1, 1980.

JIMMY CARTER

Economic Assistance for Pollution Control

Memorandums From the President.
August 2, 1979

Memorandum for the Administrator of the Environmental Protection Agency

In my Environmental Message of August 2, 1979, I recognized that most Americans benefit directly from the healthier and more agreeable environment that results from our pollution control programs. I also noted that unfortunately these programs have been a factor that has contributed to a limited number of closures of already marginal industrial plants. Although there are a number of federal assistance programs available which can aid those who have lost their jobs and the communities in which they reside, the existing programs are not being widely used.

Therefore, I am directing you to take the following actions:

- Establish an Economic Assistance Program, including the designation of economic assistance officers at headquarters and in the field, whose purpose is to ensure that economic adjustment assistance is both understood by all eligible parties and made quickly available to those who qualify for it.

- Expand the Environmental Protection Agency's "Economic Dislocation Early Warning System" so that it includes more information on potential disruptions to communities and groups of workers, as well as to businesses and so that it is operated in such a way that possible economic disruptions are identified as early as possible and that relevant agencies are quickly notified.

Please give these assignments your immediate attention.

JIMMY CARTER

Memorandum for the Secretary of Agriculture, the Secretary of Commerce, the Secretary of Housing and Urban Development, the Secretary of Labor, the Administrator of the Environmental Protection Agency, the Administrator of the Small Business Administration, the Chairman of the Council on Environmental Quality, the Director of the Office of Management and Budget

In my Environmental Message of August 2, 1979, I recognized that most Americans benefit directly from the healthier and more agreeable environment that results from our pollution control programs. I also noted that these programs unfortunately have been a factor that has contributed to a limited number of plant closures. Although there are a number of federal assistance programs available that can help firms avoid closure, and, when it is unavoidable, aid both those who have lost their jobs and the communities in which they reside, the existing programs are not being widely used.

Therefore, I am directing each of you together with the Council on Environmental Quality and the Office of Management and Budget to take the following actions:

• The Environmental Protection Agency shall have responsibility to inform affected parties of available assistance where it could ease adverse effects of pollution control laws, to notify the agencies offering such assistance of impending disruptions, and to work with both to encourage the effective, coordinated delivery of assistance; EPA shall report to me on June 30, 1980, and annually thereafter on the agencies' efforts to coordinate and improve the delivery of their economic assistance programs for this purpose.

• Each federal agency will cooperate closely with the Environmental Protection Agency and with other agencies to ensure that their various economic assistance programs are coordinated effectively.

• Each federal agency shall ensure that it responds effectively and expeditiously to specific adverse economic problems resulting from the implementation of pollution control laws.

• Each federal agency will recommend to me ways in which the existing assistance programs should be modified, if necessary, to enable the government to respond more effectively to economic adjustment problems that may occur in the future.

Please give these assignments your immediate attention.

JIMMY CARTER

Urban Noise Program

Memorandum From the President.
August 2, 1979

Memorandum for the Secretary of Commerce, the Secretary of Defense, the Secretary of Energy, the Secretary of Housing and Urban Development, the Secretary of Transportation, the Administrator of the Environmental Protection Agency, the Administrator of the General Services Administration, the Chairman of the Council on Environmental Quality, the Director of the Office of Management and Budget, the Chairman of the Interagency Coordinating Council

In my Environmental Message of August 2, 1979, I recognized that city noise is an integral part of a vibrant city lifestyle, reflecting city patterns of commerce that must be preserved and enhanced, but that much urban noise is harmful to urban living and could be abated.

I am initiating today a program to reduce urban noise by making existing programs work better through interagency and intergovernmental cooperation. I am directing you, in consultation with other federal agencies, to:

- initiate programs to achieve sound-proofing and weatherization of noise-sensitive buildings, such as schools and hospitals;

- promote the use of quiet-design features in the planning, design, and operation of proposed urban transportation projects;

- encourage noise-sensitive developments, such as housing, to be located away from major noise sources;

- help federal, state and local agencies buy quiet equipment and products; and

- support neighborhood self-reliance efforts seeking to identify and address local noise problems.

The Federal Interagency Committee on Noise, chaired by the Administrator of the Environmental Protection Agency, shall coordinate the implementation of this program. The Chairman of my Interagency Coordinating Council will assist the Interagency Committee and other intergovernmental cooperative efforts to assure that this program is carried out fully and promptly, including consultation with state and local governments.

The Administrator of the Environmental Protection Agency will report to the Chairman of the Council on Environmental Quality and the Director of the Office of Management and Budget on the progress of this new program on February 1, 1980, and on August 1, 1980.

JIMMY CARTER

World Forests

Memorandums From the President.
August 2, 1979

Memorandum for the Secretary of State

In my Environmental Message of August 3,[1] 1979, I expressed concern about the rapid disappearance of the earth's forests, especially in the tropics and subtropics. I believe there is much that the United States can do in cooperation with other nations to contribute to environmentally sound care and management of the earth's forests and to the well-being of people affected by them.

I am directing you to give high priority to the following matters in your budget and program planning:

- improved monitoring of world forest trends, particularly tropical forests, including use of satellite observations;

- research on necessary preservation of natural forest ecosystems and their rich complex of plant and animal life;

- research on multiple uses of highly diverse tropical forests, including management of natural stands, development of ecologically sound forest plantations, and combined agriculture and forestry;

- studies on increasing yields in family-scale tropical agriculture, to relieve pressures on forest lands that are not suitable for cultivation;

- demonstration of integrated projects for reforestation, more efficient fuelwood use, and alternative energy sources;

- examination of how U.S. citizens and U.S.-based corporations may be encouraged to support sound forest management practices.

---

[1] EDITOR'S NOTE: The correct date is August 2.

I am asking you to ensure that the inter-agency task force on tropical forests, chaired by the Department of State, submit to me by November 1979 its report and recommendations on U.S. goals, strategies, and programs to help protect and conserve world forests.

I am asking you to work with the Department of Agriculture, the Council on Environmental Quality and other relevant federal agencies, and with other nations and international organizations, to give full support and assistance to the international program of activities for conservation and wise utilization of tropical forests to be developed under the sponsorship of the United Nations Environment Programme.

I am also asking you to encourage and support high-level international conferences on forest problems in regions where forest losses are severe, to raise awareness and understanding both of the complex problems and possible solutions.

Finally, I am asking you and the Chairman of the Council on Environmental Quality to report to me within six months on the best ways to designate "ecological and natural resources of global importance" under Executive Order 12114, so that proposals for major federal actions significantly affecting these resources will be reviewed before a decision is made.

Please give these assignments your immediate attention.

JIMMY CARTER

Memorandum for the Secretary of Agriculture

In my Environmental Message of August 2, 1979, I expressed concern about the rapid disappearance of the earth's forests, especially in the tropics and subtropics. I believe there is much that the United States can do in cooperation with other nations to contribute to environ-mentally sound care and management of the earth's forests and to the well-being of people affected by them.

I am therefore directing you to give high priority to the following matters in your budget and program planning:

- improved monitoring of world forest trends, particularly tropical forests, including use of satellite observations;

- research on necessary preservation of natural forest ecosystems and their rich complex of plant and animal life;

- research on multiple uses of highly diverse tropical forests, including management of natural stands, development of ecologically sound forest plantations, and combined agriculture and forestry;

- studies on increasing yields in family-scale tropical agriculture, to relieve pressures on forest lands that are not suitable for cultivation;

- demonstration of integrated projects for reforestation, more efficient fuel-wood use, and alternative energy sources;

- examination of how U.S. citizens and U.S.-based corporations may be encouraged to support sound forest management practices.

I am also asking you to work with the Department of State, the Council on Environmental Quality, and other relevant federal agencies, and with other nations and international organizations, to give full support and assistance to the international program of activities for conservation and wise utilization of tropical forests to be developed under the sponsorship of the United Nations Environment Programme.

Please give these assignments your immediate attention.

JIMMY CARTER

Memorandum for the Chairman of the Council on Environmental Quality

In my Environmental Message of August 2, 1979, I expressed concern about the rapid disappearance of the earth's forests, especially in the tropics and subtropics. I believe there is much that the United States can do in cooperation with other nations to contribute to environmentally sound care and management of the earth's forests and to the well-being of people affected by them.

I am therefore asking you to work with the Departments of State and Agriculture and other relevant federal agencies, and with other nations and international organizations, to give full support and assistance to the international program of activities for conservation and wise utilization of tropical forests to be developed under the sponsorship of the United Nations Environment Programme.

In addition, I am asking you and the Secretary of State to report to me within six months on the best ways to designate "ecological and natural resources of global importance" under Executive Order 12114, so that proposals for major federal actions significantly affecting these resources will be reviewed before a decision is made.

Please give these assignments your immediate attention.

JIMMY CARTER

Memorandum for the Director of the National Science Foundation

In my Environmental Message of August 2, 1979, I expressed concern about the rapid disappearance of the earth's forests, especially in the tropics and subtropics. I believe there is much that the United States can do in cooperation with other nations to contribute to environmentally sound care and management of the

earth's forests and to the well-being of people affected by them.

I am therefore requesting that you give high priority in your budget and program planning and research support programs to forests and to the following areas of basic and applied research:

- research on the ecology of tropical forests;
- improved monitoring of world forest trends, particularly tropical forests, including use of satellite observations;
- research on necessary preservation of natural forest ecosystems and their rich complex of plant and animal life;
- research on multiple uses of highly diverse tropical forests, including management of natural stands, development of ecologically sound forest plantations, and combined agriculture and forestry;
- studies on increasing yields in family-scale tropical agriculture, to relieve pressures on forest lands that are not suitable for cultivation;
- identification of research methods to define the ecological disturbance in tropical forests from human activities, and to predict recovery of stressed forest systems.

Please give this assignment your immediate attention.

JIMMY CARTER

Memorandum for the Administrator of the Agency for International Development, the Director of ACTION

In my Environmental Message of August 2, 1979, I expressed concern about the rapid disappearance of the earth's forests, especially in the tropics and subtropics. I believe there is much that the United States can do in our development assistance to other nations to contribute to environmentally sound care and management of the earth's forests and to the wellbeing of people affected by them.

I am directing you to evaluate your development assistance programs in light of the following objectives and to give high priority to programs which would advance these objectives:

- necessary preservation of natural forest ecosystems and their rich complex of plant and animal life;
- multiple uses of highly diverse tropical forests, including management of natural stands, development of ecologically sound forest plantations, and combined agriculture and forestry;
- increasing yields in family-scale tropical agriculture to relieve pressures on forest lands that are not suitable for cultivation;
- developing integrated projects for reforestation, more efficient fuelwood use, and alternative energy sources.

Please give this assignment your immediate attention.

JIMMY CARTER

Acid Rain Research Program

Memorandum From the President.
August 2, 1979

Memorandum for the Secretary of Agriculture, the Secretary of the Interior, the Secretary of Energy, the Secretary of Commerce, the Secretary of State, the Administrator of the Environmental Protection Agency, the Director of the National Science Foundation, the Chairman of the Council on Environmental Quality, the Director of the Office of Science and Technology Policy

In my Environmental Message of August 2, 1979, acid rain was identified as a major global environmental problem.

However, our knowledge of possible effects and specific causes of acid rain are inadequate for determining what kinds of controls would best mitigate the problems caused by acid rain. It is important that we undertake efforts to describe the magnitude of acid rain effects, to develop a more thorough understanding of its causes, and to identify measures which can mitigate acid rain impacts.

To meet these goals, we must establish a comprehensive federal acid rain research program. In order to increase the program's effectiveness as well as to reduce its costs, research should be coordinated with states and private research efforts, particularly large industry efforts. Finally, in undertaking the federal acid rain research program, we should work closely with Canada, Mexico, other nations, and international organizations which are concerned about acid rain.

I therefore direct that:

• A standing Acid Rain Coordination Committee be established comprised of policy representatives from each of your agencies.

• The Committee shall be co-chaired by the Department of Agriculture and the Environmental Protection Agency. The Council on Environmental Quality shall serve as the Executive Secretary of the Committee.

• The Committee shall plan and manage a comprehensive acid rain assessment program. A Federal Acid Rain Assessment Plan shall be completed by January 1, 1980. The Plan shall identify necessary coordination mechanisms to ensure that the results of the assessment program will be incorporated in agency planning and decisionmaking.

• The Committee shall seek cooperation of state and private research efforts, particularly industry research programs, which are conducting acid rain research so that to the extent possible duplicative research is eliminated and research is jointly planned and conducted.

• Through the Secretary of State the federal acid rain research program shall be coordinated to the extent possible with similar efforts in Canada and Mexico as well as with other Nations and international bodies.

• Consistent with established procedures of the agencies chairing the Committee, the Committee shall actively solicit public involvement in its planning and reviews of the research results of the Committee's program; workshops, public hearings, and other techniques should be utilized.

• The Committee shall prepare and submit to the President by September 15 of each year an annual report which shall present the results of the acid rain assessment program and make recommendations as appropriate. This report shall serve as a planning document for focusing agency programs to meet the objectives of the acid rain research program.

JIMMY CARTER

United States-Turkey Treaty on Extradition and Mutual Assistance in Criminal Matters

Message to the Senate Transmitting the Treaty.   August 2, 1979

To the Senate of the United States:

With a view to receiving the advice and consent of the Senate to ratification, I transmit herewith the Treaty on Extradition and Mutual Assistance in Criminal Matters between the United States of America and the Republic of Turkey, signed at Ankara on June 7, 1979.

I transmit also, for the information of the Senate, the report of the Department of State with respect to the treaty.

The treaty is one of a series of modern extradition and mutual assistance treaties being negotiated by the United States. At the request of the Turkish side, the subjects are combined into one treaty. The treaty is self-executing and utilizes existing statutory authority.

The extradition portion of the treaty replaces the current treaty between the United States and Turkey which was signed in 1923. It greatly expands the list of extraditable offenses to include narcotics offenses, aircraft hijacking, bribery, and obstruction of justice, as well as many other offenses not now covered by our existing treaty. Upon entry into force, it will terminate and supersede the existing Treaty of Extradition. The new treaty will have only limited retroactive effect. American citizens are not extraditable to Turkey under the present treaty, although they are under the new treaty. Under the new treaty, however, they will not be extradited for extraditable offenses under the present treaty committed prior to entry into force of the new treaty. Also, the new treaty provides that extradition shall not be granted for an offense committed before this treaty enters into force which is not an extraditable offense under the present treaty.

The mutual assistance portion of the new treaty provides for a broad range of cooperation in criminal matters. Mutual assistance available under the treaty includes (1) executing requests relating to criminal matters; (2) taking of testimony or statements of persons; (3) effecting the production, preservation and authentication of documents, records, or articles of evidence; (4) returning to the Requesting Party any objects, articles or other property or assets belonging to it or obtained by an accused through offenses; (5) serving judicial documents, writs, summonses, records of judicial verdicts and court judgments or decisions; (6) effecting the appearance of a witness or expert before a court of the Requesting Party; (7) locating persons; and (8) providing judicial records, evidence and information.

I recommend that the Senate give early and favorable consideration to the treaty and give its advice and consent to ratification.

JIMMY CARTER

The White House,
   August 2, 1979.

United States-Turkey Treaty on Penal Judgments

Message to the Senate Transmitting the Treaty.   August 2, 1979

To the Senate of the United States:

With a view to receiving the advice and consent of the Senate to ratification, I transmit herewith the Treaty between the United States of America and the Republic of Turkey on the Enforcement of Penal Judgments which was signed in Ankara on June 7, 1979.

I transmit also, for the information of the Senate, the Report of the Department of State with respect to the treaty.

The treaty would permit citizens of either nation who have been convicted in the courts of the other country to serve their sentences in their home country; in each case the consent of the offender would be required.

This treaty is significant because it represents an attempt to resolve a situation which has inflicted substantial hardships on a number of citizens of each country and has caused concern to both govern-

ments. It also represents a significant element in the modernization of our relations with Turkey in the field of international judicial cooperation.

I recommend that the Senate give early and favorable consideration to this treaty.

JIMMY CARTER

The White House,
   August 2, 1979.

Department of Health, Education, and Welfare

Remarks at the Swearing In of Patricia Roberts Harris as Secretary.   August 3, 1979

THE PRESIDENT. This is a happy day for our country. It's a great honor for me to be here as President and to have the chance as the leader of our Nation to select and to appoint a person who is so superbly qualified to head the agency that she will be leading.

It's a time of thanksgiving, I think, among those who look to the Department of Health, Education, and Welfare for a new or sustained chance in life. I've known Pat Harris for a long time. When I formed my Cabinet almost 3 years ago, there was one major department in Government that had not adequately performed its function. It had been far short of its potential after 8 years of Republican administration. The Department of Housing and Urban Development was one that was formed with a clear recognition of a great need—poor were homeless, cities were destitute. They reached toward Washington with disappointment and frustration. The Department was poorly organized, and its effectiveness was severely in doubt.

Pat Harris came as Secretary of HUD, and with her superb management capabilities, she transformed this weak department into one of the most strong and able and effective and sensitive in government.

Hers has been a sterling performance as a manager with a heart. All who know her realize that she is bold, strong, outspoken. Anyone who looks to Pat Harris as a "yes woman" would be both foolish and ill-advised. [*Laughter*] I have never been that foolish, and I have never been advised. [*Laughter*]

She fights for her beliefs, and her beliefs are sound and she wins her fights. She has a big heart. With her background and with her experience, with her innate sensitivity and compassion, she has brought to that agency a superb record of performance. And if there's one area where my own political fortunes have been enhanced tremendously by the actions of a Cabinet officer, you could certainly not overlook the new confidence that local and State officials have in our Government, who have to deal with housing, urban development, the reconstitution, the rebuilding of our communities, and the provision of housing for those who often suffer by the lack of it.

She's now coming to serve the needs in health, education, and welfare. She will be following a good man, a man who has the same kind of concern and compassion for those who are served by this agency.

There is no doubt in my mind that there will be no slackening of effort, no lessening of commitment, no deviating from a path of superior service. And I know Pat Harris well enough to look forward with great anticipation to her ability, once a path has been described and delineated, that she can work harmoniously with every other member of the Cabinet, all the other Federal agencies, the local government, the State government officials, the constituency groups, the Congress in an effective way. She's got a superb batting average on the hill in getting legislation passed.

We now have great challenges in the Congress, hospital cost containment, the only specific piece of legislation before the Congress this year positively to deal with the increasing threat of inflation. Its passage hangs in the balance, and it's going to require an absolutely superb team effort to get it passed. I have no doubt that Pat Harris can lead that team effort.

I'm dedicated to passing through the Congress and implementing in a carefully phased and responsible way a comprehensive health program. And I will look to Secretary Harris to work with the Congress, particularly Senator Kennedy, to work with the labor organizations, the constituency groups, to make sure that our comprehensive health program is indeed passed by the Congress and is implemented.

We have a crying need to enhance the status of education in our country. The new department of education can provide this role if it's effectively founded in law, adequately staffed by me with the support and the nurturing from Secretary Harris.

And the final thing I'd like to say about her is that she has a special relationship with the poor, the homeless, the disadvantaged, the black, those who can't speak English very well, the aged, and others who will be and have been looking for succor and nourishment and a helping hand and a dependable hand from the Federal Government. Her heart is in the right place.

With all those characteristics, there could not possibly be a better person to head this important agency, and I am grateful to her for being willing to serve me as President, you as leaders of our Nation, and particularly those who will benefit from her service as the Secretary of HEW.

Pat, I thank you.

And now, I would like to introduce Justice Thurgood Marshall, who will administer the oath of office to our new Secretary of Health, Education, and Welfare.

Thank you.

[At this point, Associate Justice of the Supreme Court Thurgood Marshall administered the oath of office.]

SECRETARY HARRIS. *Mr. President, Mr. Justice, and friends:*

It is an honor for me to be before you today as the Secretary of the Department of Health, Education, and Welfare. And may I say that for some of us, it is really a great day when Justice Thurgood Marshall swears in Pat Harris, because the Justice and I first met—I remember him from that meeting because he was a great man, I was just a young whippersnapper who had been sent over by Elmer Henderson, who's out there someplace—when we were sitting at the Department of the Navy trying to get them to do right, as we did so often—we were on the other side. That really makes it a great day.

When President Carter asked me to serve as Secretary of Health, Education, and Welfare, I had deep concerns. But after careful consideration, I agreed to do so. I agreed because I believe that there are no issues of our time that are more important than those dealing with the young, the poor, the handicapped, the infirm, and the aged. These are the people I served at the Department of Housing and Urban Development, and the President did me and HUD great honor by saying that we had done our job well and that he wished me to transfer my concern, my skills, and my time to doing the same kind of job on a much broader scale at HEW.

It will be a difficult and an arduous task, but I shall do my best. And I am confident that with the help of the people who share the President's concern and our concern for the most vulnerable Americans, we will succeed.

Although we live in the mightiest, the wealthiest, and the most powerful nation on Earth, all of our accomplishments are called into question and challenged by the reality of poverty, inadequate education, and deficient health care that torment and trap so many of our fellow Americans. But I see these great problems to be the challenge of our time, and Americans have never been afraid of challenge. It is at the core of our identity, and it is at the center of our national purpose. The Department of Health, Education, and Welfare is at the center of the great national challenge and debate over these issues.

I want to assure everyone in this room and all others who view or hear this event that I will work tirelessly and resolutely to establish a separate department of education, to control the cost of hospital care, to bring reform and dignity to the American welfare system, and to enact national health insurance. We're going to do them all.

Furthermore, this member of the Cabinet, and other members as well, have an interest in the general well-being of the people that goes beyond our specific responsibilities of office. Therefore, we will be working diligently on such things as the President's concern and the concern of all of us about the cost of energy and home heating fuels for poor and moderate income Americans. These concerns can only be met by the passage of the windfall profits tax, and I believe with the help of the American people, these things will come about.

By nature, Americans are optimistic, but as the President noted in his televised address, the events of the past decade and a half have shattered much of that confidence. In November of 1976, however, nearly 41 million Americans said, "Jimmy Carter is the man to help restore that confidence and to help redefine our own sense of national purpose." The American people elected Jimmy Carter so that we could restore confidence in government, so that we could bring peace to the troubled spots of the world, so that we could make the Government more caring and more determined to meet the acute needs of our most vulnerable citizens. And I intend to work as hard as I can over the next 18 months so that all of us in this administration can fulfill our promise to the American people to get these things done, and I am convinced that this will happen.

My friends, judgments and controversy are a part of public life, if you didn't know. [*Laughter*] They come with the turf; they go with the territory. We who choose public life can neither fear them nor avoid them. Like Gibbon, we must believe that the winds and waves serve the ablest navigators, though they may overwhelm those without purpose or direction.

You who know me know the source of my purpose and direction. They are rooted in a strong belief in our system of government and optimism about our future, a confidence in our ability to get the job done, and a deep concern for those we are called on to serve. But I sincerely doubt that anyone in public life can withstand the realities of public life without the support, advice, and assistance of good friends. I need, welcome, and cherish your advice and assistance just as today I thank you for the assurance that your support by your presence here has given me.

Now, I've behaved very well. The President was very optimistic before I came over. He said, "You are going to say a few words, aren't you?" [*Laughter*] As he has said, he said I was outspoken, I'm sure he has frequently thought, but not by

many. [*Laughter*] So, for all of you, some of whom have known me for decades, that take us to 30 years—I see Judge Parker, whom I met when we were both students at the University of Chicago in the forties; we won't say when, Barrington—but I want to say it will either reassure you or frighten you or make you say, "I told you so."

High office really hasn't changed me, and with all that that means for those of you who know me, I leave on that note, my good friends, saying thank you for being here today.

NOTE: The President spoke at 1:17 p.m. at the ceremony in the East Room at the White House.

Federal Trade Commission

Nomination of Patricia P. Bailey To Be a Commissioner.   August 3, 1979

The President today announced that he will nominate Patricia P. Bailey, of Washington, D.C., to be a Commissioner of the Federal Trade Commission for a term expiring September 25, 1980. She would replace Elizabeth Hanford Dole, resigned.

Bailey is executive legal assistant to the General Counsel at the Merit Systems Protection Board.

She was born June 20, 1937, in Fort Smith, Ark. She received a B.A. from Linderwood College in 1959, an M.A. from the Fletcher School of Law and Diplomacy, Tufts University, in 1960, and a J.D. from the American University Law School in 1976.

From 1961 to 1966, Bailey was with the Agency for International Development as an assistant desk officer for the Dominican Republic, then Haiti; desk officer for Trinidad-Tobago and Guyana; and executive assistant to the coordinator of the Alliance for Progress, Latin American Bureau. In 1967 and 1968, she was a staff assistant to Representative F. Bradford Morse. In 1968 she worked on then-Governor Nelson Rockefeller's presidential campaign.

In 1972 and 1973, Bailey worked for the National Women's Political Caucus. In 1976 she was active in the Rockefeller for President campaign, then in the President Ford Committee. From 1977 to 1979, she was at the Justice Department, serving as special assistant to the Assistant Attorney General for Improvements in the Administration of Justice. From 1978 to 1979, she was on special detail to the Attorney General to work on Federal judgeships. She has been at the Merit Systems Protection Board since March of this year.

Civil Aeronautics Board

Nomination of George A. Dalley To Be a Member.   August 3, 1979

The President today announced that he will nominate George A. Dalley, of Washington, D.C., to be a member of the Civil Aeronautics Board for a term expiring December 31, 1982.

Dalley is Deputy Assistant Secretary of State for Human Rights and Social Affairs.

He was born August 25, 1941, in Havana, Cuba, and is a naturalized American citizen. He received a B.A. in economics and history from Columbia College in 1963, an LL.B. from Columbia University School of Law in 1966, and an M.B.A. from Columbia University Graduate School of Business, also in 1966.

From 1967 to 1969, Dalley was with the Metropolitan Applied Research Center, Inc., and from 1970 to 1971, he was an attorney with the firm of Stroock & Stroock & Lavan. From 1971 to 1972, he was assistant counsel to the U.S. House of Representatives Committee on the Judiciary.

From 1972 to 1977, Dalley was administrative assistant to Congressman Charles Rangel. He has been Deputy Assistant Secretary of State for Human Rights and Social Affairs since 1977, and is responsible for the formulation of U.S. human rights policy on the human rights and social issues which arise in the United Nations system.

Federal Maritime Commission

Nomination of James V. Day To Be a Commissioner.   August 3, 1979

The President today announced that he will nominate James V. Day, of Kennebunk, Maine, for reappointment as a Commissioner of the Federal Maritime Commission for a term expiring June 30, 1984.

Day, 65, has been a Federal Maritime Commissioner since 1962. He is a former national director of public affairs for the American Legion and vice chairman of its Merchant Marine Committee.

International Joint Commission, United States and Canada

Nomination of Jean L. Hennessey To Be a U.S. Commissioner.   August 3, 1979

The President today announced that he will nominate Jean L. Hennessey, of Hanover, N.H., to be a Commissioner on the part of the United States on the International Joint Commission, United States and Canada.

Hennessey, 52, is director of the New Hampshire Council of Management and Budget in the Office of the Governor, where she has established a Revenue Forecasting Council and a Property and Debt Management Council.

1395

She is a consultant on foundation, corporate, and individual philanthropy, and was for 10 years executive director of the New Hampshire Charitable Fund and Affiliated Trusts, a statewide community foundation.

She is active in civic affairs, particularly those concerned with environmental issues, and serves as a trustee of the Environmental Law Institute and the New England Natural Resources Council.

United Nations

Designation of James E. Baker as Deputy U.S. Representative on the Economic and Social Council.   August 3, 1979

The President today announced that he has designated James E. Baker, of Santa Rosa, Calif., as Deputy Representative of the United States on the Economic and Social Council of the United Nations.

Baker, 44, is now adviser to the Economic and Social Council at the U.S. Mission to the U.N.

He has been a Foreign Service officer since 1960 and has been at the U.N. since 1974.

Digest of Other White House Announcements

The following listing includes the President's public schedule and other items of general interest announced by the White House Press Office and not included elsewhere in this issue.

July 28

The President declared a major disaster for the State of Texas as a result of severe storms and flash flooding caused by Tropical Storm Claudette, beginning on or about July 24, which caused extensive property damage.

July 30

The President returned to the White House from Camp David, Md.

The President met at the White House with Senator Robert Morgan and members of the North Carolina State Legislature.

July 31

The President met at the White House with:

—Zbigniew Brzezinski, Assistant to the President for National Security Affairs;

—Frank B. Moore, Assistant to the President for Congressional Liaison.

The President declared a major disaster for the State of Indiana as a result of severe storms and flooding, beginning on or about July 25, which caused extensive property damage.

The President transmitted to the Congress the 1977 Annual Coal Mine Health and Safety Report of the Department of the Interior.

August 1

The President met at the White House with:

—Dr. Brzezinski;

—the Republican congressional leadership;

—Mr. Moore;

—Robert R. Bowie, Deputy Director, National Intelligence, Central Intelligence Agency, and Dr. Brzezinski;

—Vice President Mondale;

—Representative   Norman   E. D'Amours of New Hampshire.

August 2

The President met at the White House with:

—Dr. Brzezinski;

—members of the United Democrats of Congress;

—Mr. Moore;

—Senator Lloyd Bentsen of Texas;

—Senator Donald Stewart of Alabama;

—Mrs. Carter, for lunch;

—Secretary of Energy-designate Charles W. Duncan, Jr.

The White House announced that applications for the 1980–81 White House Fellowships are now available and must be requested by November 15, 1979. The program was established by President Johnson in 1964 to give outstanding individuals early in their career firsthand experience in governing the Nation. It is open to all U.S. citizens except those in civilian Federal Government positions. Fellows are assigned for 1 year to a Cabinet officer, the Vice President, or a senior member of the President's staff. Although their job assignment is the core of their year, they also participate in educational seminars with top Government officials, leading scholars, journalists, and others who deal with the National Government. There are no occupational, age, sex, racial, political, or religious restrictions. Minority groups and women are encouraged to apply. Application materials and additional information can be obtained from the President's Commission on White House Fellowships, Box 7737, Washington, D.C. 20044 (202/653–6263). Requests for applications must be postmarked no later than November 15, and completed applications no later than December 1, 1979.

August 3

The President met at the White House with:

—Vice President Mondale, Secretary of State Cyrus R. Vance, Secretary of Defense Harold Brown, Dr. Brzezinski, and Mr. Jordan;

—Mr. Moore;

—Lyle Gramley, member of the Council of Economic Advisers;

—Polish American leaders.

NOMINATIONS SUBMITTED TO THE SENATE

The following list does not include promotions of members of the Uniformed Services, nominations to the Service Academies, or nominations of Foreign Service officers.

Submitted July 31, 1979

ALBERT TATE, JR., of Louisiana, to be United States Circuit Judge for the Fifth Circuit, vice a new position created by P.L. 95–486, approved October 20, 1978.

WILLIAM L. BEATTY, of Illinois, to be United States District Judge for the Southern District of Illinois, vice a new position created by P.L. 95–486, approved October 20, 1978.

HUGH GIBSON, JR., of Texas, to be United States District Judge for the Southern District of Texas, vice Finis E. Cowan, resigned.

GEORGE J. MITCHELL, of Maine, to be United States District Judge for the District of Maine, vice a new position created by P.L. 95–486, approved October 20, 1978.

Submitted August 2, 1979

MOON LANDRIEU, of Louisiana, to be Secretary of Housing and Urban Development.

NEIL GOLDSCHMIDT, of Oregon, to be Secretary of Transportation.

Submitted August 3, 1979

PATRICIA PRICE BAILEY, of the District of Columbia, to be a Federal Trade Commissioner for the unexpired term of 7 years from September 26, 1973, vice Mary Elizabeth Hanford, resigned.

1397

NOMINATIONS—Continued

Submitted August 3—Continued

GEORGE A. DALLEY, of the District of Columbia, to be a member of the Civil Aeronautics Board for the remainder of the term expiring December 31, 1982, vice Alfred Edward Kahn, resigned.

JAMES V. DAY, of Maine, to be a Federal Maritime Commissioner for the term expiring June 30, 1984 (reappointment).

JOHN R. EVANS, of Utah, to be a member of the Securities and Exchange Commission for the term expiring June 5, 1983 (reappointment).

PHILIP A. LOOMIS, JR., of Maryland, to be a member of the Securities and Exchange Commission for the term expiring June 5, 1984 (reappointment).

JERRY L. BUCHMEYER, of Texas, to be United States District Judge for the Northern District of Texas, vice William M. Taylor, Jr., retired.

ALAN N. BLOCH, of Pennsylvania, to be United States District Judge for the Western District of Pennsylvania, vice Herbert P. Sorg, retired.

JEAN LANDE HENNESSEY, of New Hampshire, to be a Commissioner on the part of the United States on the International Joint Commission, United States and Canada, vice Kenneth M. Curtis, resigned.

CHECKLIST OF WHITE HOUSE PRESS RELEASES

The following listing contains releases of the White House Press Office which are not included in this issue.

Released July 30, 1979

Announcement: nomination of Albert Tate, Jr., to be United States Circuit Judge for the Fifth Circuit

Announcement: nomination of William L. Beatty to be United States District Judge for the Southern District of Illinois

Announcement: nomination of George J. Mitchell to be United States District Judge for the District of Maine

Announcement: nomination of Hugh Gibson, Jr., to be United States District Judge for the Southern District of Texas

CHECKLIST—Continued

Released July 31, 1979

Advance text: remarks at the Cane Run generating station of the Louisville Gas & Electric Company in Louisville, Ky.

Advance text: remarks at a town meeting in Bardstown, Ky.

Released August 2, 1979

Advance text: remarks at the annual convention of the International Platform Association—by Zbigniew Brzezinski, Assistant to the President for National Security Affairs

News conference: on the President's message to the Congress on environmental priorities and programs—by Stuart E. Eizenstat, Assistant to the President for Domestic Affairs and Policy, and Gustave Speth, Chairman of the Council on Environmental Quality

Fact sheets: the President's message to the Congress on the environment (two releases)

Released August 3, 1979

Transcript: remarks on the Congress August recess—by Vice President Walter F. Mondale

Announcement: nomination of Jerry L. Buchmeyer to be United States District Judge for the Northern District of Texas

Announcement: nomination of Alan N. Bloch to be United States District Judge for the Western District of Pennsylvania

---

ACTS APPROVED BY THE PRESIDENT

Approved July 30, 1979

H.R. 3661_____ Public Law 96–40
An act to increase the authorization of appropriations under the Act of December 22, 1974 (88 Stat. 1712).

H.R. 2154_____ Public Law 96–41
Strategic and Critical Materials Stock Piling Revision Act of 1979.

Approved July 31, 1979

H.R. 4712_____ Public Law 96–42
An act to delay conditionally the effective date of certain rules of procedure and evidence proposed by the United States Supreme Court, and for other purposes.

Approved August 2, 1979

S. 961_____ Public Law 96–43
Speedy Trial Act Amendments Act of 1979.

ACTS APPROVED—Continued

Approved August 2—Continued

H.R. 2729_____ Public Law 96–44
National Science Foundation Authorization
Act for Fiscal Year 1980.

Approved August 3, 1979

H.J. Res. 373_____ Public Law 96–45
A joint resolution recognizing the anniversaries of the Warsaw uprising and the Polish
resistance to the invasion of Poland during
World War II.

PRESIDENTIAL DOCUMENTS

Week Ending Friday, August 10, 1979

Department of Justice

Exchange of Letters on the Resignation of Griffin B. Bell as Attorney General. August 3, 1979

To Attorney General Griffin Bell

I accept with genuine regret your resignation as Attorney General of the United States.

As a dedicated and independent professional, as a wise and judicious administrator, as a fair and compassionate public servant and as a valued personal friend of the President you have served our country well. Your accomplishments have been a source of pride for me and for others who have assessed the accomplishments of the Department of Justice under your leadership. You have left a good heritage of personnel and policy which will serve to perpetuate the advantages of your good work.

You have my best wishes and sincere thanks as you return to private practice, and I look forward to having your advice and support in the months ahead.

Give my love (and thanks) to Mary.

Your friend,

JIMMY CARTER

———

August 2, 1979

Dear Mr. President:

As we have discussed, I hereby formally tender my resignation as Attorney General of the United States, which will be effective upon the appointment and qualification of my successor. I do so with gratitude to you for affording me the opportunity to serve as Attorney General.

As a lawyer and citizen, this has been the highest privilege of my life. For 30 months I have been the lawyer for the people of the United States. The work has been hard; the challenges have been great; and I have given my best effort. It is an experience that I will cherish for all of my days.

When you asked me to undertake this responsibility, I told you I would stay on the job until I could warrant to you that the Department of Justice was strong, running well, and an institution of which you and the American people could be proud. In asking you earlier this year for my release to return to the private sector, I gave you that representation, and I now leave the Department knowing that it is in the hands of good and strong men and women whom you have placed in its top leadership positions and that it is staffed by professionals.

You have been a bulwark of strength to me in leading the Department. I have carried out your direction to develop traditions of excellence and independence in the Department and you, indeed all Americans, can have the satisfaction of

1401

knowing that these traditions will be demanded practices for many years to come.

Finally, I simply want to state that serving in your Cabinet has been a great personal honor. I value my friendship with you, and I hope that you will call upon me whenever I can be of service.

Warm personal regards.

Sincerely,

GRIFFIN B. BELL
Griffin Bell

[The President, The White House]

NOTE: The texts of the letters were made available on August 4.

Department of the Treasury and the Federal Reserve System

Remarks at the Swearing In of G. William Miller as Secretary of the Treasury and Paul A. Volcker as Chairman of the Board of Governors of the Federal Reserve System. August 6, 1979

THE PRESIDENT. One of the enjoyable and gratifying aspects of being President of our great country is to be able to call upon distinguished Americans to serve our country. The two most important economic posts in our Government are the Secretary of Treasury and the Chairman of the Federal Reserve System. And I don't believe that anyone whom I have read and listened to very closely in the last few days have contradicted the fact that we have two superbly qualified men who will be serving in these two important posts in the days ahead.

Our country is facing troubled times economically. We've now experienced more than a decade of persistent inflation, which has sapped away the confidence of American people in the future, which has put an additional and unnecessary burden on the shoulders of our people of all kinds, and which has been a discouraging thing for economists and for the Congress and for Presidents and other administrative officials at all levels of government.

This inflationary problem has been exacerbated in recent months by the extremely rapid increase in energy costs. In the last 6 months, OPEC has raised energy prices 60 percent, and the retail price of energy in our country has increased more than that in the last 4 months alone.

How to deal with this serious problem of inflation, how to keep a sound dollar, how to keep a strongly growing economy in our Nation, how to deal with the problems of housing and unemployment, and to meet the social needs of our people is indeed a challenge that is great, not insurmountable, but requires the best leadership and the best minds and the most intense and sincere dedication.

I think all of us know that there must be experience in these two posts. There must be competence and there must be dedication. There's no doubt that Paul Volcker and Bill Miller exemplify these characteristics to an utmost degree—an unchallenged, uncontradicted degree.

In addition, it's important for our country that the leadership in our economic community have the confidence of America, of people who labor at all levels of employment—at the business executives, bankers, the financiers, government officials. These two men must have the confidence of our Nation, and they do.

It's also extremely important for everyone who lives in our country to know that the Secretary of Treasury and the Chairman of the Fed have the confidence of the financial world, because the stability of the dollar, the persistent attack on the problems of inflation are absolutely crucial to maintaining the leadership that our country must maintain—and also that there be a stable purpose of our Nation exemplified by these two men and others, like myself, who will work with them.

I'm determined to maintain a steady course, to maintain a sound fiscal policy. I'm determined to maintain a responsible policy concerning our monetary systems, and also a sound and conservative budget policy. Now is no time to change course. Now is no time to deviate from the purposes that we have espoused, that we have described to the American people and to the rest of the world.

I am absolutely confident that Bill Miller and Paul Volcker will join me in that commitment, and I am gratified to have them as partners with me, with the other administration officials, and with the Congress and the American people in pursuing this steady course based on a responsible fiscal, monetary, and budget policy.

The first to be sworn in will be William Miller, who has served in a distinguished way as Chairman of the Federal Reserve Board, who has a superb record as a corporate leader, who is a clear and evocative spokesman, both in public and in private counsels, who has shown already his ability to deal with the problems that I've outlined concerning inflation, a strong economy, employment, the meeting of our social needs in our country. And I'm grateful and honored as President to ask Judge Leon Higginbotham to administer the oath of office as Secretary of the Treasury to a fine American and a distinguished public servant, William Miller.

Judge Higginbotham.

[*At this point, Judge A. Leon Higginbotham of the Third Circuit administered the oath of office.*]

I'd like to say in introduction that Bill Miller will serve not only as Secretary of the Treasury but also as the chief economic spokesman of my administration and the economic coordinator of my administration.

Bill Miller.

SECRETARY MILLER. Mr. President, it seems I was standing in this very spot on a similar occasion not so long ago, about 17 months. At that time, I would have predicted that I would serve out my term as Chairman of the Federal Reserve Board and then return to private life. I only hope my economic forecasts prove to be more accurate.

Many of my friends have been puzzled by my move from the secure and independent halls of the Federal Reserve to an insecure and exposed seat in the Cabinet. There should be no mystery. In these difficult times, every American should be willing to serve his President and his country to the best of his abilities. If each does his part, the total impact will have a powerful influence on our effectiveness and on our confidence.

Today, in dealing with the economic conditions we face, we have a towering challenge. We have inherited the most distressing economic environment in 50 years. Inflation is a clear and present danger. It has struck at our Nation's vitality. If it is not checked, then it will threaten our democratic system itself.

Never in its history has America experienced peacetime inflation of such magnitude and such duration as we've seen during the decade of the seventies. It is unprecedented.

This virulent cancer of inflation has built up over some 15 years. Its incubation period coincided with larger events which divided our Nation and weakened our resistance to this dread disease. As a consequent, inflation has become deeply embedded in our economic structure. We can no longer effect a cure by cyclical treatment. We must attack the root causes and totally eradicate the basic sources of the malady.

Because inflation has built up over such a long period, it will not easily or quickly be dislodged. What is needed is a comprehensive, sustained, and total war against inflation. What is needed is an integrated strategy marshaling all the policy weapons at our command until we achieve unconditional surrender.

As I have often said in my former role as Federal Reserve Chairman, monetary policy certainly cannot do the job alone. But a disciplined monetary policy is a key element. President Carter has made an excellent choice in Paul Volcker as my successor. He is superbly qualified. I am sure that Paul and the other able and dedicated Governors of the Federal Reserve and the Presidents of the Federal Reserve Banks who serve on the Open Market Committee can be counted on in their independence to maintain the proper monetary stance.

At the same time, those of us with responsibility in the administration must apply ourselves with full diligence to implementing the other elements of the President's economic strategy—a disciplined fiscal policy, a program for moderation of wage and prices, commitment to a sound and stable dollar, expansion of exports, balance in our international accounts, a comprehensive energy program to reduce our dependence on imported oil, to conserve energy in every way, and to develop alternate energy sources within our borders.

And certainly the President's program on energy should be enacted as promptly as possible, including the windfall profits tax.

And we must pursue the other elements—reduction of unnecessary Government regulation and other cost-raising Government actions.

We must encourage employee training, capital investment, and the research and development and the other initiatives that are essential to increase our productivity.

Of course, economic activity is not of itself the essence of our national purpose. There are higher aspirations concerning the spiritual and humanistic values of American life and human society. But it is not likely that these higher goals can be attained in the complex and interdependent world without a sound economy.

Employment opportunities for every American, production of the goods and services we need at stable prices, advances in science and technology, molded in humane application, all are a precondition.

Without a vigorous economic system, we cannot assure the adequacy of our national security. We cannot provide sufficiently for the poor and the aged and the infirm and the veterans who have served this country. We cannot revitalize our cities. We cannot guarantee proper shelter or education or medical care for all Americans. We will be handicapped in maintaining American leadership in a fragile world.

A sound economy is thus the basis for pursuing our national goals. The government must lead the war against inflation, but the campaign most surely will succeed only if every American plays his full part.

Support of all our citizens is needed to endure a period of austerity, fairly shared, so that we may again be able to enjoy the bounty of this great land. We must have the compassion to cushion the burden in these austere times from those least able to protect themselves. It is a period of testing. Do we have the will, the determination, the character to persevere?

Watching the struggle of the boat people to find a true light in a darkened corner of the world, watching their extreme risk to find an American refuge, watching their sacrifice, speaks more eloquently than I can of the living reality of the American dream.

My purpose, Mr. President, friends, Americans, will be to serve as your Secretary of Treasury in doing my very best to assure the lasting vitality of our economic system, to fight and to win the war against inflation, to reinforce the preeminence of Americans at home and abroad, and to keep alive that great American dream.

Thank you.

THE PRESIDENT. Next, Judge Higginbotham will administer the oath of office to Paul Volcker as Chairman of the Federal Reserve System.

Mr. Volcker is a man who has devoted his entire professional career to dealing successfully with the complexities of monetary theory and practice and international finance.

I consulted with many people when I was deciding whom to ask to serve in this most important position. And the more people who talked to me, the more the choice became obvious.

Internationally, Paul Volcker is well known. His experience in the Federal Reserve Bank in New York and also within the Treasury Department itself has been a demonstration of not only sound management but incisive analysis and leadership. Among his notable peers, he is recognized as being superb in the ability to understand the complexities of a fast-changing monetary world, protecting the interest of our Nation, and making incisive decisions that were honored as their results were observed.

When I met with Paul Volcker to discuss his appointment with him, he made it clear to me, and I instantly agreed, that both he and I and Bill Miller, who was present, would honor the independence and the integrity of the Federal Reserve System.

We also recognize the need to exchange ideas and to share responsibility in a completely appropriate way between the Government—the executive branch, the Congress, and the Federal Reserve—and the private enterprise system of our Nation.

I am extremely grateful that Paul Volcker is willing to serve. He takes this position with some financial sacrifice, but with an awareness of the possible benefits to our country in broadening and expanding his responsibility in his area of service.

I have never made an appointment, I don't believe, that was received domestically and internationally with any more uniform approbation. And so for that reason, also, I am grateful to Paul Volcker for being willing now to accept the oath of office and then the responsibilities as Chairman of the Federal Reserve System of our country.

Paul.

[At this point, Judge Higginbotham administered the oath of office.]

MR. VOLCKER. Mr. President, ladies and gentlemen, that's not the first time I've taken that oath. And every time I've done so, I end up with a little lump in my throat at the end, because it really is a great privilege for me to be asked to serve in public office and, most of all, the one I'm undertaking today.

It's obvious to all of you from what's been said today that we're face to face with economic difficulties really unique in our experience. And we've lost that euphoria that we had 15 years ago, that we knew all the answers to managing the economy.

But somehow knowledge of our limitations seems to me the beginning of wisdom, and I for one am convinced we can make progress now that we have the problems in clearer perspective.

And I've been particularly encouraged, Mr. President, with the forthrightness with which you have reiterated the priorities on inflation, on energy, on the budget, and all the rest—priorities and objectives that I am sure are shared not just by me but by the Federal Reserve generally and indeed by the citizens of this country.

Now, we in Federal Reserve, I suppose, are always a little sensitive about our special niche within the Government. But I assure you, we also know we operate within the framework of government. There's no moat around that marble palace on Constitution Avenue to impede communication in every direction, and particularly with the administration, with the Congress. And I look forward to maintaining those communications.

I've spent a fair amount of my life now within the Federal Reserve, and it looks as though it will be a little more. I cherish its integrity. I cherish its professionalism. And I only hope that as I take office that reputation can be maintained and, over time, even enhanced, as it was with my predecessor, whom I'm so happy and proud to share this platform today. I appreciate the chance to try to do my part.

Thank you very much.

NOTE: The President spoke at 3 p.m. at the ceremony in the East Room at the White House.

Baltimore, Maryland

Remarks Following a Tour of Neighborhood Rehabilitation Projects.   August 7, 1979

As all of you know, our country is determined to win the energy war and I believe the people here on East Biddle Street can help me. Do you agree? [*Applause*]

A couple of Sundays ago I made a speech to the Nation about the strength of our country and about our need to have a strong and united effort in our Nation, not only to have a good economy, with jobs for people, good housing, but also to stop the waste of energy and to let our Nation be dependent on ourselves and not on the OPEC countries.

Behind me, you see several panels on the top of this house that are going to be all over the Nation in the future. There's no way for them to embargo the sunshine, right? [*Applause*]

Baltimore is showing the way. You've got a great mayor in Don Schaefer. And you have worked with him to make sure that your city is becoming a better place to live.

Two and a half years ago, almost three, I came to Baltimore to see the fine housing programs that were in effect here, where people who did not have jobs were given jobs to make old homes new and to let people live in decent housing for a change, quite often with a family that was going to live in a house doing a major part of the work.

Now we have a fine weatherization program underway in Baltimore. This year, we will have 3,000 homes completely weatherized, not with expensive workers, but with CETA workers, who were formerly unemployed. They are doing a superb job. It only costs, for each home, about $275 to make sure that the doors, the windows, the hot water heaters do not waste energy. This money comes back in saved heating bills in less than 2 years, and then for the rest of the life of the home, there's a tremendous savings in dollars and a warmer house and a better place to live which will be of benefit to you, to the city, to your neighbors, and to our country.

This year, 3,000 homes, next year, 4,000 more homes, more jobs, and one of the good things, one of the good things is that these young workers who were formerly unemployed are learning a good trade and they are going from this program into private employment with a lot higher salary level and a stable life for the future. That's what I call cooperation. That's what we need all over the country.

I don't know if you know it or not, but 40 percent of all the energy in our country goes into the heating and the cooling of homes and other buildings—40 percent. And because we are so wasteful now, between 30 percent and 50 percent of all that heat is wasted. It costs our country in energy security. It makes us too dependent on foreign oil. It takes jobs away from our Nation and imports inflation. If we can just cut down on the waste of energy in our homes, this would be a tremendous program now and in the future.

In 1977 I proposed to the Congress and the Congress passed a bill that gives $300 in tax credits for any homeowner who will weatherize a home to cut down energy waste and $2,200 for any home that will install solar heat for the house itself or for hot water or sometimes even for cooling. This is a program just getting started, and we have now proposed to the Congress an additional program that will let the power companies, the gas companies, the electric light companies, give a loan to a family or to the owner of a house that's rented to make sure that the house is weatherized and made efficient and that loan will not have to be paid back until the house is sold. This will save a half million barrels of oil every day and, again, will provide tremendous savings

for the homeowners and the working people of our Nation.

It's very important that this program be understood not just by those of you assembled here on North Patterson and East Biddle Street but also by the people all over our country. We are making good progress toward giving our people a better life, and we are letting you have a part in providing for our energy security and making us free from dependence on foreign oil that might be interrupted and damage our lives and damage the country we love. Will you cooperate on this program with me? [*Applause*]

Let me add a word about the school building on my right. This building was built, I believe, in 1896. It has educated, as you know, a lot of young people. Now it's no longer used for a school building, but it's being renovated at a very low cost compared to a new building. And by December, it will be completed, and we'll have a place to live, a beautiful place to live for 19 families. This is being done in other places in Baltimore at a great savings to the taxpayers and giving good housing for all our people.

This is the kind of cooperation that you are finding now among the Federal agencies—Housing and Urban Development, which provides the funds and the know-how; Labor, which provides the CETA programs and training the young people to have permanent jobs; HEW, interested in a better life for our people in education and welfare and health; and other Federal agencies. But the most important thing is that we are working cooperatively with the State government officials and the local government officials and also private industry.

An additional thing in Baltimore is this: The people who do most of the work are the ones who live here and who want a better place to live. That's the kind of cooperation we're going to continue, and I want to say to you from the bottom of my heart that I thank Mayor Schaefer and all the government officials here in the city. I appreciate the people who are here assembled to hear my voice, and I particularly appreciate the citizens of our country who believe that our Nation is already strong and great, that it can be greater in the future and stronger, and who will do your individual part in saving energy, cutting out waste, guaranteeing our Nation's security.

I want you to make sure that Congress cooperates with me. We and the Congress will cooperate with you. We'll have energy security for our Nation and a better life for all Americans. That's what we want; that's what we're going to have.

Thank you very much.

NOTE: The President spoke at 9:35 a.m. at the intersection of East Biddle Street and North Patterson Park Avenue, in east Baltimore.

Prior to his remarks, the President toured the home of Mrs. Genitha Rhyne. The house was rehabilitated and weatherized as part of a citywide project, and also was outfitted with a solar unit for heating. The President and Jay Brodie, Commissioner of Housing and Community Development, then toured School No. 37, one of the vacant school buildings in Baltimore being renovated into apartment housing. While he was at the school, the President met with city officials and neighborhood residents to discuss the rehabilitation projects.

Baltimore, Maryland

Remarks and a Question-and-Answer Session at the National Convention of the Order of the Sons of Italy in America.
August 7, 1979

THE PRESIDENT. *Judge Montemurro, Governor Hughes, Mayor Don Schaefer, who's done so much to keep Baltimore a great city, Senator Sarbanes, Senator Mathias, Congressman Biaggi, Judge Sirica, Colonel Battaglia, delegates, mem-* bers, and friends of the Sons of Italy in America:

I'm not supposed to go to Italy until next year. Why is it that I already feel like I'm there?

I intend to visit your great mother country next year for an official state visit in Venice to meet with the other leaders of the industrialized Western nations to discuss matters important to our country and to the other nations on Earth.

I'm especially glad today that in addition to Congressman Biaggi and Judge Sirica and Father Baroni,[1] that I was able to bring with me the highest law enforcement officer in our Nation, the new Attorney General of the United States of America, Benjamin Civiletti. And I sincerely hope that you approve of this appointment.

It is very important that the government of our Nation represent and reflect the varied heritage of America. But I recognize a special claim that Italian Americans have. Some of us are very proud that our people came over in 1620 on the *Mayflower*, but not many of us can say that our people came over in 1492 on the *Santa María.* [*Laughter*]

For myself, today I came over on the train. And first of all, I want to say that I recommend this kind of trip to every American regardless of national background. Trains have always been a truly American way to travel, and I am determined to improve America's railway system. I want to demonstrate that trains represent the future and not the past in transportation in America. And I hope you'll help me with that.

In recent years there've been too many bankruptcies, too many terminations of rail service, to a great degree brought about by excessive Government regula-

---

[1] Geno Baroni, Assistant Secretary for Neighborhoods, Voluntary Associations, and Consumer Protection, Department of Housing and Urban Development.

tion. Recently, the Congress passed legislation severely reducing Government regulation of the airline industry. Many of you flew into Baltimore, and you know that passengers on airlines have saved already more than $2½ billion. The airlines have made more money, more people travel. Now we have before the Congress a proposal to do the same thing with American railroads. And if you'll help me with Congress, we'll deregulate the railroads, put them back on a sound, blue-ink basis and have a better transportation system for our country.

Amtrak must be more efficient, more comfortable, and more economical. And we are finally changing the blocked Northeast Corridor into an open passageway for millions of Americans. This is the same thing I'm determined to do with my Presidency, to keep it open by traveling frequently and freely among the people of our Nation, and that's why I'm so glad to be here with you. I thank you for giving me this opportunity.

Now, people used to call America a melting pot, but that has never really been true. The people of this country did come from all over the world. We are a nation of immigrants; we are a nation of refugees. We came here bringing with us every kind of culture and language and religion and way of life. Our ancestors all sought the same freedom, but we never got melted down into a single featureless mass where all were exactly the same. And all of us are glad that this did not happen.

Whatever our race or religion or form of nationality, we have kept some of our original character, even as we've learned to live and to work together as Americans. We are not a melting pot. We are more like a pot of minestrone. [*Laughter*]

As I said often during my campaign throughout the country, the analogy that comes closest, to my mind, to capturing the essence of America is that we are a mosaic. Each fragment of the mosaic has its own shape and its own color and its own size. And the beauty of this mosaic is to be found both because each piece is different and unique and because the pieces fit together in harmony so well.

This country is a mosaic made up of Italians and Irish and Poles and Jews and blacks and Orientals and Native Americans and even people with southern accents. [*Laughter*]

And I might say that all of us have on occasion suffered from some degree of prejudice. But the whole is greater than the sum of its parts, and we will go on adding pieces to this American mosaic as long as there is oppression and tyranny and suffering in the world which people need to escape and to come here for freedom.

The famous poem by Emma Lazarus inscribed at the base of the Statue of Liberty includes these lines which all of you know:

> Give me your tired, your poor,
> Your huddled masses yearning to
> breathe free,
> The wretched refuse of your teeming
> shore.
> Send these, the homeless, tempest-tost
> to me,
> I lift my lamp beside the golden door!

That old, beloved poem has new and vital meaning today, and we ought to think about this. The phrase about the tempest-tossed sounds almost like a prophecy of the boat people. The refugees from Indochina who have posed such a challenge to the conscience of the world, they are the tempest-tossed of 1979. The golden door of our Nation must be open to them just as it was open to the tempest-tossed parents and grandparents of almost everyone in this room and all those who live throughout the country.

There is a tendency in our Nation, even amongst some of us, to say, well, now it's different. It's not different. We must be open-hearted, and we must still be concerned for those who seek to escape persecution and to find freedom.

It's good for our Nation that you are meeting here as Italian Americans, that you are working together to preserve your heritage and your culture, because you have so much to offer. I do not mean only the cultural and artistic and musical heritage, a heritage represented by names like Michelangelo and da Vinci, Verdi and Toscanini, nor do I mean even the great individual contributions of particular Italian Americans, although, of course, we are all intensely proud of people who have held our Nation together in a time of trial and testing and great threat—men like John Sirica, Peter Rodino, and now Benjamin Civiletti.

Even more important than any American, no matter how great that individual might be, is the system of values that the Italians and the Poles and the Irish and the European Jews and other immigrants brought to our shores. I mean the devotion to family, a sense of discipline, a belief in hard work, a readiness to sacrifice so that each generation's children could have a better life, and finally a sense of concern and compassion for others. That sense of compassion is very broad, and it's evident in this room, in this organization.

On this trip, I'm discussing with Mario Biaggi the plight of the people in Northern Ireland. Peter Rodino, with his committee, is working to help the boat people. There are many in this room who are concerned about Israel, who are concerned about the poor of all nationalities, and about the elderly who live among us.

During this convention I have learned the Sons of Italy will present a check for $2 million to the March of Dimes Foundation to fight birth defects. And that money will go to help children of every racial and ethnic background. You've raised that money in your capacity as Italian Americans, but you are donating it in your capacity as Americans. That is the spirit of the United States, the same spirit that the immigrants brought to this country, of unity, patriotism, confidence, and concern.

It's the same spirit that we must now bring to the fight to achieve and to preserve American energy security.

I'm not going to describe any particular program today. We all know that we can meet our energy security threat only if we enact legislation and then pull together as Americans.

Because our Nation is not only a mosaic ethnically and culturally but also economically, we're different one from another. Some of us financially are well off, some have to struggle just to make ends meet; some of us are energy consumers, some energy producers. Some of us are from the Northeast, where we need a lot of heating oil to keep our homes warm; some of us are from the Sun Belt, where enormous differences of distance means that we need a lot of gasoline just to go to our jobs.

Too often in the past, as we tried to deal with this complicated energy problem, we have let these differences paralyze our Nation. We've been too prone to struggle and fight among ourselves in serving our own particular interest. We have let the general interest, the national interest suffer.

I'm sorry to say that until now the general interest has had a hard time of it in the halls of Congress, despite the dedication and the work of the leadership and many Members of the Congress. The Congress has yielded to the narrow interest on energy issues time and time again. I've now called on the Congress to enact a strong windfall profits tax on the oil companies to help finance a strong national effort to achieve energy security, and I need your help.

The Congress is now in recess, and its

Members are at home listening to constituents. I'm sure that the message they will hear is a clear call to enact the windfall profits tax on the oil companies. America needs the revenues from that tax to finance a vast effort to increase energy production and also to increase energy conservation.

America needs those resources, those revenues to improve mass transit. I took the train this morning, not only because it's the best way to come from Washington to Baltimore but also because I wanted to show my support for a strong mass transportation system.

The windfall profits tax will also let us build that kind of system and will help us to ease the burden of increasing energy cost that now falls on the shoulders of the poorest among us. But we cannot do any of that unless we are willing to place the common good over the narrow special interests.

This is a challenge I talked about in my Sunday night television address. It's a challenge I'm talking about from one end of this country to another. It's a challenge I'm calling on you to help me meet together, unified, with confidence in ourselves, with confidence in each other, with confidence in our Nation, in America. You can help me and the Nation that we all love by saving energy in your own lives and in your own homes and in your own communities and by getting the message across to the representatives in Congress that all of us must cooperate and to mobilize the strength of America to achieve energy security.

We have the greatest nation on Earth. Let's make it even greater. *Sempre avanti!* And now I'm ready for your questions.

QUESTIONS

NATIONAL HEALTH PLAN

Q. Mr. President, we're concerned with what you think the possibility is of having a national health insurance program passed within this administration and, if so, do you feel it will be the administration's bill or do you feel it would be the bill of, say, others who've presented bills?

THE PRESIDENT. I think it's very important that our Nation have a comprehensive health program. The differences that have been highly publicized between myself and Senator Kennedy on what shape the legislation should assume, I think, have been exaggerated. We've come a long way. There are some differences that are material, but I believe that we can overcome those differences.

The Congress is responsible for doing this. One of the comments that I made in the swearing-in ceremonies for Patricia Harris—who will be the new Secretary of HEW—is that part of her responsibility will be to resolve the differences that do exist between my own proposal—which has been very carefully considered and is a very sound proposal—and that of many others who've been interested in national health programs for a long time. So, I predict that this will be passed during this Congress, if not this year, then next year.

We've got the support of people like Abraham Ribicoff, Senator Russell Long, Senator Kennedy, and many others in the Senate, and then we have equivalent support in the House.

It's not intended by either Senator Kennedy or I that the program would be effective immediately. It would go into effect in 1983, but because of its far-reaching impact and the need to be responsible on budget matters, we want to phase it in very carefully. The first phase will be to coordinate existing Government programs. The second phase will be to pursue aggressively a prevention program to prevent disease and to build on the things we're already doing so well in that respect, and later to broaden the coverage one step at a time until all Americans, regardless of their income, have an adequate degree of health care. The total ultimate cost will not exceed, in my opinion, what the ultimate cost will be without this program, because the costs now are growing so rapidly.

The first step that I hope the Congress will pass this year, to go into effect immediately, is hospital cost containment. As you all know, because this is not a competitive industry, hospital costs have been going up twice as fast as the average cost of inflation. So, we need hospital cost containment immediately and then to implement the health program on a nationwide basis carefully, methodically, but thoroughly and with a maximum degree of cooperation between me and, as you say, others.

ETHNIC AMERICANS

Q. Mr. President, I am John Spatuzza from Chicago, Illinois. Mr. President, your predecessor had established an Office for Ethnic Affairs to demonstrate the concerns and to make available to ethnic Americans a vehicle by which they could express their concerns in their particular areas. Mr. President, does the fact that you have not chosen to establish such an office, does that in any way indicate a diminished concern for ethnic Americans?

THE PRESIDENT. I can answer that in one word—the word is "no." It does not show any absence of concern for ethnic Americans. We are now working with the leaders of this organization and others to see how we can broaden the input from different ethnic groups throughout the country into the White House where decisions are made.

I think it's very important to realize that all of us, from the President, the Vice President on down, attempt every day accurately to mirror the interest of ethnic Americans. But we do not have any lack of compassion or understanding, commitment, determination to serve ethnic American groups greater, and we have a broad range, for instance, of Italian Americans who serve at top levels in our administration. We'll continue with this. And I think you know that Vice President "Mondali"—[laughter]—is one of the representatives of the Italian Americans that I depend on very heavily, and now we have some more in the administration as well.

VISIT WITH ITALIAN FAMILY

Q. Good morning, Mr. President. I'm Josephine Falco, and I'm from Massachusetts. In your travels around our country, you have visited American families of many different backgrounds. Do you, Mr. President, plan to visit a family of our Italian heritage?

THE PRESIDENT. Yes. Nothing would please me more than to do that.

Q. Thank you, Mr. President. How about coming to 44 Beaverbrook Road, Waltham, Massachusetts? [Laughter]

THE PRESIDENT. That's a great temptation. Some of my top scheduling aides are here, and if they don't schedule me into an Italian American home, I might make some more changes in my staff. [Laughter]

FOOD AND ENERGY PRICES

Q. Florabell LaVerdi from Brownsville, Pennsylvania. Mr. President, Americans throughout our country are deeply concerned with the family budget and its ability to provide the adequate heat in their homes and the nutritious food on our tables. Do you believe that the ever-escalating costs will force us to choose between adequate heat or sufficient food?

THE PRESIDENT. I'm very pleased that in the last few months the wholesale price of food has been going down, including that of red meat. So far, the so-called middlemen and the retailers of meat have been profiting excessively in spite of the fact that the price of beef and pork and poultry to the farmer has been going down. I believe that the sum total of all this, however, is a leveling off and a starting down of the price of food, which should continue the rest of this year.

There is no way that I or anyone else can promise you cheaper energy in the future. In the last 4 months alone in our country, because of OPEC price increases, which are exorbitant and excessive, the price of energy in our country has gone up about 60 percent at the retail level. This is not going to turn around. I think it won't be nearly that steep in the future.

I've just come from a poor neighborhood in Baltimore. Mayor Schaefer has a program here depending upon CETA workers to go into low-income homes with formerly unemployed young people and to weatherize those homes, to add insulation to windows, to doors, insulation around hot water heaters, and so forth. The total average cost of that for any home is only about $275. That much can be saved in less than 2 years, and from then on, you have a saving of $150 or so in a small home every year as long as the home lasts.

In 1977 we got through the Congress—and don't many people know this—a program to give tax credits up to $300 for the insulation of a home, up to $2,200 to install solar heating. This next proposal that we've just put into the Congress, depending upon the windfall profits tax, will provide loans from the power companies, the natural gas supplying companies, the

electric power companies to all homeowners, a very low interest loan, so that you can insulate your homes and not have to pay back the cost of that insulation until the home is sold.

With this program alone, we hope to save more than a half million barrels of oil every day. So, we are moving now to compensate with your help in saving actual money on energy. Even though the price of oil itself goes up by having more efficient automobiles, using mass transit, insulating homes, setting thermostats at a higher degree level in the summer, lower in the winter, these things you must do to help yourselves.

So, food prices are turning downward; energy prices are going to go up. But your total cost of heat can go down if you take care of yourself by cooperating in these programs.

Thank you very much for that excellent question.

MEXICAN ENERGY SUPPLIES

Q. Peter Tubiolo from Covina, California, in southern California. What is your administration doing with reference to resolving the relationship between Mexico and the United States relative to the fuel import disagreements?

THE PRESIDENT. We're negotiating now on the price of natural gas. The original projection of the quantity of natural gas that Mexico planned to sell has been dropping substantially, because President López Portillo has decided to use a greater and greater quantity of Mexican natural gas in his own country. So, the amount to be sold to us is much less than we had anticipated. We are still negotiating on a price for that gas.

1413

We are already buying between 85 percent and 90 percent of all the oil that Mexico exports. So, we are already doing what a lot of Americans don't know about. We would buy 100 percent of all Mexico's exported oil if Mexico wanted to sell all their oil to just one customer. But I can understand the Mexicans' attitude. They want to have not all their eggs in just one customer's basket. So, they do sell 10 percent or 15 percent of their oil to other countries—Japan and some European countries.

So, we have an excellent relationship already with Mexico on oil; we're negotiating on natural gas. I hope that this will be a successful negotiation. I will be meeting personally with President López Portillo in Washington next month hopefully to conclude these negotiations. We've got a good relationship with Mexico, and we intend to keep it that way.

DEPARTMENT OF EDUCATION

Q. I'm Lucy Codella from White Plains, New York. Mr. President, there has been proposed a new department of education in Washington. Will this new department have any serious impact on the programing and the management of the present private, elementary, and secondary schools?

THE PRESIDENT. I would say it would have a beneficial impact. First of all, to have a separate department of education will actually decrease the Federal bureaucracy, the cost of administration, and the number of employees.

Secondly, this department will give a higher profile, a higher degree of awareness and publicity to the problems of education than you can possibly have with education buried under health and welfare.

Another thing that's important, and that is that the State and local officials and also the private school officials will have a single identifiable person with one responsibility with whom they can deal. My own belief is that this will result in a lesser interference of the Federal Government in the affairs of the State and local public schools and also the private schools. You won't have as many lawsuits and withholdings of funds and so forth if you can have a routine natural communication and consultation and cooperation between the education officials, private and public, and the Federal Government to begin with. I think we can have fewer regulations, fewer forms, fewer requirements for Federal grants.

In the last 2½ years, we have had more increase in Federal aid for education with less interference than ever before in history, even during those days in the sixties when President Johnson was in the White House. It's been a superb achievement.

We will have within the new department an assistant secretary of education just for private schools, private education. So, I have no doubt that the relationship between the private schools and the Federal Government will be better with the new department of education than it has been in the past.

U.S.-ITALIAN RELATIONS

Q. Mr. President, I'm Guy Arigo from Revere, Massachusetts. The Italian Government has been undergoing a serious governmental crisis. Is there any change in our Government's position with respect to possible changes in the Italian Government which eventually may bring a direct communistic participation in the Italian executive branch of government?

THE PRESIDENT. I'm very proud of the fact that the United States of America has an excellent relationship with the Government of Italy. We have deplored the violence and the threats of terrorism and the acts of terrorism in Italy. We have offered our services to the Government of Italy, to the people of Italy, in a cooperative way with other nations, I might add, to help stamp out the threat of terrorism. We now see a new government taking over in Italy. We've had an excellent relationship with Mr. Andreotti. We will also have an excellent relationship with the new government.

I have been very pleased at the result of the recent election which showed that the Communists, in a free and democratic election, lost substantial support from the people of Italy.

I might say three things very quickly. It would be completely inappropriate and, I think, counterproductive for our Nation to try to interfere in the electoral process of Italy. Secondly, I hope that over a period of time, and not too long to wait, that the influence of the Communists in Italy will take another drastic drop. And the third thing is, I trust the political judgment of the people of Italy.

We don't have any fear about the future of Italy being a democratic nation, allied with us, a strong NATO member, a distinguished member of the leadership with whom I meet every year at least, and obviously tied to us with the most valuable of ties, the ties of blood kinship so well represented by this group.

ITALIAN AMERICAN JUDICIAL SELECTIONS

Q. Good morning, Mr. President. I'm Charles Caputo from Pittsburgh, Pennsylvania, the Supreme Order of the Sons of Italy, or its chief legal officer.

May I say preliminarily, in 30 years of participation in activities of the Order, I've never heard anyone received with such acclaim and warmth, with one exception, than I did you this morning. The other exception is not too far away. It was exceeded before you got here when we received the Honorable Benjamin Civiletti.

With his appointment, Mr. President, you made all Americans of Italian descent throughout the United States very, very happy. I'd like to say, on a personal note, your appointment of Leonard Paletta in the city of Pittsburgh to the district court of western Pennsylvania was received very, very tremendously and gratifyingly by Americans of every ethnic descent. I'm so sorry he passed away before he could ascend the bench.

We wondered, and have discussed in many, many meetings, why, with all of the capable legal scholars and the proficient and efficient members of the bench in the various courts throughout the United States, why not one Italian has ever been appointed to the Supreme Court of the United States—and I know of only two——

THE PRESIDENT. I have wondered the same thing.

Q. —— I know of only two that presently serve in the district courts. However, Mr. President, my question is, and I finally got around to it, will this administration continue to seek out, recognize qualified Americans of Italian ancestry in its present search for Federal judicial appointments in the many vacancies that are presently looking for filling and, secondly, would the President and his committees on selection accept recommendations backed by portfolios from this organization or any other Italian ethnic organizations?

THE PRESIDENT. I think it's very easy to answer that question. The chief adviser to the President in the selection of Federal district judges and circuit court judges and Supreme Court Justices, if there ever is a vacancy, is a very distinguished person, who is present, and that's the Attorney General of the United States.

I will make you this offer. If the Sons of Italy and other distinguished groups around the country make recommendations for Federal judgeships and if you cannot get an adequate hearing in Benjamin Civiletti's office, you can come directly to me.

Q. Thank you, Mr. President. And I think we have an eloquent salesman right behind you there, Judge Frank J. Montemurro.

THE PRESIDENT. I only have time for one more question. And I'm looking forward to it.

NEW ENGLAND ENERGY SUPPLIES

Q. E. Howard Molisani of Port Washington, New York. My question deals with energy and its effect on the Northeast Corridor. In that particular corridor, Mr. President, there is a heavy concentration of Italian Americans working and living there. The energy, as far as oil is concerned, heats up our industry, gives employment, and heats up our living quarters. At the present time, I wanted to find out whether there are any special programs being initiated for that particular area, especially since that area is more afflicted than most other areas of the United States with the plague of unemployment.

THE PRESIDENT. I don't know the exact amount of money being spent on the Northeast Corridor. It's in excess of $2 billion, and we are trying to reach out in the repair of the railroad system in the Northeast Corridor to bring in opportunities for employment among those who have high unemployment rates.

We also are particularly concerned about the possible shortage of fuel for the Northeast Corridor, not only in transportation but for home heating purposes. One of the things which makes this region of northeast America so vulnerable is that about 80 percent or more of all the oil used in that region is imported, and I think about 80 or 83 percent of all the homes in the northeastern part of our country are heated with oil—very few in the South, or even here as far south as Baltimore.

We have pledged ourselves not only to meet the transportation needs—and obviously the railroads are a crucial and vital factor that will be served adequately with distillate fuels—but also to build up the reserve supplies for home heating to an adequate level.

Last year, we had at the end of October, 233 million barrels of oil in storage, in primary storage, for the heating of homes in New England. This proved to be adequate. This year I have promised to have built up by the end of October, 240 million barrels of home heating oil, more than we had last year just on the chance that that would be a more severe winter this year than we experienced in the winter of 1978, 1979.

So, we have this as one of our major concerns. We are monitoring the level of supplies every day, and I have pledged myself as President to make sure that there is no shortage of home heating oil for the Northeast area during this coming winter.

I might say that it obviously helps, no matter what the level of reserve supplies might be, if every homeowner will do his or her part not to waste energy. Forty percent of all the oil, of all the energy used in this country goes for the heating and cooling and servicing of buildings—40 percent. And the estimates that have been run by MIT and by other distinguished independent organizations have shown that between 30 percent and 50 percent of this is wasted. That not only hurts our country, but it hurts the pocketbook of every family involved.

And I hope that all of you will go back—you are leaders, I know, within the Sons of Italy organization—if all of you would go back to your local organizations and encourage every member to survey your home, to get the power company to help if they will, to see where energy can be saved with storm windows and with insulation around your hot water tank, lower the temperature of your hot water tank from 140—which most of it is, I'll bet—down to 105 degrees, which is adequately hot, to put the small restrictive valves on your hot water faucets, to drive 55 miles an hour, to form a carpool or to share a ride with a neighbor, to leave your cars home 1 day a week whenever it's possible and either walk or ride a bike or get a ride with a neighbor.

These are the kind of things—they seem like they're not very important, but they are absolutely crucial to our country.

We will provide adequate fuel for transportation and for heating in the Northeast Corridor and throughout the Northeast this winter. You can depend upon that.

But I need for all Americans in this room and listening to my voice on radio, television, and news media to do your individual part to make our Nation strong, to remove this noose of energy dependence on foreign countries from around our neck, and to let our Nation, which is already great, as I say, be even greater in the future.

You've honored me by letting me come. God bless every one of you.

NOTE: The President spoke at 11:03 a.m. in the Francis Scott Key Ballroom at the Baltimore Hilton. In his opening remarks, referred to Frank J. Montemurro, Jr., administrative judge of the Family Court Division of Philadelphia, John J. Sirica, former United States District Judge for the District of Columbia, and Frank J. Battaglia, deputy commissioner of police of Baltimore.

Meeting With President Ahmed Sékou Touré of Guinea

White House Statement. August 8, 1979

The President met for 1 hour and 10 minutes today with President Ahmed Sékou Touré of Guinea, who is in the United States on a private visit.

The discussions covered a wide range of matters of mutual interest, including African and international problems, the continuing improvement of bilateral relations, and Guinea's growing role in pan-African affairs and with the nonaligned countries.

President Touré will meet this afternoon with Secretary of State Cyrus R. Vance.

While in the United States, President Touré will also consult with top-level officials of the United Nations, the World Bank, and a number of U.S. banks and corporations interested in promoting further U.S. investment in Guinea. He will also meet with Mayor Marion Barry of Washington, D.C., Mayor Tom Bradley of Los Angeles, and other officials on a tour that will take him to Los Angeles, Denver, Pittsburgh, and New York.

President Touré is accompanied by

his wife and several ministers of his Government.

Attending the meeting on the U.S. side were the President, Secretary of State Vance, National Security Adviser Zbigniew Brzezinski; Acting Assistant Secretary of State for African Affairs William Harrop, Ambassador to Guinea Oliver S. Crosby, and Jerry Funk of the National Security Council staff.

Attending on the Guinean side were President Sékou Touré; Madame Andree Touré, wife of the President; Ismael Touré, member of the National Political Bureau and Minister of Mines and Geology; Moussa Diakité, member of the National Political Bureau and Minister of Housing, State Lands and Urban Affairs; President of the National Legislative Assembly Damantang Camara; and Guinean Ambassador to the United States Mamady Lamine Conde.

Office of the Special Representative for Trade Negotiations

Nomination of Reubin O'D. Askew To Be Special Representative for Trade Negotiations and Designation of Alonzo L. McDonald, Jr., as Acting Special Representative.
August 8, 1979

The President will nominate Reubin Askew to be the Special Representative for Trade Negotiations with the rank of Ambassador Extraordinary and Plenipotentiary. This position will continue to be considered a Cabinet-level post. Governor Askew will succeed Robert Strauss, who is resigning the post effective today. The President earlier this year named Mr. Strauss as Ambassador at Large for the Middle East negotiations. Mr. Strauss will now be able to turn his full attention to that area.

Following confirmation, Governor As-

kew is expected to assume his duties as Special Trade Representative on or about October 1. In the interim, Alonzo L. McDonald, Jr., who is now the Deputy Trade Representative, will be the Acting Special Representative for Trade Negotiations.

Ambassador Strauss has been anxious to leave these responsibilities for quite some time, and we wanted to make this transition as soon as possible.

Both Ambassador Strauss and Ambassador McDonald have pledged to work closely with Governor Askew to ensure a smooth transition. The President is, of course, pleased that Governor Askew has agreed to join the administration in a position of this importance. The President served as Governor of Georgia at the same time that Governor Askew was in office in Florida. The men came to know each other well during that time. The President has long admired Governor Askew's abilities as a leader and as an administrator.

NOTE: Press Secretary Jody Powell read the announcement at 2:43 p.m. at the regular news briefing for reporters, held in the Briefing Room at the White House.

Federal Farm Credit Board

Nomination of Two Members.
August 8, 1979

The President today announced that he will nominate two persons to be members of the Federal Farm Credit Board for terms expiring March 31, 1985. They are:

JEWELL HAALAND, of Clarkfield, Minn., a retired farmer who served on the Grain Terminal Association for 21 years and is active in National Farmers Union activities; and

DWIGHT L. TRIPP, JR., of Auburn, Maine, a dairy farmer who raises registered holsteins (reappointment).

Meeting With Foreign Minister Hans-Dietrich Genscher of the Federal Republic of Germany

White House Statement.　August 9, 1979

While here on a working visit, Vice Chancellor and Foreign Minister of the Federal Republic of Germany Hans-Dietrich Genscher met with President Carter this morning for 30 minutes in the Cabinet Room. Also present at the meeting were Secretary of State Cyrus Vance; Zbigniew Brzezinski, Assistant to the President for National Security Affairs; George Vest, Assistant Secretary of State for European Affairs; and Steve Larrabee, NSC staff. The Foreign Minister was accompanied by West German Ambassador Berndt von Staden. During the meeting the President and Foreign Minister Genscher discussed issues of mutual concern, including theater nuclear forces, SALT II, and energy.

Following the meeting at the White House, Secretary Vance hosted a luncheon in honor of Foreign Minister Genscher, which was also attended by other senior West German and U.S. officials. Prior to his departure for the Federal Republic, Foreign Minister Genscher will also meet with Secretary of Defense Harold Brown and Dr. Brzezinski.

The meetings with Vance and other American officials are part of a regular exchange of views on matters of common interest to both countries.

Director of Selective Service

Nomination of Bernard Daniel Rostker. August 9, 1979

The President today announced his intention to nominate Bernard Daniel Rostker, of Great Falls, Va., to be Director of the Selective Service System.

Rostker is Principal Deputy Assistant Secretary of the Navy for Manpower and Reserve Affairs.

He was born February 1, 1944, in New York City. He received a B.S. in education and economics from New York University in 1964, and an M.S. (1966) and Ph. D. (1970) in economics from Syracuse University. He served in the U.S. Army from 1968 to 1970.

From 1970 to 1977, Rostker was an economist with the Rand Corp. From 1972 to 1977, he was program director for Rand's Project Air Force Manpower, Personnel and Training Program.

Rostker has been Deputy Assistant Secretary of the Navy since 1977 and has been responsible for policy development and program evaluation in all areas of Navy and Marine Corps military and civilian manpower, personnel, and training.

International Seafarers Convention

Message to the Senate Transmitting the Convention.　August 10, 1979

To the Senate of the United States:

I transmit herewith, for the advice and consent of the Senate to ratification, the International Convention on Standards of Training, Certification and Watchkeeping for Seafarers, with Annex, 1978 (the Convention), done at London, July 7, 1978. The report of the Department of State is enclosed for the information of the Senate in connection with its consideration of the Convention.

This Convention establishes improved and often new international requirements for training, certification and watchkeeping for masters, officers and certain crewmembers of "seagoing" merchant ships. These requirements should provide more highly qualified personnel on board ships and thereby reduce maritime casualties and promote safety of life at sea and protection of the marine environment. Such international requirements are responsive to proposals which were made by the United States in March 1977, following a series of tanker accidents in or near United States waters. I recommend that the Senate give prompt consideration to this Convention and advice and consent to its ratification.

JIMMY CARTER

The White House,
August 10, 1979.

United States-Norway Treaty on Extradition

Message to the Senate Transmitting the Treaty. August 10, 1979

To the Senate of the United States:

With a view to receiving the advice and consent of the Senate to ratification, I transmit herewith the Treaty of Extradition Between the United States of America and Norway signed at Oslo on June 9, 1977.

I transmit also, for the information of the Senate, the report of the Department of State with respect to the treaty.

The treaty is one of a series of modern extradition treaties being negotiated by the United States. It expands the list of extraditable offenses to include aircraft hijacking and obstruction of justice, as well as other offenses not now covered by our existing treaty with Norway. Upon entry into force, it will terminate and supersede the existing Treaty of Extradition of 1893, the Amendatory Extradition

Treaty of 1904, and the Supplementary Extradition Treaty of 1938.

This treaty will make a significant contribution to international cooperation in law enforcement. I recommend that the Senate give early and favorable consideration to the treaty and give its advice and consent to ratification.

JIMMY CARTER

The White House,
August 10, 1979.

United States-Canada Convention on Northern Pacific Halibut Fishery

Message to the Senate Transmitting a Protocol. August 10, 1979

To the Senate of the United States:

I am pleased to transmit the Protocol, with Annex, Amending the 1953 Convention Between the United States of America and Canada for the Preservation of the Halibut Fishery of the Northern Pacific Ocean and Bering Sea for Senate advice and consent to ratification. The Protocol was signed at Washington on March 29, 1979.

I also transmit for the information of the Senate the report of the Secretary of State with respect to this Protocol and an exchange of Notes, done on March 29, 1979, and an Agreed Minute, done on April 6, 1979.

This agreement was negotiated to bring the 1953 Convention Between the United States of America and Canada for the Preservation of the Halibut Fishery of the Northern Pacific Ocean and Bering Sea into conformity with the terms and intent of the Fishery Conservation and Management Act of 1976, which extended U.S. exclusive fisheries jurisdiction to 200 miles off the U.S. coasts. It will allow continuation of the International Pacific Halibut Commission, and of the joint management of the halibut resource in the Pacific. The agreement contains provisions for an interim enforcement regime, to apply, pending final delimitation, to maritime boundary areas in which both Canada and the United States claim fisheries jurisdiction. It allows the uninterrupted continuation of the work of the International Pacific Halibut Commission, and provides for the continuation of recreational fishing by both countries in maritime areas in which each exercises exclusive fisheries jurisdiction. In general, it makes an important contribution to good fisheries relations between our two countries.

I believe that approval of this Protocol is in the best interests of the United States. I recommend that the Senate give early consideration to this Protocol and its advice and consent to its ratification.

JIMMY CARTER

The White House,
   August 10, 1979.

National Aeronautics and Space Programs

Message to the Congress Transmitting a Report.   August 10, 1979

To the Congress of the United States:

I transmit this report on the Nation's progress in space and aeronautics during 1978. This report is provided in accordance with Section 206 of the National Aeronautics and Space Act of 1958 as amended (42 U.S.C. 2476).

Included in this report are statements of policy designed to maintain American space leadership. This report concentrates on the most significant Federal space and aeronautical activities. These emphases have enabled us to reduce the amount of detail and number of separate agency program descriptions.

JIMMY CARTER

The White House,
   August 10, 1979.

NOTE: The report is entitled "Aeronautics and Space Report of the President—1978 Activities" (Government Printing Office, 103 pages).

Death of Jacob Potofsky

Statement by the President.   August 10, 1979

America lost one of the giants of the labor movement when Jacob Potofsky, the former president of the Amalgamated Clothing Workers of America, died on Sunday. His long and distinguished career spanned much of modern American labor history. As a teenager, just a few years after coming to America from the Ukraine, he worked with Sidney Hillman to establish the Amalgamated Clothing Workers. In 1946 he succeeded Hillman as union president, and for 26 years he worked tirelessly to create a modern, self-sufficient, democratic, and vibrant union. While never losing sight of the needs of his members, Jacob Potofsky also recognized the need for conciliation and cooperation in labor relations.

I share with his family, the Amalgamated Clothing Workers, and the thousands of Americans who were touched by his life and his example, a sense of profound sadness at his death.

NOTE: Special Assistant to the President for Consumer Affairs Esther Peterson delivered the statement to the Amalgamated Clothing Workers of America at funeral services for Mr. Potofsky.

Digest of Other
White House Announcements

The following listing includes the President's public schedule and other items of general interest announced by the White House Press Office and not included elsewhere in this issue.

August 4

The President met at the White House with Zbigniew Brzezinski, Assistant to the President for National Security Affairs.

August 6

The President met at the White House with:
— Dr. Brzezinski;
— Frank B. Moore, Assistant to the President for Congressional Liaison;
— bishops of the African Methodist Episcopal Zion Church.

August 7

The President met at the White House with:
— Dr. Brzezinski;
— former Governor Reubin O'D. Askew of Florida.

August 8

The President met at the White House with:
— Dr. Brzezinski;
— newly elected officers of the Southern Baptist Convention;
— Ambassador Ephraim Evron of Israel;
— James T. McIntyre, Jr., Director of the Office of Management and Budget.

August 9

The President met at the White House with:
— Dr. Brzezinski;

— Rev. Jesse Jackson, national president of Operation PUSH (People United to Save Humanity).

August 10

The President met at the White House with:
— Secretary of Defense Harold Brown, Deputy Secretary of State Warren Christopher, Hamilton Jordan, Assistant to the President, and Dr. Brzezinski;
— Dr. Brzezinski;
— Mr. Moore;
— a group of editors and news directors (transcript will be printed next week).

The President participated in the briefing by administration officials for Hispanic community and civic leaders held in the East Room at the White House.

The White House announced the following personnel changes in the White House staff:
— Robert J. Lipshutz, Counsel to the President, intends to resign. He will return to Georgia to serve as cotrustee with Charles H. Kirbo of the Jimmy Carter Personal Assets Trust, and he will also chair the commission that will establish the Carter Presidential Library.
— Ambassador Esteban E. Torres, currently U.S. Permanent Representative to the United Nations Educational, Scientific, and Cultural Organization, will become Special Assistant to the President, working with programs and policies important to Hispanic Americans.
— Timothy E. Kraft, Assistant to the President, is going to the Carter-Mondale Committee as campaign manager.
— Sarah C. Weddington, currently Special Assistant to the President, will become Assistant to the Presi-

dent, assuming many of the duties of Mr. Kraft as well as continuing her work with programs and policies important to women.

—Ambassador Alonzo L. McDonald, currently Acting Special Representative for Trade Negotiations, will become Assistant to the President and director of the White House staff.

The President has asked Neil Goldschmidt to assume office as Secretary of Transportation, and Mr. Goldschmidt will be sworn into office Wednesday, August 15, in Portland, Oreg. Mr. Goldschmidt will take office under the recess appointment provision of the Constitution. His nomination was submitted to the Senate on August 2, and he will go through the normal confirmation process when the Senate returns from its recess.

The President left the White House for a weekend stay at Camp David, Md.

NOMINATIONS SUBMITTED TO THE SENATE

The following list does not include promotions of members of the Uniformed Services, nominations to the Service Academies, or nominations of Foreign Service officers.

Submitted August 10, 1979

SAMUEL D. JOHNSON, JR., of Texas, to be United States Circuit Judge for the Fifth Circuit, vice a new position created by P.L. 95–486, approved October 20, 1978.

EDWARD B. DAVIS, of Florida, to be United States District Judge for the Southern District of Florida, vice a new position created by P.L. 95–486, approved October 20, 1978.

The following-named persons to be members of the Federal Farm Credit Board, Farm Credit Administration, for the terms expiring March 31, 1985:

NOMINATIONS—Continued

Submitted August 10—Continued

JEWELL HAALAND, of Minnesota, vice Alfred Underdahl, term expired.

DWIGHT L. TRIPP, JR., of Maine (reappointment).

CHECKLIST OF WHITE HOUSE PRESS RELEASES

The following listing contains releases of the White House Press Office which are not included in this issue.

Released August 8, 1979

Biographical data: Reubin Askew, nominated to be Special Representative for Trade Negotiations

Biographical data: Alonzo L. McDonald, Jr., Acting Special Representative for Trade Negotiations

Released August 9, 1979

Announcement: nomination of Samuel D. Johnson, Jr., to be United States Circuit Judge for the Fifth Circuit

Announcement: nomination of Edward B. Davis to be United States District Judge for the Southern District of Florida

ACTS APPROVED BY THE PRESIDENT

Approved August 6, 1979

H.R. 4591_____ Public Law 96–46
An act to make technical corrections and miscellaneous amendments in certain education laws contained in the Education Amendments of 1978, and for other purposes.

Approved August 8, 1979

S. 976_____ Public Law 96–47
An act to authorize appropriations for the international affairs functions of the Department of the Treasury for fiscal year 1980.

H.R. 1786_____ Public Law 96–48
National Aeronautics and Space Administration Authorization Act, 1980.

Interview With the President

Remarks and a Question-and-Answer Session With Editors and News Directors.
August 10, 1979

THE PRESIDENT. Well, it's a pleasure to have you here. I always hate to interrupt Jody. [*Laughter*] If you've got him sweating, I don't want him to stop.

One of the most enjoyable and also the most productive things that we've done since I've been in office is to have these meetings with editors and news directors from around the country. We've scheduled them every 2 weeks, and we have anywhere from 30 to 65 people at each session.

WINDFALL PROFITS TAX

I know that you're eager to get to the questions of me, but I'd like to cover one subject first. You've heard a lot about the windfall profits tax. You're going to hear a lot more about it in the future. It's extremely important to our Nation for this tax bill to be passed by the Senate. It's already been passed by the House in a fairly reponsible fashion.

It's designed, first of all, to give us an opportunity to develop new sources of energy; secondly, to improve our rapid

transit systems in their various forms; third, to guarantee equity, because without the windfall profit tax, there would be enormous unwarranted profits going to the oil companies which they have not earned. And the last—and the most important thing, perhaps, of all from a humanitarian point of view—is to give aid to low-income families who will be impacted, no matter what else happens, by the rapidly increasing price of oil and other energy forms.

We will present to the Congress either before or by the time they return from their working recess a specific proposal. But we are advocating that in this coming fiscal year that $1.6 billion be allotted to the poor families of our country, and in the following years, $2.4 billion per year—$1.6 billion this first year, $2.4 billion from then on. The only legitimate source for these funds is the windfall profits tax. And my hope and my expectation is that an aroused public will insist upon a fair action by the Congress to pass this tax itself.

We have varied needs for it, but this is one that will be put forward on its own when the Congress returns. We've obviously got the other elements of the energy program to pursue when the Congress returns, the SALT treaty to be ratified after the Congress returns, hospital cost containment, and other items of legislation.

I would be glad to answer your questions about these or any other subjects if you have questions to ask.

QUESTIONS

WINDFALL PROFITS TAX

Q. On the windfall profits thing, if it gets a compromise, if it is accepted with a compromise, do you anticipate that the compromise would give you the amount of money you need to get all of these programs through?

THE PRESIDENT. Well, if some of the compromises that have been passed in the House of Representatives should prevail, then the windfall profits tax is adequate. They, I think, unwisely made the tax terminate in 1990. I think it would be better to have the tax be permanent, because many of the energy production projects will be very long-range in nature, and they should have an assured source of funding beyond the year 1990. However, they did increase the percentage of the tax from 50 percent to 60 percent. They made some other changes. But, in general, I would say that the net income from the windfall profits tax, as passed by the House, was equivalent to what we proposed originally.

The Senate Finance Committee has mentioned some exceptions to the windfall profits tax that would gut the tax. For instance, a change in the definition of certain kinds of oil and exclusion for so-called small producers would mean that the tax would lose forty, fifty, sixty billion dollars below what we advocated. This would certainly not be acceptable.

There is some talk among some of the Senate leaders, "Well, we'll pass an in-adequate bill in the Senate"—which I think is irresponsible—"and then in conference committee we will work out the differences." I think that's a dangerous game, and I would personally oppose that.

I think the Senate ought to pass an equivalent tax to what I proposed, which is what the House proposed, because there would be no area, if the Senate passed an inadequate tax, to bargain without having substantial reductions below what we need.

PUBLIC CONFIDENCE IN THE GOVERNMENT

Q. Mr. President, one of the topics you touched on in your historic address to the Nation had to do with national confidence.

THE PRESIDENT. Yes.

Q. And I'm wondering if you still feel that you can provide that confidence. The polls have been brutal with you. And it is perhaps the key issue in many people's minds, confidence in the White House, confidence in the administration, confidence in Washington. Will you address that question?

THE PRESIDENT. I think the lack of confidence is very broad. There is a lack of confidence of people in themselves. There's a lack of confidence in what their quality of life will be in the future, compared to the present and the past. There's a lack of confidence in many institutions. The press and the Congress are two, by the way, that are lower than confidence in the White House. And there's a lack of confidence in the President, which does concern me very much.

I believe that this absence of confidence is unwarranted. Our Nation is prosperous. Our Nation is at peace. Our Nation has a fine prospect for the future. Our Nation is the strongest on Earth economically, militarily, politically. Our alliances with our friends around the world have never been any stronger. We have excellent and improving relationships with the doubtful nations of the world— the black, the poor, the new, the brown, the yellow nations—who in the past have been active enemies of ours. We have the highest reserves of energy of any nation on Earth. I think we have 24 percent of all the energy reserves known to mankind, whereas the OPEC countries all put together only have less than 5 percent, for instance. So, there's no real identifiable basis for an absence of confidence.

But it's a fact that the people have not only lost confidence in themselves now and in the future, lost confidence in our institutions, lost confidence in our Government, the free enterprise system, the press, and so forth, but they have an increasing inclination toward divisiveness.

This is the first time in history that I know about when our country has been faced with discomfort or inconvenience or more tangible and far-reaching adverse impacts on human life, without having at the same time a threat to our Nation that was cohesive in its implications. Obviously during the First World War, the Second World War, our country was bound together because we were threatened militarily. During the Great Depression, when people were inconvenienced with massive unemployment and so forth, we were bound together with an economic threat to our country. Now we don't have that tangible, identifiable threat. The threat to our national security that does actually exist from a shortage of oil supplies and an increasing and excessive dependence on foreign oil is hard for the American people to see or to quantify or to accept.

So, when this kind of thing happens, without the binding effect of an identifi-able, tangible threat, but with an inconvenience, people tend to grasp for a temporary advantage to the exclusion of others. And I think that this is something that must be first identified and addressed, as I've tried to do so far and as I'll continue to do with my travels and speeches around the country. And secondly, we need a tangible achievement to show the strength of our country, which I've outlined is there. And I think dealing with the energy question is the best and most important test of this kind.

PALESTINIAN POLICY

Q. Mr. President, so much has been said in the last few weeks about your position regarding the Palestinians, PLO, Israel, and so on and so forth. Most of the answers have been coming through the Secretary of State. I wonder if you could tell us in your own words what your position is on the creation of a separate Palestinian state——

The PRESIDENT. I'm against it.

Q.——your position on the PLO, et cetera.

THE PRESIDENT. I'm against any creation of a separate Palestinian state. I don't think it would be good for the Palestinians. I don't think it would be good for Israel. I don't think it would be good for the Arab neighbors of such a state.

I do believe that we must address and resolve the Palestinian question in all its aspects, as was agreed to by Prime Minister Begin and President Sadat and myself in writing at Camp David.

I do believe that the Palestinians should have a right to a voice in the determination of their own future, which is also specified and agreed to by Begin, Sadat, and by me at Camp David in writing.

I will not deal with the PLO unless they do two things: accept the right of Israel to exist, which they've not yet been willing to acknowledge, and accept the fact that U.N. Resolution 242 is a document binding on them. They've got to accept 242, accept the right of Israel to exist. This is a commitment we've made. We've never deviated from it. We're not going to deviate from it.

NUCLEAR POWER

Q. Mr. President, most folks in South Carolina have accepted nuclear power development as a must. My question is, our people are deeply concerned, and our Governor Riley, who's your friend, are deeply concerned if we're being adequately protected. We don't want to become the Nation's dumping ground. And our highways are becoming—we are fearful of the hazardous conditions of the transit of so much material going to and from—both Barnwell Allied Nuclear and the Savannah River project are in my backyard, 40 miles away, so you can understand how I feel.

THE PRESIDENT. And they're also, as you know, on the Georgia line. [*Laughter*]

Q. Right. What's needed, to you?

THE PRESIDENT. Well, I've been involved in the nuclear world since the early 1950's, when that was my profession, working as a student and also working as the senior officer of the precommissioning crew of the second atomic submarine ever built. At that time I had extensive training on how to handle nuclear materials, the limitations and capabilities of nuclear power, and the problems with the disposal of waste, and also the problems with the proliferation of nuclear explosives, how one might take nuclear waste or byproducts and, through reprocessing or conversion, change them into explosive materials.

Since I've been in office, I think we've addressed for the first time in 35 years the question of the handling of waste, and the Congress has passed a very fine law which we are implementing fully on controlling the proliferation of nuclear explosives.

The incident at Three Mile Island has been one that's brought to the consciousness of the American people the need to reassess for safety purposes design of nuclear powerplants, the technology of the operation of nuclear powerplants, the training of personnel who operate the nuclear powerplants, and also the supervision by the Government of the private operators of nuclear powerplants.

When the Kemeny report is made to me by the end of this month, I will assess it very thoroughly. I will obviously carry out the recommendations of the Kemeny report if they're at all practical, and I'm sure it would be a practical recommendation. At that time I think it would be incumbent on me as President to explain to the American people the situation that does exist with nuclear power.

There is no way that our country can close down nuclear powerplants. And I think it would be ill-advised to terminate the construction of nuclear powerplants that have already been approved. We now derive, I think, about 16 percent of all of our electricity from nuclear power. And in some areas, like Chicago, for instance, they get more than 50 percent of all their power from nuclear powerplants, electric power. So, it is an important element in our energy economy. We need to assess very thoroughly the capabilities and problems. The American people need to be as well educated as possible. And I, as President, working with the Congress and with the private sector, need to make sure that we take steps to even increase the safety that presently exists.

As far as the waste disposal is concerned, we have been working since I've been in office on this very complicated subject with the Congress and with others. We don't have a final solution yet. Things that had been considered in the past as the best disposal possibilities have not proven to be well-advised. One of the earliest ones was dumping in the oceans. That was stopped years ago. Another one is the burying in the ground, like at Hanford Works in Washington. Some of the containers have ruptured, and some of the nuclear materials have gotten into the underground water supply. But I think that this can be a question that's resolved.

You happen to come from the State that's been in the forefront of production of nuclear materials, with the Savannah River plant and with the Barnwell site that was designed for the disposal of wastes and for reprocessing originally. I don't know the final answer on that yet.

The other thing I'd like to say is that we have an international nuclear fuel cycle evaluation study that we initiated in the economic summit conference in London in 1977. Its report will be completed this year. It's been a report evolved by the representatives of more than 50 nations, including the Soviet Union, South Africa, all of the Western allies and so forth. And I would guess that when this report is completed that it would be at the forefront of our agenda when we have our economic summit conference next year in Venice.

Conventional energy was in the forefront of the summit conference in Tokyo. My guess is that nuclear power in all its aspects would be in the forefront next year. So, there's an international move toward the resolution of this question. And I think I've given you too long an answer. But it's a complicated subject, and I'll try to——

STEEL IMPORTS

Q. Mr. President, while imported fuel, imported oil is a big problem, imported steel in Pittsburgh is a big problem.

THE PRESIDENT. Yes.

Q. We have the trigger-pricing mechanism. But if we do get into a recession, capital orders will fall, and that could be a continuing, worsening problem. Has the administration planned anything to deal with imported steel and how it would impact a very basic industry?

THE PRESIDENT. I can't say at this point that we have a plan evolved that could be put into effect. We consider the trigger-mechanism process to be working very well. It has enough flexibility in it to accommodate anticipated changes brought about by worldwide shifts in productivity and economic growth. Bill Miller is well acquainted with the steel industry. And I think you know that the results in American production and in profits for the steel industry have been well served by the present trigger mechanism that's been put into effect. We've done this with a minimum adverse reaction from our trade allies, including Japan.

So, we'll monitor the situation. If it appears to be running into a problem, we'll use the flexibility inherent in this system and modify it if necessary. But I can't tell you that that is not needed at this point. We will be prepared for it if the time should come.

GRAIN PROCESSING STRIKE IN MINNESOTA

Q. Mr. President, the grain miller strike in Duluth-Superior has effectively shut down that port. And it's compounded the problem that's been caused by the boxcar shortage. Although the strike itself has not caught national attention, the Governor of Minnesota has felt it was serious enough to send a telegram asking for a Taft-Hartley injunction. I think that was turned over to the Labor Department, and they turned thumbs down. Does the administration see any point if that strike continues that at some point that Taft-Hartley might become a possibility?

THE PRESIDENT. That's always an option.

I think you know that the Taft-Hartley law has very tight constraints on its own implementation. You have to be able to prove in court, for instance, that the national security of our Nation is threatened. I don't remember the exact legal language, but that's one of the aspects of it.

Ray Marshall, who's quite well acquainted with the Taft-Hartley Act and its provisions, has consulted with the White House staff, my legal staff, and also with the Justice Department, and decided at this point that implementation of the Taft-Hartley Act is not justified.

We hope that the strike will be resolved quickly, and we'll continue to monitor the situation. But at this time we don't think the Taft-Hartley implementation is advised.

1980 PRESIDENTIAL CAMPAIGN

Q. Sir, assuming that you are going to seek renomination and given the crisis of confidence, so to speak, that I think you alluded to earlier, what sort of case would you make, sir, for your own renomination and reelection? [*Laughter*]

THE PRESIDENT. That's a lot of assumptions. [*Laughter*]

I don't know how to answer that question. I'd rather wait until later on this year to make an announcement of my own

decision. I think if I decide to run again, I would have a good chance to get reelected.

Q. On what basis—if I may follow up, sir, on what would you pin your strategy?

THE PRESIDENT. Well, there are only two bases that I think are legitimate. One is the record of my own administration and the description to the American people of future achievements or actions that I think would be well-advised for the next administration. I think we've got a good record.

CHRYSLER CORPORATION

Q. Mr. President, could you tell us what plans are being made to help the Chrysler Corporation?

THE PRESIDENT. I don't think I can expand any further on what Bill Miller said yesterday. My own suggestion is you get a copy of his statement. I approved this approach to the Chrysler problem. The staff in the White House and also several of the agency heads, including Cabinet officials, evolved a series of options for me. We had a meeting here in the Oval Office, and I approved the plan that Bill Miller described yesterday.

It involves two or three elements. One is a maximum dependence on the free enterprise system, including the lending institutions and Chrysler itself and others involved, to resolve this problem; secondly, that any role of the Federal Government would be adequate, but minimal, and that the Federal Government and its investment would be protected well. And I'd say the third element would be a sharing of responsibility among all those involved of any sacrifice that would be inherent in the process. I think that what Bill Miller described is adequate, if we can get the coordinated approach that he has described.

For instance, one example about sacrifice: If the Chrysler top echelon—I don't mean the four or five, but several thousand who are at the top level in earnings in Chrysler—would forgo projected salary increases and fringe benefits and bonuses, this involves tens of millions of dollars in itself. And I would think that that would be one of the kinds of things that could be done within Chrysler without decimating the company or putting it on its knees.

We look on Chrysler as a very important part of our national economy, including both productivity and the provision of jobs. But I think that's about the best I can describe in general terms. But the specifics have already been spelled out by Bill Miller.

HEATING OIL SUPPLIES AND PRICES

Q. Mr. President, one of the most pressing problems in New England is the prospect of very high prices and perhaps low availability of heating oil. What are the reports that you get, and what plans are you contemplating to help the situation?

THE PRESIDENT. I think we'll meet our goal of the 240 million barrels of oil to be in reserve by the end of October. Last year I think we had 233 million barrels in reserve and the years before that a less amount. But we've advocated the high figure just in case there is an extremely severe winter. So, the reserves, I think, will be there, and we are monitoring this daily and have no reason for concern. There are a series of options that I can execute if we start falling behind the progression toward reaching that goal.

As far as price is concerned, I can't control the price that OPEC sets. They have increased their prices in the last 6 or 8 months alone 60 percent on basic crude oil. And of course, products from crude oil have increased an equivalent amount. What we are doing to compensate for this is to advocate to the Congress special aid for low- and middle-income families that would help them pay the extra costs that are inevitable. I think the answer in the opening statement that I made would be the best answer for that. I need not repeat it.

Ms. BARIO. Thank you, sir.

THE PRESIDENT. I'll take one more question.

MOON LANDRIEU

Q. Yes, sir. If a member of the news media outside of Washington came to this town and read the newspaper or listened to reports on radio and television, he might think that the nomination of Moon Landrieu might be in trouble. Would that be an accurate observation, sir?

THE PRESIDENT. No. No, I don't think that's accurate at all. And I hope you don't get all your impressions of Washington by reading the local newspapers. [*Laughter*]

Moon is an honorable man. He went out of the mayor's office with the highest possible esteem of his own people whom he had served. All of his actions, both as mayor and since he's been mayor, have been well known and highly publicized in the press.

He'll go through the normal confirmation proceedings. The questions that have been raised about his involvement in the real estate business, since he got out of mayor, will be completely answered. And I have no concern about this at all. I trust him, and he will be an excellent Cabinet officer.

I am very glad that you are here. If you don't mind, I would like to get a photograph with each one of you individually before you go to lunch. And I think it might be best to—do we have a photographer here? I'll stand right over here by the door, and if you all will just come by on your way out and let me shake hands and thank you for coming individually. And we'll get a photograph and send it to you.

Thank you.

NOTE: The interview began at 11:30 a.m. in the Cabinet Room at the White House. Patricia Y. Bario is a Deputy Press Secretary.

The transcript of the interview was released on August 11.

Advisory Council on Historic Preservation

Appointment of Peggy Bolton as a Member. August 14, 1979

The President today announced the appointment of Peggy Bolton, of Alexandria, La., as a member of the Advisory Council on Historic Preservation for a term expiring February 28, 1984.

Bolton is active in civic affairs, particularly work on historic preservation, and is first president of the Historical Association of Central Louisiana.

President's Commission on the Holocaust

Executive Order 12151.   August 14, 1979

By the authority vested in me as President by the Constitution and statutes of the United States of America, and in order to provide additional time for the President's Commission on the Holocaust to complete its work, Section 1–401 of

Executive Order No. 12093 of November 1, 1978, is amended to read as follows:

"1–401. The Commission shall submit its final report to the President and the Secretary of the Interior not later than September 28, 1979.".

JIMMY CARTER

The White House,
   August 14, 1979.

[Filed with the Office of the Federal Register, 2:52 p.m., August 15, 1979]

NOTE: The Executive order was announced on August 15.

Food Stamp Act Amendments

Statement on Signing H.R. 4057 Into Law. August 15, 1979

I have signed into law amendments to the Food Stamp Act of 1977 which will allow us to continue program operations without cutting benefits for needy food stamp families and also will provide a series of new measures to reduce error and fraud. These amendments are needed chiefly because inflation in food prices has boosted program costs well above the ceiling on program spending contained in the 1977 act. The Congress has acted swiftly to raise the spending cap for this fiscal year and to appropriate the additional funding we need to avoid closing the program down entirely for the month of September. The legislation also includes measures to provide additional benefits for elderly and disabled households with high medical or shelter costs. I am also pleased that the Congress has included several antifraud provisions the administration has recommended.

The need for additional funding for the food stamp program is yet another signal that inflation of the price of food is increasing at an unacceptably high rate. When the Food Stamp Act of 1977 was passed, food prices were projected to increase at an annual rate of between 3 and 4 percent a year, and the ceiling on program expenditures was based on this assumption. But in the last 2 years, food prices have risen nearly 20 percent. This rate of inflation in so basic a sector of our economy not only boosts the entire cost of the food stamp program, but it also adds to the inflationary spiral that erodes the purchasing power of all consumers.

Recently, we have learned that while farm prices have fallen, the food industry may not be passing those savings on to consumers. I have met with representatives of the food industry to deal with this matter and will do everything I can to see that consumers benefit from lower farm prices in terms of lower prices in the supermarket.

Recent increases in the number of Americans participating in the food stamp program have raised costs as well. In recent years, the program has undergone sweeping reforms. Administration proposals enacted by Congress have tightened and simplified administration, imposed tough penalties for fraud, and reduced or terminated benefits for higher income households. At the same time the administration's proposal to eliminate the requirement that households buy their food stamps has brought several million new participants into the program who had previously been eligible for food stamps, but had simply been unable to afford them. Many of these people are the elderly and rural poor, whose participation rate has historically been very low.

It would be callous and shortsighted to cut food stamp benefits, which now average a modest 33¢ per person per meal, because the program is reaching larger numbers of the poorest households and because food prices have risen so alarmingly. While this administration is committed to controlling Federal expenditures, we will do so within a budget of compassion that recognizes the fundamental importance of food assistance to our Nation's poorest families.

There can be no question that these families *are* poor. More than half of the households receiving food stamps have *gross* annual incomes under $3,600. Because of the critical importance of continued food assistance to these households, I have asked Congress to lift the spending cap for future fiscal years, and to provide the funding that will be needed to avoid cutting benefits in fiscal years 1980 and 1981.

In the interest of tighter program administration, I have also asked the Congress to enact a number of measures to save food stamp funds by reducing error rates. Some of the most important of these provisions are still pending before Congress. I ask Congress to enact these provisions along with provisons to authorize adequate funding for 1980 and 1981.

Recently, teams of doctors sponsored by the Field Foundation revisited the poverty-stricken areas where they had found serious hunger and malnutrition 10 years ago. They reported the presence of "fewer grossly malnourished people in this country today than there were 10 years ago." The doctors concluded that the food stamp program "is making the most crucial difference in improving the quality of the lives of many poor people."

I intend to give this valuable program my full support, and I call upon Congress to do the same.

NOTE: As enacted, H.R. 4057 is Public Law 96–58, approved August 14.

Department of State, International Communication Agency, and Board for International Broadcasting Appropriations Bill

Statement on Signing H.R. 3363 Into Law.
August 15, 1979

Today I am signing into law H.R. 3363, which authorizes appropriations for fiscal years 1980 and 1981 for the Department of State, the International Communication Agency, and the Board for International Broadcasting. Three sections of this act require my special comment.

First, section 110 of this bill represents a victory for common sense and sound foreign policy. This is the provision that permits the United States to begin paying its 1979 dues to the United Nations and its specialized agencies. For this entire year, up until now, we have not been able to pay our dues to these organizations, despite our obligations under international treaties. This inability to pay threatened the existence of programs vital to the United States in such fields as nuclear safeguards, air safety, and international health. This situation was caused by a provision (known as the "Helms amendment") passed by the Congress at the end of the last session. Section 110 has the effect of repealing this provision.

In addition, the supplemental appropriations bill for the Department of State for 1979 restores $27.7 million intended for our assessed obligations to the United Nations system, which the Congress deleted last year. Therefore, as of today, we are able to pay our bills, and to pay them in full. I am pleased that the U.S. Government can again resume a traditional leadership role in these international institutions.

Second, last fall the Secretary of State, after lengthy study, proposed and I approved the closing of 13 U.S. Consulates. I concluded that they were no longer needed for the performance of essential functions and viewed their closing as a sound step for economizing and for reducing unnecessary American presence abroad. However, section 108 names 10 of those posts and provides that they shall not be closed or, if closed, shall be reopened as soon as possible.

Under the Constitution, the President has the power to appoint Consuls as well as Ambassadors and other public ministers. Implicit in this grant is the right to decide when and where an Ambassador or Consul should be appointed. Just as decisions associated with the appointment of Ambassadors are acknowledged to be a constitutional prerogative of the President, I believe that Congress cannot mandate the establishment of consular relations at a time and place unacceptable to the President. In order to protect this constitutional prerogative of the President, I will therefore regard section 108 as a recommendation and not a requirement.

Third, section 408 recognizes the existing power of the President to make the decision regarding the continuation by the United States of sanctions imposed by the United Nations against Zimbabwe-Rhodesia, but declares that such sanctions are to be terminated on November 15, 1979, unless the President finds that the continuation is "in the national interest." The section purports to give Congress power to overturn this determination by concurrent resolution. This provision directly violates Article I, section 7, of the Constitution, which requires that all such resolutions, if they are to have the force of law, be presented to the President for his approval or disapproval. By giving Congress an additional role in this decision without requiring the legislative process to be followed, section 408 violates the principle of separation of powers.

NOTE: As enacted, H.R. 3363 is Public Law 96–60, approved August 15.

Fishery Conservation and Management Act Amendments

Statement on Signing S. 917 Into Law.
August 15, 1979

Today I have signed into law an act to amend the Fishery Conservation and Management Act of 1976 to provide appropriations for that act for fiscal years 1980, 1981, and 1982, and for other purposes.

A major substantive amendment contained in this act establishes a procedure designed to protect whales. This amendment, initially introduced by Senators Magnuson and Packwood, provides for reductions in fishing allocations within our 200-mile fishing zone to nations which are certified by the Secretary of Commerce to be diminishing the effectiveness of the International Whaling Convention. The bill will allow the certified nation up to 1 year to remedy the conditions leading to the certification before its fishing allocation is completely terminated. Certification under this act would also result in certification under the Pelly amendment (section 8 of the Fishermen's Protective Act) which provides for embargoes of fish imports from certified nations.

I applaud Senator Magnuson, Senator Packwood, and the Members of the House who sponsored this bill. The protection and conservation of the world's dwindling number of great whales is a major environmental concern of my administration, the Congress, and the American people. I believe that it is necessary for us to demonstrate our Nation's commitment to the conservation of whales. This bill will provide a useful tool in situations where no others are available to us.

This bill also amends section 8 of the Fishermen's Protective Act of 1967 to specifically require the Secretaries of Commerce and the Interior, as appropriate, to promptly investigate and act upon any actions by foreign nations that might be cause for certification. It also provides specifically for termination of certifications once the original conditions have been rectified. These are definite improvements to the Pelly amendment.

With regard to both the Packwood-Magnuson and Pelly amendments, the Secretaries of Commerce and the Interior should work with the Secretary of State to take prompt action to ensure that all avenues of negotiation are fully exhausted before certification is made against any foreign nation. However, in those negotiations all nations will be informed of the implications of these two amendments and the determination of this Government to use them if remedial action is not undertaken. Certification under this act will of course take place only to further the purposes of this act, that is, to provide strong support for the International Convention for the Regulation of Whaling and for the conservation of the whales.

I believe it is important also that this act makes clear the original intention of the FCMA when it was passed in 1976. These amendments require that American-owned vessels engaged in harvesting fish in the Fishery Conservation Zone must be built in America in order to be entitled to harvest fish in America's fishery zone. This "American-built" requirement will protect the massive capital investment that American fishermen and shipyards have made in anticipation of the FCMA. This amendment does not encompass vessels engaged in activities other than fish harvesting, such as fish processing. Additionally, it does not change existing law with respect to the definition of fisheries, except to the extent that it expands the existing interpretation of the definition's geographical scope to the full 200-mile Fishing Conservation Zone.

Concerning section 2 of the act, it is my understanding that this amendment is not intended to affect foreign fishing under the Fishery Conservation and Management Act, the Governing International Fishery Agreements, or other fishery agreements to which we are party. It is also my understanding, in light of the provisions of the Covenant to Establish a Commonwealth of the Northern Mariana Islands, in Political Union with the United States of America, that section 2 of the act will not preclude the use of foreign-built vessels by fishermen of the Northern Mariana Islands for fishing in the Fishery Conservation Zone or the landing of catch by such vessels.

For many years now the United States has been active in trying to gain international recognition of the need to protect great whales. We are justly proud of the contributions to this effort made by many concerned citizens and conservation organizations. There is much to be done before heavily hunted species of whales again safely flourish in the oceans. The law that I am signing today demonstrates to the world America's determination to save the great whales.

NOTE: As enacted, S. 917 is Public Law 96–61, approved August 15.

United States Representative to the United Nations

Exchange of Letters on the Resignation of Ambassador Andrew Young.   August 15, 1979

To Ambassador Andrew Young

I accept with deep regret your resignation as Ambassador to the United Nations, to be effective when your successor assumes the duties of your office. Subsequently, your continuing support for the policies of our nation will be extremely valuable.

You have earned the gratitude of all Americans with your superb performance in a most difficult assignment. You have helped to prove, thanks to your dedication and sensitivity, that our country is sympathetic to the deepest social and political aspirations of increasingly awakened human beings throughout the world. You have proven that we are sensitive to the demands for world peace and racial justice, and have earned for us the friendship, trust and respect of many nations which had previously considered the United States to be suspect and unworthy of such a relationship. You have truly exemplified the finest attributes of the American character.

You can be justifiably proud of the many achievements of yourself and your assistants and staff in the United Nations.

You have my best wishes and personal thanks.

Your friend,

JIMMY CARTER

August 14, 1979

Dear Mr. President:

It has been an extremely exciting and rewarding opportunity to serve as your Ambassador to the United Nations. I have appreciated the support and encouragement from you and Secretary Vance. Your commitment to negotiated actions in this multi-lateral forum has made it possible to advance the cause of peace, human rights and economic development far beyond my expectations. I will always be grateful for my service with your administration.

I am afraid, however, that my conduct has created serious difficulties for the administration on several occasions. It has made me question my value as a continued part of your team.

I have always acted in behalf of what I felt was the best interest of our nation, though often it has been interpreted to the contrary.

I want you to fulfill the tremendous promise of your administration, and that depends to a great extent on a settlement of the situation in the Middle East.

It is therefore extremely embarrassing that my actions, however well-intentioned, may have hampered the peace process. In order to avoid any further complications, I would like to offer my resignation as the United States Permanent Representative to the United Nations.

I will be glad to continue during the month of August as President of the Security Council and also to fulfill a commitment to lead a trade mission to Africa in early September.

There is a good staff here at USUN and they are fully capable of carrying on through the General Assembly.

I will return to Atlanta and after a brief period of respite, I will begin to campaign diligently for your re-election.

It has been an honor and privilege to serve with your administration.

Sincerely,

ANDY
Andrew Young

Firefighters' Memorial Sunday, 1979

Proclamation 4671.   August 15, 1979

By the President of the United States of America

A Proclamation

Courageous firefighters have protected the lives of their neighbors from the ravages of fire since the beginning of civilization.

Volunteer and professional firefighters are members of America's most hazardous profession. More than half of the injuries in fires each year are sustained by firefighters, over 55,000 each year.

Numerous churches and many denominations have indicated a desire to participate in a designated Memorial Sunday honoring these consecrated firefighters for their ultimate sacrifices for their fellowmen.

Now, THEREFORE, I, JIMMY CARTER, President of the United States of America, do hereby designate Sunday, October 7, 1979, as Firefighters' Memorial Sunday.

Because of my grave concern for the firefighters of this country, I have urged the Federal government to undertake numerous programs aimed at reducing the dangers faced by this country's firefighters. We must do more to reverse the trend toward more injuries and deaths of firefighters.

This year the 50-year dream of a National Fire Academy became a reality. At that site, firefighters from across the Nation can receive advanced training and education in health and safety. I invite the firefighters of the country to take full advantage of this long-awaited facility.

I also call upon the members of the Joint Council of National Fire Service

Organizations, members of the International Association of Fire Fighters, members of the International Association of Fire Chiefs, the National Fire Protection Association, all other organizations concerned with fire safety, and the United States Fire Administration to provide leadership and innovation to protect the lives of America's volunteer and professional firefighters.

IN WITNESS WHEREOF, I have hereunto set my hand this fifteenth day of August, in the year of our Lord nineteen hundred seventy-nine, and of the Independence of the United States of America the two hundred and fourth.

JIMMY CARTER

[Filed with the Office of the Federal Register, 11:20 a.m., August 16, 1979]

Fire Prevention Week, 1979
Proclamation 4672.   August 15, 1979

By the President of the United States of America

A Proclamation

Fire causes more loss of life and property in the United States than all other natural disasters combined. Fire is the second most frequent cause of accidental death in the home. Volunteer and professional firefighters bear a disproportionate burden of the human costs of fire; firefighting is still America's most hazardous profession.

Last year 8,700 Americans died, 280,-000 were injured in fires and $5 billion in property was lost. America's loss to fire is among the very highest in the industrialized world.

As evidence of my strong personal concern about our fire problem, I have im-

plemented a Reorganization Plan that puts the Federal government's principal fire programs in the new Federal Emergency Management Agency. This agency now coordinates America's disaster preparedness and response efforts. But the Federal government alone cannot reduce America's fire losses. The public and private sector must do their part. Together we can lessen this unnecessary, life-threatening destruction.

NOW, THEREFORE, I, JIMMY CARTER, President of the United States of America, do hereby designate October 8–14, 1979, as Fire Prevention Week.

Because fire deaths most often occur in homes, I call upon American families and other property owners to install smoke detectors, to practice exit drills, and to be especially vigilant in guarding against fires.

I encourage the fire service, police, prosecutors, the insurance industry, and government to work together to improve arson detection and prosecution so that we can begin to eliminate this costly, often murderous crime.

I call upon every fire department in the country to teach citizens the fundamentals of basic life support, cardiopulmonary resuscitation, and to improve the delivery of emergency medical services.

I urge the fire service to fully open their profession to women, and I offer my support to the growing number of professional and volunteer women firefighters.

I encourage the fire service to take full advantage of the National Fire Academy that became a reality this year. The Academy will be an effective tool in providing training and education for the Nation's firefighters.

I support and encourage the cooperative efforts of private enterprise and government in developing low cost residential sprinkler systems that may revolutionize fire safety in the home.

Finally, I call upon members of the Joint Council of National Fire Service Organizations, members of the International Association of Fire Fighters, members of the International Association of Fire Chiefs, the National Fire Protection Association, all other organizations concerned with fire safety, and the United States Fire Administration to provide the leadership, planning and innovation necessary for an effective national fire prevention and control effort.

IN WITNESS WHEREOF, I have hereunto set my hand this fifteenth day of August, in the year of our Lord nineteen hundred seventy-nine, and of the Independence of the United States of America the two hundred and fourth.

JIMMY CARTER

[Filed with the Office of the Federal Register, 11:21 a.m., August 16, 1979]

Commission on the Review of the Federal Impact Aid Program

Appointment of 10 Members.
August 15, 1979

The President today announced the appointment of 10 persons as members of the Commission on the Review of the Federal Impact Aid Program.

This Commission was created in November 1978 to review and evaluate the operation of the Federal Impact Aid program, a program created in 1950 to provide financial aid to local education facilities when the actions of the Federal Government increase their costs.

The members appointed today are:

CHARLIE AKINS, of Elizabethtown, Ky., superintendent of the Hardin County schools and State chairman of the Kentucky Impact Aid Schools Organization;

POLLY BACA-BARRAGAN, a Colorado State senator, who serves on the board of directors of the National Mexican American Legal Defense and Educational Fund and the National Housing Assistance Council;

EDWARD C. BOLSTAD, of Minneapolis, executive secretary of the Minnesota Federation of Teachers;

ROBERT L. CHISHOLM, superintendent of schools for the Clover Park School District in Tacoma, Wash., and a member of the board of directors of the Northwest Regional Education Laboratory;

ANSELM G. DAVIS, JR., assistant superintendent of the Window Rock School District No. 8 in Fort Defiance, Ariz., and a former education specialist with the Bureau of Indian Affairs;

FRANKLIN L. LEWIS, a member of the Nebraska State Legislature and former chairman of its education committee, who has been a classroom teacher;

BARBARA ROBERTS MASON, an executive director of the Michigan Education Association and former speech therapist;

FRANK J. MACCHIAROLA, chancellor of the New York City Public Schools and a former professor of political science;

HAROLD E. ROGERS, JR., a San Francisco attorney specializing in the field of municipal law and finance;

VIRGINIA ALLRED STACEY, of San Antonio, Tex., a teacher in the Lackland Independent School District and 1978–79 State president of the Texas State Teachers Association.

Federal Government Organization and Employees

Executive Order 12152.   August 14, 1979

DIRECTOR OF THE OFFICE OF MANAGEMENT AND BUDGET

By the authority vested in me as President by the Constitution and statutes of the United States of America, including Section 301 of Title 3 of the United States Code, and in order to ensure the continued delegation of certain functions which had been previously assigned but which are now vested directly in the President by virtue of H.R. 4616 that I have signed into law today, it is hereby ordered that the functions vested in the President by Sections 305(b), 4111(b), and 4112 (a) of Title 5 of the United States Code are hereby delegated to the Director of the Office of Management and Budget.

JIMMY CARTER

The White House,
   August 14, 1979.

[Filed with the Office of the Federal Register,
   11:19 a.m., August 16, 1979]
NOTE: The Executive order was announced on August 16.

Department of Justice

Remarks at the Swearing In of Benjamin R. Civiletti as Attorney General.
August 16, 1979

THE PRESIDENT. It's indeed a pleasure and an honor for me to be here in this assembly with Griffin Bell and the other members of the establishment. [*Laughter*]

As a fellow Georgian, I was hoping that Griffin would survive the screening process in the Cabinet recently. [*Laughter*] But I think it's accurate to say that this is a time of reassessment and of congratulations and of looking to the future. Griffin has certainly made this a nonpolitical organization. He proved that with his interview with the press recently. As a matter of fact, along with the Chief Justice, Griffin has always had a superb record in getting along with the press. [*Laughter*] Griffin has gotten more mileage out of rooster pepper sausage than I

did out of the Middle East peace treaty, as a matter of fact. [*Laughter*]

In 1976, after I was elected President, I called on Griffin Bell to help me with the screening process for Cabinet officers because of his judgment, his integrity, his intelligence, his experience, and because as a long-time friend, I had absolute confidence in him. I finally decided that there was no person in this Nation better qualified to be Attorney General than Griffin Bell. It was one of the wisest decisions that I have ever made, and I want to express my thanks to him.

He was my friend then and now; but he's become a friend of the Nation, he's become a man who has earned the trust and confidence and appreciation of all those who look on the Department of Justice as a source of fairness and equity and sensitivity and compassion. And I'm deeply grateful to him for that as well.

He's brought to this Department, to his position as Attorney General, a sense of absolute integrity, of professionalism and of merit, and of justice in the finest and most all-encompassing meaning of the word.

When he arrived here, there were some difficult cases whose resolution had been long postponed. He has helped to clear up those difficult cases in a proper way. He's brought into his own top staff, his deputy and others, the Director of the Federal Bureau of Investigation, people who share and perhaps even equal his own superb characteristics.

Griffin mentioned to me a few minutes ago that he and I together have assessed, and I have already personally approved, 232 Federal judges. And by the time the process is over and the next 22 judges have been identified and approved by me, this will encompass 40 percent of all the Federal judges who serve in this country.

The selection has been made strictly on the basis of merit, with adequate attention to affirmative action—and that is apparently a conflict. But under Griffin Bell it has not been a conflict, because as we've moved out and explored the identity of those who could serve superlatively as Federal judges, among women and among representatives of minority groups who have suffered from discrimination for too long, we have never deviated from the highest possible standards of merit. And I'm deeply grateful for that achievement of the Attorney General as well.

With the ceremony today, I express my gratitude to Attorney General Griffin Bell, my regrets that he has decided to leave this post, my confidence that he will continue to help me and this country in the future to perpetuate what he's initiated here, and also to express my gratitude to the man who will be sworn in today, Benjamin Civiletti.

Under Ben Civiletti, as the new Attorney General, we will build on the standards of excellence that have been established here in the Justice Department. He will be the highest law enforcement officer in our land, entrusted, with complete confidence, with the responsibilities which I have just described so briefly: integrity, compassion, sensitivity, fairness, equity, justice as a tangible thing, but also an accurate image of it, because the people of our country, particularly those who are poor or inarticulate or deprived must have an accurate sense that the system of justice works for them and not against them. And there is no doubt in my mind that Benjamin Civiletti is eminently qualified to have both the substance of justice and an accurate image that our Nation's Government represents the essence of fairness and justice for all.

He's a courageous man, and this is a job that requires courage. And I'm very deeply grateful to him for being willing to serve.

I look forward to the ceremony, now imminent, wherein the Chief Justice of the United States will give the oath of office as Attorney General to a fine and distinguished public servant who has already proven his qualities to be exemplary, Ben Civiletti.

Thank you very much.

ATTORNEY GENERAL BELL. We are deviating from the program just the slightest bit, Mr. President.

Thank you for your remarks. We all work for you. You are really, under the Constitution—you are the Attorney General. The President, under the Constitution, is the only person charged with the duty to faithfully execute the laws. And so, as Attorney General, and as others here at the Department, our job is to assist the President in faithfully executing the laws.

Chief Justice Burger is a great friend, if not the greatest friend in our country of judicial administration. He honors us today with his presence, and before we have the swearing-in ceremony, he wants to say a few words.

CHIEF JUSTICE BURGER. Thank you, Mr. Attorney General.

Mr. President, Mr. Attorney General-to-be, Mrs. Civiletti:

I accepted the Attorney General's invitation to make a few brief remarks because I thought it might help to remind all the young lawyers in the Department of Justice that this is a pretty good place to start. It is 26 years ago that I began here, and I retain the fondest recollections of this great Department.

From the time I was a student up to the present, and when I was a student, my fellow townsman, William D. Mitchell, was appointed Solicitor General first, and then Attorney General. From that time down to the present, I have met or known, and very often known well, every Attorney General of the United States.

There has been no finer man—and I can echo the President's praise of Griffin Bell—there has been no finer man, no man more dedicated to professional excellence and professional integrity, and a fair administration of justice, than this man who has been my friend and colleague for many years, and I salute him and congratulate him on the splendid administration he's given this great Department of Justice.

And now, Mr. Civiletti, are you prepared to take the oath of office?

[*At this point, Chief Justice of the United States Warren E. Burger administered the oath of office.*]

ATTORNEY GENERAL CIVILETTI. *Mr. President, Mr. Chief Justice, Mr. Vice President, former Attorney General Bell—* [*laughter*]—*Mrs. Bell, Senator Thurmond, Chairman Rodino, Mr. Dunlap,[1] distinguished guests and officials in the Government, fellow Cabinet members, Senators, outstanding Italo-Americans, members of my former law firm, which I see back there, and friends and fellow employees, men and women in this great Department:*

First, I would like to introduce all of you to the people who have been most important in my life. You know one of them already, Gail Civiletti. I'm privileged to have my mother and father here today, Ben and Virginia Civiletti. Would you please stand? My sister, Pamela Haber. Would you please stand, Pam? My children—Ben Civiletti; Drew Civiletti, the famous Oriole baseball commentator; and Lynn Civiletti.

---

[1] Georgia attorney James Dunlap, who headed a group which presented the Department of Justice with the official portrait of Attorney General Bell. The portrait was unveiled at the swearing-in ceremony.

As the President has said, I will attempt to follow and to build on the great work that Attorney General Bell has done in this Department, as he in turn built on the foundations that were laid by Attorney General Levi. And we are aided in that process, he in his work and I will be in my work, by the fact that there are men and women in the Department who have not only been here under Attorney General Levi and Attorney General Bell, but will be here under Attorney General Civiletti, and probably many of his successors.

The leadership changes—and we can assist or accelerate, or in some sad instances, we can detract from the Department—but the heart and soul of the Department of Justice are the career men and women and lawyers who are here, year in and year out, of high competence, great ability, integrity, and little recognition. And I recognize them and believe that they truly represent the finest in the traditions which the President has mentioned.

The themes that Attorney General Bell, seems to me, has followed, and which I have had only a small part to play in developing, but which I believe in, are, one, the access to justice, increasing it, developing it, strengthening it; the professionalism and training, the competence of the lawyers, the staff, paralegals within the Department in every possible way; and, thirdly, what the President mentioned to me when he asked me to become Attorney General: the independence and integrity of the Department— as Judge Bell says, the neutral zone concept with regard to the initiation and handling of cases.

The President said that he thought one of the most important legacies of his administration to the American people would be that concept of independence and integrity of the Department of Justice in the handling of prosecutions and cases and investigations, and that he was extremely proud of Judge Bell's work in developing, strengthening that concept which has been with the Department for many, many years. And he was confident that I could carry it forward.

Of course, there are a few refinements or modifications, things that I will perhaps do somewhat differently, additional themes that I will stress. Within those themes and beyond them, I think one of the most important functions within the Department of Justice, within its many functions and duties and responsibilities, is to represent well not only all citizens of the United States but to represent the disadvantaged, whether they be minorities, handicapped, the aged, those who cannot well represent themselves, who, without the Department of Justice and the Government to look for their rights with care and attention, they will lose their rights or not know of them or not be able to exercise them.

Secondly, I believe in strong and effective law enforcement. If the Attorney General is not an advocate for strong and effective law enforcement, who can be? It is vital not only to protect public safety and the lives and property of all persons but also to safeguard the social environment just as we must protect the physical environment, because only through effective enforcement and the resulting achievement of public safety and peace can our society truly and fully engage in the pursuit of happiness.

In addition to making possible the exercise and enjoyment of all other rights, the pursuit of the right and the enforcement of personal safety and freedom from crime does not require compromise or sacrifice of constitutional rights or civil liberties. As the Department of Justice's proposed legislative charter for the FBI— which is a dominant goal and priority of our efforts in Congress—just as it demon-

strates, strengthening law enforcement and enhancing civil liberties are consistent and complementary and mutually supportive goals.

Third, a mission and duty within the Department, which is primary, is the protection and the defense of the free enterprise system, preservation of competition. And I'm happy to say that I think we're alive and well in that regard under John Shenefield's leadership of the Antitrust Division.

I think that the progress we've made in increasing the confidence and the tools by which the men and women of the Department are able to undertake these tasks has been remarkable. With the Attorney General's advocacy institute, with training programs throughout the Department of Justice, we are now training, in 1 year, more lawyers, more paralegals, more investigators than, 3 years ago, we were training in 4 years. But I think we have a way to go. We must work faster, we must decide cases and investigate them thoroughly, but with expedition—justice delayed is justice denied. And we must have the courage to end cases, to end investigations, whether it be through successful and vigorous prosecutions, or be it in closing a case that does not merit the exercise of the prosecutorial or the civil power to bring suit.

I want to thank my staff in the Deputy Attorney General's Office. I selected it over some period of time. Some people wondered if I'd ever get a staff together. But I did it with care, and they have worked with diligence, with my total respect and confidence, and they have performed, day and night, any task, either which they thought needed doing or which I assigned to them. They have kept me from many errors, and since you all know the errors I've made, you know what a hard job they've had and how well they've done.

By the way, there's an opening on that staff. The Deputy Attorney General slot is open. I don't suppose you'd be interested, Judge Bell? [*Laughter*] We need a good person in that job, a good right hand. Do a service to your country. [*Laughter*] You don't have to commit to more than about a year-and-a-half or 2 years or so. [*Laughter*]

Good to see two outstanding Italian American citizens on the stage, Chairman Rodino and Vice President "Mondali." [*Laughter*] I always thought that was spelled with an "e."

And it's particularly pleasing to see here on the stage Senator Thurmond, the ranking Republican on the great Senate Judiciary Committee, before whom I've had the privilege of appearing three times. I won't go into the number of hours that I have devoted to the Judiciary Committee. I'm pleased that I will not be appearing, at least in a confirmation proceeding, ever again before them. I look forward, though, to appearing before that committee on many matters of importance to this Department and to this country. On every occasion, Senator Thurmond has treated me, as well as all others who I've witnessed appearing before that committee, with great dignity and great respect, as well as with some vigor.

My view of the Department and my view of the mission of the Attorney General can, in part, be summed up by this quote from President Madison in the Federalist No. 51. "It is of great importance in a republic not only to guard the society against the oppression of its rulers, but to guard one part of the society against the injustice of the other part. . . . Justice is the end of government. It is the end of civil society. It ever has been and

ever will be pursued until it be obtained, or until liberty be lost in the pursuit."

I thank you, Mr. President, for giving me the opportunity to share with the men and women of the Department of Justice in the pursuit of justice. Thank you.

I now have the privilege of introducing Senator Strom Thurmond, whom I mentioned earlier, and whom all of us in the Department of Justice rely on and trust and respect.

NOTE: The President spoke at 11:07 a.m. in the Great Hall at the Department of Justice.

The press release does not include a transcript of Senator Thurmond's remarks.

General Pulaski's Memorial Day, 1979

Proclamation 4673.   August 16, 1979

By the President of the United States of America

A Proclamation

On the eleventh day of October, the people of the United States will honor the 200th anniversary of the death of the Polish patriot, Casimir Pulaski. On the bicentennial of his death, caused by wounds suffered during the Battle of Savannah, we are reminded of his heroism and his selflessness as he led his famous cavalry unit, The Pulaski Legion, in the struggle for American independence.

As we pay tribute to General Pulaski and his sacrifices for freedom, both here and in his native land, we also honor the contributions made by generations of Americans of Polish descent to the greatness of our Nation.

Now, THEREFORE, I, JIMMY CARTER, President of the United States of America, do hereby designate Thursday, October 11, 1979, as General Pulaski's Memorial Day, and I direct the appropriate government officials to display the flag of the United States on all government buildings on that day.

I also invite the people of the United States to honor the memory of General Pulaski by holding appropriate exercises and ceremonies in suitable places throughout our land.

IN WITNESS WHEREOF, I have hereunto set my hand this sixteenth day of August, in the year of our Lord nineteen hundred seventy-nine, and of the Independence of the United States of America the two hundred and fourth.

JIMMY CARTER

[Filed with the Office of the Federal Register, 10:33 a.m., August 17, 1979]

Budget Deferrals

Message to the Congress.   August 16, 1979

To the Congress of the United States:

In accordance with the Impoundment Control Act of 1974, I herewith report four new deferrals of budget authority totalling $204.5 million. These items involve economic support fund assistance for Egypt, the White House Conference on Aging, the National Alcohol Fuels Commission, and the National Commission on the International Year of the Child.

The details of the deferrals are contained in the attached reports.

JIMMY CARTER

The White House,
   August 16, 1979.

NOTE: The attachments detailing the deferrals are printed in the FEDERAL REGISTER of August 21, 1979.

Federal Mine Safety and Health Act of 1977

Message to the Congress Transmitting a Report.   August 16, 1979

To the Congress of the United States:

I transmit herewith the 1978 Annual Report of Health Activities under the Federal Coal Mine Health and Safety Act of 1969.[1]

The Report, prepared by HEW's National Institute for Occupational Safety and Health, Center for Disease Control, Public Health Service, describes the coal mine health research conducted by the Institute, as well as the Institute's medical examination program for coal miners required by the Act.

I recommend that, in order to save HEW staff resources and time, the statutory reporting requirement for this Report be changed from once every year to once every three years. All of the information contained in this Report is available to Congress during annual appropriations and oversight hearings, and HEW will inform Congress immediately of any scientific breakthroughs in the field.

JIMMY CARTER

The White House,
   August 16, 1979.

NOTE: The 11-page report is entitled "The Federal Mine Health Program in 1978: Annual Report of Health Activities Under the Federal Mine Safety and Health Act of 1977—U.S. Department of Health, Education, and Welfare, Public Health Service, Center for Disease Control, National Institute for Occupational Safety and Health, March 1979."

---

[1] EDITOR'S NOTE: As amended by the Federal Mine Safety and Health Act of 1977.

Privacy Act of 1974

Letter to the Speaker of the House and the President of the Senate Transmitting a Report. August 16, 1979

Dear Mr. Speaker: (Dear Mr. President:)

This letter forwards the Fourth Annual Report of executive branch activities covered by the Privacy Act of 1974. The report reaffirms this Administration's commitment to protecting individual privacy, illustrates steps taken to achieve this goal, and outlines agency activities in administering the Privacy Act during 1978.

I hope you will take this record of our progress into account as you consider the Administration's legislative proposals on individual privacy. This report not only documents how far we have come since the passage of the Privacy Act, but how important personal privacy is to this Administration.

Sincerely,

JIMMY CARTER

NOTE: This is the text of identical letters addressed to Thomas P. O'Neill, Jr., Speaker of the House of Representatives, and Walter F. Mondale, President of the Senate.

The report is entitled "Federal Personal Data Systems Subject to the Privacy Act of 1974: Fourth Annual Report of the President—Calendar Year 1978" (22 pages plus appendices).

United States Ambassador to Kuwait

Nomination of Francois M. Dickman. August 16, 1979

The President today announced that he will nominate Francois M. Dickman, of Laramie, Wyo., to be Ambassador Extraordinary and Plenipotentiary of the United States to the State of Kuwait. He would replace Frank E. Maestrone, who is being transferred.

Dickman has been Ambassador to the United Arab Emirates since 1976.

He was born December 23, 1924, in Iowa City, Iowa. He received a B.A. from the University of Wyoming in 1947 and an M.A. from Fletcher School of Law and Diplomacy in 1948. He served in the U.S. Army from 1943 to 1946 and 1950 to 1951.

Dickman joined the Foreign Service in 1951 and was posted in Barranquilla, Beirut, and Khartoum. From 1960 to 1961, he was at the State Department as an international relations officer, then international economist. From 1961 to 1965, he was desk officer for the United Arab Republic (Egypt) and the Syrian Arab Republic.

From 1965 to 1968, Dickman was economic officer in Tunis. In 1968–69 he attended the Army War College. From 1969 to 1972, he was counselor for economic affairs in Jidda, and from 1972 to 1976, he was Director of Arabian Peninsula Affairs at the State Department.

United States Ambassador to Lesotho

Nomination of John R. Clingerman. August 16, 1979

The President today announced that he will nominate John R. Clingerman, of Lansing, Mich., to be Ambassador Extraordinary and Plenipotentiary of the United States to the Kingdom of Lesotho. He would replace Donald R. Norland, who is being appointed to another post.

Clingerman is Deputy Chief of Mission in Lusaka, Zambia.

He was born May 9, 1931, in Doniphan County, Kans. He received a B.A. (1953) and M.A. (1957) from Michigan State University. He served in the U.S. Army from 1953 to 1955.

Clingerman joined the Foreign Service in 1957 and was posted in Katmandu, Leopoldville, and Kisangani. In 1965–66 he took African studies at the University of Paris, and from 1966 to 1969, he was Deputy Chief of Mission in Cotonou.

From 1969 to 1972, Clingerman was political officer in Brussels. From 1972 to 1975, he was at the State Department as an educational and cultural officer, then a personnel officer. He attended the National War College in 1975–76 and since 1976 has been Deputy Chief of Mission in Lusaka.

National Advisory Council on Economic Opportunity

Appointment of 14 Members and Designation of Chairman.   August 16, 1979

The President today announced the appointment of 14 persons as members of the National Advisory Council on Economic Opportunity. They are:

HANNAH HUME BAIRD, of Florence, Ky., where she is active in civic and political affairs including the Northern Kentucky Area Development District Human Services Advisory Board;

ARTHUR I. BLAUSTEIN, director of the National Economic Development Law Project at the Earl Warren Legal Institute of the University of California at Berkeley (also designated Chairman of this Council);

IRVING BLUESTONE, of Detroit, vice president of the International Union of the United Auto Workers, and director of the UAW's General Motors Department;

WILLIAM MICHAEL DALEY, a Chicago attorney;

L. C. DORSEY, of Jackson, Miss., an organizer for the Southern Coalition on Jails and Prisons with a background as a social worker;

HAZEL N. DUKES, president of the New York State Conference of the NAACP;

GEOFFREY FAUX, of Whitefield, Maine, codirector of the Exploratory Project for Economic Alternatives, a research and public education program;

EDWARD F. FEIGHAN, a commissioner of Cuyahoga County, Ohio;

LINDA HADLEY, of Chinle, Ariz., assistant director of the Navaho mental health program at Rough Rock Demonstration School;

CHRISTINE PRATT MARSTON, an instructor at the University of Washington's School of Social Work and cochair of the National Organization for Women Task Force on Women and Poverty;

PHILIP W. McLAURIN, the State of Oregon ombudsman and a former acting director of the city of Portland's training and employment division, human resources bureau;

JUAN JOSE MOLDONADO, mayor of the city of San Juan, Tex.;

RALPH M. OCHOA, assistant to California State Assembly Speaker Leo T. McCarthy, and former associate director of the Greater Los Angeles Urban Coalition;

EVELYN WATTS, of St. Petersburg, Fla., a retired nurse who is active in community affairs and serves on the Pinellas County boards of the NAACP, Council of Human Relations, and Pinellas County Opportunity Council.

National Advisory Council on Vocational Education

Appointment of 17 Members and Designation of Chairman.   August 16, 1979

The President today announced the appointment of 17 persons as members of the National Advisory Council on Vocational Education. They are:

PEGGY SUE ARMSTRONG, a junior at Iowa State University, majoring in animal science;

CHERYL J. COSTLEY, an expert on vocational education, who is director of education for Bill Knapp's Inc., of Battle Creek, Mich., where she is responsible for the development and administration of training and educational programs for all employees;

REV. JOHN R. ERWIN, senior chaplain with the Cook County Department of Corrections in Chicago, and founder of PACE Institute, Inc., a nonprofit school offering adult basic education, vocational orientation and counseling to inmates of Cook County Jail;

KAREN MARIE CORNELIUS FENTON, director of the human resources development program of the Confederated Salish & Kootenai Tribes in Pablo, Mont.;

JOSEPH R. FITTIPALDI, coordinator for education of the New Jersey Catholic Conference and a former high school teacher and administrator;

CAROL SAUNDERS GIBSON, director of the education division of the National Urban League, whom the President has also designated Chairman of this Council;

ELI GINZBERG, the A. Barton Hepburn professor of economics at Columbia University's Graduate School of Business, director of the Conservation of Human Resources Project, and chairman of the National Commission for Manpower Policy;

LAWRENCE R. HAWKINS, a member of the Florida House of Representatives, who is a disabled veteran and an active campaigner for the rights of handicapped persons;

GLORIA T. JOHNSON, of Washington, D.C., director of education and women's activities for the International Union of Electrical Radio and Machine Workers;

HERNAN LAFONTAINE, superintendent of schools for the Hartford (Conn.) public schools, an expert on bilingual education, and a former high school teacher;

JOHN M. LIPTON, of Warren, Ark., a member of the Arkansas General Assembly and chairman of the Arkansas Advisory Council on Vocational Education;

ROMAN PUCINSKI, of Chicago, a former Member of the U.S. House of Representatives, where he was chairman of the Standing Committee on Select Education and the Standing Committee on General Education, now a Chicago alderman (reappointment);

JACK B. REIHL, of West Bend, Wis., secretary-treasurer of the Wisconsin State AFL–CIO and a member of the State Advisory Committee on Trade and Industrial Education and the Wisconsin State Apprenticeship Advisory Council for Industrial Crafts;

JOHN D. ROWLETT, a professor of industrial education and technology at Eastern Kentucky University, where he is also vice president for academic affairs and research and dean of the faculties;

JACK SILVERS, master of the Washington State Grange and a Yakima Valley fruit grower;

WILLIAM ASBURY STEMBRIDGE, SR., of Macon, Ga., a businessman who is vice chairman of the State Board of Education and serves on the State Vocational Committee; and

PATRICIA M. VASQUEZ, a San Antonio attorney who has been director of the Mexican American Legal Defense and Educational Fund's Chicana Rights Project.

Counsel to the President

Appointment of Lloyd N. Cutler.
August 17, 1979

The President today announced the appointment of Lloyd N. Cutler as Counsel to the President.

Cutler is a member of the Washington law firm of Wilmer, Cutler & Pickering. He has served as counsel to the President on ratification of the SALT II treaty since earlier this year, and was the President's special representative for maritime resource and boundary negotiations with Canada from 1977 to 1979.

He was born November 10, 1917, in New York City. He received a B.A. from Yale University in 1936 and an LL.B. from Yale Law School in 1939. He served in the U.S. Army from 1942 to 1945.

Cutler was a partner in the law firm of Cox, Langford, Stoddard & Cutler from 1946 until 1962, when he joined his current firm.

Cutler is a member of the executive committee of the Lawyers' Committee for Civil Rights under Law, and is a director of the Mexican-American Legal Defense Fund. He was Special Counsel to the President's Committee on Urban Housing from 1967 to 1968. In 1968 and 1969, he was executive director of the National Commission on the Causes and Prevention of Violence, and he was chairman of the District of Columbia Committee on the Administration of Justice under Emergency Conditions.

Price Controls on Heavy Crude Oil

Remarks on Signing Executive Order 12153. August 17, 1979

To implement a program to reduce our excessive dependence on foreign oil is absolutely necessary to secure and to preserve our own Nation's security. We must at this time minimize both divisive debates and any further delay.

Our goals are, first of all, to encourage conservation to eliminate the waste of energy and, secondly, to increase production of energy in all forms in our own country. The Congress and, indeed, every single American must act both boldly and as soon as possible to carry out these two goals.

Today, as President, I'm taking action that will significantly increase production of American crude oil reserves, lifting price controls on heavy crude oil. This Executive order, which I will sign in a minute, coupled with other related actions, will increase crude oil production in our

country by 1990 by about 500,000 barrels per day. Much of this increase will occur much earlier, between now and 1985, and, therefore, will make an immediate contribution to our Nation's security.

Our Nation is blessed with approximately 10 billion barrels of crude oil reserves which are heavy oil. Much of it's in California; other substantial reserves are in Mississippi, Louisiana, Texas, and Wyoming. However, this very thick, heavy oil is expensive to produce, because it's so difficult to extract from the ground and to transport to the refineries. The combination of high cost of the production and transportation, plus the previously existing price controls, have, indeed, impeded development of this important source of American energy.

Today's action will end this problem. Finally we'll be able to take advantage of a domestic energy source which can be the equivalent of all the oil that we know of in Alaska's Prudhoe Bay reserves. Heavy crude oil is one fuel which we can provide with important production incentives without having an adverse impact on inflation. The more domestic oil we produce, the less our Nation must depend on uncertain and extremely expensive foreign sources of oil.

With this action, I have taken all of the major steps on which I can act alone to accelerate domestic production. It's now up to Congress to act on the other proposals which I made to cut our import dependence.

Pending before Congress are a number of vitally important measures that can cut our dependence on foreign oil more than half by the year 1990. The most important of these, and the basis for all the others, is the windfall profits tax. The issue is simple—who will benefit from the increased prices of oil caused by decontrol, the oil companies or the American people? I'm determined that the American people will be the ones to benefit.

As I've emphasized over and over again, we need the revenues from the windfall profits tax to increase the production of synthetic fuels, to harness solar energy, to provide the means to spur energy conservation, to develop mass transit, and to help our poorest citizens to cope with rising energy prices.

The Senate Finance Committee, however, is currently considering some very broad exemptions to the tax, loopholes big enough to sail an oiltanker through. In many cases, these exemptions will not increase American production at all. In some other cases, the exemptions or loopholes will increase American production a very small amount. The cost of that increased production will be enormous to the American people.

I've made my position clear on what should be done about energy. My proposals have been made both to the American people and to the Congress. As I travel through the heartland of America this coming week on kind of a working vacation, I intend to explain to the American people the magnitude of the choices which now are before the Congress. I'm confident that they will share my conviction that we need an effective windfall profits tax without major exceptions and without unwarranted loopholes. Only then can our Nation be assured of the resources for genuine energy security for the United States.

Thank you very much.

NOTE: The President spoke at 1:03 p.m. to reporters assembled in the Oval Office at the White House.

Price Controls on Heavy Crude Oil

Executive Order 12153.   August 17, 1979

DECONTROL OF HEAVY OIL

By the authority vested in me as President by the Constitution and statutes of the United States of America, including the Emergency Petroleum Allocation Act of 1973, as amended (15 U.S.C. 751 *et seq.*), and notwithstanding the delegations to the Secretary of Energy in Executive Order No. 11790, as amended by Executive Order No. 12038, it is hereby ordered as follows:

1–101.   Effective August 17, 1979, prices charged in the first sale of heavy crude oil are exempted from price controls adopted pursuant to the Emergency Petroleum Allocation Act of 1973, as amended. For purposes of this section, the term "heavy crude oil" means all crude oil produced from a property, but only if, during the last month prior to July 1979 in which crude oil was produced and sold from that property, such crude oil had a weighted average gravity of 16.0° API or less, corrected to 60° Fahrenheit.

1–102.   The Secretary of Energy, or his delegate, shall expeditiously conduct a public inquiry as to what other types of heavy crude oil, if any, should be exempted from price controls adopted pursuant to the Emergency Petroleum Allocation Act of 1973, as amended, in order to maintain or increase production of such crude oil. Upon completion of that inquiry, the Secretary shall make a recommendation to the President as to what other types of heavy crude oil, if any, should be exempt from price controls.

1—103.   The Secretary of Energy may pursuant to Executive Order 11790, as amended by Executive Order 12038, adopt such regulations as he deems necessary to implement this Order.

JIMMY CARTER

The White House,
August 17, 1979.

[Filed with the Office of the Federal Register,
3:32 p.m., August 17, 1979]

United States Ambassador to Nigeria

Nomination of Stephen Low.
August 17, 1979

The President today announced that he will nominate Stephen Low, of Cincinnati, Ohio, to be Ambassador Extraordinary and Plenipotentiary of the United States to the Federal Republic of Nigeria. He would replace Donald B. Easum, who is resigning.

Low is now Ambassador to the Republic of Zambia.

He was born December 2, 1927, in Cincinnati. He received a B.A. from Yale University in 1950 and an M.A. (1951) and Ph. D. (1956) from Fletcher School of Law and Diplomacy. He served in the U.S. Army from 1946 to 1947.

Low joined the Foreign Service in 1956 and was posted in Kampala and Dakar. From 1964 to 1965, he was officer in charge of Guinea-Mali affairs at the State Department, and from 1965 to 1967, he was Special Assistant to the Deputy Under Secretary of State for Political Affairs.

In 1967–68 he attended the National War College, and from 1968 to 1971, he was counselor for political affairs in Brasília. He was director of Brazil affairs at the State Department from 1971 to 1974. From 1974 to 1976, he was detailed to the National Security Council, and since 1976 he has been Ambassador to Zambia.

International Civil Aviation Organization

Appointment of Clyde W. Pace, Jr., as
Alternate U.S. Representative.
August 17, 1979

The President today announced that he has appointed Clyde W. Pace, Jr., of Arlington, Va., to be Alternate U.S. Representative on the Council of the International Civil Aviation Organization.

Pace is currently Assistant Administrator of the Federal Aviation Administration for Europe, Africa, and the Middle East Region.

Pace, 51, has been with the FAA since 1956 and is a former airport engineer.

United States Court of Military Appeals Nominating Commission

Appointment of the Membership.
August 17, 1979

The President today announced the appointment of the six members of the Court of Military Appeals Nominating Commission, established by Executive Order 12063 (June 5, 1978):

DEANNE C. SIEMER, Chairperson, General Counsel, Department of Defense;

ANTONIA HANDLER CHAYES, Under Secretary of the Air Force;

NEAL ARTHUR, manager of government relations and human resources, Rohr Industries, Inc., Chula Vista, Calif.;

STUART POLLAK, attorney, San Francisco, Calif.;

CLINTON BAMBERGER, attorney, Boston, Mass., formerly Executive Vice President of the Legal Services Corporation;

A. KENNETH PYE, chancellor, Duke University.

The President also requested the assistance of the Commission in filling the vacancy on the Court of Military Appeals which will be created following confirmation of the Honorable Matthew Perry as a United States District Court Judge for the District of South Carolina. Judge Perry is now a member of the Court of Military Appeals.

The President directed the Commission to make special efforts to consider well-qualified women and members of minority groups as possible nominees.

Labor Dispute in the Grain Industry

Statement by the President. August 17, 1979

The dispute between the American Federation of Grain Millers and the grain companies, now entering its seventh week, is a matter of great concern to me. The farmers, who are not a party to the dispute, but whose livelihoods are so deeply affected by it, have no satisfactory alternative means of getting their product to market. With the peak harvest season now upon us, the importance of an early agreement is evident.

I have directed that Secretary Bergland and Secretary Marshall monitor the situation closely and report regularly to me. I have also directed that the Federal Mediation and Conciliation Service provide whatever assistance will facilitate the strike's prompt settlement.

This evening I will meet in St. Paul with Governors Link of North Dakota and Quie of Minnesota to discuss the strike and its effect on the upper midwest.

But there should be no doubt about my own views concerning the best way to resolve this strike. It has been demonstrated repeatedly that the process of free collective bargaining is the best method

for resolving disagreements between labor and management. In exercising their rights under that process, the parties to a dispute have a special responsibility to recognize and consider the hardships their actions are imposing on others. I urge the Grain Millers and the companies to work conscientiously with the Federal Mediation and Conciliation Service to achieve an early, equitable settlement to this dispute.

In this situation, it is clear that such a settlement can occur if the local parties, who are the most sensitive to local problems and needs, are allowed to continue negotiating together. Although the impact of the strike is causing hardship in this area, the stringent legal test of Taft-Hartley requires a demonstration of danger to the health and safety of the entire Nation. That strict requirement now effectively precludes the use of this remedy.

I am confident that the Grain Millers and the companies will act responsibly and in the Nation's best interest in attempting to resolve this strike promptly and fairly.

Community Involvement in Energy Conservation

Letter to City Officials. August 17, 1979

As you know, local leaders around the country are already working hard to make their communities more energy efficient, and the people who live there more energy conscious. I am writing to pledge the full assistance of the Federal Government in your efforts and to request your most vigorous leadership in developing your own community-wide conservation plans.

Many communities such as Portland, Oregon; Clinton County, Michigan;

Davis, California; and Greensboro, North Carolina, have successfully created participating public efforts that bring together business, civic, religious and community groups to formulate energy savings.

The potential contribution from a concentrated effort by communities across the country to our nation's battle in energy security is enormous. In fact, if extensive conservation measures are implemented in residential, public and commercial buildings alone we might reduce oil imports by well over a million barrels a day. Several hundred thousand more barrels of oil a day could be saved if we expanded use of ridesharing and took simple steps to improve automobile efficiency. These measures will also reduce the cost of living for all Americans who participate by lowering utility bills and cutting the cost of transportation.

If our national efforts to conserve are to be successful, your community's imagination and creativity must be encouraged.

Along these lines, in my July 16 speech before the National Association of Counties in Kansas City, I urged those Federal officials who had not done so to work with other leaders in their community—from both inside and outside of government—to set ambitious local conservation goals and to develop action plans to meet these goals.

I have enclosed some brief descriptions from the growing number of existing local efforts. To assist you in sharing this information and in learning more about the programs of other communities I have established a special clearinghouse to serve leaders who are undertaking energy conservation initiatives. A toll-free hotline will be opened in early September. Correspondence can be addressed now to the President's Clearinghouse for Community Energy Efficiency, Suite 185, 400 North Capitol Street, N.W., Washington, D.C. 20001.

It is through the application of your citizens' initiatives and inspiration that America can win the energy war. Our nation is counting on your help and your leadership. Thank you for your efforts. I look forward to hearing of your success.

JIMMY CARTER

NOTE: This is the text of identical letters sent to more than 6,000 mayors and elected city officials throughout the Nation.

The White House Press Office also made available the enclosure detailing the local energy conservation efforts.

Digest of Other White House Announcements

The following listing includes the President's public schedule and other items of general interest announced by the White House Press Office and not included elsewhere in this issue.

August 13

The President returned to the White House from Camp David, Md.

The President met at the White House with:

—Vice President Walter F. Mondale;

—Secretary of Agriculture Bob Bergland, Stuart E. Eizenstat, Assistant to the President for Domestic Affairs and Policy, Anne Wexler, Assistant to the President, Alfred E. Kahn, Advisor to the President on Inflation, Esther Peterson, Assistant to the President for Consumer Affairs, and representatives of the food industry, to discuss food prices.

In a ceremony in the Oval Office, the President received diplomatic credentials from Ambassadors Sadek Jawad Sulaiman of the Sultanate of Oman, Bernard

Kendrick Radix of the People's Revolutionary Government of Grenada, and Sukru Elekdag of the Republic of Turkey.

August 14

The President met at the White House with:

—Zbigniew Brzezinski, Assistant to the President for National Security Affairs;

—Frank B. Moore, Assistant to the President for Congressional Liaison;

—Vice President Mondale, Stansfield Turner, Director of Central Intelligence, Hamilton Jordan, Assistant to the President, and Dr. Brzezinski.

The President participated in a briefing on the administration's programs and policies given for civic and community leaders from Texas in the East Room at the White House.

August 15

The President met at the White House with:

—Vice President Mondale, Secretary of Health, Education, and Welfare Patricia Roberts Harris, Secretary of Labor Ray Marshall, Secretary-designate of Housing and Urban Development Moon Landrieu, Secretary Bergland, James T. McIntyre, Jr., Director of the Office of Management and Budget, Jack H. Watson, Jr., Assistant to the President for Intergovernmental Affairs, and Mr. Eizenstat, to discuss domestic policies;

—Dr. Brzezinski;

—Mr. Moore;

—Ambassador Andrew Young, U.S. Representative to the United Nations.

The President participated in a briefing by administration officials on the strategic arms limitation treaty held for community leaders in the East Room at the White House.

The President announced that he will nominate Secretary of the Treasury G. William Miller to be U.S. Governor of the International Monetary Fund, Governor of the Inter-American Development Bank, U.S. Governor of the Asian Development Bank, and U.S. Governor of the African Development Fund. He also announced that he has designated Miller as a member of the Council on Wage and Price Stability, Chairman of the U.S. Section of the Joint U.S.-U.S.S.R. Commercial Commission, and U.S. Chairman of the U.S.-China Joint Economic Committee. All of these positions are normally filled by the Secretary of the Treasury.

August 16

The President met at the White House with:

—Dr. Brzezinski;

—Mr. Moore;

—Mrs. Carter, for lunch;

—Gustave Speth, Chairman of the Council on Environmental Quality.

In a ceremony in the Oval Office, the President was presented the International Mediation Medal by officials of the American Arbitration Association for his efforts in resolving the conflict in the Middle East.

The President participated in a briefing by administration officials on the strategic arms limitation treaty held for community leaders in the East Room at the White House.

August 17

The President met at the White House with:

—Vice President Mondale, Secretary of Defense Harold Brown, Deputy Secretary of State Warren M. Christopher, Hedley W. Donovan, Senior Adviser to the President, Mr. Jordan, and Dr. Brzezinski;

—Mr. Moore.

The President announced that he has appointed Paul A. Volcker to be U.S. Alternate Governor of the International Monetary Fund. This position is normally filled by the Chairman of the Board of Governors of the Federal Reserve System.

The President left the White House for St. Paul, Minn. In St. Paul he participated in a briefing on energy for city officials and citizens (transcript will be printed next week). He then boarded the riverboat *Delta Queen* for a week-long trip down the Mississippi River, to end in St. Louis, Mo., on August 24.

NOMINATIONS SUBMITTED TO THE SENATE

The following list does not include promotions of members of the Uniformed Services, nominations to the Service Academies, or nominations of Foreign Service officers.

Submitted August 16, 1979

G. WILLIAM MILLER, of California, to be United States Governor of the International Monetary Fund for a term of 5 years and United States Governor of the International Bank for Reconstruction and Development for a term of 5 years; a Governor of the Inter-American Development Bank for a term of 5 years; and United States Governor of the Asian Development Bank and United States Governor of the African Development Fund.

FRANCOIS M. DICKMAN, of Wyoming, a Foreign Service officer of Class one, to be Ambassador Extraordinary and Plenipotentiary of the United States of America to the State of Kuwait.

JOHN R. CLINGERMAN, of Michigan, a Foreign Service officer of Class three, to be Ambassador Extraordinary and Plenipotentiary of the United States of America to the Kingdom of Lesotho.

CHECKLIST OF WHITE HOUSE PRESS RELEASES

The following listing contains releases of the White House Press Office which are not included in this issue.

Released August 13, 1979

News conference: on the President's meeting with food industry representatives—by Alfred E. Kahn, Advisor to the President on Inflation

Released August 15, 1979

Transcript: remarks announcing the President's acceptance of the resignation of Ambassador Andrew Young as U.S. Representative to the United Nations—by Press Secretary Jody Powell

Released August 17, 1979

Transcript: announcement of appointment of Lloyd N. Cutler as Counsel to the President and remarks on Executive Order 12153, price controls on heavy crude oil—by Press Secretary Jody Powell

Fact sheet: Executive Order 12153, price controls on heavy crude oil

---

ACTS APPROVED BY THE PRESIDENT

Approved August 13, 1979

H.R. 4476_____ Public Law 96–49
Higher Education Technical Amendments of 1979.

H.J. Res. 19_____ Public Law 96–50
National Lupus Week.

H.J. Res. 209_____ Public Law 96–51
National Diabetes Week.

S. 1318_____ Public Law 96–52
An act to amend title 13 of the United States Code to provide a limited exemption to the Bureau of the Census from the provisions of 322 of the Act of June 30, 1932.

H.R. 896_____ Private Law 96–1
An act for the relief of Joseph J. Andrews.

H.R. 899_____ Private Law 96–2
An act for the relief of Mr. and Mrs. Aaron Wayne Ogburn.

H.R. 932_____ Private Law 96–3
An act for the relief of Doris Mauri Coonrad.

H.R. 1158_____ Private Law 96–4
An act for the relief of James C. Wilkinson.

ACTS APPROVED—Continued

Approved August 14, 1979

H.R. 3324_____ Public Law 96–53
International Development Cooperation Act
of 1979.

H.R. 4616_____ Public Law 96–54
An act to make certain technical and clerical
amendments to title 5, United States Code.

H.R. 4811_____ Public Law 96–55
An act for the relief of the city of Nenana,
Alaska, and to amend the Act of January 2,
1976, as amended, and for other purposes.

H.R. 2807_____ Public Law 96–56
An act to amend the Bankruptcy Act to provide for the nondischargeability of certain
student loan debts guaranteed or insured by
the United States.

H.R. 3914_____ Public Law 96–57
An act to amend the National Capital
Transportation Act of 1969 to remove the
limitation on the amount authorized for
District of Columbia contributions for the
cost of construction of the rapid transit system of the National Capital Region.

ACTS APPROVED—Continued

Approved August 14—Continued

H.R. 4057_____ Public Law 96–58
An act to increase the fiscal year 1979 authorization appropriations for the food
stamp program, and for other purposes.

S. 41_____ Public Law 96–59
An act to require the Secretary of Agriculture to convey a reversionary interest held by
the United States in certain lands located in
Bell County, Kentucky, to the Board of Education, Bell County, Kentucky.

Approved August 15, 1979

H.R. 3363_____ Public Law 96–60
An act to authorize appropriations for fiscal
years 1980 and 1981 for the Department of
State, the International Communication
Agency, and the Board for International
Broadcasting.

S. 917_____ Public Law 96–61
An act to authorize appropriations to carry
out the Fishery Conservation and Management Act of 1976 during fiscal years 1980,
1981, and 1982, and for other purposes.

PRESIDENTIAL DOCUMENTS

Week Ending Friday, August 24, 1979

St. Paul, Minnesota

Remarks at an Energy Briefing by St. Paul Citizens.   August 17, 1979

ENERGY

THE PRESIDENT. Mayor Latimer and all of those who've come here to help me deal with one of the most important and significant challenges that our Nation has ever faced, let me express my thanks to you.

I'm going to be on the beautiful Mississippi River for the next 7 days with about 140 fine Americans, and I know we'll make many new friends on the ship. It'll be kind of a working vacation, because I will take every opportunity to express to the American people my deep concern about the first development in the rapid changing characteristics of energy supply that have ever comprised a direct, serious threat to the security of the Nation that we love.

This is no exaggeration. We have become overly dependent on uncertain and very expensive imported oil. We import not only oil, but we import unemployment and we import inflation. I've already taken action with the help of the Congress to save 4 million barrels of oil

per day by 1990, and I propose to the Congress savings for another 4½ million barrels of oil per day.

I can pledge to you that the most oil that this country will ever import in a year was imported 2 years ago in 1977. We're going to freeze that import and start bringing it down to make our energy security something on which we can depend. The basis for it is the windfall profits tax. The basic decision there is, as oil prices go up with decontrol to encourage American production, who is going to benefit? The oil companies or the American people? I'm determined that it will be the American people, and it must be as a result of the passage of the windfall profits tax. Only your voice can make that possible.

And out of the windfall profits tax will come money to help the poorest American families bear the increased burden of inevitable increases in the price of energy. It will let us form much more effective mass transit systems. It will also mean that we can increase American production. More coal will be used, clean-burning coal; more solar energy; more production of oil and natural gas. And the most important thing of all and the cheapest thing of all—more conservation, how to stop wasting energy.

This beautiful building has been renovated so that it does become energy-efficient. Every single building in St. Paul can have the same degree of achievement. But it can only be done with the full cooperation and involvement of all the citizens of this community.

This meeting is very important, not only for you but for the entire State of Minnesota and, indeed, for the entire Nation. Because you've done such good work before I got here, and to some degree because I'm here, people will know what you're going to do, and this is very important to us all.

Today, in preparation for my visit here to St. Paul, I sent a personal letter to every senior elected official of every county and city in the United States of America, 6,000 personal letters, with an enclosure saying what certain communities have already done. And it wasn't a coincidence that one of those communities that I've used as an example was St. Paul, because you've done a good job.

Now, I came here to listen primarily, but I want to make two very quick points. There are two basic errors or misconceptions that permeate America. One is that conservation can be accomplished by government. It cannot. It must be accomplished by citizens. Secondly, that conservation is somehow painful or inconvenient. It does not have to be painful or inconvenient. It can be exciting. It can be enjoyable. And instead of dividing one American from another, it can form a basis for closeness within a family or within a community or, indeed, within a whole nation. And it saves a lot of money—not my money, not the Government's money, but your money. This must be done. And if all the communities in our Nation will do as St. Paul is planning,

then our conservation effort will be successful. That's what I hope and pray.

And now I'm eager to listen to the presentations that have been prepared. And if you don't mind, I might interrupt every now and then to ask a question if I feel the urge.

Thank you for letting me be here. It's a great honor and pleasure for me. It's going to help the whole Nation, what you're doing.

Thank you very much.

STATEMENTS

MAYOR LATIMER. *Mr. President, ladies and gentlemen:*

In preparation for this our first meeting, as you know, we have divided into five committees. We began as a committee of 100 for a 100-day effort, and we now have three times the number of people, and I hope that means one-third the number of days. But as preparation for this, Mr. President, we have asked eight people who had previously asked to serve on this committee to make presentations on different subjects.

CENTRAL HEATING PROJECT

The first presenter is Cliff Olsen, who is from the First National Bank of St. Paul. He represents the Chamber of Commerce in the energy committee, and he's a vice president of the District Heating Development Company, which is the subject which Mr. Olsen's going to speak about.

Cliff?

MR. OLSEN. *Mr. President, Mrs. Carter, Amy, Mr. Mayor, honored guests:*

Several years of effort were fulfilled in June of this year when the public and private sectors of our community joined to form the St. Paul District Heating Development Company. Its purpose is to demonstrate the technical and the economic feasibility of providing a metropolitan community such as ours with central heating through the medium of hot water produced through cogeneration in conjunction with an investor-owned electric power station. This power station, incidentally, uses only coal as its fuel. While innovative, the concept is not revolutionary. Central hot water heating systems have been used in Europe for many years. The point is that it's never been tried in the United States.

The advantage offered by this system is the almost doubling of thermal efficiency, because energy otherwise wasted in electric generation is recaptured and becomes the hot water used in the heating system. Also the oil and natural gas which is not used to heat homes and industries is saved, and it amounts, by our engineers' calculations, to be sufficient to heat some 200,000 homes. This is about twice the number of homes that we have in St. Paul.

Our efforts have been helped very greatly by the significant contributions of the Minnesota Energy Administration and the Department of Energy. Particularly, we owe a debt of gratitude to the facility at Oak Ridge. We are also most appreciative of the interest that DOE, Under Secretary John Deutch, has shown and also for the substantial financial assistance which you have tendered to us.

We are presently in the final stages of planning which will lead to the construction, we hope in early 1981, of a demonstration project, which will include the downtown central business district and also the capital building complex.

We are very pleased with our progress to date. And we recognize that it is due to the unselfish and complete cooperation of business, labor, and every level of government. Given the opportunity to compete in a truly free market, we sincerely believe that district heating is the mode of the future, and we in St. Paul are pleased to provide an example to the rest of the country.

MAYOR LATIMER. Thank you very much, Cliff.

TRANSPORTATION PROGRAMS

The second speaker is Malcolm McDonald, who manages the Space Center Buildings in St. Paul, Minnesota, and works with Operation 85, which he'll tell the people and the President about.

Malcolm?

MR. McDONALD. Mr. President, Operation 85, trades and labor, business and civic leaders who are planning the St. Paul of tomorrow. Acting in the conviction that most practical local solutions to our energy problems will be found through a productive partnership, we as citizens have tried to construct a here-and-now energy conservation program to reduce our daily energy consumption, increase our downtown air quality, and save money for all of us.

In cooperation with the city and in particular the office of the mayor, the Metro Transit Commission, and private industry, Operation 85's Committee on Commuter Alternatives has designed four energy-saving programs for cars and people. In October we will announce the first phase.

These programs for carpools, vanpools, greater bus riding, and parking at the edge of the city have as their common goals reducing the number of cars by 15 percent, reducing gasoline consumption through shorter trips, and reducing downtown traffic congestion, increasing the use of existing public transportation systems for greater efficiency, increasing revenue for our bus system to reduce its deficit, increasing our air quality, and saving money for all of us.

To make these programs happen, the public and private sectors are cooperating to provide special aims—parking and cost incentives for van- and carpoolers; properly spec'd, long-lasting equipment designed for low-speed, continuing shuttle, to reduce maintenance and operating costs; variable work hours, flex-time, to reduce peak pressure on transit facilities; encouragement for appropriate bicycle use; and rediscovering how to walk down our new pedestrian malls.

For the future, we are looking to help St. Paulites with areawide matchups for carpools, shared-ride taxis, dial-a-ride for the handicapped, additional shelters at fringe parking lots, and extensive information programs.

Our public and private cooperation comes from our common desire to build the St. Paul of tomorrow, through the best and most economical use of public and private funds and people time.

Looking further into the future, we have been considering a peoplemover; light-rail transit; computer-controlled traffic management; expanded use of buses, jitney, small bus, and schoolbus to replace car use during the middle of the day.

Mr. President, all of us have benefited from public support at the local, State, and Federal level, both in funding and in personal commitment. We look forward to continued cooperation. The private sector of business and labor here in St. Paul wants to show through all of these efforts what we can do for ourselves.

Thank you, Mr. President.

ST. PAUL ENERGY PARK

MAYOR LATIMER. Next is Allen Boyce, who is the president of the Citizens League, which, Mr. President, is an extraordinary, not-for-profit group of citizens who research every level of govern-

ment in the major issues, as well as being an employee of the Burlington-Northern Railroad. Allen will talk to us about the potential of the energy park in St. Paul.

Mr. Boyce.

MR. BOYCE. Mr. President, I'm very glad that you decided to begin your trip here in St. Paul. I think it's particularly appropriate on a trip revolving around the energy issue that you begin in a central city like St. Paul, which is inherently energy-efficient. This is because of the proximity within our city of our facilities for shopping and work, recreation, and housing.

And I think here in St. Paul we have the opportunity to take this inherent advantage one step further. What we have—and I think this is rather unique—is a site of approximately 250 acres of land right in the heart of our metropolitan area, halfway between the downtowns of Minneapolis and St. Paul, which is available for development. This area presently contains a coke plant, which has recently shut down, an under-used stadium, and a great deal of vacant land. What we see here is the potential for the development of what we call an energy park. This would be an area which would demonstrate new techniques for combining energy-efficient light industry, housing, transportation, and the production of energy itself.

We foresee a public-private corporation which would be established to develop the following types of facilities, all in one complex: high-density, energy-efficient housing; an office industrial park for energy-related industries; an energy research and development center in connection with the University of Minnesota; a solid waste recovery plant to make use of some of the wastes generated in the complex; a hot water district heating system which could potentially produce both electricity and then, through cogeneration, use some of that waste heat for district heating.

There's also potential for a cable television system which could provide special energy-saving features that would help reduce the need for people living and working in this area to travel. Also there's a possibility for further development of our mass transit facilities, and I think placing a development like this in the center of a city like St. Paul helps to begin reducing the need for people to travel long distances to work, to live, and to have their recreation. And it makes the production and the distribution of energy much more efficient because of the compactness of our central city areas.

So, I hope you'll be supportive of this energy park project in St. Paul.

Thank you.

HOME WEATHERIZATION

MAYOR LATIMER. Mr. President, as you have pointed out numerous times, the greatest burden on the poor is in fact the inflationary impact of energy costs. And that's why it's very important to us that our next speaker, Michael McAllister, is the director of energy conservation for our local CAP program, which is called the Ramsey Action Program.

Mike?

MR. MCALLISTER. Mr. President, Ramsey Action Programs in St. Paul is a community action agency serving the low-income people in Ramsey County. Among the many programs offered, the energy programs are providing a much-needed service in two Ramsey County residences.

Currently the energy programs have three main components. One, optimum weatherization research projects—this program's operation is in conjunction with the National Bureau of Standards and the Community Services Administration in Washington, D.C. This project is a thorough evaluation and a study on the cost-effectiveness of weatherization and the development of new and improved weatherization techniques and methods. This research program is determining which energy conservation measures are the most cost-effective in residential construction.

Two, the State and Federal Crisis Intervention and Emergency Energy Assistance programs. In the past 6 months, 4,554 households have received assistance because of the high energy costs. In Minnesota, this program should be expanded and the funds administered on a year-round basis. Three, home weatherization program. In Ramsey County, this program is being accomplished by a joint effort from the city of St. Paul manpower programs, the Community Services Administration, and the State department of economic security.

Recently a needs assessment on the homes in Ramsey County was completed. 45,402 eligible people for the home weatherization program were identified. Our priorities for weatherization are fuel oil users, senior citizens, and handicapped people. In addition, the study revealed that the working poor need fuel assistance and weatherization assistance. Currently they are not eligible for assistance, because their gross income is above the guidelines; however, their net income is below the guidelines.

In the past years we have weatherized over 500 homes in Ramsey County. In 1979 we expect to weatherize 453 homes, and in 1980 over 1,000 homes will be weatherized. Depending on the living habits, our studies show that energy consumption can be reduced by 30 percent with proper weatherization methods. However, there are problems with the program.

The CETA regulations, such as the average for CETA employees, has to be resolved at the national level. In addition, there is plenty of Federal funds for weatherization materials, but very few funds for labor and support costs. The people in the State of Minnesota and the community action agencies need more funds to support the energy conservation programs.

Thank you, Mr. President.

MAYOR LATIMER. Thank you very much, Mike.

INNER-CITY PROGRAMS

Mr. President, the city of St. Paul is a very strong neighborhood-oriented city. The next speaker comes from one of our great old, nearby, downtown neighborhoods, the West Seventh Street area. Her name is Becky Yust, and she also teaches at the University of Minnesota as a home economist.

Becky?

Ms. YUST. Good evening, Mr. President.

Tonight I'm representing the West Seventh Federation, an organization in an inner St. Paul neighborhood.

It is my belief that we can have simple but long-lasting solutions to affect energy consumption. Two very basic concerns that affect families the most are simply getting to work and keeping warm in their homes.

The need for efficient transportation is great. Over 40 percent of the households in our community do not even own a car. For 2 years we have investigated and proposed a light rail system or modern trolley for our community. As in most city neighborhoods, we have one main business street that serves as a corridor from downtown to the airport and suburbs. Three different bus lines intersect it, and it is a natural collecting point for residents. Light rail is a preferred transit system, because it is nonpolluting, it operates in

our severe climate, and it is not capital-intensive; plus the efficiency and technology has been proven here and in Europe.

The second problem involves heating our homes. We have very few newly constructed housing units in the inner city. The vast majority of the housing structures are existing and too expensive to replace, and because of their age, they do not have insulation. We need funds through the HUD 312 program to provide moneys to help people insulate, weatherstrip, replace rotted windows, and ventilate.

Targeting moneys to pay heating fuel bills alone will not effect the conservation of energy. We do not want to maintain the present situation. We need to change consumption so that families can have lower heating costs.

In summary, the problems of the inner city are not new. We are still trying to deal with jobs, housing, and schools. Energy just provides a different perspective on these same issues. It is my hope that as renewed attention and pressure is placed on the inner city because of energy conservation, that you will listen to the residents living there now for the solutions.

The inner-city neighborhoods have been victims of crises in the past. Policies need to be responsive to the communities they directly affect so that the quality of life does not deteriorate.

It would seem that it is easier for the Government to effect physical changes than attitudes and habits of individuals. Therefore, in neighborhoods such as ours, improvements in transportation systems like implementing light rail transit and improvements in our existing housing stock could substantially help inner-city neighborhoods and complement ongoing rehabilitation and revitalization efforts.

Thank you.

THE PRESIDENT. I've asked the mayor to let me say just a word.

We have three more presentations to make, but there are three themes that run through all these presentations. One is there is no possibility of success without a joint, cooperative effort. One person alone, a President or a mayor, Congress, can't do it. It has to be a joint effort. Secondly, every one of the programs proposed—even the cogeneration plan or the people-mover, the weatherization of homes—is already dependent upon Federal funds as kind of a core basis for a much broader, magnified effort by everyone else. And third, every one of these proposals so far doesn't make life more dismal. It makes life better. It is not a sacrifice to get to work efficiently, not to have traffic jams, to have an easy way to shop, to save heat in your homes, not to throw away heat in the generation of power, and as you well know, every time you don't burn either coal or gas or oil, air pollution goes down.

So, those three things—a cooperative effort, the Federal Government must and is helping and can help more with the windfall profits tax, and third, conservation—makes our life better and not worse. It's a good thing for us to remember, and I know you'll watch this and see if what I've said is true for the last three speakers.

Thank you, Mr. Mayor.

MAYOR LATIMER. Thank you.

The sixth speaker is Greg Haley, who is an architect, has been very active in his community, and, in particular, has been working on community planning in his neighborhood and would like to talk about that aspect of it.

Greg?

COMMUNITY PLANNING

MR. HALEY. *Good evening, Mr. President, Mrs. Carter, ladies and gentlemen:*

I am representing District 12 Community Council. District 12 is one of 17 neighborhood planning areas created to facilitate citizen participation in the city of St. Paul. The council and other neighborhood groups have been working diligently on projects that deal either directly or indirectly with energy concerns. Our plan has been developed over a 3-year period by residents and businessmen. The city will use it and other district plans to help formulate an overall city plan.

The principal element of our plan is to propose the residential and industrial development of the vacant and under-utilized railroad land that bisects our district. New housing would fill a need for university students and provide homes for families who prefer to live and work in the city. Industrial development would help stem the flow of companies to suburban industrial parks, decrease employee commuting time, and provide a centralized distribution point for goods and services.

The University of Minnesota's inner-campus transit system will pass through this redevelopment area, affording transportation to students and staff living in the neighborhood. This under-utilized railroad land and adjacent properties make up Mayor Latimer's proposed energy park. At the very least, the energy park could be a refreshing alternative to urban redevelopment. We hope it can be a stimulating learning tool and a model for other cities to emulate.

Our neighborhood is also pursuing solutions to energy-related problems on a smaller scale. We have volunteer staff in the home improvement centers who will give out information on reinsulating and renovating older homes and how to finance the work. We have formed a local development company composed of businessmen and residents to help small businessmen secure financing for capital improvements, including rehabilitating older structures for energy efficiency.

We have also actively pursued a recycling program in District 12. We now have once-a-month curbside pickup, and our goal is to have collection of separated recycling materials in conjunction with our regular weekly refuse pickup. The district planning process in St. Paul has been a highly successful vehicle in shaping the future of the city. Involving citizens in the decisionmaking process has created an impetus which is necessary to renew the vitality of our core city.

We hope District 12 has and will play an important part in the continuing revitalization. Our interests lie in many areas, and we feel that the diversity of our projects are necessary to help deal with the multifaceted energy problem. We especially look forward to working with Federal, State, and local officials on Mayor Latimer's proposed energy park.

Thank you very much.

MAYOR LATIMER. Thank you very much.

SOLAR ENERGY PROJECTS

The next speaker is Russell Doty, who is an attorney and has done considerable research professionally in solar and alternative energy sources and the kinds of ordinance and statutory changes that might be needed to adapt to the new technology.

Mr. Doty?

MR. DOTY. Mr. President, Mrs. Carter, Ramsey County has 30 to 50 solar installations, and from these projects and the 400 to 700 other operating solar systems in Minnesota, we have confirmed that Minnesota's climate is definitely suitable for solar applications. For example, one Twin City solar system was producing 90-degree tapwater on Christmas Day 2 years ago. Many of Minnesota's systems have

been working successfully for more than 2 years, and many of them are warranted for up to 10 years. But people do not yet realize that solar systems work here, and we continue to need massive amounts of money to make solar curriculum guides and resource people available to the educational projects.

The effect of education is dramatic. Your July speech created so much interest that the Minnesota solar dealers who I've talked to who have been on the verge of going broke now believe that they may even be able to make it. But interest alone does not mean that solar soon will be available to everyone who is interested.

Even though we have a low-income solar loan program administered through the Minnesota Housing Finance Agency, and even though we now have a combined Federal-State tax credit that defrays up to 50 percent of the solar systems' costs, most people cannot afford the initial investment, that two to ten thousand dollar, upfront cost of the solar system. Energy utilities finance that upfront cost of powerplants by floating bonds that are amortized over long periods. And they float tax-free bonds for some of that plant. Now, solar energy-generating plants also should be paid for by long-term financing—but financing that allows the people and not the utilities to own their energy-generating systems once the costs are amortized.

Your proposed loan grant and small energy business assistance programs have and will help, but those funding sources won't and don't provide enough money to go around. And under them, the larger established firms likely will continue to ace out smaller applicants who are just as creative. You can help solve that problem—and this is my most important point—by advocating Federal legislation to enable St. Paul and other municipalities to support the issuance of tax-exempt, low-interest-rate industrial revenue bonds.

The bonds will finance on a lease-purchase-type basis the widespread use of individual solar systems. People can then pay for the solar system over long periods of time at Btu rates equal to utility rates, and the money market, not the government's budget, will be the only limit on available funding.

For example, a $400 million bond issue will provide more than enough money to install solar tapwater heating systems on all of the housing units in St. Paul. Direct heating solar systems can now produce more Btu's per dollar invested than nuclear and coal electric generating systems.

So, continue to challenge us, Mr. President. Give solar the same money market access and fast write-off and other tax advantages that coal and nuclear power-generating utilities enjoy, and we'll insulate and solarize and do everything that we haven't done yet and should do and do our best to see that you never have to find another $400 million to clean up a plant like Three Mile Island.

Thank you.

MAYOR LATIMER. Mr. President, you probably noticed, although we believe strongly in local control and citizen participation, that the prospect of Federal moneys continues to have some interest to us. Do you get that feeling? [*Laughter*]

THE PRESIDENT. With the windfall profits tax, we will have that money

MAYOR LATIMER. All right.

Our final and perhaps our briefest speaker—[*laughter*]. You can tell, Mr. President, that in St. Paul they know the next speaker, and they know that he's not going to be brief, but he promised me he would be. His name is Tod Lefko.

THE PRESIDENT. If I miss my boat, he's going to have to swim with me. [*Laughter*]

ENERGY PLANNING PROCEDURES

MAYOR LATIMER. Mr. Lefko is important to this city, because he helped to formulate the neighborhood participation process that we have been working under so successfully. He teaches at the university. He has about all of the qualities you could look for, except he can't seem to get elected to office. [*Laughter*]

MR. LEFKO. Thanks, George.

Mr. President, and fellow citizens, how can we translate public awareness of what can be into public action or what should be? The issue of energy is before us. In St. Paul, the possibility of solutions are enhanced because of our style of decisionmaking. In St. Paul, decisions are approached in a philosophically and pragmatically different manner than many other cities.

We begin with four philosophical bases: first, a belief in local responsibility and application of pragmatic planning. We have a tradition of identifying and facing problems and not waiting for Federal action. Next, if we have a secret, it is that we are process-oriented. We have learned that issues must not be faced as a crisis, and we've developed processes for integrated decisionmaking.

Third, in St. Paul the choice is not between the new and the old. We realize that the future is a balance. There's something just and proper about talking about energy alternatives in this building. And if you want to see what the true and best demonstration of St. Paul is, here it is.

Fourth, we see energy as but a part of a larger system, tied to economic development, housing, integrated planning, education, and movement toward self-sufficiency. Even seeking self-sufficiency we realize our obligation and interdependence. In fact, Mr. President, we know that Minneapolis has always looked to us for leadership. And we have never failed them. We shall not this time, either.

Mr. President, with these bases, St. Paul has created a number of decision processes which allow us to raise awareness and action levels. These include, first, a decentralized neighborhood planning process which recently received the award as one of the best in the Nation; second, designation by your administration as the test area for the negotiated investment strategy—and a wise decision it was, sir— third, a nationally recognized mixture of foundation grants, private investment, and governmental expenditures for urban renovation; and fourth, a State and regional decision process on energy and land use. Our State department of energy has been viewed as the pioneer in energy planning and data collection.

Mr. President, we've been successful in establishing the processes. Now we must be even more creative in utilizing them. In this view, we are discussing establishment of a model citizen educational process on energy, gardening, housing, economic development, and governmental forms and functions. Next, establishment of an urban extension service tied to our neighborhood planning process is being researched. And third, creation of an expanded participatory planning process on St. Paul, the eighties and beyond, is being explored.

Mr. President, we see a city where for the first time information, education, leadership, systems planning, and investment are being integrated. Here in St. Paul awareness can and shall be translated into action.

Mr. President, look about you. You see a city with faith in itself and the ability to become even more of a model for what neighborhoods, cities, and our society can, with vision, become.

Thank you.

MAYOR LATIMER. Mr. President, I really appreciate your generosity, and that's what I call it. I might add, by the way, that I broke up my vacation to come back here, too. [*Laughter*] But I've got more little kids than you have, and I couldn't afford to bring them all back with me, and I regret that. But it was very generous for you to do this. I know that.

I do feel very strongly that you have sparked a sense of mission in dealing with the energy issue, because it will affect poor and rich alike. You've also said something else today that I have been preaching and repeating here, and that is that we are at another crossroads. And the energy problem is not merely a problem but also a productive solution, that energy is going to be a job-producing entity, that energy indeed can pull the community together, as you have pointed out.

I think that we can take a very positive approach to the solutions to energy. And I also believe we can do it locally here, as so beautifully pointed out by Mr. Lefko.

I repeat to Mrs. Carter and to Amy and to the President, thank you so very, very much for blessing our city with your own presence and the presence of your family.

THE PRESIDENT. Thank you very much.

I can truthfully say, from the bottom of my heart, this has been an enjoyable and an inspirational meeting.

We live in the greatest nation on Earth, and we are blessed beyond all people. And still I'm absolutely convinced that what I said that Sunday night in July is accurate, that our Nation is on the verge of a very serious problem. We have tended to lose confidence in ourselves, to lose confidence in one another, to come alienated or even antagonistic toward our own Government, and to fail to recognize the blessings that we have.

God's given us every possible natural and human advantage—freedom where individuality and initiative and innovation can be nourished and used to overcome any challenge, which has always been proven in the past. We've got five times more energy reserves in our country than all the OPEC nations combined.

We're the strongest nation on Earth militarily, the strongest nation on Earth economically, the strongest nation on Earth politically. We're a democracy. Our free enterprise system encourages challenge and competition and dynamism and flexibility to meet any possible obstacles that might stand in the way of American people having a better life. And I want to see the wounds that exist and the discouragement that exists healed, and I want to see the challenges that arise overcome. And I want to see the problems that present themselves solved and the questions answered. And nobody claims—certainly I don't—that all those answers and all those solutions and all those challenges can be met from Washington.

St. Paul has the kind of spirit that can make us all proud of our country. And they can bind us together in a spirit of brotherhood and sisterhood and unity that must be the basis for future progress.

I'm thankful to you. And my visit here has made me even prouder to be the President of the greatest nation on Earth.

Thank you very much.

NOTE: The President spoke at 8:03 p.m. in the lobby of Landmark Center.

Following the energy briefing, the President went to the Lambert Landing in St. Paul, where he boarded the riverboat *Delta Queen* to begin his trip down the Mississippi River.

Labor Dispute in the Grain Industry

Telegram to Industry and Union Leaders. August 18, 1979

It is apparent that the current work stoppage between the American Federation of Grain Millers and the eight grain facilities in Duluth, Minn., and Superior, Wis., is having an increasingly severe impact upon the general economy and public welfare of this geographical area as well as seriously threatening the many thousands of farmers who are now into their annual harvest with no means to ship their grain.

It is my deep concern therefore that every effort be made to bring an immediate end to this dispute.

In this regard, I am directing Wayne L. Horvitz, the national director of the Federal Mediation and Conciliation Service, to become personally involved and to provide whatever assistance he deems necessary.

In this endeavor, a meeting has been scheduled for Tuesday, August 21, 1979, commencing at 2 p.m. at the offices of the Federal Mediation and Conciliation Service in Minneapolis, Minn.

I am confident that you will participate in these meetings recognizing not only your own personal concerns, but also your responsibility to the interests of those being adversely affected by this unfortunate dispute.

This will require a total commitment by you to continue bargaining until an all-out exhaustive effort has brought about an end to this strike.

JIMMY CARTER

NOTE: This is the text of identical telegrams addressed to E. H. Ryan, Peavey Co., Minneapolis, Minn.; Anthony Corvino, Continental Grain Co., New York, N.Y.; Gerald Mattson, International Multifoods, Minneapolis; Felix Ricco, Cargill Co., Wayzata, Minn.; Donald Friborg, General Mills, Minneapolis; Harold Schuler, Con-agra, Omaha, Nebr.; Douglas Larson, Farmers Union GTA, St. Paul, Minn.; Dale Benson, Archer-Daniel-Midlands, Decatur, Ill.; Joseph Devich, American Federation of Grain Millers, Superior, Wis.; Frank Hoese, American Federation of Grain Millers, Minneapolis; and Mike Miller, American Federation of Grain Millers, Minneapolis. Copies of the telegram were also sent to David Roe, president, Minnesota AFL–CIO, St. Paul; and John Schmitt, president, Wisconsin AFL–CIO, Milwaukee.

The text of the telegram was released at Bloomington, Minn.

Labor Dispute in the Grain Industry

Telegram to the Governors of Minnesota and North Dakota.   August 18, 1979

Following our conversations yesterday aboard Air Force One regarding the current work stoppage between the American Federation of Grain Millers and the grain companies in Duluth, Minn., and Superior, Wis., I have today directed the head of the Federal Mediation and Conciliation Service, Wayne L. Horvitz, to become personally involved in these negotiations, and to provide whatever assistance he feels is necessary to help bring about an immediate end to this dispute.

In this effort I have also called upon all parties directly involved to participate in a resumption of negotiations with Director Horvitz beginning on Tuesday, August 21, in the Minneapolis offices of the Federal Mediation and Conciliation Service.

In addition, I have asked the parties to continue bargaining until an all-out exhaustive effort has ended this strike.

I share your deep concern about this lingering dispute and will appreciate any assistance you may offer, should Director Horvitz call upon you.

JIMMY CARTER

NOTE: This is the text of identical telegrams addressed to Gov. Al Quie of Minnesota and Gov. Arthur A. Link of North Dakota.

The text of the telegram was released at Bloomington, Minn.

Wabasha, Minnesota

Remarks on Arrival at the City.
August 18, 1979

THE PRESIDENT. There is no doubt in my mind that all of us enjoy the privilege of living in the greatest country on Earth. We are a nation which has indeed been blessed by God with blessings which exceed those of any other peoples on Earth. We're a nation of freedom. We're a nation of strength, of courage, of vitality. We're a nation which has always been able and eager to meet any challenge, no matter how difficult it might have been, to solve any problem, no matter how complex it might be, or to answer any question which confronts the people of the United States of America.

I'm very proud to be the highest elected official in the greatest country on Earth, and I think what you've done here this morning in Wabasha, Mayor Meisch, and all of you, is a tremendous testimony to what our country can be in the future if we are indeed united.

Sometimes we tend to forget the blessings of freedom and the blessings of living in a democracy, where every human being is important, where each one of us has a right to be different, to live where we choose, to worship as we choose, to have equal opportunity, no matter what language we might speak or how long our family may have been in this country or what color our skin might be or how wealthy our families might be, either. These kinds of differences don't make our Nation weak. They make our Nation stronger.

We have people in our country from almost every race and every nation on Earth. We have ties to all the rest of the world, and when we are faced with a tremendous challenge, like World War I or World War II or the Great Depression—when I was a young man, those challenges were easy to see and easy to understand. We felt that our Nation was threatened and our future was not certain, and with that threat our families were drawn closer together and our communities were drawn closer together, and our Nation enjoyed a high degree of unity, because we knew that our Nation was under a threat. That was when we were strongest, with a mutual commitment, because we knew that each person was important. And we had to have faith in one another, and we had to have faith in the future.

Recently our country has been faced with a series of problems which we couldn't quite understand—the Vietnam war, the Watergate scandals, 10 or 12 years of inflation, and a shortage of energy which has caused us to turn too much to foreign nations for oil. It's made our Nation overly dependent on uncertain supplies of oil from the Middle East and other places, and it's let us realize for the first time in our great country

that we do have limits, and we cannot afford to waste any more, as we have wasted, what God gave us in the past.

This is not a problem that we cannot solve. It's not a question that we cannot answer. It's not an obstacle that we cannot overcome, if we are united. But we must do two things. First of all, we must conserve energy. We must quit wasting energy. And secondly, we must increase the energy that we produce in our own country—solar energy; increased use of coal; more production of oil and gas from our own wells; the production of new kinds of energy; synthetic oil from shale rock, from coal.

These kinds of things are a great challenge to us. But they ought to unite us and not divide us, one from another. It's very important for you to have confidence in your government—in your mayor, your county officials, your State officials, your Federal officials, your President. Regardless of whether you might be Republican or Democrat or Protestant or Catholic or Jewish, that doesn't matter. In a time of stress and trial, that's the time we need to unite with a common effort.

When elections come, vote how you choose, but when our Nation is faced with a problem, every single American must say, "What can I do to make my Nation stronger and greater and more united to face a common challenge?"

There is no doubt in my mind that we can resolve our energy problem and give our Nation security so that no matter what happens in the Middle East, our Nation will not suffer, so that we can be reliant on ourselves. We now have before the Congress proposals that will solve these problems if Congress acts. A windfall profits tax will give us money derived from taxing the oil companies, to help poor families pay the increased cost of energy, to give us a way to conserve energy and to weatherize homes, to make automobiles more efficient, to give us mass transit systems, and to produce synthetic fuels.

We have the means in our hands to solve our national problem, but the most single important thing is for us to have confidence in one another, faith in ourselves, and to be unified in facing the future.

You have really thrilled me this morning and inspired me and, I think, all Americans who will see this on television and read about this in the newspaper and hear this on the radio, to know that the people in Wabasha have come here—a lot more people than live in Wabasha; I don't know where you all came from— [laughter]—to show that you believe in the strength of our country.

How many of you believe that we live in the greatest nation on Earth? [Applause] Very good.

How many of you believe that we can have energy security in the United States of America? [Applause]

This is the most difficult question: How many of you are going to do your part and a little more to save energy and to make sure our Nation is secure in the future? If you'll do your part, would you let me know? [Applause] Very fine.

One other question. How many of you think that even though we live in the greatest nation on Earth now, we're going to all combine our efforts to make it even greater in the future and have the United States of America be an even more wonderful place to live in years to come? How many of you believe that? [Applause] Very good.

Well, you've made me very happy, and I know that Rosalynn would say this is the best birthday party she has ever had. Thank you very much.

MRS. CARTER. I want to thank you, too, for this wonderful welcome, for all your birthday wishes, and for your prayers. And I want to thank you for the birthday cake, too, with the energy pledges, because as Jimmy has said, every effort helps. And when you save energy, you help not only yourselves and your community, but you help our whole country.

I'm very proud of you and proud to be here today. Thank you very much.

NOTE: The President spoke at approximately 11 a.m. near the docking site of the *Delta Queen*.

Alma, Wisconsin

Remarks on Arrival at the City.
August 18, 1979

I hope that you'll all remember what a great country we have, how strong we are, and how much God has blessed us.

We have a serious problem, as you know, right now with inflation that's been with us for 10 or 12 years and with too much dependence on foreign oil, which makes our Nation's security a cause of great concern. There's only two things we can do about it. One is to save energy, conservation, to stop wasting so much energy, and every single person in our Nation can help with that. Figure out in your own driving habits, the way you heat your home, the way you air-condition your home, the way you share automobiles, everything that you do, try to save as much energy as possible. And secondly, we need to increase the amount of energy that we produce in our own country—solar energy, increased use of coal, synthetic fuels, and the other kinds of things that we can do as a great nation.

We have now before the Congress proposals which will give us an opportunity both to save and to produce more in our own country. It must be financed by the windfall profits tax, a tax on the oil companies so that they won't take the tremendous profits and keep it for themselves, but share it through your government with you so that we can weatherize homes, give us better transit systems, and so forth.

I hope that you will contact your own Members of Congress and ask them to support the windfall profits tax, because out of that tax can come enough money from the oil companies to help poor people, those with low incomes or moderate incomes, to pay for the increased cost of energy, to provide conservation encouragement, and also to produce more fuel for ourselves in our own country.

We've got about 25 percent of the total energy reserves on Earth in our own Nation—all the OPEC countries put together only have less than 5 percent—but we need to use our energy more effectively. So, if you'll help me, I'll help you, and we'll make the greatest nation on Earth even greater in the future.

Will you help me? [*Applause*] Good.

NOTE: The President spoke at 1:55 p.m. at the docking site of the *Delta Queen*.

Minnesota City, Minnesota

Informal Exchange With Reporters at the Docking Site of the Delta Queen. August 18, 1979

Q. Learned anything today? [*Laughter*] Seriously——

THE PRESIDENT. Well, if I have a chance with the folks on the ship—[*inaudible*]. Well, I've learned that at the first stop with us in Wabasha, and I think it's obvious they are genuinely interested in saving energy and in proving that our country can be unified and that there is a good harmony among those who have different backgrounds and different interests. I think the turnout here shows a great deal of interest obviously in the office of the Presidency, and I consider it to be a nonpartisan sort of expression of support for the President himself and for this Nation's strength.

Q. Did it seem to you that people were a little bit more upbeat than you might have expected?

THE PRESIDENT. Yeah, they really are. It's been surprising. I thought in St. Paul last night the genuine excitement that they showed in that city in putting together a very far-reaching kind of a complicated approach to the energy question was also inspiring to me. And I think the general tone of the response and the attitude of people toward one another, toward our country is one of great patriotism and strength. I've been very pleased.

Q. Are you getting any rest?

THE PRESIDENT. Enough. This has just been really exciting to me.

Q. One final question. We're standing on the wet bank of the Mississippi here.

THE PRESIDENT. I noticed that. [*Laughter*]

Q. A question someone in the crowd asked, but I didn't hear you answer it. Wouldn't it be fair to call this campaigning?

THE PRESIDENT. Well, I—you know, I want the people to be reminded of the Nation's energy problems and the fact that we can solve those problems. And so, it's a vacation for us. We're enjoying every minute of it, and I think for me to give that message as we go along is very important. So, we're campaigning for a good energy program, but not on a partisan basis. I think the people that come here—I don't know whether they're Democrats or Republicans—they come because I'm President. It's not a partisan campaign for Democrats or for me. It's a campaign for a stronger country and a comprehensive energy policy.

Q. What do you think of this boat?

THE PRESIDENT. I like it. Don't you?

Q. The boat's leaving.

THE PRESIDENT. I can't believe it. The boat's going to leave me. The boat's leaving. I've got to get on board.

NOTE: The exchange began at approximately 4:30 p.m.

As printed above, the item follows the press release.

Prairie du Chien, Wisconsin

Remarks at a Picnic Sponsored by the Minnesota Mining and Manufacturing Company.   August 19, 1979

THE PRESIDENT. Hello, everybody. I'm really proud that all of you came to the picnic that Rosalynn and I and Amy have put on with you, along with 3M Company. We're glad to be your cohosts and also the guests of a very fine example of the free enterprise system of our country.

3M was the first company in our Nation that was given the national award for conserving energy. And I think what they have done is typical of what has been done throughout the State of Wisconsin.

When your former Governor, Pat Lucey, who's now a very distinguished and able Ambassador to Mexico, was in office, he initiated some conservation measures in Wisconsin which have been good as an example for the entire Nation. You as a people in Wisconsin use 20 percent less energy per person than the average throughout our country, in spite of the fact that you rank 12th in industrial production and in spite of the fact that on normal days you have cooler weather than we do in Georgia—but I think today you've equaled the Georgia climate and temperature.

But you haven't done well enough. And neither has anyone in the United States done well enough in saving energy.

Our country has a great challenge before us at this time. There is no conflict between the two things that we must do. One is to conserve energy, to stop waste, and secondly, to produce more energy in our own Nation.

Our Nation's security is threatened because we're too dependent on foreign oil. So, everyone in the United States must do as we have done in the past when our country was in danger or when it was threatened—unite with one another, instead of being divided one from another, and realize that every single American is important, cut back on waste of energy in your driving habits, obey the speed limits, join in the vanpool system that 3M is doing in other parts of the country—will soon be doing here—make sure that you don't waste energy in your home, do everything you can to save precious energy. And secondly, we'll have to use more solar power. We'll have to use more coal from within our own country, and we'll produce more oil and gas and synthetic fuels. If we do those things, there's no doubt in my mind that we can meet this present challenge.

Our country, as you well know, is the greatest nation on Earth. We're the strongest nation politically; we're the strongest nation economically; we're certainly the strongest nation militarily. And we've got something else as well. God has blessed us above all other peoples with natural resources, not only a great river, one of the best avenues for traffic and also freight and also passengers in the whole world—one of the most enjoyable trips, I think, imaginable anywhere—but, of course, we've also been blessed with energy reserves.

In our Nation we've got 25 percent of all the energy reserves in the whole world.

All the OPEC nations in the Mideast put together only have 5 percent. So, God's blessed us with a strong nation and with a nation that has enough natural resources. It's up to us.

And I've come here this afternoon to remind you that sometimes we do get too discouraged. We ought to inventory what we've got. We ought to count our blessings and figure out how you as citizens of our country, how I as the highest elected official in the greatest nation on Earth, State officials, local officials, the Congress can all work together, not separated one from another, not criticizing one another, not looking for scapegoats, but how we can make the greatest nation on Earth even greater in the future. That's what I've pledged to do. If you'll help me, we'll do it together.

Thank you very much. God bless all of you.

Mrs. CARTER. And I want to thank you for the wonderful welcome too. I've enjoyed shaking hands with you, some of you two and even three times. And thank you for the birthday wishes too.

We've had a wonderful trip down the river. The countryside is so beautiful, and the people all along the way, you have made it very special for us. We care for every one of you, and we're pleased and proud to be here.

Thank you very much.

NOTE: The President spoke at 2:25 p.m. at the picnic grounds near the plant.

McGregor, Iowa

Remarks on Arrival at the Town.
August 19, 1979

We're all delighted that we finally got to Iowa.

This last day and a half, coming down our great Mississippi River on the *Delta Queen,* has been an inspiration for our family. And we've become convinced anew, the same as I'm sure all of you have, that we live in the greatest nation on Earth. Do you agree with that? [*Applause*]

Our country has always been blessed by God with every possible advantage that we could desire—military strength, economic strength, political strength; natural resources; basic freedoms; the cherishing of an individual human being; our right to be different; our right to speak our own voice; the right for farmers and business leaders, working people, employers, blacks and whites, those who speak different languages, Protestants, Jews, Catholics, those who have no organized religious belief, in our great country, have a right to be different. But there are times when Americans feel the necessity to put aside differences and to bind ourselves together in the common purpose.

In front of me is a distinguished veteran of the First World War, with two Silver Stars and a Purple Heart, symbols of heroism and a willingness to offer his life, if necessary, for the preservation of our Union. When we have identifiable threats to our country, we always bind ourselves together. Families, communities, local, State, Federal officials, we respect one another and we try to overlook differences. We don't try to find someone to blame for a mistake or for a problem.

These days our country is threatened. But it's a different kind of threat from what we experienced in the First and Second World War, even the Great Depression. Our Nation's security is threatened because we've become too dependent on oil from foreign countries. We must restore our Nation's energy security.

We can do it in two ways. They're not incompatible; they support one another. The first is to save energy, to conserve energy, to stop wasting energy. And every single American can do this and must do this within our own homes, within our own automobiles, at our own business or workingplace, on our farms. And the second thing we can do is to increase the production of energy in our own country—oil, gas, coal, synthetic fuels, and especially solar energy, which we are enjoying today. We have tremendous opportunities for this.

I proposed to the Congress a comprehensive energy policy, long overdue, dependent on the windfall profits tax on the oil companies. It's not right for the oil companies to take enormous profits and keep them for themselves. Through the windfall profits tax, those profits must be shared with all Americans to help us with conservation, solar power, and to become energy independent. I need you to help me with that. Will you do it? [*Applause*] This is a time for unity.

The last thing I want to say to you is that Iowa is blessed especially by God's blessings—rich soil, enormous productivity, a low unemployment rate, the kind of unity of purpose that stands our Nation in good stead. And you're also blessed with one of the finest public servants I have ever known—a man who does a great job for our country, but a man who especially has his roots deep in Iowa and who represents you every day, fighting for your rights, fighting for a better life for Iowans. And I'm especially grateful to be in the hometown of John Culver, the man I'm talking about. You're lucky to have him.

Let me say this in closing. Rosalynn and Amy and I have been inspired by the friendship shown us in this first part of our Mississippi River voyage. We'll be going all the way from St. Paul to St. Louis, meeting literally thousands and thousands and thousands of people along the riverbanks, both when the ship doesn't stop, when we go through locks, and when we have a brief stop like this to visit and shake hands directly.

It's been an inspiration for us; we're grateful for it. If you'll stick with us, stick with each other, have confidence in yourselves, in your neighbors, in your communities, and in our Nation, and revere the opportunities of a free nation and a free government, the truest democracy on Earth, then there's no doubt in my mind that we can make the greatest nation on Earth even greater in the future. That's what I want; that's what we must do together.

Thank you very much.

NOTE: The President spoke at 3:10 p.m. at Triangle Park. Following his remarks, he went to the home of Senator Culver for a private luncheon. He then boarded the *Delta Queen* at Prairie du Chien.

Dubuque, Iowa

Remarks on Arrival at the City.
August 20, 1979

Mayor Wertzburger, Congressman Tauke, our good hosts yesterday, John and Ann Culver:

I wish you could have been with us for lunch. We had enough, I believe, to feed the whole crowd, but there wasn't enough left to feed two people. We had Iowa corn, we had Iowa beef, we had Iowa ham, we had Iowa apple pie, we had some homemade ice cream made out of Iowa milk. And just so I don't use all my time up, I won't tell you about the rest of the menu, but it was just great.

One of the things that has been the best for Rosalynn and me and Amy has been to meet the people who have come out along the banks of the Mississippi to express your friendship toward us personally and your respect for the office of President of the greatest nation on Earth. I'm particularly grateful to John Culver, who saw that we were not originally scheduled to stop in Dubuque, and I think he talked to Captain Martin on the *Delta Queen,* and the first thing we knew, John Culver said, "I'll meet you in Dubuque."

I have to admit that this Midwest country is just as beautiful as Georgia, and you've got the Mississippi River as a bonus. And it's really been wonderful for us.

Every time we've been through one of the locks, we've had a large crowd of people. Night before last, we got to Lock 8, I believe it was, at 3 o'clock in the morning, and there was a large group of people there to meet us—it was almost an emotional thing. And then yesterday morning at 8 o'clock, we arrived at a lock, and it was pouring down rain. And there were several hundred people there in the rain—I think there were four umbrellas with several hundred folks with little babies and children and very senior citizens who had been waiting there several hours to pay their respects to the President of our country. And I deeply appreciate the friendship you've shown us.

We've got a wonderful country. God's blessed us in every possible way. And I know that the outpouring of friendship that has been exhibited on this trip is a true indication of your respect and your thanks for the many blessings that God's given us in the United States of America. He's given us great productive land. The number one farming State in the country, as you know, is Iowa. If anyone disagrees with that, speak up. [*Laughter*] If you agree with it, speak up. [*Applause*] I believe you have the highest percentage of productive land in the whole country. And I'm very grateful to be here with you.

I want to say two things. One is that we have a very serious problem. And the second thing I'm going to say is that we have the ability to overcome it.

The problem is with energy. Our country is too dependent on uncertain foreign oil. We've now got to the point where we are importing one-half of all the oil we use. And you've seen, back in 1973 and '74, what happened to our country when that supply was interrupted from just a few countries. And you've seen this year, when the prices have gone up 60 percent in 6 months, what can be done with prices over which we have no control. We are importing inflation and we are importing unemployment every time we import foreign oil. My preference is, instead of importing a barrel of foreign oil, is to produce a barrel of gasohol in Iowa. I believe that's a better approach to our energy problem.

We've already taken action since I've been in office, with the help of the Congress, of course, to cut our dependence on foreign oil by 4 million barrels every day. We've now proposed to the Congress a way to cut another 4½ million barrels a day by 1990. But the whole process depends upon the passage of a windfall profits tax on the oil companies. The choice is whether the oil companies keep the enormous profits that come from increasing prices of oil, or whether a part of those profits shall be taken through a windfall profits tax and distributed among the people of our Nation to conserve energy, to cut out waste, to save energy, to produce other forms of energy like gasohol, solar power, and so forth. This is the important task that we have.

Every one of you can help—in your habits, driving to and from work, whether you share your automobile with others, whether you walk sometimes instead of ride, how you handle the use of heat in your homes—there are hundreds of things, literally, that you can do to cut down on the waste of oil. And I need your help and your support with the Congress to pass the windfall profits tax and give us a chance to protect our Nation's security.

So, that's one message I want to give to you. We must have a secure nation by cutting down on waste and producing more American energy.

And the second thing I want to say is that our country is strong enough to accomplish this task. Down through history—and you're part of history, right here in Dubuque—every time our Nation has had a serious problem or a challenge, we have been strong enough and united enough to meet that challenge, to overcome that problem, to answer that question. But almost always in the past, we've been able to identify the problem, like in the First World War, we knew our Nation was in danger, the Second World War, the Great Depression. And recognizing the danger to our country, we bound ourselves together. Our families became stronger, our communities became stronger, we had respect for and we supported our local officials, our State officials, our Federal officials. We didn't let a chasm open up between ourselves and the Federal Government. We felt that it was our government, and we cherished it. If we didn't like something it did, we changed it at election time, but between elections we gave it our support and our respect.

Now with the energy shortage and 12 years of inflation, Americans have tended to get discouraged. We've kind of lost confidence in ourselves and lost confidence in one another. We've tended to become divided; we've got too many special interest groups grasping for some advantage. Now's the time for us to unite again and face this serious energy problem, which directly threatens our Nation's security, together, in an unselfish attitude.

There is no doubt in my mind that we can do it, and if you will help me, I will help you to make the greatest nation on Earth even greater in the future.

And now I'd like to come out and shake hands with as many of you as I can reach. And I thank you for coming out to meet us.

BYSTANDER. Jimmy, I've been waiting since 5 o'clock!

THE PRESIDENT. I'll be right there.

NOTE: The President spoke at 9:25 a.m. at the docking site of the *Delta Queen*.

Women's Equality Day, 1979
Proclamation 4674.   August 20, 1979

By the President of the United States of America

A Proclamation

On August 26, 1920, fifty-nine years ago, the 19th Amendment became a part of the United States Constitution, guaranteeing women the right to vote.

As we celebrate the anniversary of that victory for all Americans, we applaud the courage of the women and men who struggled for generations to achieve it. But the 19th Amendment was only one step on the long journey toward full equality for women.

Through persistent and dedicated effort, women have made great strides toward achieving that equality in recent years. But the need for the Equal Rights Amendment is still compelling. Today, I reiterate my continued commitment to make the ERA a part of our Constitution.

The ERA does not legislate that men and women are the same. It simply says that the law cannot penalize women because they are female. Nor does the ERA impose new, unwanted roles on women.

Rather, it safeguards their opportunity to develop their full potential in the directions they choose. As women are freed from arbitrary barriers and stereotypes, men are liberated as well.

When passed, the ERA will provide a single, clear, comprehensive standard against which discrimination can be measured. Legal equality for women must be made a part of the Constitution.

The ERA is not a recent idea. It was first introduced in Congress in 1923. After lengthy and careful debate, Congress submitted it to the States for ratification on March 22, 1972. Now all but three of the necessary thirty-eight states have ratified it. The deadline is June 30, 1982.

The ratification of the ERA may be the single most important step in assuring American women their full equality. Gaining ratification in the remaining states will not be easy—but it will mean our country can tap the full resources and abilities of all its citizens.

Now, THEREFORE, I, JIMMY CARTER, President of the United States of America, do hereby proclaim August 26, 1979, as Women's Equality Day and do hereby urge all Americans to work to guarantee full equality for women before the 1982 deadline.

I hope that, as a part of future celebrations for Women's Equality Day, we can celebrate the passage of the 19th Amendment and the passage of the Equal Rights Amendment.

IN WITNESS WHEREOF, I have hereunto set my hand this twentieth day of August, in the year of our Lord nineteen hundred seventy-nine, and of the Independence of the United States of America the two hundred and fourth.

JIMMY CARTER

[Filed with the Office of the Federal Register, 4:45 p.m., August 20, 1979]

Fifteenth Anniversary of the Signing of the Economic Opportunity Act

Proclamation 4675. August 20, 1979

By the President of the United States of America

A Proclamation

On August 20, 1964, our Nation embarked upon its most altruistic enterprise since the Marshall Plan. President Lyndon B. Johnson signed into law an Act "to mobilize the human and financial resources of the Nation to combat poverty in the United States."

The ideal envisioned in the Economic Opportunity Act of 1964 was a Nation in which "every individual has the opportunity to contribute to the full extent of his capabilities and to participate in the workings of our society."

The proud litany of bold innovations which this legislation introduced into the Nation's vocabulary included Community Action, Head Start, Job Corps, Legal Services, VISTA, New Careers, Foster Grandparents, Upward Bound, Follow Through, Emergency Food and Medical Services, and Senior Opportunities and Services.

The experimental concepts tested in these many programs have long since left the laboratory. Along the way, we have made some important discoveries—about poverty, about ourselves and about our country. We have learned from these programs that poverty is not an isolated problem that can be overcome without changes in the larger economy. We have learned that the poor of America are by no means alone in their deep-seated desire for institutional change; in their desire for government responsiveness at all levels; in their desire for opportunities for genuine participation as members of our society. We have discovered along the way that poor and non-poor alike long for a sense of community, a share in decision-making, a feeling that the individual can be heard—in the councils of government, in corporate meetings, and in the marketplace.

All Americans should have learned in these 15 tumultuous years that changing circumstances may place any one of us in the path of common enemies: obsolete skills in an age of technological revolution; the danger of disability through injury or disease in a hazardous environment; mutual vulnerability to shrinking energy, housing, and food resources. All of us have learned that our country cannot afford to allow differences—in income, in social status, in geography, in age, in intellect or health, in color, accent, or religion—to divide and polarize us.

This generation has learned also that poverty is not a question of income alone—we can be energy-poor, even though wealthy as a Nation; we can be spiritually impoverished, even when we are materially satiated.

Let us take this occasion, then to rededicate ourselves and our country to the ideals of the Economic Opportunity Act with a renewed commitment to our Nation's goal of securing the opportunity for every individual to "attain the skills, knowledge, and motivations . . . to become fully self-sufficient."

Now, THEREFORE, I, JIMMY CARTER, President of the United States of America, do hereby proclaim and designate the next 12 months as a year of rekindled effort to open to everyone in our land "the opportunity to live in decency and dignity."

IN WITNESS WHEREOF, I have hereun-

to set my hand this twentieth day of August, in the year of our Lord nineteen hundred seventy-nine, and of the Independence of the United States of America, the two hundred and fourth.

JIMMY CARTER

[Filed with the Office of the Federal Register, 4:48 p.m., August 20, 1979]

Davenport, Iowa

Remarks on Arrival at the City. August 21, 1979

Good morning, everybody. Good morning. Did you enjoy the music? Doc Hathaway, wasn't he great? We're really excited coming back to Davenport, and thank all of you for coming out to welcome us.

This last 3 days have been very exciting for me and for Amy and for Rosalynn—to see the beautiful Midwest, to enjoy the Mississippi, and above all, to see the wonderful people that have made us feel so welcome. Thank you very much. God bless you.

We believe that we live in the greatest country on Earth. Do you agree with that? [*Applause*] Our Nation is so strong and so good to all of us. And, as you know, God's blessed us with personal freedom, a chance to live in a democracy where we can choose our own government, solve our own problems, meet our own challenges, answer our own questions, if we as Americans can be unified, can see a common problem and work together to solve it.

We do have one serious common problem—and I'm going to talk to you about that on the telephone this morning in just a few minutes. But I think that with this tremendous crowd, I would like to say that we can solve our energy problem if we work together. It's serious enough to challenge our Nation's security. And shortly before I left Washington, I took the last action that's available to me as President by decontrolling the price of heavy oil, very heavy oil. This will add about 500,-000 barrels of oil to our Nation's supply in the future without having an adverse impact on inflation.

Now the other action that can be taken by our Government must be taken by Congress. And I want all of you to help me convince the Congress—I might say John Culver is already convinced, and he's helping me—that we need to put a windfall profits tax on the oil companies. This must be done.

The choice is, do we let the oil companies keep enormous profits or do we tax them and use that money to conserve energy, to shift towards solar power, to have more gasohol made in Iowa, and to have a nation strong and free and independent of dependence on OPEC prices and OPEC oil. Will you help me with the Congress to have an independent nation? [*Applause*] Right on.

We will soon have a very fine energy experiment work—that I'll describe to you on the radio this morning—that will let our entire Nation have advice on all 50 States about how we can conserve energy. We've tried it out now for 2 years in 10 different States throughout the country. It has worked very well. And we'll have several hundred thousands of dollars available in Iowa, beginning next year, to help us plan in every local community like Davenport how we can conserve energy, eliminate waste, and make sure our Nation is better able to meet this challenge. This is a very important program that in the long run will not cost anything—it will save much more than it costs.

So, I hope all of you will work with me and the Congress to make the greatest nation on Earth even greater in the future. I'm very glad to be back in Davenport.

You were wonderful to me a couple of years ago, and as President, you've been even nicer to me. And I believe that all of us working together can make sure that our Nation stays strong, stays happy, stays united, and that we will have indeed in the rest of our lives and for our children the greatest and the strongest nation on Earth.

Thank you very much. God bless all of you.

We'll be on the radio at 9:30. Listen in, call if you can. We'll see you later.

NOTE: The President spoke at 9:10 a.m. at the Lake Davenport Sailing Club dock.

Davenport, Iowa

Remarks During a Radio Call-Out Program on KSTT/WXLP Stations. August 21, 1979

MR. JACKSON. Good morning. I'm H. L. Jackson, news director of KSTT and WXLP. Good morning, Mr. President, and welcome to the studios and the Quad Cities.

THE PRESIDENT. Good morning.

It's really a great occasion for me to be back here in the Quad City area. I've been here several times before, but I have to say that this is the biggest and most enthusiastic crowd I've ever seen around Davenport and Moline.

This is a fine opportunity also for me as President this morning to get questions from the listeners in this Quad City area, and I'm looking forward to trying to explain as best I can what our Nation is doing now and what we can do in the future with the help of all Americans to remove this threat to our Nation's energy security. So, I think this will be a good session for me to express my views, and I'm looking forward to the questions very, very much.

MR. JACKSON. Very good. Mr. President, many people have sent in postcards, wanting an opportunity to talk with you this morning.

During the next 45 minutes, we will get as many calls in as possible. All calls have been preplaced. A reminder to those who will be talking with the President: Be sure all the radios in the vicinity of your telephone are off while you're on the phone with the President. We're using a tape delay system that may tend to be confusing to you.

Now, in order to get as many people on the air as possible we will go straight to the telephones.

Mr. President, the first caller is Mr. Carl Ferrell of Rock Island, Illinois.

MR. FERRELL. This is him. Mr. President, how are you today?

THE PRESIDENT. Just fine, Carl. It's good to hear from you.

MR. FERRELL. Well, it's good to talk to you.

NATIONAL MORALE

I just want to say I think you're doing a pretty good job, and I think it's time—energy is a problem, of course, but I think a bigger problem is the morale of the American people. I think what they should be doing is concentrating and channeling their energies to conserving energy and working with the government, rather than spending all their time working against it.

THE PRESIDENT. Carl, that's a very wise analysis. The main question that we face now is how our Nation can be unified in the face of this energy threat.

In the past, in the history of our country, when we've had a serious challenge like this, it's been easy for us to see it and to recognize it, like in the First World War, the Second World War, or even the Great Depression. But with this energy threat to our basic national security, caused by our excessive dependence on foreign oil, it's hard for the average American to see it or to understand it.

We import, as you know, about half all of our oil, and there are two things we can do about it: One is to save energy, to eliminate waste, to conserve all we can, and every American can help there. And the other one is to increase American production of energy. Oil, gas, coal, geothermal—gasohol obviously would be very important to Iowa and to Illinois—and the increasing use of solar power.

These are the basic things that must be done, but you're absolutely right that people must be determined to do it. They must be unselfish, and they must work closely with local, State, and Federal Government officials and with each other.

MR. FERRELL. Well, we've got a great nation, and the American people is a large family, and that's what they've got to realize. We have to work together to survive.

THE PRESIDENT. That's a very good statement. I agree completely with you. Thank you, Carl, very much.

MR. FERRELL. Okay. I'll let you go. I know you've got a lot of people to talk to you, okay?

THE PRESIDENT. Thank you.

MR. FERRELL. Okay. Have a good trip. Bye now.

THE PRESIDENT. Goodby.

MR. JACKSON. The next caller is Debbie Brown of Davenport. Debbie?

MS. BROWN. Yes?

THE PRESIDENT. Go ahead, Debbie.

MS. BROWN. Oh, hi. Who is this?

THE PRESIDENT. I think you're Debbie Brown.

MS. BROWN. I am.

THE PRESIDENT. My name is Jimmy Carter.

MS. BROWN. Hi.

THE PRESIDENT. Do you have a question, Debbie?

DAVENPORT

Ms. Brown. Yeah. One, I'd like to know how you like Davenport.

The President. Well, Davenport is just one of my favorite places. When I was campaigning for President, I came into the Davenport Airport, and I remember we only had about 15 or 20 people there to meet me.

This morning, we had thousands of people here to meet me as President. And I've always found, whether there was a small group or a large one, that the people in Davenport are very enthusiastic and very friendly and very patriotic.

One of the most important things, though, is that Davenport seems to be a very unified community. You've never been afraid to face difficulties. And I think that you're living in one of the most productive areas of the entire world as far as farmland is concerned, has given you a sense that you contribute to a worldwide, beneficial life for other people. So, there's an unselfishness here and a friendship here and a spirit of unity here in Davenport and a spirit of patriotism that makes your community really a good place to live.

And I might say that you've got the Mississippi River as a bonus. So, you couldn't have it better.

Ms. Brown. That's Davenport.

The President. Thank you, Debbie.

Ms. Brown. You're welcome.

Mr. Jackson. The next caller is Mark Larson in Milan, Illinois.

MILITARY PAY INCREASE

Mr. Larson. Hello.

The President. Good morning, Mark. Go ahead.

Mr. Larson. Thank you, sir.

My question has to do with a subject that's a little off from the energy problem, although I am behind your proposals and I hope Congress gets behind you as quickly as the Quad City people have.

I'm on leave from the military right now. I'm in the Navy, sir, like you were. And before I left I heard that the military was going to get a 5.5-percent pay raise. Is this true, sir?

The President. Yes, that's true, Mark. We will have a 5.5-percent pay raise for the military. It's a little bit less than the inflation rate, but I think it's enough to get us by. And we hope that in a very short time, we'll be able to turn this 10- or 12-year inflation rate around and let us have a more stable cost of living.

As you know, when we import too much oil we also import unemployment and we also import inflation. So, the economic situation in our country is very closely tied in with the energy situation. One of the best things about our Nation is, however, that we have such tremendous productivity in our farming areas. We now are exporting more farm products overseas than we ever have before in history. In 1978 we also set a world record, and in 1977 we also set a record. So, each year we're exporting more farm products, which helps us control inflation, and of course, dealing with the energy question will help it as well.

But the pay increase for the military will be as you described, and I think this is certainly well deserved by all of you who serve in the Navy and the other branches of the Armed Forces.

Mr. Larson. Well, we're behind you, sir.

The President. Thank you, Mark. That means a lot to me.

Mr. Larson. Well, thank you, sir. Have a good day.

Mr. Jackson. The next caller is Chris Swanson from Tipton, Iowa. Chris, go ahead.

DECONTROL OF OIL PRICES; NUCLEAR
POWER

MR. SWANSON. Good morning, Mr. President.

THE PRESIDENT. Good morning, Chris.

MR. SWANSON. How are you this morning?

THE PRESIDENT. I'm just great. Good to hear from you. Do you have a question or a comment?

MR. SWANSON. Yes, kind of a mixture of a comment and a question. My comment is on, I think that oil and natural gas should be decontrolled immediately, all oil and natural gas. And the reason I say this—even though it might be inflationary and maybe even cause a recession immediately—wouldn't it be better to get the transfer of American dollars from the Arab countries back towards the United States? And this flow of dollars, wouldn't it offset recession by increasing jobs and reducing unemployment and plowing $40 billion back into our economy?

THE PRESIDENT. Well, obviously the increase in American production is a very good approach, but I think an immediate decontrol of oil and natural gas would not be well-advised.

The Congress has passed legislation that would let natural gas prices be decontrolled over a fairly long period of time, 7 or 8 years. And as a result of that legislation, we've already had a tremendous increase in both the amount of natural gas produced in the United States and also the amount that's transported outside the oil-producing States to States like Georgia, Iowa, and the others further north.

So, I think that the gradual decontrol of natural gas and oil is a better approach. The main thing is to let the oil companies and the American people know that it will be done in a carefully planned fashion.

We have other forms of energy also to increase. I've mentioned gasohol already, synthetic fuels. We need to increase the use of coal, and we can make it clean-burning. And in addition to that, of course, a much heavier dependence in the future on solar power.

I hope that by 1990—well, by the year 2000, we'll have 20 percent of all the energy being consumed in our Nation coming directly from solar power.

MR. SWANSON. You're not ignoring nuclear, are you?

THE PRESIDENT. No. We have a place for nuclear power. As you know, we now have a study going on with the Three Mile Island incident. That report should be to me in the next few days, and then I will assess, as President, what we can do to make the existing nuclear plants and those being designed be safer and better operated and, obviously, better designed as well.

I might say that the whole range of energy supplies is important, but the most important facet is to conserve energy, not to waste it. I think the consumption of increasing quantities of energy in our country is not good for us, but whatever we do consume we want as much as possible to be from our own Nation.

MR. SWANSON. That's a good idea.

MR. JACKSON. The next caller is Clark Scott from Moline, Illinois. Good morning, Clark.

MR. SCOTT. Hello.

THE PRESIDENT. Clark, go ahead.

NUCLEAR WASTE DISPOSAL

MR. SCOTT. I didn't really have a question for you as much as I'd like to voice my opinion on something.

THE PRESIDENT. Fine.

Mr. Scott. I think what really made this country great are the natural resources that were here when it was settled, and that my major concern about the future is our, what I think, our abuse of the country by dumping toxic wastes. And my major concern is the dumping of nuclear wastes, and I read the other day that you were thinking about importing nuclear wastes from foreign countries to be dumped here.

The President. No. I'm not thinking about that at all. We are thinking about presenting to the Congress for the first time in 35 years a proposal on how we can more safely dispose of nuclear wastes.

I know there have been some rumors around here that toxic or nuclear wastes were being brought into Rock Island, for instance, to the arsenal. That's not true. The toxic wastes that are produced on Rock Island have been handled very carefully. And we've had a reassessment made of that situation recently, and they are being taken care of properly and taken off the island for proper disposition.

But we do not intend to import nuclear or toxic wastes from foreign countries. We're trying to make sure that when we dispose of those produced in our own country, that it's done safely and wisely.

Mr. Scott. Well, I don't see how that can be done, though, because how long do they last?

The President. Well, we've been producing nuclear wastes now for 35 or 40 years, ever since we've had nuclear power-plants. They last, as far as radioactivity is concerned, for thousands of years. The problem is to try to dispose of them so that they won't have an adverse impact on our environment in the future.

And as you know, toxic wastes or toxic materials and also nuclear materials exist in very large quantities in a natural state in the ores from which uranium is derived, and also from which radium and other radioactivity is derived.

So, we're trying to straighten out a toxic waste and a nuclear waste mess that I inherited 2½ years ago. We have proposed to the Congress new legislation that requires that the manufacturers of any toxic materials would have to pay a small amount of money into a reserve fund, like an insurance fund, and after those toxic wastes are used, then that fund would be tapped to dispose of the toxic wastes properly. And if a mistake was made in their disposition in the future, that any damage that was done to an American or to a community would be paid for out of the insurance fund that would be accumulated from the toxic wastes manufacturers.

As you know, many toxic materials have to be used in our country for herbicides, insecticides, and other reasons, and we want to make sure that when they are finally disposed of, that nobody gets hurt because they are disposed of wisely, and if any damage takes place, then the damages can be paid for by those who manufacture the toxic wastes in the beginning.

Mr. Jackson. Mr. President, we have Jaye Zessar of Rock Island on the line.

Mr. Zessar. Good morning, President Carter.

The President. Good morning, Jaye.

GOALS FOR THE NATION

Mr. Zessar. My family and I want to welcome you and your family to the Quad City area. We realize that all of you are making great sacrifices in order for you to serve as President of our country, and we appreciate your efforts and dedication and wish you success with all the issues you must deal with for the sake of our country and the world's future.

My question is, if you were granted the power to independently do three things to improve the country or the world, what three things would you consider the most important to do?

THE PRESIDENT. Okay. Let me say first of all that it's not a sacrifice to serve as President. It's gratifying and it's a great honor for me, obviously. And the support that I've had from the American people since I've been in office has made the job not a burden, but an enjoyable experience for me. It's the greatest nation on Earth, and to occupy the highest elective office in the greatest nation on Earth is really a wonderful position for me to hold.

I think the first requirement, Jaye, for any President is to guarantee the security of our Nation, and I have done what I could and will continue to make sure that our Nation's defenses are adequate to discourage any possible threat to our Nation's safety or its existence. That's the number one consideration that any President must face.

Secondly, I would like to go out of office with the same record that I've got now, that is, that no American citizen in combat would ever be endangered or lose their lives. It's been a long time since this happened, that a President could serve an entire term or a time in the White House without having any service men or women have to endanger their lives in combat. So, the peace for our own Nation is also as important as protecting its own security, to avoid war.

And the third thing, of course, I'd like to have is peace in other parts of the world. This obviously goes along with our own. And I'd like to see our country have its spirit revived. We don't need to deplore what we have now, but there is a sense in our country of disunity and kind of a loss of confidence, that I described in my Sunday evening speech.

We ought to remember as Americans— and part of my responsibility as President is to remind people—that our country is the greatest on Earth. We're the strongest country in the world—militarily, economically, politically. God's given us almost unbelievable blessings as far as natural resources are concerned.

In a democracy like ours we have freedom, the right to speak as we choose, to select our own officials, to be an individual, to be different, to meet challenges using the initiative and the innovation that comes from a free enterprise system.

So, I would say that to defend our country, to have American and world peace, and to restore and to enhance the spirit of both confidence and self-sacrifice and patriotism, those are the three things that I believe are very important.

MR. ZESSAR. I think those are three very good things, and I agree with you that this is the greatest country in the world. I think that all Americans should remember that. And it's been a privilege for me to speak with the President of the United States. Thank you.

MR. JACKSON. The next caller is Leon King in Burlington, Iowa. Mr. King?

THE PRESIDENT. Leon, go ahead.

MR. KING. Good morning, Mr. President.

THE PRESIDENT. Good morning to you.

INFLATION

MR. KING My question is, I wondered, I had some property acquired through urban renewal, and I was wondering what your plans are for lower income people as far as upgrading their standards. I know I've had an awful lot of problems with it, because of the reason that the law was made in 1972, I believe. And at that time, the price of living was lower than what it is now. And they haven't upgraded the law. So therefore, when my property was acquired, I was forced into an economic situation that I was not prepared for. And I wondered if you have any feelings along these lines or thoughts in the future.

THE PRESIDENT. Yes, Leon.

MR. KING. I can't get it across like I'd like to, Mr. President, but I sure would like to spend some time with you. I have a lot I'd like to tell you.

THE PRESIDENT. Well, as you know, we'll be in Burlington later on this week, and I'll have a townhall meeting there and be able to answer some questions for a large audience in public, and perhaps I will have a chance to see you there.

MR. KING. I sure hope so.

THE PRESIDENT. We have had this problem with inflation now for 10 or 12 years. And I think most of the programs that we've got for very poor people or for retired people through social security have had a compensation built in so that as inflation goes up rapidly, the payments for the very poor, for medical programs, and for the elderly have gone up as well.

Another thing that should be remembered about inflation, which is almost all bad, is that if you did buy property in the past and now are paying for it, then the value of your property has gone up since you bought it. And in general, the interest rates several years ago when you may have bought your property are perhaps lower than the interest rates are now.

The government, including the President, must be constantly aware of ways to meet new problems. One of the new problems is the unexpected increase in the inflation rate brought about by the OPEC oil nations increasing the price of oil more than 50 percent in the last 6 months.

With the windfall profits tax that we're

trying to get the Congress to pass to put on the oil companies, we will have a reserve fund adequate to make the low- and middle-income families' pressures from increased oil prices easier to bear.

We'll also have money derived from the oil company profits to have a better transportation system in our country. And the third thing, of course, is to produce more energy for our people and also to let us conserve energy by more efficient automobiles, weatherization of homes, and so forth, so that the poor family won't be wasting heat, but on the other hand, saving it.

A lot of people don't understand how this would work. And so, 2 years ago, just after I became President, we initiated an Energy Extension Service similar to the Home Demonstration Agent in every county, and the Agricultural Extension Agent. This is an Energy Extension Service. We tried it out for 2 years in 10 different States around the country. And early in 1980, this program will be instituted in all the States in the country.[1]

---

[1] On the same day, the White House released the following information at Davenport.

The President today announced a nationwide Energy Extension Service (EES) program that will provide Federal grants to 57 States and territories to help families, owners of small businesses, and local government officials take practical steps to save energy and switch to renewable energy sources.

The program would be administered under the Assistant Secretary for Conservation and Solar Applications in the Department of Energy.

Funding for the program includes $27.7 million in grant funds and $2 million for administrative costs, subject to final congressional approval.

State energy offices are encouraged to immediately begin the 180-day planning process. All States are expected to have their EES program operating by early 1980.

As a result of a highly successful 2-year pilot program in 10 States, the EES is being ex-
(Continued)

There will be an adequate amount of money allotted to each State. I think Illinois will get about $430,000—Illinois will get about $930,000, Iowa about $430,000. It's based on population. And out of this money will come advice for you and for other families on how you can save more energy and meet this increased financial burden if it's not handled wisely.

So, in many ways we're trying to make the burden on the poor families easier in spite of inflation. And I hope that at the end of this year, we'll see the inflation rate turning around and start down again. I believe we'll see that happen, Leon.

Thank you very much.

MR. KING. Thank you, Mr. President.

(Continued)

panded to all 57 States and territories and will provide a Federal/State partnership to give personalized information and assistance on energy conservation to small-scale users of energy.

The 2-year EES demonstration began under the National Energy Extension Service Act of 1977. The 10 demonstration States—Alabama, Connecticut, Michigan, New Mexico, Pennsylvania, Tennessee, Texas, Washington, Wisconsin, and Wyoming—each received $1.5 million. The other 47 States and territories received $45,000 each to follow and learn from the demonstration.

As a result of the demonstration program many recipients have made and are planning to make more energy conservation improvements than people who were not contacted. The EES program is cost effective, because the value of the energy saved exceeds the participants' investment and the Federal costs of the program. Under the EES grant program each State decides which small-scale energy users need the most information and assistance on energy conservation, what types of services they need, and what institutions in the State can best deliver those services.

Each State plan will be designed and implemented by the State. Those interested in participating in their State Energy Extension Service program should contact the State energy office for details.

MR. JACKSON. The next caller is Nita Eagle Frink.

MS. FRINK. Yes, this is she.

THE PRESIDENT. Do you have a question, Nita?

MS. FRINK. Hi. Good morning. How are you?

THE PRESIDENT. Good morning to you. Where you from?

MS. FRINK. And I'm from Rock Island. I just saw you down at the dock, and it was wonderful.

THE PRESIDENT. That was a very large crowd and a very excited crowd.

EQUAL RIGHTS AMENDMENT

MS. FRINK. Oh, we were, really, believe me. I do want to tell you that all of us who want the equal rights for all appreciate the fact that you have always supported the equal rights amendment. And my question is, what do you intend to do to ensure ratification of the ERA before 1982?

THE PRESIDENT. We have been working on that; not only myself but my wife and my oldest son's wife works almost full time at it. We've called the members of the legislatures in the States where equal rights has not yet passed, and we very eagerly hope that it will become part of our Constitution. We've also tried to correct some of the very misleading statements that have been made against equal rights for women by those who oppose it. This is obviously a subject of intense debate.

We are now on the border between a State that has ratified equal rights—that is, Iowa—and a State that has not yet ratified the equal rights amendment, that is Illinois. We hope it will be passed, and I think questions like yours and maybe answers like mine show people that we have established equal rights for almost every other citizen in the Nation—not yet for women. And there's no doubt in my mind that the women deserve this protection under our Constitution.

Ms. FRINK. Thank you, Mr. President. We've worked very hard, and we'll continue to do so. I hope you do, too.

MR. JACKSON. The next caller is Cindy Wolf in Davenport.

THE PRESIDENT. Cindy, good morning. Go ahead.

ENERGY CONSERVATION

Ms. WOLF. Good morning, Mr. President.

I'd like to change the focus a little bit. We're talking mostly about what happens on a very large scale, and I know that's what you're concerned with. But I'm just a little person, and OPEC to me is simply a four-letter word that we talk about at the dinner table, and that's all. I need to know something that I can do very specifically. When we talk about the economy having trouble, that will affect me. But I think we will be in more trouble, the generation of today will be in more trouble, because we can't do the things that our heritage has given us because we've let it slip through our fingers.

THE PRESIDENT. Okay. I think that's a very good approach, and it's always good for us to get down to practicalities.

I think the first thing that an American citizen could do, Cindy, in one's own life and within one's own family and within one's own community is to count our blessings and to say something good about our country and, in between elections, to try to support our government officials at the local, State, and Federal level. The sense of unity and a common purpose is often missing in a nation. We have blessings in our own standard of living, the quality of our lives, that are as high or higher than any other nation on Earth. Also when a country has a problem like we have now with energy, each family should decide what it can do and each person what he or she can do.

There are many things that I can do and you can do to save energy, first of all, I think, in our driving habits. I like to walk and in fact I run every day for exercise. We can ride bikes. We can eliminate excessive trips. We can always obey the speed limit. We can share our automobiles or perhaps small vans with neighbors going to shop or going to work every day. We can try to set aside one day in the week where we don't drive at all.

There are hundreds of things that can be done around a home to make sure that a house is efficient, to eliminate the waste of heat in the winter and to eliminate the waste of air-conditioning in the summer. These things can be not only effective in helping our country, but they can be an enjoyable experience and also save us a lot of money, help to overcome the impact of inflation.

One of the great things that we can do is to increase the productivity of our farms and factories. Each American worker, whether you're on a tractor or whether you're manufacturing a product to be sold, can do just a little bit better job during the day to have the productivity of our own lives higher.

And I think the last thing, to try to abbreviate an answer that could go on for several hours——

Ms. WOLF. Right.

THE PRESIDENT. —— is to have a renewed sense of the history of our country. Morality, ethics, the standards of our own lives, deeper commitment to our religious beliefs—these kinds of things also are very important. So, you could inventory your own life, realize it's different from everyone else's, and use your own initiative instead of waiting for a public official, even a President, to tell you or others what must be done.

Presidents learn more from people than people learn from Presidents.

Ms. WOLF. As mothers do from children.

THE PRESIDENT. Absolutely. So, we're all in it together. We've got a great country. We can make it even greater.

Ms. WOLF. That's true. And I feel like I am part of the greatest country in the world. But it's gotten its greatness from my ancestors, from my very recent ancestors, because we're a young country. And I want to be part of that greatness; I want my grandchildren to say we live in the greatest country on Earth. And we waste so much. I think that's more of a problem, one of the basic problems, rather than more specific things like energy, although that is a big problem.

THE PRESIDENT. Amen. Thank you very much.

Ms. WOLF. Thank you, Mr. President.

MR. JACKSON. The next caller, Mr. President, is Mrs. Owen Gardner, and she lives in Davenport, Iowa.

THE PRESIDENT. Luella, go ahead.

MRS. GARDNER. Good morning, sir. How are you?

THE PRESIDENT. Just fine.

FOREIGN IMPORTS

Q. So nice to have you in Davenport, and we want you to know that we think you're doing a good job.

I want to get a different kind of a question in this time. We want to know if there are any new laws in—import laws—in progress that will curb so many foreign items coming in.

You know, you can't go to the store and buy American-made sweaters or shoes or TV's or cars or anything, and we'd like to go back to buying American again. Is that going to be possible?

THE PRESIDENT. Yes, of course, it is. One of the things that the Congress has just done is to pass a Multilateral Trade Negotiation bill which helps to reduce the obstacles to international trade, and it makes the competition more efficient.

We have—just take automobiles, for instance. Your first name is Luella, is it not?

MRS. GARDNER. Right.

THE PRESIDENT. Just take automobiles, for instance, since you mentioned that. We have tried in the years gone by—before I became President, of course—to encourage American automobile producers to make cars that were more efficient, smaller, lighter, safer, and also that had cleaner exhausts.

Some of the foreign nations got ahead of us, because American customers demanded the large and very expensive, very heavy, inefficient automobiles. It was a matter of customer demand, not something that was decided for us by the automobile manufacturers.

This was when oil was selling for $2 or $2.50 a barrel. Now it's almost 10 times that high. There's a rapid transformation taking place in the automobile production industry of our country, to make automobiles not only more efficient but also safer and almost equally as convenient.

So, I think that the rapid change in the buying habits of Americans to accommodate changing circumstances is going to make your wish come true. Every American who goes into a store to buy products will have a choice. And I think it would be good for us to choose American products whenever they are of high enough quality and reasonably competitive on price.

Sometimes you can buy something a little bit cheaper from a foreign country.

But I think it's good for us to try to buy American when we can. There's no doubt in my mind now that the automobiles made by American manufacturers are as good a quality and at this point are actually cheaper than some of the foreign manufactured automobiles.

That's a good point you've made. I hope everybody listening will try to buy American whenever we possibly can.

MRS. GARDNER. I hope so, too, because it would help us all in so many ways. And I thank you, and God bless you.

THE PRESIDENT. Thank you. The same to you.

MR. JACKSON. Our next caller is from Moline, Illinois. This is Oscar Zepeda.

THE PRESIDENT. Oscar, go ahead. Good morning.

MR. ZEPEDA. Good morning, Mr. President.

THE PRESIDENT. You have a question?

MR. ZEPEDA. Yes.

THE PRESIDENT. Ask it.

SUPPORT FOR THE PRESIDENT

MR. ZEPEDA. Okay. I just wanted to say that I believe in you—and——

THE PRESIDENT. That's good enough. Thank you very much.

You know, the important thing in our country—whether you're a Democrat or a Republican, or black or white, or speak English or speak a foreign language, or whether your family has been over here for 300 years or 3 years, is to recognize that public officials in our government need our support. We're all in it together. The challenges that come before us face all of us, and the opportunities for resolving those problems and meeting those challenges must include us all.

And it's very encouraging for a President to come to a place like Davenport and to Moline, the Quad City area, and

have someone like you express your confidence in me. I thank you very much. I'll try to do you a good job.

MR. ZEPEDA. I believe you, Mr. President.

Is it all right if my wife and my little girl say hi to you?

THE PRESIDENT. Of course.

MISS ZEPEDA. Hello.

THE PRESIDENT. Hello, good morning to you.

MISS ZEPEDA. Hello, Mr. President.

THE PRESIDENT. Good morning. I'm glad to talk to you. What's your name?

MISS ZEPEDA. Mary.

THE PRESIDENT. Mary, how old are you?

MISS ZEPEDA. Three.

THE PRESIDENT. That's great. Well, I wish you could come and see Amy before we leave here. Good luck to you. Is your mother there? Is your mother there? Can I speak to your mother?

MISS ZEPEDA. Yes.

THE PRESIDENT. Okay.

MRS. ZEPEDA. Yes, I am.

THE PRESIDENT. Good morning to you. You must have a wonderful family, and I thank all of you.

MRS. ZEPEDA. Thank you.

THE PRESIDENT. Good luck, have a good day.

MRS. ZEPEDA. You too.

MR. JACKSON. The next caller, Mr. President, is Teresa Shima from Eldridge, Iowa.

SOLAR HEATING

MS. SHIMA. Morning. Morning, Mr. President.

THE PRESIDENT. Good morning.

MS. SHIMA. Okay, first of all, I'd just like to say that I think you're doing a very good job, and I'll be voting for you in the next election.

And my question is, do you think that in the future there will be Federal aid for the installment of solar heating in homes like there was for the insulation?

THE PRESIDENT. Yes. There already is, as a matter of fact—and I'm glad you asked that question. We have a very good program already passed by Congress that gives those who install solar heating or other solar uses in their home a tax break. And all you have to do is—you can get up to $2,200 in tax credits for the installation of solar heat or other solar uses in your home.

Ms. SHIMA. Thank you.

THE PRESIDENT. In the future, by the way, when we get the windfall profits tax passed, we'll have additional programs that would do things like let your utility companies, either those who sell you natural gas or electricity, provide for each family home a long-term loan at reasonable interest. And you could take that loan and weatherize your house, make it more efficient, do other things that would help with the energy problem, and then the loan would not have to be repaid until the house was actually sold.

Obviously, this costs a little money, and that money would come from a tax on the oil companies. The choice is, should we let the oil companies keep all that enormous profit that comes from higher prices for oil, or should we tax part of it with the windfall profits tax, and let the money be used for Americans for more solar energy, for better and more efficient homes, and for a better quality of life?

I think we ought to get the windfall profits tax passed, and I want all of you to help me get the Congress to pass that tax so we can have a better and more energy-secure nation, including the use of gasohol from Iowa and Illinois, as well as solar power.

Ms. SHIMA. Thank you. Have a nice trip back to Washington, D.C.

THE PRESIDENT. Thank you very much.

MR. JACKSON. The next caller is Keith Royal in Davenport, Iowa.

ENERGY LEGISLATION

MR. ROYAL. Yes. Hello, Mr. President.

THE PRESIDENT. Good morning, Keith.

MR. ROYAL. Since I'm a high school debater and last year's topic was the energy crisis, I'd like to ask you two questions.

THE PRESIDENT. Okay.

MR. ROYAL. First, of all, why do you feel that Congress has delayed so long on your energy proposals? And secondly, if Congress is the major blame, why do you feel that's the problem—like, is it a problem within the party, or something like that?

THE PRESIDENT. Well, we've had a very severe energy problem, as you know, since 1973—when we had the OPEC embargo, where they stopped shipping oil to us completely, and the price went up.

We really live in two nations here as far as oil goes. One is the oil-producing States—they derive a great deal of benefit from producing oil and distributing it to the rest of the country—and the other States, of course, or the other kinds of people, are the oil-consuming people of our country.

In the past, in the Congress, the oil companies have had a tremendous influence in the Congress. Since I became President, I have tried to build up an opposing force, made up of the consumers of our country, to meet, for the first time, this oil lobby in Washington, and it's been a very difficult thing to do.

When we passed the energy bill of 1977 last November, the votes were almost exactly even in the House and the Senate.

But for the first time the oil lobby was successfully challenged by those interested in the consumers of our country.

Now we've got another major test this year. Are we going to have a windfall profits tax on the oil companies or not? If the consumers of the country, including people like you, Keith, will speak up and let your voice be heard with your own Member of Congress and with others, then we'll have the windfall profits tax, and we'll have an able country to meet the energy challenge.

This will leave, by the way, adequate amounts of money for the oil companies to go ahead and explore and produce new oil supplies and natural gas supplies in the United States. But this is the first time in the last couple of years that anyone has ever challenged the enormous authority and influence of the oil companies in the Congress of the United States. And I believe we've made good progress so far.

But this year is going to tell the tale, and if you'll help me, along with all those who are listening to my voice, it'll pick up some extra votes, we'll get the windfall profits tax passed, leave the oil companies enough profit, and have a better life for all of us in meeting the energy challenge.

Mr. ROYAL. Thank you, Mr. President.

Mr. JACKSON. Mr. President, we have no further time for callers. We will open our microphone for any final comments you'd like to make.

THE PRESIDENT. I want to say that it's been a real pleasure for me to be with KSTT and WXLP here in Davenport and Moline to talk to roughly six or seven hundred thousand listeners of these two stations. The questions have been very good. It's given me a chance to talk about the basic strength of our country, the individual responsibility that falls on the shoulders of every American, how serious our energy problem is now, and what we can do about it. If the Congress acts effectively this year, we will have made a major stride forward in meeting a problem that has not been faced in previous years.

And I might add that the government can't do it alone. There must be a dedication and a determination on the part of every single American to do one's part.

The last thing I'd like to repeat is that our country is the greatest on Earth. We've been given enormous blessings by God in every possible way. And this is one of the richest and the most blessed parts of a great nation. So, if we can all work together, there's no doubt in my mind that our greatest Nation will be even finer in the future.

I see Amy peeping in through the door. And we're all glad to be here—Amy, Rosalynn, and I—and I might say that the trip down the Mississippi so far has been an exciting part of our lives, and I want to express my thanks to everyone listening to my voice.

Mr. JACKSON. Mr. President, we at KSTT and WXLP thank you very much for being with us. The Quad Cities, of course, thank you for taking this time from your day. It is most important that the people have access to their leaders, and today we've had exactly that. I'm H. L. Jackson, KSTT/WXLP News.

NOTE: The program began at 9:43 a.m.

Following the program, the President attended a private reception for community leaders at the home of Mr. and Mrs. Lynne Chamberlin, early supporters of President Carter's 1976 campaign.

The President then went to the John Deere Administrative Center in Moline, Ill., to view an energy biomass project. Following his visit to the center, he returned to the *Delta Queen* at the Lake Davenport Sailing Club dock.

Muscatine, Iowa

Remarks on Arrival at the City.
August 21, 1979

Don't we live in a great country? [*Applause*] Good music, beautiful rivers, lovely women, rich land, democracy, freedom, unity—we've got a lot to be thankful for.

This last 3 or 4 days has been as nice as anything we've ever done in our lives, because we have seen some of the most beautiful country in the world, we've met a lot of wonderful people, both on the river in boats and on the shore, who've come out to see us, and we are deeply grateful for the hospitality and the friendship and the welcome that the people in the Midwest have given us. We thank you, very, very much.

Thank you. Is anybody here from Muscatine? [*Applause*]

I'd like to say just a couple of things to you—and we don't have much time to stay, but Rosalynn is going to go down one side and I'll go down the other, and Amy in the middle, and we'll kind of shake hands with as many folks as we can reach after I say a few words.

Don't leave. Don't leave. We're not going to go far down the fence. So don't leave. You have to hear a speech first. [*Laughter*]

Tomorrow we're going to have, in Burlington, Iowa, a townhall meeting, and there will be several hundred people there who will ask me questions, I guess for about an hour, and I imagine it'll be broadcast and telecast so you can watch and hear it. And we'll be talking about some very serious questions and issues that affect a President of a great nation.

We'll be talking about agriculture and how farmers can be made more productive, how farm income can go up, how exports of farm products can reach an alltime high year after year after year—how the quality of our land has given us a great strategic advantage to be used for peaceful influence around the world. We'll be talking about adequate farm prices, and we'll be talking about controlling inflation, and we'll also be talking about peace.

I'm very grateful that since I've been in office not a single young American has had to endanger his or her lives in any sort of combat overseas. And I want to keep it that way.

And we'll also be talking about the control of nuclear weapons. I'm determined that as long as I'm in the White House we'll do everything we possibly can to control and eventually to eliminate nuclear weapons from the face of the Earth. That's my ultimate goal.

As you know, we now have before the U.S. Senate the SALT II treaty, which has been negotiated over 6 years under three different Presidents to put new and expanded controls over nuclear weapons. That's one of the important issues that the Senate must address this year. And I need your influence in the Congress to make sure we take this major stride forward toward peace, toward enhancing our own Nation's security, and toward controlling nuclear weapons.

The other issue is equally as important for us economically, and that is the handling of another threat to our Nation's security—that is energy. We have become too dependent on the importing of oil from foreign countries. We now import about one-half all the oil we use. We not only import enormous quantities of oil, but we import inflation and we import unemployment.

We've made some progress the last 2½ years, but we still have a long way to go.

What I've asked the Congress to do—and here, again, I need your help—is to pass a windfall profits tax on the oil companies, to give us the financial resources to conserve energy, to have more efficient vehicles, to help people weatherize their homes, to expand our production of oil, gas, coal, geothermal supplies, solar energy—which is really a great need for our country—and, of course, in Illinois, and in Iowa we want to produce gasohol as well.

We need a better transportation system. We need to help the low- and middle-income families to pay for the increasing cost of energy put on us by the OPEC oil nations in the Mideast. None of this will be possible unless we have the windfall profits tax passed by the Congress this year.

I hope you'll help me with this issue before Congress.

The other thing that we can do, of course, in addition to producing more energy in our own country, is to save energy, to eliminate waste, to conserve every way we can. This cannot be done by the government, by the Federal, State, or local governments. It can only be done when millions of Americans individually resolve that you will help to save energy.

There are many dozens of ways that you can do it—in your transportation, on your jobs, in your homes, in your living habits. Figure out every way that you use energy of any kind and see if you can't save energy in the future.

So, saving energy and producing more energy in our own Nation will help to eliminate this threat to our own Nation's security, because we are too dependent on foreign oil.

The last thing I want to say is don't ever forget, any of you, that we do live in a country where we've been blessed by God with almost every possible human need and every human advantage. We do have rich land. We do have freedom. We have a good free enterprise system. We've got a democracy. We can be individuals. We can argue and debate. We can make our own voices heard. We can be different if we choose. But when a threat comes, Americans have always united.

Lately, we have not been united. We've not had as much confidence as we ought to in the strength of our country. We've got the strongest nation on Earth economically, politically, and militarily. And I want to be sure that if you will cooperate with me in solving these problems of peace and energy, then we will make the greatest nation on Earth, the United States of America, even greater in the future.

Will you help me with that? [*Applause*] Thank you very much.

And now we'll come down and shake hands as long as we can. Thank you very much.

NOTE: The President spoke at 7:30 p.m. from the deck of the *Delta Queen*.

Burlington, Iowa

Remarks on Arrival at the City.
August 22, 1979

Good morning. I didn't know you had this many people in Burlington. I'll see most of you in a few minutes at the townhall meeting. I will see a lot of you later on at the townhall meeting, and I hope if you can't be there, that you'll listen to what is asked me and what I say.

This morning we will be discussing some matters that are very important to you and to me, indeed to all people in our country and around the world. We'll be talking about issues of peace, controlling nuclear weapons. We'll be talking about the strength of our country, the unity which, when it binds us together, has always been enough to meet any challenge or to overcome any problem or to answer any question.

In the past when our country has been challenged, almost always it's been obvious to everyone. We could understand the First World War or the Second World War or the Great Depression, and we recognized that our country was in trouble, in danger, and we all worked together— our families, our communities, our Nation was unified.

Now we have a serious problem because we rely too much on foreign oil. We import about half of all the oil we use. We need to become more energy-secure, because our Nation's security is threatened. Everyone can help. We have to do two things: One is, save energy, don't waste energy. Every American can decide how to accomplish this goal in your driving, at your home, at your job—how to save energy.

And the other, of course, is to produce more energy in our own country—oil, gas, coal, geothermal supplies, gasohol in Iowa. We can also use more solar energy. These are the kind of things we can all do.

Farmers have a great opportunity to help with the energy problem, and, of course, no one can come to Iowa without realizing that you have the most wonderfully productive land on Earth and one of our greatest blessings that God's given us in this Nation, this beautiful land to produce food and fiber for ourselves and for all the world. I'm very happy to be back. I'm very happy to be back at Burlington.

Thank all of you for coming out. We love every one of you.

We have the greatest country on Earth, and together we can make it even greater in the future.

Thank you very much. Thank you.

NOTE: The President spoke at 8:55 a.m. from the deck of the *Delta Queen*.

Burlington, Iowa

Remarks and a Question-and-Answer Session at a Town Meeting.   August 22, 1979

THE PRESIDENT. First of all, I want to thank my good friend, Senator John Culver, one of the greatest representatives in the Senate, and a man who, every day, every minute of his life, is concerned about carving out a better life for the people whom he represents here in Iowa. John Culver, thank you very much.

I also want to recognize a man whom I believe to be the finest Secretary of Agriculture this country has ever known, Bob Bergland. Bob, thank you for coming.

And this will be a surprise to him, but I have to say that Burlington, Iowa, is especially blessed to have one of the finest newspapers in the United States, and one of the greatest editors, John McCormally, with the Hawk Eye.

This last 3 or 4 days has been a period in my life and in the life of Rosalynn and Amy which we will obviously never forget. It's been an inspiration to us, not only to see the beauty of the Midwest and the majesty of the Mississippi River, but also the friendship and the commitment and the interest and the unity and the dedication of the people who've come to the banks of this great river to make us feel welcome, and to express your appreciation for the Government of our country. We do, indeed, have a great nation, the greatest nation on Earth. I hope you agree with that statement. [*Applause*]

And I've been reinspired, as the highest elected officer of our country, as I've seen and met and talked to and listened to the crowds that have come down to the banks of the river to welcome us.

ENERGY

Our Nation has never been afraid to face a challenge. We have never been unable to overcome an obstacle or to meet a problem and solve it. And our country has always been able, when we were united, to answer any difficult question.

God's blessed us in many wonderful ways, with rich land, a democratic, free government, a pride in the individualism of each person, the right to be different, the right to speak our minds, the right to control our own Government, the right to unify ourselves in times of challenge—and I have to say that this is one of those times when our people must be unified.

We are seeing our country threatened, our security threatened by an excessive dependence on foreign oil. We now import about one-half all the oil we use. We must conserve energy. We must save energy. Each American can do this in our own particular way, in our transportation, our jobs, in our home. And I hope that all of you, without being told how to do it, will search out the dozens of different ways that you can eliminate waste of energy in your own lives. And the second thing we must do is to produce more energy in our own country.

The basis of this increased production and also increased conservation is the passage of a windfall profits tax on the oil companies in our country to make sure they don't keep all these enormous profits, but those profits are divided among the American people to give us a better life. And if you'll help me, we'll get that legislation through Congress and preserve our Nation's security.

This will help to guarantee that our farmers have enough fuel for tractors and homes have enough fuel for heat in the winter. It also will guarantee us that we increase production of oil and gas and coal and geothermal supplies, solar power, learn how to use it more effectively. And of course, we've got to produce more gasohol in Iowa. That's very important, too.

The last thing I'll say before I will take questions is this: It's an inspiration to anyone to see the beautiful and productive land in your part of the country; to know that we now and in the past and increasingly in the future will have a wonderful strategic weapon for peace—not only for ourselves but for the entire world—by having the breadbasket of the world here in the heartland of our country. Your productivity is increasing almost every year, and our exports of farm products set world record the first year I was in office in '77; another world record last year; another world record this year. And next year we anticipate an even greater increase in the export of corn and wheat and other farm products from Iowa, which bring a better life for you, a better, stronger economy for our Nation, and a better life for all people on Earth.

So, I particularly want to thank, as a farmer, the farmers of Iowa and those of Illinois and others around this country for the wonderful job that you do. Thank you, farmers, from the bottom of my heart.

And now I'm eager to answer questions about any matter that might be important to you or of interest to you. I've already made arrangements with Bob Bergland and John Culver to help me out if I have a question that I can't answer, and they volunteered to do it. So, I'm ready for the first question, I think on this microphone.

QUESTIONS

GRAIN PRICES AND FUEL SUPPLIES

Q. I'm Lawrence Rowe from Grandview, Iowa, and I'm a Pioneer seedcorn salesman, and I carry a lot of interest with the farmers. Now, is there going to be plenty of fuel for the farmers for this fall and next spring? And also, will the price come down to help the farmers out, along with their price of grain?

THE PRESIDENT. The answer to your first question is that there will be enough fuel if American people, including farmers, are careful about how much you use, don't waste fuel, and if we have a success in the Congress in getting our energy program through. My guess is that both these questions will be answered yes. So, my answer to you is there will be an adequate supply of fuel for the farmers in the harvest season this fall and the planting season next spring.

The answer to your other question—will energy supplies be cheaper—the answer, unfortunately, is no. It's not good for a President to mislead the people. And I cannot tell you that now or in the future that the price of oil or other energy will be going down. Inevitably, the price of fuel in the future is going to go up, because the demand is growing and the supplies are becoming more scarce.

You'll have the fuel if you conserve it. You'll probably have to pay more for it. But I hope that we—John Culver, Bob Bergland and I and others—can make sure that the income for the American farm family continues to rise because your productivity goes up. And we'll try to hold prices as strong as we can, and particularly with the Grain Reserve program that has been implemented since I've been in the White House, with Bob Bergland's help.

The farmers need to have a greater share of the prices charged for products when they get to the consumers. In the past, the middleman and the distributor has gotten too much. We want to see more of that money go into the pockets of the American farm families.

1980 PRESIDENTIAL CAMPAIGN

Q. My name is Scott Kelsay. I'm from Burlington, and I'm a student at the University of Iowa. Mr. President, wouldn't it be appropriate for you to announce your candidacy for reelection here today, since Iowa was a stronghold for you in 1976 and your first endorsement came from our local Hawk Eye editor, John McCormally?

THE PRESIDENT. That sounds like a wonderful idea—[*laughter*]—which I will consider very carefully. Thank you very much.

Q. Thank you.

THE PRESIDENT. I haven't forgotten, by the way, what Iowa did in '76. So, I'll be thinking about that question very carefully. [*Laughter*]

OIL AND TOXIC WASTE POLLUTION

Q. My name is Jean Funck, and I'm from Burlington. I'm a housewife. Recognizing the fact that the United States is a great power and as a result must use a great deal of diplomacy, what is being done to hold Mexico responsible for harming wildlife and ecology and a regional economy in south Texas? Were the situation reversed, I am sure the entire world would be chastising the United States.

THE PRESIDENT. We do not yet have an international agreement on how to handle pollution in the high seas. And as you all know, only in the last few years—really the last few months—has the world become interested in having both ships that carry oil be made safer so that the disasters don't take place nor to control the pumping of oil from the wells in the offshore regions. So, we have no way at this point of requiring another country—Mexico or others—to pay for damage that might occur from an oil spill carried to our shores.

We are discussing with other nations means by which we can control these oil spills, first of all, and make a reserve supply of funds for damage to private individuals. It hasn't happened yet.

The other part of this, of course, is the control of the spills from our own toxic materials that in the past have not been covered at all. I have sent to the Congress now a proposal which would mean that every producer of a toxic material—which would include those that we have to use every day, like herbicides and pesticides—would have to put a small amount of money into an insurance fund so that later on, maybe many years later, when a dump near a city which contain toxic materials did damage a person's property or a person's life, that they might be paid for that damage out of the reserve fund. And part of that money would be used to ensure that those toxic materials are placed so that the spill would not occur.

This is an area of government that has just begun to be explored. But we are pushing for that agreement among nations. It hasn't been reached yet.

Q. Thank you.

THE PRESIDENT. Thank you. It's a good question.

John, it's one that we need to pursue a little further.

SOUTHEAST ASIA REFUGEES

Q. Mr. President, my name is Phillip Good. I'm from Burlington, Iowa, and I'm a student at Southeastern Community College and also a part-time employee at the Hawk Eye. You said that when we import oil, we also import inflation and unemployment. Well, I'll agree with that, but isn't it also true when we bring in the boat people, we're also bringing in unemployment and inflation?

THE PRESIDENT. Thank you, Phil. That's a good question and I'm glad you asked it.

How many people here have ancestors that were Native Americans? I see two or three hands back there whose parents were Indians.

Let me remind you that the United States is a country of immigrants. We are a country of refugees. Whether your parents came here 300 years ago or whether your parents came here one generation ago or whether you've only been here a few months, the United States has always been a nation with an open heart and with open arms to receive those people who were seeking for religious freedom or seeking for a better way of life.

The refugees who are now leaving Southeast Asia were our allies in the recent Vietnam war. They are now being persecuted by a Communist government in Vietnam, which has taken away from them their basic rights. They leave that country; almost half of them drown in the ocean before they can find a place of safety. Our Nation has joined in with other nations throughout the world to receive these refugees. We've now received, I think in all—those that are here and those that are being processed—about 220,000. That is 1 refugee—man, woman, child—for every 1,000 Americans. And we are very carefully placing those refugees, when they come into our country, in areas where the unemployment rate is low.

They are entrepreneurs; they're the kind of people that work hard under the form of free enterprise system that existed in Vietnam before it was taken over by the Communists. One of the reasons they're being pushed out of Vietnam is because they believe in individual work, individual initiative, personal freedom. They are more philosophically attuned to us than they are to the Communist regime that's taken over.

I believe that a thousand Americans can support, for just a few weeks, one refugee searching for freedom, particularly when those people have proven already that they are eager to learn our language, they are eager to be self-supporting, they are hard-working, dedicated, honest people.

So, I hope that all Americans, no matter how you might feel, will realize that your family came here in generations gone by, looking for exactly the same thing that the Vietnam refugees are looking for now. There are very few of them. And I think our country ought to be proud that we still are the land of the free and the home of the brave, with an open heart and open minds and open arms to take them in.

ENERGY LEGISLATION

Q. Mr. President, my name is Linda Larkin, and I'm from Fort Madison. And my question to you is, now that you've been in office for about 3 years, and you've seen that Congress hasn't done that much to help you, what do you think you could do to improve your working relationship with them, especially with the energy legislation?

THE PRESIDENT. Last week I took the last action that I can take to improve the production of energy in our own country by moving to encourage the production of very heavy, very thick oil. It costs more to produce it. And in the past, Government redtape and regulations and low prices have kept us from producing about half a million barrels per day of that heavy, unconventional oil.

The next steps must be taken by Congress. I might hasten to add that Senator Culver's been very helpful in trying to move toward a comprehensive energy policy. So far, we've passed about 65 percent of the energy proposals that I made to the Congress in April of 1977, the first year I was in office.

The other part that hasn't been passed relates to oil. The Congress has not yet passed a single line of legislation about oil. And it's not an accident, because for many years the oil companies have had a tremendous, effective lobby in Washington to protect their interests. You can't much blame them.

But in the last couple of years the consumers of this country have got a new voice. And now it's a very close match between the oil companies on one hand, wanting to keep all the profits that they get that they do not earn, and the consumers on the other hand, that are struggling to see the Congress pass a windfall profits tax, so that those excess profits can be shared among the American people.

I can't force the Congress to take action, but all of you, and people like you around the Nation, can force the Congress to take action.

I was just informed a few minutes ago that all the members of the United Automobile Workers in the Nation are going to take 6 minutes and write a postcard to Congress supporting the energy proposals that we have made. And I hope this will make a lot of impact on the Congress.

So, Linda, I'll have to say this to you: It's not an accident that as we've drifted down the Mississippi River, having a good time, almost every time I've stopped I've talked about the need for American people to do two things: save energy in your own life, and help me induce the Congress to pass the windfall profits tax so we can have a comprehensive energy program to make our energy security guaranteed.

That's an excellent question. And I hope everybody will listen to my voice and let your Congress Member know we need to have that energy policy passed through the Congress.

CHRYSLER CORPORATION

Q. Mr. President, my name is Jim Paul. I'm a teacher and a coach from the West Burlington School System. First of all, I'd like you to equate your concept of the free enterprise system with the application of the Chrysler Corporation to the Government for a billion dollars worth of aid. And would you support the program, the aid, if Chrysler could be forced to manufacture public transportation equipment?

THE PRESIDENT. We are approaching the Chrysler question, Jim, very cautiously. And the approach that I have approved personally has a heavy dependence on the free enterprise system.

It requires Chrysler, first of all, to reconstitute their management so they can be more effective and more efficient in the future than they have been in the past. It also requires that Chrysler go, first off, to private sources of financing to get the loans that they need. The only thing I think the Federal Government ought to do is to provide some guarantee for those loans that are obtained in the private sector, but let the Federal Government in effect hold the first mortgage.

I think we ought to protect the public

interest as we help Chrysler tide themselves over a difficult time. Chrysler must change, as the other automobile manufacturers must change in our country, to make automobiles that are more fuel-efficient and also that meet our pollution standards. They are changing now as fast as they can. In the last few years, even since—since 1973, when we had the oil embargo, the American consumers have often demanded the very large, inefficient cars. Now they must make the change.

So, I would say a shared responsibility between the employees and employers of Chrysler, a heavy dependence on the private enterprise system, a minimum involvement of the Federal Government, and a maximum security for any loans that the Federal Government guarantees—that's a package that I think would be acceptable. It would keep Chrysler operating, maintain more competition in the automobile industry to hold prices down, and it would keep about two or three hundred thousand UAW workers employed who now work for Chrysler.

That'll be a good investment, I believe, if we do it that way.

TRANSPORTATION FUNDS

Q. Good morning, Mr. President.

THE PRESIDENT. Good morning.

Q. My name is Jerry Rigdon. I live here in Burlington, Iowa, and I am a professional window cleaner. Do you have any dirty windows in the White House? [*Laughter*]

THE PRESIDENT. There's a lot of—we need a lot more light in Washington. I'll say that for you. [*Laughter*]

Q. The motto of my company is: "We brighten your outlook."

Mr. President, in lieu of the fact that our counties and cities depend on road-use tax to build new streets and new roads, it is not—with road-use taxes directly related to gasoline sales—it is not in the best interest of cities or counties to develop bikepaths, efficient mass transit systems, force carpooling, and other means that would mean tremendous gasoline savings to—in our energy program—can other revenues be released to particularly aid in these efforts of the counties and the cities?

THE PRESIDENT. I don't want to claim or leave the impression that everything a city or a county or a family does in saving energy must be with the help of the Federal Government. A lot of the initiative has got to come from individuals and from local communities.

My wife recently visited a small—well, a fairly good-sized town named Davis, California. Right, Rosalynn? That community, on its own initiative, with some already prescribed Federal programs, put in biketrails and helped people to decide how they could save energy in many different ways.

They gave Rosalynn, for instance, a free gift, which she's authorized to keep, of a solar clothes drier. It was a 20-foot rope with five or six clothespins. [*Laughter*]

I try to run 4 or 5 miles every day. I did this morning, I think at Lock 18, before I came up here. And I think a lot of people would enjoy the beauty of a place like Burlington if a few times a week or maybe every day, instead of riding a half mile or a mile to work, you'd walk there and back, or ride a bike. And this kind of approach would be very helpful as an inspiration to others if it was adequately publicized.

The Federal programs are being designed more and more in housing and urban development, in community planning, in transportation, in agriculture, in almost every aspect of American life, to conserve energy. This is an area where we

are just beginning to scratch the surface. This has not been part of our lives, as you know, in our country with $2-a-barrel oil. Now with $20-a-barrel oil becoming increasingly scarce, we've got to do this together.

I think one of the best things is for local communities to take the initiative and to let that lesson be learned at the State level, and then at the Federal level, instead of depending on the Federal Government to tell you all what to do.

Your question, though, about how Federal transportation funds can be better designed to help conserve energy at the local level is a very good one.

The new Secretary of Transportation, Neil Goldschmidt, is a former mayor of Portland, Oregon. He has a special interest in transportation, and he's also done one of the best jobs in the whole country in Portland in conserving energy in the transportation area. So, I would guess that his new approach will be very beneficial to all the country and would also help to answer your question that you've raised, which is a very good one for the whole world, our whole country to know about.

We'll try to make sure the Federal programs in the future do a better job of saving energy, even at the local, county, and city level.

SYNTHETIC FUELS; FOOD PRODUCTION

Q. Mr. President, I'm Leo Talbot from Mount Union, Iowa. I'm a farmer. Part of my question was answered by the first gentleman, but I would still like to ask this question concerned about our product that we have out here with God's help and willing, we'll have for the next thousands of years as a synthetic fuel. We raise corn, and I wondered what the Government was doing, how much emphasis they are putting upon this corn product, that we can put into ethanol to make a synthetic fuel. Are they really into it great now? We've been working at it out here for several years. Are they into it great?

And the last part of my question was, of course, are you going to put the farmers on a number one priority this fall to harvest our crops?

Thank you, sir.

THE PRESIDENT. The answer to your last question is yes. Bob Bergland is nodding his head even before I had a chance to answer. And obviously from one season to another, we have varying needs for distillate fuels, which are in relatively short supply.

During the planting season, we were putting in as many as 5 million acres per day, were we not, Bob?—one of the highest rates of planting that our Nation has ever seen. We were able, with the cooperation of farmers and the ASCS Offices, Governors, and everyone else, to get enough fuel to the farmers during the planting season so there were no long delays.

We'll do the same thing in the harvest season in the fall and also in the planting season in the future, because the production of food in our country is a top priority, along with fire protection, police protection, and emergency vehicles, both the production of food on land and also the fisheries off the shores.

As far as the production of gasohol is concerned, we are now exploring every possibility for putting into operation both the very small gasohol plants that can be put on a large farm or those that are much more costly and much more extensive. We now have two major pilot projects already underway. We are preserving the exemption of the 4 cents per gallon on gasohol to encourage its production. That amounts in total to about $60 per barrel that we are helping with gasohol use.

Third, we've done all we can so far—

but we will do more in the future—to make sure that there's an extra investment tax credit of 10 percent for people who invest in a gasohol-producing plant.

Yesterday at the John Deere international headquarters in Moline, I saw a new machine that's still in the experimental stage, where they burn corncobs— where they take corncobs and burn them and they make a gas which has about 15 percent of the energy as natural gas. And then they burn that gas and make electricity, either to pump water or to provide electricity for a farm. So, the use of farm products, cornstalks, corncobs, perhaps just as important, peanut hulls, different things—[*laughter*]—can be used now to make gas.

On gasohol, the Congress, particularly including the Congress Members from Iowa, have proposed that we make available low-interest, direct loans to farmers who will put in the very small gasohol-producing plants. I have not announced this before publicly, but I would like to announce it to you—Mr. Talbot, right?— that my administration will support this move. And I believe that Congress this year, before it goes home, will have low-interest, direct loans for people who will put in small gasohol-producing plants on farms in Iowa.[1]

----

[1] On the same day, the White House Press Office released the following information at Burlington.

The President today announced support for new legislative authority to assist in the construction of small- and intermediate-scale plants for the production of alcohol fuel. He indicated that alcohol made from agricultural and forestry residues and commodities can play an increasingly important role in our fight for energy security.

An alcohol-gasoline mixture is already being marketed through more than 800 retail outlets in 28 States. President Carter noted that alcohol fuels would be especially important over the coming decade, a period of intensive research and exploration for alternative energy

(Continued)

If you think of anything else I can do to help gasohol production, you let me know and I'll do it.

Q. I'll meet you afterwards.

(Continued)

sources. One of the great advantages of this fuel is its already proven technology, although research into improved production methods will also be undertaken.

Noting the strong interest among many Members of Congress, the President indicated that he is anxious to work with them to enact new authority to promote the further development of alcohol fuels through small- and intermediate-scale plants.

He proposed a 2-year direct or guaranteed loan program to be administered by the Department of Agriculture, with a limit of $3 million per project. The loan program would be supplemented with a program of technical assistance and research and financed from the energy security trust fund. With the help of this program, individuals or groups of individuals could play an active role in lessening our Nation's dependence on foreign oil.

The President's support of this measure is the latest in a series of steps the administration has taken to further the development, production, and use of alcohol fuels, including:

• Presidential directives to:

—use gasohol in Federal vehicles, whenever feasible;

—simplify and reduce Federal reporting requirements for alcohol fuel producers.

• Presidential recommendation that the current 4-cent-per-gallon excise tax exemption for gasoline-alcohol (10 percent) blends be extended permanently.

• Implementations of a 10-percent investment tax credit for facilities that convert alternative substances or feedstocks into synthetic liquid fuels, including alcohol fuels.

• Loan guarantees of $30 million by the Department of Agriculture for two innovative pilot projects for the production of alcohol.

• An $11 million loan and grant program by the Department of Energy, the Economic Development Administration, and the Community Services Administration to assist in the construction of 100 small-scale alcohol production plants.

• Increased funding of DOE research and development of alcohol fuels from $3 million in FY 1977 to $25 million in FY 1980. Also, the USDA is programing nearly $6 million in FY 1980 for this purpose.

THE PRESIDENT. Thank you. [*Laughter*]

THE PRESIDENT'S TRIP

Q. Mr. President, I am Gertrude Gerdom from Burlington, Iowa, and I'm a housewife. And I want to tell you I think you're doing a real good job and also ask if you've caught any fish since you've been on your trip.

THE PRESIDENT. I think I've done a better job of being President than I have catching fish this trip. But we're going to try again this afternoon, and I believe we're going to catch some.

Q. Good luck. God bless you.

THE PRESIDENT. Gertrude, that's the kind of question I never get from the Washington press corps. Thank you very much. I love you. [*Laughter*]

SIZE OF THE FEDERAL GOVERNMENT

Q. I'm Emerson Cordes from Evergreen Park, Illinois. I'm retired. Many of us were heartened recently when you gave your Sunday night speech, especially setting forth two objectives that we could all get behind that would really help our country, that of controlling inflation and attacking the energy problem in all the many ways you suggested. But to reach these objectives, you're going to need all of our help and our support. And right now, we've lost an awful lot of confidence in that Washington establishment. We just don't feel it has the capability or the willingness to respond to the people's needs and expressed feelings.

And I'm wondering if you've ever thought of setting an objective, perhaps, for your administration of reducing the size of that Washington establishment by, say, 10 percent, just to show that the people still own it and that they don't own us.

THE PRESIDENT. Yes. I've thought about it a lot, and we have made some progress.

As you know, each year, the services of the Government expand. Five years ago, there was practically no bureaucracy for the energy question. Now we have a very large department, the Department of Energy, that must administer programs that encourage gasohol and encourage the weatherization of homes and design better ways of transportation and monitor more efficient automobiles and distribute scarce supplies of fuel to farmers. That kind of service is demanded by the people. It's passed by the Congress and goes into effect. In spite of that, though, since I've been in office, we've had a reduction in the number of Federal employees, just a small reduction, 2,000. And I hope that I can finish this term and not have any increase at least in the number of Federal employees.

When you start asking Americans where do you want to cut, it's a very difficult question to answer. I would hesitate, for instance, as a farmer to eliminate either the Home Demonstration Agents or the County Agents or the ASCS Office employees who do a good job on a routine basis—and 3 or 4 months ago during planting season, we had to call on them almost full-time, 24 hours a day, to give us an inventory of where distillate fuels were and where the supplies were needed.

So, there are some requirements of the Government that must be carried out: the improvement of cities with HUD and the administering of programs for the poor through HEW, increased health for our people, the elimination of cancer, the control of these kinds of diseases must be carried out. So, I don't want you to feel that just because the Government is often insensitive that it's completely wasteful. There is waste there. There was waste in my farm in Plains. And there was waste in Carter's Warehouse, and there's probably waste in all of your businesses as well. But we are doing the best we can to hold it down.

We have now put into effect, with the Congress help, the first complete revision of the Civil Service in the last 100 years. That's just gone into effect, but I believe that in the future, you'll see some great benefits flowing from it.

So, in spite of the increase in services being demanded and being delivered, we are holding down the number of Federal employees. Maybe we're not doing a good enough job, but we're trying. And I would like to emphasize one more time what's come up two or three times already, that the initiative must come from the individual American and from the individual family and individual community. And the more you do for yourselves, within a family or within a community, the less will be demanded from the Government and the more we can save taxes and the more we can have a better life for us all, because that's where the enjoyment comes in.

I'm in favor of keeping the Federal Government as small as possible, but I have to be responsible for defending our Nation, keeping us strong, keeping us free, encouraging peace around the world, and meeting the legitimate needs of the American people.

So, don't curse your Government; just work with me to make it better.

NUCLEAR POWERPLANTS

Q. My name is Michael Lamb, Burlington, Iowa. I am an educator. Mr. Carter, if this community, in the future, could become the moral equivalent of cannon fodder and the moral equivalent of war, my question regards the continued utilization of nuclear fission power.

The 1957 Brookhaven report indicated that in the event of a massive reactor catastrophe, agricultural restrictions could prevail over 150,000 square miles, an area equal to the combined areas of Iowa, Illinois, and Indiana. Now, with this, the possible consequence of a catastrophic reactor accident, why are we allowing any reactors to be built in America's farmbelt, when it seems that just one major accident at any one of these reactors could lead to us importing food as well as oil?

THE PRESIDENT. Thank you, Michael.

I don't believe you have any nuclear reactors operating in Iowa, do you, John?

SENATOR CULVER. Yes. Palo.

THE PRESIDENT. One operating.

SENATOR CULVER. Palo. But there are several along the Mississippi and Illinois, serving Chicago.

THE PRESIDENT. Right. Well, as you know, for the last 35 or 40 years our country has had a policy of producing part of our energy from nuclear reactors. We now produce about, I think, 13 percent of all the electricity in our Nation from atomic reactors. Communities like Chicago get 50 percent of all their electricity from nuclear reactors.

It would be a very serious blow to our country to close down all the nuclear reactors that we have. We do have a problem that's now being assessed, brought about by the accident at Three Mile Island, and I have asked Dr. Kemeny, who heads up this Commission, to give me a report on how the existing atomic reactors can be made more safe to operate.

I thank God that in the last 35 or 40 years we have never had a fatality or a serious injury in a commercial reactor in the United States. But I want to make sure that we don't have any in the future.

We also have not had enough attention given to the disposal of waste from the atomic reactors. Now, when this Kemeny report comes in to me—within the next few days, as a matter of fact—I will assess it and, working with the Nuclear Regulatory Commission and with the Congress, will take whatever action is necessary for better design, better training of personnel, and better operation of the existing nuclear plants to make sure that we do have as safe a nuclear program as possible.

I don't want to mislead you. Some people like Michael don't think that we ought to have any use of atomic power. I believe that it's inevitable that there will be a place for atomic power in the future in our country. But to the extent that all of us save energy, to the extent that we increase the production of oil and gas in our country, to the extent that we shift toward the plentiful supplies of coal and make coal clean-burning, to the extent that we have more efficient automobiles, that we take whatever action we can to make homes more savers of energy—to the extent that we do all these things to conserve and to increase production of other energy, we can cut down on the demand for atomic power.

During my campaign for President 2½, 3 years ago, I said that we ought to make atomic power a source of energy as a last resort. And what I mean by that is that as we conserve and produce other forms of energy, our Nation will need less atomic power.

As you know, we have not had atomic powerplants approved for new construction in quite a while. We're at a pause now, and with the Kemeny report— which I hope all of you will study—we'll see how to make atomic power, if it is used in the future, more safe for Americans and protect both lives and the land that you describe, Michael.

Thank you very much.

Q. Mr. Carter?

THE PRESIDENT. Yes.

Q. You did still not address the fact of the farming. What happens if you have one accident in the American farmbelt?

THE PRESIDENT. Well, obviously, it depends on the kind of accident that you have.

Q. Right. A major catastrophic accident, one which on ABC News stated the odds in the next 30 years could be as high as 1 in 15.

THE PRESIDENT. The only way I can answer you is that if we have a catastrophic accident that would be a catastrophe.

Q. Mr. Carter, one more point, please. There's a great deal of talk in this country about energy independence for America. The Government should not forget that Americans need energy independence also.

AMY CARTER

Q. Mr. President, I'm Jean McKinney, an orchestra teacher from here in Burlington. And I was wondering if Amy's still making good progress with her violin lessons. [*Laughter*]

THE PRESIDENT. I think Amy plays very well, considering the talent that she has. [*Laughter*]

I think you would be proud to hear Amy play. She hasn't practiced much on this trip, I have to admit. She's been concentrating on the calliope. But she's doing very well and I'm very proud of her.

LETTER FOR THE PRESIDENT

Q. Mr. President?

THE PRESIDENT. Yes.

Q. This is really important to me. I have a letter that I'd like to give to you. And I'd risk being arrested in order to give it to you, I think it's so important.

THE PRESIDENT. No, you're not going to be arrested. If you'll give it to my wife Rosalynn, right there in the green shirt, I'll get it.

Q. Thank you very much.

THE PRESIDENT. It's a pleasure.

SALE OF KEROSENE TO IRAN

Q. Mr. Carter, my name is Mary Beth Murrell, and I'm a math teacher at West Burlington. It's super-exciting to have you here, and I want you to know that we heartily support your energy program and we're doing everything we can do to help. We're biking to work and we installed a solar system in our home.

THE PRESIDENT. Very good.

Q. But my question is this: On the late news on the radio last night, they said something about that we were selling oil to Iran. Now, they didn't explain this at all. They were heavily critical of the fact that somebody was selling our oil while you were floating down the Mississippi. [*Laughter*] I would like for you to complete this report and explain to me why we are selling oil to Iran.

THE PRESIDENT. Okay.

We get from Iran, I think, about 30 million barrels of oil every month. I'm not sure about the exact figure, but that's roughly what we get. And a few months ago, because of some riots in Iran, they sabotaged a pipeline going to the refinery which makes kerosene for the Iranian people. They use kerosene in their homes like we did when I was a child to cook and for everything else. And they had a very severe shortage of kerosene. And they asked us to sell them back about two-thirds of one day's supply of kerosene to meet the needs of the families in Iran, and since they sell us more than that every day, I personally approved the sale of that much kerosene to Iran.

But it's just a small amount compared to what we use and also a very tiny amount compared to what we get from Iran, about one-fiftieth of what we get from Iran every month. And it was just a one-time proposition.

Q. Thank you.

THE PRESIDENT. We're not going to shut down any tractors because of it.

ENERGY CONSERVATION TAX CREDITS

Q. Mr. President, my name is Dan Carlson, from Middletown, Iowa. I'm a student at Quincy College in Quincy. On the housing situation, by energy conservation, the only type of tax relief that I understand is basically solar heat that you're more or less giving a tax break to. We have several other types of energy conservation methods, such as underground living, which stays at a constant temperature, between 55 and 60 degrees a year, with no heat at all. And you can take it up to a comfortable 72 degrees by using about two logs a day in a fireplace. There's absolutely no oil use there at all.

Now, there's no tax relief for anything like that. If you have a stream that goes through your property, if you'd put a water generator on that, there's no tax relief for that or anything of that sort. Could you give me any idea on that?

THE PRESIDENT. Yes. As you know, Dan, the establishment of a program on a nationwide basis for 220 million Americans, maybe 50 million homes, is a very expensive proposition, whether it's with a tax credit or a direct loan, where interest is subsidized or sometimes a grant. It's not going to be possible for us to have a major expansion or encouraging people

to conserve energy without the windfall profits tax. That will be the source of enough money to take care of poor families, who are especially hurt by increasing prices of oil; secondly, to give us a better transportation system; and third, to encourage conservation and also the production of American energy.

We already have a tax credit for the weatherization of homes, where you'd take various means to cut down on the waste of heat. I'd have to look into the law to see if it covers the placement of a home down below the ground level.[2] But I was in Baltimore recently, where they are weatherizing this year 3,000 homes in the low-income area. Next year, they have a target of weatherizing 5,000 homes in the low-income area. It only costs them in that urban area about $275 per home to make it energy efficient. They save more than that every 2 years in reduced costs of heating oil and natural gas, whatever they use.

We now are prepared to expand this program to encourage that kind of saving. But we have to have the windfall profits tax to do it. It applies not only to solar installations, which get a $2,200 tax credit already, but also to the weatherization of homes and to the production of electricity from low-head dams.

One possibility that we are exploring and which will be pursued, by the way, is

---

[2] On the same day, the White House Press Office released the following information at Burlington.

The law, proposed by the President in April 1977 and passed by the Congress in 1978, provides a tax credit of 15 percent of up to the first $2,000 of weatherization projects added to homes after April 1977. Weatherization projects are those such as insulation and caulking, and so forth. Homes, either below or above ground, are eligible for a tax credit, providing work was performed that meets the law's requirements. There is, however, no tax credit for building a home underground per se.

the series of locks and dams on the Mississippi River, some of which might be available for the production of electricity to be used at a very low additional cost. We now have pilot projects all over the Nation where a small community formerly had its own private source of electric generation, from a nearby stream that had been dammed up with a low-height dam, and we're going to put those back into operation. There'll be several thousand of those around the country.

So, we're expanding in every possible way the encouragement of the saving of heat in homes, transportation, and the cheap production of energy. But all of that program that's not already in effect would have to depend on the passage of the windfall profits tax.

At the end of this year, I believe that we'll have an adequate base for a long period of time in the future to meet the needs that you described. But there's already a tax credit available of about $300 for homes like you described, and I'll have to find out for you, if you don't mind, whether it applies to putting the home partially underground.

Q. Thank you.

THE PRESIDENT. Thank you, Dan, very much. If one of my staff would get Dan's address, we'll send you the answer. Okay?

EMPLOYMENT

Q. Good morning, Mr. President. My name is Bonnie Wilson. I'm from Burlington, Iowa, and I'm a secretary. I'm wondering what you plan to do or what you have done to assist the middle-aged woman either entering or reentering the job market.

THE PRESIDENT. Okay.

Bonnie, it's hard to single out that particular age group and the fact that they would be women. What I faced when I was running for President, when I first became President, was an unemployment rate above 8 percent. We've had a net increase in our country now of 8 million jobs, a net increase, just in the last 2½ years—those jobs being made available to young people and older people, middle-aged men and women. So, I'm sure that the middle-aged woman has benefited.

Also, in the Federal Government, for instance, we've tried to set an example for other employers in encouraging the employment of women. Although we've had a 2,000 reduction in total Federal employment, we've had a 26,000 increase in the number of women who are employed. Obviously, this is an area that can be expanded in the future.

I think Iowa now has an unemployment rate of like 4 percent. And I would guess that any able-bodied person, man or woman, that really wants a job in Iowa can get one now. But we've made good progress on the unemployment field with the help of many people.

The best place, obviously, to acquire jobs is not in the Government or even with government programs, but in the private sector. And I think a strong and dynamic economy is the best source for jobs in the future.

But I think we've made good progress in the employment field. We haven't reached our goal of no unemployment, but we are getting closer than we were.

Thank you, Bonnie, very much.

I don't think I've got time for another question. Everybody is motioning at me. But let me say this in closing. The questions that have been asked I think will help the whole country. They're the kind of questions that make me think more about what we are doing in Washington and give me guidance for the future, both in domestic affairs, in meeting the needs of the average family on transportation and housing, agriculture and saving energy, but also in international affairs.

Jean Funck asked a question, for instance, about how we could make Mexico accountable for oil spills. This is an area that already we were exploring but we haven't yet solved.

So, I thank all of you for your questions and for giving me a chance to answer them.

Let me say this in closing: If you don't remember anything else from the town-hall meeting outdoors today, remember what a great country we have and how strong we are. Almost invariably we're inclined to think about the temporary inconvenience, the disagreements that are so highly publicized between the House and the Senate, or the Congress and the President, or the States and the Federal Government, or private citizens and others in our Nation. Those transient problems come and go very rapidly. Americans have always been able to face them and to solve them.

And I have no doubt in my mind that the present problems that our country faces can be solved, because our country is so great, because we have been so blessed with natural resources—but above all, because Americans are resilient, strong when we need to be, and unified when we see a common problem. So, I would like to ask all of you to do what I said in my Sunday night speech: Every day, say something good about America. We have the greatest nation on Earth, and if you will join in with me in the future, we'll make it even greater in years to come.

Thank you very much. God bless all of you.

NOTE: The President spoke at 10 a.m. at Crapo Park.

Following the town meeting, the President attended a private reception for community officials and area residents at the home of Mr. McCormally. He then returned to the *Delta Queen*.

Hannibal, Missouri

Remarks at the Town Square.
August 23, 1979

Mayor Herman, Congressman Volkmer, and my good friend, Governor Joe Teasdale, and all the people of Hannibal and the surrounding communities in Missouri, I guess on both sides of the Mississippi:

You have come here to make us feel welcome again.

I don't believe that any person lives in our country, and very few live throughout the world, who are not familiar with Mark Twain, Tom Sawyer, Becky Thatcher, Huckleberry Finn, and also Hannibal, Missouri.

Ours is a nation which has a source of strength and a source of greatness that's unshakable. And part of that strength comes from the memories of our boyhood and girlhood days in communities like Hannibal throughout the country—some smaller than Hannibal, like Plains; some much larger than Hannibal, like the urban areas of our country.

But the stability of a family life, the love of an Aunt Polly or a mother or a father or sisters or boyhood or girlhood sweethearts, live with us as long as we are on this Earth.

Ours is truly a great country. And I hope that Hannibal won't change very much, only in the number of people that can come here to witness and to be part of the life of Samuel Clemens, who spread the good news about America in many parts of the world.

We saw translations of "The Adventures of Tom Sawyer" in the museum that went to 50 different kinds of languages so that people all over Earth can know about you and about his boyhood and about the truth of America.

He was indeed a remarkable person who saw, with a remarkable insight, what made America great. Coming down the river, Amy has been reading "Tom Sawyer" for the second time, and I've been reading "Life on the Mississippi" for the second time, or third time, or fourth time as well. It's been part of my life as it has been part of many of you.

Mark Twain, or Samuel Clemens, had one of the greatest senses of humor, I guess, of anyone who's ever lived in our country. He always had a good thing to say about America. And I hope that's part of our own lives, to say something good about our own country. I jotted down a few things that he said, and I'll be very brief.

He had a lot to say about inflation. I don't know if you know it or not, but in "Life on the Mississippi" he said that when he was a young boy, he first saw St. Louis, he said, "I could have bought it for $6 million, and it was the biggest mistake of my life that I didn't do it."

And then he commented on energy—I won't read the whole quote—but Mark Twain saw a tremendous change in the use of energy on the Mississippi.

When he was first training to be a pilot, as you know, the steamboats used wood, and the woodyards would go for miles and miles on both sides of the river near the towns. At that time there were 10,000 steamboats on the river system of our country. He was part of that life.

And the last thing I'd like to comment on is about the Federal Government. He had some good things to say about the Federal Government. And I particularly liked this because you don't hear that very much anymore. He went by one of the Federal projects, and he said, "Everything about it suggests the hand of the national government." Listen to this: "The government's work is always conspicuous for excellence, solidity, thoroughness, and neatness. The Government does its work well in the first place, and then takes care of it afterwards."

That's the good news. The bad news is this project that he was describing was a cemetery. [*Laughter*]

Well, we still live in a great country, as you well know, and times are changing, including energy. Last night, we came by one of the very few large electric powerplants on the Mississippi. We produce a very small amount of electricity now, with all this tremendous power going past Hannibal, about 165 megawatts. We have the capability already assessed to produce 2,400 megawatts of power, 15 times as much, just using the dams that are already constructed there for the locks. I'm going to instruct the Department of the Army to simplify the procedures so that these projects can be completed earlier without going through all the redtape and complication and delay that hold up such projects now.

There are so many ways in our country that we can take advantage of what we already have and have a better nation and a better life at the same time. Conserving energy or saving energy is not an unpleasant thing. It can be an exciting thing, an enjoyable thing, that saves us money, lets us be truly patriotic, lets us restore the energy security of our Nation, and binds us together in a spirit of common purpose.

So, I believe that in many ways the present crisis that we face with a shortage of energy, an overdependence on foreign oil, can be a blessing in disguise. It can give Americans a chance to prove that a tremendous challenge can be overcome, that a tremendous problem can be solved, that complicated questions can be answered by Americans who are unified.

We sometimes forget what a great nation we have. And I believe that in the solution of our energy problem, we can prove again that Americans have never faced a challenge to our country unsuccessfully. We are the greatest nation on Earth, and if we remember what we learned in our childhood, the truth that Mark Twain told to us with a great sense of humor, and remember how strong a family can be or a community can be or a nation can be when we face a problem together, there's no doubt in my mind that we can make the greatest nation on Earth, the United States of America, even greater in the future.

If we all work together, we cannot fail. I know we'll succeed. And I thank you for being so nice to us.

Thank you very much.

NOTE: The President spoke at 11:10 a.m. Before and after his remarks, the President toured historic sites in the area, including Mark Twain's boyhood home and attached museum, the Becky Thatcher Book Shop, and the Mark Twain Cave. He also watched a skit performed by the Clemens Amphitheatre Players outside Grant's Drugstore.

Hydroelectric Power Projects

Statement by the President.   August 23, 1979

In the course of the time I will be traveling on the *Delta Queen,* we will go through 27 locks and dams on the Mississippi River. The water flowing over these dams and through these locks holds tremendous promise as a source of hydroelectric power. Of all the locks and dams on the Mississippi River between St. Paul and St. Louis, only five have installed capacity. Clearly some of the other existing locks and dams have hydroelectric potential. Other Corps of Engineers and Bureau of Reclamation existing structures around the Nation hold similar potential. We must move aggressively to begin to harness this power.

On the basis of the National Hydropower Study now being undertaken by the Corps of Engineers, it is clear that various Federal dams, locks, and other water projects would be suitable sites to be harnessed to produce hydroelectric power. I am today directing the Department of the Army, in conjunction with the Bureau of Reclamation and the Department of Energy, to develop necessary legislation which would give those agencies clearer, simpler authority to exploit the energy potential of existing Federal projects without requiring them to go through the full, protracted authorization process necessary for new construction projects in cases where the addition of the necessary turbines is economically justified and would not have an adverse impact on the environment or on stream flows.

Recently, I took two other actions to greatly expand our hydroelectric activities across the country:

—At a ceremony in Des Moines, Iowa, on May 4, 1979, I announced a major new coordinated effort to identify and develop hydroelectric potential at existing dams around the country. Under that program, for each of the next several years DOE will administer a program through which communities could conduct feasibility and engineering studies of potential sites. Following an onsite review process, including DOE, the Corps of Engineers, the Bureau of Reclamation, and the FERC, the most promising sites would be encouraged to submit applications for construction grants, loans, and loan guarantees from EDA, FMFA, REA, CSA, and HUD. Over $300 million in resources have been reserved for this purpose through 1981.

The target goal of beginning construction on 100 rural hydro projects by the end of 1981 through the interagency effort will develop approximately 300 megawatts of additional capacity. Since I announced this program, several hundred local communities have expressed interest in participating. Federal field teams will be conducting onsite inspections at about 250 of the most promising prospects during August and September.

—At my direction the Bureau of Reclamation recently testified in Congress, seeking the authority for the Secretary of Interior to plan, design, and install hydroelectric facilities on 13 existing reclamation dams. This procedure will permit a much faster review for a project which is economically justified and which will not have significant adverse environmental or stream-flow effects.

The Corps National Hydropower Study included a review of thousands of Federal and non-Federal dams. Many of the more promising non-Federal dams are being subjected to onsite inspections as part of the program to reconstruct rural hydro sites, as announced in Des Moines.

Of the Federal dams included in the Corps review, many appear to be candidates for new or additional hydroelectric facilities. While the energy-generating potential of these sites varies dramatically, the total potential for increased low-cost, clean, available power through this resource at Federal sites is great. For example, the locks and dams on the Mississippi River between St. Paul and St. Louis have an installed capacity of only 165.6 megawatts, while a preliminary Corps of Engineers study suggests a potential capacity of about 2,400 megawatts. I intend to see that this great national resource is utilized.

NOTE: The statement was released at Hannibal, Mo.

St. Louis, Missouri

Remarks on Arrival at the City.
August 24, 1979

THE PRESIDENT. Good morning, everybody. Good morning. How many of you agree with me that we live in the greatest nation on Earth? [*Applause*]

For the last week, Rosalynn and Amy and I, along with the other passengers on board the *Delta Queen,* have had one of the most remarkable and enjoyable weeks of our lives. We've not only seen the beauty of the Midwest—the lovely land, the hills, the mountains—we've also seen one of the mightiest rivers on Earth that brings prosperity to this part of the country and gives us a reminder of what our history has been. But the most important thing to us has been to see the thousands and thousands of people who've come down to the banks of the Mississippi to make us feel welcome, to express your respect for our great country, and to take us into your arms and into your hearts as the President and the First Family of our Nation.

Amy has had a good time. Rosalynn has had a good time. And so have I. We hate to see the trip end, but if it has to end somewhere, it could not possibly end in a more beautiful place and a more exciting place than under this tremendous arch here in St. Louis.

It's my privilege, by the way, to announce the 10 millionth visitor to the top of the Gateway Arch, who was selected this morning immediately before we arrived at this historic St. Louis site. His name is Bill Bund from Alton, Illinois, the 10 millionth visitor to your beautiful arch. I think Bill is here somewhere. Here is the 10 millionth visitor over here. Congratulations, Bill.

I'd like to say just a few words to you now about our country. We've got so much to be thankful for. Sometimes we forget how much God has blessed us in the United States of America. He's given us some of the richest land on Earth, and we've seen it on both sides of the Mississippi River during the last week. This is indeed the breadbasket of the world. And if there's one tremendous, strategic advantage that our Nation presently has and which will always be a weapon for peace and for the good will and the well-being of people in our own country and throughout the world, it's the food and the fiber produced in this tremendous Mississippi River basin because of the wonderful land that God has given us. I've had a chance to speak to a lot of farmers on the way down and to express my thanks to them from the bottom of my heart as President of our country.

We've also seen the tremendous advantages that we have of a good transportation system with the river, and I believe in the future we can, with a good energy policy, have a much better transportation system, no matter what kind of river we want to use for goods or for people.

We also have a nation in which we can enjoy individual freedom, the right to be individuals, to be ourselves, to be different, to make our own decisions, to control our own government, and to develop in the best way that we can according to our own abilities and our own talents. This is one of the things that we sometimes forget, but I believe it's very important for us never to forget the freedom and the democracy that we have; a free enterprise system which lets us compete and lets us have innovation and lets us have new ideas to overcome problems.

So, we are blessed with the greatest nation on Earth. Unified, nothing can stand in our way to resolving problems, overcoming difficulties, and answering serious questions.

In the past our Nation has always been able to do this as we have been faced with serious trials and temptations that threaten our country. In the First World War, the Second World War, the Great Depression, Americans recognized the threat to our country. We united together and we overcame it.

Now we have a serious threat to our country that's not nearly so easy to understand and so far we've not united enough to overcome it. And that's the threat to our Nation's security brought about by excessive dependence on foreign oil. We import about half the oil we use, and along with oil that comes in from the Middle East, we also import unemployment, and we also import inflation.

We must do something about the energy challenge that faces us. There are two things that we can do. One thing is to save energy. Every American, every American can save energy in your own life, in your own family, in transportation, in your homes, on your job. This is something the government cannot do for you, but there are dozens of things that each one of you and each one of us can decide to do day in and day out that will be beneficial to our country, and will also give us, in the same process, a better life. It doesn't make it good for us or more enjoyable for us when we waste what God has given us. So, I ask all of you to help us conserve energy.

The second thing I'd like to ask you to do is to join in with me in helping to produce more energy in our own country. The Mideast OPEC nations all put together have less than 5 percent of the energy reserves in our world. The United States has 25 percent of all the energy, energy reserves in the world. So, what we must do is to produce more of our Nation's energy—oil, gas, coal, geothermal, with our tremendous cropland for gasohol, use more solar power. This can make us secure in energy.

Now the Congress has before it a windfall profits tax, which is being opposed by the oil lobby and which must be passed. Oil prices are going up in the future, and the basic question is: Who is going to get the tremendous profits that come in that are unearned? The oil companies have not earned this profit, but they want to keep it. So, with a windfall profits tax we can take these profits and give them back to the American people for a better transportation system, to help the low- and middle-income families pay the increased cost of fuel, to insulate our homes, to have

a better way to produce synthetic fuels—all these benefits can come to us when the Congress passes a windfall profits tax.

We can have energy security. So, I want to ask you to do two things in summary: One is save energy, and the other one is work with me and the United States Congress to overcome the oil lobby, to pass the windfall profits tax, to make our Nation energy-secure.

With a strong nation we can stay at peace; we can keep our Nation secure. And if you'll help me, I will help you and the Members of Congress here with me to pass a windfall profits tax, to make the greatest nation on Earth even greater in the future. Will you do that? Will you help me? [*Applause*]

Thank you all very much, thank you.

Rosalynn, do you want to say a word? Rosalynn would like to say just a word.

MRS. CARTER. We've had a wonderful trip on the beautiful Mississippi River. The countryside is spectacular. I believe and I wish that every person in our country could take the trip that we have had and just see what we have in our country. It is so beautiful. We've enjoyed it. Amy has enjoyed it. The people along the way, you, too, have made it very special for us.

It's a week that Jimmy and I both will never forget. Thank you all for coming out today. We love you.

THE PRESIDENT. Amy? Say hi. All you have to do is say one word.

AMY CARTER. Hi. Hi.

THE PRESIDENT. How's that for a short speech? Thank you very much, everybody. We love every one of you. Thank you.

We'll come down and shake a few hands—the ones we can reach.

NOTE: The President spoke at 9:10 a.m. at the docking site of the *Delta Queen.*

Department of Energy

Remarks at the Swearing In of
Charles W. Duncan, Jr., as Secretary.
August 24, 1979

THE PRESIDENT. There's no way to over-emphasize the importance of this event, because of the significance to every American, in fact, every person, almost, throughout the world, accrued from the performance of duty as Secretary of Energy.

Fifteen years ago, the average American didn't think much about the problems that might arise from the energy question or the energy situation. But recently, in the last few years, this has become a burning issue for every person.

Our country has been well served, and I would like to ask James Schlesinger first to come to the stage.

No one who hears my voice could argue with the statement that Jim Schlesinger is a man of intelligence, competence, and also the utmost integrity. He's a man who served our Nation well in one of the most difficult jobs imaginable, that is, the formation of and the administration of the Department of Energy. He's done this to the credit of himself, my own administration, the United States Government, and the people of our country.

In addition to that, he has served well in other posts of extreme importance to our country. In time of peace and in time of war, Jim Schlesinger has always been available to a President who needed his superb capabilities to meet a difficult issue or to answer difficult problems or to solve difficult questions.

Jim has been the Secretary of Defense, as you well know, and his statements then and his actions, his recommendations have proven in the last few years of recent history to have been wise and sound.

I particularly want to congratulate him for his service as our chief intelligence officer when he was Director of Central Intelligence.

In 1953, President Harry Truman initiated an award which I would like to make to Jim Schlesinger. This is the National Security Award, given to a person who has contributed notably to our Nation's security in the intricate, highly secret realm of intelligence. I'd like to read the citation:

"The United States of America to all who shall see these presents, greeting. This is to certify that the President of the United States of America has awarded the National Security Medal to James R. Schlesinger for outstanding contribution to the national intelligence effort. Given under my hand in the City of Washington, this 24th day of August, 1979." Signed Jimmy Carter, President of the United States of America.

Jim, congratulations to you.

I see an expression of approval and appreciation on the faces of those who observe the ceremony, and I see an expression of relief and anticipation on Jim Schlesinger's face—[*laughter*]—as we approach the next ceremony.

One of the very early acts of my unofficial life after I was elected President was to invite Jim Schlesinger to come down to Plains and talk to me about the very serious problem that our Nation was experiencing in not having a national energy policy, in having more than 50 separate agencies of the Federal Government responsible for the administration of various, sometimes conflicting energy laws. We didn't have a Department of

Energy, and I have to tell you that it was not Jim Schlesinger's first choice as a Cabinet officer to be the Secretary of Energy. He recognized the complexity and the challenge of it, and also the uncertainty of proposing to the Congress the creation of a major new Cabinet-level department. But he agreed to serve, and he has served well.

Last November after a year and half of intense effort in the Congress, we had approved about 65 percent of the energy legislation that had been proposed. At that time Dr. Schlesinger came and said that he thought it was time for him to step down since he had done that job, that he had scars on him from all directions and that he thought it was time for someone, perhaps, to take over with a fresh approach, and I asked him to stay on longer.

Last January, he came back to me at the beginning of the session and said, again, that he was ready to step down, that he thought he had done his job as well as he could. Since we had not passed any legislation then or even evolved a followup proposal concerning oil, I asked him to stay again until we could evolve a program concerning oil and avoid the increasing delay that was hurting our Nation at that time. He agreed to do so. And now that we've proposed to the Congress a very fine proposal for dealing with the oil issue, I have finally agreed to let Jim Schlesinger step down in this post.

Obviously the choice of his successor is one that has been a very important one for me, and I've chosen someone who fulfills every possible requirement for the job. This is an issue that is becoming of ever more important consideration for Americans.

When I made my Sunday evening speech July 15th, I said that the strength of America lay ultimately in the inexhaustible resource of the American people.

I've just finished a 7-day trip down the Mississippi River, and I have been reinspired with the commitment of Americans to deal in a confident way with the future, to unite among themselves, to conserve energy to the utmost of their own ability and also to see hammered out here in Washington a comprehensive series of legislative proposals that will give us a sound basis for a complete energy policy in the future.

There is no limit, in my opinion, to what we in our country can do if our people are united. I've just written all 6,000 chief executive officers of the cities and towns and counties of our Nation. Many have acted on their own initiative; more will do so in the future.

Our energy security is threatened. As you know, we still import too much oil from foreign countries, about half the oil that we use. So, we must conserve; we must produce more oil and other forms of energy in our country—solar energy; we must also increase, as you know, the production of geothermal supplies, synthetic fuels, including gasohol; make sure that nuclear power is produced in a safe fashion; and insist upon a better transportation system and a means by which we can deal with the poor families, who are especially afflicted by the rapidly increasing and uncontrollable cost of oil.

The inflation figures issued just in the last few hours, when broken down by component parts, show that about one-half of the increase in our inflation rate is caused by increase in energy costs. This is such a challenging and complex issue that we absolutely must have the finest possible administrator for this increasingly important position.

I think the prices of oil and gas must go toward the market price. We have taken steps in the Congress to decontrol the prices of both natural gas and oil in a carefully phased, predictable way. This has resulted and is resulting in a fairly rapid increase in the cost of energy to mirror worldwide considerations over which we have no control.

I know that many of you here today represent the energy industry, and I would like to call on you this afternoon to put aside differences and to join with me and with the new Secretary of Energy and with the Members of Congress in supporting the proposals that we have laid before the Congress for the benefit of our country. I would like to ask the representatives of the oil and natural gas industry, and others, to support the windfall profits tax, which has been carefully devised for equity and fairness, which will give us a basis for becoming more energy-secure.

I know that you have and all Americans have a great confidence in Charles Duncan, who will now be sworn in as Secretary of Energy. He has served in the most distinguished way in the private enterprise system of our country, a superb manager, sound judgment, great intelligence, a good educational background, one who understands the complexities of our social and economic system throughout this country. In addition to that, in Government, he has built an admirable record as a Deputy Secretary of Defense. His own boss, the Secretary of Defense, Harold Brown, has told me many times

that Charles Duncan was completely qualified to be the Secretary of Defense or for any other job including, he has told me, the President of the United States. [*Laughter*] I'm not sure which job Harold Brown placed on top. [*Laughter*]

But I am grateful to Charles Duncan, who is here this afternoon to be sworn in to this important position.

And now, Judge Patricia Wald will administer the oath of office to Charles Duncan as the Secretary of Energy for the United States of America. I'm very proud to participate in this ceremony. Thank you very much.

[*At this point, United States Circuit Judge Patricia M. Wald administered the oath of office.*]

SECRETARY DUNCAN. *Mr. President, Judge Wald, distinguished guests, and ladies and gentlemen:*

Thank you, Mr. President, for those very kind remarks, and I want to thank all of you for having joined my family and me on this most significant day in my life.

As I look around the room, I see so many people that I know so well that it's impossible to make the personal comments that I'd like to, but I'd be very remiss if I didn't say to my former colleagues in the Department of Defense, so many of whom are here, that the last 2½ years have been the most interesting that I've spent. The Nation is indeed fortunate to have so many capable and dedicated men and women, both military and civilian, managing our national defense. And I say to you, Harold Brown, my mentor and my friend, that my relationship with you and the personal pleasure of working with you has exceeded my greatest expectations.

And I would also be remiss if I didn't say to the many people here from the Department of Energy that I look forward to working with you and all of your excellent associates. I'm especially pleased to see Jim Schlesinger here. The President has articulated very well the American attitude towards Jim Schlesinger. Jim has done an outstanding job during a very difficult period. He has had to organize a complex new department while simultaneously attacking one of the most difficult problems facing our Nation. We're all indebted to Secretary Schlesinger.

There are also many of my personal friends here, and many of these people have traveled a long way. My family and I are most appreciative to all of you for being here.

Mr. President, I'm deeply honored to have been selected by you to be your Secretary of Energy. This is a terribly important responsibility, and I accept it with humility. The problems are enormous. We must reduce our dependence on imported oil. We must move forward aggressively on programs of conservation and energy efficiency. We must utilize the genius of American technology to make use of the Sun and other renewable resources, and we must and can find environmentally sound ways to utilize our tremendous domestic energy resources.

In trying to do these things, Mr. President, and implementing your energy policy, I plan to maintain an active and an open dialog with all elements of American society that have an interest in energy matters, with public interest groups, consumer groups, environmental groups, labor groups, industry and business groups, all interested publics.

This is an effort that cannot be accomplished by the Secretary of Energy alone or by any single department of government. This is an effort that requires the closest possible cooperation within your total Administration, with the Congress and, most importantly, it requires the continuing cooperation and support of the American people.

The energy problems directly impact all Americans. They affect the very fabric of our economic structure. The successful management and resolution of these problems requires the involvement of individual Americans making millions of individual decisions, to understand the importance of conservation, the importance of energy efficiency, and the importance of developing alternative energy sources.

The problems and the responsibilities are huge, but I want you to know, Mr. President, that I approach my assignment with a sense of optimism, dedication of purpose, enthusiasm, and with a commitment to do my very best. I'm convinced that we can find the right balance in our answers to these problems to assure all Americans a safe and secure energy future.

And lastly, Mr. President, I thank you for giving me this opportunity to serve my country. Thank you very much.

THE PRESIDENT. And now since we've had the thermostat turned so low for this ceremony, we can turn it back up. [*Laughter*]

All of you are welcome to come over to the reception, where you can personally shake hands with Charles and Anne and his family.

Charles, if you don't mind, you might follow me through the door so that you can stand in place so that all of you can express your congratulations and your pledge of support to him.

Thank you very much.

NOTE: The President spoke at 3:39 p.m. in the East Room at the White House.

Id al-Fitr

Message of the President.   August 24, 1979

On this joyous holiday of Id al-Fitr, ending the fast of Ramadan, Rosalynn and I extend our warmest good wishes to all of our fellow citizens of the Muslim faith.

The observance of your traditional religious ceremonies strengthens the moral and spiritual values of your Faith and thereby deepens our nation's commitment to our highest principles.

At this critical time, we join together in praying for a lasting peace that will bring justice and freedom to all people.

JIMMY CARTER

Digest of Other White House Announcements

The following listing includes the President's public schedule and other items of general interest announced by the White House Press Office and not included elsewhere in this issue.

August 20

The White House announced that the President will answer questions from the public in a live, 2-hour radio broadcast from the Oval Office on Saturday, October 13. The program will be produced by National Public Radio and will be heard on most NPR member stations from 1 to 3 p.m. (EDT) on October 13. Anyone who wishes to talk with the President is requested to send a postcard to: "Ask the President," P.O. Box 19369, Washington, D.C. 20036, listing name, address, and telephone number. The questions a caller would like to ask should *not* be given on the card. Just prior to the broadcast, NPR will choose callers at random from the postcards and connect the persons selected with the President as lines become available. Susan Stamberg, cohost of "All Things Considered," will anchor the program for NPR and will introduce each caller to the President and the radio audience.

The White House announced that Ray Jenkins, editor of the Montgomery Advertiser and Alabama Journal, will join the White House staff in early September as a Special Assistant to the President. He will work in the Press Office and will assist the President and the Press Secretary in the full range of responsibilities of the Press Office.

August 24

The President returned to the White House following his trip down the Mississippi River. Later in the afternoon, the President went to Camp David, Md.

NOMINATIONS SUBMITTED TO THE SENATE

The following list does not include promotions of members of the Uniformed Services, nominations to the Service Academies, or nominations of Foreign Service officers.

Submitted August 20, 1979

PAUL A. VOLCKER, of New Jersey, to be United States Alternate Governor of the International Monetary Fund for a term of 5 years, vice G. William Miller.

NOMINATIONS—Continued

Submitted August 20—Continued

STEPHEN Low, of Ohio, a Foreign Service officer of Class one, to be Ambassador Extraordinary and Plenipotentiary of the United States of America to the Federal Republic of Nigeria.

CHECKLIST OF WHITE HOUSE PRESS RELEASES

The following listing contains releases of the White House Press Office which are not included in this issue.

Released August 20, 1979

Biographical data: Ray Jenkins, appointed as Special Assistant to the President

CHECKLIST—Continued

Released August 21, 1979

News conference: on the Middle East trip of Ambassador Robert S. Strauss, Personal Representative of the President to the Middle East peace negotiations—by Secretary of State Cyrus R. Vance and Ambassador Strauss

ACTS APPROVED BY THE PRESIDENT

NOTE: No acts approved by the President were received by the Office of the Federal Register during the period covered by this issue.

PRESIDENTIAL DOCUMENTS

Week Ending Friday, August 31, 1979

Campobello Conference on Peace and Human Rights

Message Accepting the Conference's Human Rights Award Medal.   August 25, 1979

I am deeply honored to accept this fine medal and regret that I cannot greet each of you in person who are participating in the Second Annual Armand Hammer Conference on "Peace and Human Rights—Human Rights and Peace." There is no cause with which I am prouder to be identified than that of fostering human rights for all people. I accept this honor not as a personal tribute, but as an affirmation of our effort to support the brave and decent people everywhere who struggle for human dignity, often against daunting odds.

It is especially fitting that your meeting this year is on a beautiful island, forever associated with Franklin D. Roosevelt and his wife Eleanor. Their lives and works embodied a selfless quest for peace and human rights, not only for their fellow Americans, but for all humankind.

Last December, the month of the first Armand Hammer Conference in Oslo, we celebrated the 30th Anniversary of the Universal Declaration of Human Rights, the work of the United Nations Commission on Human Rights chaired by that great humanitarian, Eleanor Roosevelt. On that occasion I described the Universal Declaration as a beacon—a guide to a future of personal security, political freedom and social justice. The Universal Declaration remains, as Mrs. Roosevelt said, "a common standard of achievement of all peoples of all nations."

Organizations such as the International Institute of Human Rights have helped to ensure that this beacon has remained an undimmed source of hope and inspiration of our fellow humans suffering deprivation and repression. No group of individuals has contributed more to the achievement of these standards over the years than the men and women participating in this Campobello Conference. Nobel Prize winners, distinguished statesmen and women, parliamentarians, scholars, international civil servants—all have been tireless participants in the struggle to achieve the great dream of universal human rights.

But human rights cannot flourish in a world at war or threatened by war, and so peace remains a crucial goal for all who seek human rights for all people. Last June in Vienna President Brezhnev and I signed the second Strategic Arms Limitation Treaty. This is a key instrument for strengthening the prospects for peace and for increasing the vitally important understanding between the nuclear superpowers. Doctor Hammer and others have worked arduously for many years to foster that understanding.

You have my warmest good wishes for a successful conference. I know your deliberations will do much to advance both human rights and international peace, and I salute you for your devotion to these noble causes.

JIMMY CARTER

NOTE: The conference was held at the International Peace Park on Campobello Island, New Brunswick, Canada. On August 25, Dr. Lincoln Bloomfield of the National Security Council staff read the President's message to conference participants and accepted the medal on the President's behalf.

Death of Lord Louis Mountbatten

Statement by the President.   August 27, 1979

I am profoundly shocked and saddened by the tragic and violent death of Earl Mountbatten. In peace and in war, he was a leader of monumental ability.

Here in the United States, his memory is enshrined for the paramount role he played in achieving victory for the Allied Forces during World War II. We mourn his passing and that of the two youngsters who died with him this morning.

I have expressed my sincere condolences and those of the American people to Her Majesty the Queen, to Prince Philip, and to Prime Minister Thatcher in this time of great loss.

NOTE: Earl Mountbatten of Burma, military strategist, statesman, and member of the British Royal Family, was killed when his fishing boat was blown up off the coast of northwest Ireland by members of the Provisional IRA. His grandson and another youth were also killed in the explosion.

Budget Deferrals

Message to the Congress.   August 27, 1979

To the Congress of the United States:

In accordance with the Impoundment Control Act of 1974, I herewith report three new deferrals of budget authority totalling $30.1 million. These items involve human development services in the Department of Health, Education, and Welfare, emergency refugee and migration assistance in the Department of State, and the National Commission on Social Security.

The details of the deferrals are contained in the attached reports.

JIMMY CARTER

The White House,
   August 27, 1979.

NOTE: The attachments detailing the deferrals are printed in the FEDERAL REGISTER of August 30, 1979.

United States Citizens Living Abroad

Letter to the Speaker of the House and the Chairman of the Senate Foreign Relations Committee.   August 27, 1979

Dear Mr. Speaker: (Dear Mr. Chairman:)

The enclosed report, prepared in compliance with Section 611 of Public Law 95–426 identifies six Federal statutory and regulatory provisions which discriminate against United States citizens living abroad. The Executive branch has evaluated those provisions and has concluded that changes are warranted in order to resolve certain inequities involving citizenship and veterans and social security benefits. The report also reviews twenty-eight other issues raised by some Americans living abroad concerning their rights and obligations as U.S. citizens.

This report is the result of a painstaking and earnest review of the many legal provisions affecting our citizens residing abroad. The test for discrimination used was to compare the effect of those provisions on U.S. citizens residing abroad with U.S. citizens living in the United States.

I believe the report responds in a responsible manner to the concern about the situation of Americans residing abroad. I am aware that section 407 of H.R. 3363 just recently enacted, broadens the scope of the report to include the "competitive disadvantage" of Americans abroad compared to nationals of other major trading partners and extends the report's transmittal date until January 20, 1980. Because this report was completed and awaiting my transmittal at the time section 407 was enacted, I believe it best to transmit it now to the Congress for its consideration. I have, moreover, requested the Secretary of the Treasury to prepare an additional report on the taxation of American citizens living abroad compared to the treatment by our major trading partners of their citizens living abroad and to identify any competitive disadvantages that may ensue.

The Administration will continue to work to resolve discriminatory provisions in regulations and in agency procedures affecting Americans living abroad; I am hopeful that inequities which are subject to legislative remedy will likewise be resolved.

Sincerely,

JIMMY CARTER

NOTE: This is the text of identical letters addressed to Thomas P. O'Neill, Jr., Speaker of the House of Representatives, and Frank Church, chairman of the Senate Foreign Relations Committee.

The 27-page report is entitled "Equitable Treatment of United States Citizens Living Abroad."

Employment and Training Report of the President

Message to the Congress Transmitting the Report.   August 27, 1979

To the Congress of the United States:

I am transmitting to you the 17th annual report pertaining to employment and occupational requirements, resources, uses, and training, as required by section 127(a) of the Comprehensive Employment and Training Act (CETA) Amendments of 1978.

This *Employment and Training Report of the President* also includes a report on how social services, vocational education, and other programs administered by the Secretary of Health, Education, and Welfare are being integrated into State and local CETA activities, as required by section 127(b) of the 1978 CETA Amendments; a number of special reports that respond to additional reporting requirements in the amended CETA; a report on services for veterans, as required by the Vietnam Era Veterans' Readjustment Assistance Act; and a response to the requirements of section 4(f)(2)(B) of the Full Employment and Balanced Growth Act of 1978.

JIMMY CARTER

The White House,
    August 27, 1979.

NOTE: The report is entitled "Employment and Training Report of the President" (Government Printing Office, 398 pages).

United States Ambassador to the Kingdom of Tonga and Tuvalu

Nomination of John P. Condon.
August 28, 1979

The President today announced that he will nominate John P. Condon, currently

U.S. Ambassador to the Dominion of Fiji, to serve concurrently as Ambassador to the Kingdom of Tonga and to Tuvalu.

Department of State

Nomination of Thomas M. Tracy To Be an Assistant Secretary.   August 28, 1979

The President today announced that he will nominate Thomas M. Tracy, of Fort Lauderdale, Fla., to be Assistant Secretary of State for Administration. He would replace John M. Thomas, resigned.

Tracy is currently counselor for administration at the American Embassy in Bonn, Germany.

He was born July 8, 1936, in Great Barrington, Mass. He received a B.A. from Colgate University in 1958, an M.A. from Stanford University in 1959, and an M.B.A. from Columbia University in 1973.

Tracy joined the Foreign Service in 1960 and was posted in Juarez, Birmingham, London, and at the State Department. From 1973 to 1975, he was administrative officer in Brussels. He was counselor for administration in Moscow from 1975 until 1978, when he became counselor for administration in Bonn.

National Advisory Council on Adult Education

Appointment of 10 Members. August 28, 1979

The President today announced the appointment of 10 persons as members of the National Advisory Council on Adult Education. They are:

LILY LEE CHEN, director of special projects and resource development for the Los Angeles County Department of Public Social Services;

REVA CRAWFORD, of Tahlequah, Okla., director of adult education for the Cherokee Nation;

ANDREW G. DONALDSON, associate director of the State University of New York Educational Opportunity Center in Manhattan;

DON DUTTON, professor and coordinator of adult and continuing education at the University of Arkansas;

MAXIE C. JACKSON, JR., director of the Center for Urban Affairs and assistant professor in the department of urban and metropolitan studies at Michigan State University's College of Urban Development;

MILDRED T. NICHOLS, supervisor of the Career Counseling Service of the Rhode Island Department of Education;

BERNADETTE PARDO PHILLIPS, public affairs producer for WPLG Television in Miami, Fla.;

LEONARD SCHNEIDERMAN, dean of the school of social service at Indiana University;

BOBBIE L. WALDEN, director of the Community Education Project and In-Service Training in Adult Competency Education for the Alabama State Department of Education; and

JAMES A. WOODS, dean of Boston College Evening College of Arts, Sciences, and Business Administration.

Advisory Panel on Financing Elementary and Secondary Education

Appointment of 15 Members and Designation of Chairman.   August 28, 1979

The President today announced the appointment of 15 persons as members of the Advisory Panel on Financing Elementary and Secondary Education. They are:

CHARLES S. BENSON, a professor of education at the University of California at Berkeley, an expert on the economics of education;

THEODORE M. BLACK, SR., a retired Army lieutenant colonel who serves on the New York State Board of Regents;

JOHN E. COONS, a professor of law at the University of California at Berkeley, and co-principal investigator on the Childhood and Government Project at Berkeley;

JOSEPH O. GARCIA, director of the California School Finance Reform Project at San Diego State University School of Education;

ROBERT GRAHAM, Governor of Florida, who was chairman of the Florida Senate's education committee from 1972 to 1975 and has also served as a member of the National Commission to Reform Secondary Schools;

TERRY HERNDON, executive director of the National Education Association;

EDWARD T. HUGHES, auxiliary bishop of Philadelphia, Pa., and former chairman of the Association of School Superintendents of the U.S. Catholic Conference;

VICTORIA LEDERBERG, a professor of psychology at Rhode Island College and member of the Rhode Island General Assembly (also designated Chairman of this Panel);

DOROTHY L. MATTISON, a public school music teacher with the Sullivan County (Tenn.) school board and a member of the Bristol, Tenn., city council;

JAMES A. MCDERMOTT, a Seattle, Wash., psychiatrist and consultant to the Washington State Department of Social and Health Services Division of Juvenile Rehabilitation and King County Juvenile Court;

ALBERT SHANKER, president of the American Federation of Teachers and a vice president of the AFL–CIO;

CARL SHARIF, assistant to Mayor Kenneth Gibson of Newark, N.J., a former consultant on the development of Neighborhood Education Development Centers (storefront schools);

WILLIAM SIMMONS, superintendent of Wayne County (Mich.) Intermediate School District, and an adjunct professor of education at Wayne State University;

MARGARET C. SIMMS, chairman of the economics department at Atlanta University and director of the Institute for Urban Affairs;

CAROLYN WARNER, State superintendent of public instruction for the State of Arizona.

International Exposition on Energy

Message to the Congress Transmitting a Proposal for Federal Participation. August 28, 1979

To the Congress of the United States:

In accordance with statutory requirements, I am transmitting to you my proposal for Federal participation in the International Exposition on Energy to be held in Knoxville, Tennessee from May through October 1982. The Congress has already received an FY 1980 budget amendment request, in the amount of $20.8 million, to support Federal participation. The Department of Commerce is submitting the authorizing legislation as well.

It is my determination that Federal participation is in the national interest. The Exposition will provide for an international exchange of ideas on energy development, innovative energy technology, energy conservation, solar energy, synthetic fuels and other subjects important to the national interest. Moreover, the Exposition will stimulate tourist travel to the United States, thereby improving our balance of trade, promote international cultural exchange and accelerate capital growth and investment in the Knoxville area.

My proposal includes all statutory requirements:

(1) assurance that the Exposition meets all criteria for recognition and has been recognized;

(2) a statement that the Exposition has been registered by the Bureau of International Expositions on April 27, 1977; and

(3) a plan prepared by the Commerce Department and other interested

departments for Federal participation.

The plan for Federal participation provides for construction of a pavilion and preparation of energy-related exhibits.

I urge that this plan be given prompt and favorable consideration by the Congress.

JIMMY CARTER

The White House,
    August 28, 1979.

Death of Samuel I. Newhouse

Statement by the President.   August 29, 1979

With the death of Samuel I. Newhouse, this country has lost a dedicated and enterprising publisher whose work in the business of news spanned most of his 84 years.

He was born in a tenement to parents who were immigrants to this country, but created one of the largest publishing and communications organizations in the United States. He exemplified those qualities which make this country great.

Rosalynn and I extend our sympathies to his wife and the other members of his family.

Columbus Day, 1979

Proclamation 4676.   August 29, 1979

By the President of the United States of America

A Proclamation

Four hundred and eighty-seven years have passed since an Italian navigator in the service of Spain left the Old World to find the New. Christopher Columbus was determined to test an audacious theory: to reach the East, sail west. On the morning of October 12, 1492, with ninety men in three small ships, he sailed into immortality.

The voyage of this intrepid explorer marked the convergence of American and world history. His discovery opened a new age—an age that gave the world a new center.

We are the inheritors of Columbus' legacy. As a nation which has always striven for the same qualities as the Great Navigator, we must continue the search for new horizons.

It is fitting that, on the observance of this October 12, we once again recall to mind Columbus' extraordinary voyage and, in the spirit of that undertaking, rededicate ourselves to that which is best and most courageous in us.

In tribute to Columbus' achievement, the Congress of the United States of America, by joint resolution approved April 30, 1934 (48 Stat. 657), as modified by the Act of June 28, 1968 (82 Stat. 250), requested the President to proclaim the second Monday in October of each year as Columbus Day.

Now, THEREFORE, I, JIMMY CARTER, President of the United States of America, do hereby designate Monday, October 8, 1979, as Columbus Day; and I invite the people of this Nation to observe that day in schools, churches, and other suitable places with appropriate ceremonies in his honor.

I also direct that the flag of the United States of America be displayed on all public buildings on the appointed day in memory of Christopher Columbus.

IN WITNESS WHEREOF, I have hereunto set my hand this twenty-ninth day of August, in the year of our Lord nineteen hundred seventy-nine, and of the Independence of the United States of America the two hundred and fourth.

JIMMY CARTER

[Filed with the Office of the Federal Register, 12:08 p.m., August 30, 1979]
NOTE: The text of the proclamation was released on August 30.

Leif Erikson Day, 1979

Proclamation 4677. August 29, 1979

By the President of the United States of America

A Proclamation

From time immemorial, explorers have sought new frontiers to explore and new worlds to conquer. Their insatiable curiosity, their willingness to face new challenges remain inspirations to the modern world.

Few people can surpass the courage and accomplishments of Leif Erikson, a remarkable representative of a remarkable people. His voyage west to uncharted waters epitomized the virtues of bravery, skill and imagination.

In honoring this great Norseman, we honor the representative of a people whose respect for law and whose early devotion to representative government mirrors our own commitments. We honor, too, Americans of Scandinavian descent, who have made such notable contributions to the development of the United States.

To express our respect for the accomplishments of Leif Erikson and his followers, the Congress of the United States, by joint resolution approved September 2, 1964 (78 Stat. 849, 36 U.S.C. 169) designated October 9 in each year as Leif Erikson Day.

NOW, THEREFORE, I, JIMMY CARTER, President of the United States of America, do hereby proclaim Tuesday, October 9, 1979, as Leif Erikson Day, and I direct the appropriate government officials to display the flag of the United States on all government buildings that day.

I also invite the people of the United States to honor the memory of Leif Erikson on that day by holding appropriate ceremonies in suitable places throughout the land.

IN WITNESS WHEREOF, I have hereunto set my hand this twenty-ninth day of August, in the year of our Lord nineteen hundred seventy-nine, and of the Independence of the United States of America the two hundred and fourth.

JIMMY CARTER

[Filed with the Office of the Federal Register, 12:09 p.m., August 30, 1979]
NOTE: The text of the proclamation was released on August 30.

White Cane Safety Day, 1979

Proclamation 4678. August 29, 1979

By the President of the United States of America

A Proclamation

Most of us take it for granted that we can walk unaided through a crowded store or street. We give little thought to our freedom to come and go as we please, yet there are over six million Americans whose vision is so impaired that every corner is a place of danger.

For many of these people, help comes in the form of a white cane. This eight-ounce, long white stick is as useful as it is simple. For a blind person, it is a kind of beacon. In the hands of someone trained in its skillful use, the white cane becomes an extension of the body, providing assurance that the path ahead is clear.

Upon encountering someone using a white cane, those of us who are fortunate enough to see well should slow our pace for a moment to notice if the person seems to need assistance. Offering an arm to a blind person crossing the street or guiding him or her around a barrier requires only a few moments. Indeed, just yielding the right of way to a blind person can make the difference between a pleasant and safe excursion or a frustrating and possibly hazardous one. Motorists, cyclists, and joggers should be especially alert to the person with a white cane.

To heighten public awareness of the importance of the white cane to the independence and safety of blind and visually handicapped Americans, the Congress, by a joint resolution approved October 6, 1964 (78 Stat. 1003; 36 U.S.C. 169d) has authorized the President to proclaim October 15 of each year as White Cane Safety Day.

Now, Therefore, I, Jimmy Carter, President of the United States of America, do hereby proclaim October 15, 1979, as White Cane Safety Day.

On this occasion, I urge all Americans to consider the needs and accomplishments of those who successfully overcome the difficulties imposed by visual disability and blindness. Such individuals merit recognition and respect for the special efforts they must make to function independently in a world where the ability to see is taken for granted.

In Witness Whereof, I have hereunto set my hand this twenty-ninth day of August, in the year of our Lord nineteen hundred seventy-nine, and of the Independence of the United States of America the two hundred and fourth.

Jimmy Carter

[Filed with the Office of the Federal Register, 12:10 p.m., August 30, 1979]
note: The text of the proclamation was released on August 30.

Labor Day

Statement by the President.   August 30, 1979

Labor Day has traditionally been a time of rest and relaxation, the last long weekend of summer. But it is also a time to reflect on our accomplishments and challenges.

We can be thankful and proud of the hard work that has built the most productive economy in world history. We can be thankful for the brave men and women in American labor whose past struggles won fundamental rights for American workers. They strengthened our democratic system and enlarged the freedom of opportunity for succeeding generations.

Today is an appropriate time to acknowledge our recent accomplishments. This is the third Labor Day of my Presidency. In these years, we have strengthened important health, safety, pension, and minimum wage protections for American workers.

Today, almost 100 million men and women have jobs in our Nation—8½ million more than when I took office. This dynamic expansion of our economy has made a crucial difference for those who suffer most from unemployment—minorities, women, and young people.

Nonetheless, we still face difficult challenges that threaten to erode some of these hard-won gains. The most serious challenge is inflation—which erodes the paychecks of all working Americans. Working together, we can forge a long-term partnership that will reduce inflation and keep it down. We must also face our energy challenge, conserve the energy we use now and develop new supplies of energy to fuel our farms and factories, to move our goods and people, to provide the warmth and light for our homes.

Our Nation can surmount these problems. Throughout our history, American workers have overcome challenges in ways that brought new progress and prosperity. By confronting our current challenges we can provide better lives for all Americans.

Americans value work and the opportunity to contribute to their communities and their Nation. Let us pause today to give thanks for the abundance of our blessings and to rededicate ourselves to meeting the challenges of our time.

Federal Civilian and Military Pay Increases

Message to the Congress Transmitting the Federal Pay Comparability Alternative Plan. August 31, 1979

To the Congress of the United States:

Under the Pay Comparability Act of 1970, an adjustment in Federal white collar pay will be required on October 1, 1979.

I have reviewed the report of my Pay Agent and recommendations of the Advisory Committee on Federal Pay relative to a pay adjustment. Their findings indicate that an average 10.41 percent increase, at a cost of about $6 billion, would be required to achieve full comparability with the private sector.

However, pay comparability for Federal civilian employees and the military must be viewed in the light of the current economic situation. Inflation continues to be the single greatest threat to our economy and is a national problem of foremost concern. In considering last year's Federal pay increase, I relied heavily on the pay standards the Administration was considering to guide decisions of all employers in determining pay increases. I am continuing that practice for this year's increase.

Accordingly, under the authority given to me by the Pay Act to propose an alternative pay adjustment which I consider appropriate in the light of "economic conditions affecting the general welfare," I have determined that an alternative plan consisting of an overall 7 percent increase and a partial exemption from the full effect of the limitation for the lowest-salaried civilian employees is appropriate for the Federal increase. This increase will be within the pay standard being developed by the Council on Wage and Price Stability that will apply to all employees in the country for 1980. It is somewhat higher than the increase anticipated by my 1980 budget. However, last January when my budget was submitted, we expected significantly lower rates of inflation than we have actually experienced. I believe that the loyal and outstanding service given to the country by the Government's civilian and military personnel warrants recognition of that changed circumstance and of the new pay standards for 1980.

Accordingly, I strongly urge the Congress to support the alternative plan which is attached.

JIMMY CARTER

The White House,
August 31, 1979.

FEDERAL PAY COMPARABILITY
ALTERNATIVE PLAN

Because of economic conditions affecting the general welfare, I hereby transmit to Congress the following alternative plan, in accordance with 5 U.S.C. 5305(c)(1):

The adjustment in rates of pay of each Federal statutory pay system to become effective on the first day of the first applicable pay period that begins on or after October 1, 1979, shall be limited to a 7 percent increase at each grade in lieu of the adjustment determined under the comparability procedure set forth in 5 U.S.C. 5305(a)–(b); *Provided, however,* that the full adjustment determined under the comparability procedure shall take effect to the extent it does not increase any rate of pay to an amount of more than *$8,902* per year.

In accordance with 5 U.S.C. 5382(c), and subject to any applicable statutory restrictions on the availability of appropriated funds, the following rates of basic pay for the Senior Executive Service shall become effective on the first day of the first applicable pay period that begins on or after October 1, 1979:

ES–1	$47, 889
ES–2	49, 499
ES–3	51, 164
ES–4	52, 884
ES–5	54, 662
ES–6	56, 500

Federal Civilian and Military Pay Increases

Announcement on the President's Proposal.
August 31, 1979

President Carter proposed to Congress today a pay increase of 7 percent affecting 3.5 million military and civilian employees. The President's proposal would raise the pay of 1.4 million Federal civilian workers and 2.1 million members of the armed services.

The law governing Federal civilian white-collar pay requires that the Bureau of Labor Statistics conduct an annual nationwide survey of salaries paid private sector employees who hold jobs similar to their Federal counterparts. This private sector salary data is then compared with Federal salaries by a body called the President's Pay Agent: the Secretary of Labor and the Directors of the Office of Management and Budget and the Office of Personnel Management. This year the Pay Agent found that an average increase of 10.41 percent would raise Federal white-collar salaries to the level of private sector counterparts.

The law provides the President authority to propose the lower increase because of "national emergency or economic conditions affecting the general welfare."

The President believes strongly that a 7-percent increase is required this year. The 1980 budget had provided for a 5.5-percent increase. The President recognizes, however, that employees are faced with a higher cost of living than when he submitted his 1980 budget. For example, current forecasts of CPI increases have risen 3.2 percentage points for 1979 and 2.0 percentage points for 1980 over those used in the budget.

By recommending 7 percent instead, the President's action will add a little less than $1 billion to the $60 billion that the budget already provides for these workers' annual salaries.

"Inflation continues to be the single greatest threat to our economy and is a national problem of foremost concern," the President said in his message to the

Congress. The average 10.41-percent increase that would be required under the comparability act is far beyond the standard of the Council on Wage and Price Stability for this year, and exceeds any standard under consideration for the coming years.

The President's proposal recognizes that low-paid employees have felt more than others the impact of inflation and provides that employees earning less than $8,900 per year will receive larger increases. Further, to ease the burden of the limitation on the military, the President has decided that there will be no reallocation of the increase from basic pay into the allowances for quarters and subsistence.

Digest of Other White House Announcements

The following listing includes the President's public schedule and other items of general interest announced by the White House Press Office and not included elsewhere in this issue.

August 28

The President transmitted to the Congress and the Comptroller General the reports of the United Nations Joint Inspection Unit during 1978.

August 29

The President returned to the White House in the afternoon, following his stay at Camp David, Md.

August 30

The President left the White House for visits to Atlanta, Ga., and Tampa, Fla. In the evening, he went to Plains, Ga., for the Labor Day weekend.

NOMINATIONS SUBMITTED TO THE SENATE

The following list does not include promotions of members of the Uniformed Services, nominations to the Service Academies, or nominations of Foreign Service officers.

Submitted August 27, 1979

JAY JANIS, of Florida, to be a member of the Federal Home Loan Bank Board for the remainder of the term expiring June 30, 1981, vice Robert H. McKinney, resigned.

Submitted August 28, 1979

THOMAS M. TRACY, of Florida, a Foreign Service officer of Class one, to be an Assistant Secretary of State, vice John M. Thomas, resigned.

JOHN P. CONDON, of Oklahoma, a Foreign Service officer of Class one, now Ambassador Extraordinary and Plenipotentiary of the United States of America to the Dominion of Fiji, to serve concurrently and without additional compensation as Ambassador Extraordinary and Plenipotentiary of the United States of America to the Kingdom of Tonga and as Ambassador Extraordinary and Plenipotentiary of the United States of America to Tuvalu.

THOMAS A. CLARK, of Florida, to be United States Circuit Judge for the Fifth Circuit, vice a new position created by P.L. 95–486, approved October 20, 1978.

NATHANIEL R. JONES, of Ohio, to be United States Circuit Judge for the Sixth Circuit, vice John W. Peck, retired.

ARTHUR L. ALARCON, of California, to be United States Circuit Judge for the Ninth Circuit, vice a new position created by P.L. 95–486, approved October 20, 1978.

HARRY PREGERSON, of California, to be United States Circuit Judge for the Ninth Circuit, vice a new position created by P.L. 95–486, approved October 20, 1978.

STEPHANIE K. SEYMOUR, of Oklahoma, to be United States Circuit Judge for the Tenth Circuit, vice a new position created by P.L. 95–486, approved October 20, 1978.

ALCEE L. HASTINGS, of Florida, to be United States District Judge for the Southern District of Florida, vice a new position created by P.L. 95–486, approved October 20, 1978.

SCOTT E. REED, of Kentucky, to be United States District Judge for the Eastern District of Kentucky, vice a new position created by P.L. 95–486, approved October 20, 1978.

1531

CHECKLIST OF WHITE HOUSE PRESS RELEASES

The following listing contains releases of the White House Press Office which are not included in this issue.

Released August 28, 1979

Announcement: nomination of Thomas A. Clark to be United States Circuit Judge for the Fifth Circuit

Announcement: nomination of Nathaniel R. Jones to be United States Circuit Judge for the Sixth Circuit

Announcement: nomination of Arthur L. Alarcon to be United States Circuit Judge for the Ninth Circuit

Announcement: nomination of Harry Pregerson to be United States Circuit Judge for the Ninth Circuit

Announcement: nomination of Stephanie K. Seymour to be United States Circuit Judge for the Tenth Circuit

CHECKLIST—Continued

Released August 28—Continued

Announcement: nomination of Alcee L. Hastings to be United States District Judge for the Southern District of Florida

Announcement: nomination of Scott E. Reed to be United States District Judge for the Eastern District of Kentucky

Released August 31, 1979

News conference: on the President's proposal for a 7-percent increase in Federal civilian and military pay—by John P. White, Deputy Director, Office of Management and Budget, and Alan K. Campbell, Director, Office of Personnel Management

ACTS APPROVED BY THE PRESIDENT

NOTE: No acts approved by the President were received by the Office of the Federal Register during the period covered by this issue.

Editor's Note

The President's Trip to Georgia and Florida

On Friday, August 31, the President was in Plains, Ga. Releases and announcements issued during his visit to Georgia and Florida will be printed next week.

Atlanta, Georgia

Remarks at the Presidential Energy
Technology Seminar.   August 30, 1979

THE PRESIDENT. Thank you, everybody. It's good to be home.

SUMMARY OF FIRST SESSION

DR. PRESS. Mr. President, we have convened this energy technology seminar at your request. We've gathered the Nation's leading experts to brief you on how American science and technology can contribute in the years ahead to help alleviate our energy problems. The Government research and development budget in energy is of the order of $4 billion per year, and the energy security trust fund will increase this substantially. Industry, universities are making substantial investments in energy research and development.

This, then, is a report on what the dividends of these research and development investments are likely to be. I believe you will see that domestic sources of energy can become available in the years ahead that will help reduce our energy dependence on foreign imports, will strengthen our economy, and will improve our national security.

So far, we've been running some 2 hours

in these energy briefings, and I would like to spend a few minutes summarizing what has already been said this morning.

Energy conservation plays a key role in our energy strategy. It reduces our dependence on imported oil. It is cost-effective. It yields results more quickly than developing new energy supplies.

Dr. Edward Jefferson, who's the vice president of duPont Company—Dr. Jefferson, would you stand?—gave us a presentation this morning on the remarkable progress in conservation by American industry. In the past 4 years, there has been a saving of some 1 million—the equivalent of 1 million barrels of oil per day due to industrial conservation. And the chemical industry has one of the best records in conservation.

This is important, because the chemical industry uses some 8 percent of our total energy consumption. In 1978 alone, that industry has saved 130 million barrels of oil through conservation, and their goal is to effect a 30-percent reduction in energy required per pound of product by 1985.

And Dr. Jefferson described some of the measures that that industry has taken to achieve this goal; for example, the cogeneration of power and steam. In the generation of electric power, there's been a lot of waste heat. That waste heat is

1533

now converted into steam and used by the industry. They have better instruments to control the generation of power. And with more research and development, they will be able to substitute raw materials derived from coal and shale oil to replace as the feedstock for that industry the oil that is currently being used.

Our second speaker was Dr. Henry Linden, who's president of the Gas Research Institute. The U.S. energy consumption is of the order of 80 quads, and one-quarter of that today comes from natural gas. Dr. Linden suggested that the contributions of natural gas will grow in the next 20 years from 20 quads to 30 quads, and that's equivalent to an addition of 5 million barrels per day.

The largest source of this growth will come from the so-called unconventional natural gas. These are resources that are plentiful, perhaps as plentiful as the conventional gas that we've been used to, but they haven't been tapped in the past because of technological or economic reasons. Much of this gas occurs in tight formations, formations which are so impermeable that the gas doesn't flow readily to the producing wells. As a result of research and development programs, methods have been developed to fracture rocks, to make rocks more permeable so that the gas is more readily available in the future.

Dr. Linden estimates that there may be as much as 1,200 quads of natural gas, conventional and unconventional, available to us, and this is of the order of 40 to 50 years of supply at the current rates of usage.

Our third speaker was Dr. Lawrence Ybarrondo, who's Director of Water Reactor Research at the Idaho National Engineering Laboratory of the Department of Energy. He is an expert on nuclear reactor safety.

Nuclear energy accounts for some 13 percent of our electric power generation. And in some places, such as Chicago, 50 percent of the electric power comes from nuclear energy. In 1978 this was equivalent to about 1.6 million barrels of oil per day. However, nuclear reactor safety is the key element to the future of nuclear power. And Dr. Ybarrondo described how science and technology can further increase the safety of existing reactors and facilities. For example, he proposes to implant more sensors in the reactor and in the plant so that we can have better knowledge of the state of the facility on a continuing basis. These larger numbers of sensors, measuring the physical properties, the temperatures, the pressures, and the flow rates and so on, will be monitored by computerized systems which collect, organize, and display the data instantaneously on the state of the plant.

The computers can verify the plant readiness to cope with any potential emergency. In the case of an emergency, this system would allow the operators to make constructive choices of what to do, and the computer would predict the outcome of all of these various choices.

This technology is actually state of the art; it's being done today in other industrial sectors—the aerospace industry and so on. It's being done today on test reactors in Idaho. So, this is certainly an important avenue for improving our reactor safety.

The fourth speaker this morning was Dr. Douglas Balcomb, who is in charge of solar programs and conservation at the Los Alamos National Laboratory. Some 30 percent of our energy use goes to heat and cool residential and commercial buildings and to provide hot water, so conservation and the use of the Sun in this area is extremely important.

Dr. Balcomb showed us some remarkable examples of residences in which conservation and the use of the Sun in a passive way has led to clean, cost-effective energy use. These technologies, he points up, are available now. They make use of all sorts of new materials and devices and new design concepts in building homes. The investments in conservation and passive solar can lead to extremely attractive residences, and these investments will save sufficient energy to pay the homeowner back in 10 years.

The fifth speaker, and the last speaker in the morning session, was Dr. Norman Hackerman, who's president of Rice University and Chairman of the National Science Board. He spoke about enhanced oil recovery.

Some 450 billion barrels of oil have been identified in place in the United States, but only one-third can be recovered by present technology. We leave two-thirds of it behind in the ground by present methods. That's 300 billion barrels of oil that's left behind. That's more oil than Saudi Arabia possesses, and that's all in the ground in this country. If we can find ways to produce this oil, to induce it to move through the ground to the producer wells, we would gain an enormous additional source of energy. Dr. Hackerman believes that research and development will enable us to recover perhaps 10 percent of this immobile oil. And if we do this well—and that's only 10 percent of what we leave behind—this would be equivalent to three to four Alaskan oil fields.

And he told us about the different techniques we might use; for example, the injection of water and gases, such as carbon dioxide, increasing the temperature of the rock formations to make the oil flow more readily, and then injecting chemicals to loosen this immobilized crude oil so that we could pull it out.

This is a brief summary of the papers that have already been presented, and if you want to question or if any of the panelists or recipients of this briefing want to question some of these speakers, now would be an appropriate time.

INDUSTRIAL ENERGY CONSERVATION

THE PRESIDENT. I'd like to ask Dr. Jefferson how the other industries are doing in our country? I know that you spoke for the chemical industry, but is this a unique achievement, or are the other generic types of industries doing an equivalent job?

DR. JEFFERSON. Well, Mr. President, most of the industries have met or surpassed the goals that were set in the program developed by the Federal Energy Administration and the Department of Commerce 4 years ago. So, in essence, most industries are doing well.

THE PRESIDENT. Do you think the 30-percent goal by 1985 is the optimum that you all can achieve? Is that goal high enough?

DR. JEFFERSON. Well, that goal relates only to energy conservation. As you know, the chemical industry uses a great deal of petroleum and natural gas as raw material. The savings that can be achieved in the raw material area are additive to this as are, also, savings that would accrue from moving away from the scarcer petroleum and natural gas over to more plentiful fossil fuels. And all these three are getting attention.

THE PRESIDENT. I presume, since you've been so enthusiastic about it, that one of the motivations is cost-effectiveness and it has been a matter of saving for you in production costs and——

DR. JEFFERSON. Yes, sir.

THE PRESIDENT. It's been a profitable thing?

DR. JEFFERSON. Yes.

THE PRESIDENT. Thank you very much. I might have some other questions later.

UNCONVENTIONAL GAS

Dr. Linden, one of the most doubtful issues that I had to face a few months ago when we were putting together our energy proposal for Congress was the unconventional gas production. We had estimates all the way from half a million barrels a day by 1990, up to 2½ million barrels a day by 1990.

Within the constraints of predictable cost for production, compared with present projections, what would be your best estimate of how much we might realize from the unconventional gas sources by 1990? My parameters may not be good ones.

DR. LINDEN. The two resources, Mr. President, that are the most immediately developable are the Devonian shales in Appalachia and the tight sands in the Western Rocky Mountain States. Nearly all estimates that have been made indicate that there are on the order of 200 trillion cubic feet or quads of gas in these two sources, available at prices somewhere between $4 to $5 a million Btu at the wellhead and—which is equivalent to something like $24 to $30 a barrel, which is a price which we are afraid will soon be reached in terms of OPEC oil imports.

Several studies done for DOE and for us have indicated that somewhere between 5 and 8 trillion cubic feet from these sources alone could be produced as early as 1990 and, perhaps, as late as 2000. So, we're talking about supplements in the 2½-million-barrel-a-day to 4-million-barrel-a-day range. Your particular initiative, the oil import reduction program, calls only for ½ to 1 million barrels a day equivalent by 1990.

I am very confident that we will meet this goal, in view of the legislative actions and regulatory actions that have been taken or proposed by you. So, we are quite confident that this will be exceeded under current conditions.

THE PRESIDENT. That was the most conservative estimate that we made, and it was done deliberately because of the doubt about the effort that would be underway. What is the degree of effort now being explored in getting these unconventional gas sources realized?

DR. LINDEN. We have large well drilling programs, wells of opportunity, and, actually, research wells in all of the four resources.

In the Devonian shale, there is a large drilling program jointly by industry, DOE, and my own organization. In the western tight sands, some very extensive stimulation work, hydraulic fraction work is underway.

In the geopressured zone, gas in the gulf, we have a 10-well drilling program underway, and you, I think, participated in launching of a project to recover gas from coal seams for rural development. So, we are making good progress. And DOE is currently spending on the order of $65 million a year on unconventional gas R&D, and we have proposed that it should be boosted to something on the order of $100 million.

But with these initiatives and the very heavy involvement of industry, as well, on a cooperative basis, I think we are well launched to realizing these targets.

THE PRESIDENT. So, to summarize, you would say that by 1990 we have an excellent chance to have, say, 2 million barrels of oil equivalent per day at prices at least competitive with synthetic fuel costs?

DR. LINDEN. Absolutely.

THE PRESIDENT. That's much higher than we had anticipated or projected.

DR. LINDEN. Thank you.

THE PRESIDENT. Thank you, Dr. Linden.

NUCLEAR SAFETY

Mr. Ybarrondo, I just had one question to ask. To what degree are you working with Dr. Kemeny and his committee? They'll be coming to me now, within the next month, with recommendations derived from the Three Mile Island incident about how nuclear power can be made more safe and operating and design features might be incorporated. Are you, or others associated with you, working with them on it?

DR. YBARRONDO. Indirectly, Mr. President. Some of the technical staff members to the Kemeny Commission have contacted us, and they have asked us to examine various options, for example, that the operators took during the course of the Three Mile Island incident.

Primarily, they're addressing the what-if questions—"What if the operator did this in lieu of something else?" And we have been asked to make some computer code calculations for them. Those calculations are in process.

THE PRESIDENT. Is the computer control technique cost-effective? Does it replace enough personnel so that a power company looking for cost savings would initiate it?

DR. YBARRONDO. I'm not sure that it would specifically reduce the personnel enough to result in significant cost savings. But the use of the computer to look at potential defects and to allow them to operate the plant more efficiently, to decrease the downtime of plants due to mechanical failures or human errors would certainly be cost-effective.

THE PRESIDENT. One of the major problems with nuclear power now is the percentage of downtime, is it not?

DR. YBARRONDO. Yes, sir. It is.

THE PRESIDENT. What does that run— 30, 40 percent, that high?

DR. YBARRONDO. On the order of that. The availability of the plant is not as high as it could be.

THE PRESIDENT. So, if the Kemeny report should recommend—I'm not anticipating—increased personnel from which could be derived increased safety, then the computer use would be more attractive under those circumstances, would it not?

DR. YBARRONDO. I believe so.

THE PRESIDENT. Thank you very much.

DR. YBARRONDO. You're welcome.

ENERGY CONSIDERATIONS IN BUILDING DESIGN

THE PRESIDENT. I'd like to ask Mr. Balcomb one question. I'm not putting all the burden on you, but it seems that one of the major unfulfilled opportunities is to get the AIA—with all the architects in the Nation and the major builders—to commit themselves in just standard designs of homes and public buildings to incorporate energy-saving features. To what degree is this being done? It's one of the things that I advocated in, I think, a national meeting of the architects in Atlanta when I was Governor. But I just wonder if the architects as a group are pursuing this without the customer asking for it necessarily. Can you answer that for me?

DR. BALCOMB. The AIA themselves have instituted a small program of seminars, directed specifically at their members, to teach them about passive solar design and energy conservation options. There are other signs. The recent April issue of Progressive Architecture, which is the leading magazine in that field, was entirely devoted to energy-conscious design, both related to energy conservation and solar applications.

In looking at the response to other seminars and information, instructional media and so forth, the response of the architects has been very good. A lot of this is coming from public demand. They are getting a lot of people walking in the door who want to do it. So, I think it is happening, yes, sir.

THE PRESIDENT. Well, there's no question that the customer is well served with an increase in insulation or decrease in window space or thickness of walls and so forth, with increasing prices of energy, right?

DR. BALCOMB. No, that is certainly not questioned. I have not seen an example where it's been done where it was not cost-effective.

THE PRESIDENT. That's one of the things that I and other public officials might do, including yourself, is to get this to be just a routine sort of thing for new building designs, instead of it being a hit-or-miss proposition. I may be underestimating what's already been done, but it seems that that's the right field for initiating these kinds of energy savings in buildings—at the initial stage of design and construction.

DR. BALCOMB. A survey of current practices done in '75 indicated that there is quite a good response—and everyone was surprised at the extent to which there is an increase in the standards which buildings are being built in response to the situation.

THE PRESIDENT. Thank you very much.

ENHANCED OIL RECOVERY

Mr. Hackerman, I had one question. I'm sorry I came in late. I probably would have gotten this from you if I had been here. You said that—part of Dr. Press' summary—that 10 percent of the oil could be recovered. Is that 10 percent of abandoned fields or is that an increase of 10 percent in a field that's under productivity?

DR. HACKERMAN. Well, either way, it's 10 percent of what would be left after full depletion.

THE PRESIDENT. Could you go back into an abandoned field and then still get that 10 percent?

DR. HACKERMAN. That's right, Mr. President.

THE PRESIDENT. Would that be cost-effective?

DR. HACKERMAN. Yes, at the way things are going, it would be cost-effective.

THE PRESIDENT. I see. [*Laughter*] That's the good news and bad news in one sentence. [*Laughter*]

Thank you.

COAL SYNTHETICS

DR. PRESS. The first speaker of this second half of our seminar, Mr. President, is Dr. Lawrence Swabb, who's vice president of the Exxon Research and Engineering Company and is one of the experts in our country on synthetic fuels derived from coal.

DR. SWABB. *Mr. President, Secretary Duncan, Dr. Press, ladies and gentlemen:*

I will discuss the technology for converting coal to synthetic fuels. And I also have some good news and some bad news. The good news is that the technology for commercial-size plants is available to change coal to gaseous products, such as synthetic natural gas, and into liquids, such as gasoline and fuel oil. In addition, research is moving ahead to develop even better technology.

The bad news is that the cost of these synthetic fuels will be higher than the prices we are now paying; just how much higher is uncertain.

Direct burning is the most efficient way to use the energy in coal, but gaseous and liquid fuels are cleaner and much more convenient to use. Our modern society has a large demand for these kinds of fuels—for transportation, for heating our homes, and for industry. With the large reserves of coal in the United States, coal synthetics represents a potentially large contribution to supplying these needs over the next 50 to 100 years.

Research on coal synthetics has increased dramatically in the 1970's. In my talk, I will cover the objectives of this research. These are: one, to lower the cost of making synthetics; two, to increase our ability to use most U.S. coals; three, to produce the products needed by consumers. In dealing with this third objective, I will briefly describe how coal synthetics are made. The fourth research objective is to ensure that environmental standards can be met as the synthetics industry is built. My final remarks will include an outlook for the impact of new research results.

Coal synthetics will be expensive. A typical commercial-size plant would cost one-and-a-half to three billion dollars if it were built today. A coal liquids plant of this size would be capable of supplying the gasoline and home fuel oil needs of a city of about 1 million people. The estimated cost of the products can vary over a wide range, depending on a number of factors such as plant size, the type of coal, financing method, and many others.

It appears that synthetic natural gas would cost much more than today's maximum price for new natural gas. If produced today, synthetic gas from a rela-

tively low-cost western or gulf coast coals would be 15 to 30 percent higher than the price of imported crude. Methyl alcohol made from these coals would be in the same cost range, and the cost of other coal liquids would be higher.

About half of the cost of the synthetics is related to the large investment for facilities and equipment. About 20 to 25 percent is the cost of coal. Another 20 to 25 percent is the cost of other expenses such as wages, utilities, and supplies.

One item that contributes to the operating cost is the fact that one-third to one-half of the energy in the coal is used in the operation of the plant. Now, these costs are only estimates. The actual costs of synthetics will not be known until specific plants have been designed, built, and operated. Obviously, the high estimated costs are a barrier to building these plants.

Coal is located in many places in the United States, and almost every deposit is unique. Bituminous coals, shown in red, are found in Appalachia, the Midwest, and the Southern Rocky Mountain regions. Sub-bituminous coals, shown in blue, are found primarily in the West. Lignite, indicated by the green areas, are in the West and the gulf coast. One of the technical challenges is to be able to convert this wide variety of differing quality coal into synthetics. To do this, we need to learn more about the chemical structure of the coal and how it reacts to form gases and liquids. Coal scientists are learning more about these areas by using modern, sophisticated research equipment and techniques.

In gasification, coal is reacted with oxygen and steam at high temperatures. The products are carbon monoxide, hydrogen, and some methane and other gases. After removing impurities, the gas can be used directly as fuel or raw materials for industry. To make synthetic natural gas, the carbon monoxide and hydrogen can be reacted together in an additional step to make more methane. This then can be mixed with natural gas for home heating.

Coal can be gasified either underground, where the coal naturally occurs, or on the surface after the coal is mined. In underground gasification, oxygen and steam are compressed and injected into the coal deposit. The product gas finds its way to a production well, and it flows to the surface where it is purified. Underground gasification will be most useful for deep coal deposits which cannot be mined by conventional methods. This technology is still in a very early stage of development.

Surface gasification is being used on a commercial scale in other countries. Several different types of gasifiers are used. Each has its own set of advantages and disadvantages. For example, some will work better with certain coals and not with others. In general, all of them gasify the coal with steam and oxygen in specially designed reaction vessels, and the coal ash is discharged either dry or as a molten slag. Product gases are purified before they can be used as fuel. Gasification research is aimed primarily at improving these gasifiers by various techniques and approaches.

In coal liquefaction, there are two types of processes. They are called indirect and direct. Both will produce either all liquids or a mixture of gaseous and liquid products.

In an indirect process, the coal is first gasified, then some of the product gases are reacted to form either liquid hydrocarbons or methyl alcohol, also known as methanol. The liquid hydrocarbons make good diesel and jet fuel, but the gasoline component is low in quality. Methanol is

a potential transportation fuel. To use it widely, however, would require changes in engines and fuel supply systems. Therefore, a new process is being developed to convert methanol into gasoline. Methanol would also be an excellent fuel for gas turbines used to generate electricity. The technology for commercial-size plants is available today to make both indirect liquids and methanol.

Direct liquefaction is not fully developed. But progress is being made in several large research projects. Direct liquefaction involves grinding coal to a small size, mixing it with oil from the process, and reacting it with hydrogen at high temperatures and pressure. The liquid products make an excellent gasoline component and acceptable heating oil and fuel oil. Direct liquefaction also requires gasification of the residue to make the hydrogen needed for the process.

The samples in the bottles illustrate the quantity of gasoline and fuel oil that can be obtained from this amount of bituminous coal in the direct liquefaction process. These liquids were actually obtained as products from a small pilot plant.

Overall, about 100 gallons of liquids can be produced from 1 ton of coal. Both indirect and direct liquefaction processes will be needed in the future to use the various kinds of coal and to produce different kinds of liquid products.

Synthetic fuels plants will be large and complex installations. In many respects, they will be similar to petroleum refineries. Plants producing either liquids or gas will likely be located near coal mines to minimize the cost of moving the coal from the mine to the plants. However, air quality, water supply, ash disposal, and physical size requirements will also play a major role in determining where these plants will be located.

The technology to meet today's environmental standards is available for cleaning up the gas in water discharge streams, also for controlling dust, and for disposing of the solid waste. This technology is already in use in refineries and electric powerplants and improved technology is the subject of a number of research programs. We've estimated that the cost for environmental protection would be roughly 15 to 20 percent of the total synthetics plant investment.

Finally, I would like to comment on the outlook for new technology. At the present time there is a substantial research program in this country on coal synthetics. A large program will continue to be needed because of the diversity of the coals, the locations, and the products. The primary target will continue to be cost reduction. Realistically, I believe a 20- to 30-percent lower cost, exclusive of inflation, can be expected over the next 20 years. This will not be easy to achieve, but improvements in gasification and liquefaction technology as well as in the purification steps can be expected.

New catalysts are the best hope for these improvements. Also, we can expect gradual improvements in equipment design, materials of construction, and process control systems as coal synthetics plants are built and operated. The best technology available will be used in a never-ending striving for lower costs.

In summary, coal synthetics are costly, but they are an important option for high-quality fuels, particularly for transportation and home heating. Large coal resources have the potential to supply U.S. needs for synthetics for many decades. Costs can be reduced through advancing technology, and progress is being made.

Thank you, Mr. President.

THE PRESIDENT. I think it might be better for me to wait until after the presentations.

BIOMASS

DR. PRESS. Shall we move next, then, to Dr. Thomas Stelson. Dr. Stelson, whom you know, is vice president of research at Georgia Tech, and he will tell us about biomass and its contribution to our energy needs in the future.

DR. STELSON. *Mr. President, distinguished guests, ladies and gentlemen:*

I'm delighted to have this opportunity to speak a little bit about the energy potential of biomass. Even though oils and gases and coals vary in character, biomass varies even more. It's a general name for a complex and diversified group of materials that are produced by living organisms. And these organisms have the capability of converting solar energy and other materials into forms of stored energy. In fact, on a geologic timescale, biomass is the source of coal and oil and gas as well.

On a short timescale all biological materials can be converted into energy, and they can be converted into all forms of energy—gas, liquid, or solid. So, the possibilities are enormous. There are literally millions of materials and many possible projects that could convert them into useful energy forms.

The two characteristics that are probably different is that biomass, like solar, is a renewable energy source. But it's a little better than direct solar in that it's stored in biological form, and it can be used without the daily or annual cycles that create problems in solar energy utilization. The other thing that's, I think, very interesting about biomass possibilities is that it's very small-scale in its opportunities, and it can be very labor-intensive and can contribute more than any other form, except possibly conservation, to job opportunities and employment.

First slide, please.

Any material—wood, grass, grain—can be converted to energy and generally can be converted fairly efficiently. So, biomass is energy stored in living organisms that then die, and can be used. And it's a very distributed source; it's not like certain highly localized sources where you have to drill or mine the material. It's generally distributed across the country and is similarly correlated with agricultural production opportunities or forestry production opportunities.

Next slide.

Typical examples are agricultural residues. In the harvesting of grain, the straw or the stalks and leaves are potential biomass energy sources. Forest residues are particularly fruitful opportunities, because in typical harvesting in a forest, about one-half of the material is left as residue on the forest floor.

There can also be developed specialized energy crops, woody materials, that have particularly good and desirable energy characteristics. And specific crops can be developed for specific types of energy products, just like specific crops are developed for specific grains.

The opportunities for research and science and technology here are enormous, because there are great unknowns.

Next slide.

This is what I'm talking about with respect to residues. Many people immediately assume when you talk about biomass that the Earth is going to be completely denuded, and particularly they might fear a similar occurrence to what has happened in the sub-Sahara area. But, for example, in the State of Georgia, where there is fairly good data, we grow here about 6 quads of biomass per year. The State uses in all forms of energy—coal,

natural gas, hydrofuel oil, and wood— about 1 quad of energy a year.

Our goal in the near term in this State is to develop about one-quarter of a quad from biological materials or biomass. This would only be about 4 percent of what's grown. So, it would be a very small portion of the total growth.

Next slide.

There are very good near-term possibilities. Probably the best is forest residue, and that is where the greatest success has been achieved so far. The agricultural wastes are also a very good opportunity, and particularly damaged material— spoiled grain, grain that is damaged in any form by vermin or by chemicals—is essentially the same as a feedstock for energy.

So, there is a national estimate that about 20 percent of all grain is damaged to the point where its use is reduced, and this is a great opportunity for utilization.

Next slide.

One of the characteristics of biomass is just like agriculture and forestry. It's very regional, and the solution for one section of the United States is probably not going to be a good solution for another section. Thus, national programs that would be uniformly applied across the country probably aren't useful.

There is a great need for fine-scale technological development that accommodates the peculiarities of each region.

Next slide.

To illustrate the two—the secure and the labor-intensive characteristics of biomass, the State of Georgia again, where we have fairly good data, imports about $3 billion of energy a year. By "import" I mean across State boundaries—coal, oil, natural gas. If we could displace within 5 years about one-quarter of this with biomass, this would be a new industry in this

State having a value of products of $750 million with a very large employment possibility.

This we consider a big new industry, one that has a $30 million annual activity. So, the economic possibilities on a local scale are tremendous.

Next slide.

Currently about 1½ to 2 quads of biomass are being utilized by industry. Quite a bit more is being used in residential energy development, but there's not really a good data base for that. It's probably around a half a quad. So, on the total there would be something like 2 to 2½ quads currently in use.

Almost all of the industrial use is in forest-based industries, where they use much of their own waste material on where they have large acreages of forest materials.

Next slide.

THE PRESIDENT. Would that include wood-burning stoves?

DR. STELSON. This does not include wood-burning stoves or any residential utilization; only industrial. The residential is probably somewhere around another half quad.

Biomass can be converted probably most easily into space-processed heat or for direct combustion for power or any other purpose or in the gasification of it.

Now, generally when you gasify biomass you cannot ship it long distances in pipelines, because it has in it heavy constituents that would condense and gum up the pipeline. So, typically we're talking about gasification at the point of use. Also, of course, biomass can be and is a very good source of liquid fuels for transportation use; that is, ethanol and methanol. And gasohol is now a very popular development.

Next slide.

This is just an illustration of what can be done. This is a textile mill in Alexander City, Alabama. It converted from fuel oil to wood, wood chips. And even though, because of unknowns in the technology, they essentially converted coal equipment to wood use and they way overdid the air pollution control system, so that the actual effluent is below 10 percent of allowable standards—in spite of some of these difficulties, the full capital cost was recovered in about 4 years. And there are literally hundreds of thousands of opportunities like this that could be repeated across the country.

Next slide.

This shows you the delivery of wood chips. This mill uses about 400 tons a day. They come in in a truck like this, which is tilted into their supply bin.

Next slide.

In the near term, in 5 or 10 years, the potential from wood—and that's the highest potential area—is from about 3½ to 5 quads. And from grains, which is more limited and which provides also competition with food sources, the potential is about ½ to 1½ quads, and that is more uncertain, because it depends upon the price of grain which fluctuates more.

Next slide.

The long-term—and by that I mean approximately 20 years—the wood potential is—these are what I would call reasonable, conservative estimates—is about 5 to 7 quads, grain about 1 to 2 quads, and others. By others, I mean aquatic biomass, special plant material, energy plantations, and things of that type. And that's perhaps 2 to 4 quads.

So, you can see the potential in 20 years is about 8 to 13 quads. And if the national use were 100 quads, this would be 8 to 13 percent, which is quite a significant development in the energy picture.

Thank you.

THE PRESIDENT. In general, I'll defer questions, but what's the estimated cost in barrels of oil equivalent? I know it varies widely, but what kind of range—say, the plant in Alabama?

DR. STELSON. It would be, right now in that plant—the cost was less than half of the cost of oil. Now, of course to the owner of the plant, he was interested in the rate of return on his capital investment, because he had to add capital to get that, so on and so forth. But in terms of fuel—gasification of wood, for example, in the southeastern part of the United States is probably competitive with natural gas right now.

THE PRESIDENT. What's the holdup?

DR. STELSON. Well, it's sort of a chicken-and-an-egg situation, in that if you're an industry that doesn't have a lot of wood, you're rather hesitant to invest capital to put in a wood-utilization facility, because you don't know if the supply system is going to be there. And if you're in the supply business, you're not going to invest in a lot of delivery mechanisms if you don't have any customers.

And so, I think it's got to be worked up at a fine scale, where you start plants like this and you build a supply-and-demand system that then escalates into a big energy industry.

THE PRESIDENT. Don't hesitate to let Charlie Duncan know what we can do to help. [*Laughter*]

DR. STELSON. Thank you.

FRONTIER OIL REGIONS

DR. PRESS. Our next speaker, Mr. President, is Dr. Bill Menard, who is Director of the United States Geological Survey and one of the world's leading marine geologists. He will describe some new frontier oil regions.

DR. MENARD. Thank you.

Good morning, Mr. President, ladies and gentlemen. I'd like to speak to you about the contribution that can be made to our oil problems by the discovery of what might be called unconventional oil fields. They're just unconventional because they're in places we haven't drilled. And one of the reasons we haven't drilled is that many of them are much deeper, in fact, than we can drill at present.

Of course, any energy scenario assumes that we will find more oil. It's assumed that we will find thousands or tens of thousands of tiny oil fields within the contiguous 48 States, where we've explored so much. It's assumed that we will find larger fields in the overthrust belt in the Rockies that's now opening up. It's assumed that we'll find giant fields in the Continental Shelves and in Alaska.

You'll notice that the less we know about the area the greater the fields you expect to find. And the reason for that, in fact, is that when you begin to explore an area, you find the big fields early. And as time goes on and you explore more, you find smaller ones.

Well, those assumptions are made. I want to talk to you about a region that isn't included in the energy scenarios, a region that nonetheless offers great promise. The region is the oil potential of the deep sea beyond the Continental Shelf. Hollis Hedburg, a distinguished oil geologist, and colleagues have recently summarized their estimates, and I think there's a growing consensus to this effect of the potential of this region.

They find in a general way that there is about the same amount, the same area, the same amount of potential oil-bearing sediments in the deep sea in the adjacent Continental Slope as we have in the oil-bearing basins of the United States.

Estimating how much oil is in a region you haven't drilled yet is a very chancy business, which I'll touch on when I try to make a more detailed estimate. But in a very general way, the best you can say is that one volume of sedimentary rock that is known to have hydrocarbons in it has as good a chance as another. If you were to make the only kind of guess you could make about what's out there, there's probably as much in the deep sea in the adjacent Continental Slope in the way of oil as there is in the areas we've already explored in the United States. Now, that doesn't mean you can get it out, because of course it has to be in very large fields to have any potential for economic development.

How do we know very much about this region? It's because for the last 30 years, the United States and other countries, the United States oceanographers funded by the Office of Naval Research and the National Science Foundation have been out making sub-bottom profiles of the sea floor with increasing degrees of sophistication and penetration. In addition, for the last 10 years, we've been drilling, through the JOIDES program and its followups, down through several thousand feet of sediment in the deep sea. So, we know something about the potential source rocks out there, and we know a great deal about the sub-bottom structure.

The oceanographers drilling out in the deep sea have never drilled in the regions where the greatest oil potential exists, the edges of the Continental Margin. They haven't drilled in the deep Gulf of Mexico, except one preliminary hole. They haven't drilled in the promising places where the sediment is thickest and the oil potential is great. That might seem irresponsible of the oceanographers, and as one of them I would have to accept that. But it really isn't. The reason they haven't drilled is that the deep sea drilling ship, the *Glomar Explorer,* does not have a

potential to drill safely in places where you expect oil and gas. They don't have blowout preventers, they don't have the risers and so on.

So, the region is unexplored by scientists for the very reason that they think there is some potential for oil and gas there. The advisory committees won't permit drilling. At the same time, industry has been extending out from the Continental Margin from the very shallow water out deeper and deeper, and it can now drill out in depths of—there's drilling right now off New Brunswick at a depth of 4,875 feet, I think it is, varying with the tide. And it has a potential to go out even greater.

We have reached a point now where the oceanographic information about the potential of the deep sea is overlapping the potential to develop that industry has brought out at increasing cost into deeper water. What would be ideal now would be to find a potential site for drilling, a prospect which would give us opportunity to evaluate the entire deep sea in a way that would encourage us to go out at greater cost into deeper water.

Ideally for our country, such a prospect would be clearly under U.S. jurisdiction. It would have the characteristic that it could be explored by existing commercial equipment, it could be explored relatively quickly, if we wanted to, and it could be explored at reasonable cost. And if the exploration was promising, it should have the characteristic that it's capable of very large yields at reasonable prices, and within a decade.

Now, there appears to be such a prospect in the area of the mid-Atlantic region which is off the—or the so-called Baltimore Canyon. I'll show you some illustrations in a moment—not quite yet—show you what this prospect is like.

The prospect is a giant reef. Now, there isn't any reef in the area now, but there used to be. There used to be a reef in this area at the same time that there were reefs in the Reforma and the Campeche bank areas off of Mexico, the same general period which we can sum together as the Mesozoic period, which, for those of you who aren't geologists, is more or less when there were dinosaurs around. A hundred to 140 million years ago is this particular period. At that time, there was a reef that ran along the edge of the Continental Shelf, just as it does now in the Great Barrier Reef off Florida.

That reef is not known to have been continuous—because we don't have that much data, because the oceanographers weren't looking for this. They just found it while studying the general characteristics of the Continental Margin. There may be gaps. In fact, there certainly are gaps we don't know about in Central Mexico. But where we do have the information, it looks as though a reef extended from these highly petroliferous new discovery areas in Mexico, around through the Gulf of Mexico, and up the Atlantic Coast.

It comes up in the mid-Atlantic region, the Baltimore Canyon region, into water that's only 6,000 feet deep. It lies there under sediments that are themselves about 6,000 feet deep. The reef is about 20,000 feet thick in the region, which means, of course, since the reef always forms at sea level, that while the reef was forming, the sea floor sank by 20,000 feet, and the sediment accumulated as it did so. The reef is about 15 miles wide in this area; it's 150 miles long, and of course, it keeps going out of the area in both directions, since it runs intermittently all the way down from Mexico to Canada.

The oil-bearing potential we do not know for sure. If the reef was elevated at

any time so that it was deeply weathered, cavernous channels were cut into it, then the oil potential would be very high. There's no evidence that the area was elevated due to plate tectonics or the movement of the continents. So, if it was elevated, it was because sea level sank, and that means that the whole reef that existed at that time was exposed and the whole thing at that time would have been eroded. And you would have had a vast cavernous system as a potential storage place for oil. But we don't know that happened. Since it's at sea level and sea level does go up and down, it's reasonable, but we don't know that it happened.

We don't know that the temperature of the potential source beds, which have been discovered by the oceanographic drilling, ever got high enough to mature a large quantity of the oil. On the other hand, we do know from the drilling that has gone on in the Baltimore Canyon area that oil and gas are present there, and so we know that the temperature somewhere in the region got high enough to be productive.

Now, I'd like to show you a series of five slides, and then try to give you some evaluation of the prospect for the site. The first slide will show you the North American Continent and how the sea floor would look if you took the water away. Actually, it wouldn't be these colors on the sea floor, because mapmakers tend to make everything out there blue. Parts of it would be red and parts white, but the relief would look the way this shows.

I think North America looks clear enough. The great deposits of sediment that Hollis Hedberg and the other oil geologists and the oceanographers have identified lie—the ones we're particularly interested in, in here, and a great thickness in the Gulf of Mexico because of the sediment, the mud and sand that pour out of the Mississippi River and have done so for the last 140 million years. The little bumps out here are saltdomes, they occur out in the deep sea, as well as in Louisiana and Texas, and other regions, and, of course, they are the sites of a great deal of production of oil.

This is the Baltimore Canyon area in here, the mid-Atlantic region. We're going to focus on it.

Next, please.

Just to show you what a modern reef looks like—this is in the Bahamas, actually—the Great Barrier Reef would extend on in a straight line much farther, but this is the shallow reef. Waves are breaking. Just about at sea level, you find an occasional gap, a pass where water goes in and out, deep on this side, shallow here. And in ancient reefs comparabe to this one in almost every way, except that there were different animals living in them, and plants, large oil fields have been discovered in association with the crest of the reefs on the deep side and on shallow side.

Next, please.

This is the leasing area, the mid-Atlantic region. The blue areas show areas that we've already leased, tracks. The line running down here is the edge of the Continental Shelf, where the sea floor begins to—instead of being almost flat, begins to slope off in the Continental slope.

The Continental slope will look quite steep in the next illustration I'll show you, which is the profile along here, but that's because there's vertical exaggeration. The actual slope is a matter of 2 to 5 degrees in most places. You wouldn't have any trouble walking up it.

These COST holes—they do cost, but that stands—it's an acronym for Continental Offshore Strategraphic Test—and these are holes where oil companies band together. They get permission from the Government to drill. And anyone who

wants to get the information that's acquired can do so, and if a discovery is made of oil or gas, why, then we make an announcement of it. If there isn't a discovery, why then, only those who bought the information get to know what's in there.

A discovery was made here. Now, that's rather strange, because these holes are drilled away from structures where you expect to find oil and gas. It's only after the oil companies and the geological survey have agreed that that's about the last place you'd find oil or gas that you're allowed to drill. [*Laughter*] And nonetheless, gas was found here in more than measurable quantities. So, it does look to be quite a promising area.

Of course, there was gas announced by Texaco and by Tenneco here—and oil by Tenneco. The yellow is this Mesozoic reef. The first figure we saw that had yellow on it, we tended to call it the yellow reef. But it sounds a little too much like the yellow road in the Wizard of Oz. So, we took to calling it the Mesozoic reef.

Next please.

This is a profile, an actual geophysical record showing the sub-bottom, and it's one of thousands of such records we have around the continental margins. The oil companies must have tens of thousands. The characteristic of these records is every year they get better and every year you wish that all the old ones you had were capable of showing you what the new ones do. By this time you acquire the information in a very complicated way that gives you a lot of signals at once, and then you do signal processing and computer enhancement and a lot of things that nobody could dream of very long ago.

With these records, you can see these lines in here and they are reflectors, and some of them, Cretaceous and Jurassic together, are just more details of the Mesozoic. So, this is what I'm talking about, this period in here when all these rocks were deposited. This being a reef, this yellow area, this means since the reef animals grow only at sea level, this used to be at sea level. It's down 20,000 feet now. The top of it, as you can see, is about 10,000 feet. The sea floor here is about 6,000. Over here it's 4,900, and that's about the depth that is now being commercially drilled. This is where the same drilling apparatus is capable of drilling right now.

This is how deep it can drill—in fact, a little farther out with small modifications which are in the mill at present.

Next, please.

This shows the reef that I told you about. It extends from—this is the Campeche region, where the offshore discoveries are going on one after another with what the Mexicans must look upon as quite satisfactory monotony—another oil field is discovered every time you drill.

This is the Reforma area, and the reef in fact splays out in here. The reefs aren't all at the same time, mind you, some are— we've got from 100 to 140 million years— is a 40-million-year span. But the reef we just looked at in that profile was around for a large part of that time. And then here are the Golden Lane fields, of some of the first fields discovered in Mexico. The most productive wells ever known were in this area—240,000 barrels in 1 day. Of course, they didn't last forever.

Then there's a gap in here, and then we can trace the reef—fair continuity, it goes out here and it's lost. And here it is off the east coast of the United States and is last seen going off Canada.

That's the end of the slides. Thank you. Lights, please.

How do we evaluate this track? Well, let me say, to begin with, that the art of evaluating—or again, that the art of eval-

uating is fairly poor. In the best known area of the United States, the chances of finding an oil field, a commercial oil field, with an exploratory wildcat drill is now 1 in 7. That's the area we really know a lot about. The chance of finding a field that has 100 million barrels in it is 1 in 2,000. It might sound as though oil finders aren't very confident, but the reverse is true. It's because they've been exploring the region for 100 years and they've found everything that they now have such difficulties. If they didn't have difficulties now, they would have been incompetent for 100 years.

So, the odds of finding something out in deep water, even though unexplored, may be considerably better than that, and especially the odds of finding a giant field, because the odds of finding a giant field in the dry United States, 48 States, are very close to zero. These may be high odds, but they must be acceptable. We don't hear very much about oil companies going broke. [*Laughter*]

The only way we can guess what's in that reef, evaluate it, is to compare it with regions that have been drilled, such as the ones in Mexico and Texas and the other giant reefs around the world. We have done that recently, and it's our estimate that in the yellow area, the Mesozoic reef that you saw off the Baltimore Canyon region, there is something like 1 to 6 billion barrels of oil, produceable oil; that is, we heard earlier you leave half to two-thirds of the oil in the ground, and so we assume there's twice to three times that much. But produceable oil, 1 to 6 billion barrels.

Dr. Press. Dr. Menard, one more minute, please.

Dr. Menard. Yes, I know. For the whole region along the Atlantic Coast we estimate 2 to 15 billion barrels. If it's elevated, the amounts would be larger.

If the oil was never mature enough, there may be none. But those are the best estimates we can give. We estimate the cost of producing, if you could do it right now, would be $15 to $20 a barrel. Tests can be made within 12 to 15 months if rigs are available, the rigs exist.

It costs twelve to fifteen million dollars a well. The exploration can be done by industry in a program comparable to the COST well program drilling cooperatively by industry. And we're offering the area for lease almost immediately, or it can be done by a consortium of universities and the Government in the way it's been done in the deep sea. Or, of course, it can be done in some combination.

Thank you.

THE PRESIDENT. Is it going to be done? You said it can be. Are the plans made for the exploratory wells to be drilled?

DR. MENARD. It will take—we cannot do it with the existing oceanographic equipment. The oil companies can do it right now. They have the option of doing it. But whether they will or not is their option. If the Government chooses to pursue it by itself, it could be done either by leasing the same drilling ships that industry would use, the entire area could be tested in a matter of a few years, with the first holes, 10 holes, something of that sort, or you could modify the *Glomar Explorer,* a ship which the U.S. Government already owns. It's lying idle for lack of a suitable project. At a cost of about $70 million, the ship could be outfitted, refitted and outfitted in something in 2 to 4 years. So, it could drill indefinitely at almost any depth you would want in the ocean. It could test the Gulf of Mexico as well as this reef.

THE PRESIDENT. Is the technology available to control ruptures at that depth?

DR. MENARD. Yes.

THE PRESIDENT. Spills?

DR. MENARD. There is not technology to produce below about 5,000 feet yet, but with the decade—after the initial discoveries, with a decade to extend out from 5,000 to greater depths, I'm sure that could be developed.

THE PRESIDENT. Thank you, sir.

DR. PRESS. Mr. President, we are working with the Department of Energy and the National Science Foundation, with OMB, and investigating seriously the possibility of converting the *Glomar Explorer* for this kind of a drilling.

AUTOMOTIVE ADVANCES

Our next speaker will be Dr. Dale Compton, who's vice president for research of the Ford Motor Company, and he will tell us about automotive advances.

DR. COMPTON. *Mr. President, Secretary Duncan, Dr. Press, and ladies and gentlemen:*

I'd like to cover three main topics in my discussion with you this morning: First, a brief review of what has already been accomplished by the domestic automobile manufacturers in terms of reducing the energy of their products; second, some of the technical developments that should make further vehicle fuel efficiency improvements possible; and third, a quick look at some questions that must be answered if we're going to accomplish that.

Could I have the first slides, please?

During recent years substantial improvements have been made in the efficiency of the power trains used in our motor vehicles. At the same time, the average weight of domestically produced cars has been reduced by about 650 pounds.

The combined effect of these two actions has produced the improvement in

1549

the fuel economy shown on this slide, a dramatic increase of over 40 percent. The use of these vehicles by the American public has already saved over 500 million barrels of oil. Of course, this saving will continue to grow as new fuel-efficient vehicles replace older cars and as even more fuel-efficient cars are introduced in the years ahead.

Frankly, I believe no other industry in the world has yet demonstrated such exceptional energy-saving progress. Before considering the opportunities for further improvement in vehicle fuel economy, I'd like to comment briefly on what I think is a common misconception, namely, that foreign-built cars are technically ahead of U.S.-built cars in terms of fuel economy.

This chart, which plots the combined city urban cycle fuel economy, the so-called metro highway fuel economy, as a function of vehicle inertia weight. You will note that—and this is EPA data for the year 1979, as published by them—note that the dotted curve representing imports lies below the line for the American-built cars, except at one inertia weight where they are essentially equal.

Let me now turn to a consideration of the technical opportunities that may exist for further improvement in fuel economy. As a basis for this discussion, I will use plots similar to the previous one of fuel economy versus vehicle inertia test weight.

The line represents the average fuel economy of the 1979 U.S.-made gasoline-powered cars, as published by the EPA. A change in weight moves one along the line, a change in power-train efficiency moves one vertically away from the current technology line. And thus a new power-train technology that works for all engines in all inertia weight vehicles would move us above the current line.

Please note that a point on this line gives the fuel economy of a vehicle at a specified weight. This graph cannot be used to determine or project corporate average fuel economy, because the sales mix of small, medium, and large cars is such a dominant force in determining this.

Now, several technical changes can be expected to provide improvements in the average overall efficiency of the present power train. For example, better fuel control, better combustion chamber design, increased use of electronic control systems, turbocharging with reduced engine displacement while maintaining constant performance, and improved transmissions through the use of torque converter lockups in overdrive will also contribute. And if these improvements could be used for all vehicle weight classes, this would lead to fuel economy improvements shown here by the upper curve—an increase of about 15 percent over current power trains. Of course all of these improvements will not be possible on every weight class, and neither is it likely that all of these improvements could be introduced simultaneously.

I've carried forward to this plot the dark line from the earlier side and have marked it "current conventional." Now, there are two other piston engine technologies that may become available in reasonable quantities by 1985—the diesel and the stratified charge gasoline engine. In both of these engines, the fuel is injected into the combustion chamber. The first of these I will discuss is the gasoline version of the stratified charge engine, which at Ford is called PROCO, for program combustion. The slide shows this, and my associate is presenting you with a model of this combustion chamber.

You'll see that there is an injector for the fuel at the center, for directly injecting the fuel into the combustion chamber; you see that the piston has a unique cup design; you see that there are two spark plugs per cylinder. The process is controlled in such a way that the combustion is initiated in the cup, and then spreads out into the total chamber.

A higher compression ratio and a very lean air-fuel ratio provides a 15- to 20-percent improvement in fuel economy over the current conventional engine. This is indicated by the upper curve. This engine type also has the capability of meeting the 1981 Federal statutory emission levels for hydrocarbons, carbon monoxide, and oxides of nitrogen, and it has a particulate emission level below the proposed 1983 standard. The earliest practical introduction date by Ford is '84, assuming a successful pilot production run in 1980.

The second piston engine technology is the diesel engine. This slide shows the combustion chamber of the Oldsmobile 5.8-liter diesel engine that is just now going into production. In this case, the fuel is injected into a prechamber down into the combustion chamber, which will ride below here. The model will show that a bit clearer.

This is a high-compression engine, of course. In terms of its fuel economy, the middle line on this chart indicates the fuel economy that present diesel engines achieve, assuming that the vehicle has the same performance as a gasoline-powered vehicle at the same inertia weight.

The line is essentially the same as the line shown on the previous slide for PROCO fuel economy improvements in the range of 15 to 20 percent. But many of the diesel-powered vehicles available today do not achieve the same performance as their gasoline-powered counterparts. And the top line represents the fuel economy achievable by some currently available diesel-powered vehicles whose performance, as measured by acceleration, is 50 percent worse than a comparable gasoline-powered vehicle.

You see the improvement in fuel economy that's achieved by the reduction in the performance. It should be noted that diesel engine manufacturers have testified that current diesel engines cannot simultaneously achieve the '81 Federal statutory emission levels for hydrocarbons, carbon monoxides, and oxides of nitrogen, and also meet the proposed levels for particulates in all weight classes.

Unless new control technology can be developed which does not have a major effect upon fuel economy, diesel usage may be restricted to vehicles of very low inertia weight, in this region and to the left. It can be expected, however, that the excellent fuel economy of both PROCO and diesel can in time be further improved through many of the same actions mentioned in conjunction with the improved conventional engine that we discussed earlier.

THE PRESIDENT. Dr. Compton?

DR. COMPTON. Yes, sir.

THE PRESIDENT. Is the reduction in performance so onerous or unpopular that the motorists would not buy it at this time? That's one part of the question. Is that how the so-called Moody Mobile gets its increased performance, or is it a different change?

DR. COMPTON. Well, there are two parts to that question, Mr. President. These four points represent the vehicles that are being sold in the United States today. And so there is a market for them, and people are buying them. Whether that is a performance level that the average consumer will accept, I think, is unclear.

THE PRESIDENT. Well, is that just low acceleration?

DR. COMPTON. Low acceleration, yes, sir.

THE PRESIDENT. I see.

DR. COMPTON. In the case of the Moody Mobile, there is an additional change that's made in that. That is a turbocharged engine, and it's down-sized. As a result, it will get somewhat better fuel economy than this. I might just add, though, that in our studies and as reported by the EPA, we have been unable to meet the emission standards with that type of vehicle. We call it the 3,000-pound vehicle, and we have not been able to reduce the emissions to the level that it could be certified.

THE PRESIDENT. Is that apparently an insurmountable obstacle or something that——

DR. COMPTON. We continue to work on it. It is not clear to us, though, that it is possible within the current levels, within the current restrictions imposed by the certification process.

Now, beyond these versions of the piston engine, several alternative power-plants are under development. The nearest term prospect appears to be the electric. While currently available batteries severely limit the size and range of such vehicles, extensive research programs are underway that have the prospect of providing a much improved range under reasonable driving conditions. Vehicles with a range between 70 and 100 miles may be available by the late 1980's. Cost, durability, and safety of electric vehicles are all issues that must be resolved.

Other alternatives include the high-temperature gas turbine and the Sterling. And both are currently under development with the assistance of funds from the Department of Energy.

This is a slide of the Chrysler automotive turbine engine that's been jointly developed with the Government—and while we have a model, it's very difficult to carry that to you for you to examine, but you can see the principal elements of it, there's a compressor, there are turbine wheels, there are diffusers.

The next generation of such turbines, if they are to find extensive usage in automobiles, will require ceramic components. We have a couple examples of those. These are the stator turbine wheel, made from ceramics. Of course these are in the very early stages of development and are far from ready for consideration for production. While progress is being made on both of these engines, it appears unlikely that either can be in large-scale production before the late 1990's or the early 2000's.

But we recognize that vehicle weight is as important to fuel economy as is power-train efficiency. This is the trend that can be expected to occur in the use of materials. Note the increases expected in plastics, aluminum, and high-strength steel. This, coupled with some further vehicle down-sizing, will probably reduce average vehicle weights by another 500 pounds by 1985 for a further increase in fuel economies of about 10 percent. We believe that weight reductions beyond this level, beyond the 1985 level, will not be possible using conventional materials unless the utility of the vehicle is very seriously reduced. Therefore, space age materials are being investigated that may allow further reductions without a change in utility.

Prominent in this research is the study of graphite fiber reinforced plastics, and here are two examples. The first example—I'll show you another in a moment—demonstrates the potential weight savings of these compounds, 73 percent in this one case. Presently the cost of these materials is prohibitive, and the available supply is insufficient to allow consideration for large-scale use. But if these and other problems can be solved, the use of this material could allow several hundred pounds more weight to be removed from a vehicle, thus allowing further weight reductions while maintaining utility. It appears unlikely, however, that the graphite fiber reinforced materials can achieve significant usage before the year 1990.

THE PRESIDENT. Because of cost or what?

DR. COMPTON. Because of cost and availability.

Now, there are many substantial technical and economic questions that must be answered as we proceed to improve fuel economies. First and foremost is cost. Ford estimates that the cost of the average vehicle will have to increase by $600 to $800 just to incorporate those technologies that we think can be in production by 1985, and that's in '79 dollars. Investments totaling many billions of dollars will be needed.

Equally important is functional utility. We must not destroy the vehicle characteristics that make the cars and trucks useful to people. We must not reduce the size to such an extent that the utility suffers. Then there is the continuing concern over the health effects of engine emissions, especially those from diesel engines. Will certain engines be precluded from use or will controls be needed whose cost and fuel economy penalties make those engines unattractive? Ways must be found to ensure vehicle safety without increasing vehicle weight, for as I've said repeatedly, increased weight reduces fuel economy. Concern also exists about the maintenance and serviceability of the power train, the increased complexity could further raise the cost of maintenance.

And finally, there's the question of timing. It has been Ford's experience that 5 to 7 years is the minimum time needed to put a new engine or transmission of reasonably conventional design into production. Further, if each of the automobile manufacturers in the country were to decide today to replace all of its engine and transmission facilities, it would take about 10 years to accomplish this task because of the very real capacity limits of our machine tool suppliers.

The availability of alternative fuels deserves special mention. In reducing national dependence upon imported petroleum, fuel economy improvements must be coupled with a vigorous program to increase the availability of liquid fuels from alternative sources. While other speakers have addressed this issue in some detail this morning, I want to emphasize that a specific synthetic fuel may be best suited to a particular engine, and the sooner that we know what fuels will be available and in what timeframe, the better each vehicle manufacturer will be able to do its job of having the proper engine available for the use of that fuel.

It is also important to come to grips with the issue of how to measure energy efficiency of cars and trucks. Since various fuels have energy contents per gallon that are greatly different from gasoline, the simple measure of miles per gallon will not continue to be an adequate measure of efficiency. For example, we may need to use something like Btu's per mile.

Lights, please.

What is the fuel economy future? Customer demand for good fuel economy stimulated by rising and realistic energy prices and availability concerns will keep fuel economy at the top of our product priorities. And over the longer term, continued efforts in basic research related to automotive technology, hopefully, will increase the opportunity for major improvements in vehicle efficiency.

This of course is the basis on which we and others in the industry and Dr. Press' office are working together in an effort to formulate an industry-government automotive research program that will concentrate on some of these fundamental research issues.

To conclude, our industry's products will have achieved a 100-percent improvement in efficiency by 1985. I believe that significant improvements in fuel efficiency will indeed continue beyond that. But we must recognize that the gains will probably be gradual, that there are some high technical risks, and that progress will be increasingly expensive.

Thank you, sir.

THE PRESIDENT. I know we're running a little short of time, but is there any work being done on what are the possibilities for the burning of gases that are presently emitted?

DR. COMPTON. There has been research. You are speaking of the exhaust gases or gases as a fuel?

THE PRESIDENT. Both. I was particularly thinking about the correlation between cutting down emissions, undesirable emissions.

DR. COMPTON. The problem with using gases as a fuel, such as hydrogen, is not so much with the vehicle as it is with providing a distribution and storage facility nationwide. There are also weight penalties associated with carrying it on board the vehicle.

The combination of those appears to us to make it unattractive as a mobile source of fuel.

THE PRESIDENT. Theoretically, it's possible.

DR. COMPTON. It is certainly possible. There is not a theoretical limit to burning hydrogen on board a vehicle. It is a question, though, of whether the overall system is better served to use the hydrogen in other ways than for the vehicle.

PHOTOVOLTAICS

DR. PRESS. Our last speaker this morning, Mr. President, is Dr. John Goldsmith, vice president of the Solarex Corporation, and formerly in charge of solar photovoltaics research at NASA's Jet Propulsion Laboratory, and he will tell us about photovoltaics.

DR. GOLDSMITH. Good morning, Mr. President, ladies and gentlemen. It is indeed a pleasure to be here this morning. In my presentation this morning, I'll try to brief you very quickly on the status of photovoltaics, where it is at the present time—technologically, economically, in the world, and what might be done in terms of improving that technology so that it might in the future become a contributor to our national energy needs.

To get into the topic, I'd like to very briefly describe for those in the audience who may not be familiar with photovoltaics. If one takes a very common material, which is—what is made up of this particular wafer that I have in my hands, you note that it's about 3 inches in diameter and about ten thousandths of an inch thick. This is made of silicon, the second most common element in the crust of the Earth. If impurities are placed in this, tiny amounts of phosphorous and boron, this material becomes electrically active, that is, that when photons, light is emitted and is impinging upon this piece of material, it activates the electrons inside of this silicon, and the solar cell becomes an energy producer, it converts the sunlight into electricity. And it does it directly, which is very different than any other form of solar energy conversion technology that certainly we talked about today.

Now, that principle of direct solar energy conversion means that it does this without any moving parts, without any emissions, without any pollution, without any vibration, and because it does it electronically, meaning that there is no chemical reactions going on within it, its lifetime is indefinite; it can go on for many, many years.

I have a very brief demonstration of what photovoltaic technology may be. This is a very simple illustration of this principle. This material has now been made into a solar cell by the addition of those impurities. It's placed in the top of this cube, and wires have been now placed from the top and the bottom of the solar cell to a little electric motor inside the cube. And if we turn on the light, which would simulate the Sun, we see that there is a direct conversion that goes on. And by simply cutting off the light, the electricity stops.

This principle has been developed, it's very modular in nature—the more solar cells we add together, the more power we derive. There is no complex interaction between the solar cells, which makes it look like as we increase the number of solar cells, we're going to get less power than you would anticipate; quite simple, electrical summations of these solar cells together.

Now, I have some slides I'd like to very quickly show you to further develop this thesis.

In this first slide we see a cutaway of what a solar cell really is. This is a very simple, thin piece of material covered with a window in order to protect the surface of it from contamination, dust, and make it easy to clean. A solar cell by itself, as we have seen, is not in itself able to sustain a complete system, that is, that when the Sun goes away. Of course, we must have energy in order to provide the energy in the evening, for instance. And this is done by a conventional technique such as a storage battery.

A solar cell, such as this, plus some means of controlling the amount of energy which is coming out to charge the battery, is something that we would conventionally

be able to use, for instance, in our home. And this is one of the very interesting aspects of what photovoltaics may offer. That is the distributed form of energy conversion that people may put on to their houses. It would take, for instance, about 500 square feet of a solar array on a south-facing roof in order to provide enough energy to power a typical American home.

At present cost today, it costs on the order of around $50,000 for that size of a power system, and therefore, in today's technology and today's economics, that's, of course, quite impractical. But it doesn't have to be there, and we'll develop this thesis further.

The technology of solar cells became quite developed during the space age, and one of the best examples of that technology was in the use of solar cells in powering our Skylab space station. This was nominally a 24-kilowatt power system. It was in orbit for over 6 years, and in that period of time it was the only source of power for the entire Skylab—a much more complicated kind of a power system than ever we would need in our home.

In that 6 years, there was unmeasurable degradation of that power system in the hostile environment of space.

Solar cells since 1973 have had a great interest in its application relative to terrestrial purposes, and here we see it being used on a tower in the Gulf of Mexico for navigation aids in order to operate lights, to blow horns, and to warn oncoming ships about its presence.

It's used frequently in isolated areas, such as this particular system which is in the Mojave Desert, which is used by the California Highway Patrol for radio relay purposes. It is being used quite successfully. It is being used now in developing countries. In this particular application, it is being used in Senegal in order to pump water, where people in the past have had to carry the water on their heads many miles to the village.

It's being used in the United States for water pumping—in this particular case, on a Navajo Indian reservation in Arizona. An even more sophisticated application of photovoltaics is coming along again on an Indian reservation in Arizona, the Papico Indian reservation, in which a photovoltaic array is providing a great deal of the energy requirements of this particular Indian tribe, not only for water pumping but, as indicated here, for refrigeration, for operating lights, for their communications, and so forth.

Progress in the use of photovoltaics has been very good and has been stimulating a great deal of interest in terms of looking at it for near-term types of needs when the price comes down further than it is at the present time. We'll talk about that price in just a minute. Such things, for instance, as large irrigation purposes. This is a 25-kilowatt system which is being studied in Meade, Nebraska, in order to irrigate these cornfields, which are immediately behind this photovoltaic array.

I'd like to now talk a little bit about what has happened in terms of photovoltaic technology and begin to develop a dialog associated with why we believe that that technology can be improved and why it may eventually reach a point where it might be useful for large scale terrestrial applications.

To summarize, however, before we get to that one point. This generally tells us about the major characteristics of what photovoltaics are. It's the direct conversion of Sun's radiation to electricity. Its intrinsic reliability seems to be very well demonstrated by the many applications that it has been experiencing over the past 20 years since it became of very serious interest. That it is modular, as we have indicated, that there is a relative absence

of environmental impacts, in fact, particularly a silicon photovoltaic array would be amongst the most benign of all types of power systems that we could consider. It has a large technology base, it has based a lot of its technology on the billions of dollars which have been developed and invested in the semiconductor industry over the past 30 years.

What has happened as far as price is concerned? And what we see is a very complex type of a graph. It is what we call, in engineering terms, a log-log plot. It's something that we have to be very careful about interpreting, but it's plotted in order to try to show what kind of relationships have existed between the price of the product and the quantity of the solar arrays which have been produced and commercially sold in the United States. And when we plot them on a log-log plot, we see that there's a relatively straight line being formed. The question, of course, is can that line continue?

We note that this is now a number when it is plotted in constant 1975 dollars, it is a cost now which has gone from the space type solar array systems which were greater than maybe $300 per watt, to prices now less than $10 per watt. But the question is, is how far down can you extrapolate that kind of a technology. Do we really believe that it can go much further than it is at the present time? And I think that the likelihood that it can with existing technology is not good.

That things have progressed greatly because of the advent of mass production, larger quantities of sales have indicated the value of significant investments in mass production kinds of equipment and those things have been primarily responsible for the kinds of improvements that we've got. But in order for us to go much further, we're going to have to bring on new technologies, technologies which are not at the present time extrapolations from the semiconductor technology which has been the base of this thing up to the present time.

Another important and interesting point about this is that in the United States we have, or we are dominant in both the industry and the technology, and of the market of solar arrays being produced and sold in the world, the United States exports 50 percent of all those uses of photovoltaics around the world. Let me rephrase that.

Of the total number of sales of photovoltaics which are primarily made in the United States, 50 percent of them are outside the United States, which then gives us some additional incentives in terms of this technology relative to our balance of payments.

I'd like to very simply try to utilize the basic information that's on this graph, but plot it in a different way in accordance with a time base.

Now, we see here a plot of the reduction of solar power or solar photovoltaic power to the present time. And we are going to use that same extrapolation down to a continuum. That curve, which I have indicated, is the learning curve that has been developed so far in photovoltaics, is very analogous to the learning curve that has been used in the electronics industry.

There's a good likelihood that that kind of a learning curve can be sustained. And if we do continue along that kind of a path and we plot against that the utility price for energy which would be derived from a utility system for a distributive-like power system, like for a particular home, and put it in the context of what a photovoltaic array might have to be in order for it to be competitive with that utility power, we find that our most optimistic curve intersects that line around 1986.

So, when might photovoltaics become a significant contributor? When might it reach a point where it might compete with utility power? We believe the optimistic curve, the fast-growth curve for that. We may begin to be able to see it around this 1986 time period. Certainly not everyone agrees with that kind of a number. I think that there is very good agreement that the likelihood for continued reduction of photovoltaic prices is very good. When it will reach this particular point in competition with utility power, it certainly could be sometime longer than that, and it will depend upon the innovation and the invention of American industry, I believe.

Now to try to understand very quickly why I believe that the technology can be improved, I will in a very short manner try to acquaint you with the way that photovoltaics are made at the present time. Those wafers that I had indicated in my earlier remarks are made in a very tedious kind of way. One takes very highly pure silicon and melts it at 1,600 degrees Fahrenheit. Then one drops a seed of silicon into that molten silicon and begins to withdraw it with a meniscus of that silicon attached, and then very slowly, at the rate of around 2 inches per hour, one withdraws the seed and rotates it in one direction while you rotate then the pot of molten silicon in the opposite direction.

So, after several days of growth perhaps, one has several feet of ingot of silicon that one then takes and very carefully cuts wafers from it.

Now, that particular technology can be significantly improved, we believe. There are ways of pulling faster. There are ways of growing the ingots larger. There are ways of cutting much more efficiently; in fact, even with this technology, it may be possible to even reach the goals that we're talking about.

But suppose instead we are able to cast the silicon as a brick, as one would cast in a foundry, or instead be able to pull a ribbon of silicon directly out of the melt. Or perhaps, even better than that, suppose we are able to make a photovoltaic material that we could spray, literally spray on to low-cost, perhaps a glass substrate, and that in itself could make a photovoltaic device.

In fact, all of those technologies are viable, and they're all being demonstrated in various ways, and they're all being worked on in many programs throughout the United States.

In this last viewgraph, I have tried to indicate the various kinds of what I will call the leading technologies that we're investigating as far as photovoltaics is concerned. The bellwether is the Czochralski technology, showing an 18-percent commercial approach which is presently commercialized.

The next one in terms of its commercial readiness is what we call an uncrystalline or semicrystalline ingot, which is a cast technology, where we literally cast bricks. That has just been newly commercialized. There are some cadmium sulfite technologies which are potentially going to be commercialized in the near future, which are thin, film-spray types of approaches.

The potential of having so many approaches all pointed towards our same goals, all having the viability, many of them having the viability of reaching our objectives, gives us some confidence that we may be able to get photovoltaics into the ballpark of being a competitive energy system for our long-range electrical needs.

So, in conclusion, photovoltaics continues to look promising as a possible alternate energy source. Perhaps as early as 1986, some impact may begin to be seen.

And, in the meantime, it is finding a growing world commercial application. It works; it's reliable, particularly in areas where utility power has not yet penetrated, photovoltaics is finding its greatest interest.

Thank you, Mr. President.

THE PRESIDENT. Dr. Goldsmith, there's been a lot of publicity this past week—and I'm sure you noticed—about the chemical process for producing the silicone single crystal. I understand that it's been done from several sources, but it didn't show up on your last chart. Does it have a breakthrough potential, or is it just one of many with approximately equal potential?

DR. GOLDSMITH. Well, the process, I believe, that has been given the most publicity during the past week was the process which was reported by the Stanford Research Institute.

THE PRESIDENT. Yes.

DR. GOLDSMITH. I personally am not that familiar with that particular process to be able to comment that it really offers the breakthrough potential that we're looking for. However, there are other very interesting technologies which are very similar in nature, that is, that it has great breakthrough potentials coming from other organizations that I do know about that look quite encouraging.

For instance, the Union Carbide approach looks to me to be a very interesting, and an approach that deserves a great deal of attention, as well as a similar kind of a technology at the Tell Memorial Institute.

So, I don't think we're hurting for techniques for purifying silicon, which is the Stanford Research Institute technology.

THE PRESIDENT. Is the purification of silicon in the production of the crystal the most expensive part of the process? Is that where the breakthrough on price is likely to come?

DR. GOLDSMITH. It's one of the most important—when we try to do an analysis of where the cost elements are in growing or making a solar array, we would find that about one-third of the price will be wrapped up in this—when we get to the point where it's a competitive alternate system—that one-third of the price will be wrapped up in that purified silicon material.

DR. PRESS. Mr. President, the report had indicated that silicon accounted for 20 percent of the material cost of solar cells now, and with this, the new development that you were referring to, it would be reduced from 20 percent to 2 percent.

THE PRESIDENT. Thank you very much.

My first reaction is one of appreciation to Dr. Press for setting this seminar up, for Joe Pettit and those at Georgia Tech, for making it possible for us to assemble here, for Charles Duncan, who has enormous new responsibilities, for promising me that he'll carry out all the opportunities that have been presented, and especially for the panelists, who've given what I consider to be an exciting and extremely interesting presentation of some of the possibilities in resolving our energy problems.

I don't think there's any argument with the fact that the cheapest and best way to meet our goals of reduced dependence on imported oil is through conservation, and this is an area that has not been adequately explored.

The technology is present, the primary obstacle has been convincing people that it's a worthy effort. I've spent a good bit of time the last 2 or 3 days talking to Members of Congress, who are home in their districts or in their States all over the Nation, and almost invariably, when I've called the Members of Congress in

the House and Senate, they say that there's sometimes a startling new realization and interest on the part of the American people that we do have an energy problem and that it can be solved if we all work together.

It's not been possible in the last 2 years to convince American people that it's a worthy subject for them to explore and for which they can make a contribution. So, I think conservation is something that we need to emphasize, first of all. There's obviously an exciting possibility that within existing natural resources that our Nation possesses, that we can increase productivity both in the percentage of the materials that we extract in coal mining, oil production, natural gas, geothermal, and also in new methods of producing materials which, in the past, have not been economically feasible, but with the new higher prices of energy on an international basis, that they are, indeed, competitive and which can use technologies long extant.

We also, of course, are interested in, and I think the public is completely sold on, the possibility for solar energy use and that of replenishable supplies. One of the most intriguing to me was that Georgia now produces 6 quads of energy in biomass. And I've got several acres of— [*laughter*]—of scrub oak trees that I would like to contribute to the process at a minimum cost. This is the kind of thing that I believe is worthy of greatly escalated exploration.

New England, obviously, has done a great job in publicity surrounding the use of wood-burning stoves, which is one use of biomass, but the conversion of waste products is an exciting possibility.

I was given some data the last time I went up to New England that just the waste from their forests that's left on the ground could meet a substantial portion of their energy requirements in New England. And, as you know, they are very heavily dependent on imported oil at a rapidly increasing cost.

There is no way that I can see that many of these possibilities can be explored—ranging all the way from biomass, the insulation of low-income families' homes, the scientific and research developments that must be a prerequisite for advances in new techniques, the promotion of these procedures in the public's mind—without the passage of proposals to the Congress for financing. The windfall profits tax, which would leave an adequate reservoir of funds for the oil companies to explore for conventional gas and oil, has to be the basis for these scientific and other opportunities. And I hope that all those who are interested, including the oil companies themselves, other producers of energy, the consumers, the Members of Congress, interested public officials, will join in without further divisive debate or delaying tactics, and get the energy package passed. We've been long overdue on it.

And my own belief is, my conviction is that our Nation has the scientific and technological ability. Our free enterprise system, with its innate competitiveness and innovation, is ready, and I think we can forge a very enlightened relationship between Government, with the initiative of guaranteed prices, guaranteed markets, for new synthetic fuels that would be very productive.

The proposals that we've made to the Congress would involve a minor Government involvement, for instance, in the production of new kinds of fuel, synthetic fuels. I think out of 80 possible projects that would be included in the new energy production corporation, a maximum of 3 out of the 80 would be operated potentially by the Federal Government, and if any of those 3, or all of the 3, were viable projects for the private sector, then the Government would defer to the private sector for the production of those synthetic fuels. The reason for including just that small number was that some are likely to be so experimental in nature and so distant from cost-effectiveness, if they are even successful, that there must be some limited Government role.

But the desire that I have as President to see government and private industry, scientists, technicians, engineers, our free enterprise system, both in production and experimentation, working with an enlightened American public is very important.

I hope that the press, who are represented here today, will make a maximum effort to report to the American public what has been delivered to us.

Many of these reports are fairly basic. I was acquainted with some of the data before I came, but it's very important for the American people in general to be well educated on what the possibilities are.

There's no reason for discouragement. I'm convinced that our Nation has the capability of overcoming the energy challenge, and to the extent that we can succeed with conservation, with solar energy of all kinds, with the extraction of existing American supplies of natural gas and oil, increased use of coal in an environmentally acceptable fashion, we can minimize our dependence on those technologies that might have potential adverse economic effects—synthetic fuels, nuclear power, and so forth.

So, I think the ordering of priorities and an enlightened public, a comprehensive energy policy approved by the Congress, and the cooperation of all Americans, particularly between the private sector and government, in my opinion, are a very hopeful prospect for the future.

I'd like to again express my thanks to the distinguished panelists who have been so kind as to acquaint us with some few facets of energy technology potentials for the future and also to express my thanks to all those who participated with this.

I will personally follow up with Dr. Press, my science and technology adviser, with Charles Duncan, the new Secretary of Energy, the other members of my administration, in the ideas that have been presented here, and others that come to me.

And I'm very grateful for the chance to live in a country that's been so generously endowed with natural resources and with the free enterprise system, and a system of society that lets the innovation of individuals contribute collectively to reaching an exalted and very important goal.

The rest of the world is watching us. I think many of the less developed nations and even the advanced Western nations will naturally defer to us in some of these areas, and when I meet with other leaders, in economic summit conferences and on a bilateral basis, I always explore the possibility for cooperation. There's no restraint on the exchange of basic research data even when it applies to automotive design, for instance, which is a highly competitive field. And I found them to be very excited about it.

The solvent refining processes for coal that might be explored in the near future in West Virginia and Kentucky, for instance—at least in West Virginia—will be jointly financed by Japan and Germany. This shows that there can be an exchange of both financing and scientific and technical data across international boundary lines. So, the possibilities are broad, and I think we can legitimately keep our hopes up that we will triumph in this very challenging test of our Nation's will and capability.

Thank you all for letting me be part of it. I've learned a lot. I know everyone here has, too.

Thank you very much.

NOTE: The portion of the energy seminar which the President attended began at 10 a.m. in the Fred B. Wenn Student Center ballroom at the Georgia Institute of Technology.

Following the seminar, the President met with the executive committee of the National Conference of Democratic Mayors at the student center.

Atlanta, Georgia

Remarks at Emory University.
August 30, 1979

As I'm sure all of you have surmised, coming back to Georgia and to this setting returns to me overwhelming memories of my past. As I sat here on this delightful day, I was reminded of the cottonfields in Sumter County during August when I was a boy, but Emory has added a new dimension—I particularly appreciate this delightful, insulated robe that they've provided for me to give this speech. [*Laughter*]

President Laney, I'm delighted to be here on your campus and the campus of the faculty and students and the alumni of a great university. It's always good to go to a college campus and know that the president is popular. I was overwhelmed with the degree of popularity when, at the luncheon which I attended—not quite long enough to eat—President Laney got almost as much applause when they mentioned his name as when they mentioned the name of Coca-Cola. [*Laughter*] That is my tribute, indeed.

My good friend Chairman D. W. Brooks reminded me of my stature as President. He talked about fishing, and then he was kind enough to mention rabbits in the same comment. [*Laughter*]

He joined with Chairman Henry Bowden in pointing out that when he had been to have lunch with me at the White House, that he had always had just a sandwich. And Henry Bowden pointed out that I had not changed my habits, that when he had lunch with me the last week that I was Governor, he also had just a sandwich. [*Laughter*]

Bishop Cannon did much better. As you can well imagine, being the gracious man of God that he is, he did not overlook an opportunity to pay true tribute to the highest elected officer of our land. He carefully chose, among all the events of my past, my interview with Playboy and described it—[*laughter*]—with some degree of relish and enthusiasm. It was indeed a delightful lunch for me.

I'm truly honored by Emory, an institution which, to a Christian, cannot fail but have a special meaning, an institution which is great in its own right, which is dynamic in its attitude toward the present and the future, an institution which, in a modern, fast-changing, technological world, would set aside the time and invite the President to a special occasion, that is, the dedication of a church, a place to worship God.

I'm going to make my speech brief. Former Attorney General Griffin Bell has given me a report, which may be apocryphal, about an event in the life of John Wesley. When asked what estate he would leave for posterity, he replied, "Just four silver teaspoons, and the Methodist Church." One of the persistent and most difficult challenges in our lives is to balance values, the transient against the permanent, and the less important against

those which are vital.

In breaking ground for the William R. Cannon Chapel and Religious Center, we honor the things in life that are most precious, things that cannot be seen and which cannot be measured. We can measure the grandeur of a person's house or the size of a bank account or the acreage of one's land, or how fast one's net worth increases each year. We tend to dwell too much on such things, for they tell us very little about the real meaning of life. For that, we must turn to things which cannot be seen or which cannot be measured, to things like honesty, integrity, the strength of conscience, the love of God, service to others, humility, wisdom.

These things are invisible. They're beyond measurement, but they comprise life's true wealth. In these things, Bishop Billy Cannon is a very rich man, and his life has also brought richness and meaning to the lives of thousands of others, including my own.

I happen to be a Baptist, but I've been surrounded by Methodists all my life— my mother, my wife, some people. And when I was enjoying the highest official day of my life, being inaugurated as President of the United States of America, I chose, to give the invocation, a Georgian, Bishop Billy Cannon.

What's true in measuring values for an individual is also true for a nation. We can measure gross national product, imports and exports, the growth of industry and manufacturing. We can see with our own eyes how many tanks we have, how many nuclear warheads in our arsenal. We can be thankful for such strength and grateful for material blessings. But we know that these are not the most important characteristics of a nation's life. They do not hold us together as a unique people. They are not the essence of what makes us Americans.

The real meaning of America is not encompassed in the material wealth and the military power of our country, for we know that wealth and power can be a potential for evil as well as for good. We measure the real meaning of America, as in a human life, in our intangible values, values which do not change—our care for one another, our commitment to human freedom, our search for justice, our devotion to human rights and to world peace and the patriotism and the basic goodness of the people of our Nation.

These qualities cannot be measured. They're invisible. Yet, these are the true strengths of America which channel our wealth and our strength, not for evil, but for good.

These are the things that have drawn so many oppressed and friendless people to our shores and that have made America a beacon of freedom for millions of people around the world who have never met an American face to face. And these are the qualities that give hope and moral sustenance to many here at home in our own country for whom the ideals of America are still imperfectly realized— the poor among us, the minorities, those who may not speak English, those who lack proper education or adequate health care or who have talents which are yet unawakened.

We are the greatest and, I believe, the most free nation on Earth. Yet all of us know that we still have a long journey ahead before the powerful, transcendent ideals of America are fully translated into reality in the daily lives of all people in our country.

But if the history of America shows anything, it shows that America is capable of change. America is capable of change because we have the courage and because the conscience of America is strong.

All of the great movements of American history, from the Revolution to the abolition of slavery, from the struggle for women's suffrage to the peaceful crusade for civil rights in our own generation, all these movements and others like them have called upon the conscience of America. And we have found that because of that conscience, America changes, America makes progress, America comes ever closer to the realization of the majestic ideals on which this country was founded.

The conscience of America is rooted in its institutions and it's rooted in the ethics of the Judeo-Christian tradition. That tradition has many expressions, but within our religions, it's not enough. It's also rooted in our secular life as well, and that gap can constantly be bridged by human beings who search for the correlation of the two. It's varied expressions are as diverse as we American people ourselves, but underlying that diversity is a basic unity of belief and purpose.

I've spoken recently of a crisis of confidence in this country and a need for unity. Of course, we are proud of our diversity. Our pluralistic society is an important source of vitality and creativity of American life. And I would guess that the American society is the most diverse in the entire world. But we must not permit diversity to degenerate into division.

In a time of trial, we must not permit the legitimate contest of competing views to become a war of group against group, special interest against special interest, and finally, each of us against all the others.

The motto of our country, as you know, is "E Pluribus Unum"—"Out of Many, One." We must, of course, continue to cherish the many—but the multifaceted nature of our people is exemplified in many. But in this time of crisis, both material and spiritual, we must learn to place greater emphasis on the "one"—on the shared values and the shared interests that unite us. For in a varied nation like our own, those transcendent values and that concern for the common good are the sole and indispensable basis for harmony and social cohesion.

In international councils, we can share with others this vision of a common humanity based on humanistic views.

I'm very sorry that Andrew Young, as President of the United Nations Security Council, was called back today to New York and was not able to be with us. He went to the United Nations 2½ years ago at a time when many countries, especially in the developing world, looked upon the United States with fear and mistrust. His work has helped millions of poor and oppressed people throughout the world to understand that we support their longing for justice and for a better life.

He speaks from the heart, he speaks out of a deep commitment, he speaks out of religious conscience, and he speaks with a preacher's eloquence. The commitment to social justice and human rights that Andy Young has brought to his work as an American diplomat will continue to guide us in the months and years ahead.

As Andy leaves the United Nations, our common task as Americans is to look ahead with a sense of caring and concern for the social fabric of our own Nation and for the more peaceful, more fair, and more just world around us.

Controversial and sensitive issues must continue to be addressed with courage by our Government. Every American has a right, even a duty, to debate all public issues, including issues of foreign policy. Open debate and the free exchange of ideas are the heart and the soul of our

political system. But differing political views, when and if they do exist, must not become the occasion for deep and damaging divisions between groups of citizens in our country.

Black Americans and Jewish Americans have worked side by side for generations in the service of human rights, social justice, and the general welfare. Both groups have a particular call on the conscience of each other and on the conscience of all of us. Both groups have suffered too much pain, too much persecution, too much bigotry to compound that suffering in any way. And both groups are part of something larger—the totality that we call America.

I spoke earlier of the need for unity, for a greater emphasis on the oneness of our Nation. Many nations today, as we well know, are in danger of being torn apart by ethnic divisions, by political rivalries, and by religious conflicts. We must seek resolution of differences, and we must stand with each other to prevent all these quarrels of the world from being imported into our own national life.

With the guidance of God we can be successful in this search for the accommodation of differences. We in the United States have learned to accommodate the diversity of our people, because all of us hold fast to our common identity, our identity as Americans. It's especially important to do that today, for we live in a time of wrenching change.

As we strive to meet the challenges of the energy crisis and of inflation, as we search for peace in a nuclear age, we must shape our national life in the light of those fundamental principles which do not change.

The well-known historian Arnold Toynbee teaches that civilizations grow in a rhythm of challenge and response, challenge and response. When civilizations reach their highest goals, he said, it's difficult decisions, difficult conditions rather than easy conditions that produce great achievements. And Toynbee further holds that great nations most often fail and fall not because of material weaknesses, but because of complacency and a failure to meet new challenges creatively.

I do not fear for the future of the United States. If there is one thing we are not, it's complacent. If sometimes we are confused, if sometimes we think we may have lost our way temporarily, it's because we are struggling to apply our transcendent values to new challenges of awesome complexity which no other peoples on Earth have been able to meet successfully. We are most likely in the forefront. The basic strength and creativity of our values remain undiminished, and as long as our national roots are imbedded in that rich soil, we prosper and we will triumph.

Throughout our history—I would like to say in closing—crisis has been the occasion for rethinking, for redirection, and resurgence. In the early and middle years of the 1700's, much of Western civilization languished in a crisis of the spirit. War and social upheaval had robbed many people of both will and purpose.

In the midst of that widespread moral depression came an international spiritual revival lead by men like John and Charles Wesley and George Whitefield. The subsequent moral upsurge began in the churches; they spilled over into the streets and found lodging in political movements in Europe and here among the American colonies.

Out of that movement of the spirit, based on spiritual things in the colonies, came our independence. The effect was so profound that years later John Adams would write, and I quote from him, "What do we mean by the American Revolution? Do we mean the American war? The Revolution was effected before the war commenced. The Revolution was in the minds and the hearts of the people— a change in their religious sentiments of their duties and obligations . . . . This radical change," he said, "in the principles, opinions, sentiments and affections of the people—that was the real American Revolution."

That crisis brought awakening; awakening brought creative and fresh directions. I pray that from our present material and spiritual crises, which are well recognized, that there may come a new sense of awakening and a new pursuit of more fulfilling ways to live and to work together as Americans.

Let us confess our failures; let us marshal our inner resources and move on, upward. If we are guided by the best of our common mandates, renewal of American spirit will come.

We in America will find a way to solve our material problems, and as we do, we can rejuvenate the spirit and the confidence of our country. And then may history record that our generation of Americans heeded the words that you have just heard in Isaiah 61—that we brought good tidings to the afflicted, proclaimed liberty to captives and comfort to all who mourn, that we repaired the ruined cities and the desolations of many generations, and that through us the Lord God will cause righteousness and praise to spring forth before all the nations.

That's my prayer. I know it's yours. Thank you very much.

NOTE: The President spoke at 2:14 p.m. at the groundbreaking ceremonies on the Quadrangle. In his remarks, he referred to James T. Laney, president of Emory University, D. W. Brooks, chairman of the Emory Committee of One Hundred, and Henry Bowden, chairman of the board of trustees of Emory University.

Prior to the ceremony, the President attended a luncheon in Cox Hall on the university's campus.

Tampa, Florida

Remarks and a Question-and-Answer Session at a Town Meeting.　August 30, 1979

THE PRESIDENT. During 1975 and 1976, my wife, Rosalynn, spent 75 days in Florida; and I spent almost as many, and I learned a lot about our country from you, because not only is Florida a dynamic and aggressive State with confidence and God's beauty, which attracts people from all over the world, but Americans from every State assessing our Nation very carefully to find the garden spot are inclined to move to Florida to spend their productive years after they become senior citizens.

ADMINISTRATION POLICIES

I had a chance during those months to listen a lot and to talk some. And I heard about the need for a social security system that was sound, and I heard about the fact that the unemployment rate was over 8 percent. But I also heard about the need to maintain peace and to make sure that no young American might lose his or her life in combat. And so far, God's blessed us, and I hope that when I leave the White House we'll still have that record.

And a lot of people here from Jewish families, and from others, said the most important single issue that threatens world peace is the Mideast conflict, where four wars in 30 years and hundreds of years of antagonism and hatred create a cancer and needs to be addressed. And we've made some progress there.

There have been many issues on which we have succeeded so far. There have been other issues that are too difficult to solve in 2½ years, and there have been other issues where one cannot find a solution until the American people get aroused and committed to joining in an effort to find a solution to it. Obviously, we're trying.

We've now got a SALT agreement with the Soviets to put a very tight constraint over any increase in nuclear weapons that threaten the world; and the Soviet Union, if the SALT treaty is passed, will have to cut back their nuclear arsenal, their numbers of launchers by 10 percent. We won't have to cut back any. But this will lead to further progress in the future, and to constrain nuclear weapons is a very burning issue now before the United States Senate.

Inflation has been with us 10 or 12 years. It goes up and down, primarily because of the price charged for imported oil. We had a very high inflation rate, 12 or 13 percent back in 1973, 1974. We've got a very high inflation rate now, because the OPEC countries have increased the price of oil over 50 percent in the last 6 or 7 months.

Inflation is tenacious. It's got to be addressed. We're doing the best we can. We're holding down Federal spending. We've already cut the budget deficit more than 50 percent. We're going to have tight management of the Federal bureaucracy. We've got civil service reform, but the key issue on which inflation depends is that excessive importing of foreign oil.

We now import 50 percent of all the oil we use, and we not only import oil, we import unemployment and we import inflation. So far, the Congress has acted on about 60 or 65 percent of the energy proposals that I sent to them in April of 1977, almost 2½ years ago, and we've already cut down our dependence on imported oil for the future about 4 million barrels a day.

Now we've got to take action to cut down 4½ more million barrels a day by passing a comprehensive energy policy through the Congress, based on the windfall profits tax. I'll be very quick to describe what it means.

The price of energy—I don't want to mislead you—the price of energy is going to go up, because the world is demanding more and more, and the world is producing not much more or even less. We have very little control over the price of energy, and as it goes up, enormous profits are going to be realized. The question is, should those unearned profits stay in the hands of the American oil companies, or should we have a windfall profits tax and let those profits be used to produce more oil and gas, yes, but also to insulate homes, to provide solar power, to have new kinds of energy, to help poor people and low- and middle-income families bear the increased cost of energy, to give us a better rapid transit system and transportation system? That's the basic question.

And I want to ask all of you to join in with me and encourage the United States Congress to pass a windfall profits tax to give our Nation energy security in the future. Will you help me do that? [*Applause*] Very good.

I want to say two other things very quickly. The first thing is this: We're all in it together—Democrats, Republicans, southerners, Yankees. I don't care who it is, we're in it together.

And the second thing is that no matter how difficult the problem, our Nation is strong enough and great enough and courageous enough and blessed by God enough to meet the energy challenge successfully if we unite and if we work together. And I have no doubt about the future of this country if we tap the tremendous strength that we have within us now.

I came here because you've already done a good job on energy conservation. The Thomas Jefferson High School has saved, just since last October, $40,000 in energy bills because of effective conservation programs; and Hillsborough County, I understand, has cut energy consumption by 15 percent. If everybody in the United States would do as well as you have done, we would have a great blessing for all of us in this country.

Now I want to answer your questions. I had the pleasure of reading the front page of, I think, the Tampa Tribune today, and the editorial page, and they said that I was welcome—almost welcome—[*laughter*]—and that the questions ought to be tough. And I'm ready for some tough questions. And I'll start with you.

Thank you very much.

QUESTIONS

KEROSENE SALE TO IRAN

Q. Hello. My question pertains to Iran.
THE PRESIDENT. Good.

Q. Thank you. The Iranian officials say that they don't need the oil that we sell them. Do you think that they'll sell the same stuff back to us at a higher price, or by doing this gesture of friendship, will they lower the prices of oil in the future?

THE PRESIDENT. That's a good question, and it's one that's been highly publicized around the country. Let me give you the facts.

We buy from Iran about 750,000 barrels of oil every day. We're heavily dependent on Iranian oil. The reason for the gas lines in California and on the east coast earlier this year were because the revolution in Iran interrupted supplies, and we lost about 100 million barrels of oil that ordinarily we would have bought from Iran. So, we have a good relationship with Iran as far as buying oil is concerned.

About 2 months ago—I don't remember the exact date—the Iranian officials sent word to our Government, and it eventually got to me, that they had had sabotage in a plant that makes kerosene. When I grew up on a farm during the Depression, about everything we had was kerosene. We cooked with kerosene or wood, and we used kerosene lamps. A lot of the Iranian families do this. And the Iranian Government asked if we would sell them back a million barrels of kerosene, because they had run out of refined korosene. You take crude oil to make kerosene out of it. I agreed to do it. That's as much oil as they sell to us, like every day and a half. It was a one-shot proposition.

I don't know whether Iran needs that oil or not. It was done through a company, an American oil company, a refinery. And they told me, the company sent me word that if we had a shortage of kerosene or home heating oil in the winter, that that company would buy extra kerosene or heating oil in other markets around the world and replace it for Americans.

So, there's no chance that we'll come up short. The oil was sold to Iran, I understand, at the market price, and if Iran should not need it, then it would probably be sold right at the market price.

I have not known about that statement until it happened today. But I will be sure that Americans don't come up short on kerosene or home heating oil, and the company that sold the oil to Iran has pledged to help me with that.

We sold it to Iran because they said they had a hardship case. And I think it was a good investment, because had we not cooperated with them—I can't claim that Iran would have cut off all oil sales to us, but they sell us a lot of oil every day.

This is a one-shot proposition amounting to about a day and a half of the oil we get from Iran.

WAYS TO CONSERVE ENERGY

Q. Welcome to Tampa, Mr. President. I'd like you to know that I've heard a lot of people say that they don't plan to cut back on energy consumption because they don't want to be the first ones to make the initial sacrifice. Until they see everyone else doing his part to conserve energy or until they're somehow forced to, they won't take action. How do you as leader and President plan to impress upon each and every individual of our country the importance and the real need to rally behind you and your energy guidelines? Thank you.

THE PRESIDENT. Let me say, first of all, that it's absolutely imperative that we do two things. One is for all Americans to save; there's no way that the Government can save for you. That's got to be something that 220 million Americans join in doing.

The second thing is that energy saving is not a sacrifice. For a family to drive the speed limit not only saves energy, but it saves lives and it's in accordance with the law. For a family to take a little money, either through a government loan or, if they can afford it, out of their own money, and insulate their homes so it doesn't take as much to cool it in the summer or heat it in the winter is an excellent investment, because you get back what you invested in less than 2 years and your home still maintains the same temperature; you just don't waste as much heat.

For a family to use a bicycle, if that's convenient, or maybe to walk sometimes. I jog every day for exercise. You know, I think it's a very good and pleasant thing to do.

A business has a tremendous cost-effectiveness; in other words, it's a profitable thing to save energy. I had a seminar this morning at Georgia Tech—and the chemical industry has already cut about

20 percent the amount of energy that they use to produce 1 pound of chemicals, and that means, in effect, 19 percent of their energy savings is going in to increase profits for them.

So, I think that a proper conservation effort, either in the proper design of a building, driving habits, habits around the home or around your job, is not a sacrifice. It can be a very pleasant thing to do, and it saves you money, because wasting energy costs money.

The cumulative effect of American savings can be a tremendous benefit to us all. In California, for instance, when they had the very serious gas lines, in just a few weeks the Californians changed their driving habits. And I would like to ask you when you drive home from this meeting today if you're in a car, see how many cars you meet only has one person or, at the most, two people. And, you know, for people to join together in going to work 5 days a week, 50 weeks a year, obviously saves money if you share an automobile.

So, I think it's something that everyone has got to do. This problem is not going to go away. And for everybody to sit back and say, "I'll wait for my neighbor to do it," is not only improper for your own life and costs you money, but it's unpatriotic. And this is the cheapest and easiest and most pleasant way to be a patriotic American I can think of. I hope everyone here will help me.

ENVIRONMENTAL STANDARDS

Q. Mr. President, recently Florida Power and Light was allowed to begin the use of high-sulfur fuel at the Parish plant in Manatee County with the permission of our Governor and the White House, over objections from residents and governments of Sarasota County. Florida Power and Light was trying to threaten us

with blackouts, and I think with the recent fuel adjustments that we may have already had our blackout in a way, because fuel bills for many of our retired citizens are so high.

Also soon to be considered by the Senate, of course, is your energy and water development bill, H.R. 4388, which would exempt certain energy projects from environmental regulations and the Tellico Dam, which will, of course, undermine our Endangered Species Act.

In light of these, do you think we really need an energy mobilization board to further exempt energy projects and projects such as the Tellico Dam? How can we really preserve high environmental quality with the development of oil shale and synthetic fuels when we can't even preserve the present environmental standards with the present use of nuclear power, oil, and coal?

THE PRESIDENT. The Environmental Protection Agency has not lowered air pollution standards for Florida Power and Light, to my knowledge. They would be violating the law if they did. They have now set standards of 1.2 pounds of sulfur emissions per million Btu's, which is a very strict standard. Florida, when I was Governor—Florida derived about 85 percent, I think, of your electricity from oil. Georgia, which went to coal much earlier, derived about 85 percent of our electricity from coal.

It's important now that there be a shift away from oil toward natural gas in some instances—and we're trying to negotiate with Mexico to get more natural gas from them—and coal, providing it is burned under circumstances that it can meet environmental standards set by law and rigidly enforced.

I do not approve of an energy production board law that would let that production board violate or change the provisions of law. The reason for the energy production board is to expedite a decision, one way or the other.

Instead of waiting 4 or 5 years to decide whether a refinery should be built or whether a gas pipeline should be built, or whether an electric power company generating plant should be built, that decision ought to be made expeditiously. And I don't want the law changed so that it can be built when it violates the law. So, I'm very insistent on the fact that environmental laws will be followed.

Now, I know that you are concerned about the quality of life here in Florida. So am I. And I can assure you that I will not do anything to lower the environmental standards in order to permit the burning of dirty fuel. I've been to a plant that burns soft coal just recently in Bardstown [Louisville],[1] Kentucky. And they've got scrubbers there that work. And we've authorized in the burning of low-sulfur coal the use of dry scrubbers. But with the use of scrubbers, which clean up the exhaust, I think that we can shift to coal without violating legal standards, EPA standards, or your standards on what the quality of the air should be.

You mentioned the Tellico Dam. I would not favor the passage of a law on the energy production board that would let them authorize a dam, through their action, that the law specifically prohibited.

Q. Right. Yes, sir. Also, sir, would you approve the Northern Tier pipeline proposed from Washington to the Midwest if that was exempted from environmental regulations?

THE PRESIDENT. Well, as you know, that pipeline is now prohibited from being constructed because of an amendment that won't let oil be unloaded in Puget Sound. And I am not in favor of the pro-

duction board being able to change the law.

I am in favor of giving the production board adequate authority to expedite a decision and to shorten the procedure through which either a "go" or "no-go" questions. I think I have one.

DEFENSE BUDGET

Q. Mr. President, we're glad to have you here, and I know you like tough questions. I think I have one.

THE PRESIDENT. Right on.

Q. In the spirit of your 1976 campaign statements and, I think, almost pledge to transfer some of the billions from defense to meeting human needs, I wonder if it wouldn't be a good idea to urge Congress now to take, say, 10 percent of the defense budget and transfer it to government research in solar energy so that we might develop a true public utility that would uncover and make available at minimal cost to the public, solar energy resources, so that we'd be less dependent on foreign oil or nuclear power, which might lead to cataclysmic holocaust of war or nuclear accident?

THE PRESIDENT. Let me be really frank with you about this question. The windfall profits tax, if passed—and I believe it will be passed—will give us over the next 10 years an average of $14 billion that we can spend for solar power, the insulation of homes, the caring for poor families, better mass transit, synthetic fuels, and so forth. Combined with what we already have committed to solar power and other sources, my belief is that that will be adequate.

Our target is to have 20 percent of all the energy that we consume in this Nation come directly from the Sun by the year 2000. And with the windfall profits tax passed, there will not be financial limits on how fast we move to solar power.

---

[1] Printed in the transcript.

The other part of your question: We have cut considerable fat and waste out of the Defense Department budget. But let me say this: The most important single responsibility that I have on my shoulders, above energy, above inflation, above anythink else, is to guarantee the security of our Nation. And I cannot promise you that a single dollar that I spend on defense will ever be used—will ever be used—in combat.

I pray that our Nation will stay strong enough so that any potential adversary who might want to challenge us in a war would refrain from doing so. And I hope that the tanks and the submarines and the nuclear missiles and the airplanes that we produce for our Defense Establishment will never be used in combat and that we can stay at peace. But I want everybody to know that our Nation not only has the will and the unity and the strength and the commitment to protect freedom, to protect our own people, to protect our principles, but also that we have the military power that if anybody should challenge us, they would be committing suicide.

ENERGY PRICES

Q. Good evening, Mr. President. With the price of energy going up——[2]

THE PRESIDENT. Go ahead.

Q. Mr. President, with the cost of energy going up and the economic plight of the poor, especially as reflected in the very high unemployment rate of blacks going down, what, sir, do you plan to do to help the poor of this Nation cope? And, finally, sir, if part of that plan depends on the passage of the windfall profit tax measure, do you have a backup plan if that should fail?

THE PRESIDENT. It's a free country.

---

[2] The speaker was interrupted by a disturbance in the audience, which continued throughout his question.

The question is—I had a little trouble hearing—but I believe that the question was, what plans do I have to help the poor families as the energy costs go up, both to pay for the cost of heating and air conditioning and also to provide better transportation?

Q. The question was that, and also, if part of your plan depends on passage of the windfall profit tax measure, do you have a backup if that should fail?

THE PRESIDENT. Okay. The primary hope that we have adequately to meet the increased cost of energy for the poor families and the low- and middle-income families is with the windfall profits tax, because it's going to take a good bit of money. We have proposed $2.4 billion per year for 10 years to cover those costs and also a special allotment of a little over a billion dollars a year to improve metropolitan transportation systems. If the windfall profits tax does not pass, then we would not have nearly that much money to take care of those needs.

In the last few winters since I've been President, we've allotted about between $100 million and $200 million every winter to meet the special needs of very low income families, those that qualify for food stamps, if they had a very high cost of energy. And, of course, we've probably done more since I've been in office than any other administration in improving the quality of the rapid transit or mass transit systems.

But I don't want to mislead you. If the windfall profits tax does not pass, my answer is we will not have an adequate amount of money to take care of the families about whom you are concerned. We need the windfall profits tax.

MEETING WITH THE PRESIDENT

Q. Mr. President——

Q. [*Inaudible*]——

THE PRESIDENT. Now, I'm not going to referee about who has the next question.

Q. I wasn't chosen to speak, but I've been trying to get to you since March of '77.

THE PRESIDENT. Why don't you—I will be glad to see you after the meeting's over if you let the lady ask the question.

Q. Yes.

THE PRESIDENT. Fine. Check with one of my staff members. Stu,[3] would you let one of the staff members bring the lady around, and I'll be glad to see her after the meeting.

FOOD PRICES

Q. President Carter, we're glad to see you. I want one thing to say is, and I'm sorry we had such rude people that had to come here to do this to your program. Second, I'd like to say, personally I'd like to thank you very highly for the pictures that you sent to our home of you and Rosalynn. They're on my TV set, and they'll stay there. And I know that you're here to talk about the energy crisis. And I cannot talk very much about that in the way that you talk about it. But I got one thing I want to say.

Will you please do something about our food prices, because every time us ladies go to the store, they're higher this week, next week they'll be higher than next week. And I would like to see you do something for us about our food prices. Can you or will you be able to freeze those prices so they will not go up any higher than they are today?

THE PRESIDENT. I think I can tell you that the last few weeks, for the first time, the retail food prices have begun leveling off, and the projections are that they will go down. We've got a very high production of pork and poultry, and those two

---

[3] Stuart E. Eizenstat, Assistant to the President for Domestic Affairs and Policy.

meat supplies will help to force the price of beef down.

About 2 or 3 weeks ago, I met with the meat processors and distributors—as a matter of fact, pork prices peaked; they got to their highest point in February. Beef prices got to their highest point in April, to the farmer. But the people that process that meat and distribute it to the stores have been making too much profit. They have not passed on those low prices to the consumer.

They told me there was always a lag between the time the farmers' price dropped and the time they could pass it on to the consumers. But I think 4 months is too long a lag. Also, last winter when the price of pork and beef was going up, there wasn't much lag. I mean, they passed those prices on to the consumer pretty fast. But I can predict to you that the price of food is leveling off and will begin to go down shortly.

I'm not in favor of putting price controls, mandatory price controls on. It's been tried in the past with farm products. It has never worked. But we've got a tremendous production in this country of food. One of your biggest export items, as you know, is food. And I think that we'll see, with the increasing production on the farm, a moderation in food prices.

Our main concern now is the rapidly increasing price of energy. Food's going to get better.

Q. May I say something else, please?

THE PRESIDENT. Yes, ma'am.

Q. I'd like to say I think it's wonderful for the turnout that you have here today——

THE PRESIDENT. I do too.

Q. ——not of only the older people, but I think you should give a little credit to these young generation that we have here, because one of these days they're going to be standing where you are and talking about things like they are to energy, the welfare, the schools, and everything else. But Tommy and I say God bless you, and thank you for coming and being here with us.

THE PRESIDENT. Thank you, ma'am.

I might say the young people in the back that had the banner which I couldn't read—it was already torn when I saw it—you know, this is a free country. And I'm President, and I think it's very good—even when people express themselves that way—I'm not embarrassed by it. I think the reaction of all of you, because you were disturbed, did its job. There's no need for me to embarrass them. So, I think it's a proper place in our country for people to raise a banner or to ask the President a difficult question or to shout out a criticism.

I don't have any problem with that. It's a free country. I want to keep it that way.

SOLAR ENERGY

Q. President Carter, first I'd like to say I'm getting a little tired of everybody giving you such a hard time in the press, you know. I think they need to—I think you've been doing a great job, and if you just hang in there, I think things will be a lot better for you.

THE PRESIDENT. Thank you.

Q. But one of the things——

THE PRESIDENT. You don't have to ask a question. That's good enough. [*Laughter*]

Q. No, I have to.

One of the things I'd like to show you that I did read in the paper was that you declared war on energy. What I've been doing with a few people—Warren Wether, Steve Cook, Mike Flanders was in 1976, these two architect students at Florida University developed a passive solar house that won the State of Florida competition and went to the finalist position in the United States. We've been working on that project for 3 years. We've done numerous things and talked to nu-

merous governmental agencies. I went to Washington with a friend of mine, and we gave a piece of paper that I have here, I want you to read also—I have a little something I want you to take home, I think you'll find interesting to read. [*Laughter*]

I went to Washington and I went to 220 Congress and Senate offices, and I gave a piece of paper to each one, each aide or representative or someone. And out of 220 people that promised to write me a letter asking for more information about my solar houses, it was people like Congressman Gibbons and Senator Stone that wrote. Senator Stone and Congressman Gibbons have been doing a lot of help, but I'd like to know why, if we have these 220 people who are so concerned, why they don't even write me a letter to find out about this house that was the finalist position we've been working on for 3 years?

I think that we have a solution, a major solution to the energy housing problem. I've spent hundreds of dollars on phone calls. I've talked to numerous agencies. Everybody passes a buck; it's a total runaround system. I went to the Small Business Administration here; they told me they wouldn't even give me an energy-related loan. The man further suggested that I take my project to Saudi Arabia and sell it to Saudi Arabians.

Not only that, when I was in Washington, I talked to a few aides—which I won't ever name. They suggested that I don't fool with the Government—the Government's a waste of my time, it's too much redtape—and I go out and find private investors. Well, you need money for private investors, because I don't want to go to jail with the SEC problems. We have spent $9,000 in 6 months on this project. The project is completed. We are ready to build the first prototype. We have no funds to build it.

You declared war on energy, and I

1573

agree it is a very big problem. Anytime—my feelings are when somebody declares war on energy, you put all the money and all the effort into solving that immediately. We have right now a solar house. I won't quote anything on it, but I believe that I have the best design for a passive solar house that had so many things to offer people. Nowadays, people my age can't even dream of buying a house.

That I was on TV, we got 15 calls; people wanted to buy our house. I had to tell every one of them, "I'd like to sell you a house, but I can't sell it to you because we don't get any Government support." The governmental agencies pass the buck, the people want the house, and I—you know, it's gotten to the point where the project is ready. Today we can start on the prototype; next year we can offer passive solar houses using the greenhouse effect. That was a finalist position. So many wonderful things that I just don't understand what's wrong. [*Audience reaction*] Well, I'm sorry. I've worked so long on this project, and it's very depressing.

And it's gotten to the point where I'm beginning to wonder exactly what is happening in the Government when we can't even offer something to the people; when billions of dollars are spent on research and all we're talking about is just a very small amount of money to build our first prototype.

THE PRESIDENT. Let me ask you one question.

Q. The question is——

THE PRESIDENT. Let me ask you one question, and then I'll give you an answer. Do you think it's a good idea?

Q. Yes, sir. I do. The American Institute of Architects judged it a winner in the Florida competition and a finalist in the United States.

THE PRESIDENT. If you will come to the White House, I will look it over myself. And then I'll try to use my influ-

ence—[*laughter*]—to get you an appointment with the Secretary of Energy, Charles Duncan.

Q. Yes, sir.

THE PRESIDENT. And then I'll ask him to refer you to the Small Business Administration. [*Laughter*] I don't think you're going to have to go any further. If you've got a good idea, I guarantee you that you will get every hearing, including from me.

Q. When can I be up there to see you? [*Laughter*]

THE PRESIDENT. Whenever you want to come. Keech [4] right here will make an appointment for you. Okay?

Q. I'd like to give you also something to take with you, if I could.

THE PRESIDENT. I will also read your material on the way home tonight.

Q. Thank you.

ENERGY CONSERVATION

Q. Hello. Mr. President, with regards to the energy problems that we're facing today in America, I don't feel that the problem is in the quantity, but rather in the attitudes of the American public. I feel that no matter how much energy sources we have available, if they're not used wisely, we'll always be wanting. And my question to you is, what can be done, short of expensive advertising, to help the American public see the true cost of energy? And when I say the true cost, I'm not speaking only of the dollar amount but of the—as far as conservation, as far as to our wildlife, to the resources, to the air, to everything.

What can be done short of advertising, the way that we've been doing before, to push different things that are very worthwhile? What can be done to help the American public see that this is a worthwhile effort and if we don't take steps today, the few people that do have energy today because they can afford it, won't

---

[4] Keech LeGrand, White House staff advance person.

have energy tomorrow, because they will have wasted it all?

THE PRESIDENT. That's good.

In addition to advertising, there are many other things that can be done. I spent yesterday and the day before yesterday on the telephone calling different Members of the Congress around the Nation, just to see how they had spent their home working vacation, talking to people and listening. And for the first time in the history, I guess, of our Nation, the people believe that there is an energy problem. In the past, it's been very frustrating, because as you probably know, I've been on television, I made speeches to the Congress, and it was hard to get people to realize or to believe that we ought to do something. Now people believe it.

When I went down the Mississippi River the other day, I made, I think, 48—somebody said—little short speeches on energy to let people know that we have a problem and that doing something about it can be productive and pleasant and good for an American.

The reason I came to Tampa was because in Hillsborough County there are many buildings that have been designed in a very efficient way to save energy, including this school building and others that I won't name. The whole county has saved energy, and I wanted the American people, through the national press that's covering this meeting, to know that some communities in our Nation are already doing a good job.

The President's voice in a forum like this can convince people that every one of you ought to go home and sit down with your wife or your husband or mother, father, children, and say, "What can we do in our family to save energy and also, at the same time, to save money and also, at the same time, to help my country?"

The first and easiest way to cut down on oil imports, which rob us all, is to save. Then, the next thing is to turn toward the kinds of energy that never give out. The most obvious is solar power. Another one is derived from solar power. That's the production of energy from growing crops or from lumber or waste timber products.

We had a session this morning at Georgia Tech, all morning. People came there from all over the Nation, about 400 people, to describe to me new ideas about energy. And Georgia grows three times more energy in our woods every year than we use in the whole State, and if we just took the pine tree tops and the pine needles and the bark and changed that into energy, we could more than meet that we waste—I mean the waste part. We'd have more energy than we need, and the same with animal products. So, I think the thing is to, secondly, turn toward renewable energy supplies.

The third way to turn is to energy supplies that we have an awful lot of. We've got enough coal to last us 600 years, and we're now finding ways to burn coal cleanly so it doesn't mess up the air. And we ought to turn to coal. We've got additional supplies of oil and natural gas that we've not yet found in our country, so we don't have to import. We need to turn to those. Geothermal supplies—underneath the ground itself there's extremely hot steam and water. We can tap that. We're already doing that. So, that's the next thing to do.

The last way to do is to turn toward things that cost a lot but that might be used to fill in the gap, like synthetic fuels. It costs a lot of money. You can make oil out of shale rock and make oil out of coal, but to the extent that we save and use solar power and turn to our renewable supplies, we can cut down on the amount of synthetic fuels we use.

But for the American people to get educated and to believe we've got a problem is the first major step. But we will do what you say, but we'll also advertise and not only voluntary public service advertising that the radio and newspapers and television might do as a public service, but also we'll have some paid advertising to tell you and your families specifically this is what you can do.

I might add one other point. Almost every agency in the Federal Government now and many local governments are sending out little pamphlets like in welfare checks or social security checks, saying, "These are the things that you can do in your own home to save energy."

And last week—week before last—I sent every chief executive, every mayor and every chairman of every county commission in the whole United States, 6,000 of them, a letter, and I gave them ideas on what they could do in their own county to save energy. I used a few examples of people that are already doing a good job. And one of those few examples that I used was this county, because the leaders have already done it.

We've got a long way to go. We can get there.

SUPPORT FOR THE PRESIDENT

Hello.

Q. Mr. President, I voted for you in 1976. I campaigned for you, and I'm going to vote for your reelection in 1980.

THE PRESIDENT. Thank you. No answer yet.

Thank you.

WAYS TO CONSERVE ENERGY

Q. You see, I ride my bicycle to school every day. I was wondering, how else can we conserve energy?

THE PRESIDENT. What's your name?

Q. Patricia Kirby.

THE PRESIDENT. Okay. How old are you, Patricia?

Q. Eleven and a half.

THE PRESIDENT. Eleven and a half.

I hope you all heard. Patricia rides her bike to school every day, and she wants to know what other ways she can save energy. Well, I think you can talk to your parents and make sure that your mother and father—do you have any brothers and sisters old enough to drive?

Q. No.

THE PRESIDENT. Well, encourage them all to obey the speed limit.

Also, I think you might plan 1 day a week, the whole family get together, and say, "What can we do 1 day a week when we don't even use the automobile?," like going on a picnic, you know, or doing something—the whole family together—taking a hike, or maybe get your mother and daddy to go on a bike ride with you, like on a Saturday, instead of driving all over the place.

Another thing that you can do is to make sure that the lights in your home are turned out when they're not being used. And encourage your folks to set the thermostats as they should be—in the summertime not any lower than 78 degrees, and in the wintertime not any higher than 65 degrees. We've been doing that in the White House ever since the first day I got there.

And you can tell your mother and father that if they want to insulate their home that there's a tax credit that they can get to help them pay for that cost of making their home, your home, more efficient. And if they want to put in a solar heating unit to heat water in your house, then there's another tax credit of $2,000 that you can get for that.

So, there are a lot of little things that you can do around the house. One thing that you might do instead of using an electric clothesdrier, you might rig up a clothesline in the back of the yard and let the Sun dry the clothes, see?

So, I think the best thing for a family

like yours to do is just to sit down some night and just go down and see who can think of the best ways in your house to save energy. And you can say, "The President told me to do these things." But see if you can come up with a better idea than the ones I've given you. Okay?

Thank you.

You're the same age as Amy. She'll be 12. She's a little more than 11½. She rides a bike. [*Laughter*]

Thank you very much, Patricia.

Q. Well, there's one other thing I was——

Q. Mr. President—[*inaudible*]—very poor situation. Then they ask, after me. My question is not—[*inaudible*]. I'm not going to take the whole time. [*Inaudible*]—of vital importance to me and my friends.

THE PRESIDENT. Why don't you—Phil?[5] We're almost out of time, and, Patricia, can I let the lady in the back ask another question, because she hasn't had one yet and she's been waiting. Thank you, beautiful.

Yes?

CONGRESSIONAL ACTION ON ENERGY

Q. Thank you, Mr. President. I'd like to welcome you to our State and to our city, and to tell you that I am also a native Georgian. And I am a Carter before I married. Glad to have you here.

THE PRESIDENT. I'm always glad to meet my kinfolk. [*Laughter*]

Q. I want to compliment your staff. I have met with some of them. I see Keech over there. And they are a wonderful advance staff, and I was greatly pleased to have met with some of them.

Now, first, I'll make a statement, and then my question.

THE PRESIDENT. Okay.

Q. Since most Congressmen have been

---

[5] Phillip J. Wise, Jr., Appointments Secretary to the President.

into Washington much longer than you have, and our problems have not arisen in the last 2 or 3 years, it seems we should start placing the blame for our problems on the shoulders of those who have helped create them.

Ever so many of our problems have been created by the lack of self-serving Congressmen sitting in Washington for many, many, many years.

Now, our question, Mr. President. Since oil and natural gas are finite elements, do you think you and we, the people, can get the Congress to listen to you and to us and help get us an energy program that will keep us the richest and the greatest and the freest nation on Earth?

Thank you.

THE PRESIDENT. First of all, let me say that there's enough blame to go around—the American people, former Governors, like I was during 1973 and 1974, Presidents, the Congress, the oil companies—there's enough blame for all of us. But I think the time has come for us not to throw rocks at each other and not try to find a place for a scapegoat, but to see what can we do in the future.

The House of Representatives, for instance—the Members of the House of Representatives have already passed the windfall profits tax. Now it's in the Senate, and it's up to the Senators to decide. But in the Senate the oil companies are concentrating an enormous lobbying effort.

In the past, the oil companies have had pretty much a free ride in Washington, because there never was a voice there of consumers, of average Americans. For the first time in the last 2½ years, there's been an intense struggle, with my proposals on one side, which I think represent what the consumers need, and the oil companies on the other. The Congress has not yet been able to pass a single line of energy legislation concerning oil.

To answer your second question, I believe that before the Congress adjourns this year, they will pass the windfall profits tax and they will pass a law setting up a production corporation to produce synthetic fuels and others that we need, and also the production board that will make the decisions quickly on major energy projects.

So, let's don't blame one another now. Let's look to the future, and I believe the Congress will act this year, provided, *provided* all of you let the Members of Congress know how you feel.

I don't have time for another question.

Q. I want to give you something to take back. I've mailed them to the White House twice.

THE PRESIDENT. And they sent them back to you?

Q. And nobody will take them over there. May I give them to someone?

THE PRESIDENT. Of course.

Q. You should have them, believe me.

THE PRESIDENT. Yes, I'll be glad to take them.

Let me say this in closing. This has been a good session for me. I've learned from you, and I hope you've learned a little from me. And I think the main feeling that I have is that there's a belief that if we all act together, we can have a better life, a happier life, a more productive life, our country's security can be greater, our Nation can be unified more, families can be closer together.

So, it may be that facing this particular crisis or challenge of energy can go a long way toward healing some of the problems that our Nation has had too long.

I think for us to recognize that we've got to save and not waste is really compatible with what the Bible teaches. God doesn't want us to waste what He gives. I think the fact that we have to now share with each other is a very good principle on which to base a family's style of living.

And I believe that Florida will prosper. I was talking to your Governor, who rode down with me in the plane from Atlanta, he and his wife, Adele. And the tourist industry, I don't believe, will suffer, because people know that with more efficient automobiles and better transportation systems and more care in preserving what we do have, that we can have that enjoyable life. And my guess is that over a period of time, work habits and work hours will be modified to give us more leisure time.

So, it may be that out of all of this struggle and strain and debate and argument and casting rocks at one another, we'll come up with an energy policy that will be adequate, that will give America a better life, and make—as I said many times on the river—and make the greatest nation on Earth, the United States of America, even greater in the future.

NOTE: The President spoke at 5:36 p.m. in the Thomas Jefferson High School gymnasium.

Following the town meeting, the President met privately with two of the questioners.

Tampa, Florida

Question-and-Answer Session With Florida Newspaper Editors. August 30, 1979

THE PRESIDENT. I think I will wait to the end of the session to shake hands with everybody.

You say you may not want to? [*Laughter*]

Let me say first of all that I am thankful that all of you would come here to meet with me this afternoon. This has been one of a series of visits that I have made to different communities outside of Washington in the last 6 weeks or 2 months. The main purpose of the visit is to dramatize the need for citizen interest in and understanding of the energy question, particularly the aspects that are part of their own lives and also, of course, legislation before the Congress.

I think that the present awareness by

the public that we do have a problem in energy is welcomed and also a recent development. For a year and a half, in spite of numerous TV appearances and addresses to the Joint Session of Congress and all the publicity that I could arouse about legislative proposals, the public still didn't show, in public opinion polling, that they believed there was a problem and didn't accept the fact that we imported any oil, a majority of them. So, I think it has been productive.

I thought the session today was perhaps the most enthusiastic, most exciting that I have had. There was a lot of spirit there. I don't know if you all had a chance to watch it on television.

But I will be glad to answer any questions you might have on any subject that you choose.

ENCOUNTER WITH RABBIT

Q. Mr. President, I am fascinated by the amphibious attack by the rabbit. [*Laughter*]

THE PRESIDENT. Are you? Okay.

Q. I wish you would tell us about what happened, if you would. I would appreciate it.

THE PRESIDENT. I will try to say this without castigating the press. [*Laughter*] I have lived all my life on the farm, except when I was in public office recently or in the Navy, and I have grown up with wild animals, including rabbits. I was out fishing on a small pond in Webster County, I think in April. I am not sure about the month. I was by myself in the boat, and I saw this animal swimming across the pond toward me. I thought it was a beaver at first, since there are beaver and otter in that particular pond. And when it got closer, I saw that it was not either one of the two animals, but it was what appeared to be a rabbit.

When it got close enough that I could see that the rabbit was going to come in the boat with me, I took the boat paddle and hit water at the rabbit, and he eventually and reluctantly turned away and went to the shore.

And to be frank about it, I didn't think about it anymore until the Secret Service said, "What was that animal that was trying to get in the boat with you?" I said, "It was a rabbit." Immediately all my Georgia friends said rabbits don't swim, it is impossible for it to be a rabbit.

About a week or two later, it appeared that a White House photographer who was on the bluff overlooking the pond had taken a photograph. When we looked at the photograph, I knew it was a rabbit, but it was hard to tell in the photograph. So, I had him blow the photograph up. It was plainly a rabbit.

The rabbit, I don't think, was trying to attack me. My guess is that the rabbit had been startled by some dogs or something and had jumped in the pond and was just looking for a dry place to crawl.

PALESTINE LIBERATION ORGANIZATION

Q. Mr. President, if we can turn the conversation to a lighter topic. [*Laughter*] This business of not talking to the PLO is not your policy, and yet you are following it. We have seen that that policy has caused the departure of one of your most devoted and apparently an official to whom you are most devoted.

THE PRESIDENT. Yes.

Q. How long are you going to continue observing this policy, and does it make any sense in a country which prides itself on open discussion of all issues with all parties that you are continuing to ban from negotiation with the PLO?

THE PRESIDENT. Our commitment, made by Secretary Kissinger, as you know, to the Israelis at the time they were negotiating Israeli withdrawal from Egypt, was that we would not recognize nor negotiate with the PLO until they did two things. One was to acknowledge Israel's right to exist and secondly to espouse U.N. Resolution 242. We will stick to that commitment. It was made when Nixon was President. Ford, when he was in office, reconfirmed our national commitment to the Israelis, and when I became President, I also committed our Nation to adhere to this commitment.

I have met with the leaders of Jordan, Syria, Saudi Arabia, Egypt, and in every instance when I have met with them, at least on my initial meeting with them, I have asked them to induce the PLO to recognize Israel's right to exist and to recognize 242. In most instances those Arab leaders said they thought they could accomplish that. They have not been able to.

So, we will not negotiate with nor recognize the PLO until after they recognize Israel's right to exist and the efficability of U.N. 242.

Q. This is not your policy, but you apparently think it is a proper policy.

THE PRESIDENT. It was not my policy. I have endorsed the policy, and I will carry it out.

TOURISM AND ENERGY

Q. Mr. President, back to energy for a second, sir. Some people, after one of your speeches, got the idea, seemed to get the idea that even vacation trips would not be patriotic—to tour States like Florida, California, Arizona, others we could name. What is the proper role of tourism in society that is no longer energy rich?

THE PRESIDENT. I think it is very important. I think the last answer I gave to the group at the townhall meeting, I tried to emphasize then that there was a very important role for vacations in an energy-conserving society. I think the structure of our lifestyle, as it does change, with, for instance, a 10-hour work day with 4 work-ing days, that's the kind of thing toward which we might move, would enhance the possibilities of tourism and recreation, give us more time, more days to enjoy life.

Also, the development of more efficient automobiles would make vacations possible under the same level of an individual family budget—and the improvement of transportation systems in general, particularly mass transportation systems, which let vacations and tourism be a greater part of American life. So, I consider a vacation to be a very important part of my existence, and I would hope the energy shortage would encourage people to conserve enough so that vacations in an individual family's life would be appropriate.

WHITE HOUSE STAFF

Q. Mr. President, you are engaged in a tough campaign to try to get America to tighten its belt. You're asking business to take fewer profits; you're asking labor to accept lower wages. How do you reconcile that symbolism with the $56,000-a-year staff chief for Mrs. Carter? Isn't that a problem for you in image?

THE PRESIDENT. I can't claim that any part of the White House staff would not be a problem. The totality of the White House staff under my administration is considerably below what it was in previous administrations. I think 25 to 28 percent fewer people work in the White House for me and Rosalynn combined than worked for, say, President Ford and Betty Ford, or Nixon and Pat, and so forth.

There is a tremendous responsibility on not only a President but, of course, the First Lady. I would guess that Rosalynn gets 3,000 letters a week which have to be answered, some by her personally, some by her staff. She has a heavy responsibility for taking care of the visitors that come to the White House, not only state visits, but we have large numbers of groups that come into the White House every week to talk about SALT, to talk about inflation, to talk about hospital cost containment, different issues that are important. Rosalynn doesn't arrange those meetings in the initial stages, but she is responsible as the hostess to make sure that when they are there that they have maybe light hors d'oeuvres or some lemonade or tea or something of that kind.

She has under her all of the persons who take care of the official visits. The State Department pays for the actual cost of a state banquet, for instance, but Rosalynn's staff members are the ones that arrange the banquet, decide on the menu, arrange for entertainment, and so forth.

We have picnics on the grounds for all the Members of Congress on occasion, or for certain other groups. For instance, Monday we will have between 1,000 and 2,000 labor representatives who will come there to celebrate Labor Day. It will be a picnic type. Her staff has to do all of those things in addition to taking care of her travel and other minor things of that kind. So, she needs somebody that is competent.

I think if you would compare—and I wish you would take the occasion to do it—if you would compare the size of her staff with her predecessors, you would find that it is modest. It is probably smaller than any recent First Lady's staff in spite of the fact that she is probably the most active of the ones who have served there in the last 12 or 15 years. So, I don't have any apology to make for it. The pay scales are set, as you know, by civil service and Government standards. But we have cut the staff considerably.

Q. Do you think that level job is the same as Hamilton's and Brzezinski's—I mean, that's the same pay as Hamilton Jordan?

THE PRESIDENT. That is correct. That is the top-level staff. I have a certain number of assistants.

SENATOR EDWARD M. KENNEDY

Q. Mr. President, Ted Kennedy has never said that he wanted to be President, and for 10 years the country seems to have had a fascination with him in the White House. He insists he is not running for President, and still he leads in all the polls. When you see all of that, read that in the newspaper, what do you think the country's fascination with him is?

THE PRESIDENT. I have heard Senator Kennedy say that his avowed commitment not to run was one of the things that made him attractive—being reluctant to be a candidate is an attraction in itself. I have heard him say that if he should announce as a candidate—which he doesn't intend to do—that his standing in the polls would undoubtedly drop a good bit.

There is also a great admiration and appreciation and respect throughout this country—particularly among Democrats, but I think among all Americans—for what the Kennedy family has done, with their older brother being killed in the war and with President Kennedy being assassinated in office and with Robert Kennedy being assassinated in the last stages of the primary campaign in 1968. And I think Edward Kennedy has done a superb job as Senator.

He is the last remaining brother, and I think all of these reasons—his own reluctance, the admiration and respect for his entire family, and his own competence and attractiveness as a political figure—would accrue to his benefit. I don't begrudge him that admiration and that respect.

1980 PRESIDENTIAL CAMPAIGN

Q. Mr. President, you have been reported as making a statement saying quite explicitly what you would do to Senator Kennedy if he should run against you. I am wondering if you have made the same statement in regard to Jerry Brown?

THE PRESIDENT. I can't deny I made the statement. I made it in a small group with five or six people sitting around the table with no intention for it to be publicized.

I have never let the identity of or the size of opponents in a political campaign deter me, and if I should be a candidate and if Senator Kennedy or Governor Brown or anyone else should decide to run against me, then I believe that I would triumph, to express it in more diplomatic terms.

I have no concern about that. I made my plans to run for President originally beginning early in 1972, and at that time, my presumption and my conviction was that I would be running against Wallace and Kennedy. And it was not until November of 1974 that Senator Kennedy announced that he would not be a candidate. And I had no fear then of running against those two very popular men, and now I would have no fear of any group of opponents or any single opponent if I should decide to run again.

Q. Senator Kennedy not only could certainly discourage these draft movements in Florida but in other States?

THE PRESIDENT. I can't answer that question.

FLORIDA AND THE 1980 PRESIDENTIAL CAMPAIGN

Q. Mr. President, in 1976 campaign, Florida was a rather key State in your strategy. Would you foresee it to be equally critical in 1980 if you should be a candidate?

THE PRESIDENT. Yes. I don't think there is any doubt about that. The country's eyes will be on Florida for the same reasons that they were in 1976. Florida is a large State; it's a State within which

have been sharp contests in recent years, at least between Democrats and Republicans, the congressional seats are contested. It's a State that's looked upon as a blend of both cosmopolitan and parochial interests, rural and urban, and where people come from all over the country. It has a heavy population of senior citizens, a high population of minority groups, and issues are sharply drawn. I think just the nature of Florida and the character of the State makes it a highly interesting political location, and the early nature of the contest enhances all those factors.

So, yes, it will be important for any candidate for President as it was in 1976.

FOREIGN OIL SALES

Q. Mr. President, you got a lot of softballs in your town meeting tonight. One of the hardest, attempt to be hard, came in the matter of the kerosene to Iran.

THE PRESIDENT. Yes.

Q. I wonder why you don't simply admit that it's paid in blackmail?

THE PRESIDENT. I don't——

Q. My question: Aren't we going to have to pay more of it, and what if the Arab nations really put the squeeze on us, how much blackmail are we willing to pay? And will we go to more if necessary to get the oil that we need?

THE PRESIDENT. I don't know how to characterize that question.

Q. Soft.

THE PRESIDENT. Well, I think it's an extremely biased sort of question. I'm not going to sit here and acknowledge that our Nation has been blackmailed——

Q. You would not answer whether this country would go to war in order to get oil?

THE PRESIDENT. The basic presumption of your question is that our Nation and I personally have been blackmailed. That is not an accurate statement, and if you remove that presumption, then I will be glad to answer the question.

We have not been blackmailed. There was no threat, whatsoever, issued to me or implied through the Iranians or any other intermediary. When they requested that we sell them from a private, free enterprise refinery that was located, I believe, in the Caribbean, at that time a million barrels of kerosene, they sent word to me through Jim Schlesinger—I was at Camp David at the time, it was during the period when I was preparing my energy speech. And he called and said that the Iranians had requested that we send them a million barrels of kerosene on a one-time basis, because through sabotage or other interruptions—I believe it was sabotage—a refinery in Iran, that produced kerosene from their unlimited supplies of crude oil, had been disrupted and that many of the people in Iran, relatively poor——

Q. Yeah, I heard your answer.

THE PRESIDENT.——depend upon kerosene as a fuel for their families. This was a problem Iran faced during the revolution—the most serious problem that Iran faced during the revolution, economically speaking, was a shortage of kerosene. And they asked me if I would supply them in effect about 1 day's worth of crude oil back in the form of kerosene. The company, which I think is—Rex,[1] do you remember?—Amerada Hess?

MR. GRANUM. It is.

Q. I have a feeling that you want to evade the question.

THE PRESIDENT. I am not trying to evade the question.

Q. The real part of the question—because most of us have heard your explanation—would you answer this question: It does seem to me that whether you call it blackmail or what, we are in

an extremely vulnerable position, and you have so said yourself.

THE PRESIDENT. I certainly admit that.

Q. That is the purpose, you say, of this visit. My question to you then is, are we willing to take the extreme measure of going to war if the Arab nations should cut off our supply, which they are perfectly capable of doing?

THE PRESIDENT. I am not going to answer your question directly, because it is too hypothetical in nature.

We had an Arab boycott, as you know, in 1973 and 1974. Our Nation did not have to go to war, because we got oil from other sources. We conserved and we got larger supplies of oil from places like Ecuador, Indonesia, Venezuela, Nigeria, and other sources.

I would take whatever action is necessary to defend the security of this country, but I would have to make a judgment if an interruption of the oil supplies from some of the Mideast countries was endangering the security of my country.

We have analyzed all options. If you study the straight military aspects of it—which has been done by my predecessors, and which I have reviewed—it is a very difficult military question. If a country, country X, said we will not send any more oil to the United States, and then if our country said we will go in and take the oil, to destroy those oil fields or to blow up a refinery would be so easy for terrorists or saboteurs, or for that government itself if they were threatened with invasion, that it adds a complicating factor to it that I cannot address right now.

But I am trying to get our Nation in the posture, first of all, with reasonable friendship toward the OPEC nations, including the Arab nations, which we have, including Iran, and secondly, to increase

---

[1] Deputy Press Secretary to the President.

production in our own country, and third, to conserve energy that we would be energy independent. But I cannot tell you that we would go to war in that case. I would do everything I could to avoid a war, but at the same time my number one responsibility is to protect the security of our Nation.

I can tell you this in addition. You keep using the word "blackmail." Since I have been in office, there has never been any allegation made to me or any insinuation made to me by an Arab or other foreign leader that "if you don't do so and so, we will cut off your supply of oil." I have never been the subject of a threat, and I have the same attitude now that we had when the Barbary pirates were in war: "Millions for defense, but not one cent for tribute." I wouldn't let you blackmail me, and I would not let an Arab country blackmail our Nation. We don't have to take that.

MIDDLE EAST OIL PRODUCTION

Q. Mr. President, a few months ago when the Saudis agreed to temporarily increase production of oil by a million barrels a day, is it your understanding that there was a linkage of that increase in production to a progress on the Mideast peace settlement, and might that production be backed off if there is no progress?

THE PRESIDENT. I can tell you that there was no linkage. I can tell you that there was no linkage ever mentioned with the Saudi diplomats in Washington or with our Ambassador in Saudi Arabia. And I might say that the increase in oil production was announced at that time to be a temporary increase.

There are two things that it is important to remember: Now the OPEC nations as a group are producing more oil than they want to produce. The Saudi Arabians would be very pleased if I and Giscard d'Estaing and Helmut Schmidt and others would, say, "Why don't you lower your production, 9½ million barrels of production down to 4 million," because 4 million barrels a day is about all the income that they can possibly use. They would rather keep the oil in the ground. They are producing the extra oil in effect as a favor to the rest of the world, to provide world stability, which helps them.

Iran is the same way. They don't need 4 million barrels worth of oil income per day. And the same with some of the other countries like Iraq that have some very close relationship with France, no diplomatic relationship with us. Other countries are now producing oil at a rate that they cannot sustain.

So, inevitably OPEC oil production on a worldwide basis is going to go down. I cannot anticipate the Saudis doing anything in the future except having a lower production. We had hoped once they might go up to 12 million barrels a day. They don't want to. That is one thing.

The other thing is the price is going to be determined eventually by the price of alternate energy sources—synthetic fuel, photovoltaic cells supplying electricity, nuclear powerplants in most nations of the world, including our own. Competitive prices of energy is what is going to determine ultimately the level of oil prices. And I think they are going to go up in price until that stabilizing point is reached.

So, you know, we are dreaming when we think that there is some tremendous reservoir of oil out there in the OPEC nations that they are waiting to sell. Inevitably their production of oil is going to go down, either because they are running out of oil, which many of them are, or because they would really prefer to have less production. There is no reason for the Saudis, to repeat myself, to produce 9½ million barrels of oil every day for 5 or 6 million people. You know, they know that the best investment they could have is to keep that oil in the ground.

Q. Isn't it being used as a political weapon to spur the Mideast peace talks?

THE PRESIDENT. No. I can't say that they don't want the Mideast situation—I have never met an Arab leader that in private professed a desire for an independent Palestinian state. Publicly, they all espouse an independent Palestinian state, almost all of them, because that is what they committed themselves to do at Rabat. But the private diplomatic tone of conversations is much more proper than is often alleged by the press and by others. Really, it would be a very great surprise to me for Crown Prince Fahd to send through our Ambassador, John West, to me a message: "If you don't expedite the resolution of the Palestinian question, we will cut off your oil."

There's a great stabilizing interrelationship between ourselves and the Saudi Arabians. They see us as their ultimate, not quite protective, but stabilizing factor, and they don't want to sever their relationships with us. They have an abhorrence of the Soviet Union because it's atheistic and because it's Communist and because they encourage, sometimes, radicalism and turmoil and violence. And they know that we are a religious nation, and they know we are a democratic nation; we know our attitude toward them is benevolent, and they know our basic policy is one of espousing stability. And all those factors, and others that I could name, are attractive to the Saudi Arabians.

So, they want our friendship and our good will just as much as we want theirs. I cannot imagine their ever coming for-

ward, "If you don't do this with the PLO we will cut off your oil."

Q. Mr. President——

THE PRESIDENT. I promised her.

OIL PRICES

Q. Mr. President, there has been a strong feeling that in addition to the shortage of oil, because of the import situation, that there are inhouse oil companies who were taking advantage of the situation just to raise prices. And all the time the oil at the gasoline stations was being raised in price, "Just wait until it reaches a dollar a gallon, there will be all the oil available you want." Would you care to comment on that?

THE PRESIDENT. I know. I hear all those allegations. The flow of oil from the producers to the ultimate consumers is a mighty tide that has an inexorability about it. It's a very large quantity, 52 million barrels a day. You can hold up that tide for a little while, perhaps like a few days. But it's got to move. What goes in one end of the pipeline has to go out the other.

I've had reports made to me that off the coast of the United States, there were hundreds of ships waiting until the price went up to unload. We had the Coast Guard make a survey of the coast. We sent helicopters out and airplanes; there were no ships out there. But it was a viable story that was reported in many news media, and many people believed it. I don't think that the oil companies, with the exception of small fluctuations, can hold back the normal flow of oil in order to wait until the price goes up.

My philosophy has been to get the Government's nose out of everything we possibly could when I feel that the free enterprise system and adequate competition can prevail. And I have induced the

Congress under the most difficult circumstances to deregulate the price of natural gas. It's a phased deregulation over a long period of time to deregulate the price of oil, and oil-controlled prices will be off in September of 1981, in 28 months after we initiated it.

We have deregulated the airline industry to the great advantage of Florida. You all have really benefited. The tourism rate has gone up, and a lot of people are using airplanes and so forth. We are trying to get the Government's nose out of business.

I think the oil companies have needed to have some predictability, because the darn thing was in a furor 2½ or 2 years ago. Nobody knew what was going to happen next. Now the oil companies, if they got natural gas, now know in 1984, January 15, that the degree of regulation and the price are going to be such and such, and they can make their plans accordingly.

One other point. I had the president of Atlantic Richfield Company come up to Camp David to give me advice on the energy speech I made that Sunday night. He said just the fact I had decontrolled the price of oil had encouraged that particular company, which is fairly large, to double their rate of exploration of oil above any level that they had ever had in the past. And that board of directors had met just before he came to Camp David. They had never spent more than a billion dollars a year for oil exploration. They decided for 5 years continuing they would spend $2 billion per year on searching for oil.

So, I think just the predictability about what the price and the degree of regulation of oil is a very attractive feature, and I don't believe that the oil companies

can deliberately hold back large quantities from the market for a long period of time in order to wait for a higher price.

AMBASSADOR ANDREW YOUNG

Q. Mr. President, what is your reaction to the ABC News story that the Government bugged Andy Young's apartment?

THE PRESIDENT. That story is absolutely false. ABC came to the Attorney General, reported that story to the Attorney General, asked him if it was true. He gave them a flat statement on his word of honor that it was a false story. ABC then came to the White House, talked to Jody Powell, and Jody told them that it was a false story. They ran the story anyhow, which I thought was a very irresponsible demonstration of journalism.

I saw it on television. I was called about it, and I had it replayed so I could watch it. I then called the Attorney General last night and told him to get a direct written statement from every single intelligence agency about that subject. They all have assured me that there has been no electronic surveillance of Andy Young's apartment, no bugging of Andy Young's apartment, no tap on Andy Young's telephone by any intelligence agency of our country. And I don't know what ABC is going to do about it. They knew the story was denied by the White House and the Attorney General.

It is a serious crime, it is a felony to put a tap on an American citizen's telephone, to bug an American citizen without a written permission from the Attorney General or the President. Obviously there was no written permission.

So, it is a false story. I don't think any of it should have been published.

One other question.

STRATEGIC ARMS LIMITATION

Q. Mr. President, I would like to know what your response is to the statement from the Senators today about Russians agreeing to certain reservations of the SALT treaty? Do you think that the Russians actually have done this?

THE PRESIDENT. I don't know. If you studied the reservations which Senator Biden and others described, they consist primarily of the inclusion in the SALT treaty itself of agreements that have already been negotiated very carefully and accepted by both sides, plus an agreement that the Senate is certainly likely to request, that the protocol which is designed to last a limited period of time will not have any presumption of extension. Do you follow me? So, those are the kinds of things that have already been negotiated very carefully with the Soviet Union.

Some of them are not in the text of the treaty, and if the Senate should—I am not advocating this, but if the Senate should say in the ratification agreement, "We approve SALT II provided it is understood that the protocol will not be extended and that the production rate of Backfire bombers will not exceed 2½ per month," which is 30 per year and so forth, then I think that the Soviets might accept it. But I can't speak for them. They were not willing during the negotiating phase to include those things in the document, in the treaty document itself. But they have agreed to those understandings, equally binding them.

Q. Your negotiators didn't get everything they could get?

THE PRESIDENT. We have the agreement from them, and if I discovered, for instance, through various means—aerial surveillance and other means—that the Soviets were producing four Backfire bombers per month, I would consider that an adequate cause for abrogation of the treaty itself, because it would be a violation of the solemn commitment of the nations and its leaders.

I consider those ancillary agreements to be just as binding as the agreements within the text of the treaty. And Brezhnev does, too. You cannot imagine— I bet you we spent more time on the verbal agreement concerning the Backfire bomber than we did at any other single issue that is included within the SALT treaty. And it was at the last minute in Vienna when Brezhnev finally acknowledged that the limit was 30 Backfire bombers per year. They had not been willing to do that up until then, because Brezhnev himself had taken the position at Vladivostok, negotiating with President Ford, that the Backfire bombers were not a legitimate subject for negotiations, since it was not a strategic arms. It was a very sensitive thing to them. And we really had to go to the wall to get them to agree that they were producing at a rate of 30 and they would not exceed it.

AIRLINE MERGER

Q. Mr. President, would you permit a local question, please? On the merger of National Airlines, are you inclined now to permit such a merger? Do you have the final say in that, with either Pan Am or Eastern?

THE PRESIDENT. I can't respond to that until it comes to me. I have to let the CAB and the State Department and others assess the consequences of it. They make a recommendation to me, and then I make the final decision.

Q. There is only one recommendation made, I believe, by the CAB, recommending Pan Am. Eastern has not been heard yet. The question is in concept.

THE PRESIDENT. My point is I am not familiar enough with it now to answer your question. When I get it on my desk, then I will study it and understand it. But I am not familiar with it yet.

Q. Mr. President?

THE PRESIDENT. I have to go. I am sorry. Let me thank you all. I tried to answer all of your questions.

I am sorry but we didn't agree on the basic premise.

Q. You did very well after you got going. [*Laughter*]

THE PRESIDENT. After we got around the allegation of blackmail, we did pretty well.

But I would like, if you don't mind, to have a photograph made with each one of you, and it will take just about 5 minutes. Then I will be on my way to Georgia, to Plains for the first time in quite awhile. I thank you again.

Q. Mr. President, I understand this is all on the record?

THE PRESIDENT. Everything I said is on the record, yes.

NOTE: The question-and-answer session began at 7:35 p.m. in the Pinellas Room at the Host International Hotel. The transcript was released on August 31.

Prior to the meeting, the President attended a private reception at the hotel for Florida State representatives and officials of the Florida State Democratic Party.

As printed above, the item follows the press release.

United States Representative to the United Nations

Nomination of Donald F. McHenry. August 31, 1979

The President today announced that he will nominate Donald F. McHenry to be United States Permanent Representative to the United Nations. Ambassador McHenry previously served as U.S. Deputy Representative to the U.N. Security Council.

Coming from a background of extensive study of international law and organizations, he joined the Department of State in 1963. For 8 years, he served in various positions there that were related to U.S. policy on questions arising in international organizations. In 1966 he received the Department of State's Superior Honor Award.

In 1971 Ambassador McHenry went on leave from the State Department to serve as a guest scholar at the Brookings Institution and an International Affairs Fellow of the Council on Foreign Relations. During that period, he also was a professorial lecturer in the School of Foreign Service at Georgetown University.

Ambassador McHenry resigned from the State Department in 1973 and joined the Carnegie Endowment for International Peace in Washington, D.C., where he directed humanitarian policy studies. Also during that period, he was a professorial lecturer at American University in Washington, D.C.

Before coming to the U.S. Mission to the United Nations, Ambassador McHenry worked on the Carter administration's State Department transition staff. His international organization experience includes: serving as both an adviser and alternate representative to the U.N. Trusteeship Council, alternate representative to the U.N. Seminar on Apartheid and Racial Discrimination, delegate to the U.N. International Conference on Human Rights, and a consultant to the U.S. congressional delegation to the Interparliamentary Union in 1966.

Ambassador McHenry has also been the chief U.S. negotiator on the question of Namibia, as a member of the U.N. Western Five Contact Group.

Prior to joining the State Department, Ambassador McHenry taught English at Howard University in Washington, D.C., from 1959 to 1962. At the same time, he continued to pursue postgraduate studies at Georgetown University.

He is author of "Micronesia: Trust Betrayed" (Carnegie Endowment, 1975) and has had numerous articles published in journals and newspapers.

Born in St. Louis, Mo., 42 years ago, Ambassador McHenry was raised in East St. Louis, Ill. He is a 1957 graduate of Illinois State University and received his master of science degree in 1959 from Southern Illinois University.

Ambassador McHenry is a single parent of one son, who recently completed graduate studies at Oxford University in Great Britain, and two daughters, who reside with him and attend school in New York City.

NOTE: The announcement was released at Americus, Ga.

Plains, Georgia

Informal Exchange With Reporters.
August 31, 1979

THE PRESIDENT. Good morning.

Q. Good morning, Mr. President. If you'd only let us know, we wouldn't have come out at 7 o'clock.

Q. Or woken up at 7 o'clock.

THE PRESIDENT. Did you wake up at 7?

Q. None of us.

Q. Close enough for me—for me it was close.

Q. Let me ask you a question. Does it concern us that there are the Russian troops in Cuba? What is your information?

THE PRESIDENT. Well, Secretary Vance is going to make a statement in Washington about that today. I've discussed it with him this morning. I think I'll let his statement stand.

Q. Is it a very serious matter?

THE PRESIDENT. Well, I'll let Secretary Vance's statement stand today, Sam [Sam Donaldson, ABC News].

Q. But, to, I mean, kind of forestall any other questions, you are making the decisions on this, though? It is not Secretary Vance——

THE PRESIDENT. That's right.

Q. ——because that would be tomorrow's question.

THE PRESIDENT. I understand. Secretary Vance and I've discussed it, and he'll make a statement today for me.

Q. Do you have something to say about your new United Nations Ambassador, Mr. President?

THE PRESIDENT. Have they announced the——

Q. Eleven o'clock. Yes, several minutes ago in Americus.

THE PRESIDENT. Yes. I will say something about him. He's a highly qualified professional, thoroughly familiar with the major issues that confront the United Nations, and I have complete confidence in him.

I've consulted with a lot of people before making the selection, and Ambassador Don McHenry fulfills all the requirements, I think, for a superb appointment. He's been highly recommended to me by Ambassador Andrew Young and by Secretary Vance and many others. His whole life has been devoted to ambassadorial or diplomatic service. And I've had a thorough discussion with him earlier this week about the major issues that confront the United Nations—North-South relationships, southern Africa, Mideast, and others—and I have got complete confidence in him.

Q. Let me try the Cuban thing from a different angle.

THE PRESIDENT. I'm not going to answer questions about Cuba. I'm going to let Secretary Vance make the statement.

Q. With regard to its potential impact on SALT, would you comment on that aspect of it?

THE PRESIDENT. No. Let's let the Cuban thing be handled by the State Department. I've instructed them what to say, and I think it's best to let them say it.

Q. What is your information about this allegation that Richard Harden may have perjured himself in the Vesco matter?

THE PRESIDENT. I don't know anything about it.

Q. There are stories to the effect that Phillip Heymann apparently told some members of the grand jury that he felt that was the case, although I think he has not commented on it.[1]

Q. He apparently said this in July.

THE PRESIDENT. I don't know anything about it.

Q. Mr. President, I understand you gave some serious thought to Leonard Woodcock as U.N. Ambassador. Is that correct?

THE PRESIDENT. We considered a lot of people. Leonard Woodcock was one of them. But it's so important right now that we have a continuation of our present policy with the People's Republic of China

that I think he's better qualified to stay there for the time being.

Q. Did you make your decision before the Kennedy Airport confrontation this week,[2] and were you persuaded one way or the other by that?

THE PRESIDENT. Well, I made a final decision after I met with Ambassador McHenry in Washington a couple of days ago. But McHenry was recommended to me as the first choice of a lot of people, and he's a man that I have known very closely since I've been President—because of his work in southern Africa in particular. He's really an expert on the Far East, including the Pacific region, but he's acquired probably the best working knowledge of southern African problems of anyone we have.

Q. Was he Andy Young's first choice?

THE PRESIDENT. Let me not get into that.

Q. What effect will his appointment have on U.S. relations with Third World and developing countries, Africa particularly?

THE PRESIDENT. I think they would guarantee that our present relationships, which I consider to be an improvement over the past, will be continued.

Q. I hate to replow the whole ground at the risk of a second-day denunciation of ABC. Is it a possibility that the Israelis bugged Ambassador Young's apartment, or some other intelligence service other

---

[1] News reports had stated that Assistant Attorney General Heymann's remarks allegedly were made in connection with Special Assistant to the President for Information Management Richard M. Harden's testimony during an investigation into charges that White House aides had attempted to interfere illegally in U.S. efforts to extradite Robert Vesco from the Bahamas. The financier had left the United States to avoid facing charges of fraudulent business activities.

[2] Following the defection to the United States of her husband, dancer Aleksandr Godunov, during a tour of the Bolshoi Ballet, his wife, Lyudmila Vlasova, sought to return to the Soviet Union. Her flight was detained for 3 days at Kennedy International Airport, where she was eventually interviewed by U.S. officials, including Ambassador Donald F. McHenry, Deputy U.S. Representative in the Security Council of the United Nations, to determine if she was returning voluntarily. She then was allowed to depart the United States.

than the United States intelligence service?

THE PRESIDENT. There's no way for me to certify to that kind of thing, but in our key spots, like the Oval Office and the U.N. Ambassador's residence, there is a routine sweep of the premises designed to detect any sort of surreptitious listening devices. And my guess is that if any nation should try to bug the telephone or the premises of the U.N. Ambassador, it would be detected quite early. And there have been no detections of any such devices.

Q. Did you have an account of Ambassador Young's interview with Mr. Terzi [3] before the State Department generated through Ambassador Young an account?

THE PRESIDENT. No.

Q. Did you have it?

THE PRESIDENT. No.

Q. In other words, our intelligence services from whatever source had not developed, to the best of your knowledge, an account of that meeting?

THE PRESIDENT. Well, I can't answer that question because I don't know. I haven't investigated that. But I did not have an account of it.

Q. In other words, if they did, then it had not been brought to you?

THE PRESIDENT. That's correct. And there are many ways to get a report of a conversation. It may be that one of the principals involved repeated it to many people, and those reports may have been collected in some fashion. I think the problem with the ABC report was that you all assumed that if a conversation was reported that it had to come from listening devices or bugging equipment, which is absolutely not the case.

Q. As I understand our story, we believe we had sources that told us this, rather than just assuming it. The sources may have been wrong. We may have gotten it wrong. But we didn't just assume it, sir.

THE PRESIDENT. I don't think there's much doubt about that. The thing that concerned us about it was that when ABC went to the Attorney General, he denied it absolutely with his word of honor at stake. ABC then checked with Jody Powell at the White House, and Jody said it was a story that was not sound and should not be reported. In spite of that, before the evening broadcast ABC went with it as though it was a fact, and that was the thing that concerned us.

Q. I was not aware of that. I had been told by my people——

THE PRESIDENT. I think the reporter was named O'Brien [Timothy A. O'Brien, ABC News], although I don't know that.

Q. ——and I'd been told that in fact before the broadcast that the Attorney General had not spoken—I mean, Mr. Civiletti.

THE PRESIDENT. No. I believe that O'Brien met personally with Terry Adamson [4] and Civiletti before the broadcast, and a flat denial was made about the accuracy of the story before the broadcast.

Q. All right. I will certainly not argue with you, but one of us has been misinformed about that.

THE PRESIDENT. That's fine. I can't certify that.

Q. What were your political soundings yesterday in Florida, in that that's an early primary State next year? How did you find your own stock?

THE PRESIDENT. Well, I didn't make any poll or anything, but I thought the

---

[3] Fehdi Labib Terzi, Palestine Liberation Organization observer at the United Nations.

[4] Director of Public Information, Department of Justice.

reception of the crowds and the public officials and others was very good.

Q. The Governor says that you're going to win that straw poll in November.

THE PRESIDENT. Oh, really?

Q. Now, he's a long-time supporter of yours, if I remember right. Didn't you support him also?

THE PRESIDENT. Not in the primary. I didn't take any position in the primary. But after he was nominated, of course we supported him as a Democratic nominee, and he is a fine Governor.

Q. Mr. President, one more question on the Vesco matter.

THE PRESIDENT. Yes, Bettina [Bettina Gregory, ABC News].

Q. What about the charges, that there has been some coverup, by the foreman of the grand jury who resigned? Have you spoken to the Attorney General or anybody about that?

THE PRESIDENT. No. But you know any allegation that the Attorney General of the United States would try to cover up a fact or a truth in the presentation to a grand jury is obviously false. There's no inclination to cover up anything. All we want in any case is to have the facts come out and to be presented in accordance with the law. There's too much at stake for a President or an Attorney General deliberately to try to subvert the legal system in our country, no matter who's involved. And that's obviously a false report.

Q. We've seen those things happen in past years. [*Laughter*]

THE PRESIDENT. I know that. I understand that. But, you know, it would be politically suicidal for me to permit anything of that kind or for Griffin Bell to have done anything of that kind or for Ben Civiletti to do anything like that. That's something that's inconceivable.

Q. I don't think a lot of people understand, if it was reported correctly, why way back then you wrote a note to Attor-

ney General Bell saying, "See Spencer Lee." Did you write such a note?

THE PRESIDENT. Yes.

Q. I don't think I know why you did that. Could you tell me?

THE PRESIDENT. I have a very hazy memory of it, and I've already given testimony to the law enforcement agencies about it. The report was made to me that Spencer Lee had a report concerning Vesco. We were trying to have Vesco extradited, and when I found that Lee had some information about it, I wrote a note to the Attorney General to see him.

Q. So, if there was some improper approach, you did not know about it?

THE PRESIDENT. No. No, I didn't.

Q. Harden did not come to you and say, "Mr. President, it's an improper approach here" or something?

THE PRESIDENT. No.

Q. Mr. President?

THE PRESIDENT. Yes?

Q. Thank you very much.

THE PRESIDENT. Okay. Now I can walk down the street. Thank you. I enjoyed it.

Q. Oh, by the way—the rabbits. Are you going fishing today, sir?

THE PRESIDENT. I might. [*Laughter*]

Q. Are you going to take an oar?

Q. Same pond?

THE PRESIDENT. Same pond.

Q. Can you give us your version of what happened?

Q. Yes, would you like to clear your good name? [*Laughter*]

Q. Have you talked to the rabbit and get his story?

THE PRESIDENT. I gave a report yesterday I think that was transcribed. I don't know if it's available to you all or not.

Q. Yeah, we got it.

THE PRESIDENT. Did you? Well, that's accurate.

Q. It said it was a timid rabbit or a——

THE PRESIDENT. It was just a fairly robust looking rabbit who was swimming without any difficulty, and he was apparently disturbed by some predator, maybe dogs or a fox. And he jumped in the far side of the pond. I didn't know what kind of animal it was at first. I thought it was probably a beaver or an otter. We have seen beaver and otter in that particular pond. But as he got closer to me I saw that it was not either one of those kinds of animals. So, I had a paddle in the boat, and when the rabbit got close enough to the boat for me to recognize it and I saw that it was going to attempt to climb in the boat with me, I thought that that would be an unpleasant situation for me and the rabbit.

Q. One of you would have to get out.

THE PRESIDENT. That's right. [*Laughter*]

Q. Did you do him in?

THE PRESIDENT. No, I never did hit the rabbit. I just splashed water toward him, and he finally veered his course and went over to the bank and climbed up on the bank.

Q. We have a Freedom of Information Act going to get that picture, by the way. We have filed a suit. [*Laughter*]

THE PRESIDENT. This picture is very clear. A lot of people doubted my veracity when I came back from the pond that a rabbit was swimming. But rabbits swim, and that one was swimming without any difficulty at all. I could certify to that. [*Laughter*]

Q. Thank you.

Q. Well, will you catch more fish than rabbits the next time?

Q. I think being able to swim in ponds is a fine thing, don't you think?

THE PRESIDENT. I think so, yes.

Q. And on that note—we'll not cross that bridge today.

NOTE: The exchange began at approximately 11:15 a.m. during the President's walking tour of the town.

Labor Day

Remarks at a White House Picnic.
September 3, 1979

Rosalynn and I just came back from Georgia. We escaped from all the killer rabbits down there—[*laughter*]—just in time to join you for a delightful picnic and some wonderful entertainment.

We've had a good vacation. We have been down the Mississippi River. We had a few days at Camp David. We went down to Atlanta, to Tampa, to Plains. And everywhere I went, my confidence in this Nation was strengthened. I began to see more and more clearly that my basic belief in the strength of our country is well justified—not only our military and economic strength and political strength but our ethical and moral strength. The spirit of our country is still intact.

Every time we had a chance to talk to a few people, even some tonight as I came through the crowd, there was a hope that our Nation might be more unified. Sometimes when a country or a community or a family experiences a difficulty or an inconvenience, people try to grasp for some special advantage for themselves just to make sure they don't get left out. And in the process, we lose sight of the overall benefit to us if we work together, if we are just a little more unselfish during a time of trial or tribulation or test or doubt, as we are today.

We've got a great country, and part of that greatness has been that every time we've been tested in the past, we've been drawn closer together. And I can say that the working people of our country, the labor movement, the trade unions, have always been in the forefront when there was a dynamic struggle to make our Nation greater in time of peace, especially in time of war.

1593

One of the most difficult peacetime struggles that ever took place in perhaps any country was the great civil rights movement in our own generation. And in the forefront of that movement, helping the minority groups, was the enlightened civil rights and labor movement, working together. And, of course, nowadays the labor leaders and the members of organized unions again are in the forefront of the changes that are dynamic and are difficult in our country.

Times are not easy. Neither our Founding Fathers nor our immediate mothers and fathers ever promised us that freedom would be easy. But they have told us that in a country like ours the struggle for freedom is worthwhile. Freedom itself, individual liberty, the strength of our country, the cohesion of our country, the progress of our country, the kind of life that we have, our individualism, the right to be free, the right to be different is worth whatever struggle it might require from us.

A few weeks ago I was at Camp David trying to decide in my own mind, as President of our country, what was the essence of the test put on us by the energy question. And Lane Kirkland [1] was sitting in a conference room at Camp David on my left, and he summed it up, I think, better than anyone that came to Camp David, about 150 people. He said, "Mr. President, the issue is freedom."

Our country now has its own basic security threatened because we have become excessively dependent on foreign oil. It's something that kind of happened. We didn't plan it that way. And we've now finally begun to face up to it. We get about half our oil from overseas. And you saw what happened to us back in 1973, 1974, when some of the oil-producing countries declared an embargo against us. And now

---

[1] Secretary-treasurer of the AFL–CIO.

we're even more dependent on foreign oil than we were in 1973.

But the Congress has begun to act slowly, but I think with courage, and this year my hope is that the President and you and the Congress can prevail and that we can have for the first time in our Nation's history a comprehensive energy policy, one of which we can be proud, one that spells out a road down which we can march together, with our basic freedoms intact and our Nation's security restored.

We can do it in two ways, very simple. One is to save energy, to conserve, to quit wasting energy. And that's something that the Government can't do. We can help. But that requires every American figuring out in one's own mind, "What can I do in my life, in my transportation, in my home, in my job, to save energy?" And the other thing is to produce more energy in our own country—oil, gas, coal, solar energy, geothermal supplies, synthetic fuels.

The production of that energy in our country would let us cut down on the importing of oil from overseas. And in this effort the labor movement is increasingly involved and increasingly supportive, because we not only will become energy-secure but will have funds with the windfall profits tax to take care of those poor families or middle-income families that find the burden of increased energy costs too severe, and in the process we can have a better transportation system and a better life.

I don't look on conservation or saving energy as a burden or an unpleasant sacrifice. It can be an inspirational thing. It can be an enjoyable thing. It can bring families together. It can bring communities together. It can make us proud of ourselves. It can restore patriotism, because when we do this, we help ourselves, we save a lot of money, it requires cooperation, and it helps our Nation.

We also have other things that I'll mention very briefly. We want peace. I thank God that in the last 2½ years we've not had a single American lose his or her life in combat anywhere in the world. And I would like to go out of office after I've served as President with that record still intact. We want peace.

We also want to control nuclear weapons. And I'm very grateful that the great labor organizations represented here have endorsed the SALT II treaty, which the Senate is now considering.

We also need a national health insurance program. And I know that you know that this has been something that every President has espoused or at least talked about since Harry Truman was in office. It hasn't yet come into being, but the Congress now has a proposal which, when passed, will have implemented by 1983 a national health insurance program, comprehensive health coverage for our Nation. It's a major social challenge.

Well, the point I'm trying to make is that there has to be a degree of harmony, a degree of cooperation. And in all the enlightened social progress for which we have struggled in the past and for which we are struggling now, none of which is easy, the labor movement has been in the forefront. I'm grateful for your help and grateful for your support.

I listen very carefully. A few minutes ago I was on the telephone with Mr. George Meany,[2] my friend. I wish he could be here tonight. He was planning to come, but he has just a slight virus attack. He had a little fever last night, and because it was threatening rain, he and I both agreed it might be better for him not to come out tonight.

But he's a fine man. He was kind of reading me my report card on the telephone. [*Laughter*] He said if I wouldn't

---

[2] President of the AFL–CIO.

tell what was on it, he wouldn't tell either. [*Laughter*]

But there are three things that a President always has in mind, you know—national security, always present; the Congress, always present; President George Meany, that's the third one. [*Laughter*]

And I think he and the other great labor leaders have been a stabilizing and an inspirational factor for all the Presidents who have served, either Republican or Democrat. And I'm sorry he's not here tonight, but it is a great time, I think, for all of us maybe to express our admiration of President George Meany by a round of applause. And I'm sure that Lane Kirkland will tell him about it. [*Applause*]

Now I just want to introduce two more people. One is a great Secretary of Labor, Ray Marshall. Ray, we are proud to have you tonight.

And the other one is the young man who's going to entertain us tonight. I was in Hannibal, Missouri, with Rosalynn and Amy and a group of folks on the *Delta Queen* a couple of weeks ago, and we were watching a little skit put on by Tom Sawyer and Becky Thatcher and Aunt Polly and Huckleberry Finn. And one of the things that Tom Sawyer did was kind of philosophize. And he said that work was something that a body is obliged to do, and recreation is something that a body does when he is not obliged to do it.

Well, I think one of the great things about the trade union movement that has made you great are the things that you were not obliged to do. And I've been impressed with your unselfishness, the fact that many times you would take a stand or espouse a cause or fight a battle when there's not any direct benefit in it for you, but there's a benefit for others who are not quite so secure or quite so organized or quite so prosperous. But you fight those battles and join those struggles, because you know that it'll make our Nation even greater. And as President of a wonderful country, we wanted to have, Rosalynn and I, this picnic just to express the thanks of a grateful nation to you. Thank you and God bless you.

Now I know you're all going to enjoy hearing Stephen Wade, a fine young man, give us some entertainment, part of which is about Mark Twain and Huckleberry Finn or Tom Sawyer. I haven't seen it yet, but I hear he is really great, and we're all delighted to have him. Stephen Wade.

Thank you very much. Have a good time.

NOTE: The President spoke at 7:30 p.m. on the South Lawn of the White House to representatives of labor organizations.

Executive Schedule

Executive Order 12154.   September 4, 1979

LEVELS IV AND V OF THE EXECUTIVE SCHEDULE

By the authority vested in me as President by Section 5317 of Title 5 of the United States Code it is hereby ordered as follows:

1–1. *Executive Schedule Positions.*

1–101. The following positions are placed in level IV of the Executive Schedule:

(a) Senior Adviser to the Secretary, Department of State.

(b) Deputy Under Secretary for International Labor Affairs, Department of Labor.

(c) Administrator, Alcohol, Drug Abuse and Mental Health Administration, Department of Health, Education, and Welfare.

(d) Special Assistant to the Special

Representative for Trade Negotiations, Office of the Special Representative for Trade Negotiations.

(e) Deputy Adviser for Labor-Management, Council on Wage and Price Stability.

(f) Deputy Adviser for Congressional Affairs, Council on Wage and Price Stability.

(g) Deputy Adviser for Government Operations, Council on Wage and Price Stability.

(h) Deputy Adviser for Regulatory Policies, Council on Wage and Price Stability.

1–102. The following positions are placed in level V of the Executive Schedule:

(a) Deputy Assistant Secretary of Defense for Reserve Affairs, Department of Defense.

(b) Executive Director, Pension Benefit Guaranty Corporation, Department of Labor.

(c) Executive Assistant and Counselor to the Secretary of Labor, Department of Labor.

(d) Commissioner on Aging, Department of Health, Education, and Welfare.

1–2. *General Provisions.*

1–201. Nothing in this Order shall be deemed to terminate or otherwise affect the appointment, or to require the reappointment, of any occupant of any position listed in Section 1–1 of this Order who was the occupant of that position immediately prior to the issuance of this Order.

1–202. Executive Order No. 12076, as amended, is hereby revoked.

JIMMY CARTER

The White House,
     September 4, 1979.

[Filed with the Office of the Federal Register, 5:08 p.m., September 4, 1979]

National Grandparents Day

Proclamation 4679.   September 6, 1979

By the President of the United States of America

A Proclamation

As we seek to strengthen the enduring values of the family, it is appropriate that we honor our grandparents.

Grandparents are our continuing tie to the near-past, to the events and beliefs and experiences that so strongly affect our lives and the world around us. Whether they are our own or surrogate grandparents who fill some of the gaps in our mobile society, our senior generation also provides our society a link to our national heritage and traditions.

We all know grandparents whose values transcend passing fads and pressures, and who possess the wisdom of distilled pain and joy. Because they are usually free to love and guide and befriend the young without having to take daily responsibility for them, they can often reach out past pride and fear of failure and close the space between generations.

The Congress, by joint resolution (H.J. Res. 244), has authorized and requested the President to designate the first Sunday of September following Labor Day of each year as National Grandparents Day.

Now, THEREFORE, I, JIMMY CARTER, President of the United States of America, do hereby designate Sunday, September 9, 1979 and the first Sunday following Labor Day in each succeeding year as "National Grandparents Day."

I urge officials of Government at the national, State, and local levels, and of voluntary organizations to plan appropriate activities that recognize the importance and the worth of the 17 million grandparents in our nation. I urge all Americans to take the time to honor their own grandparents or those in their community.

IN WITNESS WHEREOF, I have hereunto set my hand this sixth day of September, in the year of our Lord nineteen hundred seventy-nine, and of the Independence of the United States of America the two hundred and fourth.

JIMMY CARTER

[Filed with the Office of the Federal Register, 1 p.m., September 6, 1979]

Puerto Rican Nationalists

Announcement of the President's
Commutation of Sentences.
September 6, 1979

President Carter today commuted the sentences of four Puerto Rican Nationalists to time served. These individuals have been serving prison terms for Federal convictions stemming from their participation in shootings that occurred at the Blair House in 1950 and the U.S. House of Representatives in 1954.

The four individuals are Oscar Collazo, 67; Rafael Cancel Miranda, 49; Irving Flores Rodriguez, 54; and Lolita Lebron, 59.

Mr. Collazo has been eligible for parole since April 1966, and Mrs. Lebron has been eligible since July 1969. Both Messrs. Cancel Miranda and Flores Rodriguez became eligible for parole in July 1979. However, none has applied for parole because of their political beliefs.

The President based his decision on a favorable recommendation of the Attorney General to commute the sentences of these individuals to time served. The Attorney General's letter of advice to the President cited the following reasons in support of the recommendation:

1. Each of the four has served an unusually long time in prison, and the Attorney General believes that no legitimate

1597

deterrent or correctional purpose is served by continuing their incarceration. Mr. Collazo has served over 28 years; Ms. Lebron and Messrs. Rodriguez and Miranda have each served over 25 years. Bureau of Prison reports show that in recent times only three inmates have served more time in Federal custody than these four.

2. Humane considerations militate against retaining in custody persons who have served (according to Bureau of Prison records) prison terms of far greater length than the terms normally served by those convicted of equally or even more heinous offenses.

3. It is the consensus of the law enforcement officials consulted that commutation would be appropriate and would pose little substantial risk of the defendants' engaging in further criminal activity or becoming the rallying point for terrorist groups. To the extent that clemency might, under other circumstances, be viewed as evidence of leniency toward terrorists, no such conclusion could be drawn here in light of the length of the sentences served.

In addition, the President concurred with the judgment of the Secretary of State that the release of these four prisoners would be a significant humanitarian gesture and would be viewed as such by much of the international community.

The four prisoners will be released from Federal prison immediately upon completing routine administrative discharge procedures for their release.

World Conference on Religion and Peace

Remarks at a White House Reception for Conference Participants.   September 6, 1979

Let me say, first of all, that it's a great honor for me and my wife to have the representatives from many nations here to visit us in the White House. Is there anyone here from Japan? [*Laughter*] Raise your hand if you're from Japan. Good. Very good.

Anyone here from India? Very fine. Canada? The Federal Republic of Germany? People's Republic of China? China. Very good. The Soviet Union? And 40 other nations, I understand.

Your organization and the purpose of it, the fact that you are meeting in the United States, warms my heart. Our Nation's motto is "In God We Trust." And we believe in separation of church and state. We don't permit our Government to dominate nor to interfere in the right of each individual person to worship as he or she chooses.

The Bible says, "Let me hear what God will speak, for He will speak peace to His people." And I would guess that each holy book or thesis or statement of ethical principles would encompass the same philosophy.

Our religion is based on peace. And the Bible also says, "Depart from evil, do good, seek peace, pursue it—pursue it actively, search for peace." This has not been a characteristic of all those who profess faith or all those who are related to or committed to a religion.

Many wars have been caused by and fought under the banners of religious beliefs. Suffering, divisions have occurred; sometimes with no noble purpose, often because people of slightly different religious beliefs were jealous of one another and struggled for dominance because they could not communicate, they did not understand each other, they were not filled with a desire for peace, there was no sense of love.

Even in our present time many nations are divided within themselves and against one another because of irreconcilable religious beliefs and a lack of a desire to understand one another. Terrorism is the professed motivation for many with deep religious beliefs. Our country now sees throughout the world large numbers of refugees as a result of religious wars.

It's encouraging indeed to have people assembled here from 45 or so nations, worshiping God in many different ways, working together for peace, for the survival of human beings with noble purposes, one of which is to educate leaders—religious leaders, also government leaders. And I am grateful for it.

The control of nuclear weapons, the control of conventional weapons, the opening up of avenues of communication and understanding, the alleviation of hunger, suffering, poverty, disease, are all common purposes regardless of our particular religious commitment. And I believe that this conference—I believe your third; the first in Japan, the second in Belgium, you've honored us with your third—can have increasingly far-reaching beneficial effect throughout the world.

I know that in your own deliberations at Princeton you've reached a new level of humility, a realization that none of us knows all the answers, that we benefit from listening to one another, and that there is a place for us to become brothers and sisters without regard to national boundaries and without regard to religious differences. And this doesn't mean that we have to abandon or weaken our own deep faith or our own patriotism or our own love and affection for our own kind. We can be individuals, we can be proud of our country, we can be fervent believers in our own religion and still work for peace and harmony, good will, love, a sense of brotherhood throughout the world. And because of these noble aspirations that you have, I am very proud as the President of a great country, a country where many different faiths are represented—all of your faiths are represented among Americans—to welcome you here.

God bless you. I hope that in your own way that you will remember me and other world leaders, who are responsible for many of the world's ills and perhaps the future alleviation of those ills, that you will remember us in your prayers.

Thank you very much.

NOTE: The President spoke at 4:06 p.m. in the East Room at the White House.

MX Missile System

Remarks Announcing the Configuration for Basing the Missile System. September 7, 1979

Good morning, everybody. I have a statement to make about the new strategic deterrence system which I consider to be quite significant. Some analysts would equate it with two other major decisions made by Presidents in this century: The first, to establish the Strategic Air Command itself under President Truman, and the subsequent decision by President Kennedy to establish the silo-based Minuteman missile system.

For nearly 30 years now our Nation has deterred attack and has kept the peace through a complementary system of land, sea, and airborne nuclear forces, commonly known as the strategic triad. By maintaining the special strengths and the advantages offered by each of the three separate forces, we make it impossible for any enemy to counter all of them.

My administration is now embarked on a program to modernize and to improve the ability of our entire strategic triad, all three systems, to survive any attack. Our bomber force is being strengthened with nuclear-tipped cruise missiles. Our strategic submarine force is being upgraded by Trident submarines and Trident missiles. However, as a result of increasing accuracy of strategic systems, fixed land-based intercontinental ballistic missiles or ICBM's located in silos, such as our Minuteman, are becoming vulnerable to attack. A mobile ICBM system will greatly reduce this vulnerability.

Therefore, I decided earlier this year to proceed with full-scale development and deployment of a new, large, mobile ICBM known as the MX. I made this decision to assure our country a secure strategic deterrent now and in the future. The MX will enable us to continue with a modernized, unsurpassed, survivable strategic deterrent ICBM, submarine-launched, and heavy bomber triad—ICBM's, submarine-launched ballistic missiles, and the heavy bomber triad, armed with cruise missiles.

Clearly, the way we base the MX to enhance its own security from attack is vital to the ability it has to defend our country. At the time that I made the decision to build the MX, I established five essential criteria which the basing system would have to meet. First, it must contribute to the ability of the strategic forces to survive an attack. Second, it must be verifiable so as to set a standard which can serve as a precedent for the verifiability of mobile ICBM systems on both sides. Third, it must minimize the adverse impact on our own environment. Fourth, its deployment must be at a reasonable cost to the American taxpayer. And fifth, it must be consistent with existing SALT agreements and with our SALT III goal of negotiating for significant mutual reductions in strategic forces.

In light of these criteria and after full consultation with Secretary of Defense Harold Brown and my other principal advisers, I've decided upon the following configuration for basing the MX missile system. The MX will be based in a sheltered, road-mobile system to be constructed in our western deserts, the total exclusive area of which will not exceed 25 square miles. This system will consist of 200 missile transporters or launchers, each capable of rapid movement on a special roadway connecting approximately 23 horizontal shelters.

Let me point out how this meets the criteria that I've established. First, it increases the survivability of our missiles by multiplying the number of targets which would have to be attacked, because not knowing in which of the 23 shelters the missile was located, all 23 shelters would have to be targeted in order to be sure to attack the missile.

The capacity of the missiles to move rapidly ensures that no attacker will be able to find out ahead of time where the missiles might be located and attack just those locations only. In fact, the missiles would be able to change shelters during the flight time of an enemy ICBM. Moreover, the system is flexible enough so that we can adjust the scale of deployment either up or down in response to a future enemy threat, or to progress on future SALT negotiations.

Secondly, the system is adequately verifiable. The special roadways will be confined to designated areas, and the associated missile transporters will be incapable of moving other than on those designated roadways.

The shelters will be designed so they may be opened in order to demonstrate that no extra missiles are hidden within them. These and other features will make this system adequately verifiable.

Third, the system minimizes the impact on the environment. The shelters are flush with the ground. The public will retain access to the area. Only the shelters themselves will be fenced off. The entire system, as I said earlier, will take only about 25 square miles of land out of public use.

Fourth, the system is affordable. The projected cost over the full 10-year period, total cost to develop, to produce, and to deploy, is $33 billion in 1980 dollars. While this acquisition cost may vary somewhat as the program proceeds, it's important to recognize that the cost of this system, in constant dollar terms, will be no greater than the cost of any one of the original three legs of our strategic triad, either the B–52 force or the Polaris-Poseidon force or the Minuteman ICBM system.

Finally, this system is compatible with existing SALT agreements and with our objectives for SALT III. Deploying this system will make it clear to the Soviet Union that they will gain no strategic advantage out of continuing the nuclear arms race. This is a fundamental precondition to more effective arms control agreements. Equally important, this system points in the direction of reductions of strategic arms, because we are giving better protection with a force of fewer missiles. Without such a mobile shelter system, the only way we could maintain our deterrent would be to increase greatly the number of our strategic systems or nuclear missiles.

In the course of making the series of decisions that led to this announcement, I carefully studied the potential threat to our Minuteman force. That threat is real. The system I've outlined this morning does the best job of meeting that threat, while also fulfilling the conditions that I specified at the outset. The system is survivable, it's verifiable, it has a minimum impact on the environment, it's affordable in cost, and it's consistent with our SALT goal of deep reductions in strategic arms.

In sum, this system will enhance our Nation's security, both by strengthening our strategic deterrent and by offering the prospect of more effective arms control. This system is not a bargaining chip. It's a system that America needs and will have for its security. I'm confident that the American people will support its deployment.

Unhappily, we do not yet live in the kind of world that permits us to devote all our resources to the works of peace. And as President, I have no higher duty than to ensure that the security of the United States will be protected beyond doubt. As long as the threat of war persists, we will do what we must to deter that threat to our Nation's security. If SALT II is ratified and SALT III is successful, then the time may come when no President will have to make this kind of decision again, and the MX system will be the last weapon system of such enormous destructive power that we will ever have to build. I fervently pray for that time, but until it comes, we will build what we must, even as we continue to work for mutual restraint in strategic armaments.

Secretary Brown is with us, and he is willing to answer your questions. Thank you very much.

NOTE: The President spoke at 10:51 a.m. to reporters assembled in Room 450 of the Old Executive Office Building.

Following the President's remarks, Secretary of Defense Harold Brown held a news conference on the President's announcement.

Federal Emergency Management Agency

Nomination of Gloria Cusumano Jimenez To Be an Associate Director.   September 7, 1979

The President today announced that he will nominate Gloria Cusumano Jimenez, of Durham, N.C., to be an Associate Director of the Federal Emergency Management Agency (FEMA). Her area of responsibility would be insurance and hazard mitigation.

Jimenez has been Acting Associate Director of FEMA since last April.

She was born July 1, 1932, in New York City. She received an LL.B. from Brooklyn Law School in 1954. From 1955 to 1966, she practiced law in New York, and in 1965 and 1966, she also served as district aide to Congressman Richard Ottinger. From 1968 to 1970, she was director of housing and urban programs for the North Carolina Department of Local Affairs.

From 1971 to 1974, Jimenez was a housing consultant and assistant director of the Low Income Housing Development Corporation in Durham, N.C. She was deputy commissioner and general counsel of the North Carolina Department of Insurance from 1975 to 1978.

In 1978 Jimenez was appointed Federal Insurance Administrator. She was appointed Acting Associate Director of FEMA after the Federal Insurance Administration's insurance and hazard mitigation functions were transferred to FEMA under Reorganization Plan No. 3 of 1978.

United Nations Children's Fund

Appointment of Marjorie Craig Benton To Be U.S. Representative on the Executive Board. September 7, 1979

The President today announced that he has appointed Marjorie Craig Benton to be the Representative of the United States on the Executive Board of the United Nations Children's Fund.

Benton, 46, of Evanston, Ill., is currently a member of the United States National Commission for the International Year of the Child.

Soviet Combat Troops in Cuba

Remarks to Reporters.   September 7, 1979

I want to take a few minutes to speak to you about the presence of the Soviet combat brigade in Cuba. The facts relating to this issue have been carefully laid out by Secretary Vance, both in his public statement and in his testimony before the Congress. The facts, in brief, are as follows:

We have concluded, as the consequences of intensified intelligence efforts, that a Soviet combat unit is currently stationed in Cuba. We have some evidence to indicate that such a unit has been in Cuba for some time, perhaps for quite a few years.

The brigade consists of 2,000 to 3,000 troops. It's equipped with conventional weapons, such as about 40 tanks and some field artillery pieces, and has conducted training as an organized unit.

It is not an assault force. It does not have airlift or sea-going capabilities and does not have weapons capable of attacking the United States.

The purpose of this combat unit is not yet clear. However, the Secretary of State spoke for me and for our Nation on Wednesday when he said that we consider the presence of a Soviet combat brigade in Cuba to be a very serious matter and that this status quo is not acceptable.

We are confident about our ability to defend our country or any of our friends from external aggression. The issue posed is of a different nature. It involves the stationing of Soviet combat troops here in the Western Hemisphere, in a country which acts as a Soviet proxy in military adventures in other areas of the world, like Africa.

We do have the right to insist that the Soviet Union respect our interests and our concerns if the Soviet Union expects us to respect their sensibilities and their concerns. Otherwise, relations between our two countries will inevitably be adversely affected. We are seriously pursuing this issue with the Soviet Union, and we are consulting closely with the Congress.

Let me emphasize that this is a sensitive issue that faces our Nation, all of us, and our Nation as a whole must respond not only with firmness and strength but also with calm and a sense of proportion.

This is a time for firm diplomacy, not panic and not exaggeration. As Secretary Vance discusses this issue with Soviet representatives in the coming days, the Congress and the American people can help to ensure a successful outcome of these discussions and negotiations by preserving an atmosphere in which our diplomacy can work.

I know I speak for the leadership in Congress, with whom I have met this afternoon, as well as for my own administration, when I express my confidence that our Nation can continue to show itself to be calm and steady, as well as strong and firm.

Thank you very much.

NOTE: The President spoke at 4:15 p.m. in the Briefing Room at the White House.

Digest of Other White House Announcements

The following listing includes the President's public schedule and other items of general interest announced by the White House Press Office and not included elsewhere in this issue.

September 3

The President declared a major disaster for the Commonwealth of Puerto Rico as a result of Hurricane David, beginning on or about August 29, which caused extensive public and private property damage.

The President returned to the White House from Plains, Ga.

September 4

The President met at the White House with:

—Zbigniew Brzezinski, Assistant to the President for National Security Affairs;

—Frank B. Moore, Assistant to the President for Congressional Liaison;

—Vice President Walter F. Mondale.

The President participated in a briefing on hospital cost containment legislation given for community leaders in the East Room at the White House.

The White House announced that the U.S. delegation representing President Carter at the funeral of Lord Mountbatten will be headed by W. Averell Harriman. Ambassador Harriman will also serve as the personal representative of the President. Other members of the delegation, which departed for London this morning, are:

PAMELA HARRIMAN;

KINGMAN BREWSTER, JR., U.S. Ambassador to the United Kingdom of Great Britain and Northern Ireland;

CLAIBORNE PELL, U.S. Senator from Rhode Island;

ADM. THOMAS B. HAYWARD, USN, Chief of Naval Operations;

JANE BYRNE, mayor of Chicago;

ADM. JOSEPH P. MOORER, JR., USN, Commander in Chief, U.S. Naval Forces, Europe;

GEORGE S. VEST, Assistant Secretary of State for European Affairs;

DR. CORTES F. ENLOE, former flight surgeon, First Air Commando Force (CHINDITS), Annapolis, Md.;

EUGENE HAYTOW, chairman of the board, Amalgamated Savings and Trust, Chicago, Ill.;

DR. RAJENDRA PRASAD, chairman of the National Council of the Associations of Indians in America, San Mateo, Calif.;

JAMES ROOSEVELT, business consultant, Los Angeles, Calif.;

ADM. ELLIOTT BOWMAN STRAUSS, USN, Washington, D.C.;

GEN. A. WEDEMEYER, USA, retired, Boyds, Md.;

WYNELLE WATSON WHITE, Washington, D.C.

September 5

The President met at the White House with:

—Dr. Brzezinski;

—Mr. Moore;

—the Democratic congressional leadership.

The White House announced that in keeping with the invitation from President Carter to President López Portillo of Mexico at their meeting in February, the two Presidents will meet in Washington on September 28 and 29 to review bilateral and international issues and to strengthen U.S.-Mexican relations.

The President transmitted to the Congress the Report to the President on Disease Control Programs, prepared by the Department of Health, Education, and Welfare in accordance with Public Law 94–317.

September 6

The President met at the White House with:

—Dr. Brzezinski;

—Mr. Moore;

—Dale Emmons, president of the Young Democrats of America;

—Mrs. Carter, for lunch;

—Stansfield Turner, Director of Central Intelligence, and Dr. Brzezinski.

In a ceremony in the Oval Office, the President was presented with the Special Conservation Award of the Florida Wildlife Federation by federation representatives.

The President participated in a briefing on the administration's programs and policies given for civic and community

leaders from Mississippi in the East Room at the White House.

September 7

The President met at the White House with:

—Dr. Brzezinski;

—Vice President Mondale, Secretary of State Cyrus R. Vance, Secretary of Defense Harold Brown, Hedley W. Donovan, Senior Adviser to the President, Hamilton Jordan, Assistant to the President, and Dr. Brzezinski;

—Mr. Moore;

—Charles L. Shultze, Chairman of the Council of Economic Advisers;

—a group of editors (transcript will be printed next week).

The White House announced that President Mobutu Sese Seko of Zaire will call on President Carter at the White House on September 11, in connection with his private visit to the United States. He will also meet with other executive branch officials and with Members of Congress to discuss a range of issues of mutual interest. President Mobutu will meet with American business executives in Washington and New York, and plans to visit Florida before returning to Zaire.

NOMINATIONS SUBMITTED TO THE SENATE

The following list does not include promotions of members of the Uniformed Services, nominations to the Service Academies, or nominations of Foreign Service officers.

Submitted September 5, 1979

R. ROBERT RUSSELL, of California, to be Director of the Council on Wage and Price Stability, vice Barry P. Bosworth, resigned.

Submitted September 7, 1979

GLORIA CUSUMANO JIMENEZ, of North Carolina, to be an Associate Director of the Federal Emergency Management Agency (new position).

BERNARD DANIEL ROSTKER, of Virginia, to be Director of Selective Service, vice Byron V. Pepitone, resigned.

CHECKLIST OF WHITE HOUSE PRESS RELEASES

The following listing contains releases of the White House Press Office which are not included in this issue.

Released August 30, 1979

Advance text: remarks at groundbreaking ceremonies at Emory University, Atlanta, Ga.

Released September 3, 1979

Advance text: remarks at the Labor Day picnic on the South Lawn of the White House

Released September 7, 1979

Transcript: remarks to a group of editors and news directors on Soviet-Cuban relations— by Zbigniew Brzezinski, Assistant to the President for National Security Affairs

CHECKLIST—Continued

Released September 7—Continued

News conference: on the basing for the MX missile system—by Secretary of Defense Harold Brown

---

ACTS APPROVED BY THE PRESIDENT

Approved September 6, 1979

H.J. Res. 244_____ Public Law 96–62
National Grandparents Day.

S. 1146_____ Public Law 96–63
An act to extend for three fiscal years the authorizations for appropriations under the Safe Drinking Water Act.

PRESIDENTIAL DOCUMENTS

Week Ending Friday, September 14, 1979

Interview With the President

Remarks and a Question-and-Answer Session With a Group of Editors.   September 7, 1979

THE PRESIDENT. I'd like to spend a few minutes with you.

This is an interesting day for you to be in Washington. We have, as usual, an accumulation of both domestic and foreign issues to be addressed by me and by my associates, with whom you've met already.

It is a coincidence that we have already had a major announcement on the deployment of the MX missile in a mobile form this morning, and in just a few minutes, about 4 o'clock, I will make a statement to the Nation concerning the Soviet troops in Cuba.[1]

I've talked to Dr. Brzezinski since he met with you and have read a transcript of his answers and your questions concerning those troops.

ADMINISTRATION POLICIES

At the same time, we are pursuing our goal of peace for our country, its enhanced security, the honoring of our commitment to our allies and friends, the mutual disarmament and the reduction of the threat of a nuclear confrontation, the control of the proliferation of nuclear explosives among nations that don't pres-

---

[1] See page 1602 of this volume.

ently have them, our focused peace efforts in the Middle East, in southern Africa, and in other places, and also domestic issues that are well known to you and very important to me.

We've had excessive inflation in our country now for more than 10 years. This is a matter of constant concern to us. We are trying to address the basic roots of it with increased agricultural productivity and the other provision of goods for ourselves, more stable marketing techniques, the reduction of the Federal budget deficit, a constant policy on Government expenditure restraint, reduction of Government intrusion into business affairs, the elimination of unnecessary forms and Government regulation, the provision of a stable dollar.

We have a massive effort ongoing to establish an energy policy for the first time in our country, although it's long overdue. We've already had success in the Congress and with my own executive actions to reduce the projected importation of foreign oil by about 4 million barrels per day. Our presentations to the Congress will result in an additional saving of 4½ or so million barrels in the future.

I need not go into detail about that. I'll be glad to answer any questions for you.

At the same time, we have budgets, appropriations, authorizations of every facet of American life that all come to my attention and on which I have to make basic decisions, in addition to legislation that would enhance the control of hospital costs, give the mental health facilities in our Nation a boost, improve the relationship between the Federal Government and local and State officials, and deal effectively in strengthening our private enterprise system.

On occasion, we have a major event at the White House, both social and political meetings, and also we expect later on this winter to have a major White House Conference on Small Business.

It would be impossible for me to describe all the different responsibilities that a President has, and I think the best thing for us to do now is to let me answer your questions on these or other issues. I think it would probably save you time if you didn't repeat questions that have already been answered by my staff members, unless you were dissatisfied with their answer.

We have a very close and tight and, I think, well-organized interrelationship here in the White House. Dr. Brzezinski, for instance, on foreign affairs, and my domestic advisers can speak accurately for me. But I'd be glad to answer any questions.

Yes.

QUESTIONS

PUERTO RICAN NATIONALISTS

Q. Mr. President, I'm Jack Skelly of El Nuevo Día, San Juan, Puerto Rico. Your action yesterday in commutation of the four nationalists' prison terms was against the recommendation of the Governor of Puerto Rico, who had asked you in a letter to have them sign some kind of guarantee that they were sorry. My question has two parts: One, did you consult with the Governor at all before this decision was made—I mean, re-

cently? And, two, in view of the fact that they are part of some, what you would call terrorist movement, or have been in the past, do you plan to campaign in the primary down there next year? Have you been advised one way or another?

THE PRESIDENT. I haven't decided to announce my candidacy yet, so I won't comment on campaigning in the primary. [*Laughter*]

I have been thoroughly familiar with the attitude of the Governor on this issue, but also the attitude of other Puerto Rican leaders—his predecessors, the representatives in Congress, and political leaders in all factions and, I think, the sentiment of the Puerto Rican people. That was obviously assessed. And I regret that on this particular issue, the Governor and I don't agree. On most issues we do. I had to make the judgment on the basis of my best assessment of justice and the best interests of my country and, obviously, the best interests of the Puerto Rican people.

These persons had been adequately punished. They've been in prison longer than almost anyone in the Federal system. They've never asked for clemency, but their attorneys, with their knowledge, participated in the proprieties of making their views known. They have been model prisoners. And my own assessment, based on information derived from other sources through the Attorney General, is that they will not be a threat to the security of Puerto Rico and are highly unlikely to engage in terrorist activities there. I can't guarantee that—for them or any other person.

But I think the forces of justice were honored. And that's a decision that I had to make alone, after consulting with your Governor and with many other people. My decision, contrary to his inclinations, was no indication of my lack of respect for him or for his opinion. I had to assess his opinion, among others, and made what I believe firmly is a right decision.

Q. Mr. President——

Q. Excuse me, could you answer the second one, Mr. President?

THE PRESIDENT. Well, if I decide to become a candidate, the decision on these released prisoners would not affect my presence in Puerto Rico. I would expect that among the majority of the people of Puerto Rico that the decision would be an attractive one, but I've not run a poll on it.

GRAIN INDUSTRY

Q. With two railroads in bankruptcy and one on strike, there's a definite feeling in the Midwest that we are going to have a real crisis this fall in the moving of grain. Are you doing anything to perhaps help head that off, say, move in, for example, on the Rock Island strike, or take any action to get them back to work?

THE PRESIDENT. Yes, I've talked to the Federal negotiator, Wayne Horvitz, since I've come back to Washington this week. I think to reveal my conversation with him or his plans or the prospects would not be conducive to helping resolve the strike.

I am completely aware of the high yield of crops this year and the need to move them to market. We're participating in some States with the Governors, and with secretaries or commissioners of agriculture through Bob Bergland, and through the Department of Transportation, to build up a reserve supply of transportation facilities to get grain both to elevators, to the barge system, when it's appropriate, and from the elevators to the international shipping points, if required.

I can't guarantee there won't be some bottlenecks—there always have been—but I hope that they can be handled both

with country elevator storage and with the substantially increased quantity of farm storage that we have put into effect.

Q. You're not considering, say, invoking the Taft-Hartley Act?

THE PRESIDENT. In my judgment, and in the judgment of the Attorney General and the Department of Labor, the Taft-Hartley Act is not appropriate in this case.

WINDFALL PROFITS TAX

Q. Mr. President, in regard to the important windfall profits tax measure—my name is Jim Barbieri from Bluffton, Indiana, by the way. I'd like to ask, in your talk since Congress has returned, can you give any indication of any timetable or any—what the potential is now on this legislation, toward getting it enacted in substance without being watered down too much by loopholes?

THE PRESIDENT. Well, as you know, the House has already passed an acceptable windfall profits tax. It deviated from my proposal in one important aspect, in that it terminates in 1990. I think it ought to be permanent.

I heard Senator Byrd say today that Senator Long intends to honor his commitment to me to have on my desk a windfall profits tax that would be "pleasing" for the President to sign. And I think that the goal of the Senate Finance Committee is still the first of October, although this information is best derived from Senator Long.

I don't think there's been any delay on the consideration of the tax bill. During the recess period, Senator Muskie, who's the chairman of the Budget Committee, specifically requested that the Congressional Budget Office and his committee staff be given time to determine the impact of the windfall profits tax on 1980 and subsequent years' budgets. So, during the interim of August, the Senate Budget Committee and all the related staffs were working on this matter. And I don't see any reason for concern about delay.

I am concerned about the ultimate content of the tax. If it's watered down by any substantial degree, we will not reach our goals on energy, and our Nation's security will be damaged. And we just absolutely must have a way to reduce our dependence on foreign oil, and the windfall profits tax is a key to this assurance.

ENERGY

Q. Mr. President, before you announced your energy program, a consortium of five utilities have already spent $4 million on the study of the possibility of a plant in North Dakota to convert lignite coal to gas. Secretary Andrus has endorsed this wholeheartedly as being in line with your energy aims. A judge of the Federal Energy Regulatory Commission has recommended that it be turned down, because the utilities plan on providing about 25 percent of the costs which would be assumed by shareholders.

Now, the decision comes before the full Commission sometime in October. Would this hinge on congressional action or could this proceed as a pilot plan under your energy program?

THE PRESIDENT. I don't know. I'm not familiar with their particular status. You're talking about the Federal Energy Regulatory Commission is considering it——

Q. Their decision on a go-ahead in October. There is a bill before the Congress on endorsing loans.

THE PRESIDENT. I see. I can't answer that question.

The energy production board* would, if passed into law—and I hope it will be—will expedite that kind of decision on powerplants, refineries, pipelines, synthetic fuel production plants, and cut through the redtape and the procedural delay which hamstrings a great portion of our energy program. It wouldn't decide whether a plant was warranted or not or whether a site was proper or not. It would just ensure that that decision was made to "go" or "no go" without unnecessary delay.

If a plant is environmentally acceptable and is needed and is financially reasonable and is located properly, I'd like to see the decision made and get the plant built and operating. If it's not acceptable, let the people who propose it know. But I think that would be expedited by congressional action.

Q. Thank you.

THE PRESIDENT. And I'll check with Cecil Andrus about this. I think if the Secretary of Interior has endorsed the project——

Q. He's endorsed it—[*inaudible*]——

THE PRESIDENT.——this would probably remove most of the potential obstacles that I can envision.

I promised the gentleman on the end. I'll get you next.

STRATEGIC ARMS LIMITATION

Q. Dean Conklin from Racine, Wisconsin. Your National Security Adviser expressed concern about linkage of the SALT II consideration with other events. My question is, how can the American people be expected to separate Soviet behavior in Africa or with the Mideast or Cuba from its feeling related to SALT II?

---

*The President meant the Energy Mobilization Board. [Printed in the transcript.]

THE PRESIDENT. I'm convinced that SALT II ought to be passed on its own merits. I'm convinced that SALT II contributes to the security of our country, and I'm convinced that SALT II enhances the prospect for world peace. I'm convinced that the rejection of SALT II would cause each one of the inevitable, competitive interrelationships between ourselves and the Soviets in the future to be magnified in their importance and become a much more critical problem than would that same incident with SALT II.

There's no way that we can avoid peaceful competition with the Soviets as we deal with countries in Africa or Asia or the Mideast or Eastern or Western Europe. And without a SALT agreement limiting strategic nuclear weapons, each one of those differences, which are going to be with us for many, many years, is much more likely to become a major threat to our Nation's peace.

So, SALT II is so beneficial on its own merits—I think the Senate has accepted the basic proposition that it is adequately verifiable—to link it with some action or inaction of the Soviets, or for them to link it with some action or inaction of ours, I think, would not be in the best interest of the American people.

My own hope is that my own convictions, which are now being translated to the Senate after detailed hearings, will ultimately be accepted by the American people. But I don't presume to speak for them, and I certainly can't force the American people to accept the position.

It's so obvious to me that I don't have any doubt about it. I hope that obvious benefit of SALT II will become clear to the American people.

Q. But there was that same kind of expectation, I think, with the Panama Canal and——

THE PRESIDENT. Yes.

Q.——I think there are many American people who still react negatively to that.

THE PRESIDENT. I understand that they do.

Q. It's accomplished, but not accepted.

THE PRESIDENT. I understand. I think in the long run, though, it will be accepted.

As you know, it was difficult, almost impossible, to get two-thirds of the Members of the Senate to become convinced, on its own merits, that the Panama Canal [Treaty] [2] was in the best interests of our country, in spite of the fact that the overwhelming portion of our own constituents at home did not favor the Panama Canal Treaty. I think in the SALT case, a substantial majority of the American people basically approve the signing of a treaty between ourselves and the Soviets to limit nuclear arms.

So, you've got that difference. The American people are basically for SALT, they were basically against the Panama Canal Treaty.

I don't think we'll have as great a selling job in the Senate on SALT as we did the Panama treaty. But I don't underestimate the difficulty; I live with it every day.

FOREIGN POLICY

Q. I'm Bill Pace from Indianapolis. This is a general question about our overall defense posture. In this tug-of-war with the Soviet Union, it seems that their posture is one of aggressiveness and, generally, ours is one of a defensive posture.

In the belief that one of the best defenses is an offense, would it not be wise for us to try to counter some of their offensive moves psychologically, to try to balance the scales?

THE PRESIDENT. When I assess in my

---

[2] Printed in the transcript.

own mind the trends in Soviet influence the last 10 or 15 years, say—just to get out of my own administration and to make it a bipartisan thing—versus the Soviet Union, I'm very encouraged.

The Soviets did win an advantage in Afghanistan. That Soviet-endorsed government is in substantial danger, and that's significant. But when you compare that with our new relationship with India, compared to what it was 5 years ago, or our new relationship with Egypt, the strongest and most powerful Arab country, compared to what it was during the time of the Aswan Dam construction, when Egypt was absolutely committed to the Soviet Union and was dependent on the Soviet Union for military and economic aid, and now are completely friends with us and have prohibited Soviet technicians and others from coming into the country—that's a major change in the Mideast itself.

The People's Republic of China, a fourth of the people on Earth—it wasn't long ago that they were endorsed and supported by and were the closest of allies with the Soviet Union. Now we have a new and burgeoning friendship with the people of the People's Republic of China, and we have not lost our financial and economic and friendly relationships with the people on Taiwan.

I could continue to go, but those are major countries. There have also, obviously, been some setbacks. I don't deny that.

I think that the present commitment that I have given to defense has reversed a longstanding trend. For 15 years, our country was making no real increase in defense expenditures. In fact, when I came into office, our real commitment to defense was less than it was in 1963. This year, the current fiscal year, we have accommodated all the impact of inflation,

and we have at least a 3-percent growth in defense expenditures.

I think we have restrengthened NATO, which was very weak, not only militarily but politically. There's a new spirit and a new dynamism and a new cooperation in NATO that did not exist before.

On strategic weapons systems—if you take our sea-based missiles and you assess the dramatic progress being made with the Trident submarines and the new Trident missiles, that's a quantum step forward. The air-breathing leg of our triad, with the new generations of cruise missiles coming along—that's a major technological and strategic breakthrough. And with the MX missile that I announced this morning on land-based, silo-type missiles—this is the first time that we have ever seen a single missile acquire such a tremendous importance. And it not only gives our country a better defense or attack capability, it also contributes to stability, because you've got a lot more defense with a lot fewer missiles.

So, I think that if you look at other factors—our espousing human rights, the economic strength of our country, our overall trade relationships—in almost every measure, I do not see our country as being affected detrimentally, as contrasted with the Soviet Union.

We recognize that they are a military nation; they put a lot more emphasis on military weaponry than do we. And we are much more inclined to support the status quo, to put down regional conflagrations and conflicts than are the Soviet Union. They espouse a revolutionary political thesis, and to them the change of governments quite often is in their advantage. We generally are inclined to support the government that's in power, unless it is so obnoxious to our own standards and principles that we cannot accept it.

So, the Soviets are inclined to stir up

trouble; we're inclined to try to dampen trouble and to provide peace. That's one thing that gives them an advantage when there is trouble. But I think we have stood up well against them, and I think we can continue to do it in the future on a peaceful, competitive basis. There's no doubt in my mind that the ideals and the principles and the basic strengths of America can prevail and have prevailed.

Ms. BARIO. Thank you, sir.

THE PRESIDENT. One more question.

AMBASSADOR ANDREW YOUNG

Q. Mr. President, I'm from East St. Louis, Illinois. My name is Clyde Jordan. In view of the fact that Andrew Young has been credited with bettering our relationships with many countries in Africa and other Third World nations, do you have any plans to use him in any other governmental position?

THE PRESIDENT. I agree with your assessment that Andy has greatly enhanced our relationships. And one of the advantages that we've got over the Soviet Union in the less-developed world is because of Andy Young.

Andy hasn't made any plans yet about future governmental involvement. Andy left early this week to go on a seven-nation trip with the President of the Eximbank and also with about 20 top American business leaders to see about investments and to let the African nations which he will visit know that there is a continuity in our relationship with the less-developed countries of the world. Andy and his wife, Jean, and their little son both spent the night with me at the White House the night before he left, and I talked to him briefly about his future plans.

I think Andy intends, for the time being at least, to establish himself in private life. He's never had an opportunity to have any income. He's been a very sacrificial person, as you know. I think he would like to let his influence be felt in the private sector of our country for a while. He's interested in politics; he's very supportive of me, and his voice will be heard. I think he's looking forward to his new role for the months ahead. What he will do after that, I have not heard him say, and I don't think he knows himself. But I would welcome Andy in any major position because I have such confidence in him.

Let me take this opportunity to thank you for being here, and I'd like to get a photograph with each one of you, if you'd permit me that pleasure. Let me stand over here and maybe if you come around this way and just let me shake hands and get a photograph, we'll send it to you.

And I'm glad you were up here today. It was kind of an exciting day for me; the decisions have been important ones for our country, and you've kind of seen how Government worked, a little more actively, at least in defense matters, than would ordinarily be the case. I hope you've had an enjoyable and a productive day.

Thank you.

NOTE: The interview began at 2:35 p.m. in the Cabinet Room at the White House. Patricia Y. Bario is a Deputy Press Secretary.

The transcript of the interview was released on September 8.

Home Heating Oil

Telegrams to the Heads of Major Oil Companies. September 8, 1979

I applaud your leadership in initiating Texaco's program to alleviate home heating oil prices and supply hardships this winter.

Members of my staff have already met with Texaco representatives to assure that federal and local activities are coordinated with Texaco's program. In addition, I have sent a telegram to other oil companies asking that they take similar action.

Sincerely,

JIMMY CARTER

NOTE: The telegram was sent to Maurice F. Granville, Jr., chief executive officer of Texaco Inc.

I commend to you the program one of the major oil companies (Texaco Inc.) announced yesterday on home heating oil prices, emergency supplies and credit terms. We are working to maximize the assistance this plan can provide to consumers, particularly the low-income and the elderly.

This program is: (1) holding the line on home heating oil prices; (2) providing emergency supplies of heating oil to needy households, whether or not they are regular Texaco customers; and (3) improving credit terms to wholesalers, who in turn are asked to ease credit terms to retail customers.

I applaud this initiative and urge you to take similar action to help keep heating oil prices stable and to assist in meeting emergency supply and credit needs. I assure you of my strong support in these efforts, and I will continue to work with Congress to make emergency funds available in time for this winter.

I have asked Secretary Duncan to work with you in every way possible to alleviate home heating oil price and supply hardships this winter.

Sincerely,

JIMMY CARTER

NOTE: This is the text of identical telegrams sent to: Richard I. Galland, director, chairman of the board, and chief executive officer, American Petrofina, Inc.; John E. Swearingen,

chairman of the board and chief executive officer, Standard Oil Co. (Indiana); Orin E. Atkins, chief executive officer and chairman of the board, Ashland Oil Inc.; Robert O. Anderson, director, chairman of the board, and chief executive officer, Atlantic Richfield Co.; Alton W. Whitehouse, Jr., chairman of the board, Standard Oil Co. (Ohio); William T. Smith, president, Champlin Petroleum Co.; H. J. Haynes, chairman of the board, Standard Oil Company of California; Robert V. Sellers, chairman of the board and chief executive officer, Cities Service Co.; Robert G. Reed, chief executive officer, Clark Oil and Refining Corp.; Oscar S. Wyatt, Jr., chairman of the board, Coastal States; R. E. Bailey, chairman of the board and chief executive officer, Conoco, Inc.; Henry A. Rosenberg, Jr., chairman of the board, Crown Central Petroleum Corp.; Clifton C. Garvin, Jr., chairman of the board and chief executive officer, Exxon Corp.; John F. Anderson, president, Farmland Industries Inc.; Harold E. Berg, chairman of the board, Getty Oil Co.; Jerry McAfee, chairman of the board, Gulf Oil Corp.; Leon Hess, chairman of the board and chief executive officer, Amerada Hess Corp.; McClaran Jordan, president, Kerr-McGee Refining Corp.; Charles Koch, chief executive officer, Koch Industries, Inc.; H. D. Hoopman, president and chief executive officer, Marathon Oil Co.; Rawleigh Warner, Jr., director, chairman of the board, chairman of executive committee, and chief executive officer, Mobil Oil Corp.; W. F. Martin, chairman of the board and chief executive officer, Phillips Petroleum Co.; John F. Bookout, Jr., chief executive officer, Shell Oil Co.; Theodore A. Burtis, chairman of the executive committee, chairman of the board, and president, Sun Oil Company, Inc.; James L. Ketelsen, chairman of the board, chief executive officer, and president, Tenneco, Inc.; Morton M. Winston, chief executive officer and president, Tosco Corp.; and Fred L. Hartley, president and chairman of the board, Union Oil Company of California.

Gospel Music Association

Remarks at a White House Performance. September 9, 1979

Hello, everybody. How many of you know the significance of a fifth Sunday? Not many. Well, in country churches, as you all may know, the preachers would preach four Sundays, but then once every quarter there was a fifth Sunday. That was the Sunday, particularly in the summer and fall, when people would get together for an all-day singing, and dinner on the grounds, and great local and even distant gospel groups would come, quartets and others, as a time to bridge the gap between churches and between denominations, between communities, and let people reach down, into down-to-earth singing and kind of lift the spirit up to heaven.

Rosalynn and I, when we came home to Plains from the Navy, always looked forward to the summer months, when we could visit different places around near our home and participate in those all-day singing events.

I'm particularly glad this afternoon that the Gospel Music Association, Jim Myers, president, was willing to put together what I believe will be a remarkable program. It's going to last 3 hours, which is going to seem like too short a time for you when it's over. And what we want you to do is just to relax here on the White House grounds, enjoy yourself, get to know one another, and listen to some of the most delightful music that anyone could hear.

Gospel music is really rural music from the country. It has both black and white derivations; it's not a racial kind of music. And this afternoon you'll hear remarkably talented groups who happen to be both black and white.

But I think it's important to recognize that gospel music is derived from deep within the heart of human beings—it's a music of pain, a music of longing, a music of searching, a music of hope, and a music of faith. And you'll hear all those expressions, I am sure, this afternoon in this remarkable performance.

I'm very proud that all of you could

come. We have been to Waycross, Georgia, where they have all-day singing; by that I mean 24 hours. We've been down to Bonifay, Florida, where they have 24-hour sings, and we apologize for cutting this one short. [*Laughter*] But we'll try to make up for it by the quality, and I'm sure that you will enjoy it very much.

I don't know who's going to introduce the first group. Am I going to?

The first group is the Archers. This is my next to the last performance; this is an afternoon of gospel music and not preaching. So, I'm going to end the preaching and turn you over to the Archers, the first group, who will give us a delightful afternoon of gospel music. I'm sure you'll all enjoy it. We're really looking forward to it and to having you here.

Thank you very much, and God bless you all.

NOTE: The President spoke at 2:11 p.m. on the South Lawn of the White House.

Academy of Television Arts and Sciences

Remarks Honoring Don Harris, Robert Brown, and Bill Stewart.   September 9, 1979

Good evening.

Every citizen who carries into the world the standard of truth carries the banner for which this country stands.

For those who bring us the facts on which we make our judgments as a nation, pursuit of the truth is especially dangerous. Finding the center of the news was not only the profession of Don Harris, Robert Brown, and Bill Stewart— it was their passion. Their gift to us was knowledge.

They were killed by some who would suppress the truth and by others who were merely ignorant. But when all the dictators and all the fanatics have come and gone, it's always the truth which remains.

It is no accident that the root meaning of the word "martyr" is "to witness." In Guyana and Nicaragua, these three men were our witnesses, and they were our martyrs. For as they died in the service of a free press, they died in the service of us all.

In this moment of remembrance, even as we are repelled by the horror of their deaths, let us recall the service of their lives.

Whatever differences that might exist within our own country, let us join together tonight in honor of Don Harris, Robert Brown, Bill Stewart, and their families, by renewing our pledge to the standard which they upheld—our common faith as Americans that it is the truth which sets all people free.

NOTE: The President spoke at approximately 9:13 p.m. from the Oval Office at the White House. His remarks were broadcast live during the Academy's Emmy Awards program.

Don Harris and Robert Brown of NBC were killed in November 1978 by members of the People's Temple, while accompanying Representative Leo J. Ryan on his investigation of the People's Temple commune in Jonestown, Guyana.

ABC news correspondent Bill Stewart was killed in June 1979 while covering the civil war in Nicaragua.

United States Ambassador to Botswana

Nomination of Horace G. Dawson, Jr.
September 10, 1979

The President today announced that he will nominate Horace G. Dawson, Jr., of Washington, D.C., to be Ambassador Extraordinary and Plenipotentiary of the United States to the Republic of Bot-swana. He would replace Donald R. Norland, who has been transferred to another post.

Dawson has been counselor for political affairs in Manila since 1977.

He was born January 30, 1926, in Augusta, Ga. He received an A.B. from Lincoln University in 1949, an M.A. from Columbia University in 1950, and a Ph. D. from the State University of Iowa in 1960. He served in the U.S. Army from 1944 to 1946.

Dawson was an instructor of English at Southern University from 1950 to 1953, and associate professor and director of public relations at North Carolina Central University from 1953 to 1962.

He joined the International Communication Agency (then USIA) in 1962, and was posted in Kampala, Lagos, and Monrovia. In 1970–71 he took the Senior Seminar in Foreign Policy at the Foreign Service Institute, and from 1971 to 1973, he was cultural affairs adviser in Washington.

From 1973 to 1977, Dawson was Deputy Assistant Director for Africa, then Assistant Director for Africa, at USIA in Washington.

United States Ambassador to Canada

Nomination of Kenneth M. Curtis.
September 10, 1979

The President today announced that he will nominate Kenneth M. Curtis, of Cape Elizabeth, Maine, to be Ambassador Extraordinary and Plenipotentiary of the United States to Canada. He would replace Thomas O. Enders, who has been transferred to another post.

Curtis is a Portland, Maine, attorney and former Governor of Maine.

He was born February 8, 1931, in Leeds, Maine. He received a B.S. from Maine Maritime Academy in 1952 and a J.D. in 1959 from Portland University School of Law (University of Maine). He served in the U.S. Navy from 1953 to 1955.

Curtis was assistant to Congressman James C. Oliver from 1959 to 1961, and was with the Legislative Research Service of the Library of Congress in 1961. From 1961 to 1964, he was State Coordinator for the Commerce Department's Area Redevelopment Administration.

From 1965 to 1967, Curtis was secretary of state for Maine. He was Governor of Maine from 1967 to 1975. From 1975 to 1977, he practiced law with the Portland firm of Curtis, Thaxter, Corey, Lipez and Stevens. From 1977 to 1978, he was director of the Democratic National Committee. Since 1978 he has returned to his law practice and has also served as United States Commissioner on the International Joint Commission—United States and Canada.

United States Ambassador to Guyana

Nomination of George B. Roberts, Jr.
September 10, 1979

The President today announced that he will nominate George B. Roberts, Jr., of Philadelphia, Pa., to be Ambassador Extraordinary and Plenipotentiary of the United States to the Cooperative Republic of Guyana. He would replace John Richard Burke, resigned.

Roberts has been Deputy Chief of Mission in Vientiane since 1977.

He was born May 25, 1930, in Philadelphia, Pa. He received a B.A. (1952) and M.A. (1953) from Yale University. He served in the U.S. Navy from 1953 to 1957.

Roberts joined the Foreign Service in 1957. He took Thai language and area training at the Foreign Service Institute and was posted in Bangkok and Vientiane. He was at the State Department from 1962 to 1966, and took Swahili language training in 1966–67.

From 1967 to 1969, Roberts was political officer in Dar es Salaam, and from 1969 to 1973, he was Deputy Chief of Mission in Kingston. He was special assistant to the Deputy Secretary of State from 1973 to 1974.

From 1974 to 1976, Roberts was Director of Thai-Burma Affairs at the State Department. In 1976–77 he took the Senior Seminar in Foreign Policy at the Foreign Service Institute.

United States Ambassador to the Ivory Coast

Nomination of Nancy V. Rawls.
September 10, 1979

The President today announced that he will nominate Nancy V. Rawls, of Belair, Fla., to be Ambassador Extraordinary and Plenipotentiary of the United States to the Republic of the Ivory Coast. She would replace Monteagle Stearns, resigned.

Rawls has been Deputy Assistant Secretary of State for Personnel since 1978.

She was born January 24, 1926, in Clearwater, Fla. She received an A.B. from Shorter College in 1947.

Rawls began her career at the State Department as a clerk in 1947 and then served as administrative assistant in Vienna and consular officer in Hamburg, then Montreal. In 1957–58 she took economic studies at the University of Wisconsin, and from 1958 to 1960, she was a foreign affairs officer at the State Department.

Rawls served as economic officer in Hamburg from 1960 to 1963, supervisory commercial officer in Monrovia from 1963 to 1967, and economic and commercial officer in Nairobi from 1967 to 1970. She attended the National War College in 1970–71.

From 1971 to 1974, Rawls was Director of the Policy Planning Staff of the Bureau of African Affairs. From 1974 to 1976, she was Ambassador to the Republic of Togo. From 1976 to 1977, she was Alternate Representative of the U.S. for Special Political Affairs in the United Nations. From 1977 to 1978, she was a Foreign Service inspector at the State Department.

United States Ambassador to Switzerland

Nomination of Richard David Vine.
September 10, 1979

The President today announced that he will nominate Richard David Vine, of Santa Rosa, Calif., to be Ambassador Extraordinary and Plenipotentiary of the United States to Switzerland. He would replace Marvin Warner, who has resigned.

Vine has been Principal Deputy Assistant Secretary of State for European Affairs since 1977.

He was born December 10, 1925, in New York City. He received a B.S.F.S. from Georgetown University in 1949 and an M.A. from Yale University in 1960.

He served in the U.S. Army from 1943 to 1946.

Vine joined the State Department in 1948 and was posted in Bonn, Tel Aviv, and Paris. From 1960 to 1963, he was officer in charge of European integration affairs at the State Department, and from 1963 to 1965, he was political officer in Bonn. From 1965 to 1969, he was counselor for political affairs in Brussels (USEC).

From 1969 to 1972, Vine was Deputy Chief of Mission in Bern. From 1972 to 1974, he was Director of Western European Affairs at the State Department, and from 1972 to 1977, he was Deputy Assistant Secretary of State for European Affairs.

United States Ambassador to Tanzania

Nomination of Richard N. Viets.
September 10, 1979

The President today announced that he will nominate Richard N. Viets, of Hyde Park, Vt., to be Ambassador Extraordinary and Plenipotentiary of the United States to the United Republic of Tanzania. He would replace James Spain, who has transferred to another position.

Viets has been Deputy Chief of Mission in Tel Aviv since 1977.

He was born November 10, 1930, in Burlington, Vt. He received an A.B. from the University of Vermont in 1955. He served in the U.S. Army from 1950 to 1952.

Viets was a public affairs assistant at the International Communication Agency (then USIA) from 1955 to 1957. He was assistant exhibit manager for the

Department of Commerce from 1957 to 1960, and was with Mobil International Oil Co. from 1960 to 1962.

Viets joined the Foreign Service in 1962 and was posted in Tokyo, Madras, and New Delhi. From 1972 to 1973, he was an international relations officer at the State Department, and from 1973 to 1974, he was Director of the Executive Secretariat at State. From 1974 to 1977, he was Deputy Chief of Mission in Bucharest.

National Science Foundation

Nomination of Francis Severin Johnson
To Be an Assistant Director.
September 10, 1979

The President today announced that he will nominate Francis Severin Johnson, of Dallas, Tex., to be an Assistant Director of the National Science Foundation. He would replace John B. Slaughter, resigned, and his area of responsibility would be astronomical, atmospheric, Earth and ocean sciences.

Johnson is the Cecil H. and Ida M. Green honors professor of natural sciences at the University of Texas at Dallas and also serves as executive dean of graduate studies and research.

He was born July 20, 1918, in Omak, Wash. He received a B.S. in physics from the University of Alberta (Canada) in 1940, and an M.A. (1942) and Ph. D. (1958) in meteorology from the University of California at Los Angeles.

From 1946 to 1955, Johnson was head of the High Atmosphere Research Section of the U.S. Naval Research Laboratory. From 1955 to 1962, he was manager of space physics research at Lockheed Missiles and Space Co. From 1962 to 1964, he was head of the atmospheric and space

sciences division of the Southwest Center for Advanced Studies in Dallas. He was director of the Earth and Planetary Sciences Laboratory from 1964 to 1969.

Johnson has been a professor of natural sciences at the University of Texas since 1969. He has also served as acting president of the university from 1969 to 1971, and as director of the Center for Advanced Studies there from 1971 to 1974. From 1968 to 1972, he also served as director of the Space Sciences Center at Southern Methodist University.

Johnson's area of research is upper atmosphere and space physics, planetary science, solar radiation, and synoptic and physical meteorology. He has been a consultant to a number of NASA and NSF committees and has received NASA's Exceptional Scientific Achievement Medal.

National Science Foundation

Nomination of William Klemperer To Be an
Assistant Director.   September 10, 1979

The President today announced that he will nominate William Klemperer, of Watertown, Mass., to be an Assistant Director of the National Science Foundation. He would replace James Krumhansl, resigned, and his area of responsibility would be mathematical and physical sciences and engineering.

Klemperer is a professor of chemistry at Harvard University and is known for his research in molecular spectroscopy.

He was born October 6, 1927, in New York City. He received an A.B. from Harvard University in 1950 and a Ph. D. from the University of California at Berkeley in 1954. He served in the U.S. Navy Air Corps from 1944 to 1946.

Klemperer has been on the faculty at Harvard since 1954 and has been a full professor since 1965. He was elected to the National Academy of Sciences in 1969 and is a member of numerous professional associations.

National Lupus Week, 1979

Proclamation 4680.   September 10, 1979

By the President of the United States of America

A Proclamation

Lupus erythematosus is an increasingly serious connective tissue disease, affecting 500 thousand Americans, mostly young women. There are an estimated 50,000 new victims each year stricken by this disease.

In the systemic form, lupus attacks the entire body and its diverse organ systems, destroying connective tissue in the kidney, heart, and other vital organs. A major feature of the disease is redness of the skin, particularly the appearance of a butterfly-like rash that is often sensitive to light. Additional manifestations of lupus include fever, arthritis, pleurisy, pneumonia, blood abnormalities, heart disease, and central nervous system dysfunction. As its name suggests, this "lupine" disease ravishes the total body in a relentless clinical course and frequently costs its victims their lives in early adulthood.

Although the cause of lupus is not known, the prognosis for patients has vastly improved in recent years. In 1955 the survival rate for lupus victims was 50 percent four years after diagnosis. Now, more than 80 percent of lupus patients are treated successfully during the ten years after their disease has been identified. This increased survival is due to a number of factors including greater awareness of the disease, better diagnostic methods, and development of more effective drug therapies.

The outlook is far from bleak, but greater awareness of the disease and new approaches for improved treatment and diagnosis are needed in order to eliminate lupus as a cause of human suffering and to improve the quality of life in our society for its victims.

Now, THEREFORE, I, JIMMY CARTER, President of the United States of America, do hereby proclaim the week of September 16 through September 22, 1979 as National Lupus Week. I invite the Governors of the States, the Commonwealth of Puerto Rico, and officials of other areas subject to the jurisdiction of the United States to issue similar proclamations.

I urge the people of the United States and educational, philanthropic, scientific, medical, and health care organizations and professions to provide the necessary assistance and resources to discover the cause and cure of lupus erythematosus and to alleviate the suffering of all persons struck by this disorder.

IN WITNESS WHEREOF, I have hereunto set my hand this tenth day of September, in the year of our Lord nineteen hundred seventy-nine, and of the Independence of the United States of America the two hundred and fourth.

JIMMY CARTER

[Filed with the Office of the Federal Register, 2:51 p.m., September 10, 1979]

Strategic and Critical Materials

Executive Order 12155.   September 10, 1979

By the authority vested in me as President of the United States of America by the Strategic and Critical Materials

Stock Piling Act, as amended (50 U.S.C. 98 *et seq.*), and by Section 301 of Title 3 of the United States Code, and in order to provide for the performance of certain functions previously performed by agencies pursuant to their own authority, it is hereby ordered, effective July 30, 1979, as follows:

1–101. The functions vested in the President by Section 3 of the Strategic and Critical Materials Stock Piling Act, as amended, hereinafter referred to as the Act, (50 U.S.C. 98b), are delegated to the Director of the Federal Emergency Management Agency.

1–102. The functions vested in the President by Section 6 of the Act (50 U.S.C. 98e) are delegated to the Administrator of General Services.

1–103. (a) The functions vested in the President by Section 8(a) of the Act (50 U.S.C. 98g(a)) are delegated to the Secretary of the Interior.

(b) The function vested in the President by Section 8(b) of the Act (50 U.S.C. 98g(b)) are delegated to the Secretary of Agriculture.

1–104. The functions vested in the President by Section 10 of the Act (50 U.S.C. 98h–1) are delegated to the Administrator of General Services.

1–105. The functions vested in the President by Section 11 of the Act (50 U.S.C. 98h–2) are delegated to the Director of the Federal Emergency Management Agency. The Secretaries of the Interior and of Agriculture and the Administrator of General Services shall submit biannually a written report to the Director. The report shall detail their performance of functions under the Act and this Order.

1–106. Section 4–101 of Executive Order No. 12148 is revoked and the following new Sections 4–205 and 4–206 are added thereto:

"4–205. Effective July 30, 1979, the functions vested in the President by Section 4(h) of the Commodity Credit Corporation Charter Act, as amended (15 U.S.C. 714b(h)), are hereby delegated to the Director of the Federal Emergency Management Agency."

"4–206. Effective July 30, 1979, the functions vested in the President by Section 204(f) of the Federal Property and Administrative Services Act of 1949, as amended (40 U.S.C. 485(f)), are hereby delegated to the Director of the Federal Emergency Management Agency.".

JIMMY CARTER

The White House,
  September 10, 1979.

[Filed with the Office of the Federal Register, 2:52 p.m., September 10, 1979]

Federal Emergency Management Agency; Department of Energy

Executive Order 12156.   September 10, 1979

CORRECTIVE AMENDMENTS

By the authority vested in me as President by the Constitution and statutes of the United States of America, and in order to correct references in two prior Executive Orders, it is hereby ordered as follows:

1–101. Section 5–211 of Executive Order No. 12148 of July 20, 1979, is corrected and amended to read:

"Section 1–102 of Executive Order No. 12083, as amended by Executive Order No. 12121, is further amended by adding in alphabetical order "(z) The Director of the Federal Emergency Management Agency".".

1–102. Section 1(c) of Executive Order No. 12038 of February 3, 1978, is corrected and amended to read:

"(c) Executive Order No. 11912, as amended, relating to energy policy and conservation, and Proclamation No. 3279, as amended, relating to imports of petroleum and petroleum products, are further amended by deleting "Administrator of the Federal Energy Administration", "Federal Energy Administration", and "Administrator" (when used in reference to the Federal Energy Administration) wherever those terms appear and by substituting "Secretary of Energy", "Department of Energy", and "Secretary", respectively, and by deleting "the Administrator of Energy Research and Development" in Section 10(a)(1) of Executive Order No. 11912, as amended.".

JIMMY CARTER

The White House,
    September 10, 1979.

[Filed with the Office of the Federal Register,
    2:53 p.m., September 10, 1979]

International Energy Conservation Month, October 1979

Proclamation 4681.   September 10, 1979

By the President of the United States of America

A Proclamation

The United States is the largest user of energy in the world and since 1978 has become increasingly dependent on imported oil to meet its domestic needs.

While considerable progress has been made in reducing the rate of growth in demand for energy, much more remains to be done if the United States is to meet its responsibility to reduce its demand for petroleum on the world market.

Energy problems facing us in the United States are similar to those facing other industrialized nations, as well as many of the world's less developed countries. The fundamental problem domestically and internationally is that demand for petroleum is increasing faster than the capacity to produce it.

As the world's major consumer of energy, it is essential that the United States become a leader in conserving energy by curtailing unnecessary and wasteful uses, by improving the efficiency with which we use energy for essential purposes, and by switching from increasingly scarce petroleum and petroleum products to more abundant alternate sources.

To this end, I have announced a program of import quotas to see that the commitment we made at the Toyko Summit will be achieved.

We must also reduce our imports through vigorous and sustained conservation of energy. This task has already begun. The National Energy Act I proposed, which was enacted last November, includes:

—a $300 residential energy conservation tax credit, which the taxpayer can claim for the purchase of insulation and other energy-saving measures;

—a residential insulation service which local utilties must provide beginning in the fall of 1980, to provide energy evaluations of homes and to arrange loan financing for installation of insulation;

—a 10% investment tax credit for equipment used to conserve energy by improving the efficiency of industrial plants;

—weatherization grants for low-income households;

—a 5% reduction in annual energy use

by each Federal department, including mandatory building temperature standards and a 10% reduction in automobile fuels;

—a $900 million grant program to provide 50% of the cost of energy conservation measures for schools and hospitals;

—a $65 million grant program to provide technical assistance and energy audits for local government and other public buildings;

—mandatory non-residential building temperature restrictions;

—mandatory automobile fuel economy standards for each model year through 1985; and

—a "gas guzzler tax" on automobiles failing to meet fuel efficiency standards, beginning with the 1980 model year.

I also have proposed, and Congress will consider:

—a major program to make residential and commercial buildings more energy efficient;

—$16.5 billion in new Federal funding over the coming decade for mass transportation systems and improved automobile efficiency. These latter programs will be funded by the proposed Windfall Profits Tax.

The effectiveness of our efforts to conserve energy in the years ahead will have substantial impact on both the Nation's ability to meet future energy needs at home and on the stability of social, political and economic institutions around the world.

In response to the recognized need to conserve energy, the 20 member countries of the International Energy Agency, including the United States, have designated the month of October 1979 as International Energy Conservation Month. The objectives of International Energy Conservation Month are: 1) to provide an international focus for national efforts to stimulate greater public awareness of the continuing and long-term need for energy conservation; 2) to underline the extent to which industrialized nations are cooperating to conserve energy; and 3) to give member countries an opportunity to plan events which will either culminate during the month or use the month as a springboard for continuing programs.

Now, Therefore, I, Jimmy Carter, President of the United States of America, in full support of this international program, do proclaim October 1979 as International Energy Conservation Month in the United States and call upon all Americans to join me in observing it. During the month let us as a Nation focus our attention on energy conservation through our actions and deeds. Let us view that month as the springboard to a more energy-efficient, energy-reliable future.

I call upon State and local governments to join me in proclaiming October as International Energy Conservation Month and to undertake activities in support of its objectives.

I urge all citizens, corporations, labor unions, trade associations, the media, and groups and organizations of all types to participate in this international energy conservation program at home, at work, while traveling and in all daily activities.

In Witness Whereof, I have hereunto set my hand this tenth day of September, in the year of our Lord nineteen hundred seventy-nine, and of the Independence of the United States of America the two hundred and fourth.

Jimmy Carter

[Filed with the Office of the Federal Register, 11:23 a.m., September 11, 1979]

Superior Court of the District of Columbia

Nomination of Henry Kennedy, Jr., and Frank Schwelb To Be Associate Judges. September 10, 1979

The President today announced that he will nominate Henry Kennedy, Jr., and Frank Schwelb to the vacancies on the District of Columbia Superior Court, caused by the resignations of Judges Joyce Green and William Pryor. Green was recently named to the United States District Court, and Pryor was elevated to the District of Columbia Court of Appeals.

Kennedy, 31, has served for the last 3 years as one of three Federal Magistrates on the United States District Court. Prior to that time, he worked for the United States Attorney's office in Washington. He attended Princeton University and Harvard Law School.

Schwelb, a graduate of Yale College and Harvard Law School, has worked in the Civil Rights Division of the Department of Justice since 1962, and for a number of years headed the Division's fair housing office. He is 47.

Independent Truckers' Strikes

Announcement of Followup Actions by the Administration. September 10, 1979

Following the negotiated end of the independent truckers' work stoppage 2 months ago, the President directed that the administration work actively with representatives of the independent truckers and State leaders to find solutions to serious and longstanding problems facing the independent trucker. The President also recently requested that as a followup, members of his administration report to him on those actions. Based on progress reports prepared by Secretary of Transportation Neil Goldschmidt, Secretary of Agriculture Bob Bergland, and Interstate Commerce Commission Chairman Daniel O'Neal, Jack Watson, Assistant to the President for Intergovernmental Affairs, is issuing today the following summary of actions being taken to deal with independent trucker problems:

—The Interstate Commerce Commission (ICC) has notified each of the 17,-000 regulated carriers of their obligation to pass through the fuel surcharge to owner-operators and to comply with leasing rules. The Commission has vigorously enforced these provisions in response to complaints from truckers. Several hundred carriers have been investigated and most are now complying.

—The Department of Transportation (DOT) and the Department of Energy (DOE) have set up a mechanism for locating fuel supplies and directing truckers to them. DOE's field staff also is able to arrange transfers of fuel to areas where shortages exist.

—The ICC continues to update its weekly fuel surcharge programs, begun June 15, to reflect escalating costs at the pump. The surcharge is now 9.5 percent, and the program will continue.

—Several States have put into effect temporary increases in allowable truck size and weight. When these approached their expiration dates, DOT urged State governments to extend them in view of the fact that Congress was considering enacting Federal legislation to provide uniform limits during a declared fuel shortage.

—The Department of Agriculture (USDA) is issuing weekly bulletins on rates paid to truckers for hauling produce and a monthly report on the cost per mile of operating refrigerated trucks. Arrangements have been made to have both truck rate and cost information available by phone to truckers at 48 USDA Market News Service offices and posted at almost 1,000 truck stops.

—Legislation giving the President authority to mandate uniform size and weight standards for trucks on the Interstate System during periods of fuel shortage has been introduced in both Houses of Congress. The administration supports early congressional action. Secretary Goldschmidt, during his confirmation hearings on September 5, 1979, emphasized to the Senate Commerce Committee the need for this legislation. The administration will continue to push hard for its passage.

—The Bureau of Motor Carrier Safety is developing a way to respond to truckers' complaints about safety enforcement activities. The ICC has expanded its truckers' complaint hotline (800–424–9312), adding several more toll-free lines, and has satisfied hundreds of owner-operator complaints.

—The Bureau of Motor Carrier Safety has already begun considering changes in logbooks and hours-of-service regulations. The Bureau has promised to work with truckers to make certain that any complaints, suggestions, or opinions they have are formally considered during the rulemaking process.

—USDA is developing legislation to standardize hauling contract provisions. Such provisions would end much of the uncertainty truckers now face and help safeguard their rights in the market. The provisions could also ease the problem of unfair unloading practices ("lumping") and increase truckers' available driving time by placing loading and unloading responsibilities on the shipper and receiver.

—A joint ICC–DOT–Small Business Administration (SBA) task force, in liaison with USDA, is developing literature and seminars to aid owner-operators in sharpening management skills, reducing maintenance costs, and increasing operating efficiency.

—The ICC is considering penalties for shippers who intentionally overload trucks.

—The ICC is considering permitting owner-operators to trip-lease in their own names, in order to gain greater revenues. The Commission also is studying the relationship between owner-operator costs and carrier rates, and has initiated a rulemaking process to permit carriers hauling exempt agricultural commodities to backhaul regulated goods.

International Wheat Agreement, 1971

Message to the Senate Transmitting Protocols for the Fifth Extensions of the Wheat Trade Convention and the Food Aid Convention. September 11, 1979

To the Senate of the United States:

I transmit herewith, for Senate advice and consent to ratification, the Protocols for the Fifth Extension of the Wheat Trade Convention (WTC) and Food Aid Convention (FAC) constituting the International Wheat Agreement, 1971. The Protocols were adopted by a conference which met in London on March 21–22, 1979 and were open for signature in Washington from April 25 through May 16, 1979.

I transmit also, for the information of the Senate, the report of the Secretary of State with respect to the Protocols.

The WTC Protocol extends that Convention until June 30, 1981, maintains the framework for international cooperation in wheat trade matters, and continues the existence of the International Wheat Council.

The FAC Protocol extends until June 30, 1981, the parties' commitments to provide minimum annual quantities of food aid to developing countries.

Declarations of Provisional Application of both Protocols were deposited by the United States on July 15, 1979, thus permitting the United States to continue full and active participation in the International Wheat Council and Food Aid Committee. This step was necessary to reduce the risk of expiration of the International Wheat Agreement. The WTC Protocol requires deposit of instruments of ratification or declarations of provisional application by June 22, 1979, on behalf of governments of wheat-exporting member nations holding at least 60 percent of the exporter votes and on behalf of importing member nations holding at least 50 percent of importer votes for the extension to enter into force on July 1, 1979. The FAC Protocol requires entry into force of the WTC Protocol and deposit of instruments of ratification or provisional application by all Parties by June 22.

I hope that the Senate will give early and favorable consideration to the two Protocols so that ratification by the United States can be effected at an early date. Doing so will demonstrate our continued commitment to cooperation on international wheat trade matters and to providing food aid to needy developing nations.

JIMMY CARTER

The White House,
    September 11, 1979.

National Hunting and Fishing Day, 1979

Proclamation 4682.   September 11, 1979

By the President of the United States of America

A Proclamation

The millions of hunting and fishing licenses issued each year reflect a widespread appreciation of the healthy recreation, peaceful solitude and closeness to nature these pursuits offer.

America's hunters and fishermen have long been leaders in the conservation movement. They understand the importance of clean air, good water and adequate habitat for wildlife. They support those goals through the purchase of licenses and the payment of taxes on hunting and fishing equipment. They and the organizations that represent them are also effective leaders in the promotion of firearm and boating safety.

It is appropriate that we recognize all of these contributions by the observance of a National Hunting and Fishing Day.

Now, THEREFORE, I, JIMMY CARTER, President of the United States of America, do hereby designate Saturday, September 22, 1979, and the fourth Saturday of September in each succeeding year, as National Hunting and Fishing Day.

I urge all of our citizens to join with outdoor sportsmen in the wise use and management of our natural resources.

IN WITNESS WHEREOF, I have hereunto set my hand this eleventh day of September, in the year of our Lord nineteen hundred seventy-nine, and of the Independence of the United States of America the two hundred and fourth.

JIMMY CARTER

[Filed with the Office of the Federal Register, 2:40 p.m., September 11, 1979]

Child Health Day, 1979

Proclamation 4683.   September 11, 1979

By the President of the United States of America

A Proclamation

For over 50 years, this Nation has observed Child Health Day. By setting aside this special day each year, we reaffirm our commitment to the improvement of the health of our children. Excellence is the only standard that is acceptable in our efforts to promote good health, prevent disease and disability, and improve conditions that interfere with the ability of each child to reach his or her potential.

In this International Year of the Child, we have accelerated our assault on infant mortality, childhood accidents, acute and chronic diseases and handicapping conditions. I am determined to assure that children receive the expert care they need and to which they are entitled. My goal continues to be excellence in providing for the health needs of our children.

Now, THEREFORE, I, JIMMY CARTER, President of the United States of America, do hereby proclaim Monday, October 1, 1979, as Child Health Day.

I ask that you join me as we pledge our continuing attainment in the pursuit of excellence of health care for our Nation's children.

IN WITNESS WHEREOF, I have hereunto set my hand this eleventh day of September, in the year of our Lord nineteen hundred seventy-nine, and of the Independence of the United States of America the two hundred and fourth.

JIMMY CARTER

[Filed with the Office of the Federal Register, 2:41 p.m., September 11, 1979]

Jewish High Holy Days

Message of the President.   September 11, 1979

My Fellow Americans:

As you celebrate Rosh Hashanah, the beginning of the High Holy Days, Rosalynn and I send our warmest greetings to you as you gather together in homes and synagogues to welcome a new year.

I know that your liturgy for this sacred season includes prayers for reconciliation between neighbors and affirmation of life and recommitment, and at this time you reflect on eternal questions concerning life and death. The words of these services echo universal human concerns.

With you, we recommit ourselves to cherish the freedom of all peoples and to strive peacefully for its realization. With you, we pray, not for an escape from challenges, problems and decisions, but for the wisdom, insight and courage to choose wisely and bravely.

Let us strive to make common cause with decent people of all faiths and nations. Let us strive to preserve the values of our democracy and to broaden the areas of its blessings. Your religion, like mine, seeks to help all people learn to live in harmony with one another and with God. May the coming year bring us closer to the just and lasting peace for which we have yearned and prayed so long and bring to each of you new strength of faith and purpose.

JIMMY CARTER

Meeting With President Mobutu Sese Seko of Zaire

White House Statement.   September 11, 1979

The President met this afternoon for 25 minutes in the Cabinet Room with President Mobutu Sese Seko of Zaire, who is in Washington on a private visit connected with meetings of the International Monetary Fund (IMF).

The two Presidents discussed the situation in Zaire. President Mobutu informed President Carter of the progress that Zaire is making in dealing with its economic and security problems. President Carter restated our strong support for Zaire and the importance that we attach to the ongoing process of reforms in Zaire. He welcomed President Mobutu's description of progress that is being made in these regards.

Also attending the meeting were Secretary of State Cyrus Vance; Under Secretary of State for Political Affairs David D. Newsom; Dr. Zbigniew Brzezinski, the President's National Security Adviser; Thomas Thornton of the NSC staff; Zairean State Commissioner for Foreign Affairs and International Cooperation Nguza Karl-I-Bond; and Ambassador of Zaire to the United States Kasongo Mutuale.

Panama Canal Treaties

Announcement of Vice President Mondale's Trip to Panama for Ceremonies Marking the Entry Into Force of the Treaties. September 11, 1979

President Carter today announced that, in response to an invitation from President Royo of Panama, Vice President Walter F. Mondale will represent the United States at the ceremonies in Panama on October 1, marking the entry into force of the Panama Treaties of 1977. He will be accompanied by Secretary of State Vance and other distinguished Americans.

President Carter attaches great importance to this event, which will signify a

new partnership based on mutual respect between Panama and the United States. For that reason, he has asked the Vice President to represent him at these ceremonies.

National Advisory Committee on Oceans and Atmosphere

Designation of Evelyn F. Murphy as Chairman.   September 11, 1979

The President today announced that he has designated Evelyn F. Murphy to be Chairman of the National Advisory Committee on Oceans and Atmosphere (NACOA).

Murphy has been a member and Vice Chairman of NACOA since 1978. She replaces the late Donald L. McKernan as Chairman. Murphy is a fellow at the Institute of Politics of Harvard's Kennedy School of Government. She is a former secretary of environmental affairs of the Commonwealth of Massachusetts.

Defense Budgets

Message to the Congress on the Fiscal Year 1980 and 1981 Budgets.   September 11, 1979

To the Congress of the United States:

I am sure you agree with me that we cannot effectively safeguard U.S. legitimate interests abroad nor pursue safely peace, justice and order at home unless our national security is protected by adequate defenses. The fundamental responsibility of the President—a responsibility shared with Congress—is to maintain defenses adequate to provide for the national security of the United States. In meeting that responsibility, this Administration moved promptly and vigorously to reverse the downward trend in U.S. defense efforts. This is demonstrated by an examination of the trends in real defense expenditures since the mid 1960s. At NATO Summits in May 1977 and 1978 we persuaded our allies to join with us in endorsing a goal three percent real annual growth in defense outlays and an ambitious Long Term Defense Program for the Alliance. Together these represented a turning point, not only for the United States, but the whole Alliance.

For our part, we moved promptly to act on this resolve. We authorized production of XM–1 tanks; we greatly increased the number of anti-tank guided missiles; we deployed F–15s and additional F–111s to Europe, along with equipment for additional ground forces. We reduced the backlog of ships in overhaul and settled contractual disputes that threatened to halt shipbuilding progress. In strategic systems, we accelerated development and began procurement of long range air-launched cruise missiles, began the deployment of Trident I missiles, and have begun the modernization of our ICBM force with the commitment to deploy the MX missile in a survivable basing mode for it.

These and other initiatives were the building blocks for a determined program to assure that the United States remains militarily strong. The FY 1980 budget submission of last January was designed to continue that program. In subsequent months, however, inflation has run at higher levels than those assumed in the cost calculations associated with that defense program. Accordingly, I plan to send promptly to the Congress a defense budget amendment to restore enough funds to continue in FY 1980 to carry out the Administration's defense program based on our current best estimate of the inflation that will be experienced during the fiscal year. Although the detailed calculations

needed to prepare an amendment are still in progress, I expect that the amount of the amendment will be about $2.7 billion in Budget Authority above the Administration's January 1979 budget request.

Correcting for inflation is not enough in itself to assure that we continue an adequate defense program through FY 1980. We must also have the program and the funds authorized and appropriated, substantially as they were submitted. Therefore, in the course of Congressional consideration of the second budget resolution, I will support ceilings for the National Defense Function for FY 1980 of $141.2 billion in Budget Authority and $130.6 billion in outlays. I will also request that the Congress support the Administration's FY 1980 defense program and, in particular, that the Appropriation Committees actually appropriate the funds needed to carry it out.

Furthermore, in FY 1981 I plan a further real increase in defense spending. The Defense Department is working on the details of that budget. It would, therefore, be premature to describe the features of that budget beyond noting that it will continue the broad thrust of our defense program, and that I intend to continue to support our mutual commitment with our NATO Allies.

While this defense program is adequate, it is clear that we could spend even more and thereby gain more military capability. But national security involves more than sheer military capability; there are other legitimate demands on our budget resources. These competing priorities will always be with us within the vast array of budget decisions both the Congress and the President are called upon to make. Defense outlays are actually lower in constant dollars than they were in 1963, and a much lower percentage of the gross national product (5% compared with 9%). There are those that think this has caused a decline in American military might and that the military balance has now tipped against us. I do not believe this to be so, but I am concerned about the trends. I believe that it is necessary for us to act now to reverse these trends.

The Secretary of Defense will be presenting to the Congress over the coming months the highlights of our defense program in terms of the goals we think we should achieve and the Five-Year Defense Program we plan to achieve them. In this context he will point out, among many other items, how MX and our other strategic programs will contribute to the maintenance of essential equivalence between the central strategic forces of the United States and Soviet Union, how we plan to modernize theater nuclear forces in cooperation with our NATO allies, how our general purpose forces programs contribute both to our military capability to support our NATO allies and rapidly to deploy forces to defend our vital interests elsewhere. That presentation can serve as the basis for future discussions (including open testimony) that will allow us to build the national consensus that is the fundamental prerequisite of a strong and secure America.

JIMMY CARTER

The White House,
    September 11, 1979.

Hartford, Connecticut

Remarks and a Question-and-Answer Session at the National Issue Forum of the National Retired Teachers Association and the American Association of Retired People. September 12, 1979

President Johnson, President Hughes, Governor Grasso, Senator Weicker, Congressmen Cotter, Dodd, and Ratchford:

It is a distinct honor for me to be here with these two combined distinguished groups of retired Americans. As much as I admire you as retired Americans, I must admit that I'm not yet tempted to join your ranks anytime soon. [*Laughter*]

For much of this century, you've seen our Nation through its major crises—two World Wars, a great depression, severe shortages, tragic assassinations, political scandals, embarrassments to our Government, and social upheavals changing the racial interrelationship of our country. You've helped to bring us through all of that, and you've helped to build the most powerful, free society in history, with both material power and also with spiritual power.

These are achievements of which all of you can be very proud, and I as President am deeply grateful to you for this wonderful achievement for all of us. Thank you very much.

But there are some things that trouble us about the future of our great Nation. And I cannot think of any group more qualified to discuss our Nation's future than you who have so positively shaped its past and its present.

My greatest responsibility, above everything else as President of the United States of America, is to protect the security of the United States. Excessive imports of foreign oil—listen very carefully—threaten the security of our country. We not only import about one-half of all the oil we use, but with that oil, we also import excessive inflation and unemployment.

Listen to this: Without including energy, the inflation rate would only have gone up this year about one-fourth of 1 percent—without energy. Energy prices, however, have forced up the consumer price index, because they have increased 60 percent this year.

You know that our country has had

severe problems with gasoline this summer. But throughout that difficult period of shortage, which bothered motorists, when tempers ran even higher than the gas tanks ran low, my top concern was to prepare for this winter.

The morning after my Sunday night address about the crisis of confidence in our country, I flew out to Kansas City, where I set forth the specifics of our energy plan for the Nation. And I said then, and I quote, "We must have adequate heating fuel to prevent suffering next winter." Today, I am pleased to tell you that we will have necessary fuel to see us through this winter. You need not doubt that any longer.

Our heating oil stocks will reach 240 million barrels in October. At this moment, we are 2 million barrels ahead of where we were last year at this time, and we are now producing 330,000 barrels every day more than we were producing this time a year ago.

Another of the actions that I pledged to you was better management of the supplies that we have. It won't be enough to have 240 million barrels of oil in storage somewhere if there is an emergency shortage where you live. Therefore, I've created a special heating oil management group to assure steady and predictable deliveries throughout this winter. The group will involve the Departments of Energy and Agriculture, Transportation—and even the Coast Guard and the Army Corps of Engineers, in case we have severe transportation problems because of excessive icing or excessive snow. And they'll work closely with the industry and with State and local governments. Special emphasis will be placed on coordination with Governors. The headquarters of this group will be in Boston, and the team will go into action on September 15.

With OPEC jacking up its prices by more than 60 percent just since last December, we know all too well that the price of heating oil has gone up all too much. As a nation, we simply must face up to the true cost of energy. And I cannot mislead you; there is no prospect of any reduction in energy prices anytime in the foreseeable future.

You can understand when it's time for this country to face hard realities, because you yourselves, in the past, led us to face hard realities and to overcome them. Given this hard reality of high prices, we're going to reduce the burden of these increased costs on those Americans, many of them the elderly, who are least able to bear them. We will reduce those burdens from the shoulders of those for whom you have deep concern.

Last week, one of the major oil companies, Texaco, announced that it would hold the line on home heating oil prices, that they would provide emergency supplies of heating oil to needy households, and that they would improve credit terms for wholesalers and for retail customers. I'm asking the other 27 major oil companies to act in a similarly responsible manner, to freeze prices and to give adequate credit to help us through this winter with heating oil.

I've launched a continuing major investigation to make sure that no oil companies profiteer from our energy problem. If one inescapable truth has emerged from the whole energy crisis, it is that all of us—oil executives, gas station owners, farmers, renters, homeowners, truckers, retirees, Members of the Congress, Governors, and Presidents—all of us share this problem together, and we must all pull together to beat this problem so it will not beat us all.

There is so much more that we can do if we are ever again to have an adequate energy security for our Nation, on which our own well-being depends. All of us must save energy, stop wasting energy, to hold down the total amount we use and to minimize competition for available supplies and, therefore, hold down the price.

Tax credits are now available to every family in our country for insulating of homes. And we have seen through observation that the simple matter of spending a few hundred dollars on better insulation of homes will cut consumption of fuel by as much as 50 percent. And, obviously, everyone can set your own thermostats to either save energy or to waste energy. We must, however, in addition to this, give special help to the elderly and others who live on low incomes.

I'm today asking the Congress to provide $1.6 billion this winter and $2.4 billion next year and thereafter to ease the burden of rising energy costs on people who most need assistance. This financial help will be for everyone in our country who's the most needy. I know you'll appreciate that. The Congress must act, and you must help me induce the Congress to act.

The program has two basic propositions, and I'll be very brief.

First, a special program which will make cash assistance available to all low-income households. The average benefits nationwide will be about $200, but, of course, there will be higher payments for parts of the country like New England, where the coldest weather prevails. And there will be a second crisis assistance program, that we've had in the last 2 years since I've been in office, that will be greatly expanded to help the States give needy households, in energy emergencies that are dangerous to health, extra help.

I'm asking the Congress to take $400 million for the crisis assistance program this winter out of general revenues—that's

out of existing tax programs now—to prevent tragedies and to avoid delays.

The Congress must also act quickly on the windfall profits tax on the oil companies' unearned profits to pay for the special program for over 7 million needy households in our country.

In structuring this program, we've done several things to ensure that the elderly benefit as much as possible. For example, States will be required to take special steps, which Governor Grasso is already taking, to ensure help for the nearly 2 million elderly who are expected to participate in the special program this winter.

The price rise of heating oil is a perfect example of why this Nation must have a windfall profits tax now. Once we have it—and I predict that we will have it this year—then 50 percent of any increase in the price of oil will be recaptured for low-income assistance, for conservation, for mass transportation, and for developing alternative fuels to reduce our dependence on uncertain crude oil supplies from overseas.

I'll be working also with the Congress to explore every additional way possible to help Americans meet this energy challenge.

The simple truth is that this country is going through a hard transition—from energy so cheap that we didn't even have to think about it, to fuel so dear that it's hard to think about anything else.

Year after year, we have put off the tough decisions on energy. This summer, it became clear to many Americans, who were previously doubtful, that we no longer have a choice, that we have a real energy problem. This winter we must be prepared to face this truth together.

To summarize, we've built up our fuel stocks; we're preparing for emergency distribution of available fuel supplies; we have assistance for needy families; we have an adequate, financial, encouraging program to insulate your homes; we are shifting from oil to more available fuels— natural gas in some instances up here. The most important thing we must do now is to ensure that the windfall profits tax passes, so that it can give us energy security. We can put the era of gas lines and precarious winters behind us.

Of all the groups in this country, you are the best equipped to teach America how to endure and how to prevail. You're the best trained troops we have for winning the energy war.

Look just for a moment, in closing, at the victories we've already won together. Before I became President, as I traveled around our country, the main concern expressed to me by elderly Americans was the fear that the social security system was in danger of bankruptcy, the Disability Insurance Trust Fund was to be depleted, bankrupt in 1979, and the Old Age and Survivors Insurance Trust Fund would be bankrupt by 1983.

With Nelson Cruikshank's [1] help and with your strong support in the Congress, we now have legislation which assures the soundness of the social security system, and we will keep the social security system secure. You can depend on that.

This is a fight we've won together. It was not easy. Members of the Congress who voted for this program have suffered politically, but it was the right thing to do; it was the courageous thing to do.

This is not the only victory we've won. We've won protection against unwarranted mandatory retirement when I signed last year the Age Discrimination in Employment Act. We have won better and more efficient Government services when I signed last year the Comprehensive Older Americans Act, a landmark

---

[1] Counselor to the President on Aging.

piece of legislation that helps every retired person in our country. And we've also won important victories in pension reform, housing for the elderly, rural clinics, mental health care, food stamps, and helping the elderly handicapped. This is a good record. We can be proud of it. And today I want to pledge that together we're going to add two more vital victories to that record in the field of health care.

The first victory which you and I are going to win together is to establish in this country a comprehensive national health insurance plan for which this country has been waiting all our lives. Ever since Harry Truman was President, we've been talking about it; now's the time to do it.

Under this health care program, the 24 million older Americans now receiving Medicare will, for the first time, have a limit on out-of-pocket expenses. After the very first day of hospitalization, senior citizens will be entitled to an unlimited number of fully subsidized hospital days.

There will also be doctor fees publicly set for physicians for both Medicare and Medicaid, for health services rendered. Senior citizens will not face doctors' bills beyond those covered by Medicare.

In addition, over 10 million poor Americans will be given health coverage for the first time. Pregnant mothers, newborn children will be covered. Catastrophic medical bills will be covered for all Americans. We are ready to enter a new era in the United States in health care. If you'll help me, we'll implement this program in the Congress.

And finally, I'm absolutely determined to get hospital cost containment passed through the Congress. The key votes are going to come in the next few days. I hope every one of you will help in every way possible. My proposal to control the skyrocketing increases in hospital costs, increases that fall so heavily on older Americans with fixed incomes, is a crucial part of the health program and the program to control inflation. The States represented here in New England already have such plans, and they're working well.

I'd like to remind you that in the year 2000, the Americans born in the first year of social security will turn 65. They will owe a great debt to you. It's not too much to ask the rest of us that we repay some of this debt now. You who have strengthened this country, changed our society, and have yourselves endured, know that we still live in the greatest and most free democracy in the world. Your will can be made our Nation's will if you make it known to your elected representatives.

I trust you to do that now, as you always have done in the past. I trust you to fight for a just distribution of the resources of this great country, from windfall profits to social security. And, above all, I trust you to help me prove that this land is big enough, rich enough, and humane enough for it to be both free and fair.

To summarize, we must carry forward our vision of a greater America. We must work together for a rebirth of the American spirit. We must restore confidence in ourselves, our neighbors, and in our country. We must revitalize basic human values, which do not change. We must regenerate a sense of unity among the different people in this country. And we must define new and exciting goals for America. Together, that's the kind of nation we will continue to build. Together, that's the kind of land we will leave our children.

Your courage and your commitment, your experience and your wisdom will help to see this dream of a greater America come true. As we have in the past, our Nation will still depend on you.

God bless you. And now, I'd like to answer some questions.

QUESTIONS

NATIONAL HEALTH PLAN

Q. Mr. President.

THE PRESIDENT. Yes, sir.

Q. I'm Jim Peace from Cape Cod in Massachusetts. Your hospital cost containment bill is having a difficult time; we will help you get that through. However, why introduce piecemeal legislation that is inflationary, rather than the entire package as contained in the Kennedy bill?

THE PRESIDENT. For the last 20 or 30 years, the Congress has been assessing, with frequent proposals, how to get passed a comprehensive, nationwide health insurance program. We have assessed the possible means of implementing this nationwide insurance program in every possible way.

I've spent hours with Senator Kennedy, with Senator Long, with Senator Ribicoff, and others. There's no doubt in my mind that the proposal we put forward will not only be less costly but has enough support in the Congress finally to pass. Its ultimate results will be equal to at least the coverage described in any health insurance program. And it's focused upon a phased implementation, which will meet the most urgent needs that I've outlined this morning.

First, both proposals, mine and Senator Kennedy's, have a lot in common. Both will be first implemented in 1983. The difference, in my opinion, is that mine can pass. And as the propositions go through the Congress, I have no doubt that there'll be negotiations, decisions by subcommittees in the House and Senate, and that we'll eventually come out with a plan that I support, that previous Presidents have advocated—none have been able to get through—and that the Congress and the House and Senate, including Senator Kennedy, will be proud to see implemented in our country.

We're working together. There are a few differences. Both plans are good. I believe mine can and will pass.

HEALTH INSURANCE

Q. Mr. President, my name is John J. Stevens of Amherst, New Hampshire. We've had reports that you had a meeting this morning with a number of insurance executives in this insurance city. Are we to understand that you assured them that any national health plan which you plan to propose to Congress will not interfere with their business? [*Laughter*]

THE PRESIDENT. I have not met with any insurance executives. I will meet with them after this meeting, and I will not give them that assurance.

Q. Thank you, Mr. President. [*Laughter*]

NATIONAL HEALTH PLAN

Q. Mr. President, I'm Delbert Smith. I'm from central New York, a little town named Eaton. Would it not be less expensive and more practical, less costly, to have a complete coverage, such as they have in some of the other nations, than to try to bolster up the present system, which I understand your present plan calls for?

THE PRESIDENT. Our plan is a complete one. It is phased to be implemented step by step. It's the kind of proposal that has already aroused substantial support from people who in the past have blocked the passage of any health legislation, as I said, since the time of President Truman.

The final plan, which we have presented to the public and to the Congress, is nationwide. It is comprehensive, it is adequately all-inclusive, it's fiscally sound. And it has an excellent chance to pass though the Congress. I have no doubt that the judgment that I've made on it is the proper one for you, for me, and for the country.

NURSING HOME CARE; SCOPE OF COVERAGE

Q. I'm Patricia Barey from Windsor, Connecticut. And I would like to ask if the national insurance plan would cover elderly patients in nursing homes and, also, to ask, why is it so difficult now for the patients to obtain hospital coverage?

Thank you.

THE PRESIDENT. No, none of the comprehensive national health insurance plans include the long-term care in nursing homes, neither mine, Senator Kennedy's, nor any others, so far as I know. We all agreed that the best way to handle that is through a more comprehensive proposal dealing with different facets of financing, the licensing of nursing homes, and the Medicaid-Medicare extension to chronic care, including drug programs.

As far as the coverage of persons— that's a difficulty that you described—I believe that the program that we've put forward to the Congress will be all-inclusive for certain categories and, obviously, will include all Medicaid and Medicare patients in the future. There would be no exclusion at all.

Let me pause to ask Nelson Cruikshank if there's a special consideration that I need to describe.

MR. CRUIKSHANK. No, that's correct, Mr. President.

THE PRESIDENT. Nelson says that my answer's correct. I'm glad to hear it.

Q. Thank you, Mr. President.

THE PRESIDENT. He's my expert on the subject.

MEDICARE

Q. Mr. President, I'm Marcella Spigelmire, president of the Maryland Retired Teachers Association. I'm from Baltimore, Maryland. Having filed many Medicare forms for myself and my relatives, and always wishing afterward that I had the foresight to select a doctor who would accept the assignment and whose fees met the requirements of being not greater than reasonable and proper, I wonder if you have anything in your plan to alleviate the redtape and rigidity of the present requirements.

THE PRESIDENT. Yes. The whole plan is designed to minimize the redtape and rigidity, because now there are so many different, nonrelated facets of health care. Each person, almost, in our country, each small group of people in our country are in a separate category, and much of that paperwork is designed to identify or to define a person's right for coverage.

The reason that we put forward this comprehensive plan to the Congress is so that as it's phased in, each broad class of people would be completely covered. There would be a minimum amount of paperwork—I would hope no more than you experience with your social security, routine payments. And this is what we hope for, and I believe that we can achieve that.

Q. Thank you, Mr. President.

THE PRESIDENT. Thank you. The comprehensive nature will help to decrease the paperwork.

INFLATION RATE

Q. President Carter, my name is Thomas Canzillo from Monroe, Connecticut. The rate of inflation has been increasing in the last month or so. From all our economic indicators, do you expect the rate of inflation to go up or go down?

THE PRESIDENT. I expect the rate of inflation to go down the rest of this year. As I pointed out earlier, the 60-percent increase in fuel costs imposed on the rest of the world by OPEC is a prime cause of the rapid growth in the inflation rate this year.

Yesterday, I had my economic advisers give me a summary of what the inflation rate would be without energy. And as I said earlier, throughout this whole year the inflation rate would only have changed about one-fourth of 1 percent without energy. With energy included, the inflation rate has changed 4 or 5 percent, because energy has gone up at an annual rate of about 100 percent.

We do not anticipate—although I cannot control this—we do not anticipate any further increases by OPEC this year. So, the rate of increase, even in energy, is likely to level off. And that's why we're working so closely with Texaco and, hopefully, with other oil companies, to get them now to level off their price increases so that we can have a decrease in the inflation rate by the end of this year. I predict that that will happen.

NATIONAL HEALTH PLAN

Q. Mr. President, Bernard Hartspak, Campbell Hall, New York. We have come here from all over this great Nation to listen and also to be listened to. I was told to make my presentation short for lack of time. All one needs to do is look at the seniors in this room to see there is not much time. [*Laughter*] If you'll bear with me, I would like to make part of this presentation, and I'll leave the full text with you.

THE PRESIDENT. I don't agree with that last statement you made. It looks to me like they have a lot of time.

Q. A comprehensive national health plan must and should be put into operation with all due haste. Some of the reasons are: When a nation spends over a hundred billion dollars a year for medical expense—excuse me, I can't see too well with my age—[*laughter*]—we'll get to the question, relax—for medical expenses, still, the American people cannot afford medical attention without the fear of additional expense, is a national disgrace. When a President talks about fair and equal treatment for all, is it fair and equal when the President, Senator, Congressmen, diplomats, heads of state, heads of foreign states, members of their family receive medical treatment at the taxpayers' expense? It would be fair and equal treatment only when all people receive the same treatment.

When a nation serves the medical needs of welfare recipients, drug addicts, alcoholics, prisoners, at the taxpayers' expense, fair and equal treatment for all Americans will apply only when all people are included, when illness strikes.

Now, the question, because time is—[*laughter*]—relax. How much longer will the American people have to wait for a complete national health plan for all Americans?

Thank you very much.

THE PRESIDENT. Thank you. It depends as much on all of you assembled in this room as it does on me.

We have evolved and presented to the Congress, worked closely with the chairman of the Ways and Means Committee, Al Ullman, closely with the chairman of the Finance Committee in the Senate, Russell Long, and with Senator Kennedy and with Jim Corman and others, to propose a comprehensive, nationwide health insurance program. The Congress passing of that program will be dependent on how much they are convinced of your interest in it and the need of the country for it.

I'm convinced that your interest in it is acute and that you will work on it. And I'm convinced that the Nation needs it. And I'm determined to make sure that it comes into being. The implementing date of the health insurance program that we put forward and also, coincidentally, the one that Senator Kennedy put forward, is 1983. If the Congress acts this year or early next year, that's the earliest that a complicated program like this can be implemented.

So, your answer is—I agree with your basic concerns and your basic purposes. If we can get the Congress to act, this program will start to be implemented in 1983. And it will be comprehensive, all-inclusive, and adequate to meet your needs.

HOSPITAL COST CONTAINMENT

Q. President Jimmy, I'm Frank Pezzick from Nutley, New Jersey. I'm going to try to make my question shorter than the preceding speaker, because I'm a Jerseyite and all these other speakers have been New Englanders. [*Laughter*]

Every homemaker in this country knows that when she goes to the store, the price on a can of beans or the price on a steak is higher today than it was yesterday, and it'll be higher tomorrow than it was today, and so on. You and Governor Grasso have pointed out that the price of fuel is going up constantly. We know—and Senator Weicker's drug company can substantiate this—that the price of medicines goes up constantly.

Now, you say that you're going to contain hospital costs. Every delivery a hospital gets of food for its patients is up higher than it was the day before. Every jar of intravenous solution is up, constantly——

AUDIENCE MEMBERS. Question!

Q. The question—quiet, you listened to the other one, now you can listen to me. [*Laughter*]

THE PRESIDENT. But you promised to be briefer. Right?

Q. The question is, simply, what are you going to do to contain hospital costs in view of circumstances like I just mentioned?

THE PRESIDENT. Okay. Let me point out that our system of economy is based on the free enterprise system, where competition helps to control prices even in times of inflation. In the last few years, where hospital cost containment did not exist, hospital costs have gone up about twice the rate of inflation, because there is not adequate competition in hospital care.

Quite often, a person pays hospital insurance for years, if they are fortunate and are well. All of a sudden they feel badly. Their inclination is to go into the hospital, to stay a few days, if possible, to get a good physical examination, to get at least as much care as they need, and partially to recoup what hospital insurance premiums they've paid.

The hospital administrators quite often are very eager to keep the beds full, because the more beds are full, the more profits are made. It's more convenient for a doctor to treat a group of patients in the hospital than a group of patients outside the hospital. In many cases, the doctors are the ones that own the hospitals and derive a profit when the hospitals are full.

Quite often, patients can be treated much more cheaply with generic drugs and much more cheaply in their own homes and with out-patient care than they can incarcerated in a hospital. And what we're trying to do is to make sure that hospitals don't profit from the ab-

sence of competition that I've described for you, and that they do be given an adequate means to pass on the inflation rate that prevails in the rest of the society, but not to continue to have excessive charges above and beyond what the inflation rate would normally warrant. That's the reason for hospital cost containment.

In the States that have it, it has worked. The quality of hospital care has not gone down. The profits are still there, and the patients and the whole society profits.

This hospital cost containment proposal, if passed, would save the American people $56 billion in the next few years; the Federal Government, $22 billion; local and State governments, $6 billion. And the hospital care would still be adequate; the profits for the hospitals would still be adequate. I think we need it; I'm going to fight for it and get it if we possibly can.

Q. A lot of the things you've said are wrong, but we'll talk about that some other time.

THE PRESIDENT. Thank you. This will have to be the last question.

NATIONAL HEALTH PLAN

Q. Mr. President, I'm Bonnie Berstein, director of senior services for West Hartford, Connecticut. When you spoke about your national health plan, you said that doctors' fees will be publicly set, that elderly will not face doctors' bills not covered by Medicare. Who will pick up that tab of the bills that are higher than those "publicly set"?

THE PRESIDENT. Well, we'll do several things in that. One, of course, is that the fees charged by the doctors will be publicly posted; and insurance companies and the general public, the President's Advisory Committees and others, the Health, Education, and Welfare Department will monitor those fees.

If doctors charge different fees under the health care program than they do private patients, say, higher or more abusive, they would be revealed. And that doctor will either be prohibited from participating in the plan or castigated in public as someone who's trying to cheat his patients or her patients.

Let me say this in closing: I'm very proud to have a chance to come and be with you. In almost every forum of this kind we spend our time—mine in my opening speech, yours in asking questions, mine in answering questions—talking about the problems that we face, the differences that exist among us, the disappointments, the challenges, the debates, the controversial issues—that's part of our system, and I wouldn't want to change it.

But as President, I'd like to remind you of this: The problems that we face, compared to the blessings that we have, are very few and far between. God has given us in this great country uncounted, sometimes unremembered opportunities and blessings. We are free, we can be individuals, we can speak our mind, we can criticize the President, we can let our Congress know what we want and demand, we can shape our own government. We can sustain ethical and moral standards and commitments in a time of transient, fast-changing, technological progress. We can repair a nation when it's injured; we can unite if we choose when a nation's in danger. We've got ideals and commitments we can spread around the world.

So, I'd just like to remind you not to forget that our country, in spite of its problems—and they're here, they are manageable—in spite of its problems, it's still the strongest and greatest nation on Earth. Militarily, economically, politically, morally, spiritually—we still live in the greatest nation on Earth. And with your help as free human beings, we can make it even greater in the future.

Thank you very much.

NOTE: The President spoke at 10:30 a.m. in the Hartford Civic Center assembly hall. In his opening remarks, he referred to J. Leonard Johnson, president of the American Association of Retired People, and Frank Hughes, president of the National Retired Teachers Association.

Following his appearance at the forum, the President met with insurance executives at the Sheraton-Hartford Hotel to discuss energy issues.

Low-Income Energy Assistance Program

Statement Announcing Proposed Legislation. September 12, 1979

I am today announcing that my low-income energy assistance program is being sent to Congress. The program would provide $1.6 billion in aid this winter, and $2.4 billion per year thereafter.

This proposal will address a critical need—alleviating the impact of higher energy prices on those who are suffering most from higher energy prices. Our energy policy must be compassionate. Without a substantial program such as this one, our most needy households, including many of the elderly on meager fixed incomes, will face almost impossible pressures on household budgets which already go entirely for the necessities of life.

The proposal has two components: an energy crisis assistance program, which will provide $400 million this year to the States to operate flexible programs to help low-income households faced with health-threatening energy emergencies; and a special allowance program which will provide $1.2 billion this winter and $2.0 billion next year and thereafter, in cash assistance to all poor households. When fully implemented the special allowance program would be available to all households with incomes below 125 percent of the Federal poverty threshold. That threshold is currently $7,160 for a family of four.

While revenues from the proposed windfall profits tax will be necessary to fund this program, I am asking the Congress to move immediately to make general revenues available for the $400 million emergency program this winter. When the windfall tax is passed, its revenues will be used to reimburse the $400 million spent from general revenues. With prompt congressional action on the windfall tax and on my low-income assistance program, and close cooperation between the Federal and State Governments, we can provide help to over 7 million needy households this winter—and avoid tragedies which might otherwise occur.

Steubenville, Ohio

Remarks and a Question-and-Answer Session at a Townhall Meeting.　September 12, 1979

THE PRESIDENT. It's great to be here at Big Red.

Senator John Glenn, Congressman Doug Applegate, distinguished leaders of Ohio government, local officials, and my friends from Steubenville and the surrounding communities:

I've come as President today to say a few words to you at the beginning and then to spend what time we have to-gether with your commenting to me and asking me questions about our Nation and our Government, our present and our great future.

I'm convinced that we live in the greatest nation on Earth.

And I'm convinced that the steel industry, being so crucial to our Nation, is strong now and will be increasingly strong and beneficial to our people in the future.

And I'm convinced that with good leadership in government and in the private sector of American life, that that partnership—free people, democratic government, free enterprise—can be successful in overcoming even the most difficult obstacles, answering the most difficult questions, resolving the most difficult problems.

ADMINISTRATION POLICIES

When I became President a little more than 2 years ago, the steel industry was in serious trouble. Profits were nonexistent. Losses on a nationwide basis were very high. Plants were closing down. People were being laid off. Excessive, unfair imports were taking away our markets. Only 78 percent of the capacity of our steel plants in this country was being utilized.

I established a task force. I was part of it, Bob Strauss was part of it, John Glenn was part of it, Doug Applegate was part of it. We had officials from your area and throughout the country, from the Congress, in all States that produce steel. And we tried to devise some comprehensive approach dealing with all the many problems of the steel industry.

It was a voluntary program. No steel executive, no steelworker was required to participate. But we approached each other in a spirit of mutual trust, without looking for scapegoats, without condemning one another, without being fearful about the future, without having lost the spirit of America, and I think we've been remarkably successful.

We set up a trigger price mechanism to cut out illegal dumping of foreign steel. We appropriated $14 million for modernization programs to make sure that obsolescent steel plants had a new incentive to modernize and to save jobs. We also introduced, for the first time, in a friendly way, the steel industry to the Environmental Protection Agency, so they could understand one another for a change and kind of work together to accommodate the law's requirements, but not to put handcuffs on the steel industry itself.

The 78-percent utilization rate of all our steel capacity has now grown to more than 90 percent. Those constant annual losses in 1977 changed in 1978 to $1.3 billion in steel industry profits that can go to new hiring, distribution of profits to owners, and new improvements to keep our steel industry vital. In 1979 my understanding is that the profits will be even higher than they were last year.

We now have 465,000 steelworkers on the job. And early this summer, the steel industry as a whole had a $1 billion payroll, the highest payroll the steel industry has ever seen in the history of our country. These kinds of achievements have been accomplished through cooperation and through using the tremendous advantages that God has given us in this country. It shows, I think, in a vivid way what we can do when we face a challenge together and with confidence in ourselves, in each other, in our Nation. It shows that there's room for jobs, there is room for profits, there's room for environmental quality, the quality of our lives, there's room for productivity, for community de-

velopment, there's room for cooperation between Government and citizens.

Now we've got another challenge, and I need you to help me with that. I believe that it's better for us instead of importing more foreign oil, to use more Ohio coal. And very briefly let me tell you why, in case you need convincing.

We import about 50 percent of all the oil we use. We import, along with that oil, inflation. We import unemployment. We will send overseas this year from our country about $70 billion that we ought to keep here. We've got enough coal to last us 600 years, but in the past, in the last number of years, there has not been that dedication of industry, employees, and the Government working together. We've already made some progress. We're going to make some more.

The years ahead, I predict, will see a tremendous improvement in the utilization of American coal, including Ohio coal, and a restoration of the security of our country, because it's not good for us to have our Nation in danger because we are overly dependent on oil from an uncertain source and at an uncontrollable price. As you know, the OPEC oil prices have increased in the last few months, since December, 60 percent. That's an annual rate of inflation in energy of about 100 percent. This has got to stop, but I need your help with it.

I believe that by 1995, we can triple the amount of coal used in this country. We can honor, in the process, environmental laws. We could have an increasing sense of unity among Americans. We can enhance our Nation's security. We can have more jobs in our country, less unemployment, less inflation. Three-fourths of all the synthetic fuels that we anticipate producing in the coming years will be from coal. And the windfall profits tax, when it passes, it'll bring in about $88 billion for energy purposes over the next 10 years; $75 billion of that will be spent on coal.

This is the kind of vision that I have for the future, but it's going to require action by the Congress. And your Congressmen and your Senators support this, but are dealing with the question in a confident and courageous way. In the process, we have enhanced mine safety and the health of miners, and I believe there's a growing sense of cooperation between mineworkers and mineowners.

Our country is strong enough to withstand any challenge if our people are willing to do two things: make a common sacrifice, not losing our confidence, and work in a spirit of unity. The synthetic fuel process is going to take a good while, 8, 10 years. In the meantime, we need to save energy, stop wasting energy, use more coal, which you've already got. And I believe with that kind of program, we will prevail.

Now I would like to answer the questions that you've prepared for me. I have no idea what they are. I'll do the best I can in answering them.

And I am very glad to be with you. Thank you for coming.

Now, the first question.

Questions

ENERGY PRICES

Q. Mary Albritton, project director from the city nutrition program in Jefferson County. I would like to know what are you going to do about the utility bills for the seniors in the low-income in this area? We do not have any funds at this time for that purpose.

THE PRESIDENT. We're doing several things, the first one of which is to continue our crisis financing program that we've had in the last 2 years since I've been in the White House to give low-income families some help with their energy bills if they were too high. In the last 2 years, working through the State governments, we've allocated $250 million for that purpose. If the family's health was in danger, because they were going to get too cold and couldn't afford the bills, that's been helped. We intend to expand that this coming winter by a hundred and fifty more million dollars.

And in addition to that, we are asking for a special program, because energy costs have gone up so much—home heating oil, for instance, is likely to double in price. Propane is likely to double in price. Under the windfall profits tax, we'll have additional funds available to help those families that can't afford to pay for their rapidly increasing bills.

The most important thing for all families in our country is this: We've already approved a tax credit, up to $300 per home, for you to insulate and to make your own homes more efficient.

I was in Baltimore just a few days ago—a few weeks ago, and they have winterized or weatherized or insulated 3,000 homes in that one city; next year, 5,000 homes. The average cost per home was only $175. They'll save that much on their heating bill the first year, or if the house was pretty well insulated to start with, it might take 2 years. But if you do that, you have a direct tax credit when you pay your income tax to pay that back to you.

So, saving through winterizing your homes, help for low-income families to overcome a very high, uncontrollable energy bill, plus your need to save in every way you can what energy you consume, in the setting of your thermostats, the closing off of unused rooms in your house, and that sort of thing, I believe, will help us get through the winter.

And, of course, we need to keep the lowest possible kinds of energy used. The EPA and the Jay Rockefeller Coal Commission report have identified 100 electric powerplants in our country that ought to shift and can shift from the burning of fuel oil over to coal. And that will be continued in the future as rapidly as we can.

Those three things, very briefly, are part of the steps that you can take and we can take to get us through a difficult winter.

In the second microphone.

FUEL SUPPLIES

Q. Scott Campbell from Steubenville. With the energy crisis so severe, why do we supply other products to other foreign countries so cheaply, when they are only holding the fuel while we are holding their food products and other type of products? Also, with the energy crisis so severe, why can't the EPA loosen some of their regulations so that we can move more coal through this area and get the steel production going a little bit more burning Ohio coal and not to raise the unemployment here? We'd get a few more people employed in this area.

THE PRESIDENT. Those are good, I think, three questions, and I'll try to answer them briefly.

First of all, I think it's to our advantage whenever we can sell American coal overseas to do it, and I hope to increase exports of American coal in the future.

In the past we've had good markets in Japan. Three or four years ago those markets were lost. Now we're trying to get them back and to get other markets for our coal. We've got enough to use and also to export. If there ever comes a time when we don't have enough for both

purposes, obviously we would meet our own needs first.

There's been some—you may be referring to the sale of a million barrels of home heating oil to Iran. Let me explain that to you.

Iran had an interruption of the production of their home heating oil because of sabotage or because one of their plants broke down. They asked us to let them have a million barrels, because, as was the case when I was a child growing up on the farm and didn't have electricity, they use kerosene or home heating oil for almost everything, for lamps and for heat, for cooking. So, we let them have a million barrels of home heating oil. They sell to us every day 750,000 barrels of crude oil. And I thought it was a good idea for humanitarian purposes and to make sure we keep that market for us open.

Last spring, when we had serious shortages of fuel oil, heating oil, gasoline, distillate for trucks, it was because they had a revolution in Iran and that supply was interrupted. Now they produce about 4 million barrels each day. We get about 20 percent of that.

The EPA standards—I think it's best for me to be frank with you—there are laws that bind the entire Nation on air pollution standards and water pollution standards. I don't think you would want to see those laws stricken down. Forty-nine of the States have submitted and have had approved an environmental program. One State in the Nation has not had an environmental program approved. That State happens to be Ohio.

It's much better for the enforcement of environmental laws, or any other law, when you can have the cooperation of the State government and let basic management of a program be done by local and State officials instead of by the Federal officials. But the law requires that until the State gets an approved plan, the Federal Government has to be involved in it almost a hundred percent. We don't like this. I'll be eager to see Ohio have an approved plan very shortly, I hope, just like the other 49 States have already done.

We have interpreted in the EPA—it's an independent agency, I can't control it—but we've interpreted that law as best we can within the legal framework to permit the continued and increased use of Ohio coal.

I was in a plant in Kentucky recently that uses very high sulfur coal. It's a modern plant, meets all the standards, has no problem with EPA, because they've made the change to a more efficient use of the coal in the scrubbing in the smokestacks.

Now, we have had some problems recently, as you know, with Cleveland Electric, and they are now authorized to burn high-sulfur Ohio coal. Most of the plants in Ohio have shifted so that they are qualified to burn Ohio coal. Others will be qualified by October 19. We'll do all we can, within the bounds of the environmental standards, to let Ohio coal be used. I hate to see Ohio importing coal for your own electric power production, and I'm as eager as you are to obey the laws, which I'm sworn to uphold, to turn over the responsibility to the State and local officials to enforce the environmental laws and to see a maximum use of Ohio coal. I think my goal and yours in that respect are identical.

Thank you very much for that question.

ENERGY PROGRAMS

Q. Mr. President, my name is David Hawkins, and I'm from Mingo Junction, Ohio. And my question is, what steps or procedures do you hope to see implemented within the upcoming year to reduce unemployment due to the energy problems we are experiencing?

THE PRESIDENT. We've proposed to the Congress three things on energy. One is the passage of the windfall profits tax. This is a tax that will be levied on the unearned profits of the oil companies. Oil prices are going up. The oil companies are getting a higher price for their oil. The question is, who's going to get that money? We believe that enough should be left for the oil companies to increase their production of American oil and American natural gas. But we think that about half of that money ought to come to be used for synthetic fuels, for conservation, for solar energy, for the improvement of our rapid transit systems, or mass transit systems, and also to help families to overcome the difficulties of increased costs of energy. And it's imperative for the energy program for the windfall profits tax to pass.

Secondly, we are setting up a corporation, a security corporation that will have the authority to implement 80 new projects all over this country to produce synthetic fuels, to work on solar power, to do things concerning conservation, which will generate tremendous numbers of new jobs. And in the process of having energy produced in our own country and stopping the sending of $70 billion, like this year, overseas, we'll generate more jobs for Americans, not only in synthetic fuels, solar power, the weatherization of homes, but also in the increased production of coal. And I think that this new energy program is a very effective way to deal with potential unemployment and to keep our country strong.

The other thing that has hurt us in the past has been the unnecessary delay in making decisions. We expect to institute in the Congress—and we got good news from one of the major committees this morning—a board, a mobilization board that will cut through redtape. Now when you have a decision to make about building a new powerplant or a new oil refinery or a place to produce electricity or a pipeline, you have to wait 5 or 6 or 7 or, sometimes, 8 years to get a decision to either build it or don't build it. What we are trying to do is to get the Congress to shortcircuit that long delay and let the decision be made without delay. If it ought to be built, build it. If it ought not to be built, don't build it. But the thing is to make the decision and get moving.

Our country's basic security—I'm not exaggerating this—is in danger. So, we've got to have a stronger America, we've got to cut down our overdependence on foreign oil, and we've got to make sure at the same time that American jobs are created and American energy is used to give our country back its strength, its confidence and its unity and its prosperity and a good life. That's what we're trying to do, not only for energy but for jobs and also inflation at the same time.

It's a good program. I need you all to help me with it. Will you help me with it? [*Applause*] Thank you.

COAL SUPPLIES

Q. Mr. President, I'm a mineworker from Hyatt Point, Ohio, North American Coal Number 6, Local 1810. And my mine's been shut down since August 31—there's 900 people employed down there—and the reason, on account of our stockpiles are too big; they're not burning our coal.

And all your plans seem fine, you know, for the future, but us coal miners, we want to work now, not 10 years from now. And I'd like to suggest that you put a task force to solve the steelworkers' problems, put a task force together now to solve our problems, because we want to work. We're proud people down here.

Thank you.

THE PRESIDENT. Is this particular mine shut down because Cleveland Electric is ordinarily buying the coal from your mine?

Q. Our contract's with Cleveland.

THE PRESIDENT. That's right. Now, Cleveland Electric has promised us in writing that they would purchase the coal derived from your mine. We understand that the shutdown is likely only to last about 4 weeks. That may or may not be true. I'm not vouching for that. That's the information I got this morning. And we are very eager to remove every obstacle so that within the law, of course, on environmental quality, that Cleveland Electric, its two plants, and all the other plants can begin to use more and more Ohio coal.

We are going through a changing time, because for years these particular questions have not been addressed and the energy industry—oil, coal, natural gas, and others; coal miners, coal workers, powerplants, electric-generating plants—have not known what to expect next. We've never had an energy policy in this country. But I believe that after this year, after the Congress acts and after we work out a relationship with the State of Ohio and the power companies, that you won't have this off-again, on-again kind of production of coal.

I would like to see your mine working full-time, all the mineworkers employed, Cleveland Electric using your coal on a sustained, permanent basis, with a clear working-out of the problems that presently exist.

We're working on it. It can't be done instantaneously, but I guarantee it will not take 10 years to do it if we all work together.

EMPLOYMENT IN THE COAL INDUSTRY

Q. Mr. President, Kathleen Jones from Bellmont, Ohio. Do you consider over 4,000 Ohio coal miners out of work a minimal effect, as the U.S. EPA has stated is their reason not to invoke Section 125 of the Clean Air Act?

THE PRESIDENT. You know, I don't want to see any Ohio coal miners or other employees out of work.

I noticed in the statistics concerning the Steubenville area that the unemployment rate has gone down in the last 12 months, and I'm very glad to see that. The unemployment rate in Ohio is fairly good. And I think the combined employment opportunities for both coal and steel have been greatly improved since I've been in the White House.

I don't claim to you that we have solved all the problems with coal, but we are working out the environmental problems in spite of the absence of an agreement with the State government of Ohio. I hope that'll be solved soon. I'm not criticizing anybody.

Secondly, as I said earlier, we'll have $75 billion, about 3 or 4 billion dollars a year, once the windfall profits tax is passed, to take coal and use it for new things that we presently do not use it for, either finely pulverized coal to be burned as it is, coal to be refined so that it is very clean-burning, coal to be used in electric powerplants that presently use crude oil or oil, and other means.

I believe that by 1995, as I say, we will triple the use of coal, and that obviously has to come from Ohio as well as other places.

I'm very concerned about the unemployment rate among coal miners, but I believe that they are getting in better shape now. And I will devote my full time working on this energy question with John Glenn, Doug, and others in Washington. I need you all to help me, though, to get this program through the Congress.

Let me add one other thing that you didn't ask me about, but it's important for you to understand. I really govern two countries, as far as energy is concerned. One is a producing nation on oil, and the other is a consuming nation on oil.

In the past, in Washington, whenever there was an argument about energy, the oil companies won. They had the best lobbyists; they were the most effective; they were well-organized; and nobody ever challenged them, until 2 years ago. And now there's an aroused interest on the part of the coal industry and other energy-producing areas, and also consumers.

We've made good progress. We've already cut our potential imports of foreign oil by 4 million barrels—got still a long way to go. But if we don't get the windfall profits tax passed on the oil companies, we won't have a synthetic fuels program; we won't have a conservation program; we will not have a program to help poor families overcome a high energy cost in their homes. We will not have an ability to change over into coal-burning plants instead of oil-burning plants. The whole thing depends on action by the Congress.

I predict to you that we will win this fight. But it's not a sure thing. And I hope that all of you realize that it's not the time for scapegoats or to blame me for what I've not done or what my predecessors have not done. Now's the time for us to marshal our efforts. And I believe that we can be just as successful in Ohio coal areas with new uses and presently known uses as we have been in steel—

perhaps even more. But it's going to require that same degree of cooperation.

I'll do the best I can, but I really need for all of you to help me with this challenge to the oil companies. They do not want to see the windfall profits tax passed. They want to keep all the money themselves. They have not earned the money. We need that money for other purposes, including coal.

Help me. We'll prevail. And I think that you will see inevitably the present unemployment rate in the coal mining area go down sharply.

NUCLEAR ENERGY

Q. Hi. I like your smile. I'm Peggy Wilt from Bratenahl, Ohio, and I have an energy-related question. But first I'd like to ask you another question. I believe in your commitment to the people of the United States and to the people of Ohio to hear them out. And on September 8 and 7, hundreds of telegrams were sent to you from the tiny village of Bratenahl, and I'm wondering if you're intending to respond to the people there.

My energy-related questions are, since it appears that uranium ore located in the United States will probably be depleted between 1985 and 1990, and since the Federal Government is still encouraging the building of nuclear powerplants, will not the United States become doubly dependent on foreign sources of energy? And also, would you support the creation of a nuclear ombudsman program?

Thank you.

THE PRESIDENT. I will reply to the telegrams.

We will not see our uranium supplies depleted anytime this century. We've got enough uranium to last us probably through the next century.

Until the Kemeny report is in to me—

and that'll be later on this month—concerning the causes of the incident that we had at the Three Mile Island plant in Pennsylvania, it will not be possible for us to make a policy decision on the use of nuclear power in the future.

We want to be sure that as nuclear power is an integral part of our energy production society now, that it will be in the future, but the design of plants, the training of personnel, the operation standards, the modification of existing plants will be adequate to reassure the people that they are safe.

I was in Connecticut earlier this morning. About 60 percent of all their electricity comes from nuclear powerplants; in Chicago, more than 50 percent. We can't close down those nuclear plants, but we need to make them safe.

I think that other nations will move much more aggressively and quickly toward the dependence on nuclear power than we will in order to escape from dependence on OPEC oil. Because we are so fortunate—we have geothermal supplies; we have natural gas supplies; we have enormous coal supplies; we have very good crude oil supplies in our country; we've got the highest developed scientific and technology base to move into new areas, like photoelectric cells and so forth, of any country on Earth; and we've got a free enterprise system and free people who can be innovative and show a lot of initiative on our own to deal with changing circumstances.

So, I would say that we are very likely to escape any sort of major disappointment or increasing dependence on the OPEC countries in the future. I think if we work together, the plan that I've laid out to the Congress will work and we will be successful. I don't have any doubt about that.

Q. What about the nuclear ombudsman program? Would you support something like that?

THE PRESIDENT. Yes. I think that at this moment the Kemeny Commission, which has got full authority from me, is looking into the entire nuclear question. At the end of that, I will assess their recommendations and then make a full report to the American people about what I will and will not do. The ombudsman idea is a good one. But let me reserve judgment on making that promise to you. There will be someone in the Government at a high and identified level who will be responsible for answering any questions asked about nuclear power or resolving any problems that exist for an American citizen concerning nuclear power, or receiving suggestions on how the use of nuclear power can be made more acceptable. Whether we call it a separate ombudsman, I can't say yet.

COAL AND ENVIRONMENTAL STANDARDS

Q. President Carter, I'm Sondra Downend from Orville, Ohio. I'm the wife of a small coal mine operator, and I'm the secretary and bookkeeper for our company. We spent 2 months without shipping coal, and I spent a lot of sleepless nights and sent you lots of letters. I got one back from the Department of Energy that spoke of Federal leases on Federal land and spoke of western coal. But my letter came from Ohio. And I wasn't interested in western coal, nor federally leased lands.

You talked about how slow Ohio was in presenting their clean air act. And I spoke with them because I was interested in next month what's going to happen to our mine, because we're afraid that we won't have any place to ship our coal. And in talking with them, he told me that they felt that the Federal law was too restrictive and they didn't have proof.

So, they wanted to take their time and not make the mistakes the Federal bureau had made and that they had made in the past, and go very slow and do their modeling and their monitoring and measuring. He told me of places that they have in the State of Ohio where they measure the air control. And they have measured the air quality from utilities and other industries, and they feel that Ohio can still burn the high-sulfur coal and still come within the numbers required by the Federal EPA.

And, I'd like to ask, then—the Ohio EPA that I talked to was so certain that their plan now meets everything the Federal would require of them, I would like to ask, why won't the Federal EPA approve Chapter 3745–18 of the Ohio Administrative Code and allow the utilities to burn the high-sulfur coal?

And this is something that is causing a great deal of concern to us, a lot of anxiety. We're trying to stay in business. We're trying to ship the coal. We lost our orders to Ohio Edison because of the high sulfur in our coal. We have two customers now. And in meeting with the Wash plant, they tell us that next month they don't know if they'll be able to take our coal or not because of the Clean Air Act.

THE PRESIDENT. Let me try to answer as best I can. [Representative] Doug Applegate is coming to Washington Friday morning at 10 o'clock to meet with my staff and some members from EPA and the Department of Energy. Doug, could you bring her with you to Washington?

Q. Thank you. I love ya.

THE PRESIDENT. I think the obviously sincere way that you've described the problem and asked the question would be very helpful to us in Washington.

Q. I'll do everything I can. [*Laughter*]

THE PRESIDENT. Secondly, let me point out to you that I'm not trying to criticize the State of Ohio; I don't want anybody to get that impression. But, you know, with a given Federal law which the Congress is highly unlikely to change, it's much more advantageous for you and for your husband and for your coal mine to have a cooperation between the Federal and State Government, as we have in all the other 49 States, rather than to have a continued confrontation. And I believe that the best thing to do to alleviate problems and to make sure we've got a real local input when a decision is made is to have the Ohio environmental program approved and implemented. If there are some differences between the Federal requirements under the law and Ohio will just have to——

Q. Just work them out.

THE PRESIDENT. ——they'll just have to work them out, or Ohio will have to amend it's proposal.

But it doesn't help anything for 2½ years to go by and for Ohio still to maintain, "We don't like the Federal law, therefore we're not going to comply." What it means is that there's no State input, and you're faced with well-meaning people from Washington who are trying to administer that law. In all the other States, we've got State people who understand your problems much better— who might know you personally—working alongside of the Federal administrators to ensure compliance.

So, I believe that if you will come to Washington and meet with Stu Eizenstat and others and also use your influence to encourage the State of Ohio and I'll encourage EPA to work together, we'll make a great stride forward.

That's one of the reasons, by the way, that I wanted to come to Steubenville. It's not an accident that I came here. I'm proud of what we've done in steel. I'm concerned about what we have not yet accomplished on coal, and you are a

highly motivated, very knowledgeable group about both these areas of American life. And I think your kind of question is very helpful to me as President. It'll be helpful to you and your coal mine in a personal way; I think it'll be helpful to the whole country, and I thank you for it.

COAL PRODUCTION

Q. Mr. President, my name is Bob Houston, and I'm a UMWA coal miner from Local Union 1810. Effective August 31, as Larry Bussey's told you, our mine was shut down. But in your energy message you have declared the moral equivalent of war in your energy policy, and coal was included in that policy.

However, in the State of Ohio, mines are being shut down because of the U.S. EPA standards. I have attended these EPA hearings; I've testified, as well as many other coal miners. And we have always stated that we thought that the answer, the solution to this problem was a compromise. But we seem—our words have never been heard, because our mine shut down and there are approximately 5,000 coal miners laid off in the State of Ohio. And what we would like to know is, when can we expect some concrete solutions to these sulfur dioxide problems, and to get 5,000 coal miners back to work and the energy program on the road to make us energy independent from foreign oil sources?

THE PRESIDENT. I don't think I need to repeat what I've already said about the proposal. But let me make one point more clear.

My proposing an energy policy to the Congress is just the first step. Until the Congress adopts it, we don't get the benefits from it. And the Congress has not yet passed a single line of legislation concerning oil because of the power in the past of the oil companies. I think now it's about an even contest in the Congress, in Washington, between the oil companies' influence and the influence of the rest of the country. I'm not particularly trying to criticize the oil companies, but the fact is that the Congress has not yet acted on the energy proposal that I described Monday morning in Kansas City after my Sunday night address. As soon as the Congress acts, we'll have all the benefits that I described then for the increased use of coal.

In the meantime, we've got to depend on two things—conservation and shifting away from fuel oil use onto the use of coal. That will help a great deal. The President's Coal Commission had some good recommendations. One, which has already been approved by EPA, by the way, is to transform a hundred electric utility companies away from using oil to the use of coal. And every time in our whole Nation you start using more and more coal, you create more and more jobs for United Mine Workers, and I believe we make that progress. But this cannot be done instantaneously, because it's been too long in getting America aroused about energy.

I made that speech about the moral equivalent of war in April of 1977, and as you probably noticed, the news media mostly made fun of it—there was a lot of fun made of it—and said that it's too serious, we're just not going to get serious. It was really this summer, when the gas lines started developing in California and on the east coast, that the people got aroused. You, as a coal miner, have been aroused for a long time.

I think the settlement that was made between UMW and the coal operators is a very major step forward. I'm not trying to predict what's going to happen in the future. I'll knock on wood. But the shutdown and the uncertainty of delivery of coal has now been substantially alleviated, and people who want to depend on coal permanently don't have to worry about frequent interruptions of production. I think it's a much more stable industry. That's been accomplished in the last 2 years.

We are making progress, got a long way to go, but I feel like you and I are partners in making that progress. I'll help you if you'll help me.

Q. You have my help, sir.

THE PRESIDENT. That's a deal.

RENEWABLE ENERGY SUPPLIES

Q. Hello, Mr. President. I'm Peter McGee from Steubenville, Ohio. I'm a social studies instructor at the Jefferson County Joint Vocational School, and I asked my students to submit to me some questions that they would ask you of energy. And I picked one from here to ask you.

This is from a student named David Ramsey. He would like to know, why isn't gasohol and other agricultural fuels being researched and used more extensively?

THE PRESIDENT. It is being researched, and it is being used more extensively than it was 3 months ago or 6 months ago or 12 months ago or 2 years ago. There's a great deal of interest in gasohol and other energy from so-called biomass, replenishable supplies.

Biomass is a resource in our country that's not yet been tapped, except to a very minor degree. It consists of growing things and what energy you can get from those products.

I'll give you one example. Georgia has about 65 percent of its area covered with trees. We produce in Georgia just with growing trees three times as much energy as we use, all put together. And when we harvest pine trees to make lumber and paper pulp, and so forth, we presently waste in some plots of timberland one-half of all the parts of a tree that we don't use now. So, we've got a potential there to produce energy from growing plants.

One obvious example is gasohol, where you make ethanol from corn—you can use other products as well—mix it with gasoline, and make gasohol. There's a great deal of interest in it. We are encouraging that in every possible way with research and development.

The Iowa legislature, for instance, has passed a bill that encourages individual farmers to put in a gasohol plant on their farm. At first it would be too expensive to use sound, marketable grain for the production of ethanol. Good corn costs too much. But the waste corn, the corn that's been contaminated with crotalaria seeds or with weevils or that has rotted, and so forth, is very good for making ethanol. And in Iowa, in many communities, you can go there and buy gasohol.

We have no Federal tax on gasohol. The total amount of present supplement in a gallon of ethanol is about $60 a barrel. It's good that we are interested in it. In other countries, like Brazil, they use, I think, cassava roots, which are grown very cheaply and which have a very high substance to them. And about 10 percent of all their fuel in automobiles is presently alcohol from those cassava roots, or from sugarcane byproducts. We are moving in that direction very rapidly.

Gasohol will be a major industry, in my opinion, in this Nation in the future.

ENERGY-EFFICIENT AUTOMOBILES

Q. My name is Bill Lane, and I'm from Wheeling, West Virginia. And, Mr. President, my question: Although the large, poor mileage automobiles are not selling very well right now, I think that when the gasoline becomes more available, I'm afraid that people are going to start buying them again. I just wonder if you favor any heavy luxury tax to put on these cars.

THE PRESIDENT. No, I don't think it's going to be necessary. I don't believe that we will ever see a time in our Nation when gasoline is both plentiful and cheap. And the problem that we have now in our automobile production industry—with GM and Ford and Chrysler and American Motors—is that they have not shifted toward a more efficient automobile.

Chrysler today is in serious trouble. They could sell hundreds of thousands of small Chrysler automobiles if they had planned accordingly, but they've insisted on producing the large, so-called gasguzzling automobiles. I don't think we'll ever go back to a time in the future when those large, inefficient automobiles are popular.

I had a meeting, within the last month, with Tom Murphy, who's the president—or chairman of the board of General Motors. In the past, they have fought the requirement of more efficient automobiles, that they would have to have 27½-miles-per-gallon average by 1985. He came to tell me that they're giving up that fight; they're going to meet that standard and then some. And this year, we'll have an average nationwide of 1-mile-per-gallon more efficiency just because the American public is more energy conscious and is shifting toward the smaller and more efficient automobiles.

What I would like to do is to see American producers of automobiles stay with the efficient cars. And I believe we can meet anybody in competition and therefore cut down the dependence that Americans presently have on imports.

I believe that's the avenue of the future. I don't believe that we will go back, in the American preference, for the large, gas-guzzling, inefficient automobiles. So,

I don't think we'll need any luxury tax on them. We've got standards now that they'll meet. I think the American industry, American free enterprise system, can meet this challenge and have new prosperity and keep our United Automobile Workers employed and also meet the needs of the American people.

There's a change taking place in our country, and if you will think back 2 or 3 years ago at your habits and what bothered you and what questions you asked political leaders and what you wrote Congress about and what you heard discussed in the evening news, now it's completely different. Our country has become aware of the fact that for the first time we have a limit on what God has given us and what we have a right to waste.

I believe that conservation is not an unpleasant chore for Americans, but is an exciting and enjoyable opportunity. It is a challenge, yes, but it tests American ingenuity and commitment on an individual basis. Everybody in here can help with conservation. If you will, in your own home, sit down with your children, your 6-year-old children, or your grandmother and say, "What can we do in our family to save energy in our driving habits, in our homes, in our jobs" and just make a list of the things you can do.

Every time you save energy, you save money. Every time you save energy, you cut down on the cost of the energy that you are using, because you have less competition for it and the price is going to be cheaper. And every time you save energy, you're doing a patriotic thing. And in a test like this, which took place in World War I, World War II, the Great Depression, there's a tendency for divided Americans to be unified. Families will be closer together; communities will be closer together; our Nation will be more united.

I have no doubt in my mind at all that we can meet any challenge with the ingenuity and the commitment and the courage and the freedom and the cooperation and the free enterprise system of our Nation.

And I would like to remind you in closing that our Nation is so great, it's so powerful, it's so strong. We're so blessed that we're still the strongest nation on Earth militarily—no one can challenge us there. We're the strongest nation on Earth economically. We're the strongest nation on Earth politically. We're the strongest nation on Earth morally, ethically, and we have the greatest freedom. And when we talk about problems—with the coal mine shutdown, serious; with the steel industry challenge, serious; with increased inflation, serious, yes—but we're the kind of people that can meet those serious challenges.

I just want us never to forget the blessings that God has given us in the greatest nation on Earth. Let's keep it that way. I will if you will.

Thank you.

NOTE: The President spoke at 3:05 p.m. in the Steubenville High School auditorium.

Following the townhall meeting, the President attended a reception for Democratic State representatives and officials of the State Democratic Party at the Fountain Restaurant in Steubenville.

Department of Energy

Nomination of George M. Fumich, Jr., To Be an Assistant Secretary.   September 12, 1979

The President today announced his intention to nominate George M. Fumich, Jr., of Arlington, Va., to be Assistant Secretary of Energy for Fossil Energy. Fumich is the first person nominated for this position.

He is currently Program Director for Fossil Energy at the Energy Department.

Fumich was born December 8, 1917, in Calamady, Pa. He received an A.B. from West Virginia University and a J.D. from West Virginia University College of Law in 1948.

From 1948 to 1961, Fumich was an attorney for the Christopher Coal Co. in Osage, W. Va. From 1961 to 1963, he was Director of the Office of Minerals Exploration at the Department of the Interior.

From 1963 to 1975, Fumich was Associate Director, then Director, of the Office of Coal Research. He was on the senior staff in fossil energy at the Energy Research and Development Administration from 1975 until 1977, when ERDA was merged into the Department of Energy and he assumed his present position.

Department of Energy

Nomination of Ruth M. Davis To Be an Assistant Secretary.   September 12, 1979

The President today announced his intention to nominate Ruth M. Davis, of Silver Spring, Md., to be Assistant Secretary of Energy for Resource Applications. She would replace George S. McIsaac, who has resigned.

Davis is Deputy Under Secretary of Defense for Research and Advanced Technology.

She was born October 19, 1928, in Sharpsville, Pa. She received an M.A. and Ph. D. from the University of Maryland.

Davis was a lecturer at the University of Maryland from 1955 to 1957, and at American University from 1957 to 1958. From 1958 to 1961, she was in research management at David Taylor Model Basin.

From 1961 to 1965, Davis was involved in research management at the Defense Department. From 1967 to 1970, she was director of the Lister Hill National Center for Biomedical Communications and Associate Director for Research and Development at the National Library of Medicine, National Institutes of Health. Since 1977 she has been Deputy Under Secretary of Defense.

Department of Energy

Nomination of John C. Sawhill To Be Deputy Secretary.   September 12, 1979

The President today announced that he will nominate John C. Sawhill, of New York City, to be Deputy Secretary of Energy. He would replace John O'Leary, resigned.

Sawhill is president of New York University.

He was born June 12, 1936, in Cleveland, Ohio. He received an A.B. from Princeton University in 1958 and a Ph. D. from New York University in 1963.

Sawhill was with Merrill, Lynch, Pierce, Fenner & Smith in Washington from 1958 to 1960, and was associate dean of New York University School of Business Administration from 1960 to 1963. He was director of credit research and planning for Commercial Credit Corporation in Baltimore from 1963 to 1965.

From 1965 to 1968, Sawhill was senior associate with McKinsey & Company in Washington. He returned to Commercial Credit from 1968 to 1973 as senior vice president for planning.

In 1973 and 1974, Sawhill was Associate Director of the Office of Management and Budget for Natural Resources, Energy and Science. He was with the Federal Energy Administration in 1974 as Deputy Administrator, then Administrator. He has been president of New York University since 1975.

Department of Energy

Nomination of William Walker Lewis To Be an Assistant Secretary.   September 12, 1979

The President today announced his intention to nominate William Walker Lewis, of Washington, D.C., to be Assistant Secretary of Energy for Policy and Evaluation. He would replace Alvin L. Alm, who is resigning.

Lewis is Principal Deputy Assistant Secretary of Defense for Program Analysis and Evaluation.

He was born March 29, 1942, in Roanoke, Va. He received a B.S. in physics from Virginia Polytechnic Institute in 1963 and a Ph. D. in theoretical physics from Oxford University in 1966.

From 1966 to 1969, Lewis was with the Office of the Assistant Secretary of Defense (Systems Analysis), where he served as Director of the NATO and General Purpose Force Analysis Division, and Director of the Strategic Concepts, Command and Control Division. From 1969 to 1971, he was associate provost for resource planning and a lecturer in public and international affairs at Princeton University.

From 1971 to 1973, Lewis was director of the office of analytical studies at the University of California at Berkeley. From 1973 to 1977, he was with the World Bank, serving as senior operations officer of the Industrial Development and Finance Division, Eastern Africa Region, and senior programing officer of the Programing and Budget Department.

In 1977 Lewis joined the Defense Department and served briefly as Deputy Assistant Secretary, then as Principal Deputy Assistant Secretary for Program Analysis and Evaluation.

Department of Energy

Nomination of Hazel Reid Rollins To Be Administrator of the Economic Regulatory Administration.   September 12, 1979

The President today announced his intention to nominate Hazel Reid Rollins, of Washington, D.C., to be Administrator of the Economic Regulatory Administration, Department of Energy. She would replace David Bardin, who is resigning.

Rollins has been with the Washington accounting firm of Coopers & Lybrand since last May, as a firm principal for energy.

Prior to joining Coopers & Lybrand, she was Deputy Administrator of the Economic Regulatory Administration.

Rollins was born May 17, 1937, in Newport News, Va. She received a B.A. from Fisk University in 1959 and an LL.B. from Rutgers University Law School in 1966. After graduation from law school, she served as deputy attorney general for the State of New Jersey, as coordinator of the Community Action Workshop in Newark, as assistant director of the Essex County Legal Services Corporation, and as assistant prosecutor in Essex County. She also maintained a private law practice.

Rollins joined the Federal Government in 1972, serving at the Cost of Living Council as Director of the Self-Administered Industries Division, as deputy to the counselor to the Director, CLC, and as Director of the Public Services Division.

From 1974 to 1976, she was Director of the Office of Consumer Affairs/Special Impact in the Federal Energy Administration (FEA). She left that position to become General Counsel of the Community Services Administration, and returned to the FEA in 1977 as Assistant Administrator for Conservation and Environment.

The FEA was merged into the Department of Energy on October 1, 1977.

Department of Energy

Nomination of Edward Allan Frieman To Be Director of the Office of Energy Research. September 12, 1979

The President today announced his intention to nominate Edward Allan Frieman, of Princeton, N.J., to be Director of the Office of Energy Research, Department of Energy. He would replace John M. Deutch, who has resigned.

Frieman is deputy director of the Princeton University Plasma Physics Laboratory and professor of astrophysical sciences at Princeton University.

He was born January 19, 1926, in New York City. He received a B.S. in engineering from Columbia University and an M.S. and Ph. D. in physics from the Polytechnic Institute of Brooklyn. During World War II, Frieman served with the U.S. Navy and participated in the Bikini A-bomb tests. After the war, he taught at the Polytechnic Institute of Brooklyn.

In 1952 Frieman joined Princeton University's controlled thermonuclear research project, now known as the Princeton University Plasma Physics Laboratory. In 1953 he was appointed the head of the laboratory's theoretical division. In 1964 he was awarded a National Science Foundation senior postdoctoral fellowship and assumed the position of associate director of the Plasma Physics Laboratory. In 1970 he received a John Simon Guggenheim Fellowship.

Frieman has served as a consultant to

a number of government agencies, and is the author of numerous articles in scientific journals, particularly in the areas of MHD theory, statistical mechanics, plasma transport theory, and plasma stability.

Embargo Regulations Under the Trading With the Enemy Act

Memorandum From the President. September 12, 1979

Memorandum for the Secretary of State, the Secretary of Treasury

Subject: Determination Extending the Exercise of Certain Authorities Under the Trading With the Enemy Act

Under Section 101(b) of Public Law 95–223 (91 Stat. 1625; 50 U.S.C. App. 5 note), and a previous Determination made by me on September 8, 1978 (43 *Fed. Reg.* 40449 (1978)), the exercise of certain authorities under the Trading With the Enemy Act is scheduled to terminate on September 14, 1979.

I hereby determine that the extension for one year of the exercise of those authorities with respect to the applicable countries is in the national interest of the United States.

Therefore, pursuant to the authority vested in me by Section 101(b) of Public Law 95–223, I extend for one year, until September 14, 1980, the exercise of those authorities with respect to those countries presently affected by: (1) the Foreign Assets Control Regulations, 31 CFR Part 500, (2) the Transaction Control Regulations, 31 CFR Part 505, (3) the Cuban Assets Control Regulations, 31 CFR Part 515, and (4) the Foreign Funds Control Regulations, 31 CFR Part 520.

The extension of the authorities with respect to the People's Republic of China is in connection with implementation of the Agreement Concerning the Settlement of Claims entered into between the Government of the United States and the Government of the People's Republic of China on May 11, 1979.

This Determination shall be published in the FEDERAL REGISTER.

JIMMY CARTER

[Filed with the Office of the Federal Register, 12:16 p.m., September 12, 1979]

Embargo Regulations Under the Trading With the Enemy Act

Letter to the Speaker of the House and the President of the Senate.   September 12, 1979

Dear Mr. Speaker: (Dear Mr. President:)

Today I issued a Determination that the extension for one year of the authorities currently exercised under Section 5(b) of the Trading With the Enemy Act, 50 U.S.C. App. 5(b), with respect to the countries indicated below, is in the national interest. This Determination was issued pursuant to Section 101(b) of Public Law 95–223, December 28, 1977, 91 Stat. 1625.

The Foreign Assets Control Regulations, 31 CFR Part 500, prohibit persons subject to the jurisdiction of the United States from engaging in unlicensed commercial or financial transactions with North Korea, Vietnam, Cambodia or nationals of these countries. The Regulations prohibit importation or dealing in merchandise of these countries or transactions in blocked assets of these countries or their nationals absent a license from the Office of Foreign Assets Control, Department of the Treasury.

In the case of the People's Republic of China (PRC), Chinese assets have remained blocked under the Regulations but current commercial or financial transactions are authorized except for the control of strategic items.

On December 15, 1978, I announced that the United States and the PRC had agreed to recognize each other and to establish diplomatic relations as of January 1, 1979. As part of our resumption of normal relations, the United States and the Government of the PRC entered into an Agreement Concerning the Settlement of Claims, signed on May 11, 1979.

Under the Agreement, the Government of the PRC agreed to pay to the Government of the United States $80.5 million in settlement of claims of United States nationals arising out of expropriation losses in China. The Government of the PRC will pay $30 million of the total on October 1, 1979, and the remainder in five equal annual installments.

Under the Agreement, the United States will unblock Chinese blocked assets by October 1, 1979. Along with the general unblocking of Chinese assets, the United States will impose a twelve-month moratorium on the transfer of blocked Chinese assets to state custodians of abandoned property under state laws providing that abandoned or unclaimed property is to be transferred to their custody. The moratorium is designed to facilitate Chinese recovery of this class of assets.

The Transaction Control Regulations, 31 CFR Part 505, are Treasury regulations which prohibit U.S. persons from engaging in unlicensed sales of strategic goods located abroad to almost all Communist countries.

The Cuban Assets Control Regulations, 31 CFR Part 515, are parallel to the Foreign Assets Control Regulations in content. However, foreign subsidiaries of U.S. firms may engage in certain non-strategic types of trade with Cuba under Treasury license.

The Foreign Funds Control Regulations, 31 CFR Part 520, continue to block the property of Czechoslovakia and the German Democratic Republic pending a claims settlement of private American property following World War II. The Regulations also continue to block such assets of Estonia, Latvia, and Lithuania as a reflection of the U.S. policy of nonrecognition of the forcible incorporation of those countries into the USSR.

I have determined that the authorities for these four regulatory programs should be extended because the results attendant upon the lapse of these authorities would be unacceptable in light of present U.S. foreign policy objectives. Their extension would be in the national interest of the United States for the following reasons.

(1) Current trade and financial embargoes against Cambodia, Cuba, North Korea, and Vietnam should continue until such time as the policies of those countries make it appropriate for us to modify our restrictions on trade and financial transactions with those countries.

(2) The Transaction Control Regulations are needed to support controls to which we have agreed with our allies with respect to the export of strategic goods to Communist countries.

(3) Freezing of Vietnamese and Cuban assets and controls over the remaining World War II assets of the German Democratic Republic and Czechoslovakia should continue until American claims against these countries are settled. Controls over the remaining World War II assets of the Baltic States should continue as a reflection of the U.S. policy of nonrecognition of the forcible incorporation of these countries into the USSR.

(4) To implement the US–PRC Claims/Assets Agreement, authority for administration of blocked PRC assets should continue through the period of the extension of the authorities.

In light of these considerations, pursuant to Public Law 95–223, I have extended the exercise of these authorities for another year, until September 14, 1980.

Sincerely,

JIMMY CARTER

NOTE: This is the text of identical letters addressed to Thomas P. O'Neill, Jr., Speaker of the House of Representatives, and Walter F. Mondale, President of the Senate.

United Nations Day, 1979
Proclamation 4684.   September 13, 1979

By the President of the United States of America

A Proclamation

Thirty-four years after its founding "to save succeeding generations of mankind from the scourge of war", the United Nations remains mankind's last best hope for building a world community based on justice, tolerance for diversity and respect for the rule of law.

The United Nations has no magic formula for solving the increasingly complex problems of our revolutionary age. Yet it remains the symbol, and the standard, of mankind's desire to turn away from ancient quarrels and live in a world in which all people can share in the fruits of prosperity and peace.

More than ever, the international community is challenged by problems of global dimension which can be solved only through world-wide cooperation and dialogue. The 100 new nations which have joined the United Nations since its founding are a symbol of the increasingly complex and diverse world which the United Nations confronts today.

Protecting international peace and security is still the United Nation's greatest contribution and responsibility, but that political stability is only the precondition for fulfilling the larger aspirations of mankind. For all its imperfections, the United Nations remains the principal forum for the pivotal dialogue among the nations of the world on constructing a more stable, equitable, and productive economic order. It plays a leading role in the global management and allocation of vital natural resources. It offers an increasingly important channel for providing development assistance to many nations in the world. It offers a forum, and often a timely and effective mechanism for protecting basic human rights. The leadership of the United Nations in responding to the present refugee crisis, and the recent Geneva Meeting on that problem, represents one of the proudest examples of that world body's ability to harness world cooperation in the cause of human dignity.

The United States has historically been one of the United Nations' most active and dedicated supporters, and I have been proud to continue and expand on that support as President. Not a single day goes by when we in the United States do not call upon the United Nations, or one of its affiliates, to help deal with a problem of global dimensions. I join with many other Americans and citizens of all nations in expressing my sincere support for this unique world body on the thirty-fourth anniversary of its founding.

Now, THEREFORE, I, JIMMY CARTER, President of the United States of America, do hereby designate Wednesday, October 24, 1979, as United Nations Day. I urge all Americans to use this day as an opportunity to better acquaint themselves with the activities and accomplishments of the United Nations.

I have appointed O. Pendleton Thomas to serve as 1979 United States National Chairman for United Nations Day, and the United Nations Association of the U.S.A. to work with him in celebrating this very special day. And I invite all the American people, and people everywhere, to join me on this thirty-fourth anniversary of the United Nations, in strengthening our common resolve to increase its effectiveness in meeting the global challenges and aspirations that we all share.

IN WITNESS WHEREOF, I have hereunto set my hand this thirteenth day of September, in the year of our Lord nineteen hundred and seventy-nine, and of the Independence of the United States of America, the two hundred and fourth.

JIMMY CARTER

[Filed with the Office of the Federal Register, 3:07 p.m., September 13, 1979]

United States Ambassador to Ghana

Nomination of Thomas W. M. Smith. September 13, 1979

The President today announced that he will nominate Thomas W. M. Smith, of Readfield, Maine, to be Ambassador Extraordinary and Plenipotentiary of the United States to the Republic of Ghana. He would replace Robert P. Smith, who has transferred to another position.

Smith has been Director of the Office of West African Affairs at the State Department since 1975.

He was born April 18, 1930, in Boston, Mass. He received an A.B. from Harvard

College in 1951, a B.A. (1953) and M.A. (1956) from Cambridge University, and an M.A. from the University of Wisconsin in 1970. He served in the U.S. Marine Corps from 1953 to 1956.

Smith joined the Foreign Service in 1956 and was posted in Tunis, Paris, and Lagos. From 1968 to 1971, he was Chief of the Division of United Nations Economic Affairs, then an international economist at the State Department. In 1971–72 he attended the National War College.

From 1972 to 1975, Smith was economic and commercial officer in London.

Board for International Broadcasting

Nomination of Thomas H. Quinn To Be a Member.   September 13, 1979

The President today announced that he will nominate Thomas H. Quinn for reappointment as a member of the Board for International Broadcasting.

Quinn, 41, has been a member of this Board since 1974. He is a general partner in the Minneapolis-Washington law firm of O'Connor & Hannan, specializing in the field of administrative practice with emphasis on financial institutions policy matters.

Chief of Protocol for the White House

Nomination of Abelardo Lopez Valdez for the Rank of Ambassador.   September 13, 1979

The President today announced that he intends to nominate Abelardo Lopez Valdez for the rank of Ambassador while serving as Chief of Protocol for the White House.

Valdez has served as Assistant Administrator of the Agency for International Development (AID) for Latin America and the Caribbean since 1977.

He was born August 31, 1942, in Floresville, Tex. He received a B.S. in civil engineering from Texas A&M College in 1965, a J.D. from Baylor Law School in 1970, and an LL.M. from Harvard Law School in 1974.

Valdez served in the U.S. Army as a lieutenant from 1965 to 1967, and served as military aide to President Johnson for that period. He was an attorney for the Federal Power Commission from 1970 to 1971 and for the Overseas Private Investment Corporation from 1971 to 1973. Valdez served as General Counsel of the Inter-American Foundation from 1973 to 1975. He was a partner in the Washington law firm of Purcell, Hansen & Valdez from 1975 to 1977. In 1977 he also was a member of the faculty of the John F. Kennedy Institute of Politics at Harvard University, where he taught a seminar on critical issues in U.S.-Latin American relations.

Secretary of the Navy

Nomination of Edward Hidalgo.
September 13, 1979

The President today announced his intention to nominate Edward Hidalgo, of Washington, D.C., to be Secretary of the Navy. He would replace W. Graham Claytor, Jr.

Hidalgo has been Assistant Secretary of the Navy for Manpower and Logistics since 1977.

He was born October 12, 1912, in Mexico City, Mexico, and has been a U.S. citizen since early childhood. He received a B.A. from Holy Cross College in 1933 and a J.D. from Columbia Law School in 1936. In 1959 he received a degree in civil law from the University of Mexico. He served as a lieutenant in the U.S. Naval Reserve from 1942 to 1946.

Hidalgo served as a law clerk to the Second Circuit Court of Appeals in 1936 and 1937, and was an associate with the law firm of Wright, Gordon, Zachry & Parlin (Cahill, Gordon & Reindel) from 1937 to 1942. From 1942 to 1943, he was assigned to the State Department as a legal adviser to the Ambassador to the Emergency Advisory Committee for Political Defense in Montevideo.

From 1943 to 1945, he served as an air combat intelligence officer on the carrier *Enterprise,* and he was a member of the Eberstadt Committee, which reported to the Secretary of the Navy on unification of the military services in 1945. In 1945 and 1946, he served as Special Assistant to the Secretary of the Navy.

From 1946 to 1948, Hidalgo was a partner with the law firm of Curtis, Mallet-Prevost, Colt & Mosle, in charge of their Mexico City office. He was a founder in 1948 and a senior partner until 1965 in the Mexico City law firm of Hidalgo, Barrera, Siquieros & Torres Landa.

From 1965 to 1966, Hidalgo was a Special Assistant to the Secretary of the Navy, and from 1966 to 1972, he was a partner in the law firm of Cahill, Gordon & Reindel, in charge of their European office. In 1972 he served as Special Assistant for Economic Affairs to the Director of USIA, and from 1973 to 1976, he was General Counsel and Congressional Liaison of the Agency.

National Employ the Handicapped Week, 1979

Proclamation 4685.   September 13, 1979

By the President of the United States of America

A Proclamation

The past decade has been marked by significant advances for handicapped people.

Such laws as the Rehabilitation Act of 1973 protect many handicapped individuals from discrimination in employment and services. Handicapped workers have made great progress in entering the job market, and those already in the labor force are moving up to better jobs. More of our Nation's buildings and public transportation systems are being made accessible. Many handicapped individuals have been moving out of institutions into homes, apartments, and community facilities which facilitate independent living. As handicapped individuals move into the mainstream of society, more and more of their fellow citizens are overcoming their prejudices and seeing handicapped individuals as people.

Yet much remains to be done. Many qualified handicapped people, including many disabled veterans, are unemployed or underemployed, and others are not promoted because of discriminatory attitudes rather than an inability to perform. Many buildings still have thoughtless architectural barriers that prevent handicapped persons from getting jobs and education. Public transportation is still not available to all handicapped individuals.

This country needs the creativity, skill and participation of all our citizens. To affirm our commitment to equality for the handicapped members of our society, the Congress, by joint resolution of August 11, 1945, as amended (36 U.S.C. 155), has called for the designation of the first full week in October each year as National Employ the Handicapped Week.

Now, THEREFORE, I, JIMMY CARTER, President of the United States of America, do hereby designate the week beginning on October 7, 1979, as National Employ the Handicapped Week. I urge all Governors, Mayors, other public officials, leaders in business and labor, and private citizens at all levels of responsibility to help remove all barriers which prevent handicapped individuals from obtaining productive employment and from participating fully in other aspects of American life.

IN WITNESS WHEREOF, I have hereunto set my hand this thirteenth day of September, in the year of our Lord nineteen hundred seventy-nine, and of the Independence of the United States of America the two hundred and fourth.

JIMMY CARTER

[Filed with the Office of the Federal Register, 1:59 p.m., September 14, 1979]

Welfare Reform Legislation

Statement on Action by the House Ways and Means Committee.   September 13, 1979

I congratulate the members of the House Committee on Ways and Means for their favorable action today on welfare reform. I especially commend the leadership and diligence of Chairman Al Ullman and of Representative Jim Corman, chairman of the Public Assistance Subcommittee.

Our Nation can afford to help its most needy, and we can do so with a welfare system that encourages work, while providing decent levels of assistance for those who cannot work. Our programs can and must be simpler, more efficient, and more equitable. This bill is not the entire or the final solution, but it does make important progress. Combined with the other half of my welfare reform package, which will expand work and training opportunities, Congress itself has a precious opportunity to make welfare reform a reality. We can help millions of people and do so in a fiscally responsible manner.

Welfare reform has been a decade-long legislative struggle, and this important action today is the most positive step in this area in recent years. I applaud the Ways and Means Committee, and urge the other key committees and the Congress as a whole to move promptly to complete action on welfare reform.

Congressional Hispanic Caucus

Remarks at the Annual Dinner.
September 13, 1979

Mr. Speaker, Chairman Garcia, distinguished Members of Congress, members of my own administration—both those who speak Spanish and the few who don't—[laughter]:

It is a real pleasure for me as President of our country to be present at this Second Hispanic Caucus Dinner.

I have never known such a small caucus to have so many friends and so much power and so much influence. And the friends, power, and influence are all growing every day, and I'm thankful for it. I'm sure it's because the members of the Congressional Hispanic Caucus have hearts that are pure, and they certainly have a cause that is just.

Mrs. Roybal just told me that Ed [1] is feeling very well. His message was one of great encouragement to us, and I am looking forward to continuing my work with him as soon as he is released from the hospital, perhaps tomorrow.

Tonight we are enjoying good food, good hospitality, good friendship, good company, and good plans for the future and good memories of the past. But as we gather together in a spirit of celebration and good fellowship, we must never forget that we are here because of something that's larger and much more important.

Everyone in this room is a part of three great struggles, struggles that have defined the history of our time. I'm talking about the struggle for human rights at home and abroad. I'm talking about the struggle for basic social and economic justice, and I'm talking about the struggle for a peaceful Earth.

The actions that I take as President of the United States of America are aimed at advancing, with you, these three great causes. The lives of many in this room have literally been dedicated to these causes. And in these battles, the members of the Congressional Hispanic Caucus have been, as you know, just where they belong, always in the frontlines of the struggle. I've been proud to stand with you for the last 2½ years, and I'm proud that we've stood together in a common cause.

Ed Roybal and his colleagues—Bob Garcia, Baltasar Corrada, and Kika de la Garza, and others who have joined the Spanish Caucus—have made their voices heard far beyond their own districts. They've fought for the rights of all Hispanic Americans, whether their background is Mexican or Cuban, Puerto Rican, Central American, or South American. They've fought for jobs, for political participation, for better education, and for an end to prejudice, discrimination, and bigotry.

All Americans, not just those who happen to speak Spanish, have benefited from their efforts. And on behalf of all Americans, I thank them, and I thank you.

The road we travel together is long and it is hard, but we are moving. And we are going to keep on moving and keep on pushing until the magnificent ideals of this Nation are a reality for all who live within its borders.

Tonight, I want to report to you very briefly on the progress we have made together within this Government and within this Nation in the cause of liberty, of justice, and of peace.

This Nation was founded on a passionate commitment to basic human rights, but for too many years our Government, our Nation, has seemed to have lost touch with this basic source of strength. It's been said often, and said rightly, human rights begin at home. And I'm determined that the provisions of the United States Constitution and the laws of our land shall apply to all who live within the borders of our country, whether they are citizens or not.

Months ago I urged all the Governors of our country, and I have now signed an order to all of the heads of the departments and agencies in our own Government, directing them to see that undocumented aliens are treated fairly and humanely in every instance. And I'm directing Federal officials to give full cooperation to officials of other nations who seek their help in investigating any allegation of discrimination or deprivation of those basic human rights which we hold so dear.

We have not yet stamped out all the vestiges of bigotry and brutality in our

---

[1] Representative Edward R. Roybal of California.

country, but we must do so. These have been the goals of Leonel Castillo as Director of the Immigration and Naturalization Service. Leonel has made the INS more efficient and more responsive, so that suffering people, trying to obey the law, would not have to wait years for a simple answer to a basic question. He took on one of the toughest, most thankless jobs there is in the United States, and he did it well. And all of us ought to thank him for it.

I know that Leonel is disappointed at some things which have not yet been done in the not much more than 2 years that he has served so well, but I am very proud of his accomplishments.

For too long both the legislative and the executive branches of Government have ignored our immigration policies and the problems that were building up throughout our land. Undocumented aliens have feared that any solution attempted would be at their expense, and a great many other people have just found it easier not to think about this problem as long as it was others who suffered and not themselves.

Together in the last few months, we have tried to face up to these difficult problems and to seek real solutions. We are making some progress. We've not yet gone far enough. And we are consulting closely with the Mexican Government officials for the first time, and other countries who are involved. And I promise you that this effort which has been initiated so well by Leonel Castillo, by the Immigration and Naturalization Service, will not terminate with his departure. He will continue to help us, and the progress that he started will continue as well.

Some parts of our policy are very controversial—human rights at home also means justice, tempered with mercy.

Last week, I commuted the sentences of the last four Puerto Rican nationalists who attacked President Truman and wounded five Members of Congress more than 25 years ago. I did this for humane reasons.

AUDIENCE MEMBER. Why?

THE PRESIDENT. I'll tell you why. I did this for humane reasons and because I agreed with Congressmen Garcia and Corrada and with Franklin Lopez and others here tonight, that the time that they had served, more than 25 years, was long enough.

I'd like to make it clear that an important principle was involved. These nationalists were imprisoned for criminal conduct, not for their political views. Like other Americans, they're entitled to the freedom of speech guaranteed by the Constitution. And I can say to you that our country is strong enough so that we can honor the principle of freedom of speech, and we need not fear those who speak out with ideas with which we may disagree.

On the important issue of the future status of Puerto Rico, I will support whatever decision is made by the people of Puerto Rico because I believe—[applause]—because I feel that Puerto Ricans have enough judgment to make a decision about their own future for themselves, and I will honor their judgment.

We must look now to the present and its needs, and to a better future for all Puerto Rican citizens, whether they live on the island or whether they live here on the mainland. And we seek to fulfill human rights here at home, and we will continue to speak out for human rights abroad.

From the day that I took office, I have sought to place at the top of my agenda and to awaken the conscience of the world and to bring that conscience about human rights to bear on the world's leaders. We have created an atmosphere that I believe has made significant progress on human rights throughout our hemisphere. Many prison doors have swung open, repression of the poor and the weak and the helpless has been eased in many countries. Democratic government or civilian government has been rescued and has replaced military governments and autocratic governments, where people had little voice.

The struggle for human rights is basic and so is the struggle for the economic and the social justice which permits human beings to enjoy those rights once they have been obtained with dignity. That struggle cannot be won unless the Government of this country, which we love, is peopled with men and women of courage, ability, sensitivity, and the knowledge of the special problems which many of you in this room know so well.

I will have two superb new leaders to help me in the near future. One of them is Abelardo Valdez, who is now administering our AID program and who will soon be the United States Chief of Protocol. The other is a fine man, one of the most competent men I know in government, who happened to have been born in Mexico City, has practiced law there for 19 years, who served our Nation well, and who will now be the Secretary of the Navy of the United States of America, Edward Hidalgo. I think Abelardo and Edward are here. Are they here? Stand up if you will, new Secretary of Navy. He was not only my first choice, he was first choice of the former Secretary of Navy, now the Deputy Secretary of Defense. And I am very proud of you, Edward, and what you've already done for our country.

As you know, in order to advise me on personnel and other important affairs, Esteban Torres, who came here with me tonight, has joined my White House staff. Ambassador Torres has distinguished himself both in government and also as a labor leader.

As United States Ambassador to UNESCO, his ability to make friends was demonstrated by his election to the UNESCO Executive Board. Our country is not always unanimously popular in the United Nations. But when Esteban ran for the Executive Board of UNESCO, out of 130 countries voting, he got 127 votes.

He's going to be giving me advice on many things, one of which is how to get votes. [*Laughter*]

Ambassador Torres is working closely with me, also, on the upcoming visit of President López Portillo of Mexico. And he will make sure that your voice is heard every day when policy is made within the White House. Assisting him will be Gilbert Colon.

All of those that I've named, and many others, are working very closely with our new Attorney General to root out any element of racism or discrimination in our system of criminal justice. And a special advisory committee is being set up, with Esteban's help and the help of the Attorney General, of Hispanic Americans to make sure that this goal, which has not been accomplished in the past, will be accomplished in the future.

We also know that accurate information about our country is a fundamental weapon in the struggle for social justice. In this connection, the 1980 census is a major opportunity and a personal challenge to me and to everyone in this room. If Hispanic Americans are to be full partners in all aspects of American life and to share in its full benefits, we must have an accurate count of how many Hispanic

Americans live in the United States of America.

I have for the first time directed the Census Bureau to hire bilingual census takers, to print questionnaires in Spanish, and to work with community groups and leaders who understand their own community, to encourage cooperation. It's important, because of the sensitivity of some people's lives who live here, that the confidentiality of individual census information will be protected. And I have directed, without equivocation, that this be done.

I cannot look at the individual information, your Congressman cannot look at it, and no other Government agency can look at this individual confidential information that will give us accurate information. An accurate count will mean better Government funding for areas that have a high population of Hispanic Americans and better political representation. And a much larger Congressional Hispanic Caucus will result from better counts of those who live in our country. That in turn will put much more muscle behind the efforts that all of you tonight in this room will espouse for the benefit of those in our country who speak Spanish.

With your help, we've increased funds for bilingual education already, in just a little over 2 years by 50 percent. And I've requested funds for a special program for bilingual vocational education. And I strongly support, by the way, the legislation which has already passed the Senate to give the Southwest Border Commission authority to award construction grants to ease severe overcrowding in schools in the Southwest, in heavily Hispanic areas.

Just as we carry on the struggle for human rights and social justice, we're struggling to build peace and security in this hemisphere and throughout the world.

In the Western Hemisphere, among our American neighbors, we believe in peace. We believe in a policy of nonintervention. We respect the other American states as equals and as individuals. We work closely with our friends in political and diplomatic matters. We consult closely with them, because we know that their advice, their counsel, their cooperation is crucial to us to make the right decision on the policy and the motivations and the actions of our own Government that affect those who live in the Caribbean, in 'Central and South America.

We're promoting economic development and building stronger trade relationships. We are committed, along with the other free countries and free peoples of this hemisphere, to minimize the spread of totalitarian and atheistic Communist influence among the free people of this hemisphere.

I'm very proud that we are rebuilding the world's faith in all these and other American commitments.

Together, with a sense of wisdom and of fairness, we fought and we won a victory for peace and for human rights—that was not politically popular with the Panama Canal treaties. The Senate of the United States took courageous action, and you and I, as full partners, were able to do what was right, because we stood together. I believe that this will be recognized in history as an action that spared this half of the world of possible conflict between peoples that have always in the past been friends, but which would have shattered this friendly relationship forever.

The Congress still must take action on the Panama Canal treaties. And I plead with all of you to use your influence for favorable consideration of the implementation legislation for the Panama Canal treaties, so that we will not be embarrassed by violating the word of honor of our Nation and mistreating the heroic and the generous and the good friends that we have who live in Panama and throughout the southern part of this hemisphere.

In the tragic wake of the recent Hurricane David, the American people responded immediately and with open hearts to the needs of the people of Dominica and the Dominican Republic. Governor Romero and the people of Puerto Rico have been especially helpful. And the people of Miami, under Mayor Ferre's leadership, also deserve our congratulations for their donations of food and medicines for the people of the Dominican Republic.

This month, here in Washington, I will meet with President López Portillo of Mexico, and I expect this meeting to further the balanced relationship that I seek with our near neighbor and our friend.

There are many issues of great importance to both nations that we can only manage—because they have been so long ignored—through continual, careful, and close consultation between the United States and Mexico. We'll be discussing energy and trade and border issues, as well as other matters on which we are now negotiating with the Mexican Government. These negotiations are now and will continue to be frank, fair, and mature. They are conducted within a framework of mutual respect and with a conviction that both nations will benefit from them. That's how it should be, and with your continued support, that's how it always will be.

Our relations with Mexico are among the most important that we have in the entire world. And I will never let the inevitable problems and differences of opinion that may arise, deflect us from the mutual respect, friendship, cooperation, and sensitive attention to our proper duties which we share with President López Portillo and the Mexican people.

In closing let me say this: These are just a few items on a big agenda, but I know that we can do this together. Our goals are the same—to bring all Americans, no matter in which country we live, into full partnership in every aspect of our lives, with full justice, economic opportunity, and political participation. If that day is to come down, and come down to us soon, we must work together to bring it about. It will not come automatically. I cannot do it alone; no President could. Government cannot do it alone. You cannot do it alone. But together, if we have a common goal, mutual respect, courage, and respect for one another and for the principles that bind us together, we can make it happen.

To close my remarks I would like to use for a few seconds our Nation's second language.

Tenemos que trabajar juntos para garantizar la participación total en todos aspectos de la sociedad americana para todos miembros de la comunidad hispana, para el futuro de nuestros hijos, para el futuro de la comunidad hispana, y para el futuro de nuestra nación. Muchas gracias a todos. [We have to work together to guarantee the total participation in all aspects of the American society for all members of the Hispanic community, for the future of our children, for the future of the Hispanic community, and for the future of our Nation. Thank you very much.]

NOTE: The President spoke at 9:38 p.m. in the International Ballroom at the Washington Hilton Hotel.

Undocumented Aliens

Memorandum From the President.
September 13, 1979

Memorandum for the Heads of Executive
Departments and Agencies
Subject: The Human Rights of Undocumented Aliens

Protection of the basic rights of all persons in our land is a vital part of our commitment to a just and humane society. This Administration's policy on human rights can only be effective if we assure the rights of all persons in the United States, whether or not they are citizens of this country.

I will continue to enforce vigorously this nation's immigration laws. Those found in violation will be dealt with as the law prescribes. But persons accused of being undocumented aliens must be treated fairly and humanely. No one in our country should be vulnerable to mistreatment or exploitation because he or she is afraid to secure protection of the law.

Since many of the problems in this area are under state and local jurisdiction, I sent letters to the Nation's Governors on May 4, asking for their concern, assistance and advice in dealing with these problems. In those letters, a copy of the text of which is attached, I also described some of the significant efforts the Federal Government has made in this area.

The work of each of your departments and agencies touches upon some aspects of the treatment of undocumented aliens in the United States. I will not dwell on all Government activities in this message but will mention some issues of particular importance.

A number of Federal, or Federally-assisted, social welfare and medical pro-grams by law must exclude specifically persons who are not citizens or legal permanent residents of the United States. In such cases, I ask that the concerned agencies review their policies and practices in implementing these requirements to ensure that they are clear, equitable, adequately disseminated and understood and compassionately applied within the limits of the law, and that they are carried out with respect for the basic dignity and privacy of all persons concerned.

I urge you to give full cooperation to Consular and other officials of Mexico and other countries who, in the discharge of their duties in the United States, seek your help in investigating possible incidents of abuse involving their citizens. I also ask you to work closely with the Department of State and the working groups of the U.S.-Mexico Consultative Mechanism.

I urge you to continue to keep this Administration's commitments in mind as you develop and carry out your programs and I would particularly welcome your recommendations of possible remedies for additional problems in this area of which you may be aware.

JIMMY CARTER

NOTE: The text of the memorandum was released on September 14.

United Nations

Nomination of U.S. Representatives and
Alternate Representatives to the 34th
Session of the General Assembly.
September 14, 1979

The President today announced the nomination of four persons as Representatives and three persons as Alternate Representatives of the United States to the 34th Session of the United Nations General Assembly, to be held in New York beginning September 18. They are:

Representatives

DONALD F. McHENRY, United States Representative-designate to the United Nations

BENJAMIN S. ROSENTHAL, U.S. Representative from New York

LARRY WINN, JR., U.S. Representative from Kansas

ESTHER L. COOPERSMITH, president of the United States-Egyptian Cultural Committee

Alternate Representatives

RICHARD W. PETREE, Alternate Representative of the United States for Special Political Affairs in the United Nations

WILLIAM L. DUNFEY, president of Dunfey Hotels of Hampton, N.H.

HOWARD T. ROSEN, a Newark, N.J., attorney.

President's Management Improvement Council

Executive Order 12157.   September 14, 1979

By the authority vested in me as President by the Constitution of the United States of America, in accordance with the Federal Advisory Committee Act (5 U.S.C. App. I), and in order to improve the management effectiveness of Executive agencies, it is hereby ordered as follows:

1-1. *Establishment of the Council.*

1-101. There is hereby established the President's Management Improvement Council.

1-102. The Council shall be Cochaired by the Director of the Office of Management and Budget and the Director of the Office of Personnel Management. The Council's membership shall consist of representatives from Executive agencies and from the non-Federal sector; such as

business, industry, organized labor, foundations, universities, and State and local governments. The members shall be appointed by the President.

1-2. *Functions of the Council.*

1-201. The Council shall advise the President on significant and critical management problems and issues affecting Executive agencies and Government programs.

1-202. The Council shall work cooperatively with the Comptroller General, senior program management and administrative officials, and Inspectors General to provide advice and guidance on specific management improvement projects involving one or more Executive agencies.

1-203. Where feasible, the Council shall advise the Executive agencies in the development of management systems or management techniques to improve the effectiveness and responsiveness of Federal programs.

1-204. The Council shall advise the Executive agencies of solutions to critical management problems, as well as the constraints on management effectiveness.

1-205. In developing its recommendations, the Council shall utilize the experience of the public and private sectors. The Council shall also identify and facilitate the application to Federal programs of appropriate successful systems and techniques which have been used elsewhere in public and private sectors.

1-206. The Cochairman shall report to the President on the performance of the Council's functions.

1-3. *Administrative Provisions.*

1-301. The Director of the Office of Personnel Management shall, to the extent permitted by law, provide the Council with administrative and staff services, support and facilities as may be necessary for the effective performance of its functions.

1–302. Each member of the Council, who is not otherwise a full-time employee of the Federal Government, shall receive no compensation from the United States by virtue of their service on the Council, but all members may receive the transportation and travel expenses, including per diem in lieu of subsistence, authorized by law (5 U.S.C. 5702 and 5703).

1–4. *General Provisions.*

1–401. Notwithstanding the provisions of any other Executive order, the functions of the President under the Federal Advisory Committee Act (5 U.S.C. App. I), except that of reporting annually to the Congress, shall be performed by the Director of the Office of Personnel Management in accordance with guidelines and procedures established by the Administrator of General Services.

1–402. The Council shall terminate on December 31, 1980, unless sooner extended.

JIMMY CARTER

The White House,
    September 14, 1979.

[Filed with the Office of the Federal Register, 3:15 p.m., September 14, 1979]

President's Management Improvement Council

Memorandum From the President.
September 14, 1979

Memorandum for the Heads of Executive Departments and Agencies

Subject: President's Management Improvement Council

One of the highest priorities of my Administration has been, and remains, improving the management and performance of the Federal government. Together we have made some significant progress toward that end. Civil Service Reform, regulatory reform, cash management improvements, paperwork reduction, Federal grant reform, and our efforts to prevent fraud and waste are producing substantial improvements in the operations of the Federal government.

I recognize that you are already doing many things to improve management in your departments or agencies. Yet as I meet and talk with individual citizens and groups, I am constantly reminded that there continues to be widespread distrust of government, and widespread dissatisfaction with how well the Federal government does its job. I believe that there are further management improvements which need to be undertaken, and I seek your commitment to take a fresh look at management problems in your agency.

I would urge you to give special attention to the problems of delivery of service to the public. There continue to be many instances throughout government of slow response to client needs, backlogs of work, overly complicated procedures, and insensitivity or indifference in dealing with the public. In many cases improvements can be made in practical, down-to-earth ways by line managers and supervisors, if they have your strong backing to do so.

As part of this renewed commitment to Federal management, I have, by Executive Order, established the President's Management Improvement Council. This Council, co-chaired by the Directors of the Office of Management and Budget and the Office of Personnel Management, consists of representatives from Federal agencies and State and local government, executives from the private sector and labor organizations, and academic leaders. Its purpose is to work with you in a renewed effort to bring all of our collective expertise, experience, and knowledge to bear to generate the highest level of performance in the Federal government.

I am convinced that there is much that we can learn—and must learn—from sources outside the Federal government to improve the efficiency of our operations and our delivery of public services. The Council brings us an added dimension to help identify and solve the difficult and persistent problems of managing complex government institutions. I have asked the Council to focus its attention especially on the more practical problems affecting the delivery of services to the public. In turn, I am asking you to view the Council as a resource to advise and assist you in addressing your critical management problems.

The Council will keep me informed of its activities and will bring significant problem areas to my attention. I urge you to seize the opportunity which the Council represents and renew your commitment to an efficient and responsive Federal government.

JIMMY CARTER

President's Management Improvement Council

Appointment of 19 Members and Designation of Cochairpersons. September 14, 1979

The President today announced the appointment of 19 persons as members of the President's Management Improvement Council. He also announced that Alan K. Campbell, Director of the Office of Personnel Management, and James T.

McIntyre, Jr., Director of the Office of Management and Budget, will be Cochairpersons of the Council.

The President's Management Improvement Council consists of leading representatives of Federal, State, and local governments, private industry, labor organizations, and academic and professional organizations. The role of the Council will be to advise the President on management problems and issues in the Federal Government and to assist in efforts to improve Federal Government management and program performance.

The Council holds its first formal session at 11:30 a.m. today in the Federal Home Loan Bank Board building immediately following a brief introductory ceremony in the White House. At the session, the Council will consider management issues involving the General Services Administration, the Health Care Financing Administration, Federal debt collection, and reduction of Federal travel costs.

The persons appointed to the Council today are:

ROBERT P. BILLER, professor and dean of the School of Public Administration at the University of Southern California;

DOLPH BRISCOE, JR., former Governor of Texas, now chairman of the board of the First State Bank of Uvalde (Texas) and the Security State Bank in Pearsall, Tex.;

ALAN K. CAMPBELL, Director of the Office of Personnel Management;

HUGH A. CARTER, JR., Special Assistant to the President for Administration;

W. GRAHAM CLAYTOR, JR., Deputy Secretary of Defense;

JOSEPH E. CONNOR, chairman and senior partner of Price Waterhouse and Co., the New York accounting firm;

ALAN L. DEAN, vice president for administration of the United States Railway Association;

ROBERT GRAHAM, Governor of Florida;

DOROTHY GREGG, corporate vice president of communications of Celanese Corp.;

JOHN A. KOSKINEN, president of Victor Palmieri and Company, Inc., a Washington, D.C., asset management firm;

JOHN A. McCART, executive director of the AFL–CIO's Public Employee Department in Washington, D.C.;

JAMES T. McINTYRE, JR., Director of the Office of Management and Budget;

RUSSELL E. PALMER, managing director and chief executive officer of Touche Ross and Co., the New York City accounting firm;

MARION O. SANDLER, vice chairman of the board of Golden West Financial Corp. and World Savings and Loan Association in Oakland, Calif.;

GEORGE R. SCHRADER, city manager of Dallas, Tex.;

ELMER B. STAATS, Comptroller General of the United States;

DOROTHY L. STARBUCK, chief benefits director of the Veterans Administration;

WAYNE E. THOMPSON, senior vice president of Dayton Hudson Corp. and chairman and chief executive officer of Dayton Hudson Foundation in Minneapolis; and

WILLIAM H. WYNN, international president of the United Foods and Commercial Workers International Union.

Day-to-day operations of the Council will be managed by a small staff headed by Charles Bingman, Executive Director.

National Diabetes Week, 1979

Proclamation 4686. September 14, 1979

By the President of the United States of America

A Proclamation

Diabetes mellitus affects the lives of 10 million Americans. Each year, 35,000 Americans die from this disease, and many times that number fall victim to heart at-

tack, stroke, kidney failure, blood vessel disease and blindness related to diabetes. Diabetes now costs the country more than $6 billion annually in health care expenses, disability payments and lost wages.

A major national effort is underway among Federal agencies, State and local governments, academic institutions and voluntary health organizations to combat diabetes and its complications, which so often compromise the quality of life of its victims. There is optimism in the scientific community that research is leading to greater understanding and improved methods of treatment for diabetes and its complications. We must continue to focus attention on the needs of the many victims of diabetes in the United States if we are ever to reduce the impact of this disease as a source of human suffering in our Nation.

The Congress, by Joint Resolution enacted August 13, 1979 (Public Law 96–51), has authorized and requested the President to designate the week of October 8 through October 14, 1979, as National Diabetes Week.

NOW THEREFORE, I, JIMMY CARTER, President of the United States of America, do hereby proclaim the week of October 8 through October 14, 1979, as National Diabetes Week.

I call upon public and private agencies and organizations to recognize and observe it appropriately. I invite the Governors of the States, the Commonwealth of Puerto Rico and officials of other areas subject to the jurisdiction of the United States to issue similar proclamations.

IN WITNESS WHEREOF, I have hereunto set my hand this fourteenth day of September, in the year of our Lord nineteen hundred seventy-nine, and of the

Independence of the United States of America the two hundred and fourth.

JIMMY CARTER

[Filed with the Office of the Federal Register, 3:14 p.m., September 14, 1979]

Mobile, Alabama

Remarks Prior to an Inspection Tour of Areas Damaged by Hurricane Frederic.
September 14, 1979

THE PRESIDENT. I would like to say, first of all, that the entire Nation is deeply concerned about the damage caused by the recent hurricane here in Alabama and also in Mississippi and Florida.

Because of extremely good cooperation between the Federal and State agencies and local volunteers and others, the evacuation that took place ahead of Hurricane Frederic, so far as I know, was the most massive evacuation in the history of our country. About 500,000 people were moved out of the area that was later damaged by the storm.

This was a very severe hurricane, equal in its damage potential to Hurricane Camille about 10 years ago. Early estimates, as a matter of fact, show that the property damage might exceed what occurred with Hurricane Camille.

Ten years ago, 250 people lost their lives, but because of the evacuation techniques and the quick action on the part of Governor James and the other Governors involved, we've had serious loss of life, but so far as I know, only nine people. This is too much, obviously, but it's much better than the 250 that could have occurred had this action not been taken.

The Federal agencies and the State agencies are now, have been, and will continue to work with the closest possible coordination. All Federal agencies are working under the direction of John Macy, the head of FEMA. Our aid to this area has been approved by me—I think the quickest declaration of an emergency that I've ever had since I've been President—and we will continue this aid, not just for a few days or a few weeks but on a long and sustained basis, until the damage caused by this hurricane has been repaired.

This might take not only months but several years, but we will be here working with local and State officials to make sure that the damage is repaired as best we can and also that adequate aid is provided. With mobile homes, unemployment compensation, loans for homes and businesses, farmers, and as we repair this damage, we hope that working with local citizens and with officials at the State and local level as the damage is repaired that we can take much more effective steps to minimize any future damage than was taken 10 years ago.

I think it's accurate to say that the gulf shore region of our country is susceptible to fairly frequent, all too frequent storm damage, and I think in the design of buildings, in the orientation of transportation systems, and the organization of local volunteers, with building codes and otherwise, we can make sure that future storms have less damage to property and to our people than this one did.

My overwhelming sense here is one of concern, dedication to provide maximum service, but above all, my admiration, my appreciation, and thanks to Governor Fob James and others in this area who helped to minimize damage with their timely action and the unselfish volunteer work that has been so evident here in Alabama.

Governor, I thank you, and we are very eager to cooperate in every way we can.

GOVERNOR JAMES. Thank you, Mr. President.

We appreciate very much your being here and caring about what's going on down in Alabama. Thank you.

THE PRESIDENT. We will take a flight in the helicopter at low altitude to observe and to assess the damage. We'll have with us people who have already been through the area, and we'll probably be landing briefly in Mississippi. We'll be then going to Florida. And as a result of this trip, I hope that I can better coordinate the efforts of the Federal Government. And I also, of course, came down here to make sure that the people in this area know that the whole Nation cares and that the whole Nation is deeply grateful for the timely action and the unselfish work that has been done.

GOVERNOR FINCH. Mr. President, we're proud of you, proud of the speedy method that you've handled everything, not only here but the Easter floods that Governor James and Governor Graham and all of us, citizens and all, have faced in the last few months. I haven't seen anybody respond as expeditiously and certainly show your concern and love for your fellow Americans as you have. We all want to tell you we appreciate this. We're just grateful that you took these few hours to come to Alabama, Mississippi, and Florida to show us your real concern.

GOVERNOR GRAHAM. Mr. President, your observation, too, is when we rebuild them, we rebuild them to stay, is so very valid. Just in the design of the understructure of these beach dwellings makes a lot of difference.

THE PRESIDENT. Yes.

Perhaps the press has a couple of questions. I'd be glad to answer. I'll probably refer them to——

Q. [*Inaudible*]

THE PRESIDENT. Yes, we did. But we came in fairly high. And we will use the helicopter primarily to examine from a lower height.

Q. Is there any possibility of airlifting food to the area—[*inaudible*]?

THE PRESIDENT. Yes. We'll bring in whatever food is necessary that needs to be brought in. And we are also beginning to assess the placement of mobile homes throughout the southeastern area, and they'll be moved in to provide places for people to live when they move out of the emergency shelters. I understand twenty or thirty thousand people are still in the emergency shelters in these three States.

Q. President Carter—[*inaudible*].

THE PRESIDENT. You mean gasoline? Do you have a shortage?

GOVERNOR GRAHAM. Yes.

GOVERNOR FINCH. We have agreed to bring it in, Mr. President.

THE PRESIDENT. Both Governors say that that's being taken care of satisfactorily. We will obviously help if they ask us to.

GOVERNOR FINCH. They have responded, and they have brought it in to you.

THE PRESIDENT. Very good.

Along with me, in addition to the head of our entire operation, is the manager, Vernon Weaver, of the Small Business Administration. In addition to loans for farmers, we also, of course, have loans available under new legislation for homeowners, 3-percent loans, up to $55,000, and for businesses, loans at the interest rate of 5 percent. For people who have second homes, like vacation homes, then the interest rates would be about 7⅝ percent. But those loans will be available, and we'll have people moving in here to take care of those needs immediately.

I might point out coincidentally that although Hurricane Camille took place 10 years ago, the Small Business Administration still has 22 people in this area taking care of the loans that were extended to people in Alabama and Mississippi back in those years.

Does anyone else have a question? If not, we'll go and take a look around.

I want to thank the Red Cross for the good work you all have done and the other volunteer workers. Thank you very much. Well, we're all in it together, and we're here to provide help with the taxpayers' money, and I just am glad to be partners with such a fine group as this.

Thank you very much, Fob.

NOTE: The President spoke at 11:17 a.m. at Bates Field.

Pascagoula, Mississippi

Remarks Following an Inspection Tour of Areas Damaged by Hurricane Frederic. September 14, 1979

THE PRESIDENT. I'd like to say one other thing just for the benefit of the people of Mississippi. I think that it is indeed a catastrophe here, about which the whole Nation is concerned, and I come on behalf of all the other people in the Nation, who feel that you have done admirably. Governor Cliff Finch and all of the officials here, the Members of Congress and others have prepared well, and had we not prepared, we could very well have several hundred people's lives having been lost in Mississippi.

And I believe that the degree of cooperation between the Federal Government and the local and State governments and also the people at large has been remarkable. It's difficult to induce people to leave their homes, even when you tell them there's a danger coming. And I think that the strong leadership that has been shown here has helped us to minimize the damage.

And the other thing that I'd like to say is that we will be here on a long-term basis, because the repair that's got to be done to the community structure is not going to be quickly resolved. And I hope that the people who are farmers will know that we've got assistance available for them; businesses, large and small, that have been shut down, we've got unemployment compensation, and we'll have extra people that have been here from the Labor Department to process those claims. And if anything should arise in the future that's a problem for you, or is delayed in being delivered, in delivery of services, if you'll let Bill Simpson know, or Jack Watson, or me directly in the White House, we'll take care of it without delay.

BYSTANDER. Mr. President, may I say, if I may: You've been concerned about unemployment. Here in this country, we're one of the largest employers in the Southeast United States; right here in the shipyard alone, 16,000 people, and they're not all from Mississippi. They come from other States in the Union. So, we make a real contribution to the total economy, and we need to get our people back to work as fast we can.

We have 40 other industries of national prominence. And with your help, that you just mentioned, it's just like a Godsend to us, and we want to thank you from the bottom of our hearts for what you're doing for us.

THE PRESIDENT. It's a very difficult thing for a President or for anyone who lives in Washington to forget about Pascagoula Shipyards with Senator Stennis present. [*Laughter*]

SENATOR STENNIS. We all work together.

BYSTANDER. We are proud of what you have done. Thank you for coming, sir.

GOVERNOR FINCH. One thing, Mr. President, we're going to set up a Governor's office here on the coast where Defense and the State and local people will all be working together. So, my office will be here, and we'll be in touch with Jack, I know, somewhere along the line. But we want to, firsthand, move into the location like you have, to come here and see it. But we're going to set up our office here and use it, Senator, for the benefit of all the people here at Gulf Coast Marine Research Center, that is also funded by the Feds and State, thanks to our leadership in Washington.

THE PRESIDENT. Good luck to you.

NOTE: The President spoke at approximately 12:30 p.m. at the Ingalls Shipyard, a division of Litton Industries.

Pensacola Naval Air Station, Florida

Remarks Following an Inspection Tour of Areas Damaged by Hurricane Frederic. September 14, 1979

I would like to say just a word that I think is important, not only to you who are assembled here in Pensacola and in Florida and those who might hear my voice later on in Alabama and Mississippi but for the entire Nation.

Our hearts go out to those who have suffered so much in Hurricane Frederic, but I think that the most overwhelming sense that we have is one of gratitude that in spite of one of the most severe hurricanes which has ever hit our Nation, because of the close working cooperation between local and State and Federal officials and many volunteers and citizens who came forward, that the loss of life has been minimal. My reports have shown and my observations have also proven to me that this is perhaps even more a destructive hurricane than was Hurricane Camille 10 years ago, when about 250 people lost their lives. But because we had a massive evacuation effort, when 500,000 people moved further inland, we have minimized, thank God, the loss of life.

The damage has been severe. I just flew in from Pascagoula, over Dauphin Island and down the gulf shore area. And hundreds and hundreds of places where homes formerly existed, there are no homes at all, and it's impossible even to tell where the building lots were located. Mobile has suffered very severe damage.

We have a fine organization already in place, with all the Federal agencies being administered from a single place and with the closest possible cooperation from Governors and other State officials, from mayors and county officials in every community involved.

The damage is extremely severe, and the Federal commitment to helping all of you and all those who were damaged repair what has been done and restore the quality of your lives is complete and it's permanent. The repair of this damage is going to take a long time. It can't be accomplished in a few weeks or even a few months. But we are dedicated to provide unemployment compensation for those who are not presently employed because of the loss of their jobs because of damage, low-interest loans for homes, low-interest loans to repair businesses, help for farmers who've lost their crops. And we'll try now to restore the vital services, transportation, electric power, telephones, working with the private organizations for power and telephones that are doing so well.

I'd like to point out that after a few days the intense concern and the unselfish attitude and the cooperative spirit might tend to fade away. I hope that you all won't let that happen. We're going to have to have a sustained effort of taking care of one another. Government can do just a limited amount. The vast contribution of repair and human care must come from volunteers. This is the character of our Nation, and when we are tested as a country, we always respond successfully.

I hope that as we rebuild the areas of our gulf coast, which have in many cases been completely destroyed, that we'll be looking forward to the future with caution, building on our experiences. Camille was 10 years ago, and we don't know whether a year from now or 10 years from now we'll have another severe hurricane. As we do rebuild and repair, we ought to have in mind how we can minimize damage in the future.

I think the early warning that came to you was a tremendous achievement. We now have the ability to track hurricanes and to predict their course. Sometimes you may have to move from your home and the hurricane didn't strike. I hope that the next time the Governor asks you to move, you'll do it immediately, because I have seen many places that had people not responded, not knowing for sure that the hurricane would strike, they would have lost their lives. They've lost their homes.

The last thing I want to say is this: We ought not be discouraged. We are sensitive about your needs. We'll be available when we can to help you. And I would like to congratulate every Member of the Congress, every Governor, every State official, every local official, every Red Cross worker, every volunteer who has accommodated so far the intense need of many people and have minimized the damage which has come to us.

We have many things for which we can be thankful, and the saving of human life is one of the most important.

The country will not forget you, those people who were not severely injured in this storm. We'll be partners with you in the days and weeks ahead. And I pray that this damage can be minimized and that your own lives might be restored very quickly to a normal state so that we can enjoy the privileges and the honor of living still in the greatest country on Earth.

I've appreciated the aid and the help and the reports that I've gotten from many officials. Those lined up behind me come from almost every community around here. Some are in charge of school systems; some, transportation systems; some, administering cleanup operations. And they've come to let me as President know, in some cases we are doing well, in some cases we need certain things. But together, as partners, we've done a good job so far, and I have no doubt that in the future we'll continue to do so.

Thank you very much. You have my admiration and my appreciation, my pledge of support, my congratulations. May God bless all of you.

Thank you very much.

NOTE: The President spoke at 1:35 p.m. at Forrest Sherman Field.

United States Ambassador to Chad

Nomination of Donald R. Norland.
September 14, 1979

The President today announced that he will nominate Donald R. Norland, of Grantham, N.H., to be Ambassador Extraordinary and Plenipotentiary of the United States to the Republic of Chad. He would replace William G. Bradford, resigned.

Norland has been Ambassador to the Republic of Botswana, the Kingdom of Lesotho, and the Kingdom of Swaziland since 1976.

He was born June 14, 1924, in Laurens, Iowa. He received a B.A. (1948) and M.A. (1950) from the University of Minnesota. He served in the U.S. Navy from 1943 to 1946.

Norland was an instructor at Iowa State Teachers College from 1949 to 1951, and a teaching fellow at the University of Michigan in 1951–52. He entered the Foreign Service in 1952 and was posted in Rabat and Abidjan and served at the State Department.

From 1961 to 1963, Norland was political officer in Paris. In 1963–64 he was detailed to the Air Command and Staff College at Maxwell Air Force Base under the State-Defense Department exchange program. From 1964 to 1969, he was posted in The Hague as political officer, then counselor for political affairs.

Norland was a State Department fellow at Stanford University in 1969–70 and served as Deputy Chief of Mission in Conakry from 1970 to 1972. He was a political-military affairs officer at the State Department from 1972 to 1973, and a personnel officer from 1973 to 1975. From 1975 to 1976, he was Deputy Director for Management Operations in the Office of the Under Secretary for Management.

Laurent is senior vice president of McElvain-Reynolds Co., a Chicago mortgage banking firm, where he is in charge of the multifamily government-insured loan division.

He was born May 11, 1937, in Evanston, Ill. He received a B.A. from Fisk University in 1960.

Laurent was with Johnson Publications in Chicago from 1960 to 1961, and was a housing inspector with the Evanston Department of Health from 1962 to 1964. He entered the mortgage banking business in 1964 as a loan officer with Salk, Ward & Salk, Inc.

From 1969 to 1970, Laurent was assistant vice president of Percy Wilson Mortgage and Finance Corp. He joined McElvain-Reynolds Co. in 1970 as vice president, and has been senior vice president since 1972.

Laurent is former president of the Illinois Mortgage Bankers Association and a former lecturer at the Mortgage Bankers Association School of Financing. He served on the HUD Task Force on the Future Role of FHA. He was on the board of directors of the Chicago Committee on Urban Opportunity and was a panel member of the Community Revitalization Clinic, sponsored by the Illinois League of Savings and Loan Associations.

Government National Mortgage Association

Nomination of Ronald P. Laurent To Be President.   September 14, 1979

The President today announced that he will nominate Ronald P. Laurent, of Chicago, Ill., to be President of the Government National Mortgage Association. He would replace John Dalton, who has resigned.

Digest of Other White House Announcements

The following listing includes the President's public schedule and other items of general interest announced by the White House Press Office and not included elsewhere in this issue.

September 8

The President met at the White House with Zbigniew Brzezinski, Assistant to the President for National Security Affairs.

September 10

The President met at the White House with:

—Dr. Brzezinski;

—the Cabinet;

—James T. McIntyre, Jr., Director of the Office of Management and Budget;

—Secretary of Agriculture Bob Bergland and the Voluntary Agency Partners in the Combined Federal Campaign.

The President announced that he has designated Richard R. Rivers as Acting Special Representative for Trade Negotiations.

September 11

The President met at the White House with:

—Dr. Brzezinski;

—members of the Senate Energy Committee;

—Frank B. Moore, Assistant to the President for Congressional Liaison;

—Secretary of Energy Charles W. Duncan, Jr., and members of the New Coalition and the State and Local Energy Task Force.

The President participated in a briefing by administration officials on the strategic arms limitation treaty given for community leaders in the East Room at the White House.

The President announced the appointment of the following three persons to the American National Red Cross Board of Governors:

PATRICIA ROBERTS HARRIS, Secretary of Health, Education, and Welfare;

JOHN W. MACY, Director of the Federal Emergency Management Agency; and

ROBERT B. PIRIE, JR., Assistant Secretary of Defense for Manpower, Reserve Affairs and Logistics.

The President has signed an order designating three positions for membership on the Emergency Management Council. They are the Assistant to the President for National Security Affairs, the Assistant to the President for Domestic Affairs and Policy, and the Secretary to the Cabinet and Assistant to the President for Intergovernmental Affairs.

September 12

The President met at the White House with Dr. Brzezinski.

The President participated in a breakfast briefing by administration officials on the strategic arms limitation treaty given for a group of religious leaders in the State Dining Room at the White House.

September 12

The President met at the White House with:

—Dr. Brzezinski;

—a group of Senators to discuss energy;

—Mr. Moore;

—representatives of the Women's Sports Foundation, including Carol Mann, professional golfer; Janet Guthrie, race car driver; Lacey O'Neal, former Olympics track and field contender; and Donna E. de Varona, member of the President's Advisory Committee for Women and Olympic gold medal winner;

—Al Rubin and a delegation from the National Planning Council for the International Year of Disabled Persons;

—the heads of ABC, CBS, NBC networks and the presidents of their parent organizations, and Gerald M. Rafshoon, Assistant to the President for Communications, to discuss energy.

The President declared major disasters for Alabama, Florida, and Mississippi because of extensive public and private property damage caused by Hurricane Frederic.

The President attended a reception for members of the Conference of National Volunteer Organizations held in the East Room at the White House.

September 14

The President met at the White House with:

—Vice President Walter F. Mondale, Secretary of State Cyrus R. Vance, Secretary of Defense Harold Brown, Hamilton Jordan, Assistant to the President, Hedley W. Donovan, Senior Adviser to the President, and Dr. Brzezinski;

—John M. Craig, a participant in the Tampa, Fla., town meeting.

The President participated in a briefing on the administration's programs and policies, given for civic and community leaders from Florida in the East Room at the White House.

The White House announced that the President has signed two Presidential determinations under the Foreign Assistance Act of 1961. One states his determination that $4.8 million should be appropriated to provide assistance to the victims of Hurricane David in the Caribbean. The other authorizes furnishing $10 million to Yugoslavia from the fiscal year 1979 Economic Support Fund. These funds will be used for reconstruction following the earthquake there.

The President announced that he has appointed Hugh Carter, Jr., Special Assistant to the President for Administration, to be a member of the President's Commission on Executive Exchange. This Commission runs an executive interchange program between the Federal Government and private industry.

The President left the White House for a weekend stay at Camp David, Md.

The President declared a major disaster for the State of Maryland as a result of severe storms, tornadoes, and flooding on September 5 and 6, which caused extensive property damage.

NOMINATIONS SUBMITTED TO THE SENATE

The following list does not include promotions of members of the Uniformed Services, nominations to the Service Academies, or nominations of Foreign Service officers.

Submitted September 10, 1979

NEIL GOLDSCHMIDT, of Oregon, to be Secretary of Transportation, to which office he was appointed during the last recess of the Senate.

DONALD F. McHENRY, of Illinois, to be the Representative of the United States of America to the United Nations with the rank and status of Ambassador Extraordinary and Plenipotentiary, and the Representative of the United States of America in the Security Council of the United Nations.

HORACE G. DAWSON, JR., of the District of Columbia, a Foreign Service information officer of Class one, to be Ambassador Extraordinary and Plenipotentiary of the United States of America to the Republic of Botswana.

KENNETH M. CURTIS, of Maine, to be Ambassador Extraordinary and Plenipotentiary of the United States of America to Canada.

GEORGE B. ROBERTS, JR., of Pennsylvania, a Foreign Service officer of Class one, to be Ambassador Extraordinary and Plenipotentiary of the United States of America to the Cooperative Republic of Guyana.

NANCY V. RAWLS, of Florida, a Foreign Service officer of Class one, to be Ambassador Extraordinary and Plenipotentiary of the United States of America to the Republic of Ivory Coast.

RICHARD DAVID VINE, of California, a Foreign Service officer of Class one, to be Ambassador Extraordinary and Plenipotentiary of the United States of America to Switzerland.

RICHARD NOYES VIETS, of Vermont, a Foreign Service officer of Class two, to be Ambassador Extraordinary and Plenipotentiary of the United States of America to the United Republic of Tanzania.

NOMINATIONS—Continued

Submitted September 10, 1979

Francis Severin Johnson, of Texas, to be an Assistant Director of the National Science Foundation, vice John B. Slaughter, resigned.

William Klemperer, of Massachusetts, to be an Assistant Director of the National Science Foundation, vice James Arthur Krumhansl, resigned.

Henry Harold Kennedy, Jr., of the District of Columbia, to be an Associate Judge of the Superior Court of the District of Columbia for a term of 15 years, vice Joyce Hens Green, elevated.

Frank Ernest Schwelb, of the District of Columbia, to be an Associate Judge of the Superior Court of the District of Columbia for a term of 15 years, vice William Cornet Pryor, elevated.

Submitted September 12, 1979

Reubin O'D. Askew, of Florida, to be Special Representative for Trade Negotiations, with the rank of Ambassador Extraordinary and Plenipotentiary, vice Robert S. Strauss, resigned.

Submitted September 13, 1979

Thomas W. M. Smith, of Maine, a Foreign Service officer of Class one, to be Ambassador Extraordinary and Plenipotentiary of the United States of America to the Republic of Ghana.

John C. Sawhill, of New York, to be Deputy Secretary of Energy, vice John F. O'Leary, resigned.

Thomas H. Quinn, of Rhode Island, to be a member of the Board for International Broadcasting for a term expiring April 28, 1982 (reappointment).

The following-named persons to be Representatives of the United States of America to the Thirty-fourth Session of the General Assembly of the United Nations:

NOMINATIONS—Continued

Submitted September 13—Continued

Donald F. McHenry, of Illinois
Benjamin S. Rosenthal, United States Representative from the State of New York
Larry Winn, Jr., United States Representative from the State of Kansas
Esther L. Coopersmith, of Maryland

The following-named persons to be Alternate Representatives of the United States of America to the Thirty-fourth Session of the General Assembly of the United Nations:
Howard T. Rosen, of New Jersey
William L. Dunfey, of New Hampshire
Richard W. Petree, of Virginia

CHECKLIST OF WHITE HOUSE PRESS RELEASES

The following listing contains releases of the White House Press Office which are not included in this issue.

Released September 8, 1979

Transcript: interview with a group of editors—by Zbigniew Brzezinski, Assistant to the President for National Security Affairs

Released September 10, 1979

Fact sheet: Labor Surplus Area Outreach program

ACTS APPROVED BY THE PRESIDENT

Approved September 14, 1979

S. 1646_____ Public Law 96–64

An act to amend the International Banking Act of 1978 (Public Law 95–369) to extend the time for foreign banks to obtain required deposit insurance with respect to existing branches in the United States.

PRESIDENTIAL DOCUMENTS

Week Ending Friday, September 21, 1979

First Anniversary of the Camp David Agreements

Statement by the President.
September 17, 1979

One year ago today, on September 17, 1978, Prime Minister Begin of Israel, President Sadat of Egypt, and I returned from Camp David with an agreement establishing the Framework for Peace in the Middle East. We believed then that we had reached an historic turning point in the bitter history of that long-suffering region. One short year later, that belief has become a firm reality.

After 30 years of hostility and war, Israel is truly at peace with its largest Arab neighbor. The relations between them are improving daily. The provisions of the treaty of peace are being carried out precisely and on schedule.

This peace is no longer words on paper. It is now facts on the ground and faith in the hearts of millions of people. This remarkable change—from war to peace, from hostility to friendship—was clearly visible in the recent visit by President Sadat to Haifa, where he was received with genuine warmth and enthusiasm by the people and the leaders of Israel. Such events, which would have seemed amazing, even unthinkable, until the very recent past, are now accepted almost as routine. That is itself a measure of how far we have traveled along the road to peace.

So it is worth remembering on this occasion what an extraordinary change in attitudes has taken place. The successes of Egypt and Israel so far in overcoming three decades of animosity give us renewed confidence in facing the difficult tasks which remain.

Our goal has always been the establishment of a comprehensive peace in which Israel could at last live in security and tranquillity with all its neighbors. The Camp David accords are a long step on that path. We do not underestimate the difficulties that lie ahead, but we knew from the outset that the road would be hard and rocky. And looking back today at the solid achievements of the past year, we are justified in keeping our eyes firmly on the goal of peace rather than in heeding the inevitable cries that say peace cannot be achieved.

The peace process outlined at Camp David 1 year ago is alive and well. The talks on full autonomy for the West Bank and Gaza are proceeding on schedule, in an atmosphere of good will and serious cooperation. I am confident those talks will succeed. Their progress is a tribute

1681

to the vision and courage of President Sadat, Prime Minister Begin, and the people of their two great nations.

Over the coming months it will be our common task to continue demonstrating that peace does work and, by the evidence of our deeds, to convince other nations and leaders to join with us in this quest for lasting peace, security, and the opportunity for productive lives for all the people of the Middle East.

NOTE: On the same day, the White House announced that the President had received messages from Prime Minister Begin and President Sadat. As printed below, the messages follow the texts made available by the White House Press Office.

On this the first anniversary of the Camp David agreement signed in Washington on September 17th I vividly recall the wonderful hospitality which you and your gracious lady accorded to my wife, my colleagues and myself during those 13 days of the momentous conference. I remember well the sessions, the strong debates, the mutual convincing, the difficulties we all had to overcome, the weighing of every sentence and word and ultimately the joy of achieving the understanding which became the basis of an historic agreement. Out of it the treaty of peace between Egypt and Israel, certainly a turning point in the annals of the Middle East emerged and the positive concept of full autonomy for the Palestinian Arabs, inhabitants of Judea, Samaria and Gaza District was brought forth.

You, Mr. President did your utmost by your own hard work to make these agreements possible, allow me, therefore, on this memorable anniversary to thank you from the heart for the great assistance rendered to both Egypt and Israel in achieving a rapprochement between two countries which for thirty one years, were in a state of war, and which have now concluded peace, the first step towards a general and comprehensive settlement in the Middle East.

There are people who do not yet appreciate the value of this moral international achieve-

ment, but many millions of women and men of goodwill will rejoice together with us in this accomplishment. Their blessings are our joy and the source of satisfaction.

Accept, Mr. President, my deepest gratitude for all you have done with such great devotion in the service of peace.

Yours respectfully and sincerely,

MENACHEM BEGIN

This afternoon I have issued a presidential statement expressing my views on the first anniversary of the signature of the Camp David agreements. On this occasion I wish to express my deep feelings and thanks for your personal contribution to this historical event. I am confident that these agreements, which have been the first steps toward a comprehensive peace, will help bring a solution to the Palestinian question in all its aspects. The role of the U.S. as a full partner in the peace process will remain a key element in our mutual efforts to achieve a just and lasting peace in the Middle East.

Sincerely,

ANWAR EL-SADAT

Federal Council on the Aging

Nomination of Five Members.
September 17, 1979

The President today announced that he will nominate five persons as members of the Federal Council on the Aging. They are:

AARON E. HENRY, president of the Mississippi State Conference of the NAACP and chairman of the National Black Caucus on the Aging;

CYRIL HILARY CARPENTER, president of the Minnesota Farmers Union;

JOHN B. MARTIN, legislative consultant to the American Association of Retired Persons and the National Retired Teachers Association and former Special Assistant for the Aging to President Nixon (reappointment);

MARY C. MULVEY, supervisor of adult education for the Providence (R.I.) public schools and a lecturer on preparing for retirement at the University of Rhode Island Extension Division; and

JEAN JONES PERDUE, medical director of the Office of Health Services of Metropolitan Dade County, Fla., and a specialist in internal medicine and cardiology since 1934.

Council on Wage and Price Stability

Message to the Congress Transmitting a Report.   September 17, 1979

To the Congress of the United States:

In accordance with Section 5 of the Council on Wage and Price Stability Act, as amended, I hereby transmit to the Congress the eighteenth quarterly report of the Council on Wage and Price Stability. The report contains a description of the Council's activities during the first quarter of 1979 in monitoring both prices and wages in the private sector and various Federal government activities that may lead to higher costs and prices without creating commensurate benefits. It discusses Council reports, analyses, and filings before Federal regulatory agencies. It also describes the Council's activities of monitoring wages and prices as part of the anti-inflation program.

The Council on Wage and Price Stability will continue to play an important role in supplementing fiscal and monetary policies by calling public attention to wage and price developments or actions by the government that could be of concern to American consumers.

JIMMY CARTER

The White House,
September 17, 1979.

Railroad Retirement Board

Message to the Congress Transmitting a Report.   September 17, 1979

To the Congress of the United States:

I hereby transmit the Annual Report to the Railroad Retirement Board for fiscal year 1978.

The report summarizes the Board's operations to assist the railroad sector during the year. Under the Railroad Retirement Act, 1,100,000 recipients were paid $4 billion in retirement and survivor benefits, and under the Railroad Unemployment Insurance Act 175,000 beneficiaries were paid almost $200 million in unemployment and sickness benefits.

I note with concern that the Board has advised me that the balance in the Railroad Retirement Account continues to decline as benefit payments exceed income for the eighth consecutive year.

The Board's most recent actuarial valuation indicates a serious and growing actuarial deficit which requires short term remedial action, a judgment also concurred in by the General Accounting Office. This Administration's budget for fiscal year 1980 includes even-handed legislative proposals to restore to solvency the railroad industry pension fund which will assure the interests of current and future railroad retirement beneficiaries. We also invite the view of railroad labor and management on our proposal to provide sound financing of the industry pension component by the railroad industry without added Federal subsidies.

The Board is currently preparing its 14th Triennial Actuarial Valuation of the industry pension, which should provide a more accurate, up-to-date analysis of the financial condition of the fund. The forthcoming actuarial valuation will project the condition of the fund based on strict current law basis as well as under the normal requirements of the Employee Retirement Income Security Act (ERISA). Both estimates will use the economic assumptions in the most recent Social Security Trustee's Report. These additional perspectives will help assure that changes to restore the solvency of the industry pension are based on information under a variety of economic and legislative assumptions.

JIMMY CARTER

The White House,
    September 17, 1979.

NOTE: The report is entitled "Railroad Retirement Board—1978 Annual Report for Fiscal Year Ending September 30" (Government Printing Office, 94 pages).

First Anniversary of the Camp David Agreements

*Remarks of the President, Vice President Muhammad Husni Mubarak of Egypt, and Foreign Minister Moshe Dayan of Israel Following Their Meeting.
September 17, 1979*

THE PRESIDENT. First of all, I'd like to introduce to the press some very famous gentlemen who are almost as well known in our country as am I: the Vice President of Egypt, Mr. Mubarak; the Foreign Minister of Israel, Moshe Dayan; the Defense Minister of Israel, Ezer Weizman; and General Ali, who is the Director of Defense of Egypt; and the two Ambassadors from Egypt and Israel.

As you know, this is the first anniversary of the signing of the Camp David accords. During that year we have seen realized, because of the courage and the conviction and the vision and the determination of President Sadat and Prime Minister Begin, the hopes and dreams that were present among us a year ago. Although the Camp David accords is a document made of words, the peace progress that has been made in the last year has been in the hearts and minds of the people of Israel and Egypt.

It's obvious that both countries, both peoples, both leaders are determined that this process will be successful and that we will indeed have peace in the Mideast, based on a comprehensive settlement of the differences that have divided the Arabs and the Israelis for so many years. It's with a great sense of thanksgiving and confidence that I assess what has been done so far and what will be done in the future.

I'd like to introduce now Vice President Mubarak of Egypt, representing President Sadat. I talked to President Sadat and Prime Minister Begin this morning. They sent their best wishes to the American people and their thanks for the foundation that was laid a year ago for this comprehensive peace.

Mr. Vice President.

THE VICE PRESIDENT. Thank you. Mr. President, friends, this is a fine moment for those who are committed to the cause of peace.

A year ago today, the leaders of the three countries—the three great nations— signed the Framework for Peace in the Middle East. It was an historic step of tremendous significance, but it remains a first step. Much remains to be achieved in the months ahead. We are all committed to continue our efforts until we reach a comprehensive settlement that tackles all aspects of the problem. First and foremost, it must address itself to the heart and the core of the entire conflict— namely, the Palestinian question.

It's very significant that we are in Washington on the 17th of September to follow up our efforts and build on what was achieved in Camp David.

In the months ahead we'll be working tirelessly together until we reach that goal for the good of world peace and security. This is an unwavering commitment which we share and are determined to honor. Thus, we should refrain from any rash act that would jeopardize the prospects of peace at this crucial stage. Acts of defiance and negativism should be avoided. The policy of confrontation and fait accompli is contrary to the spirit of Camp David.

Mr. President, under your leadership the American people are playing the role which is worthy of a great nation—the role of the peacemaker. This is a source of confidence and reassurance. Never before has there been so much promise and hope for the future. Never before has there been such awareness of the necessity for tackling the Palestinian question. Never before has there been such confidence in the United States as an honest and full partner in peace in the Middle East.

Much of the credit for all these positive developments goes to you, Mr. President. Through your determination and courage, we were able to overcome the most difficult problems, able to overcome the most difficult problems. With your vision and a deep sense of commitment, we were able to heal the wounds of the unhappy past and focus on the future. With your compassion and understanding, we were able to put the problem in the proper perspective.

We are also indebted to each and every American in the United States. No other nation showed so much interest in peace in the Middle East. No other nation has devoted so much effort and the energy to help friends build a great structure for peace. We count on your continued help and commitment.

I bring you greetings from President Sadat and the 41 million Egyptians. Let us now remain together until we reach our common goal. God willing, we shall reach it.

Thank you.

THE PRESIDENT. And now I'd like to introduce Foreign Minister Moshe Dayan, who played such a crucial role in the negotiations at Camp David and since that time, as we wage peace, not war, in the Middle East.

THE FOREIGN MINISTER. Mr. President, I want to thank you very much on behalf of the Israeli Government and the Israeli people on this splendid meeting here today and on the event for this meeting, on reaching peace with our neighbors in Egypt. Had it not been for you, we couldn't have done it, and we wouldn't be here today celebrating the anniversary of this day.

You said, Mr. President, that, of course, when you turn provisions written on paper into reality, you come against difficulties, which is true. And one of the problems that we have to face, we shall be trying to solve tomorrow and the day after. But allow me to say that, on the other hand, we did come surprisingly against pleasant, unexpected events during the implementation of the peace treaty. And I mention just one of them.

When we were sitting down here and in Camp David and working out the peace treaty, we were very worried about what we called the process of normalization, and we all looked forward with great anxiety about the day when an Egyptian Ambassador would have to come to Israel and an Israeli Ambassador would have to go to Egypt. But what happened in the meantime with the visits of President Sadat to Israel and the feeling that he was met with when he came to Israel, and the visits of Prime Minister Begin to Egypt, and the visits of hundreds of Israelis and many Egyptians to both countries, not only with no incidents but with warm feeling, meeting the people of the other country. And anyone who was not in Haifa when President Sadat was there recently cannot imagine the spirit, the moving spirit of the joy of the Israelis, not only about the meeting but about what that meeting represented—the peace between the two countries.

I know, Mr. President, that for the last few months you did not deal that much with our problems like you used to do before, and I assume that you did have other business to attend to. But though I do hope that we shall reach an agreement with the current negotiation—and I want to remind my friends, Vice President Mubarak and General Ali, that the gap that we had between the two of us when we started the negotiation, believe me, it was wider than the gap that we have between us and the Palestinians when we talk now about autonomy. So, I am hopeful about that. Still, what I want to tell you, Mr. President, besides thanking you again, to remind you that you are a party in this business. And if somehow we shall come against major difficulties, we might ask you to extend your hand, your guiding hand, to be involved again in the process of peace so that we shall achieve it.

Thank you very much.

THE PRESIDENT. Let me say in closing that one of the most gratifying and somewhat surprising developments has been the burgeoning friendship and the growing respect and cooperation that has developed directly between President Sadat and Prime Minister Begin. This accurately mirrors, in my opinion, the genuine feeling that exists between the people of Egypt and the people of Israel.

Good progress is being made. But, Mr. Foreign Minister, as you suggested, in the future, if an apparently insurmountable obstacle should be confronted in the negotiating process, then I would be deeply committed to becoming personally involved again. In the meantime, however, Ambassador Bob Strauss, Secretary Vance, and others can adequately represent the United States in adding our good offices to the negotiating process.

We believe that a firm foundation now exists for major progress to be made between Egypt and Israel and, in the future, among others that will join the peace process who live in the Mideast.

Thank you all for the constructive work that's already taken place. God bless you in future endeavors, which I'm sure will be successful in bringing the peace that we all cherish and for which we all hope with all our hearts.

Thank you very much.

NOTE: The President spoke at 4:19 p.m. on the South Lawn of the White House.

National Forest Products Week, 1979

Proclamation 4687.   September 18, 1979

By the President of the United States of America

A Proclamation

Our Nation's forests are one of our greatest resources, covering nearly one-third of our land. The forests are "lands of many uses" providing wood for a multitude of products, protection of watersheds, forage for livestock, food and shelter for wildlife, wilderness areas, and a tremendous range of recreation opportunities for people of every age and income.

In these times of worldwide inflation and energy shortages, we can turn to our forests for relief. Forests offer numerous opportunities for low-cost vacations.

Forest products can have even greater inflation-fighting and energy-saving roles. I recently directed two Federal agencies to examine their forested lands to see what could be done to provide more timber so that the cost of housing could be reduced.

Discoveries from forest product research are being applied to help fight inflation and save energy. A new house developed by Forest Service scientists will allow us to build houses with 30 percent less structural lumber than is used now for similar structures. New processing techniques reduce the amount of energy needed to make paper and also allow manufacture of more paper from less wood.

In addition, America's forests make direct contributions to reducing our dependence on foreign sources of energy. This country once ran on the energy provided by burning wood, and we can obtain energy from that resource again. Every year, more and more Americans are turning to efficient wood-burning stoves and furnaces to help in their fight against rising energy costs.

Wise use of our Nation's forest products results in turn from wise and efficient management of the forests themselves. Planning carefully for all forest uses, minimizing waste, and replenishing harvested trees will sustain our forests and insure the continuity of this tremendous renewable asset.

In recognition of the value of forests for energy, wood products, and recreation, Congress has designated the third week of October as National Forest Products Week. It is important that we pause to reflect upon the value of our forests to our national well-being.

Now, THEREFORE, I, JIMMY CARTER, President of the United States of America, do hereby proclaim the week of October 21 through October 27, 1979, as National Forest Products Week and ask all Americans to demonstrate their awareness of the value of forests through suitable activities.

IN WITNESS WHEREOF, I have hereunto set my hand this eighteenth day of September, in the year of our Lord nineteen hundred seventy-nine, and of the Independence of the United States of America the two hundred and fourth.

JIMMY CARTER

[Filed with the Office of the Federal Register, 2:29 p.m., September 18, 1979]

Veterans Day, 1979

Proclamation 4688.   September 18, 1979

By the President of the United States of America

A Proclamation

No Americans have done more to win and protect the peace than the men and women of our Armed Forces, past and present.

Veterans Day affords each of us the opportunity to join our fellow citizens, in communities across the Nation, in honoring those whose love of country knew no bounds—those to whom patriotism was principle, not mere sentiment. Without the sacrifices which our brave veterans made so freely and so generously, our cherished freedom would long ago have vanished.

On this historic day, let us resolve anew to keep faith with those who have done so much to shape this Nation with their honor and valor. The flag under which they served is the emblem of our unity, our power, our purpose as a Nation. It has no other character than that which we give it from generation to generation.

Now, THEREFORE, I, JIMMY CARTER, President of the United States of America, do hereby invite citizens everywhere to join with me in observing Veterans Day on Sunday, November 11, 1979. Let the past and present unite in prayer that America will ever seek the ways of peace, and, by her example at home and throughout the world, hasten the return of goodwill among men.

This is a particularly appropriate time to remember with respect and affection our sick and disabled veterans. I urge their families and friends to visit with them and reassure them of their country's enduring gratitude.

I call upon the press, radio and television and other media of public information to participate in this observance to help realize the full purpose and meaning of this important commemoration.

I ask that Federal, State and local government officials arrange for the display of the flag of the United States on this day, and encourage the public's involvement in appropriate ceremonies throughout our land.

IN WITNESS WHEREOF, I have hereunto set my hand this eighteenth day of September, in the year of our Lord nineteen hundred seventy-nine, and of the Independence of the United States of America the two hundred and fourth.

JIMMY CARTER

[Filed with the Office of the Federal Register, 2:30 p.m., September 18, 1979]

Presidential Scholars

Executive Order 12158.   September 18, 1979

AWARDS FOR SPECIAL CAPABILITY IN THE VISUAL AND PERFORMING ARTS AND IN CREATIVE WRITING

By the authority vested in me as President by the Constitution and statutes of the United States of America, Section 2 of Executive Order No. 11155 is hereby amended by adding thereto the following paragraph:

"(5) In addition to the Presidential Scholars provided for in paragraphs (3) and (4) above, the Commission may choose other Presidential Scholars not exceeding twenty in any one year. These Scholars shall be chosen at large, from the jurisdictions referred to in paragraph (3), on the basis of outstanding scholarship and demonstrated ability and accomplishment in the visual and performing arts or in creative writing.".

JIMMY CARTER

The White House,
    September 18, 1979.

[Filed with the Office of the Federal Register, 10:48 a.m., September 19, 1979]

Archbishop Iakovos of the Greek Orthodox Church in North and South America

Remarks at a White House Reception Honoring the Archbishop. September 18, 1979

THE PRESIDENT. Rosalynn and I are very delighted that not only the East Room but the entire White House is filled with admirers and friends and lovers of Archbishop Iakovos. We are very proud that you are here. It's an honor for us to participate in honoring him.

I would like to say that we have Members of the Congress here; we have distinguished educators here, distinguished religious leaders from every faith. We also have people who've come as personal friends—those from the business community, from other elements of government, from all over the Nation—to listen to the beautiful music of the Metropolitan Singers and to take part in this celebration of one of the important anniversaries in the Greek Orthodox Church.

As all of you know, the Greek Orthodox Church has been the repository and the avenue through which the culture and the values of Hellenic society have been transmitted and enhanced from one generation to another, in the service of one another and in the service of Jesus Christ.

Our own Nation is a nation of immigrants. We've brought here some of the finest aspects of the lives and the customs, the achievements and the hopes and aspirations of people throughout the world. But our heritage from Greece is indeed extraordinary, because from that great country, the mother country of many in this room, we have derived the basis for American principles and government—liberty and democracy. And we thank all of you and your ancestors for that noble gift.

We could not have a better exemplification of the finest aspects of human life than His Eminence Archbishop Iakovos. His life is one which has been dedicated to the pursuit of the broadest possible realm of basic civil rights, basic human rights, not just in this country but throughout the world.

As you know, this is the 20th anniversary of his enthronement as a spiritual leader of North and South America. Although he only has 3 million communi-cants who look to him with direct religious conviction, and a common, narrowly defined religious conviction, he has many millions of other Americans who look to him for spiritual inspiration and who admire his great contributions to our country and to the kingdom of Christ.

His small gestures have exemplified not only humaneness but also courage. In 1965, when it was not an easy thing to do, this great man walked shoulder to shoulder with Martin Luther King, Jr., holding the hand of a small black girl in Selma, Alabama. He didn't have to do it. His church did not demand it. Had he not been there, few would have noticed his absence. But he was there. And this simple act was not extraordinary in his life, because it's one of many similar acts that have exemplified his public and his private and his religious service. He has always sought justice for the poor.

He's also been a world leader in many organized religious efforts—twice president of the World Council of Churches. He's had the breadth of vision to transcend religious boundaries, which often are very difficult to cross. One of his major achievements has been that he was the first Archbishop in 350 years, 3½ centuries, to meet with the Pope, representing the Roman Catholic Church. And not only in this connection between Greek Orthodox and Roman Catholic Churches but among Protestant and other religious orders, this fine leader has helped to bridge a chasm that separates human beings.

He's been an adviser for many. He's been an adviser for me, and I thank God for it. Not too long ago I was at Camp David, considering our Nation, some of its problems, some possible solutions for it. I needed counsel on government, politics, energy, taxation, economics. But, above all, I needed counsel on our country's spirit—who we are, what we are, what we should be. I asked him to come to Camp David and meet with me, and he graciously consented.

We talked about a vision of a greater America. We talked about the need for a rebirth of the American spirit. We talked about how we might, as Americans, revitalize the basic human values on which our country was founded and which are part of the ethics and the morals on which the church itself premises its service to human beings. We talked about the need for a new sense of unity, which he, throughout his own life of public service, has exemplified so well. And we talked about the definition of new and even higher goals for our country and for all Americans, who live here together. That could not possibly be a greater demand on a person's understanding and sensitivity and intellect and experience than to give a President counsel on these kinds of important things.

I'm a great personal admirer of his. And since I've been President, I have given two awards—one to Jonas Salk, who helped to eliminate the threat of polio from the world, and the other one to Martin Luther King, Jr. And I would like to announce to this group that I will present to Archbishop Iakovos the Presidential Medal of Freedom later on this year. This will give me a chance to invite some of you back for an additional ceremony. [*Laughter*] And it will also give the Nation a chance to be reminded of the remarkable achievements of this fine man, my friend and your friend.

And now I would like to ask our dear friend to say a few words here to his friends.

Thank you very much.

THE ARCHBISHOP. *Mr. President, Mrs. Carter, fellow clergymen, ladies and gentlemen:*

For a long time now I have pondered my 20 years of service; I have examined and reexamined my record of service countless times. And yet I have never felt so inadequate. Who am I? What have I done to deserve recognition of such magnitude and spiritual significance? Even if I have achieved anything noteworthy, was it not my dutiful responsibility? Is it not Jesus, our Lord and Savior, who admonishes us to say, when we are thanked for something, "We are merely servants. We have done no more than our duty."

In His name, Mr. President, I have endeavored to offer some small services to my church, to the church of Christ in general, to education, and to my fellow man. And most especially, my heart and soul have been touched and moved to cry out for the oppressed and for those who have suffered and continue to suffer because of social injustice in the world. Indeed, I have walked hand in hand with a small black girl in Selma, next to the great Martin Luther King. But is it not true that marching forward is a solemn duty and obligation for me at all times and under all circumstances?

I have always considered myself to be a servant, and I pray to be a faithful one. It is a singular honor to be in the service of the Servant of Servants. He has taught me to serve and lead the way for all who wish to serve. I am conscious of my faults and my failures, which cause me considerable pain. But I am also conscious of an ongoing incentive within me to do better, for I carry a triple legacy—an American, a Hellenic, and the Christian legacy. I pray God may ever show me the wisdom to correct my faults and grant me the strength to ever glorify Him in deed and word.

I view this magnanimous and obliging gesture of yours, Mr. President, as a mandate, for through this event, you once again remind me of the unfinished task which lies ahead: the reunion of all Christians into the one holy, catholic, and apostolic church that may serve and save the world; the restoration of the image of God in man by our renewed and concerted effort to reinstate respect for human dignity and justice; the spiritual reawakening of our society in the face of the ugly realities of today, which may lead us to the recapturing of the modern spiritual values of Christianity; the stirring of the human soul and thought, so that it may once again attain and grasp God's truth and love, through which peace in the world may be advanced. All of these sacred causes and many more place formidable demands upon me and upon all of us.

We who are privileged to share this great moment with you, Mr. President and Mrs. Carter, will ever treasure the beauty and meaningfulness of it. From the depths of my heart, I thank you, Mr. President, and your beloved wife, our First Lady, Rosalynn.

And on behalf of all of us, please accept, Mr. President, Mrs. Carter, our fervent prayer. May God, our Father, grant you your heart's desire and crown all your plans for our country and the world with triumphant success.

NOTE: The President spoke at 4:36 p.m. in the East Room at the White House.

Energy Legislation

Statement by the White House Press Secretary on Congressional Actions.
September 19, 1979

Last night and this morning, there have been two very encouraging actions on the Hill on energy.

The Senate Energy Committee has approved, by substantial bipartisan margins, amendments that give them now an energy mobilization bill that is very close

to the proposals the President sent up and which we are very happy with. The President asked that I convey publicly his appreciation to the leadership shown in that committee by the chairman, Senator Jackson, also to the leadership and hard work from Senator Johnston of Louisiana, and his appreciation for the bipartisan support for this legislation.

In addition, the Conference Committee on Rationing—although at my last check they had not quite finished their work; there were still some issues to be resolved—appears to be well on their way to a good and acceptable rationing bill. We expect that that progress will continue and that the result will be a good rationing bill.

NOTE: Press Secretary Jody Powell spoke at 2:45 p.m. at his regular daily briefing in the Briefing Room at the White House.

Environmental Protection Agency

Nomination of Inez Smith Reid To Be Inspector General.   September 19, 1979

The President today announced that he will nominate Inez Smith Reid, of New York City, to be Inspector General of the Environmental Protection Agency.

Reid is Deputy General Counsel for Regulation Review at the Department of Health, Education, and Welfare.

She was born April 7, 1937, in New Orleans. She received a B.A. from Tufts University in 1959, an LL.B. from Yale University in 1962, an M.A. in political science from the University of California at Los Angeles in 1963, and a Ph. D. from Columbia University in 1968.

In 1963–64 Reid was a lecturer in criminal law at the École Nationale de Droit et d'Administration in Congo-Kinshasa. In 1964–65 she was an assistant professor of African studies and political science at the State University of New York at New Paltz. In 1965–66 she was a lecturer in political science at Hunter College in New York.

From 1966 to 1971, Reid was on the faculty at Brooklyn College, moving from instructor to associate professor of political science. She has been on the faculty of Barnard College, Columbia University, since 1971 and was on leave in 1972 and from 1976 to 1979.

From 1972 to 1976, she practiced law in New York City. From 1976 to 1977, she was general counsel of the New York State Executive Department, State Division for Youth. She has been Deputy General Counsel of HEW since 1977.

Peace Corps

Nomination of William G. Sykes To Be Deputy Director.   September 19, 1979

The President today announced that he will nominate William G. Sykes, of Baltimore, Md., to be Deputy Director of the Peace Corps. He would replace Thomas Houser, resigned.

Sykes is deputy secretary of the Maryland Department of Human Resources.

He was born December 5, 1926, in Halifax, Va. He received a B.S. from Hampton Institute in 1956 and an M.S.W. from Howard University in 1962. He served in the U.S. Army from 1956 to 1957.

From 1957 to 1960, Sykes was a caseworker for the city of Baltimore, and from 1960 to 1961, he was a probation officer for the criminal division of the Supreme Bench of Baltimore. From 1961 to 1964, he was a school social worker for the Baltimore City Department of Education.

From 1964 to 1966, Sykes was project supervisor for the Baltimore Youth Services Project of the National Committee for Children and Youth. From 1966 to 1967, he was training director for the National Committee for Children and Youth. He was chief social worker for the Baltimore City Health Department in 1967 and 1968.

Sykes was with the Baltimore Model Cities Agency from 1968 to 1973, as health coordinator, acting director, and then director. From 1973 to 1975, he was assistant to the mayor of Baltimore and director of the mayor's Office of Human Resources. He has been deputy secretary of the Maryland Department of Human Resources since 1975.

Senior Executive Service

Memorandum From the President. September 19, 1979

Memorandum for the Heads of Departments and Agencies

Subject: The Selection and Development of the Senior Executive Service

The Senior Executive Service, the keystone of the Civil Service Reform Act, was inaugurated on July 13. The SES offers one of the most promising avenues for improving the management of the Federal government. I know that you share my satisfaction and pleasure that over 96 percent of those eligible to join the Senior Executive Service did so. It is essential that we take advantage of this demonstration of confidence in the Service and maintain the momentum which it has created.

I know that you will take a continuing interest in the SES and in the development of those who will join the Service in the future. One of the most important ways of accomplishing this is by establishing a strong Executive Resources Board in your organization to oversee the administration of the Senior Executive Service. This Board will also direct executive development systems to identify and train candidates for future membership in the SES.

The people who serve on these Boards hold the key to the future of the SES. It is imperative that you impress upon the Chairperson and members of your Executive Resources Board the importance this Administration places upon executive selection and development.

The Office of Personnel Management has established criteria for executive selection and development programs. I believe these criteria provide the flexibility you need to devise a system which meets the specific characteristics and needs of your organization. Central to every program must be the identification and selection, in advance, of top performers who have executive potential and whose talents should be developed to enable them to take top-level responsibilities. This will involve both wide competition and a very careful selection for the executive development programs required by the Reform Act. I also want to make certain that women, the handicapped, and members of minority groups are given full consideration when selections are made.

We have the opportunity, now, to establish systems that will provide an effective, motivated, and exemplary corps of career executives to serve the needs of our Nation in the years to come. There are no more important actions we can take to provide long-term benefit to Government and more efficient delivery of services to the public.

JIMMY CARTER

National Meals on Wheels Week, 1979

Proclamation 4689.   September 19, 1979

By the President of the United States of America

A Proclamation

This year marks the twenty-fifth anniversary of the Meals on Wheels programs which make nutritious food available to aged and ailing persons in their homes. Since 1954, thousands of volunteers in these programs have made it possible for many of the Nation's elderly to reside at home rather than in institutions and to live healthier, happier and more independent lives.

In recognition of the outstanding contributions of these volunteers, the Congress, by House Joint Resolution 367, has designated the week beginning September 16, 1979, as National Meals on Wheels Week.

Now, THEREFORE, I, JIMMY CARTER, President of the United States of America, do hereby proclaim the week of September 16 through September 22, 1979, as National Meals on Wheels Week.

In accord with the congressional resolution, I invite the Governors of the several States, the chief officials of local governments and the people of the United States to observe this period with appropriate ceremonies and activities.

IN WITNESS WHEREOF, I have hereunto set my hand this nineteenth day of September, in the year of our Lord nineteen hundred seventy-nine, and of the Independence of the United States of America the two hundred and fourth.

JIMMY CARTER

[Filed with the Office of the Federal Register, 4:44 p.m., September 19, 1979]

National Day of Prayer, 1979

Proclamation 4690.   September 19, 1979

By the President of the United States of America

A Proclamation

The history of our country is a history of triumph over adversity. Time after time, we have overcome threats from within and without. Over the generations, wars, depressions, and internal differences and bigotry in various forms have struck at the foundations of our society. As we have met these challenges together, the bonds between us as Americans have grown stronger.

We endure and remain a land of hope because of the basic goodness and strength of our people and because the God of us all has shown us His favor.

The decisions we make today on arms, economics, social justice and global responsibilities echo into the future of the world. We accept our responsibilities and make our choices with all the will and determination at our command, but always in the full knowledge that we are finally in the hands of God. In the words of the prophet Zechariah, "Not by might, not by power but by my spirit saith the Lord of Hosts." (4:6)

Recognizing this, the Congress by joint resolution approved April 17, 1952 (36 U.S.C. 185; 66 Stat. 64) has called upon the President to set aside a suitable day each year as a National Day of Prayer.

Now, Therefore, I, Jimmy Carter, President of the United States of America, do hereby proclaim Wednesday, October 3, 1979, as a National Day of Prayer. I ask all Americans to join with me on that day to recommit ourselves to God, to each other and to the towering ideals of truth, justice, fairness, brotherhood, and love which our Nation has cherished and

protected. Let us pray for the will and wisdom to create a world in which all people can live with each other in peace. Let us pray that careful stewardship of today's opportunities will protect and enlarge the inheritance of liberty and security we give our children.

In Witness Whereof, I have hereunto set my hand this nineteenth day of September, in the year of our Lord nineteen hundred seventy-nine, and of the Independence of the United States of America the two hundred and fourth.

Jimmy Carter

[Filed with the Office of the Federal Register, 4:46 p.m., September 19, 1979]

National School Lunch Week, 1979

Proclamation 4691.   September 20, 1979

By the President of the United States of America

A Proclamation

Active, growing youngsters need good food to do well in school. And since the eating habits established in childhood affect later tastes and practices, school meals also provide a unique opportunity to understand and enjoy good nutrition. The National School Lunch Program, established in 1946, now provides nourishing lunches to 26 million school children each school day. The United States Department of Agriculture sets nutritional standards to these meals but the quality and appeal of school lunches depend on another vital ingredient: people who care.

Therefore, I want to pay special tribute to the thousands of people—parents, teachers, principals, school food service workers, State and local officials—who make the school lunch program work in

94,000 schools across the country. They determine whether the cafeteria is a pleasant and welcoming place, whether the food served is actually eaten, whether children come to think of good nutrition as punishment or pleasure.

In recognition of the School Lunch Program's contribution to America's youth, the Congress, by a joint resolution of October 9, 1962 (76 Stat. 779; 36 U.S.C. 168), has designated the week beginning the second Sunday of October in each year as National School Lunch Week, and has requested the President to issue annually a proclamation calling for its appropriate observance.

Now, THEREFORE, I, JIMMY CARTER, President of the United States of America, do hereby urge the people of the United States to observe the week of October 14, 1979, as National School Lunch Week and give special attention to activities that will promote good nutrition for America's youth.

IN WITNESS WHEREOF, I have hereunto set my hand this twentieth day of September, in the year of our Lord nineteen hundred seventy-nine, and of the Independence of the United States of America the two hundred and fourth.

JIMMY CARTER

[Filed with the Office of the Federal Register, 2:29 p.m., September 20, 1979]

Emergency Board To Investigate a Railway Labor Dispute

Remarks Announcing Establishment of the Board.   September 20, 1979

I have an announcement to make about the Rock Island Railroad.

I'm today appointing an emergency board, under the Railway Labor Act, to intervene in the labor dispute that has crippled the Rock Island Railroad since August 27.

This strike is having a severe, adverse economic effect on farmers throughout the Central United States. Processing mills for grain are already shutting down, and within 2 weeks the marketing of what promises to be a record grain crop could be genuinely threatened. If the grain does not begin to move on schedule with the harvest, not only would there be economic loss to the farmers and an employment loss in the grain-processing industry, but ultimately the consumers would be affected by higher food prices as well.

The purpose of this action is to get the trains rolling again in a matter of days and to start moving grain that has already been piling up in the large areas of the Midwest served by the Rock Island Railroad line.

Because the Rock Island is critically short of cash, it's probable that the railroad will not be able to restore service on its own, even with this action. To meet that difficulty, I'm asking the Interstate Commerce Commission to take the steps needed to permit other railroads to employ Rock Island employees and workers to maintain service.

I'm taking these strong actions, because we absolutely must mobilize all our transportation resources for the movement of grain during this period of record-breaking grain harvests and also record-breaking demands for grain exports. Not only our farmers but also the consumers of grain—both here within our own country and, indeed, throughout the world—simply must be protected.

I've acted because the normal process for settling labor disputes has broken down, primarily as a result of the likelihood that Rock Island will not be able to reorient its services because of financial difficulties. And we must restore this service of financial support if a settlement is to be reached and carried out.

As an additional step, I directed the Secretaries of Transportation, Labor, and Agriculture to work closely with the State officials and also with the Chairman of the Interstate Commerce Commission in solving the inevitable day-to-day problems involving safety and operation of the railroad, in getting this Rock Island line rolling again across the grain belt.

We must now move quickly beyond this immediate problem and work to restore all our Nation's rail services to a high degree of efficiency and financial stability.

The current situation on the Rock Island is symptomatic of the problems that confront the entire United States rail industry. To prevent further problems such as those I've confronted with the Rock Island, I call upon the Congress to pass without delay the rail deregulation proposal to break the strangulation of outmoded, unnecessary economic regulations, which will help the industry to generate the revenues it needs and to maintain and to improve its services. Only by such fundamental action can we avoid further bankruptcies and further dislocations in our rail industry throughout the country.

Such a deregulation reform bill will be a victory for the hard-pressed rail industry, for the shipping and the consuming public, and for the taxpayers, who are increasingly having to subsidize the rail industry.

Now I'd like to ask Neil Goldschmidt and the other officials with me on the stage to answer questions from you. And I'm sure that the people in the Midwest will be well served by this action.

NOTE: The President spoke at 1:30 p.m. to reporters assembled in the Briefing Room at the White House.

Following the President's remarks, Secretary of Transportation Neil Goldschmidt and other administration officials held a news conference on the labor dispute.

Emergency Board To Investigate a Railway Labor Dispute

Executive Order 12159.   September 20, 1979

CREATING AN EMERGENCY BOARD TO INVESTIGATE DISPUTES BETWEEN THE CHICAGO, ROCK ISLAND, PACIFIC RAILROAD & PEORIA TERMINAL COMPANY AND BROTHERHOOD OF RAILWAY, AIRLINE & STEAMSHIP CLERKS, FREIGHT HANDLERS, EXPRESS AND STATION EMPLOYEES; AND THE UNITED TRANSPORTATION UNION

Disputes exist between the Chicago, Rock Island, Pacific Railroad & Peoria Terminal Company and certain of its employees represented by both the Brotherhood of Railway, Airline & Steamship Clerks, Freight Handlers, Express and Station Employees; and the United Transportation Union.

These disputes have not heretofore been adjusted under the provisions of the Railway Labor Act, as amended; and

These disputes in the judgment of the National Mediation Board threaten substantially to interrupt interstate commerce to a degree such as to deprive a section of the country of essential transportation service:

Now, THEREFORE, by the authority vested in me by Section 10 of the Railway Labor Act, as amended (45 U.S.C. 160), it is hereby ordered as follows:

1–101. *Establishment of Board.* There is established a board of three members to be appointed by the President to investigate these disputes. No member of the board shall be pecuniarily or otherwise interested in any organization of railroad employees or any carrier.

1–102. *Report.* The board shall report its finding to the President with respect to these disputes within 30 days from the date of this Order.

1–103. *Maintaining Conditions.* As provided by Section 10 of the Railway Labor Act, as amended, from this date and for 30 days after the board has made its report to the President, no change, except by agreement, shall be made by the Chicago, Rock Island, Pacific Railroad & Peoria Terminal Company, or by its employees, in the conditions out of which these disputes arose.

JIMMY CARTER

The White House,
    September 20, 1979.

[Filed with the Office of the Federal Register,
    2:52 p.m., September 20, 1979]

Emergency Board To Investigate a Railway Labor Dispute

Appointment of the Membership.
September 20, 1979

The President today announced the appointment of the three members of the Emergency Board to investigate the Chicago, Rock Island, Pacific Railroad & Peoria Terminal Company labor dispute. They are:

James J. Reynolds, of Washington, D.C., to serve as Chairman of the Emergency Board. Reynolds was president of the American Institute of Merchant Shipping until his retirement in 1978. He served as Assistant Secretary of Labor and Under Secretary of Labor in the Kennedy-Johnson administrations. He has also served as a member of the National Labor Relations Board.

Ida Klaus, of New York City, an arbitrator and mediator with more than 40 years' experience in the labor relations field. She has served as special arbitrator under the U.S. Steel Agreement since 1975. She has also served as Solicitor for the National Labor Relations Board and,

from 1962 to 1975, as executive director of the Office of Labor Relations and Collective Bargaining of the New York City Board of Education.

Nicholas H. Zumas, of Washington, D.C., an attorney and arbitrator who has been in private practice since 1965. He is a member of the District of Columbia Board of Labor Relations. He has also served as counsel for the House Special Subcommittee on Education, Committee on Education and Labor, and assistant to the Under Secretary of Health, Education, and Welfare.

Department of State

Nomination of Roberts Bishop Owen To Be Legal Adviser. September 20, 1979

The President today announced that he will nominate Roberts Bishop Owen, of Washington, D.C., to be Legal Adviser of the Department of State. He would replace Herbert J. Hansell, resigned. Owen is a partner in the law firm of Covington & Burling.

He was born February 11, 1926, in Boston, Mass. He received a B.A. in 1948 and an LL.B. in 1951 from Harvard University, and a C.L.S. from Cambridge University in 1952. He served in the U.S. Navy from 1943 to 1946. Owen has been with Covington & Burling since 1952.

President's Advisory Committee for Women

Appointment of Four Members.
September 20, 1979

The President today announced the appointment of four persons as members of

1697

the President's Advisory Committee for Women. They are:

JACK T. CONWAY, senior vice president of United Way of America, former president of Common Cause and the Center for Community Change, and former executive director of the American Federation of State, County and Municipal Employees;

CHARLES GUERRIER, executive director of the Women's Law Fund in Cleveland, Ohio, and a member of the board of trustees of the Women's Resource and Policy Development Center in Columbus, Ohio;

NANCY A. HUMPHREYS, president of the National Association of Social Workers and an assistant professor at the Graduate School of Social Work at Rutgers University;

ESTELLE RAMEY, professor and director of graduate studies at the School of Medicine, Georgetown University, and a nationally known lecturer on women's health issues.

American Education Week, 1979

Proclamation 4692. September 20, 1979

By the President of the United States of America

A Proclamation

Our nation has come a long way toward realizing the Founders' dream of having an educated electorate, so that all our people might share fully in freedom, justice and opportunity. In this International Year of the Child, as we join with other nations to understand and meet the needs of children around the world, we are especially aware of the importance of education.

The theme of this year's American Education Week, "Teach All the Children", acknowledges both our goal and what must be done to accomplish it. The responsibility for educating our children lies not just with the schools, but with parents and communities as well.

Every American has a responsibility to make sure that our children do not merely pass through school systems, but actually receive the education they need. To do that, we must find ways to reach every child—regardless of race, sex, religion, national origin or economic background, and responding to particular needs because of physical or mental handicaps or special talents. We must respect and nourish each child's unique potential.

NOW, THEREFORE, I, JIMMY CARTER, President of the United States of America, do hereby designate the week beginning November 11, 1979, as American Education Week.

I ask for the support of every American in helping to create challenging educational opportunities that will help develop the diverse abilities of children, and to help nurture in each a sense of excellence and respect for all mankind.

I urge individuals and groups to work with schools in their communities to ensure that they are able to "Teach All the Children" well.

IN WITNESS WHEREOF, I have hereunto set my hand this twentieth day of September, in the year of our Lord nineteen hundred and seventy-nine, and of the Independence of the United States of America the two hundred and fourth.

JIMMY CARTER

[Filed with the Office of the Federal Register, 10:35 a.m., September 21, 1979]

Panama Canal Treaties

White House Statement on Disapproval of Implementing Legislation by the House of Representatives. September 20, 1979

The President deeply regrets that the House of Representatives did not adopt the legislation proposed by the House-Senate conference to provide for the operation of the Panama Canal under the treaties that enter into force on October 1. We understand that the new conference will meet again soon, possibly as early as tomorrow.

The administration will make every effort to obtain the necessary legislation. The United States must have legislative authority by October 1 to exercise our rights to operate the canal. It is inconceivable that the Congress would allow the Panama Canal to be closed even for a short time.

The President is confident that the Government of Panama will respond to this development with the dignity and restraint which has characterized it during the long deliberations on the canal treaties and the implementing legislation in the Congress.

Regulatory Reform of the Telecommunications Industry

Message to the Congress.   *September 21, 1979*

To the Congress of the United States:

I am today announcing my support for efforts in Congress to reform the regulation of telecommunications. Legislation is needed to eliminate needless regulatory controls, encourage competition and innovation, and keep telephone service affordable throughout the country.

Regulatory reform is one of my highest national priorities. Where the marketplace can work, we must get the government out of making marketplace decisions. Where regulation is needed, we must ensure it is well managed.

Last year the Administration and Congress worked together to deregulate airlines, introducing competition that already has saved over $2.5 billion for passengers while increasing air travel and airline revenues. This year we have submitted to Congress far-reaching regulatory reform proposals affecting trucking, railroads, banking, drugs, and regulatory procedures.

The 45-year-old regulatory charter for telecommunications also needs revisions. This industry can provide more and better services while cutting many costs. It can help fight inflation and promote growth. We cannot afford to have this progress frustrated by unwarranted regulation. We must ensure that competitors fight through their salesmen in the marketplace rather than through their lawyers in government hearings.

Telecommunications is crucial to our society. This industry—which includes the telephone companies and the firms which provide satellite communications, computer links, and other specialized services—has more than one million employees and annual revenues of over $50 billion. The availability of nationwide, high-quality communications is vital to the economy, national security, and the quality of our lives. Sophisticated new communications systems are providing better services, lower costs, and improved productivity in an economy that depends more and more on information transfers.

Telecommunications firms are regulated by the Federal Communications Commission under the Communications Act of 1934. That Act was designed at a time when technology made monopoly the logical structure for telecommunications. That system, assisted by the rural telephone loan program, has nearly achieved the national goal of universal service—96 percent of all households and nearly all businesses have telephone service.

Two critical changes have occurred since 1934. First, there have been extraordinary technological advances. In addition to the wired network, the telephone companies and new, competing firms are using satellites, lasers, microwaves, and

1699

miniature computers to provide more and more systems and services for business and homes. The new technology makes it possible to hold meetings, transmit messages, do research, bank, shop and receive a widening variety of information and entertainment—all through electronics. In the process, the technology has invalidated the old assumption that all aspects of telecommunications service are natural monopolies. Second, FCC and court actions over the last decade opened portions of the industry to competition. Despite these far-reaching developments, the statutory framework has remained unchanged, and regulatory changes have come slowly.

Outmoded regulatory controls and slow procedures are harming new competitors, established telephone companies, and the users of telephone and other telecommunications services. Regulatory delays and uncertainties discourage firms from entering new markets and offering new services. In a dynamic industry, these delays can mean that the product or service offered is obsolete by the time the regulatory proceeding ends. Innovation is hobbled by uncertainty and by the need to respond to artificial regulatory conditions instead of real consumer demand.

Consumers are the final beneficiaries of competition, through lower prices and wider choices. The competition already allowed in the telecommunications industry is producing benefits. For example, the market for telephone sets and other terminal equipment recently was opened to competition. Consumers now can shop around for good prices, choose from a wide variety of products, and decide whether to buy or lease. Competition is also providing more choices among sophisticated, new services, such as those that combine data processing and transmission.

The choice is clear. Competition is a fact of life in this industry. It cannot and should not be rolled back, and we should not allow it to continue developing haphazardly. That approach means delay and uncertainty, and it poses a long-run danger to the health of our telecommunications system. Instead, we need both legislation and well-planned action at the FCC. The task is to create a structure that will give consumers the benefits of competition and deregulation wherever they make sense while keeping telephone service reliable and affordable.

The FCC under Chairman Charles Ferris is working hard on this effort, but the Act itself needs change. The House and Senate Communications Subcommittees are now working on legislation to meet this challenge. I urge Congress to press forward and enact a bill that incorporates the following basic principles:

• *Competition should be encouraged and fully competitive markets should be deregulated.* The bill should set a policy of encouraging competition wherever it is workable and of eliminating needless regulation. Deregulation makes sense for competitive markets, such as terminal equipment, and for small firms that cannot dominate markets. Many communications and equipment offerings should be deregulated now, and legislation is needed to avoid endless litigation over the FCC's authority to do so. Of course, some communications markets, such as the local exchange, may remain regulated monopolies indefinitely. The legislation should not, however, preclude competition in any market.

As the industry moves toward competition and deregulation, some continued controls will be needed because one firm dominates the telecommunications industry and others have local monopolies. Firms should be prevented from using monopoly power and revenues in some markets to gain advantage over competitors in others. Any monopoly facilities used in providing competitive services should be available to all competitors at the same rates and terms. In addition, changes in companies' structures will be needed, such as mandating fully separate subsidiaries. Where such changes are made, the employment, pension, and union rights of the employees should be protected.

• *Restrictions based on out-of-date market divisions should be removed.* The line between telecommunications and data processing has become blurred; new equipment and services involve both. Existing controls based on this distinction have produced years of regulatory proceedings and are delaying the use of new technologies. In addition, the rules that divide some communications services between domestic and international companies are outmoded and need change. These problems should be solved through open competition by all, without extending the scope of regulation. To ensure fair competition, creation of fully separate subsidiaries, including separate accounts and marketing, will be needed, and some of the restrictions on international service will have to be removed gradually.

• *Universal availability of basic telephone service at affordable rates must be maintained.* Overall long-distance revenues currently contribute to keeping some local and toll rates affordable. This is done through complex accounting processes largely determined by the telephone industry. Because of the developments of the last decade, this system is in trouble. The industry is considering changing it in order to match the new competitors' rates, and that could mean significant rate increases in some rural areas.

These are important public policy decisions and should not be left solely to the industry. We need a new system, which would be administered openly by public officials. The legislation should provide for a charge on all long-distance services—including those of the new competitors—which use local exchanges. This "access charge" would cover the actual cost of using local facilities, provide support for local service, and finance protection for rural residents against large toll rate increases.

These provisions should be drawn to encourage the FCC, state regulators and the telephone companies to take long-term steps to support universal service. Such steps include prices based on actual use; low "lifeline" rates for basic service; and use of new technologies that can provide low-cost service over long distances.

In addition, the rural telephone companies and cooperatives should be encouraged to help extend to rural Americans the benefits of all the new communications technologies. As my policy statement on rural communications said last January, the current rules that restrict rural telephone companies from offering cable TV services should be removed.

• *Appropriate jurisdictional boundaries should be set.* The current boundary between Federal and state regulatory jurisdictions—the state line—is inconsistent with technological realities. The bill should set new, clear boundaries: service within local exchanges should be regulated by the states, while service between exchanges should be under Federal control.

• *The FCC should be given the authority to develop efficient means of assigning non-broadcast frequencies.* Many of the new telecommunications systems use radio frequencies, such as satellite links, microwaves, and mobile radio. The FCC currently assigns many of these frequencies through "comparative hearings" which impose months or years of delay and waste FCC resources. Under the current system, once a frequency is assigned there is no incentive to use it efficiently. That is a problem because growing numbers of users, here and abroad, are crowding the limited space in the radio spectrum.

We need assignment systems that are fast, flexible, and that provide incentives to use the spectrum efficiently. The legislation should give the FCC authority to design new procedures which use marketplace forces, such as auctions, leasing, and re-sale. These procedures will help ensure that the spectrum is used sensibly, just as similar tools are employed for oil leases and other limited natural resources.

• *The antitrust laws should remain applicable as before.* It should be explicit that the legislation is neutral as to pending and any future litigation.

• *The technical quality of the telecommunications network should be protected.* The legislation should not impede cooperation between the carriers to plan and manage national systems. To provide for technical quality, national security, and·emergency preparedness needs, the FCC should retain authority to set technical standards and ensure that facilities are capable of interconnection where appropriate.

• *Public participation in regulatory decision making should be encouraged.* Effective participation by the users of telecommunications services will help the FCC and state regulators make their difficult decisions. Such involvement should be encouraged through open proceedings and by providing funding for groups that

could not otherwise afford to participate and that represent an important interest that would not otherwise be heard.

————

I congratulate Chairman Lionel Van Deerlin of the House Communications Subcommittee and Chairmen Howard Cannon and Ernest Hollings of the Senate Commerce Committee and the Communications Subcommittee and their colleagues for the extensive and informative hearings they have held and the thoughtful bills they have introduced covering the issues I have outlined and other important communications matters. My Administration will continue to provide assistance on specific provisions. I urge Congress to move forward with this important effort.

JIMMY CARTER

The White House,
    September 21, 1979.

Interstate Commerce Commission

Nomination of Reginald E. Gilliam, Jr., To Be a Member.   September 21, 1979

The President today announced his intention to nominate Reginald E. Gilliam, Jr., to be a member of the Interstate Commerce Commission.

Gilliam is legislative assistant to Senator John Glenn.

He was born December 29, 1944, in New York City. He received an A.B. from Lincoln University in 1965 and a J.D. from Harvard Law School in 1968.

From 1968 to 1969, Gilliam was a staff attorney in Utica, N.Y. He was an assistant professor at the State University of New York in Albany, N.Y., from 1969 to 1972. From 1972 to 1975, he was assistant dean of Williams College. He has been legislative assistant to Senator Glenn since 1975.

United States-Mexico Agreement on Natural Gas

Remarks Announcing the Framework for an Agreement.   September 21, 1979

I'm pleased to announce that we have just reached an agreement with the Government of Mexico which will permit the purchase of Mexican natural gas by United States buyers.

This is a significant step toward providing a new source of energy supplies for our country. Just as important, the agreement is a breakthrough in building the relationship of equity and mutual respect which we seek with the government and the people of our great southern neighbor.

Under the terms of this agreement, the United States purchasers will be able to buy 300 million cubic feet of natural gas each day. This gas will be in excess of Mexico's national demand and will meet our own needs which are not covered by our present supplies. The price is a fair one for both countries.

This natural gas agreement represents an important first step toward a deeper and broader relationship, and it will be of great benefit both to the people of Mexico and to the people of our own country.

I've expressed to President López Portillo today my pleasure that we've reached an understanding with respect to natural gas sales and that we will have a chance to discuss more important issues—other important issues when we meet in Washington next week.

Thank you very much.

NOTE: The President spoke at 3:58 p.m. to reporters assembled in the Briefing Room at the White House.

United States-Mexico Agreement on Natural Gas

Joint Announcement.   September 21, 1979

The Governments of Mexico and the United States of America have reached an understanding on a framework for the sale of 300 million cubic feet per day of natural gas by Petroleos Méxicanos, the Mexican State Oil Company, to U.S. purchasers.

Pursuant to the understanding reached, the Governments of the United States of America and the Mexican States have agreed to authorize and support as a matter of policy commercial transactions which are within the following framework:

—The initial volume of natural gas deliveries will be 300 million cubic feet per day, commencing as soon as contracts are signed, regulatory approvals obtained, and gas is available for delivery.

—The initial price will be $3.625/million btu as of January 1, 1980. This initial price is subject to reconsideration prior to January 1, 1980, if the price for natural gas from comparable sources exceeds that amount prior to said date.

—The arrangement shall continue without limitation subject to the understanding that the gas to be supplied is surplus associated gas in excess of Mexican national demand, that the gas being purchased is to meet U.S. needs not covered from other sources, and that therefore the contractual provisions will provide that either nation, on the basis of its own determination of its national interest, taking into account its domestic supply and demand for natural gas, may cause the termination of the arrangement upon 180 days notice to the other nation.

—The initial price will be adjusted quarterly by the same percentage as the change in world crude oil prices pursuant to a specific formula to be agreed upon by the contracting parties.

The way is now clear for the negotiation of commercial contracts between Petroleos Méxicanos and U.S. purchasers on terms which both governments regard as mutually beneficial. Such contracts will be subject to appropriate governmental approvals in each Country.

The two governments will review from time to time the terms of this arrangement as well as other energy issues of mutual interest.

Advisory Council on Historic Preservation

Appointment of Mrs. S. Henry Edmunds as a Member. September 21, 1979

The President today announced the appointment of Mrs. S. Henry Edmunds, of Charleston, S.C., as a member of the Advisory Council on Historic Preservation.

Edmunds is executive director of the Historic Charleston Foundation and recipient of the highest award of the National Trust for Historic Preservation for her work in preservation and restoration in Charleston.

Digest of Other White House Announcements

The following listing includes the President's public schedule and other items of general interest announced by the White House Press Office and not included elsewhere in this issue.

September 17

The President returned to the White House from Camp David, Md.

The President participated in a meeting of the Policy Review Committee at the White House and conducted a National Security Council review of the situation concerning Soviet troops in Cuba.

The President met at the White House with:

—Zbigniew Brzezinski, Assistant to the President for National Security Affairs;
—Vice President Walter F. Mondale;
—a group of Senators to discuss energy.

The President participated in a briefing by administration officials on the strategic arms limitation treaty given for community leaders in the East Room at the White House.

The President has declared a major disaster for the Virgin Islands of the United States as a result of Hurricane David and Tropical Storm Frederic during the period of August 29 through September 7, which caused extensive public and private property damage.

The President transmitted to the Congress the second annual report on the Status of Health Information and Health Promotion.

September 18

The President met at the White House with:

—Dr. Brzezinski;
—the Democratic congressional leadership;
—Frank B. Moore, Assistant to the President for Congressional Liaison.

September 19

The President met at the White House with:

—Vice President Mondale, Secretary of Agriculture Bob Bergland, Secretary of Commerce Juanita M. Kreps, Secretary of Health, Education, and Welfare Patricia R. Harris, Secretary of the Interior Cecil D. Andrus, Secretary of Transportation Neil Goldschmidt, James T. McIntyre, Jr., Director of the Office of Management and Budget, Stuart E. Eizenstat, Assistant to the President for Domestic Affairs and Policy, and Jack H. Watson, Jr., Assistant to the President for Intergovernmental Affairs, to discuss domestic policies;

—Dr. Brzezinski;

—Mr. Moore;

—Mrs. Carter, for lunch.

In a ceremony in the Oval Office, the President presented the Boy of the Year Award to Danny Rolett, 16, of Little Rock, Ark. Also attending the ceremony were representatives of the Boys Club, which sponsors the award.

September 20

The President met at the White House with:

—Dr. Brzezinski;

—a bipartisan group of Senators and Representatives to discuss the presence of Soviet troops in Cuba;

—Senator Pete V. Domenici of New Mexico;

—Mr. Moore;

—members of the United Democrats of Congress.

The President participated in a briefing by administration officials for leaders of the National Conference of State Legislatures held in Room 450 of the Old Executive Office Building.

The President transmitted to the Congress the 1978 Report to the President on Disease Control Programs and the Second Annual Report on the Administration of the National Sickle Cell Anemia, Cooley's Anemia, Tay-Sachs, and Genetic Diseases Act.

The President announced the reappointment of Douglas Fraser, president of the United Auto Workers, and Lloyd McBride, president of the United Steelworkers, as members of the Advisory Committee for Trade Negotiations for 2-year terms.

September 21

The President met at the White House with:

—Dr. Brzezinski;

—Vice President Mondale, Secretary of State Cyrus R. Vance, Secretary of Defense Harold Brown, Hamilton Jordan, Assistant to the President, Hedley W. Donovan, Senior Adviser to the President, and Dr. Brzezinski;

—Mr. Moore;

—Charles L. Schultze, Chairman of the Council of Economic Advisers;

—Gov. Brendan Byrne of New Jersey, chairman, and members of the National Citizens' Coalition for the Windfall Profits Tax;

—a group of editors and broadcasters (transcript will be printed next week).

NOMINATIONS SUBMITTED TO THE SENATE

The following list does not include promotions of members of the Uniformed Services, nominations to the Service Academies, or nominations of Foreign Service officers.

Submitted September 17, 1979

DONALD R. NORLAND, of New Hampshire, a Foreign Service officer of Class one, to be Ambassador Extraordinary and Plenipotentiary of the United States of America to the Republic of Chad.

RONALD P. LAURENT, of Illinois, to be President, Government National Mortgage Association, vice John Howard Dalton, resigned.

NOMINATIONS—Continued

Submitted September 18, 1979

The following-named persons to be members of the Federal Council on the Aging for the terms indicated:

For terms expiring June 5, 1981

CYRIL HILARY CARPENTER, of Minnesota, vice Mrs. John William Devereux, term expired.

JOHN B. MARTIN, of Maryland (reappointment).

MARY CROWLEY MULVEY, of Rhode Island, vice Harry Holland, term expired.

JEAN JONES PERDUE, of Florida, vice Nat T. Winston, Jr., term expired.

For a term expiring June 5, 1982

AARON E. HENRY, of Mississippi, vice Frell M. Owl, term expired.

Submitted September 20, 1979

WILLIAM G. SYKES, of Maryland, to be Deputy Director of the Peace Corps, vice Thomas J. Houser.

INEZ SMITH REID, of New York, to be Inspector General, Environmental Protection Agency (new position).

ROBERTS BISHOP OWEN, of the District of Columbia, to be Legal Adviser of the Department of State.

Submitted September 21, 1979

ROBERT S. STRAUSS, of Texas, for the rank of Ambassador during the tenure of his service as Personal Representative of the President of the United States of America.

JAMES F. LEONARD, of New York, for the rank of Ambassador during the tenure of his service as Chief of the United States Mission to the Middle East Peace Negotiations.

CHECKLIST OF WHITE HOUSE PRESS RELEASES

The following listing contains releases of the White House Press Office which are not included in this issue.

Released September 17, 1979

News conference: on his review of the Department of Energy's preliminary report on oil industry supplies—by Stuart E. Eizenstat, Assistant to the President for Domestic Affairs and Policy

CHECKLIST—Continued

Released September 17—Continued

Advance text: remarks to the World Jewish Congress in New York City—by Zbigniew Brzezinski, Assistant to the President for National Security Affairs

Released September 20, 1979

News conference: on the Rock Island railway labor dispute—by Secretary of Transportation Neil Goldschmidt

Released September 21, 1979

News conference: on regulatory reform of the telecommunications industry—by Alfred E. Kahn, Advisor to the President on Inflation; Richard Neustadt, Assistant Director, Domestic Policy Staff; Dale Hatfield, Associate Administrator for Policy Analysis Development, National Telecommunications and Information Administration, Department of Commerce; and Mr. Eizenstat

News conference: on the United States-Mexico agreement on natural gas—by Warren M. Christopher, Deputy Secretary of State; Julius L. Katz, Assistant Secretary of State for Economic and Business Affairs; Leslie Goldman, Deputy Assistant Secretary of Energy for Policy and Evaluation; and Mr. Eizenstat

Fact sheet: United States-Mexico agreement on natural gas

ACTS APPROVED BY THE PRESIDENT

Approved September 19, 1979

H.J. Res. 367_____ Public Law 96–65
A joint resolution to authorize and request the President to proclaim the week of September 16 through 22, 1979, as "National Meals on Wheels Week".

Approved September 21, 1979

H.R. 2774_____ Public Law 96–66
An act to authorize appropriations for fiscal years 1980 and 1981 under the Arms Control and Disarmament Act, and for other purposes.

S. 109_____ Public Law 96–67
An act to amend the International Development and Food Assistance Act of 1978 and the Foreign Assistance and Related Programs Appropriations Act, 1979, by striking out certain prohibitions relating to Uganda, and for other purposes.

Interview With the President

*Remarks and a Question-and-Answer Session
With Editors and Broadcasters.
September 21, 1979*

THE PRESIDENT. I'm very glad to have you here. I believe that since I've been in the White House this is the 48th group of editors from outside Washington who've come to meet with me and Dr. Brzezinski, Jody Powell, and others, depending upon the current event emphasis of that particular week. There obviously are a broad range of responsibilities that I have to face each day with a great deal of enthusiasm and enjoyment, sometimes with some degree of concern.

ADMINISTRATION POLICIES

This has not been a good week for us in the Congress. But I had a meeting last night with about 100 Members of the Congress—of the House—concerning key issues—the Panama Canal implementation legislation, which must be passed by the 1st of October; the debt limit, which must be changed and raised by the 1st of October; and also the second budget resolution, which also must be passed if the budget process is going to be successful. And now, of course, that must be done as well.

We've had good progress recently in the evolution of our overall energy policy, concerning rationing standby authority, concerning the windfall profits tax, concerning the security corporation to develop synthetic fuels, and concerning the production board, which is designed, as you know, to—the mobilization board, as it's called—which is designed, as you know, to expedite decisions to be made concerning energy projects. This is an extremely complicated subject, multifaceted, with broad-ranging responsibilities in the House and Senate. But I think we've had good success this year and, particularly, this last week.

There's a momentum building up in the House and Senate, and it's very gratifying to me. And I think this is derived directly from an increasing interest among the American people that I and the Congress must act on energy this year. The prime responsibility that I have as President is to guarantee the security of our country, and I see our Nation directly threatened in its security by an excessive dependence on imported oil.

The House and the Senate have many other items to consider—the Senate, obviously, involving itself with consideration of SALT. The Cuban-Russian troop item has been a matter of extra concern for us the last 2 or 3 weeks, and the size of the defense budget is being negotiated with the Senators. This is just a range of subjects that we have in legislation.

In addition, as you know, it's important for me to have as good a working relationship as I possibly can with other interest groups around the country, particularly mayors, Governors, and others in positions of authority. And of course, we have a broad range of foreign policy issues that come before me literally every day.

I think the best thing that I can do at this moment is to answer your questions about any matter that might be of interest, and I'll try to answer them.

QUESTIONS

DULUTH-SUPERIOR GRAIN MILLERS STRIKE

Q. I want to ask you about the Duluth-Superior grain millers strike. I know before you started your trip down the Mississippi, you met with Governor Link and Governor Quie about the strike. A lot of people back in the Dakotas and Minnesota and northwestern Wisconsin are wondering, since you stepped into the Rock Island situation—and that was obviously a major part of grain transportation in the Midwest—wondering why similar action hasn't been taken in the Duluth-Superior strike.

Today the port director of Duluth is saying that if the strike is not settled here, maybe over the weekend or early next week, no more grain would move out of Duluth. And that's about 5 percent of the exports, and it's the third agricultural port in the country.

If you could, sir, could you characterize the differences in the situation between your intervention in the Rock Island situation and the stand you've taken as far as the grain millers in Duluth is concerned?

THE PRESIDENT. Well, there are some common features, one of the most notable of which is that I hope the both of them are rapidly settled. There are obviously some additional features, in that employers and employee negotiations are ongoing.

There are differences in law. The Federal laws relating to railways give the President special responsibility and authority to deal with the transportation interruption. And this is an act under which I have recently proposed a resolution of the issue to get the railroads moving again.

The Rock Island Railroad is on the verge of bankruptcy. And it's obvious to me that if a settlement even is reached between the owners and the employees, that the settlement is unlikely to be implemented because of an absence of funds, if I don't act.

In the Duluth elevator question, we have provided, under the law, maximum Federal assistance and participation. The Federal negotiator has been directly involved with an increasing degree of emphasis since I visited the St. Paul area, and we have seen spasmodic indications of progress. Some days we have very good reports that progress is being made, even tentative settlements having been reached; other days not.

It's inappropriate, according to the legal rulings that I have from the Attorney General and Labor Secretary and others, that the Taft-Hartley Act is legally applicable to the Duluth grain elevator strike. The security of our Nation has to be in danger. And it would be difficult to prove in court—and the burden of proof would be on us—that this one strike is, indeed, threatening the crippling of our Nation and its security state or is a danger to the health of the Nation.

But we're doing everything we can to resolve both issues. I have much more authority on the Rock Island Railroad than in the Duluth.

COAL SUPPLIES

Q. Mr. President, Glen Moyer from WOAI Radio in San Antonio, Texas. The conversion to coal is a well-known prophecy or directive of yours as a part of your national energy program.

The city of San Antonio, a couple of years ago, made that conversion and now owns and operates municipally—or owns a municipal electrical power-generating plant that is coal burned. The problem that we are facing is continuous rate increases being granted by the Interstate Commerce Commission to, particularly, the Burlington Northern Railroad. Since January their price increases have increased by 18 percent. In fact, just this morning the Commission upheld yet another rate increase that now raises the price more than $19 a ton to get coal from Wyoming to San Antonio. The city has even looked at the possibility of importing from overseas, coal from Australia, at a more economical rate than we could use American coal.

I have somewhat of a two-part question, if I might. First of all, does your administration have any plans for getting involved or intervening in any way in that pricing situation? And if not, how then can the administration continue to urge the conversion to coal in order to limit our need for oil imports, which you, a few moments ago, said is in some ways a threat to our security?

THE PRESIDENT. We're doing all we can, through legislation and through administrative action, to encourage a shift from oil to coal. And of course, the com-petitive price of the two fuels is one that is of great concern to me.

As you know, the Interstate Commerce Commission is an independent agency, and I have no authority over that agency in directing them to establish a particular rate for the hauling of coal. That's done in a judicial forum, where the customers and also the railroads have a right to present their cases. And I presume the ICC has made a reasonable judgment in it.

We also are pursuing the option for coal delivery using slurry lines. The railroads are fighting this proposal, and of course, you have the additional problem involving environmentalists, that it may be an excessive use of water if the origin point has a scarce supply of water. But this is something that we've put forward, we're trying to fight through the Congress, to give the appropriate agencies the right to require rights-of-way under railroads if the coal slurry pipeline needs to travel in that direction.

We will make every effort, through public statements and otherwise, to influence the ICC and the railroads to restrain their rate increases. I would presume that the railroads and the coal miners know that if coal should get to a price level, including transportation costs, that's non-competitive, that they would lose very important and very large customers.

I don't know the details of the San Antonio area, but I think it's worthy of my inquiry now that you've raised the question.

AGRICULTURE EXPORTS

Q. Mr. President, a number of congressional leaders from the Midwest have mentioned that it would be feasible for this country to use the agricultural products, primarily wheat, beef, corn, to other nations to establish more of a balance of trade, import-export, especially with Japan and China. What's your stand on that? Do you plan to go more to that?

THE PRESIDENT. We've already done that, and we are pushing that as hard as we possibly can.

One of the prime campaign issues when I ran for President in '75 and '76 was the repeated grain embargoes that had been implemented under former Secretary of Agriculture Butz and under both Nixon and Ford, and I pledged that this would not be done unless our own Nation's security was directly threatened. We have sustained this commitment and have massively increased agricultural exports.

Our exports this year in volume, not counting even price, will probably be 60-percent greater than any year's exports in history, before I became President. We have set new United States and even world records every year on the total volume of agricultural exports. And I would presume that 1980 would show an even faster rise in exports of American grain to foreign customers.

There's a fairly good crop of grain in China and some other areas of the world. There's a fairly short crop of grain in the Soviet Union. And of course, we will have a bumper crop of grain this year. So, we have really emphasized this ability.

I want to make two other quick points. The second thing that we've done is to set up, within the Agriculture Department, export promotion centers, I believe in six foreign cities, where grain is purchased at that point, to encourage additional customers of our grain that wouldn't ordinarily, maybe, turn to us for grain. It's a highly competitive area.

And the second thing we've done is to greatly increase the quantity of grain that can be stored on the farm. In the past, farm storage was minimal, and quite often the farmers had to sell their grain at the most depressed price level—that is, during harvest season—and any fluctuations later in the grain market, the profits ordinarily went to the middlemen. We have now increased substantially the amount of farm-stored grain, which gives us a chance to let the farmers participate in any improvement in the price, but also to stabilize grain prices, so that you don't have the wild fluctuations that did exist in the previous two administrations before mine.

I think all of these efforts have been very fruitful. And we've got a good reserve supply of grain on hand, rapidly increasing exports, additional emphasis overseas to broaden the customer range that we presently enjoy, increased participation by the farmers in seasonable profits.

PROJECT SEAFARER

Q. Mr. President, Dave Rood, the Delta Reporter, Gladstone, Michigan. When you were campaigning for the Presidency 3 years ago, you made the commitment at that time that you would not put in Project Sanguine, Seafarer, ELF, the Extremely Low Frequency——

THE PRESIDENT. Seafarer.

Q. ——Seafarer against the will of the people of the Upper Peninsula. Yet there still persists—ELF is still alive. What is your position on that now? Would you still reiterate what you said before?

THE PRESIDENT. Well, my commitment was not to proceed with Seafarer against the will of the people. We have greatly modified the Seafarer proposal in every possible way. We have brought Michigan officials in to the Defense Department, and we've had people go out to explain to them what modifications were taking place. We're looking for every alternative to what was considered a threat to the Michigan, and—I think primarily the

Michigan environment—and I will still be very reticent about violating the desires of the Michigan people.

Having departed almost completely from the Seafarer proposal, which was my pledge, if we can find a successful alternative to that—and I consider it to be necessary for the security of our country—then I would have to make that decision to defend our country. But we are still assessing it, still working with the people in Michigan and other States to try to find a reaonable alternative to any objectionable use of this very low frequency communications system.

STORAGE OF CHEMICAL WEAPONS

Q. Mr. President, I'm Rob Rule from KJQ Radio in Ogden, Utah. The Army is planning to move some 900 Wet Eye nerve gas bombs into Utah to be stored. These are bombs that were manufactured in the early fifties and obviously have never been used against an enemy. I have a two-part question. Number one, do you see any reason why these weapons and other weapons like them shouldn't be neutralized tomorrow? And number two, why does Utah have to be the storage ground for these terrible weapons and for so many nuclear waste piles, too?

THE PRESIDENT. We have successfully, I think, concluded a negotiation with the Soviets on the prohibition against radiological weapons—that is, using radioactivity. We've not yet been successful in working out an agreement with the Soviet Union to abolish chemical warfare weapons, but we are actively pursuing that.

I don't believe it would be good for our country unilaterally to take this action. If we did, there would be no possible means in the future to induce the Soviets to join in with us and remove the threat of chemical warfare from the world. The major unresolved difficulty is how to verify compliance with such an agreement.

I cannot tell you the reasons why the Defense Department has concluded that Utah is a better place to store it. I think, as you know, we've got destructive weapons and caustic materials and potentially dangerous operations possibly existing in every State in the Union. And sometimes a particularly offensive weapon might be stored in Utah; sometimes it would be stored in Georgia. We manufacture at the Savannah River plant, just on the border between Georgia and South Carolina, substantial quantities of radioactive material. We have, as you know, in Tennessee, ever since 35 or 40 years ago, manufactured plutonium. We're doing the same thing in Ohio. And I think you can go down the gamut of States, and you'd find in almost every State there are some objectionable things taking place, to certain groups. One was just mentioned here in Michigan.

Q. Wouldn't we look very good to the world community, though, if we said, regardless of what the Soviets are going to do, that the United States makes a commitment never to use one of these weapons, regardless?

THE PRESIDENT. We would look very good to some people in the world if we unilaterally disarmed and prostrated ourselves and said to the Soviets, "Come in and walk over us." But I don't feel that that's an appropriate position for me as President to assume.

KU KLUX KLAN

Q. Mr. President, I'm Milton Reid, the Journal and Guide Newspaper in Norfolk, Virginia. Mr. President, there's a two-part question here. There has been a general rise of the Klan in the South and in the Nation. More recently there's been an organizing of the Klan in the Navy.

THE PRESIDENT. In the Navy?

Q. In the Navy, in Norfolk, with the blessings of one admiral, who said that there was room in the Navy for the Klan as well as anybody else.

THE PRESIDENT. I've never heard that. I'll check on this right after this meeting. When was it?

Q. It was on Monday, Monday morning of this week that the admiral said this in Norfolk.

THE PRESIDENT. Well, what I consider—the Ku Klux Klan and everything it stands for is absolutely abhorrent to me and, I think, to our Nation. My assessment as a southerner is that the acceptability and the presence and the influence and the threat of the Ku Klux Klan is minimal. These are erratic people who have earned the contempt of the rest of the Nation and also of their immediate neighbors in every community in the South with which I am familiar.

There are certain rights of free speech, however, under our constitutional system that protects even obnoxious groups like the Klan in having a right to voice their views and even to march down a public street or, as you know, in the Chicago suburbs, to get the right under the court-ordered system to participate in a public park. We have to face that kind of thing in an absolutely free society.

But I think that the condemnation of our country concerning the Klan, which was anti-Semitic, anti-Catholic, anti-black, and shrouded in understandable secrecy, is pretty much a thing of the past as far as having any real import.

But I certainly would not approve of any sort of imprimatur of acceptability for the Klan in the armed services. And I'll check on this right after I adjourn this meeting.

PUBLIC OPINION POLLS

Q. Mr. President, maybe a philosophical question. I'm Charles Davis from Iowa Falls, Iowa. The press and politicians seem to pay a lot of attention to public opinion polls. Given the complexity of international-domestic politics, the economy, and everything else, is it reasonable to expect a President under these conditions to rate very high with the majority of the people in the public opinion polls?

THE PRESIDENT. My guess is, in this present political environment it is almost impossible. There are times of euphoria that sweep the Nation immediately after an election or after an inauguration day or maybe after a notable success, like the Camp David accords, when there's a surge of popularity for a President. But most of the decisions that have to be made by a President are inherently not popular ones; they're contentious.

There is not a single vote to be derived from the evolution of a national energy policy. It's down all the way, because the highly motivated consumers groups, for instance, or environmentalists, and so forth, can never be satisfied with any acceptable proposal that has a chance to be approved by the Congress, and the oil companies and all those who are from producing States can never be satisfied with a compromise that's acceptable to Congress and is able to be passed. And for the President to espouse a balanced program naturally arouses the condemnation, certainly the opposition, criticism at least, of those highly motivated opinion-shapers.

In addition, there are times when you have to take a stand that you know is unpopular. A case that comes to my mind as I sit here is the Panama Canal treaties. When we got to the conclusion of the Panama Canal negotiations, after 14 years of negotiating, knowing that this is in the best interest of our country, there was a public opinion poll run, I think, by Gallup under the Foreign Affairs Institute—it was not a Government poll—that showed that only 8 percent of the American people favored a new Panama Canal treaty. But my predecessors, ever since President Johnson, all the knowledgeable people in the State Department—mine and the previous administrations—knew that we had to have a new Panama Canal treaty. And for me to espouse that and to work with a great deal of commitment to get two-thirds vote in the Senate was patently a losing political proposition.

Also, when you have uncontrollable things happen—I could control it; I could have avoided it. I didn't have to put forward an energy policy. When you have an uncontrollable situation like inflation—inflation has been with us for 10 years. It's fluctuated between about where it is now, which is about the same as it was in 1974, down to maybe 6½ or 7 percent. The President is naturally held to be responsible for the state of the economy. I think the fluctuations in the state of the economy are one thing which hurt President Ford just before the election in November of 1976.

But a President is responsible for the inconveniences or the disappointments or the concerns of the American people. And you're constantly involved in contention and debate. And as you know, the press—and without criticizing the press—is not going to emphasize the successes or the agreements or the cooperative attitudes or the achievements.

The first year I was in office, for instance, I put forward maybe 15 major programs in which I was personally involved. I guess at the end of the year, we had gotten 9½ or 10 of them passed, but the emphasis was on the ones we didn't get. And even those that we got passed, the emphasis was on—when a subcommittee would vote no, it would be a headline on the front page. If, the next day, the full committee voted yes and then the bill passed, there would be no notice of it.

Another thing is that you have achievements that are not recognized—and this is the last thing I'll say about this. When Kennedy was President, I think it's generally accepted that in all the domestic achievements that he had, a trade bill— where trade barriers were stricken down and an ethical standard for promoting trade was passed—was his major achievement. We passed one this year that is broader and, I think, superior in every way to the one that was passed in 1962 or 1963. In the Washington Post, which is a major focal point here for the promotion of news stories, there was not a single word when the Congress passed that bill.*

So, you know, it's hard to mold an approving public when you have those kinds of varied responsibilities to meet. I'm not saying this to deplore the situation, but to tell you that this is the way it is, particularly in an off year. Now, when we face an election year, it'll be time for the American people to make an assessment, an inventory of what has been done—and I think we've got a superb record—a projection of what we hope to accomplish in the future, and then, of course, your own character assessment, the reputation that you have for being steady in an emergency, the organizational structure or commitment of your supporters. Those things become much more important than the relatively transient public opinion polls.

---

*The President meant there was no separate news story. Passage of the trade bill was given two paragraphs on page 3 in the congressional digest for that day. [Printed in the transcript.]

The last point is this: Where I come from, which is southwest Georgia, if you ask these days, "How do you think the county school superintendent is doing?", if somebody says, "I think he's doing a fair job," that is a high approbation. But in most of the public opinion polls, for instance—there are, I think, I don't know, I won't name the public opinion polls—they've got excellent, good, fair, and poor. And excellent and good are considered positive; fair and poor are considered negative.

There are a lot of complications about public opinion polls. I look at them; I'm concerned about them. I would like to be highly popular in our country. I'd like to have a 75-percent favorable rating; that would be very nice. But I remember that a week after I was an announced candidate for President, Gallup ran a poll and listed 36 people—Ralph Nader, Julian Bond, and 34 others. My name was not on the list. But I became the President.

So, public opinion polls are interesting. I think they are a guide on how the public feels, but, I think, have relatively little significance about the outcome of an election that might be held next year.

SOVIET TROOPS IN CUBA

Q. Mr. President, I'm Dale McIlwain from the Washington Star. I wanted to know what steps you might have in mind to get the Russian brigade out of Cuba.

THE PRESIDENT. I think it's better for me not to talk at this moment about specifics on that.

Secretary Vance made a statement, which I later followed and basically repeated, that, I think, goes as far as I want to go as far as a President. I said this was a matter of great concern to us,

that the status quo was not acceptable, and that we would be working with the Soviet Union to change the situation in a manner that would be acceptable to us. If this effort should be unsuccessful, then I would have to take appropriate action. And I think to go into further detail than that would be inappropriate.

We are meeting with the Soviet Union, assessing our intelligence data, understanding clearly what is the status quo, and I'll have to make a judgment on what to do about it within the near future.

Ms. BARIO. Thank you, Mr. President.

Q. Mr. President?

THE PRESIDENT. Yes, one more question.

COAL

Q. The lack of specific incentives to develop anthracite coal is of particular concern in my area. I'm from Wilkes-Barre, Pennsylvania, the Scranton area. We're sitting on a mountain of coal, and the production is now at 6 million tons, when it was at nearly a hundred million tons a year in the 1930's. The people in our area would like to know, are you prepared to support tax credits to encourage the use of anthracite coal? Are you prepared to support government stockpiling to create a market for anthracite coal?

THE PRESIDENT. I believe the answer to both those questions would be no. I don't have any plans to do either of the two. We are taking other action, however, to increase the use of coal, and I think anthracite, in some instances, would be affected. My guess is that by 1985, we'll have a substantial increase in the use of coal, perhaps even doubling the present use and maybe before the end of this century to triple what we are presently using in the way of coal.

There are some uses for coal which are not particularly related to the original characteristics of the coal. One is obviously the derivation of synthetic oil and gas from coal supplies. My own expectation would be that as we get the windfall profits tax passed and establish a security corporation and set up production plans, that we would want to have them disbursed so as to assess, in the broadest possible way, every energy resource that we have. Knowing of the enormous reserves of anthracite, a major emphasis will be on how to use anthracite in this process.

We expect over a 20-year period to spend about $88 billion on the synthetic fuels program. I believe that 75 billion of that 88 billion is designed for use in synthetic fuels from coal. And so, I would say that in every way the increased use of coal for broad purposes to replace oil and natural gas, eventually, and the use of coal for new synthetic purposes would guarantee that all forms of coal would have a better opportunity to be used in the future.

Let me say in closing that I appreciate your presence and your questions. It gives me a good chance to know what is of interest to you. And I always enjoy these exchanges.

If you don't mind, I'd like to get a photograph with everyone here, and I'll stand right back—right back here?—and let you all come by and let me have a handshake and a photograph and send it to you.

NOTE: The interview began at 1:15 p.m. in the Cabinet Room at the White House. Patricia Y. Bario is a Deputy Press Secretary.

The transcript of the interview was released on September 22.

United States Representative to the United Nations

Remarks at the Swearing In of Donald F. McHenry.   September 23, 1979

THE PRESIDENT. One of the great challenges and opportunities of a President is to analyze the problems which confront our Nation and to try to choose the best possible partners to work with him in the resolution of those problems and in the meeting of those challenges.

The problems, of course, and the responsibilities are broad-ranging: how to make our cities better places in which to live, how to give economic justice and support and a new opportunity in life for the poor and those who have felt the burden of discrimination, how to provide for the health needs of our country, how to provide a sense of unity in a nation which struggles against the divisive elements of a modern-day world, how to have a strong defense, which is a prerequisite on a super power like ours, to maintain peace for ourselves and for our allies and friends and all nations.

I've chosen allies like that—Eleanor Holmes Norton and Pat Harris and Clifford Alexander and others, who've worked closely with me with a special sensitivity about the problems of those that have, in the past, been deprived. We've made some progress. We all still have a long way to go.

There's another commitment, and that is one to maintain the standards of a basic morality, to honor the ethics and the principles on which this Nation was founded, not only among the Americans who are blessed to live in this great country but as an example to other people as well—the principles of human worth, freedom; the preservation and the enhancement of basic human rights; the spread of democracy in societies which have known the heel of totalitarian governments; the welcoming of refugees who, like our own ancestors, have found a better life in America; this bridging of gaps between our own Nation and other people, which have been long existent and where, in the past, very few attempts have been made to build those bridges.

In our Ambassador to the United Nations, we find that opportunity for me to form a partnership. And more than 2½ years ago, I formed a good partnership with a great American, who has served his country well and who will continue to serve it well in whatever role he chooses to play—my friend and the friend of the world, Andy Young. And I thank you, Andy.

I might say in passing that any claims or allegations that American Jewish leaders or anyone else urged me to ask Andy for his resignation are absolutely and totally false, and neither did anyone urge Andy to resign. He made his judgment on what was best for our country and him. And his role in the future, in my judgment, to help his Nation will be undiminished.

When Andy and I had a private discussion about his future, one of the questions that came up was about a successor. I wanted someone to carry on, in an undiminished way, the thrust of what has been achieved in the last 2½ years. There was an instant realization that such a successor was at hand—a man who is a foreign policy professional in the finest sense of the word; a man who has been at the United Nations, working in a very top position in the most sensitive areas of international life; a man whose moral character is unstained, who's proven his ability in times of strain and with the focus of public attention on him, as was the case recently in a New York airport; a man

who will take this position, I believe, with the highest degree of personal knowledge of the inner workings and the hidden mechanisms and the ultimate purposes and the challenges and the solutions of the United Nations than anyone who's ever served there.

And with the choice of Don McHenry, which has been almost unanimously, so far as I know, unanimously approved, four messages will go out in a very clear tone. One is that we are continuing to bridge the gap between the developed nations of the world, like our own, and the developing nations of the world, who search for friendship, understanding, and a better life for their people; secondly, to let the world know that we staunchly are committed as a nation and as a government to ending racism and apartheid in southern Africa and we will never yield on this point; third, that our commitment to human rights and basic human freedoms is an accurate commitment that expresses the will of 220 million Americans and that this will never cease so long as our country exists; and that we are a nation committed to peace, a strong nation committed to peace.

In the Middle East, we've made good progress. The sensitivities there are perhaps as complex as any which have ever confronted negotiators or diplomats. The progress that has been made in the last 13 or 14 months is far beyond anything that we had dreamed. We still have a long way to go. But we have a man in the United Nations who understands those sensitivities, and our Ambassador there will be able to contribute greatly to what I am able to accomplish—Secretary Vance, Ambassador Bob Strauss, and others—in bringing peace to that troubled region. I am indeed grateful that Don McHenry has accepted this position.

And now I would like to ask Andy Young to say just a brief word and to introduce, at the close of his words, Judge Parker, who will administer the oath of office to Don McHenry. And then, if Don has no objections, I would like for him to respond to you.

Andy Young.

AMBASSADOR YOUNG. Thank you very much, Mr. President, Mr. Vice President, Mr. Secretary.

It really gives me great pleasure to be here to see, in some sense, the passing on of a baton. In a very real sense, I think, I ran my part of the race, and while I wasn't getting tired, my time was probably over. [*Laughter*] And I really and truly have no regrets. In fact, I'm quite proud to be able to pass on the baton of responsibility at the United Nations to Don McHenry.

Let me hasten to say that I didn't recommend Don for this job, not because I have any reservations about his competence or the fact that, as the President says, he does bring more knowledge of the United Nations and of our foreign policy to this job than perhaps any other person we've ever had in the position, but because I happen to know how rough the next General Assembly is going to be. And I really didn't feel free to wish that on a friend of mine. [*Laughter*]

But one thing about being Ambassador to the United Nations—and maybe this is also true for the first time in our Nation's history—never has the United Nations had the kind of commitment from the President of the United States and from the Secretary of State and the entire State Department that it has in this administration. And there has been a commitment to doing many of the things that are in the national interest of this great Nation through the multilateral diplomatic forum of the United Nations.

And there has been a tremendous amount of teamwork that has existed between the staff at the United Nations and the Assistant Secretaries. In fact, even in passing on to Bob Strauss, the former Deputy Permanent Representative of the United Nations, Cy Vance suggested that there was a sense of continuity and interrelationship between the United Nations and the rest of the decisionmaking apparatus of our foreign policy. And so, Don will move in as a very important part of what I feel to be a very great team.

And it's my pleasure at this time to ask Judge Parker if he will administer the oath of office to my good friend, Don McHenry.

[*At this point, United States District Judge Barrington Parker administered the oath of office.*]

AMBASSADOR McHENRY. *Mr. President, Mr. Vice President, Judge Parker, friends:*

I am very proud of this moment. I feel in one sense as if I am continuing a journey for which I have prepared for a long time, and at the same time I am very conscious of that warning which Andy gave and of which I am well aware. We probably face the most difficult General Assembly that we've ever faced in the last 10 years or so.

I should say that I approach this opportunity and this responsibility with every intention of doing the best I can, with a very competent and dedicated staff and supported and working with the other members of the foreign policy team here in Washington.

I do not expect that in our time, the immediate time, that we will be able to magically come up with solutions to all of the problems which face us. Indeed, we will be lucky if we can come up with the solution to a very few. But I believe in the importance of diplomacy. I believe in the importance of trying very hard, with imagination and hard work, to resolve problems, to bring people to devote their best efforts to the resolution of those problems.

The United Nations today is not the United Nations of 34 sessions ago, yet I believe it is a reflection of the world in which we live. And anyone who wishes to accomplish anything in that forum or, indeed, if we wish to resolve many of the foreign policy problems which face us, we have to live and deal with the United Nations of today and the world of today, and not the ideal which we may have set many years ago.

Yet, the ideal is important. And I look upon the Charter of the United Nations very much as I have always looked upon the Constitution of the United States: It is something that we work toward. And as long as, it seems to me, that there is a commitment toward the goal of those principles set down in the Charter or those principles set down in the Constitution, I am prepared to devote my best efforts to achieving those goals—frustrated sometimes, to be sure; angry sometimes, more than the press realizes, to be sure—[laughter]—but nevertheless trying as best I can to move ahead and always recognizing that no accomplishment in our lives is that of a single individual.

Many of you here have worked very long and very hard with me over the 19 or so years that I have been in Washington and working in foreign affairs. On some occasions, I cannot say that I enjoyed some of the things that I have done, but I hope that I have learned the full measure of the responsibilities which I will need in the days ahead.

I am heartened by an observation which, I think, Ambassador Young has made, but which I would like to make also. In the many years that I have observed American foreign policy, I know of no instance where we have gotten such strong support in the United Nations, in

our efforts to live in the world as it is today, than we have gotten from the President of the United States and the Secretary of State.

It has been with that support that we have been able, in the last 2½ years, to turn our image in the United Nations from one in which everyone knew what we were against, but very few people knew what we were for. We are no longer the abominable "no man." [Laughter] We stand for and work for positive goals in the United Nations.

And I hope that the partnership which was formed 2½ years ago and which consisted, in many instances, of Andy Young on the outside and Don McHenry on the inside—I hope that that partnership will continue outside in a new place. But nevertheless, I look forward to the support which Ambassador Young and all of you can give us in this responsibility which we are about to undertake.

And so, may I conclude by thanking you, Mr. President, for the confidence which you have shown in me, and thanking you, the American people, for the confidence which you have shown, and reminding you that I can't do it alone.

Thank you.

NOTE: The President spoke at 2:08 p.m. in the East Room at the White House.

Departments of Transportation and Housing and Urban Development

Remarks at the Swearing In of Neil Goldschmidt as Secretary of Transportation and Moon Landrieu as Secretary of Housing and Urban Development. September 24, 1979

THE PRESIDENT. This is really a happy day for me and for the country. Don't you agree? [Applause]

I think if we searched the Nation over, which I did, it would be impossible to find two men who are more conversant with the crucial issues that face our country in the area of transportation and the development of better communities—men who've got experience, men who know how to work with others, men who have a respect for the concerns and problems and doubts and fears, but, at the same time, of the aspirations and hopes and dreams of the American people, in communities of all sizes, both urban and rural, throughout the country.

There is a need to break down the barriers which exist between government and people, but also to break down the barriers that exist among different levels of government. I think we've made a lot of progress in that respect, and Moon Landrieu and Neil Goldschmidt have been in the forefront of that effort.

The problems tend to multiply, and they interrelate one with another. It's almost impossible to solve the problems of housing and education, of health, of the spirit of America, as long as we don't have national policies that provide a framework for the resolution of problems and the discussion of issues, as it relates to energy or transportation.

In the last 2½ years, we have hammered out a basis on which these policies can now be firm and understood. We've not yet finished on energy. We'll make a major stride this year; we've been making excellent progress the last few days. We've not yet forged a comprehensive policy on transportation, but we are determined to do so. I think we've made a major stride in the evolution of an understandable urban policy, and we are now approaching the time of announcement of an equally comprehensive and effective rural policy.

I need, at my shoulder, leaders who can carry on this good work. And as you can well see, standing behind me, I've been successful in finding leaders of that kind.

Our country changes so rapidly. We are in a transition period now. I think when we look back on this from a historical perspective, we'll see that the emphasis on the elements that comprise a happy American's life are changing at this time.

We are facing, for the first time really, the realization that the resources that God gave us have limits and that we can't be wastrels in the future. To me, this is not a negative development. It's a basis on which we can be excited and innovative, preserve our individualism, but still work in a united fashion to have a better life, families closer, communities closer, a pride in taking individual steps to conserve and to save those precious things, which in itself is a patriotic contribution.

Neil Goldschmidt, as a mayor, has been in the forefront of the evolution of a practical demonstration of what transportation can mean to a city. He knows about crosstown transportation, but he also knows about crosscountry transportation of all kinds.

He's been on the job now, as you know, for several weeks, and he's begun to confront, in a successful way, problems that have been here for a long time, dealing with Rock Island Railroad, dealing with Westway, dealing with the allocation of resources for public transportation, highways, automobile efficiency, air pollution, airbags. The breadth of his responsibilities is awe-inspiring, and he's already begun to deal with those problems in a comprehensive and effective fashion.

I think Neil also knows how to interrelate the quality of life and participation of citizens in hammering out a successful answer to a complicated question. He's proven this.

1719

Moon Landrieu has earned the admiration of every mayor and public official in our country with what he's done in New Orleans—a city of ancient history, a city of a wide range of ethnic groups, diverse points of view—with a desire to preserve the precious, but the need to resolve differences.

Moon has been in the forefront of some evolutionary changes that almost became revolutionary changes, and I have observed with admiration and have learned from him how he's dealt with the basic question of civil rights, human rights. When it wasn't easy in the South, Moon Landrieu stood firm and said there's no longer any place for discrimination or racism. And he did this in such a way that he marshaled the support of his entire community and won an overwhelming victory and, I think, had he wanted to, could have been mayor for a long time.

And he was successful in revitalizing an area that I hope will always retain its character, because it's one of America's fine possessions. And in the process, he let the people of New Orleans feel that the future was not dismal or discouraging, but exciting and promising.

So, for these reasons and for many others, I'm very grateful to have this opportunity to introduce to the Nation and to have join my Cabinet these two men.

And I see former mayors of New York here, who remember very well when New York City was in a dangerous condition and there needed to be some broad-based national support for New York's effort to save itself. And Moon Landrieu traveled the country to marshal the support of other people in Georgia and in Louisiana and in Kansas and in California to support New York City. He convinced me, along with Mayor Beame and others, that this should be done. And I made

that commitment as a candidate, and we've carried out that commitment.

And now I don't think anyone could deny that what Moon Landrieu espoused as a mayor of New Orleans, joining with his partner and partners throughout the country, including New York, that our great city of New York has a new life. I hope he'll do that with every city, ranging from New York City down to Plains, Georgia, and I have confidence that he will.

Now I'd like to ask Margaret Goldschmidt and Judge Steinbock to come forward to administer the oath to Neil Goldschmidt as Secretary of Transportation.

[*At this point, Louisiana Supreme Court Justice Irving Steinbock administered the oath of office.*]

And now I'd like to ask Moon and Verna and Judge Calogero to come forward for the oath. And Moon, it would be nice if your family joined you. I hope the photographers have a wide-angle lens. [*Laughter*] I might say that—well, I think I'll say that I'm not sure that Moon's family will grow this fast the next 5 years. [*Laughter*]

[*At this point, Louisiana Supreme Court Justice Pascal Calogero administered the oath of office.*]

I won't give them another introduction, but I'd like for Neil Goldschmidt and then for Moon to say a word to the group.

Secretary Goldschmidt. *Mr. President, Mr. Vice President, Mrs. Carter, friends:*

I cannot think of a nicer occasion than to come to the service of my country with a good friend like Moon Landrieu.

It is a wonderful feeling that among so many fine public servants who have been elected to high office, including many who are mayors, and the staffs who have supported us and worked so hard—it's a pleasure to be here on all of their behalfs.

I did not travel a particularly long road to come here. My age, I think, is witness to that fact. But I come through a very, I guess, traditional route. I am a graduate of public education in the United States, a public education afforded by the taxpayers of my communities and the communities all over our land. To a Congress which has, for so long, appropriated the funds to make it possible for people like myself to go to school and to aspire to high office and to serve my country, you have my deep thanks. To my family, which has come with me today and to whom I owe so much, I guess they already understand how I feel.

I hope that the promise of these years can be fulfilled. And I have given the President my pledge, and I will give it to all of you—friends and those that I hope to meet as I travel and move about the United States on the President's behalf— that I will do everything in my power to make life in the United States a good one for all of those to whom I owe a best effort.

There has been much written about how difficult these times are. And for those of us who got our education not on the battlefields of Europe, but on the battlefields of Mississippi, those of us who got our understanding of higher education in the free speech movement in California, and for those of us who have had our beliefs challenged by Vietnam, everything in the future looks bright, looks hopeful, and looks possible.

And I look forward to working with everybody in this country who feels as I do—and I think that's just about everybody—that they wouldn't live anyplace on the Earth before they'd live in America, to keep building, to keep growing, and keep loving.

Thank you.

THE PRESIDENT. And now the Secretary of Housing and Urban Development.

SECRETARY LANDRIEU. *Thank you, Mr. President, Mrs. Carter, Mr. Vice President.*

Neil Goldschmidt has always had a great capacity for brevity and for expressing precisely what's on his mind. I've never had that particular talent. [*Laughter*]

Mr. President, first I want to thank you for giving me the opportunity to serve once again. It's a great privilege to be back in the Government and to be working with those who are laboring to rebuild urban America. And I couldn't be more honored myself than to be sworn in with a man such as Neil Goldschmidt, a man whom I admired from the first moment that I met him. He bristles with energy and intelligence and with commitment.

It always struck me as a marvelous thing that Neil Goldschmidt, as a young man far removed from the South, took time out from his duties to go into the freedom marches during the great civil rights crusades. We've been very, very warm friends, and I'm honored to be serving with you, Neil. As a matter of fact, he's probably the outstanding mayor in the country, unless you walked in the audience and shook hands with John Rousakis or with John Olivier from Sunset— [*laughter*]—or with the 50 or so other mayors who are out there.

Just one word about urban America. I read the other day on a plaque that Secretary Weaver had placed on the HUD building when it was dedicated, and this is what he said, and I think it's important to recollect this. He said, "Today we're engaged in rebuilding the urban areas of the United States, a task so large that it amounts to recreating them, a task as ambitious as any nation has ever set for itself." That was said in 1966. It was only in 1965 that this child of a department was founded, and I think we can date from that moment the kind of formalization of our war against urban decay that this Nation undertook. And it occurred to me that that is only about 13 years ago or 14 years ago, not even one-half the life of an average home mortgage, and yet we've done much in that period of time, despite our impatience.

Each President, each Congress, each Secretary of this Department has added new tools to the urban workbox. We developed model cities and general revenue sharing, community development block grants, aid to mass transit, and, of course, under the leadership of President Carter, the most significant urban statement of all—the development of a national urban policy and the beginning of the formation of a partnership between those of us in public office and the private sector, and the recognition by him that we, the politicians, did not build America, but rather it was built by the private sector. And as our cities are rebuilt, it will be rebuilt by the private sector, but hopefully in an atmosphere created by the public sector, one of assistance and aid, one of encouragement, permitting the private enterprise system to do what it knows how to do best, to build and to move and to create.

So, Mr. President, I'm very, very honored to be with you in that movement, and I'm very pleased that I have the chance to serve with so many distinguished public officials who serve in your Cabinet.

In closing, I would like to thank the rather substantial number of people who came up from New Orleans, very much like the Peanut Brigade, Mr. President, who followed you around the country. I've been fortunate in having some very dear and close friends. I also thank the many mayors and county execs and housing officials and others from the constituency groups who are here. I'll give you my best.

Thank you.

NOTE: The President spoke at 10:37 a.m. in the Rose Garden at the White House.

Meeting With Members of the Nicaraguan Junta

White House Statement.   September 24, 1979

The President met today in the Cabinet Room with three members of the Nicaraguan Junta on their way to New York to lead the delegation of the Government of Nicaragua to the United Nations General Assembly. The discussion centered on ways to strengthen the basis for a cooperative relationship between the United States and Nicaragua based on mutual respect.

The Nicaraguan delegation included Junta members Daniel Ortega, Sergio Ramirez, and Alfonso Robelo, Minister of Foreign Affairs Miguel D'Escoto, and Ambassador-designate to the U.S. Rafael Solis. Present from the U.S. Government, in addition to the President, was the Vice President, Deputy Secretary of State Warren Christopher, National Security Adviser Zbigniew Brzezinski, Assistant Secretary of State for Inter-American Affairs Viron P. Vaky, U.S. Ambassador to Nicaragua Lawrence A. Pezzulo, Ambassador Henry Owen, and NSC staff member Robert Pastor.

United States Jaycees

Remarks at a Meeting With Members of the Executive Committee and State Presidents. September 24, 1979

That's the same kind of reception I get from the Washington press corps at my press conferences. [*Laughter*]

President Bechtol and distinguished leaders of the U.S. Jaycees:

It's an honor and a pleasure for me to welcome you here. I owe you a lot. Not only have you helped me in extremely difficult times, such as the passing of the Panama Canal treaty legislation last year, but you've been in the forefront of many other challenging issues, because you've got a lot of courage, you're well-organized, you're dynamic and aggressive, you're strong and patriotic, and as Jaycees you're united in serving your country. And I'm grateful to you for it.

Also, I would not be living in this house had I not, as a young, budding student of Georgia politics, gone to the State Jaycee conventions to see how the elections were conducted. [*Laughter*] Last election, in '76, when the going got tough, I remembered those days, and the memories came flooding back to me. And I was able, in those final, elbowing phases of the campaign for President, to win, because I remembered what I'd learned from you.

Tomorrow you'll get a briefing on the SALT treaties from Dr. Brzezinski and perhaps others, but today I want to talk to you about a challenge that's as serious as any that has faced our country. We've got a strong nation and a great nation, as you so well know and as you so well represent. And as you also know, down through history our country, when it's been challenged, has responded successfully. We have never failed to meet a difficult challenge or to overcome an obstacle or to answer a question or to solve a problem, provided we could detect and understand the challenge to our country.

As I said many times on my trip down the river to small and large groups that assembled along the shoreline, in World War I, World War II, even the Great Depression, Americans could see the challenge to our country. And in understanding the challenge, we responded. We put aside differences. We developed a respect for our own governments. Families united, communities united, and in spite of adversity, America became a nation which could work together. Now we've got a challenge that's not so easy to see. It's just as important.

My prime responsibility as President, above all others, is to guarantee the security of my country, your country. And our security is threatened now, because we are overly dependent on imported oil. We import about one-half the total oil we use. We export about $70 billion this year— American money—to pay for that oil, and along with the oil, we import inflation and unemployment and dependence on an uncertain supply at an uncontrollable price. The last 3 or 4 months, for instance, the inflation rate would have been almost exactly constant. It would not have changed a quarter of 1 percent had it not been for energy. But oil, because of OPEC decisions, is going up, this last 3 months, at an annual rate of inflation of 100 percent.

Our country has never had an energy policy. Decisions have always been made in the Congress primarily as the oil companies chose—and I don't criticize them because of it—because there never was a reason until recently for others, consumers, to rally and say something has got to be done to give our Nation a clear concept of where we go in the future on energy.

The basic thrust of what we're trying to do depends primarily upon conservation—the saving of energy, the elimination of waste. That's it, as far as the number one priority is concerned. It's something that every single American can do, every single American has to do. It's something that can bring our people together. It is not an onerous task. It need not cause us concern about the future. It's a challenge that can be met effectively and pleasantly. And the benefits accrue to each American who acts to save energy, and it's a patriotic gesture at the same time.

So, conservation is first. We've made some progress already; we've got a long way to go. We also need to turn toward replenishable supplies of energy, energy that can be restored every year or every minute. Solar energy, energy derived from growing plants—these kinds of things can become a major element in our life in the future. And we predict, if our programs are put into effect, that by the year 2000, 20 percent of all our energy will be derived directly from solar sources.

Georgia produces enough biomass, growing crops, growing trees, to produce three times as much energy as the total that we consume in our State. And we now waste about one-third or sometimes one-half of our total timber products, because of ill-advised harvesting techniques. We're trying to move on those areas.

We need to increase the amount of oil and gas produced in our country from conventional sources. And we are giving to the oil companies tremendous increased income under my own proposals that will let them have that amount of revenue which they require.

But the other sources that we need to tap—synthetic fuels, the increased use of coal, geothermal supplies, unconventional gas, unconventional oil—not yet have we made adequate progress in these areas. But we've got now in the Congress—recently making very good progress because the people are finally aroused—an energy policy proposal that is adequate and which will restore to our country energy security.

Recently we had a vote in the Senate Energy Committee, 15 to 3, to set up an energy mobilization board, a board designed to cut through redtape and to expedite a decision on whether or not a particular energy-producing project would be built or would not be built. It's not designed to cut through State law or Federal law or to change Western water law. It's designed to cut through government redtape and delay and obfuscation and unnecessary regulations.

If a plant is well advised, if it's got a good site, and if it doesn't violate laws, it's acceptable on the basis of assessing its merits, it ought to be built. And if it's got a defect in it—the wrong place at the wrong time or the wrong concept—it ought not to be built. But the thing is, a decision ought to be made, yes or no. Now sometimes it takes 7 or 8 years just to get that exact same answer, either yes or no. But by the time the decision is made, the cost of the plant is tripled or quadrupled, the factors involved in financing the plant have changed, the people have been discouraged, and we've been deprived of a necessary element in our energy society.

We also are trying to set up an energy security corporation, not a Government agency, an extra-Government agency like the one designed to produce synthetic rubber during the Second World War or to put the communications satellite in orbit. This would be authorized to have 80 ongoing projects, at any one time, to produce synthetic fuels. The Government would just provide a reservoir of guaranteed purchases at a guaranteed price so that the private enterprise system, without interference from the Government, could go ahead and begin the production of synthetic fuels, knowing that they would have a market when their product was finally produced.

And, of course, the basis for all this is the windfall profits tax, a well-balanced tax. The House has already passed it. The Senate is now considering what form it should take. We cannot afford to see this tax decimated or aborted or changed in nature.

This comprehensive approach will give us an energy package which will reward the private enterprise system, reduce government intrusion, give the oil companies and other energy companies a chance to increase production of available United States supplies, cut down on our torrent of foreign oil coming into this country, give us jobs in our Nation, instead of overseas, and give us energy security. That's a package that we need. That's a package that we're going to have, provided I can get some good partners who have the courage and the dedication and a patriotic motivation to fight with me.

My question to you is: Will you join me as partners in getting a comprehensive energy policy for our country that will guard our Nation's security and give us a greater America, even than the one we've already got, which is already the greatest nation on Earth? Will you do that for me? [*Applause*]

NOTE: The President spoke at 2:13 p.m. in the East Room at the White House. In his opening remarks, he referred to Terryl Bechtol, national president of the Jaycees.

United Nations

Nomination of William J. vanden Heuvel To Be Deputy U.S. Representative.
September 24, 1979

The President today announced his intention to nominate William J. vanden Heuvel, of New York City, to be Deputy Representative of the United States to the United Nations with the rank of Ambassador Extraordinary and Plenipotentiary. He would replace James F. Leonard, who has been appointed Chief of the U.S. Mission to the Middle East Peace Negotiations and Deputy to Ambassador Robert Strauss.

Vanden Heuvel has been Representative of the United States to the European Office of the United Nations since 1977.

He was born April 14, 1930, in Rochester, N.Y. He received a B.A. in 1950 from Cornell University and an LL.B. in 1952 from Cornell Law School.

From 1952 to 1957, vanden Heuvel was an associate in the law firm of Leisure, Newton and Irvin. In 1953 and 1954, he was executive assistant to Ambassador to Thailand William J. Donovan. In 1958 he served as special counsel to Gov. Averell Harriman.

From 1959 to 1961, vanden Heuvel was an associate in the law firm of Javits, Moore and Trubin. In 1963 and 1964, he was special assistant to Attorney General Robert F. Kennedy. He served as Acting Regional Administrator for the Office of Economic Opportunity in 1964 and 1965.

Vanden Heuvel was with the New York law firm of Stroock and Stroock and Lavan from 1965 to 1977. In 1967 he was vice president of the New York State Constitutional Convention. He served as chairman of the New York City Board of

Correction from 1970 to 1973, and as chairman of the New York City Commission on State-City Relations from 1971 to 1973.

United States Ambassador to Rwanda

Nomination of Harry Roberts Melone.
September 24, 1979

The President today announced that he will nominate Harry Roberts Melone, of Auburn, N.Y., to be Ambassador Extraordinary and Plenipotentiary of the United States to the Republic of Rwanda. He would replace T. Frank Crigler, transferred.

Melone is foreign affairs coordination officer in the Bureau of Intelligence and Research at the State Department.

He was born June 30, 1928, in Auburn, N.Y. He received an A.B. from Dartmouth College in 1950.

Melone joined the Foreign Service in 1951 and was posted in Tabriz, Tehran, Yaounde, and at the State Department. He was Deputy Chief of Mission in Bangui from 1961 to 1963, and in Niamey from 1963 to 1964. From 1964 to 1966, he was international relations officer in the Bureau of African Affairs at the State Department.

From 1966 to 1968, Melone was adviser for African affairs at the U.S. Mission to the United Nations. He was counselor for political affairs in Conakry from 1968 to 1969, and international relations officer at the State Department from 1969 to 1970.

Melone attended the National War College in 1970–71. He was an international relations officer at the State Department from 1971 to 1973, and served as political officer in Paris from 1973 to 1977. Since 1977 he has been foreign affairs coordination officer in the Bureau of Intelligence and Research.

Environmental Protection Agency

Nomination of Eckardt C. Beck To Be an
Assistant Administrator. September 24, 1979

The President today announced that he will nominate Eckardt C. Beck, of Holmdel, N.J., to be an Assistant Administrator of the Environmental Protection Agency. He would replace Thomas Jorling, resigned.

Beck is Regional Administrator of EPA for New Jersey, New York, Puerto Rico, and the Virgin Islands.

He was born May 21, 1943, in Oceanside, N.Y. He is a graduate of Emerson College in Boston, where he was an assistant graduate professor while working toward his masters in communications in 1968–69. He received an M.P.A. in 1972 from New York University, where he is currently a doctoral candidate.

From 1969 to 1972, Beck was air pollution control officer with the city of Stamford, Conn. From 1972 to 1973, he was director of air compliance for the State of Connecticut. From 1973 to 1975, he was deputy commissioner of the Connecticut Department of Environmental Protection. He also established and directed the Connecticut Energy Agency and served as the Governor's chief adviser on energy policy.

From 1975 to 1978, Beck was Deputy Assistant Administrator of EPA for Water Planning and Standards. He has been Regional Administrator for New Jersey, New York, Puerto Rico, and the Virgin Islands since 1978.

As a Regional Administrator of EPA, Beck has served as Chairman of the Federal Regional Council. He also serves as a commissioner of the Tri-State Regional Planning Commission and is involved in international environmental activities as working group chairman of the Water Management Committee and as U.S. delegate to the Environment Committee, Organization for Economic Cooperation and Development.

National Advisory Council on the Education of Disadvantaged Children

Appointment of Nine Members and Designation of Chairman. September 24, 1979

The President today announced the appointment of nine persons as members of the National Advisory Council on the Education of Disadvantaged Children. They are:

FRED L. BANKS, JR., of Jackson, Miss., an attorney and member of the Mississippi House of Representatives who serves as associate counsel for the Mississippi NAACP Legal Defense and Educational Fund and as a consulting attorney to the Mississippi Association of Educators;

DON DAVIES, chairman of the Department of Systems Development and Adaptation and director of the Institute for Responsive Education at Boston University's School of Education;

CONSTANCE E. GOMES, a public education specialist and legislative advocate with Rhode Island Legal Services, where she acts as a liaison with low-income community groups concerned with public education;

JOHNNY L. JONES, superintendent of schools for Dade County (Florida) public schools;

ROBERT H. KOFF, professor of education and psychology and dean of the College of Education at Roosevelt University in Chicago;

JOSEPH P. MCELLIGOTT, director of the Division of Education of the California Catholic Conference, chairman of the California Executive Council for Nonpublic Schools, and a commissioner of the California Equal Education Opportunities Commission;

M. HAYES MIZELL, associate director of the Southeastern Public Education Program of the American Friends Service Committee (designated Chairman of this Council);

RACHEL B. TOMPKINS, director of Citizens' Council for Ohio Schools, an organization concerned with desegregation, finance, exclusion, and citizen participation in schools;

ELUID HECTOR ZAMORANO, a counselor and foreign student adviser at Richland College, Dallas County (Texas) Community College District, an expert on bilingual education, and a consultant to the U.S. Office of Education's Migrant Division.

President's Export Council

Appointment of Robert B. Washington, Jr., as a Member. September 24, 1979

The President today announced the appointment of Robert B. Washington, Jr., of Washington, D.C., as a member of the President's Export Council.

Washington, 36, is a partner in the Washington law firm of Danzansky, Dickey, Tydings, Quint & Gordon. He serves on the board of directors of the Metropolitan Washington Board of Trade and is chairman for legislative affairs of the Legislative/Fiscal Bureau of the Board of Trade.

National Advisory Council on Economic Opportunity

Appointment of Ruby Duncan as a Member. September 24, 1979

The President today announced the appointment of Ruby Duncan, of North

Las Vegas, Nev., as a member of the National Advisory Council on Economic Opportunity.

Duncan is president of the Clark County (Nevada) Welfare and Economic Rights Organization and executive director of Operation Life, Inc., a self-help community project.

Department of Education Legislation

Statement on Senate Approval of the Conference Report. September 24, 1979

The Senate's approval of the conference report on the department of education bill is a major step toward improved government efficiency. Placing Federal education programs in a separate department will allow us to manage these programs in a more effective, commonsense manner. It will cut redtape, reduce manpower levels, and save tax dollars. It will also mean better service—at less bureaucratic cost—for the State and local institutions which provide education in our country.

I would like to thank Senator Ribicoff for his excellent leadership in bringing this reorganization to final Senate passage.

Country Music Month, October 1979

Message of the President. September 24, 1979

Every year at this time the harvest season is celebrated throughout the hills and valleys of rural America, where country music has its roots. Country music chronicles the richness and fullness of American

life, the hopes and dreams, joys and sorrows of those who have raised a great Nation from a bountiful land.

Because it expresses the simple human emotions we all share, country music is in tune with our everyday experiences, whether we live on a farm or in the city. This authentic American art form has grown to be one of the most popular styles of music in our Nation today.

It is fitting, therefore, that October be designated as "Country Music Month." I commend the Country Music Association for its contribution to this annual observance, and I invite all Americans to join me in saluting the talented performers who have given us so many hours of listening pleasure through country music.

JIMMY CARTER

Financial Reform Legislation

Statement on the Senate Banking Committee's Approval of the Legislation. September 24, 1979

I am deeply gratified by the Senate Banking Committee's approval of my financial institutions deregulation legislation.

For the past decade, the Federal Government has imposed a ceiling on the interest rates that savers can receive on their deposits in banks and savings institutions. Those ceilings have cost the American people billions of dollars in lost interest annually, and they have become increasingly unfair to the small saver. Especially during a period of high inflation, it is simply unacceptable for the Government to force the small saver with a passbook account at a commercial bank to accept a $5\frac{1}{4}$ percent yield when large and sophisticated savers may receive more than 11 percent.

I would like to thank Chairman Proxmire for his leadership on this bill, and I will continue to work closely with the Congress to assure final action on this important legislation.

International Trade Functions

Message to the Congress Transmitting Reorganization Plan No. 3 of 1979. September 25, 1979

To the Congress of the United States:

I transmit herewith Reorganization Plan No. 3 of 1979, to consolidate trade functions of the United States Government. I am acting under the authority vested in me by the Reorganization Act of 1977, chapter 9 of title 5 of the United States Code, and pursuant to section 1109 of the Trade Agreements Act of 1979, which directs that I transmit to the Congress a proposal to restructure the international trade functions of the Executive branch.

The goal of this reorganization is to improve the capacity of the Government to strengthen the export performance of United States industry and to assure fair international trade practices, taking into account the interests of all elements of our economy.

Recent developments, which have raised concern about the vitality of our international trade performance, have focused much attention on the way our trade machinery is organized. These developments include our negative trade balance, increasing dependence upon foreign oil, and international pressures on the dollar. New challenges, such as implementation of the Multilateral Trade Negotiations (MTN) agreements and trade with non-market economies, will further test our Government trade organization.

We must be prepared to apply domestically the MTN codes on procurement, subsidies, standards, and customs valuation. We also must monitor major implementation measures abroad, reporting back to American business on important developments and, where necessary, raising questions internationally about foreign implementation. MTN will work—will open new markets for U.S. labor, farmers, and business—only if we have adequate procedures for aggressively monitoring and enforcing it. We intend to meet our obligations, and we expect others to do the same.

The trade machinery we now have cannot do this job effectively. Although the Special Trade Representative (STR) takes the lead role in administering the trade agreements program, many issues are handled elsewhere and no agency has across-the-board leadership in trade. Aside from the Trade Representative and the Export-Import Bank, trade is not the primary concern of any Executive branch agency where trade functions are located. The current arrangements lack a central authority capable of planning a coherent trade strategy and assuring its vigorous implementation.

This reorganization is designed to correct such deficiencies and to prepare us for strong enforcement of the MTN codes. It aims to improve our export promotion activities so that United States exporters can take full advantage of trade opportunities in foreign markets. It provides for the timely and efficient administration of our unfair trade laws. It also establishes an efficient mechanism for shaping an effective, comprehensive United States trade policy.

To achieve these objectives, I propose to place policy coordination and negotiation—those international trade functions that most require comprehensiveness, influence, and Government-wide perspective—in the Executive Office of the President. I propose to place operational and implementation responsibilities, which are staff-intensive, in line departments that have the requisite resources and knowledge of the major sectors of our economy to handle them. I have concluded that building our trade structure on STR and Commerce, respectively, best satisfies these considerations.

I propose to enhance STR, to be renamed the Office of the United States Trade Representative, by centralizing in it international trade policy development, coordination and negotiation functions. The Commerce Department will become the focus of non-agricultural operational trade responsibilities by adding to its existing duties those for commercial representation abroad, antidumping and countervailing duty cases, the non-agricultural aspects of MTN implementation, national security investigations, and embargoes.

THE UNITED STATES TRADE REPRESENTATIVE

The Trade Representative, with the advice of the Trade Policy Committee, will be responsible for developing and coordinating our international trade and direct investment policy, including the following areas:

Import remedies. The Trade Representative will exercise policy oversight of the application of import remedies, analyze long-term trends in import remedy cases and recommend any necessary legislative changes. For antidumping and countervailing duty matters, such coordination, to the extent legally permissible, will be directed toward the establishment of new precedents, negotiation of assurances, and coordination with other trade matters, rather than case-by-case fact finding and determinations.

East-West trade policy. The Trade Representative will have lead responsibility for East-West trade negotiations and will coordinate East-West trade policy. The Trade Policy Committee will assume the responsibilities of the East-West Foreign Trade Board.

International investment policy. The Trade Representative will have the policy lead, regarding issues of direct foreign investment in the United States, direct investment by Americans abroad, operations of multinational enterprises, and multilateral agreements on international investment, insofar as such issues relate to international trade.

International commodity policy. The Trade Representative will assume responsibility for commodity negotiations and also will coordinate commodity policy.

Energy trade. While the Departments of Energy and State will continue to share responsibility for international energy issues, the Trade Representative will coordinate energy trade matters. The Department of Energy will become a member of the TPC.

Export-expansion policy. To ensure a vigorous and coordinated Government-wide export expansion effort, policy oversight of our export expansion activities will be the responsibility of the Trade Representative.

The Trade Representative will have the lead role in bilateral and multilateral trade, commodity, and direct investment negotiations. The Trade Representative will represent the United States in General Agreement on Tariffs and Trade (GATT) matters. Since the GATT will be the principal international forum for implementing and interpreting the MTN agreements and since GATT meetings, including committee and working group meetings, occur almost continuously, the Trade Representative will have a limited number of permanent staff in Geneva. In some cases, it may be necessary to assign a small number of USTR staff abroad to assist in oversight of MTN enforcement. In this event, appropriate positions will be authorized. In recognition of the responsibility of the Secretary of State regarding our foreign policy, the activities of overseas personnel of the Trade Representative and the Commerce Department will be fully coordinated with other elements of our diplomatic missions.

In addition to his role with regard to GATT matters, the Trade Representative will have the lead responsibility for trade and commodity matters considered in the Organization for Economic Cooperation and Development (OECD) and the United Nations Conference on Trade and Development (UNCTAD) when such matters are the primary issues under negotiation. Because of the Secretary of State's foreign policy responsibilities, and the responsibilities of the Director of the International Development Cooperation Agency as the President's principal advisor on development, the Trade Representative will exercise his OECD and UNCTAD responsibilities in close cooperation with these officials.

To ensure that all trade negotiations are handled consistently and that our negotiating leverage is employed to the maximum, the Trade Representative will manage the negotiation of particular issues. Where appropriate, the Trade Representative may delegate responsibility for negotiations to other agencies with expertise on the issues under consideration. He will coordinate the operational aspects of negotiations through a Trade Negotiating Committee, chaired by the Trade Representative and including the Departments of Commerce, State, Treasury, Agriculture and Labor.

The Trade Representative will be concerned not only with ongoing negotiations and coordination of specific, immediate issues, but also—very importantly—with the development of long-term United States trade strategies and policies. He will oversee implementation of the MTN agreements, and will advise the President on the effects of other Government policies (e.g., antitrust, taxation) on U.S. trade. In order to participate more fully in oversight of international investment and export financing activities, the Trade Representative will become a member of the National Advisory Council on International Monetary and Financial Policies and the Boards of the Export-Import Bank and the Overseas Private Investment Corporation.

In performing these functions, the Trade Representative will act as the principal trade spokesman of the President. To assure that our trade policies take into account the broadest range of perspectives, the Trade Representative will consult with the Trade Policy Committee, whose mandate and membership will be expanded. The Trade Representative will, as appropriate, invite agencies such as the Export-Import Bank and the Overseas Private Investment Corporation to participate in TPC meetings in addition to the permanent TPC members. When different departmental views on trade matters exist within the TPC as will be the case from time to time in this complex policy area, I will expect the Trade Representative to resolve policy disagreements in his best judgment, subject to appeal to the President.

THE DEPARTMENT OF COMMERCE

The Department of Commerce, under this proposal, will become the focal point of operational responsibilities in the non-agricultural trade area. My reorganization plan will transfer to the Commerce Department important responsibilities for administration of countervailing and antidumping matters, foreign commercial representation, and MTN implementation support. Consolidating these trade functions in the Department of Commerce builds upon an agency with extensive trade experience. The Department will retain its operational responsibilities in such areas as export controls, East-West trade, trade adjustment assistance to firms and communities, trade policy analysis, and monitoring foreign compliance with trade agreements. The Department will be substantially reorganized to consolidate and reshape its trade functions under an Under Secretary for International Trade.

With this reorganization, trade functions will be strengthened within the Department of Commerce, and such related efforts in the Department as improvement of industrial innovation and productivity, encouraging local and regional economic development, and sectoral analysis, will be closely linked to an aggressive trade program. Fostering the international competitiveness of American industry will become the principal mission of the Department of Commerce.

IMPORT REMEDIES

I propose to transfer to the Department of Commerce responsibility for administration of the countervailing duty and antidumping statutes. This function will be performed efficiently and effectively in an organizational setting where trade is the primary mission. This activity will be directed by a new Assistant Secretary for Trade Administration, subject to Senate confirmation. Although the plan permits its provisions to take effect as late as October 1, 1980, I intend to make this transfer effective by January 1, 1980, so that it will occur as the new MTN codes take effect. Commerce will continue its supportive role in the staffing of other unfair trade practice issues, such as cases arising under section 301 of the Trade Act of 1974.

COMMERICAL REPRESENTATION

This reorganization plan will transfer to the Department of Commerce responsibility for commercial representation abroad. This transfer would place both domestic and overseas export promotion activities under a single organization, directed by an Assistant Secretary for Export Development, charged with aggressively expanding U.S. export opportunities. Placing this Foreign Commercial Service in the Commerce Department will allow commercial officers to concentrate on the promotion of U.S. exports as their principal activity.

Initially, the transfer of commercial representation from State to Commerce will involve all full-time overseas trade promotion and commercial positions (approximately 162), responsibility for this function in the countries (approximately 60) to which these individuals are assigned, and the associated foreign national employees in those countries. Over time, the Department of Commerce undoubtedly will review the deployment of commercial officers in light of changing trade circumstances and propose extensions or alterations of coverage of the Foreign Commercial Service.

MTN IMPLEMENTATION

I am dedicated to the aggressive implementation of the Multilateral Trade Agreements. The United States must seize the opportunities and enforce the obligations created by these agreements. Under this proposal, the Department of Commerce will assign high priority to this task. The Department of Commerce will be responsible for the day-to-day implementation of non-agricultural aspects of the MTN agreements. Management of this function will be a principal assignment of an Assistant Secretary for Trade Policy and Programs. Implementation activities will include:

- monitoring agreements and targeting problems for consultation and negotiation;
- operating a Trade Complaint Center where the private sector can receive advice as to the recourse and remedies available;
- aiding in the settlement of disputes, including staffing of formal complaint cases;
- identifying problem areas for consideration by the Trade Representative and the Trade Policy Committee;
- educational and promotion programs regarding the provisions of the agreements and the processes for dealing with problems that arise;
- providing American business with basic information on foreign laws, regulations and procedures;
- consultations with private sector advisory committees; and
- general analytical support.

These responsibilities will be handled by a unit built around the staff from Commerce that provided essential analytical support to STR throughout the MTN negotiation process. Building implementation of MTN around this core group will assure that the government's institutional memory and expertise on MTN is most effectively devoted to the challenge ahead. When American business needs information or encounters problems in the MTN area, it can turn to the Department of Commerce for knowledgeable assistance.

Matching the increased importance of trade in the Department's mission will be a much strengthened trade organization within the Department. By creating a number of new senior level positions in the Department, we will ensure that trade policy implementation receives the kind of day-to-day top management attention that it both demands and requires.

With its new responsibilities and resources, the Department of Commerce will become a key participant in the formulation of our trade policies. Much of the analysis in support of trade policy formulation will be conducted by the Department of Commerce, which will be close to the operational aspects of the problems that raise policy issues.

To succeed in global competition, we must have a better understanding of the problems and prospects of U.S. industry, particularly in relation to the growing strength of industries abroad. This is the key reason why we will upgrade sectoral analysis capabilities throughout the Department of Commerce, including the creation of a new Bureau of Industrial Analysis. Commerce, with its ability to link trade to policies affecting industry, is uniquely suited to serve as the principal technical expert within the Government on special industry sector problems requiring international consultation, as well as to provide industry-specific information on how tax, regulatory and other Government policies affect the international competitiveness of the U.S. industries.

Commerce will also expand its traditional trade policy focus on industrial issues to deal with the international trade and investment problems of our growing services sector. Under the proposal, there will be comprehensive service industry representation in our industry advisory process, as well as a continuing effort to bring services under international discipline. I expect the Commerce Department to play a major role in developing new service sector initiatives for consideration within the Government.

After an investigation lasting over a year, I have found that this reorganization is necessary to carry out the policy set forth in section 901(a) of title 5 of the United States Code. As described above, this reorganization will increase significantly our ability to implement the MTN agreements efficiently and effectively and will improve greatly the services of the government with regard to export development. These improvements will be achieved with no increase in personnel or expenditures, except for an annual expense of about $300,000 for the salaries and clerical support of the three additional senior Commerce Department officials and a non-recurring expense of approximately $600,000 in connection with the transfers of functions provided in the plan. I find that the reorganization made by this plan makes necessary the provisions for the appointment and pay of a Deputy Secretary, an Under Secretary for International Trade, and two additional Assistant Secretaries of the Department of Commerce, and additional members of the Boards of Directors of the Export-Import Bank and the Overseas Private Investment Corporation.

It is indeed appropriate that this proposal follows so soon after the overwhelming approval by the Congress of the Trade Agreements Act of 1979, for it will sharpen and unify trade policy direction, improve the efficiency of trade law enforcement, and enable us to negotiate abroad from a position of strength. The extensive discussions between Administration officials and the Congress on this plan have been a model of the kind of cooperation that can exist between the two branches. I look forward to our further cooperation in successfully implementing both this reorganization proposal and the MTN agreements.

JIMMY CARTER

The White House,
September 25, 1979.

REORGANIZATION PLAN No. 3 OF 1979

Prepared by the President and transmitted to the Senate and the House of Representatives in Congress assembled, September 25, 1979, pursuant to the provisions of chapter 9 of title 5 of the United States Code.

REORGANIZATION OF FUNCTIONS RELATING TO INTERNATIONAL TRADE

SECTION 1. *Office of the United States Trade Representative*

(a) The Office of the Special Representative for Trade Negotiations is redesignated the Office of the United States Trade Representative.

(b)(1) The Special Representative for Trade Negotiations is redesignated the United States Trade Representative (hereinafter referred to as the "Trade Representative"). The Trade Representative shall have primary responsibility, with the advice of the interagency organization established under section 242 of the Trade Expansion Act of 1962 (19 U.S.C. 1872) (hereinafter referred to as the "Committee"), for developing, and for coordinating the implementation of, United States international trade policy, including commodity matters and, to the extent they are related to international trade policy, direct investment matters. The Trade Representative shall serve as the principal advisor to the President on international trade policy and shall advise the President on the impact of other policies of the United States Government on international trade.

(2) The Trade Representative shall have lead responsibility for the conduct of international trade negotiations, including commodity and direct investment negotiations in which the United States participates.

(3) To the extent necessary to assure the coordination of international trade policy, and consistent with any other law, the Trade Representative, with the advice of the Committee, shall issue policy guidance to departments and agencies on basic issues of policy and interpretation arising in the exercise of the following international trade functions. Such guidance shall determine the policy of the United States with respect to international trade issues arising in the exercise of such functions:

(A) matters concerning the General Agreement on Tariffs and Trade, including implementation of the trade agreements set forth in section 2(c) of the Trade Agreements Act of 1979; United States Government positions on trade and commodity matters dealt with by the Organization for Economic Cooperation and Development, the United Nations Conference on Trade and Development, and other multilateral organizations; and the assertion and protection of the rights of the United States under bilateral and multilateral international trade and commodity agreements;

(B) expansion of exports from the United States;

(C) policy research on international trade, commodity, and direct investment matters;

(D) to the extent permitted by law, overall United States policy with regard to unfair trade practices, including enforcement of countervailing duties and antidumping functions under section 303 and title VII of the Tariff Act of 1930:

(E) bilateral trade and commodity issues, including East-West trade matters; and

(F) international trade issues involving energy.

(4) All functions of the Trade Representative shall be conducted under the direction of the President.

(c) The Deputy Special Representatives for Trade Negotiations are redesignated Deputy United States Trade Representatives.

SECTION 2. *Department of Commerce*

(a) The Secretary of Commerce (hereinafter referred to as the "Secretary") shall have, in addition to any other functions assigned by law, general operational responsibility for major nonagricultural international trade functions of the United States Government, including export development, commercial representation abroad, the administration of the antidumping and countervailing duty laws, export controls, trade adjustment assistance to firms and communities, research and analysis, and monitoring compliance with international trade agreements to which the United States is a party.

(b)(1) There shall be in the Department of Commerce (hereinafter referred to as the "Department") a Deputy Secretary appointed by the President, by and with the advice and consent of the Senate. The Deputy Secretary shall receive compensation at the rate payable for Level II of the Executive Schedule, and shall perform such duties and exercise such powers as the Secretary may from time to time prescribe.

(2) The position of Under Secretary of Commerce established under section 1 of the Act of June 5, 1939 (ch. 180, 53 Stat. 808; 15 U.S.C. 1502) is abolished.

(c) There shall be in the Department an Under Secretary for International Trade appointed by the President, by and with the advice and consent of the Senate. The Under Secretary for International Trade shall receive compensation at the rate payable for Level III of the Executive Schedule, and shall perform such duties and exercise such powers as the Secretary may from time to time prescribe.

(d) There shall be in the Department two additional Assistant Secretaries appointed by the President, by and with the advice and consent of the Senate. Each such Assistant Secretary shall receive compensation at the rate payable for Level IV of the Executive Schedule, and shall perform such duties and exercise such powers as the Secretary may from time to time prescribe.

SECTION 3. *Export-Import Bank of the United States*

The Trade Representative and the Secretary shall serve, ex officio and without vote, as additional members of the Board of Directors of the Export-Import Bank of the United States.

SECTION 4. *Overseas Private Investment Corporation*

(a) The Trade representative shall serve, ex officio, as an additional voting member of the Board of Directors of the Overseas Private Investment Corporation. The Trade Representative shall be the Vice Chair of such Board.

(b) There shall be an additional member of the Board of Directors of the Overseas Private Investment Corporation who shall be appointed by the President of the United States, by and with the advice and

consent of the Senate, and who shall not be an official or employee of the Government of the United States. Such Director shall be appointed for a term of no more than three years.

SECTION 5. *Transfer of Functions*

(a)(1) There are transferred to the Secretary all functions of the Secretary of the Treasury, the General Counsel of the Department of the Treasury, or the Department of the Treasury pursuant to the following:

(A) section 305(b) of the Trade Agreements Act of 1979 (19 U.S.C. 2515 (b)), to be exercised in consultation with the Secretary of the Treasury;

(B) section 232 of the Trade Expansion Act of 1962 (19 U.S.C. 1862);

(C) section 303 and title VII (including section 771(1)) of the Tariff Act of 1930 (19 U.S.C. 1303, 1671 *et seq.*), except that the Customs Service of the Department of the Treasury shall accept such deposits, bonds, or other security as deemed appropriate by the Secretary, shall assess and collect such duties as may be directed by the Secretary, and shall furnish such of its important records or copies thereof as may be requested by the Secretary incident to the functions transferred by this subparagraph;

(D) sections 514, 515, and 516 of the Tariff Act of 1930 (19 U.S.C. 1514, 1515, and 1516) insofar as they relate to any protest, petition, or notice of desire to contest described in section 1002(b)(1) of the Trade Agreements Act of 1979;

(E) with respect to the functions transferred by subparagraph (C) of this paragraph, section 318 of the Tariff Act of 1930 (19 U.S.C. 1318), to be exercised in consultation with the Secretary of the Treasury;

(F) with respect to the functions transferred by subparagraph (C) of this paragraph, section 502(b) of the Tariff Act of

1930 (19 U.S.C. 1502(b)), and, insofar as it provides authority to issue regulations and disseminate information, to be exercised in consultation with the Secretary of the Treasury to the extent that the Secretary of the Treasury has responsibility under subparagraph (C), section 502(a) of such Act (19 U.S.C. 1502(a));

(G) with respect to the functions transferred by subparagraph (C) of this paragraph, section 617 of the Tariff Act of 1930 (19 U.S.C. 1617); and

(H) section 2632(e) of title 28 of the United States Code, insofar as it relates to actions taken by the Secretary reviewable under section 516A of the Tariff Act of 1930 (19 U.S.C. 1516(a)).

(2) The Secretary shall consult with the Trade Representative regularly in exercising the functions transferred by subparagraph (C) of paragraph (1) of this subsection, and shall consult with the Trade Representative regarding any substantive regulation proposed to be issued to enforce such functions.

(b)(1) There are transferred to the Secretary all trade promotion and commercial functions of the Secretary of State or the Department of State that are—

(A) performed in full-time overseas trade promotion and commercial positions; or

(B) performed in such countries as the President may from time to time prescribe.

(2) To carry out the functions transferred by paragraph (1) of this subsection, the President, to the extent he deems it necessary, may authorize the Secretary to utilize Foreign Service personnel authorities and to exercise the functions vested in the Secretary of State by the Foreign Service Act of 1946 (22 U.S.C. 801 *et seq.*) and by any other laws with respect to personnel performing such functions.

(c) There are transferred to the President all functions of the East-West Foreign Trade Board under section 411(c) of the Trade Act of 1974 (19 U.S.C. 2441 (c)).

(d) Appropriations available to the Department of State for Fiscal Year 1980 for representation of the United States concerning matters arising under the General Agreement on Tariffs and Trade and trade and commodity matters dealt with under the auspices of the United Nations Conference on Trade and Development are transferred to the Trade Representative.

(e) There are transferred to the interagency organization established under section 242 of the Trade Expansion Act of 1962 (19 U.S.C. 1872) all functions of the East-West Foreign Trade Board under section 411 (a) and (b) of the Trade Act of 1974 (19 U.S.C. 2441 (a) and (b)).

SECTION 6. *Abolition*

The East-West Foreign Trade Board established under section 411 of the Trade Act of 1974 (19 U.S.C. 2441) is abolished.

SECTION 7. *Responsibility of the Secretary of State*

Nothing in this reorganization plan is intended to derogate from the responsibility of the Secretary of State for advising the President on foreign policy matters, including the foreign policy aspects of international trade and trade-related matters.

SECTION 8. *Incidental transfers; interim officers*

(a) So much of the personnel, property, records, and unexpended balances of appropriations, allocations, and other funds employed, used, held, available or to be made available in connection with the functions transferred under this reorganization plan as the Director of the

Office of Management and Budget shall determine shall be transferred to the appropriate agency, organization, or component at such time or times as such Director shall provide, except that no such unexpended balances transferred shall be used for purposes other than those for which the appropriation originally was made. The Director of the Office of Management and Budget shall provide for terminating the affairs of any agency abolished herein and for such further measures and dispositions as such Director deems necessary to effectuate the purposes of the reorganization plan.

(b) Pending the assumption of office by the initial officers provided for in section 2 of this reorganization plan, the functions of each such office may be performed, for up to a total of 60 days, by such individuals as the President may designate. Any individual so designated shall be compensated at the rate provided herein for such position.

SECTION 9. *Effective date*

The provisions of this reorganization plan shall take effect October 1, 1980, or at such earlier time or times as the President shall specify, but not sooner than the earliest time allowable under section 906 of title 5 of the United States Code.

The Cyprus Conflict

Letter to the Speaker of the House and the Chairman of the Senate Foreign Relations Committee. September 25, 1979

To Speaker Tip O'Neill (To Chairman Frank Church)

In accordance with the provisions of Public Law 95–384, I am submitting the following report on progress made during the past 60 days toward the conclusion of a negotiated solution of the Cyprus problem.

In my last Cyprus report to the Congress, dated July 25, I noted that UN Secretary General Waldheim and his staff were seeking to bring the two parties back to the conference table. Unfortunately, the recess in the intercommunal talks continues, largely because the two sides still have major differences both with regard to their approach to this negotiation and to the content of a final settlement of the Cyprus problem.

The UN Secretary General, through his staff, is continuing to consult informally with the parties. He has had some success in creating a foundation on which the talks might resume. We are giving strong and continued support to this effort. We have frequently discussed the situation on Cyprus in a frank manner with all parties, reminding them that negotiation is preferable to stalemate, and that their broad interests would be served by a return to the conference table. Other interested third parties have made similar points to them.

Despite the difficulties, we continue to believe that a way can be found to end the present impasse and to permit the two sides to commence a serious negotiation of the Cyprus problem.

This Administration will continue to strive for progress in that direction. In pursuit of this goal, we shall remain in close touch with the United Nations, the parties to the Cyprus dispute, and our close European allies.

Sincerely,

JIMMY CARTER

NOTE: This is the text of identical letters addressed to Thomas P. O'Neill, Jr., Speaker of the House of Representatives, and Frank Church, chairman of the Senate Foreign Relations Committee.

August Consumer Price Index

White House Statement.   September 25, 1979

Once again, the increased cost of energy was the major factor in an unacceptably high inflation rate during the month of August, and once again, this fact underscores the importance of following through on the President's energy and anti-inflation programs. In fact, the cost of energy and the cost of buying and financing a home were exclusively responsible for pushing the Consumer Price Index into a double-digit annual rate.

We were, of course, gratified that grocery prices remained stable during the month. And outside of food and the troublesome areas of energy and housing, other consumer prices rose at a much lower, though still too high, annual rate of 8.5 percent.

For the second time in 6 years, our Nation is suffering severely from both higher inflation and higher unemployment because of a sudden and massive increase in world oil prices. The need to reduce our dependence on foreign oil is driven home each time the CPI comes out.

We simply cannot allow the huge increases in the prices of energy and housing to set off double-digit inflation in wages and other prices. To prevent that from happening, we need restraint on two fronts:

1. continuing to pursue a tight Federal budget as the President has proposed, and
2. observing the President's voluntary wage-price standards, which, skeptics to the contrary, have been keeping double-digit inflation at bay, outside of energy and housing.

New York City, New York

Remarks at the Annual Convention of the American Public Transit Association. September 25, 1979

Senator Moynihan, Governor Hugh Carey, Mayor Ed Koch, Secretary of Transportation Neil Goldschmidt, Members of Congress from this State and from others, Lieutenant Governor Mario Cuomo, Chairman Harold Fisher, my good friend and partners with me in a great future for mass transit, rapid transit, public transportation, public transit:

We're all in it together, and we're going to prevail.

Thank you. I'm glad to be with you. I'm particularly glad to be back in New York—this great city which has, among so many other superlatives, the title of the "mass transit capital of the world." With 45 percent of all the riders of public transportation in our Nation, it's obvious that I should come here, first of all, and say that there is absolutely no way that New York would lose Federal funds for public transportation because of any technicality or lack of adequate preparation between the Federal Government and New York, and no one need worry about that.

And I'm glad to be in the same room with so many people, from all over this Nation, who agree with me that public transit is one of the keys to the future of the United States of America.

We can no longer afford to think of public transportation as something that we might some day get around to developing adequately for the people who look to me and you for public leadership, once all the superhighways and cloverleafs have been completed. We must address the problems of public transportation now, and we will address those problems together.

This has always been a problem and a challenge. But this Nation is now in the throes of an energy crisis, a crisis of dangerous overdependence on foreign oil—a challenge and overdependence which directly threatens the security of our very Nation, a crisis that affects every single person who lives in this country. In a few blunt words, that is why public transit is important to all citizens of this country, regardless of where they might live.

In cities and small towns, among suburbanites and rural dwellers, subway riders and pickup truck drivers—we all have an interest in public transit—even though some may not ever ride in a public transportation vehicle—because we all have an interest in solving the problem of energy. And we will solve that problem. The subways, the buses, and the trolleys of America will help to carry America to a time of energy security.

In my first energy speech to America, I told the American people bluntly that the era of cheap and abundant energy and wasteful consumption was gone. I was warned that this would not be good politics. Nobody likes bad news. And when I made that evening address to the American people, I said in that talk that it would undoubtedly cost me 15 percent in the public polls. That was the underestimation—[*laughter*]— of my first year.

I called the energy crisis the moral equivalent of war, a statement that was ignored by some and ridiculed by others. But I was determined then and I'm determined now to level with the American people. It has not been easy to get that message across, but today, 2½ years after that speech, millions of Americans now know from hard experience and careful analysis that I was not exaggerating.

Not too long ago the United States was a net exporting country for oil. By 1973, when the OPEC nations' oil embargo hit with a massive increase in prices, we were importing about one-third of all the oil we used, sometimes at less than $2 a barrel. But we failed to come to grips with the underlying problem that OPEC began to exploit. We were given fair warning; we did not listen. Instead, through a complicated system of price controls, we tried to insulate ourselves from the realities of a global economic change.

This policy, or absence of a policy, did not work. In fact, it encouraged our illusions about cheap energy and actually made our dependence worse, so that this year we are importing about one-half all the oil we use. And because OPEC has taken advantage of this industrial world's thirst for oil at any price, OPEC has continued to jack up the prices. The dollars have flowed out even faster than oil has flowed in. In 1973, for instance, we were paying in American dollars, for foreign oil, $7 billion. Next year we will pay $70 billion—a tenfold increase.

When those billions of dollars flow out of our country, American jobs flow out with them. And when those millions of barrels of foreign oil flow in, we import inflation. Without the astronomical rise in energy costs, in fact, the inflation rate would be at least one-third lower than it is now. The last 3 months, the inflation rate would have increased only one-fourth of 1 percent, if you don't count energy. But energy has been increasing in price at an average of 100 percent per year.

Our economic well-being is at stake and so is our political freedom of action. We are vulnerable to interruptions in oil supply at any time from very uncertain sources, and we are mandated to pay whatever prices are asked. And the competition for oil supplies tends to weaken our political alliances, because we and our friends are in competition to buy the same scarce and expensive barrel of oil.

The production of oil by the OPEC nations is highly unlikely to increase. The trend is probably going to be downward because of several reasons. Some OPEC nations are now producing more oil than they would like to produce for their own benefit and for the benefit of their people. Other OPEC nations have recently begun to reduce oil exports because their supplies are running out. And others, as you well know, tend to use oil as a political weapon, attempting, unsuccessfully so far, to blackmail or to attempt blackmail by the threat of withholding their oil from the world market.

So, dependence on foreign oil threatens our economy, and it also threatens our security. It threatens our very future. Therefore, we must stop and then reverse this growth in imported oil. And public transit can help us do that.

Thirty-five years ago, at the close of the Second World War, this country could claim some of the finest public transit systems on Earth. Those transit systems were more than just a way to get people from one place to another. They helped to structure a compact and efficient pattern of land development where people lived, where people worked, and this contributed to a sense of community, of unity, of sharing, of interrelationships, a feeling that brought neighbors together in a common sense of place. Our transit systems were a vital connecting link that helped to form our own way of life.

But in the years after World War II, we let that connecting link begin to erode. Because we did not recognize its worth, we valued it too little; because we did not measure its contribution to our lives, we ignored it too much; and because we

could not imagine its absence, we hardly noticed its decline in quality.

As we turned our attention to the construction of a vast network of superhighways, we began to operate on a set of unspoken, unacknowledged, untenable assumptions. We assumed, for instance, that the United States was afloat on a sea of 20-cent-a-gallon gasoline. We assumed that bigger always meant better and that nothing could be better than a long, chrome-plated convertible with a gas-guzzling V–8 engine under the hood. We assumed that urban sprawl was a law of nature, not a logical outcome of transportation and development policies. We assumed that the only respectable way to get a 160-pound human from point A to point B was to wrap him in 2 tons of metal with an engine powerful enough to drive an army tank.

So, we began to lose our public transportation systems. One by one, city by city, the systems fell prey to decay and to neglect.

Now we know that was a mistake. Now we recognize the value of mass transit, and now, as the battle for American energy security is joined, we stand committed to the rediscovery and the revitalization of America's public transportation systems. You and I together have embarked on that rediscovery. We have begun that revitalization. Federal support for public transportation now stands at the highest point in history.

I proposed, and the Congress passed, the most far-reaching surface transportation bill in our history, giving it a higher priority than it has ever had before.

Under our comprehensive urban policy, which many of you helped to evolve—the Nation's first, by the way—cities and towns are now working along with private enterprise and with the Federal Government to make transit an integral part of urban development and urban redevelopment. There's a good example just a few blocks from here at the Grand Central Terminal, where a $10 million Federal grant will help tie in several forms of public transit with a new mall, a new hotel, and a surrounding area of shops and offices.

During the fuel shortage this summer, which shook our Nation up, we kept the trains running and the buses fueled and rolling. And we will keep them rolling in the future if we have additional energy shortages. America's public transportation systems will continue to have the fuel that they need.

When I was looking for a new Secretary of Transportation, some of you came forward and made suggestions which I took. I looked all over America for a person who could come to Washington as a strong advocate of public transit and who understood very clearly the role that public transportation must play in the life of a community. I found that person in Neil Goldschmidt, who worked as a leader in our Nation's transportation problems, working with other mayors and local and State officials all over this country, and whose commitment to mass transit produced extraordinary results in Portland during his term as mayor.

And since he's been there, he's made some very wise decisions, one of which I'm pleased to announce today. And that is that the new administrator of our urban mass transit program will be Ted Lutz, who's one of you. And he was chosen, as a matter of fact, the Rail Man of the Year. And I'm very proud of him, because he's got practical experience on how to coordinate government programs with local needs, how to cut through redtape, how to get to the heart of a program and a problem and to find a resolution and an answer.

We've made a strong start, but I'm here today, after 2½ years in office, to tell you that we've got a long way to go, a lot more to do, much more.

Our Nation's investment in public transit during the 1970's came to a total of $15 billion, and now we must take a quantum jump. With the energy proposals that I have presented to the Congress, the Nation, our Nation, will invest $50 billion in public transportation during the decade of the 1980's. We need it, and we will have it. Our goal during that time is to add 15 million passengers per day to the buses, the streetcars, and the trolleys and subways of our cities and our communities.

We will double the production of buses, the only form of mass transit in 97 percent of America's cities. We will step up the modernization and the refurbishment of existing rapid transit systems. For example, New York: Its subway system is the senior citizen of underground rail travel. The IRT is 75 years old this year. It has survived, and we are proud of our senior citizens. But when Ed Koch and Harold Fisher and I get through with it, with the tools we are fighting to get from the Congress, it's not going to look a day over sweet 16. [*Laughter*] And we will also speed up the construction of new rail lines already approved or underway in other major American cities.

We'll build subways and elevated trains, trolleys, people-movers, commuter trains. We'll repair track beds, modernize stations, improve signaling and control stations, replace aging railcars, expand the size of fleets, extend lines into new areas and encourage new technologies. In short, we will reclaim and we will revitalize America's transit systems.

Over the long term—and this is very important—the energy savings will be massive. Those savings will result not only from getting folks out of cars and onto buses and trains but also from the patterns of development that the public transit system can encourage.

Public transit means good living for people in downtown areas and more efficient housing development patterns, which in turn means less waste of energy for fuel and also for heating and cooling. And better mass transit will give us an insurance policy against the lack of mobility in the future. If gasoline crunches come— and I think they will surely come—better mass transit will help us attack a whole range of critical, interrelated problems, not just energy but also inflation, unemployment, the health of our environment, and the vitality of our cities.

Public transit means cleaner air. Public transit means less noise. Public transit means stronger, more livable cities. It means more mobility and more opportunity for everybody, and especially those who need it most—the poor, the aged, the young, the handicapped, minorities.

And public transit means jobs, a lot of jobs. The energy mass transit initiative that I've proposed to the Congress will put Americans to work. I'm not talking about a few hundred jobs for bureaucrats in Washington, along with administrators, but I'm talking about an average of at least 40,000 jobs a year, at all levels of skills, throughout the 1980's.

Clearly, public transportation is a critical part of the overall assault that I've directed against this Nation's energy dilemma. And just as clearly, our transit investments cannot do the job alone. Those investments must be a part of a comprehensive program. And that's exactly what I've proposed—a program that develops alternative forms of energy, especially those plentiful ones that are ours to control, such as coal, and the most plentiful source of all, the Sun; a program

that lets vital energy projects be built without endless redtape and confusion and delay and also without compromising our commitment to a clean environment and a good quality of life; a program that offers some help for the poor among us, on whom the most cruel blows of skyrocketing costs inevitably fall. And public transit can encourage people to do the most important thing of all—stop wasting energy.

Conservation must become a part of our lives, and this need not be an onerous part or an unpleasant part of our lives. It can be an exciting and enjoyable thing to stop wasting what God has given us. It can bind families together. It can make us look around and see how we and our neighbors can have a more productive and more enjoyable life. And at the same time, we can contribute greatly to the health and well-being of our country. It's a patriotic gesture.

This program, along with our transit initiative, can take us to our energy goal of energy security. But for all this program to succeed, the Congress absolutely must approve the one major element, which Chairman Fisher has already named—the windfall profits tax.

A train needs an engine. A bus needs an engine. A pickup truck needs an engine. And the windfall profits tax will be the engine of American energy security. Through it, we will use the unavoidable rises in oil prices as a lever, as kind of a crowbar, to pry ourselves loose from the dilemma that our overreliance of oil got us into in the first place.

Right now lobbyists are swarming all over Capitol Hill, working to devastate the windfall profits tax. In fact, their proposed amendments would put a total of well over $100 billion in the pockets of the oil companies. And what would they do with this money? Would they develop renewable energy sources? Would they push for a national energy conservation program? Would they winterize homes? Would they help poor people pay their fuel bills? Would they devote $13 billion to public transportation? Of course not, of course not.

These crucial steps are not their business, but they're the public's business. They're the Nation's business. And the Nation needs these funds to make our energy future secure.

I have traveled the length and the breadth of this country, fighting for a tough, permanent, fair windfall profits tax, and I will continue to fight for it. I do not intend to lose this fight, and if you will help me, we will not lose.

And finally, I would like to say this: I deeply appreciate the support that the American Public Transit Association has given me in this fight so far. Today I call upon you collectively, as an association and as individuals, to redouble your support as the crucial votes in the Senate, and then the Senate and House, on windfall profits draw near. With your help, we can gain this tax and drive our program forward.

Cutting our reliance on foreign oil will curb inflation, strengthen the dollar, stimulate new jobs, give Americans a better life. Public transportation is part of this chain of support—saving energy, adding jobs, and improving the overall quality of life in our Nation's history— one of the most important challenges that we have faced in our Nation's history.

We're about to enter a new decade, carrying with us the lessons of the past, the good lessons and the bad lessons, and the hopes and the dreams and aspirations of all Americans.

The choices ahead are difficult, and we cannot avoid making them, but Americans have never looked for an easy way out when we were faced with a challenge that threatened our country. I believe in the decency and in the courage of the American people. I believe that we have the material and the moral and the spiritual strength to meet any challenge.

Together, in the years ahead, we can seize control again of our own destiny, and we can make sure that America will remain what America is today—the greatest nation on Earth.

Thank you very much.

NOTE: The President spoke at 3:55 p.m. in the Grand Ballroom at the New York Hilton Hotel. In his opening remarks, he referred to Harold Fisher, chairman of the New York Metropolitan Transit Authority and chairman of the American Public Transit Association.

Urban Mass Transportation Administration

Nomination of Theodore C. Lutz To Be Administrator.   September 25, 1979

The President today announced his intention to nominate Theodore C. Lutz as Administrator of the Urban Mass Transportation Administration, Department of Transportation.

From November 1976 to May 1979, Mr. Lutz served as general manager of the Washington Metropolitan Area Transit Authority (METRO) in Washington, D.C. From 1973 to 1976, he served as Deputy Under Secretary of the Department of Transportation. From 1968 to 1973, Mr. Lutz was a budget examiner in the Office of Management and Budget.

He was born September 24, 1945, in Philadelphia, Pa. He received a B.A. degree from Carleton College in 1967 and an MPA degree from Syracuse University, Maxwell Graduate School of Citizenship and Public Affairs in 1968.

NOTE: The announcement was released at New York City, N.Y.

New York City, New York

Remarks at a Reception for Community Leaders. September 25, 1979

That's one of the best speeches I've ever heard Ed Koch make. Thank you very much. [*Laughter*]

Senator Pat Moynihan and Governor Hugh Carey, Governor Brendan Byrne, distinguished Members of the Congress, public officials representing New York City and New York State, and my friends:

I'm very glad to be back with you again.

The first time I came to New York, after I announced that I was a candidate for President, I told my wife when I got back home that it was a city that had lost its spirit. There was a sense of despair among many, but a sense of dedication and resolution and courage and a sense of unity that was a core of the strength that would tide New York City over a time of crisis.

I formed a partnership with New York City in my mind. And I've never headed toward this great place without a sense of warmth and friendship and pleasant anticipation, and I have never been disappointed. And I thank you for that.

I think in the last 2½ or 3 years, we've come a long way. We still have a long way to go. The Congress has responded well to superb leadership.

And one day when I was in the Cabinet Room with Tip O'Neill and was, in a way, bragging about what we had done for New York City, he said, "Mr. President, I don't want to take anything away from you. You're a great man and a gentle person and a beautiful man. But," he said, "the Congress passed the bill establishing Federal credits for New York City loans because they had confidence in Ed Koch." And I said, "Well, that's the— [*applause*]——

But it's obvious that the entire New York delegation and Mayor [Governor] Hugh Carey and many friends throughout the Congress worked hard to make it possible for New York to get itself back on the side of strength and confidence in the future—and tangible accomplishments already. There can be no retreat from this course that we've set out together, because we still have a long way to go.

In public transit—I just spoke to the national convention of those who are intensely interested as professionals in public transit—we've made a lot of progress. I think the next 4 years, compared to the previous 4 years, will show at least a 50-percent increase in the allocation of Federal funds for public transit in your city. And we'll have continued improvements in other areas of life as well.

I've not been in office long—sometimes it seems like a long time—but just since I was inaugurated, we've had a 33-percent increase in the amount of Federal funds coming in aid of all kinds to New York City—a $700 million increase, net. However, this has not been confined to any special thing. It's been broad-gauged in its effect, and it has had to find a ready reception here and an eagerness among people to look forward to the future with confidence.

In education, in transportation, in housing, in recreation, in health, we're working with a close spirit of common purpose. On occasion there have been some instances of inadequate communication, recently between the Department of Transportation and Governor Carey. But that's a transient thing, and there's no problem in working that out.

And as I told those interested in public transportation, New York will not lose any Federal funds because we or the city or the State have failed to meet the technicalities of the law. We will make sure you get your money.

And these are also not cosmetic changes. I think that following the 1976 July Fourth great ships parade and then followed by another great event, the Democratic convention of 1976, I could see a new spirit in the city—*[laughter]*—that I think will be mirrored again next summer, when the Democratic convention comes back here.

And I would like to say in closing that we have proposals in the Congress now that will add a great deal more in opportunity for your city and your State to make even greater progress in the years to come.

Welfare reform has cleared the House Ways and Means Committee, and Pat Moynihan is working hard to get it through the Senate Finance Committee. Our proposal under the windfall profits tax will mean a tremendous increase in help for poor families to deal with the inordinately rising costs of energy, to give a better mass transit system, and to make our Nation energy-secure in the future.

We have an opportunity, I think, to be sure that there is a continued sense of common responsibility for your city and for your State. Every one of you in this room is a constituent of mine, and your well-being and the quality of life among those who look to you for leadership I consider to be my direct responsibility. I was not elected President to tell New York City to drop dead, and I will obviously never do so.

The political and the financial health of the greatest city on Earth is a sure sign of the political and the financial health of the greatest nation on Earth. And this Nation is my responsibility. And what you do here will have a direct effect on the quality of life throughout the whole Nation.

I want to recognize Mayor Abe Beame,[1] who I understand is here. Stand up, Abe. Abe's always too modest to stand up. Thank you very much, Abe. *[Laughter]*

Let me say this in closing: As this button says, I love New York.

Thank you very much.

NOTE: The President spoke at 4:55 p.m. in the Trianon Room at the New York Hilton Hotel. The reception was hosted by Mayor Edward I. Koch of New York City.

New York City, New York

Question-and-Answer Session at a Town Meeting With Residents of the Borough of Queens.   September 25, 1979

THE PRESIDENT. *Senator Pat Moynihan, Mayor Ed Koch, Lieutenant Governor Mario Cuomo, President Don Manes, President Saul Cohen, and my friends from Queens and from New York City:*

I am very glad to be back with you.

First of all, I want to thank the Queens Symphony Orchestra for a tremendous reception.

I was going to make an opening statement or speech. I've decided that since so many people are here, and I know you have a lot of questions, that I will not do so. So, if you will not be timid with your questions, I will not be timid with my answers. Let's get on with the question-and-answer period.

PRESIDENT'S JOGGING HABITS

Q. Mr. President, this is a great honor. My name is Nicholas Gray. I live in Manhattan, and I own a store there called Gray's Papaya. *[Laughter]* We're famous for our better filet mignon frankfurters.

---

[1] Abraham D. Beame, former mayor of New York City.

THE PRESIDENT. My name is Jimmy Carter. I'm President of the United States. [*Laughter*]

Q. I am a fan of yours, and I was told to tell you this.

THE PRESIDENT. I know. Great.

Q. Mr. President, welcome to New York City.

THE PRESIDENT. And I grow peanuts, you know, so eat peanut butter. [*Laughter*]

Q. Welcome to New York City, Mr. President. You look great. There are many millions here who stand firmly behind you and who look forward to your reelection.

My question is friendly and personal. I wonder if you'd take a couple of minutes to tell us about your jogging habits and how you are feeling in general since your race in Maryland last week? [*Laughter*]

THE PRESIDENT. I'd like to answer all the questions, including this one. Thank you, Mr. Gray, for your welcome.

I've been running in college. I've been running for the State Senate, and then for Governor, and then for President—[*laughter*]—still have running on my mind.

I run about 3 or 4 miles a day on the average—sometimes as much as 12 miles, sometimes as little as 2 miles, and enjoy it very much. My wife runs from 2 to 5 miles with me each day. It helps me to be by myself, enjoy a conversation with my wife, and I look forward to it very much. And I stay in good shape, ready for running in the future.

Q. Thank you, Mr. President. You look great.

THE PRESIDENT. Thank you.

PRESIDENT'S 1976 CAMPAIGN PROMISES

Q. Good evening, Mr. President. My name is Stewart Weinberg. I'm 22 years old, from Bayside, Queens, and I'd sure like to thank you for making me feel almost as if I'm in touch with my Government. I think it's great. I really do.

THE PRESIDENT. Thank you.

Q. I want you to know that in 1976 I worked very hard for your election campaign. [*Laughter*] Just cool it people, just cool it. I worked very hard, and I'd like you to take that into consideration when I ask you this question. [*Laughter*]

Consider your 1976 election campaign promises, and consider how those ideas and programs have progressed. Consider that the American dollar has been plummeting. Consider the rise in inflation, the oil crisis, the gas lines, the tremendous cost of home heating oil. Consider the tumultuous nature of your ever-changing Cabinet. Consider how we have added more destruction to our ecosystem with nuclear energy and oil spills. Consider that we really don't have a comprehensive national energy or health program. And consider that I am a college-educated young man who has been unemployed for 3 months, and I'm very unhappy about that.

Evaluating what I've pointed out, please explain why I should support you for your reelection. What makes you think your first term merits a reelection? I want to know if I should work for you a second time, and why.

THE PRESIDENT. Thank you, Mr. Weinberg.

I've now been President for a little more than 2½ years. We've had some notable achievements and we've had some disappointments. I think in trying to go down the list of things that you described—and I'll confine myself to that and not talk about the good things, okay?—to be fair to you.

Employment—when I was elected President and inaugurated, the unemployment rate was 8 percent. Now it's 6 percent. We've had a net increase in jobs in this country of 8 million, a net increase in jobs. This record has mirrored itself in New York City, where the unemployment rate has dropped about 2 percent.

I would like for every college graduate, like you, and also for every person in our country who hasn't had the advantages of college, to have a job. It's not possible to give a job to everyone. I think we've made reasonable progress.

On inflation—we've had inflation with us for about 10 years, 11 years. It's been as high as 12 or 13 percent in 1973 and '74, when OPEC raised their prices. It's up to that level now because OPEC has raised their prices.

In the last 3 months, for instance, the inflation rate, not counting energy, has gone up one-fourth of 1 percent. In that same time, because of action taken by OPEC, over which I have no control, the inflation rate in energy is going up 100 percent per year. And obviously, when that's mixed in with the other costs, the inflation rate is high; it's too high. I wish I could get it down.

You point out that we have no energy policy. We are hammering out a comprehensive, excellent energy policy which I believe and predict flatly will be on the law books by the time this year is over.

We have not ever had before any semblance of an energy policy. And in spite of my efforts for the last 2½ years, the Congress has yet not passed one word relating to oil.

In the past, the oil lobbies have permeated the influence on the Hill in Washington, because consumers had no strong voice. And I have to admit, at that time that oil prices were relatively low. Now it's just about an even thing. But I still predict to you that we will add on to a very good legislative program last year, a complete energy policy this year. It's long

overdue, but there's only so much that you can do in 2½ years.

The second thing I'd like to say is that so far we've already saved, because of actions taken within the last 12 months, about 4 million barrels of imported oil that we will not have to import by 1990. My additional proposals, which will pass this year, will save an additional 4½ million barrels of oil.

I know how serious the problem is. I don't know how you reacted in April of '77 when I went to the people on evening television and said this is the moral equivalent of war. Very few citizens, perhaps even including you, rallied to my side and said, "I agree with you, Mr. President. We will fight for an energy policy." But I fought for it, and a lot of people in this country thought it was a ridiculous thing to say. And now we are seeing that we have a serious energy problem that really endangers the security of our Nation.

You mentioned the Cabinet changes. I went 30 months and did not make a single change in my Cabinet. And then I decided that that level of the Cabinet had done some extraordinary things. They had initiated good programs—like Jim Schlesinger, for instance, and put through a major part of the energy program and also set up a Department of Energy, and his time had expired. He wanted to step down.

So, I've now got Charlie Duncan in there—highly qualified, administrator, manager—who can take over an existing department and make sure it functions smoothly.

I've appointed a man as head of HUD, Housing and Urban Development, Moon Landrieu, an accomplished mayor, a mayor of New Orleans. And those of you who keep up with the history of New York City know that just a few years ago, not too long ago, when New York City was on the verge of bankruptcy and despair, there was one mayor in this country who left his city and traveled all over the Nation with 11 other mayors to tell everybody in Georgia, in Washington, in Oregon, in Iowa, "We have got to save New York City." You know who that was? Moon Landrieu, who's now the Secretary of HUD.

And we've got another good man named Neil Goldschmidt, who's taken over now the Transportation Department, an experienced man.

I have no apology for keeping my original Cabinet 30 months, and I have absolutely no apology for making a change when I see fit. It's a prerogative and a responsibility of a President to have his own Cabinet.

I'll say one more thing. This is a long answer, but I think it covers a lot of questions that might have been asked later.

You mentioned national health insurance. I am for national health insurance. We have not had legislation passed through the Congress to improve our health system in any degree for the last 30 years. We need to have it passed. President Truman called for a comprehensive, nationwide health insurance program; we don't have it. Senator Kennedy has been in Congress now for 16 years. His major premise, his major goal has been to establish a comprehensive, national health insurance policy for our country. He's the chairman of the Health Committee in the Senate. He has never gotten a comprehensive national health bill out of his subcommittee. It is not easy.

But I'm determined to get a national health insurance program for our country, and I believe that I now have enough support in the Congress to do it before this term is over. So, we are making some progress, we're making some progress.

Q. I would just like to say one thing.

THE PRESIDENT. Yes.

Q. That is, you might just get me to work for you a second time.

THE PRESIDENT. That's a deal. Thank you.

UNEMPLOYMENT AND INFLATION

Q. Mr. President, my name is Barbara Miles, and I'm glad to hear you say you want the hard questions, because I have one for you.

THE PRESIDENT. Great.

Q. I represent a new coalition of religious and community organizations called the Crusade for Work. And I think you can infer from the name what our major interest is.

I think you also will realize that unemployment is dehumanizing and life-threatening, and I'm very glad to hear you say that you've been able to bring the unemployment rate down by 2 percent. But I want to dwell on that a little bit, because we're very disturbed now by your new monetary policies, as articulated by G. William Miller and by Paul Volcker, because those policies, as I understand them, threaten to raise the unemployment rate back up to 8 percent again, while there's no evidence as far as I can ascertain that you will be successful in curbing inflation. So, in view of the risk and the painfulness of this process, then why are you willing to take such a large gamble?

THE PRESIDENT. I have the same feeling you do about unemployment. This is very important.

[At this point, there was an interruption from the audience.]

THE PRESIDENT. Now, it's okay. It's okay. It's all right. It's a free country.

[The interruption continued.]

THE PRESIDENT. If you all can hear me, I'll go ahead with my answer. *[Applause]*

Miss Miles, I'm as concerned as you are about the high rate of inflation. But one of the things that we have to remember is that inflation at a high level and unemployment at a high level are directly related. And one of the reasons that we have the prospect of higher unemployment in the future is because we have not been able to control the inflation rate. Most of the cause of that has been because of uncontrollable OPEC prices. But there has to be some dealing with inflation and its root causes.

Every poor person, whether employed or not, is robbed much more severely by inflation even than those who are more wealthy and more able to accommodate their basic needs and may have to do away with some of the luxuries because inflation strikes their family.

We are trying to maintain employment levels high, to target programs. We now have two programs before the Congress: one that would provide additional aid to a locality, perhaps where you live, if the unemployment rate gets above 6½ percent. There's another triggering device, separate program, that would give jobs, above and beyond the ones we have now, on a nationwide basis, if the unemployment rate gets above 6½ percent. That's a kind of an insurance policy for the future. But in the meantime, I'm determined that we will not waste money.

I have been able, since I've been in office, to cut the Federal deficit more than 50 percent. I think this is important. We've increased services. For instance, since I've been in office, we've increased the amount of money given to education, primarily for the poor, by 60 percent. We've never had that increase before. We've given aid to New York City, $700 million increase, since I've been in office. We've still cut the budget deficit down by 60 percent. At the end of next year, we'll

have 20,000 fewer Federal employees, doing a much better job, I think, of administering what we've got.

So, there has to be a combination of restraint on inflation, and it has to be consistent, at the same time more narrowly focusing job opportunities on those who need them most. And I gather from what you say that you represent those who are poor, perhaps minority groups, perhaps even the young, who are most heavily afflicted by unemployment.

We are not ignoring them, and we've made some progress. We still have a long way to go. I will not ever use inflation as a means to wring out our economy and make the poor or the unemployed suffer.

LEADERSHIP QUALITIES

Q. Mr. President, I appreciate the opportunity to ask you this question. My name is Elizabeth Howie. I'm a social studies teacher in Jamaica, Queens, Dominican Commercial High School.

My question is, I believe both you and Senator Kennedy are in essential agreement on most of the basic issues confronting our country today. Many believe the nomination and election will be decided on the question of leadership. And in view of our apparent, as you call it, crisis of confidence, how do you intend to lead, how do you define leadership, how do you intend to inspire us?

THE PRESIDENT. Okay. First of all, I want to say that neither Senator Kennedy nor I are announced candidates. We will have—[laughter]—I will have plans to announce later on this fall. I think on October 13, there will be a preliminary political skirmish between myself and Senator Kennedy in Florida, and we look forward with great anticipation to that encounter. I have no way to know how it's going to come out.

On the subject of leadership, I think the records have to be examined. Let me just not refer to him, because he can speak for himself. But I've never been afraid, since I've been in office, to tackle a difficult issue, even if I knew it was going to cost me votes. I'll give you just two or three quick examples.

I think this is one example of leadership: In the Panama Canal treaties, this had been negotiated for 14 years, and when we ran a public opinion poll—I didn't run it, Gallup Poll did it independently of me—only 8 percent of the American people were in favor of it. But I felt that it was in the interest of our country to go ahead and consummate the treaty and to have it ratified, which has now been done. I could have ignored it.

When I made my speech to the Nation in April of 1977 on the evening television, I said that when I go to the country with an energy policy the consumers are going to be dissatisfied, the producers are going to be dissatisfied, there is no way to win politically—I'll probably lose 15 percent in the public opinion polls. I grossly underestimated my loss in the public opinion polls, but I think this needed to be done.

And I won't go down the list of things. We have had a country at peace. We've not had a single person wounded or killed in combat since I've been in office. That's a sign. In addition, we've had some crises where it required a steady hand and a careful and deliberate decision to be made. I don't think I panic in a crisis.

I'm willing to fight for what I believe in. I was willing to challenge the Republican incumbents in 1975 and 1976 and prevailed. I'm an incumbent President. I think that my record has got to be examined very closely, what we've achieved and what we haven't achieved.

We've made good progress in finally getting a SALT treaty. It must be ratified.

It's in the best interest of our country to control nuclear weapons. There has been a 7-year effort to get the treaty completed, unsuccessfully; I was fortunate enough to get it done. I've already mentioned some of the things that we've done on unemployment.

The Mideast is an area where the hearts and the minds and the souls of Americans went out to an area tortured by constant war, not just the last 30 or so years when four wars have been fought and thousands of people have been killed, but literally for hundreds of years. And I think it required some degree of leadership, against the advice of all my diplomats, against the advice of all my political advisers—"Do not go to Camp David," "Do not go to the Far East—to the Mideast, because you are doomed to failure." But I had confidence in Prime Minister Begin and President Sadat, and we made some progress.

That's the kind of thing that I've tried to do. But we've had some disappointments. And I will have to face the music for those disappointments and try to point out to the American people what might be accomplished in the next 4 years if my announcement later on this fall is as a candidate.

Q. I wish you luck. Thank you, Mr. President.

THE PRESIDENT. Thank you.

ISRAELI SECURITY AND DEFENSE

Q. Good evening, Mr. President.

THE PRESIDENT. Good evening.

Q. My name is Zahava Teitelbaum, and I'm a housewife and I work for a program for new immigrants. I just came back last week from a trip to Jerusalem, the beautiful and divided capital of the Israeli Government.

My question is, I know the United States would never tolerate terrorist attacks from Cuba, and I wanted to know why the President opposes Israel's right to defend itself on its northern borders against the PLO terrorist incursions into Israel.

THE PRESIDENT. I don't. I think any nation has a right to defend itself; obviously, including Israel. Let me recapitulate just for a moment what has happened.

Two years ago, I met with Prime Minister Rabin and then with Prime Minister Begin and also with President Sadat and others. There was a conviction in their minds that never in their lifetime would they have direct communication with one another and no chance to negotiate a peace treaty between them.

A year ago, almost exactly, we went to Camp David and came down with the Camp David accords, which set out not only a basis for peace between Israel and Egypt but also a basis for a comprehensive peace settlement for the entire Middle East, including all of Israel's neighbors.

Six months ago, we concluded the Mideast peace treaty. And a lot of people say, you know, "What have you done lately?" Well, the fact is that now we are looking to President Sadat and Prime Minister Begin to negotiate directly. They have developed a very good respect for one another. And it was a thrilling thing for me to see Sadat sail into the Haifa Harbor recently in an Egyptian yacht, escorted by American and Israeli warships and American and Israeli airplanes, and see him received so well in Haifa.

A basis of the Camp David accords was the right of Israel to defend itself, a right of Israel to be secure. And along with that was a commitment made by President Sadat and myself and Prime Minister Begin that the Palestinian question in all its aspects would be resolved, that the Palestinian people have a right to a voice in the determination of their own future. But, at the same time, Sadat agreed on behalf of many Arabs that Israel would have a right to defend itself. And I have never questioned Israel's right to defend herself against terrorism from the north or against her neighbors from the east or from the south.

The second thing I'd like to say is that we give Israel—as a good investment for our own security, because we derive great benefits from Israel being strong and free and at peace—great aid, the most aid we give any other nation on Earth, because we believe in Israel having the ability to defend itself. In addition to that, as a result of the Camp David accords and the Mideast peace treaty, I advocated to the Congress, and the Congress agreed to increase that aid by $3 billion. And we're now working out with Defense Minister Weizman, who was in Washington in my office last week, how to spend that money to give Israel the means by which they can defend themselves.

But this Government and this President will never abandon Israel. We will always support Israel, and we will always make sure that Israel has the means by which to defend themselves.

I want to say one more thing, and then I'll close this answer. Israel's got one sure friend, and that's the United States of America. And I look with great concern and disgust at a growing clamor around the world, even making the ridiculous charge that Zionism is the same as racism. That's an outrage and a disgrace to human beings.

And I'm not asking you—Miss Teitelbaum, right?—I'm not asking you to give me your support or to approve everything I do. But let me say this: It's important for Israel, for a President like me, to have your support in carrying out the agreements made at Camp David and with the treaty. I need your help and I need your support.

God knows that politics is secondary to me when it comes to the defense and the strengthening and the peace and the security of Israel. But I think that our Government, which has already done so much—working with Sadat and Begin and others to make this major move toward peace—really needs the unity and the support and the understanding of making further progress. Condemnations and criticisms during these transient times, I don't believe help Israel. I don't want you to approve everything I do, but I need your support and your prayers that my future efforts, along with those of the Israelis and Egyptians, will be as successful as they have been in the last 12 months.

NUCLEAR POWERPLANT SAFETY

Q. Mr. President, my name is Barbara Glick. I live in Forest Hills, and I just graduated from York College as of June and, at the moment, am an aspiring, unemployed journalist. And my question centers around a concern that a lot of New Yorkers feel is quite relevant to them.

It has been reported that if a nuclear accident were to occur at Indian Point, depending on the direction of the wind, radiation could spread over a 30-mile radius, causing thousands of deaths, tens of thousands of eventual deaths resulting from cancer, with hundreds of thousands becoming ill.

My questions are these: What requirements are you going to enact, as President, to see that the Three Mile Island syndrome doesn't occur at populous plants such as Indian Point? And B, can you force these plants to come up with adequate emergency plans concerning proper evacuation procedures, which are lacking at the present time?

THE PRESIDENT. Are you referring to the plant in Virginia, where we had the little incident today?

Q. No. I was referring to Indian Point.

THE PRESIDENT. Indian Point, okay. We have—by the way, there was an incident today in Virginia, and I've gotten a report from it just a few minutes ago. I don't know the name of the plant. But it is under control, and they are shutting it down. And I understand there are no—there's no danger to it.

Now, we will have a report from the Kemeny Commission on the Three Mile Island accident, I think, within the next month. Until that time, the Nuclear Regulatory Commission is acting with extreme caution, waiting for Kemeny and his committee and the NRC and others to decide what was the cause of that accident, whether it was a design failure or an installation failure or an absence of training or improper operating techniques.

When that report is made, I will examine it very thoroughly to see what can be done to ensure in the future that nuclear powerplants are safe. If they aren't, then I would certainly not approve them. There is no guarantee, obviously, of what the Kemeny report will advocate.

We now have in this country about 13 percent of all our energy coming from nuclear powerplants—in Connecticut, I think, 60 percent; in Chicago, maybe 50 percent. And to require those plants to shut down would be ill-advised, and I am not going to do it. But we will do what we can in the future to enhance the security of the plants that might be operating in years to come.

Q. What about as far as evacuation procedures regarding Indian Point? There are none.

THE PRESIDENT. I think that will probably be part of the Kemeny report. And on that basis, we will do what we can.

As you know, the States have a right to decide whether or not a nuclear powerplant can be located within its borders. Some of the States have forbidden, through referenda and through action by the State legislatures, the installation of nuclear powerplants in their State. There is one plant in Georgia that was built while I was Governor. And we have taken action to encourage States to evolve evacuation plans.

And I think that what you have asked and what the people of New York decide is a very important consideration. For the Federal Government to mandate, however, that the nuclear powerplants in New York should be shut down under present circumstances, I think, is an unwarranted encroachment on the local prerogatives. And I would not favor that, and neither would the Congress do it.

Q. Thank you very much.

THE PRESIDENT. Thank you.

Q. And by the way, I love you.

THE PRESIDENT. Thank you.

SOVIET TROOPS IN CUBA

Q. Mr. Carter, my name is Fred Feingold. I'm from Hollis Hills, here in Queens, and I'm a sales representative. I was going to ask you a question about inflation, but that subject has been gone over a bit. I then was going to ask you a question about national health care, but that question, I think, was pretty well done. [*Laughter*] I was then going to speak about Israel, and that question—[*laughter*]—was covered. Therefore, to avoid repetitious questions, I'm going to ask you about the Russian troops in Cuba.

In the event that all diplomacy fails, we do everything we can diplomatically— which I'm sure you're doing now—do you foresee another Russian missile crisis if nothing works and the troops just stay there?

THE PRESIDENT. First of all, let me say that this is not the same thing as the 1962 missile crisis. At that time, the Soviets had within Cuba missiles, that could reach our own Nation, that had nuclear warheads. There was a direct threat to our country, and millions of people could have been killed from those launching pads. Our country was threatened with an offensive attack.

The present brigade of Soviet troops in Cuba is not a threat to the security of our country. There are about 2,500 troops there. They do have 40 tanks and a few field pieces; they have no offensive weapons that can reach our shores. They have no capability for a seaborne invasion; they have no capability for an airborne invasion. So, it's not a threat to our security.

The thing that concerns us, however— and this is a serious matter, and the status quo is not acceptable to us—is that it's a combat unit. The Soviets deny it has combat status. But it is a combat unit located in a country in this hemisphere, in a country that is totally dependent on the Soviet Union.

Cuba, in effect, is a puppet of the Soviet Union, and they act completely in accordance with Soviet foreign policy. A hundred percent of all their weapons are given to them by the Soviet Union. The Soviet Union gives Cuba about $8 million every day to sustain it economically. They pay five times the world price, for instance, for all Cuba's sugar. They provide them with all their oil. And in response to that or in trade for that, Cuba acts, in effect, as a Soviet surrogate in many nations around the world.

In 1975, as you know, they moved thousands of troops into Angola. Since

I've been President, they've moved thousands of troops into Ethiopia. They have troops in many other countries in Africa. So, because of the combination of Soviet support and Cuba acting as a Soviet puppet, this does create a great concern for us. There is, however, no threat to our Nation's security.

We are now trying, through diplomacy, to get the Soviets to eliminate the combat nature of this unit, and I don't know yet whether we will succeed. If we do not succeed, we will take appropriate action to change the status quo.

Q. Thank you, Mr. President.

PRESIDENT'S REELECTION CAMPAIGN

Q. My name is Anthony Cerami. I'm a senior in St. John's University in New York.

THE PRESIDENT. What was your name?

Q. Anthony Cerami. I was a 1976 Carter supporter. Off the record of your administration, I totally expect to support you again in 1980 if you decide to run. I think you've made some tough, sometimes unpopular decisions for the good and the great and long-range good for the American people.

THE PRESIDENT. Thank you very much, Anthony.

Q. My question is——

THE PRESIDENT. I was hoping you wouldn't ask a question. [*Laughter*]

Q. ——if you run again, do you intend to emulate your 1976 strategy of running in every Presidential primary? Because there has been talk that if you lose—in some of the newspapers—that if you lose some of the early Northeastern primaries, you will drop out. Will you run in every primary? Because there's a lot of people out here who want to support you.

THE PRESIDENT. I have never backed down in the face of adversity. I won some

primaries and lost some primaries in 1976. And if I become a candidate later on this year, I would intend to run in every primary.

Q. Thank you very much. Good luck.

THE PRESIDENT. Thank you.

UNEMPLOYMENT IN THE CONSTRUCTION INDUSTRY

Q. Good evening, Mr. President. Welcome to the Borough of Queens. My name is Noel Casey. I am a resident of Woodside, Queens. I'm an active member of the Carpenters Union, Local 608.

I would like to know what your administration is going to do about the high unemployment in the construction industry in New York City, in projects such as the South Bronx, Westway, Battery Park, and the convention center. Now that we're going to have the 1980 Democratic convention in New York, we don't even have a convention center. That's my question, Mr. President.

THE PRESIDENT. I see. Well, Mr. Casey, it's hard to answer your question specifically, but in the construction industry, we have seen employment increase about 25 percent in the last 2½ years. I don't claim credit for all of that, but I think we have had a massive program for public works, for local public works, and as you know, we've had an average of more than 1.8 million homes built each year since I've been in office.

What we would do in the future is hard now to ascertain. We have a broad range of things that can be done. If we see the unemployment rate begin to go up dramatically in the construction industry or others, I'm not predicting that we'll do any of these things, but we could obviously repeat the great success we had in 1977 with local public works programs.

The first 2 years I was in office, we reduced taxes about $28 billion, which did stimulate the economy to some degree. We have the focused countercyclical bills for jobs under the Government, CETA jobs and otherwise, which provide several hundred thousand jobs in communities that are most highly impacted because of unemployment.

But I think so far we've got a fairly good record. We'll monitor it very closely and decide in the future what to act on, but I would guess that our future actions would be based on the successes that we've had in 1977 with that stimulus program. That's the best answer I can give.

Q. Last year you came to the South Bronx.

THE PRESIDENT. Yes.

Q. And you promised Federal money for the South Bronx, and yet today the South Bronx is still the same way.

THE PRESIDENT. I didn't promise to rebuild the South Bronx in 6 months. I promised to work with the local and State officials and start the rejuvenation of South Bronx.

We've spent an awful lot of time and effort and, so far, allocated substantial financial resources in the South Bronx. I don't remember the exact amount of money that we put in there extra to try to start making progress, but it's been substantial. And I don't claim, standing here before all of you, that we have cleaned up the South Bronx or put the South Bronx back in a profitable or a successful state. I can't claim that, but we've made good progress.

And I think, as you know, your own local officials, on one major proposal for the South Bronx, decided not to go ahead with it. I don't believe in a philosophy of government that lets the Federal Government come in and take over and run things in contradiction to your locally

elected officials. And I'll ask my good friend Ed Koch to be responsible to you for the rejuvenation of the South Bronx in the future.

SOVIET TROOPS IN CUBA

Q. Good evening, Mr. President. My name is Pete Reilly, from Syosset, Long Island. I'm a student at C. W. Post College. I'm studying economics and acting. [*Laughter*] I want to be a politician.

I would like to challenge you on your answer about the Soviet troops in Cuba.

THE PRESIDENT. I don't know which is worse right now, to be an economist or a politician. [*Laughter*] Go ahead and challenge.

Q. You said that the status quo is unacceptable——

THE PRESIDENT. That's right.

Q. ——and you'll take appropriate measures to alter it.

THE PRESIDENT. That's correct.

Q. What are "appropriate measures?"

THE PRESIDENT. I would rather not spell out at this point what we will do.

There are two ways to change the status quo. One is by the action of the Soviet Union. If the Soviets fail to act, then the other way to change the status quo is by action on the part of the United States. And I will report to the Nation, probably within the next week, after we get through with our negotiations with the Soviet Union, what action I will take. But it would not be appropriate tonight for me to give you the details of what we might do.

Q. I understand that.

THE PRESIDENT. Okay, go ahead, Pete.

Q. What I wanted to say was, you know, you're trying to separate the SALT II issue from the Cuban issue.

THE PRESIDENT. Yes, they ought to be separated. There ought not to be any connection.

Q. Okay. But I want to tell you, the assumption of the SALT II treaty is that—we're laying the groundwork for peace between the Soviet Union and America. Why do they have troops in Cuba? For that matter, why do the Soviets back troops if they want peace? Why are they eating up Southeast Asia? Why are they in Africa? Why do they denounce peace in the Middle East? Where are we going to draw the line? Our measures have got to be effective.

THE PRESIDENT. You put me in the position of defending the Soviet Union, which I have no inclination to do. [*Laughter*] But let me say this: There have been troops in Cuba for a long time.

Q. I understand.

THE PRESIDENT. In 1962 there were 22,000 troops in Cuba. Evidence is that ever since that time, there have been substantial numbers of Soviet troops in Cuba.

We, this year, began to monitor that situation much more closely. In the past Cuba was not a high priority for us to monitor with our surveillance systems on a concentrated basis. We were looking at the Soviet Union to make sure they complied with the provisions of SALT I; we were monitoring Vietnam during that war, and we, this year, earlier, focused our attention more on Cuba to monitor what the Soviet troops were doing. My judgment is that the number of Soviet troops is less now than it was in 1963, for instance, months after all the missiles had been moved out of Cuba in October, I believe, of 1962.

The question is whether this is a combat unit—we're convinced it is—and whether that combat status should change. I might point out to you that the United States has troops in several coun-

tries around the world, some of them very close to the borders of the Soviet Union. This is part of a normal interrelationship between major powers, like ours, and the Soviet Union. We have troops in South Korea, we have troops in Japan, we have a few troops in Turkey, we have had some troops in Iran, and so forth. And so, this is not a new thing.

But we want the Soviets to understand that the American people are exceptionally sensitive about Soviet combat troops in this hemisphere, particularly in a country like Cuba, which acts, in effect, as an arm of the Soviets in adventurism and intervention in other countries.

How to deal with this successfully is not an easy task, but we'll do the best we can. And I believe that you will be satisfied when I make my report to the country within the next week.

Q. One departing remark. Thanks a lot. That's the first time I ever spoke to a President. [*Laughter*]

THE PRESIDENT. This is your last question. [*Laughter*]

Q. Yes. I just want to say a departing remark. I'm just worried about the principle of the matter, not the threat of invasion. Thanks, President Carter.

THE PRESIDENT. Thank you very much.

OIL PRICES

Q. My name is Lori Kober, and I'm a student at Saint Mathias School, and I'm 11 years old. This is my question. There are four kids in my family, and my parents just bought a house. This house is to use oil heat, and my mom says that oil is very expensive. Is there anything you will do to help about these high prices?

THE PRESIDENT. Thank you. Your first name is Laura?

Q. No. Lori.

THE PRESIDENT. Lori, okay. It's very difficult for me to answer your question, because there's a limit to what I can do.

Throughout the entire world, Lori, the price of oil is going up. It's increased 65 or 70 percent, almost doubled, in the last 8 months. In the last 5 years, the price of oil has gone from $2 a barrel to almost $30 a barrel. It costs 15 times as much as it did in 1973. And as the price of oil goes up, which everybody has to pay, then the price of gasoline and diesel oil and home heating oil and kerosene also go up.

What we are trying to do now is to cut down or reduce the amount of oil that we buy from overseas. We buy about half our oil from foreign countries. This is what we are trying to correct with our new energy policy.

Next year we'll send about 70 billion American dollars overseas to pay for foreign oil. And we import, with the oil, high inflation—which is what bothers your mother—and also unemployment.

We have made some progress. Earlier this year, we thought that there would be a shortage of home heating oil this winter. I think we've now got the oil companies to produce enough oil to take care of the needs of people who live in New York and the States further north.

One thing that you and your family can do is—since the oil companies now have enough oil for the winter—is to cut down on the amount that you use. The less oil people use, the more we save; the less we waste, then the cheaper the price is going to be, because you have a certain amount of oil, and if people don't buy as much as you have in the past, then there will be more competition and people will have to sell their oil at a lower price.

We've also gotten a few of the oil companies—Texaco and seven or eight more—to agree not to raise their prices any more in the next number of weeks, as the winter comes on us. The prices have already gone up too much. We want to make sure they don't go up any more.

And the other thing that we are doing is providing help for poor families, who are the first ones to suffer when the price of energy goes up, particularly oil. We will have the Congress pass this year $400 million worth of aid for families that are poor to help them pay their heating bills. And we've asked, in the windfall profits tax, which I hope the Congress will pass without delay, a tax on the oil companies, another $1.6 billion to take care of tax credits for poor families as well.

So, we're trying to get the oil companies to hold down the price. We're asking people to save oil and not waste it, to hold down the price. And we're going to provide financial help, direct grants, that the Governor will administer, for families that are poor and who cannot afford to pay for oil.

But I don't think there's any need to— I don't want to mislead you, Lori—the price of oil is going to continue to go up in the future no matter what I do or what anybody else does, because all over the world it's getting scarcer and people are demanding more. We're going to move toward solar energy. We're going to move toward a greater use of coal, and we're going to move toward a greater development of our own energy supplies. And I think that will help us a great deal in the future.

But our country waited too long to start acting to get an energy policy. Now we are moving. And as I predicted earlier, by the end of this year we will have a good energy policy passed into law by our Congress, which will help you and your family in the future.

That's a great question and I thank you for it.

I can take one more question, I understand.

TAX REDUCTIONS

Q. Mr. President, I'm Kathleen McGilloway. I'm a housewife, and this is also the first time I've ever spoken to a President.

THE PRESIDENT. I'm glad to talk to you, Kathleen.

Q. But it has generally been acknowledged that our present tax structure is grossly unbalanced, penalizing married working couples and middle-income families. They pay high taxes while many large corporations pay little or none. Do you plan to rectify this situation?

THE PRESIDENT. I could hear you, Kathleen.

That's one of the failures that we've experienced since I've been in office. When I was here in New York in August of 1976 and made my acceptance speech at the Democratic National Convention, I pointed out then that the tax system in this country is a disgrace to the human race. It still is. It's not fair.

We've made some changes in it, very minor changes, because the pressure groups and the lobbyists in Washington are almost beyond comprehension. And when you start trying to make corrections to the tax laws, quite often the Congress goes in the opposite direction and opens up more loopholes for those who are powerful enough and influential enough to have active lobbyists there.

We have had some reduction in taxes since I've been in office, about $28 billion. We may have to have some more in the future. But I cannot tell you that we have made any substantial progress in that respect. And it's only going to be when an aroused public demands action by individual Members of the House and the U.S. Senate that we will ever have substantive tax reform. I wouldn't say it's hopeless, but it hasn't happened so far.

Two years ago we could not get the public to demand an energy policy. It looked hopeless. And now we see progress. And I think the same thing applies to the Middle East, and the same thing applies to SALT, and so forth. You just have to take one thing at a time until the public is genuinely interested, and then you can make progress.

But I hope and pray that in the future we will change the tax structure to make it fairer to the average citizen and take away the gross loopholes that reward the powerful and the rich, who can pay lobbyists to protect their interests in Washington. I'm with you. I have not been able to do anything yet.

Let me say one other thing in closing. I think your questions have been very good, and I've enjoyed them and enjoyed the chance to answer them. I learn a lot from you, by knowing what is of interest to you and having a chance to explain what I have done and what I have not done, the successes we've achieved and the failures that we've achieved so far.

We're in it together. If I'm successful as a President, then you have a better country. When I fail in my duties, because of obstacles that I just cannot overcome, it hurts you as well. But I think we all ought to remember this: No matter what your political affiliation or no matter what your special interest might be, we tend to dwell in this country on the transient inconveniences and disappointments, and we remember very vividly the things that divide us one from another and the intense debates and the times when we've failed to overcome a challenge the first try. But what we forget is the manifold blessings that we have in this country and how many things bind us together and the principles of freedom in a democracy, which make us able, in the future, to achieve success where we haven't yet done it.

And I would like to remind you in closing that not only is this a nation that believes in free speech, but we are also the greatest nation on Earth. And if you help me, we'll keep it that way.

Thank you very much.

NOTE: The President spoke at 7:35 p.m. in the Charles S. Colden Auditorium at Queens College. In his opening remarks, he referred to Donald R. Manes, president of the Borough of Queens, and Saul Cohen, president of the college.

Energy and Water Development Appropriation Act, 1980

Statement on Signing H.R. 4388 Into Law. September 25, 1979

It is with mixed reactions that I sign H.R. 4388, the energy and water development appropriations bill.

With one major exception, this is a sound and responsible bill. It recognizes the need to hold down spending. It does not commit to unacceptable future expenditures. It provides for sound water projects and for energy development. It represents a commendable step by the Congress in the direction I have been urging through my water resources development and energy policies. It does not fund water projects which, at my request, were terminated in past appropriation bills, and it generally reflects restraints in water project funding.

On the other hand, this bill mandates the completion of the Tellico project on the Little Tennessee River. This project has been halted because of conflicts with the Endangered Species Act. A decision was made through a deliberative process to deal with these conflicts. A special

Cabinet-level committee, authorized by the Congress, unanimously concluded that the project should not be completed, on economic grounds.

This action by the Congress overturns that decision and directs the flooding of the Little Tennessee River Valley. I am satisfied, however, that the Congress clearly confronted this issue and settled on its action with clear majority votes in both Houses. I accept, with regret, this action as expressing the will of the Congress in the Tellico matter. I am also convinced that even if I vetoed this bill, Tellico exemptions would be proposed repeatedly in the future.

Nevertheless, I believe firmly in the principles of the Endangered Species Act and will enforce it vigorously. I do not consider that the action by Congress on the Tellico matter implies congressional intent to overturn the general decision process for resolving conflicts under that act. I am convinced that this resolution of the Tellico matter will help assure the passage of the Endangered Species Act reauthorization without weakening amendments or further exemptions.

I also expect the Congress to move vigorously to solidify progress in water resources policy. Prompt action is needed to authorize and appropriate funds for the Water Resources Council water project review function, so that proper technical analysis can ensure executive branch recommendations for sound water projects. I believe firmly that my decision on the bill I am now signing will further progress on obtaining a strong Water Resources Council.

As President I must balance many competing interests. With many important national issues before the Congress—including energy, SALT, the department of education, the Panama Canal implementing legislation, the Endangered Species

Act, and water resources policy—I believe that avoiding a divisive veto battle will helps focus congressional efforts on priority concerns.

NOTE: As enacted, H.R. 4388 is Public Law 96–69, approved September 25.

Federal Consumer Programs

Remarks on Signing Executive Order 12160. September 26, 1979

Thank you. First I'll do my duty, and then I'll explain why.

[At this point, the President signed the Executive order.]

Congressman Rosenthal and Esther Peterson, distinguished representatives of consumer groups from all over the Nation:

I've just signed an Executive order entitled "Providing for Enhancement and Coordination of Federal Consumer Programs." This is a result of a lot of work by me and by 50 leaders in our Government, who represent the major agencies, by many consumer groups throughout the country, by Members of Congress, who have been in the forefront of the fight for consumer rights, and, I think, above everyone else, by Esther Peterson, who deserves and who has the gratitude of everyone here.

The longer I've been in the White House as President, the more I have recognized the importance of each individual person in our country. Traveling around the Nation during the long campaign years and since then, it's been a striking thing for me to have brief encounters with and conversations with Americans. Quite often, as they touch a President's hand or pass me in a corridor or on the street, they impart to me, in that brief, rare moment, their deepest thoughts. And quite often I'm struck with how distant they are from government and how many of the decisions of government that are made that impact that person's life are never known or understood by them. They have no direct representative within an agency or within a decisionmaking body that's relatively obscure but vital.

I think it's particularly important that their voices be heard in government on a continuing, sustained basis, and that's the reason for this Executive order.

As you know, the first year I was in office I proposed to the Congress, and we fought to the last vote, to get an independent agency established—an independent office established to protect consumers' rights. We have not yet been able to get that legislation passed. It is still absolutely important. And this Executive order does not supplant the need for a coordinated, single consumer protection agency. It's important for all of us to remember that. But at the same time, I've had to turn to alternative means by which I, as President, could help to protect consumers' interests in the most effective way.

I asked Esther Peterson to join my staff. She is at my right hand. She works with other members of the White House staff and with every agency in this Government in the most highly effective way. She's been assisted by large numbers of volunteers, who have confidence in her and who share her determination to protect the consumers in our Government.

We have now come to a point of realization that her presence in the White House, no matter how effective, is not enough. There are so many agencies in the Government. And I asked her a few months ago to consult with the Office of Management and Budget, with the agencies themselves, to see how we could expand her influence. And the result of all that work is this Executive order, which is now effective.

It prescribes a standard for the protection of consumer interests throughout Government—a single, carefully drafted, comprehensible standard that will provide coherence and unity and a better understanding of the purposes that we want to accomplish. And it also establishes a strong leader within each agency, who will be designated by the head of each agency, to protect consumer interests.

Esther, of course, will continue to represent me directly in these relationships. But in this process of evolving the Executive order, I think we've aroused to a high pitch of interest the leaders throughout Government who will be affected by the order itself.

OMB is extremely reluctant to expand the bureaucracy or to make an ineffective Government effort possible, and they are extremely important to save taxpayers' funds. They are enthusiastic supporters of this Executive order, because they see that this is a contribution to the efficiency of Government and does not create additional bureaucracy nor delay decisions in their final judgments.

I might add one other thing, and that is that recent trends in Government have been very disturbing to me, particularly on Capitol Hill. The attacks that are being made against the Federal Trade Commission, the recent effort in the Senate to have every regulatory decision be subjected to proof in court before it can go into effect, the efforts to block sections of bills that would directly give consumers a stronger voice in Government, the trend toward increasing one-house vetoes over decisions made by agencies responsible for protecting consumers' rights—these kinds

of trends are a bad omen. And I would like to ask all of you to monitor very carefully what goes on in Government to prevent these unwarranted encroachments on the basic rights of every American citizen.

We have worked together in the past. Many of you have been in the forefront of battles to make the civil service system more effective. You've helped me greatly in the progress that we've made so far in hospital cost containment, to reduce the inflationary pressures on American citizens, and of course, you've helped me with the evolution of the concept of the cooperative bank and many other items on which we share a major interest. We are in this fight together. And I welcome your support and the partnership that we share.

And I'm particularly grateful to your leader and to my leader, Esther Peterson, who will continue the fight, with us as her army. And I'm very grateful to serve in this capacity under one of the greatest leaders in Government. And now I'd like to introduce to you Esther Peterson.

NOTE: The President spoke at 11:50 a.m. in Room 450 of the Old Executive Office Building. Following his remarks, Esther Peterson, Special Assistant to the President for Consumer Affairs, spoke to the group.

Federal Consumer Programs

Executive Order 12160.   September 26, 1979

PROVIDING FOR ENHANCEMENT AND CO-ORDINATION OF FEDERAL CONSUMER PROGRAMS

By virtue of the authority vested in me as President by the Constitution of the United States of America, and in order to improve the management, coordination, and effectiveness of agency consumer programs, it is ordered as follows:

1–1. *Establishment of the Consumer Affairs Council.*

1–101. There is hereby established the Consumer Affairs Council (hereinafter referred to as the "Council").

1–102. The Council shall consist of representatives of the following agencies, and such other officers or employees of the United States as the President may designate as members:

  (a) Department of Agriculture.
  (b) Department of Commerce.
  (c) Department of Defense.
  (d) Department of Energy.
  (e) Department of Health, Education, and Welfare.
  (f) Department of Housing and Urban Development.
  (g) Department of the Interior.
  (h) Department of Justice.
  (i) Department of Labor.
  (j) Department of State.
  (k) Department of Transportation.
  (l) Department of the Treasury.

Each agency on the Council shall be represented by the head of the agency or by a senior-level official designated by the head of the agency.

1–2. *Functions of the Council.*

1–201. The Council shall provide leadership and coordination to ensure that agency consumer programs are implemented effectively; and shall strive to maximize effort, promote efficiency and interagency cooperation, and to eliminate duplication and inconsistency among agency consumer programs.

1–3. *Designation and Functions of the Chairperson.*

1–301. The President shall designate the Chairperson of the Council (herein-after referred to as the "Chairperson").

1–302. The Chairperson shall be the presiding officer of the Council and shall determine the times when the Council shall convene.

1–303. The Chairperson shall establish such policies, definitions, procedures, and standards to govern the implementation, interpretation, and application of this Order, and generally perform such functions and take such steps, as are necessary or appropriate to carry out the provisions of this Order.

1–4. *Consumer Program Reforms.*

1–401. The Chairperson, assisted by the Council, shall ensure that agencies review and revise their operating procedures so that consumer needs and interests are adequately considered and addressed. Agency consumer programs should be tailored to fit particular agency characteristics, but those programs shall include, at a minimum, the following five elements:

  (a) *Consumer Affairs Perspective.* Agencies shall have identifiable, accessible professional staffs of consumer affairs personnel authorized to participate, in a manner not inconsistent with applicable statutes, in the development and review of all agency rules, policies, programs, and legislation.

  (b) *Consumer Participation.* Agencies shall establish procedures for the early and meaningful participation by consumers in the development and review of all agency rules, policies, and programs. Such procedures shall include provisions to assure that consumer concerns are adequately analyzed and considered in decisionmaking. To facilitate the expression of those concerns, agencies shall provide for forums at which consumers can meet with agency decisionmakers. In addition, agencies shall make affirmative efforts to inform consumers of pending proceedings and of the opportunities available for participation therein.

(c) *Informational Materials.* Agencies shall produce and distribute materials to inform consumers about the agencies' responsibilities and services, about their procedures for consumer participation, and about aspects of the marketplace for which they have responsibility. In addition, each agency shall make available to consumers who attend agency meetings open to the public materials designed to make those meetings comprehensible to them.

(d) *Education and Training.* Agencies shall educate their staff members about the Federal consumer policy embodied in this Order and about the agencies' programs for carrying out that policy. Specialized training shall be provided to agency consumer affairs personnel and, to the extent considered appropriate by each agency and in a manner not inconsistent with applicable statutes, technical assistance shall be made available to consumers and their organizations.

(e) *Complaint Handling.* Agencies shall establish procedures for systematically logging in, investigating, and responding to consumer complaints, and for integrating analyses of complaints into the development of policy.

1–402. The head of each agency shall designate a senior-level official within that agency to exercise, as the official's sole responsibility, policy direction for, and coordination and oversight of, the agency's consumer activities. The designated official shall report directly to the head of the agency and shall apprise the agency head of the potential impact on consumers of particular policy initiatives under development or review within the agency.

1–5. *Implementation of Consumer Program Reforms.*

1–501. Within 60 days after the issuance of this Order, each agency shall prepare a draft report setting forth with specificity its program for complying with the requirements of Section 1–4 above. Each agency shall publish its draft consumer program in the FEDERAL REGISTER and shall give the public 60 days to comment on the program. A copy of the program shall be sent to the Council.

1–502. Each agency shall, within 30 days after the close of the public comment period on its draft consumer program, submit a revised program to the Chairperson. The Chairperson shall be responsible, on behalf of the President, for approving agency programs for compliance with this Order before their final publication in the FEDERAL REGISTER. Each agency's final program shall be published no later than 90 days after the close of the public comment period, and shall include a summary of public comments on the draft program and a discussion of how those comments are reflected in the final program.

1–503. Each agency's consumer program shall take effect no later than 30 days after its final publication in the FEDERAL REGISTER.

1–504. The Chairperson, with the assistance and advice of the Council, shall monitor the implementation by agencies of their consumer programs.

1–505. The Chairperson shall, promptly after the close of the fiscal year, submit to the President a full report on government-wide progress under this Order during the previous fiscal year. In addition, the Chairperson shall evaluate, from time to time, the consumer programs of particular agencies and shall report to the President as appropriate. Such evaluations shall be informed by appropriate consultations with interested parties.

1–6. *Budget Review.*

1–601. Each agency shall include a separate consumer program exhibit in its yearly budget submission to the Office of Management and Budget. By October 1 of each year the Director of the Office of Management and Budget shall provide the Chairperson with a copy of each of these exhibits. The Chairperson shall thereafter provide OMB with an analysis of the adequacy of the management of, and the funding and staff levels for, particular agency consumer programs.

1–7. *Civil Service Initiatives.*

1–701. In order to strengthen the professional standing of consumer affairs personnel, and to improve the recruitment and training of such personnel, the Office of Personnel Management shall consult with the Council regarding:

(a) the need for new or revised classification and qualification standard(s), consistent with the requirements of Title 5, United States Code, to be used by agencies in their classification of positions which include significant consumer affairs duties;

(b) the recruitment and selection of employees for the performance of consumer affairs duties; and

(c) the training and development of employees for the performance of such duties.

1–8. *Administrative Provisions.*

1–801. Executive agencies shall cooperate with and assist the Council and the Chairperson in the performance of their functions under this Order and shall on a timely basis furnish them with such reports as they may request.

1–802. The Chairperson shall utilize the assistance of the United States Office of Consumer Affairs in fulfilling the responsibilities assigned to the Chairperson under this Order.

1–803. The Chairperson shall be responsible for providing the Council with such administrative services and support as may be necessary or appropriate; agencies shall assign, to the extent not inconsistent with applicable statutes, such personnel and resources to the activities of the Council and the Chairperson as will enable the Council and the Chairperson to fulfill their responsibilities under this Order.

1–804. The Chairperson may invite representatives of non-member agencies, including independent regulatory agencies, to participate from time to time in the functions of the Council.

1–9. *Definitions.*

1–901. "Consumer" means any individual who uses, purchases, acquires, attempts to purchase or acquire, or is offered or furnished any real or personal property, tangible or intangible goods, services, or credit for personal, family, or household purposes.

1–902. "Agency" or "agencies" mean any department or agency in the executive branch of the Federal government, except that the term shall not include:

(a) independent regulatory agencies, except as noted in subsection 1–804;

(b) agencies to the extent that their activities fall within the categories excepted in Sections 6(b) (2), (3), (4), and (6) of Executive Order No. 12044.

(c) agencies to the extent that they demonstrate within 30 days of the date of issuance of this Order, to the satisfaction of the Chairperson with the advice of the Council, that their activities have no substantial impact upon consumers.

JIMMY CARTER

The White House,
    September 26, 1979.

[Filed with the Office of the Federal Register,
    4:56 p.m., September 26, 1979]

Consumer Affairs Council

Memorandum From the President.
September 26, 1979

Memorandum for the Heads of Executive Departments and Agencies

I hereby designate Esther Peterson, my Special Assistant for Consumer Affairs, to be Chairperson of the Consumer Affairs Council established by Executive Order 12160, which I issued today.

JIMMY CARTER

Saudi Arabian Crude Oil Production

White House Statement.   September 26, 1979

We have received official confirmation of today's reports that the Government of Saudi Arabia intends to continue production of 9.5 million barrels of oil per day— 1 million barrels above its established limit—for 3 more months.

President Carter welcomes this decision as "a constructive complement to the efforts of the oil-importing nations to curb consumption and switch to other fuels."

"I hope no one will take this news as a signal to relax the effort that each citizen must make to ease our demand on a limited world supply of oil," the President said.

Continued high production by Saudi Arabia and several other countries will relieve concern about the adequacy of oil supplies this winter. It will permit full restoration of oil inventories drawn down after Iranian oil exports were halted last winter and subsequently reduced to about half their usual volume. It should help to stabilize prices in the world oil market.

Democratic National Committee

Remarks at a Fundraising Dinner.
September 26, 1979

Are we going to win in 1980? [*Applause*] Right on. Thank you very much.

Thank you, Governor Jim Hunt, for that very good introduction, and thank all of you who are here for letting us participate in the largest, most successful single fundraising event in the history of the greatest political party on Earth. Thank all of you very much.

We've already recognized the Governors, the Cabinet, the Members of the Congress, who do give me remarkably good support, the last 2 days. And I thank you for it. [*Laughter*] Last week was just one of those weeks best to forget about. But we're correcting all our mistakes. [*Laughter*]

But I'd like to recognize one special Democrat, who means as much to me as anyone that I have known since I've been involved in politics. He represents the essence of the Democratic Party, the kind of principles and achievements and ideals and accomplishments that make every Democratic chest swell with pride. I'd like for all of us to express our appreciation and admiration to Averell Harriman. Averell. [*Applause*]

He's helped to carve out the history of our country in the past. He's helping to forge the history of our country now. And he provides the guidance for an even greater America in the future.

We have a lot to be thankful for. We are here tonight because we know, as Harry Truman said in September, 26 years ago, the principles and the programs of the Democratic Party are exactly what's best for the United States of America. We still have that relationship with our country, and we are going to keep it that way.

I'm sorry I wasn't here early enough to eat supper with you. Rosalynn and I will stop on the way home and get some ice cream. [*Laughter*] And I would like for there to be no political analysis made of the fact that I still eat ice cream. [*Laughter*]

Jim Hunt complained about the $1,000-a-plate supper. I understand that it costs a thousand dollars just to eat lunch with John Connally, the famous friend of the few—[*laughter*]—which reminds me of one of those few, Bob Strauss, who's already been introduced. [*Laughter*]

Bob finished his job helping me control inflation, and then he's now working in the Middle East. [*Laughter*] He's taken the same kind of dedication and modesty to the Middle East that he used to fight inflation. [*Laughter*] If there's one thing you can say about Bob Strauss, he's always loyal to the Democratic Party, and I thank him very much.

Sometimes he goes too far. I had a call this morning from Prime Minister Menahem Begin, who said—he said, "Mr. President, I am willing to take on new friends, to meet with President Sadat, who was an enemy of mine for the last 20 years." He said, "I am willing to give up the Sinai, because you and President Sadat asked me to." He said, "I am willing to put my political future on a piece of paper, the treaty between us and Egypt. But I am not willing to buy a table to the DNC fundraising banquet this evening." [*Laughter*] He said, "As you well know, the people of Israel have never had any interest in United States politics." [*Laughter*]

I'm also glad that Senator Bob Byrd is going to play his fiddle for us tonight. He's a wonderful man, a close friend, and a great supporter of mine in the Senate. I meet with him regularly. Rosalynn can always tell when I'm in trouble in the United States Senate. Every time I come back from a leadership breakfast on Wednesday morning with another $25 worth of fiddle records—[*laughter*]—she knows I'm still trying to buy influence. [*Laughter*] But it works.

And I would like to express my thanks, particularly tonight—if I don't do it all the way through my speech—to the tremendous Democratic Congress, which means so much to our country.

The Members of the Congress have just recently returned from their home work period with their constituents, where they listened to hear expressions of concern, even fear, but a modicum of hope. And I, too, have been visiting with the same people, who are also my constituents, from one end of this country to the other. During that August recess period, I made about 60 speeches about the greatness of our country and the need for a new energy program. I've listened, I've debated, I've answered questions, I've talked, and I've learned. And the Congress and I came back to Washington filled with, in some ways, with a feeling of being refreshed, even inspired. But in other ways, we came back concerned and reflective.

The people tell me and they're telling the Congress that this is a crucial time in the history of our country. And that means, for you and me, that it's a crucial time for the Democratic Party, because there's no way to separate the two. Our very way of life is literally being transformed. Historians will prove that this is true. Rapid, uncontrollable, unpredictable changes confront us on every hand.

Many Americans are genuinely filled with troubled souls and doubt about the future. But this is not the first time this has happened in the history of our country, and time and again, we Democrats have been called upon to lead the American people through times like these. We Democrats are not crippled by fear or trepidation or doubt. That's a characteristic of our party which has prevailed in every time of trouble and strife and challenge. And we have always met that challenge successfully, and I guarantee you that we always will.

We brought the Nation through a great depression as a united Democratic Party. We fought and we won World War II and saved the world for freedom and forged a long peace that followed, as a united Democratic Party. We got the country moving again in the 1960's, and we made an enduring commitment to the poor and to the people struggling for basic human rights, as a united Democratic Party. In 1976 America turned to us again, and now we must meet the challenges of the 1980's as a united Democratic Party.

Those 8 years of Republican rule could not erase what we had begun to build in this country, but 8 years of Republican rule could and did damage the faith of American people in our own government and in the very institutions of democracy. It's hard to remember clearly now how seriously our Nation was afflicted 3 or 4 or 5 years ago. We inherited illegalities and embarrassments, confusion, deprivation, and deep unemployment. But we've never confronted any of those tough issues which we inherited and flinched from our duty. We have never avoided a single difficult issue, no matter what the political consequences might be.

Our Federal, State, and local officials, I guarantee you, in an unprecedented way are now working as a team. This was not the case before. Our party, as Tip O'Neill pointed out so well, is putting America back to work. We created 8 million new jobs. We increased job programs for the poor and the minorities to a level 10 times greater than that of the Ford administration budget, and we have knocked the unemployment rate down by 25 percent.

We've increased education aid by 60 percent. We've added massive improvements in housing, public transportation, agriculture. We've cut the unwarranted intrusion in the private enterprise system by government and eliminated regulations and cut out redtape. We've boosted business profits. And as Tip said, again, at the same time, in spite of all those better services for our people, we have slashed the Federal deficit by more than 50 percent.

We've not yet solved all the problems of our country. For more than 10 years now, our Nation has faced a serious problem of inflation, a problem that wracks our economy, that frightens our people, and which is at the top of our legislative and the national agenda. But we have refused to take the road that some would suggest to lick inflation by sacrificing jobs and employment opportunities. The Democratic Party never has and will not now turn its back on the working men and women of America.

We've listened to Americans who are concerned about the way government works, about the growing impersonality of government bureaucracies. We didn't just listen; we acted.

We put through the first reform of the civil service system in a hundred years. It's paying off. And it will help all Americans, those who work inside government as employees full-time and those who receive the benefits of government service for the next hundred years.

We've begun to reorganize the structure of the Federal Government. Let me just give you one recent example of what that means to the American people. This reorganization plan, so far as I know, never got any media attention. But earlier this month, three Governors in the gulf coast region called me about the damage being done by Hurricane Frederic. Because we had reorganized our emergency services—eight different programs now into one; five agencies now into one, under one solid and competent administrator—we were able to guarantee effective assistance for their States in minutes. In the past, it could very well have taken weeks or more, and then the assistance would not have been well coordinated or effective.

We've faced up to the problem of a social security system that was headed down the road toward bankruptcy. And again, at some considerable political cost, we put the social security system back so it was secure again, and we kept faith with millions of hard-working Americans, both young and old, who had their faith shaken during the '74, '75, and '76 period.

We're delivering on another promise, too—the promise that we would maintain an America that is strong and an America at peace. NATO is revitalized. Our alliances are strengthened. And under this Democratic administration and under this Democratic Congress, not one single American life has been lost in combat, and I thank God for that. And we've maintained this peace without retreating 1 inch from our responsibility to America or to our allies—not with saber-rattling rhetoric, but with calm, reason, and persistence.

And we've made historic progress toward peace in the Middle East. A year ago, we had the Camp David accords; 6 months ago, a Mideast peace treaty. It's imperative that all of us—and these days, especially, American Jews and American blacks—must unite in securing peace and justice in that historically troubled land. This is no time for division; it's no time for criticism. It's a time for searching together for a common ground.

We've created a new and beneficial relationship with one-fourth of all the human beings who live on Earth, in China. We've taken the lead, and we continue the Democratic Party's tradition, of seeking to prevent the proliferation of nuclear weapons. We've dared to put the issue of human rights on the permanent international agenda. Only the history books will ever record how many jail doors are open and how many formerly oppressed people, who lived under a totalitarian regime, now know the benefits of human freedom and a chance to choose their own leaders.

Our concern with human rights, which is a foundation of the Democratic Party, begins here at home. We've chipped away at decades of neglect, and we've tried to root out examples of blatant prejudice. We've placed minorities, qualified in every way, in many decisionmaking jobs in the Federal Government. We've whacked away subtle forms of discrimination. We've improved the enforcement of Federal equal opportunity laws. We've brought more minorities and more women into our judicial system than in all the rest of American history combined. And we are not through yet. And we have waged an intense State-by-State effort for the adoption of the equal rights amendment. And we are not through yet.

I could go on and on about the achievements of this administration and this Democratic Congress. It's a record of courage and of dedication and of leadership. But the truth is that, despite our record of accomplishment, much of what we do here in Washington too often seems confusing and irrelevant to millions of Americans. You who are in the Congress share that problem. You know that your constituents may love you as a person, but they think poorly of the institution of which you are a part and which you represent.

You know how easy it is for us to reap the benefits of the Democratic Party and our own incumbency in high office and, at the same time, to attack in a subtle way the system or the government in order to derive transient political advantage. It's the simplest job for us to tend to a certain home base or some narrow constituency, while giving national interests less attention. And because of this temptation, party unity sometimes goes lacking and our Nation suffers, because national priorities are sometimes met at a snail's pace.

Look, for example, at the energy problem. Is it real? It certainly is. But it's taken 2½ years—I'm not exaggerating—2½ years to get the people of this country to face the fact that our very Nation's security is in danger. Is the energy problem understood? My mail says that, to an increasing degree, it is understood by the the American people and that the American people are crying out now for action, bold action, and action without any further delay.

Americans will not long permit and not long suffer those who do permit the drain of billions of dollars going overseas to pay for oil—next year $70 billion sapped out of the American economy. Along with those dollars go jobs, and with those millions of barrels of oil every day, we import inflation. United Democrats can now and are making good progress toward giving our Nation, finally, after long years of neglect, a comprehensive national energy policy that will heal our troubled land, bind us together in a spirit of unity and accomplishment and also hope and confidence to the future, cut down on inflation, put our people back to work, and

let our Nation be secure. I'm proud of the progress made so far.

I'm also convinced that Americans want nuclear weapons controlled. The SALT treaty must be ratified. And I tell you, it is easy to find a reason, if one is a U.S. Senator, not to support SALT.

I could have written a better SALT treaty had I done it unilaterally, without consulting the Soviet Union. This treaty was hammered out over 7 years by three Presidents. It's fair; it's balanced. It contributes to our Nation's security. It lets us monitor what the Soviets are doing. It puts a limit and an actual decrease of 10 percent on Soviet missile launchers. It keeps us in a role of leadership for the Western World. It holds NATO together. It contributes to world peace. It gives us authenticity and influence in preventing non-nuclear weapons from turning toward that horrible option.

But if SALT is rejected by the U.S. Senate, that will be a terrible blow to our country and to our party and to our security and to our unity and to our influence in the world and to our alliances and to our own future and to world peace. It is extremely important. And I hope that every single Democrat who listens to my voice will put the ratification of the SALT II treaty at the top of your priority and help me get this done. We must not betray Americans who want peace. We must not betray Americans who look to us for leadership. We must not play politics with nuclear arsenals.

I know that Americans want a nation at peace and a strong America. A strong America is the best guarantor of peace for our own country and for the world. I tell you quite frankly, I believe in a united nation, and I believe in a strong defense. And as long as I'm in the White House, this Nation is going to have a strong defense. And you can depend on it.

I'm sure you would agree with me when I say that it's not easy these days to be a President or to be a Governor or to be a Member of the Congress or to be a mayor. But through unity, we can share the responsibilities that fall so heavily on our shoulders, and we can enjoy the honor and the pleasure and the gratification of effective public service.

This is a time of testing, for us and for our country. It's time to make the American people understand what we are doing and understand government and, therefore, to trust and respect and support government in difficult times. How? By beginning to speak to one another, to work with one another, and to reason more closely together, by spelling out a common vision of and for America, a vision that our party has always had and a vision that we are now bringing into reality.

Our party has always represented the best in American thoughts and ideals and values. Our party has had the ability to deal with change, change without timidity and without fear. There are others, not Democrats, who long for the past, who resent the present, and who fear the future. That's not the story of the Democratic Party. Our theme song isn't "Auld Lang Syne" or some funeral dirge. Our theme song is "Happy Days Are Here Again."

Let me say in closing that it's time now to shape the Democratic Party for the 1980's. We, the Democratic Party, have the biggest stake of all in making government work, because we intend to be the majority party permanently.

The people give us their confidence, but they also give us a great responsibility. It's a greater responsibility than a Republican has. We must understand that unless we make government work well, some day it may not work at all. We must recognize and we must understand the impatience and the frustration with government that is so common in our Nation. We must fight the splintered special interest and single issue politics that tend to dominate our national debates.

The challenge that we face is to build a party for the rest of this century that's strong enough to be effective and broad enough to be representative, a party that speaks the meaning to the people of what democracy is, what compassion is, what truth is, what peace is, what harmony is, what unity is, what freedom is, what leadership is. That's our responsibility, and together we can do it. But with selfish divisions among ourselves, our voice is fractured, and it cannot be clearly heard.

This forthcoming year will be filled with campaigns and caucuses, conventions and debates, and we look forward to it. There will be disagreements, and there must be. We will argue about the issues among ourselves, and we ought to. But we can make the system work. We can sharpen our focus on the common agenda items which pull us together, which unite us as Democrats.

We must join together in the fight for SALT II, for hospital cost containment, for better environment, for healthy and growing and happy cities, for a national health plan, for welfare reform, for a windfall profits tax on the oil companies to finance energy security for our country. We've got a lot to do. Let's do it together.

In my speech on July 15, a Sunday night speech, I spoke of a crisis of confidence and a lack of unity in America. The outpouring of mail and telephone calls to the White House after that speech was overwhelming. The professionals that have been there 25 or 30 years said they have never seen so many letters or had so many telephone calls on any single incident, in wartime or peacetime. Tens of thousands of people, literally, from all over the country wrote similar letters. "You're right," they said. "Tell us how we can help." Sometimes it's hard for that person, who probably wrote their first letter to a President, to find an avenue to the core of American Government. That avenue is through you and through other members of the Democratic Party.

I say to you tonight what I've said to them: The answer to the crisis of confidence is action, and the answer to fragmentation and doubt is unity. It's this belief that holds us together here tonight—that we believe in working together as a great party, that we can shape the destiny of a great nation—the faith that as a free people we can join together to improve our own lives and the lives of others not nearly so fortunate as any single person in this room, that as a strong nation we can build a community of nations at peace. These are not just dreams. They are the long-term agenda that gives purpose to our Democratic Party.

We believe with William Faulkner that mankind will not merely endure, but will surely prevail. So, let us think and consider and rededicate ourselves tonight to the simple truth of that conviction. We shall prevail, we shall overcome, together.

Thank you very much.

NOTE: The President spoke at 10:25 p.m. in the International Ballroom at the Washington Hilton Hotel.

Hospital Cost Containment Legislation

Statement on Action by the House Interstate and Foreign Commerce Committee. September 26, 1979

I am very pleased by the action of the House Commerce Committee today in favorably reporting, 23 to 19, with bipartisan support, the administration's bill to contain hospital costs. Since the Ways and Means Committee has already reported similar legislation, the full House will at last have an opportunity to act on one of the Nation's most serious problems—soaring hospital costs.

Although it promises to be a close vote, it is inconceivable that a majority of the House would refuse to join in this effort to attack directly one of the primary causes of inflation and to save billions of Federal and State taxpayers' dollars. This is undoubtedly the single most important anti-inflation and budget-saving bill the Congress will face this session. Every Member's seriousness in dealing with excessive inflation and wasteful Federal spending will be judged—correctly—in large part by his or her vote on this issue. I am confident the full House will follow the lead of the Senate during the last Congress and act favorably at long last to restrain soaring hospital costs.

I am grateful for the leadership of Commerce Committee Chairman Harley Staggers and Health Subcommittee Chairman Henry Waxman in seeing the bill successfully through the committee.

Budget Deferrals

Message to the Congress. September 27, 1979

To the Congress of the United States:

In accordance with the Impoundment Control Act of 1974, I herewith report four new deferrals of budget authority totalling $61.9 million and a revision to one previously transmitted deferral increasing the amount deferred by $3.8 million. These items involve the Departments of Agriculture and Commerce and the Railroad Retirement Board.

The details of each deferral are contained in the attached reports.

JIMMY CARTER

The White House,
  September 27, 1979.

NOTE: The attachments detailing the deferrals are printed in the FEDERAL REGISTER of October 2, 1979.

President's Commission on the Holocaust

Remarks on Receiving the Final Report of the Commission.   September 27, 1979

Mr. Chairman, the beauty of your words and the solemnity of your thoughts and the importance of the work of this Commission are all very impressive.

Eight months ago, I asked Elie Wiesel and a distinguished group of Americans, some from the Congress, to take on an awesome responsibility. Jim Blanchard of Michigan and others said they couldn't be here because there is a vote pending in the House, but they have served well, along with a broad cross-section of Americans who have gone into this effort with a great deal of dedication and who have produced a report that will solve problems and picture for us proper actions in the future.

This is an awesome responsibility that you have performed. I asked this group to recommend a fitting memorial in the United States to the victims of the most unspeakable crime in all of human history—the Holocaust. Rarely has a Presidential commission faced a more sobering or a more difficult or a more totally important challenge. This event of the Holocaust, the crime against humanity itself, has no parallel in human history. A philosopher wrote that human language

itself breaks down when confronted with the monstrous challenge of describing this evil.

So, I want to pay a special tribute, on behalf of our Nation, to all those who have contributed to this effort and for the tremendous service that you've performed.

Your very work as a commission is part of a living memorial to the victims of the Holocaust. Your grappling with the meaning of this event has helped bring new understanding and moral vision to all who must confront this question. Your historic trips to the concentration camps in Eastern Europe and to Babi Yar in the Soviet Union have helped to arouse the conscience of the world and to remind us once again that we must never forget. And I know our country appreciates the fact that many of you went on those trips, not at Government expense, but at your own expense.

Out of our memory and understanding of the Holocaust, we must forge an unshakable oath with all civilized people that never again will the world stand silent, never again will the world look the other way or fail to act in time to prevent this terrible crime of genocide.

In addition to the Jewish people who were engulfed by the Holocaust simply because they were Jews, 5 million other human beings were destroyed. About 3 million Poles, many Hungarians, Gypsies, also need to be remembered. To memorialize the victims of the Holocaust, we must harness the outrage of our own memories to stamp out oppression wherever it exists. We must understand that human rights and human dignity are indivisible. Wherever our fellow human beings are stripped of their humanity, defiled or tortured or victimized by repression or terrorism or racism or prejudice, then all of us are victims. As

Americans, we must and we always will speak out in defense of human rights at home and everywhere in the world.

And I might add that as Americans we must share the responsibility for, 40 years ago, not being willing to acknowledge that this horrible event was in prospect.

And I think that the action of this Holocaust Commission is long overdue, because we've not had a constant center which could be visited by Americans of all faiths and all races to be reminded of our omission in the past, to have the memory of this horrible event kept vivid in our minds, to prevent a recurrence of such an action anywhere on Earth in the future.

In view of the 6 million Jewish victims of the Holocaust, it's particularly appropriate that we receive this report during the High Holy Days, just prior to Yom Kippur, the Day of Atonement. Yom Kippur is a day and a time for looking back. It's a time for reflection. It's a time for remembrance. But it's also a time for the reaffirmation of life, a time for looking ahead.

So, I will consider this report most carefully and will respond personally to this Commission and to the people of our Nation with my personal prayer that the memory of the Holocaust shall be transformed into a reaffirmation of life. And as President, I can pledge to you that I will do everything in my power to carry out the recommendations of this report.

The Members of the Congress will be intensely interested in arousing support in our Legislature. And I'm sure the people of this country will be looking with anticipation to this reminder of the victims and also a warning that this horrible event will never again occur on Earth.

Thank you very much, Mr. Chairman, and all the members of the Commission.

NOTE: The President spoke at 2:15 p.m. at the ceremony in the Rose Garden at the White House. Prior to the ceremony, the President met with Mr. Wiesel, Chairman of the Commission, in the Oval Office.

Department of Defense

Nomination of Robert W. Komer To Be Under Secretary for Policy.
September 27, 1979

The President today announced that he will nominate Robert W. Komer, of Alexandria, Va., to be Under Secretary of Defense for Policy. He would replace Stanley R. Resor, resigned.

Komer is Advisor to the Secretary of Defense on NATO Affairs.

He was born February 23, 1922, in Chicago, Ill. He received a B.S. from Harvard College in 1942 and an M.B.A. from Harvard Graduate School of Business Administration in 1947. He served in the U.S. Army from 1943 to 1946.

Komer was with the Central Intelligence Agency from 1947 to 1961, and served as alternate National Security Council Planning Board member and staff assistant from 1958 to 1961. From 1961 to 1965, he was a senior staff member on the National Security Council.

From 1965 to 1966, Komer was Deputy Special Assistant to the President for National Security Affairs, and from 1966 to 1967, he was Special Assistant to the President. From 1967 to 1968, he was Deputy to the Commander of the United States Military Assistance Command, Vietnam.

From 1968 to 1969, Komer was U.S. Ambassador to Turkey. He was a consultant with the RAND Corp. from 1969 to 1976, and a consultant to the Secretary of Defense during 1977.

Department of the Interior

Nomination of William E. Hallett To Be Commissioner of Indian Affairs.
September 27, 1979

The President today announced that he will nominate William E. Hallett, of Broomfield, Colo., to be Commissioner of Indian Affairs. He would replace Ben Reifel, resigned.

Hallett is Assistant Regional Administrator of the Office of Indian Programs for Region VIII in Denver.

He was born May 18, 1942, in Red Lake, Minn. He received a bachelor's degree in business administration from Bemidji State College in 1965.

From 1965 to 1967, Hallett was a personnel technician for the Chicago Police Department. From 1967 to 1968, he was director of housing and manpower programs for the Red Lake Band of Chippewa Indians, where he set up and directed the Tribal Home Construction Co.

From 1968 to 1970, he was director of industrial development for the National Congress of American Indians. During 1970 Hallett was a consultant to the National Council on Indian Opportunity and the President's National Advisory Council on Minority Business Enterprise.

From 1970 to 1975, Hallett was special assistant to the Regional Administrator for Indian Affairs for Region VIII. He has been Assistant Regional Administrator since 1975.

Department of Health, Education, and Welfare

Nomination of William B. Welsh To Be an Assistant Secretary.   September 27, 1979

The President today announced that he will nominate William B. Welsh, of Annandale, Va., to be an Assistant Secretary of Health, Education, and Welfare. He would replace Richard Warden, resigned, and his area of responsibility would be legislation.

Welsh is Assistant Secretary of Housing and Urban Development for Legislative Affairs and Intergovernmental Relations.

He was born September 18, 1924, in Munfordville, Ky. He received an A.B. from Berea College in 1949 and an M.A. from the University of Kentucky in 1952. He served in the U.S. Army from 1943 to 1946.

Welsh was legislative assistant to U.S. Senator Herbert H. Lehman from 1952 to 1956, and research director of the Democratic National Committee from 1957 to 1958. From 1959 to 1967, he was administrative assistant to U.S. Senator Philip Hart.

In 1967 and 1968, Welsh was administrative assistant to Vice President Hubert Humphrey. From 1969 to 1971, he was executive director of the Democratic National Committee. From 1972 to 1979, he was executive director for governmental affairs of the American Federation of State, County, and Municipal Employees.

National Highway Safety Advisory Committee

Appointment of 12 Members.
September 27, 1979

The President today announced the appointment of 12 persons as members of the National Highway Safety Advisory Committee. They are:

PETER J. ALLEN, owner of Allen's Home Furnishings in San Jose, Calif., where he is active in civic and political affairs;

RALPH V. DURHAM, director of safety and health for the International Brotherhood of Teamsters;

FRANCES H. GOODWIN, an associate judge of the Municipal Court of Dallas, Tex. (reappointment);

JOHN C. LANDEN, vice president of 3M Co. for traffic control products;

WILLIAM L. MALLORY, majority floor leader in the Ohio House of Representatives and an adjunct professor at the University of Cincinnati;

DANIEL F. PORTIS, of Lepanto, Ark., director of the Portis Mercantile Co., and a past member of the Arkansas Highway Commission;

DEBORAH D. RICHARDS, founder, board chairman, and manager of Action for Child Transportation Safety, Inc.;

PETER W. RODINO III, assistant county counsel for Essex County, N.J., and an attorney in East Orange, N.J.

CARL E. SERNA, director of the Project Development Division of the New Mexico State Highway Department;

ADELE D. SPIELBERGER, chief of the Bureau of Highway Safety, Florida Department of Administration, and Governor's highway safety representative for Florida;

LAWRENCE H. STERN, president of Sterns Transport, Inc., an ICC common carrier, and past president of the New Jersey Motor Truck Association;

PATRICIA F. WALLER, associate director for driver programs at the University of North Carolina Safety Research Center.

education. Billions of dollars were being spent, but education programs continued to be denied the full-time attention from a Cabinet Secretary that would make these programs perform effectively. That is why I proposed a separate department of education and why I have made it one of my highest legislative priorities over the past 2 years.

With a separate department of education, we will finally have a single agency and a single Cabinet official responsible full-time for the effective management of Federal aid-to-education programs. As a result, the American people will now have a much clearer picture of what the Federal Government is doing in education and who is in charge of those activities.

I would like to especially thank Chairman Brooks and Speaker O'Neill for bringing this important measure to final passage. I would also like to thank Senator Ribicoff for his successful leadership on this matter in the Senate. I look forward with great pleasure to signing the bill that these congressional leaders have helped pass.

Department of Education Legislation

Statement on House of Representatives Approval of the Legislation.
September 27, 1979

The House's vote today approving the creation of a department of education is a significant milestone in my effort to make the Federal Government more efficient. We will now have a single Cabinet department which can provide the coherence and sense of direction needed for Federal education programs.

When I came to Washington, I was convinced that the Federal Government had failed to deliver adequately on its limited, but important role in American

Panama Canal Act of 1979

Statement on Signing H.R. 111 Into Law.
September 27, 1979

I am pleased to sign into law the Panama Canal Act of 1979, which implements the Panama Canal Treaty of 1977.

The Panama Canal Treaty and the Neutrality Treaty were the result of 13 years of careful negotiations. They have been hailed throughout this hemisphere as a model for equitable negotiations between ourselves and our smaller neighbors. As I said when I signed the treaties, they express the commitment of the United States to the belief that fairness, and not force, should lie at the heart of our dealings with nations of the world.

The treaties also protect our economic and security interests. We will continue to operate the canal until the end of the century through the Panama Canal Commission, an agency of the United States in which Panama will have a minority voice. We will maintain military forces in Panama until that date. After the year 1999, Panama will assume responsibility for operating the canal. A regime of permanent neutrality is established under which both nations have the right to act against any aggression or threat directed against the canal. The Panama Canal Act provides a framework in which the United States can exercise its rights to operate and defend the canal in a manner consistent with our responsibilities and obligations under the treaties.

I particularly want to thank Senators Stennis and Levin and Congressmen Murphy, Bowen, and Derwinski for their outstanding leadership in resolving the many difficult issues embodied in this act.

In signing this act, I want to assure Members of Congress and the Government of Panama that this legislation will be interpreted and applied by the executive branch in strict conformity with the terms and the intent of the treaties. In this respect, I believe that certain technicalities in several sections of the act require comment.

Section 1503 requires congressional approval for transfers of property to Panama. Section 1504 grants such approval subject to a 180-day notice requirement and a prohibition against transfer of the canal itself before termination of the treaty. It remains the position of the administration that the treaty is self-executing with respect to the transfer of property, and thus no additional legislative authorization is required. With regard to the condition contained in Section 1504 (c) concerning transfer of the canal, I note that this does not preclude other discretionary transfers during the lifetime of the treaty, as provided for in Article XIII, paragraph 2(b) and 2(c) of the treaty.

Section 1341(e) lists certain costs which must be paid prior to any contingent payment to Panama under paragraph 4(c) of Article XIII of the treaty. It is my understanding that costs listed in this section are identical to those which will be included in the tolls base under Section 1602 of the act. These costs are related to the operation and maintenance of the canal and are thus properly considered as "expenditures" under paragraph 4(c) of Article XIII, to be paid before any surplus is due to Panama under that provision.

NOTE: As enacted, H.R. 111 is Public Law 96–70, approved September 27.

Anti-Inflation Program

Remarks Announcing a National Accord Between the Administration and the American Labor Leadership. September 28, 1979

In my Sunday night speech to the Nation in July, I said that the people of our country want to see government and our great institutions pull together to face the complex challenges which confront us as a people. Inflation is the most persistent challenge to our economy, primarily fed by escalating energy costs, which are predominantly controlled by others in foreign countries. Inflation tends to pit our people and our institutions against each other and contributes to a sense of frustration and doubt and concern, which is so worrisome to our people. Ultimately, if not curbed, inflation will sap our confidence as a nation, will erode our faith in the future, and will threaten those basic human values which make our country great.

I've called for our institutions and our people to regain a sense of shared purpose and shared cooperation and to join in a successful fight against inflation. Today, I'm very pleased to announce that enormous progress toward that goal has been made. I'm pleased and proud to announce that this administration has achieved a new national accord with the broadest possible impact in order to fight against inflation.

This accord is represented by a statement of principles which we've been pursuing since July in discussions with representatives of organized labor. Parallel discussions have also been held with the leaders in the business community.

The communication from President George Meany—that the AFL–CIO executive council has today endorsed the statement of principles—means that for the first time in history, such an accord has been reached on a voluntary basis. I'd like to say that President Meany, who's announced that he will not seek reelection today, has contributed with his heart and his mind, his experience, his inspirational leadership to the reaching of this agreement, and I'm deeply grateful to him.

I also want to commend especially Secretary William Miller and the members of my economic policy group, the key leaders, in addition to Mr. Meany, of our major labor organizations, and representatives of the business community for working so constructively together in search of this understanding.

As part of our national accord, we will be establishing a Pay Advisory Committee and a Price Advisory Committee. Organized labor leadership has agreed to serve on the Pay Advisory Committee, and I'm counting on business leaders to join it also.

This Committee, which will play an important role in assuring restrained but equitable pay increases, is to be made up of 15 members—five each from labor, business, and the public. John Dunlop has accepted my invitation to serve as

Chairman of this Pay Committee, and other members will be announced in the near future. The Price Advisory Committee will consist of five public members whom I will name in a few weeks.

I want to emphasize again that if substantial progress is to be made to reduce inflation in this country—and this will obviously take time and sustained effort— we will need the active and dedicated support for Government of both business and labor.

The developments of today provide us the initial framework for such an effort, and I pledge to do my utmost to follow through and to make this initiative a significant forward step in our continuing and determined fight against inflation in the United States.

I would like now to introduce the Secretary of Treasury, William Miller, who, along with others on the stage with me, will be glad to answer your questions.

Bill Miller.

NOTE: The President spoke at 1:47 p.m. in Room 450 of the Old Executive Office Building. Following his remarks, Secretary Miller, Alfred E. Kahn, Advisor to the President on Inflation, and Lane Kirkland, secretary-treasurer of the AFL–CIO, held a news conference on the national accord.

Anti-Inflation Program

Executive Order 12161.   September 28, 1979

SECOND YEAR OF THE ANTI-INFLATION PROGRAM

By the authority vested in me as President and as Commander in Chief of the Armed Forces by the Constitution and statutes of the United States of America, including the Council on Wage and Price Stability Act, as amended (12 U.S.C. 1904 note), and the Federal Property and Administrative Services Act of 1949, as amended (40 U.S.C. 486(a)), and in order to supplement the anti-inflation program established on November 3, 1978, Section 1–102 of Executive Order No. 12092 is hereby amended to read as follows:

"1–102. Anti-inflationary wage and price behavior shall be measured by the following standards:

(a) For prices, anti-inflationary price behavior of a company is a current rate of average price increase no greater than its historical rate of price increase during 1976–77, except where the company experiences uncontrollable increases in the prices of the goods and services it buys, and subject to the provisions of paragraphs (c) and (d).

(b) For pay, anti-inflationary pay behavior is the holding of pay increases to not more than 7 percent annually above their recent historical levels, subject to the provisions of paragraphs (c) and (d).

(c) These standards, which shall be further defined or modified by the Chairman of the Council on Wage and Price Stability, shall be subject to limitations and exceptions as determined by the Chairman and shall be administered so as to take into account any inequities that may have been created by the standards during the past year.

(d) The Council is directed to reconstitute in accordance with the Federal Advisory Committee Act, as amended, a Pay Advisory Committee and a Price Advisory Committee in order to provide greater participation by the public in the anti-inflation program. The Pay Advisory Committee and the Price Advisory Committee will advise the Council on developing policies that encourage anti-inflationary pay and price behavior by private industry, employers, and labor, that decelerate the rate of inflation and that provide for a fair and equitable distribution of the burden of restraint. To the extent permitted by law, the Council is directed to provide the Pay and Price Advisory Committees with all information required to perform their duties.".

JIMMY CARTER

The White House,
    September 28, 1979.

[Filed with the Office of the Federal Register, 4:40 p.m., September 28, 1979]

Department of Agriculture

Nomination of James C. Webster To Be an Assistant Secretary.   September 28, 1979

The President today announced that he will nominate James C. Webster, of Madison, S. Dak., to be Assistant Secretary of Agriculture. He would replace Dale Hathaway, who has been appointed Under Secretary of Agriculture.

Webster has been director of the Office of Governmental and Public Affairs at the Agriculture Department since 1977.

He was born February 9, 1938, in Grand Island, Nebr. From 1961 to 1963, he was South Dakota manager for UPI, and from 1963 to 1968, he was managing editor of the Madison Daily Leader. From 1968 to 1969, he was editor of the East River Guardian.

From 1970 to 1973, Webster was director of public relations for the American Public Power Association. From 1973 to 1975, he was legislative assistant and press secretary to Senator George McGovern. From 1975 to 1977, he was chief clerk and press secretary of the Senate Committee on Agriculture and Forestry.

Gasoline End-User Allocation

Executive Order 12162.   September 28, 1979

AMENDMENT TO EXECUTIVE ORDER 12140

By the authority vested in me as President by the Constitution and statutes of

1779

the United States of America, including the Emergency Petroleum Allocation Act of 1973, as amended (15 U.S.C. 751 *et seq.*), Executive Order No. 12140 is hereby amended by deleting the first sentence in Sec. 1–105.

JIMMY CARTER

The White House,
    September 28, 1979.

[Filed with the Office of the Federal Register,
    4:50 p.m., September 28, 1979]

Budget Deferral

Message to the Congress.   September 28, 1979

To the Congress of the United States:

In accordance with the Impoundment Control Act of 1974, I herewith report a routine revision to a previously transmitted deferral for the Department of Transportation. This revision increases the amount deferred by $5.0 million. The details of this revised deferral are contained in the attached report.

JIMMY CARTER

The White House,
    September 28, 1979.

NOTE: The attachment detailing the deferral is printed in the FEDERAL REGISTER of October 3, 1979.

Procurement of Grain in Nicaragua

*Memorandum From the President.
September 28, 1979*

Presidential Determination No. 79–17

*Memorandum for the Administrator,
Agency for International Development*

Subject: Determination and Authorization under Section 614(a) of the Foreign Assistance Act of 1961, as amended, for

Procurement in Nicaragua of Rice, Sorghum, Beans and Corn

Pursuant to the authority vested in me by section 614(a) of the Foreign Assistance Act of 1961, as amended (the Act), I hereby

A. Determine that the use of approximately $5.0 million in funds available in FY 1979 for the procurement in Nicaragua of rice, sorghum, beans and corn, without regard to the requirements of section 604(e) of the Act, is important to the security of the United States; and

B. Authorize such use of approximately $5.0 million in funds for the procurement in Nicaragua of rice, sorghum, beans and corn.

This determination shall be published in the FEDERAL REGISTER, as required by law.

JIMMY CARTER

[Filed with the Office of the Federal Register,
    4:51 p.m., September 28, 1979]

Thanksgiving Day, 1979

Proclamation 4693.   September 28, 1979

*By the President of the United States
of America*

A Proclamation

Thanksgiving Day was first celebrated in this land not in a moment of unbridled triumph, but in times of great adversity. The colonies of Massachusetts and Virginia had few material possessions to help them face the dangers of the wilderness. They had no certainty that the harvests for which they gave thanks would be sufficient to carry them through a long winter. Yet they gave thanks to God for what they had and for the hope of this new land.

In the darkest hour of the American Revolution, when the young Republic faced defeat by the strongest military power on Earth, our forefathers also saw fit to give thanks for their blessings. In the midst of a devastating Civil War, President Lincoln proclaimed a day to express gratitude for our "singular deliverances and blessings."

The ensuing years have multiplied our nation's blessings. We have been delivered from repeated perils, and we have been blessed with abundance beyond the imaginings of those who offered thanks in the chill of approaching winter more than three-and-one-half centuries ago.

Succeeding generations have broadened the freedom they cherished and the opportunity they sought, and built a mighty nation on the strong foundations they laid. In this two hundred and fourth year of our independence, we have good reasons for gratitude: for liberty in a world where repression is common, for peace in a world of threats and terror and war, for a bounteous harvest in a world where hunger and despair still stalk much of mankind.

Like those who came before us, we come to give thanks for our singular deliverances and blessings, in a time of both danger and great promise. May we be thankful in proportion to that which we have received, trusting not in our wealth and comforts, but in the strength of our purpose, that all nations might be similarly blessed with liberty and abundance and live in peace.

Now, THEREFORE, I, JIMMY CARTER, President of the United States of America, do proclaim Thursday, the 22nd of November, 1979 as Thanksgiving Day. I ask all Americans to give thanks on that day for the blessings Almighty God has bestowed upon us, and seek to be good stewards of what we have received.

IN WITNESS WHEREOF, I have hereunto set my hand this twenty-eighth day of September, in the year of our Lord

nineteen hundred seventy-nine, and of the Independence of the United States of America the two hundred and fourth.

JIMMY CARTER

[Filed with the Office of the Federal Register, 11:32 a.m., October 1, 1979]

Visit of President López Portillo of Mexico

Toasts at the State Dinner. September 28, 1979

PRESIDENT CARTER. President López Portillo, we welcome you and your lovely wife, Carmen, and your personal family and your official family back to the White House. Tonight we're determined to make the result of our toasts better than they were when I was in Mexico City. [*Laughter*]

You represent a great democratic nation, growing in world influence. And, Mr. President, your depth of insight and your breadth of vision match the past and the future achievements of your great country.

Your speech yesterday at the United Nations on the future of the world as it relates to energy was indeed one of the most profound and the most beautiful speeches I have ever read. This can lay the groundwork for discussions among all nations on Earth—as you said, democratic nations and socialist nations, developed nations and undeveloped nations—which can lead to the resolution of one of the most difficult challenges of our time. This is typical of your personal leadership, Mr. President, and the leadership of your great country.

It's an honor and a privilege and an exciting experience for us to have you again in our country for serious discussions that will affect your people and mine.

1781

Our nations are linked by both border and by destiny, by blood kinship and by a love of freedom. Both of us have thrown off colonial rule. Our ancestors know what it means to go from oppression to liberty. The relationships between our two countries have not always been happy, nor always peaceful. Some differences in the past, unfortunately, have even been settled by bloodshed. Some differences even in our own lifetime have been too long ignored or hidden. Now I believe that these troubled and uncertain times between our two countries are gone forever. If we lead well, we can write a new and a long history of peace, friendship, cooperation, and understanding between our people.

We are determined that our dialog will always be creative, that our negotiations will be frank and fair and mature and productive, that we will solve problems so that our people will have a better quality of life, and that together, through leadership, we can benefit the people of other nations.

When I had the honor to speak to the members of the Mexican Congress, I quoted the words of your great leader, Benito Juarez, that are inscribed on the walls of the Chamber of Deputies. The people of your country—through television, thanks to you—heard these words, but I would like the citizens of my country to hear them tonight here in the White House. *Entre los individuos, como entre las naciónes, el respeto al derecho humano es la paz.*

INTERPRETER. Between individuals, as between nations, respect for the rights of others is peace.

PRESIDENT CARTER. Very good. [*Laughter*] I might say that that is a perfect translation. [*Laughter*]

And in that spirit, ladies and gentlemen, that between nations and between individuals there can be a perfect peace, I would like to offer a toast—without wine, but with water, and we'll drink wine later on—to the President of Mexico, to the family which he has brought here, both official and personal, to peace between our two countries, to better understanding throughout the world, and to the people of Mexico.

[*At this point, there was a brief pause as wine was served.*]

If I could have your attention again, just to make sure that the toast is authenticated—[*laughter*]—I would like to again offer a toast to the President of a great country and to the people of Mexico. Welcome to our Nation.

PRESIDENT LÓPEZ PORTILLO. *Mr. President of the United States and Mrs. Carter:*

For me, for my family and the members of my party, it is a great honor to meet again for the third time.

Our two peoples feel great security in the fact that since we are neighbors, the two Presidents of the two countries can meet as frequently as we do. To communicate is actually to open up the possibility of a peaceful coexistence, to live together. Communication is a guarantee of human coexistence.

For me, it is a great satisfaction to communicate with the President of the United States for the third time, to be able to once again witness the enormous values that he holds in himself as a human being—his generosity and his braveness. For me, President Carter, it is a great pleasure to see you again and a great honor to take up, once again, the very serious matters in the very open way in which we have dealt with them.

Today we could see that we were not mistaken when we decided upon a certain way of work between the two countries. It was a new system that had some problems in taking off, but which is now working very well. We were right, President Carter, and I am very happy that we were. We can now analyze in depth the bilateral problems that, perforce, have to come about when two countries are neighbors.

Life is risk; life is a solution of problems. As we say in my homeland, it is only the dead that do not make noise. [*Laughter*] Noise is life, and our two countries are very vital countries. They are both located in the same continent, but they have two different roots.

We are learning to live together. It is a great guarantee for us that we have this possibility of living together at a time when the head of the Government of this great country is a person like Mr. Carter. He has been very generous, as he always is, when he referred to the proposal that we made yesterday in my address before the General Assembly of the United Nations. In this proposal, we stand on opposite sides.

The United States is the powerful nation, perhaps the most outstanding expression of this kind of a nation in the world. Mexico is a developing nation. There is a border between us 3,000 kilometers long, and perhaps this is the best expression of the north-south relationship.

If we can understand the facts of our reality as a problem, if we can state our facts as a problem within this climate of mutual respect, which has prevailed today and which has prevailed always when we have met, we can then prove that we can win out, and we can transcend the differences between the north and the south, between developing and the developed. That is why I have high hopes that at the only universal forum that we men have been able to create, and which we sometimes tend to ignore as if it had just fallen upon us from Mars—since the real fact is that we created that forum ourselves and it will be whatever we want it to be, at that forum, no doubt, we can bring up problems that are of interest to all.

I am obsessed with the problem that I consider to be fundamental for the future of humanity, the problem of energy. We have this energy supply in Mexico. We have hydrocarbons, but we know that it is a depletable resource. I would like to transmit to you the need to create an awareness in all of mankind, so that they will understand that the generation that is represented here tonight is the generation that will see the end of the era of oil and will witness the beginning of a new era or the end of them all. With this thought in mind, we have come to the United Nations, and now we have come to the United States to present our reflections to Mr. Carter, in order to be able to win the political will of the United States.

We have many times said that to be strong means great responsibilities towards humanity. I am fully convinced that if the United States expresses its political will to put order into the world of energy sources, but within a framework of responsibility that will comprise all of humanity and not through bilateral agreements, bloc agreements, or unilateral struggles, in order to become independent—I am convinced that we can survive, that we can go ahead, that we can cross a bridge that connects one era with another.

However, sometimes I reflect, and I think that what is reasonable and simple is not always what is possible. Many times, unfortunately, humanity seeks absurd solutions. Perhaps it is because what is absurd does not require great discipline. But I feel that humanity can become disciplined, and it can go from one style of energy into another lifestyle which requires another energy source. And I insist, once again, if the United States expresses its political will in this direction, this will be made possible.

The objective is a very simple one. The proposition is a very simple one. Let us prepare to go from one era into another era by putting order into a resource, into the exploration, exploitation, distribution, and consumption of the resource we have now, and let us prepare to use another one later on, because if we do not, life will no longer be possible.

Mexico is willing to do whatever it can do. Before all the nations of the world, it has expressed its political will to take on a commitment. We consider that it is indispensable to commit ourselves. We must think about our children and our children's children and the world we're going to leave behind for them to live in. Will it be an orderly, peaceful world, or will it be the world of the apocalypse? Will it be a disorderly world? I believe that it is not a difficult selection. I forgive for insisting upon this idea once and again, I beg your forgiveness.

It is with this idea in mind that we have come to the United States in order to have the satisfaction to review, within the framework of that very intelligent instrument that was established by President Carter and myself, the state of our relationship, to seek your solidarity, to solve a problem that is everyone's problem, and to recommend what I would consider to be a very simple remedy.

During my political campaign, I insistently said that the solution is to be found in all of us. I believe, in the case of energy sources and ever so many other matters that are very serious for mankind, we must constantly think that the solution is to be found in all of us.

To these values that are common to all of our democracies, the friendship of our peoples, with the hope that our communication lines will be always open between us, and to the happiness of the United States and, particularly, the Carter family, I ask you to join me in a toast.

NOTE: President Carter spoke at 8:15 p.m. in the State Dining Room at the White House. President López Portillo spoke in Spanish, and his remarks were translated by an interpreter.

Earlier in the day, President Carter and President López Portillo held a meeting in the Cabinet Room at the White House to discuss bilateral issues.

Digest of Other White House Announcements

The following listing includes the President's public schedule and other items of general interest announced by the White House Press Office and not included elsewhere in this issue.

September 23

The President and Mrs. Carter hosted a dinner for Members of Congress at the White House.

September 24

The President met at the White House with:

—Zbigniew Brzezinski, Assistant to the President for National Security Affairs;

—Frank B. Moore, Assistant to the President for Congressional Liaison;

—the Bee Gees, a musical group.

The President met in the Oval Office with Lou Brock, an outfielder for the St. Louis Cardinals professional baseball team, to congratulate him on achieving his 3,000th career hit. Other participants included Mr. Brock's family, Vice President Walter F. Mondale, and Members of Congress.

September 25

The President met at the White House with:

—Dr. Brzezinski;

—members of the Congressional Suburban Caucus;

—Mr. Moore.

The President declared a major disaster for the State of Texas as a result of severe storms and flooding, beginning on September 17, which caused extensive property damage.

The President declared a major disaster for the State of Louisiana as a result of severe storms and flooding, beginning on September 19, which caused extensive private property damage.

September 26

The President met at the White House with:

—Dr. Brzezinski;

—Vice President Mondale, Secretary of the Treasury G. William Miller, Charles L. Schultze, Chairman of the Council of Economic Advisers, James T. McIntyre, Jr., Director, and John P. White, Deputy Director, Office of Management and Budget, Stuart E. Eizenstat, Assistant to the President for Domestic Affairs and Policy, Alfred E. Kahn, Advisor to the President on Inflation and Chairman of the Council on Wage and Price Stability, John N. Gentry, Deputy Adviser on Inflation and Counselor on Labor-Management Relations, Council on Wage and Price Stability, and Landon Butler, Deputy Assistant to the President;

—a group of Democratic Representatives to discuss the department of education legislation;

—Vice President Mondale, Paul A. Volcker, Chairman of the Board of Governors, Federal Reserve System.

Secretary Miller, Mr. Schultze, Mr. McIntyre, and Mr. Kahn.

September 27

The President met at the White House with:

—Dr. Brzezinski;

—Mr. Moore;

—Gov. Edward King of Massachusetts.

The President transmitted to the Congress the annual report on the Alaska Railroad for fiscal year 1978, prepared by the Secretary of Transportation.

September 28

The President met at the White House with:

—Dr. Brzezinski;

—Vice President Mondale, Secretary of State Cyrus R. Vance, Secretary of Defense Harold Brown, Hedley W. Donovan, Senior Adviser to the President, Lloyd N. Cutler, Counsel to the President, and Dr. Brzezinski;

—Mr. Moore.

The President attended a reception for officers of the National Education Association held in the East Room at the White House.

NOMINATIONS SUBMITTED TO THE SENATE

The following list does not include promotions of members of the Uniformed Services, nominations to the Service Academies, or nominations of Foreign Service officers.

Submitted September 25, 1979

HARRY ROBERTS MELONE, of New York, a Foreign Service officer of Class two, to be Ambassador Extraordinary and Plenipotentiary of the United States of America to the Republic of Rwanda.

ECKARDT C. BECK, of New Jersey, to be Assistant Administrator of the Environmental Protection Agency, vice Thomas Cash Jorling, resigned.

NOMINATIONS—Continued

Submitted September 28, 1979

ROBERT W. KOMER, of Virginia, to be Under Secretary of Defense for Policy, vice Stanley R. Resor.

WILLIAM BROWNLEE WELSH, of Virginia, to be an Assistant Secretary of Health, Education, and Welfare, vice Richard D. Warden, resigned.

WILLIAM EDWARD HALLETT, of Colorado, to be Commissioner of Indian Affairs, vice Ben Reifel, resigned.

WARREN JOHN FERGUSON, of California, to be United States Circuit Judge for the Ninth Circuit, vice a new position created by P.L. 95–486, approved October 20, 1978.

DOROTHY WRIGHT NELSON, of California, to be United States Circuit Judge for the Ninth Circuit, vice a new position created by P.L. 95–486, approved October 20, 1978.

TERRY J. HATTER, JR., of California, to be United States District Judge for the Central District of California, vice a new position created by P.L. 95–486, approved October 20, 1978.

MILTON LEWIS SCHWARTZ, of California, to be United States District Judge for the Eastern District of California, vice a new position created by P.L. 95–486, approved October 20, 1978.

ROBERT H. HALL, of Georgia, to be United States District Judge for the Northern District of Georgia, vice a new position created by P.L. 95–486, approved October 20, 1978.

DALE EMERSON SAFFELS, of Kansas, to be United States District Judge for the District of Kansas, vice a new position created by P.L. 95–486, approved October 20, 1978.

HAROLD ARNOLD ACKERMAN, of New Jersey, to be United States District Judge for the District of New Jersey, vice George H. Barlow, deceased.

DICKINSON RICHARDS DEBEVOISE, of New Jersey, to be United States District Judge for the District of New Jersey, vice a new position created by P.L. 95–486, approved October 20, 1978.

H. LEE SAROKIN, of New Jersey, to be United States District Judge for the District of New Jersey, vice Lawrence A. Whipple, retired.

ANNE ELISE THOMPSON, of New Jersey, to be United States District Judge for the District of New Jersey, vice a new position created by P.L. 95–486, approved October 20, 1978.

NOMINATIONS—Continued

Submitted September 28—Continued

NEAL P. McCURN, of New York, to be United States District Judge for the Northern District of New York, vice a new position created by P.L. 95–486, approved October 20, 1978.

FRANK HOWELL SEAY, of Oklahoma, to be United States District Judge for the Eastern District of Oklahoma, vice Joseph W. Morris, resigned.

LEE ROY WEST, of Oklahoma, to be United States District Judge for the Western District of Oklahoma, vice a new position created by P.L. 95–486, approved October 20, 1978.

THOMAS RUTHERFORD BRETT, of Oklahoma, to be United States District Judge for the Northern District of Oklahoma, vice a new position created by P.L. 95–486, approved October 20, 1978.

JAMES OLIVER ELLISON, of Oklahoma, to be United States District Judge for the Northern District of Oklahoma, vice Allen E. Barrow, deceased.

GEORGE WASHINGTON PROCTOR, of Arkansas, to be United States Attorney for the Eastern District of Arkansas for the term of 4 years, vice Wilbur H. Dillahunty, term expired.

DENNIS P. McAULIFFE, of New Jersey, to be Administrator of the Panama Canal Commission (new position).

CHECKLIST OF WHITE HOUSE PRESS RELEASES

The following listing contains releases of the White House Press Office which are not included in this issue.

Released September 22, 1979

News conference: on their trip to Africa to promote U.S.-African trade relations—by Ambassador Andrew Young, U.S. Representative to the United Nations, J. Bruce Llewellyn, President and Chief Executive Officer, Overseas Private Investment Corporation, and John L. Moore, Jr., President and Chairman, Export-Import Bank of the United States

Transcript: interview with a group of editors—by Zbigniew Brzezinski, Assistant to the President for National Security Affairs

Released September 25, 1979

Fact sheet: reorganization of the Federal Government's international trade functions (Reorganization Plan No. 3 of 1979)

CHECKLIST—Continued

Released September 25—Continued

Advance text: remarks at the annual convention of the American Public Transit Association in New York City

Transcript: remarks on the signing of the Energy and Water Development Appropriation Act, 1980—by Press Secretary Jody Powell

Released September 26, 1979

News conference: on the Interstate Commerce Commission order concerning the Rock Island Railroad—by Vice President Walter F. Mondale, Secretary of Agriculture Bob Bergland, A. Daniel O'Neal, Chairman, Interstate Commerce Commission, and John M. Sullivan, Federal Railroad Administrator, Department of Transportation

Fact sheet: Executive Order 12160, Federal consumer programs

Transcript: remarks on Executive Order 12160, Federal consumer programs—by Esther Peterson, Special Assistant to the President for Consumer Affairs

Released September 27, 1979

Advance text: remarks to the Alumni Association of the School for International Affairs—by Dr. Brzezinski

Released September 28, 1979

Announcement: nomination of Warren John Ferguson to be United States Circuit Judge for the Ninth Circuit

Announcement: nomination of Dorothy Wright Nelson to be United States Circuit Judge for the Ninth Circuit

Announcement: nomination of Terry J. Hatter, Jr., to be United States District Judge for the Central District of California

Announcement: nomination of Milton Lewis Schwartz to be United States District Judge for the Eastern District of California

Announcement: nomination of Robert H. Hall to be United States District Judge for the Northern District of Georgia

Announcement: nomination of Dale Emerson Saffels to be United States District Judge for the District of Kansas

Announcement: nomination of Harold Arnold Ackerman to be United States District Judge for the District of New Jersey

Announcement: nomination of Dickinson Richards Debevoise to be United States District Judge for the District of New Jersey

CHECKLIST—Continued

Released September 28—Continued

Announcement: nomination of H. Lee Sarokin to be United States District Judge for the District of New Jersey

Announcement: nomination of Anne Elise Thompson to be United States District Judge for the District of New Jersey

Announcement: nomination of Neal P. McCurn to be United States District Judge for the Northern District of New York

Announcement: nomination of Frank Howell Seay to be United States District Judge for the Eastern District of Oklahoma

Announcement: nomination of Lee Roy West to be United States District Judge for the Western District of Oklahoma

Announcement: nomination of Thomas Rutherford Brett to be United States District Judge for the Northern District of Oklahoma

Announcement: nomination of James Oliver Ellison to be United States District Judge for the Northern District of Oklahoma

Announcement: nomination of George Washington Proctor to be United States Attorney for the Eastern District of Arkansas

News conference: on the national accord between the administration and the American labor leadership in connection with the anti-inflation program—by Secretary of the Treasury G. William Miller, Alfred E. Kahn, Advisor to the President on Inflation, and Lane Kirkland, secretary-treasurer, AFL–CIO

Fact sheet: the national accord between the administration and the American labor leadership in connection with the anti-inflation program

List: participants in the President's meeting with President José López Portillo of Mexico

News conference: on the President's meeting with President López Portillo—by Jerrold Schecter, Press Secretary, and Guy Erb, staff member, National Security Council

Report: Consultative Mechanism between the United States and Mexico

News conference: on the national accord between the administration and the American labor leadership in connection with the anti-inflation program—by R. Robert Russell, Director of the Council on Wage and Price Stability, and Mr. Kahn

Fact sheet: Executive Order 12162, extension of delegation of end-user gasoline allocation authority

ACTS APPROVED BY THE PRESIDENT

Approved September 24, 1979

H.R. 4392_____ Public Law 96–68
Departments of State, Justice, and Commerce, the Judiciary, and Related Agencies Appropriation Act, 1980.

Approved September 25, 1979

H.R. 4388_____ Public Law 96–69
Energy and Water Development Appropriation Act, 1980.

ACTS APPROVED—Continued

Approved September 27, 1979

H.R. 111_____ Public Law 96–70
Panama Canal Act of 1979.

Approved September 28, 1979

S.J. Res. 105_____ Public Law 96–71
A joint resolution to provide for a temporary extension of certain Federal Housing Administration authorities, and for other purposes.

PRESIDENTIAL DOCUMENTS

Week Ending Friday, October 5, 1979

Visit of President José López Portillo of Mexico

Remarks Following a Meeting.
September 29, 1979

PRESIDENT CARTER. I would like to say to the press that President López Portillo and I have had very friendly and constructive and profitable discussions this last 2 days. We have prepared a joint communique to outline the results of our discussions.

But I believe that this visit has been not only a delightful one for us but has served to convince the people of our two countries that we live in a state of harmony, of mutual purpose, and of friendship and of cooperation. And I'm deeply grateful to President López Portillo for his contribution to the outcome of this meeting.

Thank you.

PRESIDENT LÓPEZ PORTILLO. Thank you very much, Mr. Carter.

Yes, actually, I do want to say that our meetings have been very good ones. I'm very grateful to President Carter.

The meetings have taken place within the framework within which they have taken place during our other two previous times. There's a framework of friendship and deep understanding. They have served to prove that the lines of communication are alive and working. And this is the only way that it can be and the way that it should be. This is the only way in which we can guarantee our constant contact, communication, for harmonious coexistence and the only manner in which all the countries of the world can live within a system of dignity and peace.

Thank you.

NOTE: President Carter spoke at 11:27 a.m. on the South Lawn of the White House. President López Portillo spoke in Spanish, and his remarks were translated by an interpreter.

Visit of President López Portillo of Mexico

Joint Press Statement.   September 29, 1979

President Carter and President López Portillo met at the White House September 28–29 for the third in a series of reviews on the status of bilateral relations and consideration of regional and global issues of mutual interest.

At their second meeting the Presidents had agreed to a restructuring of the Consultative Mechanism and had requested their Secretaries of State and Foreign Relations to report on the matter. The first order of business at this meeting, accordingly, was to review that report. The Presidents expressed satisfaction with the intensive effort made by the working groups of the Consultative Mechanism and the substantive progress achieved in those groups. They concluded that the Mechanism has proven to be an effective vehicle for coordinating and further defining bilateral relations. They therefore instructed their Administrations to continue working through the Mechanism in the areas of mutual interest already identified.

President Carter and President López Portillo reviewed the status of bilateral consultations in the energy field and expressed their pleasure at the successful conclusion of governmental negotiations for the sale of Mexican surplus associated natural gas to the United States. They considered this agreement advantageous to both countries. Regarding another energy source, the Presidents expressed their hope that ongoing negotiations for electric energy interchanges along their common border may also be satisfactorily concluded in the near future.

Both Presidents noted that the common border offers unique opportunities for close collaboration in many areas. They expressed their interest in enhancing the environment along the border and preserving the quality of life in the region. Presidents Carter and López Portillo agreed on the need for both countries to prevent events or actions on one side of the land or maritime boundary from degrading the environment on the other

side. They also instructed their Administrations to give a high priority to such questions. They also agreed to work within the Consultative Mechanism to determine if it is possible or appropriate to conclude agreements for measures by both countries to lessen or eliminate environmental damage in the future.

The Presidents recalled that last February they had instructed the International Boundary and Water Commission to recommend measures that might be adopted within the context of existing agreements to achieve further progress towards a permanent solution to border sanitation problems. The Presidents reviewed the recommendations submitted by the Commission, and found them satisfactory as a basic agreement for solution of border sanitation problems. The Presidents asked the Commission to proceed as soon as possible to conclude the supplementary recommendations for completion of the works required to provide the good quality water which they had recognized in February to be so important for the health and well being of the citizens of both countries living and traveling in the border area.

The Presidents paid special attention to the phenomenon of the migratory flow between Mexico and the United States, including specific issues that arise therefrom on both sides of the border. They recognized that, as they had agreed last February, it is essential to know with greater precision and detail all aspects of the matter.

The President of Mexico accordingly outlined the purposes and first partial results of the national survey of emigration to the northern border and the United States, undertaken by the Department of Labor and Social Welfare. This large-scale study, which is in an advanced stage, will provide more precise information on the size and nature of emigration, including data on the number of emigrants who annually enter the United States, how many return to Mexico, their contribution to the U.S. and Mexican economies, and the degree to which they draw upon and contribute to social services in the United States. President Carter agreed on the importance of statistical consistency in approaching questions of migration and was pleased to learn of the progress of the survey.

President Carter described the steps he has taken to ensure that all Departments and Agencies of the United States Government give priority to the protection of the human rights of all persons in the United States, whether or not they are American citizens.

Both Presidents repeated their commitment to combat the smuggling of undocumented persons, which constitutes a serious threat to human rights.

Following their review of bilateral matters, President López Portillo and President Carter discussed recent developments in Central America and agreed that progress toward a democratic government in Nicaragua had improved the prospects of peace in the region and a greater respect for human rights. They committed their governments to continue supporting the Nicaraguan Government of National Reconstruction with a view toward assisting it in the task of economic and social recovery. Both Presidents exchanged points of view on the Caribbean.

President Carter congratulated President López Portillo on his proposal to the United Nations on rationalized production and consumption of energy, both in the industrialized countries and the developing countries, saying that it was a bal-

anced presentation, positive in tone. President Carter also referred to the energy plan proposed to the U.S. Congress and agreed on the need to devote increased efforts to alternative sources.

Finally, there was a review of the latest developments on the Middle East and SALT II Treaty.

Trade With Argentina

Proclamation 4694.   September 29, 1979

STAGED REDUCTION OF RATES OF DUTY ON CERTAIN PRODUCTS TO CARRY OUT A TRADE AGREEMENT WITH ARGENTINA

By the President of the United States of America

A Proclamation

1. I have determined, pursuant to section 101(a) of the Trade Act of 1974 (the Trade Act) (19 U.S.C. 2111(a)), that certain existing duties of the United States are unduly burdening and restricting the foreign trade of the United States and that one or more of the purposes of the Trade Act would be promoted by entering into the trade agreement with Argentina identified in the third recital of this proclamation.

2. Sections 131(a), 132, and 133 of the Trade Act (19 U.S.C. 2151(a), 2153, and 2154) and section 4(c) of Executive Order No. 11846 of March 27, 1975, have been complied with.

3. Pursuant to Title I of the Trade Act (19 U.S.C. 2111 *et seq.*), I have, through my duly empowered representative, on August 10, 1979, entered into a trade agreement with Argentina, effective Octo-

ber 1, 1979, pursuant to which United States rates of duty on certain products would be modified as hereinafter proclaimed and as provided for in the annexes to this proclamation, in exchange for certain measures which will benefit United States interests.

4. In order to implement the trade agreement referred to in the third recital of this proclamation it is necessary to modify the Tariff Schedules of the United States (TSUS) (19 U.S.C. 1202) as provided for in the annexes to this proclamation, attached hereto and made a part hereof.

5. Pursuant to the Trade Act, I determine that the modifications or continuance of existing duties hereinafter proclaimed are required or appropriate to carry out the trade agreement identified in the third recital of this proclamation.

Now, THEREFORE, I, JIMMY CARTER, President of the United States of America, acting under the authority vested in me by the Constitution and the statutes, including sections 101, 105, 109, and 604 of the Trade Act (19 U.S.C. 2111, 2115, 2119, and 2483), do proclaim that—

(1) Part 2B and part 5A of schedule 1 of the TSUS are modified as provided in Annexes I and II to this proclamation.

(2) Each of the modifications to the TSUS made by this proclamation shall be effective as to articles entered, or withdrawn from warehouse, for consumption on or after October 1, 1979.

IN WITNESS WHEREOF, I have hereunto set my hand this twenty-ninth day of September, in the year of our Lord, nineteen hundred and seventy-nine and of the Independence of the United States of America the two hundred and fourth.

JIMMY CARTER

[Filed with the Office of the Federal Register, 11:33 a.m., October 1, 1979]

NOTE: The annexes are printed in the FEDERAL REGISTER of October 2, 1979.

Administration of Foreign Assistance and Related Functions

Executive Order 12163.   September 29, 1979

By virtue of the authority vested in me by the Foreign Assistance Act of 1961, Reorganization Plan No. 2 of 1979, the International Development Cooperation Act of 1979, and section 301 of title 3 of the United States Code, and as President of the United States, it is hereby ordered as follows:

1–1. *United States International Development Cooperation Agency*

1–101. Establishment of the United States International Development Cooperation Agency. Sections 1, 5, 6, and 8 of Reorganization Plan No. 2 of 1979 are declared effective and the United States International Development Cooperation Agency (hereinafter referred to as "IDCA") is hereby established.

1–102. Delegation of Functions. (a) Exclusive of the functions otherwise delegated, or reserved to the President, by this order, and subject to the provisions of this order, there are hereby delegated to the Director of IDCA (hereinafter referred to as the "Director") all functions conferred upon the President by:

(1) the Foreign Assistance Act of 1961 (22 U.S.C. 2151 *et seq.*); (hereinafter referred to as the "Act");

(2) the Latin American Development Act (22 U.S.C. 1942 *et seq.*);

(3) section 402 of the Mutual Security Act of 1954 (22 U.S.C. 1922);

(4) section 413(b) of the International Security Assistance and Arms Export Control Act of 1976 (22 U.S.C. 2431); and

(5) title IV of the International Development Cooperation Act of 1979 (22

U.S.C. 3501 *et seq.*) (hereinafter referred to as the "IDC Act of 1979").

(b) The functions under sections 116 (e), 491(b), 491(c), 607, 627, 628, 630 (3), and 666 of the Act, and section 403 (e) of the IDC Act of 1979, delegated to the Director shall be exercised in consultation with the Secretary of State.

(c) The functions under section 125 (b) of the Act delegated to the Director shall be exercised in consultation with the Secretary of the Treasury and, with regard to the United Nations Development Program, in consultation with the Secretary of State.

(d) The Director shall exercise the functions of the President under sections 301(a), 301(e)(1), 301(e)(3), and 305 of the Act only insofar as they pertain to the United Nations Development Program, UNICEF, the Organization of American States Technical Assistance Funds, the United Nations Capital Development Fund, the United Nations Educational and Training Program for Southern Africa, the United Nations/Food and Agriculture Organization World Food Program, the Food and Agriculture Organization Post-Harvest Losses Fund, the United Nations Disaster Relief Organization, and any other international programs whose purpose is primarily developmental.

(e) In carrying out the functions under section 653 of the Act that are delegated to the Director, the Director shall consult with the Director of the Office of Management and Budget.

(f) To the extent practicable, the Director will exercise functions relating to Foreign Service personnel in a manner that will assure maximum compatibility among agencies authorized by law to utilize the Foreign Service personnel system. To this end he shall consult regularly with the Secretary of State.

(g) In exercising functions under the Act arising from later-enacted amendments to any law specified in subsection (a) of this section that relate directly to matters of foreign policy, the Director shall consult with the Secretary of State to determine whether such function should more appropriately be exercised by the Secretary or reserved to the President.

1–103. Agency for International Development.

(a) The Director shall continue within IDCA the Agency for International Development, heretofore established in the Department of State.

(b) The Agency for International Development shall be headed by an Administrator appointed pursuant to section 624(a) of the Act.

(c) The officers provided for in section 624(a) of the Act shall serve in the Agency for International Development.

1–104. Office of Small Business. The Office of Small Business provided for in section 602(b) of the Act shall be in the Agency for International Development.

1–2. *Department of State*

1–201. Delegation of Functions. (a) Subject to the provisions of this order, there are hereby delegated to the Secretary of State (hereafter in this Part referred to as the "Secretary") all functions conferred upon the President by:

(1) sections 239(g), 301(a), 301(b), 301(c), 301(e)(1), 301(e)(3), 302 (a)(1) as it relates to the Presidential certification concerning the United Nations Relief and Works Agency, 302 (a)(3), 305, 481, and 502B of the Act;

(2) section 495F of the Act, insofar as they relate to policy decisions pertaining to refugee programs under such section;

(3) sections 504(a), 505(a) relating to other provisions required by the Presi-

dent, and 505 (d), (e), and (g) of the Act;

(4) sections 505(a) (1) and (4) of the Act relating to consent;

(5) section 505(b) of the Act to the extent that it pertains to countries that agree to the conditions set forth therein;

(6) chapter 4 of Part II of the Act, insofar as they relate to policy decisions and justifications for economic support programs under such chapter, including determinations of whether there will be an economic support program for a country and the amount of the program for each country. Such functions shall be exercised in cooperation with the Director.

(7) section 533(b) of the Act;

(8) chapter 6 of part II of the Act;

(9) section 601(b) (3), (4), and (6) of the Act;

(10) section 614(b) of the Act, except that the function of determining which provisions of law should be disregarded to achieve the purpose of the provision is reserved to the President;

(11) section 620 (b), (c), (e), (f), (g), (i), (j), (q), and (s) of the Act;

(12) section 620C(d) of the Act;

(13) section 625(d) of the Act, insofar as it relates to personnel in the Department of State;

(14) section 625(k) (1) of the Act;

(15) section 634B of the Act, insofar as it relates to functions delegated to the Secretary under this order;

(16) sections 617 and 653 of the Act, insofar as they relate to chapter 8 of part I and part II of the Act (other than chapter 4 thereof);

(17) sections 657 and 668 of the Act;

(18) other provisions of the Act that relate directly and necessarily to the conduct of programs and activities vested in or delegated to the Secretary;

(19) the Mutual Defense Assistance Control Act of 1951 (22 U.S.C. 1611 *et seq.*);

(20) section 8(d) of the Act of January 12, 1971 (22 U.S.C. 2321b(d)); and

(21) section 607 of the International Security Assistance and Arms Export Control Act of 1976 (22 U.S.C. 2394a).

(b) The functions under sections 239 (g), 620(e), 620(g), 620(i), 620(j), 620(q), 620(s), and 625(k)(1) of the Act delegated to the Secretary shall be exercised in consultation with the Director.

(c) The functions under section 653 of the Act delegated to the Secretary shall be exercised in consultation with the Secretary of Defense, insofar as they relate to functions under the Act administered by the Department of Defense, and the Director of the Office of Management and Budget.

(d) The Secretary may redelegate to the Director or to any other officer or agency of the Executive branch functions delegated to the Secretary by this order.

1–3. *Department of Defense*

1–301. Delegation of Functions. Subject to the provisions of this order, there are hereby delegated to the Secretary of Defense:

(a) The functions conferred upon the President by Part II (except chapters 4 and 6 thereof) of the Act not otherwise delegated or reserved to the President.

(b) To the extent that they relate to other functions under the Act administered by the Department of Defense, the functions conferred upon the President by sections 602(a), 605(a), 625(a), 625(d) (1), 625(h), 627, 628, 630(3), 631(a), 634B, 635(b) (except with respect to negotiation, conclusion, and termination of international agreements), 635(d), and 635(g) of the Act.

(c) Those functions under section 634A of the Act, to the extent they relate to notifications to the Congress concerning changes in programs under part II of the Act (except chapters 4 and 6 thereof), subject to prior consultation with the Secretary of State.

(d) The functions under sections 627, 628, and 630(3) of the Act delegated to the Secretary of Defense shall be exercised in consultation with the Secretary of State.

1–302. Reports and Information. In carrying out the functions under section 514 of the Act delegated to him by section 301 of this order, the Secretary of Defense shall consult with the Secretary of State.

1–4. *Institute for Scientific and Technological Cooperation*

1–401. Establishment of Institute for Scientific and Technological Cooperation. There is established within IDCA the Institute for Scientific and Technological Cooperation (hereinafter referred to as the Institute).

1–402. Establishment of the Council on International Scientific and Technological Cooperation. There is established the Council on International Scientific and Technological Cooperation pursuant to section 407(a) of the IDC Act of 1979.

1–403. There are hereby established two additional positions in the Institute pursuant to section 406(c) of the IDC Act of 1979. The officers appointed to these positions shall perform such duties and exercise such powers as the Director of the Institute may prescribe.

1–5. *Other Agencies*

1–501. Department of the Treasury. (a) There are delegated to the Secretary of the Treasury the functions conferred upon the President by:

(1) section 301(e)(3) of the Act as it relates to organizations referred to in section 301(e)(2) of the Act;

(2) section 305, insofar as it relates to the International Bank for Reconstruction and Development, the International Development Association, the International Finance Corporation, the Inter-American Development Bank, the Asian Development Bank, the African Development Fund, and the International Monetary Fund;

(3) the second sentence of section 612 (a) of the Act; and

(4) section 502 of the Mutual Security Act of 1954 (22 U.S.C. 1754).

(b) The Secretary of the Treasury shall continue to administer any open special foreign country accounts established pursuant to former section 514 of the Act as enacted by section 201(f) of Public Law 92–226 (86 Stat. 25) and repealed by Section 12(b)(5) of Public Law 93–189 (87 Stat. 722).

(c) The functions under section 305 of the Act delegated to the Secretary of the Treasury shall be exercised in consultation with the Director, as provided in Executive Order No. 11269 of February 14, 1966, as amended.

1–502. Department of Commerce. There is hereby delegated to the Secretary of Commerce so much of the functions conferred upon the President by section 601(b)(1) of the Act as consists of drawing the attention of private enterprise to opportunities for investment and development in less developed friendly countries and areas.

1-503. Office of Personnel Management. There is hereby delegated to the Director of the Office of Personnel Management the function of prescribing regulations conferred upon the President by the proviso contained in section 625(b) of the Act.

1-504. International Communication Agency. The International Communication Agency shall perform all public information functions abroad with respect to the foreign assistance, aid, and development programs of the United States Government.

1-505. Development Loan Committee. There is hereby established a Development Loan Committee in accordance with section 122(e) of the Act which shall consist of the Director of IDCA, who shall be Chair, the Administrator of the Agency for International Development, the Chairman of the Board of Directors of the the Export-Import Bank of the United States, the Assistant Secretary of State for Economic Affairs, the Assistant Secretary of the Treasury dealing with international finance, the Assistant Secretary of Commerce for Industry and Trade, and the officer of the Agency for International Development dealing with development financing.

1-506. Development Coordination Committee. (a) In accordance with section 640B of the Act, there is hereby established a Development Coordination Committee (hereinafter referred to as the Committee). The Committee shall consist of the Director of IDCA, who shall be Chair; the Administrator of the Agency for International Development, the Director of the Institute for Scientific and Technological Cooperation; the Under Secretary of State for Economic Af-

fairs; the Under Secretary of the Treasury for Monetary Affairs; the Under Secretary of Commerce; the Under Secretary of Agriculture; the Under Secretary of Labor; the Under Secretary of Energy; a Deputy Special Representative for Trade Negotiations; an Associate Director of the Office of Management and Budget; a representative of the Assistant to the President for National Security Affairs; the President of the Export-Import Bank of the United States; and the President of the Overseas Private Investment Corporation.

(b) Whenever matters within the jurisdiction of the Committee may be of interest to Federal agencies not represented on the Committee under subsection (a) of this section, the Chair of the Committee may consult with such agencies and may invite them to designate representatives to participate in meetings and deliberations of the Committee.

(c) The Chair of the Committee may establish subcommittees of the Committee and designate the chairs thereof.

(d) Subject to the foreign policy guidance of the Secretary of State, the Committee shall advise the President with respect to coordination of United States policy and programs affecting the development of developing countries, including programs of bilateral and multilateral development assistance.

(e) All agencies and officers of the Government shall keep the Committee informed in necessary detail as to the policies, programs and activities referred to in subsection (d) of this section.

(f) Nothing herein shall be deemed to derogate from the responsibilities of the Secretary of State or the Secretary of the Treasury, or from responsibilities vested elsewhere by law or other Executive orders.

1–6. *Additional Delegations and Limitations of Authority; Consultation*

1–601. General Delegation of Functions. There are hereby delegated to the heads of agencies having responsibilities for carrying out the provisions of the Act all functions conferred upon the President by:

(a) section 654 (except as reserved to the President) ; and

(b) those provisions of acts appropriating funds under the authority of the Act that relate to the Act, or other acts authorizing such funds, insofar as they relate to the functions delegated by this order.

1–602. Personnel. (a) In carrying out the functions conferred upon the President by the provisions of section 625(d) (1) of the Act, and by this order delegated to the Director of IDCA, the Director shall authorize such of the agencies that administer programs under the Act as he may deem appropriate to perform any of the functions under section 625 (d)(1) of the Act to the extent that the said functions relate to the programs administered by the respective agencies.

(b) Persons appointed, employed, or assigned after May 19, 1959, under section 527(c) of the Mutual Security Act of 1954 or section 625(d) of the Act for the purpose of performing functions under such Acts outside the United States shall not, unless otherwise agreed by the agency in which such benefits may be exercised, be entitled to the benefits provided by section 528 of the Foreign Service Act of 1946 in cases in which their service under the appointment, employ-

ment, or assignment exceeds thirty months.

1–603. Special Missions and Staffs Abroad. The maintenance of special missions or staffs abroad, the fixing of the ranks of the chiefs thereof after the chiefs of the United States diplomatic missions, and the authorization of the same compensation and allowances as the chief of mission, class 3 and class 4, within the meaning of the Foreign Service Act of 1946 (22 U.S.C. 801 *et seq.*), all under section 631 of the Act, shall be subject to the approval of the Secretary of State.

1–604. International Agreements. The negotiation, conclusion, and termination of international agreements pursuant to the Act, title IV of the IDC Act of 1979, or section 402 of the Mutual Security Act of 1954 shall be subject to the requirements of 1 U.S.C. 112b and to applicable regulations and procedures.

1–605. Interagency Consultation. Each officer to whom functions are delegated by this order, shall, in carrying out such functions, consult with the heads of other departments and agencies, including the Director of the Office of Management and Budget, on matters pertaining to the responsibilities of departments and agencies other than his or her own.

1–7. *Reserved Functions*

1–701. Reservation of Functions to the President. There are hereby excluded from the functions delegated by the foregoing provisions of this order:

(a) The functions conferred upon the President by sections 122(e), 298(a), 451, 504(b), 613(a), 614(a), 620(a), 620(d), 620(x), 620A, 620C(c), 621(a), 622(b), 622(c), 633(a), 633(b), 640B, 662(a), and 663(b) of the Act.

(b) The functions conferred upon the President by sections 402, 405(a), 406 and 407 of the IDC Act of 1979.

(c) The functions conferred upon the President by the Act and section 408(b) of the Mutual Security Act of 1954 with respect to the appointment of officers required to be appointed by and with the advice and consent of the Senate and with respect to the appointment of officers pursuant to sections 233(b) and 624(c) of the Act.

(d) The functions conferred upon the President with respect to determinations, certifications, directives, or transfers of funds, as the case may be, by sections 303, 481(a), 505(d)(2)(A), 505(d)(3), 506(a), 515(f), 604(a), 610, 614(c), 632(b), 633A, 659, 663(a), 669(b)(1) and 670(b)(1) of the Act.

(e) The following-described functions conferred upon the President:

(1) Those under section 503(a) that relate to findings: *Provided,* that the Secretary of State, in the implementation of the functions delegated to him under section 505(a)(1), (a)(4), and (e) of the Act, is authorized to find, in the case of a proposed transfer of a defense article or related training or a related defense service by a foreign country or international organization to a foreign country or international organization not otherwise eligible under section 503(a) of the Act, whether the proposed transfer will strengthen the security of the United States and promote world peace.

(2) Those under section 505(b) in respect of countries that do not agree to the conditions set forth therein.

(3) That under section 614(b) with respect to determining any provisions of law to be disregarded to achieve the purpose of that section.

(4) That under the second sentence of section 654(c) with respect to the publication in the FEDERAL REGISTER of any findings or determination reserved to the President: *Provided,* that any officer to whom there is delegated the function of making any finding or determination within the purview of section 654(a) is also authorized to reach the conclusion specified in performance of the function delegated to him.

(f) Those with respect to determinations under sections 103(b) (first proviso), 104, and 203 of the Mutual Defense Assistance Control Act of 1951 (22 U.S.C. 1611b(b), 1611c, and 1612b).

(g) That under section 523(d) of the Mutual Security Act of 1954 (22 U.S.C. 1783(d)).

(h) Those under section 607 of the Foreign Assistance and Related Programs Appropriations Act, 1979 (92 Stat. 1591, 1601), with respect to findings.

1–702. Subsequent Amendments. Functions conferred upon the President by subsequent amendments to the Act are delegated to the Director only insofar as they do not relate directly and necessarily to the conduct of programs and activities that either the President or an agency other than IDCA is authorized to administer pursuant to express reservation or delegation of authorities in a statute or in this or another Executive order.

1–8. *Funds*

1–801. Allocation of Funds. Funds appropriated or otherwise made available to the President for carrying out the Act shall be deemed to be allocated without any further action of the President, as follows:

(a) There are allocated to the Director (1) all funds made available for carrying out the Act except those made available for carrying out Part II of the Act (other than chapter 4 thereof), section 481 of the Act, and section 637(b) of the Act, and (2) all funds made available for carrying out title IV of the IDC Act of 1979.

(b) There are allocated to the Secretary of Defense funds made available for carrying out Part II of the Act (except chapters 4 and 6 thereof).

(c) There are allocated to the Secretary of State funds made available for carrying out sections 481 and 637(b) and chapter 6 of Part II of the Act.

1–802. Reallocation of Funds. The Director of IDCA, the Secretary of Defense, and the Secretary of State may allocate or transfer as appropriate any funds received under subsections (a), (b), and (c), respectively of section 1–801 of this order, to any agency or part thereof for obligation or expenditure thereby consistent with applicable law.

1–9. *General Provisions*

1–901. Definition. As used in this order, the word "function" includes any duty, obligation, power, authority, responsibility, right, privilege, discretion, or activity.

1–902. References to Orders and Acts. Except as may for any reason be inappropriate:

(a) References in this order or in any other Executive order to (1) the Foreign Assistance Act of 1961 (including references herein to "the Act"), (2) unrepealed provisions of the Mutual Security Act of 1954, or (3) any other act that relates to the subject of this order shall be deemed to include references to any subsequent amendments thereto.

(b) References in any prior Executive order to the Mutual Security Act of 1954 or any provisions thereof shall be deemed

to be references to the Act or the corresponding provision, if any, thereof.

(c) References in this order to provisions of any appropriation Act, and references in any other Executive order to provisions of any appropriation Act related to the subject of this order shall be deemed to include references to any hereafter-enacted provisions of law that are the same or substantially the same as such appropriation Act provisions, respectively.

(d) References in this order or in any other Executive order to this order or to any provision thereof shall be deemed to include references thereto, respectively, as amended from time to time.

(e) References in any prior Executive order not superseded by this order to any provisions of any Executive order so superseded shall hereafter be deemed to be references to the corresponding provisions, if any, of this order.

1–903. Prior Executive Orders. (a) The following are revoked:

(1) Executive Order No. 10973 of November 3, 1961, as amended;

(2) section 2(a) of Executive Order No. 11579 of January 19, 1971; and

(3) Executive Order No. 10893 of November 8, 1960.

(b) The following are amended:

(1) section 3(a) of Executive Order No. 11846 of March 27, 1975, as amended, by adding the following new paragraph (12) after paragraph (11):

"(12) The Director of the United States International Development Cooperation Agency";

(2) section 1–202 of Executive Order 12065 of June 28, 1978, by striking out "The Administrator, Agency for International Development" and inserting in lieu thereof "The Director of the United

States International Development Cooperation Agency";

(3) section 2(a) of Executive Order No. 11958 of January 18, 1977, by striking out "the Administrator of the Agency for International Development" and inserting in lieu thereof "the Director of the United States International Development Cooperation Agency";

(4) section 3 of Executive Order 10900 of January 5, 1961, by adding thereto the following new subsection:

"(d) The Secretary of State may redelegate to the Director of the United States International Development Cooperation Agency, or to any other officer or agency of the Executive branch, functions delegated to such Secretary by this order.";

(5) section 4 of Executive Order 11223 of May 12, 1965, by inserting immediately following "the Secretary of State" the words "or the Director of the United States International Development Cooperation Agency (with respect to functions vested in or delegated to the Director)"; and

(6) the President's memorandum of October 18, 1961, entitled "Determination Under Section 604(a) of the Foreign Assistance Act of 1961" (26 FR 10543) is amended by inserting after "the Secretary of State" each time it appears in such memorandum the words "or the Director of the United States International Development Cooperation Agency (with respect to non-military programs administered by such Agency)".

(c) Any reference in any other Executive order to the Agency for International Development or the Administrator thereof shall be deemed to refer also to the International Development Coop-

eration Agency or the Director thereof, respectively.

(d) As authorized by section 403(c) of the IDC Act of 1979, the reference in Executive Order No. 11223 of May 12, 1965 to "the performance of functions authorized by this Act" shall be deemed to include the performance of functions authorized by section 403 of the IDC Act of 1979.

1–904. Saving Provisions. Except to the extent inconsistent with this order, all delegations of authority, determinations, authorizations, regulations, rulings, certificates, orders, directives, contracts, agreements, and other actions made, issued, or entered into with respect to any function affected by this order and not revoked, superseded, or otherwise made inapplicable before the date of this order, shall continue in full force and effect until amended, modified, or terminated by appropriate authority.

1–905. Effective Date. The provisions of this order shall become effective as of October 1, 1979.

JIMMY CARTER

The White House,
    September 29, 1979.

[Filed with the Office of the Federal Register, 11:34 a.m., October 1, 1979]

Multilateral Development Institutions

Executive Order 12164.   September 29, 1979

By the authority vested in me as President of the United States of America by the Bretton Woods Agreements Act, the International Finance Corporation Act, the Inter-American Development Bank

Act, the International Development Association Act, the Asian Development Bank Act, Public Law 95–118, Reorganization Plan No. 2 of 1979, and Section 301 of Title 3 of the United States Code, it is hereby ordered as follows:

1–101. Executive Order No. 11269, as amended, is further amended in Section 1(b) by adding "the Director of the International Development Cooperation Agency," after "the Chairman of the Board of Governors of the Federal Reserve System,".

1–102. Executive Order No. 11269, as amended, is further amended as follows:

(a) In Section 3(a)(1) insert ", subject to the provisions of Section 7 of this Order," after "Authority".

(b) Add at the end of Section 3(a)(2) the following new sentence: "Such authority, insofar as it relates to the development aspects of the policies, programs, or projects of the International Bank for Reconstruction and Development shall be exercised subject to the provisions of Section 7 of this Order.".

(c) In Section 3(e), add ", subject to the provisions of Section 7 of this Order" before the period.

1–103. Executive Order No. 11269, as amended, is further amended in Section 4(a)(2) by adding: ", the Director of the International Development Cooperation Agency," after "the Council" each time it appears.

1–104. Executive Order No. 11269, as amended, is further amended by adding the following new Section 7:

"Section 7. Functions of the Director of the International Development Cooperation Agency. As the principal international development advisor to the President, the Director of the International Development Cooperation Agency shall advise both the Secretary of the Treasury and the appropriate United States representatives to the International Bank for Reconstruction and Development, the International Development Association, the International Finance Corporation, the Inter-American Development Bank, the Asian Development Bank, and the African Development Fund on the development aspects of matters relating to those institutions and their activities.".

1–105. This Order shall be effective as of October 1, 1979.

JIMMY CARTER

The White House,
    September 29, 1979.

[Filed with the Office of the Federal Register,
    11:35 a.m., October 1, 1979]

Budget Rescission and Deferrals

Message to the Congress.   October 1, 1979

To the Congress of the United States:

In accordance with the Impoundment Control Act of 1974, I herewith propose rescission of $113,673 in unneeded funds appropriated to the International Communication Agency, and report 31 deferrals of fiscal year 1980 funds totalling $1,003.2 million. The deferrals are primarily routine in nature and do not, in most cases, affect program levels.

The details of the rescission proposal and each deferral are contained in the attached reports.

JIMMY CARTER

The White House,
    October 1, 1979.

NOTE: The attachments detailing the rescission and deferrals are printed in the FEDERAL REGISTER of October 5, 1979.

Peace and National Security

*Address to the Nation on Soviet Combat
Troops in Cuba and the Strategic Arms
Limitation Treaty.   October 1, 1979*

Good evening.

I want to talk with you about the subject that is my highest concern, as it has been for every President. That subject is peace and the security of the United States.

We are at peace tonight, as we have been at peace throughout the time of my service in this office. The peace we enjoy is the peace of the strong. Our national defenses are unsurpassed in the world. Those defenses are stronger tonight than they were 2 years ago, and they will be stronger 2 years from now than they are tonight, because of carefully planned improvements that are going forward with your support and with the support of the Congress.

Our program for modernizing and strengthening the military forces of the NATO Alliance is on track, with the full cooperation and participation of our European Allies. Our strategic nuclear forces are powerful enough to destroy any potential adversary many times over, and the invulnerability of those forces will soon be further assured by a new system of powerful mobile missiles. These systems are designed for stability and defense.

Beyond these military defenses, we are on the threshold of a great advance in the control of nuclear weapons—the adoption of the second strategic arms limitation treaty, SALT II.

This evening, I also want to report to you about the highly publicized Soviet brigade in Cuba and about its bearing on the important relationship between our Nation and the Soviet Union.

This is not a simple or easy subject. The United States and the Soviet Union are the two most powerful nations on Earth, and the relationship between us is complex, because it involves strong elements of both competition and cooperation.

Our fundamental philosophies conflict; quite often, our national interests conflict as well. As two great nations, we do have common interests, and we share an overwhelming mutual concern in preventing a nuclear war. We must recognize therefore that nuclear arms control agreements are vital to both our countries and that we must also exercise self-restraint in our relations and be sensitive to each other's concerns.

Recently, we obtained evidence that a Soviet combat brigade has been in Cuba for several years. The presence of Soviet combat troops in Cuba is of serious concern to us.

I want to reassure you at the outset that we do not face any immediate, concrete threat that could escalate into war or a major confrontation—but we do face a challenge. It is a challenge to our wisdom, a challenge to our ability to act in a firm, decisive way without destroying the basis for cooperation that helps to maintain world peace and control nuclear weapons. It's a challenge to our determination to give a measured and effective response to Soviet competition and to Cuban military activities around the world.

Now let me explain the specific problem of the Soviet brigade and describe the more general problem of Soviet-Cuban military activism in the Third World.

Here is the background on Soviet forces in Cuba: As most of you know, 17 years ago in the era of the cold war, the Soviet Union suddenly attempted to introduce offensive nuclear missiles and bombers into Cuba. This direct threat to the United States ended with the Soviet agreement to withdraw those nuclear weapons and a commitment not to introduce offensive weapons into Cuba thereafter.

At the time of that 1962 missile crisis, there were more than 20,000 Soviet military personnel in Cuba. Most of them were withdrawn, and we monitored their departure. It was believed that those who stayed behind were not combat forces, but were there to advise and train Cubans and to perform intelligence functions.

Just recently, American intelligence obtained persuasive evidence that some of these Soviet forces had been organized into a combat unit. When attention was then focused on a careful review of past intelligence data, it was possible for our experts to conclude that this unit had existed for several years, probably since the mid-1970's, and possibly even longer.

This unit appears to be a brigade of two or three thousand men. It is armed with about 40 tanks and other modern military equipment. It's been organized as a combat unit. Its training exercises have been those of a combat unit.

This is not a large force, nor an assault force. It presents no direct threat to us. It has no airborne or seaborne capability. In contrast to the 1962 crisis, no nuclear threat to the United States is involved.

Nevertheless, this Soviet brigade in Cuba is a serious matter. It contributes to tension in the Caribbean and the Central American region. The delivery of modern arms to Cuba and the presence of Soviet naval forces in Cuban waters have strengthened the Soviet-Cuban military relationship. They've added to the fears of some countries that they may come under Soviet or Cuban pressure.

During the last few years, the Soviets have been increasing the delivery of military supplies to Cuba. The result is that Cuba now has one of the largest, best equipped armed forces in this region. These military forces are used to intrude into other countries in Africa and the Middle East.

There's a special relationship between Cuba and the Soviet Union. The Cubans get their weapons free; other Soviet satellite countries have to pay for their military supplies. The Communist regime in Cuba is an economic failure that cannot sustain itself. The Soviet Union must send to Cuba about $8 million in economic aid every day.

Fidel Castro does not pay money for Soviet arms; the Cuban people pay a much higher price. In every international dispute, on every international issue, the Cuban regime automatically follows the Soviet line. The Soviet brigade is a manifestation of Moscow's dominance of Cuba. It raises the level of that dominance, and it raises the level of responsibility that the Soviet Union must take for escalating Cuban military actions abroad.

Now I want to report further on what we are doing to resolve these problems and to counter these activities.

Over the past 3 weeks, we've discussed this issue at great length with top Soviet officials. We've made it clear that the presence of a Soviet combat unit in Cuba is a matter of serious concern to us.

The Soviet Union does not admit that the unit in question is a combat unit. However, the Soviets have made certain statements to us with respect to our concern: that the unit in question is a training center, that it does nothing more than training and can do nothing more; that they will not change its function or status as a training center. We understand this to mean that they do not intend to enlarge the unit or to give it additional capabilities.

They have said that the Soviet personnel in Cuba are not and will not be a threat to the United States or to any other nation; that they reaffirm the 1962 understanding and the mutually agreed upon confirmation in 1970 and will abide by it in the future. We, for our part, reconfirm this understanding.

These assurances have been given to me from the highest level of the Soviet Government.

Although we have persuasive evidence that the unit has been a combat brigade, the Soviet statements about the future noncombat status of the unit are significant. However, we shall not rest on these Soviet statements alone.

First, we will monitor the status of the Soviet forces by increased surveillance of Cuba.

Second, we will assure that no Soviet unit in Cuba can be used as a combat force to threaten the security of the United States or any other nation in this hemisphere. Those nations can be confident that the United States will act in response to a request for assistance to meet any such threat from Soviet or Cuban forces.

This policy is consistent with our responsibilities as a member of the Organization of American States and a party to the Rio Treaty. It's a reaffirmation in new circumstances of John F. Kennedy's declaration in 1963 "that we would not permit any troops from Cuba to move off the island of Cuba in an offensive action against any neighboring countries."

Third, I'm establishing a permanent, full-time Caribbean joint task force headquarters at Key West, Florida. I will assign to this headquarters forces from all the military services responsible for expanded planning and for conducting exercises. This headquarters unit will employ designated forces for action if required. This will substantially improve our capability to monitor and to respond rapidly to any attempted military encroachment in this region.

Fourth, we will expand military maneuvers in the region. We will conduct these exercises regularly from now on. In accordance with existing treaty rights, the United States will, of course, keep our forces in Guantanamo.

Fifth, we will increase our economic assistance to alleviate the unmet economic and human needs in the Caribbean region and further to ensure the ability of troubled peoples to resist social turmoil and possible Communist domination.

The United States has a worldwide interest in peace and stability. Accordingly, I have directed the Secretary of Defense to further enhance the capacity of our rapid deployment forces to protect our own interests and to act in response to requests for help from our allies and friends. We must be able to move our ground, sea, and air units to distant areas, rapidly and with adequate supplies.

We have reinforced our naval presence in the Indian Ocean.

We are enhancing our intelligence capability in order to monitor Soviet and Cuban military activities—both in Cuba and throughout the world. We will increase our efforts to guard against damage to our crucial intelligence sources and our methods of collection, without impairing civil and constitutional rights.

These steps reflect my determination to preserve peace, to strengthen our alliances, and to defend the interests of the United States. In developing them, I've consulted not only with my own advisers but with congressional leaders and with a bipartisan group of distinguished American citizens as well. The decisions are my own, and I take full responsibility for them as President and as Commander in Chief.

I have concluded that the brigade issue is certainly no reason for a return to the cold war. A confrontation might be emotionally satisfying for a few days or weeks for some people, but it would be destructive to the national interest and to the security of the United States.

We must continue the basic policy that the United States has followed for 20 years, under six administrations of both parties, a policy that recognizes that we are in competition with the Soviet Union in some fields and that we seek cooperation in others—notably maintaining the peace and controlling nuclear arms.

My fellow Americans, the greatest danger to American security tonight is certainly not the two or three thousand Soviet troops in Cuba. The greatest danger to all the nations of the world—including the United States and the Soviet Union—is the breakdown of a common effort to preserve the peace and the ultimate threat of a nuclear war.

I renew my call to the Senate of the United States to ratify the SALT II treaty.

SALT II is a solid treaty. Ensuring compliance with its terms will not be a matter of trust. We have highly sophisticated, national technical means carefully focused on the Soviet Union to ensure that the treaty is verifiable.

This treaty is the most important step ever taken to control strategic nuclear arms. It permits us to strengthen our defense and to preserve the strategic balance at lower risk and lower cost. During the past few years, we have made real increases in our defense expenditures to fulfill the goals of our 5-year defense plan. With SALT II, we can concentrate these increases in areas where our interests are most threatened and where direct military challenge is most likely.

The rejection of SALT would seriously compromise our Nation's peace and security.

Of course we have disagreements with the Soviets. Of course we have conflicts with them. If we did not have these disagreements and conflicts, we would not need a treaty to reduce the possibility of nuclear war between us.

If SALT II is rejected, these disagreements and conflicts could take on a new and ominous dimension. Against the background of an uncontrolled nuclear arms race, every confrontation or dispute would carry the seeds of a nuclear confrontation.

In addition, SALT II is crucial to American leadership and to the further strengthening of the Western Alliance. Obviously, a secure Europe is vital to our own security. The leaders of our European Allies support SALT II—unanimously. We've talked to a number of those leaders in the last few days. I must tell you tonight that if the Senate fails to approve the SALT treaty, these leaders and their countries would be confused and deeply alarmed. If our allies should lose confidence in our ability to negotiate successfully for the control of nuclear weapons, then our effort to build a stronger and more united NATO could fail.

I know that for Members of Congress this is a troubling and a difficult issue, in a troubling and difficult time. But the Senate has a tradition of being the greatest deliberative body in the world, and the whole world is watching the Senate today. I'm confident that all Senators will perform their high responsibilities as the national interest requires.

Politics and nuclear arsenals do not mix. We must not play politics with the security of the United States. We must not play politics with the survival of the human race. We must not play politics with SALT II. It is much too important for that—too vital to our country, to our allies, and to the cause of peace.

The purpose of the SALT II treaty and the purpose of my actions in dealing with Soviet and Cuban military relationship are exactly the same—to keep our Nation secure and to maintain a world at peace.

As a powerful nation, as a super power, we have special responsibilities to maintain stability even when there are serious disagreements among nations. We've had fundamental differences with the Soviet Union since 1917. I have no illusions about these differences. The best way to deal with them successfully is to maintain American unity, American will, and American strength. That is what I am determined to do.

The struggle for peace—the long, hard struggle to make weapons of mass destruction under control of human reason and human law—is a central drama of our age.

At another time of challenge in our Nation's history, President Abraham Lincoln told the American people: "We shall nobly save, or meanly lose, the last best hope of earth."

We acted wisely then and preserved the Nation. Let us act wisely now and preserve the world.

NOTE: The President spoke at 9 p.m. from the Oval Office at the White House. His remarks were broadcast live on radio and television.

Meeting With President William R. Tolbert, Jr., of Liberia

White House Statement.   October 2, 1979

President Carter met this morning for an hour in the Cabinet Room with President William R. Tolbert, Jr., of Liberia. They had a warm and comprehensive exchange of views on bilateral and regional issues.

President Carter expressed the importance of the United States special relationship with Liberia and our desire to enhance and promote it. The two Presidents agreed to consider the visit of a group of distinguished Americans to Liberia in the near future. The group will work towards strengthening U.S. ties with Liberia and focus on economic and development cooperation in the public and private sectors.

The two Presidents had an extensive discussion of President Tolbert's role as Chairman of the Organization of African

Unity (OAU) and the OAU meeting last July. President Carter complimented President Tolbert on his leadership as head of the OAU and praised President Tolbert's efforts to resolve outstanding problems in the region.

Those attending the meeting were:

U.S. Side

The President

Deputy Secretary of State Warren Christopher

David Aaron, Deputy Assistant to the President for National Security Affairs

Richard Moose, Assistant Secretary of State for African Affairs

Ambassador Robert Smith, U.S. Ambassador to Liberia

Parker Borg, Director of West African Affairs, Department of State

Jerry Funk, National Security Council staff member

Liberian Side

President William R. Tolbert, Jr.

Foreign Minister Cecil Dennis

Ambassador Francis Dennis, Liberian Ambassador to the United States

J. Bernard Blamo, Minister of Education

D. Franklin Neal, Minister of Planning and Economic Affairs

William Bull, Counselor, Embassy of Liberia

ing profession. You bear a great responsibility in a free society. Our people depend on you to bring them the facts on issues and problems that affect their lives and the future of our nation. Their opinions are often based as much on your interpretation of events, what you point out as important and relevant, as on the events themselves. The pressure of deadlines is compounded by your desire to get all the facts. I am sure the satisfaction you derive from doing a good job and meeting those constant challenges is in proportion to the obstacles.

The variety of your concerns, the breadth of your knowledge, the quality of understanding that you bring to the task of finding out what is happening is important to our nation. Just as we in government have a sworn duty to serve the people, you have a professional duty to uphold their right to know. Our Founding Fathers considered that duty as basic to our freedom as the structure of government. We share a duty to serve and be accountable to the people, just as we share a need to retain our humility and compassion in the face of heavy responsibility and great power.

I commend you for your commitment to a proud tradition which has served our nation with honor and distinction. Each of you has my best wishes for continuing success.

JIMMY CARTER

National Newspaper Week, October 7–13, 1979

Message of the President.   October 2, 1979

On the occasion of National Newspaper Week, I am pleased to greet the men and women who gather and report the news.

Yours is indeed a noble and challeng-

Special Representative for Trade Negotiations

Remarks at the Swearing In of Reubin O'D. Askew.   October 2, 1979

THE PRESIDENT. Well, after 3 years of effort, I have finally gotten Reubin Askew to join my Cabinet. Immediately after the election, almost 3 years ago, Governor Askew was one of the first people I called, to ask if he would join my Cabinet in almost any capacity. He said he had an obligation to the people of Florida, and he would finish out his term of office. But I've called on him many times in the meantime to help me with difficult assignments, and he's always responded enthusiastically and well.

There are great men and women who have served as Governors and who still serve in those capacities, but I think it's generally accepted among those who have known Reubin Askew that he is one of the leaders among those leaders. He was the chairman of the National Governors' Conference, as it was known then, and set a standard of achievement and leadership and inspiration which was an example to us all, a degree of quietness, modesty, personal integrity that provided a basis for others to trust him and to give him a deserved degree of high admiration. He comes to take on a very important responsibility.

When I became President and first met with the leaders of the other Western nations, they immediately told me that the Tokyo Round of the Multilateral Trade Negotiations was dead and it was beyond resurrection. I thought for a while, and then I finally thought of Bob Strauss, because I knew that he could bring something back to life. And he undertook that responsibility and resurrected this tremendous effort successfully and concluded it.

And then the Congress passed this year the Trade Agreements Act, which is the most far-reaching and comprehensive trade act ever passed in this country. I thank both Bob Strauss and Al McDonald

and Alan Wolff [1] and others who worked with him to bring that about. I thank the Members of Congress, represented by Al Ullman, chairman of the Ways and Means Committee, who were responsible, in face of great difficulty, in getting this bill passed almost unanimously. It was a tremendous demonstration of harmony and cooperation and a searching for a noble goal, in spite of the most extreme difficulties.

Now, to administer this act will require somebody with a knowledge of statesmanship and experience and superb leadership qualities, and that's why I've asked Reubin Askew to take on this job. I think he has the background for it.

As a Governor, in addition to the achievements which I've already outlined so briefly, he made trade missions to Europe, to the Far East, and to South America to bring into his own State the benefits to be derived from international trade. He did this successfully.

He's a man who has headed up the selection committee to help me choose every Ambassador whom I've appointed since I've been President. In doing this, he had not only to study the character and the qualifications of all those who sought to be or were willing to be Ambassadors, but he also had to learn the needs of individual countries. He became an avid student of even the most remote part of the world. So, he's learned through that process, long months of unpublicized hard work, about the world and what it is

---

[1] Alonzo L. McDonald, Jr., Assistant to the President and former Deputy Special Representative for Trade Negotiations, and Alan W. Wolff, Deputy Special Representative for Trade Negotiations.

now, an awareness of what it can be in the future.

He's able to span chasms that sometimes exist between people, and his intense devotion to duty and his superb knowledge of our country and his ability to bring disparate groups together in a spirit of common purpose will stand our Nation in good stead. I'm very grateful to Reubin for being willing to do this.

One of his first assignments will be to alleviate the problem of Mexican tomatoes—[*laughter*]—competing with Florida tomatoes. [*Laughter*] I see Bob Strauss smiling broadly, and we've almost taken the smile off Reubin Askew's face. But this is one among many very detailed but very important issues which can serve to bind our Nation together very closely with other nations, and I'm deeply grateful for Reubin Askew's willingness to take on this assignment.

And now Judge Joseph Hatchett, newly appointed to the Court of Appeals, Federal Court of Appeals, will administer the oath of office, while my friend, Donna Lou, holds the Bible for Reubin Askew.

Judge Hatchett.

[*At this point, Judge Joseph W. Hatchett of the Fifth Circuit administered the oath of office.*]

AMBASSADOR ASKEW. *Mr. President, Mrs. Carter, distinguished guests, my family, and friends:*

This is a happy day for me, to say the least. Public service is a high calling, and I'm truly happy that I've been called once again.

I want to begin my brief remarks by thanking President Carter for giving me this opportunity to serve the people of the United States of America in this challeng-

ing assignment and to the United States Senate for its confirmation.

I want to thank my predecessor, my very dear friend, Ambassador Robert Strauss, for all that he's meant to me over these years and for all he's done and continues to do for our country. I think the Almighty made only one Bob Strauss, and I'm sure that makes some people glad and other people sad. [*Laughter*]

In addition, I want to thank all the members of the STR staff for their capable assistance during these past several weeks in what promises, I believe, to be a smooth and successful transition; to the Members of the Congress and their staffs for their continued counsel and encouragement and support, for I am not unmindful that I also work for them as well; to the Governors of this Nation—two of my very closest friends, Governor Busbee, who rearranged his schedule from the Southern Governors' Conference to come up here, to Governor Milliken, who has been one of my very closest friends for many years—and for the role that the national Governors are playing and continue to play in this vital area; and also again to the President for the privilege of working with the other members of his Cabinet, almost all of whom I know very well and look forward very much to working with, and their staffs.

I'm grateful, too, for the support I've received and the experiences I've shared with many of you here today, for, Mr. President, I stand here with a great deal of emotion, because I see so many good friends in this audience, for some of you have traveled long distances at some sacrifice just to be with me and my family. I know that you know that I appreciate it. Seeing your faces once again inspires many fond memories. Your friendship and support through the years has made it possible for me to stand here today. More important, your hard work and your loyalty to the dreams we've shared together have led to many accomplishments and have made it possible for me to dream now of still greater accomplishments in the service of this Nation we all love so much.

I'm grateful also to my family—to my mother and mother-in-law, who were not able to be here today, to my brother and sisters, to my children, Angela and Kevin, but most of all to my wife, Donna Lou, who knows only too well the many sacrifices that a life of public service demands, for this is an area that I have in common with you, Mr. President, for we're both indeed fortunate to be given the privilege to share our lives with two people like Rosalynn and Donna Lou.

And above all I'm grateful to my Creator for favoring me with such friends and such a family, and the privilege to live in such a nation, and with this and all the many opportunities I've had to help my fellow man. And I pray for His continued guidance in fulfilling the responsibilities I assume today.

Those responsibilities are not small by any means. More and more we are coming to realize the crucial importance of international trade to the economy and to the future of the United States and, yes, to the world.

With the personal leadership of President Carter and despite imposing obstacles—for when he says that the MTN was all but considered dead when he took over as President, I'm telling you he is exactly right. Bob Strauss knows he's right. Bob Strauss and his group visited seven capitals in 2 days, even to the point of getting Prime Ministers to come to airports, trying to emphasize the importance of doing this, and doing this in a meaningful way, and of the personal commitment of the President of the United States.

And when he talked to me about assuming this responsibility, it was a high priority that he placed in this area, for he stated time and time again that one of his highest legislative priorities was the passage of the trade agreements. And frankly, it was a foresight initiative of the Congress of the United States and preparing it in such a way that it could take place like it did.

So, I feel that I have the privilege to come here in a success story. And I really do, frankly, get a little disturbed that it's not better understood of what exactly this success story can mean and will mean to the United States. And without the tenacity of Jimmy Carter and Robert Strauss it simply would not have happened.

This accomplishment is a tribute to this country, for what you have seen—you have seen a Congress that, over the years, has worked so hard in this area. You saw a legislative branch of government and an executive branch of government come together, joining the private sector in what I believe is really an example of how this country should and can work. For as I told the Trade Advisory Committee a few moments ago, the single biggest thing that sticks out in my mind, over this whole effort, has been the meaningful input of the private sector of this country. And so, I want to commit myself, not only to the Congress but to the private sector of this country, that we're going to continue this relationship. And as the President's Trade

Representative, we're going to do our very best to keep faith with those who labored so hard to make it possible.

But for all that we know of these recent accomplishments, however impressive, we know that they're only the beginning, they're only the prelude to the challenges which await—challenges which compel an enlightened policy, dedicated to fair trade in every expanding global marketplace. We have such a policy in this administration.

That policy may be summarized as follows: The United States must be more ambitious, more aggressive, more assertive, more imaginative, and more resourceful in matters related to international trade. We must win for the people of this Nation a larger share of the overall world marketplace for goods and services, even as we retain our commitment to fostering increased trading opportunities for all the nations.

Stop and think of history, my friends. Where at any point in history has a nation done a better job of helping others than what this country did in the Marshall plan for the European Community and what it did for Japan? And yet for all that it's done to them in improving their situation to the point of making it difficult, sometimes, competitively on the marketplace, the fact of the matter is, had we not done it, do you realize where we would be?

And so, we have seen over this history of time the leadership of the United States of America. And when you hear people talking about problems—while every person, I'm sure, is proud of their country— what other place in the world would you rather live, and what other person has tried harder to do right by this world and by its own people than has the United States of America? For it's been Jimmy Carter who has understood what these agreements will mean in terms of jobs for our people, in terms of a standard of living, yes, in terms of competition.

This country should not ever fear fair competition, because we also want to be fair to the consumers in order to promote the best possible price for our people. It will lead to broader choices for them. It will lead to an easing of inflation, through a more favorable balance of trade. It could lead as well to a lessening of tensions among nations, as we come to depend more and more on one another in a very interdependent world.

And so here again, we must learn in this area, when people expect us as the United States of America, as one country, to so manipulate our own economy that we have no problems, they do not understand the free enterprise system. The free enterprise system anticipates there would be good times and bad times. If government tries to make every bad time a good time, the system breaks down. And yet, it has been this system of free enterprise, through private ownership of property, that has brought the Western World to the standard of living that it now enjoys. And that's what we're recommitting ourselves, under the President of the United States, in this whole area of trade.

This policy requires fair international trading rules, rules which can be assured through timely implementation, a scrupulous enforcement of the new agreements of the Tokyo Round. And I want to tell you, the day is past when we can afford to make sure that we always assume our obligations without asserting our rights. And I want to tell you, one of the first things the President of the United States told me is that whatever we told the people of this country that was in it for them, to the extent that it presented balanced trade throughout the world, that's what my job was. And that's what I'm committed to do.

And one of the unique things about this area that has pleased me so much has been the very nonpartisan approach of this whole issue. I want to tell you, if there's one area that must remain nonpartisan, it's this area. And I want to give tribute to the minority in both Houses of this Congress for the role that they have played in making it possible, because sometimes they themselves have set a standard for us to try to follow. So, it's important not only that the Congress and the Executive work together; it's important also that we continue a nonpartisan effort together with the private sector.

The policy of which I speak requires an institutional response in furthering the trade interests of our country, a goal which can be attained by the approval of the trade reorganization plan submitted to the Congress by the President. This policy requires continued cooperation among the agencies and branches of government and, in addition, continued cooperation between government, business, and agriculture and labor in fashioning a coherent and creative presence for the United States in the world marketplace. And this policy requires, as well, the avoidance of unnecessary impediments to increased exportation of American goods and services to other nations of the world.

In closing, let me say, crucial to this achievement of the important ends of our trade policy is a substantial increase in American exports. We must encourage ex-

ports in every appropriate way, and this administration is committed to a continuing review in all of those that some might classify as export disincentives. To the extent possible, we have to free up the American business man and woman to compete in the foreign marketplace. We must marshal every ounce of American ingenuity, every device of American technology, and every reserve of American enterprise in a renewed effort to sell American skills, American products around this world. We must make America the forceful competitor it should be in the world marketplace.

As I assume this responsibility, I'm reassured, particularly by the key leadership in both the majority and the minority in the Congress and key positions, as well as the key Cabinet members, for I've come to know them, in particular to know Cy Vance and Warren Christopher, who's acting in his place now as the acting Secretary of State. There's no finer person in American Government than Cyrus Vance. I've worked closely with him, and worked with him in the dedication of the people in that Department, with the people in Treasury, the people in Commerce, as you move to every facet of American Government.

But I want to tell them, parenthetically, that I come as a trade advocate—and which I intend to assert fully to every extent possible, the trade interest of the United States as contained in that legislation—but will work with them to make sure that all that we do has a constructive result and effect upon this country.

I believe in the policy of this administration. I believe in the better life and the lasting prosperity this Nation can get under it. I look forward to the months ahead.

I thank you again, Mr. President. I value our continued personal relationship, because I think you know that I feel that you've done an outstanding job, Mr. President. And I am proud to become part of your Cabinet and to join you as you continue to make this Nation secure and an even better place for us to live and our children's children.

Thank you.

The President has a pressing commitment that he has to immediately return to his office. But I would like the privilege, since so many of you have come from so far away, for Donna Lou and I to stand down the halls, so I might personally have a chance to say hello to each one of you.

NOTE: The President spoke at 2:35 p.m. in the East Room at the White House.

National Wild and Scenic Rivers and National Trails Systems

Message to the Congress Transmitting Reports and Proposed Legislation. October 2, 1979

To the Congress of the United States:

In my Environmental Message of August 2, 1979, I proposed legislation to add a number of rivers and trails to the National Wild and Scenic Rivers and National Trails Systems.

Enclosed are reports and draft legislation that would add the following three river segments to the National Wild and Scenic Rivers System as federally administered components:

—Gunnison River, Colorado

—Encampment River, Colorado
—Priest River, Idaho

I am reaffirming my support for designation of a segment of the Illinois River in Oregon for which legislation was submitted to the Congress last year. I am also reaffirming my support for the following four river segments proposed in my last Environmental Message for inclusion in the System:

—Bruneau River, Idaho
—Dolores River, Colorado
—Upper Mississippi River, Minnesota
—Salmon River, Idaho

In addition, I am transmitting to you new study reports on eight rivers which have been found to qualify for inclusion in the National Wild and Scenic Rivers System as State-administered components. Each of the States in which the rivers are located has expressed an interest in administering these rivers as components of the national system. The rivers are:

—Pine Creek, Pennsylvania
—Buffalo River, Tennessee
—Youghiogheny River, Pennsylvania- Maryland
—Shepaug River, Connecticut
—Kettle River, Minnesota
—Lower Wisconsin River, Wisconsin
—Housatonic River, Connecticut
—Illinois River, Oklahoma

In my 1977 Environmental Message, I proposed 20 additional river segments for study as potential additions to the National Wild and Scenic Rivers System. Several of those rivers have already been designated. Except for rivers where subsequent development has affected the river's qualification for designation, I continue to support legislation authorizing the study of these rivers. Moreover, I am submitting legislation to add the North Umpqua River in Oregon to the list of those rivers to be studied.

In order to assist full congressional deliberation on the proposed Upper Mississippi Wild and Scenic River, I have directed the Secretary of the Interior to complete, with full public participation, a conceptual master plan for the river which will set forth the specific requirements for lands or interests in lands to protect the river corridor and provide public access, campgrounds and other recreational facilities. This is to be completed by April 1980.

My recent Environmental Message also contained a number of proposals relating to the National Trails System. The system is still in its fledgling stage and should be expanded to meet widespread public interest. With this objective in mind, I have directed the Federal land managing agencies to enlarge the National Recreation Trails System. In addition, I am transmitting the study report and legislation to designate the 513-mile Natchez Trace National Scenic Trail through Tennessee, Alabama and Mississippi. I am also resubmitting proposed legislation to establish the Potomac Heritage Trail through Pennsylvania, Maryland, West Virginia, Virginia and the District of Columbia. Furthermore, I am reaffirming my support for the enactment of legislation to create the North Country Trail from the State of New York to North Dakota. Legislation to create this 3,200-mile trail has already passed the House of Representatives in the form of H.R. 3757.

Finally, I am transmitting a report from the Secretary of the Interior recommending that a 13.6-mile segment of the Big Thompson River in Colorado not be added to the National Wild and Scenic Rivers System. This river segment is located entirely within the Rocky Mountain National Park and is managed and protected by the National Park Service. Further, approximately 80% of this 13.6-mile river segment is in a wilderness proposal now before the Congress. Therefore, I believe that the protection afforded by the National Wild and Scenic Rivers Act is unnecessary.

I urge that the Congress promptly act on my recommendations in order to protect these rivers and trails for the recreational and aesthetic enjoyment of all Americans.

JIMMY CARTER

The White House,
    October 2, 1979.

Owyhee River in Idaho and Oregon

Message to the Congress Transmitting a Report and Proposed Legislation. October 2, 1979

To the Congress of the United States:

I am transmitting herewith draft legislation to add two segments of the Owyhee River in Idaho and Oregon totalling 178 miles to the National Wild and Scenic Rivers system. These segments would be administered by the Secretary of the Interior as units of the national system.

I also recommend that an additional 14-mile segment of the river be administered by the State of Oregon under its Scenic Waterways program.

These recommendations are based on the accompanying report prepared by the

Secretary of the Interior under section 5(a) of the Wild and Scenic Rivers Act.

JIMMY CARTER

The White House,
    October 2, 1979.

NOTE: The 175-page report is entitled "Owyhee Wild & Scenic River Study—Final Report/Environmental Statement."

The text of the proposed legislation is included in the press release.

Tuolumne River in California

*Message to Congress Transmitting
Proposed Legislation. October 2, 1979*

To the Congress of the United States:

Pursuant to Section 4(a) of the Wild and Scenic Rivers Act (P.L. 90–542), I am transmitting to the Congress my recommendations and proposals with respect to the designation of the Tuolumne River in California.

The Tuolumne River has been jointly studied by the Departments of Agriculture and Interior. Of the 92 miles which were studied, 82 miles have been found eligible to be added to the national system of Wild and Scenic Rivers. The study proposes that if added to the national system, the river would be jointly managed by the Departments of Interior and Agriculture.

On the basis of information now available, I concur with the findings of the study and recommend that the mileage found to be eligible to be added to the system should be designated as a Wild and Scenic River as part of the national system. A draft bill to accomplish this is attached.

The final printed version of the study has not yet been prepared. In order to meet the statutory deadline of October 2, 1979, however, I am transmitting this rec-

ommendation. I intend that the study of the river be finalized and I shall have it transmitted to you when it is complete. Should any other pertinent information become available however, which would call for a different recommendation, I shall transmit a revised proposal to you along with the completed study.

JIMMY CARTER

The White House,
    October 2, 1979.

NOTE: The text of the proposed legislation is included in the press release.

National Advisory Community Investment Board

*Appointment of Clanzel Thornton Brown as
a Member. October 2, 1979*

The President today announced that he will appoint Clanzel Thornton Brown, of Jacksonville, Fla., as a member of the National Advisory Community Investment Board.

Brown, 47, is president of the Jacksonville Urban League. He serves on the Downtown Development Authority of Jacksonville, the Private Industrial Council, and the University of North Florida Affirmative Action Committee.

President's Council on Physical Fitness and Sports

*Appointment of Alton M. White as a
Member. October 2, 1979*

The President today announced that he will appoint Alton M. White, of Tampa, Fla., to be a member of the President's Council on Physical Fitness and Sports.

White, 39, is executive director of public housing in Tampa and a former administrative assistant to the mayor. He is a former high school health and physical education teacher and is active in sports. He is a member of the board of directors of the Boy Scouts of America in Tampa and a former member of the Florida Committee on Athletics.

Country Music Gala

Remarks at the Fundraising Performance for Ford's Theatre.   October 2, 1979

I am really glad to be here tonight to enjoy with you and to celebrate country music. Some people call it, some experts call it indigenous American music, but when I grew up in Plains, Georgia, when we asked for music, we got country music.

Musicians coming out of the South, like the late Mother Maybelle Carter, brought with them songs that had been sung and played for centuries. These were songs that were played for entertainment by people who had to sing them themselves. They were songs that came out of the people's own hearts. Some of those tunes, even some of the words, had been with them since medieval times; others were composed in this country as people walked through the southern mountains or rode a horse or in the back of a mulewagon or sat beside a campfire in the western plains.

The good songs were passed down from generation to generation, because they told stories of how ordinary people lived and felt and loved. As people moved to the cities, they wrote different songs about their own new feelings and new experiences, but even in our day country music has remained people music. Now it's sometimes composed on kitchen tables or in a hotel room or even riding along in a pickup truck or on Greyhound buses or in an 18-wheeler.

Today all kinds of people listen and love country music. Country music is about all kinds of experiences—sad times and bad times, wasted lives, dashed dreams, the dirty dog that took advantage of you. But it also celebrates the good and the permanent times, home and family, faith and trust, love that lasts for a lifetime and sometimes, I admit, love that lasts just for one good time. [*Laughter*] It's as universal as tears and as personal as a baby's smile.

The country in country music is America. Like jazz and the blues, country music has become a bridge of understanding and good will and friendship from our country to other nations, and so have many of its top talent and top artists.

I want to thank the great performers who've come here tonight to benefit Ford's Theatre. Many of these performers come from cities and towns that are large and as cosmopolitan as Plains, Georgia. [*Laughter*] And right now I'm going to turn over the program to one of those—from Sevierville, Tennessee, Miss Dorothy Parton.[1]

NOTE: The President spoke at 7:21 p.m. at Ford's Theatre.

15th Anniversary of the Service Corps of Retired Executives

Message of the President.   October 2, 1979

On the fifteenth anniversary of the Service Corps of Retired Executives, I want to congratulate the 8,000 SCORE volunteers who provide valuable assistance to small businesses all over the country.

As a former small businessman, I know

---

[1] Popularly known as Dolly Parton.

from first-hand experience how important this SBA program really is.

SCORE volunteers have guided and counseled hundreds of thousands of small businesses over the past fifteen years. Their efforts have helped our nation maintain the healthy small business community that is the backbone of national stability and confidence.

On this occasion I salute SCORE volunteers and their associates at the Small Business Administration who have helped SCORE grow in numbers, spirit and accomplishment. All Americans can be proud of what this milestone represents.

JIMMY CARTER

NOTE: The text of the message was released on October 3.

Urban Park and Recreation Recovery Program

Announcement of Grants to 44 Cities and Counties.   October 4, 1979

The White House today announced grants to 44 cities and counties, totaling $17.1 million, under the Urban Park and Recreation Recovery (UPARR) program. The program is part of the President's urban policy legislative program and offers direct matching grants to eligible local governments to rehabilitate urban park and recreation systems.

The UPARR program is a key element in the administration's plan to revitalize American cities. The program is designed to revitalize neighborhood recreation opportunities in the Nation's most distressed cities, while encouraging local and State governments to make greater use of their own resources for urban recreation.

The grants announced today are the first in a series to be awarded over a 5-year period. The 44 jurisdictions announced today were selected from over 200 applications, whose proposals totaled more than $90 million. Cities and counties whose applications were not selected for funding this time will automatically be held over for consideration in the next funding cycle.

Factors considered in the selection of projects were: the expansion of neighborhood recreation opportunities and the extent to which a project would provide jobs for minorities, youth, and low- and moderate-income neighborhood residents. Other factors were the quality of local recreation system planning, the degree of need, and the applicant's ability to match Federal funds with private and local contributions.

The program was approved by the 95th Congress as title X of the National Parks and Recreation Act of 1978 (Public Law 95–625). It is administered by the Interior Department's Heritage Conservation and Recreation Service.

The 44 cities and counties whose grants are being announced today are Birmingham, Ala., Tucson, Ariz., San Francisco, Calif., San Jose, Calif., Bradenton, Fla., Dade County, Fla., Savannah, Ga., Chicago, Ill., Bloomington, Ind., Alexandria, La., New Orleans, La., Boston, Mass., Cambridge, Mass., Lowell, Mass., Detroit, Mich., Minneapolis, Minn., Pascagoula, Miss., St. Joseph, Mo., Camden County, N.J., Essex County, N.J., Hoboken, N.J., Irvington, N.J., Perth Amboy, N.J., Plainfield, N.J., Bernalillo County, N. Mex., New York, N.Y., Syracuse, N.Y., Utica, N.Y., Cincinnati, Ohio, Cleveland, Ohio, Cuyahoga County, Ohio, Lincoln Heights, Ohio, Steubenville, Ohio, Warren, Ohio, Lawton, Okla., Portland, Oreg., Memphis/Shelby County, Tenn., Galveston, Tex., Laredo, Tex., Portsmouth, Va., Richmond, Va., Seattle, Wash., Tacoma, Wash.

Department of Commerce

*Exchange of Letters on the Resignation of
Juanita M. Kreps as Secretary.
October 4, 1979*

To Secretary Juanita Kreps

With the greatest reluctance and regret, I accept your resignation. I wish it were possible for you to remain, for your absence will be a great loss for our administration.

Not only have I valued your advice on a broad range of economic matters but under your leadership your department has built an impressive record.

Also, in the growing area of international trade, your accomplishments have earned the department the major new role it will soon begin to play. You have begun the essential process of increasing the awareness of our country of the advantages of increased trade and exports. The Trade Agreement you negotiated during your visit to the People's Republic of China marks an historic step in establishing normal relations with one-quarter of the people who live on earth. In Europe, the Middle East, in the Soviet Union and other countries you have been a splendid emissary for the United States.

Finally, with love and genuine friendship I wish you well. We shall miss you. It is my hope that we shall have the continuing benefit of your advice and counsel in the future.

Sincerely,

JIMMY CARTER

October 3, 1979

Dear Mr. President:

It is with deep regret that I offer my resignation as the Secretary of Commerce. My reasons are altogether personal.

Nearly three years ago, when we first met to discuss the economic issues that would face you as President, we were acutely aware of the problems before the Nation. Unemployment was high, the recession dragged on, and business confidence lagged. Threats of protectionism were widespread. Under your leadership, jobs have been created and the unemployment rate lowered significantly; businesses have prospered; new trade agreements promise larger markets for our producers and higher levels of living for the American people.

We now face the critical issues of rapidly rising energy costs and the inflation they generate. We must implement the trade agreements. In order to take advantage of widening world markets, we must find ways to increase our productivity and competitive strength. For the resolution of these longrun problems we shall need the most imaginative approaches, the most realistic assessment of alternatives.

While I am pleased with the progress we have made, I should have liked to continue with the work we have begun. You have my wholehearted support and my great admiration.

Sincerely,

JUANITA

[The President, The White House, Washington, D.C. 20500]

Health Planning and Resources Development Amendments of 1979

*Statement on Signing S. 544 Into Law.
October 4, 1979*

I am pleased to sign S. 544, the Health Planning and Resources Development Amendments of 1979.

This legislation extends the health

planning program which has become a crucial element of our national effort to reduce wasteful health care spending. It complements my proposed hospital cost containment legislation.

The success of health planning has depended upon the voluntary participation of over 50,000 citizens in all parts of the country. A renewed health planning program will enable these and other citizens to more effectively and efficiently allocate resources to meet the health needs in their own communities. This bill also recognizes the critical role that States must play in the planning process. An important new authority will provide Federal assistance to permit closure of excess hospital beds or their conversion to more appropriate and needed uses.

This legislation was enacted after a long and difficult passage through the Congress. I am disappointed that the bill contains amendments which may weaken the authority of planning agencies to control unnecessary spending and continues unneeded construction authorities. Yet the health planning structure remains intact and, with enactment of this legislation, has been given new life. I now look forward to a period of solid accomplishment as we move toward the goal of assuring all Americans equal access to quality health care at reasonable cost.

NOTE: As enacted, S. 544 is Public Law 96–79, approved October 4.

Energy Mobilization Board Legislation

Statement on Senate Approval of the Legislation.   October 4, 1979

I want to commend the Senate for its overwhelming vote today approving an energy mobilization board. That vote represents a major step forward in the joint effort of the Congress and my administration to achieve energy security for our Nation.

The bill that passed today substantially reflects the proposal I made to the Congress in July. This board will have the power to cut through unnecessary procedural delays in order to ensure that priority energy projects will be expeditiously considered and constructed, while environmental values and State and local decisionmaking are preserved.

I want to express my appreciation for the diligent bipartisan efforts of Senators Jackson, Johnston, Hatfield, and Domenici. I call upon the House to follow the Senate's actions promptly, so the board can soon begin its important tasks.

United Nations Educational, Scientific and Cultural Organization

Nomination of Barbara W. Newell for the Rank of Ambassador While Serving as U.S. Permanent Representative.   October 4, 1979

The President today announced that he will nominate Barbara W. Newell for the rank of Ambassador during her service as U.S. Permanent Representative to the United Nations Educational, Scientific and Cultural Organization (UNESCO) in Paris. She replaces Esteban Torres, who has been appointed Special Assistant to the President.

Newell has been serving as Representative to UNESCO in a consultant capacity since earlier this year. She was previously president of Wellesley College and a professor of economics there.

She was born August 19, 1929, in Pittsburgh, Pa. She received a B.A. from Vassar College in 1951 and an M.A. (1953) and Ph. D. (1958) from the University of Wisconsin.

From 1951 to 1959, Newell was a research assistant, then teaching assistant, at the University of Wisconsin, then the University of Illinois. She was an assistant and associate professor of economics at Purdue University from 1959 to 1965 and served as assistant to the chancellor of the University of Wisconsin from 1965 to 1967.

From 1967 to 1971, Newell was at the University of Michigan, where she served as assistant to the president, acting vice president for student affairs, special assistant to the president, and then associate professor of economics. She was associate provost for graduate study and research and professor of economics at the University of Pittsburgh in 1971–72. She was at Wellesley from 1972 to 1979.

Newell is a member of the Institute of International Education and was U.S. delegate to the OAS Conference on Women's Education in Buenos Aires. She is the author of several books and numerous articles.

United States Arms Control and Disarmament Agency

Designation of McGeorge Bundy as Chairman of the General Advisory Committee.
October 4, 1979

The President today announced that he has designated McGeorge Bundy as Chairman of the General Advisory Committee to the Arms Control and Disarmament Agency.

Bundy has been a member of the Com-

mittee since 1978. He is president of the Ford Foundation and served as Special Assistant for National Security Affairs to Presidents Kennedy and Johnson.

National Council on Educational Research

Designation of Harold Howe as Chairman.
October 4, 1979

The President today announced that he has designated Harold Howe as Chairman of the National Council on Educational Research.

Howe has been a member of the Council since 1978. He is vice president for education and research of the Ford Foundation and served as United States Commissioner of Education from 1965 to 1968.

Department of Health, Education, and Welfare

Nomination of Billy M. Wise To Be an Assistant Secretary. October 5, 1979

The President today announced that he will nominate Billy M. Wise, of Vienna, Va., to be an Assistant Secretary of Health, Education, and Welfare. He would replace Eileen Shanahan, resigned, and his area of responsibility would be public affairs. Wise has been Assistant to the Secretary of Housing and Urban Development for Public Affairs since 1977.

He was born November 1, 1936, in Shawnee, Okla. He received a B.A. in journalism from the University of Oklahoma in 1958. He served in the U.S. Air Force from 1958 to 1960.

From 1960 to 1961, Wise was a reporter for the Tulsa Tribune. He was with Life magazine from 1961 to 1969, serving as a reporter in New York, a correspondent in the Washington and Paris bureaus, and Mideast bureau chief in Beirut, Lebanon. From 1969 to 1977, Wise was press secretary to Senator Birch Bayh.

European Communities

Nomination of Thomas O. Enders To Be U.S. Representative.   October 5, 1979

The President today announced that he will nominate Thomas O. Enders, of Waterford, Conn., to be the Representative of the United States to the European Communities, with the rank of Ambassador Extraordinary and Plenipotentiary. Enders has been Ambassador to Canada since 1976.

He was born November 28, 1931, in Hartford, Conn. He received a B.A. from Yale University in 1953, an M.A. from the University of Paris in 1955, and an M.A. from Harvard University in 1957.

From 1958 to 1960, Enders was an intelligence research specialist at the State Department, and from 1960 to 1963, he was visa officer, then economic officer, in Stockholm. He was a supervisory international economist in the Bureau of European Affairs from 1963 to 1966.

From 1966 to 1968, Enders was special assistant in the office of the Under Secretary for Political Affairs. He was Deputy Assistant Secretary for International Monetary Affairs from 1968 to 1969 and Deputy Chief of Mission in Belgrade from 1969 to 1971.

From 1971 to 1974, Enders was Deputy Chief of Mission in Phnom Penh. From 1974 to 1976, he was Assistant Secretary

of State for Economic and Business Affairs.

United States Sinai Support Mission

Message to the Congress Transmitting a Report.   October 5, 1979

To the Congress of the United States:

I am pleased to transmit herewith the Eighth Report of the United States Sinai Support Mission. It covers the Mission's activities during the six-month period ending October 1, 1979. This Report is provided to the Congress in conformity with Section 4 of the Public Law 94–110 of October 13, 1975.

The Peace Treaty which Egypt and Israel signed in Washington on March 26, 1979 calls for the United States to continue monitoring responsibilities in the Sinai until January 25, 1980, when Israeli armed forces withdraw from areas east of the Giddi and Mitla Passes. This mission will be completed on schedule.

Trilateral talks in Washington on September 18 and 19 resulted in tentative agreement for the United States, using the Sinai Field Mission, to verify force levels specified in Annex I of the Treaty, in the area of the Sinai west of the Interim Buffer Zone. Administration officials have been in touch with appropriate Congressional committees on various aspects of the U.S. undertaking and will provide Congress with all agreements and understandings to which the United States is a party.

This year's funding of the Sinai Support Mission is authorized under Chapter 6, Part II of the Foreign Assistance Act, "Peacekeeping Operations." A request has been made to Congress to restore $6.1 million of the Sinai Support Mission funds for FY 1980, to cover anticipated outlays associated with the new U.S. undertaking in the Sinai.

The American peacekeeping initiative in the Sinai has been highly successful. I know the Congress will continue its support of the Mission, as part of United States efforts to meet our goal of permanent peace in the Middle East.

JIMMY CARTER

The White House,
    October 5, 1979.

NOTE: The report is entitled "Report to the Congress—SSM: United States Sinai Support Mission" (19 pages plus annexes).

Uranium Enrichment Capacity

Message to the Congress Transmitting a Report. October 5, 1979

To the Congress of the United States:

In accordance with Sections 103 and 104(c) of the Nuclear Non-Proliferation Act of 1978, I hereby transmit to Congress the U.S. Uranium Enrichment Capacity Annual Report.

This Report has been prepared by the Department of Energy in conjunction with the Department of State, the Arms Control and Disarmament Agency and the Office of Management and Budget and submitted to me as required by law. The Report discusses the need for additional U.S. uranium enrichment capacity and addresses the desirability of and options for foreign participation in new U.S. uranium enrichment facilities.

JIMMY CARTER

The White House,
    October 5, 1979.

NOTE: The 11-page report is entitled "Need for Additional U.S. Uranium Enrichment Capacity and Desirability of and Options for Foreign Participation in New U.S. Uranium Enrichment Facilities."

Treaty on the Limitation of Strategic Offensive Arms

White House Statement on a Senate Select Committee on Intelligence Report. October 5, 1979

The principal findings of the Senate Select Committee on Intelligence speak for themselves. They confirm that the SALT II treaty can be monitored to a degree that justifies the administration's conclusion that the treaty is adequately verifiable.

The committee expressly finds that the SALT II treaty enhances the ability of the United States to monitor those components of Soviet strategic weapons forces which are subject to the limitations of the treaty. Additionally, the committee has found that in the absence of the SALT II treaty, the Soviets would be free to take more sweeping concealment and deception measures, which could make monitoring of Soviet strategic forces even more difficult.

Thus, we believe the Senate can proceed to vote on the SALT II treaty with the full confidence that the issue of verification has been satisfactorily resolved.

We welcome this Intelligence Committee report and look forward to the Senate Foreign Relations Committee testimony of Chairman Bayh and Senator Goldwater next week. In addition, the President intends to meet personally with both Senators Bayh and Goldwater to discuss the report in more detail.

Digest of Other White House Announcements

The following listing includes the President's public schedule and other items of general interest announced by the White House Press Office and not included elsewhere in this issue.

September 29

The President met at the White House with Zbigniew Brzezinski, Assistant to the President for National Security Affairs.

The President met in the Roosevelt Room with members of his advisory panel on the Soviet troops in Cuba, including George Ball, Roswell Gilpatric, Henry Kissinger, John McCone, Dean Rusk, Brent Scowcroft, McGeorge Bundy, Averell Harriman, Sol Linowitz, David Packard, James Schlesinger, Clark Clifford, Nicholas Katzenbach, John McCloy, and William Rogers.

The President declared a major disaster for the State of Florida as a result of severe storms and flooding, beginning on or about September 14, which caused extensive property damage.

The President declared a major disaster for the State of North Carolina as a result of severe storms and flooding, beginning on September 21, which caused extensive property damage.

The President declared a major disaster for the Commonwealth of Virginia as a result of severe storms and flooding, beginning on September 21, which caused extensive private property damage.

The White House announced that Robert J. Lipshutz, Counsel to the President since his inauguration, formally submitted his resignation to President Carter and announced that he is returning to Atlanta to join the law firm of Haas, Holland, Levison and Gibert on November 1. In his new private practice, Mr. Lipshutz will be President Carter's personal attorney and cotrustee of his personal trust, as well as chairman of the proposed Carter Presidential Library commission.

The White House announced that the President has signed a determination that withdraws the designation of Ethiopia as a beneficiary developing country for purposes of the Generalized System of Preferences.

The President left the White House for a weekend stay at Camp David, Md.

October 1

The President returned to the White House from Camp David.

October 2

The President met at the White House with:

—Dr. Brzezinski;

—Frank B. Moore, Assistant to the President for Congressional Liaison.

The President attended a luncheon for country music performers, held in the State Dining Room at the White House.

October 3

The President met at the White House with:

—Dr. Brzezinski;

—Vice President Walter F. Mondale, Secretary of Health, Education, and Welfare Patricia R. Harris, Secretary of Transportation Neil Goldschmidt, Secretary of Labor Ray Marshall, Secretary of Housing and Urban Development Moon Landrieu, Alonzo L. McDonald, Jr., Assistant to the President, Stuart E. Eizenstat, Assistant to the President for Domestic Affairs and Policy, and Jack H. Watson, Jr., Assistant to the President for Intergovernmental Affairs, to discuss domestic policies;

—Secretary of Commerce Juanita M. Kreps;

—Mr. Moore;

—State Democratic Party chairmen and cochairmen;

—Stansfield Turner, Director of Central Intelligence, and Dr. Brzezinski;

—Mrs. Carter, for lunch.

October 4

The President met at the White House with:

—Dr. Brzezinski;

—Mr. Moore;

—representatives of the Rural Coalition;

—Vice President Mondale;

—U.S. Ambassador to the Soviet Union Thomas J. Watson, Jr., and Mrs. Watson.

The President participated in a briefing by administration officials on the strategic arms limitation treaty given for community leaders in the East Room at the White House.

The President declared a major disaster for the State of Connecticut as a result of a tornado and severe storms, beginning on October 3, which caused extensive property damage.

October 5

The President met at the White House with:

—Dr. Brzezinski;

—Vice President Mondale, Secretary of Defense Harold Brown, Deputy Secretary of State Warren M. Christopher, Hedley W. Donovan, Senior Adviser to the President, Hamilton Jordan, Assistant to the President, Lloyd N. Cutler, Counsel to the President, and Dr. Brzezinski;

—Mr. Moore;

—officers of the Leif Ericson Society International;

—Frank I. Hamilton, commander of the American Legion;

—Charles L. Schultze, Chairman of the Council of Economic Advisers.

The President met in the Oval Office with Carl Yastrzemski, an outfielder for the Boston Red Sox professional baseball team, to congratulate him on achieving his 3,000th career hit. Other participants included Mr. Yastrzemski's family and friends.

NOMINATIONS SUBMITTED TO THE SENATE

The following listing does not include promotions of members of the Uniformed Services, nominations to the Service Academies, or nominations of Foreign Service officers.

Submitted October 1, 1979

JAMES C. WEBSTER, of South Dakota, to be an Assistant Secretary of Agriculture, vice Dale Ernest Hathaway, elevated.

Submitted October 5, 1979

THOMAS O. ENDERS, of Connecticut, a Foreign Service officer of the Class of Career Minister, to be the Representative of the United States of America to the European Communities, with the rank and status of Ambassador Extraordinary and Plenipotentiary.

BARBARA W. NEWELL, of Massachusetts, for the rank of Ambassador during the tenure of her service as the United States Permanent Representative to the United Nations Educational, Scientific, and Cultural Organization at Paris, France.

BILLY M. WISE, of Virginia, to be an Assistant Secretary of Health, Education, and Welfare, vice Eileen Shanahan, resigned.

CHECKLIST OF WHITE HOUSE PRESS RELEASES

The following listing contains releases of the White House Press Office which are not included in this issue.

CHECKLIST—Continued

Released September 29, 1979

News conference: on the administration's recent accomplishments on domestic issues—by Stuart E. Eizenstat, Assistant to the President for Domestic Affairs and Policy, and Frank B. Moore, Assistant to the President for Congressional Liaison

Announcement: resignation of Robert J. Lipshutz as Counsel to the President

Released October 1, 1979

Advance text: address to the Nation on peace and national security

---

ACTS APPROVED BY THE PRESIDENT

Approved September 29, 1979

S. 737_____ Public Law 96–72
Export Administration Act of 1979.

H.R. 3996_____ Public Law 96–73
An act to amend the Rail Passenger Service Act to extend the authorization of appropriations for Amtrak for 2 additional years, and for other purposes.

H.R. 4393_____ Public Law 96–74
Treasury, Postal Service, and General Government Appropriations Act, 1980.

ACTS APPROVED—Continued

Approved September 29—Continued

H.R. 5380_____ Public Law 96–75
An act to continue in effect any authority provided under the Department of Justice Appropriation Authorization Act, Fiscal Year 1979, for a certain period.

S. 230_____ Public Law 96–76
An act to amend title VIII of the Public Health Service Act to extend through fiscal year 1980 the program of assistance for nurse training, and for other purposes.

H.J. Res. 406_____ Public Law 96–77
A joint resolution to extend by one hundred and twenty days the expiration date of the Defense Production Act of 1950.

H.R. 5369_____ Public Law 96–78
An act to provide for a temporary increase in the public debt limit, and to amend the Rules of the House of Representatives to make possible the establishment of the public debt limit in the future as a part of the congressional budget process.

Approved October 4, 1979

S. 544_____ Public Law 96–79
Health Planning and Resources Development Amendments of 1979.

S. 275_____ Private Law 96–5
An act for the relief of Leah Mi Cohen.

Visit of Pope John Paul II

Remarks at the Welcoming Ceremony.
October 6, 1979

THE PRESIDENT. *Members of Congress, members of the Supreme Court, members of the Cabinet, ladies and gentlemen:*

Niech będzie Bóg pochwalony!—which, for those of you who do not speak Polish, means "May God be praised!"

This is a day for praising God. On behalf of every American of every faith, I'm pleased and honored to welcome you, Pope John Paul, to the Capital City of the United States of America. Welcome.

In our souls, there is a special feeling which we may call solemn joy. This historic day brings forth such a feeling as we mark another milestone in the long, intertwined history of our country and its faith in God.

But the moment is also historic because the currents that flow below this brief ceremony reach into the very depths of individual lives and even to the breadth of the relationship among sovereign nations. Your journey among us has helped us to see those currents as part of one great river of effort to alleviate human needs and to realize the hunger for spiritual aspirations.

You've moved among us as a champion of dignity and decency for every human being and as a pilgrim for peace among nations. You've offered us your love, and we as individuals are heartened by it. You can be sure, Pope John Paul, that the people of America return your love.

As you've traveled our city streets and our country roads, you've met and touched the vast and rich diversity of America. We cherish our independence of religious thought and our tradition of the separation of church and state, but we are all grateful that we can stand together upon the common ground of shared beliefs.

Sustained by a broad base of mutual understanding, we must seize four unique opportunities which have been dramatized by your visit.

As the first opportunity, we can renew our spiritual lives—in our individual lives, in our families, in our Nation, in our world. During the past few days, you've made us reexamine ourselves. For all the attraction and the sometimes necessity of material things, you've reminded us of the value of human life, and that spiritual strength is the most vital resource of people and of nations. Caring for others makes us strong and gives us courage, while blind pursuit of selfish purposes—of *having* more instead of *being* more—only leaves us empty and depressed, lonely and fearful.

We often see tragic results among those we love—disillusionment, cynicism, alienation—sometimes leading to self-debasement, crime, and violence. This does not have to be. These times of rapid and complex change demand that we turn to that which does not ever change—the spiritual strength to grow together; to find unity as a nation, as a human family—and I believe we will.

Our second opportunity is to recognize that our values, our beliefs, our faith are forged and made meaningful only through action. We must be prepared— both as individuals and as a society—not only to deplore poverty, injustice, and the smothering of human aspirations, but to end them.

We know that material values and spiritual values are interrelated and that inequality of opportunity in life breeds disillusionment and sometimes even strife among human beings. We Americans can act on that knowledge both within our country and beyond our borders—and I believe that we will.

Our third opportunity is to remember that the enhancement of human rights is the compelling idea and goal of our time. Through your own example, you've shown the world that the power of the human spirit cannot be subdued by the power of the state. Your courage inspired your native land, and it now inspires the world.

You've shown how we can find meaning within ourselves by reaching out to others in a shared humanity. We believe that the worthy goals of a society call upon us to help others in a common pursuit of freedom and human rights.

This, for us, has been the meaning of America for more than two centuries. The Pilgrims of New England, the Quakers of Pennsylvania, the Catholics of Maryland, the Jews, and many members of other faiths and denominations who've found safety in America have all been witnesses to a fundamental fact—that where religious faith is free, human liberty, equality, and justice may grow. This is a message which is as vital today as it was 200 years ago when our Nation was founded.

As a nation of faith and vigor, we are committed to deliver the message of human freedom throughout the world— and, Your Holiness, that we will.

Our fourth opportunity is peace. We are dedicated to the belief that the natural and proper desire of all human beings is peace.

We seek a peace in Rhodesia, in Nicaragua, in Northern Ireland, in the Middle East. We are committed to peace in every part of the world. We are a great nation that through self-confidence and faith must share with others the security and the beneficial influence which God's blessings have offered to us.

We have the will to limit the growth and spread of nuclear arms. We can bury hatreds and heal political divisions and control the terrible instruments of mass destruction on behalf of humanity. It is our duty and our destiny to walk with those others like yourself who would guide the world in the ways of peace—and we will, because this Nation is not and never can be afraid of peace.

Your Holiness, this is what your historic journey has meant to us. It's fitting that your path through America has brought you at last to our Nation's Capital.

I welcome you to the White House, the symbolic home of all our people. And on behalf of every American of every faith, I also welcome you into our Nation's heart. God bless you for coming to our country. We are proud to have you here.

THE POPE. Mr. President, I wish to express my most sincere thanks for your kind words of welcome to the White House. And also, if I could say, my congratulations for your Polish language.

It is indeed a great honor for me to meet with the President of the United States during a visit of which the aims are spiritual and religious in nature. May I convey at the same time to you, and through you to all your fellow Americans, my profound respect for all the Federal and State authorities of this Nation, for its beloved people.

In the course of the last few days, I have had the opportunity to see some of your cities and rural areas. My only regret is that the time is too short to bring my greetings personally to all parts of this country, but I want to assure you that my esteem and affection go out to every man, woman, and child without distinction.

Divine Providence in its own designs has called me from my native Poland to be the successor of Peter in the See of Rome and the leader of the Catholic Church. It gives me great joy to be the first Pope in history to come to the Capital of this Nation, and I thank Almighty God for this blessing.

In accepting your courteous invitation, Mr. President, I have also hoped that our meeting today would serve the cause of world peace, international understanding, and the promotion of full respect for human rights everywhere.

Mr. Speaker and honorable Members of Congress, distinguished members of the Cabinet and of the judiciary, ladies and gentlemen:

Your presence here honors me greatly, and I deeply appreciate the expression of respect which you thus extended to me. My gratitude goes to each one of you personally for your kind welcome, and to all I wish to say how profoundly I esteem your mission as stewards of the common good of all the people of America.

I come from a nation with a long tradition of deep Christian faith and with a national history marked by many upheavals; for more than a hundred years Poland was even erased from the political map of Europe. But it is also a country marked by a deep veneration for those values without which no society can prosper—love of freedom, cultural creativity, and the conviction that common endeavors for the good of society must be guided by a true moral sense.

My own spiritual and religious mission impels me to be the messenger of peace and brotherhood and to witness to the true greatness of every human person. This greatness derives from the love of God, who created us in His own likeness and gave us an eternal destiny. It is in this dignity of the human person that I see the meaning of history and that I find the principle that gives sense to the role which every human being has to assume for his or her own advancement and for the well-being of the society to which he or she belongs.

It is with these sentiments that I greet in you the whole American people, a people that bases its concept of life on spiritual and moral values, on a deep religious sense, on respect for duty, and on generosity in the service of humanity—noble traits which are embodied in a particular way in the Nation's Capital, with its monuments dedicated to such outstanding national figures as George Washington, Abraham Lincoln, and Thomas Jefferson.

I greet the American people in their elected representatives, all of you who serve in Congress to chart, through legislation, the path that will lead every citizen of this country towards the fullest development of his or her potential, and the Nation as a whole towards assuming its share of the responsibility for building a world of true freedom and justice. I greet America in all who are vested with authority, which can only be seen as an opportunity for serving your fellow citizens and in the overall development of their true humanity and in the full and unimpeded enjoyment of all their fundamental rights.

I salute the people of this land also in the members of the judiciary, who are servants of humanity in the application of justice and who thus hold in their hands the awesome power of profoundly affecting, by their decisions, the lives of every individual.

For all of you I pray to Almighty God that He may grant you the gift of wisdom in your decisions, prudence in your words and actions, and compassion in the exercise of the authority that is yours, so that in your noble office you will always render true service to the people.

God bless America.

NOTE: The President spoke at 1:57 p.m. on the North Lawn of the White House.

Following the ceremony, the President hosted a private reception for the Pope in the Blue Room at the White House. They then met in the Oval Office.

Visit of Pope John Paul II

Remarks at a White House Reception. October 6, 1979

THE PRESIDENT. My friends, fellow Americans of every faith, I greet you here with a mixture of both pride and pleasure. We've been privileged to meet today at the White House with a truly extraordinary man—John Paul—one who will mean even more to us in the future as we in this world move in this century to meet the complex challenges which inevitably will confront us and all others who live on Earth.

Our Nation was not founded to deny human beings a life of the spirit, but to welcome the spiritual into our lives, and I join all Americans in welcoming Pope John Paul II with open hearts into the lives of our Nation. You are welcome with us, Your Holiness.

As you know, he comes to us as a pastor, as a scholar, as a poet, as a philosopher, but I think primarily as a pastor. [*To the Pope*] Do you agree? As a pastor?

THE POPE. You are right.

THE PRESIDENT. He has decided not to dispute the word of the President. [*Laughter*]

Regardless of our faith, we look on him as a pastor, and he's come to know us and to talk to us about gentleness, about humility, about forgiveness, and about love. You've taught us, our beloved guest, that we in the United States are not perfect, that we in the United States are responsible for our own behavior. You show in your life and in your teachings a particular concern for human dignity. You know that many people are fearful, but that a person with faith need not be afraid. Our religious faith is, indeed, relevant to a modern world.

We've been greatly blessed in this country. We know from the holy word that to whom much has been given, much will be required. You've reminded us, indeed, of our own responsibilities.

Our America was founded to give a home to all those who sought religious freedom. For us today, religious freedom is not just a valued relic of a bygone age or a source of national pride. It's a practical necessity for our Nation's forward course into the future, for as we face difficult, painful, often disheartening changes and transformations in our own lives, now as never before, our Nation needs all the spiritual strength that has been gained and nurtured through the long history of a nation of freedom.

Long before he became Pope, Karol Wojtyla, as a priest in his native Poland, wrote these words of poetry: "We stand in front of our future . . . which opens and closes at the same time."

This afternoon Pope John Paul and I met alone in the Oval Office and discussed the future—the future of faith, the future of people, the future prospects for peace. We share a belief that "the Church must in no way be confused with the political community, nor bound to any political system." But we also spoke of opportunities we might pursue together.

We will work to renew our spiritual strength that can bear us beyond the blind materialism which brings no joy and change that into true caring for one another—in our families, in our communities, in our nations, in our common world. We will pursue this goal through action, not just through words.

I join His Holiness in urging all individuals and nations of the world to alleviate the hunger of people and the homelessness of refugees—not as political acts, but as acts of humanitarian concern. We cannot profess to love humanity and watch hundreds of thousands of men, women, and children die in human tragedy, which we ourselves can help, as a nation and as people, to prevent. It's our responsibility to provide prompt and generous aid to them through action of our own.

In another area of opportunity—concern and action on behalf of human rights—we have long shared a common purpose. As His Holiness has written, "The essential sense of the State, as a political community, consists in that the society and the people composing it are master and sovereign of their own destiny."

We call on all people and all nations to look beyond ancient hatreds, beyond differences in race and customs, traditions and beliefs, to see the shared humanity of every other human life on Earth. Whenever state and religion can do that together, then violations of the human rights of any person anywhere in the world—whatever cause may be claimed in justification of those deprivations—will be seen to be, as Your Holiness has so accurately described them, "warfare on humanity" itself.

It's abhorrent in our time to allow differences in the way God's children worship the same Father to wound each other, when our common faith could do so much to heal each other.

All of us share full responsibility for seizing another opportunity: In a world filled with weapons there can be no more urgent human passion than to wage and to win the struggle for peace—for the sake of every living thing on Earth.

We must, above all, wrest the fateful lightning of nuclear destruction from the hands of man. We must successfully conclude our nuclear arms agreements, and in this continuing effort we must find a way to end the threat of nuclear annihilation in every nation on Earth. The age of nuclear weaponry can either be long or short, as we choose.

We must continue the common struggle—the church and governments—for peace.

In closing, let me repeat the phrase from your poem: "We stand in front of our future."

Fellow Americans, in the presence of this good man, as we pause quietly for these few moments in our sometimes frantic pace, we ask ourselves: What is important? What is progress? What are we creating which we need fear? In his last words [hours] Jesus prayed for his disciples, "Holy Father, keep them in Thy name, which Thou hast given me, that they may be one, even as we are one." And we are also reminded: "God is love."

Let all of us here of every faith stand as one—under God—for peace and justice and for love.

Let us vow that what our Creator has made—human life and human spirit—that we ourselves shall not destroy.

Let us simply choose to change the world as best we can, each one of us in our own particular place, but towards the common purposes of just societies on a peaceful planet.

Our new friend, the people of my country have waited a long time for this meeting. As human beings, each acting for justice in the present and striving together for a common future of peace and love, let us not wait so long for ourselves and for you to meet again.

Welcome to our country, our new friend.

THE POPE. Mr. President, I am honored to have had, at your kind invitation, the opportunity for a meeting with you; for by your office as President of the United States of America, you represent before the world the whole American nation, and you hold the immense responsibility of leading this nation in the path of justice and peace. I thank you publicly for this meeting, and I thank all those who have contributed to its success. I wish also to reiterate here my deep gratitude for the warm welcome and the many kindnesses which I have received from the American people on my pastoral journey through your beautiful land.

Mr. President, in responding to the kind words which you have addressed to me, I take the liberty of beginning with the passage from the Prophet Micah that you quoted at your inauguration: "You have been told, O man, what is good; and what the Lord requires of you, only to do right, and to love goodness, and to walk humbly with your God." In recalling these words, I wish to greet you and all the authorities in the individual States and the Nation who are committed to the good of the citizens.

There is indeed no other way to put oneself at the service of the whole human person except by seeking the good of every man and woman in all their commitments and activities. Authority in the political community is based on the objective ethical principle that the basic duty of power is the solicitude of the common good of society and that it serves the inviolable rights of the human person. The individuals, families, and various groups which compose the civic community are aware that by themselves they are unable to realize their human potential to the full, and therefore they recognize in a wider community the necessary condition for the ever better attainment of the common good.

I wish to commend those in public authority and all the people of the United States for having given, from the very beginning of the existence of this Nation, a special place to some of the most important concerns of the common good. Three years ago, during the Bicentennial celebration, which I was fortunate to participate in as the Archbishop of Kraków—as you say it, as a pastor, with many implications—several implications—it was obvious to everyone that concern for what is human and spiritual is one of the basic principles governing the life of this community. It is superfluous to add that respect for the freedom and the dignity of every individual, whatever his origin, race, sex, or creed, has been a cherished tenet of the civil creed of America, and that it has been backed up by courageous decisions and actions.

Mr. President, ladies and gentlemen, I know and appreciate this country's efforts for arms limitation, especially of nuclear weapons. Everyone is aware of the terrible risk that the stockpiling of such weapons brings upon humanity. Since it is one of the greatest nations on Earth, the United States plays a particularly important part in the quest for greater security in the world and for closer international collaboration. With all my heart I hope that there will be no relaxing of its efforts, both to reduce the risk of a fatal and disastrous worldwide conflagration and to secure a prudent and progressive reduction of the destructive capacity of military arsenals.

At the same time, by reason of its special position, may the United States succeed in influencing the other nations to join in a continuing commitment for disarmament. Without wholeheartedly accepting such a commitment, how can any nation effectively serve humanity, whose deepest desire is true peace?

Attachment to human values and to ethical concerns, which have been a hallmark of the American people, must be situated, especially in the present context of the growing interdependence of peoples across the globe, within the framework of the view that the common good of society embraces not just the individual nation to which one belongs but the citizens of the whole world. I would encourage every action for the reinforcement of peace in the world, a peace based on liberty and justice, on charity and truth.

The present-day relationships between peoples and between nations demand the establishment of greater international cooperation also in the economic field. The more powerful a nation is, the greater becomes its international responsibility; the greater also must be its commitment to the betterment of the lot of those whose very humanity is constantly being threatened by want and need. It is my fervent hope that all the powerful nations in the world will deepen their awareness of the principle of human solidarity within the one great human family.

America, which in the past decades has demonstrated goodness and generosity in providing food for the hungry of the world, will, I am sure, be able to match this generosity with an equally convincing contribution to the establishing of a world order that will create the necessary economic and trade conditions for a more just relationship between all the nations of the world, in respect for their dignity and their own personality. Since people are suffering under international inequality, there can be no question of giving up the pursuit of international solidarity, even if it involves a notable change in the attitudes and lifestyles of those blessed with a larger share of the world's goods.

Mr. President, ladies and gentlemen, in touching upon the common good, which embodies the aspiration of all human beings to the full development of their capacities and the proper protection of their rights, I have dealt with areas where the church that I represent and the political community that is the state share a common concern: the safeguarding of the dignity of the human person and the search for justice and peace. In their own proper spheres, the political community and the church are mutually independent and self-governing. Yet, by a different title, each serves the personal and social vocation of the same human beings.

For her part, the Catholic Church will continue her efforts to cooperate in promoting justice, peace, and dignity through the commitment of her leaders and the members of her communities and through her incessant proclamation that all human beings are created to the image and likeness of God and that they are brothers and sisters, children of one Heavenly Father.

May Almighty God bless and sustain America in her quest for the fullness of liberty, of justice, and peace.

NOTE: The President spoke at 4 p.m. on the South Lawn of the White House.

Visit of Pope John Paul II

White House Statement.   October 6, 1979

President Carter welcomed His Holiness Pope John Paul II to the White House October 6, 1979. The Pope's visit to Washington concluded an historic week-long papal journey to six American cities.

In their private talks, the President and the Pope discussed, in particular, situations of concern to world peace and justice. They also reviewed ways of best serving the cause of peace, freedom, and justice in the world.

Sharing the belief that respect for human rights and the dignity of the individual must be the cornerstone of the domestic and international policies of nations, the Pope and the President underlined their support for international covenants on human rights and for international organizations and entities which serve the cause of human rights. They agreed that the international community must mobilize its concern and resources to deal with the problems of refugees, to protect human rights, and to prevent hunger and famine.

The President and the Pope urged all states to support humanitarian efforts to deal with the plight of starving people and refugees.

The Pope and the President agreed that the cause of peace in the world is served by international efforts to halt the proliferation of armaments and to eliminate the weapons of war.

The President discussed the importance of the Camp David accords and his efforts to end the bitter conflict in the Middle East. He emphasized the determination of the United States to seek a comprehensive peace, including resolution of the Palestinian and Jerusalem questions, the

establishment of peace and stability in Lebanon, and genuine security for all countries in the Middle East. The Pope reiterated the special interest which the Holy See attaches to the Middle East peace process and to the need for an internationally acceptable solution to these grave problems.

The Pope and the President discussed the tragic situation in Northern Ireland. They jointly condemned resort to violence, by any party for any reason, and recalled the appeals which both have recently made for a peaceful solution.

The Pope reviewed his trips to Poland and to Mexico and stressed the universal longing for human dignity and freedom, which he had encountered during his pilgrimage.

The President and the Pope also discussed recent developments in southern Africa, Asia, and Latin America. The President noted that the United States seeks conditions of stability, prosperity, and peace in all these areas in the belief that these will promote human rights. The President emphasized that the international community, and especially the industrial nations, must undertake a greater effort to assist less developed countries to achieve a better way of life for their peoples. The Pope and the President agreed that efforts to advance human rights constitute the compelling idea of our times.

During the Pope's private talks with the President, Vice President Walter Mondale chaired a meeting of principal papal and U.S. advisers. On the Vatican side there were present: His Eminence Agostino Cardinal Casaroli, the Papal Secretary of State, His Excellency Archbishop Eduardo Martinez Somalo, the substitute Secretary of State, His Excellency Archbishop Jean Jadot, Apostolic Delegate in the United States, Monsignor Audrys Backis, the Undersecretary of the Council for Public Affairs of the Church, and others.

On the United States side there were present: Secretary of State Cyrus Vance, the President's National Security Adviser, Dr. Zbigniew Brzezinski, Deputy National Security Adviser David Aaron, Anne Wexler, Assistant to the President, the President's personal envoy to the Vatican, Ambassador Robert F. Wagner, Assistant Secretary of State for European Affairs George Vest, and others.

In addition to the topics discussed in the Oval Office, this meeting in the Cabinet Room reviewed the status of the SALT II treaty and the implementation of the Helsinki Final Act, to which both the Holy See and the United States are signatories. They viewed compliance with the provisions of the Final Act, to be examined at the 1980 Review Conference in Madrid, as essential for enlarging human rights and, in particular, freedom of conscience throughout the world.

The Nation's Economy

White House Statement on Actions by the Board of Governors of the Federal Reserve System. October 6, 1979

The administration believes that the actions decided upon today by the Federal Reserve Board will help reduce inflationary expectations, contribute to a stronger U.S. dollar abroad, and curb unhealthy speculations in commodity markets.

Recent high rates of inflation, led by surging oil prices, other economic data, as well as developments in commodity and foreign exchange markets, have rein-

forced the administration's conviction that fighting inflation remains the Nation's number one economic priority.

The administration will continue to emphasize a policy of budgetary restraint. Enactment of effective national energy legislation to reduce dependence on foreign oil is vital to long-term success in this effort.

The administration believes that success in reducing inflationary pressures will lead in due course both to lower rates of price increases and to lower interest rates. ·

NOTE: Earlier in the day, the Board of Governors had announced that measures would be taken to increase the discount rate, the interest rate the Federal Reserve charges member banks when lending them money, from 11 percent to 12 percent; to require that banks set aside an 8-percent reserve of moneys received from foreign and other sources; and to take greater direct control over the supply of the Nation's money.

National Port Week, 1979
Proclamation 4695.   October 6, 1979

By the President of the United States of America

A Proclamation

Virtually every major metropolitan region of the United States centers around a port, or is closely linked by rail or highway to a port. As waterborne trade in the United States approaches 2 billion tons of cargo per year, the rippling economic effects of expanding port activities will continue to generate employment, revenues, and community development.

Local control and administration of our Nation's port system has fostered the development of some 170 commercial seaports and numerous inland ports on our navigable inland waterways. As the world's leading trading country, the United States depends upon local port expenditures, modernizations and expansions to accommodate expected growth in trade and improvements in transportation technology. But the benefits extend to the national economy, as well as to local communities.

Since 1946, local port agencies have invested more than $5 billion to construct and modernize our pier and wharf facilities. These local public expenditures have essentially been matched by the investments of private marine terminal owners, while the Federal Government helps provide channel and navigation improvements. For the years 1973–1978, these local port expenditures reached $1.8 billion. Projections for the next five years total an estimated $3 billion. These local investments are the vital streams of our foreign and domestic waterborne commerce.

Now, THEREFORE, I, JIMMY CARTER, President of the United States of America, in order to remind Americans of the importance of the port industry of the United States to our national life, do hereby designate the seven calendar days beginning October 7, 1979, as National Port Week. I invite the Governors of the several states, the chief officials of local governments, and the people of the United States to observe such week with appropriate ceremonies and activities.

IN WITNESS WHEREOF, I have hereunto set my hand this sixth day of October, in the year of our Lord nineteen hundred seventy-nine, and of the Independence of the United States of America the two hundred and fourth.

JIMMY CARTER

[Filed with the Office of the Federal Register, 10:39 a.m., October 9, 1979]

NOTE: The text of the proclamation was released on October 7.

Department of Labor

Nomination of John N. Gentry To Be Under Secretary. October 9, 1979

The President today announced that he will nominate John N. Gentry, of Reston, Va., to be Under Secretary of Labor. He would replace Robert Brown, resigned.

Gentry is the principal labor-management relations adviser to Alfred Kahn, the President's Advisor on Inflation and Chairman of the Council on Wage and Price Stability.

Gentry was born May 16, 1930, in Williamsport, Pa. He holds an undergraduate degree in economics from the University of Maryland and a J.D. from Georgetown University Law Center.

He served in a number of positions at the Labor Department, including Deputy Assistant Secretary for Labor-Management Relations and executive assistant to the Under Secretary of Labor.

In 1970 he entered private practice as a member of the Washington firm of Wirtz & Gentry, a law and public interest consulting firm. Gentry also served as president of the National Manpower Institute. In 1978 he served as Chairman of President Carter's board of inquiry under Taft-Hartley to investigate issues in the bituminous coal strike.

THE PRESIDENT'S NEWS CONFERENCE OF OCTOBER 9, 1979

THE PRESIDENT. Good afternoon.

Ms. Thomas [Helen Thomas, United Press International].

STRATEGIC ARMS LIMITATION; SOVIET TROOPS IN CUBA

Q. Mr. President, do you think that you

PHOTOGRAPHIC PORTFOLIO

President Jimmy Carter

Overleaf: Service for the American hostages in Iran at the National Cathedral in Washington, D.C., November 15. *Left:* At the home of Mr. and Mrs. Marvin Porterfield in Martinsburg, W. Va., July 13. *Below left:* With troops of the U.S. Army 122d Signal Battalion at Camp Casey, Republic of Korea, June 30. *Below:* With Western and Japanese leaders during the Tokyo Economic Summit Meeting, Japan, June 28.

bove left: Following remarks at
he Congressional Hispanic Caucus
inner in Washington, D.C., Septem-
er 13. *Below left:* Ceremonies com-
nemorating the 10th anniversary of
he Apollo 11 Moon landing, in the
tose Garden, July 20. *Above:* Near
he city of Prairie du Chien, Wis.,
uring a trip down the Mississippi
tiver, August 19.

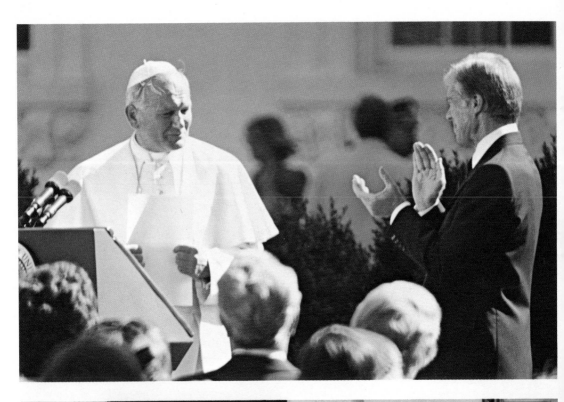

Left: Welcoming Pope John Paul II to the White House, October 6. *Below left:* Meeting with foreign policy advisers on the American hostages in Iran, in the Cabinet Room, November 20. *Right:* During the National Public Radio call-out program, in the Oval Office, October 13. *Below right:* News conference, in the East Room, November 28.

Right: State dinner for Prime Minister Thatcher of the United Kingdom, in the State Dining Room, December 17. *Below:* Following his announcement of candidacy for the 1980 Democratic Presidential nomination, in the East Room, December 4.

have diffused the problem or issue of the Soviet brigade in Cuba and satisfied those who seek a bigger defense budget enough now to win SALT ratification this year, and if so, how?

THE PRESIDENT. I believe SALT will be ratified this year basically on its own merits. It's obvious to me that the SALT treaty is in the best interest of our country. It enhances the security of the United States; it contributes to world peace; it will strengthen our own alliances; it will preserve our place as a leader of the Western World; it will let it be more easy for us to control the spread of nuclear explosives all over the world.

In my opinion, we have answered the question of the Soviet combat unit in Cuba adequately. I think we've isolated any threat from that unit. We'll increase our surveillance there, and I believe that this obviously has been an important issue for us to address. I believe it's been addressed adequately.

As far as the defense budget is concerned, that still must be resolved. I'm committed to a 3-percent real growth in our defense. I've maintained that position for the last 3 years. It's important to us, to our allies, to American strength. If I see a need for increased defense programs, I would not hesitate to recommend them to the Congress.

THE NATION'S ECONOMY

Q. Mr. President, are you prepared to persevere in your support of tight money policies even if it begins to hurt you politically during the primaries?

THE PRESIDENT. Yes. It's obvious that there are three entities in our Government which have been meticulously isolated either under the Constitution or the law and made independent. One is the Federal Reserve Board, which has a right, through various means, to determine the supply of money by changing interest

rates, the reserve moneys that have to be retained by banks that cannot be lent, and so forth. The Congress has the ultimate responsibility on taxation, and the President has the best responsibility on preparing and submitting the budget to the Congress.

There's no doubt in my mind—and this is corroborated by my long discussions the last few weeks with labor, in reaching a labor accord—that I and labor and business and all those who are interested, including the Congress, agree that the number one threat to our national economy is inflation. And I intend to maintain it as a top priority and continue to work against inflation. So, whatever it takes to control inflation, that's what I will do.

I recognize that the inflationary impact falls much more heavily on those who are least able to afford the basic necessities of life. And I also recognize that there are some elements of inflation over which I have no control. The price of energy levied on the world by OPEC in the last 10 months has been an increase of 60 percent. Had it not been for energy price increases, for instance, the inflation rate during this summer would have been the same as it was in 1978 and 1977. So, I can't control energy prices levied on the world by OPEC.

But we'll continue to fight against inflation as a top economic priority.

U.S.-SOVIET RELATIONS

Q. Mr. President, what is your reaction to Dr. Kissinger's statement that the Soviet troops in Cuba are the first organized hostile force in this hemisphere since the Monroe Doctrine that we've accepted? And also, Mr. President, do you feel that the Soviet troops in Cuba symbolize the growing expansionism of the Russians, the Soviet Union?

THE PRESIDENT. The troops in Cuba have been there for a long time. I've not read Secretary Kissinger's speech; I've read news reports of it. Its basic premises are compatible with my own: that the presence of a Soviet combat unit there is a serious matter, which I think we have addressed as best we could; secondly, that this is not the most important matter of all, that above and beyond that, it's important to recognize and to do what we can to contain Cuban interventionism or adventurism around the world. As you know, this began primarily with the entrance of more than a 10,000 body of troops from Cuba into Angola in 1975, before I was President.

We do look upon this as a major threat. I have not seen any reports that Secretary Kissinger recommended different moves from the ones that I outlined to the Nation on the evening of October 1. So, we do share a common concern. I think that our response was measured and appropriate. I do not favor the Soviets extending their arm of influence to the Cubans or anyone else around the world.

This has been part of the history of the Soviet Union. We attempt to meet them and compete with them adequately, in my opinion, on a peaceful basis. And in my judgment, if we can control the military expenditures and have equality, have arms control, in my judgment, we can compete with the Soviets on a peaceful basis with an excellent prospect for victory.

The Soviets represent a totalitarian nation; we are committed to peace and freedom and democracy. The Soviets subjugate the rights of an individual human being to the rights of the state; we do just the opposite. The Soviets are an atheistic nation; we have deep and fundamental religious beliefs. The Soviets have a primary emphasis on the military aspect of their economy; ours is much more broadly based to give the benefits of economic growth to individual human beings. So, I believe that in addition to that, our raising a standard of human rights and the honoring of national aspirations, not trying to interfere in the internal affairs of other countries, gives us an additional advantage in a peaceful competition with the Soviets.

So, I don't have any fear of or any trepidation about that intense competition with the Soviets on a peaceful basis. I obviously want the same thing that President Brezhnev wants, that is, the avoidance of a nuclear war. So, we have some things in common, the avoidance of war. We have other things in common, a willingness to compete.

We've got advantages over them that I hope to utilize in the future as we have in the past.

JESSE JACKSON; FLORIDA CAUCUSES

Q. Mr. President, how do you think you'll fare in Florida? And also a second question——

THE PRESIDENT. I didn't hear the first one.

Q. How do you think you will fare in Florida for the Florida caucus poll? And also, will you plan on talking to Reverend Jesse Jackson in response to his meetings with Yasser Arafat?

THE PRESIDENT. Do I have my choice between those two questions? [*Laughter*]

Q. I'd like you to answer both, if you would, sir.

THE PRESIDENT. I have no plans to talk to Reverend Jackson—I presume you mean about his recent trips to the Middle East. He has, or will make a report to Ambassador Strauss, who is our Mideast negotiator.

In Florida, I don't know how the caucus results will come out. This is one of the evidences of an increasingly early attention focused on a Presidential race. I don't think it is in the best interests of our country to start so early. The importance of the Florida caucuses, I think, will be assigned by the press, not by anything that I do. I don't intend to go down there to campaign. We do have people working for me in Florida, which I appreciate. And I think that since this is a first test between myself and other candidates who also are mounting an effort among their supporters, it will be significant.

But I cannot predict the outcome of the caucuses. I've seen no polls, have no indication about what the outcome might be.

VISIT OF THE POPE

Q. Mr. President, clearly the Pope on his visit to the United States and in Washington left an extraordinary impression beyond simply the religious.

THE PRESIDENT. Yes.

Q. Have you reflected on the meaning of the Pope's visit to the United States?

THE PRESIDENT. Yes.

Q. Could you discuss that?

THE PRESIDENT. In addition to being with him in public and when we met with the members of my family in the White House, I had an extensive private conversation with the Pope, and we discussed this particular question. We were both surprised at the degree of warmth and enthusiasm among American people in welcoming the Pope. I expected the welcome to be warm and friendly, but I had no idea that it would be that enthusiastic and that large a number of people, and neither did he.

I think there's an innate hunger in our country for moral and ethical and religious principles, things that do not change during a time of rapid change brought about by a technological revolution throughout the world. I believe there's a hunger for things that are decent and honest, for principles of which we can be proud. I think the Pope as a religious leader accurately mirrors for many people those aspirations and hopes.

I think it shows that this hemisphere is the most deeply religious, perhaps, in the world, certainly the most deeply religious Christian population in the world. We had long discussions about what this meant in other nations, the threat of atheism as espoused and enforced by the state against the inherent desire of people for religious belief.

But I believe this was one of the most dramatic and, I think, potentially the most beneficial visits we've ever had from a leader in the world. I was very thrilled to meet him and believe that his visit will have benefits for our country.

DEPLOYMENT OF U.S. FORCES

Q. Mr. President, in your speech on Cuba the other night, you spoke about wanting to increase the capabilities of our rapid deployment force.

THE PRESIDENT. Forces.

Q. Forces. I wondered if you could say under what circumstances you would be willing to intervene militarily in the Middle East.

THE PRESIDENT. I see no prospect at this point for our intervention militarily in any place in the world. That would be a judgment that I would only make if I thought the security of our country was directly threatened.

SENATOR EDWARD M. KENNEDY

Q. Mr. President, the other night in Queens, in the context of answering the question about your leadership and Senator Kennedy, you said you had never panicked in a crisis. Now, there was some interpretation that this was a reference to Senator Kennedy's behavior at Chappaquiddick. And you subsequently, or Jody subsequently denied it.

Let me ask you specifically, do you think Chappaquiddick indicates that President Kennedy's character is somewhat flawed, and will this be a continued issue in the primaries if he enters?

THE PRESIDENT. I think it was Senator Kennedy to whom you refer. [*Laughter*]

I did not refer to Senator Kennedy's experience at Chappaquiddick in Queens, and I have no desire to comment on it now.

INTERNATIONAL MONETARY POLICY

Q. Mr. President, further on the Fed tight money policy, figures such as the West German Finance Minister Emminger [1] and Democratic Party Presidential candidate Lyndon LaRouche have charged that this is leading us rapidly towards the Crash of '79. Will you move to stabilize the dollar in the economy by collaborating with Europe on their moves to demonetize gold as LaRouche and others have suggested?

THE PRESIDENT. I doubt that that's in prospect, certainly not for this year. We do cooperate with our allies and friends and trade partners in order to stabilize the worldwide monetary system, including at times the interrelationship between currencies from one country and another and sometimes the basic metals. I don't see any threat to the well-being of any

---

[1] Otmar Emminger is president of the Deutsche Bundesbank, the Federal Republic of Germany's equivalent of the U.S. Federal Reserve System.

American because of a rapidly increasing price of gold, except those who have sold early or bought late. But as far as the average citizen's concerned, the price of gold, whether it's $200 an ounce or $400, has very little impact.

Recently, the Federal Reserve Board has decided to raise interest rates and take other steps concerning the reserve supply of money to be kept on hand by banks. This has resulted in a strengthening of the dollar, which had already begun to strengthen. And I believe that it's well within the bounds of management; it's stable. I noticed an analysis that showed that in the last year the price of the dollar, the value of the dollar, as compared to currencies of all our trade partners, has increased substantially. Among the OPEC nations and their trade partners the value of the dollar, even before we made this recent move, had increased 8 percent over the last year.

So, I believe the dollar is stable, I believe the world economy is stable, and I see no prospect of shifting to a rigid price of gold and a gold standard.

1980 PRESIDENTIAL CAMPAIGN

Q. Sir, two more political questions in light of Senator Kennedy's prospective challenge of you. One, as you did in 1976, would you be willing to debate the Senator and other candidates in the primaries? And two, if you lost, would you support the Democratic nominee actively? And if you won, would you expect your opponents to do the same for you?

THE PRESIDENT. That's a lot of conjecture. We don't have any candidates yet who have declared. I look forward to the campaign with a great deal of anticipation and confidence. And I think the normal routine interrelationships among candidates would probably prevail in 1980, as they did in 1976.

There were no official debates, as such, until the general election in 1976, when President Ford and I, as a nominee, were given that opportunity. But I feel at ease about it. I will protect my record, which I think is a good one. And as I say, I look forward to the campaign with anticipation and confidence.

Q. Mr. President, may I follow up? Will you support the winner of the convention?

THE PRESIDENT. Yes. My presumption is——

Q. And second, your opponents support you if you win?

THE PRESIDENT. My presumption is that I would support whatever Democrat gets the nomination. I have always voted Democratic.

ECONOMIC POLICY

Q. Mr. President, wholesale prices continue to increase, indicating that there will be further inflation at the retail level throughout the rest of this year and perhaps longer. Most of the predictions that you've made and your economic advisers have made about the economy have proved to be on the low side and are constantly being revised upward, especially with regard to inflation.

Don't you think it's about time for some kind of reevaluation of your economic programs and policies? Are you going to just continue to go along on the same course, or do you think any kind of reexamination of your policy is indicated?

THE PRESIDENT. I think so far the program has been well conceived, and I think it has some very beneficial results. We are all surprised at the rate of inflation, brought about primarily, as I said, by an annual rate of increase of energy prices the last few months of more than 100 percent per year. Also, as I said earlier, if you could discount those energy increases, the rate of inflation would be the same this year as it was the preceding 2 years.

We have cut the budget deficit by $36 billion since I've been elected. We have reduced the total number of employees in the Federal Government. We've reduced the percentage of the gross national product being spent by the Government by 2 full percent, from 23½ down to 21½. We've cut paperwork by 15 percent. We've begun a strong move to deregulate, that is, to get the Government's nose out of the private business sector and the lives of private people. We've had a very stringent effort made to eliminate unwarranted spending, and we've moved when necessary to stabilize the value of the dollar.

We've also proposed to the Congress for the first time a means by which we could reduce the inflationary impact of importing 50 percent of our oil. This has been a long, slow, tedious process, but I think when the Congress does complete its work this year on an energy package, this will remove the single major factor that has been causing excessive inflation.

I don't intend to change our basic policy, and I believe that we've had maybe inadequately assessed results even from the wage-price guidelines.

The wage increases, for instance, this year, the first 9 months of this year, have been lower than they were in 1978. We've had more than a million union workers who have signed contracts within the wage guidelines. And the price standards have also been very effective. For instance, the items that come under price standards have been increasing at only one-half the rate of those that cannot be controlled, like OPEC oil prices.

So, I think in general our policy is an adequate and a good one, and I intend to maintain the thrust of it.

MINORITY EMPLOYMENT

Q. Mr. President, I think earlier this year, you had a memo to the agencies and departments which discussed black institutions and contracts and awards. It seems as though that memo has lost some of its teeth in the process. Is there any way that that could be regenerated so that the employment of minorities in the country and through the colleges can increase?

THE PRESIDENT. We've had some success with the unemployment rate among minorities. Even this past month, as you know, the unemployment rate among women, teenagers, and minorities dropped. And we've been pleased at the average rate of unemployment throughout the country. It's still extremely high, however, comparatively speaking, among, say, black teenagers or other minority teenagers.

In addition to that, we have helped the Congress write a law so that public works projects, when assigned to individual communities, would include at least 10 percent of the total money going into contracts with minority-owned businesses. I set as a goal for our administration a tripling in 1 year of the portion of Federal purchases from minority businesses. It was a billion dollars. I set as a goal for the end of this year $3 billion. I think we'll hit a little below my goal, about $2½ billion.

Also, I think in other ways, like the hiring of black employees or the minority employees, we've done a good job. I think I've appointed more judges, for instance, who are black than all the other Presidents in the history of our country

combined. It's not been adequate, but we've made a major step forward. And we are assessing any failures that we've experienced—for instance, in purchasing, where I wanted to reach $3 billion, and we will only reach $2½ billion. I have gotten identified now those agencies that did not meet the tripling goal that I set for them, and they are being especially encouraged by me to meet their goals next year.

We are making progress—not enough.

Judy [Judy Woodruff, NBC News].

THE NATIONAL SPIRIT

Q. Mr. President, Senator Kennedy has suggested that instead of complaining about, I believe, what you call the malaise that the country is experiencing, that what the President should do now is ask the people to roll up their sleeves to try to pull the country out of its problem. And in effect, he spoke of a can-do spirit that harkens back to the 1960's.

THE PRESIDENT. Is this a campaign speech for him or—[*laughter*].

Q. No, sir.

THE PRESIDENT. Okay.

Q. What merit, if any, do you see in that suggestion that he made, and also, how vulnerable do you think you are on the issue of leadership?

THE PRESIDENT. Obviously there is a degree of malaise in the country. People are discouraged about the current situation. They are doubtful about the future; they are saving less than they ever have been in the past; and they have a serious concern about confidence in one another and sometimes about the Government itself.

When I made my speech to the Nation, I think, on July 15, on a Sunday evening, I pointed this out. But I said that our country is inherently strong, capable, and able, that there is no need for us to be discouraged or disillusioned or divided or doubtful about one another or about our Government processes. We're the strongest nation on Earth—economically, politically, and militarily. We're going to stay that way.

And what I prescribed as a major test of American will and confidence was the evolution of and the passage of an energy program, which had never been done in the history of our country, that would be adequate to meet the challenge before us. I think the Congress has made good progress so far. I predict that before they adjourn this year, that we will have this test of our Nation's will successfully achieved.

So, I believe that through the process of helping one another, having confidence, working on major projects, and letting the Government show that it can be competent to deal with a major problem like this, we can resolve the malaise that has existed in our country. I'm not discouraged. I believe that we can succeed.

1980 PRESIDENTIAL CAMPAIGN

Q. Mr. Carter, a few moments ago you said that you thought you probably would like to be the Democratic nominee, in reference to the question on debating. Why are you waiting until December to announce, in view of the fact that Senator Kennedy is probably about to run? Why don't you tell us now that you're going to run?

THE PRESIDENT. I said I was going to make an announcement December 4. I didn't say what it would be yet.

I think that that's not too late. I want to do all I can without being an announced candidate to work with the Congress to get controversial issues decided and also to make plans for the initiation of a campaign year.

There's a tendency in our country to want to move that campaign date earlier and earlier. I believe that what I have decided on a date is compatible with past history. Also, of course, there is a limit to how late one can wait. There are some States that require filing, I believe, around the middle of December.

And so, I think that's late enough to give me a chance to do what I can with this year's Congress; not too late to miss any filing dates if I decide to meet them.

ROSALYNN CARTER

Q. Mr. President, fairly or unfairly, the polls suggest that one of your major political problems is a perceived lack of leadership. At the same time, Mrs. Carter is very visible these days. She's traveling and speaking on your behalf. She's almost on television as much as you are these days.

Do you think it's possible that her high profile in some strange way might ironically exacerbate your political problem? And secondly, is it true that some of your advisers believe that she has too high a public profile and would like her to be a little less visible?

THE PRESIDENT. I believe that if you would compare my wife's schedule now with what it was, say, a year ago, it wouldn't be materially different. The difference is that now the press is paying attention to where my wife goes and what she says.

Rosalynn has always been very close to me personally as well as to consult with me on matters of interest to me and to her. In some areas of public life, she plays a very strong role. She's interested in mental health, which he has been since even before I became Governor of Georgia.

She's always been extremely interested in the problems of older Americans, and this has been a historic interest for her. And I think since this last year, perhaps, she's especially been encouraging people within communities to act on their own initiative to work together to correct local problems, not to wait for the Federal Government or the State or local government to do everything for them. And those things are not incompatible.

In addition, she is a very effective political campaigner. In 1976 and also in 1970, 1966, 1962, when I've had my other campaigns, Rosalynn has always played a substantial role. And I would imagine that she would continue that as long as she and I share a partnership and I'm in politics.

But I don't think her profile is too high. She's very knowledgeable; she is sensitive about American people's beliefs and feelings. She would never abuse her role as a wife or even the wife of a President. I have confidence that she will do the right thing.

KAMPUCHEA

Q. Mr. President, by all accounts, it appears that in the coming months, a million or more people could die in Cambodia of starvation. I know that you talked about this with the Pope the other day. What, if anything, can this Government do in combination with other groups?

THE PRESIDENT. We've been encouraging the humanitarian granting of aid, particularly food aid, to the people of Cambodia, hundreds of thousands of whom, maybe millions of whom are starving. We are trying to work out with the uncertain leaders of that country—uncertain because it's contested through war—a mechanism by which the United Nations primarily, the Red Cross, and UNICEF could get food into those people who are within Cambodia.

There's also a legal problem in refugee funds, because it hasn't yet been determined legally if a person who hasn't left the country is still identifiable as a refugee. The fact that the country's divided by war creates a complication.

But we are ready and eager to join in with other countries to provide humanitarian aid to all the people of Cambodia who are starving, and we will move on that without any further delay as soon as it's possible to join other countries in this effort.

VICE PRESIDENT MONDALE

Q. Mr. President, have you had any second thoughts as to who your running mate would be? Will it definitely be Walter Mondale?

THE PRESIDENT. Fritz Mondale and I have a very good partnership, and I have no plans whatsoever to change it.

ARMS LEVELS IN EUROPE

Q. Mr. President, going back to your comments about competition with the Soviet Union with regard to arms, would you support NATO deployment of the Pershing missile to counter the SS–20? And if I could add another question there, do you have any reaction to President Brezhnev's conditional offer, too, on arms reduction in Central Europe?

THE PRESIDENT. Our allies and we are carefully assessing the significance of President Brezhnev's statement. However, I'd like to point out that what he's offering in effect is to continue their own rate of modernization as it has been, provided we don't modernize at all.

They have had an actual reduction in launchers the last few years. They've been replacing the old SS–4's and SS–5's with the SS–20, not on a one-for-one basis, but the SS–20 has three warheads, the old missiles only had one warhead. The SS–20 has a much greater range. It can reach our Western Allies' countries as a target even if it's located in the central part of Russia. It's three to six times as accurate as the old missiles which it replaced. And in addition to that, it's mobile; that is, it can't be located specifically and destroyed with a preemptive strike if that should become a desire on the part of allies. They also have replaced older airplanes with the Backfire bomber.

So, it's not quite as constructive a proposal as at first blush it seems to be. I think it's an effort designed to disarm the willingness or eagerness of our allies adequately to defend themselves.

In my judgment, the decision ought to be made to modernize the Western Allies' military strength and then negotiate with full commitment and determination mutually to lower armaments on both sides—the Warsaw Pact and the NATO countries—so that we can retain equivalency of military strength, equity of military strength, and have a lower overall level of armaments. This is what we hope to achieve.

I might point out that Chancellor Schmidt said, I believe yesterday or day before, that a prerequisite to a decision by our NATO Allies to take these steps, which he considers to be vital for the security of NATO, is the passage of SALT II.

So, if we can be successful in controlling existing strategic Soviet and United States atomic weapons through SALT II, then we'll move in the next step to reducing the nuclear weapons which don't have intercontinental range. And along with that, we'll continue with our mutual and balanced force reduction effort to reduce conventional arms.

It's an interesting proposal; it's one that might show promise. We're assessing it carefully, but it's not as great a step as would ordinarily be judged at first.

HAMILTON JORDAN

Q. Mr. President, do you have any intention at all of asking Hamilton Jordan to step down as Chief of Staff if a special prosecutor is named? And secondly, is there any thought in your mind, sir, that his departure might at all benefit your Presidency and your chances for reelection, or would they hurt them?

THE PRESIDENT. I'd like to remind you, first of all, that the President is the chief law enforcement officer of the land. And I don't think it would be appropriate for me to comment on guilt or innocence of anyone. Secondly, I'd like to point out that the appointment of a special prosecutor has no insinuation in it at all that the person investigated is guilty.

I believe it would be better for me not to go further than that, because I would ordinarily wait until the Attorney General made a report to me and then seek his advice on what the proprieties would be about my own public statements. I think, though, I've described my position adequately to answer your question.

PALESTINE LIBERATION ORGANIZATION

Q. Mr. President, a question on the Middle East. Do you agree with those such as former Ambassador Andrew Young and George Ball and others who say that it is now time to do away with the restrictions put on our foreign policy by Henry Kissinger and open up a dialog with the Palestinians and the PLO?

THE PRESIDENT. No, I do not. We will not negotiate with the PLO. We will not recognize the PLO until after the PLO recognizes Israel's right to exist and endorses United Nations Resolution 242 as a basis for Middle East peace.

FRANK CORMIER [Associated Press]. Thank you, Mr. President.

NOTE: President Carter's fifty-second news conference began at 3:30 p.m. in Room 450 of the Old Executive Office Building. It was broadcast live on radio and television.

United States Ambassador to Mexico

Exchange of Letters on the Resignation of Patrick J. Lucey. October 9, 1979

Dear Pat,

With deep regret I accept your resignation as Ambassador to Mexico as of November 1, 1979.

During your years in Mexico you brought political skills and personal stature to one of America's most important and difficult diplomatic assignments. These years were but the latest example of your dedication and commitment to public service.

Your leadership has contributed significantly to a new frankness and balance in our cooperation with Mexico. The recently concluded visit of President López Portillo was a reminder of how much we have accomplished. Formal agreements on natural gas sales, prisoner exchanges, civil aviation, and improvements in the mechanisms through which we manage major United States-Mexican issues have advanced the vision of our relationship with Mexico that you and I have shared since the outset of my Administration.

Since the time that we began our service as Governors together, I have valued the courage, effectiveness, and good judgment that you bring to public policy. The Secretary of State joins me in thanking

you and in wishing you all success as you return to Wisconsin.

Rosalynn and I especially appreciate the advocacy of efficient and humane government that we know we can count on from Pat and Jean Lucey.

Sincerely,

JIMMY CARTER

[The Honorable Patrick J. Lucey, American Ambassador, Mexico City]

October 8, 1979

Dear Mr. President:

For almost two and a half years now, I have served as this country's ambassador to Mexico. It has been a stimulating experience for me, and I hope it has been constructive for the policies and the peoples of both countries. I have enjoyed my work here and my working relationship with you and Secretary of State Vance. However, I now have decided to resign from this position, effective November 1, 1979, and to return to Wisconsin.

I leave not with regret but with a sense of satisfaction because it is clear that Mexico and the United States have accomplished a great deal together since your Administration took office. The strength and the importance of the relationship between the two countries has perhaps never been more apparent than over the last month. As the successful meetings between you and President López Portillo just a few days ago demonstrated, it is a relationship based on mutual respect and appreciation. In addition, the new intergovernmental agreement on the guidelines for a natural gas contract has been well received in both countries. That agreement has more than symbolic importance—it offers real potential for helping us solve our energy problems. But these are only the most recent achievements.

In 1977, Mexico and the United States entered into the Prisoner Transfer Treaty that, since its ratification, has permitted more than 400 young Americans to complete prison sentences in their own country. While Vice-President Mondale was in Mexico last year, he signed the most comprehensive commercial aviation agreement ever negotiated between any two countries, and the impact of this agreement on tourism in the United States as well as in Mexico has been dramatic. Moreover, the joint decision to expand and strengthen the Consultative Mechanism, announced on your trip to Mexico City earlier this year, has generated negotiations that promise major bilateral agreements in many other areas.

There have been significant, if less obvious, improvements in this country's perception of Mexico and in this government's ability to help shape a relationship that is productive for both countries. Through the presidential policy review process, the efforts of the Department of State, and our emphasis on working with the Congress, there is a greater public and governmental awareness of our relationship with Mexico and the impact that seemingly unrelated domestic and foreign policies can have here. Bob Krueger in the new position of Ambassador-at-Large will provide a great service to both countries as he continues to expand the interdepartmental coordination and cooperation that already have begun.

In Mexico City, the U.S. Embassy itself, the nation's largest diplomatic mission, has played an increasing role in the formation and conduct of our policies. For example, the Embassy was directly involved in the formation and early deliberations of the Askew Committee. While massive undocumented immigration will confront our two countries for many years, that committee will provide constructive new proposals in this difficult area. With the State Department's encouragement and cooperation and the creative application of zero based budgeting, we now have a lean, more efficient and highly professional staff at the Embassy and its constituent posts. I will miss working with the people here, but my successor will find his or her job less difficult because of their presence and their dedication.

There is a common theme in much of what has happened over the last few years, Mr. President. It is the gradual recognition that Mexico seeks no favors from us, no "special" relationship, but that, instead, Mexico seeks our friendship as the mature, responsible, independent, and rapidly-developing nation that it has become. That friendship will continue to reward both countries in the years ahead. And it is that friendship that will enable Mexico and the United States to resolve the difficult, persistent and shared problems that remain.

I submit my resignation to you only after a great deal of deliberation. I do believe, however, that after two and a half years in Mexico City, it is time to return to Wisconsin where I began my public service more than 30 years ago, and I believe that this is a logical and appropriate time to do so. Jean and I very much appreciate the personal kindness that you and Rosalynn have shown us and the public trust that you have placed in us. Thank you.

With warm regards,

PATRICK J. LUCEY
Patrick J. Lucey
United States Ambassador

[Hon. Jimmy Carter, The White House, 1600 Pennsylvania Avenue, Washington, D.C.]

Federal Civilian and Military Pay Increases

Executive Order 12165.   October 9, 1979

ADJUSTMENTS OF CERTAIN RATES OF PAY AND ALLOWANCES

By the authority vested in me as President by the Constitution and the laws of the United States of America, it is hereby ordered as follows:

1-1. *Adjusted Rates of Pay and Allowances.*

1-101. *Statutory Pay Systems.* Pursuant to the provisions of subchapter I of Chapter 53 of Title 5 of the United States Code, the rates of basic pay and salaries are adjusted, as set forth at the schedules attached hereto and made a part hereof, for the following statutory pay systems:

(a) The General Schedule (5 U.S.C. 5332(a)) at Schedule 1;

(b) the schedules for the Foreign Service (22 U.S.C. 867 and 870(a)) at Schedule 2;

(c) the schedules for the Department of Medicine and Surgery, Veterans Administration (38 U.S.C. 4107) at Schedule 3; and

(d) the rates of basic pay for the Senior Executive Service (5 U.S.C. 5382) at Schedule 4.

1-102. *Pay and Allowances for Members of the Uniformed Services.* Pursuant to the provisions of Section 1009 of Title 37 of the United States Code, the rates of monthly basic pay (37 U.S.C. 203(a) and (c)), the rates of basic allowances for subsistence (37 U.S.C. 402), and the rates of basic allowances for quarters (37 U.S.C. 403(a)) are adjusted, as set forth at Schedule 5 attached hereto and made a part hereof, for members of the uniformed services.

1-103. *Executive Salaries.* The Executive Salary Cost of Living Adjustment Act (89 Stat. 419, 28 U.S.C. 461) provides for adjustments in the rates of pay and salaries as set forth at the schedules attached hereto and made a part hereof, for the following:

(a) The Vice President (3 U.S.C. 104) and the Executive Schedule (5 U.S.C. 5312-5316) at Schedule 6; and

(b) Congressional Salaries (2 U.S.C. 31) at Schedule 7.

1-2. *General Provisions*

1-201. *Effective Date.* The adjustments in rates of monthly basic pay and allowances for subsistence and quarters for members of the uniformed services shall be effective on October 1, 1979. All other adjustments of salary or pay shall be effective on the first day of the first applicable pay period beginning on or after October 1, 1979.

1-202. *Superseded Orders.* Executive Order No. 12087 of October 7, 1978, is superseded.

JIMMY CARTER

The White House,
    October 9, 1979.

[Filed with the Office of the Federal Register, 10:33 a.m., October 10, 1979]

NOTE: The schedules are printed in the FEDERAL REGISTER of October 11, 1979.

The Executive order was announced on October 10.

United States Ambassador to Zaire

Nomination of Robert B. Oakley.
October 10, 1979

The President today announced that he will nominate Robert B. Oakley, of Shreveport, La., to be Ambassador Extraordinary and Plenipotentiary of the United States to the Republic of Zaire. He would replace Walter Cutler, who is being reassigned.

Oakley has been Deputy Assistant Secretary of State for East Asian and Pacific Affairs since 1977.

He was born March 12, 1931, in Dallas, Tex. He received a B.A. from Princeton University in 1952. He served in the U.S. Navy from 1952 to 1955.

Oakley joined the Foreign Service in 1957 and was posted in Khartoum, Abidjan, Saigon, Paris, at the United Nations, and at the State Department. From 1971 to 1974, he was political officer in Beirut, and in 1974 he was an international relations officer at the State Department.

From 1974 to 1977, Oakley was assigned to the National Security Council.

United States Ambassador to Mali

Nomination of Anne Forrester Holloway. October 10, 1979

The President today announced that he will nominate Anne Forrester Holloway, of Washington, D.C., to be Ambassador Extraordinary and Plenipotentiary of the United States to the Republic of Mali. She would replace Patricia M. Byrne, who is being transferred to another post.

Holloway has been special assistant and director of the office of the Ambassador to the United Nations since 1977.

She was born June 2, 1941, in Philadelphia, Pa. She received a B.A. from Bennington College in 1963, an M.A. from Howard University in 1968, and a Ph. D. from Antioch/Union Graduate School in 1975.

From 1963 to 1966, she was a history teacher at Northfield School, East Northfield, Mass. She was a lecturer at Howard University in the African studies program in 1968–69 and was director of Drum and Spear Press, a publishing house, from 1969 to 1970.

In 1970–71 Holloway was visiting assistant professor in the black and African studies program at the State University of New York at Buffalo. From 1971 to 1972, she was associate director for legislative affairs of the Southern Christian Leadership Conference.

From 1972 to 1975, Holloway was executive director of the Black Student Fund. From 1975 to 1977, she was legislative assistant for foreign affairs to then-Congressman Andrew Young.

Federal Magistrate Act of 1979

Statement on Signing S. 237 Into Law. October 10, 1979

I have today signed the Federal Magistrate Act of 1979. This act will expand the jurisdiction of United States magistrates in both civil and criminal cases, and will ensure that magistrates are appointed on merit. It will also improve the capabilities and efficiency of the Federal court system, while at the same time preserving parties' rights and reducing the expense of litigation.

I congratulate Congressmen Kastenmeier, Rodino, and Railsback, and Senators DeConcini, Kennedy, and Thurmond for their leadership on this bill. Without their able efforts its passage would not have been possible.

On February 27 of this year, I sent a message to Congress in which I supported six judicial reform measures to increase the efficiency, cut the cost, and maintain the integrity of the Federal court system. The Federal Magistrate Act of 1979 is the first of these six measures to have passed Congress. I ask the Congress to act promptly on the remaining measures, which will benefit our Federal court system and the public.

NOTE: As enacted, S. 237 is Public Law 96–82, approved October 10.

Office of Federal Procurement Policy Act Amendments of 1979

Statement on Signing S. 756 Into Law.
October 10, 1979

I have this day signed S. 756, a bill which authorizes appropriations for the Office of Federal Procurement Policy for fiscal years 1980 through 1983.

In addition to its other provisions, the legislation clarifies the authority of the Administrator for Federal Procurement Policy to issue policy directives for improving the supply systems and processes of the executive branch. The legislation also calls for the development of a proposal for a Uniform Procurement System to be submitted to the Congress within 1 year. This will serve as successor to the National Supply System project, which I approved August 9, 1979.

NOTE: As enacted, S. 756 is Public Law 96–83, approved October 10.

United States-Denmark Fishery Agreement

Message to the Congress Transmitting the Agreement.   October 10, 1979

To the Congress of the United States:
In accordance with the Fishery Con-

servation and Management Act of 1976 (Public Law 94–265; 16 U.S.C. 1801), I transmit herewith a governing international fishery agreement between the United States and Denmark and the Faroe Islands, signed at Washington on September 5, 1979.

This agreement is one of a series to be negotiated in accordance with that legislation. I urge that the Congress give favorable consideration to this agreement at an early date. Since 60 calendar days of continuous session, as required by the legislation, may not be available, I recommend that the Congress consider issuance of a joint resolution to bring this agreement into force.

JIMMY CARTER

The White House,
October 10, 1979.

United States Travel Service Appropriations Bill

Statement on Signing S. 233 Into Law.
October 10, 1979

I have decided to sign S. 233, which authorizes appropriations for the United States Travel Service.

At the beginning of the year I recommended that the Service be eliminated, for its function can and should be performed by the private sector. I have not changed my view.

I have signed S. 233, however, because the appropriations for the Travel Service have already been enacted as part of a separate bill. I will work to restructure the Federal Government's travel program in order to conform its operation with what I believe to be an appropriate Federal role in tourism promotion.

NOTE: As enacted, S. 233 is Public Law 96–85, approved October 10.

Department of Health, Education, and Welfare

Nomination of Nathan J. Stark To Be Under Secretary. October 10, 1979

The President today announced that he will nominate Nathan J. Stark, of Pittsburgh, Pa., to be Under Secretary of Health, Education, and Welfare. He would replace Hale Champion, resigned.

Stark is vice chancellor for health professions at the University of Pittsburgh and president of the University Health Center of Pittsburgh.

He was born November 9, 1920, in Minneapolis, Minn. He received a B.S. from the U.S. Merchant Marine Academy in 1943 and a J.D. from Chicago Kent College of Law in 1947. He served in the U.S. Merchant Marine from 1942 to 1945.

From 1953 to 1954, Stark practiced law, and from 1954 to 1959, he was vice president of the Rival Manufacturing Co. From 1959 to 1974, he was senior vice president of Hallmark Cards, Inc. From 1971 to 1974, he was chairman of the board and chief executive of Crown Center Redevelopment Corp. He has been at the University of Pittsburgh since 1974.

Stark was treasurer of the Kansas City Area Hospital Association from 1950 to 1967 and chairman of the Kansas City Metropolitan Hospital Planning Council from 1957 to 1967.

Stark has served on a number of national panels concerned with health services, including the Secretary of HEW's Task Force on Medicaid and Related Programs. He has been a consultant to several university medical schools and other organizations.

Kirtland Air Force Base, New Mexico

Remarks on Arrival. October 10, 1979

New Mexico is indeed one of the most beautiful places on Earth, and I am very glad to be back here with you.

New Mexico is not only beautiful, but you have superb leaders in Bruce King, Mayor David Rusk, and others who have served and are serving with them, among people who are also so friendly that I'll never forget the first time I came here.

Bruce was talking about the 3 inches of snow that I just left in Washington. The first time I came to Albuquerque, I was going with Alice King to the State Fair, and it rained 3 inches on us and she and I had to swim out of the State Fairgrounds' gates. That was all the rain you got that year in 1974. It came on me in one afternoon.

This is an airport full of New Mexico hospitality. And I'm here to meet with the Governors of the Western States, with Bruce King as the host, to talk about some issues that are very important to everyone here. We're going to talk about a way to preserve the quality of life of the people who live in this beautiful State, not only now but throughout eternity.

I believe in the preservation of the beauty of your State, and I believe in the purity of air and the quality of water. And I'm convinced that this Nation, working with you here, can have prosperity, stable but steady economic growth, a cooperation between local and State and Federal employees and leaders and people and, at the same time, tap the tremendous offerings that you have for yourselves and for the rest of the country.

This is the land of opportunity. You've

1851

been blessed by God not only with beauty but with great human and natural resources, with oil, with coal, with gas, with uranium, and with the greatest of all, the Sun. And how this great treasure is utilized by people now and in the future will be primarily up to you.

Your choice of wise leaders, your working closely with them, your demand that we maintain the highest possible standards of service and accountability to you will determine whether our decisions are wise or ill-considered. We're determined to make the wise decisions. And I'm glad that you've got forceful leaders like Bruce King that will speak up when there is a danger to what you hold to be so precious.

Our country faces difficult challenges, tough problems, confusing issues, hard questions to answer—but we've always had within us a strength and the courage and the unity when it was needed to meet any challenge, any threat to our country successfully.

We now face a threat to our own Nation's security that's very serious and about which all of you should be aware, and that is the threat of overdependence on imported oil for our country. We now import half the oil we use, and along with all that oil that we import, we also import inflation and we import unemployment.

Next year we expect to spend on foreign oil $70 billion—money that we could use here in our own country to give us a better life, to correct the defects in our society, and to let us have confidence and vision for the future. We must finally address this difficult issue, and that will be the main subject of discussion tonight when I meet for 2 or 3 hours with the Governors representing the Western States.

I have no doubt that we can meet this challenge successfully if our country is united and if we don't forget our great heritage and the great promise of the future.

I'm very proud also that we have common goals and common purposes and common standards, ethics, morality, religious beliefs, of which we can be truly proud.

Many things change in a modern technological world. Sometimes those changes are so fast, so rapid that it disturbs our lives. But this past week with the visit of Pope John Paul, we were reminded vividly of things that don't change—love, honesty, families caring for one another—these things don't change. And I think the tremendous reception that we gave to this distinguished and beloved visitor is a true picture of the character of the American people.

We've got a wonderful country because of you, because of our people, and because of the character that we have always exhibited in a moment of test or trial. And I hope that you will stand united and never lower your standards and never forget that our Nation is, our governments are what you are and what you demand. Together, all of us, we can make the greatest nation on Earth even greater of the character that we've always exwhat I pray for. And I know you join with me in this hope and this dream and this expectation.

Thank you very much. God bless you all.

NOTE: The President spoke at 6:23 p.m.

Following his remarks, the President went to the Four Seasons Hotel in Albuquerque to attend a meeting of the Western Governors' Policy Office.

Albuquerque, New Mexico

Remarks at the National Association of Development Organizations' Dinner. October 10, 1979

Jack Watson just came up and gave me some advice about my opening statement. He suggested that I apologize for substituting for him as your speaker this evening. [*Laughter*] As a matter of fact, if there's one group with whom I feel at home, it would be those of you who've been involved in economic development throughout our country in the last number of years.

One of the first things I did as a young man involved in public service was to organize an eight-county area planning and development commission. I did not have an executive director. I had to act as that myself. [*Laughter*] My eight counties suffered severely from it until I finally got a professional. But it was a turning point in my life.

We had 30 towns and small villages that I served, and we began to bridge the chasm that existed even in front of the county line, and to let people who were competent and eager and filled with the true spirit of America begin to assess the advantages that God had given them, and to make plans for the future that would give their children and grandchildren a better life.

I felt that I was a part of the growth of America. And I felt responsible for the retention of its qualities, and I recognized the rapid changes that took place in the lives of the people that I was trying to serve, and I felt responsible for them, and vice versa. And to lead the life which many of you do as professionals in serving others in this way is a characteristic and a commitment which I admire very deeply.

I graduated from the area planning and development commission to the President of the United States. But I haven't forgotten what I've learned, and as Vernon would know—Vernon Martin was a good friend of mine, even in those days—as he would know, the responsibilities which fall on the shoulders of a Governor or a President are very similar to the responsibilities that fall on the shoulders of those assembled here in this meeting and those whom you represent throughout the country: how to correlate conflicting interests; how to preserve environmental quality and at the same time take advantages of economic growth; how to make sure that each person, no matter how large or small a status in life is occupied, can feel part of a community and not estranged from it; how government can be made effective; how the delivery of services to a human being in need can be as effective as the original vision was at the inception of a law; how to deal with rapidly changing, sociological interrelationships to let people who are different live in harmony with one another; how to realize limitations on our lives, limitations of energy, limitations of wealth, limitations of health care, limitations of housing, transportation—all those limits that they have—how to either accommodate them and make the best of them if they're inevitable or to eliminate them or minimize them if something can be done about them.

You live truly challenging lives, and as we evolve programs for economic development or local public works for dealing with housing, transportation, education, welfare, health, I need your partnership in making our great country even greater.

I met your newly elected president, President Kuhn, who will take office, I think, in January. He'll have another exciting challenge before him, and I wish him well. And I hope that in the next number of months, as we deal with the problems that confront us all, particularly in evolving an energy policy for our Nation, that we will keep in mind the common goals and the common purposes that bind us together.

I just spent a little more than 2 hours with the Governors of the Western States trying to study the special problems of this beautiful part of the Earth and how many of our energy needs can be met from the oil and natural gas and uranium and coal and solar, opportunities that exist here, and how on a permanent basis we can meet the needs of our country in the future.

Each region is different, each county is different, each tiny part of the Earth is different from the others, and I think you have a special insight into how these tiny portions of America can be combined together to make the greatest nation on Earth even greater in the future.

I'm pleased to be with you and I'm honored. I met Aliceann Fritchler Wholberuck earlier tonight. You have an excellent executive secretary. She's worked, as you know, with the county organizations in the past, and I think that she will be a good one to bridge whatever gap might still remain between those of you who are responsible for development of the finest things of life and those who've been elected to serve at the local level of government, which by far is the most important level.

I hope that you will not ever be timid in letting your views be known to me and to the members of my administration with whom you work, who want to do a good job for you, and I know you want to do a good job for the same nation that I serve.

Thank you for letting me interrupt your meeting. God bless you, everyone.

NOTE: The President spoke at 9:30 p.m. in the International Ballroom at the Albuquerque Hilton Inn.

Water Resources

Statement by the President.   October 10, 1979

State systems for allocating and managing water resources have evolved over decades in the Western United States. These systems recognize the high value and relative scarcity of water. Their continuation is essential to stability and equity in the West. With the exception of unique Federal and Indian water rights, the States must allocate their water resources in the manner best suited to themselves.

I have proposed a major domestic energy production effort which we as a nation must undertake to reduce our reliance on imported oil. We hope to establish an energy mobilization board to ensure that decisionmaking on energy projects does not get tied up in redtape. At the same time, I strongly believe that we must preserve the essential and historic role of the States in the process of allocating water among competing needs. I have and will continue to support legislative language to make it clear that federally supported energy development should be accomplished without preemption or change of State water laws, rights, or responsibilities.

With proper planning and sensitivity to all of the human and natural resource problems associated with energy projects, we can produce the energy we need without jeopardizing agricultural and community water use. We can also maintain, as we must, the high quality of the Western environment.

We must respect the rights and responsibilities of our State governments—and when the issue is priorities of water use in a State, the State must and does have the ability to say no through existing State water allocation systems. This right must and will be protected in the energy proposals now pending before the Congress.

NOTE: The statement was released at Albuquerque, N. Mex.

Interview With the President

Remarks and a Question-and-Answer Session With Editors and Broadcasters.
October 10, 1979

THE PRESIDENT. We've had more than [almost][1] 50 sessions with leading news executives and news men and women from outside Washington since I've been President, an average of every 2 weeks. I think between 1,500 and 2,000 have come here for private meetings with my staff and with me and, on occasion, with my wife and some members of the Cabinet.

It's been very helpful to us, and what I ordinarily do is just outline some of the important concerns or projects that are ongoing that are my direct responsibility and then spend the time we have together answering your questions.

ADMINISTRATION POLICIES

We had a leadership breakfast this morning with the Democrats from the House and Senate. I do this twice a month. Once a month I have a leadership breakfast with the Republican leaders of the House and Senate. This morning we discussed the top priority of the year, which is to get SALT II ratified; secondly, to get the energy package completed. We got about 65 or 70 percent of it last year. This year we're dealing with the subject of oil. And then the third thing is to deal directly with inflation, primarily the hospital cost containment.

There are obviously many other pieces of legislation that are important, concern

[1] Printed in the transcript.

ing appropriations, budget, and reduction of regulations, and so forth. But those are the three top priorities—SALT, energy, and hospital cost containment.

We've had a good record with the Congress since I've been in office. The percentage of important proposals that I've made to the Congress which has been passed has been as high as any recent administration in the first 3 years. President Johnson's term is probably the only time that there was a better percentage of success. And some of the things we haven't passed in the years gone by, months gone by, like the portions of the energy bill, we're coming back again and again until we get them passed by the Congress.

I have in addition to legislative responsibilities those of foreign policy and defense, and I believe we've had a good session so far in the General Assembly of the United Nations.

Secretary Vance has been up there almost 2 full weeks, which gives him the chance to participate in the debates, emphasize particular aspects of foreign policy, like peace in Lebanon, and to have literally dozens of private sessions with the heads of state or foreign ministers of countries around the world. The United Nations environment is a very good forum through which for 15 minutes or for several hours the Secretary of State can deal with foreign leaders in a convenient fashion and also a fairly private fashion.

I have been up there once for 2 or 3 days and, I think in those 2 or 3 days, met 24 heads of state who came there, some to meet with me, others on routine business.

We have, in addition, ongoing negotiations on Namibia, on Rhodesia, on the Middle East, and constant relations on a daily basis with our allies around the world—military, politics, economics—and are trying to alleviate suffering among refugees and starving people and in hu manitarian things, which is part of the greatness of our country.

I would be glad to answer any questions that you might have on specific issues.

QUESTIONS

MEETINGS WITH THE PRESS

Q. Mr. President, I appreciate it— thank you.

Mr. President, while this type of format with visiting editors may be somewhat helpful to you and somewhat heady for the editors who are here, it does not allow for the aggressive interrogation that characterizes your press conferences with the reporters assigned to Washington.

THE PRESIDENT. Please be aggressive. [*Laughter*]

Q. Okay. Nor does it result in the wide- spread dissemination of your views such as the press conferences do. For instance, yesterday's press conference was at least two front-page stories on many of our na- tional newspapers. Yet, your press con- ference yesterday was the first one since July 25, and there are indications that you have abandoned your campaign pledge to hold two per week—or two per month, I mean—sorry.

Do you consider this format to be an adequate substitution for those press con- ferences?

THE PRESIDENT. No. I've been in office now, I think 32 or 33 months. I've had over 100 [50] [2] press conferences—I think 52 of them with the White House press corps exclusively; the others on a regional basis, either in Atlanta or Miami or Des Moines or Hartford, Connecticut, or wherever. At those regional press confer- ences I ordinarily give the White House correspondents half the questions. If I'm in Seattle, Washington, I'll ask the Seattle newspeople, to give them a chance for one

[2] Printed in the transcript.

question, then I give the White House correspondents who travel with me the second question, and alternate back and forth. So, this is an average of press con- ferences, more than three a month, about three a month.

In addition, I've had 12 or 14—I've forgotten the exact figure—townhall meetings, where I have anywhere from a thousand to 3,000 people and—just in arbitrary ways, without my having any knowledge or influence over the ques- tion—answer questions from the public. I'll have my second telephone call-in show this Saturday. And, as I said, this is, I think, my 51st or 52d meeting with out-of- town editors.* I would guess that in its totality, my relationship with the public has been more than any other previous President.

My own belief is that this mixture is better than to exclusively have just a re- lationship with the White House press corps, but that's a judgment that I myself make. And when I decided to cut down on the twice-per-month relationship with the White House press corps, that's when I decided to go out once a week or once every 2 weeks, either for a regional press conference or for a townhall meeting.

There's a much wider diversity of ques- tions. I think they are much more sub- stantive in nature on the average, and they also give me an insight into parochial questions, you know, what is important to the people of the Northwestern part of the United States or to the Northeast or the Deep South. And I don't think there's any robbing away of interest in even inter- national affairs. If I go to a press confer- ence in Iowa, I get about a third of the questions on international matters.

* The President has met with such editors' groups in Washington 49 times and in Florida once. [Printed in the transcript.]

So, I think this is a good balance, and I've not tried to withdraw into a shell. I think I've been more open maybe the last few months than even before.

U.S. POLICY TOWARDS ISRAEL

Q. Mr. President, Simon Weber, Jewish Daily Forward, New York. As an ethnic newspaper, we have a special interest in Israel——

THE PRESIDENT. So do I.

Q. ——and of course we are concerned with all the problems of the United States. But there is a feeling in the Jewish community your administration is kind of pressing hard on Israel, in the case of Lebanon, in the case of the Palestinians. Would you explain that?

THE PRESIDENT. Yes, I will. I think I would prefer to let Foreign Minister Dayan speak for me. I'm sure you're familiar with the comment that he made.

Q. Yes.

THE PRESIDENT. And he has a good clear insight into the relationships, both public and in the private negotiations between Israel and the United States. I could not have said it better. Neither could Jody Powell have said it better.

We have opened up public discussion and public debate and private negotiation on matters that were previously avoided because they are controversial. But I think it's well to remember that about a year ago, we had the Camp David accords signed, not just by me, not just by President Sadat, but by me, Begin, and Sadat. And then about 6 months ago, we had the Mideast peace treaty signed and approved by all three of us. The progress has been sometimes faltering, sometimes epitomized by dispute, sometimes by allegations that the United States has been unfair to Israel or unfair to the Arab countries or unfair to Egypt or unfair to the Palestinians or unfair to Lebanon.

I think we've had a well-balanced approach. We have, as a primary concern—primary concern—the security of Israel, the existence of Israel, leading toward peace for the people who live in Israel with not just Egypt but all their neighbors. That's our first concern. And along with that, of course, is to seek for a comprehensive agreement between Israel and all her neighbors. I think we've had good progress so far.

We believe that there can be no permanent peace without a resolution of the Palestinian question in all its aspects, to use the language that Prime Minister Begin himself adopted in the Camp David accords. And I think as far as Lebanon is concerned, we deplore violence in the northern part of Israel and the southern part of Lebanon, no matter where it originates. We abhor the use of terrorism by some of the Palestinians to effectuate their cause. We think this is a sad and deplorable mistake. And we hope to see a relationship between Israel and the people of Lebanon, including Palestinians, which would lead to a peaceful relationship.

But we don't put any pressure on Israel. It would be counterproductive if we did. And I believe that Prime Minister Begin would join in with Foreign Minister Dayan in certifying that our approach has been responsible and fair.

I can't deny that there have been occasions when the Israelis have felt that we took a biased position, and I can't deny either that there have been times when the Arab countries feel that our position is biased toward Israel. But I describe to you the same order of priorities that I would describe to Sadat: first of all, the existence and security of Israel; secondly, the effectuation of peace between Israel and her neighbors, all her neighbors; and third, a recognition that a resolution of the Palestinian question has to be a prerequisite to a permanent peace in the Mideast.

FUEL SUPPLIES

Q. Mr. President, Doug Breisch from KDTH Radio in Dubuque. People out in the sticks are having a hard time believing anybody on this energy matter. We've heard that there's plenty of middle distillates available for the home heating season coming up and for the harvest season. And harvest season is upon us, and the Energy Department says we've got plenty of middle distillates; they're all at the refineries so that we can keep track of how much we've got. And the mechanism is ready to get that out to the farmer, but we want to keep it at the refinery as long as possible so we know how much we have.

What is going on? What is happening in order to get this fuel out to the farmer? Are they going to have enough for harvest season? Are we going to have enough to heat our homes for winter?

THE PRESIDENT. We lost about 100 million barrels of oil that we would ordinarily have acquired the first few months of this year because of the Iranian revolution and the cessation of Iranian shipments to us. Ordinarily they now produce about 4 million barrels a day, and that production was interrupted completely. Because of that, we had potential shortage of tractor fuel during the planting season, which we weathered successfully. We did have some shortages of gasoline on the highways in some areas of our country, as you well know, and we had the threat of a severe shortage of home heating fuel for the Northeast, the entire northern part of our country, during this fall.

We have replenished our stocks of home heating fuel. Our target was to reach 240 million barrels on hand in primary stocks during October. We will meet that target. Some predicted at first that we would not. Now with that supply assured, we are shifting the emphasis on the middle distillates toward diesel fuel for both trucks and tractors, and my prediction is that we will have adequate supplies for the harvest season.

The sum total of all the discussion, however, is for us to have in place a comprehensive national energy policy that is predictable and where we are not so heavily dependent on imported oil, which can be interrupted, as you know, at any time and where the prices have increased inordinately, lately and as far back as 1973. Last year we got about 65 percent of the energy proposals that we put to the Congress. We didn't get anything on oil. This year, with the windfall profits tax, the security corporation, the production board, and with the rationing standby plan, we'll have a fairly good proposal.

The other thing that's important, though, is to meet the needs of the poor people, who are being so heavily impacted by the rapidly increasing prices of home heating oil, which is compatible with all the energy prices. And we have asked the Congress already for $400 million to take care of those needs, plus $1.2 million more that would be available, increasing to a total of 2.4 million in the next fiscal year. I hope the Congress will act expeditiously on this.

But I can predict to you that we'll have an adequate supply, barring some further interruption. But the key to it is conservation and an increase in the production in our own country of energy supplies. All of our thrust for the last 2½ years has been oriented toward that goal.

I think we had better move on just to give the other folks a chance.

WAGE AND PRICE GUIDELINES

Q. I'm Scott Goodfellow from WJZ, Baltimore. When might we anticipate some revision in the wage-price guideline? I'm especially interested in the upward revision of the wage structure, however slight, if at all.

THE PRESIDENT. We're setting up a pay board, pay advisory board, headed by John Dunlop, who's the chairman, and I have not yet appointed the other members of the board. We're consulting with both business and labor to get their advice to me before I make the final selections on the pay advisory board. We have not changed the standard established by the Council on Wage and Price Stability earlier this year. That's the basis for our present wage policy.

When the pay policy board, advisory board, goes into effect and begins to function, they have the directive or will have, from me, to make recommendations on how to administer pay policy or wage policy. The final judgment will be made by the Chairman of the Council on Wage and Price Stability. But the presumption would be that the advice of this pay board would have a heavy weight, both with me and with COWPS, Council on Wage and Price Stability.

The price standards have already been set, beginning on the 1st of October, because corporations cannot make their price changes retroactive. Once you've sold something, you can't go back and charge a higher price. It's very difficult to give refunds. And they wanted to have before this quarter again the price standards which have been stable and haven't changed.

I might point out that in spite of some degree of flexibility derived from the difference in the cost-of-living adjustment, the pay standards will be maintained on an equitable and sustained basis without any abrupt changes. They've had excellent results. Among the wage earners, the wage increases have been less in 1979 in the first 9 months than they were in 1978, which is an accomplishment not yet recognized by the press.

Secondly, among items that have been under the price standards, the rate of increase of the prices for those items has been one-half the rate of inflation for other items that we cannot control.

So, we've had good results so far. The new national accord that has been worked out with labor and with the help of business, I think, will let us be much more effective in the future even than we have been in the past. So, I can't say that there won't be any modifications, but the modifications will be based on a careful analysis of how to change our present policy. There won't be any abrupt changes, and changes will be made reluctantly.

Labor, by the way, certifies with us— and you might want to read over the accord, which is brief and written in laymen's language—labor certifies with us that the prime responsibility is to control inflation, which I think is a major step forward. We're pleased with it, and I think it will have far-reaching, beneficial effects.

CRIME

Q. JoAnne Young from Casa Grande, Arizona. What does your administration plan to do about the rising crime rate in this Nation?

THE PRESIDENT. Well, the crime rate goes up and down. For a while, since I've been in office, it's gone downward, and lately, in some cities at least, it's gone upward. We have tried to work more closely with the local and State officials. The primary responsibility for the enforcement of the law in a given community lies with local officials, first of all, State officials secondly, and with the Federal Government coming in to participate in some types of crime which involve interstate violations of the commerce laws or the violation of basic civil rights.

We've had remarkably good success, I think, in trying to interrupt and reduce the flow of illicit drugs coming into our country, particularly from Mexico. And now we're increasing our efforts to cooperate with Colombia, with Peru, and other Latin American countries, in addition to our good success with Mexico.

So, the effort to prevent white-collar crimes, to enforce the antitrust laws and others, I think, have been very successful. We've prosecuted and concluded longstanding cases involving illicit surveillance of citizens and other sensitive matters that were left over from previous administrations adequately. So, I think that's the best analysis I can give you.

We still have a serious problem with crime. One of the factors that's impossible to assess is how much a better reporting system affects the number of crimes reported. My guess is that there's a much more efficient way now to have an accurate count of the number of crimes committed. I say none of this with apology for the excessively high crime rate, but we're doing the best we can under difficult circumstances.

JEWISH AND BLACK AMERICANS

Q. Mr. President, I would like to ask you about the—my name is Gabriel Cohen. I'm with a national Jewish newspaper, the National Jewish Post and Opinion, which you do not read. [*Laughter*] I would like to ask you——

THE PRESIDENT. How do you know I don't read it?

Q. I already asked that question. [*Laughter*]

THE PRESIDENT. Oh, I see, but I didn't answer. Go on.

Q. I'd like to ask you about the rupture between the black and Jewish communities, but before that, I'd like to ask you a personal question.

THE PRESIDENT. All right.

Q. I understand you are from Georgia, and my wife and I met in Atlanta. And we now have eight children, and I thought maybe you know something that we don't know. [*Laughter*]

THE PRESIDENT. Well, I've only got four children, but I'm working on grandchildren now. [*Laughter*]

Q. The question I have about—there is a deep concern in the Jewish community, a very deep concern, and I don't know that it comes to you.

THE PRESIDENT. Yes, there's a concern in the White House, too, if I anticipate your question correctly. Go ahead.

Q. I know you have methods and people through whom you do consult. But the charge, for instance, that the Jews control the press, that has been made by Mr. Jackson—well, you probably know better than anybody that Jews do not control the press. Another charge is that dual loyalty, we call it dual loyalty, but it means that the Jews are more loyal to Israel than they would be to the United States. And the thought occurred to me, if you will forgive me, that perhaps—well, I know you've already spoken out on it, and I know that you have stated that the Jews were not responsible for the Young resignation.

THE PRESIDENT. That's correct.

Q. But perhaps you have in mind convening a group of Negro and—or black and Jewish leaders, and maybe not so much the leaders and trying to resolve this. It's a very dangerous situation, because Jews have never forgotten the Holocaust.

THE PRESIDENT. I know.

Q. And I can tell you of times when, on my honeymoon, I went to a country club and put down my golf clubs on the first hole and went in to register, and there was a sign that says, "No Jews allowed." And so the fellow said, "It's off season. You can go ahead and play." And I said, "Oh, no I can't," and I left. But that incident is not so much apparent today.

THE PRESIDENT. Well, as you know, blacks have suffered the same kind of discrimination and other minority groups have in our country.

I'm sure you realize I don't associate myself with the statements that you made earlier, that people allege that Jews control the press or this or that. I don't associate myself with that. And the dual loyalty, I have no question about the innate loyalty of American Jews for our country. I also have a deep commitment to Israel, which I hope accurately mirrors the deep feelings of the Jewish Americans who share the same concern. I've expressed that in answer to an earlier question.

I am concerned about the division between black and Jewish Americans. I might say that none of the blacks who travel to the Mideast do it as a representative of mine. We have myself, the Vice President, the Secretary of State, and Bob Strauss, who are authorized to negotiate from time to time, all under my direct supervision. And we don't call on private citizens to negotiate for us with other national leaders throughout the world.

Secondly, I don't have any authority, nor do I want to have any authority, to interrupt or to interfere with the right of American citizens to travel where they choose and to meet with whom they choose. I would not want that authority;

I think it would be a violation of the basic constitutional rights that are precious to our Nation.

We have talked—I have talked privately with people like Elie Wiesel and with Ed Sanders and with Ted Mann and others about the best way to bring about an understanding between black Americans and Jewish Americans concerning the complicated interrelationships and sensitive matters concerning the Mideast. Bob Strauss is the one on whom I depend primarily, not only for Mideast negotiations but for the alleviation of misunderstandings and tensions between blacks and American Jews. I and the Vice President also do what we can to alleviate these tensions.

My advice so far from American Jewish leaders is not to inject the White House into the dialog that ought to take place or is sometimes taking place between the two minority groups. But I would be willing to do that in the future if necessary. I believe a better understanding between the two would help to identify and to define common ground. And there may be some irresolvable differences because of points of view—that shouldn't create a schism between the two groups in our country who've suffered most from discrimination.

Ms. BARIO. Thank you, sir.

NATIONAL SPIRIT AND THE 1980
PRESIDENTIAL CAMPAIGN

Q. Mr. President, my name is Luke Feck from Cincinnati. When you were at Camp David you identified a malaise in the American countryside, and when Assistant Secretary of Treasury Brill resigned, he talked about America's interest in immediate self-gratification. The polls show a decline of confidence in all institutions. The American people, are they becoming more difficult to govern, and if they are, what effect will that have in the campaign of 1980?

THE PRESIDENT. I've read a lot of history since I've been in this house. And when I compare the present difficulty of governing with what it was under previous administrations, I don't think there's a remarkable difference. Obviously, under President Hoover and Roosevelt and Kennedy and Truman and Johnson and Nixon and Ford, there were extreme difficulties, some the same that I have inherited; others change from one decade or generation to another.

The thing that does concern me, however, is the tendency among our people to alienate themselves, one from another: the evolution of special interest groups, with a narrowly focused grasping for advantage; the inability that our country has so far exhibited to deal with a major threat to our national security, that is, an overdependence on foreign oil; and a general lack of confidence in the future as revealed by public opinion polls and an absence of saving habits. And I described this as best I could in the speech in July on Sunday evening, after coming back from Camp David.

In spite of all that evidence, which is available to anyone, I have a firm and growing awareness of the basic strength of our country, which is unshaken. Militarily, politically, economically, morally, ethically, our country is still extremely strong, the strongest nation on Earth, in my opinion, in every one of those categories that I have just outlined. I think in any sort of peaceful competition we can prevail over any other power on Earth because of the qualities of American beliefs and principles.

I also believe that our system of government is admirable and worthy of emulation. Our belief in stability on Earth, the absence of war, the enhancement of peace, the independence of other nations,

their right to be free of foreign intrusion from us or anyone else, is appealing to other countries.

Militarily, I'm determined to keep our Nation as strong as any on Earth. I don't ever want to see our country be second to the Soviet Union or any other country in military strength.

I feel that our Nation can be unified if in a few test cases we can prevail and the Government can show its ability to deal with a controversial issue effectively. The ratification of SALT will be a major step forward. The passage this year of the energy package will show Americans that we have a clear vision of the future and that we can make sacrifices when necessary. We can accommodate changing times even though it's inconvenient and there is a possibility of triumph in a time of difficulty through national unity, even though the threat to our Nation's security is not so obvious as a war or a worldwide depression. I expressed all this as clearly as I could.

The campaign, to close my answer and refer to the last part of your question, I think is an excellent opportunity for candidates and for American people to assess and to debate these controversial issues. I will be trying to present to the American people as clearly as possible the achievements of our country during the last 3 years, the unmet needs, my own proposals for meeting those needs, and, in the give-and-take with other candidates and with the media and with private citizens, let these controversial issues be explored. And I think the American people will be educated in the process, which is always a case with the campaign.

So, I look forward to the 1980 campaign, not with trepidation or doubt, but with anticipation and pleasure—and, I might say, confidence—and believe that the American people will benefit from it.

I don't see any deleterious consequences of open debate and sharp expressions of opinion even when they differ. I think that the more American people are involved in the evolution of decisions and the establishment of policies for our country, domestically or foreign, the less likely we are to make a serious mistake.

We've made some serious mistakes in recent years with Vietnam and Watergate and CIA violations of the law and so forth, because the American people were excluded from the process or because they were told lies, even by people who worked in the Oval Office. And I want to make sure that never happens again. I think had the American people known the truth from the beginning, those deep embarrassments for our country, which shocked the consciousness of our Nation and contributed to the disunity and the doubt, would have been avoided.

So, I feel that that's part of my responsibility, to correct past mistakes, to deal fairly with the American people, and to prevent future mistakes. And I think the political campaign season is a good opportunity for that.

Let me say in closing that I've appreciated the chance to talk to you. By the way, we do get a very good coverage from these editors meetings in the national news media. There is hardly a Saturday evening or a Sunday that goes by that two or three items, sometimes front-page stories, don't come out of this session. We make a transcript of all my answers. The questions are quite often probing and different kinds of questions, and we give you—I think they explained the ground rules—we give you a chance to use the answers for a number of hours before they are made public. But there are a lot of good news stories that come out of these editorial sessions that I think are probably other than what I would get in a White House press conference.

Thank you again. If you don't mind, I'd like to get an individual photograph with each of you before you leave. And I'll stand right over here, and if you'll come by, we'll just take a handshake.

NOTE: The interview began at 11 a.m. in the Cabinet Room at the White House. Patricia Y. Bario is a Deputy Press Secretary.

The transcript of the interview was released on October 11.

Albuquerque, New Mexico

Remarks at a Meeting With Civic and Community Leaders. October 11, 1979

Governor Bruce King, it's a great honor for me to come to meet with this distinguished bipartisan group this morning. [*Laughter*] The only thing I can say is that the people in Albuquerque get up pretty early. And I'm very proud to be with the most effective and distinguished mayors in the city, David Rusk. David celebrated his 39th birthday this week—yesterday? Yesterday. I've celebrated 16 of those 39th birthdays. [*Laughter*]

It's good for me to come back to be with you. As I walk down the rope—and I'll shake hands with everyone here before I leave—I was reminded of the times I've been to New Mexico before and the friendship that you've always extended to me, which is typical of the hospitality and the character of those of you who live in this beautiful State.

I do have a lot of responsibilities on my shoulders, but it's one of the most challenging and, certainly, the most exciting jobs on Earth. And it's one that I am thinking very seriously about keeping for a while if you'll help me. [*Laughter*]

This past week, we had an experience that I think will live in the history of our Nation and in the memories of all Americans—and I'm glad that Archbishop

Sanchez is here, because it has been a thrill for me as a Baptist, for others of all kinds of faiths, to see the tremendous outpouring of love and respect that was paid to Pope John Paul.

He came here not as a statesman, although he is; he came here as a man of God. And when I had a private conversation with him, he said that he was absolutely amazed at the tremendous reception that he got. I was, too. I knew that they would have tens of thousands of people, maybe hundreds of thousands of people who would come out to meet him, but to see literally millions of people assembled on the streets of Chicago and Boston and Philadelphia and New York and even in the rural area of Iowa and, of course, in Washington, was a pleasant surprise and an exciting surprise for me.

I think there's a hunger in our country for decency and commitment, for the binding of wounds, for unity, for mutual respect, for compassion, and for love; and this to me is heartening. And I think the reception that he got transcended any kind of minor religious differences we have, because we worship the same God. And this, I think, is a good solid base for Americans to meet any possible challenge to us.

We are so strong—our country is. Sometimes we get bogged down in the daily news programs—where we are reminded of the problems and the differences and the debates and the temporary failures and the inconveniences—and we forget to stand back for a moment and assess the blessings that we have.

We live in the greatest and the strongest nation on Earth. It's the strongest nation on Earth militarily. We need fear no one, and we will never be second to any other country in military strength. And, of course, we are the strongest nation on Earth economically, because God blessed us with such great natural resources. In the past, we've not always handled them carefully. We've not been constant good stewards of what we've inherited. But I really believe that the recent reminder that there is a limit to how much waste Americans can accept in our society is healthy for us.

I met last night, 2 hours, with the Governors of the Western States. It was one of the most productive and exciting meetings I've ever had. And I told the Governors at the conclusion of the meeting that I wished that every person in America, with TV cameras or otherwise, could have seen what went on there, because it was a vivid demonstration of the system of federalism at work.

There was a frank exchange of ideas and a searching for common ground. And when we got through, I can tell you that the differences among us were almost nonexistent and we had been brought together. It would not have been that way a year ago or 2 years ago, but now we see common problems and we see common solutions. And we see a binding together of officials at the local, State, and Federal levels of government to deal with the particular problem of energy that, in my opinion, will be carried over in future years, to deal with other crises or challenges or problems that we've not yet had to address.

You in this part of the world live in a relatively untouched environment. You begin to see, though, an enormous explosion in population as people move from other parts of the country here. And how to deal effectively with the growth, both in population and economically, and the utilization of your natural resources, and at the same time keep the beauty of your place and the quality of your life, is indeed a challenge. And I think this new relationship between the State and Federal Government in dealing with the energy crisis is going to provide a basis of communication and consultation and partnership that will stand us in good stead in the future.

It's the way our Nation ought to work. And it's the way our Nation has always worked if we had a crisis or a challenge or a threat that we could see clearly. The threat of the First World War, the threat of the Second World War, even the threat of the Great Depression touched every American's life. And so, at that time we were unified; our families came together; our communities came together; people had more respect for public officials. We were like a team meeting the challenge. And it's not been possible for us in the past to marshal our great strength and to unify ourselves to meet a challenge that was not quite so easy to see—the threat to our security from the importation next year of $70 billion worth of foreign oil. We're importing oil; we're importing unemployment; we're importing inflation.

The inflation rate now is boosted 4 percentage points just by energy increases foisted on us by OPEC. And if we can cut down the level of our imports through the prices of the energy program I've put to Congress, we can cut down severely on inflation. But that's hard to see, and we've got to unify our efforts to deal with it— that was the purpose of my visit out here. And we can do the same thing with inflation, and we can hold constantly those cherished personal values in America through that same process.

You've got such a great State. I've depended on New Mexicans to help me, on a per capita basis, in Washington perhaps more than any other State in the whole Nation. Graciela Olivarez came out with me on the plane. She handles the Community Services Administration, to deal with people who are most deprived. And she does a superb job with tens of millions of dollars, carefully placed to alleviate the most severe hardships in our country. She's got a special sensitivity. She knows what it means to be from a community which is not only poor but also where the people don't speak English well. And I think that's a special insight that the Federal Government ought to have.

And Alex Mercure has been of great help to me. I happen to be a farmer, and to have him as Assistant Secretary of Agriculture gives a special insight into the problems of agriculture for your region.

Fabian Chavez, as you know, has helped me in the Department of Commerce. He's here among you again now. But these kinds of contributions are very good. And last and perhaps least—I won't mention everyone—Tim Kraft—[*laughter*]—and Chris Brown [1] helped me in special ways as well.

And you also have the greatest amount of solar energy, per capita. So, you've got a lot to be thankful for. But I think the main thing that I would like to say this morning in closing is that I appreciate your friendship and the strength and the pioneer spirit that still exemplifies the people who live in your beautiful part of the country. And I hope that we can form this closer relationship in the future to deal with challenges that will inevitably arise. And I have absolutely no doubt that we can meet any challenge or answer any question or resolve any problem if Americans have confidence in one another and confidence in our system and, also, if we can unify our efforts toward common goals. That's one of the responsibilities of

---

[1] Carter/Mondale Presidential Committee campaign manager and campaign manager for the New England area, respectively.

a President, and I feel a partnership with every one of you here.

Thank you for letting me be with you. God bless every one in this room.

NOTE: The President spoke at approximately 8 a.m. in the Rio Grande Room at the Sheraton Old Town Hotel.

San Diego, California

Remarks at the Annual Convention of the Building and Construction Trades Department, AFL–CIO.   October 11, 1979

President Bob Georgine and my good friends in the building and construction trades:

It's good to be here with you, the men and women who are building America's future.

It's an honor and a pleasure, and I'm grateful that yesterday one of the finest Secretaries of Labor who ever served was able to address you. I understand he made my speech for me, and I wonder if he did all right. Did he do okay? [*Applause*] Thank you very much.

It must be very reassuring to you, as it is to me, to have a man as Secretary of Labor who understands what it means to work for a living. Yesterday, I understand Ray said it would make us feel more at home if you had sawdust on the floor— [*laughter*]—but we understand you and believe that our Nation will be better in the future because of you.

I'm going to violate protocol, too, and repeat something that my introducer has already said. I don't want to change the text of my speech. It shows that great minds move in the same direction. [*Laughter*] As a matter of fact, I want to tell you three brief stories.

Back in 1976, at the Democratic National Convention, as Bob Georgine said,

I had a long private talk with him, as the new Democratic nominee for President. As he said, I asked him, "What can I do, Bob, for the building trades?" And I never forgot his quick answer. He was clear, to the point; he didn't equivocate. He said, "Governor, my people need jobs." I've not forgotten it. We were in the midst of what was nothing less than a depression for the construction industry.

When I took office, unemployment among the building and construction trades was averaging 15 percent, in some areas 25 or 30 percent. It had been that way for a long time. I felt then and I feel now that we formed a partnership. With your help, I was elected President, and working with a Democratic Congress and with you, we have created, since January 1977, a net increase of 8½ million jobs in the United States, an unprecedented achievement in the history of our country. I thank you for it. That partnership has really paid off.

For all American workers, we've cut the unemployment rate about 25 percent, and I'm proud of that. But I'm even prouder of the remarkable achievement among those who look to you for leadership, for the total unemployment rate has dropped more than 40 percent. As a matter of fact, among those 8½ million jobs, 1 million—more than a million have been new construction jobs in just 30 months. There are more construction workers on the job today than ever before in history. Bob, we have delivered together, and we're not through yet.

In spite of some economic obstacles which you and I recognize together, I intend to preserve those construction jobs and to get some more. That's the first story I wanted to tell you about.

The second story involves another labor leader who also happens to be here with us today, and he was with me at

Camp David in July. While I was searching for a clear approach to the very complicated subject of energy, not knowing quite how to address a longstanding, unanswered question in our society, Lane Kirkland [1] called for boldness with a simple and startling answer about what to do concerning energy. "Mr. President," he said, "the issue is freedom."

Now, there's a third story with even deeper dimensions—about our Nation's basic values and how we can reassert those values and how I believe we've already begun to do so.

Last week, I watched the television arrival of His Holiness Pope John Paul II. When he came down from his plane, he knelt to kiss the earth of our country, and then my wife, Rosalynn, greeted him. And he made a brief but powerful and eloquent statement about America the beautiful.

He said essentially that he respects us individually as a nation and that we are good people and that he loves us. It was a rare moment in our lives, an emotional moment, a moment for history.

But immediately, the TV commentator turned to his colleagues and said, "It was a gracious speech, gentlemen, but there was nothing new in it. Did you think so?" And another one said that the Pope looked very tired, and then the third comment was, "I don't believe he can speak English well enough to carry on a conversation."

For television viewers, a beautiful and significant moment was kind of glossed over and made trivial. But that was a transient damage, because the character of John Paul and our Nation's hunger to restore the unchanging ethical and spiritual standards as a part of American life has made his visit to the United

---

[1] Secretary-treasurer of the AFL–CIO.

States of America a triumph, not only for him as a great spiritual leader but also for us. It brought out for all the world to see the finer elements of our character as Americans.

These three episodes, one with Bob Georgine, one with Lane Kirkland, one with the Pope's visit to our country, contrast the powerful forces that face us in our day-by-day lives as Americans and the choices that we have to make, both as individuals and as a nation. These choices are between cynicism and faith, between despair and confidence, between weakness and courage.

These are basic choices in our personal lives. They're also basic choices in our economic and political lives as a nation. They are choices that I discussed with you and other Americans in my television address that Sunday evening in July when I came back from Camp David. In that speech, I outlined my vision of a rebirth in American values and American spirit.

As President, I have a chance to think a lot and to talk a lot and to listen a lot to people who understand our country. And I recognize the problems of America, but I also recognize our strength. I know that we can meet those challenges, I know that we can answer those difficult questions, and I know that we can solve those tough problems. But first we must restore our confidence in one another and our faith in the future. All else pales in importance when compared to this absolute necessity for us to have confidence in one another and confidence in the future of our Nation.

Second, we must revitalize our basic human values like freedom, patriotism, duty, trust, family, compassion, love. Our outpouring of affection for the Pope showed how deep and strong those values are within the souls and the hearts of Americans.

And third, we must regenerate our sense of unity. We must draw again from that deep reservoir of spirit that's always been available to us when our Nation was in danger or when we faced a serious challenge. And today we do face some of the most serious economic and international challenges in history. Energy, employment, inflation, world peace are of special concern to me as President.

In the last few months, I believe we have turned a corner. I see a growing willingness to pitch in, to recognize problems, to face them courageously, and to try to solve those problems together. The labor movement has helped to lead this change.

We are finally building up good momentum in the Congress after long years of delay in major energy legislation.

Last year, with your help, we passed part of an energy bill that can reduce imported oil by 2½ million barrels a day by the end of this coming decade. But even with those huge savings and the savings that we expect to get from increased conservation, if we do nothing more, we will be importing more oil by 1990 than we import today. We've still got a long way to go. And we will not accept this threat to our Nation's very security.

At Camp David, I also turned to Marty Ward, to Jack Lyons, and they told it to me straight: "This country needs a new energy base, Mr. President, and we've got to start right away." And I have a clear message from Bob Georgine, from Charlie Pillard, Bill Sidell, Jay Turner. They tell me that we must stop exporting American jobs and stop importing inflation. And they also tell me that there's some construction workers in this country ready to fill those new jobs when we create them.

Americans are ready and we will save much more energy in the future than we have ever tried to save in the past. But we also have got to build and produce more. We need more American oil, American gas, American coal, American solar power, American nuclear power, American synthetic fuels to run our homes and factories, and we're going to produce them without further delay—American energy for American people, for American jobs, and to cut inflation. If you'll help me, we will not fail.

I want to tell you this: This will not be an unpleasant sacrifice on the part of Americans. It will be and can be a pleasant thing, a notable achievement. We'll get from it a sense of patriotism.

We must have an energy security corporation financed by a windfall profits tax on the unearned profits of the oil companies. I'm determined to get it. If you'll help me, we will not fail on that.

This will finance—and this might be of interest to you—one of the biggest construction projects in the history of the world—a brand-new American industry—American industry—with American technology and American jobs on a scale which will even exceed the construction of our Interstate Highway System. Without even counting any indirect benefits, in construction alone, it will create more than 145,000 jobs.

But I need your help with the windfall profits tax in the Senate, because the oil companies are pushing for loopholes that could give them nearly $100 billion of this proposed tax and which would only produce only a small increase in American oil and American gas. This would all be at the expense of programs to help the poor pay rapidly rising energy costs, to give us a better transportation system, to develop synthetic fuels. This we cannot permit, and I want to know, would you help me stop this attempt by the oil companies to get this $100 billion for themselves? Will you help me with that? [*Applause*] Right on.

I know you've helped me before, and I appreciate it, but now's the time to help again, without delay. Importing just 1 barrel of oil per day—1 barrel of oil per day—costs our country $8,000 a year. This is more than many workers in our country make in an entire year. Next year, we will import not 1 barrel of oil, but 8½ million barrels of oil every day. We will send out of the United States next year $70 billion. Just imagine how many American jobs could be created with $70 billion. That's why we need the windfall profits tax, because we're going to build a new energy future for our country. And the building and construction workers are going to build it.

But we're not going to stop there. As Bob Georgine says, the unemployment rate is still too high. Our goal is full employment, and to me this means full employment for construction workers as well.

In fighting inflation, we do not sacrifice construction jobs. While interest rates have been rising, because of decisions made by the Federal Reserve Board, to high levels in order to cool inflation, we've taken special financial measures to sustain credit for construction.

In the past, as you well know, when interest rates went up, building dropped to practically zero. It was the first industry to suffer. This has not been the case. Interest rates are too high, inflation is too high, but we've tried to build into the system protection for construction workers and especially housing construction.

I reject the advice of those who think the only way to cure inflation is to throw millions of people out of work. This has

been done in the past by administrations before mine, but I guarantee you that I will not fight inflation with your jobs.

I've worked with President George Meany and Bob Georgine and others on this platform up here to make sure that American workers never again have to suffer such a loss because of a cruel and unnecessary policy.

Let me add that your strength today is a tribute to the dedication of President George Meany to a free, democratic, patriotic, and responsible labor movement, not just in the United States but all over the world. Every American owes President George Meany a debt of gratitude.

I told him last January that in fighting inflation, that we would make labor, probably for the first time, full partners. I assured him that labor would be at the table when my administration made any major decisions about economic matters. And I've delivered on that promise.

As you may know, we've just concluded, with your leadership, with the help of Lane Kirkland and others, the new economic pact between my administration and organized labor—the national accord is what it's called—the national accord—which amounts to an economic charter for the 1980's, a decade that can be a time of stable prices, steady expansion, and growing employment. Labor, business, and the public will all be represented on the pay committee which is envisioned in the national accord. The chairman will be a man who is a special friend of yours and in whom we all have confidence, John Dunlop.

For the first time—and this is very significant, in my opinion—the national accord makes full partners of those people whose well-being and standards of living are at stake in the fight against inflation— the working men and women of America.

The national accord commits us to protect jobs, it commits us to aid the poor as they struggle with inflation. The national accord also obligates us to continue what we begin—action to ensure capital for the housing industry, and especially to make available adequate financing for low- and middle-income families who are seeking homes.

Now, we all know that we must pursue a policy of fiscal discipline, with protection for the poor and the disadvantaged. We cannot spend our way out of this inflation. Austerity is unavoidable and inevitable. We all recognize that. Labor, business, and government leaders, we can no longer postpone it.

If we all continue shoving each other to get more, we will only get more inflation and, ultimately, less of everything. But if we respect each other's needs and capabilities and needs and if we restrain ourselves and cooperate with one another, we can have both less inflation, more jobs, and a steadily expanding economy.

Let me add that I count as an obligation something not written into the labor accord. That's my pledge to you to oppose in the Congress antilabor legislation and to support positive labor legislation, such as common situs picketing and labor law reform. My own experience is that you can't always get from the Congress everything you want the first year, but I've never been one to give up, and I don't intend to give up on this.

That's the positive action that we want from the Congress. But we've also seen this year seven different attempts in the Congress to gut the Davis-Bacon act. We've turned back all seven attempts, and I stand with you to turn back all such future attempts. And you can depend upon it.

It's clear that protecting the rights of workers is essential to any sort of energy, economic plans or contracts. So, when somebody begins to complain about inflation, for instance in the Congress, and then attacks labor, I say that all they want to do is to put the sacrifice, all the sacrifice, on the shoulders of the working men and women of this country. And this we cannot and we will not permit. The sacrifice must be shared.

We've got some problems that are difficult to resolve. There's no question about that. As you know, I'm the fourth President to have to deal with the problem of continued high inflation. But missing from every previous approach to resolve the problem of inflation has been this voluntary compact, negotiated freely, with a broad consensus of support, including, as an essential element, labor. For the first time, we have such an accord now in the national accord. It's because of you that we have it, and I thank you deeply for it.

And I might add that within a few moments after the AFL–CIO executive council approved the national accord, President Frank Fitzsimmons sent me word that I could count on the Teamsters, and, President Fitzsimmons, I thank you for that.

In closing, let me point this out—it's important to you and me: Our energy and economic and other domestic efforts are closely tied to our international challenges, for it's our national strength and our national resolve and our world leadership that helps to promote peace.

We are at peace in the world. While I've been President, not one single American has lost a life in combat, and I thank God for it.

This is a peace based on strength, on determination, a peace based on vigilance. We've strengthened our NATO commitment, and it becomes stronger every day. We've reversed the long decline in real spending for national defense. My number one responsibility, above everything else, is our Nation's security. And as long as I'm President of the United States, you can count on our Nation having military forces second to none.

I don't deny that we have challenges, but we face our challenges calmly because we have confidence in America. We've established an essential balance between security and peace.

While strong and at peace, we must never lose sight of the need to eliminate the threat which has hung over our heads for the last 30 years, the threat of nuclear annihilation. I say to you today what American labor has said for a long time: The Senate must ratify the SALT II treaty.

SALT II represents 7 years of detailed negotiations under three different Presidents, both parties. It's a fair treaty; it's a balanced treaty. It's a treaty that can be verified; it's a treaty that lets us monitor what the Soviets are doing. It's a treaty that maintains our role as a leader of the Western World. It's a treaty that exemplifies America's desire for peace through strength. It's a treaty which permits our Nation to put its precious financial resources where they pay the greatest dividend for American quality of life. It's a treaty that enhances world peace. This is a responsibility that we must fulfill for our own children and for future generations.

SALT II will lead to further arms reductions so that we can maintain equivalency of military strength and use the tremendous advantages that America has to compete with the Soviet Union all over the world.

We are a nation that believes in freedom, individuality, liberty, democracy; the Soviets don't believe in those things. We think a person should never be sub-

jugated to the state; the Soviets put the state first. We are a nation with deep ethical standards and religious beliefs; the Soviets are an atheistic nation. We believe in the rights of other countries; the Soviets inject themselves directly or through Cuban surrogates into the internal affairs of other countries and disrupt the societies there.

We have tremendous advantages that can be marshaled to prevail and to make friends and trade partners with nations throughout the world, provided the SALT II treaty is passed. We don't fear anyone, but we believe that we can prevail through peaceful competition. Our allies must have confidence in us. They look to us to negotiate successfully. They look to us to control the nuclear threat to themselves. We cannot betray this confidence of our allies.

And the SALT II treaty permits us as well to contribute to a world that will let us expand everywhere the scope of our belief in human rights. I'm proud that we've put this issue, including trade union rights, on the international agenda.

We in America will never lower the banner of human rights. We want the benefits of a peaceful world for ourselves and for others. We have worked hard for this.

We've made historic progress toward peace in the Middle East. A year ago, we had the Camp David accords. Six months ago, we had the Middle East peace treaty between Israel and Egypt. And now we hope to reach a permanent solution to the terrible conflict that has dominated the history of this troubled corner of the world. We are determined not to fail in bringing peace to Israel and to the Middle East.

At times, this has been a lonely struggle, but throughout this effort, I have drawn strength and support and encouragement from the labor movement. You're always with me when peace or freedom are at stake. I know I can count on you; I have never been disappointed.

In wartime, during the struggle for civil rights in our own country, in meeting our economic challenges, no matter how severe they may have been, whenever our well-being or our basic values are at stake, labor is in the front line.

The visit of Pope John Paul has given us a chance to reflect on our basic values and the challenges to them. We cannot permit this chance to slip away. Let's seize this opportunity and make the most of it.

Perhaps the greatest gift the Pope gave us in his brief visit to our country was a chance to rethink what these four words mean, "One nation, under God." He lifted our eyes from petty concerns, sometimes selfish concerns, from the cynicism and the indifference that sometimes divides Americans one from another, to show us that we can unite for common purposes, as Americans, as children of God, or as citizens of a fragile world.

Now let us rededicate ourselves to a simple truth that together we can shape a bright future, together we can improve our own lives, that as a strong nation together, we can build a community of nations at peace.

We have within us the ability to make these dreams a reality. And I ask you, the building and construction workers of America, to help me make these wonderful dreams come true.

Thank you very much.

NOTE: The President spoke at 10:08 a.m. in the Convention Tent at the Islandia Hyatt House.

San Diego, California

Remarks at a Reception Hosted by the San Diego County Board of Supervisors. October 11, 1979

Congressman Van Deerlin and his beautiful and very wise, dedicated, competent, friendly constituents:

I'm glad to be with you. As a matter of fact, it's nice for me to come back home. As some of you may know, during the time of the Korean war, my wife, Rosalynn, and I and my older son, Jack, and Chip lived here in San Diego. Coronado was looked on as the retired naval officers' heaven, and I never quite reached that high and exalted position. I had to take second best, President of the United States—*[laughter]*—but it's not too late. It's not too late.

I was serving on the U.S.S. *Pomfret,* Submarine SS 391, and we tied up not at a dock, but at a submarine tender. And the only bad thing about where I lived was that I had to get up at a quarter to four every morning to catch a ride down to the pier to get a boat that didn't travel on a regular schedule out to the Navy tender and then get on a submarine to be there on time. And that's almost my most vivid memory of San Diego. [*Laughter*] That's right.

And I understand that they put a *freeway* through the house where I used to live. I cannot believe—[*laughter*]. It must have been under a Republican administration. [*Laughter*]

We had a good life there. Most of our neighbors spoke Spanish, and it gave me and Rosalynn a chance to learn that language. And we had an overwhelming expression of friendship for me and my wife and my two little children.

I went from there to be the only officer, as a matter of fact, on the first ship that the Navy built after the Second World War. And I went from that antisubmarine submarine to serve on one of the two nuclear-powered submarines, the first ones ever built. So, I had a good launching for my naval career from San Diego. I'm glad to be back.

This is a good trip for me also to express in the clearest possible ways to the Building and Construction Trade Union—they're having their annual convention here—some of the challenges, some of the problems, some of the opportunities which our Nation has to face together.

As I said in that talk, our Nation is strong. We need not fear the present or the future if we accurately assess the blessings which we've been given in this country, have confidence in one another, and have faith in the future. We can meet anything that arises. The rest of the world looks to us for leadership not only in material things—economic and military strength, political influence—but also, I hope and believe and pray, in ethical and moral standards, the things that have always been the core of American strength.

We've grown, I think, in the last 200 years. We've not gone backward. The vision that our Founding Fathers had in establishing this country are being realized more and more as each generation of Americans have a chance to serve our country together. We've opened up the processes of government to more and more people, to young people, to women and the others, which we didn't have before. Now Americans elect our U.S. Senators directly. Formerly, just State legislators made that choice. We've guaranteed rights to black citizens, to those who don't speak English well, to those recent newcomers to our country.

And I'm always reminded, as President,

trying to assess on a daily, sometimes an hourly basis, our strengths and our problems, that we are a nation of immigrants—we are really a nation of refugees. Our ancestors came here some 300 years ago, some, 3 years ago, to find a greater degree of freedom, a chance to be an individual, a chance to be different, a chance to assess our own God-given talents and to use them in the most productive and exciting way. And I hope we never dampen that sense of Americans being individuals when we choose, but also unifying in a time of challenge and testing.

It's obvious that we can unify ourselves and put aside petty differences and put aside unselfishness when we can see clearly that our Nation is threatened by a Great Depression of the thirties or by the First World War, the Second World War. Then families, communities become close to one another, and we honor our government, and we kind of minimize the mistakes that public officials make. And we say, "Our system is the best, I'm going to make it work," rather than withdrawing from it because of something we don't like on a transient basis.

And sometimes we forget, in the excitement of reading the news, where you only see the small failures and the transient inconveniences and the debates and the setbacks, we forget about the strengths and the blessings. And I believe that Americans are hungry now for a restoration and a reminder of those standards that never change, those commitments that never change, those human qualities that are always cherished in spite of temporary challenges.

We can overcome the energy challenge. It does threaten our security. I'm not exaggerating that. We buy now half the oil we use from foreign countries, from an uncertain source, and they change the price, and we can't control it. Four percentage points of our inflation rate are due directly to the increase in the price of oil charged to us by OPEC because we buy so much of it.

Next year we will send $70 billion of American money overseas—as I said in my speech earlier today—and not only does this make us dependent on foreign countries, but if that supply should be interrupted, it would cause severe problems for our economic structure.

You experienced that very slightly earlier this year with gasoline lines and temporary shortages of fuel for your automobiles, and it created semipanic in some communities. People spent half their time sitting in gasoline lines. Just with a slight interruption, we lost about 100 million barrels of oil because Iran had a revolution. They only produced about 3 million barrels a day out of over a hundred million in all in the world, but that little, slight interruption caused us to have severe problems.

What I'm trying to do now, with your help, is to get an energy program established for our Nation that will make us secure and to let us produce American oil and American gas and use American coal and depend on solar power and things that can be replenished and don't waste away. It's not easy. I'm the first President that ever tried it. After being bogged down in it for the last 2½ years, I can well understand why my predecessors did not do it. [*Laughter*]

As Congressman Van Deerlin would certainly certify, this is the most difficult and divisive issue perhaps that the Congress has ever addressed in the last 200 years of our existence. On every vote on natural gas or whatever, not only was the House and Senate exactly divided, but within the House and within the Senate and within the conference committees, almost a precise 50–50 division. But now consumers' voices are being heard more clearly, and the oil companies and others are beginning to see that the Nation's well-being must be put first. And in doing that, everyone will be better off. It's not a time for selfishness, it's not a time to gouge others, it's not a time even to find scapegoats or to try to blame those who might be responsible. We ought not to forget about that.

Inflation has been with us 10 or 11 years. We're trying to address it calmly and persistently. I have a fairly conservative philosophy about economics. We have cut the Federal deficit by $36 billion since I've been in office, more than 50 percent, almost 60 percent.

We have less Federal employees now than we had when I took office. We'll have less next year than we have now, in spite of tremendously increased government services available for our people because we are more efficient now than we used to be.

We're spending with the Federal Government a lower percentage of our gross national product than we did before. It was 23½ percent when I took office; now it's down to 21½ percent. We're trying to get government's nose out of the private and internal affairs of individual citizens and also out of the affairs of the free enterprise system.

When I got off the plane at the San Diego Airport, one of the first people that met me there was the president of a major airline that serves your State. He said, "Airline deregulation is the best thing that ever happened to the airline industry. We have not only reduced air fare sharply below what it formerly did, but we've got more paying passengers and our profits are higher." And when I met with the President of Mexico 2 weeks ago, he pointed out to me that tourists now are able to travel so much more cheaply that the number of tourists traveling to and from Mexico on airplanes have gone up 60 percent. So, deregulation and getting the Government's nose out of our business has paid off, and eventually, those things will help us with inflation.

I just want to mention two other things briefly. As I said to the construction workers, it is absolutely necessary that the Senate ratify SALT II. I need every one of you to help me with this. Alan Cranston is really one of the leaders in fighting for SALT II. We need both Senate votes. And I hope you'll use your own influence. Whether you're Democrats or Republicans is of no concern of mine on this particular issue. It's a bipartisan issue.

This treaty has been negotiated by three Presidents over a period of 7 years. If SALT II should be rejected, the consequences would be a severe blow to our country. We would have no way to monitor what the Soviets are doing. They could do everything they wanted to secretly, and every time we got a rumor of a new weapon for the Soviet Union or a new breakthrough for the Soviet Union or additional weapons for the Soviet Union, we would have to suspect the worst. It would create an enormous nuclear arms race, exactly the opposite of what we want, and the balance between ourselves and the Soviet Union would not be changed. It would just greatly escalate both of us in the percentage of our resources spent on nuclear weapons. We don't need that.

And also our allies in Europe look upon us as being responsible for containing and reducing the nuclear threat to them. And if the Soviets have accepted the treaty, which they have, and then the United States rejects it, it would be a clear signal to our own allies that we can-

not be trusted anymore to represent the Western World in controlling these terribly devastating weapons.

We couldn't control proliferation of nuclear explosives in other countries, because it would be very embarrassing for me to go to the Prime Minister of, say, India, or Pakistan—the President of Pakistan—and say, "Don't build a single nuclear explosion," and they would look at me and say, "You've got thousands, and you cannot even agree to limit additional thousands." It would mean that many countries would probably shift toward more and more dependence on a nuclear world.

So, I ask you to help me with this, and of course, we'll keep a strong defense. It's important to San Diego and to California and the Nation that we have a strong defense, not only a strong defense in general but especially a strong navy. That's one of my prime interests.

Let me say in closing that Congressman Van Deerlin and the board of supervisors here have been very gracious to let me come. I do have a challenging job to represent 220 million people well and to lead the greatest country on Earth. But it's a job that's not only challenging and sobering but also exciting and gratifying, because the strength that comes not from the office itself but from the interrelationship with literally tens of thousands, hundreds of thousands, millions of Americans who share with me a dream of an even greater America, a more peaceful world, a place where the quality of life can be maintained, where people can live in closer harmony, one with another, and where we together, under a democratic system, believing in freedom, committed to human rights for everyone, can make the greatest nation on Earth, our Nation, even greater in the future.

That's what I want. With your help, we'll do it.

Thank you.

NOTE: The President spoke at 11:05 a.m. in the Hotel del Coronado ballroom.

San Diego, California

Exchange With Reporters on Departure From Lindbergh Field. October 11, 1979

Q. [*Inaudible*]

THE PRESIDENT. No one can control the stock market or predict what it's going to do.

Q. [*Inaudible*]

THE PRESIDENT. I hope not. We've done everything we could in spite of high interest rates to hold up employment in the construction industry. And as I told the construction workers, ordinarily the first part of our economy which feels adversely high interest rates has been the homebuilding industry.

Since I've been in office, we've had an average, I think, and still maintain of about 1.8 million homes being built every year. But we've changed economic policy to accommodate that problem. I think we'll minimize unemployment.

Q. [*Inaudible*]—if the interest rate situation does begin to hit, can the construction industry be—[*inaudible*].

THE PRESIDENT. Yes, we are assessing it constantly. But I think right now our economic policies are sound and well-advised.

Q. Are we headed for a deeper recession because of the higher interest rates?

THE PRESIDENT. I don't believe so—we've been—but I think the degree of recession has been less than we had anticipated earlier this year.

Q. Why did the markets do what they have done for the past few days?

THE PRESIDENT. I can't comment on the market. I don't know anything about them.

Q. [*Inaudible*]

THE PRESIDENT. My first priority is to deal with inflation.

NOTE: The exchange began at approximately 12 noon.

Advisory Commission on Intergovernmental Relations

Appointment of Jason Boe as a Member. October 11, 1979

The President today announced the appointment of Jason Boe as a member of the Advisory Commission on Intergovernmental Relations for a 2-year term.

Boe is president of the Oregon State Senate. He replaces John Briscoe, whose term has expired.

Select Commission on Immigration and Refugee Policy

Appointment of Rev. Theodore Hesburgh as a Member and Chairman. October 11, 1979

The President today announced the appointment of Rev. Theodore Hesburgh as a member and Chairman of the Select Commission on Immigration and Refugee Policy. He replaces Reubin Askew, who has resigned from the Commission.

Father Hesburgh, 62, is Chairman of the U.S. Delegation to the United Nations Conference on Science and Technology for Development. He was president of the

University of Notre Dame from 1952 to 1977.

He was born May 25, 1917, in Syracuse, N.Y. He attended the University of Notre Dame from 1934 to 1937 and received a Ph. B. degree in 1940 from Gregorian University in Rome. He attended Holy Cross College from 1940 to 1943 and received an S.T.D. degree in 1945 from Catholic University. He was ordained to the priesthood in 1943.

From 1943 to 1944, he was chaplain for the National Training School for Boys in Washington, D.C. From 1945 to 1947, he was chaplain to veterans at the University of Notre Dame, and from 1948 to 1949, he was assistant professor of religion, then head of the department of religion. He was executive vice president of Notre Dame from 1949 to 1952.

The Select Commission on Immigration and Refugee Policy was created by law to "study and evaluate existing laws, policies and procedures governing the admission of immigrants and refugees to the United States and to make such administrative and legislative recommendations to the President and to the Congress as are appropriate." The Commission's final report is due on September 30, 1980.

The law creating the Commission was signed October 5, 1978. It is a 16-member commission. Four of the members are appointed by the President, four by the Speaker of the House from the membership of the House Judiciary Committee, and four by the President pro tem of the Senate from the membership of the Senate Judiciary Committee.

The other four members are the Secretary of State, the Attorney General, the Secretary of Labor, and the Secretary of Health, Education, and Welfare. The President appointed his four members March 22, 1979. They were Askew (Chairman), Rose Matsui Ochi (execu-

tive assistant to Mayor Tom Bradley, Los Angeles), Joaquin Francisco Otero (international vice president of the Brotherhood of Railway and Airline Clerks), and Cruz Reynoso (associate justice of the Third Appellate District in Sacramento, Calif.).

Energy Security Corporation

White House Statement on Senate Energy Committee Approval of the Legislation. October 11, 1979

The President welcomes the overwhelmingly favorable action by the Senate Energy Committee in establishing an energy security corporation. The legislation embodies the three elements which the President has said are essential to a synthetic fuels program: a long-term commitment to a substantial synthetic fuels effort, an independent entity to carry out this commitment, and the authority and immediate funding for a strong start.

The President is grateful to Chairman Jackson and Senators Johnston and Domenici, as well as to the other committee members, for the dedication and effort that led to the Committee's favorable vote. The President hopes the Senate will promptly follow the Energy Committee's vote so the Nation can soon begin the important task of producing synthetic fuels and reducing our need for foreign oil.

Home Heating Oil Supplies

Remarks to Reporters. October 12, 1979

I am pleased to announce that our 7-month effort to build up adequate home heating fuel oil stocks has succeeded. Figures released yesterday indicate that our stocks today are in the range of 235 million barrels. We are well ahead of last year at the same time, and it's clear that we're now at the point of achieving our goal of 240 million barrels in primary reserves.

This is a gratifying achievement which ensures that we will have enough home heating oil to meet our needs this winter. Having achieved this goal of primary heating oil stocks, our primary effort now will shift toward distributing these supplies as they are needed throughout the different regions of our country.

I've instructed Secretary Charlie Duncan of the Department of Energy to work with the major refiners and suppliers to assure proper distribution now as a first priority. The positive action already taken by the fuel distributors must be continued and expedited. No one needing fuel should be left unserved as the cold months approach. The Department of Energy will deal expeditiously when extraordinary circumstances might possibly cause temporary spot shortages.

Last April, our primary stocks were down to about 113 million barrels, which were 25 million barrels below the 1978 levels. At that time, I set as a goal the reaching of 240 million barrels in primary reserves. I want to commend the refiners for their cooperation and also applaud all Americans who've cut back on the waste of energy and increased their efforts to conserve energy to reduce overall demand for oil.

I urge continued restraint in energy consumption by all Americans, which will tend to hold down prices and also to prevent spot shortages. I'm also calling upon refiners to take the following steps: first, to maintain heating oil and diesel production at high levels to assure a continued flow of adequate supplies throughout this winter; also to distribute as much heating oil as possible now to sections of the country which might be visited by early snow and heavy snows or also early freezing of waterways used to transport fuel oil to the places of consumption.

We also want them to increase allocations to marketers, to accelerate deliveries to wholesalers and retailers before the full onset of the heavy heating season during the winter, and to maintain historical credit practices so that consumers will have an opportunity to purchase oil on the same credit terms as they have enjoyed in previous years.

I know that the increase in the price of oil will cause a hardship on some consumers and particularly those on low and fixed incomes. I urge the Congress to adopt without delay the measures I have proposed which will make $1.6 billion available this winter to assist the poor and the aged and others who are unable to meet the rapidly increasing energy costs. I have today sent the Congress a supplemental appropriations request for $1.2 billion to achieve this purpose.

With the passage of the windfall profits tax we will have the assurance each year, for the next 10 years, of $2.4 billion at least to accomplish the purposes of alleviating the heavy financial burden on the low-income families because of increased prices of energy. In addition. I have instructed the Small Business Administration to ensure that there is adequate assistance available to small suppliers who are in need of credit to make purchases for major supplies of home heating oil.

We are doing everything we can to prevent interruptions of supply, to make sure that supplies are adequate, to reduce the heavy burden on the poor families of increased energy costs, and to make sure that distributors have adequate credit to keep their supplies on hand during the coming months of the winter.

I'd like now to introduce the Secretary of Energy, who will answer questions from the media if you have details which you would like to have explored.

Charlie.

NOTE: The President spoke at 12:05 p.m. in the Briefing Room at the White House. Following his remarks, Secretary of Energy Charles W. Duncan, Jr., held a news conference on the President's announcement.

Federal Emergency Management Agency

Nomination of Frank A. Camm To Be an Associate Director. October 12, 1979

The President today announced that he will nominate Frank A. Camm, of Arlington, Va., to be an Associate Director of the Federal Emergency Management Agency. His area of responsibility would be plans and preparedness.

Camm has been Deputy to the Director of Central Intelligence since 1977.

He was born March 13, 1922, in Fort Knox, Ky. He is a graduate of West Point and holds masters degrees from Harvard University in civil engineering and George Washington University in international affairs.

Camm was commissioned in the Army Corps of Engineers, and early in his career served at the Pentagon and worked on the Manhattan Project. In 1969 he was promoted to brigadier general and took charge of the Corps of Engineers construction on Army and Air Force bases west of the Rockies and on river and harbor and civil emergency work in a similar area. In 1972 he became Assistant General Manager for Military Application in the Atomic Energy Commission.

In 1973 Camm became military director for the civilian Army Materiel Acquisition Review Committee. In 1974 he joined the Army staff to supervise strategic plans and operations, organization, materiel needs, command-control, and help in domestic emergencies.

In 1975 he was promoted to lieutenant general and became deputy commanding general of the U.S. Army Training and Doctrine Command. He retired from active duty in 1977.

Federal Energy Regulatory Commission

Nomination of Charles B. Curtis To Be a Member, and Designation as Chairman. October 12, 1979

The President today announced that he will nominate Charles B. Curtis for reappointment as a member of the Federal Energy Regulatory Commission for a term expiring October 1, 1983. He also announced that he would redesignate Curtis as Chairman of the Commission on confirmation. Curtis has been a member and Chairman of the Commission since 1977.

He was born April 27, 1940, in Upper Darby, Pa. He received a B.S. from the University of Massachusetts in 1962 and an LL.B. from Boston University Law School in 1965.

From 1965 to 1967, Curtis was a staff attorney, then supervising staff attorney in the Office of the Comptroller of the Currency. From 1967 to 1971, he served on the Securities and Exchange Commission as special counsel to the Division of Trading and Markets, Chief of the Branch of Regulation and Inspections, and attorney-adviser (finance).

Curtis was counsel to the House Committee on Interstate and Foreign Commerce from 1971 to 1976, with special emphasis on energy and securities regulation. From November 1976 to January 1977, he worked for the Carter-Mondale transition team as liaison to the Federal Energy Administration.

Curtis was with the Washington law firm of Van Ness, Curtis, Feldman & Sutcliffe from January 1977 until August 1977, when he became Chairman of the Federal Power Commission. He became Chairman of the Federal Energy Regulatory Commission in October 1977, when it was created by the Department of Energy legislation.

Interstate Commerce Commission

Designation of Darius W. Gaskins, Jr., as Chairman. October 12, 1979

The President today announced that he will designate Darius W. Gaskins, Jr., as Chairman of the Interstate Commerce Commission, effective January 1, 1980.

Gaskins has been a member of the ICC since earlier this year. He replaces Daniel O'Neal as Chairman, who has announced his resignation, effective December 31, 1979.

Gaskins, 40, of Washington, D.C., is an economist with regulatory experience. He has served as Deputy Assistant Secretary of Energy for Policy Analysis, Director of the Office of Economic Analysis of the Civil Aeronautics Board, Director of the Bureau of Economics of the Federal Trade Commission, and as a professor of economics at the University of California at Berkeley.

Agency for International Development

Nomination of Genta A. Hawkins To Be an Assistant Administrator. October 12, 1979

The President today announced that he will nominate Genta A. Hawkins, of Huntington Park, Calif., to be an Assistant Administrator of the Agency for International Development (AID). She would replace Jean P. Lewis, and her area of responsibility would be legislative affairs.

Hawkins has been legislative management officer for foreign aid in the Office of Congressional Relations at the State Department since 1978.

She was born September 3, 1940, in Anadarko, Okla. She received a B.A. from the University of Southern California in 1962, and took graduate studies in international relations at the London School of Economics and Political Science in 1962–63.

From 1964 to 1966, Hawkins was director of AID's "Self-Help" program in Abidjan, and from 1966 to 1968, she was liaison officer for U.S. and international voluntary agencies in the Office of the Special Assistant to the Secretary for Refugee and Migration Affairs at the State Department. From 1968 to 1970, she was special assistant to the U.S. Ambassador to France. In 1970 she was secretary of the U.S. Delegation to the Committee of the Conference on Disarmament in Geneva.

From 1972 to 1973, Hawkins was deputy public affairs officer at the regional Office of Economic Opportunity in New York. She took economic studies at the Foreign Service Institute and served as a loan officer in the State Department's Office of Development Finance from

1973 to 1974. From 1974 to 1977, she was chief of the economic/commercial section and AID liaison officer at the American Embassy in Nassau. From 1977 to 1978, she was a Congressional Fellow, serving as legislative assistant to Senator Gary Hart and Congressman David Obey.

Highway Safety and National Traffic and Motor Vehicle Safety Acts of 1966

Message to the Congress Transmitting Two Reports.   October 12, 1979

To the Congress of the United States:

The 1966 traffic safety legislation which initiated a cohesive national effort to curb deaths, injuries and accidents on the Nation's highways also requires that annual reports be rendered to the Congress on the administration of the Acts. This is the 12th year these reports have described the problems and the remedies that have been applied to ameliorate them.

The report on motor vehicle safety includes the annual reporting requirement in Title I of the Motor Vehicle Information and Cost Savings Act of 1972 (bumper standards). An annual report also is required by the Energy Policy and Conservation Act of 1975 which amended the Motor Vehicle Information and Cost Savings Act and directed the Secretary of Transportation to set, adjust and enforce motor vehicle fuel economy standards. Similar reporting requirements are contained in the Department of Energy Act of 1978 with respect to the use of advanced technology by the automobile industry. These requirements have been met in the Third Annual Fuel Economy Re-

port, the highlights of which are summarized in the motor vehicle safety report.

In the Highway Safety Acts of 1973 and 1976, the Congress expressed its special interest in certain aspects of traffic safety which are addressed in the volume on highway safety. The annual reporting requirements set forth in the Highway Safety Act of 1978 will be covered in future editions of this report as may be appropriate.

JIMMY CARTER

The White House,
    October 12, 1979.

NOTE: The reports are entitled "Highway Safety 1978: A Report on Activities Under the Highway Safety Act of 1966 as Amended, January 1, 1978–December 31, 1978—U.S. Department of Transportation, National Highway Traffic Safety Administration, Federal Highway Administration" (Government Printing Office, 67 pages plus appendices) and "Motor Vehicle Safety 1978: A Report on Activities Under the National Traffic and Motor Vehicle Safety Act of 1966 and the Motor Vehicle Information and Cost Savings Act of 1972, January 1, 1978–December 31, 1978—U.S. Department of Transportation, National Highway Traffic Safety Administration" (Government Printing Office, 57 pages plus appendices).

Digest of Other White House Announcements

The following listing includes the President's public schedule and other items of general interest announced by the White House Press Office and not included elsewhere in this issue.

October 6

The President met at the White House with Zbigniew Brzezinski, Assistant to the President for National Security Affairs.

The President and his family met with Pope John Paul II in the Residence.

October 9

The President met at the White House with:

—Dr. Brzezinski;

—Frank B. Moore, Assistant to the President for Congressional Liaison.

The President met in the Oval Office with Manny Mota, an outfielder for the Los Angeles Dodgers professional baseball team, to congratulate him on breaking the major league record for pinch hits.

The President participated in a briefing on the administration's programs and policies given for civic and community leaders from Iowa in the East Room at the White House.

October 10

The President met at the White House with:

—David L. Aaron, Deputy Assistant for National Security Affairs;

—the Democratic congressional leadership;

—Mr. Moore;

—Vice President Walter F. Mondale;

—Gen. Bernard W. Rogers, Supreme Allied Commander, Europe, and Commander in Chief of U.S. Forces in Europe.

The President participated in a briefing by administration officials on energy legislation and the windfall profits tax given for civic and community leaders in the East Room at the White House.

October 11

The White House announced that the President and Mrs. Carter have accepted the invitation of Prime Minister Clark to visit Canada on November 9 and 10. President Carter will be accompanied by a party of senior officials. During the visit the President will address a joint meeting of the Senate and the House of Commons.

The President transmitted to the Congress the 1977 and 1978 annual reports of the Civil Service Commission.

October 12

The President met at the White House with:

—Dr. Brzezinski;

—Vice President Mondale, Secretary of State Cyrus R. Vance, Secretary of Defense Harold Brown, Hedley W. Donovan, Senior Adviser to the President, Hamilton Jordan, Assistant to the President, and Dr. Brzezinski;

—Mr. Moore;

—Senator William V. Roth, Jr., of Delaware;

—James T. McIntyre, Jr., Director of the Office of Management and Budget;

—Joseph M.A.H. Luns, Secretary-General of the North Atlantic Treaty Organization.

In a ceremony in the Oval Office, the President received diplomatic credentials from Ambassadors John Tzounis of Greece, Enriquillo Antonio del Rosario Ceballos of the Dominican Republic, Raoul Schoumaker of Belgium, Joshua Luyimbazi Zake of Uganda, and Ricardo Crespo Zaldumbide of Ecuador.

The President participated in a briefing by administration officials on the strategic arms limitation treaty given for community leaders in the East Room at the White House.

NOMINATIONS SUBMITTED TO THE SENATE

The following list does not include promotions of members of the Uniformed Services, nominations to the Service Academies, or nominations of Foreign Service officers.

Submitted October 9, 1979

RUTH M. DAVIS, of Maryland, to be an Assistant Secretary of Energy (Resource Applications), vice George S. McIsaac, resigned.

NOMINATIONS—Continued

Submitted October 9—Continued

WILLIAM WALKER LEWIS, of the District of Columbia, to be an Assistant Secretary of Energy (Policy and Evaluation), vice Alvin L. Alm, resigned.

JOHN N. GENTRY, of Virginia, to be Under Secretary of Labor, vice Robert J. Brown, resigned.

Submitted October 10, 1979

ANNE FORRESTER HOLLOWAY, of the District of Columbia, to be Ambassador Extraordinary and Plenipotentiary of the United States of America to the Republic of Mali.

ROBERT B. OAKLEY, of Louisiana, a Foreign Service officer of Class one, to be Ambassador Extraordinary and Plenipotentiary of the United States of America to the Republic of Zaire.

Submitted October 11, 1979

NATHAN J. STARK, of Pennsylvania, to be Under Secretary of Health, Education, and Welfare, vice Hale Champion, resigned.

ANDREW L. JEFFERSON, JR., of Texas, to be United States Circuit Judge for the Fifth Circuit, vice a new position created by P.L. 95–486, approved October 20, 1978.

CECIL F. POOLE, of California, to be United States Circuit Judge for the Ninth Circuit, vice a new position created by P.L. 95–486, approved October 20, 1978.

WILLIAM O. BERTELSMAN, of Kentucky, to be United States District Judge for the Eastern District of Kentucky, vice a new position created by P.L. 95–486, approved October 20, 1978.

PETER HILL BEER, of Louisiana, to be United States District Judge for the Eastern District of Louisiana, vice a new position created by P.L. 95–486, approved October 20, 1978.

L. T. SENTER, JR., of Mississippi, to be United States District Judge for the Northern District of Mississippi, vice Orma R. Smith, retired.

JAMES T. GILES, of Pennsylvania, to be United States District Judge for the Eastern District of Pennsylvania, vice Herbert A. Fogel, resigned.

LUCIUS DESHA BUNTON III, of Texas, to be United States District Judge for the Western District of Texas, vice John H. Wood, Jr., deceased.

HARRY LEE HUDSPETH, of Texas, to be United States District Judge for the Western District of Texas, vice Adrian A. Spears, retired.

NOMINATIONS—Continued

Submitted October 11—Continued

CHARLES FREDERICK CARSON RUFF, of the District of Columbia, to be United States Attorney for the District of Columbia for the term of 4 years, vice Earl J. Silbert, resigned.

TERRY LEE PECHOTA, of South Dakota, to be United States Attorney for the District of South Dakota for the term of 4 years, vice David V. Vrooman, resigned.

CHECKLIST OF WHITE HOUSE PRESS RELEASES

The following listing contains releases of the White House Press Office which are not included in this issue.

Released October 6, 1979

Advance text: remarks at the welcoming ceremony for Pope John Paul II

Advance text: remarks at a White House reception for the Pope

Released October 10, 1979

Advance text: remarks at the annual convention of the Building and Construction Trades Department, AFL–CIO, in San Diego, Calif.

Released October 11, 1979

Announcement: nomination of Andrew Jefferson, Jr., to be United States Circuit Judge for the Fifth Circuit

Announcement: nomination of Cecil F. Poole to be United States Circuit Judge for the Ninth Circuit

Announcement: nomination of James T. Giles to be United States District Judge for the Eastern District of Pennsylvania

Announcement: nomination of William O. Bertelsman to be United States District Judge for the Eastern District of Kentucky

Announcement: nomination of L. T. Senter, Jr., to be United States District Judge for the Northern District of Mississippi

Announcement: nomination of Peter Hill Beer to be United States District Judge for the Eastern District of Louisiana

Announcement: nomination of Harry Lee Hudspeth to be United States District Judge for the Western District of Texas

Announcement: nomination of Lucius Desha Bunton III to be United States District Judge for the Western District of Texas

Announcement: nomination of Charles F. C. Ruff to be United States Attorney for the District of Columbia

CHECKLIST—Continued

Released October 11—Continued

Announcement: nomination of Terry Lee Pechota to be United States Attorney for the District of South Dakota

Advance text: remarks at the Kasimir Pulaski memorial dinner in Savannah, Ga.—by Zbigniew Brzezinski, Assistant to the President for National Security Affairs

Released October 12, 1979

News conference: on the President's remarks concerning home heating oil supplies—by Secretary of Energy Charles W. Duncan, Jr.

ACTS APPROVED BY THE PRESIDENT

Approved October 6, 1979

H.J. Res. 303_____ Public Law 96–80
A joint resolution authorizing and requesting the President of the United States to issue a proclamation designating the seven calendar days beginning October 7, 1979, as "National Port Week".

S. 721_____ Public Law 96–81
Civil Rights Commission Authorization Act of 1979.

ACTS APPROVED—Continued

Approved October 10, 1979

S. 237_____ Public Law 96–82
Federal Magistrate Act of 1979.

S. 756_____ Public Law 96–83
Office of Federal Procurement Policy Act Amendments of 1979.

H.R. 3920_____ Public Law 96–84
An act to amend the Unemployment Compensation Amendments of 1976 with respect to the National Commission on Unemployment Compensation, and for other purposes.

S. 233_____ Public Law 96–85
An act to amend the International Travel Act of 1961 to authorize additional appropriations, and for other purposes.

Approved October 12, 1979

H.J. Res. 412_____ Public Law 96–86
A joint resolution making continuing appropriations for the fiscal year 1980, and for other purposes.

H.R. 5419_____ Public Law 96–87
An act to authorize the Secretary of the Interior to provide for the commemoration of the efforts of Goodloe Byron to protect the Appalachian Trail, and for other purposes.

"Ask the President"

Remarks During a Telephone Call-out
Program on National Public Radio.
October 13, 1979

ANNOUNCER. From National Public Radio in Washington, this is "Ask the President," a live, 2-hour broadcast with President Jimmy Carter. President Carter will be speaking with Americans by telephone from the Oval Office. The questions will not be screened before they are put to the President. For technical reasons, listeners cannot call in to the White House or National Public Radio. NPR will call out to questioners. For several weeks now, on radio, television, and in newspaper ads, Americans have been notified of this broadcast. They were invited to send NPR their names and phone numbers if they wished to ask Mr. Carter a question. The names are being selected at random, and National Public Radio staff members are now placing the calls.

Here now in the Oval Office with President Carter, NPR's Susan Stamberg, your host for "Ask the President."

Ms. STAMBERG. Good afternoon, President Carter. It's good to have you with us.

THE PRESIDENT. Thank you, Susan. I'm looking forward to it.

Ms. STAMBERG. This is a format that you enjoy a lot, isn't it, this radio-telephone business?

THE PRESIDENT. It is. I've not only done it here in the Oval Office, but for instance, when I went down the Mississippi River on a paddle-wheel steamboat——

Ms. STAMBERG. That's right.

THE PRESIDENT. ——we stopped and had a telephone call-in show. And in addition to that, whenever I have a chance, I go out into the country and, with several hundred or sometimes several thousand people present, take questions from the audience in an unrehearsed way. You get a lot different kind of question that relates more directly to people than just the ordinary political questions, very good——

Ms. STAMBERG. Do you think they are as intense—the questions that you get from citizens—as the sort that you would get from the Washington press corps?

THE PRESIDENT. Without exhibiting prejudice, I think they're much more intense and much more heartfelt. It's a rare thing for a citizen to have a chance to ask a question directly to a President, and quite often that remark or that question is the most important thing in a person's life, at least at that moment. Sometimes there's just a friendly exchange, you know, people saying, "Glad to talk to you, Mr. President, wish you well." But ordinarily the questions asked are extremely important to that person.

Ms. STAMBERG. Well, let's get to some of those questions.

Before we take the first call, I have a few cautionary notes to make to our callers. Please, folks, keep your questions short, no speeches, no filibustering, or I'm going to have to cut you off. And the reason for this is not that I'm rude, it's that we want to get a chance to have as many of you on the line as possible. Also, when you are speaking with the President, stay on the phone as he is giving you his answer. In case you have any followup questions that you want to ask, you'll have that opportunity.

All right, Mr. President, the first call is from David A. MacIver, in Springfield, Massachusetts. Go ahead, Mr. MacIver.

INCOME TAX REFORM

MR. MacIVER. Good afternoon, sir.

THE PRESIDENT. Hello, David.

MR. MacIVER. I'd like to ask about possible income tax reform and the guides to the inequities between filing as a married person versus a single person. Being married and with two incomes, presently we pay more than two comparable single persons would. Also, I'd like to know why a certain amount of interest couldn't be earned before taxing it, as an incentive to the small saver.

THE PRESIDENT. Thank you, David.

We've attempted, as you know, since I've been in office, to have some income tax reform measures passed and have been partially successful. One of the major issues that has been addressed, on which I've talked with the chairman of

the Finance Committee in the Senate and the Ways and Means Committee in the House, is to remove that inequity between a married couple and two individuals who are single. Now there is a penalty against marriage, in effect, and I think it would be a good step to remove that inequity.

We at this time are concentrating on controlling inflation, which is our biggest single economic threat, and we are not working on any income tax reductions for the time being.

In the future, if we do go to an income tax reduction proposal, one of the considerations would be to encourage saving, as you've described, and also to encourage investment to make sure we have additional jobs available in the future. Another one is to provide more equity or fairness among people who have to pay income taxes, and of course, another one would be to reduce inflation itself. There are some types of income tax reductions which could contribute to reduced inflation.

We've been successful in reducing income taxes since I've been in office. I think next year, for instance, the income tax reductions that we've already initiated will amount to about $40 billion, and at the same time, we've cut the Federal deficit down by $36 billion. So, we are making some progress, still have a long way to go.

The suggestions that you made are very interesting and, I think, good ones.

Ms. STAMBERG. Mr. MacIver, anything else that you wanted to ask?

MR. MacIVER. No. Thank you very much.

Ms. STAMBERG. Good. Thank you so much.

The next caller, Mr. President, is Mrs. Mary Tingle, in Louisville, Kentucky.

Go ahead, Mrs. Tingle; you're on the line with President Carter.

PRAYER IN SCHOOLS

MRS. TINGLE. President Carter, first, we love you, your family, and Miss Lillian. And the question is, our Nation was built on trust in God, and a lot of our young people don't know Him. And why can't we have prayer in school?

MS. STAMBERG. Mrs. Tingle, we had a little bit of trouble hearing you.

THE PRESIDENT. I think I understood her. She said, "Why don't we have prayer in school?"

MRS. TINGLE. Yes.

THE PRESIDENT. Mary, as you know, I'm a Christian and a Baptist, and I believe very strongly in the separation of church and state, which is guaranteed under our Constitution.

MRS. TINGLE. I know.

THE PRESIDENT. I am in favor of voluntary prayer in school and the right of each person to worship God in his or her own way at any time one is motivated. I pray frequently in my own daily life as President, more so now than I used to, I might say.

I don't believe, though, that it's proper for a government entity, either the Federal Government or local government or even a school board, to require that children worship in school. And sometimes even a small child would be embarrassed if, for instance, there are different faiths represented in the classroom. Sometimes the children don't worship God at all; sometimes they might be Jewish or Christian, sometimes Catholics and Protestants, sometimes in our modern-day society even those who are Moslems. And I think that to mandate or to require a person to worship in school is not proper.

The Supreme Court has ruled on this,

and the Supreme Court ruling is basically in accordance with what I've just described to you as my preference.

MS. STAMBERG. Thank you very much, Mrs. Tingle.

The next caller is Mrs. Annette Lantos, and she's calling from Hillsborough, California. Good morning. It's morning for you, isn't it, Mrs. Lantos? You're on the line with President Carter.

RAOUL WALLENBERG

MRS. LANTOS. Mr. President, when my husband and I were youngsters in Hungary during World War II, our lives were saved through the intervention of a Swedish diplomat named Raoul Wallenberg. We later learned that Mr. Wallenberg, who also saved the lives of thousands of other Jewish people like us, was acting in behalf of the American State Department. But unfortunately, Mr. Wallenberg was arrested at the end of the war by the Russians and has been in a Russian prison ever since. And although the Russians claim that he died, there is an overwhelming amount of evidence which indicates that he's still alive in a Soviet prison. Could you do something, Mr. President, to help him get released?

THE PRESIDENT. There's a limit to what I can do. We have inquired into the Wallenberg case with the Russians, both when I was in Vienna this year with President Brezhnev and other Russian leaders, and through the Soviet Ambassador here in Washington and also our Ambassador in Moscow. On occasions, when Secretary Vance has met with Foreign Minister Gromyko, we've also inquired about the Wallenberg case, along with the cases of many others.

The Soviets maintain their claim that Mr. Wallenberg is no longer alive, but we are not forgetting about this case and will continue our efforts.

MRS. LANTOS. Thank you very much, Mr. President. I hope you will.

MS. STAMBERG. Thank you, Mrs. Lantos.

The next caller is in Jacksonville, Florida. It's Mrs. Carol A. Whitcomb. Go ahead, Mrs. Whitcomb, you're on the line with President Carter.

ADDRESSING THE PRESIDENT

MRS. WHITCOMB. President Carter?

THE PRESIDENT. Good morning.

MRS. WHITCOMB. I just want to say that this is really an honor to talk to you, and I'm so thrilled. I want to tell you also, I went down to Tampa on August 30 to see you, and I really enjoyed your speech. But my question is really a complaint about the news media, how they always tend to call you Mr. Carter. And to me, I think they should show you the respect that is due to you by calling you President Carter. And that is really the only thing I have to say except that I just wanted to talk to you.

THE PRESIDENT. Well, thank you very much, Carol. I hope I can meet you personally sometime.

MRS. WHITCOMB. I hope so, too, President Carter. And also, is there any way I can get a letter saying that I talked to you, so I can have it to show to my children?

THE PRESIDENT. Well, there are literally hundreds of thousands of people listening to us, and I will also write you a letter.

MRS. WHITCOMB. Thank you, sir, I really appreciate it.

THE PRESIDENT. Let me comment on your comment, first of all, before we quit. I hope you don't forget to go to the caucuses today; everybody in Florida ought to participate.

MRS. WHITCOMB. Yes, sir, I saw that.

THE PRESIDENT. Good. And the second thing is that I believe we ought to have the President addressed by "Mr." It's perfectly all right.

When Washington became the first President, there was a move made to give him some sort of title, and he objected to this. And there was some doubt about how he should be addressed during his term of office, and also John Adams. When Thomas Jefferson became President, he insisted that everyone call him "Mr. Jefferson."

And so, I don't have any objection to that. The President ought not to be honored any more than just being able to hold the office, and so "President Carter" or "Mr. President" is also very good. And when I drive down the streets—for instance, recently in Tampa for a townhall meeting—and the children and everybody yell "Hi, Jimmy," I also am thrilled by the friendship. But I think "Mr. Carter" or "President Carter" are both appropriate.

MS. STAMBERG. Thanks very much, Mrs. Whitcomb.

The next call comes from Jerry Johnson, and he's calling from Flint, Michigan. Go ahead, Mr. Johnson, you're on the line with President Carter.

STRATEGIC ARMS LIMITATION

MR. JOHNSON. Good afternoon, Mr. President.

THE PRESIDENT. Good afternoon, Jerry.

MR. JOHNSON. How are you?

THE PRESIDENT. Fine.

MR. JOHNSON. Okay, I have a question here concerning the SALT treaty.

THE PRESIDENT. Okay.

MR. JOHNSON. All right. If it's rejected by the Senate—and I know there's doubts right now—what are your future options concerning arms reductions? And is verification really the chief obstacle to its ratification right now?

THE PRESIDENT. Jerry, if the SALT II treaty is rejected, this would be a severe blow to our country, to our Nation's security, and to the prospects for world peace. SALT II is a treaty that's been negotiated over a 7-year period by three different Presidents—two Republicans and myself as a Democrat. It's a carefully negotiated treaty that is in the best interest of our own country and also, I might add, in the best interest of the Soviet Union and all those who want peace on Earth.

We have adequate means to verify compliance with the SALT II treaty. We do not depend on trusting the Soviet Union. We have our own national technical means that we can use to make sure that the Soviets do honor every provision in the SALT II treaty. If we should detect in the future—and we have that ability— any evidence that the Soviets are violating the treaty, then we have the right under the terms of the treaty itself to terminate the treaty at that moment.

Another thing that I'd like to point out to you are the consequences of rejection. It would end, really, a 30-year process toward controlling nuclear weapons throughout the world, particularly in our country and the Soviet Union. If that was ended, it would be very difficult to recommence it, and if we did start another 2- or 3- or 7-year negotiation, the chances are very high that the final product would be almost identical to what we have negotiated this time.

In addition, a lot of countries around the world—our allies, like those in Europe, Japan, the less developed countries, nonaligned nations like India, for instance— look upon us and the Soviet Union as having a major responsibility to negotiate successfully. We have negotiated successfully. The Soviets have, in effect, adopted the treaty, because they don't have democratic processes, but we still have to get the approval of the Senate.

If the Senate should vote no on SALT, this would be a clear signal to the people all over Earth that our country is not indeed committed to the control of nuclear weapons adequately, and the Soviets would be given a tremendous and undeserved propaganda weapon to use against us. They would say, falsely, that they are a nation committed to peace and the control of nuclear weapons, but that we, because the Senate rejected SALT II, are a nation that's not inclined toward peace and the control of nuclear weapons. That would be a false claim, but it would be a very powerful political weapon that the Soviets could use.

What I want to do is to maintain equivalency and equality of nuclear capability, reduce sharply in the future atomic weaponry, and then compete with the Soviet Union on a peaceful basis, because we've got all the advantages on our side—democracy, freedom, respect for human rights, basic ethical standards, deep religious commitments. On a peaceful basis, we can compete and win. We don't want to compete on a warlike basis, but we're going to stay strong enough to deter any potential aggressor from daring to attack us. SALT II would accomplish all these worthy goals.

MS. STAMBERG. Mr. Johnson, does that answer your question?

MR. JOHNSON. Yes, it does.

Mr. President, I'd like to know if you're coming back to Flint next—well, I hope you do come back to Flint next year. I remember you were here in '76.

THE PRESIDENT. I hope, too, yes.

MR. JOHNSON. Yes. Thank you.

MS. STAMBERG. Thank you, Mr. Johnson.

President Carter, Senator Frank Church has said that he wants to attach an understanding to the SALT treaty which, in effect, says it won't go into effect until you can provide him with some assurances that that Soviet troop problem in Cuba has been solved. Do you think that's feasible? Is that a reasonable request?

THE PRESIDENT. I don't think it's necessary. My own belief is, Susan, that the SALT II treaty ought to be accepted or rejected on its own merits. Does it indeed enhance the security of our Nation? It's obvious to me that it does. Does it indeed contribute to world peace? And I think there's no doubt that it does. Is the treaty fair? The answer is yes. Can it be verified? The answer is yes.

The Senate will go into the debate on SALT II, hopefully, around the first of November, and I don't have any doubt that there will be some requests by the Members of the Senate for clarification of its terms or maybe for some requirements on us in the future. Those will be carefully considered, but my own judgment now is that those kind of amendments and so forth are not needed. If they come, we'll just have to assess them on an individual basis.

Ms. STAMBERG. Thank you.

Before we take the next question, I want to remind our listeners that what you're hearing is a live, 2-hour telephone program with President Carter from the Oval Office at the White House. National Public Radio welcomes your participation, but, alas, you cannot call us; we have to do the phoning out to you. For some weeks now, citizens have been sending NPR cards with their names, addresses, and phone numbers on them, and the cards are now being chosen at random. The calls are being placed from Washington. So, please don't call us; we'll call you.

The next call is from Mrs. Jeanette Lindstrom in Sun City, Arizona. Go ahead, Mrs. Lindstrom.

U.S. MARINES IN GUANTANAMO

MRS. LINDSTROM. President Carter.

THE PRESIDENT. Yes, Jeanette.

MRS. LINDSTROM. Yes. I'm so thrilled to be talking with you. I'm just getting over a bad cold, so you'll have to excuse my scratchy voice.

THE PRESIDENT. It sounds beautiful. And I'm glad to talk to you, too.

MRS. LINDSTROM. I'm so thrilled to be talking with you; I'm so excited.

I'm concerned about the Marines in Guantanamo. I lost a brother in World War II. He was a Marine, and this has got me quite upset about the Marines being down there. Can you assure me, Mr. President, that they are not there for any other purpose than what the media is telling us?

THE PRESIDENT. Yes, I can assure you of that. We have a perfect right to be in Guantanamo and to have a military base there. This is in accordance, Jeanette, with a 1903 treaty. This treaty was reconfirmed by the Cuban Government in 1934, and after Fidel Castro became the head of the Cuban Government, he reconfirmed to us the right of the United States to have this small military base. From time to time, as a matter of routine military maneuvers, we've put in more troops there for a few days or a few weeks and then take them out just to practice on military affairs, as is common for all nations on Earth.

There is no prospect for a war or for conflict or for combat. It's a very safe thing to do. We're going to stay in Guantanamo in accordance with our negotiated rights, and there need be no concern on your part.

Mrs. LINDSTROM. Oh, thank you, and I feel better about that. And God bless you, President Carter.

THE PRESIDENT. Well, I hope your cold's better soon.

Mrs. LINDSTROM. Thank you.

Ms. STAMBERG. Thank you, Mrs. Lindstrom.

The next call is Mr. Adrian Boles, and he's on the line with us from Madison, Wisconsin. Go ahead, Mr. Boles.

ENERGY AND THE NATION'S ECONOMY

MR. BOLES. Good afternoon, Mr. President.

THE PRESIDENT. Hello, Adrian.

MR. BOLES. The reason why I'm calling is, you like to hear what people feel like. And when I go to a bank, the interest rates have gone up, and when I go to the food store, that has gone up. And, you know, inflation has really affected the country, especially when it comes down to me personally. And, you know, I've had loans on my car—and luckily, I got them years ago, because I'm still paying for the car. But the problem is that everything has gone up, Mr. President. And I know you're trying to do the best you can, but, you know, when you have—I think it's a Democratic Congress, I believe, you're working with?

THE PRESIDENT. That's correct. Adrian, this is one of the biggest responsibilities that I have and the biggest problems that I have as President.

I'm the fourth President now who's tried to deal with excessive inflation. Most of the inflation is uncontrollable, at least in the short term, and a great portion of it has been caused by the, I think, unnecessary and excessive increases in energy costs put on us by the OPEC countries, both in 1973, when they quadrupled the price of oil, and even in this last 8 or 9 months,

when they've increased energy prices or oil prices by 60 percent. For instance, if we didn't have energy, if we could remove the energy part of the inflation picture, then during this past summer, say, June, July, August, we would have the same inflation rate that we had a year ago or 2 years ago. And now about 4 percent of the inflation rate is caused by these increases in oil prices.

What we're trying to do is to deal with inflation on a long-term and consistent and persistent basis. We're not going to back down on it. Obviously, a major unmet need is to have an energy policy in our country that reduces dependence on imported oil.

We not only import about 8½ million barrels of oil from foreign countries every day, but we import along with it inflation and unemployment. Next year we'll send overseas $70 billion in American money to pay for oil that we are importing. That's why we've needed so long and the Congress is now working so hard on getting a national energy policy. This would depend primarily on conservation, and we're trying to encourage every American to cut back on the waste of energy of all kinds, to save energy.

We're going to shift toward the kinds of energy in our country that's so plentiful, for instance, solar power and replenishable supplies of energy that come from wood and growing plants—gasohol is one evidence of that—geothermal heat underneath the surface of the Earth that we've just begun to tap. We've got a lot of coal that would last six or seven hundred years. We're going to increase the use of it and have it in such a form that it wouldn't create low-quality air or violate our environmental standards.

These kinds of things will let us cut back on the future dependence of imported oil, I would say at least two-thirds by the year 1990, and at the same time help to control inflation.

There's no way that we can avoid, at this time, having high interest rates, because interest rates go with inflation, and the best way to get the interest rates down is to reduce inflation.

One other comment I might make very quickly is that we've tried to do it through Government action as well. For instance, we've cut the Federal budget deficit since I've been in office more than 50 percent, by $36 billion. We have about 20,000 fewer Federal employees now than we had in 1976, in spite of the fact that we are delivering more services. And we've cut down the portion of our gross national product, everything America produces, that's being collected and spent by the Federal Government. These kinds of things in the long run will have a good impact on inflation.

So far, we are dealing with it on a broad base. I believe that the inflation rate will turn downward during the end of this year and, I hope, continue downward in the years ahead.

MR. BOLES. Okay. I like that answer, Mr. President, because, you know, like I said, my apartment where I live is insulated. So, that has really cut down the cost as far as heating. And a lot of people are saying, well, that costs too much and this and this. But you've got to have that because it saves a lot on heating bills.

THE PRESIDENT. I think in the long run our awareness that energy supplies might be short and the prices very high will encourage Americans to do what we've always needed to do, that is, stop waste of energy and have conservation efforts on our own.

I hope that every American listening, by the way, to my voice now, every family will kind of get together before the day is over and decide how that particular family can cut back on the waste of energy in their homes, on their jobs, or traveling. That will be the biggest single one thing that we can do to control inflation in the future.

MR. BOLES. Just like me, personally, I will drive to work every day—and I don't live too far from my job—but in the wintertime I will drive, too. But if there was some mass transportation, I wouldn't have to depend on my car. We have buses. But when I leave at 1 o'clock in the morning to go home, then there's no buses anymore, and I don't want to take my chances.

THE PRESIDENT. That's a good point. I hope you've got more than one person in your car when you go to work.

MS. STAMBERG. Mr. Boles, thank you so much for joining us today. We appreciate it.

President Carter, that sparks a question from me, and that is, there are nations in Europe, also Japan, where they're paying $2 a gallon for gasoline.

THE PRESIDENT. Or even more, $2.70.

MS. STAMBERG. Or more, yeah. But their inflation is lower than ours and their unemployment rate is lower than ours. Why can't we do that?

THE PRESIDENT. Let me tell you why. In the past our gasoline prices have— say, just even in recent months, have been 90 cents. If gasoline prices all over the world go up 10 cents a gallon, and ours go from 90 cents to $1, that's about an 11-percent inflation rate. Are you with me so far?

MS. STAMBERG. Sort of.

THE PRESIDENT. But say in a foreign country—Italy or France—if the price of gasoline to begin with was $2.40 and the price only went up 10 cents, then the inflation rate in percentages would be much, much less, like 3 percent or less. So, since their prices have always been so high on energy to start with, and ours have been much lower, any increase in the price of energy shows up much greater in our inflation rate than it does in other countries around the world.

I represent and lead, really, two nations, as far as energy is concerned. We have the greatest energy-consuming nation on Earth, and our Nation produces as much energy as any nation on Earth. So, we are a consumer and a producer.

In the past, the Congress has been influenced very heavily by the oil producers, the oil companies, and only since I've been in office, the last few months, have we seen consumers having an equal voice in the Congress. And my prediction to you is that by the end of this year, when the Congress adjourns, we will have on the law books of our country a comprehensive energy policy that will really benefit our Nation in the future.

Ms. STAMBERG. The public sometimes gets the feeling, though, that it's taken an awfully long time for this to come through.

THE PRESIDENT. It has. We've never had it before.

Ms. STAMBERG. Why is that?

THE PRESIDENT. Well, the longer I've been involved in the energy question, the more I can understand why my predecessors in this office didn't try to do anything about it. It is a losing proposition politically.

When I spoke to the country in April of 1977 in an evening television address, I told them that just opening up the energy problem would probably cost me 15 points in the public opinion polls. I underestimated the problem; it's cost me a lot more than that, because the oil-producing States think we have hurt the oil industry, and many consumers think we have not done enough for them.

But just to address this problem and to make Americans realize that we do have a problem and start cutting down on the unnecessary oil imports will help every American in the future. And it also en-

hances our Nation's security, because we are subject now to blackmail, and we are subject to having a major portion of our energy supplies interrupted in countries over which we have no control. And obviously, every time they jack up prices, the more oil we're importing, the more it costs American consumers.

So, we'll shift toward more conservation, more use of American energy of all kinds. That's the best approach.

Ms. STAMBERG. Let's get to the next question from a listener, although it would be nice to continue chatting. Robert O'Connor is on the line from Elkader, Iowa. Am I pronouncing Elkader properly, Mr. O'Connor?

MR. O'CONNOR. That's Elkader, Iowa; that's in northeast Iowa.

Ms. STAMBERG. Oh, thank you very much.

ENERGY RESOURCES AND CONSERVATION

MR. O'CONNOR. Good morning, Mr. President.

THE PRESIDENT. Good morning, Robert.

MR. O'CONNOR. And I appreciate you calling me.

Basically, I sort of want to continue a little bit on the line of the energy program. It seems that the part of the program or the general trend is towards trying to satisfy America's energy addiction, rather than curbing it. It seems like you're continuing to advocate the use of nuclear power, contrary to the campaign promise, and also, recently, this inefficient and perhaps environmentally dirty synthetic fuel program. And I was wondering—it all seems to try to be towards avoiding the purchasing of foreign oil, but it seems like the area that's still, you know, in the end result is still being avoided is the use of renewable fuels. And some of these conservation measures don't seem to actually be happening, and I'm just wondering, why hasn't a greater emphasis been put on these things?

You know, maybe I'm being impatient or something, but it seems like more of an emphasis can be put on some of these other things, rather than synthetic fuel, which seems to be oriented just towards trying to keep it just in America. And, you know, I think it's okay to use some of the foreign fuels, but why not put more emphasis on conservation and renewable fuels right here, that we have?

THE PRESIDENT. Well, our number one reliance on correcting the energy problem, Mr. O'Connor, is conservation. That's the cheapest and best way to cut down on imports. And as I said earlier on this program, I hope that every American will do everything possible within one's own life to be more efficient in the use of energy. The Government's doing its share as well. And the things we've already done will save about 2½ million barrels of oil per day by 1990.

In addition to that, we are trying to shift toward more renewable supplies of energy. Solar power is one that you mentioned, and I'll comment on that specifically. We've set as a goal for ourselves by the end of this century to have 20 percent of the total energy used in this country coming directly from the Sun. This is a tremendously ambitious goal, but I believe that we can meet it.

In order to do that, for instance, we are setting up a solar bank that will give loans to people who will take actions to increase their own use of solar power. We've put into effect tax credits for families throughout the country if they will insulate their homes, for instance, or put in solar heat. They can get tax credits and reduced income tax payments because of that.

We have, in addition, a major move toward using the kinds of growing plants

that can produce energy and be replenishable every year, deriving their substance indirectly at least from the Sun. For instance, I was in Georgia recently at a seminar at Georgia Tech, where we discussed innovative ways to resolve our energy problems. It was pointed out that Georgia's growing plants produced twice as much energy every year, just 1 year's growth, as the entire State uses. And we now waste throughout our forests in this country about 30 percent or 35 percent of the total tree that grows. And this kind of waste can be used in the future. Burning wood is obviously the most well known way, in stoves.

MR. O'CONNOR. I burn wood myself.

THE PRESIDENT. So, these are the kind of things we are pursuing.

As a last resort, we'll have to have some additional supplies of energy. And coal is not, in some forms, a clean-burning product, and so the synthetic fuels program is designed primarily to get clean-burning fuels, like gas and oil, out of coal and shale, which is of tremendous importance in our country. And nuclear power is an integral part of our energy supplies, too. But I think we ought to minimize nuclear power and, as I said during the campaign, have it as a last resort, just to make up the difference between what we can produce and save from other sources compared to what we totally need.

MS. STAMBERG. Thank you, Mr. O'Connor, for posing your question to President Carter.

A quick reminder that you're listening to "Ask the President" on National Public Radio, and our callers are being selected at random from postcards sent in over the past few weeks. Please do not call National Public Radio, don't call the White House, and don't call your local public radio station. If your card has been chosen, we'll do the calling, and we'll call you.

We have just called, and on the line with us now, a 10-year-old named Shanie Ridge in Colorado Springs, Colorado. Shanie, are you there? Go ahead. The President's on the line with you.

VIEWS ON THE PRESIDENCY

Miss Ridge. Mr. Carter?

The President. Yes, Shanie.

Miss Ridge. Do you like your job?

The President. Yes, I like it very much. I like the White House and the life there; so does Amy, by the way. And I like my job. It's the best job in the greatest country on Earth.

Miss Ridge. That's what you think?

The President. That's what I think. Would you like to be President some day?

Miss Ridge. Oh, I don't know, I guess so.

The President. Well, good. You might have to run against Amy; I don't know.

INFLATION

Miss Ridge. And my other question is, what could I do to help stop inflation?

The President. I don't know if you've been listening to the program or not, Shanie, but I think one of the things is that you could help to save energy, and around the house you could observe ways to keep doors closed, to make your parents insulate their home better to prevent heat from escaping. You could keep the thermostat set fairly high during the summer and low during the winter so you don't waste heat. You could cut off electric lights and other electrical appliances when they're not in use.

And when you're driving along the road with your parents, you could certainly make sure they obey the speed limit. And I think that when your father or your mother go to work, for instance,

you could try to get them to join in a carpool so that one automobile could be filled before it rides up and down the highways with just one person in it.

We're doing all we can on this end, but there are a lot of things that a 10-year-old can do. Around the school, you ought to get together with other kids in your class, for instance, and try to share ideas with each other about what you can do in addition to those things that I've already described.

As far as buying things is concerned, if you see a product that's going up in price too much or if your mother sees one going up in price, shop around and try to get lower priced products that give you the same service, like food or clothing and so forth. Good shopping, I think, will also help to control inflation.

I wish you well. It's really good to see a 10-year-old interested in public affairs. And you can help me as much as anyone in this country can to cut down on energy waste and hold down inflation.

Ms. Stamberg. Thank you, Shanie, for your question.

Mr. President, the next caller is Michael Del Coro, and he's calling from the Bronx, New York. Go ahead, Mr. Del Coro.

SOLAR ENERGY

Mr. Del Coro. Hello, Mr. President.

The President. Yes, Michael.

Mr. Del Coro. I'd like to ask you, do you believe in solar energy?

Ms. Stamberg. Mr. Del Coro, would you say your question again, please? We didn't understand you.

Mr. Del Coro. Do you believe in solar energy?

The President. Solar energy—yes, very much so. I think people forget how much solar energy we already use. A great portion of the heat that we use in homes, for instance, comes through the windows and through the walls and through the roof of homes, even if you don't have a solar collector, as such, on the roof. And, of course, the Sun provides ultimately all the heat that we use on this Earth, either by stored, Sun-produced products in the past that make oil and coal or through the generation of hydroelectric power by water that's been taken to the mountains by Sun's evaporation, and so forth.

So, I believe very deeply in solar energy and believe that in the future, Michael, that we can use a lot more of it.

POTENTIAL WARS OVER OIL

MR. DEL CORO. Yes, I am—[inaudible]—to ask you about that. Now, the second question is this, that is there any possibility of any war for oil?

MS. STAMBERG. Any war for oil.

THE PRESIDENT. I don't believe so. Obviously, there's always a possibility that other nations would try to interrupt supplies of oil for us. We're trying to improve our Nation's security by cutting down on the amount of oil that we have to import and become more self-reliant, that is, produce more oil of our own.

I think that in 1973, it was, some of the Arab countries and OPEC countries had an embargo against our country and did not send us oil for a while. I don't believe that's likely in the future. We have a much better relationship now with those countries than we did in the past. And I believe that the prospect for war over oil would be very, very remote.

MR. DEL CORO. Okay. Now, this is——

MS. STAMBERG. Mr. Del Coro, I'm so sorry, I'm going to have to interrupt you. I think two questions is about the limit for each caller. Thank you very much, Mr. Del Coro.

THE PRESIDENT. Good luck to you.

MS. STAMBERG. We're going to go on to the next call. It's from Samuel Scott Rosenburg, in Key Biscayne, Florida. Go ahead, Mr. Rosenburg.

ALCOHOL FUEL

MR. ROSENBURG. Hello, Mr. President.

THE PRESIDENT. Yes.

MR. ROSENBURG. Greetings from Key Biscayne. How are you today?

THE PRESIDENT. Just great.

MR. ROSENBURG. Good. I'm real excited to be able to speak to you today, because I have good news, rather than a question regarding our energy, which is really in response to what's going on. It would take about 30 seconds to tell you. May I?

THE PRESIDENT. Yes, it suits me fine.

MR. ROSENBURG. Sure. One of the ways, you know—on the farm alcohol stills in America more and more are showing us that 100-percent alcohol is used as a motor fuel in today's engines, as well as the recent announcement by Brazil to agree to produce 650,000 alcohol-powered cars by 1982. In fact, their President said it's their key weapon in the fight against rising oil prices.

Now, I myself, personally, have a simple, coordinated strategy not only to bring down the cost of fuel to under $1 at the pump, but obviously it would cool inflation as well. And, frankly, I'd like to share it with you.

As we all know, Thanksgiving time is here, and we really have to take stock and be thankful we are Americans. We're the envy of the world. There's nothing that we can't do. We gave the world electricity, lights——

MS. STAMBERG. Mr. Rosenburg.

MR. ROSENBURG. ——telephones, airplanes, and if that doesn't seem unreal, we even put a man on the Moon. And then——

Ms. STAMBERG. Mr. Rosenburg, excuse me, I'm going to have to interrupt. I think you're either filibustering or making a speech; I'm not sure which. Could you get to the question for President Carter, please?

MR. ROSENBURG. Yes, I will. What I was simply saying is that rather than a question, I would like to just advocate more alcohol fuel, and I have a plan laid out, blueprints and books. So, as I say, I don't want to filibuster, but I would like to meet with you or your people in the White House and show you what it is I'm talking about.

THE PRESIDENT. Mr. Rosenburg, send me a letter up here and mark on the front of the envelope that you are one of those who called me on the telephone. I get about 50,000 letters a week, and I want to make sure yours gets to me personally. And I'll refer you to someone up here who can discuss it with you, okay?

MR. ROSENBURG. Yes, sir. And by the way, prior to your becoming President, I was one of your rooters for you, and I had gotten a letter from one of your top people in Washington, which I also have, as well as having been invited to your Inauguration.

THE PRESIDENT. Good luck to you, and thank you for your friendship.

MR. ROSENBURG. Thank you, sir.

Ms. STAMBURG. Thank you very much, Mr. Rosenburg.

President Carter, next on the line, Judy Caufeld, in Pittsburgh, Pennsylvania. Go ahead, Ms. Caufeld.

EQUAL RIGHTS AMENDMENT

Ms. CAUFELD. President Carter.

THE PRESIDENT. Yes, Judy.

Ms. CAUFELD. I've always been a supporter of the equal rights amendment.

THE PRESIDENT. So am I.

Ms. CAUFELD. What type of positive action are you going to take to ensure its ratification by June of 1982?

THE PRESIDENT. I'll work as a partner with you, Judy, and others around the country who believe that women do need equal rights and deserve them. My wife is also very active in the equal rights amendment movement, and of course, my daughter-in-law, Judy, my oldest son's daughter [wife], travels nationwide to work with equal rights proponents to try to get those reluctant States to ratify the amendment.

So, I'm a partner with you. I believe in it, and I believe that your question and my answer might help to convince some of those State legislators who still are not convinced that the equal rights amendment is best for our country as well as, of course, best for all women.

Ms. CAUFELD. Okay. Thank you.

THE PRESIDENT. Thank you.

Ms. STAMBERG. Thank you, Judy.

Mr. President, I wonder what you think of the kind of economic boycotting that's going on against cities and States which are not getting behind the ERA.

THE PRESIDENT. Well, you know, I can't be a proponent of boycotts. But I believe that the political season is going to come this year, and if women who suffer most from hiring discrimination, wage discrimination, would let their voices be heard by State legislators who will make the judgment or decision, that's the best approach.

Quite often working women are not as highly organized or as highly motivated as some of the nationwide women's groups, and I think that when women who do have a job and who see the discrimination against them become aroused, they prevail, and this is the best approach to it.

Ms. STAMBERG. Good. Let's take another call now. This is from Elizabeth Gamble, in Everett, Washington. Mrs. Gamble, go ahead, please; you're on the line with President Carter.

PRESIDENTIAL TERMS OF OFFICE

MRS. GAMBLE. Hello, Mr. President.

THE PRESIDENT. Hello, Elizabeth. Go ahead.

Ms. STAMBERG. Go ahead.

MRS. GAMBLE. Hello, Mr. President.

THE PRESIDENT. Hello, I hear you very well.

MRS. GAMBLE. I'm honored to be called. Now my question is this: What do you think of one 6-year term for the Presidency instead of two 4-year terms? Under the present law, a President is forced to spend time and energy in the first term working for reelection—unfortunately, this year, sooner than usual.

THE PRESIDENT. I agree with you.

MRS. GAMBLE. Good.

THE PRESIDENT. Since I've been in this office, I've become more and more convinced that one 6-year term would be better. We have too much of an emphasis by the news media, in my opinion, on political motivations of a President, almost as soon as a President takes office.

And I've seen and talked to and studied the situation where other Presidents in countries in this hemisphere, like Mexico and Venezuela, for instance, have one 6-year term. I think they're much more likely not only to act in a nonpolitical basis or a nonpartisan way but also to have the recognition among people, including the news media, that when they do take a difficult stand or do make a public statement or take action, that it is not politically motivated.

And I think the injection of politics so early in the election year—already, as a matter of fact—is unfortunate.

MRS. GAMBLE. Well, that is my opinion. Do you think that there's any possibility of there ever being—the law ever being changed?

THE PRESIDENT. I think it's quite remote, because it requires a tremendous and concerted effort all over the Nation to make a change in the U.S. Constitution. And I don't see the issue being so sharply of interest to American people that this high motivation would ever be marshaled any time in the near future.

MRS. GAMBLE. Well, I don't wish to take up too much time, but before closing, I wish to say I think that Rosalynn is the ideal American woman.

THE PRESIDENT. I know she's the ideal wife. Thank you very much.

MRS. GAMBLE. Thank you, Mr. President.

Ms. STAMBERG. Thank you, Mrs. Gamble.

On the line now, from Fairbanks, Alaska, Mr. President——

THE PRESIDENT. Very good.

Ms. STAMBERG.——is John Jacques. Go head, Mr. Jacques.

ALASKAN PUBLIC LANDS

MR. JACQUES. Yes. Good morning, Mr. President, how you doing this morning?

THE PRESIDENT. Good morning. I hear you perfectly well. I'm glad to hear from you.

MR. JACQUES. Well, Mr. President, I have an Alaskan question to ask you. With your imposition of the Antiquities Act and the National Monuments a year ago, you have locked up a few acres, matter of fact, millions of acres of land here in Alaska, taken this control away from the State government——

THE PRESIDENT. No, that's not——

MR. JACQUES. I was——

THE PRESIDENT. Go ahead.

MR. JACQUES. I was wondering—with the energy crisis, we can't explore on this land, and there's no way that we can explore on this land. I was wondering why you have taken the State control and put it in the Federal Government's hands.

THE PRESIDENT. Well, I think you've got it a little bit backwards, John. This is not State land that we've taken away from the State of Alaska; this is Federal land that we're retaining for the use of all Americans. It's, in effect, being put in a protected status—very carefully chosen, about 115 million acres, which is a tiny portion of the total acreage in Alaska. And we very carefully excluded whenever possible those areas of Alaska that did have promise as far as major energy production is concerned.

As you know, Alaska has become a great oil-producing State, natural gas-producing State, which we hope to bring down to our country through a new gasline, and obviously has other minerals of value as well. But as has been the case throughout our country, the land is first owned by the Federal Government and then a portion of it, either almost all or very little, is turned over to the State. Some is preserved for the entire American population if it's especially beautiful or especially precious, and that's the kind of land that I have preserved for posterity, for Americans of all 50 States and Alaska.

I think it was a very wise decision. It has not interfered with the Alaskan ability to produce energy.

MR. JACQUES. But don't you feel that we can't explore on this land, if there's oil and natural resources on this land?

THE PRESIDENT. Well, I might say that there are certain circumstances under which oil exploration can be done even on some of this land. Some of it is too valuable and too precious to have exploration. But there is plenty of land in

Alaska for any time in the years immediately ahead to completely use all the oil exploration capability that we have in this country.

MR. JACQUES. Okay. Thank you, Mr.

THE PRESIDENT. Thank you, John.

MS. STAMBERG. Thank you, Mr. Jacques.

A reminder again that you are listening to "Ask the President" on National Public Radio. This is a live, 2-hour telephone program from the White House Oval Office. President Carter is answering questions from citizens across the country, and for technical reasons you cannot phone us with your question. NPR instead is phoning out to randomly selected listeners.

And here comes one now. It's Mrs. Moila Roundy, in St. Joseph, Missouri. Go ahead, Mrs. Roundy; you're on the line with the President.

ENVIRONMENTAL LAWS

MRS. ROUNDY. Good morning, Mr. President. I feel very fortunate to speak with you. My question is, is there some way that we can get the Clean Air Act of 1977 amended or rescinded?

THE PRESIDENT. I would not be in favor of rescinding it.

MRS. ROUNDY. But—*[inaudible]*—amend it. The EPA has become such a monster, and it's costing us and wasting so much of our energy unnecessarily. They placed a burning ban on us here in St. Joseph, and we are mostly made up of senior citizens on fixed income. And we are in annexed areas, so large with all of this waste. We can't afford to buy bags, pay the minimum wage to have it cut up, and pay to have it hauled off to these landfills, which pollute much worse our soil and our water tables. It's costing an awful hardship on us here in St. Joseph, and we're fighting. We have over 8,000 signatures to try to get this amended.

THE PRESIDENT. I don't know which particular provision of the law you refer to, but I think in general the environmental laws are very important.

MRS. ROUNDY. But our air isn't that dirty. It comes from agriculture and from the State of Kansas and the two Kansas Cities and the airports. And our burning of our leaves and yard waste and garden waste, seasonal, will not add to this pollution.

THE PRESIDENT. I understand. Sometimes when a city has a very high air pollution to begin with, because of many factors, including factories and automobiles and so forth——

MRS. ROUNDY. Well, we don't have that.

MS. STAMBERG. Mrs. Roundy——

MRS. ROUNDY. They seem to think burning yard waste—but the monitors were inaccurate. We found that out. So, we're trying to get another way of monitoring our air.

THE PRESIDENT. I understand. I know in Atlanta, when I was living there as Governor, the air pollution got very high, and everybody was encouraged to take their yard wastes—for instance, fallen leaves and branches and things of that kind—and make mulch out of them, which is a very nice thing that all farmers have done since I've been a farmer, and then use that mulch for fertilizer. It solves the problem of excessive burning and air pollution and also gives you a very valuable product at the end.

MRS. ROUNDY. That's true. I do some of that. But these people who have 5 to 40 acres and are senior citizens, they just can't do these things. And it's going to take all of our money for our heating bills. Now, Mr. President, last year my oil, my heating bill was $183 to $235 per month.

THE PRESIDENT. Yes.

MRS. ROUNDY. And that was less than half the price it is today, even though I set my thermostat at 65 and 55. So, this is going to exceed the income of these senior citizens, and what will they do for taxes, food, and other utility bills?

THE PRESIDENT. That's a very good question and a different question. I think that, obviously, the two——

MRS. ROUNDY. Well, I think it ties in, Mr. President, because we'll be using all this extra oil to buy bags, this extra oil to transport our garden waste to these landfills. And I think that's unnecessary when we could burn them.

THE PRESIDENT. Let me answer your question. I think one thing that can be done if your house has a wood stove is to use some of that waste for fuel. I do it in my own home in Plains and also in the White House.

The second thing is that we're trying to provide some financial assistance for people like you to help pay those extra energy costs this winter. I've just sent to the Congress this week, for instance, a request for $1.2 billion, to be added to $400 million we already have, to help pay those high costs. And I'm also asking the Congress to set aside about $2½ billion every year for the next 10 years to give people some help on the very high energy bills.

You have put your finger, however, on the best way to start solving the question, and that is to save the amount of energy that we have been wasting in the past.

MRS. ROUNDY. That is what we must do, is to save, conserve, yes.

THE PRESIDENT. I think all three of those things are important: to save energy, to start with; to use fuels that are available to us, like wood in your case; and for us to help with some financial help, which will be coming to you later on this winter.

MRS. ROUNDY. Well, I'm a commission member on aging in this area and in the city, too, and these problems come to me all the time. We must do something for our senior citizens. And they say that our rights, our human rights and all are being taken away from us due to this EPA monster, and I agree.

MS. STAMBERG. Mrs. Roundy, thank you so much for joining us and participating in this program today.

Our next caller, Mr. President, is in Springville, Alabama. It's Lew Windham. Mr. Windham, go ahead, please.

ENERGY PRICES

MR. WINDHAM. Mr. President?

THE PRESIDENT. Good morning, Lew.

MR. WINDHAM. We're in the petroleum business here, in an area of the country that I'm sure you're familiar with. We own two LP gas companies that supply these rural people with propane for heating; at the same time we're in the oil-jobbing business.

We find it extremely hard to explain to our customers why every time they buy a petroleum product that it is higher. Now, we cannot see any evidence that the Department of Energy is doing anything. Now, I feel that the majority of the people in this country need a very good explanation as to what the Department of Energy is doing to put the lid on these producing companies.

THE PRESIDENT. Well, that's not an easy question to answer, Lew, because there's very little that the Department of Energy or a President can do to prevent foreign countries from raising their price of oil. And the basic thrust that we are pursuing is to cut down on that imported oil.

As you know, this past month the rate of increase of energy was more than a hundred percent per year on an annual basis, and as I said earlier, about 4 percent of our inflation rate is derived directly from energy costs. This is a very serious

matter, and I think you've noticed, if you've listened to this call-in show, how many people have raised this same question.

MR. WINDHAM. Yes.

THE PRESIDENT. We are concerned about home heating oil in the Northeast, but I think many people forget that in the area where you live and where I live, that the isolated farm families and families in small towns also have to heat their homes, and most of them do use propane. And the cost of propane is derived from natural gas prices and goes up also, along with oil and coal and everything else.

I can't give you any easy answer. There's no reason for me to sit here in the Oval Office and try to mislead the American people. There are only three ways that we can deal with this question: one is to use as little energy as possible through conservation, savings; second, to use more of the energy that we produce in our own country than we have been doing in the past; and third, provide Federal and other assistance for the low-income families to make sure that they do have enough fuel to heat their homes and to cook with, and so forth, and also so that they can have enough money to pay those bills.

But there's no way that I can mislead you. The prices are high now; they're going to get higher in the future than they are already. And unless our Nation unites itself and deals with this very serious threat, we're going to be worse off in the future than we have in the past.

I inherited this problem. I'm not complaining about it, but it has been an extremely difficult thing to get the Congress to pass any legislation on this issue, because it's so controversial. We have still not passed a single line of legislation in the Congress dealing with oil. This year we have a very good prospect of finally getting those laws on the book, which will help you and me and all your customers and people like them throughout the country.

It's been slow in coming, but we're now making some progress. It's not really fair to blame the Department of Energy, because they don't have the authority to control energy prices charged by foreign countries. We've just got to do what I've just told you as the best way to deal with this problem.

Mr. WINDHAM. Mr. President, I would like to congratulate you and the Congress on the move that you have put forth to help these needy people in this crisis we're in, because I feel that that is one answer, and you're to be congratulated on that move.

THE PRESIDENT. Thank you. This will amount, by the way, I think, between $100 and $200 per family, to help them with the fuel bills this winter. So, if they combine that help, if they're a poor family, with saving as much energy as possible, I think we can get people through the winter.

Mr. WINDHAM. Thank you.

THE PRESIDENT. Good luck, Lew, and thank you.

Ms. STAMBERG. Thank you, Mr. Windham.

The next call is from Lancaster, Kentucky, Mr. Carter, Mr. President Carter, and it's from Robert Gordon. Go ahead, Mr. Gordon, you're on the line with President Carter.

SUGGESTION FOR PRESIDENTIAL CAMPAIGN

Mr. GORDON. Yes, Mr. President. Well, first off, I'd just like to say I love you very much. I'm praying for you, and my friends are praying for you.

THE PRESIDENT. Thank you.

Mr. GORDON. You've got quite a responsibility. May I make a suggestion, Mr. President?

THE PRESIDENT. Please.

Mr. GORDON. Well, what I would like to just suggest and encourage, sir, is that when politicking time comes, cut that time in half and spend it on your knees seeking the Lord Jesus Christ, because, sir, Jesus is more important than this country. He will give you the answers, sir. He will give you the answers to lead, as it is His will—excuse me, I'm a little nervous.

THE PRESIDENT. That's all right.

Mr. GORDON. But the Lord Jesus that puts a man in power—and if you spend your time on your knees, seeking His will, and if it's His will that you stay in power another 4 years, then He'll put you in power.

Mr. President, again, I'm praying for you. I love you. And this is going to seem a little silly, but I was wondering if you could send me your autograph, sir.

THE PRESIDENT. Yes, I'll be glad to. I'll do that.

Ms. STAMBERG. Thank you very much.

THE PRESIDENT. Good luck, and thank you for those good wishes and advice.

Ms. STAMBERG. The next question comes, Mr. President, from Mrs. Colleen Porter, and she is joining us from Provo, Utah. Go ahead, Mrs. Porter.

GOVERNMENT-SPONSORED DAY-CARE CENTERS

MRS. PORTER. Yes. I'm married, and I'm a full-time mother. We've got two children, and we hope to have a few more. And I really love my job, and I'm concerned about the prospect of Government-sponsored day-care centers, because it seems to me it's logical that the increased taxation necessary to keep these running would force our economy into even more of a two-income economy—and there's us on our one-income budget—and force me to work. And that's not really far-fetched, because I think you know what the tax rates are in some of the Scandinavian countries and places that have these really nifty Government-sponsored day-care centers. And I wondered how you felt about that.

THE PRESIDENT. Okay. My own basic philosophy, Colleen, is that anything that can be done by the private individuals of our Nation or private institutions, churches and others—certainly the private enterprise system ought to be first, and that the Government should inject itself into the lives of American people in a minimal way, only as a last resort to meet a need that can't be met otherwise.

There are many communities around the country where there is no private offering of day-care services. In those instances I think the Federal Government has a role to play. I don't think it ought to abuse the right or the duty, and I think that even in that case, there ought to be as much care and consideration, not only for the children but for the sensitivities of the parents and the community as possible.

Many women, for instance, and, I guess, on occasion some men could not possibly work and would be permanent welfare recipients if there was not a place to leave a small child and to have that child cared for. And also, of course, with the Head Start program and other more permanent programs during the year, small children on the pre-first-grade level start to get a good education. So, I think that this is a partial answer to your question.

The other one is, we don't anticipate any massive increases in Federal day-care programs that would put an additional burden on the taxpayers of our country. This is a fairly well established program. I don't anticipate any substantial changes in the future.

MRS. PORTER. Well, you're so, just so in favor of the equal rights amendment, and——

THE PRESIDENT. Yes, I am.

MRS. PORTER.——most of the people that are in favor of the equal rights amendment, the women's groups, are also very strongly in favor of massive day-care centers. And I just hope you'll keep your convictions about where to draw that line.

THE PRESIDENT. Okay. They're not necessarily related, but I agree that some people do relate them.

MRS. PORTER. Yes, most of them. And also, I'd just like to say that when you, if you ever did get in the situation to cut down on the role of the family, not only are you going to put out tax money for day-care centers but for more prisons, for more welfare, for more drug and alcohol rehabilitation. And I think if I can just stay home and raise my kids, they're going to be good citizens.

Thank you.

THE PRESIDENT. That sounds like a good thing to do if that's your preference. Good luck to you.

MRS. PORTER. Thank you.

MS. STAMBERG. Thank you so much, Mrs. Porter.

President Carter, at this point we're going to take a 1-minute break. During that time our stations across the country can identify themselves, and you can get a 4½-inning stretch; so can I.

THE PRESIDENT. Very good.

MS. STAMBERG. Then we will be back with another hour of "Ask the President," from NPR, National Public Radio.

———

This is Susan Stamberg, back again at the Oval Office in the White House for National Public Radio's live broadcast, "Ask the President."

President Carter is answering questions by telephone from citizens across the country. The questions are not being screened, but the questioners are being chosen on the basis of geographic distribution. We're kind of strolling around the country by phone, and we're doing it for the reason that citizens from many parts of the Nation want to have a chance to speak with the President. We want to give them that chance.

To explain, again, this curious procedure, you cannot call us; we have to do the calling out to you. For several weeks now, in newspaper ads and on the radio and television, citizens have been invited to send us their names, their addresses, phone numbers, to put it all on a postcard if they wanted to ask a question. Those names are being chosen at random now, and we are placing the calls—all this for technical reasons.

There will be another hour of questions and answers with President Carter, which will be followed by a half-hour analysis of the President's statements by National Public Radio reporters.

Mr. President, you ready for the next call?

THE PRESIDENT. All set.

Ms. STAMBERG. It's from Al Sheahen, and he's in Van Nuys, California. Go ahead, Mr. Sheahen.

DEFENSE SPENDING AND NATIONAL
SECURITY

MR. SHEAHEN. President Carter?

THE PRESIDENT. Yes, Al.

MR. SHEAHEN. We admire your courage and enthusiasm for running for the 10-kilometer races, and I hope you'll keep it up.

THE PRESIDENT. I will.

MR. SHEAHEN. The reason I'm calling, the question I had—we all know that inflation is caused by deficit spending, and we've got a $30 billion deficit this year, I think you said.

THE PRESIDENT. This coming year, yes.

MR. SHEAHEN. The largest expenditure by the Government is defense spending,

military spending. One out of every two of our income tax dollars goes for defense. In 1976 when you campaigned, you said you'd try to cut the defense budget by five to seven billion dollars, and yet right now it's about $40 billion per year more than when you first took office. And now you're asking for an MX missile, which is going to cost anywhere from $30 billion to $90 billion. Experts say we don't need it. My question is, why don't you try to stop inflation by stopping the unnecessary military spending and put that money to work in our economy?

THE PRESIDENT. Al, let me say that we have cut more than six or seven billion dollars out of the Defense Department by increased efficiency.

But I need to make a point very clear to you and to other Americans. The number one responsibility on my shoulders, above everything else, is to guarantee the security of our country. And I don't make any apology for it.

We spend now a very small portion of our gross national product on defense, about 5 percent. Other countries like the Soviet Union spend often much more. The Soviet Union spends maybe 13 to 15 percent of their GNP on defense. For the last 15 or 20 years, they have increased their defense expenditures by about 3 or 4 percent per year in real terms, like compound interest. We spend now less than we did 15 or 20 years ago, in real dollars, on defense. We've tried to make up that difference and to retain our strength by more efficient expenditure of funds and to tap the basic strengths of our country in politics and economics and otherwise.

We have at this time the strongest nation militarily on Earth. And we've tried to enhance our strength by making sure that our NATO Alliance, our alliances with other countries around the world stay sound and that there is a mutual sharing of responsibility and an enhanced trust between us.

We are moving toward a possibility of drastically reducing nuclear weapons in the future if we can get SALT II ratified. Both President Brezhnev and I, I think the people of America and the people of the Soviet Union want to see drastic cuts made in nuclear armaments below what they are now, even below what they will be under SALT II.

We have in addition—and the last point I'd like to make—a major responsibility on Earth. People look to us to maintain stability and to prevent war. We have been at peace for the first term, I might say, of a President in 40 years. No American has lost a life in combat since I've been here in the Oval Office. I pray that that might be the record that I leave here when I have finished my service as President.

But we cannot afford to become weak. The surest way to end peace and to cause war is for a potential adversary of our country to believe that we are weak in military strength or in the will to protect ourselves.

I hope that the expenditures that we presently are making on armaments, on military personnel salaries, even the future expenditures will be a good investment. And a good investment is a weapon which is never fired. I hope that no person ever dies because we get into a war.

MR. SHEAHEN. We certainly appreciate the job that you're doing in keeping peace. It's an enormous job. I can't even imagine how difficult it is.

But can't you—you mentioned that the United States only spends 5 percent of our gross national product on defense, which is true. But I understand that Germany spends substantially less, 3 percent, Switzerland only 2 percent, Japan less than 1 percent. Isn't it time for them

to—why should we assume this tremendous burden? Why can't our allies take care of some of it?

THE PRESIDENT. Well, I can't comment on those exact figures. Japan is the one that I do know about. When we occupied Japan after the Second World War, under General MacArthur and Harry Truman, who was President, we required the Japanese to limit themselves on military capability strictly to an ability to defend their own country. And at that time there was established a limit on how much would be spent on armaments.

We have some troops in Japan, not a large number, and we provide part of the protection for Japan. I think this is a good and stabilizing factor. And of course, they, in addition to their own forces, pay a substantial portion of the cost of maintaining American troops in Japan.

It's a complicated thing, Al; it's not simple. But I believe that over a long period of years the trend has been distinctly downward in our own country in the portion of our wealth that we spend on defense. I personally believe that what we are spending now is an excellent investment, and I don't see any way that we could possibly lower our resolve or our commitment to a strong defense. That would be the best way to lead toward a war, which would cause an enormous explosion in defense expenditures. I think this is an insurance policy that really pays rich dividends for our country.

MR. SHEAHEN. Thank you, Mr. President.

MS. STAMBERG. Thank you, Mr. Sheahen.

A call now, a little closer to home, President Carter, from Baltimore, Maryland, Dr. Edward Davens. Go ahead, Dr. Davens.

DR. DAVENS. Good afternoon, Mr. President. This is Dr. Ed Davens in Baltimore.

THE PRESIDENT. Go ahead, Doctor.

NUCLEAR ENERGY

DR. DAVENS. You've already referred to nuclear power, which is what my question is about.

THE PRESIDENT. Yes.

DR. DAVENS. But I'd like to have you pursue it just a bit more. Will you please state clearly your policy on the development of nuclear power? My impression is that you're convinced that going full steam ahead is essential for the good of the economy. Am I wrong about that?

THE PRESIDENT. During my own campaign for President and since I've been in office, I've taken a position on nuclear power that I think is a proper one—first of all, that there is a place in our energy industry for nuclear power. It's already been established, and I think that it would be very difficult if not impossible to root it out. For instance, I was in Hartford, Connecticut, not long ago. Connecticut derives about 60 percent of all their electricity from nuclear powerplants; Chicago, for instance, about 50 percent; and so forth.

However, as I said earlier, I think that the nuclear power portion and also the synthetic fuel portion can be minimized by those who fear it or those who want to avoid it, to the extent that we can have conservation, the increased production of other forms of energy in our own country.

We will get back, probably around the end of this month, a report from the so-called Kemeny Commission on the Three Mile Island accident. At that time I will analyze that Commission report very thoroughly and make a report without delay to the American people about its recommendations and whether or not we can carry out those recommendations and the extent to which we can remove present doubts about the safety or advisability of nuclear power in the future.

I think our country is possibly, probably going to rely on nuclear power less in future years than other major nations about which I happen to know. In Japan, in Germany, Great Britain, even oil-producing countries like Iran and Saudi Arabia, they're moving much more rapidly toward nuclear power than are we. We are blessed with a broad diversity of energy sources, not only solar, with the technical ability to use it, but also coal, geothermal supplies, oil, natural gas, shale deposits, and many others, hydroelectric power.

So, I think there is a place for nuclear power. It ought to be safe; the American people ought to understand all the facts about it; and its use can be minimized to the extent that we save energy and shift to other sources of energy. But I don't want to mislead you. I think there will be a place for nuclear power in the future. It's my responsibility along with many others to guarantee that it is safe.

DR. DAVENS. Your background is in nuclear engineering; mine is in pediatrics. I would like to urge you to look very carefully at the evidence that nuclear radiation is simply not a viable thing for the survival of the race on this planet, and I hope you will pay real attention to the Kemeny Commission and other advice you may get on minimizing this dangerous pollution of the environment.

Thank you very much.

THE PRESIDENT. Doctor, I will. I don't want to lose that point without making, however, a clarification. I have done graduate work in nuclear physics and nuclear engineering at the beginning of its use back in the early 1950's, and I'm familiar with the dangers of radiation.

I would like to point out that in the production of power in our country, using nuclear power, there has never been a person killed or a life lost. And this is not to say that we should not be extremely cautious about nuclear power in the future. In coal-burning plants, even hydroelectric plants and other kinds, there have been numerous deaths.

But we've done a good job so far in setting standards for operation and design and installation to enhance to a maximum degree, so far, safety standards. I think we can do a better job in the future, and I'm looking forward with a great deal of anticipation and a sober expectation to the Kemeny report. I think that we can make corrections in past mistakes and make even more effort in the future to make sure that nuclear power is safe.

I'll add one other point. I think that the economic considerations and others that I've already described, that I need not repeat, will permit our country to minimize the use of nuclear power in the future, compared to some other countries.

DR. DAVENS. I hope so. This is no place to argue the issue, but I'm not completely satisfied with your answer.

Thank you.

THE PRESIDENT. I didn't think you were.

MS. STAMBERG. Thank you very much, Doctor.

President Carter, I'd like to ask you something about what you've just said, that argument about no lives lost. It's pretty much the standard argument of the nuclear industry. Is that really the point? You're not going to see an instant death. You may see some problems from cancer 10, 20, 30 years down the line.

THE PRESIDENT. I think the answer is accurate, including radioactivity. There have been some people injured, even killed, in experimental nuclear powerplants in very rare occasions. But in the standard designed and operated nuclear powerplants to produce electricity in our country, there has never been an incident

that led, so far as we know, to a human death. At the same time, there have been numerous deaths involved in boiler explosions with plants that burn oil or coal and so forth.

That's not to say that I'm not concerned about safety. I am deeply concerned, and I am determined to act accordingly. And I believe that the incident, which could have been very serious, at the Three Mile Island plant in Pennsylvania gives us a cautionary signal to stop, to think, to study, to analyze, and then to make decisions based on what our country should do in the future.

I have no idea what the Kemeny Commission is going to recommend. But I will read and very carefully analyze that report myself, and if they make recommendations on the design of powerplants using atomic energy, the installation, the operation, the training of personnel, preparations for a possible accident that are feasible for us to carry out, then I will make sure they are carried out. And if they point out some inherent defect in nuclear powerplants that can't be corrected, obviously that would be cause for termination of such approvals in the future.

I think the best thing, though, that can happen is for American people to know the facts, not to be excessively afraid and also not to be excessively at ease. And it's part of my responsibility as President not only to act but to educate in cases of this kind. And it was my decision to appoint the Kemeny Commission itself to make sure that they, on a completely unbiased and free basis, made an analysis.

No Federal official has tried to influence the outcome of the Kemeny report. We've given them every assistance. They have been given authorization by Congress to deliberate in private without any sort of interference from outside, and I believe that their report will be a full one and also will be accurate. And I hope that every American who's interested will study the report and join with me in analyzing where we go from now.

There's a role for nuclear power. As I've described, we need to emphasize and correct any defects that might exist now, in the past, or in the future.

Ms. STAMBERG. We'll get to the next call in a moment. But again, a reminder that this is a live, 2-hour broadcast from National Public Radio in Washington. President Carter is speaking by telephone with Americans. None of the questions are screened, but for technical reasons, you cannot phone in with your questions. Please do not call NPR, don't call the White House, don't call your local public radio station. Instead, National Public Radio is phoning out to randomly chosen listeners who have written to say that they wish to "Ask the President."

Here's one of those listeners now, President Carter. It's Kimberly Powell from Hyannis, Massachusetts, and I'm told that Kimberly is 13 years old. Go ahead, Kimberly.

VISIT TO BARNSTABLE MIDDLE SCHOOL, MASSACHUSETTS

MISS POWELL. Hi, Mr. President.

THE PRESIDENT. Good afternoon.

MISS POWELL. My name is Kim Powell, and I'm from the Barnstable Middle School, Red House Team II. As you already know, our team of eighth graders sent out an invitation, a note for you to come and teach a history lesson to our school in any way possible that would be convenient to you. We did get a response, but they didn't give us a definite answer. We would like to know if you are really considering to come and when your visit will be? It will be greatly appreciated.

THE PRESIDENT. Well, thank you, Kimberly. I have seen news reports that you all were inviting me to come to Hyannis and to visit your school. I don't know whether I can do it or not. I'll be coming up to Massachusetts again on the 20th of this month to join in dedicating the library of former President John Kennedy, but whether I can visit Hyannis, I don't know. I'll check with my schedulers after this program's over, and we'll let you know directly whether or not I can be there.

MISS POWELL. Okay, thank you. I would also like to ask you a question.

THE PRESIDENT. Okay.

INFLATION

MISS POWELL. Do you have any idea what inflation will be when I get out of school, like, you know, when I'm 18?

THE PRESIDENT. I hope it will be much less.

MISS POWELL. Me, too.

THE PRESIDENT. If every American will help with it, then it'll be much less.

We've had, by the way, Kimberly, pretty good luck with our wage and price guidelines that we've established about a year ago. And now we've got a new thing that's never been formed in the past in our country, and that is an agreement that we reached voluntarily with labor and with business so that government, labor, and business will all join in together in a common effort to hold down inflation. In the past, the Government has passed a law and, in effect, forced on the working people and business, standards for wages and prices. I think this new so-called national accord or agreement will be a major step forward.

And we've already discussed on this program the things that we can do about buying habits and energy waste and so forth, that would help.

So, I think the inflation rate's going to be down considerably by the time you get out of school.

MISS POWELL. Okay. Thank you very much.

THE PRESIDENT. Good luck to you.

MISS POWELL. All right. Bye.

MS. STAMBERG. Thank you, Kimberly.

President Carter, over the last weekend, your administration took some dramatic steps to help hold down inflation. One of those steps was raising the prime interest rate to 14½ percent. To a lot of people, that seems like a gigantic leap of faith. Is it going to work, and are you going to get behind it and back it up? Where does it go from here?

THE PRESIDENT. Well, the Federal Reserve raised, in effect, the interest rates 1 percent, which was a clear signal not only to our country but to the rest of the world that we do consider inflation to be the number one economic threat to our lives and to the quality of our life. I think that this analysis, or this decision was applauded by both liberal and conservative economists, and I believe there's no question about the fact that we have got to deal with inflation. The interest rates really go with inflation, and the only way to get interest rates down is to get inflation down.

We must have a stable dollar. When the dollar values go down in foreign countries, it hurts us directly. We can't export our—we can't have as much trade as we would like, to produce American products and to sell them. In addition to that, the reputation of our country is extremely important on a worldwide basis.

We have taken action since I've been in office to minimize the damage to employment with high inflation. We, in the past, have seen, whenever the interest rate went up, an immediate nosedive in housing construction. As a matter of fact, since

I've been in office, because of energy prices, inflation has gone up, but we've had a 50-percent growth in the rate of production of homes for people to live in. And we've been maintaining this very high rate of home construction.

Another point is that we've kept people at work since I've been in office. Again, working with the Congress and in spite of inflation, which is too high, we've had a net increase of 8½ million jobs in this country. It's never been accomplished before. And we've cut the unemployment rate down by a full 25 percent. So, so far, in spite of these pressures for inflation, which have been with us more than 10 years, we have been successful in keeping people at work.

MS. STAMBERG. Yes, but I think some of your own advisers—Stuart Eizenstat, William G. [G. William] Miller—have said that they expect that unemployment rate to go a bit higher next year, up to 6.6 or 7 percent.

THE PRESIDENT. It might go a bit higher. Well, it was 8 percent or more when I came in office. And we've added, as I say, over 8 million new jobs, and the labor force has grown in our country. Another factor that people forget in looking just at the unemployment rate, which has come down very gratifyingly, is that when a teenager, for instance, sees a neighbor get a job, that teenager goes and puts his or her name on the employment rolls and starts looking for a job. So, as people are put to work—and we've increased teenage employment about 26 percent in the last 2½ years—you have more people registering for jobs, which tends to make the unemployment rate look like it's rising.

But I think in general, that's one of the most notable achievements of the last 2½ years, that in spite of energy costs, in spite of high inflation, in spite of increased

1909

interest rates, we have still improved Americans' ability to get jobs.

Ms. STAMBERG. Let's take another question from a listener. Mr. President, this is Kenneth Morris, in Chatham, New Jersey. Go ahead, Mr. Morris.

GRAIN EXPORTS

MR. MORRIS. Well, it's quite an honor, I must admit, to be talking to you, Mr. President. I have two questions, I guess. I'm doing the family bills, and I have to admit I'm worried about inflation. Why can't the U.S. Government put more muscle in support of American business in dealing with the OPEC countries and sit down on a government-to-government level and negotiate oil for barrels of wheat or even form an agreement with other major grain-producing countries, like Argentina, or even perhaps consider certain exemptions to the antitrust laws. That's a mouthful, I suppose.

THE PRESIDENT. Kenneth, this is a frequent proposal made, that our Nation exchange a bushel of wheat for a barrel of oil, something of that kind. It has an immediate appeal to people, but it's just not practical.

The oil-producing countries, like Saudi Arabia, for instance, which produces about 9½ million barrels a day, have a very small population, and they, therefore, import very little food although they don't produce it themselves. Any other country that's of any size at all, like France, in Europe, or other European countries or countries in Latin America, would be eager to provide those small quantities of grain to the oil-producing countries if we decided not to. And it would be a very serious mistake for us to try, through a wheat embargo, to cut out food supplies to those foreign countries.

One of the most important gifts that God has given us is fertile land and a free enterprise system, which gives us food and grain and other products to sell to others. I would say that we have a better advantage in producing food, which will last, hopefully, forever, than the oil-producing nations overseas have with depleting oil supplies. The greatest strategic advantage that I see that our country will have in years to come is food, which can be made available in a very beneficial way to all the people on Earth who need food.

Secondly, we have derived from this much better and more stable markets in our own country. Since I've been in office, for instance, we've increased the amount of grain that's stored on farms, we've improved the quality of life, and the income of farm families is near the peak that it's ever been in history now. And every year we have set records, unprecedented on Earth, for the export of American products.

So, just as Saudi Arabia or Iran or Nigeria or Venezuela benefit from their sale of oil to other countries, we benefit on a permanent basis, hundreds of years, from the export of food products. And if we should interrupt the sale of those grain products overseas, as was done quite frequently when Secretary Butz was running the Agriculture Department and the Republican administration was in office, we would make our potential buyers of American products very uncertain about our ability to supply them.

We have not had grain embargoes since I've been in office, and we're not going to have them. So, we can deal with the energy imports in other ways—which we are doing—without stopping the export of our equally valuable product, even more valuable product, and that is food.

INFLATION

MR. MORRIS. I guess the second question is related to inflation. That is, how can you persuade families to hold down on consumer spending when they know that 6 months from now things will be so much more expensive?

THE PRESIDENT. Well, my daddy always said, "If you don't need something, it's not cheap, no matter what you buy it for," and he had to warn my mother about this quite often when they went to auction sales around home. I think prudent buying is obviously an important element of any family's existence, unless one is so wealthy that you don't have to worry about what you spend for.

And also, of course, what we forget about is that when we save and don't waste things, if there's a given supply, the competition to sell to customers will force the price down. I hope this will happen, for instance, with the most significant product that I hear about now, and that's home heating fuel. We've got adequate supplies on hand, for instance, in our country for home heating oil—240 million barrels have now been put in the primary reserves.

If the families throughout our country will, through thermostat settings and very careful living habits, reduce the amount of energy that they use this winter, compared to previous winters, then there'll be much more competition among oil suppliers to get those customers' business—and they don't want to carry over those oil stocks until next winter. So, prudent use of energy supplies can be a major factor in forcing down prices in a competitive free market system.

So, there are many different elements of the issue that I could discuss—I've tried not to repeat things that I've said earlier in the program. But that's one that I hadn't

mentioned previously that I think is an important factor. Prudent buying, no matter what the item is, can help us control inflation.

MR. MORRIS. Thank you very much, Mr. President, and good luck.

THE PRESIDENT. I've enjoyed talking to you. Thank you, Kenneth.

MS. STAMBERG. Thank you, Mr. Morris.

A reminder again to listeners that you cannot call into President Carter. National Public Radio is doing the phoning to citizens who have been chosen at random and have written in advance to "Ask the President."

The next question will come from Bruce Hallock, Mr. President, and he's on the line from Austin, Texas. Go ahead, Mr. Hallock.

U.S. SPACE ACTIVITIES

MR. HALLOCK. Hello, Mr. President.
THE PRESIDENT. Hello, Bruce.

MR. HALLOCK. What is your view of mankind's future in space for the long term and for right now?

THE PRESIDENT. I think we have a very bright future, Bruce. We're moving into a new era of the use of space that will be quite different from what we've known in the past. We've had the highly publicized exploratory flights into space, not only to the Moon with men—Americans on the Moon—but also in trips with our space vehicles through the different planets themselves.

Now we are shifting to a more routine use of space flights with the shuttle, that will be launched for the first time next year. This will permit us with a space vehicle to launch relatively cheaply a major load of equipment and other things into space—both from our Government, from other governments who are friendly to us, and from private enterprise as well—for experimental purposes or for commercial purposes, and then have that vehicle returned back to Earth to be used over and over again. And, as you know, on the Florida coast we'll launch for basic flights east and west, and from the California coast region we'll launch for basic flights that will go over the poles.

And so, we're going into an era now where all of the technological advances that have been made with previous space flights can be used for direct benefits. And we've derived, in my opinion, tremendous personal benefits from the experiments and the innovations that went into earlier space flights. We're now ready to capitalize on that in the future—both in the quality of our life, with weather, with geothermal analyses, photography and experiments in space, an absence of an atmosphere, direct observations of stellar things for astronomical observations—there are so many that it's almost mind-boggling. But I think that now we're going into a more routine space use—quite a transformation from previous experimental flights.

MR. HALLOCK. Well, does it bother you that now we're at the dawn of this bright future, that we seem to be cutting back with NASA's budget while the Russians are proceeding methodically with their manned space programs?

THE PRESIDENT. I don't believe that that's an accurate comparison. I believe that the space shuttle will be a major innovation. In effect, now, the Soviets are just following along with what we've done many years ago.

MR. HALLOCK. Thank you.

MS. STAMBERG. Thanks very much, Mr. Hallock. Thank you for joining us.

The next question will come from Ann Williams, President Carter, and she is on the line with us from Indianapolis, Indiana. Go ahead, Ms. Williams.

INHERITANCE TAXES

MS. WILLIAMS. Mr. Carter.

THE PRESIDENT. Yes, Ann.

MS. WILLIAMS. The very rich are able to protect their wealth with trusts and various other means and are able to pass their wealth down from generation to generation, whereas the average people, who really cannot afford to set up such expensive tax-saving devices, are taxed so heavily on inheritance taxes. This is a socialistic program which only benefits those who do not accumulate wealth in their lifetime.

Why don't you propose increasing the estate deduction to a much higher dollar amount than the present level, or eliminate inheritance taxes altogether?

THE PRESIDENT. Well, Ann, I think that your question provides two different views of the same subject. The inheritance taxes fall much more heavily on the extremely wealthy, and we have tried and are still trying to close loopholes in how those trusts can be used. I think there are still some gross abuses—where people put a large estate into a foundation, for instance, that's ostensibly to be used for the benefit of other people and then, through various loopholes in the law, provide very high salaries for members of that family to continue to benefit from the trust itself.

We have, I believe, a need from time to time to increase the amount of a person's inheritance left to children and to other members of the family that is excluded from taxation. As land values go up, for instance, it's very damaging to a farm family to have to sell even a relatively small farm in order to pay inheritance taxes, instead of letting the children take that farmland and continue to use it.

So, we are making modifications in the size of inheritance that is excluded from inheritance taxes to preserve relatively small estates. And I hope that we'll continue to close loopholes for the very wealthy. I agree with your basic premise.

Ms. WILLIAMS. Thank you very much.

Ms. STAMBERG. Thank you, Ms. Williams.

On the line now from St. Paul, Minnesota, is Cassandra Johnson. Go ahead, Ms. Johnson.

HUMAN RIGHTS

Ms. JOHNSON. Thank you. Good morning, Mr. President. I have a question involving human rights that I would like you to answer. I first of all would like to say that I'm really pleased that you've made that an issue and that you have raised the consciousness level throughout not only our own country but throughout the world. My question involves three countries which we support—South Korea, Chile, and the Philippines—who are gross violators of human rights to their own people in their own country.

I would like to know, is there any way that we as a country and you as a President who is for human rights can put more pressure, especially on the Philippines, to ease the tension and release the political prisoners in those countries?

THE PRESIDENT. Cassandra, we utilize every legitimate means to influence both leaders and governments of other countries to move toward a deeper honoring of human rights. There have been some substantial indications of progress in this hemisphere and, indeed, throughout the world in recent years, I think possibly because of our emphasis on human rights. Literally tens of thousands of prisoners

have been released from incarceration, and we've seen major moves away from totalitarian governments toward more democratic forms of government.

Just yesterday, for instance, I welcomed here the new Ambassador from Uganda, who has spent a lot of time in our country when Idi Amin, supported by the Soviet Union, was violating human rights in the grossest and most obnoxious way. Now the new government is much more inclined toward honoring human rights.

In the Philippines, there has been a good bit of progress made—still they don't measure up to standards that we ourselves would espouse in this country. And I visited South Korea not too long ago and had some very strong and heart-to-heart talks with President Park, letting him know that the relationships between his country and ours would be severely damaged with any indication of violation of human rights. Following that visit, large numbers of prisoners were released. But recently, as you've seen in the legislative body of South Korea, the opposition party members have resigned in protest because one of their leaders was excluded, a Mr. Lee.*

So, we are trying to encourage and sometimes even force other countries, as best we can legitimately, to shift toward a greater honoring of human rights. In international lending institutions, for instance, we don't vote for economic aid—except for the most narrowly defined humanitarian purposes, like food for starving people—unless that country does honor human rights as assessed by us. And I'm required each year to give to the Congress a report on every country with whom we deal at all, concerning the de-

---

*The President later said that he had intended to refer to Mr. Kim Yong Sam. [Printed in the transcript.] See page 1919.

gree of their compliance with our own human rights standards.

This is sometimes a cause of major diplomatic protests from those countries, but we do it. And I think that their awareness that they are being assessed by us and by Amnesty International and other countries are very important factors. I doubt now in the last 2½ years that there is any government leader on Earth, either in totalitarian countries or democratic countries, including myself, who don't frequently stop and say, "What are we doing that would cause the condemnation of the world to come on us because we are violating human rights?"

We're making some progress; but still have a long way to go.

INDIAN RESERVATIONS

Ms. JOHNSON. Along with that question, Mr. President, I'd like to ask about, you know, the Indians. I've been aware— 'cause this is an area that we've got reservations, in Minnesota and throughout the Midwest area and South Dakota and such—that with the energy crunch as it is today, that the energy companies—oil, electricity—are coming into some of these reservation lands and in some way trying to get hold of the land and take it over to produce energy, whatever that—you know, uranium, especially, I'm thinking of, in the Black Hills area in South Dakota.

Can there be any assurances that those treaties that were made with the Indians will not be violated by the Federal Government?

THE PRESIDENT. Yes, the assurance lies under the constitutional guarantees of honoring civil rights or human rights of those Indians. And as you probably have noticed in the last few years, the Federal courts have been much more inclined to honor the Indians' rights, even though they were derived from very ancient treaties. They were violated for many generations. Now I think there's a substantial movement toward honoring those original treaties.

Ms. STAMBERG. Thanks very much, Ms. Johnson.

Let's move on now, President Carter, to another question. This one from Peg Ormsby, in Weston, West Virginia. Go ahead, Ms. Ormsby.

DAM AND WATER PROJECTS

Ms. ORMSBY. Hello, President Carter; we're grateful for the chance to talk to you.

THE PRESIDENT. Thank you. I'm honored to have a chance to talk to all of you.

Ms. ORMSBY. You're asking us to make sacrifices in the name of the energy crisis and to help control inflation, and you said that the Federal Government is doing everything it can to help with these problems. But here on the local level, in Lewis County, West Virginia, we're fighting to keep the Federal Government from building the expensive Stonewall Jackson Dam.

Now, this dam would destroy existing coal, oil, and gas reserves as well as using an enormous amount of energy in its construction. Alternatives to the dam exist, but they haven't been explored.

President Carter, this dam was never reviewed under your water projects criteria. EPA has challenged its justification. So, how can you tell us here on the local level, who feel the results of Federal projects and Federal dictates, that the Government itself is doing everything it can to save energy and fight inflation?

THE PRESIDENT. Peg, I can't say that the Government's doing everything it can; I say we're doing a lot, and we're trying as best we can.

One of the things that I've done since I've been in office, that's been one of the most difficult things and most controversial things, is to try to eliminate the construction of unnecessary dam or water projects and to preserve the analysis rights of the Federal Government to screen out, in the future, projects that are not needed.

In many cases—I'm not sure about the project to which you refer—but in many cases, these decisions to construct such a project were made many years ago and ostensibly with the support of not only the Federal Government but your own Members of Congress and local officials who had to participate, including, I presume, your own Governor and your own State legislature. It's extremely hard, although we've been successful in some cases, to cancel a project—even though it's ill-advised—if it has a lot of commitment already made to be completed.

The environmental element is one factor involved. We are trying now to get installed for the first time a permanent screening group that would look at each of these dam construction projects on its own merits and in a much more objective and fair way and to eliminate politics or local chamber of commerce support from it. I think that in any particular construction project that the best way to stop it, if it's once begun and once a commitment is made, is through a delegation of your Members of Congress or your Governor or your State legislature or from the local level.

We're doing our share here, but it's very hard to reverse standards and procedures that have been in existence in our Government for generations. We've made a lot of progress, though. I think anyone would admit that.

Ms. ORMSBY. Yeah, I agree that you've made a lot of progress, and we certainly applaud your efforts. This is a very old project. The problem is that the Federal Government itself, not just Congress, has a role—every agency from EPA to the Fish and Wildlife people. They're not doing their share in their honest evaluation. It's too easy to always pass the blame onto your Congressman, and we're working on the local level to ensure a change here. But we still need the help of the Federal agencies whose job it is to watchdog over these kinds of projects.

THE PRESIDENT. I agree with you. I was not trying to put the blame on Congress.

Ms. ORMSBY. No, I know that, although they shoulder their share.

Thank you very much.

THE PRESIDENT. Yes, there's plenty of blame to go around.

Ms. STAMBERG. Thank you, Ms. Ormsby.

Dr. George Bergstrom joins us now. He's on the line from Fallbrook, California. Go ahead, Dr. Bergstrom.

U.S.-SOVIET RELATIONS

DR. BERGSTROM. Good morning, Mr. President.

THE PRESIDENT. Good morning. Doctor.

DR. BERGSTROM. As an American who's spent much of the last 19 years traveling and living in Asia and Europe, I'm greatly concerned with the rather serious growth of Russian military and political influence in not only Asia and Europe but in various other parts of the world as well. Your proposed SALT treaty appears to be, I think, a positive step forward towards meeting this challenge. Can you comment on how SALT will strengthen America's position vis-a-vis Russia?

And secondly, I think one of the most strategic, long-range actions of your administration has been the establishment of working relations between America and

China. Can you expand on some of the specific programs you plan to establish which will increase cultural and business relations between America and China?

THE PRESIDENT. Yes. And I'll try to be brief, although your question is very deep and a penetrating one and hard to answer in a few words.

There's no doubt in my mind that the SALT II treaty will enhance our relative military strength with the Soviet Union. For instance, the Soviets will be required to dismantle or destroy about 10 percent of all the nuclear missile launchers that they have. We will not be required to dismantle any of them. And this will mean that over a period of time, we'll maintain equivalency with the Soviet Union in strategic or nuclear armaments and, at the same time, have a chance to take our great reservoir of financial and natural resources and our human resources and orient them either toward conventional defense capability or toward a better life for our people.

If we can maintain military strength adequate to defend our country—and that's what I'm committed to do—then we put the competition with the Soviet Union on a peaceful basis where, in my opinion, we have all the advantages.

For instance, the Soviet Union is a totalitarian government; ours is a free government, a democratic government. The Soviets believe that the citizen ought to be subject to the mandates of the state; we believe that citizens as individuals ought to be honored and that the citizens ourselves should control the government. We believe in individual initiative and in the worth of the human beings; the Soviets believe that the state should dominate in every respect. Ours is a country that's founded on a free enterprise system, where innovation and new ideas, through a competitive society, have a chance to

succeed, and it inspires the rapid development of research and development.

I think if you'd look at the Nobel prizes given out in health or chemistry or physics and so forth in the past number of years, America takes a tremendous number of those because this is an advantage that we have.

One of the most important advantages, however, is that we have moral and ethical standards, human rights standards that make us competitively superior over the Soviet Union in the peaceful competition for the friendship, the hearts and the minds, the trade relationships of uncommitted or nonaligned people around the world.

We value also the independence of other governments, even in small or weak or new nations. The Soviets often try to subvert those governments and take over control of the affairs of people.

So, in a peaceful competition with the Soviet Union, I think we have all the advantages to prevail. That is an important element of the SALT treaties.

On the China question—if you look at the last number of years, we have made tremendous strides, in my opinion, in this peaceful competition for the friendship of those around the world. It wasn't too long ago that the closest ally that the Soviets had was the People's Republic of China, a fourth of the population of the entire Earth. That's changed dramatically now.

It wasn't too long ago that, under Mrs. Indira Gandhi, India was closely allied with the Soviet Union and quite antagonistic toward us. That has been completely changed.

It wasn't too long ago that Egypt, the largest and most influential and important Arab country, was closely aligned with the Soviet Union and diametrically opposite and opposed to us. That's changed.

In Africa the largest black nation and the most influential and powerful black nation in the African continent is Nigeria. It wasn't too long ago that Secretary Kissinger couldn't even get permission to go inside Nigeria, because they were antagonistic toward the United States. I've visited there myself. Now they're one of the best friends and allies we have.

We haven't been successful in every instance. But in general, in our peaceful competition with the Soviet Union, we are making out very well. And I think this gives us an opportunity—with China and other countries—to benefit Americans in the future.

Ms. STAMBERG. Thank you, Dr. Bergstrom.

U.S. STRENGTHS

President Carter, I noticed when you answered that question outlining our relations with the Soviets, your answer was very similar to one that you gave earlier in the week at a news conference. And it begins to sound like a kind of litany, a list that you're doing really of a definition of what the Soviet Union is about, as compared to what the United States stands for. Why are you doing that right now? Is this some sort of escalation of rhetoric?

THE PRESIDENT. No, no. I think it's good for our country to be reminded of our strengths. We're the strongest nation on Earth militarily. We're the strongest nation on Earth economically. We're the strongest nation on Earth politically. I think we're the strongest nation on Earth when you compare ethics and moral standards and a commitment to basic human freedoms. It does give us an advantage that Americans ought not to forget about.

Quite often we read in the news media, watch television, listen to the radio, and all we hear about are the temporary inconveniences and the differences that exist in Washington between the President and the Congress or between the House and the Senate, the arguments and the debates and the temporary setbacks and the failures. But in general, the progress of our country is absolutely superb. It's something that we ought to remember—how much we've been blessed, what a superior opportunity we have in life, and how influential our country is among the community of nations in the world.

And I believe that to point out these basic advantages strengthens the ability of Americans to overcome temporary setbacks and to meet challenges and to answer questions and to resolve problems, whereas on the other hand, we often tend to become discouraged. And I think that a part of my duty as President is not to mislead anyone, but to remind Americans of how strong and how great our country is now and can be in the future.

Ms. STAMBERG. Interesting that you're saying this. Now, a few months ago you were telling us about the malaise that you were perceiving across the country.

THE PRESIDENT. Exactly.

Ms. STAMBERG. Has now that disappeared?

THE PRESIDENT. No, it hasn't disappeared. But part of that malaise that I pointed out and a lack of confidence in the American people is what I'm trying to address. If we'll just stop and inventory what we have, there is no need for us to be discouraged or divided or antagonistic toward our own Government or discouraged about the strength of America, now and in the future. We need that confidence, and we need—not only that—to respect each other.

When we have gasoline lines or even when we have a serious problem like increased home heating costs, we tend to overemphasize those inconveniences and those problems. They are serious, and our

Nation is able to address them. But for us to use those temporary or transient inconveniences or serious problems as an excuse to lash out at one another and to try to grasp a selfish advantage for ourselves or to turn against our own Government or to turn against our own free enterprise system and condemn ourselves, that's what I deplore.

And so, I think we do have a serious problem in our country with a lack of confidence in the future and some tendencies toward disunity. But when we analyze the reasons for unity and the need for us to work together and the blessings that we have, I think that's an accurate means for Americans to derive an honest opinion of our own country.

PRESIDENT'S LEADERSHIP QUALITIES

Ms. STAMBERG. President Carter, to what extent does that lack of confidence that you say we're exhibiting in the future of the country depend on a confidence in you and your ability to govern?

THE PRESIDENT. A lot.

Ms. STAMBERG. You've seen your ratings in the polls are very low, and real questions are being raised about your own leadership abilities.

THE PRESIDENT. Sure. I think that has a lot to do with it. It's not only a lack of confidence in the President but an even lower confidence, for instance, in the Congress and a very low confidence in the news media, in the churches, in the schools. And people have become more uncertain, as I pointed out in my Sunday night speech in July.

A part of it is because of present inconveniences and divisions and competition. Part of it, however, is derived from historical events—Vietnam war, Watergate embarrassments, and so forth—that America is now beginning to heal. But I think the fact that we have been able to weather the leaving of this office, in which we are sitting, by an incumbent President under embarrassing circumstances, the fact that we have been willing to face the first experience in American history when we were not successful in a war, in Vietnam, and still have a strong country is a sign that we ought not to be discouraged, but that we ought to be encouraged.

Our basic institutions that we sometimes doubt—government, the Presidency, the Congress—have survived and have prevailed. And I don't think our system of either economics or our social system or our government system has any equal anywhere on Earth. We ought to remember that.

Ms. STAMBERG. But are you saying, though, that your low ratings in the polls are a result of general public lack of confidence in the institution itself, or in your own ability to be President, to provide leadership?

THE PRESIDENT. I think both. I don't think that all of my low ratings in the polls are attributable to a general lack of confidence. Part of it is because of people's opinion about me.

This has not been a unique circumstance. All previous Presidents have had very low ratings in the polls at one time or another. Without being apologetic about it, we have never failed. And I hope I never fail, as long as I'm in this office, to address a necessary and difficult question just to avoid criticisms or a lower rating in the poll.

There's no way to benefit, for instance, from addressing the energy question. You're condemned by producers of oil, you're condemned in some ways by consumers who, once the issue is raised, say, "Well, why doesn't the President do something about it?" We're trying. And I think that this is inherent in this office.

I didn't come here looking for glory or looking for everyone to approve what I did; I came here to do a job for our country. And if it results in either temporary or permanent criticisms or lower opinion among American people, if I think I'm right and doing what is best for this country, I'm going to do it.

I believe that this next year, 1980, a presidential election year, will serve as a time for presentation to the American people of what I have done as President, the problems that still remain, and what I can propose to the American people in the future to correct those problems. And if I can build up at that time adequate confidence in me, when the issues are clearly addressed and that accurate inventory is made, then perhaps the people will change their opinion.

Ms. STAMBERG. President Carter, we're almost at the end of our time, but we do have time for perhaps a few more callers' calls.

This is Mrs. Sue Eik, and she's in Philipsburg, Montana. Go ahead, Mrs. Eik.

HOSPITAL COST CONTAINMENT

MRS. EIK. Thank you.

Mr. President?

THE PRESIDENT. Yes. Go ahead.

MRS. EIK. I'm very pleased to be able to speak with you. Speaking of something closer to all of our hearts and on the homefront, I recently, due to personal experiences within the family—I'm concerned with rising medical costs and care of the elderly. I guess until you get involved in it yourself you just pretty much take it for granted. You're aware of these high costs, but when you really get down to it and you're trying to figure out adequate means for your family to get good health care, do the best you can for them, then you come down to figuring out how you're going to pay for it. It really is a concern to each and every one of us.

I have in-laws that are in very poor condition, and I'm doing everything I can

for them. But in this last month, I have come to see very good cases of good health care, and in the same instances I feel that as great of a nation as we are, we're really handling things very poorly.

THE PRESIDENT. Mrs. Eik, let me see if——

MRS. EIK. There are great strides in medicine, and yet it doesn't seem like we have very much interest or care in our aging people. We're doing great things with heart surgery and transplants.

Ms. STAMBERG. Mrs. Eik, let me interrupt you for a moment, because our time is running short. Why doesn't President Carter go ahead and answer you?

THE PRESIDENT. One of the best things that we can do about all the problems that you've described, Mrs. Eik, is to have the Congress pass the hospital cost containment legislation that's before them. Last year the Senate passed it, and now it's before the House and the Senate again. The lobbyists are trying to oppose this legislation, and it must be passed. It would cut down on the amount that Americans will spend for hospital care in the next 5 years by $53 billion. It'll not only cut your future hospital bills by roughly $500, but it'll also leave the hospitals adequately profitable and will not reduce the level or quality of health care.

Hospital cost containment is extremely important. We hope to get it finally passed.

KIM YONG SAM

I would like to correct one thing I said earlier, if you don't mind.

Ms. STAMBERG. Okay.

THE PRESIDENT. When I was in Korea I met with Kim Yong Sam, who is the opposition leader in the legislature that was expelled. I think I inadvertently said Mr. Lee. But it's Kim Yong Sam whom I met there. I didn't want to leave an error.

Ms. STAMBERG. Thanks for the correction. Thanks very much.

We have no more time, I'm afraid——

THE PRESIDENT. Oh, sorry.

Ms. STAMBERG.—— President Carter. We've come to the end of it. Thank you so much for taking part in this broadcast.

THE PRESIDENT. Well, I've thoroughly enjoyed it, Susan. I hope we can do it again.

Ms. STAMBERG. I want to thank the thousands of citizens who wrote in asking to speak with the President and thank all of you who did get a chance to pose questions. "Ask the President" was made possible with funds provided by the Corporation for Public Broadcasting. Stay with us for some analysis of the President's remarks in a few moments.

This is NPR, National Public Radio.

NOTE: The program began at 12 noon.

Kennedys-King Day Dinner

Remarks at the Annual Dinner Honoring John F. Kennedy, Robert F. Kennedy, and Martin Luther King, Jr.   October 13, 1979

Thank you, my good friend Walter Fauntroy, Mayor Barry, who spoke so eloquently about future plans for the city and for mine and his relationship, Mrs. King, distinguished guests, fellow Democrats, and fellow citizens of the District of Columbia:

I've been reading lately about Mayor Barry's attempts to find a house to live in. [*Laughter*] He has my sympathy. I understand his problem. It took my wife and me 2 solid years—[*laughter*]—of hard work to get the exact house we wanted in the District. [*Laughter*] And we could not have succeeded without the help of many of you. And I have particularly enjoyed the high quality of the garbage collec-

tion—[*laughter*]—in our residence, Mr. Mayor.

It's especially appropriate that the Democratic Party of this District should honor the recent heroes of our country, for it was only recently that your own struggle for the right to vote was honored. The early days of that struggle were shadowed by the cruel and heart-rending deaths of John F. Kennedy, Robert F. Kennedy, Martin Luther King, Jr. They championed the cause of the voiceless—people whose silent pain became an ocean roar that swept across our Nation, helping to wash away ancient hatreds and prejudice and discrimination and fear.

Their success was made possible by the people who stood with them, their closest loved ones, like Coretta Scott King, who spoke on this platform a few minutes ago. We finally won some of the battles which they began. And, as you know, old barriers have been falling so that many people can now share more fully the life in a nation dedicated to freedom and equality. This has been especially true here in the District. Yet for all of our victories, the right for full citizenship must continue.

Our strong District Democratic Party, represented by this enormous crowd tonight, is proof of some of those victories. You won the right to vote for President in 1964. It took you 10 years to win the right to vote for local officials, in 1974. You've got a good record. In 1964, 1968, 1972, you cast at least or almost 80 percent of your votes for the Democratic candidate for President. This is the kind of careful, balanced political judgment that I really admire. [*Laughter*] This District is truly the most Democratic place in our country and, therefore, a good place to live. And it inures a great deal of justifiable credit to you.

In 1976 you were able to improve even on that remarkable early record, casting

82 percent of your votes for the Carter-Mondale ticket, and I thank you for it. And I hope that you all do even better in 1980—*[laughter]*—for all the Democrats who run.

You yourselves have produced outstanding political leaders: your able representative to the United States Congress, Walter Fauntroy; your dynamic and nationally admired young mayor, Marion Barry; the effective leader of your local Democratic Party, Bob Washington; your distinguished national committeeman and committeewoman, John Hechinger and Sharon Dixon.

And, in addition, this great city has provided many outstanding people to serve with me in the administration of the affairs of the United States of America: people like Pat Harris, Cliff Alexander, Geno Baroni, Sterling Tucker; Tyrone Brown, the FCC; Emmett Rice, the Federal Reserve; Senator Joe Tydings, Ruth Prokop, the Merit Systems Protection Board; Edith Barksdale Sloan, the Consumer Product Safety Commissioner; Bunny Mitchell; Wiley Branton at Conrail; Marjorie Lawson, Kennedy Center; Jim Dyke; Pauline Schneider, and many others—I don't have time to name them all. But this forces the Federal Government to recognize you, to recognize your hopes and your dreams and your problems and your aspirations. And it also gives the District, which has a highly motivated and consummately, politically educated electorate, to have a great and beneficial effect on the rest of our country.

The party that produced this tremendous array of talent also nurtured the District's image as a vigorous local entity, separate and apart from the seat of our Federal Government. As a matter of fact, as you well know, there are really two Washingtons: one, of the Federal city, which is a national and an international center; and hometown Washington, where 700,000 local people live and work and make a good city function. When I campaigned, I often mentioned the mistakes of the Federal Government, and I have even had a few things to say about that since I have been living here. But I have never confused the two cities, and I have only had good things to say about hometown Washington.

This city enjoys the special beauty and the cultural advantages of being the Nation's Capital. And you've coped well with the special responsibilities of being an international center. But hometown Washington must also correct or prevent problems that you share with other cities throughout this country—such as urban decay, poverty, crime, and unemployment. You manage this and you manage it well, because you have a special kind of determination which has sustained this community despite generations of deprivation of basic human rights.

As far as hometown Washington is concerned, I have the same commitments tonight that I had when I was a candidate for President.

More than 2 years ago, I asked Vice President Walter Mondale to bring together a group, a high-level task force of local officials, officers from our own administration, Members of Congress, and to work with me and to work with you to carry out those campaign commitments and make sure that the basic problems of the District were not only identified but resolved.

First, I'm determined to reduce Federal intrusion into the local affairs of the District of Columbia. I've already ended Presidential review of local decisions where there is no significant Federal interest involved, and I support similar elimination of congressional review of such local matters. I will never treat the

District as merely an extension of the Federal Government. I'm committed to complete home rule for the District of Columbia.

This is an easy thing to say; it's a difficult thing to do. But you have a partner here who will work with you in every single opportunity to bring about what I have just described, because until these goals can be reached, we must press for decisions in the meantime that are speedy, simple, and fair to your people.

Secondly, I'm determined to establish a sound financial relationship between the District and the Federal Government.

I support increasing the authorized Federal payment and appropriating the full amount authorized, with a formula to make this process both orderly and predictable. I want to remove the Federal Government from the budgetmaking process for the District, because I think budgets ought to be made by the people who pay them.

There is a fact unknown by the rest of this Nation, that the bulk of your budget comes from local taxes. Other cities get Federal help and they still have a right to make their own budget decisions, and I believe so should the District of Columbia.

We have ended the last vestige of colonialism in Latin America on October 1, when the Panama Canal Treaty was implemented. And I want to end the last vestige of colonialism in America by passing the voting rights amendment in the 38 States of this country to make it law.

With your mayor, with other political leaders, with Walter Fauntroy, I am eager to cooperate mutually, to consult with one another, to lay a political strategy and to help to carry it out, because there is an awful lot of misinformation around this country about the composition of the District—its people, your qualifications, and the cheating that has taken place under present constitutional provisions, and the tinge of racism which has colored the reluctance to make this decision which is so long overdue. Fundamental justice requires that all citizens have not only a voice but also a vote in Congress.

The right to win congressional approval of this amendment was not easy, but for the first time in history—and this can make a difference—a President is supporting full voting representation for the District.

We received the necessary bipartisan support in Congress, because we all worked as a team. We made it attractive for both Democrats and Republicans to support this controversial issue. Had we not, it could not have passed the House or the Senate of the Congress. Many people deserve credit for that victory, but we all owe a special debt of gratitude to the man who never stopped letting us dream the impossible dream—Walter Fauntroy.

That success has been one of the most gratifying victories that's taken place during my administration. But we cannot rest until we have full congressional representation in the House and Senate for the citizens who live in the District.

Early in his administration, Mayor Barry visited me in the Oval Office, and we discussed ways that we could work together to form an even better partnership between him and me, his administration and mine, to solve other problems that involve the District and the Federal Government. Since then, our offices have been working closely together—constantly—to cement and to utilize this partnership.

It hasn't been long yet, but we've already seen significant results.

Working together, we're going to complete the Metro system. The Federal Government has now placed its total monetary commitment to Metro on the table. Now it's up to the surrounding jurisdictions to fund their share of the system—and Washington needs the full 101 miles of the Metro system—and working together as partners, we're going to get it.

Until tonight I believe that that was the plan. We might have to cut maybe a mile or two off, Mr. Mayor, to get a few more garbage trucks. We'll see about that in the future. [*Laughter*]

Also working together, we've developed a plan to transfer authority to prosecute local crimes from the United States attorney's office to the District Government. Legislation to bring this transfer about will be a top priority for my administration. Other cities have control over their local criminal justice system, and so should the people who live in the District of Columbia.

I'm committed as well to having the mayor appoint local judges. This district is the only jurisdiction in the United States where local judges must be appointed by the President. The right to make decisions affecting your life is crucial to you, but the District also has special problems and it needs special help.

We recently approved grants totaling $58 million for the District. These funds came from you in Federal income taxes paid, and they will go to construct new sewage treatment systems, to complete urban renewal projects, to modernize the public housing development, to provide financial aid and home weatherization for the elderly and low-income people, and to pay for various health improvement programs. The partnership between me and the mayor, my administration and his, is already paying off.

And now I'd like just to add a personal note: This is not just your city, it's my city, too. My whole family enjoys living in this exciting and beautiful place. As you know, we came from a small town, and as you know, one of the things that we have been is part of this community. We don't get to do enough of the simple things along with you that we enjoy, most of all, because of the pressures of the office I hold. But without publicity and without fanfare, we walk around the Tidal Basin to see the cherry blossoms, and we run along the canal towpath, and we visit some of the churches around the District—not with publicity, but quietly—St. Matthew's, St. John's, St. Patrick's, Washington Cathedral, National Cathedral, Warner Presbyterian, Zion Baptist, Metropolitan AME, my own First Baptist Church, and others.

As parents of a student in the public schools, in Stevens Elementary and now at Hardy Middle School, we are personally interested in the quality of education in the District for Amy Carter and for your children, too.

In private homes which we visit, in stores, in restaurants and theaters and art galleries and museums, at the memorials commemorating the lives of famous Americans, we share the culture and excitement with tourists and with other residents of the District. Like you, we watch the Redskins and the Bullets play ball.

And Rosalynn has visited and worked with you in many places. I'd like to name just a few so you will know what my wife has been and is doing—the Children's Hospital, the Green Door, D.C. General Hospital, where she has led Jaycees and others to remodel that hospital and to get certification for nurses; immunization centers for children; the D.C. Village, Home for Older Americans, at Jubilee House, Friendship House; employment seminars for the well, employment seminars for the handicapped; at the Federal

City Club to inspire the business community to work more closely together to make this a truly great city; at Terrell Junior High School, at the Children's Museum, and many others. She has been there, and she works with you on projects.

We've tried to learn about the Nation's problems by learning about yours and to learn about some solutions to those problems by trying to solve yours and mine—how to improve health care, how to have better public housing, how to care for alcoholics, how to care for the mentally afflicted, how to promote employment, how to enhance the beauty of the city.

And we've invited literally hundreds of people like you to come to join in with us at the White House, and we've invited volunteers who work with Rosalynn, and other workers, to come to the White House so we could thank them and encourage them to be better citizens of the District of Columbia.

We're one of you, and we're part of the city, and I don't want you to ever forget that you've got official friends and personal friends who live at 1600 Pennsylvania Avenue.

Washington does share the problems of other cities, but Washington is also unique. Washington should be a model of how problems can be solved creatively and compassionately so that every citizen of the District will have a share in both the present and the future, not just of this city, but of our Nation. And I think we've got a tremendous untapped resource in the Congress. And I think you and I collectively ought to encourage the Members of the Congress to get to know more about the District, not just the places of entertainment and where to eat, but also to learn about the life of people who live here who are not rich, but who are struggling for a place under the Sun in life.

I believe it would help you all over the country if they were invited specifically to visit some of the places that I've just named, where Rosalynn goes and many others where she has not yet been. We cannot have a Federal city of affluent officials, lobbyists, lawyers, and others, serving in the midst of another city, a very different city of the poor, the lonely, the sick, the homeless, the jobless, the old—a city of disadvantaged citizens and disfranchised citizens.

This city has already proved a major point for our country: that black and white citizens can live and work together and can build an effective Democratic Party together, yes, but also you've proven that you can build a greater community together. You are building a community that proves what America—the land of opportunity—really means.

Because of you, this unique national city—international center and hometown—is a vigorous community, ready to accept the full responsibilities—along with the full rights—of citizenship.

Like you, I'm proud to be a Democrat, and I am also proud to be a Washingtonian.

Thank you very much.

NOTE: The President spoke at 10:10 p.m. in the International Ballroom at the Washington Hilton Hotel.

Aid for Kampucheans

Statement Announcing United States Relief Effort Pledge.   October 15, 1979

A human tragedy of horrifying proportions is unfolding in Kampuchea, with millions of people facing illness or death from starvation. Every member of the international community has a duty to help avert further mass suffering in Kampuchea. This is beyond politics. It is a matter of simple and urgent humanitarian concern.

Two respected agencies—the International Committee of the Red Cross (ICRC) and the U.N. Children's Fund (UNICEF)—have been acting as agents for concerned governments and the United Nations in launching a major relief program to get food and medicine to the people of Kampuchea before it is too late.

I am today announcing an initial United States pledge of $7 million to this effort: $2 million from the United States Emergency Refugee and Migration Assistance Fund, plus 10,000 tons of food, worth $5 million from Food for Peace. This is in addition to the more than $1.2 million we have already devoted to feeding and caring for people along the Thai-Kampuchean border. I hope we can do more once the food and medicine begins to flow to those who need it, and I am eager to work with Congress to that end. Subsequently, we expect that the United Nations World Food Program, which is taking a leading role in mobilizing international food assistance, will draw upon U.S. pledges already made.

Secretary-General Waldheim has appealed to U.N. member states to support this effort with money and food. Japan, the Federal Republic of Germany, Australia, Britain, and the European Economic Community, have already responded. I urge others to follow their example.

I want to commend the private voluntary agencies which have moved so quickly to deal with this emergency. During Pope John Paul's visit to the White House, he and I discussed the need to act swiftly. I know that his concern is shared by religious groups of many denominations.

A heavy responsibility rests on the regimes and fighting armies causing so much of the misery in Kampuchea. I call on those who are supplying them the weapons of war to use all their influence to assure that humanitarian relief reaches the people.

Kansas City, Missouri

Remarks at the Annual Convention of the National Conference of Catholic Charities. October 15, 1979

Bishop Sullivan, Father Dunn, Monsignor Corcoran, Governor Carlin, Congressman Skelton, distinguished volunteers who combine together, and have for 251 years, in our Nation to make us proud of benevolence and unselfishness through Catholic charities:

I was at Sunday school yesterday morning, and someone said to me, "Mr. President, you're spending an awful lot of time with Catholics lately." [*Laughter*] And one of my Baptist friends, who was standing there said, "It hasn't hurt you a bit." [*Laughter*]

After inviting Pope John Paul to come to the United States and, 10 days ago, having the great honor to receive him as my personal guest, I thought for the Nation how unprecedented an event it was to have the President of the United States welcome the spiritual leader of the world's Roman Catholics to our Nation's Capital for the first time, to the White House, the symbolic home of all Americans. For me personally, this occasion ranked as one of the best experiences of my Presidency.

There was a glow of warmth and friendship with the outstretched arms of millions of Americans to welcome our distinguished visitor. He and I had a delightful private conversation, quite extended. I told him I was surprised. He said he was, too. I knew that the welcome would be warm, but the overwhelming nature of it was indeed one of the most remarkable events of the entire world.

He and I talked about many things. We talked about weapons. We talked about peace. We talked about Ireland, and we talked about the Middle East. We talked about China. We talked about hunger. We talked about charity. We talked about abortion. We talked about families. We talked about communism. We talked about freedom. We talked about the role of the church in this hemisphere and the spread of the gospel in countries where missionaries are now excluded. We talked about the relationship between the church and the state and how the efforts of public and private lives might be harnessed in common causes.

Pope John Paul's visit merits our continuing thoughts and reflections. His message to America was first and foremost a spiritual message. In his address to Catholic University, he said, "Materialistic concerns are never sufficient to fill the heart and mind of a human person. A life reduced to the sole dimension of possession of consumer goods, of temporal concerns will never let you discover and enjoy the full richness of your humanity."

The Pope's message and his visit stirred our Nation's Capital and, indeed, the entire world, and it stirred particularly the lives of our countrymen whenever he visited a streetcorner or a community or a small or a large church.

Looking for truth in a time of doubt, people have found in this good man a reaffirmation of those values that hold our society together—the fundamental values of love, unity, charity, family. In normal circumstances, we Americans have a very difficult time expressing our sentiments about these kinds of things. But they are as real as any of our more tangible concerns. John Paul's visit showed that these feelings are always within us.

People were waiting for someone to say, "God bless America." And it sounded, I believe, particularly good coming from the lips of a world leader whose life is devoted to the service of God—Pope John Paul II.

I spoke to the Nation about this great underlying sense of community and patriotic values in my July address on Sunday evening, following a long period of consultation and meditation at Camp David. I believe such values are as important now as they were to our mothers and fathers and our ancestors when they first arrived in this country—either 3 years ago, 30 years ago, or perhaps 300 years ago—immigrants to a new land, determined to build a new life in what Pope John Paul has christened our "continent of hope."

If Pope John Paul left our Nation with one central message, it was this: We need to put our deep moral beliefs into action. And that's what you do, and I'm proud of you for it. "The poor," he said, "are our brothers and sisters." Instead of throwing them "crumbs," we should treat them like "guests at our family table."

Your great organization, the National Conference of Catholic Charities, personifies this standard of compassion. For 250 years, you've put your faith and your values into action. You've translated your vision of mankind and your philosophy into a working, living reality.

It's hard to imagine how differently our Nation would have grown had it not been for your own historic commitment. Generations ago, when government welfare programs were scarce or nonexistent, it was your organization and others like it that provided welcome and initial nourishment to millions of immigrants who reached our shores. To the huddled masses, it was not the government, but the church and voluntary charitable groups that one had to look to for help.

And for many immigrant groups— from Ireland and Italy and Poland and Latin America—it was the Catholic Church that stood as the one institution that gave them an immediate sense of belonging to American society. The church helped new arrivals put down roots socially and economically, as well as spiritually. In the process it helped not only to build lives, but it helped to build our Nation.

Today your organization remains at the cutting edge of our Nation's great social commitment. Without your voluntary action, without generous participation of other private citizens in communities, churches, and organizations, we would live in a society without a soul.

All the grants-in-aid, all the income maintenance programs of the Federal Government, and all the well-intentioned and effective efforts of dedicated Federal and other government employees could never replace this heartfelt, voluntary effort that covers our Nation like they do. But neither can voluntary agencies do the job alone. To meet our society's needs, we need to foster a true partnership, one which involves government at all levels, private enterprise, and unselfish volunteers.

This partnership of public and private interest is a major element in my own administration's domestic policy. It's also been illustrated vividly in the resettlement in our country of many thousands of Indochinese refugees. This step would not have been possible without the help of the voluntary agencies and, especially, Catholic charities.

There is now developing, to the horror of the world, a tragedy of profound consequence in Cambodia, known now as Kampuchea. Today I announced a

United States pledge of $7 million, which will be increased in the future, to help feed the tens of thousands of starving human beings.

We have difficult obstacles to overcome in the distribution of this food. And this effort will be carried out by private charities and by organizations of the United Nations, and together we must succeed. If obstacles arise between the starving and the food we offer, those obstacles need to be highly publicized so that the officials of south Vietnam will not dare perpetuate the horrible circumstances which they themselves have created.

These steps in Southeast Asia and in other places around the world would not have been possible without the help of the voluntary agencies. On behalf of all Americans, I thank you for your service and salute your tremendous humanitarian work in this area.

I might mention here another example of successful public and private partnership—in the fine work that your own president-elect, Monsignor Fahey, has been doing as my appointee on the Federal Council on the Aging.

There's one aspect of our national life where we need to put our partnership to even better use—and I talked about it when I was with you 3 years ago, in 1976—that is the problem of the families. This is a subject of pivotal concern to all of us and was especially during Pope John Paul's American visit. Families are the foundation of a healthy and a vibrant society. They carry out the timeless tasks of nurturing, supporting, and caring for their own members, in many different cultures and many different communities. They provide irreplaceable strength and shelter for one another.

Today, what Pope John XXIII called "the first and essential cell of human society"—that is, a family—is in trouble.

Many families have already been strained to the breaking point by social and economic forces beyond their own control. Some families indeed have broken. The tragic results are all around us, in alcoholism, drug addiction, social alienation, and crime.

Three years ago in Denver, I told you there was a gap in the way our country makes public policy—the lack of an explicit, conscious concern for how government policies and activities affect families. I said at the time that a nonpolicy toward families by government has the same adverse consequences as an antifamily policy would have.

I promised that my administration would make a conscious commitment to strengthen the American family, and I promised to consult with you and your own officials so that I might have the proper guidance. We set to work on that commitment, and in every policy area, economic and otherwise, we have sought to assist and to support families. We recognize that spiritual uplift for a person can only follow if the bare necessities of life are provided.

I'm proud of my administration's record in pursuing this approach. We've added, for instance, more than 8 million new jobs to combat perhaps the greatest twin threats to the family—unemployment and poverty.

We've undertaken to reform our Nation's ineffective, inefficient welfare programs, programs that for too long have been antiwork and antifamily. We've finally gotten this legislation out of the Ways and Means Committee in the House, and I need for you to help me get it the rest of the way through the Congress. Only by building up public awareness and public support for a proposal like this can it overcome the inertia of the Congress and arouse the support that will

encourage the Members of Congress to give it their support.

We've greatly increased funding for social services, for health, for housing, and for education, and we are today working to pass comprehensive health insurance, another long overdue aid to families. I also hope to implement major improvements in our policies and programs concerning foster care and adoption. Such programs, if poorly administered, have often hurt rather than helped children and families.

In dozens of other ways, we've sought to build a strong commitment to preserve and protect American families in all their diversity.

We've worked for the passage of important new legislation to combat child abuse, sexual exploitation of children, and discrimination in employment because of pregnancy. We've extended Head Start, we've begun new programs to deal with adolescent pregnancies, and we've expanded the Foster Grandparents program.

With your help, we've reformed the food stamp program to eliminate fraud and to make it more available to poor families by eliminating the requirement to pay cash for food stamps.

We've strengthened the social security system and put it on a sound basis, and we've removed some of its antimarriage features.

We've enacted new laws and regulations to promote part-time employment and flexible time schedules, both of which will permit employees to adjust their workday to fit today's family responsibilities.

I've also asked Congress to appropriate $1.6 billion this year to ease the burden of rising energy costs on poor people, who most need this assistance, and then I've also asked the Congress to provide $2.4 billion annually for the next years for this purpose. With your help, we can win approval of the windfall profits tax on the unearned profits of the oil companies, which will help to finance this and other programs to help the low-income families.

We've worked on all of these projects in partnership and shoulder to shoulder with you.

We're making final plans now, after a very careful and, I think, well-placed preparation, for a White House Conference on the Families. This conference will involve the public in long overdue assessment of how actions by the government, and major private institutions as well, sometimes help or hurt or neglect American families.

The White House conference will not limit itself to what Washington officials think is important, but we will learn what American families believe is important to them. We'll look at the real and important changes that have taken place in American family life and discuss what we as a nation can do to support and to strengthen families.

Instead of a single Washington event, which has always in the past been the case, we will have three separate White House conferences on families next summer— one in Baltimore, one in Minneapolis, and one in Los Angeles. These conferences will bring together families, or those who speak for them, in the widest possible geographic diversity and will encourage the broadest participation in setting an agenda for action on behalf of America's families.

Just as previous White House conferences have really helped to generate ideas and to prepare an agenda on behalf of the young, the old, the handicapped, and others, this set of conferences—the first of its kind—can help bring concern for families to the center of national policymaking, where it deserves.

I might emphasize here that the prob-

lems of American families cover almost the entire gamut of responsibilities of public and private service. Some of the issues are extremely sensitive and controversial, as you well know, but I believe that they should no longer be ignored. And only if we are all willing to come together to discuss in a frank fashion the acknowledged problems of the family, to let those who are affected speak up and be heard throughout the country, and then in a common way seek solutions to those problems, can we ever hope to arrest the downward slide of the strength of families in our country. And as you know, the strength of families is equivalent exactly to the strength of the moral character of our Nation.

And I urge you and the people whom you serve to get involved in this important initiative, in the hearings that are now going on in the State conferences and the three White House conferences next summer. I hope that you will be there.

You and Catholic charities have already a great voice in the direction of the conference on the families. Your past president, the man who greeted me so warmly when I spoke to you in 1976, Rashey Moten, is on the Conference Advisory Committee. And if you don't like the way the conference is doing, see Rashey Moten. After getting to know him at your conference 3 years ago and since then, at my request he is engaged, along with others, in one of the most important and challenging tasks ever undertaken by a group of Americans.

I can assure you that this conference on the family will not simply produce another one of those government reports which all too often go on the shelf and then becomes forgotten. Because the needs of families is so deeply ingrained in my own consciousness and within the lives and hearts of people like you and others around the country, this report cannot be forgotten.

The conference will serve as a catalyst for continuing and expanding action on family issues in the Federal Government. To ensure this development, I've today directed all Federal departments and agencies to support and to cooperate with the conference's activities.

And I'm also announcing today that Health, Education, and Welfare Secretary Patricia Harris is creating for the first time an office for families within HEW. I know you agree with me that this is long overdue.

But I want to make sure that this office is not only involved in the preparation for the conference and helping to make the conference a success, but after the conference work is completed, this office, a permanent entity within HEW, will be there as a focal point to carry out the recommendations of the conference itself. It will be deeply involved in implementing those recommendations and also generating new thoughts and new ideas on a continuing basis after the conference adjourns, because Americans' social life and the problems of the families changes from one year to another.

I'd like to add that Rosalynn shares my interest in the success of the administration's program for the American family, and my whole family will be involved in making sure that this entire effort is successful. Once my mother and Rosalynn and Amy get involved in something all together, you can be sure that we will not permit this effort to fail. [*Laughter*]

As I said at the beginning of my remarks, family values are not the only reason for national concern. In my July speech to the Nation, I spoke about the crisis of the spirit that I saw brewing in America. I listened carefully to the prayer a few minutes ago, and this message to God, this request for help by God, mirrored the same concern.

I warned in July, and I have been saying ever since, that we are threatened with the loss of that fundamental trait which has characterized Americans since the foundation of our country—optimism, confidence in one another, and confidence in the future.

The response to that speech was overwhelming. Those who have worked in the White House for 25 or 30 years say the response was unprecedented. We received tens of thousands of letters and hundreds of telephone calls, all sounding similar themes. "You're right," they said, "now tell us what we can do to help."

My answer to those thousands of Americans is the same as my message to you. The answer to the crisis of confidence is action. The answer to alienation from one another or from government is participation. The way we solve our problems is through unity and partnership.

You in this room typify, personify the best in America. Your network of social services, the largest in our country, is composed of tens of thousands of Americans united by faith, dedicated to the ideal of serving others, and determined to translate that ideal into action for the benefit of others. You've chosen to light a candle and not to curse the darkness, and the flame of compassion lights the road for all of us to follow.

Let us carry on our own the tasks outlined so eloquently by Pope John Paul. Let us preserve and enhance the partnership between government and the private sector, which serves our people well, and let us make every effort to strengthen our families.

Finally, let us share the prayer of the American poet Stephen Vincent Benet: "Grant us brotherhood," he said, "not only for this day, but for all our years—-a brotherhood not of words, but of acts and deeds." With this kind of generous spirit, we can strengthen our Nation and bring new enrichment in every way to the lives of the people we love.

NOTE: The President spoke at 1:09 p.m. in the Imperial Ballroom at the Radisson Muehlebach Hotel.

Kansas City, Missouri

Remarks at a Reception for Business and Civic Leaders. October 15, 1979

First of all, I want to thank our host, Mr. Baumgardner, for that good introduction and also to tell you that for any President it's both an exhilarating and a sobering experience to come to the home of President Harry Truman.

As you know, President Truman is a man who has grown in stature with historians and with American people and with those throughout the world who know history—the more we have a chance to assess what his contributions were.

He was a tough political infighter. He was highly partisan. He told me—rather, he said once, and I've read his comments—that "When somebody comes and tells me they're bipartisan, I know I've lost a vote. They're not going to vote with me." And I've still got in the Oval Office an exact replica—I tried to get the original, but Mrs. Truman and Margaret wouldn't let me have it—of his sign, "The buck stops here." And I think about that a lot as I carry on the affairs of our great Nation.

Times change from one President to another, from one generation to another—challenges, problems, questions, change. But there's a surer realization as history progresses that our Nation is so strong, so powerful, that there is no challenge we cannot meet, there is no problem we can't resolve, there is no question that we can't answer, if we have confidence in one another and if we are united in a common purpose.

I'm the fourth President, for instance, who's dealt with 10 or 11 years of inflation, which is too high. But if Americans are willing to work together, to have confidence in one another, we can get inflation under control.

We've never had an energy policy for our country, because for too long we had extremely cheap oil—a dollar and a half or so a barrel—and we didn't have to worry about it, and we became addicted to—a highly dependent society on—foreign oil.

We import about half the oil we use now. Next year we'll send overseas $70 billion in American money that could provide jobs for our people. And as we import 8½ million barrels of oil per day, we also import inflation, and we import unemployment.

These are just a few of the questions or problems that I have to face along with problems of defense and the search for peace. But it's a wonderful job to have because it's the greatest elected office in the greatest nation on Earth.

And President Truman said another thing that I've noticed, particularly lately. He said, "If a President ever becomes timid because he's worried about public opinion polls or what newspaper columnists say might be the results of the next election, then he's not worthy to lead this great country." So, I remember that. I'm not concerned. I look to the future with great confidence in myself, in politics, and also in this country. I base that confidence on what I know our Nation is.

I just spoke to the national convention of Catholic charities, a group that's been involved in volunteer work for other people for more than 250 years in our country. And I mentioned to them about the profound impact of the visit of Pope John Paul II to our country. It was kind of an outpouring of awareness of the kind of ethical and moral and spiritual characteristics which never change in the hearts and minds of American people, but sometimes get buried under the transient or the temporary problems or inconveniences that we, as extremely fortunate people, have in our country.

And I think that was a good reminder that we ought not to be discouraged, that we ought to be inspired to look to the future with confidence, and to reach our hand out to a neighbor and say, "Let's work together to make the greatest nation on Earth even greater in the future."

Thank you very much for letting me be your President and for letting me visit you here.

NOTE: The President spoke at 1:53 p.m. at the Jackson County Courthouse.

Chicago, Illinois

Remarks at a Fundraising Dinner for Mayor Jane Byrne.   October 15, 1979

This is unbelievable. When Jane Byrne raises a crowd, I'm always eager to come and speak. I've never seen such a tremendous outpouring of support and Democratic enthusiasm and harmony and commitment and courage and anticipation for the future as you've demonstrated here tonight.

You might feel bad about sitting in this room—you'll be hearing the speeches on television later on—but it took me and Rosalynn and many of you 2½ years to get the place we wanted to live in in Washington, D.C. So, maybe before 2½ years you'll be moving up to the next floor. [*Laughter*]

I predict that if Jane Byrne stays as your mayor, and I think she will, this outpouring of affection and appreciation which you have demonstrated for her will continue.

This afternoon I was in Kansas City— Kansas City, Missouri—in a county courthouse, Jackson County. It's a famous courthouse, because 8 years before he became President, Harry Truman was a county judge.

As I stood there this afternoon in a small crowd on the main floor of the courthouse, I thought about him as President and what he meant as a Democrat. Harry Truman believed in Democratic Party unity. Harry Truman stayed close to the people. Harry Truman was plainspoken. He said what he thought, and the people listened. Harry Truman was not always popular, because he did what was right, regardless of public opinion polls. Harry Truman was a man of his word. When he said something, you could believe it.

Harry Truman recognized that we had a nation, during the last part of the Second World War and during the few years afterwards, which was shot through with very serious problems, but he never gave up. He tapped the reserves not only of the Democratic Party but of the people of our country.

He believed in families; he believed in neighborhoods; he believed in communities. And he saw that, in spite of problems which change from one day to another or divisions among people which cause hot debates in a free country, that there was an undercurrent, a reservoir, a foundation, a base of innate courage among the American people, and there were principles which never change, principles of honesty, integrity, dedication, concern about one another, steel strength when our country was in danger, and compassion and love among American people.

And his ability as a President to tap these tremendous resources come daily for me in the White House as a reassuring fact, because I know that the same characteristics that existed when he became President, when he served, still exist among people in our country today.

A few days ago in Grant Park, you had assembled for a great visitor probably the largest crowd of human beings ever assembled in the United States, perhaps even the world, in history—about a million and a half people, who came not out of curiosity, but to demonstrate that there was a hunger among us to preserve the finest characteristics that permeate our lives, fill our hearts and our souls. You recognized that there are things eternal and that there are things in a modern technological world that do not change.

We Democrats must remember that, although all parties have deep religious faiths. But we should remember that our country also is strong, ethical, morally, spiritually, that we don't change inside, that we have an obligation to one another. And the strength of our party and of our country lies in our belief in one another, our confidence in the future, and our determination, which we will never yield, that we will make together the greatest nation on Earth, the United States of America, even greater in the future. If you'll help us, we'll help you realize this dream.

Thank you very much. I'll see you on television in a few minutes.

[*The President spoke at 8:09 p.m. in the Banquet Annex Hall at the McCormick Place Convention Center. He then went to the Don Maxwell Hall, where he delivered the following remarks at the main dinner at 9:05 p.m.*]

My good friend Mayor Jane Byrne, Chairman Dunne,[1] *Michael Howlett,*[2] *State officials, Members of Congress, distinguished leaders of Chicago and Cook County, both Democratic and those who've not yet been converted to our party—[laughter]—and especially more than 12,000 of Jane Byrne's closest friends:*

I know where to come the next time I want a quiet, restful evening to spend alone. [*Laughter*]

Just a few minutes ago, I went down and spoke to five or six thousand people, and I was on the way back to my hotel when Jane said, "Wait, you haven't seen anything yet." And this is an absolutely unbelievable sight. I'm proud to be here.

In the last few years, this is my third visit to this great city on an occasion when the mayor of Chicago is honored. A President has many interesting and exciting experiences, but I don't believe any more interesting or exciting than to be here tonight.

I've been doing a lot of different things lately. When I was at Sunday school yesterday morning, one of my friends said, "Mr. President, I know what you've been doing the last week or so. What are you going to do next?" And I said, "Well, I'm going to Kansas City tomorrow morning to speak to the National Conference of Catholic Charities, and then tomorrow night I'm going to Chicago to a large testimonial dinner to Mayor Jane Byrne." And they looked at me for a while and said, "You've been spending an awful lot of time with Catholics lately." And another Baptist friend standing nearby said, "Well, it hadn't hurt you at all. Keep it up."

---

[1] Cook County Democratic chairman.

[2] Master of ceremonies for the dinner.

I am glad to be with you, members of all political parties, members of all faiths. I speak to you tonight as President of the greatest nation on Earth, and I also speak to you as a friend of your mayor. I also speak to you as a Democrat.

This enormous attendance is proof indeed of the enthusiasm and the dedication and the unity and the commitment and the confidence of people who live in Chicago, and it's also proof of the tremendous leadership of your mayor, Jane Byrne. You've made a wise choice, and I'm proud of it.

We are here to honor the mayor, to provide her with the support and the help she needs in a very difficult job and to recognize the fine performance which she has already exhibited to the rest of the Nation in the short time she's held this exalted office.

I want to thank you for this support for her personally and to encourage you to keep it up. The lifeblood of politics and effective government is good and loyal people ready to work, ready to contribute talent, ability, and care for one another. Your mayor is depending on you, and your President is depending on you, also.

God must have loved Democrats because he made so many of us. However, he always leaves us short of money. Our opponents can almost always outspend us. Since we don't like to lose elections, we work harder to raise money, and we do a better job in office after we are elected. Your mayor has proven that. This extraordinary determination and fighting spirit and better performance all in our party make sure that our party is the first choice of Americans. By earning the loyalty and the support of the American people, we have been the majority party for the last 50 years, and my determination is to keep it that way.

Mayor Richard Daley understood the basis for party strength. He was proud of the people of Chicago. He dedicated his life, as you know, to serving you. He earned the loyalty of the people of this city, no matter what your party preference might be. In doing that, he made Chicago synonymous with economic progress and with workable government.

What I admired most of all and what kept him in office so long was that his government, your government, was one with a human side. He understood that politics is a two-way street that loyalty comes to an officeholder only if we give good government to the people who vote, and bring into the political system working people—immigrants, minorities, the old, the needy. Then they'd know they are better off to be inside the political system rather than outside as an alienated and lonely American citizen.

So, when we honor Jane Byrne tonight, we also honor the tradition of Chicago and the people who helped to make her become your mayor—I might add, with an unbelievable 82 percent of the vote. And we also honor the people who have made Chicago one of the great success stories in the entire world.

From the time Chicago was founded, people came here in search of better lives. They came here to work and to build together. That's what still distinguishes Chicago today. You are a city of builders—builders of new industries and great enterprises and the most superb architects on Earth. There is no better symbol of this than the Chicago skyline—nothing like it in the world.

This afternoon I and Rosalynn and Jane Byrne, George Dunne, and others flew down the lakeshore and looked at the skyline from a helicopter. It was a thrilling sight, and I get a thrill as President and as an American every time I see it. And there's another side to Chicago that I also admire, which I mentioned earlier—its human dimension. This is a city of families. This is a city of neighborhoods, where churches and community life and traditions are important.

When His Holiness Pope John [Paul] [3] II came here, he did not visit just the great cathedrals. He went to the neighborhoods, and he went to their churches. He went to the South Side, to Marquette Park, to Pilsen, to the Five Holy Martyrs Church, and the Visitation Church. He was in the different communities of this city, where unique heritages and customs stay strong and vital.

Sustaining that neighborhood life has been a chief goal of Mayor Jane Byrne. She's fighting for the well-being of neighborhoods in Chicago, and I can assure you that she's fighting for Chicago in Washington as well. And she is winning her fight in both places—here and in Washington.

With a good partnership between your mayor and your President, Chicago is leading the country in Urban Development Action Grants, above any other city in the Nation. We expect this money to stimulate $300 million in private investment, creating 5,000 new and permanent jobs in Chicago. In addition, we've approved block grants for Chicago of $127 million for this 1 year. We've just reached an agreement with Mayor Byrne, who is a tough negotiator, that will preserve over 1,300 federally funded city government jobs.

My urban policy means making government work better together—Federal, State, and local. In Chicago, we have had an opportunity to ensure that a major national and international travel

---

[3] Printed in the transcript.

system is not stifled in its necessary development and expansion.

I'm very pleased to report to you tonight that after 10 years of waiting and after several months of work with Mayor Byrne, we have finally reached an agreement in principle to relocate some defense facilities at O'Hare Airport, which will permit the much-needed expansion and modernization of your international air terminal.

This is good news for Chicago, and it's good news for the millions of people who fly in and out of O'Hare Air Terminal, and it's good news to me, because it represents precisely that kind of creative Federal-local cooperation that's so important to our mutual success and lets our Nation realize its great strength.

I don't want to recite a long list tonight. I just want to emphasize to you at this special evening banquet that Jane Byrne is working hard for this city in the same tradition as her great predecessors. And I can also say that if we had more congressional delegations like Chicago's, we would be moving even more vigorously to rebuild all our cities and also to rebuild our national economy even more rapidly.

I've worked closely with Senator Adlai Stevenson, with Danny Rostenkowski, with Frank Annunzio, and all the rest of the Chicago delegation. When I say that Chicagoans are builders, I mean that you also send that same building spirit to Washington.

When I took office as President and the times called for rebuilding a stagnant economy, I called on the Democratic Congress and Chicagoans in that Congress to get the job done. We've done that job—together—and we can be proud of it.

We've increased our commitments to Democratic programs—social security, housing, education, and health. Corporate profits are up 50 percent. Farm exports have broken world records in 1977, 1978, and again in 1979. Taxes have been cut. In 1980 you will realize tax savings of over $40 billion. We've had good luck in getting away from unnecessary regulations. We have cut 1,000 OSHA regulations off the books. Paperwork is down 15 percent, and the budget deficit has been slashed 60 percent by $36 billion. Those things are important. They are kind of a measure of what we have tried to do in this country and what we've accomplished.

In 30 months, we've created 8½ million new jobs in America, a quarter million of those jobs right here in Chicago. We've brought the national unemployment rate down by 25 percent. And in Chicago, because of your extra good leadership, unemployment has been cut almost 30 percent.

Throughout the country, we created a million new jobs for black workers, over 1,000* of those jobs for black citizens here in Chicago. We've created 700,000 jobs for teenagers in America, 17,000 of those jobs here in Chicago. We've created over a million jobs for construction workers, 30,000 of those jobs here in Chicago. The country's never had before so many new jobs in such a short time, and we are still hard at work.

Americans in 1976 also wanted to rebuild our cities, our older cities. I knew that with the right policies older cities could be rebuilt, a new spirit could be engendered, past defects could be corrected, our urban dwellers could be given a better life.

With your help, we launched the Nation's first comprehensive urban program. We changed old and existing Federal pro-

---

*The President meant to say 100,000. [Printed in the transcript.]

grams so that for the first time they really began to give better services to our people. Now downtown and inner-city communities are reviving all over the Nation. As in Chicago, the building spirit has revived, and people are putting hard work and new life back into our cities.

There's plenty to be done. It will not be easy, but we are off to a good start. And I pledge to keep this progress going. Our cities in America must be rebuilt. If you'll help me, we will succeed with that job.

And we are now devoting that same American spirit—individualism, innovation, dedication—to our energy problem, to free us from dangerous overdependence on imported oil. We now import more than half the oil we use from foreign countries. Next year, we will spend $70 billion on foreign oil. We are importing oil; we are exporting jobs, we are importing inflation.

We've begun to act after too long a delay. We've already cut imports by 2½ million barrels per day by 1985, but we know that this will not be enough. We must do better.

I have now sent to Congress, in July, a program to conserve more energy and to produce more American energy. I proposed a windfall profits tax on the unearned income of the oil companies of this country to help poor families pay high energy bills, to build a better transportation system, and to produce synthetic fuels, solar power, and other energy in our own country.

It will amount to the most ambitious peacetime undertaking in our history, on the same massive scale as we saw when we built the Interstate Highway System throughout the United States. It's the kind of program Chicagoans like. It builds on American strengths. It harnesses American ingenuity. It provides American jobs.

We can cut our oil imports by one-half by 1990. We can reassert American leadership. We can achieve energy security. All it takes is a spirit of common enterprise and determination, and that's what we've got.

Energy price increases are now the main force driving inflation. Oil price increases have caused 4 percent of our own inflation rate. Without energy, the inflation rate this past summer—this summer—would be no higher than it was in 1978 or 1977.

Clearly, no economic problem today is more important than the 10 years of high inflation, and I intend, with your help, to bring it under control.

We took a big step forward just a few weeks ago by forging a historic national accord. It's a broad agreement with labor on economic and domestic policy, with direct participation on wage and price stability. For the first time ever, we've made full partners of those who suffer most from inflation—the working men and women of America.

The national accord acknowledges that we all have to tighten our belts. We've recognized inflation as the number one threat economically to our country.

The national accord acknowledges that we can succeed. We can and we will do it fairly. We can and we will protect jobs. We can and we will protect the poor and the disadvantaged. That's what the national accord is all about. It's not just to make life comfortable for the few. It is to bring economic justice and security to all Americans.

There's nothing easy about this inflation fight for you or for me. In fact, I'm the fourth consecutive President to confront this same problem. Presidents before me have tried mandatory controls, and they've also tried the deepest recession since the 1930's. Neither worked. I believe

they didn't work because we've never before had a comprehensive energy policy, and we've never before had a national accord where the tackling of the inflation problem would be a joint effort among government, business, and labor.

The national accord gives us all an historic opportunity to bring inflation down without massive unemployment and suffering. It's a program that can appeal to our finest instincts and can bring about the best in Americans.

We face other challenges and opportunities. As President, my first and my foremost responsibility is to keep America strong and to maintain peace for our people. We are also helping to bring peace to our friends in the Middle East, who've been enemies for centuries and at war almost continually for the last 30 years.

We're determined to control nuclear weapons. The Senate must ratify the SALT II treaty.

And as Americans, we will always hold high the banner of basic human rights throughout the world.

We are indeed maintaining America's leadership among all nations on Earth. This is not an easy role, but we will not fail.

Let me add this about inflation and jobs and world peace and our other challenges: When I became President, I decided to confront the fundamental problems of our country. I decided to do it forcefully and directly, no matter what the political impact might be, no matter what the public opinion polls might be.

Whatever the future may hold, I want the personal satisfaction to know that we did not duck problems, that we did not settle for half-hearted approaches, that we always put the interests of this country first. We owe that debt to the Democratic Party. We owe that debt to the people of this country, and I owe that debt to myself.

As a Democrat and as President, I'm not afraid; in fact, I look forward to tough political fights—and with your help, we will not lose those fights ahead. This has been the approach of the Democratic Party, and this has been the approach of our country to major challenges in the past.

Whenever our Nation has been in danger, whenever we have seen our Nation being tested, Americans have put aside differences, have put aside trepidation and fear, have reached our hands out to one another, have joined in together and have approached the future with determination and with confidence. That must always be our commitment, as it must be in times like these.

The energy crisis, the inflation crisis, is not as easy to see as the First World War or the Second World War or the Great Depression. But at the same time, our Nation's security is in danger.

At times serving as President can be a lonely job, but a President, particularly a Democratic President, does not stay lonely on a trip to Chicago, especially when you're with Jane Byrne and 12,000 friends of hers and great leaders on your own.

I'll still be with you when I'm back in Washington. I'll still be working with Mayor Byrne, with George Dunne, with Frank Annunzio, Danny Rostenkowski, and all the other good Democrats and Republicans who are here representing Chicago.

We'll be working together to tap that great reservoir of strength in America— the same spirit that's brought us together in time of war and depression, that can reunite us again to meet any challenge and to prevail.

When Pope John Paul spoke to a million and a half Chicagoans in Grant Park,

he saw in you a picture of America—a nation formed of many people, each with a different history, but together creating something new each day. I share that beautiful vision of Chicago and of America. And our common prayer will be that we will return to the basic and unchanging values that have made this country great.

I pledge to you as President to lead this Nation—all of our people—to realize that vision so that our most fervent prayers for each other and for our great country will be answered as God has answered them in the past.

Thank you very much. God bless all of you.

NOTE: The following morning, the President attended a private reception at the residence of Mayor Byrne.

Commissioner of Patents and Trademarks

Nomination of Sidney A. Diamond.
October 15, 1979

The President today announced his intention to nominate Sidney A. Diamond, of Tucson, Ariz., to be Commissioner of Patents and Trademarks. He would replace Donald Banner, who has resigned from the Commission.

Diamond, 64, is currently counsel to the New York City firm of Kaye, Scholer, Fierman, Hays & Handler and vice president of the International Patent and Trademark Association, the American group of the International Association for the Protection of Industrial Property.

He was born October 17, 1914, in New York City. He received an A.B. from Dartmouth College in 1935 and an LL.B. from Harvard Law School in 1938.

Diamond practiced law in New York

City from 1938 to 1941 and in Washington from 1941 to 1943. From 1943 to 1946, he was with the Justice Department as special attorney and special assistant to the Attorney General. He has practiced law in New York City since 1946, first with Roosevelt, Freidin & Littauer, then since 1956 with Kaye, Scholer, Fierman, Hays & Handler.

Diamond has served as chairman of the American Bar Association's section of patent, trademark and copyright law and as vice president of the Copyright Society of the U.S.A. He has written numerous articles in legal and other journals on trademark and copyright matters.

White House Conference on Families

Memorandum From the President.
October 15, 1979

Memorandum for the Heads of Executive Departments and Agencies

In July, the National Advisory Committee of the White House Conference on Families held its first meeting. The Committee adopted a plan of action for the Conference, which includes hearings, state activities, and White House Conferences at several sites throughout the country.

A major goal of the White House Conference on Families, which I called for in my campaign for the Presidency, is to identify public policies which strengthen and support families as well as those which harm or neglect family life, and to recommend appropriate changes. To accomplish this goal, the Conference must have the support and assistance of every Department and Agency within the government.

I am, therefore, directing Department and Agency heads to cooperate fully with the staff of the White House Conference on Families. Such cooperation should include, but not be limited to, the following: Identifying and cataloging programs, policies and research studies which impact on family life; analyzing the impact of selected policies and programs; publishing studies, reports and other informational materials relating to families; providing detailees, logistical assistance, meeting facilities and other resources for Conference activities; earmarking discretionary funds for projects which support the goals of the White House Conference on Families, and informing employees and constituent groups about Conference activities.

To demonstrate this Administration's commitment to the goals of the WHCF, I am requesting Agency and Department heads to be available to make presentations at the hearings which will be held this fall and at the White House Conferences scheduled for June and July of next year. To coordinate government-wide participation in the Conference, an Interagency Task Force will be established. Please designate one of your Special Assistants or an Assistant or Deputy Assistant Secretary for Policy or Planning who has knowledge of family-related programs and a capacity to draw on the resources within your Department to serve on this Task Force. Notification of this appointment should be sent to John Carr, Executive Director of the White House Conference on Families (472–4393) by October 25, and your designee should plan to attend the first meeting of the Interagency Task Force scheduled for November 1.

Thank you for your assistance in helping strengthen and support our nation's families.

JIMMY CARTER

NOTE: The text of the memorandum was released on October 16.

Dolton, Illinois

Remarks and a Question-and-Answer Session at a Townhall Meeting.   October 16, 1979

THE PRESIDENT. First of all, I want to thank my good friend, Marty Russo, for that wonderful introduction.

In 1974, a little bit earlier in the year than this, I was Governor of Georgia, and this district had an incumbent Congressman. I won't say which party he represented. But I heard way down in Georgia about a fine young man who was running for Congress for the first time. And I left Georgia and came up here and went to the VFW club just a couple blocks from here. They told me they may not have but 50 or 75 people there—it was a fairly small building—but there were six or seven hundred local citizens packed in that place, not to see me, because I was an unknown Governor, but to see Marty Russo. You've been good to him, and he's been good to this district and good to the country.

The most important thing I know of as President is, in times of trouble and challenge, in times when our Nation might even be in danger, in times when people's lives are changing very rapidly and people are concerned about their own families, to tap the tremendous strength of this country, the strength that comes from a knowledge of one another, a confidence in our neighbors, and a confidence in the future. And it's very important—[*interruption from the audience*]. Free country. I think you can hear me okay. It's very important for us in this country when we do have trials to rally together.

I was in Chicago last night standing on the decks of *Delta Queen No. 2* with a great mayor, and we had one of the most remarkable political events that I have ever known about—12,000 people came to show their confidence in local government, their confidence in a superb new mayor, and an appreciation of what Chicago has been in the past, is now, and will be in the future.

I've come to listen to your questions and to give you the best answers I can. It's a pleasure to be here. You've honored me by letting us meet together. And now, I'd like to turn to the first questioner, and if you'll give me your name and the question, I'll be glad to try to answer.

QUESTIONS

POPE JOHN PAUL II

Q. My name is Father Al Pizza. I'm from St. George, in Tenley Park. First of all, I just feel fortunate to be able to tell you I think you're doing a fantastic job. I think you have an impossible job, and I would wish sometimes that the news media would give you an even break.

My question has to do with—it's an easy question for you, I think.

THE PRESIDENT. You can stop right there to be safe. [*Laughter*]

Q. It has to do with the Pope's visit. He drew millions of people around our country, and I was wondering what your personal thoughts would be about the effects he's going to have in the long range around the world with, especially, maybe in Communist countries. Do you think he is going to be able to change people or change the attitudes, maybe lift the apathy and the cynicism and things like that, along those lines? If we could just maybe hear your thoughts on that.

THE PRESIDENT. Obviously, as President, I was extremely interested in having the Pope come here to begin with. I extended him a personal invitation last spring and was delighted when he decided to accept it.

When I had a private meeting with the Pope in the Oval Office, following the North Lawn reception and before the South Lawn speeches, he and I discussed his visit. He and I were both surprised, pleasantly surprised, at the tremendous, unanticipated outpouring of affection and love for him, exemplified by the enormous crowds. I doubt that there's ever been a larger crowd assembled, for instance, than there was in Grant Park in Chicago, to see His Holiness there.

It was a great testimony, I believe, to a hunger among the American people to be reminded of and to remember those characteristics of human beings that never change—truth, integrity, humility, gentleness, the strength of families, compassion, concern, unselfishness, love. Those kinds of things we don't talk much about in public life, but the Pope, in speaking of them, aroused in American people a response that was truly remarkable and very good for all our country, no matter what faith an American might espouse in his own religion or her own religion.

In our private conversations we talked about many things. We talked about families. We talked about abortion. We talked about the truth that exists in open societies and the threat of communism to stamp out peoples' deep religious beliefs. We discussed his recent trip to Poland, which is a Communist Government, but where the church is undoubtedly stronger than the government itself. We talked about the overwhelming Christian nature of the people who live in both North and South America. We talked about parts of the world where it's very difficult for the Christian message to be promulgated—in China, for instance, or in some other places throughout the world. We talked

about the shift toward secularism in Western Europe and the concern that the Pope has about that development.

There was a great belief expressed by him, which I certainly share, that we've got to put our religious faith to action, that we can't just talk about gentleness, we can't just talk about compassion, we can't just talk about love, and overlook the deep needs of our immediate neighbors and those who suffer from hunger or lack of clothing or lack of shelter throughout the world.

So, I believe that the message he brought, both publicly and privately, was an inspiration to me as President. It was also an inspiration to our whole country. I think his beneficent influence throughout the world has been well established, not only in his trip to free countries like ours and Mexico's but also behind the Iron Curtain in Poland.

I might say one thing finally about that. It was an unprecedented thing to have the Pope visit the White House. This has never been done before. But I hear from all kinds of religious faiths—Jews, Protestants, even those who belong to the Islamic faith. I've not had any criticism at all, so far as I know, from any of those other religious faiths because the Pope did come to our country, because they all see that his ministry and his message was one that tapped the best in America. And I'm very proud that he could come, and I invited him back. He said he wanted to rest up first. [*Laughter*]

THE NATION'S ECONOMY

Q. Good morning, Mr. President.

THE PRESIDENT. Good morning.

Q. By the way, welcome to Dolton.

THE PRESIDENT. Good to be in Dolton.

Q. The thing that seems to be foremost in everyone's minds now is the fact that your economic program isn't working real well. We still have runaway inflation, and the only prices that seem to be coming down are gas-guzzling automobiles and pork. [*Laughter*]

Do you think that it might be time for a change in your policies, such as strict wage and price controls?

THE PRESIDENT. I think the policies that we have established are the best, and I believe that they're going to pay off. What we've had in the past 11 years is excessive inflation. I'm the fourth President who's tried to deal with inflation. So far we've not been successful. Mandatory wage and price controls were attempted by President Nixon. They were very quickly abandoned. And we still suffer with high meat prices because of those mandatory price controls on farm products.

We also went through a time of deep recession, almost a depression, approaching the problems of the 1930's. That also did not cure inflation.

What I've tried to do is to deal at the roots of it. For instance, we've just formed a national accord, an agreement between the government, business, and labor, to work together now to hold down both wages and prices. We've been remarkably successful already with our wage and price guidelines. For instance, the wage increases in 1979 have been no higher at all than the wage increases in 1978. And the prices over which we do have some authority in our voluntary price controls have been going up in price only one-half as much as those over which we do not have control, like energy. We've never had this before, a voluntary cooperative effort.

Energy is the main threat and the main cause of high inflation. The oil prices raised by OPEC have caused 4 percent of our inflation rate. If it weren't for energy,

if you could just set aside energy and count everything else put together—food and everything else—this past summer of 1979, the inflation rate would be no higher at all than it was in 1978 and 1977. But OPEC oil prices have increased more than 60 percent since last December. The approach to that is to have an energy policy that cuts down on oil imports. We now import half the oil we use. We also import, along with that, inflation and unemployment.

The Congress is finally addressing, after long years of delay, this energy problem. We're trying to reduce imports, increase oil production in our own country, gas production, coal production, use of solar power, synthetic fuels, and also have a major emphasis on conservation.

If we can cut down on the amount of oil we import, that'll be a major step toward controlling inflation. And I predict to you that before this year is over, you will see the inflation rate begin to go down because of the action we've already taken.

The last point to a very complicated answer is that we have tried in this process not to have jobs fall off. In the first 30 months of my term—I've only been in office now less than 3 years—we have had a net increase—not decrease, but a net increase—of 8½ million jobs in this country: a million construction jobs, 700,000 jobs for black people; a quarter of a million of those increased jobs are in Chicago alone. So, at the time we've had high inflation and high interest rates, we've also had the highest employment level in the history of our Nation.

We've tried to protect people from high job losses that have always come along in the past with high inflation. And if we turn the inflation rate down—and I'm predicting that we will—and hold those jobs up, I think it'll be a good step in the right direction. And controlling those energy costs and having cooperation between labor and business with government, I think, is a good policy.

I might say that we've done all we could at the Federal Government level. We've restricted spending programs, but given our people better lives. We've cut the deficit by 60 percent. Corporate profits are up 50 percent. We've got 20,000 fewer Federal employees now than we had when I took office. We've cut down paperwork by 15 percent. We've gotten the Government's nose out of the private sector by deregulating airlines. We're now moving on other sectors.

So, I believe our total package of economic policies is the best we can have. And I think with a little patience, which everybody must have, and a little realization that it's a common problem, not one caused by any particular person or party, I think with that understanding and strength of our country, having confidence in it, we'll succeed.

So far, we've got problems; we can solve them together.

U.S.-CUBAN RELATIONS

Q. Mr. President, my name is Joe Penn, from Riverdale. I'm a semi-retired pharmacist, and it is indeed an honor and privilege, most sacred as far as I'm concerned, to be able to speak to the President of the United States. I'm actually awed, and therefore, I have to read my question.

The gentleman before me stole the thunder, and you answered it very well. I was going to ask you about putting an immediate freeze on wage, prices, et cetera. So, my alternate question is in regards to Cuba.

In view of the fact that we've finally come to recognize Communistic countries such as Russia, Red China, and others, why can't we accept the fact that our neighbor Cuba and its form of government is here to stay and end the futile and useless embargo once again and give Monroe Doctrine a chance to work?

THE PRESIDENT. Okay. I'll be glad to answer that. I'll be glad to answer that.

We are not at war with Cuba. We have no intention of being antagonistic toward the people of Cuba. The fact is that Cuba's policies, within their own nation and relating to other countries, make them a very difficult government to recognize officially. Also, they are almost completely subservient to the Soviet Government. They're kind of a surrogate of the Soviets. The Cubans have over 45,000 troops in countries overseas where, in my opinion, they have absolutely no business. It's the most highly militarized country on Earth per capita.

They are constantly interfering in the affairs of adjacent countries or other people, for instance, Puerto Rico. The Puerto Rican people voluntarily choose the form of government they want. They are now a commonwealth of our country. They may prefer to be a State, the 51st State; they may prefer to be independent. Whatever the Puerto Rican people want suits me fine. Castro is constantly trying to stir up the people of Puerto Rico to seek independence from the United States, which the Puerto Rican people do not want. He points out the advantages of independence. But when people leave one country and go to another, the people leave Cuba and go to find a better life in Puerto Rico.

I think we've got to have a firm policy on Cuba.

The last point is this: There's no way that Cuba could survive economically, with their Communist experiment 90 miles from our country, without the Soviets propping them up. Every day the Soviet Union sends to Castro $8 million just to keep the Cuban people alive economically and to keep Castro in power. And they send them large quantities of arms, military weapons—and don't even charge Cuba for it. All the other satellite countries in Eastern Europe, for instance, when they get arms from the Soviet Union, they have to pay for it.

So, I believe that until Cuba can bring their own troops back from unwarranted involvement in the internal affairs of other countries, until they release the hundreds and hundreds, even thousands of political prisoners they have in jail—and some of them have been there over 20 years—and until they stop interfering in the internal affairs of countries, even in this hemisphere, we will not recognize Cuba. After that, we'll consider it.

Q. Thank you, Mr. President.

THE PRESIDENT. Thank you, Doctor, very much.

OIL IMPORTS AND GRAIN EXPORTS

Q. Hello, Mr. President, my name is Harvey Harris, and I attend school here at Thornridge High School.

THE PRESIDENT. Right on. [*Laughter*]

Q. The question that I would like to ask you is, what do you plan to do about the rising prices of gasoline, and what do you plan to do about the OPEC nations keep raising the prices of barrels of oil? Do you plan to raise the price of wheat or the imports that go over there?

THE PRESIDENT. I see. We don't have any control, Harvey, over the prices that are charged to us for oil from overseas. What we must do is to cut down on our overdependence on that oil. So, what we want to do is to cut down on imports and produce more energy in our own country.

The most important thing that we can do, everyone in this room can do, is to save energy. The more we save, the more our families benefit and the more the security of our country is protected.

Every family represented here, I hope, later on today will meet together, either at suppertime or at lunch, and just talk over how you, in your own homes, on your own jobs, traveling back and forth, can cut down on the consumption of energy. The more we save, the better off we all are.

We're also trying to shift toward the use of energy sources that never give out—solar power—and the use of growing crops like trees or farm crops, like to make gasohol out of. If we can do that, then year after year, for thousands of years, we'll have an adequate supply of energy.

Another thing that we can do is to use the kinds of energy in our own country that we have most of. The number one State in the Nation on coal reserves—you know what it is?

AUDIENCE. Illinois.

THE PRESIDENT. Illinois, right. And we can increase the use of coal. So, the more we can move away from dependence on those foreign countries, the better off we are.

You mentioned wheat and corn. I would rather have what God has given us, in the way of land and the ability to produce food, than I would to have all the oil deposits in Saudi Arabia and all the OPEC countries put together, because we've got a permanent, very fine strategic export that the rest of the world needs, they will get, and is profitable for us.

The number one State in the export of farm products—you know what it is?

AUDIENCE. Illinois.

THE PRESIDENT. Illinois. Right. Very wise audience.

And every year since I've been in office, we have tried to increase the exports of grain. We set world records in 1977, world records in 1978, world records in 1979. I believe in 1980, next year, we'll set world records again on the total amount of grain exported.

We don't want to punish our farmers by raising the prices of our grain so it cannot sell on foreign markets. The OPEC countries have very small populations; they don't buy much food. And if we cut off all our shipments of wheat and corn to the OPEC countries, they could very easily get that wheat or corn from France or from European countries or from Argentina or some other country aside from us. It would only hurt our farmers. So, I would rather see our exports be sure, so customers could depend on us and to have this tremendous benefit from getting new customers for our grain.

When I ran for President, I promised that there would never be any grain embargoes put on the farmers as there were several times just before I became President. So, I think for us to export our beautiful product of food and to import less oil from overseas because we save and produce more energy at home, is the best approach. That's what we're doing. I need all of you to help me with it.

Thank you very much, Harvey.

DEFENSE AND NATIONAL SECURITY

Q. Mr. President, my name is Gerald Reilly. I reside in South Holland, Illinois. I would like to add my words of welcome to you for coming to our area and express my appreciation for the wonderful job you are doing under conditions as they exist today.

THE PRESIDENT. Thank you, sir.

Q. Mr. President, do you feel that the money appropriated for defense in your 1980 budget is really for defense or a step towards the possible conflict with another nation?

THE PRESIDENT. I'll be glad to answer that.

The most important responsibility that I have as President is to guarantee the security of our Nation. It comes above everything else—above inflation, employment, energy, agriculture—to preserve the security of our country, because unless our Nation is secure, unless our Nation is free from the constant threat of a successful attack by other countries, then everything that we stand for would be lost.

I have no apology for the defense budget request. I believe in a strong defense, and as long as I'm President, the strength of our military forces will be second to none. I want to be sure that if any other country is tempted to attack the United States, that they will realize that they are committing military suicide.

We only spend about 5 percent of our gross national product on defense. In the past, this is the lowest we've ever spent. In the past, we've spent 8, 9, 10, 11 percent. The Soviet Union spends 13 percent of their gross national product on defense. Our military is still better than theirs, and we're going to keep it that way. But I hope that every American will realize that it's not a sacrifice when we pay our military personnel a good salary, when we give them high training, when we give them the best weapons.

What I want to be sure of is that all of our nuclear submarines, all of our airplanes, all of our tanks, all of our artillery pieces, are never used—are never used—and the way to do this is to let the world know that we are strong, not only in weapons and service people but also in our national will.

If the other countries on Earth—our allies, our friends, our potential adversaries—know that the United States is a strong country, then we'll have peace. If they ever believe that the United States is weak, either because we don't have adequate weapons or because we don't have the courage and the unity to defend ourselves, that's when we'll have to use our weapons and that's when we'll have loss of life.

One of the greatest things that I've experienced as President—the first time in 40 years—is that since I've been in the White House, we have not lost a single life of a young American in combat, and I pray to God that we'll have that record when I go out of office.

So, to summarize: peace with all nations on Earth, through strength here at home.

DEPARTMENT OF EDUCATION

Q. Good morning, Mr. President.

THE PRESIDENT. Good morning.

Q. I'm Pershing Broome, of Phoenix, Illinois. I'm also on the faculty here at Thornridge High School. And I, too, would like to welcome you to Thornridge.

THE PRESIDENT. It's a pleasure.

Q. I believe during your campaign for the Presidency some 3 years ago, you proposed to take the "E" out of HEW. I also believe that the Congress has voted to do just that. Do you plan to sign the bill to make this effective?

THE PRESIDENT. Absolutely. I'm very proud of that legislation. I'll tell you why, just briefly.

When I was in State politics, my main interest was in education. When I was elected to the State Senate, I had one request when I got to Atlanta. That was to be put on the education committee. I was on a local school board for 7 years before I went to the State Senate. And when I became Governor, I spent about 25 percent of my time trying to make sure that education for our students was improved.

Since I've been President, that has not been the case. Education in Washington

gets lost. I doubt that 2 percent of the people in this room could tell me who is specifically responsible for better education from the Federal point of view.

So, I believe that a separate department that can focus not on social programs, not on arguments and so forth and lawsuits, but on better classroom education is a very important step forward.

The second thing is this: We wrote into the law a requirement that the bureaucracy be reduced. The law says that we've got to have 500 fewer employees in the new department of education than we have now. With increased efficiency, we can do that. The law also requires that no increase in personnel in the new department can be approved unless the President, the Office of Management and Budget, and also the Congress specifically votes to increase personnel. So, we've tried to build in there a protection against increased bureaucracy.

The third thing that the law says is that local people, not the Federal Government, shall have control over the policy and the curriculum of the schools. I want to keep the Federal Government's nose out of the business of the local school system.

So, I'm proud of the new law, as you can well see, and I believe it's going to be better for education all over the country.

Thank you, sir.

SCHOOL BUSING

Q. Mr. President, I am Marcella Kuersten, of South Chicago Heights. And it is indeed a privilege to be here today.

THE PRESIDENT. Thank you, ma'am.

Q. Young families, when they buy homes or go out to rent, usually buy a home that is near a school. Then they find out when their children go to school, they are bused maybe on the other side of the city or to other parts of the county. Now, you mentioned a few minutes ago, we should learn how to cut back on our gas situation. Do you think it's feasible to continue the busing of students? And it's also a tremendous tax burden on the taxpayer.

THE PRESIDENT. My own experience has been and my own belief is that mandatory busing ought to be minimized.

There are requirements under the law, as you know, against any sort of discrimination or preventing students from getting the same quality of education within a given city or within a given school district. That's got to be honored.

My hope is that the present dispute concerning the integration of the schools or the elimination of discrimination in the schools in the Chicago region can be solved harmoniously. And I don't know where the best place might be to do it.

I have a feeling that to have the decision made by the local Federal court might very well be better for Chicago and the preservation of its neighborhoods and the honoring of the civil rights of people than to have it as a debate between the local school system and the Department of HEW. I'm not sure; that's my belief. I don't know what will come out.

We are operating under Federal laws concerning school districts and busing and integration, the elimination of deprivation of basic civil rights, and we're trying to work out an agreement. If that agreement can't be worked out between HEW and the local school board, then the normal transfer would be to the Federal court. And I've seen the Federal courts in the South, 10, 15 years ago, do outstanding jobs in trying to relieve these conflicting tendencies and pressures for the best interests of the students. I have confidence that that will be done in this case.

I don't have any authority over it, as you know, as President. But I believe that everyone wants to work it out so that there can be a satisfactory solution for black parents, for those who speak Spanish or other languages, for those who have strong ethnic commitments, and for those who want to preserve neighborhoods, those who want higher quality education.

So, what happens in the future will be very closely observed by me, and I'll do the best I can to reach the ultimate goal of honoring people's rights and having better education. But don't consider it to be a catastrophe if the case is moved into court. I think there it can be considered very calmly, very carefully, and I believe that ultimately the solution will be satisfactory to you.

FINANCIAL ASSISTANCE FOR HIGHER EDUCATION

Q. Good morning, Mr. President.

THE PRESIDENT. Good morning.

Q. I'm Arlene Zuiker, from Dolton, Illinois. And as an elementary schoolteacher, on behalf of the children, I'd like to thank you for coming to Dolton so they can see participatory democracy in action.

THE PRESIDENT. Thank you very much.

Q. Mr. President, my husband and I are both employed, and our combined incomes put us in the above-average group, which does not allow for grant-in-aid eligibility for our four college-age children. Yet by the time we pay tuition for these four children, our income drops to the poverty level, practically. Question: Is there any hope in this inflationary period to have a tax credit for educating our most important natural resource, the youth of America?

THE PRESIDENT. The question is not whether to give assistance to a family with college-age children, but what form that assistance should take.

I decided—before I became President, as a matter of fact, but after long experience in education and financing—that the best approach was the one that we've taken. We've increased the Federal contribution to education, in the first 2 years I was in office, by 60 percent above what it had been in the past. We implemented last year, 1978, a $12 billion* increase in aid to make sure that every family in this country, even one like your own, would have an opportunity to put their children through college, if the students are academically qualified and do their work.

We've approached it on a broad base. First of all is direct grants to students if their parents don't have the financial ability to put them through; secondly is a loan program to guarantee that the students, on their own initiative, can finance their college tuition and other costs and then repay afterwards when they are able to sustain their own income; and the third one, of course, is a work-study program, where the students can work part-time and go to school part-time or go to the classroom part-time, combining those two efforts so that the work part of their life is related in some way to the actual courses that they are taking. But we've tried to increase this tremendously.

The problem with going to tax credits is that we have not found any formula by which you could help the low- and middle-income families. You have a much greater financial benefit to the very wealthy families at the expense of the other taxpayers. So, this direct focusing of help on grants, loans, and work-study programs is a much better and fairer way to guarantee that the students can go to college.

---

*The President meant to say $1.2 billion. [Printed in the transcript.]

I believe that if you have a thorough knowledge of what we do offer that there won't be any reason for all four of your children or the ones that you might have in the future—I don't know how many that would be—[not] to go to college and get a good education.

Good luck in the future and also now.

HOUSING CONSTRUCTION AND FINANCING

Q. Good morning, Mr. President.

THE PRESIDENT. Good morning.

Q. I'm Pat Adamski, and I live here in Dolton. My question——

THE PRESIDENT. What's your first name?

Q. Pat.

THE PRESIDENT. Pat.

Q. My question this morning is—as you know, the mortgage market is getting very tight. Fourteen States now either are running short of or have no money. How are you going to ease this problem, because this is going to affect people countrywide—real estate agents, builders, and people who buy and sell.

THE PRESIDENT. It's hard to answer that question about the future. My hope is that interest rates have peaked, along with inflation, and will now be going down.

High interest rates are caused by high inflation. It's very difficult to have interest rates lower than the inflation rate. So, the best attack on interest rates is to do what I've described earlier—to get the inflation rate back down, with high yield of farm products, adequate farm storage, the working relationship between labor, business, and government, for a change, to hold down wages and price increases, and to decrease the imports of oil.

As far as the homebuilding is concerned, we've taken some action since I've been President that has paid off very well. In the past, when interest rates got up above 9 or 10 percent, the homebuilding industry took a nosedive, because it was almost impossible to get financing. That has not happened. I can't say that in the next few months it may not happen, but so far we have sustained a remarkable record of home construction. We've averaged about 1.8 million homes per year in this country so far, in spite of high interest rates, because we've made available to homebuilders and to families new sources of financing for homes.

I don't know what will happen in the future. I can't guarantee that there won't be some dropoff in that level, but it set records for the first 2 years, even in spite of high interest rates. In my opinion, the purchase of a home is still a good investment for a young couple that can afford the monthly payments.

I think real estate, including land, homes, and other things, will continue to go up at least a moderate rate, and I believe that when we get inflation under control with the policies that I've described, we'll alleviate that pressure. But we are doing everything we can with savings and loan bankers, the people who help us with finances, Government programs for low- and middle-income families, FHA, Farm Home Administration loans, to make sure that there is no dropoff in home construction or availability of homes. There may be local problems. I'm not trying to mislead you, but we have really held down the historic dropoff in home construction.

I might say, as another indication of that—I spoke to the building and construction workers union meeting in San Diego this past week—and since I've been in office, we've put an extra million construction workers on the job; we've cut the unemployment rate in that industry down by 40 percent. That's another indication that homebuilding and other construction is still a very strong element in our society.

I hope it will stay the way it has been. So far, we've got a good record. I just pray it'll hold.

ENERGY

Q. Good morning, Mr. President.

THE PRESIDENT. Good morning.

Q. My name is Christopher Stevo. Could you please tell me how we are progressing in developing new energy sources?

THE PRESIDENT. I couldn't hear you. Come up here a minute. [*Laughter*]

When I get supporters and allies his age trying to help me resolve the energy question, I think we're on sound ground and we've got the right road filled out for us.

We're doing several things at one time.

First of all, the Congress has very wisely required that all the automobiles produced now and in the future would have to be much more efficient, get a lot more miles for every gallon. That's the first step. By 1985 all the automobiles produced in our country would have to average 27½ miles per gallon, a big improvement over what we have had in the past.

Secondly, automobile buyers, with the high gasoline prices and with the few gasoline lines that took place this summer, have rapidly shifted toward the smaller and the more efficient automobiles.

All of you can help. I said earlier that I hope the families would have a consultation about how you can save energy.

When you go home from this meeting, look at how many cars you meet on the road that only have one passenger—sometimes two, very rarely three or four. And if you would change your driving habits, and five people could ride in your car to and from work, instead of five automobiles going to and from work, that saves a tremendous amount of fuel.

Another thing that we can do is to shift toward the use of gasohol and other automobile fuels that come not from oil, which is going to run out on Earth, but which can be sustained on a permanent basis. We've made a move in that direction in the Congress in the last year, and it's going to have tremendous influence. Brazil, for instance, now produces about 10 percent of all its automobile fuel from growing plants, through gasohol, and I think our country is moving very rapidly toward that.

We're also encouraging automobile manufacturers to shift toward other kinds of propulsion. You've probably noticed that one of the major automobile producers, the biggest one in the world, has just come out with an experimental automobile that uses batteries that can run 30,000 miles on one set of batteries, about a hundred miles before it has to be recharged. You can drive your car a hundred miles during the day, put it in the garage, plug it into the plug in your garage; the next day you can go a hundred more miles. And you can do that 300 times before you have to change batteries.

So, new design of automobiles, more efficient driving habits on the part of Americans, and new forms of energy, like gasohol, can all help to make sure that we have a better efficiency in the future and that we use our fuel more wisely.

That was a great question, and I thank you for it very much.

I might say that it doesn't hurt people to ride bicycles instead of cars. I was out early this morning before the Sun came up, and I ran 4 miles. And it doesn't hurt people to walk to work every now and then.

And I hope that you'll see, in general, that when our country faces a problem like energy shortages, that we need not shrivel up and be fearful about the future

or start lashing out against one another and try to take some selfish advantage. It may be that the new awareness on the part of Americans that we have limited amount of energy will be the best thing that ever happened.

I think our country can be stronger, not weaker. I think our family life might be coordinated rather than more fragmented. I think neighborhoods might be preserved a little bit more. I think people might be healthier, because they get more exercise. And we might pause a little bit in our lives and enjoy the beauty of the places that we live, instead of dashing from one place to another and not even recognizing what God's given us. So, I think in general we might be a better people because of it.

FEDERAL-LOCAL RELATIONS

Q. Good morning, Mr. President. My name is Ralph Spencer. I'm from Calumet City, Illinois. I am involved there in local politics, somewhat. I'm an alderman in Calumet City, and being involved in the local politics, I do get concerned and have a lot of people asking, is the return and the balance of money that goes into Washington from a particular area and the amount that comes back to this—particularly Illinois.

One of the things that is very important in the financing of local government is Federal revenue sharing. It has developed into a very, very important function or very, very important source of revenue. I understand that very shortly Federal revenue sharing, as it stands right now, is destined to cease.

What is your feeling, and what is your stand towards balancing out the payments to the local people, and what is the future of Federal revenue sharing?

THE PRESIDENT. I don't believe there's

any chance that Federal revenue sharing would be in danger for local governments. That answers part of your question.

Secondly, when you start balancing how much Federal money comes back into a community, compared to how much goes from that community to the Federal Government, you get into some very complicated economics.

The best way I know to make sure you get more money back than you pay in is not make so much money yourself, to start with, because the rich communities, where the people have high income and pay more income tax, don't ever get back as much as you paid in, whereas a poorer community, with income very low or perhaps very serious problems on housing and a high unemployment rate, they're the ones that do get Federal money back to let their lives be better. So, I think you live in one of those very fortunate communities, apparently, where you have a fairly good life and a fairly high income, fairly high employment, not any serious housing problems, and so forth.

We have always believed that the Federal Government should provide aid and have a minimum control over the lives of people. One of the best things that we can do to control inflation, by the way, that I have not mentioned so far, is to get the Federal Government's nose out of the affairs of private citizens or out of the affairs of the free enterprise system. We've tried to do this, and we've been successful in some areas. I'll give you one quick example.

We made a move to deregulate the airline industry. It was opposed by almost every airline company in the Nation, but Marty Russo and others helped, and we got that legislation passed. It's been a great benefit. Airline fares have dropped remarkably low. The airplanes now, instead of their being a quarter full, are almost filled to capacity, passengers have gone up in number tremendously, and the profits of the airlines have also gone up. We're trying to do the same thing now with other elements of the American free enterprise system.

In some cases, too many cases, the Federal regulatory agencies that are supposed to regulate an industry have become protectors for that industry at the expense of the American people. And I think the more we can get the Federal regulatory agencies' nose out of the business of the free enterprise system and let competition work, the better off our country will be.

So, there are many ways that you can make sure that the Federal Government does have a more effective relationship to the people in your own community.

One other thing that I've tried to do is to cut the Federal deficit. We've slashed the Federal deficit by more than 60 percent, $36 billion, and at the same time, we've cut down on the percentage of our total Nation's income that's collected from people and spent by the Federal Government. When I became President, it was about 23½ percent. We've cut that down now to 21½ percent, and we've got it going in the right direction.

So, we're trying to cut the Federal deficit, balance the budget, reduce the amount of your money that the Federal Government collects and sends back to somebody, and also, we're trying to get the Federal Government's nose out of your business. All those things, in the long run, will pay off.

TRAFFIC STOP SIGNS

Q. Mr. President, my name is Larry Kast, and I'm a mechanical engineer. I live in Dolton, and I work for the Metropolitan Sanitary District of Greater Chicago. I'm going to address myself to conservation of energy. I know it's a very good subject of yours.

Four-and-a-half years ago, I was picked by the late Mayor Daley to run for Cook County commissioner, and Mayor Jane Byrne, at that time, was our chairman of the nominating committee. And I ran. But during the campaign, I made a study on where are we wasting energy or where can we save energy, and I found out that we— I addressed myself to the 1,200,000 cars, automobiles that are in use today on a day-by-day basis, 110,000 trucks that are running around every day, mostly 8 hours a day, and I addressed myself to kinetic energy, which is energy of motion.

And when you see these automobiles with a 2-ton vehicle coming to a stop sign, an unnecessary stop sign, and stopping, to get that car going 30 miles again requires an awful lot of energy, not to mention a 78,000-pound truck, approximately 40 pounds [tons] fully loaded, 40 miles an hour coming to a stop light, an unnecessary stop light, or a stop sign, and then to get that car or that truck going again, 40 tons, 40 miles an hour, you eat gasoline or fuel up by the gallons. And this is where we are losing or wasting fuel.

I also make these statements, and I have calculations to prove it. Four-and-a-half years ago, during that campaign, I calculated it. And would you believe, by the time I——

THE PRESIDENT. I think the people are going to want you to ask a question.

Q. All right, fine. I took kinetic energy, I converted it to Btu's; Btu's to gallons of gas; gallons of gas to crude oils; crude oils to number of barrels. And it came out to be we could conserve 7 million barrels a day—fantastic—exactly what we were importing 4½ years ago. Today it's 8.3 million or more barrels.

All right, my question is: Do you think that system of reducing or eliminating one-third of the stop signs has merit across the country?

THE PRESIDENT. Good question. It was a long question, but I think it's worthwhile, because this is one of the few questions that I get for which I'm not responsible. [*Laughter*] Nobody can accuse me of putting in those extra stop signs, right? [*Laughter*]

You know, I believe that this is one area that we have not adequately addressed. And I will relay your question to the Secretary of Transportation, Neil Goldschmidt, and tell him, in working with local people and also in the Federal highway system, to see if we can't reduce the number of unnecessary stop signs. And I think that that is a very worthy suggestion.

We get a lot of good thoughts and a lot of good ideas from coming out to meet with people like you, and I think the sense that I get is that we are all partners. Every one of your constituents, as a local official, is also my constituent, and every one of Marty Russo's constituents in this district is my constituent. We represent the same people. And what I do as President that benefits our Nation is exactly what you want, whether you're a Democrat or a Republican. You want the President to do a good job.

I don't have time for another question, I'm sorry. But I would like to say this in closing.

When we read the local newspapers or see the evening television or listen to the radio, what we get at that moment of that day is a picture, most often an accurate picture, of the problems of our society. The inconveniences are multiplied in their importance, and the debates that take place on controversial issues, like taxes or housing or interest rates or inflation or legislation concerning education—we see and we think about the difficulties and the arguments and the temporary failures.

What we don't see on the news, but what we ought to remember, is the blessings that we have in this country. I think we ought to be sure to inventory for our own reassurance and then just comment every now and then to people that listen to your voice about what God's given us in this Nation.

We're a nation of freedom. Our people can stand on our own feet, make our own decisions, be different, be individuals, be innovative, be hard-working, be lazy if we want to, get a good education, choose our own jobs, choose a place to live, choose our own officials, criticize the government, make comments, make suggestions, influence our neighbors. We have a country that lets each person take whatever talent we have and express that talent and let that talent grow to a maximum degree.

We also have a nation that's strong. We're the strongest nation on Earth. Militarily, we're the strongest; economically, we're the strongest; politically, we're the strongest; morally, ethically. Deep religious beliefs all exist within us. We've got our faults; we make our mistakes; we're not perfect. And as I mentioned to the Pope on the South Lawn of the White House the Saturday before last, we're responsible for our own actions. But let's don't ever forget that the United States of America is the best place on Earth to live. It's the greatest nation on Earth, and I believe that you and I together can make it even greater.

Thank you very much. God bless you all.

NOTE: The President spoke at 10:05 a.m. at Thornridge High School gymnasium.

Following the town meeting, the President attended a private reception for Democratic State representatives and officials of the State Democratic Party at the Holiday Inn in Harvey, Ill.

Pay Advisory Committee

Appointment of Chairman and 17 Members. October 16, 1979

President Carter today announced selection of 17 prominent business, labor, and public figures to serve as members of the anti-inflation program's Pay Advisory Committee. They will serve with John Thomas Dunlop, a Harvard economics professor and former Secretary of Labor, who has accepted the Chairmanship of the Committee.

The President said on September 28 that he would name a committee to broaden public participation in the development and administration of the voluntary pay standard for the second year of the anti-inflation program. It was enlarged from 15 to 18 to provide for wider participation.

The Pay Advisory Committee will advise the Council on Wage and Price Stability on developing policies that encourage anti-inflationary pay behavior by employers and labor, in order to decelerate the rate of inflation and provide for fair and equitable distribution of the burden of restraint.

The Committee will recommend any modifications to the pay standard it considers necessary and to pay exception and noncompliance decisions of the Council. It will also recommend new or revised interpretations of the pay standard.

Members of the Committee were chosen after wide consultation with representatives of labor, business, and the general public.

The Committee will hold its first meeting at 10 a.m., Wednesday, October 17, in Room 2008 of the New Executive Office Building.

Following are names of the Committee members and the sectors which they represent:

Public members

JOHN T. DUNLOP—Chairman. Mr. Dunlop is currently Lamont University professor at Harvard Business School and was Secretary of Labor from March 1975 to February 1976;

PHYLLIS WALLACE, professor of industrial relations at the Sloan School of Management of the Massachusetts Institute of Technology;

ROBBEN W. FLEMING, president of the Corporation for Public Broadcasting and former president of the University of Michigan; he has accepted subject to approval of his board;

ARVIN ANDERSON, chairman, Office of Collective Bargaining, City of New York;

LLOYD ULMAN, professor of economics, Institute of Industrial Relations, University of California, Berkeley;

ROBERT NATHAN, consulting economist and chief executive officer of Robert R. Nathan Associates, an economic consulting firm.

Labor members

LANE KIRKLAND, secretary-treasurer of the AFL–CIO;

WILLIAM WYNN, president, United Food and Commercial Workers;

JOHN LYONS, president, International Association of Bridge and Structural Iron Workers;

LLOYD MCBRIDE, president, United Steelworkers of America;

FRANK FITZSIMMONS, president, International Brotherhood of Teamsters, Chauffeurs, Warehousemen and Helpers of America;

DOUGLAS FRASER, president, United Automobile, Aerospace, and Agricultural Implement Workers Union.

Business members

R. HEATH LARRY, president of the National Association of Manufacturers;

JESSE HILL, president and chief executive officer of Atlanta Life Insurance Co.;

CHARLES R. MCDONALD, chairman, Council of Smaller Enterprises, and president, McDonald Equipment Co. of Cleveland, Ohio;

JOHN T. CONNER, chairman of the board, Allied Chemical Corp.;

NORMA PACE, senior vice president, American Paper Institute;

PHILIP M. HAWLEY, president and chief executive officer of Carter Hawley Hale Stores.

Alternates will be named later for business and labor representatives.

Carter Family Peanut Warehouse

White House Statement on the Findings of a Special Investigation.   October 16, 1979

We are, of course, carefully studying the report and will have further comment on it later.

We said from the beginning of the investigation that no moneys were diverted from the Carter warehouse into the Jimmy Carter Presidential campaign or from the campaign into the warehouse, and the report shows our statements were absolutely correct. We also said from the beginning that we would cooperate fully with the investigation, and the report shows we did exactly that.

We are very pleased by the special counsel's findings.

NOTE: On March 20, 1979, Paul J. Curran was appointed by the Department of Justice as a special counsel to investigate the financial transactions of the Carter family peanut warehouse.

International Convention on Load Lines, 1966

Message to the Senate Transmitting an Amendment to the Convention. October 17, 1979

To the Senate of the United States:

I transmit herewith, for the advice and consent of the Senate to acceptance, an amendment to the International Convention on Load Lines, 1966. The report of the Department of State is enclosed for the information of the Senate in connection with its consideration of the amendment.

The International Convention on Load Lines establishes uniform international principles governing the safe loading of ships in all seasons and waters. The purpose of this amendment is to expedite the procedure for amending the technical annexes to the Convention.

I believe that the proposed amendment is highly desirable. The Convention's present amendment procedure has made it impossible to bring into force many technical improvements to the requirements of the Convention. The new procedure will greatly facilitate and accelerate the entry into force of these essential improvements.

I recommend that the Senate give consideration to this amendment and advice and consent to its acceptance.

JIMMY CARTER

The White House,
  October 17, 1979.

Department of Education Organization Act

Remarks at the Bill Signing Ceremony.
October 17, 1979

THE PRESIDENT. The first thing I want to do is to invite into the room the real beneficiaries of the new Department of Education, a group of fourth grade students from Brent Elementary School. This morning they can stand where they want to. [*Laughter*]

In 1962 I was serving on a local school board in the Deep South and had been for 7 years. We were going through a time of sociological change, when public, elected officials, and churches, business leaders stood mute while children suffered because of ancient policies of racial discrimination. That situation changed because of schoolteachers and the courage of educators, who saw the devastating effect of continued racial policies in the South and throughout the country.

I decided to run for the State Senate to see if I could help in Georgia, based on my own experiences under those trying circumstances. And when I got to Atlanta as a newly elected senator, I had one request, and that was that I be put on the education committee. And I was.

I later ran for Governor, and my prime campaign commitment was to improve education in Georgia. And we did. I spent probably 25 percent of my time as Governor trying to deal with better education for our students.

When I became President, that situation was drastically different. There has not been in the Federal Government an adequate mechanism by which we can improve the quality of education in the United States, and I say that not in criticism of those who've served under such difficult circumstances. But I think you could interrogate local elementary and high school principals and classroom teachers, county school board members, State school superintendents, college professors, university presidents, Governors, and you would find an almost complete negative attitude toward how much support is given from the Federal Government for better education, compared with the tremendous potential that exists.

As Fritz [1] pointed out, we have increased tremendously the Federal financial contribution to education, 60 percent in 2½ years, with the help of the Congress. This has obviously been focused in a very fine way, but the interrelationship between local people—public and private

---

[1] Vice President Walter F. Mondale.

education—and State officials, who are directly responsible and ought to have control over the policy of the schools—relationship between them on the one hand and the Federal bureaucracy on the other one has been a very poor record.

I don't know what history will show, but my guess is that the best move for the quality of life in America in the future might very well be this establishment of this new Department of Education, because it will open up for the first time some very substantial benefits for our country.

There is a growing concern in our Nation about the decrease of the measurement of the quality of education through testing, through the achievement levels of our students. And it's not the students' fault, it's not the teachers' fault that there have been obstacles placed in the way of better education because of bureaucracy, too much redtape, too much confusion, an inadequate consultative process.

When I was a Governor, I didn't know where to go in Washington to get the answer to a question about education in my State. And I'll bet you very few—I'll bet you not more than two or three Governors in this Nation know who, specifically, is responsible for the educational programs in Washington. I'll bet you not 10 percent of the Members of the House and Senate know, specifically, who is responsible. In the future I hope that everyone will know—who's interested in education—this is the Secretary of Education, and that's the person that I'll go to to get the answer to a question or to resolve a problem or to overcome a difficulty. That is a great step in the right direction.

Also, I hope and I pray and I'm determined that we're going to cut out unnecessary forms, applications, redtape, regulations that have been an obstacle in the past.

It's important for us to remember that education is the biggest single national in-

vestment in the United States. Sixty million Americans are directly involved in the educational process; that is 3 Americans out of 10, who work in a direct or indirect way in education, $120 billion spent in our country every year on education. And I want to see that investment of human and financial resources pay rich dividends in the future. It hasn't in the past, not nearly up to the potential. We're going to change that.

I believe that we can have, in the future, the acknowledgement that policy, curriculum, personnel decisions should be made at the local level, as close as possible to the parents and to the students in private and public education, and that the Federal Government is there, eager to help, to bridge gaps, to consult, to remove problems. And I hope the prime focus will be on the quality of the knowledge and the future life of each student.

I think this can be a fairly narrowly focused commitment. It's not possible to have that focusing of attention in Health, Education, and Welfare, where education is buried under the enormous responsibilities of welfare, health, and other related subjects.

There can also be a substantial saving in administrative costs, and that's built into the legislation in a mandatory fashion. I won't go into details about it.

And I believe that in the future we can have a much more responsive Federal Government, where, if a problem should arise in an embryonic way, an educator can know exactly where to go to get an answer, and where there can be a bridging of a chasm that quite often in the past has separated educators from the Federal Government. It's not going to be a panacea which can resolve every problem immediately, but I'm determined to make it work.

And I'm very grateful to all of those who've been instrumental in reaching this goal after I don't know how many years of frustrated efforts. Sometimes it didn't look as though we were going to make it, and Fritz has already thanked those who have helped. Educators, local officials of all kinds, interested parents, students helped, and I think in the House and Senate, as Fritz has already said, we had superb bipartisan leadership.

I'd like to introduce now, to speak for the House, Jack Brooks, who's a formidable ally to have in a tough fight. He hates to lose, and he rarely does. [*Laughter*] And I'm very grateful to Jack Brooks, because there were times when the outcome was in doubt, and had it not been for him, we would not have prevailed. And I think what he's done for me as President, for our government, and for the children and other students in our country is a notable achievement, and I'm deeply grateful to Jack.

I might point out that [Representative] Frank Horton and the Republicans helped enormously to make sure that the Nation knew, and the votes indicated, that this is not a partisan issue, as Fritz has already pointed out.

But I would like to introduce to you my friend, with a great deal of gratitude, Jack Brooks.

REPRESENTATIVE BROOKS. Mr. President, I want to thank you. It gives me a great pleasure to be here on this occasion. We weren't always sure we'd make this trip. [*Laughter*]

But an educated citizenry is essential to the survival of a democratic form of government, to the promotion of justice and equality, and to our country's economic progress. And for the first time, our $14 billion education program will be receiving Presidential attention, and the managers can be held accountable for achieving maximum results.

So, I want to congratulate you, Mr. President, for your insight, your leadership in the field of education. This bill is a result of cooperation and teamwork between the White House and the Congress, and we're just pleased to join you here in finalizing that successful effort.

THE PRESIDENT. I don't know if [Representative] Carl Perkins is here. Is he? I wanted particularly to thank him. Well, Jack, you tell him that we missed him, and thank him especially.

And now I'd like to turn to Abe Ribicoff, who had a similar responsibility and achievement in the Senate. He, contrary to Jack Brooks, made an extremely difficult issue look easy. [*Laughter*] But I was involved in both fights on both sides, and they are great allies to have.

But I'd like to call now on Abe Ribicoff to come and say a word, if he will. Abe?

SENATOR RIBICOFF. Mr. President, in 1960 President-elect Kennedy asked me what job I'd like in the Cabinet, and I told him I'd like to go to HEW. And the basic reason for that was education. When I got in the Cabinet, I realized that the problems of health and welfare were so overriding that education was relegated to the back burner.

When I came to the Senate in 1963, the first measure I placed in the hopper was the creation of a department of education. I felt then that it was absolutely essential. If we were to take care of children such as this, we needed the organization to put into effect the huge expenditures of money that we have been appropriating. And I'm so pleased that President Carter was the first President during that interim period who realized the absolute necessity for a department of education.

So, now it's become a reality—organization is policy, the policies that we have been adopting can be put into effect. And I want to take this opportunity of thanking my colleagues in the Congress and especially you, Mr. President, for making it possible for this Nation to move forward for all its people with a Department of Education.

THE PRESIDENT. I don't think Senator Percy is here, but he was a strong right arm for Abe Ribicoff.

Is Dr. Benjamin Mays here? I've been looking around to see if I could find him. Dr. Mays, would you come here, please?

Dr. Mays probably personifies the dedication of educators as well or perhaps better than anyone I know in this country. He's been involved in education under the most trying circumstances for more than 50 years, as a teacher, as a president of a great university, as a leader in the extremely difficult sociological changes that took place under the aegis of education, which required great courage and his personal influence over many Americans, including myself. I think he personifies—just to repeat myself—the finest elements of education.

And I just thought it might be good for me to get one of the fourth graders from Brent and for Dr. Mays to stand here, just to show you how important it is to bridge the generation gap and how the beneficial effect of distinguished and dedicated educators, many of whom cannot be recognized—how their impact on the life of a child can be so beneficial to our country. So, I just want to get these two up here with me.

And now I'd like to sign the bill.

NOTE: The President spoke at 10:10 a.m. in the East Room at the White House.

As enacted, S. 210 is Public Law 96–88, approved October 17.

Department of Education Organization Act

Statement on Signing S. 210 Into Law.
October 17, 1979

Education is our most important national investment. It commands the time and attention of 60 million Americans— 3 citizens in 10. It consumes an annual public and private expenditure in excess of $120 billion. Every citizen has a vital, personal stake in this investment. Our ability to advance both economically and technologically, our country's entire intellectual and cultural life depend on the success of our great educational enterprise.

At no time in our history has our Nation's commitment to education been more justified. At no time in our history has it been more obvious that our Nation's great educational challenges cannot be met with increased resources alone.

I came to the office of the Presidency determined that the American people should receive a better return on their investment in education. I came equally determined that our Nation's formidable educational challenges should be brought to the forefront of national discussion, where they belong.

Primary responsibility for education should rest with those States, localities, and private institutions that have made our Nation's educational system the best in the world, but the Federal Government has for too long failed to play its own supporting role in education as effectively as it could. Instead of assisting school officials at the local level, it has too often added to their burden. Instead of setting a strong administrative model, the Federal structure has contributed to bureaucratic buck passing. Instead of stimulating needed debate of educational issues, the Federal Government has confused its role of junior partner in American education with that of silent partner.

The time has passed when the Federal Government can afford to give second-level, part-time attention to its responsibilities in American education. If our Nation is to meet the great challenges of the 1980's, we need a full-time commitment to education at every level of government—Federal, State, and local.

The Department of Education bill will allow the Federal Government to meet its responsibilities in education more effectively, more efficiently, and more responsively.

First, it will increase the Nation's attention to education. Instead of being buried in a $200 billion-a-year bureaucracy, educational issues will receive the top-level priority they deserve. For the first time, there will be a Cabinet-level leader in education, someone with the status and the resources to stir national discussion of critical education concerns.

Second, it will make Federal education programs more accountable. For the first time there will be a single Cabinet Secretary, responsible full-time for the effective conduct of Federal education programs.

Third, it will streamline administration of aid-to-education programs. Separating education programs from HEW will eliminate unnecessary bureaucracy, cut redtape, and promote better service for local school systems. For the first time there will be a direct, unobstructed relationship between those who administer aid-to-education programs and those who actually provide education in our country.

Fourth, a Department of Education will save tax dollars. By eliminating bureaucratic layers, the reorganization will permit direct, substantial personnel reductions. By enhancing top-level management attention to education programs, it will mean improved educational services at less cost.

Fifth, it will make Federal education programs more responsive. Placing education in a highly visible department of its own gives the American people a much clearer perspective on what the Federal Government is doing in education and who is responsible for these activities. It allows people to better decide what the Government should and should not be doing in education.

Sixth, a Department of Education will ensure that local communities retain control of their schools and education programs. That is essential if our schools are to serve their students properly, and the Department of Education will, therefore, not permit the Federal Government to begin making decisions on education policy that are best made at the local level.

The Department of Education bill will permit improved administration of the Government's health and human service programs, whose functions are closely related. It will allow the Government to focus greater attention to the needs of those Americans who need it most—the poor, the disabled, and the elderly.

Today's signing fulfills a longstanding personal commitment on my part. My first public office was as a county school board member. As a State senator and Governor I devoted much of my time to education issues. I remain convinced that education is one of the noblest enterprises a person or a society can undertake.

I would like to thank the leadership of both houses of Congress for bringing this historic measure to final passage. I would like to pay particular tribute to the leadership role of Chairman Jack Brooks, Senator Abe Ribicoff, Senator Chuck Percy, and Congressman Frank Horton. Your relentless dedication to this legislation has earned you the gratitude of every citizen.

I would like also to salute the active participation in this legislative struggle by a strong coalition of groups devoted to educational quality and equal educational opportunity. You refused to believe that education is a part-time responsibility, for the Federal Government or for yourselves.

NOTE: As enacted, S. 210 is Public Law 96–88, approved October 17.

15th Annniversary of the Job Corps

Statement by the President.   October 17, 1979

The Job Corps began 15 years ago on the premise that, if given the opportunity, young people who had grown up in poverty and frustration could become responsible, employable, and productive citizens.

With government, labor, and industry working together, this idea has become a reality for more than 700,000 young men and women who have received basic education, skills training, work experience, and health care through the Job Corps. With their new skills and pride in accomplishment, Job Corps graduates are entering the labor market, confident that they can become contributing workers with satisfying careers.

In the years to come, I know that the Job Corps will continue to assist young men and women, who might otherwise have been neglected and forgotten, to lead rewarding lives.

Department of Health, Education, and Welfare

Nomination of Joan Zeldes Bernstein To Be General Counsel.   October 17, 1979

The President today announced that he will nominate Joan Zeldes Bernstein,

of Chevy Chase, Md., to be General Counsel of the Department of Health, Education, and Welfare. She would replace Richard Beattie, resigned. Bernstein has been General Counsel of the Environmental Protection Agency since 1977.

She was born March 17, 1926, in Galesburg, Ill. She received a B.A. in economics from the University of Wisconsin in 1948 and an LL.B. from Yale Law School in 1951.

Bernstein was an associate attorney with the New York firm of Sherman & Sterling from 1951 to 1952 and with the Chicago firm of Dahlstream, Schiff, Waite & Hardin from 1952 to 1953. From 1968 to 1970, she was an associate attorney with the Washington firm of William B. Wolf, Jr.

Bernstein was with the Bureau of Consumer Protection of the Federal Trade Commission from 1970 to 1976, serving as a trial attorney, then Assistant to the Director, Deputy Director, and finally Acting Director. From 1976 to 1977, she was a partner in the Washington firm of Baker, Hostetler, Frost & Towers.

Department of State

Nomination of William G. Bowdler To Be an Assistant Secretary.   October 17, 1979

The President today announced his intention to nominate William G. Bowdler to be Assistant Secretary of State for Inter-American Affairs. Bowdler has been Director of the Bureau of Intelligence and Research at the State Department since 1978.

He was born March 27, 1924, in Buenos Aires, Argentina, and became a naturalized citizen in 1945. He received a B.A. in history from the University of Richmond in 1948 and an M.A. from the Fletcher School of Law and Diplomacy in 1949. He served in the U.S. Army from 1944 to 1946.

From 1950 to 1951, Bowdler was a research assistant at the State Department, and from 1951 to 1952, he was an international administration officer. From 1952 to 1956, he was an international relations officer in the Bureau of Inter-American Affairs. From 1956 to 1961, he was political and consular officer in Havana.

From 1961 to 1963, Bowdler was an international relations officer, and from 1963 to 1964, he was Deputy Coordinator of Cuban Affairs. From 1964 to 1968, he was executive liaison officer for Latin American affairs with the White House. From 1968 to 1971, he was Ambassador to El Salvador.

From 1971 to 1973, Bowdler was Ambassador to Guatemala. He became Deputy Assistant Secretary of State for Inter-American Affairs in 1973 and Acting Assistant Secretary in 1974. He served as Ambassador to South Africa from 1975 to 1978.

Drug Enforcement Administration

Nomination of Frederick A. Rody, Jr., To Be Deputy Administrator. October 17, 1979

The President today announced that he will nominate Frederick A. Rody, Jr., of Miami Lake, Fla., to be Deputy Administrator of the Drug Enforcement Administration in the Department of Justice. He would replace Jerry N. Jenson, resigned. Rody is Regional Administrator of the Drug Enforcement Administration for the southeast region.

He was born September 8, 1931, in Sewickley, Pa. He received a B.S. from Michigan State University in 1955. He served in the U.S. Army from 1955 to 1957.

In 1954 and 1955, Rody was assistant chief of police in Davison, Mich. In 1957 he was with the Ottawa Roughriders of the Canadian Football League.

From 1957 to 1975, Rody was with the U.S. Bureau of Customs, where his positions included Deputy Assistant Commissioner and special agent in charge of the Seattle and Laredo district offices.

Rody has been with the Drug Enforcement Administration since 1975, and has served as Acting Assistant Administrator for Enforcement, Acting Deputy Administrator, and Regional Director in the Seattle and Miami regional offices.

Federal Prison Industries, Inc.

Appointment of Two Members of the Board of Directors. October 17, 1979

The President today announced the appointment of two persons as members of the Board of Directors of the Federal Prison Industries, Inc., in the Department of Justice. They are:

DARYL F. GRISHAM, a Chicago businessman, who is chairman of the PUSH Foundation, a principal of Chicago United, and chairman of the Chicago Metro Division of the National Alliance of Businessmen;

MONICA HERRERA SMITH, a deputy probation officer with the Los Angeles County Probation Department and program coordinator for CONTACT, an exoffender employment project.

Internal Revenue Service

Nomination of N. Jerold Cohen To Be Chief Counsel.   October 17, 1979

The President today announced that he will nominate N. Jerold Cohen, of Atlanta, Ga., to be Chief Counsel of the Internal Revenue Service in the Department of the Treasury. He would replace Stuart Seigel, resigned. Cohen is with the Atlanta law firm of Sutherland, Asbill & Brennan.

He was born June 13, 1935, in Pine Bluff, Ark. He received a B.B.A. from Tulane University in 1957 and an LL.B. from Harvard Law School in 1961.

Cohen has been with Sutherland, Asbill & Brennan since 1961. He is an adjunct professor at Emory University School of Law and serves as chairman of the Atlanta Community Relations Commission.

1979 Nobel Prize in Medicine

Message of Congratulations to Allan McCleod Cormack.   October 12, 1979

To Professor Allan McCleod Cormack

Congratulations! I know that all Americans join me in applauding the tribute you have received from the Nobel Assembly.

Untold numbers of persons stand to benefit—as have thousands already—from the advanced diagnostic procedures made possible by your work on the theoretical processes underlying the development of the CAT scan. Your work has meant not only a triumph for science but also a triumph for humanitarian concerns.

It gives me great pleasure to salute you on this occasion and to send you my best wishes.

Sincerely,

JIMMY CARTER

[Professor Allan McCleod Cormack, Department of Physics, Tufts University, Medford, Massachusetts 02155]

NOTE: The text of the message was released on October 17.

1979 Nobel Peace Prize

Message of Congratulations to Mother Teresa of Calcutta.   October 17, 1979

To Mother Teresa of Calcutta

I would like to express my personal congratulations for your richly deserved award of the Nobel Peace Prize for 1979.

Your work on behalf of children, refugees, the poor and the sick has been a great inspiration for many years to those of us who cherish and espouse human rights. Mankind is in your debt for your fine contributions and for the example you have provided of selfless concern for others.

I wish you every continuing success in your service to humanity.

Sincerely,

JIMMY CARTER

[Mother Teresa of Calcutta, Missionaries of Charity, 54 A Lower Circular Road, Calcutta 16, India]

1979 Nobel Prize in Chemistry

Message of Congratulations to Herbert C. Brown.   October 17, 1979

To Professor Herbert Brown

Congratulations on your Nobel Prize in Chemistry for 1979.

I am pleased that your outstanding work in boron chemistry, which has led to the development of large molecules of enormous use to industry, is being recognized through this renowned international prize.

I know that Americans everywhere are proud of your accomplishments and join me in sending you our very best wishes.

Sincerely,

JIMMY CARTER

[Professor Herbert C. Brown, Department of Chemistry, Purdue University, Lafayette, Indiana 47907]

At a time when the economic problems of the developing world are among the most urgent problems of all mankind, it is significant and gratifying that your achievements have been recognized with this renowned international award.

I know that Americans everywhere join me in extending our very best wishes to you at this proud moment.

Sincerely,

JIMMY CARTER

[Dr. Theodore W. Schultz, Professor Emeritus, Department of Economics, University of Chicago, 5801 South Ellis Street, Chicago, Illinois 60637]

1979 Nobel Prize in Economics

Messages of Congratulations to Sir William Arthur Lewis and Theodore W. Schultz. October 17, 1979

To Sir Arthur Lewis

Congratulations on your Nobel Prize in Economics for 1979.

Your work in economic growth and development theory has had a profound effect on everyone involved in efforts to advance the lives of people in the under-developed areas of the world.

I am indeed pleased that you have long pursued your career at Princeton University, where your teaching and writing have been so admired and appreciated.

I know that all Americans join me at this time in sending you these congratulations and best wishes.

Sincerely,

JIMMY CARTER

[Sir William Arthur Lewis, Woodrow Wilson School, Princeton University, Princeton, New Jersey 08540]

———

To Dr. Theodore Schultz

Congratulations on winning the 1979 Nobel Prize in Economics.

1979 Nobel Prize in Physics

Messages of Congratulations to Sheldon L. Glashow and Steven Weinberg. October 17, 1979

To Professor Sheldon Glashow

Congratulations! I am pleased that you and your colleague, Professor Weinberg, are being awarded the Nobel Prize in Physics for 1979.

Your independent work in particle physics has brought one step closer to realization the long-standing dream of a unified field theory. Americans everywhere are proud that your accomplishments have been recognized with this renowned international prize.

On their behalf, and on my own personal behalf, I want to express our appreciation and our best wishes as we share with you this proud moment.

Sincerely,

JIMMY CARTER

[Professor Sheldon L. Glashow, Department of Physics, Harvard University, Cambridge, Massachusetts 02138]

———

To Professor Steven Weinberg

Congratulations! I am pleased that you and your colleague, Professor Glashow, are being awarded the Nobel Prize in Physics for 1979.

Your independent work in particle physics has brought one step closer to realization the long-standing dream of a unified field theory. Americans everywhere are proud that your accomplishments have been recognized with this renowned international prize.

On their behalf, and on my own personal behalf, I want to express our appreciation and our best wishes as we share with you this proud moment.

Sincerely,

JIMMY CARTER

[Professor Steven Weinberg, Department of Physics, Harvard University, Cambridge, Massachusetts 02138]

Death of S. J. Perelman

Statement by the President.   October 18, 1979

S. J. Perelman was one of the best writers of comic prose our country has ever produced. His playground was the American language, and whether he was writing the screenplay for a Marx brothers movie or a short essay for the New Yorker, his verbal gymnastics were sometimes surprising, often breathtaking, and always funny. Like Mark Twain, George Ade, Ring Lardner, and James Thurber, S. J. Perelman made a permanent contribution not only to American humor but to American literature as well.

Windfall Profits Tax Legislation

*Statement on Senate Finance Committee Approval of the Legislation.
October 19, 1979*

I am pleased that the Senate Finance Committee has approved the windfall

profits tax The committee has adopted the basic framework I proposed, dedicating the proceeds of the tax to important energy-related purposes, such as low-income assistance and public transportation, as I urged.

While I am pleased that the committee has rejected a number of major exemptions from the tax, I am also disappointed with some of the exemptions that were adopted. I do not believe they are cost-effective. They would ensure little additional crude oil production, while losing billions of dollars of revenue for the public. I will work for the elimination of these exemptions.

The committee has produced a constructive bill that we can continue to strengthen on the Senate floor and in conference.

National Transportation Safety Board

Nomination of G. H. Patrick Bursley To Be a Member.   October 19, 1979

The President today announced that he will nominate G. H. Patrick Bursley for reappointment as a member of the National Transportation Safety Board, for a term expiring December 31, 1984.

Bursley has been a member of the National Transportation Safety Board since earlier this year. He retired from the Coast Guard in 1978 as Chief Counsel, with the rank of rear admiral, after 32 years of service.

He was born April 5, 1925, in Istanbul, Turkey. He received a B.S. from the U.S. Coast Guard Academy in 1946 and a J.D. from George Washington University Law School in 1953.

Bursley had various sea and shore assignments with the Coast Guard between

1946 and 1954. From 1954 to 1958, he was district legal officer in Seattle. From 1958 to 1960, he was commanding officer of the Coast Guard cutter *Magnolia*. From 1960 to 1964, he was a district legal officer, first in San Francisco, then in Honolulu. From 1964 to 1966, he was Coast Guard liaison with the Treasury Department.

From 1966 to 1968, Bursley was assistant to the Deputy Under Secretary of Transportation. From 1968 to 1969, he was with the Office of Policy Review in the Office of the Secretary of Transportation, and from 1969 to 1972, he was chief of the Maritime and International Law Division of the Coast Guard.

From 1972 to 1974, Bursley was captain of the port for the Coast Guard in Baltimore. From 1974 to 1976, he was commander of the second Coast Guard district. In 1976 he was chief of the U.S. delegation to the International Conference on Convention for the Limitation of Liability of Maritime Claims, held in London.

From 1976 until his retirement in 1978, Bursley was Chief Counsel to the Coast Guard and Chairman of the Marine Safety Council of the Coast Guard.

Export-Import Bank

Executive Order 12166.   October 19, 1979

By the authority vested in me as President of the United States of America by Section 2(b)(1)(B) of the Export-Import Bank Act of 1945, as amended (12 U.S.C. 635(b)(1)(B)), and by Section 301 of Title 3 of the United States Code, it is hereby ordered as follows:

1–101. The function vested in the President by Section 2(b)(1)(B) of the Export-Import Bank Act of 1945, as amended (12 U.S.C. 635(b)(1)(B)), is delegated to the Secretary of State. That function is the authority to determine that a denial by the Export-Import Bank of an application for credit would be in the national interest, where such action could clearly and importantly advance United States policy in such areas as international terrorism, nuclear proliferation, environmental protection and human rights.

1–102. Before making such a determination, the Secretary of State shall consult with the Secretary of Commerce and the heads of other interested Executive agencies.

1–103. In accord with Section 2(b)(1)(B) of that Act, only in those cases where the Secretary of State has made such a determination should the Export-Import Bank deny an application for credit for nonfinancial or noncommercial considerations.

JIMMY CARTER

The White House,
    October 19, 1979.

[Filed with the Office of the Federal Register,
    4:08 p.m., October 19, 1979]

Urban Development Action Grant Program

Remarks at a White House Reception Commemorating the Second Anniversary of the Program.   October 19, 1979

MR. WATSON. It's a great pleasure to welcome all of you to the White House.

As I look around the room, I feel as though this is Old Home Week, because there are so many familiar faces here who've worked so hard on what we are here to celebrate. And I will say only with this one remark, because it will be underscored by several of the people on the platform, including the President, who will arrive shortly, we're here today, very pleased that you can join us, quite simply to celebrate a spectacularly successful program in which the Federal Government and local governments and the private sector all over this Nation have been participating now for 2 years.

It's my great personal pleasure and privilege to present to you the distinguished former Secretary of HUD, present Secretary of Health, Education, and Welfare, the shy, the retiring—*[laughter]*—the demure Patricia Harris.

SECRETARY HARRIS. *My distinguished colleagues, my particularly distinguished successor at HUD, all my friends:*

This really, you know—it's Old Home Week to be here.

Jack, many a true word is spoken in jest. Simply because you don't know that you were accurately describing me doesn't mean that you weren't. *[Laughter]*

I particularly wanted to be here today, because I wanted to go back a bit in history. The former Secretary of State entitled his autobiography "Present at the Creation." And there are few of us in this room who were present at the creation of UDAG, and I'm not sure that many people know the story of how the UDAG started, and I want to be sure that you hear it today.

Before there was an inauguration, before there was a Jay Janis or Bob Embry or even a Larry Simons at HUD, in fact, before there was a Pat Harris at HUD, but after the President said, "Pat, I'd like you to do this," I asked a group of people to join me at my former law firm and talk about where we were going in the area of community development.

I was initially very conservative. And I said, instead of changing the way in which we distributed funds under the Community Development Block Grant

formula, we ought to ask for a 1-year extension. And those three conservative characters, who are still at HUD, demure and quiet Carl Riedy, shy Ron Gatton, and quiet, agreeable Deputy Assistant Secretary Garrison, were in the room that day, and they, along with Chuck Edison, said to me, "We can do some very good things."

And they started talking about the formula for the distribution of Community Development Block Grant funds, and they started talking about a discretionary program whose purpose was to do something we all agreed we wanted to do as part of the Carter administration—give maximum discretion to the cities on how they revitalize their cities, to maintain standards for the expenditure of Federal funds, but allow the widest discretion to the cities, and finally, to bring in the private sector to aid in the development of cities in a way that would keep the private sector there, but more importantly, would have the private sector there at the beginning.

They discussed these ideas with me, and I said, "Go ye forth and till the earth and sow the seeds." Well, a lot of things happened. We had discussions with the OMB, but the President's wisdom prevailed. *[Laughter]* And we were able to go to the Congress with a plan that some people in Congress questioned. And a few people wanted to know if this wasn't too much discretion for Democratic HUD Secretaries, because after all, everybody knew HUD Secretaries were the same— Democrats or Republican. They had forgotten. And we got the UDAG.

The seed was planted, and what a harvest it's been: nearly 500 projects approved, nearly a billion dollars in grants awarded, nearly a quarter of a million permanent jobs created, more than $5½ billion in private sector commitments—

$5½ billion, I remind you—to distressed cities, stronger local tax bases, and growing confidence in our cities. That's what the Carter administration brought to the cities; that was a Carter administration creation.

And for those who tell you that an administration cannot plan what it wants to do and bring that plan to fruition, today's celebration of the anniversary of the UDAG proves that they are wrong. We can plan; that's what the Carter administration has demonstrated here. And as I've said so many times in recent weeks, you ain't seen nothin' yet in terms of the future.

And one of the reasons you ain't seen nothin' yet is the distinguished Secretary of Housing and Urban Development, Moon Landrieu. Moon.

SECRETARY LANDRIEU. I am what they say in vaudeville is a straight man. I speak between Pat Harris and the President of the United States for as many minutes as it takes. [*Laughter*] So, in a few moments I expect the President to be here.

I just came from a luncheon over at the Federal City Council, which is a group of businessmen, politicians, citizens interested in the city of Washington, D.C., as a place to live, as distinguished from the seat of government. And Mrs. Katherine Graham was the principal speaker and gave a fascinating talk on the beginning of that council, which, she pointed out, started back in 1954 as a thought of her husband's, the late Philip Graham, who, being devoted to Washington and being concerned about what he saw as a deterioration of a great city, began a series of articles in the Washington Post which began to search for ideas and for analysis of what was happening to Washington, D.C., and perhaps all cities in the United States. It just so happens that today

marked the 25th anniversary of the beginning of that effort.

And it occurred to me that many people were in the field of concern about urban America a long, long time before I ever came on the scene in the early 1970's and late 1960's. And it also occurred to me that it took some 10 years from that point—and I don't mark that as necessarily the very beginning of the effort, but at least of one effort in one city—that it took until 1965 to organize the Department of HUD, which was the first formal recognition, the first gathering together of the resources of this country for an all-out effort on what was obviously a growing urban problem.

By that time, we had already been into 400 years of physical development and redevelopment of the United States, and we had been a nation for almost 200 years. And yet it took that period of time in which to formalize our concerns in the way of a department dedicated to that purpose. And it actually took another 10 to 12 years before we could formulate a comprehensive urban policy.

There are too many people in this room to thank individually who began that program, and there are too many people in this room who are consulted in the process to thank individually. But it did result in the President of the United States, President Carter, establishing a task force to examine the possibility of creating for the first time a very comprehensive national urban policy, which would not only use the resources of the one department that was defined as an urban department but which would also use all the resources of the Federal Government to redevelop the cities of this Nation and the urban centers of this Nation.

And the cornerstone of that policy came out with the funny name of Urban Development Action Grants. And it has performed well beyond, I think, anyone's expectations, not only because it has channeled significant amounts of money into the urban areas but, most importantly, has been the key link in forming the partnership that President Carter so desperately sought between the Federal Government and local governments and between the government itself and the private enterprise system.

It was his belief that the private sector had built this country and that it was certainly capable of rebuilding it if government could create the atmosphere in which the private sector could move and to exercise its ingenuity and its capital and its desires.

And so, we're here today, marking the second anniversary of the founding of that program, and I'm so happy——

[At this point, the President entered the East Room.]

——happy to join here with so many who brought it about.

THE PRESIDENT. When I heard all of you were in town, I knew that Moon was announcing new UDAG grants today. *[Laughter]*

It's a real pleasure for a President to meet with a group who have formed an effective partnership in dealing with some of the most serious problems of our country, and I emphasize the word "successful." Sometimes an idea or a dream or a determined effort—many times those concepts are not realized. And there is a building up of hope and expectation and a forming of a partnership, the delineation of a plan, an effort through Congress, a bill is passed, money is appropriated, and then there's an embarrassed realization that the idea was not a good one. This is not the case.

In 1975 and 1976, I traveled around this country as a candidate, and there were several serious problems that I detected. I would say that one of the most persistent problems was the realization in our urban areas, our cities, our downtown central cities that their prospects for a good life or even survival was not good. This was a concept or belief that permeated our country. It was most highly publicized in New York City, but at the time of the shock of the New York City financial problem announcement, there was a general feeling around the country that "this could happen in my city next."

We began to evolve this program—Pat Harris, Bob Embry, many others that I won't name now—to try to deal with that problem, because we realized, first of all, that there was not an adequate consultation between labor, business, private investors, county officials, mayors, Governors, Members of Congress, administration officials, or the President, that there was no way to share the problem and, in effect, share the probing for a solution. But we formed one, and the outcome has been, I think, very good.

The Urban Policy Group has functioned well. Some of you in this room have been here to Washington, have been in the Cabinet Room, have been in the Oval Office 5, 6, 7, 8, 9, 10 times as we've tried to hammer out a solution to serious problems in our urban areas.

The Urban Development Action Grants, UDAG program, has been the centerpiece of what we proposed. It's new, it's innovative. And we also recognized that there would not be enough Federal money to solve the problem, but we also saw that there were many potential investments that would restore the spirit of a community and keep the responsibility where it ought to be—the people who had to pay for and administer and benefit from a major project. The ratio between

Federal moneys and private investments had been about 6 to 1, as you well know, and the results have been notable.

There is no more a feeling of isolation or despair or hopelessness or alienation from the Federal Government—quote, "from the Federal Government." I believe that mayors, county officials, local officials from all over the country now feel that there is an open reception here for you and for those that you represent. I think there's a new sense of enthusiasm.

I do some traveling still since I've been in the White House. I was in Chicago recently; I was in Kansas City recently; I was in New York City recently; Hartford, Connecticut, recently; and smaller towns as well. And I don't get the complaints that I used to get, and that's, in itself, gratifying.

There has been, in addition, an effort, because of your instigation, to bring good people into the Government. I can't say that there haven't always been good people occupying the same positions; I'm not criticizing others. But we've got in the Department of Housing and Urban Development—brought in by Pat, now with Moon Landrieu—a collection of people who understand the problems of the urban areas and who know what it means to be faced with a serious challenge and who know what it means to resolve a problem. We've got more mayors in the President's Cabinet now than we had all put together in the last 50 years, and I think that's a great achievement in itself.

I've been determined that the urban centers would, in the future, be the backbone of the social and economic structure of our country and not the Achilles heel which it has been in the past. We've moved on a broad front: CETA programs, we've doubled them; youth programs, we've added 70 percent; education programs, 60 percent in funding from the Federal Government. But in urban development, with UDAG and EDA, we have increased these commitments 3,000 percent. We're now putting 30 times as much effort and financing into the reconstitution of our urban areas as had been the case before, and it's paid rich dividends. It's let us know what could be done in housing, in social programs, in health, in education, in transportation.

As we've gone into these projects and investigated them, we've learned a lot about the community. There hasn't been a chasm that we couldn't cross. We've been there on the street, in the alleys, looking at homes, looking at people who had to be moved and where they wanted to be moved to and how they wanted to be treated. And we've learned in the process to make government, on a daily basis, much more responsible, much more responsive, much more knowledgeable about the people that we were trying to serve.

In the last 2 years, I think, we've had about $6 billion in programs. In 1980 we are asking for another $6 billion program that will engender 400,000 jobs in the private sector. Here, again, about one-sixth of the money will come from the Government itself.

Another thing that we've tried to do is to not eliminate private initiative. The initiative is yours, whether you're a mayor or county official or whether you don't hold public office. The initiative is yours. We're trying to help. And the applications don't get bogged down in interminable redtape and delay. We try to have a turnaround time, between when we get an application and when we give an answer, 60 days. And I think it's a rare occasion when people have to wait 90 days, is it not, Pat? That's extraordinary for the Government to do that way, and I say this not to congratulate myself, but to tell you that we've got people here eager to work with you, and they've been successful in it.

I might say in summary that this coming year, 1980—we're already in it—we're asking for a 70-percent increase in this program, and we're trying to focus it on pockets of poverty that exist within communities that are, basically and on the average, healthy. And we've increased the percentage that the conference committee reports are accepting up to 20 percent that can be derived from UDAG. We want to do even better in the future.

And I said earlier, I hadn't recognized all the people involved. Pat and Bob did help, but the basic concepts that I have tried to pursue as President came from officials who have served for a long time on the firing line.

And I'd like to call now on the dean of those local officials, a good friend of mine, the mayor of Milwaukee, Henry Maier, who has served in his difficult job—it's become easier, I think, the longer he's been there—since 1960. He organized the Conference of Democratic Mayors. He's been the president of the U.S. Conference of Mayors.

And in 1975 and 1976, because of his consultations and the trust that others had in him, he put together—Henry did—a kind of a picture of what the Federal Government ought to do in a comprehensive urban policy, and we have basically adopted what he and many of you that I see in this room have put together. And that's been the Government program—the program that we got from local officials. That's the way it ought to work, in my opinion.

And I'm very grateful to call now the mayor of Milwaukee, my friend.

MAYOR MAIER. Mr. President, I am overwhelmed. I thank you very much for those very kind words.

Senator Williams and Representative Ashley, our very good friends, and our other good congressional friends, whom I want to thank very much—who are here today—for all the help you've given us, and Secretary Harris and Secretary Landrieu, and distinguished audience:

I am greatly honored to speak as a mayor on this milestone occasion, and I'm particularly grateful, because I recall the days when an official national urban policy was just a dream. And as the first president of the National Conference of Democratic Mayors in 1974, I was in the long effort to spell out a first national urban policy statement to give our cities a top priority on the national agenda.

And I recall very vividly the day some 3 years ago in New York when you appeared, Mr. President, and you appeared with the other Presidential candidates before a panel of Democratic mayors in a conference that I chaired. And that day you pledged to support and actively work for a national urban policy, and you also pledged that, as President, you would institute a White House open-door policy for the mayors of America. And further, you promised that programs and the policies of your administration affecting our Nation's urban areas would be coordinated. And you have kept those promises, Mr. President, and we thank you.

And I know the leaders of the Democratic Mayors, fighting mayors like Dick Hatcher of Gary, Indiana, and Coleman Young of Detroit and Maynard Jackson, our present president of the Democratic Mayors, Bill McNichols of Denver and Kevin White of Boston, Neil Goldschmidt of Portland and Moon Landrieu of New Orleans—once a mayor, always a mayor—[*laughter*]—and my very good friend Lee Alexander, who is vice president of the Democratic Mayors, will be president next year, and is past president of the United States Conference of Mayors—these men were the men who held the eight regional hearings throughout the country in which we received testimony related to our national urban policy.

And I would say, Mr. President, that you have exceeded your pledges to the mayors of America. Your very recent appointments of our good friends and fellow mayors, Secretary Landrieu and Secretary Goldschmidt, reflect a true commitment to urban America in the full implementation of your national urban policy.

Now, I'll admit, Mr. President, that the policy that we formulated and was entered in this document, in which these gentlemen's pictures are also present, was a little, perhaps, exaggerated, and you probably couldn't agree with all of it. But the mayors have instructed me to inform Secretary Landrieu and Secretary Goldschmidt that we fully expect them to effectuate that policy. [*Laughter*] And I know I speak for my fellow Democratic mayors when I commend you and thank you for keeping the pledges and keeping the faith.

And in very concrete terms, the Urban Development Action Grant component of your national urban policy is giving our cities a basic new life in the area where our hugest tax base was in a state of decline. In Milwaukee our original UDAG grant for our downtown shopping mall was based upon an anticipated $60 million in private investment. And we have already now exceeded over $100 million as a result of the spinoffs from our UDAG grant, and we're still climbing.

As you mentioned, Mr. President, it is indeed a blue chip investment, in capital investment and in jobs and in tax dollars. We find that for every Federal dollar spent, there's a $6.10 private investment, and for every UDAG dollar, an additional 10 cents in property tax revenue. And there isn't another Federal program in

existence that has given us these kinds of fiscal tangible results. And I thank you, Mr. President, and I commend you for carrying forward the program.

Thank you.

THE PRESIDENT. As all the Members of the Congress know, and as I know very well and I'm sure all of you realize, we have a very serious conflict, basically between trying to control the Federal budget expenditures, to hold down the deficit, and to help control inflation on the one hand, and to sharply focus direct and expanded benefits when Federal moneys are expended. And this fiscal year 1980 appropriation, which has now been passed through the Congress and through its conference committee, will provide just in the construction area alone 230,-000 permanent jobs and 130,000 temporary jobs, in addition to giving people a better life in the communities involved and increasing the hope and the expectation that they can work in harmony, not only with themselves but also with their government. It restores confidence, which I think is very good.

Have the Members of Congress been recognized yet—the individuals? All the Members of Congress here that are not on the stage, would you all stand? I think you really deserve a debt of gratitude.

There are many others, obviously, in the Congress who've been in the forefront of this, and those are here today. There are others who couldn't be here, and there are many others who are now claiming credit for the program—[*laughter*]—which is very good and the highest accolade that the program could have.

But I would like to introduce two people now to make remarks, one from the House and one from the Senate, representing a bipartisan group. Since we do have a majority of Democrats, they happen to be Democrats. [*Laughter*] But I would like to point out that this is really and genuinely a bipartisan program, and I'm grateful for it.

Pete Williams, the Senator from New Jersey, is chairman of the Subcommittee on Housing and Urban Development. He's been one of those who has helped to initiate the UDAG program and has been in the forefront of housing, urban development long before I became President. I'm very grateful to Pete for not only his help with proposals that I made but also the initiative that he has shown in channeling his own ideas into the administrative process and through Congress, in legislation passed.

I'd like to introduce now, Senator Pete Williams.

SENATOR WILLIAMS. *Thank you very much, Mr. President and Secretary Harris, Secretary Landrieu, Mayor Maier, and my colleague here on the platform, Lud Ashley, and colleagues in the room, ladies and gentlemen:*

Everybody here can be called an ally in urban revitalization. It's, of course, a very, very happy anniversary—second anniversary of UDAG—celebration for all of us.

We remember 2 years ago this week that UDAG became law, signaling a new and exciting initiative in urban revitalization, a new partnership between private enterprise and government, designed to deal with one of the most complex problems our society faces, this kind of partnership, which you, Mr. President, have articulated so well in the urban policy initiatives you have presented to Congress that represents the best hope for our distressed cities. And by cities, we don't mean monolithic institutions; we're talking about people.

Mr. President, I can tell you firsthand how much UDAG does mean to people. Earlier this year, I toured Newark's neighborhood improvement program, a

UDAG project—by the end of next year, will result in the rehabilitation of 1,500 homes.

Newark had become a classic example of the decline—physical and spiritual—of a major city. But my most vivid recollection very recently in Newark is not of rebuilt buildings—and we have a lot of them—but the vividness that comes back to me is being there to observe and to feel, to sense the rebuilding of lives. Resident after resident came to me truly expressing joy. It was an outpouring of gratitude for the help that they have received. And over and over they said that this program meant the difference between continued wretched living or a life in a wholesome, decent, and, to say it again, joyful environment.

So, Mr. President, I extend to you their thanks. They are representative of people throughout our country that have had this opportunity under UDAG, in cities large and small.

So, there is a new sense of revival and progress for communities that have been plagued by economic decline. Mr. President, as you and Secretary Harris worked so hard to get this program underway, your leadership brought us all together. You can be so very proud of its achievements.

And I want to say, looking ahead, when UDAG comes up for reauthorization next year, I look forward to working with you, with Secretary Landrieu, Lud Ashley, to ensure that this vitally important tool remains available to our communities that need it so much.

THE PRESIDENT. I wish everybody could see the expression on Tom Marsaro's face. Tom, raise your hand. Raise your hand, keep it up.

Tom happens to be the young, very competent man who's in charge of the particular project in Newark—and others, too. And when Pete Williams was describing the effect on the lives of those who live in that reconstituted area of our Nation, it was gratifying to me to see Tom, with genuine pride and gratification, know that he had done a good job. And I thank you and Bob Embry and others, Pat Harris and now Moon Landrieu, who have made this project a success.

The Urban Development Action Grants—I would say, of those four words, the most important word is "action"—we don't mess around with the applications or the carrying out of those projects once they get to us. And I think that "action" word exemplifies the political life, the congressional leadership of Lud Ashley.

Perhaps the most difficult legislation which has ever faced the Congress, certainly in my lifetime, was the very complicated, comprehensive energy policy that I proposed to the Congress in April of 1977. We hope that we'll complete it this year. But when the Speaker of the House put together an ad hoc committee, comprised of the leaders of many committees in the House of Representatives, he chose Lud Ashley to head that program. And Lud is more famous, perhaps on a nationwide basis, for having dealt successfully with the energy problem in a very expeditious and effective fashion.

But I think the longest testimony to Lud's effectiveness is in the area of housing and urban development. He cares about people, and he's superb in his ability to conceive legislative programs, to get them passed by Congress, to have them financed, and then to make sure that they do apply to improving the life of a human being. And I'm very grateful at this time to introduce to you Lud Ashley.

REPRESENTATIVE ASHLEY. Well, Mr. President, if I had known I would get such an introduction from you, I promise you,

I would have written something down. [*Laughter*]

I want to take just a moment to say what I feel, which is that President Carter is the first President in the history of the United States that really has had the courage to try to articulate a policy for our cities. And you know that's true, and I know it's true. We know why it's true.

We may as well put it where it is. You know, the reason the Presidents have been a little reluctant to do this is not because they haven't recognized that cities have problems, it's because to try to articulate a policy for the cities exposes you and makes you vulnerable, because 4 years hence you can be held accountable to those strategies that you tried to articulate. Well, I kind of like to have a President that will risk that, and we have that President.

I do have to be absolutely honest with you, Mr. President. It's been my conviction, pretty much since coming to the Congress, that any initiative that comes from the White House is one that in almost every instance can be improved upon by the Congress. You understand that. [*Laughter*] The marvelous thing about the UDAG program is that that wasn't so. And don't think we didn't look, Mr. President, because we did. [*Laughter*]

But the reason that it couldn't be really improved upon is because it does combine what my associates, Pete in particular, has touched upon. You know, it starts off with a partnership concept, predicate, and it insists that there be the kind of 6-to-1 leverage that is the usual. It relies primarily on local initiative, nothing from the Federal Government. Nobody's out there saying, do this, do that—not at all. So, it's got the partnership concept, it's got the local initiative, it's got that marvelous feature—from the time of application, if successful, to the time that the pick goes in the ground, is shorter than any program of any government on the face of the Earth. It's absolutely astounding. That was certainly true in Toledo, I'll say that. [*Laughter*]

But finally—and here again, Pete Williams touched on this—revitalization is something that we all have our ideas about, and that's important. But more important—if possible—more important than the actual rebuilding of a community is the spirit of revitalization—the spirit of revitalization—because that goes on, that's got to live with us day in and day out. When applications are turned down, when they come back the second time, it's got to be the spirit of revitalization and a little knocking on doors and what have you. [*Laughter*] But it's that spirit of revitalization that I think is absolutely fundamental.

And I say to my people in Toledo, progress doesn't come in quantum leaps. You know, it's got to be regular, it's got to be constant, and, I think, on that basis. And that's why I applaud your administration, because you've given us hope, Mr. President, that we can count on a commitment from the Federal Government, that it won't necessarily come in quantum leaps, but it's going to be there. We can count on it. We can tell our constituents, we can tell our mayors, we can say this Government is committed to the continued progress and revitalization of our cities.

So, thank you, Mr. President. I appreciate it.

Mr. WATSON. Thank you. Be seated for just one more moment, please. The President asked me to do something richly deserved, actually two things. I told you this was going to be a celebration. Thank you, Lud Ashley.

I would like for the folks who work in HUD and who specifically comprise the UDAG staff please to stand in your place so that we can applaud you. [*Applause*]

I'm also pleased to say that the persons that you just saw stand comprise the total UDAG staff. [*Laughter*] Believe it or not, it's true.

The other point that the President suggested to me that I make is one also worthy of note. Though we're here really to applaud and to congratulate the Department of Housing and Urban Development, and particular staff within that Department for the program we've here been discussing, the fact of the matter is that, as a result of the President's urban policy announced now a year and a half ago, the administration and the Government at large are engaged in a way unprecedented in assessing the direct and indirect impacts and effects of Government actions on cities and towns all over the country.

There are some people in the room whom I simply want to note by name, because they represent, with respect to their departments, people who are engaged with HUD in this whole urban revitalization, small town economic development effort that we're here to celebrate.

I'm talking about people, in addition to Bob Embry and his staff, such as Larry Simons, the Assistant Secretary for Housing in HUD, Ernie Green, the Assistant Secretary of Labor, Bob Hall, the Assistant Secretary for Economic Development in the Department of Commerce, Barbara Blum, the Deputy Administrator of EPA, Mort Downey, Assistant Secretary at DOT, Alex Mercure, Assistant Secretary of Agriculture for Rural Development, and others. The Department of the Interior, virtually every domestic agency in this Government, through the Interagency Coordinating

Council and through other collaborative efforts, are engaged in this process.

Thank you all very much. We would like to invite you to the State Dining Room for a reception.

Thank you.

NOTE: The President spoke at approximately 2:30 p.m. in the East Room at the White House. Jack H. Watson, Jr., is Assistant to the President for Intergovernmental Affairs.

Digest of Other White House Announcements

The following listing includes the President's public schedule and other items of general interest announced by the White House Press Office and not included elsewhere in this issue.

October 13

The President met at the White House with David L. Aaron, Deputy Assistant to the President for National Security Affairs.

In response to inquiries on the October 12 House of Representatives gasoline decontrol vote, the White House announced that it has been the President's policy since the beginning of the administration that gasoline ultimately should be decontrolled. The President made a decision earlier this year based upon an assessment of general gasoline and economic conditions that decontrol would not be appropriate at this time. The administration does not support a congressional amendment mandating decontrol of gasoline. The President now has all the authority he needs to take this step when it is appropriate after a review of prevailing economic factors.

October 15

The President met at the White House with:

—Zbigniew Brzezinski, Assistant to the President for National Security Affairs;
—Frank B. Moore, Assistant to the President for Congressional Liaison.

October 17

The President met at the White House with:

—Dr. Brzezinski;
—Vice President Walter F. Mondale, Secretary of Health, Education, and Welfare Patricia R. Harris, Secretary of Housing and Urban Development Moon Landrieu, Secretary of the Interior Cecil D. Andrus, Secretary of Transportation Neil Goldschmidt, James T. McIntyre, Jr., Director of the Office of Management and Budget, Jack H. Watson, Jr., Assistant to the President for Intergovernmental Affairs, and Hamilton Jordan, Assistant to the President, to discuss domestic policies;
—Mr. Moore;
—members of the Pay Advisory Committee;
—Representative and Mrs. James C. Corman of California and Adam Corman;
—Stansfield Turner, Director of Central Intelligence, and Dr. Brzezinski;
—Vice President Mondale.

The President attended a reception for members of the National Minority Purchasing Council, held in the East Room at the White House.

The President transmitted to the Congress the 15th annual report on the Status of the National Wilderness Preservation System and the 1978 report of the National Cancer Advisory Board.

In the evening, the President attended the seventh and final game of the 1979 World Series at Memorial Stadium in Baltimore, Md. At the conclusion of the game he met with the Pittsburgh Pirates and the Baltimore Orioles teams and then returned to the White House.

October 18

The President met at the White House with:

—Dr. Brzezinski;

—Mr. Moore;

—Hedley W. Donovan, Senior Adviser to the President.

The President attended a reception for members of the Alliance to Save Energy, held in the East Room at the White House.

The White House announced that Prime Minister and Mrs. John M. Lynch of Ireland will make an official visit to the United States November 7–15 at the invitation of President Carter. The President and the Prime Minister will hold talks on November 8.

The White House announced that Les Francis, deputy to the Chief of Staff, will be leaving the White House to join the Carter/Mondale Presidential Committee. He will assume the post of campaign staff director, reporting directly to national campaign manager Tim Kraft, on October 22.

The White House announced the following appointments to the staff of Lloyd N. Cutler, Counsel to the President: Joseph Onek and Michael H. Cardozo, Deputy Counsels to the President; Douglas Huron, Senior Associate Counsel to the President; and Patrick V. Apodaca and Barbara E. Bergman, Associate Counsels to the President.

October 19

The President met at the White House with:

—Dr. Brzezinski;

—Secretary of State Cyrus R. Vance, Mr. Jordan, Dr. Brzezinski, and Mr. Donovan;

—Mr. Moore;

—Dr. Ruben F. Mettler, outgoing chairman of the National Alliance of Businessmen and chairman and chief executive officer of TRW, Inc., John H. Filer, incoming chairman of the NAB and chairman of AETNA Life and Casualty Co., and Assistant Secretary of Labor for Employment and Training Ernest G. Green;

—Charles L. Schultze, Chairman of the Council of Economic Advisers.

The White House announced that Prime Minister Margaret Thatcher of the United Kingdom will make an official visit to the United States on December 17 and 18, at the invitation of President Carter. The President and the Prime Minister will hold talks on December 17.

The President announced the designation of Norton J. Come as Acting General Counsel of the National Labor Relations Board, effective tomorrow. He replaces John J. Irving, who has resigned effective today. Come, 59, has been with the NLRB since 1948. He has served as Deputy Associate General Counsel since 1963.

NOMINATIONS SUBMITTED TO THE SENATE

The following list does not include promotions of members of the Uniformed Services, nominations to the Service Academies, or nominations of Foreign Service officers.

Submitted October 15, 1979

EDWARD HIDALGO, of the District of Columbia, to be Secretary of the Navy, vice W. Graham Claytor, elevated.

ABELARDO LOPEZ VALDEZ, of Texas, for the rank of Ambassador during his tenure of service as Chief of Protocol for the White House.

GENTA A. HAWKINS, of California, to be an Assistant Administrator of the Agency for International Development, vice Jean Price Lewis, resigned.

NOMINATIONS—Continued

Submitted October 15—Continued

FRANK A. CAMM, of Virginia, to be an Associate Director of the Federal Emergency Management Agency (new position).

Submitted October 17, 1979

JOAN ZELDES BERNSTEIN, of Maryland, to be General Counsel of the Department of Health, Education, and Welfare, vice Richard I. Beattie, resigned.

CHARLES B. CURTIS, of Maryland, to be a member of the Federal Energy Regulatory Commission for the term of 4 years expiring October 20, 1983 (reappointment).

N. JEROLD COHEN, of Georgia, to be an Assistant General Counsel in the Department of the Treasury (Chief Counsel for the Internal Revenue Service), vice Stuart Evan Seigel, resigned.

FREDERICK A. RODY, JR., of Florida, to be Deputy Administrator of Drug Enforcement, vice Jerry N. Jenson, resigned.

CHECKLIST OF WHITE HOUSE PRESS RELEASES

The following listing contains releases of the White House Press Office which are not included in this issue.

Released October 13, 1979

Advance text: remarks at the Kennedys-King Day dinner

Released October 15, 1979

Advance text: remarks at the annual convention of the National Conference of Catholic Charities in Kansas City, Mo.

Advance text: remarks at a fundraising dinner for Mayor Jane Byrne in Chicago, Ill.

Released October 17, 1979

Fact sheet: Department of Education Organization Act

Released October 18, 1979

Announcement: resignation of Les Francis as deputy to the Chief of Staff of the White House

CHECKLIST—Continued

Released October 18—Continued

Announcement: appointments to the staff of Lloyd N. Cutler, Counsel to the President

Released October 19, 1979

Fact sheet: Urban Development Action Grant program

ACTS APPROVED BY THE PRESIDENT

Approved October 17, 1979

S. 210_____ Public Law 96–88
Department of Education Organization Act.

Approved October 19, 1979

S. 817_____ Public Law 96–89
An act to amend the Act of July 2, 1940, as amended, to increase the amount authorized to be appropriated for the Canal Zone Biological Area.

H.R. 929_____ Private Law 96–6
An act for the relief of Eun Kyung Cho and Hei Kyung Cho.

H.R. 946_____ Private Law 96–7
An act for the relief of Maria Estela Sims.

H.R. 1153_____ Private Law 96–8
An act for the relief of Nyoman Rahmawati.

H.R. 1163_____ Private Law 96–9
An act for the relief of Gladys Venicia Cruz-Sanchez.

H.R. 1486_____ Private Law 96–10
An act for the relief of Dang Petersen.

H.R. 1628_____ Private Law 96–11
An act for the relief of Susan Katherine Adamski.

H.R. 2098_____ Private Law 96–12
An act for the relief of Antonio Rivera Aristizabal.

H.R. 3142_____ Private Law 96–13
An act for the relief of Michael Carl Brown.

H.R. 3146_____ Private Law 96–14
An act for the relief of Patrick A. and Wayne L. Thomas.

H.R. 3218_____ Private Law 96–15
An act for the relief of Rebecca Sevilla DeJesus.

PRESIDENTIAL DOCUMENTS

Boston, Massachusetts

Remarks at Dedication Ceremonies for the John F. Kennedy Library. October 20, 1979

Members and friends of the family of John F. Kennedy:

As President of the United States, I'm indeed honored to be here on this occasion, at once so solemn and also so joyous—the dedication of the John F. Kennedy Library. Like a great cathedral, this building was a long time coming. But it more than justifies the wait. Its grace and its dignity are, I hope and believe, worthy of the man whose memory it will nurture.

I never met him, but I know that John Kennedy loved politics, he loved laughter, and when the two came together, he loved that best of all.

For example, in a press conference in March 1962, when the ravages of being President were beginning to show on his face, he was asked this two-part question: "Mr. President, your brother Ted said recently on television that after seeing the cares of office on you, he wasn't sure he would ever be interested in being President." [*Laughter*] And the questioner continued, "I wonder if you could tell us whether, first, if you had it to do over again, you would work for the Presidency and, second, whether you can recommend this job to others?" The President replied, "Well, the answer to the first question is yes, and the second is no. I do not recommend it to others—at least for a while." [*Laughter*]

As you can well see, President Kennedy's wit and also his wisdom—[*laughter*]—is certainly as relevant today as it was then. [*Laughter*]

This library, this repository of facts and ideas, will feed history with a permanent record of the dreams of John Fitzgerald Kennedy, and also the realization of those dreams.

In America, the records of a great political leader will not be threatened by succeeding political regimes which might fear them, because we are a nation committed not only to freedom but also to the pursuit of truth.

A library is especially fitting as a tribute to John Kennedy, for he was not only a maker of history but a writer of history as well. His fame as an author of books foretold his fame as an author of events. He said he had few apprehensions about how his Presidency would fare in history, because he planned to write that history himself.

To our loss, we will never read the books that he would have written about his own Presidency. His death impoverished not only statecraft but literature as well. But in this building behind me, the work of reflection and evaluation of what he did can now be done very well by others.

President Kennedy understood the past and respected its shaping of the future. Yet he was very much a man of his own time. The first President born in this century, he embodied the ideals of a generation as few public figures have ever done in the history of the Earth. He summoned our Nation out of complacency, and he set it on a path of excitement and hope.

The accomplishments of this thousand days, as you well know, are notable, though his Presidency was too short for him to finish all the tasks that he set for himself. We honor him not just for the things he completed but for the things he set in motion, the energies that he released, and the ideas and the ideals which he espoused.

President Kennedy took office understanding that the texture of social and economic life of our Nation and our people was changing, and that our Nation and our people would have to change with it. "Change is the law of life," he once said. "And those who look only to the past or the present are certain to miss the future." He had a vision of how America could meet and master the forces of change that he saw around him.

President Kennedy entered the White House convinced that racial and religious discrimination was morally indefensible. Later, that conviction became a passion for him, a passion that his brother Robert shared and, as his son has so well said, carried forward.

As a southerner, as a Georgian, I saw at first hand how the moral leadership of the Kennedy administration helped to undo the wrongs that grew out of our Nation's

history. Today the problem of human rights in the United States is shifting from inequality of legal rights to inequality of opportunity. But the question of legal rights is not yet settled.

We are all Americans, we are all children of the same God. Racial violence and racial hatred can have no place among us in the South or in the North. The moral imperative of the Kennedy administration, indeed, still remains with us.

President Kennedy sought to move our foreign policy beyond the sterility of the cold war. He never failed to uphold liberty, and he never failed to condemn tyranny; yet he saw very clearly that the threat of nuclear destruction had created the need for mutual accommodation with our potential adversaries. He warned against the nation and a world turned into "a prison in which man awaits his executioner."

When the nuclear test ban treaty was signed in 1963, he voiced the hope—though he dared not yet voice the anticipation or expectation—that there would someday be controls on the numbers and the types of nuclear weapons. Now the SALT II treaty can redeem that hope. Its ratification will be a further fulfillment of the needs of all humanity.

President Kennedy knew that the future of freedom would be increasingly bound up with social, political, and economic justice in what has since become known as the Third World. His one bold expression of this vision was the Peace Corps, which, with its combination of activism, idealism, and adventure, summed up so many of John Kennedy's virtues.

I'm proud that this kind of commitment has now been vigorously renewed and that America once again holds out her hand to the poor, the silenced, and oppressed of every country in the world.

Like every President who hopes to leave the world a better place because he served in it, President Kennedy chafed under the limits of his power to act. These limits on a President still exist. As he put it during his second year in office, "There are greater limitations upon our ability to bring about a favorable result than I had ever imagined." Yet, President Kennedy persisted. He became and he still remains a symbol of human aspiration. Perhaps that's why the outpouring of grief at his death had such a special quality.

On that November day, almost 16 years ago, a terrible moment was frozen in the lives of many of us here. I remember that I climbed down from the seat of a tractor, unhooked a farm trailer, and walked into my warehouse to weigh a load of grain. I was told by a group of farmers that the President had been shot. I went outside, knelt on the steps, and began to pray. In a few minutes, I learned that he had not lived. It was a grievous personal loss—my President. I wept openly for the first time in more than 10 years—for the first time since the day my own father died.

People wept in Boston and in Paris, in Atlanta and in Warsaw, in San Francisco and in New Delhi. More than anyone had realized before that day, the spirit of this young American President had taken hold of the hearts and the imaginations of countless millions of people all over the world.

During the months that followed—in civil rights, in medical care for the aged, in greater dignity for the poor, in an increase of caring for one another—his vision was carried into the reality of our Nation's life with the help of a united Congress and a united people, united in grief, but also united in determination to fulfill the dreams which he had painted for us.

At the time, the tragedy in Dallas seemed an isolated convulsion of madness. But in retrospect, it appears near the beginning of a time of darkness. From Vietnam to Cambodia, from Los Angeles to Memphis, from Kent State to Watergate, the American spirit suffered under one shock after another, and the confidence of our people was deeply shaken.

The American people are good and strong. We've undertaken a solid commitment to heal those wounds, and at long last the darkness has begun to lift. I believe that America is now ready to meet the challenges of the 1980's with renewed confidence and with renewed spirit.

These challenges, of course, are not the same ones that confronted us a generation ago. The carved desk in the Oval Office which I use is the same as when John F. Kennedy sat behind it, but the problems that land on that desk are quite different.

President Kennedy was right: Change is the law of life. The world of 1980 is as different from what it was in 1960 as the world of 1960 was from that of 1940. Our means of improving the world must also be different.

After a decade of high inflation and growing oil imports, our economic cup no longer overflows. Because of inflation, fiscal restraint has become a matter of simple public duty. We can no longer rely on a rising economic tide to lift the boats of the poorest in our society. We must focus our attention and our care and our love and concern directly on them.

We have a keener appreciation of limits now—the limits of government, limits on the use of military power abroad, the limits of manipulating, without harm to ourselves, a delicate and a balanced natural environment.

We are struggling with a profound transition from a time of abundance to a time of growing scarcity in energy. We're only beginning to learn the new habits and to utilize the new technologies that will carry us to a future age of clean and renewable energy.

And we face these times when centrifugal forces in our society and in our political system as well—forces of regionalism, forces of ethnicity, of narrow economic interests, of single-issue politics—are testing the resiliency of American pluralism and of our ability to govern. But we can and we will prevail.

The problems are different; the solutions, none of them easy, are also different. But in this age of hard choices and scarce resources, the essence of President Kennedy's message—the appeal for unselfish dedication to the common good—is more urgent than it ever was. The spirit that he evoked—the spirit of sacrifice, of patriotism, of unstinting dedication—is the same spirit that will bring us safely through the adversities that we face today. The overarching purpose of this Nation remains the same—to build a just society in a secure America living at peace with the other nations of the world.

The library that we dedicate today is a symbol, above all, of that unchanging purpose. Through our study here of his words and his deeds, the service of President Kennedy will keep its high place in the hearts of many generations of America to come after us.

This library may be dedicated with the words of a poet from Tennessee, a contemporary of the President whose name the library will bear:

"To those who in all times have sought the truth and have told it in their art or in their living, who died in honor . . .

"To those who died in the high and humble knowledge of God . . .

"(T)o those who died in sorrow, and in kindness, and in bravery; to those who died in violence suddenly . . .

"(T)o those who died in the time of the joy of their strength. . . ." [1]

This library is dedicated to John F. Kennedy, 35th President of the United States of America.

NOTE: The President spoke at 11:25 a.m. outside the library.

Prior to the ceremonies, the President was given a private tour of the library.

Boston, Massachusetts

Question-and-Answer Session With Newspaper and Television Reporters. October 20, 1979

MR. FOELL. Hello, I'm Earl Foell of the Christian Science Monitor. With me today to interview President Jimmy Carter are Tom Ellis of Station WCVB–TV, Channel 5 in Boston, Jim Scott of WBZ, Channel 4, Mary Richardson of WNAC–TV, Channel 7, and Christopher Lydon of WGBH–TV, Channel 2. This program is being taped at Logan Airport on Saturday afternoon for broadcast at this time.

SENATOR EDWARD M. KENNEDY

Mr. President, before we get into the heavyweight questions, I think a lot of viewers are interested to hear what you had to say with Senator Kennedy before and after the ceremony at the opening of the Kennedy Library.

THE PRESIDENT. We have always been friendly toward one another and have conversations about matters before the Senate and also about politics. But today we concentrated mostly on the impact that his brother had—his brothers, as a matter of fact—on our Nation.

---

[1] Excerpts from James Agee's dedication to his first book of poems, "Permit Me Voyage."

The first thing he did was to tell my wife that the bill on mental health which she has worked 2 or 3 years to accomplish was passed through his committee. That was the business at hand. And then we had about a 35-minute tour of the library itself, looking at John Kennedy's early campaign history, his naval career. They've got a beautiful letter in there from my mother that was written to him on her 70th birthday while she was a Peace Corps volunteer in India, which I appreciated.

And I thought the whole family was extremely gracious, and I believe this is one of the most beautiful sites for the commemoration of a President's memory and to hold the records that I've ever seen. It's a place that uses a large number of visual aids. It's a human sort of environment that people will thoroughly enjoy, and I believe it's a great addition to this community and, of course, to our country.

Mr. FOELL. Tom Ellis.

1980 PRESIDENTIAL CAMPAIGN

MR. ELLIS. Thank you, Mr. Foell.

Mr. President, first I'd like to welcome you to New England again and thank you for giving us this time to ask a few questions.

There have been some political developments this week of significance, beginning with your good showing in Florida; the announcement by Senator Kennedy's people that they're about to form an organization, which most feel is tantamount to his formal announcement; the endorsement of Senator Kennedy by the Governor of Maine, the first Governor in the Nation to do that. And in view of all of that, plus the earliness of the primaries in New Hampshire and Massachusetts, I'm wondering how this will affect your own personal timetable.

Can you tell us today that you will be a candidate for reelection?

THE PRESIDENT. I'll be making an announcement on December 4.

I was pleased with this week. The Florida results were very encouraging to us. And it was a pretty hot contest with a lot of secondhand involvement. I didn't go in to campaign, neither did Senator Kennedy, but our surrogates were there, a lot of enthusiasm, a fairly high participation. And I thought the 2-to-1 margin that we achieved was gratifying.

I think the time that I'll spend in the next year on politics will be adequate, but, of course, as President, I won't have time to campaign as I did in 1975 and 1976 when it was an absolutely full-time job for me. But I look forward to it with a great deal of interest and anticipation and confidence.

HEATING OIL SUPPLIES

MR. ELLIS. One of the pressing issues here in New England—we've already had an early taste of winter—is the subject of number 2 home heating oil. We've heard you give assurances in other parts of the country that we will have adequate supplies of home heating oil this winter. The fellow I buy home heating oil from has been in business for 30 years, and he tells me that because of tight credit, allocations, and the price, quite a few of his customers won't have oil if we get a severe cold spell this winter.

I'm wondering if you can assure us here today in New England that we will have adequate supplies and that the people who can't afford to pay 90 cents a gallon for it will still be reasonably warm this winter.

THE PRESIDENT. Yes. We set two goals for ourselves late in the spring, when home heating oil supplies were very low, quite a bit below last year. The first commitment that I made in Portsmouth, New Hampshire, at a townhall meeting, was that in October we would have 240 million barrels of home heating oil on hand in storage, ready to go to homes throughout the New England area and throughout the country by the end of October. We've already reached that goal.

Last year during a fairly severe winter, we had a total consumption, I think, of 233 million barrels. So, we've got enough home heating oil on hand.

The second commitment I made was to do something about helping families to meet the rapidly increasing cost of home heating oil. We took the initiative, went to the Congress quite early. As you know, OPEC has increased prices 60 percent since last December, and it's been an extraordinary burden on the entire Nation, and it's coming on homeowners in this winter.

We've not yet been able to get the bill through Congress, but we've been pushing it day and night. And I think the arousing of interest on the part of people in New England, particularly, and the rest of the country has caused Congress lately to begin to move. I can make a flat statement predicting—as sure as anything is in politics and government—that there will be a decision made by Congress to support the proposal that we made and that people will have the help for low-income families to meet the needs that are brought about by the increased cost of oil.

We are asking this year for $1.6 billion to help low-income families, and we are also asking the Congress during the next 10 years to allocate $2.4 billion per year. And I can assure you that the Congress will act favorably on this legislation.

MR. FOELL. Jim Scott.

MR. SCOTT. Mr. President, a followup to that question.

THE PRESIDENT. Yes.

MR. SCOTT. If the Congress does act favorably and that action is late, say, at the end of winter this year, what will the people do? What happens in the interim?

THE PRESIDENT. Well, there are two different proposals that add up to the 1.6 billion. One is $400 million, which is being requested under a program that's been in existence ever since I've been in the White House. The first year I was in office, we asked for $250 million and got it. This money is allotted to families, primarily through the State government structure, Governors having a lot to do with it. That will be expanded from 250 million bucks to 400 million. And in addition to that, we're adding $1.2 billion more on to that to help the extraordinary price increase this year.

We've asked Congress to expedite the money as much as possible. Our proposal for the long run is to have the money come from the windfall profits tax, the tax on the unearned profits of oil companies, then to be put into reserve fund and used to pay for home heating oil. But since that windfall profits tax might be enacted later than we want to, we are asking the Congress in effect to expend that money out of the regular income tax collections, so that we won't have to wait for the windfall profits tax to go into effect. Later, we'll get the money through the windfall profits tax from the oil companies and repay the money that we borrow from general funds.

But to make sure that the families don't have to wait pending uncertain legislative decisions on the windfall profits tax, we'll go ahead and get that money out of regular funds for use in a timely fashion.

THE NATION'S ECONOMY

MR. SCOTT. Mr. Carter, inflation is the number one concern among many Americans, and apparently you've made it a priority. But how far will you go to curb inflation, and how lasting will your moves be?

THE PRESIDENT. The move is lasting, and I'm not going to back down in fighting inflation. And at my last press conference somebody asked me if I would stick with it even if it cost in political approval of popularity. I will.

I think in the long run our commitment to control inflation, which has been with us more than 10 years now—I'm the fourth President to have to deal with it— is a commitment that cannot be abandoned. We've had a concern that putting pressure to hold inflation down might hurt the poor and the working families of this country, who are the ones who suffer most from inflation itself. So, we focused our attention on very narrowly defined, targeted programs to maintain the employment opportunities for people in spite of our effort to control inflation. And we've been remarkably successful, more than we ever dreamed, as a matter of fact.

In the first 2½ years that I was in office, we added a net increase of 8½ million jobs in spite of very high inflation rates. And in the process, we've also made funds available for home construction, because we did not want the homebuilding industry to take a nosedive. In the past, as inflation and interest rates have gone up, the first ones to suffer were the homebuilders and the construction workers and families that need homes. But we've maintained that homebuilding rate at almost 2 million homes per year, and that rate is still holding up.

Last month, for instance, we built at a rate of 1.88 million homes per year in our country. So, we've held up job opportunities, we've held up homebuilding programs and, therefore, jobs, in spite of heavy inflation pressures.

We're going to stick with the control of inflation by doing some basic things—not wasting money, having tight fiscal policies, making sure that we cut out redtape and regulations from the Government, which holds down inflation. We've been very tight on the number of Federal employees in spite of increased services. We've cut Federal employees about 20,000, and we've tried to maintain throughout the Government a commitment toward holding the budget deficit down. In fact, we've cut the budget deficit almost 60 percent since I've been in office, about $36 billion. That combination is very difficult to maintain, but so far we've done a good job.

The last thing I want to say on a fairly lengthy answer is that it's a long-time process. We cannot expect immediate reduction of inflation that's been with us for 10 years in spite of OPEC price increases; we can't expect miracles. And the second thing is that the American people are going to have to all do our share. In home heating oil, every homeowner is going to have to conserve energy, do everything they can to keep from wasting energy, which helps them personally, also helps our country.

MR. FOELL. Mary Richardson.

1980 PRESIDENTIAL CAMPAIGN

Ms. RICHARDSON. Mr. President, on the subject of a possible Carter-Kennedy contest.

THE PRESIDENT. Yes.

Ms. RICHARDSON. Does the fact that you are here with us today, that you have given 1 hour of your time to local television, indicate that you're worried about your political standing in New Hampshire and in Massachusetts?

THE PRESIDENT. No. Chris has traveled with me a lot during 1976 and the campaign—even when my name wasn't even on the public opinion polls, I never was worried. And I was perfectly willing in 1976 to meet any candidate who wanted to run against me, and for a while, earlier than that, we thought that Senator Kennedy might be a very likely prospect. That doesn't bother me at all.

I've always made a practice, when I was Governor or when I was a candidate for President or since I've been in office, to take advantage of every reasonable opportunity to let my views be known to the public. And that's really what I want to do up here is to let the people of New England, who watch this program, know what we're doing about inflation, what we're doing about jobs, what we're doing about home construction, what we're doing about the energy shortage and home heating oil and so forth. And I believe that's the most important aspect of my relationship with you all.

I would hope that the political questions could wait until later, because neither of us are announced candidates, but, of course, the press is preoccupied with the subject and, I think, perhaps even more than the people are.

Last Saturday afternoon, I had a 2-hour telephone call-in show on public radio. I guess I got about 40 questions. There was not a single question about the political contest. The questions were about the things that government might do or not do that affect their lives. So, I think the injection of political questions almost invariably comes from the press, not by me.

Ms. RICHARDSON. Of course, Mr. Carter, we are in Kennedy country right now, and there is an obsession with politics in New England, as you know. Being pre-

occupied with it, if I can be for one more question——

THE PRESIDENT. You might.

Ms. RICHARDSON.——can you beat Senator Kennedy in Massachusetts in the primary here?

THE PRESIDENT. I wouldn't want to predict that any more than he would be likely to predict that he could beat me in Georgia. I'll do well in Massachusetts, and I think I'll win throughout the country.

I think the Florida results are a fairly good indication. Florida is a cosmopolitan State in that people from all over the Nation move to Florida. And there were just flat predictions by everyone that Dade County, Miami area, would be heavily for Senator Kennedy. We carried the delegates in Dade County almost 2 to 1. And I'm perfectly willing to meet anybody who runs against me.

I'm an incumbent President. I ran against an incumbent Republican when everybody had a chance to run. I won the election. We've got a good record, and I think the people will ultimately decide not on the basis of personal popularity or charisma or speaking ability and so forth, but on the basis of whether or not a President in office, who's a Democrat, who's done an adequate job, to be trusted to lead the country 4 more years.

And I think the opportunity for me to go throughout the Nation and for the Cabinet officers and the Vice President and members of my family and others who are interested and tell the record of what we've done and what we anticipate doing for the next 4 years is an excellent opportunity. It'll be an educational process; it'll give us a chance to learn about problems that we haven't solved and ideas we hadn't thought about, and to realize the programs that are successful and those that are not successful.

So, I don't see the upcoming political campaign as a negative thing at all or one to be feared or one to be dreaded. As I said earlier, I look forward to it with great anticipation and confidence.

Mr. Foell. Chris Lydon.

SENATOR EDWARD M. KENNEDY

Mr. Lydon. Mr. President, I have a question about the Kennedy legacy. You spoke at the library dedication of John Kennedy's inspiration in your own life. Some people have always thought you resemble him. I caught a suggestion in your speech that John Kennedy, were he alive, might be closer to the restraint in your own politics than to the expansiveness of his brother Ted.

My question is, is Senator Kennedy, by his name, any more worthy of the Kennedy legacy than you are?

The President. I don't think so. The family of Presidents is very small. And I have read a lot of history before I became President, certainly during the time I was planning to be President. Since I've been in the White House, I've become a much more avid history student, and I've seen and studied about the decisions that President Kennedy made under the most trying and difficult circumstances—when you're alone, when you have no one to turn to, and that ultimately the question comes to you in the Oval Office on that desk and you have to make a decision, quite often late at night when nobody's there to advise you.

I've also seen, as a President—he was the 35th President; I'm the 39th President—that some of the decisions he made have affected my life as a President very profoundly. I mentioned a few of those in the speech I made today.

So, I feel a political kinship with President Kennedy that's very intense and also very personal. And obviously the name and the family relationship—blood kin— is a very strong and powerful force in the minds of American people and also certainly in the minds of those who are interested in politics and who will vote in 1980.

But I think as far as political alignment and relationship and the sharing of responsibility for having governed this country in the highest elected office in the land, I feel a very close kinship with President Kennedy also.

Mr. Lydon. If I may follow. The point was bluntly stated in Massachusetts politics some years ago to the effect that if his name were Edward Moore, not Edward Moore Kennedy, his candidacy would be a joke. How far would you go in embracing that line with respect to the forthcoming Presidential contest?

The President. I wouldn't go along with that at all. That was his first political race and he was untested then. My assessment of Senator Kennedy's accomplishments and his ability as a leader is that he's excellent, and this is based not on his relatives or his family position, but on his own record.

I think he's done a good job as a Senator, and he's espoused programs with which I agree. And in most instances, the programs that I have put forward to the Senate for decision, those that were highly publicized, those that were controversial, those that were difficult and on which I took a public position, Senator Kennedy has supported almost without exception.

So, in my own relationship with him and the sharing of opinion on controversial issues and in his performance as a Senator, I think he's built a record that's very good.

There have been some areas where we disagree. I think as far as fiscal prudence is concerned, balancing the budget, holding down unnecessary spending, being cautious about what kind of new programs we've put forth that are very expensive, we are in sharp disagreement. Senator Kennedy is much more inclined toward the old philosophy of pouring out new programs and new money to meet a social need. He may be right. I disagree with him. I'm much more inclined to try to make existing programs work efficiently and start up new programs only when it's absolutely necessary.

I think in the matter of a commitment to our Nation's defense strength, I would be in favor of much stronger defense commitments than his record shows. And I think with those two exceptions, there is little real incompatibility between us in working for peace, in trying to meet the needs of unfortunate people, and moving to eliminate racial or other discrimination in our society.

I have found a complete ability to work harmoniously with Senator Kennedy. But he's got a record of his own, and I don't think he has to depend on his brother's reputation to give him the stature of a very good leader.

EMPLOYMENT

MR. FOELL. Mr. President, you just mentioned not throwing money at programs.

THE PRESIDENT. Yes.

MR. FOELL. I'd like to double back to your answer to Jim Scott's question for a moment. There seems to be some confusion still as to whether you were including all construction workers in the promise you made to the construction workers in San Diego, and, if so, what dollar figure might be put on the size program you have in mind for them and why this would not be inflationary.

THE PRESIDENT. Well, what we've tried

to do is be firm and resolute in controlling inflation and, at the same time, without wasting money or creating massive spending programs and so forth, to focus the effective Government funding and administration of programs to hold down unemployment to give people jobs.

For instance, when I became President, the unemployment rate among construction workers was between 15 and 20 percent. We added a net increase of a million construction jobs alone, and we cut the unemployment rate among construction workers by 40 percent.

We did this in various ways: local public works projects and Economic Development Administration projects. One of the most successful, for instance, has been the Urban Development Action program, UDAG we call it.

Through this program, we have put in about $6 billion and we've added over 400,000 jobs. Only one-sixth of that money is Federal money. The other five-sixths comes from private investment. But we've provided the incentive there to rebuild the deteriorating central cities of our country. We have slashed through redtape and government delay. And the Government never initiates these programs. It's initiated by local government and by private investors. They come to us with a proposal on very simple forms. We make a decision on that request within 60 days, and then a small amount of Federal money goes in there, a large amount of local money goes in, mostly from private sources, and people are put to work and people's lives are changed.

Housing programs become better, new facilities are built for the life of a city, transportation, otherwise, and that's the kind of effect we've had. That's one reason why we have such strong support, politically speaking, from the Governors and mayors of this country. We have made them full partners in the process. So, we've not created jobs in the construction industry by handing people jobs in government; we've created jobs in the construction industry and other ways by letting the private sector of our country, the free enterprise system, be given a free reign absent Federal obstructions and eliminating Federal regulations with just a small amount of taxpayers' money.

That's my philosophy of approach, and that's what I intend to continue. I can't guarantee that nobody will lose a job, whether the inflation rate won't vary at all. But within the constraints of controlling inflation, we will minimize the loss of jobs, as I described to the construction workers.

Mr. FOELL. Tom.

NATIONAL DEFENSE

Mr. ELLIS. Mr. President, you mentioned defense preparedness, and we hear reports that our military strength is falling below what would be necessary to respond adequately to a military emergency. And in view of the recent squabble we had with Cuba over the presence of Russian combat troops, which seems suddenly to have subsided quite a bit, what do you see as an immediate step that needs to be done to strengthen our Armed Forces? Would it be reinstatement of the draft, an updating of the military?

THE PRESIDENT. Well, first of all, let me say that the military strength of the United States is the greatest of any nation on Earth. And there have been some trends upward by the Soviet Union which have concerned me and have also concerned my predecessors in office and are beginning to concern the Congress as well.

In the last 7 years, for instance—I was looking at some statistics the other day—

Presidents, two Republicans and myself, have made recommendations to increase defense expenditures—$30 billion in total over 7 years, higher than the Congress has finally approved. I think that that trend has changed. This past year, for instance, that ended on the 1st of October, we had a 3-percent real growth, growth above and beyond the inflation rate. We'll have the same thing for 1980 fiscal year, which just began on the 1st of October.

We've tried again to eliminate waste and overlapping and to plan very carefully to put the defense investment where it will pay the richest dividends, by strengthening NATO, for instance, and getting our allies to come in and do the same thing we are. Those alliances are very important to us, and one American dollar, one American service person can be greatly magnified if we work harmoniously with our allies. We've strengthened the Navy, the Air Force, and now on strategic weapons. We're trying to go into new fields as well.

It's important to point out two other things, and I'll try to be brief. One is that my number one priority above anything else—above inflation, above jobs, above home heating oil, above everything else—is to guarantee the security of this country. That's number one, because we wouldn't have anything if this Nation ever becomes vulnerable to a successful attack or threat or blackmail from a foreign country. And I want to make sure that our Nation's defense commitment is so strong that any nation that might be tempted to test us militarily would realize that they are committing military suicide.

I also want to be sure that the people of this country understand that we are at peace. I'm the first President in 40 years where we haven't had a single American killed in combat in a foreign country. I'd like to go out of office, no matter how long I serve, with that record intact.

But the best way, the only way, I think, that we can preserve peace is to be strong. And as long as the Nation, ourselves, and our allies and our potential adversaries all know that our Nation is strong militarily and the will to defend ourselves, under those circumstances, we are likely to maintain peace for ourselves, and our allies. If we ever become weak and vulnerable or vacillate or divided from one another, that's when we are likely to have to go to war. And so, I have no apology to make for what we've done to try to strengthen our defense. I'm going to keep it up.

I might say that the percentage of our gross national product, what this country produces, that goes into military is very low, about 5 percent, much lower than it's been in previous years—we're more efficient now—and much lower than the Soviet Union puts in. They put in about 13 percent of their gross national product into defense, but still we're the strongest and we're going to stay that way.

SHIPBUILDING CONTRACTS

MR. ELLIS. This is strictly a local or regional question that involves the General Dynamic Shipyard in Quincy, which has lost several recent shipbuilding contracts to firms from different parts of the country when we understood that they had submitted the low bid.

What is the bidding process? How is it determined who gets that bid? And if the Government were willing to step in, for instance, and come to the aid of the Chrysler Corporation, would it also be willing, do you think, to step into the aid of a business that's important regionally as the General Dynamic Shipyard is to this economy here?

THE PRESIDENT. I have a special feeling for General Dynamics. After the Second World War, as a young naval officer, I was assigned as the only officer to Electric Boat Company then, which later became General Dynamics, to build the first ship our Nation built, a little small antisubmarine submarine. At that time, General Dynamics was building refrigerator bodies for pickup trucks. So, my history of navy yards and my interest is very strong.

I don't want to mislead you. As long as I'm in the White House, I'm not going to let politics, even the hope of getting votes in Boston, affect—or Quincy—affect the decision on contracts on what's best for our whole country. I don't interfere, for political reasons, in which military base is expanded or which one's closed down. There's a tremendous temptation to do that; I'm not going to do it. I made that clear during the campaign. I'm not going to deviate from it.

The decision on contracts at Quincy and other navy yards around the Nation are made on the basis of what's best for our country. Most recently, although Quincy lost a highly publicized contract, I understand that since then, they have gotten one equally as good—that's not quite so highly publicized when they got one. It's important to us to see the shipyards around the Nation be kept viable and open and to keep their labor force relatively intact—they can't be frozen—relatively intact, because if our country is ever threatened or needs to expand rapidly what our Navy is doing or repair our ships rapidly in time of war, we'll need those navy yards to be in operating condition and to have the skilled people there.

The contract decisions about Quincy were not made with any political considerations at all. When they lost a contract, it was not made on the basis of politics; when they got a contract later on, it was not made on the basis of politics, but what, in the opinion of our responsible defense officials, approved by me, was in the best interest of our country.

Mr. FOELL. Do any of you want to follow up on that before we go to Jim? Jim, I guess you're on.

NATIONAL SPIRIT

Mr. SCOTT. Mr. President, you said that the number one priority is national security, of course. But how do you ease the minds of the Americans who see their dollar buying less, the ones who can't afford to buy the homes anymore, and the ones who have the general feeling that the rich keep getting richer and the poor keep getting poorer. How do you ease their minds?

THE PRESIDENT. Jim, you know it concerns me that people's minds are not at ease. Mine's not at ease; I have challenges and questions and problems that I have to resolve as best I can. I think we've done a fairly good job so far, and I don't want people to believe, first of all, that controlling inflation is hurting the poor or the aged or the infirm or the unemployed. The people who suffer most from high inflation are the ones who are least able to afford it, the ones who can't change their income or can't move to a different community and who have to buy the necessities of life with a major portion of their total earnings.

Secondly, I don't want those people to feel that an adequate defense commitment is at their own expense. This is an extremely important thing, because in the past, at least, certainly in the Vietnam war, the ones who suffered most were the poor.

If we ever have any reason in the future to go to a draft system, I'm going to make sure that we do not give special privilege to a young person who's in college because the wealthy can put their kids in college, which they did during the Vietnam war, and the poor people are primarily the ones that go and fight. My oldest son volunteered to go to Vietnam, but most of the discrimination, in my opinion, in the draft in the last combat was against poor people.

The third thing is this: We've had tremendous improvements or increases since I've been in office in helping the life of those who are poor. I've already mentioned employment opportunities that have increased, housing has been extremely high. We've also had commitments made to education. For instance, we have increased, just the first 2 years I was in office, the Federal allocation of funds for education by 60 percent. And I would almost say flatly—there may be a few exceptions—that now if a young person reaches college age, if that person is motivated and is educationally qualified, that young person can go to college because we've expanded those opportunities so greatly.

I think this has got to continue. We have not cheated or deprived or ignored the people who suffer most. We have shifted, however, to an attempt to focus particular programs much more specifically on those who are deprived by letting programs be drafted in the Congress and passed to meet a particular need so that people who don't need these services don't get nearly as much of it as they used to.

So, our country is strong, not only militarily but economically, it's strong politically, and I hope—and I believe that it's strong morally and ethically—that what we stand for is, indeed, an inspiration to other people throughout the world as well as reassuring to our own people.

There need be no fear on the part of anyone in this country that their needs which are presently being met will not be met in the future or that their needs will be ignored. They are an ever-present concern to me, to Senator Kennedy, to other Members of the Congress, and to the American people.

MR. SCOTT. A followup, Mr. President. As you travel about the country and go among the people, are you confident now that they believe in you and believe the things that you just said to me?

THE PRESIDENT. That's hard to say. No, I don't think there is an adequate degree of confidence in the strength of our country. I'm convinced that there is. But as I mentioned this morning in the Kennedy Library dedication, we had a series of things in the last 15 years or more that really shook the confidence of our people in our Nation, in one another, and particularly in government.

The Vietnam war was perhaps the most important single factor. The assassination of John Kennedy and Robert Kennedy, Martin Luther King, Jr., caused people to be deeply concerned about the societal structure in which we live. I would say the Watergate embarrassment and the deposing of an incumbent President caused Americans to doubt the integrity of their own Government.

And as far as the strength of our Nation was concerned, we've always thought that we were right, that our Nation fought noble battles, and we also thought that we would never lose. There are many people who doubt that the Vietnam war was a noble undertaking, and we lost; we didn't succeed in meeting the goals.

So, those kinds of factors, combined with 10 years of inflation and a realization that now we don't have as much to waste as we always thought we did— energy is a notable example—have caused us to stop and pause and say, "Where do we go next?" But in the going-somewhere-next, we need not be afraid, because in spite of all those problems, our Government has survived; it has a basic integrity that's not going to be changed. We are sensitive about the needs of poor people and those who've been deprived in the past or have felt the rages of discrimination.

In addition to that, among the world of nations, we are reaching out. We've won new friends in the last few years that we never thought we'd get 15 or 20 years ago. Egypt, India, the People's Republic of China, Nigeria have moved toward us and away from the Soviet Union. So, we've been successful there.

And I believe that if we can resolve the energy question, which I think we can, and let people see that it's not an unpleasant experience or a great sacrifice or a permanent inconvenience when we save instead of waste, I think that our Nation can survive this present series of challenges, as we have for the last 200 years. I've got complete confidence in the people of our country and in the strength of our institutions.

MR. FOELL. Mary.

AMERICAN STANDARD OF LIVING

Ms. RICHARDSON. Mr. President, you've been talking about inflation. This past week Paul Volcker, the Chairman of the Federal Reserve Board, said that Americans must accept a lower standard of living if the inflation rate is to be controlled. Why should people be asked to accept a lower standard of living? Isn't that the job of government, to control inflation? And how can you ask people who had very little to do with the causes behind inflation to tighten their belts?

THE PRESIDENT. I don't agree with

Paul Volcker. I think I know more about the people of this country than he does. I think I know more about the Nation than he does. And I'm not sure what he meant. In my own experience, in dealing with the people through the press and making an offhand statement, quite often a statement can be taken out of context and distorted from the intention of the speaker's that the speaker had when he made it. This may be the case with Paul.

If he meant that Americans can no longer avoid saving, then I think he's right. If a person measured a standard of living by saying, "I've got to be able to drive 75 miles an hour in a large, fancy, heavy automobile by myself," then he's right. Americans are already beginning to decide we've got to use public transportation when it's available, we ought to have three or four people in a car instead of one, we ought to obey the speed limit, and we're shifting toward smaller and more efficient automobiles. So, in that case he would be right. It depends on what the person thinks is a standard of living.

Let's take another example. I think in people's homes we're talking a lot about the cost of home heating oil. The average family can do more than I can. We're going to provide about $200 to help poor families pay heating bills during the winter. It'll pay a substantial portion of the increase in cost, but that family can do a lot more than that if they insulate their homes, keep the doors shut, put weatherization on the windows, if they hold their thermostats at a reasonable level. They can save a lot more than I've just described to you with their own actions. And people might say, "Well, I don't want to cut the thermostat down, therefore, my standard of living has been decreased."

So, I believe that the American people have a strength and the resiliency to take care of these changes in our lives when we do have limits that we didn't have before without lowering the quality of a life. I like to think about families who in the future will walk more and maybe ride bicycles more, maybe stay home more, maybe go on picnics more, or maybe drive a little slower. These kind of things cannot only be enjoyable instead of a pain, but they can also be patriotic at the same time.

So, there are ways to have a good life, even a better life without wasting so much. And if Paul Volcker meant that, I agree with him; otherwise I don't.

TAX CREDITS FOR ENERGY CONSERVATION

Ms. RICHARDSON. You mentioned weatherization, and, of course, here in New England that's very important.

THE PRESIDENT. Yes, it is.

Ms. RICHARDSON. At present there are no Federal programs, there are no incentives for multiunit buildings; in other words, buildings where there are apartments, townhouses. There are plenty of incentives for the homeowner. There are presently a million dwellings in Massachusetts. Half of those are multiunit dwellings, and yet there are no incentives for the owner of an apartment building, say, to begin a weatherization process. Do you have any plans to offer programs in that area?

THE PRESIDENT. Yes, this proposal is in Congress now, and I hope it will pass. As you know, we had to walk before we could run, and a year ago, or 6 months ago, it was almost impossible to get any American citizen, much less the Congress, to agree that we really had an energy problem. But we did last year get tax credits for homeowners to insulate their homes and to get credit for it when they paid their income tax. I think about 9 percent of all the families in the United States took advantage of that opportunity last year.

My guess is that with higher heating oil brought on us by OPEC oil prices, that more families will take advantage of that in 1979 and even more in 1980. But that program should be extended so that renters of multifamily homes would benefit from the weatherization of their apartments. And I think we ought to let that program go forward. I believe the Congress will favorably consider that.

MR. FOELL. Chris.

SUPPORT FROM CONSTITUENCY GROUPS

MR. LYDON. Mr. President, 4 and 5 years ago you and I used to talk at rather great length about who was for you and against you in 1976.

In office, it has seemed that your relations have eroded with a lot of the core constituencies of the Democratic party, including the black leadership, union leadership, Jewish leadership, liberals, environmentalists, and others, particularly against Senator Kennedy in 1980.

What—in political terms that you and I have talked about before—what is the Carter coalition? Or do you think you can win without a constituency coalition, so to speak?

THE PRESIDENT. Chris, first of all, I wouldn't want the viewers of this program to be misled. The fact that you and I discussed this 3 or 4 years ago does not necessarily imply that we agreed 3 or 4 years ago.

MR. LYDON. No. [*Laughter*]

THE PRESIDENT. I would say that we disagreed more than we agreed. And I don't agree with your basic premise now. I don't think we've lost that constituency group or those groups. In some cases, maybe so.

Obviously when a President or a Governor or a mayor is in office, and there are disappointments by some people, there are programs that don't quite work, or when unforeseen or uncontrollable economic circumstances sweep across a city or a nation, the incumbent officeholder is the one to be blamed, particularly if there's no campaign underway. Then when the campaign takes place, like in Boston, or like it was in Massachusetts a year or two ago, in 1976, the people start saying, "Which one of these two people can I best trust?"

I would say, for instance, in Miami, where we just had a test vote a week or so ago, is a good example. I wouldn't say that it was an accurate mirror of the whole Nation, but there are heavy populations there of Jewish citizens, Hispanics, blacks, as well as others, and we did very well in all those constituency groups in a sharp, highly publicized test of political strength. I can't predict what will happen in the future, but I think that that shows that we've not lost those basic strengths.

And if you remember correctly, in 1976 I would say one of our most significant political victories was in Pennsylvania. All of the labor unions, the leaders and so forth, were for Senator Jackson. But we carried Pennsylvania overwhelmingly, because the workers, members of those unions and others, voted for me.

I think we've got a much better relationship now with the labor leaders and their members than we did during the 1976 campaign. They've gotten to know me; I've gotten to know them. They've seen what we've done. We've got an almost perfect record, I have as President, and my administration, on labor issues, that they've actually been able to observe for the last 2½ years.

So, I wouldn't yield to anyone on the ability to attract those really valuable constituency groups that you named.

ENVIRONMENTAL ISSUES

MR. LYDON. A quick followup. I wasn't talking about sort of the grinding disappointments of everyday life, but, for example, the more articulate disappointment of the environmental groups, with your decision on the Tellico Dam, for example, who felt not just that it was a little disappointment, but they had misjudged your whole emphasis or that you had misled them.

THE PRESIDENT. Last year, among the coalition of environmental groups, I was given the award as the outstanding environmentalist in the Nation. And it was pointed out by them—not by me, but by them—that not since Theodore Roosevelt had there been a President who had done as much to preserve environmental quality and to protect the precious qualities of life of American people. Just a couple of months ago, I was given the Environmentalist of the Year Award by the Florida Coalition of Environmentalists.

On that one decision, I can't say that it attracted the approval of environmentalists. It was a difficult thing for me. I had fought that dam for 2½ years. The Congress had passed approval of that dam over my opposition. They had already attached an amendment to a continuing resolution which I could not veto, perpetuating the Tellico Dam.

I was and am now interested in making sure that the Endangered Species Act is passed, and I believe that we picked up a lot of support that we would not have gotten because of that particular incident. Also, the small endangered fish had been transferred to another place where they are thought by the specialists to be presently protected.

In Alaska, for instance, in spite of congressional intransigence we have taken action, which is going to stand, to protect 115 million acres of valuable land from exploitation and destruction, perhaps. And I think that our environmental record is very good. I don't have any apology to make about that.

But a President has to make decisions that are close calls and which almost invariably alienate some interest group at that particular time. The totality of a record, though, is one that has to be assessed by a particular interest group, and sometimes I just have to say, well, that interest group will have to be against me. I'm doing what I think is best for this country.

MR. LYDON. Could I sneak in one quick local environmental question? You know we have enormously valuable fishing grounds off the Massachusetts coast on Georges Bank.

THE PRESIDENT. Yes.

MR. LYDON. The Interior Department is still determined to sell oil-drilling leases on October 29 against some public and private suits in the State.

The question is why the Interior Department has not taken more formal notice of the blowout in the Gulf of Mexico and why you, with the environmental sensitivities that you have or have had, have not spoken on that matter specifically.

THE PRESIDENT. If I had to choose between protecting the fisheries industry off Massachusetts or having oil exploration, I would say zero oil exploration. I would protect the fisheries industry, because it's permanent. That's not the choice we have to make. We can have both if it's handled properly.

We have very carefully assessed the regions on the Georges Bank and excluded from any leasing the most valuable areas, and I think Cecil Andrus, the Secretary of Interior, has done a very good job. I haven't studied the maps and the charts—I haven't been out there—but I trust him.

In addition, I believe, if I'm not wrong, that very well respected environmental leaders of Massachusetts have also approved what decision we have made, I believe, including the Members of the Congress, including Senator Tsongas and also Senator Kennedy.

So, I believe that we can have very carefully controlled exploration for oil and at the same time protect the extremely valuable, much more valuable fisheries industry.

U.S. FOREIGN POLICY

MR. FOELL. We've talked about defense, but we haven't talked about foreign policy on a broader scale, Mr. President. Both you and your foreign policy advisers have denied that there's going to be any impeding of your ability to conduct foreign policy because of the early start of the campaign.

THE PRESIDENT. Yes.

MR. FOELL. What incentive does a leader of another country—let's take a PLO leader, for instance—have not to wait until he sees how John Connally might do in the primaries? What incentive does an Israeli leader have not to wait and see how Senator Kennedy does in the primaries? What's to keep them from holding back?

THE PRESIDENT. It would be a mistake to think that our country is the only one that faces election or changes in leadership. This takes place all over the democratic world and sometimes in the totalitarian world as well, and it's a part of the political structure of foreign policy with which we have to live every day.

We have, I think, been successful this first 2½, going on 3 years, in dealing with some problems that were longstanding, and we will not slow down our efforts to spread the beneficent influence of this country and other countries because of a campaign.

Panama, the most difficult political challenge I have ever faced in my life— it was more difficult for me to get the Panama treaty passed and implementation legislation than to be elected President. That had been dragging 14 years. The SALT II treaty, which we signed, that had been dragging 7 years under three Presidents. Mideast peace had been dragging for 30 years, and we finally brought the two major protagonists together in a spirit of harmony and genuine, growing friendship. Opening up Africa to the good influence of our country and on a reciprocal basis, this had been never done before. We've done this in the short time I've been in office.

All those efforts and others will be continued. The strengthening of NATO, the handling of the energy shortages on a worldwide basis, the alleviation of world hunger, the dealing with the difficulties of refugees from Southeast Asia, the maintenance of peace—those kinds of things will continue through any election interval in an undisturbed way. And I might say that the prospective opponents that I might have next year are not the kind of people that would make foreign policy a major issue.

I might say that in 1968, when an incumbent President was challenged, it was because there was a deep philosophical difference between the challengers and the incumbent over whether we should or should not stay in the Vietnam war. And because of that, President Johnson decided not to run for reelection.

We don't have that kind of difference now. There are no major, deep, philosophical differences that divide me from any potential challenger. So, I don't believe that our Nation's movement toward a better influence for our country to be strong and at peace with other countries will be a factor in the upcoming election.

I think that John Connally's statements

are not the kind that would appeal to the American people. I don't think the American people would seriously consider that as a viable approach to the Mideast problem.

MR. FOELL. Tom.

GASOLINE SHORTAGES

MR. ELLIS. Mr. President, you made a statement a few moments ago that 6 months ago, it was hard to get Americans convinced that there was an energy shortage.

THE PRESIDENT. Yes.

MR. ELLIS. The CIA told us this past week that by 1981 or '82, after the recession, we would have another gasoline shortage.

My question is, if we know this far in advance that there's going to be a gasoline shortage, why does there have to be one? And why can't the administration take steps right now to head it off?

THE PRESIDENT. We are taking steps. In the first place, the gasoline shortages that did exist in California first, and then on the east coast, that was the factor that convinced American people that we had to move on energy and also was a great factor in convincing the Congress to move.

We have been trying to get authority to develop a standby rationing plan for gasoline ever since I've been in office. The Congress has not yet acted.

This week, this past week, for the first time, the Senate voted a rationing plan through. And we hope that this coming week, if things go well, that the House will also vote to give me authority to develop a standby rationing plan so that if we do have a serious shortage, we can put it into effect and go for rationing. I hope we won't need it.

If the American people will continue to conserve gasoline with their driving habits and other ways, then we won't have

the gasoline shortage that the CIA predicted. I think we can get by without a gasoline shortage. I can't maintain here or guarantee people that we will never have a localized shortage of gasoline, but we are moving toward that.

The programs that we are putting into existence now through congressional action that will be permanent have as their number one emphasis saving, conservation of energy. The second emphasis is on developing energy supplies in our own country which are permanent, from growing plants and directly from the Sun, for instance. The third emphasis is on utilizing plentiful supplies of other kinds of energy in our country, from shale oil, from coal. And the last part is, of course, to develop more rapidly and more thoroughly and to use more efficiently those common supplies of energy, like oil and natural gas, which we've already known.

We've made good progress in all those ways, and I believe that we will not have any serious gasoline shortages if American people do conserve, if we have a standby rationing plan, and if we do move away from imported oil toward a heavier dependence on our own energy sources.

MR. FOELL. Jim, we have just a few minutes left.

REVEREND JESSE JACKSON

MR. SCOTT. Mr. President, you mentioned the bringing together of the Egyptians and the Israelis after a 30-year conflict.

THE PRESIDENT. Yes.

MR. SCOTT. And now we are seeing Reverend Jesse Jackson going to both areas and talking to these leaders, most especially the PLO leaders. Could this be an embarrassing situation for you? Is it embarrassing for you?

THE PRESIDENT. I can't say that it's embarrassing. The most embarrassing thing that I can think of is for me as a

President of a free nation to try to interfere with the right of an American citizen to travel to a country of his choice and to meet with foreign leaders of his choice. This is a free. country, and I don't have any control over Jesse Jackson. And if I tried to constrain him because he's black or because he might talk to some unpopular person, then the next thing that I might want to do is to try to keep Jewish citizens from going to Israel. This is a ridiculous thing to get involved in.

He has a right to go where he chooses, to talk to whom he chooses. The foreign leaders have a right to talk to him. It's not embarrassing to me. And I think the thing that we have to depend on is the sound judgment of the American people ultimately to resolve a controversial issue of this kind. I've met with large numbers of Jewish citizens, large numbers of black citizens; they talk to me very frankly.

Jesse Jackson did not go at my instigation, he did not go to represent me, he does not represent me. I've got myself, the Vice President, the Secretary of State, and Robert Strauss specifically charged with trying to bring about permanent peace in the Mideast, to protect the security of Israel, to let that nation live in peace with its neighbors, and to legitimately solve the rights or to honor the rights of the Palestinian people. I don't need private citizens to negotiate for me, and I don't permit them to. But they have a right to do as they choose as free people, and I would protect that right.

MR. FOELL. Is Mr. Strauss making headway?

THE PRESIDENT. I think so; I believe he's making as much headway as anyone can. But now we are really, for the first time, letting, to a maximum degree, the Egyptians and Israelis negotiate with one another, which is what we wanted from

the beginning. We come in and help when they ask us to.

MR. FOELL. I'm sorry, ladies and gentlemen, but our time is up. Mr. President, thank you for joining us today.

Questioning the President have been Tom Ellis of WCVB–TV, Channel 5 in Boston, Jim Scott of WBZ, Channel 4, Mary Richardson of WNAC, Channel 7, and Christopher Lydon of WGBH, Channel 2. I'm Earl Foell of the Christian Science Monitor. Thank you for joining us.

NOTE: The question-and-answer session began at 12:50 p.m. in the Volpe International Terminal at Logan Airport. It was taped for broadcast on October 21.

The transcript of the interview was released on October 21.

Energy Emergency in Florida

Memorandum From the President.
October 19, 1979

Memorandum for the Administrator, Environmental Protection Agency

Based on a request submitted to me by the Governor of the State of Florida to extend my July 6, 1979 determination that a regional energy emergency continues to exist in the State of Florida of such severity that a temporary suspension of certain air pollution control regulations which apply to fossil-fuel fired electric generating plants under the Florida Air Quality Implementation Plan may be necessary, and that other means of responding to the energy emergency may be inadequate, I hereby extend that determination from October 15, 1979, to and including December 31, 1979. This extension is limited by the same conditions as my July 6, 1979 determination.

If, during the extension, I find that a regional energy emergency no longer exists in Florida, I will direct that this extension be rescinded, and that all suspension orders issued by the Governor be terminated on the day of that rescission. Please continue to work with State officials to monitor carefully the residual oil supply in Florida and to inform me if the emergency should cease to exist. You will continue to retain full authority to disapprove temporary suspension of regulations in Florida and to exercise your emergency powers authority under Section 303 of the Clean Air Act, when and if necessary. It is important to keep suspensions to an absolute minimum since Section 110(f) of the Clean Air Act limits each suspension to a maximum duration of 120 days.

While my determination permits the temporary suspension of certain emission limiting requirements, it in no way permits the suspension of any national ambient primary or secondary air quality standard. Protection of these national health and welfare protective standards is consistent with Governor Graham's petition, and I commend him for his past restraint in using the authority to suspend some air pollution requirements.

This determination shall be published in the FEDERAL REGISTER.

JIMMY CARTER

[Filed with the Office of the Federal Register, 3:08 p.m., October 22, 1979]

NOTE: The memorandum was announced on October 22.

Rock Island Railroad Labor Dispute

White House Statement on an Agreement. October 22, 1979

We are pleased that all parties to the Rock Island labor dispute have reached agreement. This is another positive step in the process initiated on September 20 to meet the threat of curtailed grain shipments in the Midwest.

We wish to thank both management and labor for their cooperative attitude. Special thanks should also be given to Chairman James Reynolds and Ida Klaus and Nicholas Zumas of the Emergency Board.

NOTE: The press release also included the following information.

On September 20 the President created an Emergency Board to examine the labor dispute between the Rock Island Railroad and its unions, the Brotherhood of Railway, Airline and Steamship Clerks and the United Transportation Union. Today, the Emergency Board reported that agreement among the parties has been reached.

The agreement will have no immediate effect on the Rock Island system, since that system is now being operated by another carrier—the Kansas City Terminal Company—under the directed service order issued on September 26 by the Interstate Commerce Commission. The Commission issued its order after finding that the Rock Island lacked the financial resources required for satisfactory rail performance. The accord announced today will be important, however, should the Rock Island be able to resume operations following the period of directed service.

National Farm-City Week, 1979
Proclamation 4696. October 22, 1979

By the President of the United States of America

A Proclamation

All too often we take for granted the close working relationship between our farms and cities. On this 25th anniversary of National Farm-City Week, we can again reflect with pride on this unique interdependence.

It is a crucial interdependence that requires our constant attention. It determines whether our food and fiber supply will meet the needs of our citizens, our trading partners and our international humanitarian commitments. In short, it determines our future.

National Farm-City Week is a time for our rededication to cooperation, so we as a Nation can successfully meet the challenges that lie before us.

Now, THEREFORE, I, JIMMY CARTER, President of the United States of America, do hereby designate the period, November 16 through November 22, 1979, as National Farm-City Week.

IN WITNESS WHEREOF, I have hereunto set my hand this twenty-second day of October, in the year of our Lord nineteen hundred seventy-nine, and of the Independence of the United States of America the two hundred and fourth.

JIMMY CARTER

[Filed with the Office of the Federal Register, 4:41 p.m., October 22, 1979]

United States-People's Republic of China Trade Relations

Proclamation 4697.   October 23, 1979

AGREEMENT ON TRADE RELATIONS BETWEEN THE UNITED STATES OF AMERICA AND THE PEOPLE'S REPUBLIC OF CHINA

By the President of the United States of America

A Proclamation

As President of the United States of America, acting through my representatives, I entered into the negotiation of an agreement on trade relations between the United States of America and the People's Republic of China with representatives of the People's Republic of China;

The negotiations were conducted in accordance with the requirements of the Trade Act of 1974 (P.L. 93–618, January 3, 1975; 88 Stat. 1978) ("the Act");

An "Agreement on Trade Relations between the United States of America and the People's Republic of China", in English and Chinese, was signed on July 7, 1979, by representatives of the two Governments, and is annexed to this Proclamation;

The Agreement conforms to the requirements relating to bilateral commercial agreements specified in section 405 (b) of the Act;

Article X of the Agreement provides that it shall come into force on the date on which the Contracting Parties have exchanged notifications that each has completed the legal procedures necessary for this purpose; and

Section 405(c) of the Act provides that a bilateral commercial agreement and a proclamation implementing such agreement shall take effect only if approved by the Congress;

Now, THEREFORE, I, JIMMY CARTER, President of the United States of America, proclaim as follows:

(1) This Proclamation shall become effective, said Agreement shall enter into force according to its terms, and nondiscriminatory treatment shall be extended to the products of the People's Republic of China in accordance with the terms of the said Agreement, on the date on which the Contracting Parties have exchanged notifications that each has completed the legal procedures necessary for this purpose in accordance with Article X of the said Agreement.

(2) General Headnote 3(e) of the

Tariff Schedules of the United States is amended by deleting therefrom "China (any part of which may be under Communist domination or control)" and "Tibet" as of the effective date of this proclamation and a notice thereof shall be published in the FEDERAL REGISTER promptly thereafter.

IN WITNESS WHEREOF, I have hereunto set my hand this twenty-third day of October, in the year of our Lord nineteen hundred and seventy-nine, and of the Independence of the United States of America the two hundred and fourth.

JIMMY CARTER

AGREEMENT ON TRADE RELATIONS
BETWEEN
THE UNITED STATES OF AMERICA
AND
THE PEOPLE'S REPUBLIC OF CHINA

The Government of the United States of America and the Government of the People's Republic of China;

Acting in the spirit of the Joint Communique on the Establishment of Diplomatic Relations between the United States of America and the People's Republic of China;

Desiring to enhance friendship between both peoples;

Wishing to develop further economic and trade relations between both countries on the basis of the principles of equality and mutual benefit as well as nondiscriminatory treatment;

Have agreed as follows:

ARTICLE I

1. The Contracting Parties undertake to adopt all appropriate measures to create the most favorable conditions for strengthening, in all aspects, economic and trade relations between the two countries so as to promote the continuous, long-term development of trade between the two countries.

2. In order to strive for a balance in their economic interests, the Contracting Parties shall make every effort to foster the mutual expansion of their reciprocal trade and to contribute, each by its own means, to attaining the harmonious development of such trade.

3. Commercial transactions will be effected on the basis of contracts between firms, companies and corporations, and trading organizations of the two countries. They will be concluded on the basis of customary international trade practice and commercial considerations such as price, quality, delivery and terms of payment.

ARTICLE II

1. With a view to establishing their trade relations on a nondiscriminatory basis, the Contracting Parties shall accord each other most-favored-nation treatment with respect to products originating in or destined for the other Contracting Party, i.e., any advantage, favor, privilege, or immunity they grant to like products originating in or destined for any other country or region, in all matters regarding:

(A) Customs duties and charges of all kinds applied to the import, export, re-export or transit of products, including the rules, formalities and procedures for collection of such duties and charges;

(B) Rules, formalities and procedures concerning customs clearance, transit, warehousing and transshipment of imported and exported products;

(C) Taxes and other internal charges levied directly or indirectly on imported or exported products or services;

(D) All laws, regulations and requirements affecting all aspects of internal sale, purchase, transportation, distribution or use of imported products; and

(E) Administrative formalities for the issuance of import and export licenses.

2. In the event either Contracting Party applies quantitative restrictions to certain products originating in or exported to any third country or region, it shall afford to all like products originating in or exported to the other country treatment which is equitable to that afforded to such third country or region.

3. The Contracting Parties note, and shall take into consideration in the handling of their bilateral trade relations, that, at its current state of economic development, China is a developing country.

4. The principles of Paragraph 1 of this Article will be applied by the Contracting Parties in the same way as they are applied under similar circumstances under any multilateral trade agreement to which either Contracting Party is a party on the date of entry into force of this Agreement.

5. The Contracting Parties agree to reciprocate satisfactorily concessions with regard to trade and services, particularly tariff and non-tariff barriers to trade, during the term of this Agreement.

ARTICLE III

For the purpose of promoting economic and trade relations between their two countries, the Contracting Parties agree to:

A. Accord firms, companies and corporations, and trading organizations of the other Party treatment no less favorable than is afforded to any third country or region;

B. Promote visits by personnel, groups and delegations from economic, trade and industrial circles; encourage commercial exchanges and contacts; and support the holding of fairs, exhibitions and technical seminars in each other's country;

C. Permit and facilitate, subject to their respective laws and regulations and in accordance with physical possibilities, the stationing of representatives, or the establishment of business offices, by firms, companies and corporations, and trading organizations of the other Party in its own territory; and

D. Subject to their respective laws and regulations and physical possibilities, further support trade promotions and improve all conveniences, facilities and related services for the favorable conduct of business activities by firms, companies and corporations, and trading organizations of the two countries, including various facilities in respect of office space and residential housing, telecommunications, visa issuance, internal business travel, customs formalities for entry and re-export of personal effects, office articles and commercial samples, and observance of contracts.

ARTICLE IV

The Contracting Parties affirm that government trade offices contribute importantly to the development of their trade and economic relations. They agree to encourage and support the trade promotion activities of these offices. Each Party undertakes to provide facilities as favorable as possible for the operation of these offices in accordance with their respective physical possibilities.

ARTICLE V

1. Payments for transactions between the United States of America and the People's Republic of China shall either be effected in freely convertible currencies mutually accepted by firms, companies and corporations, and trading organizations of the two countries, or made otherwise in accordance with agreements signed by and between the two parties to

the transaction. Neither Contracting Party may impose restrictions on such payments except in time of declared national emergency.

2. The Contracting Parties agree, in accordance with their respective laws, regulations and procedures, to facilitate the availability of official export credits on the most favorable terms appropriate under the circumstances for transactions in support of economic and technological projects and products between firms, companies and corporations, and trading organizations of the two countries. Such credits will be the subject of separate arrangements by the concerned authorities of the two Contracting Parties.

3. Each Contracting Party shall provide, on the basis of most-favored-nation treatment, and subject to its respective laws and regulations, all necessary facilities for financial, currency and banking transactions by nationals, firms, companies and corporations, and trading organizations of the other Contracting Party on terms as favorable as possible. Such facilities shall include all required authorizations for international payments, remittances and transfers, and uniform application of rates of exchange.

4. Each Contracting Party will look with favor towards participation by financial institutions of the other country in appropriate aspects of banking services related to international trade and financial relations. Each Contracting Party will permit those financial institutions of the other country established in its territory to provide such services on a basis no less favorable than that accorded to financial institutions of other countries.

ARTICLE VI

1. Both Contracting Parties in their trade relations recognize the importance of effective protection of patents, trademarks and copyrights.

2. Both Contracting Parties agree that on the basis of reciprocity legal or natural persons of either Party may apply for registration of trademarks and acquire exclusive rights thereto in the territory of the other Party in accordance with its laws and regulations.

3. Both Contracting Parties agree that each Party shall seek, under its laws and with due regard to international practice, to ensure to legal or natural persons of the other Party protection of patents and trademarks equivalent to the patent and trademark protection correspondingly accorded by the other Party.

4. Both Contracting Parties shall permit and facilitate enforcement of provisions concerning protection of industrial property in contracts between firms, companies and corporations, and trading organizations of their respective countries, and shall provide means, in accordance with their respective laws, to restrict unfair competition involving unauthorized use of such rights.

5. Both Contracting Parties agree that each Party shall take appropriate measures, under its laws and regulations and with due regard to international practice, to ensure to legal or natural persons of the other Party protection of copyrights equivalent to the copyright protection correspondingly accorded by the other Party.

ARTICLE VII

1. The Contracting Parties shall exchange information on any problems that may arise from their bilateral trade, and shall promptly hold friendly consultations to seek mutually satisfactory solutions to such problems. No action shall be taken by either Contracting Party before such consultations are held.

2. However, if consultations do not result in a mutually satisfactory solution within a reasonable period of time, either Contracting Party may take such measures as it deems appropriate. In an exceptional case where a situation does not admit any delay, either Contracting Party may take preventive or remedial action provisionally, on the condition that consultation shall be effected immediately after taking such action.

3. When either Contracting Party takes measures under this Article, it shall ensure that the general objectives of this Agreement are not prejudiced.

ARTICLE VIII

1. The Contracting Parties encourage the prompt and equitable settlement of any disputes arising from or in relation to contracts between their respective firms, companies and corporations, and trading organizations, through friendly consultations, conciliation or other mutually acceptable means.

2. If such disputes cannot be settled promptly by any one of the above-mentioned means, the parties to the dispute may have recourse to arbitration for settlement in accordance with provisions specified in their contracts or other agreements to submit to arbitration. Such arbitration may be conducted by an arbitration institution in the United States of America, the People's Republic of China, or a third country. The arbitration rules of procedure of the relevant arbitration institution are applicable, and the arbitration rules of the United Nations Commission on International Trade Law recommended by the United Nations, or other international arbitration rules, may also be used where acceptable to the parties to the dispute and to the arbitration institution.

3. Each Contracting Party shall seek to ensure that arbitration awards are recognized and enforced by their competent authorities where enforcement is sought, in accordance with applicable laws and regulations.

ARTICLE IX

The provisions of this Agreement shall not limit the right of either Contracting Party to take any action for the protection of its security interests.

ARTICLE X

1. This Agreement shall come into force on the date on which the Contracting Parties have exchanged notifications that each has completed the legal procedures necessary for this purpose, and shall remain in force for three years.

2. This Agreement shall be extended for successive terms of three years if neither Contracting Party notifies the other of its intent to terminate this Agreement at least thirty (30) days before the end of a term.

3. If either Contracting Party does not have domestic legal authority to carry out its obligations under this Agreement, either Contracting Party may suspend application of this Agreement, or, with the agreement of the other Contracting Party, any part of this Agreement. In that event, the Parties will seek, to the fullest extent practicable in accordance with domestic law, to minimize unfavorable effects on existing trade relations between the two countries.

4. The Contracting Parties agree to consult at the request of either Contracting Party to review the operation of this Agreement and other relevant aspects of the relations between the two Parties.

In witness whereof, the authorized representatives of the Contracting Parties have signed this Agreement.

Done at Beijing in two original copies this 7th day of July, 1979, in English and Chinese, both texts being equally authentic.

For the United States of America
LEONARD WOODCOCK

For the People's Republic of China
LI XIANG

[Filed with the Office of the Federal Register, 12:39 p.m., October 23, 1979]

United States-People's Republic of China Trade Relations

Memorandums From the President.
October 23, 1979

Presidential Determination No. 80–2

Memorandum for the Secretary of State
Subject: Determination under Section 402(c)(2)(A) of the Trade Act of 1974— People's Republic of China

Pursuant to section 402(c)(2)(A) of the Trade Act of 1974 (Public Law 93– 618, January 3, 1975; 88 Stat. 1978) ("the Act") I determine that a waiver by Executive order of the application of subsections (a) and (b) of section 402 of the Act with respect to the People's Republic of China will substantially promote the objectives of section 402.

On my behalf, please transmit this determination to the Speaker of the House of Representatives and the President of the Senate.

This determination shall be published in the FEDERAL REGISTER.

JIMMY CARTER

[Filed with the Office of the Federal Register, 4:46 p.m., November 2, 1979]

———

Presidential Determination No. 80–3

Memorandum for the Secretary of State
Subject: Determination under Section 405(a) of the Trade Act of 1974—People's Republic of China

Pursuant to the authority vested in me under the Trade Act of 1974 (Public Law 93–618, January 3, 1975; 88 Stat. 1978) ("the Act"), I determine, pursuant to section 405(a) of the Act, that the Agreement on Trade Relations between the United States of America and the People's Republic of China will promote the purposes of the Act and is in the national interest.

On my behalf, please transmit this determination to the Speaker of the House of Representatives and to the President of the Senate.

This determination shall be published in the FEDERAL REGISTER.

JIMMY CARTER

[Filed with the Office of the Federal Register, 4:47 p.m., November 2, 1979]

United States-People's Republic of China Trade Relations

Letter to the Speaker of the House and the President of the Senate.   October 23, 1979

Dear Mr. Speaker: (Dear Mr. President:)

In accordance with section 407 of the Trade Act of 1974, I am transmitting a copy of a proclamation extending non-discriminatory treatment to the products of the People's Republic of China. I also enclose the text of the Agreement on Trade Relations between the United States of America and the People's Republic of China, which was signed on July 7, 1979, and which is included as an annex to the proclamation.

The Agreement on Trade Relations will provide a nondiscriminatory framework for our bilateral trade relations, and thus strengthen both economic and political relations between the United States and the People's Republic of China. Conclusion of this agreement is the most important step we can take to provide greater economic benefits to both countries from this relationship. It will also give further impetus to the progress we have made in our overall relationship since normalization of our diplomatic relations earlier this year.

I believe that the Agreement on Trade Relations is consistent with both the letter and the spirit of the Trade Act of 1974. It provides for mutual extension of most-favored-nation tariff treatment, while seeking to ensure overall reciprocity of economic benefits. It includes safeguard arrangements to ensure that our trade with the People's Republic of China will grow without injury to domestic firms or loss of jobs for American workers.

The Agreement also confirms for American businessmen certain basic rights and facilities in establishing operations and conducting business in the P.R.C. Other provisions include those dealing with settlement of commercial disputes; financial transactions; government commercial offices; and protection for industrial property rights, industrial processes, and copyrights.

I am also enclosing a copy of my report to the Congress pursuant to section 402 (c) (2) of the Trade Act of 1974. I shall issue today an Executive order waiving the application of subsections (a) and (b) of section 402.

In the past year and a half, Chinese leaders on several occasions have called for facilitating family reunification and for simplifying the procedure for getting permission to enter or leave China. During this period we have noted a marked relaxation of Chinese emigration procedures. Processing time has been reduced for most cases and numbers of emigrants have jumped dramatically. We have re-cently had discussions with senior Chinese officials and firmly believe that Chinese statements and the marked increase in emigration reflect a policy of the Government of China favoring freer emigration.

I have reviewed the circumstances of emigration from the People's Republic of China in light of all these factors, and have determined that a waiver of the application of subsections (a) and (b) of section 402 of the Trade Act of 1974 will substantially promote the objectives of that section.

I urge that Congress act as soon as possible to approve the Agreement on Trade Relations.

Sincerely,

JIMMY CARTER

NOTE: This is the text of identical letters addressed to Thomas P. O'Neill, Jr., Speaker of the House of Representatives, and Walter F. Mondale, President of the Senate.

United States-People's Republic of China Trade Relations

Message to the Congress. October 23, 1979

To the Congress of the United States:

Pursuant to section 402(c)(2) of the Trade Act of 1974, (hereinafter, "the Act") I shall issue today an Executive Order waiving the application of subsections (a) and (b) of section 402 of the Act with respect to the People's Republic of China.

I wish to report to the Congress that I have determined that the requirements of section 402(c)(2)(A) and (B) of the Act have been satisfied.

JIMMY CARTER

The White House,
October 23, 1979.

United States-People's Republic of China Trade Relations

Executive Order 12167.   October 23, 1979

WAIVER UNDER THE TRADE ACT OF 1974 WITH RESPECT TO THE PEOPLE'S REPUBLIC OF CHINA

By virtue of the authority vested in me as President of the United States of America by section 402(c)(2) of the Trade Act of 1974 (Public Law 93–618, January 3, 1975; 88 Stat. 1978), which continues to apply to the People's Republic of China pursuant to section 402(d), and having made the report to the Congress required by section 402(c)(2), I waive the application of subsections (a) and (b) of section 402 of said Act with respect to the People's Republic of China.

JIMMY CARTER

The White House,
  October 23, 1979.

[Filed with the Office of the Federal Register, 12:40 p.m., October 23, 1979]

Low-Level Radiation Policy

Announcement of Administration Initiatives. October 23, 1979

The President today announced a series of administration initiatives to deal with the problems of low-level ionizing radiation. His decisions came after a year-long, interagency analysis to consider the need for better public information, guidelines for protection of workers and citizens, research questions, potential compensation issues, and coordination of the Government's programs. The analysis was chaired by HEW and coordinated by the Domestic Policy Staff (DPS) and the Office of Science and Technology Policy (OSTP).

The President approved the establishment of a Radiation Policy Council to advise on broad radiation policy, coordinate Federal activities that use or control the use of radiation, resolve problems of jurisdiction, recommend legislation, ensure effective liaison with States and the Congress, and provide a forum for public input. This Council will be chaired by the Administrator of the Environmental Protection Agency and will include high-level officials from the other relevant agencies. It will have a 4-year sunset provision.

The President reaffirmed the lead role of the Environmental Protection Agency (EPA) in the issuance of guidance for protection from radiation. EPA will work closely with the Food and Drug Administration (FDA), the Nuclear Regulatory Commission (NRC), and other agencies.

The President directed the Office of Management and Budget (OMB) and OSTP to assure, during the preparation of his FY 1981 budget request, a sound research program on the long-term health effects of low-level radiation. The roles of the HEW agencies (the National Institutes of Health (NIH), FDA, and the Center for Disease Control), the Department of Energy, and other agencies in the research program will be decided through the cross-agency budget review.

An Interagency Radiation Research Committee, chaired by the Director of NIH, will review the kinds of research needed and the quality of research in this area supported by the Federal Government.

In addition, a task force, already established to examine criteria for compensation for civilians exposed to unusual radiation hazards, was given the additional assignment of assessing criteria for workers and veterans.

These administration initiatives are expected to improve substantially the Government's programs to protect the American people from unnecessary radiation exposure from medical, occupational, and environmental sources and to enhance public understanding of radiation and radiation protection.

Equal Rights Amendment

Remarks at a White House Reception for Supporters of the Amendment. October 23, 1979

Rosalynn helped me write my speech this afternoon. [*Laughter*] She said she was going to introduce me and then made my speech for me. [*Laughter*]

I think all of you can look at the women behind me on the stage and see that the broadest possible support exists for ERA, not only in a peripheral or superficial way but in the deepest possible way.

Lady Bird Johnson, I think, personifies the finest in political service and the enhancement of the beauty of our lives in every possible manner in our country.

Lynda Robb—a politician in her own right, a strong ally of her husband, a forceful leader in her own life, daughter of a great President—understands the sensitivities of America and also the needs of our country, helping to give me advice as chairman of our advisory committee on women's affairs.

Liz Carpenter, a real tough infighter. [*Laughter*] Ellie Peterson, who pointed out to me that the Republican Party had ERA in their platform 4 years before the Democrats. [*Laughter*] But this is not a partisan issue. And I would like to remind this group, as Lynda Bird Robb reminded me this afternoon, that I am the seventh consecutive President who has endorsed the ratification and the passage of the equal rights amendment. This is not a transient

thing. It is a permanent, deep commitment of many people, including all of you, and a deep need for our country.

This afternoon, I met with my advisory committee. They had spent all day analyzing 10 States where we have a good opportunity to get the remaining needed States to ratify the equal rights amendment. And we've made a very important decision, which Rosalynn has already mentioned, and that is that in 1980 we are going to ratify the equal rights amendment to the United States Constitution.

This is a human rights issue. As I've told many of you before, some of you before, the first conversation I had with the Ambassador from the Soviet Union, just a get-acquainted session which lasted about an hour, we had a good exchange of ideas and views. And finally we began to talk about basic human rights, because I had made such an issue of the human rights issue itself in my Inaugural address and in my campaign. And his response, which took me aback somewhat, "You don't even have equal rights for women in the United States." Ambassador Dobrynin told me that. It's not the only time he's ever mentioned it. [*Laughter*] And I believe that this is, to a major degree, an indictment of our country.

This is not an athletic contest to see whether or not the equal rights amendment is ratified. There were those who said a few months ago that the extention of the time available to ratify equal rights was not fair, there was a violation of some dreamed up, unwritten rule.

I don't believe Americans felt that way in the 1860's, when slavery was a major issue in our country. I don't believe any reasonable person said, 7 years after our Nation was founded, "Since we still have slavery after 7 years, let's never change it." And when Susan B. Anthony was seeking the right of women to vote, I don't think she said, "Since the 7-year deadline passed and women still don't have the right to vote, let's not bring up the issue."

And when Rosa Parks and Martin Luther King, Jr., began to move for equal rights in our country without respect to race, they didn't give up after 7 years of educating the American public about the needs to eliminate the intense and debilitating racial stigma, not just on blacks but on all of us, because there had been legal discrimination still not removed completely from the consciousness of America.

And I believe that 7 years has passed. We've got an extension now, and there's the same identical issue, that is, human rights, applicable to seeking equal rights for women. I'm determined to succeed. We've been waiting long enough for it. 1980 has got to be the year.

We have this afternoon gone through a list of 10 States where equal rights can be ratified by State legislatures in 1980. I think we must go all-out to prevail in these difficult tests of strength.

On the one side: the general populus, a heavy majority of Americans, a heavy majority of Governors, seven Presidents in a row, both parties, a heavy majority in the Congress, people who know what's right and who believe in fairness—dedicated to the ratification of ERA; on the other side: a minority representing no party, not representing a majority of any elected group of people, but basing their stand on intense feelings which they exemplify in every contest, and benefiting from inertia, benefiting from delay, benefiting from confusion, benefiting from rumor, benefiting, quite often, from political timidity, benefiting, however, from a tight, close-knit, well-organized, dedicated, opposition force.

The only way to deal with that kind of opposition is to have a tight, well-knit, well-organized force to present the facts to the American people and to analyze, State by State, where are the crucial votes? How can we approach the Members of the House and Senate in these 10 States or perhaps a few more? And what can we do to let the people in those States involved know the facts about the equal rights amendment?

We've got to assess the problem. We've got to divide up the responsibility. We've got to organize our own forces effectively. We've got to share information. We've got to put aside the inclination that we all have to find a scapegoat on which to blame a temporary setback. We've got to honor the capabilities of one another. We've got to share information about progress.

And we need never to be deterred. Our course is a proper one; our cause is right. And I predict that next year we will win. I'm determined to do so if you'll help me.

Thank you very much.

NOTE: The President spoke at 6:51 p.m. in the East Room at the White House.

In his remarks, the President referred to Liz Carpenter and Ellie Peterson, honorary cochairs and founders of ERAmerica.

International Human Rights Award

Remarks on Accepting the Award from the Synagogue Council of America. October 24, 1979

First of all, I hope that before all of you leave you'll stop by, and if Ed Sanders [1] will place the acrostic here, I would like for you to know how beautiful it is. And the shofar is symbolically extremely important to me, because there's no doubt that the rest of the world needs to be awakened from its slumber about the im-

---
[1] Senior Adviser to the President and the Secretary of State.

portance of the preservation of human rights.

This is an honor for me for several reasons—not a personal honor, but an honor to the office I hold and the principles which I espouse as the leader of this country. The fact that the reformed, conservative, and orthodox Jews of our Nation, in complete harmony with one another, have decided to give me this award is extremely significant in itself. I know you represent, under the aegis of worshiping the same God, differences of views, but I think the exemplification which you bring to this ceremony is that the commitment to human rights transcends differences among American people.

I campaigned for this office for 2 years or more, and everywhere I went, with every opportunity I had, I promised that if I was President that I would emphasize, to the highest degree of my ability, our Nation's commitment to human rights. It's one reason that I was elected. When I made my acceptance speech at the Democratic Convention, when I made my Inaugural speech, human rights was a focal point for my basic summary of this Nation's foreign policy.

Human rights takes on a broad range of meanings. And we've had some notable successes in the last 2½ to 3 years: Prison doors have opened to release literally tens of thousands of those who've been incarcerated for years, even decades. We've seen a massive shift in countries around the world and particularly, I think, in this hemisphere toward giving people the basic human right of shaping their own future, of choosing their own leaders, of modifying and establishing the policies of their own government.

We've espoused the cause of human rights in trying to honor the desire of people to be free, to leave the Soviet Union, to escape persecution, to reunite families, to be able to speak without fear of restraint or punishment.

Increasingly we've extended the helping hand of a highly blessed nation to those who suffer. We've taken a leadership role in helping the refugees from Southeast Asia—and later on today, I'll be making another major announcement and commitment of our country to alleviate the hunger, which is preying so heavily on my own heart and mind, on yours, and on the hearts and minds of people throughout this country.

It has not always been easy, even in this country, to maintain a strong commitment to human rights. As Pat Derian, sitting on the front row, responsible for this position in the State Department, so well knows, there are always delegations who come to me or to her or to Secretary Vance and say, "This particular dictator has been a valuable ally of ours, and when the United States makes a critical remark about political prisoners who are being restrained or in jail or punished or executed, it tends to shake our relationship with that country." We've had to withstand those kinds of pressures, and I believe that in many instances we've been successful in that effort.

Leaders of the business community—I'm sure none of you here—have sent delegations to me with a very forceful political presentation: "How can we possibly disturb our possible sales abroad or our profits abroad by making statements about apartheid or about some other deprivation of human rights?" I hope that our Nation will always stand resolved. And I'm encouraged by your recognition that I, as President, have accurately represented what our Nation is, what we hope to be in the future, and what we expect and demand, as a matter of fact, from nations all over the world.

This has not required any courage on my part, although there have been some obstacles to overcome, which I've just described, because I know that I have the overwhelming support of the American people for our human rights policy. I hope that in the future it will never be weakened, but further strengthened. And I believe that it is accurate to say that there are very few, if any, national leaders around the world who are not reminded constantly now, because of the American position, that deprivation of human rights not only hurts them in their own country but helps to tear down the esteem and respect and influence and the well-being of their country vis-a-vis the other nations of the world.

It's a constant subject for discussion and attention no matter how the government might be, how totalitarian in its orientation or composition, or how callous they have been in the past toward basic human rights. In spite of the fact that it's a little bit difficult for us in our free Nation, under a democratic government with strong public support, we ought to recognize how extremely difficult it is, how extremely dangerous it is, how much courage is required from those who live under constant oppression to demand, in sometimes a weak and faltering voice, their basic human rights. And I believe that they will be strengthened because of the result of this ceremony.

I accept this with gratitude not because of any accomplishment of my own or courage on my part, because that's not applicable here, but because you have recognized that the President of the United States ought always to withstand any pressure that contravenes the furtherance of our basic commitments, our basic beliefs, our basic principles, our basic obligation to our fellow human beings, our basic obligation to the God we worship.

Thank you very much for honoring me in this way. I'm deeply proud to be with you.

NOTE: The President spoke at 12:01 p.m. in the Rose Garden at the White House.

The President was presented with a citation in the form of an acrostic spelling out his name and a shofar, a ram's-horn trumpet, symbolizing the President's leadership in advancing the cause of human rights.

Aid for Kampucheans

Remarks Announcing Additional Relief Efforts.   October 24, 1979

Thirty [37] [1] years ago a holocaust began which was to take the lives of more than 6 million human beings. The world stood by silently in a moral lapse whose enormity still numbs the human mind.

We now face, once again, the threat of avoidable death and avoidable suffering for literally millions of people, and this time we must act swiftly to save the men, women, and children, who are our brothers and sisters in God's family.

Five days ago, the International Committee of the Red Cross and the United Nations Children's Fund appealed jointly for $111 million in aid to help the millions of Kampucheans, formerly known as Cambodians, who are facing death from starvation during the next 6 months. We must respond to this appeal, and we must also help the related need for food and medicine and shelter for refugees who are fleeing from Kampuchea to Thailand.

Here is what we must do, and this is what we will do: First, as to the Red Cross and United Nations joint appeal, I'm today directing that $3 million in existing refugee aid funds be made available immediately to UNICEF and to the International Committee of the Red Cross, in addition to the $2 million that I ordered transferred last week.

----

[1] Printed in the transcript.

I'm urgently asking the Congress to enact a supplemental Food for Peace appropriation that will make available $20 million in commodities for use in Kampuchea, subject only to assurances that it will reach its destination, that is, the human beings who are suffering. This is in addition to the $5 million in food that I pledged for this purpose last week.

Today I'm also directing that $9 million in U.S. refugee assistance funds go to meet about one-third of the total cost of Thailand's program to help starving refugees who are entering Thailand from Kampuchea. I commend the Thai Government on its decision to admit more refugees. They have already received tens of thousands of them.

Third, I've told Chairman Zablocki in the House and cosponsors that the administration supports their proposal to authorize $30 million for the next phase of relief in Kampuchea. This would enable us, as a total, to raise our contributions to the continuing program for the alleviation of suffering in Kampuchea as high as $70 million.

The dimensions of the Kampuchean tragedy are immense, and more aid will almost certainly be needed. And I'm also asking my Commission on World Hunger, headed by Sol Linowitz, to recommend to me the next steps that we must take to meet worldwide hunger needs.

I'm certain that the American people, in addition to their Government, will want to be part of this urgent humanitarian effort. It's absolutely too important to be left to Government alone.

Standing behind me on the platform are representatives of religious and other groups who have already pledged to help in this effort, who've called on me to do what I'm announcing now, and who, I believe, sincerely said that they would match the Government effort.

Several voluntary agencies have been working all along to meet the needs of increasing numbers of refugees, and I call upon all Americans to support this work. I ask specifically that every Saturday and Sunday in the month of November, up until Thanksgiving, be set aside as days for Americans in their synagogues and churches and otherwise to give generously to help alleviate this suffering. I'm confident that Americans' responses will be matched abroad.

Many governments and international voluntary agencies are already coming forward with their pledges. The human family, those of us who have been blessed so highly with food and a relative absence of suffering, must not be found wanting in our response to alleviate this almost unprecedented mass human suffering. If a tragedy of genocidal proportions is to be avoided in Kampuchea, we must all help, both nations and governments and individuals alike.

I would now like to call on Father Theodore Hesburgh, who was the spokesman for the group, representing private entities, churches, synagogues, and others, to say a few words to you, and he and others in this room from government and from the private sector will be glad to answer your questions about this humanitarian effort.

Father Hesburgh.

NOTE: The President spoke at 1:40 p.m. to reporters assembled in the Briefing Room at the White House.

Prior to the President's remarks, he met with religious leaders and representatives of various humanitarian organizations to discuss the situation in Kampuchea. Following his remarks, Rev. Theodore M. Hesburgh, Chairman of the Select Commission on Immigration and Refugee Policy and chairman of the board, Overseas Development Council, and Ambassador Henry D. Owen, Special Representative of the President for International Economic Summits, held a news conference on the President's announcement.

President's Commission for a National Agenda for the Eighties

Executive Order 12168.   October 24, 1979

By the authority vested in me as President by the Constitution of the United States of America, and by the Statutes of the United States of America, including the Federal Advisory Committee Act, 5 U.S.C. App. I, and 3 U.S.C. 301, in order to establish an independent forum to recommend for this Nation an Agenda for the Eighties and to recommend approaches for dealing with the major issues which will confront the American people during that decade, it is ordered:

1–1. Establishment and Structure

1–101. There is hereby established the President's Commission for a National Agenda for the Eighties.

1–102. The Commission shall be composed initially of fifty members appointed by the President from among private citizens of the United States. Upon the request of the Commission, the President shall select and appoint no more than fifty additional members.

1–103. The President shall designate the Chairperson of the Commission. The Chairperson, following consultations with Commission members, shall designate no more than fifteen members of the Commission to constitute an Executive Committee.

1–104. The members of the Commission shall not receive compensation for their service on the Commission, but may receive travel expenses, including per diem in lieu of subsistence.

1–2. Functions and Reports

1–201. Under the direction of the Executive Committee, the Commission shall identify and examine the most critical public policy challenges of the 1980's. It shall examine issues related to the capac-

ity for effective Federal governance, the role of private institutions in meeting public needs, and underlying social and economic trends, as these issues bear on our public policy challenges in the 1980's. Areas to be reviewed by the Commission shall include:

(a) underlying trends or developments within our society, such as the changing structure of our economy, the persistence of inflationary forces, demands on our natural environment, and demographic shifts within our population that will shape public choices in the 1980's;

(b) opportunities to enhance social justice and economic well-being for all our people in the 1980's;

(c) the role of private institutions, including the non-profit and voluntary sectors, in meeting basic human needs and aspirations in the future;

(d) defining the role of the public sector, and financing its responsibilities in the 1980's;

(e) impediments to building policy consensus, both within government—the Executive branch, Congress, State and local government—and within the Nation as a whole.

Within this framework, the Commission shall identify the specific issues appropriate for examination.

1–202. The Chairperson of the Commission shall organize the Commission to study and make recommendations on major subject matter areas. This shall include the authority to appoint study panels and their chairpersons.

1–203. The Executive Committee shall coordinate the work and act on behalf of the Commission as necessary.

1–204. The Commission shall make every feasible effort to ensure citizen participation in the development of its Agenda and recommendations. The Commission, in preparing its recommendations, shall also consult with the Congress and with State and local officials.

1–205. The Commission shall prepare a final report setting forth its recommendations for addressing its Agenda for the Eighties and shall present the report to the President and to the Congress by December 31, 1980.

1–206. The Commission shall terminate on February 15, 1981.

1–3. Staff and Support

1–301. The Chairperson of the Commission shall appoint an Executive Director of the Commission.

1–302. To the extent permitted by law, Executive Agencies shall provide funds, facilities, support, services and assistance for the Commision and its subgroups, and such information and advice as the Commission may request.

1–303. Notwithstanding Executive Order 12024, the functions of the President under the Federal Advisory Committee Act (5 U.S.C. App. I), except that of reporting annually to Congress, shall be performed by the Director of the Office of Management and Budget with regard to the Commission and its subgroups. The Director is authorized to further delegate these responsibilities.

JIMMY CARTER

The White House,
     October 24, 1979.

[Filed with the Office of the Federal Register,
     4:08 p.m., October 24, 1979]

President's Commission for a National Agenda for the Eighties

Announcement on the Establishment of the Commission.   October 24, 1979

The President signed an Executive order today establishing an independent, nonpartisan forum to recommend a National Agenda for the Eighties.

The Presidential Commission is a direct outgrowth of the President's extensive discussions at Camp David this summer, when he determined to organize a longer term review of issues of primary priority to the country and developments that will shape them in the decade ahead.

President William McGill of Columbia University was designated Chairman of the Commission and announced that the group would begin immediately its organization planning to launch its work.

Within the framework of its broad mandate, the Commission will identify the specific issues appropriate for examination and designate panels for indepth review and discussion of these subjects. Consultative groups from the Congress and from State and local officials will be asked to exchange ideas regularly with the Commission.

Both in the makeup of the Commission itself and through its inputs from various organizations, the Commission is expected to have access to the broadest possible spectrum of our national views and thinking. The Commission will be composed initially of 50 private citizens appointed by the President. As the Commission defines and organizes its work, the President will select, at the request of the Commission, up to an additional 50 members. A partial initial list of Commission members was announced today.

To ensure the nonpartisan nature of the deliberations, the President has designated that the Commission present its report to the President and to the Congress by December 31, 1980.

The President's Executive order pledged the cooperation of all Federal agencies in the furthering of the Commission's work.

The principal White House liaison for the Commission will be through Hedley Donovan, who became a senior Presidential adviser following his retirement as editor-in-chief of Time Inc. publications. Mr. Donovan worked closely with the President in structuring the Commission, which was formally brought into being with today's Executive order.

The Office of Management and Budget will assume the responsibility for overseeing the Secretariat and providing support for the Commission's work.

John F. Kennedy Center for the Performing Arts

Appointment of Three Members of the Advisory Committee on the Arts.
October 24, 1979

The President today announced the appointment of three persons as members of the Advisory Committee on the Arts (John F. Kennedy Center for the Performing Arts). They are:

RALPH HORNBLOWER III, a Washington, D.C., attorney who has studied voice and has sung with the Washington Opera;

G. JOSEPH MINETTI, a Washington, D.C., attorney and former member of the Civil Aeronautics Board;

ANN K. REGAN, of Billings, Mont., a Montana State senator and junior high school teacher.

Friends of Carter/Mondale

Remarks at a Fundraising Dinner.
October 24, 1979

The only thing I like better than 4 more years is 5 more years. [*Laughter*]

First of all, I want to thank Fritz Mondale for that introduction and for being the finest Vice President, perhaps, that ever served this country.

His office is right near mine. There is no meeting which I attend or have ever attended from which he was excluded. He's involved in the most sensitive areas of our Nation's life, in every aspect of our Nation's life. He's a full partner of mine in every sense of the word. And there is nothing that has been described here tonight, very generously by those who've spoken before supper, that I could possibly have done without Fritz Mondale. I don't talk of him very seriously, but I want to say that.

Because of his superb leadership and help, I think I should make a direct statement about my own plans concerning him for the future. Fritz, let me put it this way: I expect you to run for reelection. I expect you to be renominated, and if so, I intend to support you. [*Laughter*] The difference between this commitment and those you may have heard before is that I really mean it. [*Laughter*]

And as you pointed out a little earlier, it is really good to have Bob Strauss on my side this time—and before the convention, even. [*Laughter*]

In the next few weeks, I will make a statement of my own concerning 1980. Tonight I won't say exactly what that statement will be, but I can say this: For all those of you who are my friends, you will not be disappointed. [*Laughter*] Because of a deep sense of propriety, that's all I can say.

Well, as a matter of fact, I can say a couple more things. I asked my Mama. [*Laughter*] For those of you who are waiting with bated breath, she said okay. [*Laughter*] Rosalynn said she would be willing to live in the White House for 4 more years. [*Laughter*] And we have already dropped these hints around a few places in the country, recently in Florida—

[*laughter*]—and so far, as is proven by this group tonight, the hints have been very well received.

I want to speak to you seriously for a few minutes, and I'll try not to repeat what's already been said. I want to say a little about myself.

Where I come from, going on two centuries now, Democrats have believed in seniority. We've developed in Georgia and in many States of the South, as you well know, a tradition that once you're elected, you get reelected. [*Laughter*] I inherited this habit. There's no way I can break it—[*laughter*]—and I'm certainly not going to start next year.

But I don't want to talk about just one person's victory or even the team's victory. I'm here to talk about a Democratic victory, a victory that we Democrats throughout the Nation deserve and we are going to win in 1980. And I want to talk to you about our party as seriously as I know how—what it has been, what it means to me, what it means to you, what it means to our country.

First of all, Fritz Mondale and I are Democrats. We are loyal Democrats. We are lifetime Democrats. Neither of us have ever in our lives voted for anything except Democrats. In 1980 [1976][1] when there was a Republican incumbent in the White House, we ran for President and won. This has been a very enlightening and a very inspiring and a very gratifying 2½ to 3 years. And since we've been in the White House, in every action that we have taken and every word that we have spoken, we've tried to live up to the highest possible principles and ideals of a Democratic Party, as described by Fritz a few minutes ago.

Democrats are not afraid of government, because we know government can

---

[1] Printed in the transcript.

work. Government can be responsive to the people's needs without interfering in an unnecessary way in people's lives. Government can help all people, all Americans, with particular attention to those who need government's help most. Government can inspire people to be better. Government can probe for weaknesses in a system that's already good and make that system better. Government can raise a banner of ideals, commitments, principles. Government can help to paint a picture of a beautiful dream and then inspire the people to work together to realize those dreams. Government can create jobs and expand economic opportunities. Government can lead the country toward peace and prosperity.

So, in times of great challenge and great crisis and great danger to our country, our people have wisely and historically turned to the Democratic Party for leadership of their government. Democrats believe in sharing that authority, that responsibility, and that power with the people. Democrats who are worthy of our party's name don't forget who put us in office.

Democrats are not afraid to face a difficult challenge, and that's where Fritz and I have been, along with many of you, the last 3 years—in the thick of our Nation's most serious challenges, almost all of which we inherited. We have never ducked; we have never hidden. We've fought the hard battles; we've stayed in the arena where, at times, political blood has been shed.

I do not want to read you a list of our accomplishments. The real achievement of the last 33 months, in my opinion, has been something quite fundamental. It's the renewal of a tradition, a tradition of service that has been reestablished now in our Nation in government after 8 years of Republican rule. I don't think I need remind anyone here about the history of those 8 years—a time of bloodshed and failure, a time of embarrassment for our country, a time of division and discouragement, a time of despair and alienation.

I think that the tradition which we cherish is now perhaps more alive in the hearts and minds of all Americans than any time in history, at least about which I know. I'd like to look at—just a few minutes—at that tradition.

I believe in hard work; Democrats believe in hard work. I and other Democrats believe that Americans have a right to a job, to support oneself in dignity and with self-respect. Working together during this last 33 months, we have realized that expectation; we've lived up to that tradition; we've helped Americans realize those hopes.

Despite the economic problems and discouragements that we inherited, we live in a country today with the highest level of employment and the highest percentage of its work force employed than any time in history. And that's a record of which Franklin Delano Roosevelt and Harry S. Truman and John Fitzgerald Kennedy and Lyndon Baines Johnson would all have been proud. It is a record that every one of us here can share, because we did it together.

And I particularly want to recognize the Democratic Congress. I'm waiting for the end of this term and the beginning of the campaign year, when the American people and the news media, for a change, will accurately assess what we have proposed, what we've fought for, and what we have achieved. And I believe that there has never been a list of more controversial and difficult proposals made to the Congress than have been made this last 3 years. And I believe that the record will show at the end of this term that even during those halcyon days when Lyndon Johnson, after a time of tragedy, became

President, that there will not have been a better record of White House and Capitol Hill cooperation and achievement for the American people than we have seen during this first 3 years of my term.

There's something else we've been working on. It's been mentioned twice tonight already, but I want to make it clear, because I happen to be the President and I want the words to come from me. For the first time in 40 years, I'm a President that has seen our Nation completely at peace, not a single loss of life, and I thank God for that. And I hope I can leave this office, which you've given to me, with that record still intact.

It is not an accident. I don't take credit for it myself. The American people are deeply committed to peace. But along with that, there has to be peace not just for Americans. We've used our strength and our influence, our national will, our political courage not only to avoid war for ourselves but to pursue fundamental human principles for ourselves, yes, and also for others.

Today, after long years of bloody and bitter warfare, Israel and Egypt are at peace. They are working together because of the United States. Who would have believed this possible 3 years ago? You cannot imagine—or perhaps you can— what a thrill goes through my soul when I see on television Anwar Sadat steaming into the harbor at Haifa in an Egyptian ship, escorted by Israeli ships and planes, American warships standing at a proper distance offshore, and tens of thousands of men, women, and children on the streets to welcome their former enemy with open arms and open hearts and a pledge of friendship, which is so valuable now to them both.

And I believe this period in the search for a permanent peace in the Middle East—it's good not to intrude ourselves in an unwarranted fashion, but to let the Israeli leaders and to let the Egyptian leaders get to know each other and feel the responsibility on their own shoulders, which they do.

And I really enjoy getting a telephone call from Anwar Sadat after Begin leaves Egypt, and he says, "Mr. President, we got along just fine. You know that Prime Minister has really changed." It's the greatest feeling.

And I think here in our own hemisphere, we've enhanced the spirit of mutual respect and national dignity by implementing the Panama Canal treaties. This was my life's most difficult political effort, with absolutely no immediate political benefit, and there's not a single United States Senator who voted for the Panama Canal treaties who could possibly have expected accolades or one extra vote because of that courageous action. And I've never witnessed in my own lifetime a demonstration of greater political courage than the U.S. Senate showed in the ratification of the Panama Canal treaties and the House recent action in implementing legislation.

It made me proud, because it was a right thing to do, it was a decent thing to do, it was a fair thing to do. And it wasn't entirely an unselfish gesture, because I say flatly to you that the United States will reap rich dividends from this action in the years ahead. We're already doing it. These treaties were, indeed, worthy of the Democratic Party and all it stands for. We really honored the Democratic Party's finest principles.

In Africa, for the first time in the history of our Nation, after 200 years the United States stands boldly and clearly on the side of justice for majority rule, for democracy, for the end of apartheid. There's absolutely no equivocation about where we stand. We don't talk out of both

sides of our mouths. We can be proud of this; we can be proud of this together.

As has been mentioned several times throughout the world, we are now known as the champion of human rights. This is good for others, and it's also good for us. In our battle for basic human rights, we will never yield, and you can depend on that.

And I might add that we've not achieved full human rights here at home. It took us a long time to abolish slavery in this country. It took us even longer to find the generosity in our political system to let women have the right to vote. I think it's time to give women equal rights by ratifying the equal rights amendment, and I hope you'll all help me with that.

We can be proud, too, of the great struggle for SALT II, which will control nuclear weapons, it will enhance our Nation's security, it will contribute to world peace. It took 7 years to negotiate it. This is a goal: nuclear weapons control, strong national security, world peace. It's obviously in the tradition of the Democratic Party.

And I want to make another thing clear. I'm a Navy man, come from Georgia, and I am for a strong defense. My position is clear, and I don't want to make any apology for it. And there may be those who say, "I wish you weren't so strongly for a powerful nation, militarily." I'm just going to take one aside to comment on why. We only spend about 5 percent of our gross national product for defense. In the past we spent much more than that. We do it more efficiently now, more effectively, better coordinated, better spirit. The Soviets spend 13 percent, 14, maybe 15 percent of their gross national product on defense.

We have been at peace. We've mentioned that several times. The only reason that we are at peace is because we have a strong nation. We are not talking about very destructive weapons. They cause me more concern than anybody in this room—the MX missile, Trident submarines, Trident missiles, cruise missiles. The best investment that we can make is in a weapon which will never be fired in anger, and the best investment we can make is in a soldier who will never die in battle.

And I think so long as our potential adversaries know that we are strong militarily and that we have the courage and the will and the unity to defend ourselves if attacked, our Nation will stay at peace, and that's the only way we can realize all the other aspirations which are so dear to our people. This is a position that the Democratic Party has maintained, and that inherited tradition is extremely important to me and to you.

The true strength of the party over the years has been its unequaled capacity to lead this Nation in times of change. As President Kennedy said—I used this same quote in Boston, Saturday—"Change is the law of life and those who look on it to the past or the present are certain to miss the future." These past 3 years, without timidity, we have plunged head on into the future with courage, with conviction, with confidence.

And today we're engaged, as you know, in a massive, unprecedented enterprise to free our Nation from a very dangerous overdependence on foreign oil. It's the most ambitious peacetime undertaking in our history, as ambitious as the Marshall plan and the space program combined, bigger than the Interstate Highway System, by far.

We'll overcome these and all the other challenges—which I don't have time to mention—but there's no shortcut. It's going to take hard work. It's going to take dedication. It's going to take unity. It's going to take perseverance, and above all,

it's going to require us to tell the American people the truth, never to mislead them, never to raise a false hope, never to lie.

We will continue to meet our Nation's needs in education, in health, in housing, better cities, transportation, agriculture, with efficiency and with carefully managed programs, not with wasteful bureaucracy, not with gimmicks.

We'll look forward in the Democratic Party, not backward. And we'll talk sense to the American people, because I believe they're prepared for it, they demand it. And it makes it doubly sure that Fritz Mondale and Jimmy Carter and all those who work with us will minimize our mistakes if, in the decisionmaking process, the American people, through full knowledge and open debate, have a voice in arriving at those conclusions. I trust the wisdom of the American people just as much as I trust their innate unselfishness and their innate patriotism, in the finest sense of those words.

We are now coming to grips with a 10-year burden of excessive inflation on the American people—fundamental challenge of our time. Recently, we moved boldly down a new road, which I believe will bring rich dividends, and that is to recruit to our side labor and business in a national accord.

In the past the Government has imposed upon the free enterprise system of our country, on the labor unions, business, and others, a mandate. It may have been a good mandate, you may have been able to defend it logically, but now we're working in harmony. We're developing our plans and the way to implement those plans jointly. Labor has a full voice; business has a full voice; the Government has a full voice. We're working to cure inflation as partners, for a change. There is no working man or woman in this country that can find fault with our administration's policy on labor.

We're backing up this accord and what I've just said by demonstrating needed Government fiscal restraint. This is not a time to waste money; it's not a time to create excessive and unneeded bureaucracies. This is not just an ideology, but it's a simple necessity of our time.

In 1976 when I ran for President, we had a budget deficit of $66 billion. I've just gotten the figures on this past year—$26½ billion.

And the last thing I want to say is this: As you may have surmised, I have confidence in America. We can meet the challenges, we can solve the problems, we can answer the question if we are united with a common purpose.

Mine is a complicated and a difficult job, but I enjoy serving in the highest and greatest elective office in the world. And I deeply appreciate the support that you've given me in the past and which you've come tonight to pledge to me in the future. The Presidency can sometimes be a lonely job, but here tonight you've helped to make it a lot less lonely.

As you well know from my fairly brief but, so far, fairly successful political career, I have never feared a political fight, and I can say truthfully to you that I look forward to 1980 with anticipation and confidence. And as I said many times in 1976, when not nearly so many people listened, if I can keep my Mama's permission—[laughter]—I do not intend to lose.

Like all the rest of you in this room, I believe in a strong nation and a good nation, where every person has a better opportunity in life. I believe in a world where people can live with one another in peace and not war. These are not just dreams, but they are permanent agenda for all of us in the Democratic Party. And tonight, here among my friends, I would like to pledge to you as President, the leader of this Nation, and as the leader of our party that with your help, I will meet that responsibility, my responsibility, to bring this Democratic agenda to completion.

I'm determined to make even greater the greatest nation on Earth.

Thank you very much.

NOTE: The President spoke at 10:15 p.m. in the Yorktown Room at the Hyatt Regency Hotel.

Prior to his remarks, the President attended a reception for Friends of Carter/Mondale in the East Room at the White House.

New Brunswick, New Jersey
Remarks at a Meeting on Energy Conservation. October 25, 1979

When they told me that Congressman Eddie Patten was going to make a speech just 1 minute long, I decided to come and hear it. [*Laughter*] And I was not disappointed. I can't believe it. I'm sure he's going to finish his speech after I'm gone. [*Laughter*]

I know all of you weren't here when I arrived at the airport and came down through this beautiful community, and I wish you could have seen the tremendous, friendly reception that I got.

I remember the turning point in Brendan Byrne's campaign. He told me when they waved at him with all five fingers he knew he had it made. [*Laughter*] That's an actual quote from Brendan. [*Laughter*] I think he used it all over New Jersey, and I can't think of a more vivid description of a turning point in a political campaign than that one.

I'm here to talk to you about a very serious matter. And you have distinguished leaders on the platform with me who are an integral part of the process of protecting the interests of our people individually and collectively and also repairing a very serious threat to the very security of our country.

We import now about half of all the oil we use—8½ million barrels a day; next year, $70 billion worth. And along with oil we import inflation and unemployment. Our inflation rate right now would be 4 percentage points lower if you didn't have to count energy. And if you just take that one factor out—energy—the inflation rate in '79 would be no higher than it was in '78, no higher than it was in '77. You see what a tremendous impact this has had on our country, and it's getting worse, not better, provided we don't act.

The best way to cut imports is not to drill for more oil or to burn more coal or even to use more advanced synthetic fuels. The best way to cut our imports is to save, to stop wasting, to conserve energy. And that's why we're here this afternoon—to talk about a special way to save energy.

There are many ways. And I hope that every family represented here, before you go to bed tonight, will get your family together, from little children 5 years old all the way up to grandparents or even great-grandparents and say, "How can we in our own lives and using our own influence in our homes, to and from jobs, on the job, cut down on the waste of energy, save energy?"

Our country's doing a fairly good job so far. We've got a long way to go. Half the oil that we use in this country is not only imported, but half of it is used in transportation. And obviously the biggest potential saving in oil is in transportation.

I got word, after I took off in Air Force One, today that the Senate Finance Committee has passed the windfall profits tax—much lower tax on the unearned profits of the oil companies than I had wanted or anticipated. And I hope that with Bill Bradley's good work and others—Pete Williams—that on the floor of the Senate we can restore to the American people what has been lost so far in the Senate Finance Committee in taxing these profits which the oil companies have not earned.

These taxes will be used for several reasons: One is to help the poor families of our Nation pay the rapidly increasing cost of energy. Another one is to improve the quality of transportation, public transportation. And over the next 10 years, we've set aside $3½ billion for research and development to make sure that we have more efficient transportation vehicles. We can save about 75,000 barrels a day for every mile per gallon that we cut off the gas-burning automobiles. There's a tremendous savings there.

But I want to talk this afternoon, just for a few minutes, about ridesharing—ridesharing. It's not anything complicated; it's carpools, vanpools, subscription buses, public transit, and so forth. This saves fuel. It preserves our environment. It maintains personal mobility, and it helps the income and the standard of living of families simply because they stop wasting the money that they earn.

Over 50 million Americans every day commute to and from work in an automobile by themselves—one passenger. And if you doubt what I say, the next time you take a trip—I'm sure your car will be full—[*laughter*]—just look at the cars you meet. This is a tremendous waste, 150 million unoccupied spaces for American riders every day—we've only got 220 million people in our country—and that's just the cars going to and from work.

These spaces, if filled, would be just as valuable as drilling a new well to find more oil. So far, about 20 percent of all the commuters share a ride or ride on public transportation, about 20 percent.

If we could just change that 1 percent—and I have no doubt that we can, with the help of people like Brendan Byrne and Tom Bradley—1. percent change in that percentage would save about 175 million gallons of gas per year—175 million. And that would take care of all the transportation in automobiles of New Jersey for 18 days.

And as you can well figure out, if one car is filled and the ride costs are shared, then a person can travel a whole week and tap the family budget for the same thing that it costs per day if one travels alone.

You've already begun some initiatives in New Jersey that are important. Governor Byrne has spoken out forcefully for vanpooling and carsharing. Local governments have already taken action. And Prudential Insurance Company, for instance, has one of the best carsharing programs in the whole Nation. Twenty-three hundred people commute to work each day in 208 vans, under the aegis of Prudential Insurance Company, in the Newark area. Johnson and Johnson has helped, AT&T has helped, Nabisco has helped, Allied Chemical has helped, and others.

This is a difficult thing to do without some high degree of coordination and help from local governments, from the State and the Federal Governments. In the past, we've really had more obstacles to ridesharing than we've had assistance or help for ridesharing programs. And I have started an initiative, encouraged by people like Brendan Byrne and Tom Bradley, to do more at the Federal level. We hope that if we can be successful, we can save as much as half a million barrels of oil per day before this next decade is over.

We'll extend the 10-percent tax investment credit to vanpools. We'll guarantee to multiple-rider vehicles that gasoline will be available if there should be shortages in the future. There will be a high priority allocation of gasoline to vehicles that have multiple riders. We'll issue an Executive order upgrading the ridesharing efforts for Federal employees.

We're already taking some very controversial steps by charging some Federal employees for parking privileges. In the past they've got free parking privileges in Washington. Space is at a premium, and this encourages, as you can well see, one passenger per car.

In our Department of Transportation, we're trying to move toward special highway lanes for commuter passengers and for public transit vehicles, and this would amount to about $250 million a year in extra help for these kinds of construction projects in this next decade. And we also anticipate granting interest-free loans for the purchase of vans.

One problem has been that the insurance companies need to reassess automobile insurance charges to make it attractive for a person to have a van or a station wagon or others that are shared by other employees going to and from work. And we'll seek model State laws, because it's very difficult to have adequate vanpooling projects if a city is near a State line, unless there is some standardization of State laws themselves.

We've also organized a National Task Force on Ridesharing, and we have, luckily, the national chairman here with us this afternoon, whom I'll introduce in just a minute. We've got an outstanding young former mayor, Neil Goldschmidt, who is now the Secretary of Transportation. I think in the city of Portland, which he served before he came into my Cabinet recently, has one of the finest energy conservation programs of which I have ever heard. And he will be working intimately with any local official group or private employer group that needs help in evolving and implementing and continuing a good rideshare program.

It's now my pleasure—I want to take two pleasures. One is to thank you for coming and for letting me be a part of this program, although I am passing through your meeting very briefly. The reception that I've received is exhilarating and very gratifying to me. We've got a great and wonderful country that's facing a difficult challenge. And I think that anyone in the Congress or perhaps any of you who try to deal with the problem of evolving a comprehensive energy program, knows that it's been a very slow, tedious, and difficult thing. There have been no accolades coming forth for those who took the initiative. There have been no votes gained. It's been a losing proposition all around politically, but it's the right thing to do.

It requires a great deal of initiative. It requires a great deal of courage. It requires a deal more unity than we've had so far among the people of our Nation. And it requires all of you who are in positions of leadership to make sure that this issue is kept in the forefront, because I tell you, from the bottom of my heart as President, that our Nation's very security is at stake.

You saw what happened this past summer with very slight reductions in oil imports—the near panic that developed around Los Angeles, where Tom Bradley is the mayor, and in some places on the east coast because there was a slight shortage of gasoline. Think what would happen—and God forbid its happening—if we had a total embargo, as heavily dependent as we are on foreign oil. It would be a devastating blow to our country. We have got to have more energy produced in our own country. We've got to have a great saving in the energy that we consume and, therefore, to reduce imports.

Every effort helps, and the effort that we are launching on a nationwide basis

this afternoon, in this courthouse in Middlesex County, in New Brunswick, can have a great beneficial effect in the future—500,000 barrels in saving per day for our Nation if this seed that we plant among you takes root and sprouts and grows. And what you do here and throughout New Jersey can be an inspiration to the rest of the country. I call on you to join in enthusiastically. We'll provide the seed money to help Brendan Byrne and local officials make this a possibility.

I thank you for coming, but I particularly want to express my thanks to Tom Bradley, the great mayor of Los Angeles, whose leadership has really been an inspiration to every other public official in this country, including the President.

Tom Bradley has volunteered to be the national chairman of the ridesharing program, because he sees the potential that can be realized. He sees the difficulty of a sustained effort, but he's the kind of leader, I'm sure, that can bring this effort to fruition and help our Nation in the process and at the same time help every American who participates.

Now I'd like to introduce my friend, Tom Bradley. Tom.

NOTE: The President spoke at 3:25 p.m. in the Jury Assembly Room at the Middlesex County Courthouse Center.

National Task Force on Ridesharing

Appointment of the Membership.
October 25, 1979

The President today announced the persons whom he will appoint as members of the National Task Force on Ridesharing. They are:

MAYOR TOM BRADLEY, Los Angeles, Calif. (Chair);

T. F. BRADSHAW, president, Atlantic Richfield Co., Los Angeles;

THOMAS W. BRADSHAW, JR., secretary of the North Carolina Department of Transportation;

ROY COUGHLIN, staff specialist, Southern New England Telephone Co., Hartford, Conn.;

JACK DERBY, statewide ridesharing coordinator, California Department of Transportation;

RICHARD H. ERICKSON, manager of safety, health, and security, Hallmark Cards, Kansas City, Mo.;

GOV. ELLA GRASSO, Connecticut;

RAY HERZOG, chairman of the board, 3M Company, St. Paul, Minn.;

DALE W. LUEHRING, general manager, Golden Gate Bridge and Transit District, San Rafael, Calif.;

JOHN A. MAHONY, manager, office services, Smith Kline Corp., Philadelphia, Pa.;

LOUIS R. NICKINELLO, State senator, Boston, Mass.;

CLARENCE SHALLBETTER, project director, Public Service Options, Inc., Minneapolis, Minn.;

DAVID J. SHERWOOD, president, Prudential Insurance Company, Newark, N.J.;

RICHARD SOMERVILLE, transportation program coordinator, Texas Medical Center, Houston, Tex.;

STAN STOKEY, Tennessee Valley Authority;

JEANNETTE WILLIAMS, city council member, Seattle, Wash.

Hungarian Americans

Statement by the President.
October 25, 1979

I want to take the opportunity of this visit to New Brunswick to salute our many citizens of Hungarian heritage. While retaining strong attachments to their 1,000-year-old homeland, Hungarian Americans have made outstanding contributions to the welfare and the cultural richness of our Nation.

Early this year we commemorated the bicentennial of the death of Col. Michael Kovats de Fabricy, a hero of our Revolutionary War who died while defending Charleston, South Carolina, from occupation by British forces. Colonel de Fabricy's heroism symbolized the centuries-old devotion of Hungarians to freedom and liberty. Many of us recall vividly the tragic events of 1956 and the spirit that inspired them 23 years ago this week.

Although we continue to have disagreements with the present Hungarian Government over many questions of political freedom and basic human and social values, our relations have improved substantially. One important move in this improvement was the return of the Crown of Saint Stephen to the Hungarian people in January 1978. As a result, the thousand-year-old crown is back in its ancestral homeland, on dignified public display where it can be seen by Hungarians and persons of Hungarian descent from around the world.

East Rutherford, New Jersey

Remarks at a Fundraising Dinner for Democratic State Legislative Candidates. October 25, 1979

Governor Byrne, Chairman Coffee, distinguished leaders of the State legislature, distinguished Members of your fine congressional delegation, Democrats, and my friends:

It's always a pleasure for me to come back to New Jersey. I like a State like yours: two Democratic Senators, a strong Democratic congressional delegation, a Democratic House, a Democratic Senate, a Democratic Governor, a Democratic President—and you know the proper role for the Republicans to play—that is a minority role. [*Laughter*] You've got to keep them that way.

And that's not the only reason I'm glad to come back to New Jersey. Somebody told me that Brendan Byrne was passing through this country, and I wanted to be here to meet him—[*laughter*]—because he's one of the strongest, best leaders I know.

I'd like to remind you of something tonight. I had a prepared speech, but I don't want to make it, because you need to be reminded of a fact. When I first began moving around this country in my campaign for President, I came to New Jersey. I was a lonely candidate; nobody cared about me; nobody thought I had a chance. I traveled in a car with one driver, and I had a chance to learn a lot about this Nation.

At that time—and you think back—New Jersey was a drastically different State. There was a great deal of discouragement in your State. There was a very high unemployment rate. There was very little confidence in government at any level. There was not a spirit of anticipation about the future.

Now it is absolutely different. I have never seen such a startling transition in the tone and quality and the vitality of a State anywhere in this Nation. And I think you all know why—it's because you have a great Democratic Governor in Brendan Byrne, and you have a great Democratic legislature that has backed him to the hilt and taken some very courageous stands.

It has not been easy for him or for the courageous Democratic leaders in the legislature. I came here fairly early in 1977, when Brendan Byrne was running for reelection. Everybody was calling him "One-Term Byrne"—you remember that. But as the people went through that campaign and assessed what had been done and the difficulty and the political conse-quences of some of his courageous stands, you made the right judgment.

I believe in this country—we have the greatest nation on Earth. And I believe in the Democratic Party, and I'd like to tell you, in a few minutes, why.

The Democratic Party is a party of compassion. We care about people. We don't believe in keeping someone down. We don't believe in giving him a constant hand of help. We believe in helping them to stand on their own feet, to meet their own needs, to live their own life, and to live a life of dignity.

The Democratic Party believes in hard work. I grew up on a farm. I know what it means to work from before sunup till after sundown, day after day, to make a crop during the depression years. And I believe that every American ought to have a right to a job, and the Democratic Party has this commitment, and always has.

You remember the mess that Franklin Roosevelt inherited in the early thirties. He put America back to work. Since I've been in office, in the last 3—almost 3 years, we have added a net increase of 8½ million new jobs in this country, because we believe in work.

It's good for our country to have its people at work, that's true. But it's particularly important to a person, a human being, to be able to do something useful with a precious life, to take whatever talent or ability God might have given that person and use it with pride and with self-confidence and a realization that you're making a contribution to your own family, to your community, and to your Nation.

The Democrats believe in work and the right of Americans to have jobs. The Democrats are concerned about the older people. We believe that they ought to live in dignity and have security in their lives, and that's what we've had to accomplish in this last 3 years.

When I was campaigning around this country, a constant question was: "What are you going to do about social security? It's on the verge of bankruptcy." It was. It's now been put into a secure status.

The Democrats believe in a strong nation, a strong defense. We believe that our Nation ought to be at peace. I'm the first President in 40 years who hasn't had a single American killed in combat overseas. I want to keep that record intact.

The reason for it is that our country has been strong, and our country must be strong to stay at peace. If we ever get weak in military strength or in the will or resolve or unity that comprises a nation's strength, that's when we'll be vulnerable to an attack by a potential adversary, and that's when our young people will be losing their lives in war. We must stay strong, and I believe in a strong defense, and the Democratic Party does. And we're going to keep it that way.

Another thing the Democratic Party believes in is harmony. Think back in the history of our country. This is a nation and you are a State of immigrants—you might even use the word "refugees." One of the great potential strengths of our country has always been that different people from all over the world come here with their own pride in their heritage, their own pride in their habits and beliefs, and still preserve those precious things in our lives, but still blend together without losing their individuality to become a strong, united nation. And the Democratic Party has always opened its arms to everyone who comes here.

The first few days or the first few weeks or the first few years a person is in this country, which party has always said, "Come and be a part of a political system of a great nation. Come and realize your right to choose your own leaders, to shape your own government, to preserve your own freedom, and to determine your own destiny?" The Democratic Party has.

And the last thing I'd like to mention is this: The Democratic Party does not believe in waste. We believe not only in a compassionate government and a confident government, we also believe in a competent government.

Now, you can have better services delivered to people not when you establish massive spending programs that are not well run and not sensitive to the needs of the people they're serving, but wasteful. And one of the things about Democrats is that we have the kind of relationship with those who need the services of government, so we understand how well those services are being provided.

In the Republican Party there's a tremendous chasm that exists between Washington on the one hand and the people who need help on the other: a local government, a county, a city, a housing project, a family, an unemployed person. There's a big chasm if a callous party supported by big shots is in office. But the Democrats have always felt a relationship, and they've been able to consult and communicate and assess what government is doing to make sure that it is efficient and effective. We do not waste money.

Next year our country will have the benefits of $40 billion in reduced taxes. At this moment, we have fewer Federal employees than we had when I became President. At the end of the next year, we'll have 20,000 fewer Federal employees than when I became President. We've had a tremendous improvement in housing, in education, in transportation, in every element of American life.

We've tried to cut down the Federal deficit. When I was running here in 1976, the deficit was $66 billion. I just got the report for this past year, that was completed the end of September—we've cut it from a $66 billion down to a $27 billion deficit already, and we're still on our way to making sure that in the future we have a balanced budget for our Federal Government. That's not a callous thing, that's a good thing for all Americans.

The last thing that I'd like to say to you is this: We need a nation with confidence in one another, confidence in our neighbors, confidence in our institutions, our churches, our schools, confidence in our Government.

A government leader can't always do what you like, but you have got to have confidence in the system of government in this country. And I know that we've had a lot of things happen to us during the 8 years before I became President that shook the confidence of America in our own government, things of which we were ashamed, unprecedented failures in government. Those times are gone.

We've still got problems. We've still got challenges. We've still got questions to be answered, but we can solve problems together. We can overcome obstacles and challenges together. We can answer difficult questions together, but there's got to be a sense of participation.

And I hope that every one of you tonight who have contributed your money—I hope you'll contribute more in the future—will also contribute your time in this next 12 days, because it would be a devastating blow to New Jersey if, through overconfidence or lack of concern about your own lives and your own government and your own State, you didn't participate to the fullest degree in making sure that Brendan Byrne still has for the next 2 years a strong Democratic General Assembly in New Jersey to back him, to make a great State even greater in the future.

I'm proud of New Jersey, because you're my State, too. I'm proud of this country. I'm proud of the Democratic Party. But working together with unity, we can make everything of which we're proud even better. You're my partners; I'm proud of you.

God bless every one of you.

NOTE: The President spoke at 6:47 p.m. in the East Room at the Stadium Club, Giants Stadium. In his opening remarks, he referred to Richard Coffee, chairman of the New Jersey State Democratic Party.

Prior to his remarks, the President attended a private reception for New Jersey State legislative candidates in the Pegasus Room at the Stadium Club.

East Rutherford, New Jersey

Interview With Dick Leone of WNET–TV. October 25, 1979

MR. LEONE. Good evening, I'm Dick Leone.

We want to welcome President Carter to New Jersey. In a little while he will speak at a fundraising dinner here at the Meadowlands Sports Complex.

HOUSING FINANCING AND CONSTRUCTION

President Carter, earlier this week a couple of friends of mine, actually a young couple, told me that after months of looking for a new house, they had to give up the search, because there's no mortgage money. And in talking to bankers in the area, I find that's generally true, with the high interest rates. What kind of hope can you hold out to people like that?

THE PRESIDENT. Well, of course, the best hope is that we'll get the inflation rate coming down, which I think will happen before the end of this year, and therefore, interest rates can go down.

We've had good luck throughout the country, Dick, and we are now making an assessment among the different communities around the Nation to see where mortgage money is short.

Up through the end of September, we had not experienced at all a reduction in new home starts, because the figures then were 1.9 million homes per year were still being built at an annual rate. We've sustained, in spite of high interest rates, so far, almost 2 million homes being built in our country per year, which is near the alltime record, and we've been very proud of this.

But Bill Miller, who's the Secretary of the Treasury, is now making a survey throughout the Nation to see where mortgage money might be scarce, and the Home Loan Bank Board is very concerned about the possible consequences of this.

So far, we've been able to reduce the unemployment rate among construction workers by more than 40 percent since I've been in office by focusing the attention of the Government to work with private sector interests to keep the construction business going well. We are concerned about this, but so far we've held up pretty well.

INFLATION AND ENERGY

MR. LEONE. I guess the more general economic question is, has the Fed gone too far in recent days in raising reserve requirements and forcing interest rates up to historically unprecedented highs?

THE PRESIDENT. That's always a question. I think the number one threat to our country, economically speaking, though is inflation. We've tried to approach it at a multiple level, that is, different ways at the same time.

As you well know, I don't have any control over the Fed, none at all. It's carefully isolated from any influence by the President or the Congress. This has been done for many generations, and I think it's a wise thing to do.

We've tried to hold down Government spending. We've cut the budget deficit considerably since I've been in office. We just got the figures for last year, for instance, and the deficit has been dropped down to $27 billion. It was $66 billion when I was running for President in 1976.

We've tried to approach the key cause of inflation after many years of delay, that is, the unnecessary and excessive importing of foreign oil. Energy is the main driving force in the high inflation rate now. As a matter of fact, energy alone, not counting anything else, adds 4 percentage points to the inflation rate and, therefore, indirectly, 4 percentage points onto the interest rates. As a matter of fact, if it were not for energy, which has been jacked up in price by OPEC because we import so much oil, our inflation rate this summer would be the same as it was in 1978, same as it was in 1977.

The Congress is approaching the end of their consideration of a package of legislation that, I believe, will be successful in the long run in cutting down our excessive oil imports. Next year we'll spend $70 billion on foreign oil. And we not only import a lot of foreign oil, but we also import inflation, which I've already mentioned, and also unemployment.

This is a long-overdue thing. It's been one of the most difficult political battles I've ever been in. But if the American people will conserve, save all they can, and we can shift toward supplies of oil and natural gas and coal that we already know about in our own country, and develop new sources of energy, like solar energy, for instance, I think in the future we'll see a much more stable economy and a much greater contribution to our Nation's security, because we won't be dependent on uncertain foreign sources of oil.

WINDFALL PROFITS TAX

MR. LEONE. In this part of the country, in the New Jersey, New York area, about 78 percent of all the energy is oil, and it's nearly all imported. So, I think people are aware of the pressures. On the other hand, while they recognize that OPEC is no friend of ours, they're more incensed than anything, I think, over the oil company profits which have, in the last week, been announced at over 100-percent increases for many of the largest companies. And I think they tend to say, "Why isn't the President doing something about those profits?"

THE PRESIDENT. Well, we've had a proposal to the Congress for more than $2\frac{1}{2}$ years, up in April of 1977, to put a tax on the oil companies, to take back part of the unearned profits that they've received, and turn that money over to the general public. We call it the windfall profits tax. And I believe that this year you'll see the Congress pass a windfall profits tax, if the people's voice can remain strong.

The House has already passed the windfall profits tax basically as we proposed it. The Senate Finance Committee has not passed an adequate windfall profits tax. It will now go to the Senate floor. I think it's accurate to say that Senator Pete Williams and Senator Bill Bradley from New Jersey are strongly in support of a good energy package, including the windfall profits tax.

When that is done, we'll cut down tremendously on the amount of profits that the oil companies will keep—roughly $270 billion over the next 10 years—and that money can be used to help poor people pay the increasing cost of energy in their own homes, to develop better forms of transportation, including public transportation, and develop synthetic fuels and other energy supplies in our own country. If that profits tax does not pass, then the oil companies would keep those profits.

I might point out that a lot of the profits that are shown by the oil companies is earned overseas. And if the Congress doesn't pass an adequate windfall profits tax, then we would have to take other steps to make sure that the oil companies don't profit off of the increased prices of energy.

But I think if we can get the windfall profits tax, we'll have a good, sound energy program. We'll leave the oil companies with enough money to explore for new supplies of oil and natural gas in our own Nation. And we'll have great benefits to the poor people, to those who want better transportation, and those who want to see our country using energy derived from the United States.

But the windfall profits tax is the key to it. And I can predict to you, I believe, on this program, that it will pass the Congress in a satisfactory fashion this year, because the American people have finally become aroused about it.

HOME HEATING OIL

MR. LEONE. Let me ask you about a related prediction. The price of home heating oil is almost a dollar a gallon now in this area. There's a lot of concern about whether it'll be available. New York and Connecticut have passed laws already to help the poor pay for it; it's under discussion in New Jersey. I know that when you were in New Hampshire recently, you made a pledge that there would be enough heating oil to get them through. Can we get a similar kind of commitment here in this part of the country?

THE PRESIDENT. Late in the spring, early in the summer—I've forgotten the exact date—I made two promises to the people of New England, in fact, the entire country.

At that time we had a very short supply of home heating oil. There was a great danger that we would have severe shortages this winter. I promised that we would have 240 million barrels of oil on hand during October. Last year the total that we used was about 233 million barrels; 240 is an adequate supply. We've reached that goal already.

The other thing that I promised was that we would do everything we could in the Government to help the poor families pay the increased cost of home heating oil. And we've asked the Congress this year for $1.6 billion to help those low-income families pay that extra cost and also to pledge the Congress, through legislation that would be permanent, that for the next 10 years we would have $2.4 billion per year to go to the families to help them pay the increased cost of home heating oil.

I believe that I can also predict to you that within the next few weeks, we will have the Congress finally pass the legislation that I put to them to provide this financial assistance for the low-income families.

POSSIBILITY OF RECESSION

MR. LEONE. Mr. President, turning to the economy again, I think one of the most frustrating things for your supporters is explaining to people that we might need a recession in order to deal with the inflation problem. It frightens people in terms of the budgets of a Newark or a New York City, and the normal Democratic constituency doesn't understand how we can get to a point where that becomes the only policy available to us. How do you answer that kind of criticism of where we are?

THE PRESIDENT. We're doing everything we can to avoid a recession, and so far we've been successful. I can't say that we won't have temporary recessionary figures coming in. But the last month, for instance, showed a 2.4-percent increase in our total Nation's productivity, our gross national product, and that's far from a recession. A recession is defined arbitrarily that you have zero growth for two succeeding 3-month periods.

In addition to that, we've had extraordinary good luck in keeping business profits up. Since I've been in office, they've gone up about 50 percent. We've added a net total increase of 8½ million jobs. We've cut the unemployment rate down by 25 percent nationwide, and in some industries, like the construction industry, we've cut the unemployment rate by 40 percent. These figures are accurate. We've got equivalent success in revitalizing the agricultural industry, the steel industry.

What we suffer from is a distortion in our economy, brought about by the fact that we import half our oil from overseas. And last month, for instance, the annual rate of increase of prices of energy was about 100 percent per year, and when you have to absorb that, because we have become too dependent on foreign oil, it's just going to take a while to get the economy straightened out again. But we're making good progress, and in the meantime we're holding up employment, growth, and the strength of our free enterprise system.

WAGE AND PRICE CONTROLS

MR. LEONE. I guess a number of people are beginning to talk about wage and price controls who didn't do so in the past, who basically agreed with you that they were a bad idea. I know that the standby authority to implement them has recently lapsed, and I wonder if you have any regrets that that instrument is not available if things get worse.

THE PRESIDENT. No, I don't have any regrets. The authority for the President to impose, without warning, wage and price controls did lapse. Nixon used it back, I think, in 1972, but I don't think that having mandatory price controls is feasible or advisable.

There is absolutely no way that the Congress would pass wage and price control authority. Just one Senator could filibuster that and prevent its being passed in the Senate, and there's an overwhelming feeling in the Congress that the mandatory price and wage controls would not work.

If the Congress started working on this, trying to pass it, then just knowing that the wage and price controls might come in a few months, in the future, would cause an extraordinary increase in the prices charged to people. I think it would make our inflation rate much greater.

I really believe that the best way to control inflation is to get at the roots of the problem: to control the Federal deficit, to have an efficient government, to cut down on our overdependence on foreign oil, to keep the supply of basic products stable, not to let our basic industries, like steel, for instance, go under, which it was threatened with for a while, and to make Americans more self-sufficient, and to generate more confidence in government. We've done all these things with fairly good success.

The inflation pressures are not only on our Nation, but they're all over the world. For instance, in Israel the inflation rate, I think, is over a hundred percent. And in Europe, where the countries have been deathly afraid of any inflation—and they have always accepted much higher unemployment, instead of inflation—now they're facing the same degree of inflation that we are.

So, I believe that we've got it under fairly good shape, if the people will be patient, not lose their confidence, work together, and help us address these basic questions.

Another thing that I didn't mention a few minutes ago is to increase American exports overseas. This helps to hold down inflation in our own country. And of course, we need to keep the dollar value stable—and the dollar values are stable. As a matter of fact, even a month ago, when the dollar seemed to be somewhat lower than the average, it had actually increased in value by 8 percent, compared to a year ago, among the things that the OPEC nations have to buy. These are very complicated matters, and it requires patience.

And I would say the crux of the whole issue of controlling inflation and keeping a strong economy is to have an adequate national energy policy, which we have never had. None of my predecessors in the White House proposed, effectively, a national energy policy. After I've gotten into it, I've seen why they postponed it until the next President each time. It's a difficult issue.

But I think I can predict, again—this is my third prediction—that before the Congress goes home this year, we will have the total package of establishing in legislation, in law permanently, a national energy policy that will help address our problems.

ENERGY CONSERVATION

MR. LEONE. I sometimes get the feeling that a successful energy policy or anti-inflationary policy requires a lot of cooperation from the American people.

THE PRESIDENT. Yes, it does.

MR. LEONE. And I think about the fact, from everything one knows of you, you are a very disciplined man. I believe if you weren't President, you would drive 55 miles an hour and turn the lights off and try very hard.

THE PRESIDENT. Yes, I would.

MR. LEONE. Do you have any sense of frustration that you don't get that kind of response from the man in the street, that he just wants to know that there's gasoline down at the corner pump?

THE PRESIDENT. I did much more 2½ years or 2 years ago or 1 year ago or 6 months ago than I do now. I think there's a growing awareness, very rapidly coming on us, among the American people that we do indeed have an energy problem and that every American needs to do something about it.

The thing that impresses me most strongly is that the conservation of energy, the saving of energy, the stopping of the waste of energy need not be an unpleasant thing; it need not be a sacrifice; it need not be something that disrupts America. It can be an exciting, positive, pleasant thing.

It's not necessary for us to drive around in automobiles that weigh 5,000 pounds, one person in an automobile, going 75 miles an hour. It's not necessary to have a house in the wintertime that's up to 80 degrees temperature or one chilled down to 55 or 60 degrees in the summer, where you have to wear a sweater.

You know, these kinds of things can give us a better life. And I think that I can say accurately that as we move toward more conservation, increased use of solar power, and the development of American energy resources, we will not have a lower quality of life. We can have an even better quality of life, safer and more enjoyable, and with the sense that

we've done something not only for ourselves and our family but also for our Nation. It will be a patriotic thing.

PRESIDENT'S POPULARITY

MR. LEONE. Let me ask a more political question. You said about a year ago, I think, in an interview with Bill Moyers, that today the President is sort of a personification of problems. And I have a sense that you believe that's one of the difficulties with, one of the explanations behind your standing in the polls or the fact that people here in Jersey and elsewhere say Senator Kennedy's ahead right now, whatever it means at this stage. Do you think that's something you can overcome, yourself, in the coming months?

THE PRESIDENT. Yes, I think so.

When I made a speech in April of 1977 about energy, for instance, one of the lines that I put in the text to the American people was that just addressing this politically sensitive issue of a better energy policy would cost me 15 percentage points in the polls. The only mistake I made was that I underestimated how much popularity I would lose. There's no way to win when you address a difficult issue like SALT, Panama Canal treaties, energy, inflation, and so forth. There's no way to win. And I think that the best assurance that I have is the sound judgment and the fairness of the American people.

One of the great things about a political campaign is that it provides a forum for incumbents like me—as it did for Brendan Byrne when he ran for Governor this last time—to actually and accurately explain to the people who are going to vote what we have been doing, why we have taken these steps, why we have taken unpopular stands.

You know, it's easy for someone to get in office and not do anything because you're afraid that you might go down in the popularity polls or because some special interest group may not like it. But I don't believe that we have ever avoided a difficult issue that we thought was best for our country, just to keep our popularity up or the polls high or to get votes.

And this series of very difficult issues— which we have addressed, I think, very well—when they're inventoried by the American people, I think, will repair a lot of the damage that has been caused to me and other incumbents. I think a perfect example is the one I used—Brendan Byrne, when he ran for reelection.

PRESIDENT'S LEADERSHIP QUALITIES

MR. LEONE. You're in a place where Byrne was way behind here, Carey in New York, Grasso in Connecticut. You've come here for encouragement, I guess.

It seems to me that the likelihood of potential Democratic challengers differing widely with you on important issues is not great. By and large they seem to be saying, "We basically agree. Jimmy Carter is well intentioned, we have not great policy differences, but he's not a strong leader." And the issue on which the campaigns seem likely to be joined, perhaps the only important one, is the question of leadership: "He hasn't been effective in moving Congress or moving the American people."

And I think you're going to have to answer the question in the course of this campaign, and I'd like you to let your imagination roam a little bit.

THE PRESIDENT. I don't have to imagine. Any objective analysis of my administration and its success with the Congress would stack up very well with any previous administration in this century, and that would include the best days of Lyndon Johnson's relationship with the

Congress immediately after the death of Jack Kennedy.

The difficulty of the legislation that I have put to the Congress, I think, is unequaled any time in my lifetime, but the percentage of the legislation that the Congress and I have have passed together is as high as it has ever been. And I believe that's one of the issues that will be assessed.

Another one is what we've achieved. You know, I don't particularly want to sit here and brag, but I'm the first President in 40 years who has served without there being a single American killed in combat. We've kept our country at peace. We've also strengthened NATO and all our alliances overseas. We're now very rapidly restoring the quality of our own forces, keeping a strong defense.

I've moved into areas that have been avoided for a long time in the past. I'm not criticizing my predecessors. But the Egyptians and the Israelis have been at war for 30 years. They've been filled with hatred for centuries. And to see now Sadat and Begin sitting down, working out a peace agreement between them, because of action that we took in this country, is gratifying, indeed.

We've raised the banner of human rights around the world to make our country proud once again. We've opened up the continent of Africa to good relations, sound relations, based on basic human rights, majority rule, democracy, freedom, equality. We've also opened up, for the first time, a good relationship with one-fourth of the total population on Earth, in China, and at the same time we've not damaged our relationships with the people who live on Taiwan.

We've passed the Panama Canal treaties, which were condemned at first, but in the long run, I think, the American people will see this is one of the greatest things that's ever happened to benefit our own country.

None of these issues were considered to be easy, and many of them were not politically attractive. And I could go down the list a lot longer, if we had a longer program. But I think those are the kinds of things that exhibit leadership, and I am perfectly willing to stand on my record. I look forward to 1980 with a great deal of anticipation and also confidence.

SUCCESS OF PRESIDENT'S PROPOSALS

MR. LEONE. I might ask—I think this is bound to come up in the campaign— what are the things you feel didn't go well—the income tax reform or welfare reform? How do you deal with those things that were a big part of the campaign in '76 and we don't have them today?

THE PRESIDENT. Well, if there's one characteristic I have, it's tenacity. You know, I don't give up, in spite of discouragement.

Last year, for instance, after a year and a half of tough debate, we only got about 65 percent of what we asked for in the energy package. We've come back this year, hopefully to get the other 30 or 35 percent. Last year we didn't get a word of oil. This year we're addressing the oil issue. We haven't gotten welfare reform yet. I think that we will get it. I can't say that it'll be exactly as we originally proposed, but I think that we'll get welfare reform.

Our major agenda items have pretty well been passed by the Congress. There's one on which we have failed, and that is tax reform. We need basic tax reform in this country, but the powerful special interest groups are so influential on Capitol Hill in Washington that it is almost impossible to have basic and good tax re-

form. And until the American people get aroused enough to let their individual Members of Congress in the House and Senate know that they demand equity and fairness, then the big shots in this country are going to continue to use their influence effectively and block basic tax reform.

With that one exception, however, I think we've had very good luck in the Congress, and the American people will benefit now and in the long run because of it.

PRESIDENT'S POLITICAL PHILOSOPHY

MR. LEONE. Let me ask you—neither you nor Senator Kennedy is an announced candidate yet, although both of you are around the country a lot talking like candidates these days. Politicians here in New Jersey and in this region say it'll be very tough for Carter to beat Kennedy; Kennedy has a mystique; there's a legend about it.

I was interested to see at the dedication of the Kennedy Library in Boston last week, you said that you felt in some ways you were closer to John F. Kennedy than Senator Ted Kennedy is. And I wonder if you could elaborate on that.

THE PRESIDENT. Well, philosophically, I think so. I don't believe that the Federal Government ought to do everything. I don't believe in establishing a whole big array of massive Federal Government spending programs to take care of the needs of our country. I believe in tight management; I believe in making the existing programs efficient. I believe in saving money; I believe in trying to have fiscal responsibility in managing the budget; and another, I believe that John Kennedy would have agreed with all those things.

In addition, I believe in a strong defense. I think the Nation can only be at peace if we are strong, that the best single way to get our Nation back into war, with massive loss of life of our own young people, is if any potential adversary ever thinks our country is weak. I believe in a strong defense.

I'm not criticizing Senator Kennedy, but I think those are going to be two of the issues. There are some others, too. In general, there's no basic, deep, philosophical difference between me and him. His voting record on issues that we've put forward and where I've taken a public stand is very good.

And you talk about the outcome of the election. We had our first skirmish in Florida. We were predicted to suffer a massive and very embarrassing defeat. We got about a 2-to-1 victory there, and I think that's a fairly good indication of the kind of response we'll get. I'm not predicting that we'll win everywhere, but I've never backed down. And when and if I get in the race, I'll be there to stay, and as I said before, I feel very confident.

NATIONAL MORALE

MR. LEONE. Let me ask you one final question. In August you made a stirring speech about energy and talked about the American people suffering from a malaise and being unresponsive. I wonder what your own assessment is of the response over the last couple of months.

THE PRESIDENT. I think the response has been good. Among the people who've worked in the White House for 25 or 30 years, the professionals who stay there as Presidents change, that speech, which I think was July 15, got the most response of anything that a President has ever done, and the response was overwhelmingly positive. People said, "You're right. We do have a long way to go in this country to have basic confidence in each other,

in our Nation, respect for our government. What can I do to help?"

I think one thing that has caused people to take some positive action to help has been, for instance, the gasoline lines. It kind of shocked people to say, "You know, we do have a problem. What are we going to do about it?" And now there is a growing interest in it. The Congress positive action this year, which I predicted, I think will have a reassuring effect. And of course, the election, with the open debates, getting the American people deeply involved and much better educated on what has been going on in our country and what's got to be done in the future, all are good factors to bring about a restoration of confidence in our country.

We've got the greatest nation on Earth. I just want to make sure we keep it that way.

MR. LEONE. Well, Mr. President, it's nice having you here in New Jersey and talking to you about these problems that are of great concern to us. I want to thank you.

And on behalf of Date Line, New Jersey, this is Dick Leone. Good evening.

NOTE: The interview began at approximately 5 p.m. at the Meadowlands Racetrack. It was videotaped for broadcast at 8:30 p.m. on October 26 on New Jersey public television.

The transcript of the interview was released on October 26.

Eradication of Smallpox
White House Statement. October 26, 1979

President Carter today welcomed the official eradication of smallpox throughout the world, announced by the World Health Organization (WHO) in Nairobi today.

Over more than a decade, the WHO brought together in a sustained battle against smallpox a group of experts, health workers, and political officials from countries throughout the many regions where the disease was endemic. The leader of that WHO effort was Dr. Donald A. Henderson, who was then an officer of the U.S. Public Health Service working with the WHO. Henderson and his successors at the Center for Disease Control were imaginative and dedicated American contributors to this worldwide success.

In addition to eradicating what was long one of the most dread diseases known to mankind, this global campaign has produced financial savings for the United States. We invested an estimated $27 million over the many years that some 300 persons from the Public Health Service filled assignments overseas related to smallpox control, and in direct financial assistance from AID and HEW. Now, routine smallpox vaccination is no longer necessary in this country, and there is no risk of smallpox to American travelers abroad. The $27 million investment is returned every 3 months in savings.

"I am proud of the results of the smallpox eradication program, and I cite this program as a giant step toward the goal of rational planning for good health throughout the world in the future," the President stated.

Meeting With Chancellor Bruno Kreisky of Austria

White House Statement.   October 26, 1979

President Carter met with Austrian Chancellor Bruno Kreisky in the Cabinet Room for an hour this morning. The two leaders exchanged views on a number of international issues, including East-West relations and the Middle East. The President reiterated the U.S. commitment to the Camp David process, which can bring a comprehensive peace settlement to the area. The conversations were constructive and friendly.

Other participants in this morning's meeting between the President and the Chancellor included:

U.S. Side

Secretary of State Cyrus Vance
Zbigniew Brzezinski, Assistant to the President for National Security Affairs
Milton Wolfe, U.S. Ambassador to Austria
James Rentschler, NSC staff member

Austrian Side

Georg Lannkh, Private Secretary to the Chancellor
Karl Schober, Austrian Ambassador to the United States
Guenter Birbaum, Minister-Counselor of the Austrian Embassy

Aid for Kampucheans

Remarks Following a Meeting With Senators Jim Sasser, Max Baucus, and John C. Danforth on Their Trip to Southeast Asia. October 26, 1979

My first comment to the press and to the American people is one of thanks and appreciation on behalf of all of our country to Senators Sasser, Baucus, and Danforth, who have just returned from a visit to Thailand and Kampuchea to represent our Nation in the analysis of what can be done to alleviate the tragedy that is taking place in that country.

It's been estimated that almost half the people of Kampuchea have lost their lives in the last few years. And at the present time, hundreds of thousands of people in that unfortunate country and some refugees that have crossed the Thai border are now at the point of death because of starvation.

Our country has been encouraging, through the United Nations and also through the International Red Cross, a means by which we could get food to those people, over the obstacles created by the Vietnamese and the Kampuchean authorities of all kinds. We have discussed this matter in the last few minutes. Senators Sasser and Baucus and Danforth have given me a report of what they observed there. They'll answer questions for you in a few minutes.

We are prepared as a nation—my own administration and the Congress—to proceed expeditiously in every possible way to alleviate the extant suffering. I will ask Dick Clark, former Senator now in charge of our refugee program, to represent me directly. The State Department and I will give him full authority and support throughout all the agencies of government to make his administration of relief to those people effective. As the Senators have just described to me, it's mandatory for effectiveness to deal with the starving people and deliver aid through the United Nations and also through the Red Cross, not on a unilateral basis.

We have had some discouraging word from the officials in Phnom Penh. We hope that this is a temporary circumstance and that because of world concern, that they would modify their positions and permit a land bridge to be formed so that food can be brought in through Thailand, over the border, to the people who are suffering so greatly, primarily by truck.

I might add one other thing, that I have agreed with the Senators that it would be important for them to talk directly to Secretary-General Waldheim of the United Nations, to give him a first-hand report and also to seek his continuing support for the effort that all of us are joining in helping.

I want to say that the Thai Government has performed nobly in preparing and permitting a haven for the starving Kampucheans and are cooperating in every possible way to get food to the refugees who now are living on the borderline of death in their own country.

I'd like to turn the podium over to Senator Sasser, who was the leader of this group, and let him make a report to you. And then he and Senators Baucus and Danforth will answer questions that you might have.

Thank you very much, Jim Sasser, for a very fine and——

SENATOR SASSER. Thank you, Mr. President.

THE PRESIDENT. ——a very fine and successful visit and also one that I think demonstrated a great degree of human courage.

NOTE: The President spoke at 2:27 p.m. to reporters assembled in the Briefing Room at the White House. Following his remarks, the Senators held a news conference on their trip.

St. Lawrence Seaway Navigation Clearance

Announcement of Extension of the Deadline. October 26, 1979

The White House announced today that the United States and Canadian Governments have agreed to extend the 1979 navigation clearance deadline in the St. Lawrence Seaway from midnight December 15 to midnight December 18. The 3-day extension of the shipping season is designed to help reduce the backlog of grain awaiting shipment from Great Lakes ports.

The backlog developed this harvest season due to a bumper wheat crop and unprecedented export demands, which severely strained the Nation's grain transportation system. Two months of labor strife at the Port of Duluth in Minnesota also disrupted grain shipments and slowed total grain exports by as much as 10 million bushels a week.

The White House expressed gratitude to the Canadian Government and stated:

"We expect the additional Seaway shipping time to help relieve the current backlog of grain in Great Lakes ports. We are hopeful that the weather will allow shippers to take full advantage of the additional time to move grain through the Seaway."

Department of Justice

Nomination of Alice Daniel To Be an Assistant Attorney General.   October 26, 1979

The President today announced that he will nominate Alice Daniel, of Washington, D.C., to be an Assistant Attorney General. She would replace Barbara A. Babcock, resigned, and her area of responsibility would be the Civil Division. Daniel has been General Counsel and Interim Director of the Legal Services Corporation in Washington since 1976.

She was born September 17, 1934, in New York City. She received a B.A. from Boston University in 1958 and an LL.B. from Columbia University School of Law in 1963.

Daniel was a teaching associate, then a research associate, at Columbia University School of Law from 1963 to 1966. She was an attorney with the New York City Investigations Commission from 1966 to 1967 and with the New York State Council on the Arts during 1967.

From 1967 to 1970, Daniel was an attorney with the California Legal Aid Society, and from 1970 to 1972, she was with the NAACP Legal Defense Fund. She was on the faculty of Hastings College of Law from 1972 to 1974 and was a director of the American Civil Liberties Union from 1974 to 1975. During 1975 she was deputy legal affairs secretary to the Governor of California.

Department of Justice

Nomination of John H. Shenefield To Be Associate Attorney General.
October 26, 1979

The President today announced that he will nominate John H. Shenefield, of Arlington, Va., to be Associate Attorney General. He would replace Michael J. Egan, resigned. Shenefield has been Assistant Attorney General for the Antitrust Division since 1977.

He was born January 23, 1939, in Toledo, Ohio. He received an A.B. from Harvard University in 1960 and an LL.B. from Harvard Law School in 1965. He served in the U.S. Army from 1961 to 1962.

From 1965 to 1977, Shenefield was with the Richmond, Va., firm of Hunton and Williams. He was Deputy Assistant Attorney General early in 1977 and has been Assistant Attorney General since September 1977.

United Nations

Nomination of Richard W. Petree To Be Deputy U.S. Representative in the Security Council.   October 26, 1979

The President today announced that he will nominate Richard W. Petree, of Falls Church, Va., to be Deputy Representative of the United States in the Security Council of the United Nations, with the rank of Ambassador. He would replace Donald McHenry, who has been appointed U.S. Representative to the United Nations. Petree has been Alternate Representative of the United States for Special Political Affairs in the United Nations since 1978.

He was born June 4, 1924, in Jamestown, N.Y. He received an A.B. from the University of Colorado in 1948 and an M.A. from Harvard University in 1950. He served in the U.S. Navy from 1943 to 1946.

From 1946 to 1947, Petree was a personnel officer with the Department of the Army. He joined the State Department in 1950 as an intelligence research analyst. From 1957 to 1960, he was principal officer in Tokyo, and from 1960 to 1963, he was principal officer in Fukuoka.

Petree was an international relations officer from 1963 to 1967 and attended the National War College in 1967–68. From 1968 to 1972, he was posted in Addis Ababa as political officer, then counselor for political affairs.

From 1972 to 1973, he was Consul General in Naha. From 1973 to 1976, he was counselor for political affairs in Tokyo. From 1976 to 1978, he was Minister-Counselor for Political and Security Affairs at the U.S. Mission to the United Nations.

National Advisory Council on Women's Education Programs
Nomination of Carolyn L. Attneave To Be a Member.   October 26, 1979

The President today announced that he will nominate Carolyn L. Attneave, of Seattle, Wash., to be a member of the National Advisory Council on Women's Education Programs.

Attneave, 59, is a professor of psychology and adjunct professor of psychiatry and behavioral sciences at the University of Washington. She has also served as director of American Indian studies at the University of Washington. She has been a member of the American Psychological Association's ad hoc committee on minority affairs and is editor of the newsletter of the Society of American Indian Psychologists.

Department of Transportation
Nomination of William J. Beckham, Jr., To Be Deputy Secretary.   October 26, 1979

The President today announced that he will nominate William J. Beckham, Jr., of Detroit, Mich., to be Deputy Secretary of Transportation. He would replace Alan Butchman, resigned. Beckham has been manager of North American government affairs for Ford Motor Co. since 1978.

He was born in Cincinnati, Ohio, on November 7, 1940. He attended Detroit Institute of Technology, Wayne State University, American University, and the University of Maryland, taking courses in political science.

Beckham worked as a Capitol Police officer at the U.S. Senate from 1962 to 1964. In 1964 he went to work for Senator Philip Hart's campaign in Detroit as a campaign assistant. In January 1965 he joined Senator Hart's staff in Washington as an aide responsible for correspondence to constituents.

From 1966 to 1970, Beckham served as an administrative aide in Senator Hart's Detroit office, where he was responsible for managing the office and establishing an additional office in Grand Rapids.

2039

Beckham served as staff assistant in Senator Hart's Washington office from 1971 to 1973, responsible for monitoring and reviewing legislative and agency actions in the areas of labor, education, housing, and hunger and malnutrition, and for coordinating the activities of the Michigan offices.

From January 1973 to November 1973, Beckham served as director of the Equal Opportunities Subcommittee of the House Education and Labor Committee.

In November 1973 Beckham joined Detroit Mayor-elect Coleman Young's transition staff as director, and from January 1974 until 1977, he was chief executive assistant and deputy mayor of Detroit. From 1977 to 1978, he was Assistant Secretary of the Treasury for Administration.

United States Mint at Denver

Nomination of Michael E. Witt To Be Assayer. October 26, 1979

The President today announced that he will nominate Michael E. Witt, of Aurora, Colo., to be Assayer of the Mint of the United States at Denver. He would replace Hildreth Frost, resigned. Witt has been Supervisor of the Survey Evaluation Section at Rocky Mountain Arsenal, Colo., since 1978.

He was born June 1, 1947, in Angola, Ind. He received a B.S. from the University of Florida in 1969 and a Ph. D. from Louisiana State University in 1973. He served in the U.S. Army from 1974 to 1976.

Witt has been with the Rocky Mountain Arsenal since 1974. From 1974 to 1976, while serving in the Army, he was Deputy Director of Product and Environ-

mental Assurance, Arsenal Quality Assurance Officer, and Acting Chief of the Material Analysis Laboratory Division. As a civilian, he has served as Chief of the Material Analysis Laboratory and as Supervisor of the Survey Evaluation Section.

United States Holocaust Memorial Council

Executive Order 12169. October 26, 1979

By virtue of the authority vested in me as President by the Constitution of the United States of America and in order to establish, in accordance with the provisions of the Federal Advisory Committee Act, as amended (5 U.S.C. App. I), a committee to begin the implementation of the recommendations of the President's Commission on the Holocaust for the establishment of a Holocaust Memorial, it is hereby ordered as follows:

1-1. *Establishment of the Council*

1-101. There is established a United States Holocaust Memorial Council. For the purpose of this Order, the "Holocaust" is the systematic and State-sponsored extermination of six million Jews and some five million other peoples by the Nazis and their collaborators during World War II.

1-102. The membership of the United States Holocaust Memorial Council shall consist of not more than 45 and not less than 25 members as follows:

(a) The President shall appoint between 15 and 35 members of the Council and shall designate one of these members to Chair the Council and another member to serve as Vice Chairman. The

Chairman may recommend to the President a member of the Council to serve as Vice Chairman.

(b) The President of the Senate and the Speaker of the House of Representatives are each invited to designate five members of their respective Houses to serve as members of the Council.

1–2. *Functions of the Council.*

1–201. The Council shall recommend to the President and to the Secretary of the Interior ways to implement the approved recommendations of the President's Commission on the Holocaust: (a) the erection of a memorial museum, (b) the establishment of an educational and research foundation, and (c) the establishment of a Citizens Committee on Conscience.

1–202. The Council shall recommend specific site locations within the Washington, D.C. metropolitan area. Criteria for choosing architectural design should be included in the site recommendations.

1–203. The Council shall propose a concept for the memorial museum, including general descriptions of the types and categories of exhibits to be displayed in the museum. Similarly, suggested functions and limitations for the educational and research foundation should be recommended.

1–204. The Council shall recommend the size, composition, and names of distinguished American citizens qualified to serve on the Citizens Committee on Conscience. It shall advise on the specific duties and limitations of such a Committee.

1–205. The Council shall also advise on the various ways to fund all of these recommendations. Funding proposals should provide that construction costs would be raised primarily from private contributions.

1–206. In addition, the Council shall recommend appropriate ways for the Nation to commemorate "Days of Remembrance of Victims of the Holocaust."

1–207. The Council shall submit a final report to the President and to the Secretary of the Interior no later than June 30, 1980.

1–3. *Administrative Provisions.*

1–301. The Secretary of the Interior shall, to the extent permitted by law, provide the Council with administrative services, facilities, support, and funds necessary for the effective performance of the Council's functions.

1–302. Members of the Council who are not otherwise employed by the Federal Government may receive compensation for each day such member is engaged in the work of the Council at a daily rate to be determined by the Secretary of the Interior. Such rate shall not exceed the amount payable pursuant to the Federal Advisory Committee Act, as amended.

1–303. Members of the Council shall be entitled to travel expenses, including per diem in lieu of subsistence, as authorized by law (5 U.S.C. 5702 and 5703) for persons in the Government service employed intermittently.

1–4. *General Provisions.*

1–401. Notwithstanding the provisions of any other Executive Order, the functions of the President under the Federal Advisory Committee Act, as amended, except that of reporting to the Congress, which are applicable to the Council, shall be performed by the Secretary of the Interior in accordance with guidelines and procedures prescribed by the Administrator of General Services.

1–402. The Council shall serve as an interim body and shall terminate on July 31, 1980, unless sooner extended.

JIMMY CARTER

The White House,
    October 26, 1979.

[Filed with the Office of the Federal Register, 10:50 a.m., October 29, 1979]

Digest of Other White House Announcements

The following listing includes the President's public schedule and other items of general interest announced by the White House Press Office and not included elsewhere in this issue.

October 20

The President declared a major disaster for the State of California as a result of an earthquake occurring on October 15, which caused extensive property damage.

Following his visit to Boston, Mass., the President went to Camp David, Md.

October 22

The President returned to the White House from Camp David.

The President participated in a briefing by administration officials on the windfall profits tax given for community leaders in the East Room at the White House.

October 23

The President met at the White House with:

—Zbigniew Brzezinski, Assistant to the President for National Security Affairs;
—Frank B. Moore, Assistant to the President for Congressional Liaison;
—the Democratic congressional leadership;
—members of the National Advisory Council on Economic Opportunity;

—Mrs. Carter, for lunch;
—Senator Patrick J. Leahy of Vermont;
—members of the President's Advisory Committee for Women.

In a ceremony in the Oval Office, the President received the first sheet of Christmas Seals, which marked the start of the 1979 Christmas Seal Campaign. Participants in the ceremony included Charles Schulz, National Christmas Seal chairman and creator of "Peanuts," Gordon Beck, president of the American Lung Association, and Jenny Chesser, 10, of Austell, Ga., Lorna Garrison, 10, of Washington, D.C., and Brian Owens, 10, of Kingsport, Tenn., representing the winners of the State Christmas Seal poster contests.

The President announced the members of the U.S. delegation to the independence ceremonies in Saint Vincent and the Grenadines, to be held October 26–29. They are:

SALLY ANGELA SHELTON, U.S. Ambassador to Barbados, Grenada, and the Commonwealth of Dominica and Minister to Saint Lucia;
ROBERT F. BOSSIE, a Manchester, N.H., attorney;
PATRICIA ANNE FRANK, a Florida State senator; and
PATRICK T. McGAHN, JR., an Atlantic City, N.J., attorney.

The President announced the designation of Clark M. Clifford as Chairman of the Presidential Advisory Board on Ambassadorial Appointments. Clifford has been a member of this Board since last March. As Chairman, he replaces Reubin O'D. Askew, who has resigned from the Board.

October 24

The President met at the White House with:

—Dr. Brzezinski;
—the Cabinet;
—Mr. Moore;

—Vice President Walter F. Mondale.

The President participated in a briefing by administration officials on the strategic arms limitation treaty given for community leaders from Kentucky, North Carolina, and West Virginia in the East Room at the White House.

The President has designated Zbigniew Brzezinski, the President's Assistant for National Security Affairs, to head the U.S. delegation to the 25th anniversary celebration of the Algerian revolution in Algiers on November 1. Dr. Brzezinski will be accompanied by Under Secretary of State for Political Affairs David D. Newsom. Other members of the delegation will be named at a later date.

October 25

The President met at the White House with:

—Dr. Brzezinski;

—Vice President Mondale, Secretary of the Treasury G. William Miller, Charles L. Schultze, Chairman of the Council of Economic Advisers, James T. McIntyre, Jr., Director of the Office of Management and Budget, Alfred E. Kahn, Advisor to the President on Inflation and Chairman of the Council on Wage and Price Stability, R. Robert Russell, Director, and John N. Gentry, Counselor on Labor-Management Relations, Council on Wage and Price Stability, Stuart E. Eizenstat, Assistant to the President for Domestic Affairs and Policy, and Landon Butler, Deputy Assistant to the President;

—members of the National Citizens' Coalition for the Windfall Profits Tax;

—Mr. Moore;

—Members of the House of Representatives to discuss hospital cost containment legislation.

The President transmitted to the Congress the 1978 annual report on Administration of the Radiation Control for Health and Safety Act of 1968.

October 26

The President met at the White House with:

—Dr. Brzezinski;

—Vice President Mondale, Secretary of State Cyrus R. Vance, Secretary of Defense Harold Brown, Hedley W. Donovan, Senior Adviser to the President, Lloyd N. Cutler, Counsel to the President, Hamilton Jordan, Assistant to the President, and Dr. Brzezinski;

—a group of editors and broadcasters from Minnesota (transcript will be printed next week).

The President participated in a briefing on the administration's programs and policies given for civic and community leaders from Washington State in the East Room at the White House.

The President transmitted to the Congress the 1978 annual report of the Federal Council on Aging.

The President left the White House for a weekend stay at Camp David.

NOMINATIONS SUBMITTED TO THE SENATE

The following list does not include promotions of members of the Uniformed Services, nominations to the Service Academies, or nominations of Foreign Service officers.

Submitted October 22, 1979

WILLIAM J. VANDEN HEUVEL, of New York, to be the Deputy Representative of the United States of America to the United Nations, with the rank and status of Ambassador Extraordinary and Plenipotentiary.

GEORGE HERBERT PATRICK BURSLEY, of Maryland, to be a member of the National Transportation Safety Board for the term expiring December 31, 1984 (reappointment).

NOMINATIONS—Continued

Submitted October 23, 1979

JUAN M. PEREZ-GIMENEZ, of Puerto Rico, to be United States District Judge for the District of Puerto Rico, vice a new position created by P.L. 95–486, approved October 20, 1978.

Submitted October 25, 1979

HAZEL REID ROLLINS, of the District of Columbia, to be Administrator of the Economic Regulatory Administration, vice David J. Bardin, resigned.

Submitted October 26, 1979

RICHARD WILSON PETREE, of Virginia, a Foreign Service officer of Class one, to be Deputy Representative of the United States of America in the Security Council of the United Nations, with the rank of Ambassador.

MICHAEL E. WITT, of Colorado, to be Assayer of the Mint of the United States at Denver, vice Hildreth Frost, Jr., resigned.

JOHN H. SHENEFIELD, of Virginia, to be Associate Attorney General, vice Michael J. Egan, resigned.

ALICE DANIEL, of the District of Columbia, to be an Assistant Attorney General, vice Barbara A. Babcock, resigned.

CAROLYN L. ATTNEAVE, of Washington, to be a member of the National Advisory Council on Women's Education Programs for a term expiring May 8, 1981, vice Mary Beth Peters, term expired.

WILLIAM J. BECKHAM, JR., of Michigan, to be Deputy Secretary of Transportation, vice Alan A. Butchman, resigned.

EDWARD ALLAN FRIEMAN, of New Jersey, to be Director of the Office of Energy Research, vice John M. Deutch, elevated.

CHECKLIST OF WHITE HOUSE PRESS RELEASES

The following listing contains releases of the White House Press Office which are not included in this issue.

Released October 20, 1979

Advance text: remarks at dedication ceremonies for the John F. Kennedy Library in Boston, Mass.

CHECKLIST—Continued

Released October 22, 1979

Announcement: nomination of Juan M. Perez-Gimenez to be United States District Judge for the District of Puerto Rico

Released October 23, 1979

News conference: on the President's meeting with members of his Advisory Committee for Women to discuss the equal rights amendment—by Lynda Johnson Robb, Chair, and Ann Richards, member, President's Advisory Committee for Women

Released October 24, 1979

News conference: on relief efforts for Kampucheans—by Rev. Theodore M. Hesburgh, Chairman of the Select Commission on Immigration and Refugee Policy and chairman of the board of the Overseas Development Council, and Ambassador Henry D. Owen, Special Representative of the President for International Economic Summits

News conference: on Executive Order 12168, establishing the President's Commission for a National Agenda for the Eighties—by Hedley W. Donovan, Senior Adviser to the President, and William J. McGill, president of Columbia University and Chairperson of the Commission

Released October 25, 1979

Fact sheet: initiatives in energy conservation through ridesharing

Released October 26, 1979

News conference: on their trip to Southeast Asia—by Senators Jim Sasser of Tennessee, John C. Danforth of Missouri, and Max Baucus of Montana

---

ACTS APPROVED BY THE PRESIDENT

Approved October 22, 1979

H.R. 1753_____ Private Law 96–16
An act for the relief of Sergio and Javier Arredondo.

ACTS APPROVED—Continued

Approved October 23, 1979

H.R. 1301_____ Public Law 96–90
An act to amend title 18 of the United States Code to allow the transportation or mailing to a foreign country of material concerning a lottery authorized by that foreign country, and for other purposes.

H.R. 898_____ Private Law 96–17
An act for the relief of Rodney L. Herold and others.

Approved October 25, 1979

S. 567_____ Public Law 96–91
An act to amend title 28 of the United States Code to allow the United States attorney and assistant United States attorneys for the Eastern District of New York to reside within twenty miles of the district.

PRESIDENTIAL DOCUMENTS

Week Ending Friday, November 2, 1979

Interview With the President

Remarks and a Question-and-Answer Session With Editors and Broadcasters From Minnesota. October 26, 1979

THE PRESIDENT. I'm grateful that you've come this afternoon. We had a previous meeting planned, and we had a conflict of schedules, and you couldn't come. I'm glad to have you here.

I want to reserve as much time as possible for your questions, not for statements from me.

ADMINISTRATION POLICIES

We are constantly at work trying to preserve the peace which our Nation enjoys. I think it's been 10 Presidents ago since we've had a time when no service people were killed in combat—a remarkable fact that I just learned this morning: 56 years ago; I think President Harding was the last one. I hope we can keep that posture. And it's dependent entirely, I think, on having a strong nation, united with resolved will and an adequate defense capability.

We want to get along well with the Soviet Union and meet with them on a peaceful, competitive basis. We are proceeding with SALT, which I think is the most important decision that's likely to be made by our Government while I serve in this office. We've strengthened NATO.

I think we've moved very firmly and aggressively to encourage new friendships around the world. India now has very good relationships with us. Under Mrs. Ghandi, they were inclined strongly toward the Soviet Union. Our new opening with China, a fourth of the nations' populations, has been very successful so far. We've not damaged our relationship, so far as anyone can tell, with the people of Taiwan. And this is a fine balancing act, which I think has been fairly successful at this point. We've also had a chance to open up the possibilities for increased benefits with relations among the African nations and ourselves.

In the Mideast we've had some limited success so far in bringing a permanent peace to that region. We are continuing this effort, with a larger dependence at this time on direct negotiations between Egypt and Israel. We play a role; we will increase our role if desired by the two major participating parties. Both of them are bound by the Camp David accords, which extend in the future toward and including a comprehensive peace, involving, of course, the resolution of the very difficult question of the Palestinian rights.

In the domestic area we are trying to deal with the chronic inflation which has been on us now 10 or 11 years. A major factor here is the resolution of the energy question and the evolution within the Congress, in perhaps the most complicated and difficult legislative challenge the Congress has ever faced, and that is an energy policy for our country. At the present time the inflation rate is comprised of about 4 percent energy, and the balance of it is nonrelated to energy. If it weren't for the energy factor alone, the inflation rate now would be the same as it was in 1978 and 1977.

I think we'll be successful this year in completing the major portion of the energy proposals that I presented to the Congress in April of 1977. This has not been an easy thing; it's been a constant challenge.

There are many other matters that I would be glad to discuss with you, concerning agriculture or social programs, health, education, housing, transportation, Federal-State-local relationships, improving the quality of life in our cities. But I think the best thing for me to do is to answer your questions. Perhaps those who haven't had an opportunity to ask questions earlier today would like to start, and then I'll open it to anyone else. Or if you've all had a chance to ask questions, then just use your own judgment.

QUESTIONS

NUCLEAR EXPLOSION IN SOUTH AFRICAN REGION

Q. President Carter, I was wondering now, what's the latest on the atom explosion in the area of South Africa?

THE PRESIDENT. A few weeks ago, we had an indication that somewhere in that region, covering literally thousands of square miles, there was an explosion. We have been and are continuing to try to follow up that initial observation. There is no certain answer yet that anyone can derive.

Q. Does it appear as though it's South Africa?

THE PRESIDENT. That's hard to say. There's a lot of ocean surrounding South Africa, and I don't think it would be possible to pinpoint it any closer than a distance of literally hundreds of miles.

So, we don't really know, except just a general area where an indication was obtained. The people that got that indication feel quite sure, but followup checks have not been successful. This doesn't prove or disprove whether or not there was an actual explosion.

WINDFALL PROFITS TAX

Q. Mr. President, yesterday, sir, you expressed dissatisfaction with the windfall profits tax as it was, so far, in the Congress. What is the rockbottom level that you're willing to settle for, and what are some of the punitive measures that you are willing to take should the version that comes out of the Congress not please you?

THE PRESIDENT. I'd rather not describe the additional measures that I would take, because I'd like to keep all my options open.

The minimum thing that would satisfy me is the proposal that we put to the Congress at the very beginning, roughly $275 billion in income from that source. I think, if anything, that figure ought to be higher, if the Congress makes a change, than lower.

The House lowered it some, a considerable amount, 12 to 15 billion dollars, and also limited the time of application from a permanent tax on the unearned profits of the oil companies to a 10-year period—where some of these projects are very long range in nature, and I think the permanent aspect of the tax is important. That was a major change the House made.

The Senate, however, slashed our proposal in half—the Senate Finance Committee did. So, we'll fight as hard as we can to restore the losses on the floor when the Senate debates and votes on this issue. And if we're not completely successful there, we'll take our battle to the conference committee and then back to the House and Senate floors for the assessment of the conference committee decision.

But if any change is made in what we originally proposed, it ought to be stronger, rather than weaker, because of subsequent events that have occurred.

WAGE AND PRICE GUIDELINES

Q. Mr. President, I believe two out of three American people holding jobs are not members of labor unions. What would you like to see for them in the year 1980 for the guideline for wage increases?

THE PRESIDENT. The most impor— Oh, I was preanticipating your question. I started to say that one of the most important things we could do is to pass the labor law reform legislation that was proposed by us to the Congress earlier in my administration.

We would like for all of the wage earners and business executives to comply with the voluntary wage and price guidelines that have been established by us. These have been and are being modified as we accumulate more information and more data. And of course, now we have what we call the national accord, a joint approach to this very sensitive question, where labor and business and the Government voluntarily work with one another, whereas previously, up until this month, the guidelines were imposed by the Government, in effect, on a reluctant labor and business community. This is a major step forward, and I think that the results will be good.

I'd like to add quickly that we've had excellent response on both prices and wages during this past year. Wage increases have been very compatible with those in previous years, in 1978, for instance. We've had good cooperation in almost every respect. On the items that can be put under the umbrella of our price guidelines, we've had very good response from business.

The major things that have broken the inflation control effort and forced prices up have been: number one, energy; secondly, things like forest products and heavy demand for homes—we've had an almost 2-million-home-per-year building rate—and, of course, food, which is impossible, in my opinion, to have prices controlled.

But on items that are sold, we've had good response from the business community as well. I think the new accord will help us in the future to make our guidelines more effective. And I hope that the same guidelines would apply equitably between members of labor unions and those who are not.

PUBLIC WORKS AND WATER PROJECTS

Q. Mr. President, in the area of public works and water projects, there's a bill in the House that's nearing the floor and one in the Senate committee that deals with cost-sharing ratios for the local units of government that are different from what you've previously said are your guidelines. Does that make it veto material that they haven't adhered to your guidelines on a higher local share of the total project cost?

THE PRESIDENT. I can't answer that question. My recollection is that the proposal we made to the Congress had at least tacit approval from State leaders and others in the country before we presented it. Subsequently, an alternative was put forward.

I would have to assess the legislation in its entirety before I could decide whether to veto or not veto it. If it was a decided improvement over what we have now and would make water projects, including dams, be built on the basis of merit and not political porkbarrel considerations, then I would probably sign the legislation. If it was of great danger to the level of expenditures in the future or would encourage unwarranted projects being built, then I would veto it.

Q. In the Minnesota area, it's the flood control projects, three of them, where you have asked for a doubling of the local effort versus what Congress has acted upon.

THE PRESIDENT. In general, the local and State officials have been amenable to that local and State effort. It gives them some authority or influence over the decisions, which they haven't had in the past. It's been almost exclusively a Federal Government bureaucracy and the administration and Congress decision. The costs are relatively low. But I think this would prevent projects being approved with the wild support of chambers of commerce and so forth, when they don't have to bear any of the cost at all at the local level. So, I think a proper sharing of responsibility and cost is the best approach, as we've put forward to the Congress.

But the thing I don't want to do is to participate in conjecture about what kind of bill might ultimately get to my desk after it goes through the tortuous legislative procedures and say I will or will not veto something that I haven't seen.

CANADIAN OIL EXPORTS

Q. Mr. President, you'll be traveling to Canada early next month. At that point will you be trying to restore some of the cutbacks we've experienced in Canadian crude oil to this country?

THE PRESIDENT. That will be on the agenda. We will be discussing environmental questions, fishing rights questions, the future supplies of oil and natural gas, maybe even some sharing of electric power that might be generated on each side of the border, and a clearer understanding of what we might experience in the future.

As you know, Canada, like our own Nation, has a very serious problem of being, in effect, two nations, one a major producing nation, and the other one a major consuming nation. And sometimes it's delineated geographically. On the east coast of Canada, there's a fairly substantial shortage of oil, as you know. On the western part of Canada, in the north, there's sometimes a surplus of oil.

My understanding from the Canadian authorities is that over a period of the next number of years, until they can hope to get tar sands and shale production, that they are going to have to be importing a little more oil than they have in the past.

So, I think for the Americans to believe that we'll have large supplies of oil coming from Canada in the future would be a fruitless hope. But that will be one of the issues Prime Minister Clark and I will discuss.

ENERGY CONSERVATION

Q. Mr. President, do you think the American people, in their daily lives and daily habits, are sufficiently aroused about the gravity of the energy shortage? Have they given up enough? What's going to excite them about getting involved in carpools?

THE PRESIDENT. Well, in the last few months, since the California gas lines and some on the east coast, there's been a new interest in and concern existing among the American people themselves. For instance, I think last year, in the winterization of homes we had about a 9-percent participation rate in getting tax credits for weatherizing homes among the families of our country.

I've been pleased the last few weeks, maybe the last few months, about the response of the American people. One indication of this is that we have measured about 1 mile per gallon higher efficiency among all the automobiles in the Nation during this summer than we had anticipated, which shows that Americans are driving more carefully, trying to save gasoline, and also shifting, as rapidly as they are available, to more efficient automobiles.

I expect there's to be a large increase in the utilization of the tax credits to winterize homes. We've spot checked Government buildings around the Nation—and this has been done by the news media in some cases—and found a fairly surprising degree of compliance with the new thermostat control settings that I advocated.

So, to answer your question in one sentence, I think that in general, lately the American people's concern about energy has mirrored itself in increased conservation—not enough yet. I think more will come in the future.

One other point that's interesting is that for the last several years, the business community—industry, primarily—has practiced better conservation than before.

In 1973, for every 1-percent increase in the gross national product, energy consumption went up about 1 percent. Now, when the gross national product goes up 1 percent, energy consumption only goes six-tenths of a percent. So, that's a substantial saving that's been brought about just by business and industry attention to profits and losses. And now that intense interest in prices of energy and its adverse effect on a family budget is beginning to have a major effect, beneficially, on conservation.

HOUSING CONSTRUCTION AND FINANCING

Q. Mr. President, you mentioned that the cost of homes is one of the chief things that have risen, contributing to the inflation problem.

THE PRESIDENT. It's primarily the interest rates.

Q. Yes. Now, I have a letter here that was addressed to you by the president of the Minnesota AFL–CIO, who is one of the main supporters of yours in Minnesota, and he's extremely critical of the Federal Reserve Board, particularly of Mr. Volcker, on raising interest rates all the time. In fact, he suggests you find a way of getting rid of Mr. Volcker. Do you have any comments on that?

THE PRESIDENT. Well, first of all, it's not possible to get rid of Mr. Volcker under the American law. And, secondly, the Federal Reserve has very wisely been isolated from political influence exerted by the White House or the Congress. It's an independent agency, and I think it ought to be independent.

Interest rates are almost directly related to the rate of inflation, and I think it would be expecting too much for the interest rates charges to be lower than the rate of inflation. The best way to get interest rates down is to lower inflation.

We've been effective in making alternative supplies of money available, which did not exist several years ago, for continued homebuilding in spite of high interest rates.

The interest rates have been fairly high, for instance, the last number of months, ever since—certainly all during this year—but the homebuilding rate in September was still near a 2-million-home-per-year mark. I think the highest it's ever been in history was a rate of about 2.3 million homes per year. We've sustained that level so far. What will happen in October, nobody can say.

Secretary Miller and the Home Loan Bank Board are now making a telephone survey for me around the Nation to see what is the degree of available money and how much has homebuilding been constrained because of the high interest rates. This is a matter of great concern to us.

I might say that in the first 2½ or so years that we've served, we have cut the unemployment rate among construction workers down by 40 percent, and I hope to keep that—the building in our Nation—at a reasonable, sustained level. But I'm also concerned about the high inflation and the attendant high interest rates, and I'm sure that Mr. Volcker is, too.

Q. Mr. President, don't the interest rates, though, contribute to and inflame inflation?

THE PRESIDENT. Yes, that's absolutely right, because the interest rates, through some strange quirk in the regulations, which is certainly an exaggeration, are applied to the Consumer Price Index as though every month every homeowner in the country had to renegotiate their home loan on the basis of the higher rates, which means that this greatly exaggerates in the Consumer Price Index the effect of high interest rates on home loans.

Obviously, many people are now paying off home loans at an interest rate of 5 or 6 percent, but within the CPI, it's as though all the homeowners in our country had just borrowed their money this past month. So, that is an exaggerated figure. But when the CPI goes up because of high interest rates at our current level, it feeds back into everything else, including the cost-of-living adjustments and other things.   •

RELIEF EFFORTS FOR KAMPUCHEANS

Q. Mr. President, you recently compared the situation in Cambodia to the Holocaust. And if it is so—and I agree it is—might it be worse because it's in a smaller population of 8 million, while there it was the European community? How do you explain the reaction, or is it adequate, of the Vatican, the Christian world, and the Western democracies, and why are we so timid in pointing out to the world who is causing the holocaust?

THE PRESIDENT. I don't think we've been timid. Have you all met with Secretary Vance yet?

Q. Yes, this morning.

THE PRESIDENT. I can get for you—I need not go into it now—just a calendar of what we have done, the voices that we've raised, our efforts in the United Nations, our condemnation, publicly and through diplomatic channels, of the authorities in Kampuchea over a period of months, beginning way back in 1978.

In the first place, it's hard to identify who is the government in Kampuchea—it's a very confused subject, the country is at war; secondly, the location of the people who are starving; and third, it's been very difficult to arouse the interest of the international community enough to force the combatant groups in Kampuchea to let food be delivered. There's no reason for us to deliver large supplies of food to a totalitarian government, who's responsible for the starvation, and have the food never get to the people who are starving. That was and has been an obstacle.

Only 5 days after we were successful in getting the United Nations, including the International Red Cross and UNICEF, to make a move, we made our pledge, and we've had our pledge on the line ever since I have known any way to get food to the starving people. We just arbitrarily said, "We'll provide a third of anything that goes to the Kampuchean starving people."

We still don't have a sure way to get the food to the people who are starving. It's been estimated that at least a third, maybe approaching a half, of the total population of Cambodia has already died, and they are still suffering very seriously.

My next meeting after this meeting with you is with the three United States Senators that have gone over there to try to convince the government in Phnom Penh to let 30,000 tons of food per month cross the Thai border and go into the area where the starving people exist, where they're trying to survive. We have food ready, on the way. We've already allocated enough money to accommodate every possible means to deliver the food.

It's one of those horrible examples of, I think, partially a deliberate attempt to decimate a population in the form of genocide. And now, I think, that the world has been aroused, I think the conflicting military groups in Kampuchea, including the Vietnamese, have been convinced that they must open up an avenue to alleviate the suffering. And we are in the forefront and have been in the forefront of making food and money and transportation capabilities available.

Mr. Eisele. Thank you, Mr. President.

The President. Thank you. I'll take one more question and then——

PRESIDENT'S LEADERSHIP QUALITIES AND ACCOMPLISHMENTS

Q. Mr. President, the question of leadership is apparently going to be a very large one in the coming Presidential campaign. And some of your critics contend that one of the problems you got into early on was that you had no grand vision of national goals, no overarching idea of what direction the country ought to go in. And they say that that's because you were an engineer and you were engrossed in details, but couldn't deal in the grand picture, particularly here in Washington. How do you react to that?

The President. You know, in many ways our country has been built by people like engineers. I think Thomas Jefferson was a scientist, for instance. I was a farmer like George Washington was. I don't think there's any exclusive kind of person who has visions or who has leadership, to the exclusion of other kinds of people. We've had haberdashers who were great leaders, we've had military generals who've been great leaders, we've had ex-Governors who were great—Presidents, I meant to say—who were great

Presidents. And I don't know how to respond to any particular categorization.

I think the fact that I was an engineer and have had some training in State government and also in science and also in agriculture—none of those things are debilitating experiences. [*Laughter*] I believe that any fair and accurate analysis of what we have proposed and accomplished would debunk that kind of allegation.

Before I was ever President, we had broad and extensive goals that we wanted to accomplish, and I think the difficulty that we've experienced with Congress originally has been because of the complexity of the proposals that we've put to them. I'll just give you two quick examples, one on the domestic scene.

We've never had an energy policy. For many years, back to Harry Truman, we've recognized that something needed to be done about energy. It's been in a crisis stage since 1973. This has been one of the most complicated and difficult political battles on the Hill that our country has ever seen. And I predict to you that before the end of this year we will have, almost in its totality, an adequate national energy policy. Had we had this earlier, we would have saved our Nation a great deal of suffering and threat to our very security.

In foreign affairs, we've had the same thing. You know, for 14 years Presidents have had the opportunity to complete a Panama Canal treaty and, for much longer than that, to open up China to trade and diplomatic relationships with our country, for even longer than that, to try to bring peace to the Mideast.

We've never flinched in any way from addressing an issue that I consider to be important to our Nation domestically or in foreign matters because of adverse political consequences. I can well understand now why some of my predecessors did not bring these issues up. [*Laughter*]

When I made my TV speech to the people of our country, I think, April 20 of 1977, on energy, I said then that I predict that my public opinion polls would drop at least 15 percent because of the energy proposals that I would make. That was one of the worst underestimations—[*laughter*]—I've ever made to the American people. But some of the things we've done have been very difficult, they've not been political winners, and we've been successful.

I might close by saying that the most difficult political undertaking I've ever had in my life, including a campaign for President, was getting the Panama Canal treaties ratified and the implementing legislation passed. When we began that effort, only 8 percent of the American people were in favor of any sort of Panama Canal treaty. And I think this will pay rich dividends for our country in the future. But it was obviously not politically attractive to do it.

So, I don't have any apology to make. We've still got problems. We haven't been 100 percent successful. But I think that when this Congress goes home, I predict to you that if you analyze what we proposed to the Congress versus what they passed, that there would not be a President in the last 20 years or more that's had a record as good as ours, and that would even include the relatively halcyon days of Lyndon Johnson's administration, immediately after the tragedy of John Kennedy's death.

We've got a good record, very difficult issues, an extremely fine, cooperative relationship between me and the Congress. And I think the facts—not just my voice, which certainly will be thought of as, perhaps, biased—the facts will show that what I've told you is accurate.

NOTE: The interview began at 1:16 p.m. in the Cabinet Room at the White House. Albert Eisele is Press Secretary to Vice President Mondale.

The transcript of the interview was released on October 27.

Republic of Korea

Letter to Acting President Choi Kyu Ha Following the Death of President Park Chung Hee. October 27, 1979

Dear Mr. Acting President:

It is with a deep sense of shock and sorrow that I have learned of the death of President Park Chung-Hee. President Park was a firm friend of America, a staunch ally, and an able leader. In particular, his role in Korea's remarkable economic development will not be forgotten.

Let me assure you, as you assume your duties as Acting President, that the United States Government will continue to stand firmly behind its treaty commitments to the Republic of Korea. Our thoughts will be with you and the Korean people during this difficult time.

Sincerely,

JIMMY CARTER

NOTE: President Park was assassinated on October 26 by Kim Chae Kyu, Director of the Korean Central Intelligence Agency, at KCIA headquarters. Also killed during the shooting incident were five of President Park's aides.

On October 30 the White House announced that the President designated Secretary of State Cyrus R. Vance to lead the United States delegation to the funeral of President Park in Seoul on Saturday, November 3. Secretary Vance was to be accompanied by the President's son Chip and a delegation of leaders from the Congress, the executive branch, the military services, and the American public.

Providence, Rhode Island

Remarks at the Northeast Summit on Energy.
October 29, 1979

Governor Brendan Byrne, Governor Grasso, other members of this group, who are distinguished leaders throughout the northeastern part of our country:

I can't think of any more appropriate subject for a summit conference anywhere in our Nation and particularly in this part of our country than you have chosen. Summits are ordinarily called when there is a matter of grave significance to a nation or to a group of nations.

I had a summit meeting with President Brezhnev in Vienna not long ago to talk about the peace of our generation throughout the world and the control of nuclear weapons. There was an economic summit earlier this year in Tokyo, when the leaders of seven industrialized and democratic nations met to talk about the future of the Western World.

And today we are addressing a subject that is equally as important, because there are two things involved: One is the well-being of the people of our country, and the other is the security of our Nation. I don't make a statement like that lightly. When a President, the Commander in Chief of our Armed Forces, says that the security of our Nation is at stake, the words should be chosen carefully, and I choose them very carefully.

Our Nation has become overly dependent on foreign oil. This is a subject of grave importance to us.

In January of 1973, oil was selling freely around the world about $2 a barrel; that's about 6 or 7 years ago. Now oil prices are more than 10 times as great; on the spot market, 20 times as great, about $40 per barrel.

We rely on an uncertain source. We import half the oil we use. Along with oil, we import inflation and unemployment. Next year we will send from our country to foreign oil suppliers $70 billion. Think of the jobs and investment and a better life for the American people that could be bought with that kind of money.

Inflation is an all-pervasive burden on the American people. The driving force behind inflation is our overdependence on oil and the high prices paid for it. Four percentage points of our present inflation rate are directly attributable to one item—energy. If it weren't for the rapid increase in energy costs in the last 6 or 8 months, the inflation rate now would be the same as it was in 1978 or the same as it was in 1977.

The people of our country are losing confidence in the future, because they see that we rely on an undependable source which provides oil for a thirsty nation at uncontrollable prices. This is a very serious subject, and the fact that all of you would assemble here is proof that you agree with me about my expression of concern.

In April of 1977, about 90 days after I had been sworn in as President, I presented to the people and to the Congress an analysis of the energy question and presented also to the Congress a proposal for a comprehensive national policy on energy. Mine was a lonely voice. I referred to the energy problem as the moral equivalent of war. This statement was ridiculed by the press, discounted by many people in our country.

And after a year and a half the Congress, after one of the most divisive and bitter and difficult debates in the history of our Nation, finally passed last year about 65 percent of the energy package that I had presented to them—not one word, however, about oil; not one word.

So, here we sit, 7 years after the first oil embargo, 2½ years after a comprehensive package has been presented to the Congress, still needing vital action by our legislative branch of the Government, and our country's still vulnerable.

There have been some beneficial changes made, however. The American people are now becoming aroused, and the Congress is beginning to take action, even on oil. I'm not discouraged about the future.

One very bright light throughout all this process has been the awareness of the Northeastern Governors and those who work with them that this was indeed a serious problem. I have had strong allies among the men and women at this table from the very beginning, and the fact that you are here indicates that their influence has been all-pervasive throughout the northeastern part of our country. You saw the dangers early, and you began to act.

One of the things that has been a serious problem, politically and otherwise, has been the artificial controls on the prices of oil and natural gas, which have caused Americans to continue to depend upon oil to an unwarranted degree, to the exclusion of conservation, the shifting toward renewable supplies of energy like solar power, and the realization among our Nation that we did have a serious problem on hand.

The most important single action that every single person in this country can take is to save energy, to conserve energy, to stop wasting energy. This is something that can be done at the national level, State, local levels of government, in private industry, in every community, in every family, in the life of almost every person.

And I hope that everyone listening to my voice here in this room or on television or otherwise will make an assessment today with family members: "What can I do as a patriotic American and to help my Nation, yes, but also to help my community, my family, and myself? What can I do to save energy in my home, going to and from work, to and from shopping, on my job?"

There are myriad different ways that Americans can save energy if we make up our minds that it's important enough to do it. And I might point out to you that this is not an unpleasant thing; it's not an unwarranted sacrifice; it will not even be an inconvenience. It will certainly not weaken our family structure, our communities, our States, our Nation. It can be an exciting and productive and positive action. It can bring families together in a closer unity. It can strengthen communities. It can strengthen our Nation. It's a patriotic gesture. It can be pleasant, not an unpleasant sacrifice.

The crux of the issue in conserving, meeting the needs of American families, developing new supplies of energy, is the windfall profits tax. The windfall profits tax is now being considered by the House and the Senate of the U.S. Congress.

The House has passed a reasonable windfall profits tax, not as strong as I advocated, not as strong as I would like. The revenues are not as great as what I proposed, and the House put a 10-year limit on the application of the tax. It should be permanent, and the lost revenues, below what I advocated, should be restored.

The Senate Finance Committee has reported out a framework only of a tax structure that can be built on the floor of the Senate, in the conference committee, and ultimately by the Congress.

The House would give back to the oil companies, as a portion of the unearned profits over a 10-year period, $151 billion. The Senate Finance Committee would give back to the oil companies, in unearned profits, $374 billion, at the present price of oil, as projected, and at the present inflation rate. This could become a $1 trillion giveaway to the oil companies.

I hope that every one of you will help me to convince the Congress that an adequate and acceptable windfall profits tax should be levied on the oil companies to take away a major portion of their unearned profits, because that would give us a reserve supply of money to be used for things that are crucial: first of all, to meet the needs of our American families, to pay the increasing cost of energy. The increasing costs are inevitable. The poor families of our Nation must have added financial help to pay those costs.

And the second need, of course, is to have a strong, consistent, permanent conservation program, to encourage Americans to do what's best for them, through tax credits, home audits, shifting away from the scarcer supplies of energy to more plentiful supplies of energy, the evolution of new kinds of energy from supplies which in our country are adequate—synthetic fuels from coal, geothermal supplies, biomass, low-level dams which have been abandoned in the past that can now be reconstituted— a heavy dependence upon insulation of homes, more efficient automobiles, research and development.

These things are all possible; in fact, in our country they're inevitable, provided we have adequate incentives. And those incentives financially must be derived and can be derived only from a windfall profits tax. It sounds so logical and so clearly to the advantage of our country that you might say, "Why the doubt; why the delay; why must the President continue to pound on this one subject for 2½ years, yet without success?"

I represent and lead, in effect, two different nations. One is the largest oil-consuming nation on Earth, and the other nation is one of the largest oil-producing nations on Earth. And in the past there has been one strong all-pervasive voice on Capitol Hill, and that has been the oil companies' lobbies. Now, in the last couple of years, we've built up an effective countervoice as the American people have become aroused to protect their own interests.

The third quarter oil company profits are adequate proof of the need for a rapid passage of the windfall profits tax in an acceptable form for me and for you.

We must meet the needs of the poor families, particularly in the northern part of our Nation. In April of this year, I made two basic pledges. One was that this winter we would have an adequate supply of home heating oil. At that time we were far below the reserve supplies needed. We've been successful with that. Our goal was 240 million barrels in reserve supply in October. We have already passed that point. We will have adequate fuel oil supplies for homes during this winter. That's a notable achievement.

But the other part of that commitment was to provide, from Federal revenues, assistance for poor families, to help meet the rapidly increasing costs of home heating oil brought about by OPEC price rises. Very quickly now, $250 million will be distributed throughout the country, particularly the Northeast, for Governors to allocate through their own mechanisms for poor families. This is a growth of a program that I established the first year I was President, with the help of the Congress. It's been effective so far.

We're advocating that this be increased substantially and that we add to the $400 million from this program another $1.2 billion to be paid out through other means to the poor families of this country. In addition to that, we've advocated $2.4 billion per year for 10 years to have a permanent, stable, predictable program to meet these high needs of the poorer families in our midst.

These revenues will come ultimately from the windfall profits tax, but in order to expedite the process and not delay the payments until the windfall profits tax is passed, they'll be paid out of general revenue funds and then repaid when the windfall profits tax is collected from the oil companies.

I'd like to remind you again, however, that the best way, the cheapest way, the quickest way to cut down on costs, to make our Nation more energy-secure, and to reduce oil imports is conservation—conservation. Every family can help. It's one of the most important and patriotic challenges that we've ever faced.

If we could just insulate, for instance, all the buildings in our country adequately, we would, in effect, have another Prudhoe Bay supply of oil, equivalent to the oil that we are deriving now from the recent discoveries in Alaska.

The tax credits for insulation of homes was passed a year ago and already in an embryonic stage of use. Of this ability for families to take credit on the income taxes to insulate their own homes—which they should do anyhow—about 10 percent of the middle- and upper-class families, the ones who pay the most income taxes, are already participating. That percentage will undoubtedly grow.

I'd like to point out one other thing to you. We have established, to make sure that energy supplies are distributed quickly and equitably in your region, a fuel oil management group. The headquarters for this group will be in Boston. It's already been constituted. It's comprised of representatives from the Department of Energy, the Department of Agriculture, the Department of Transportation, and, to make sure that in cases of heavy snowfall or icing of waterways that we can overcome those difficulties rapidly, the Coast Guard and the Corps of Engineers.

The primary coordinating effort will be through the Governors, so that if a distribution problem should arise during this winter, this group is already in existence, planning carefully to avoid mistakes and to avoid interruptions in supply, but eager to correct defects in the distribution whenever they should become apparent.

Our Nation is in a state of transition, from a time when fuel was so cheap that we never gave it a thought to a time when fuel is becoming so expensive that we can think of little else. And it's very important that all of us—leaders with an effective voice and effective influence—unite.

The delays have been unwarranted. They've damaged our country. We should have had a national energy policy 5, 6 years ago. The challenges have not been easy to overcome. The questions have not been easy to answer. The problems have not been easy to solve. But it's too late to try to find scapegoats, to try to affix blame for delays. Now is the time for us to work together, to recognize that we have a common problem, a common challenge, that we face common questions.

All the Governors on this platform and I represent the same people. We're in it together. We need not fear the future. It may be that the early warnings and the increasing prices, which were inevitable in any case, have come at a time to restore our Nation's integrity and to improve our Nation's security.

We've been blessed beyond all other nations, even in the field of energy. In its totality, our country has about 24 percent of all the energy supplies known on Earth. The OPEC nations all put together have about 5 percent. But ours are in forms that have not yet been adequately tapped—hydroelectric power, wood, coal, oil, geothermal supplies, natural gas, shale, tar sands. They are ready to be tapped by a nation that can marshal its resources in an effective way, which can unite with one another and not be divided from one another as we grasp for some selfish advantage in a time of transient shortage or transient inconvenience.

We've been blessed not only with reserve supplies of energy; we've been blessed with a form of government that makes us quickly sensitive to the needs and demands of the American people; and we've been blessed with the free enterprise system, which encourages innovation, dynamism, competition, and flexibility. So, we have everything on our side.

And with the passage of the proposals that I submitted to the Congress in April of 1977 and again in July of this year, our country will have the framework, with a comprehensive energy policy based on financing with the windfall profits tax, to meet this challenge successfully.

There is no reason for us to fear. We're going through a temporary time of inconvenience and rapid change. We were not adequately prepared for it by past action, but now we understand the problem much better.

My only plea to you in closing is this: that we not be divided one from another, that we not be confused or deluded, that we not dream of the restoration of past times when oil was plentiful and cheap. It'll never come back. The chances are, in the future, that oil will be less plentiful, and it's certain that oil will be more expensive. But we can accommodate this change, because God has given us such tremendous blessings in our free Nation, an opportunity to cooperate. And we should not be distracted by allegations of impropriety among those who occupy positions of leadership.

We all have the same motivations: to have a nation strong, competent, united, determined, concerned about those who are less fortunate than we, recognizing that we are a world leader, and recognizing that our Nation must be secure. All these goals can be achieved if we work together, and I have no doubt that you and I together and other Americans who share

our common purpose can assure, without further delay, that we will make the greatest nation on Earth even greater in the future.

Thank you very much.

NOTE: The President spoke at 9:20 a.m. in the Grand Ballroom at the Biltmore Plaza Hotel.

The summit was sponsored by the Coalition of Northeastern Governors.

Cranston, Rhode Island

Remarks at a Governor's Reception for Civic and Community Leaders. October 29, 1979

Governor Garrahy, Senator Pell, Senator Chafee, Congressman St Germain, my good friend John Pastore, ladies and gentlemen:

It's an honor for me to be here.

I think that one of the best things we can do is to learn. Senator Pastore is a man—a son of Cranston, a statesman from Rhode Island—who was elected Governor twice, elected to the U.S. Senate four times. He gave reelection a good name. [*Laughter*] He's truly an inspiration to me. [*Laughter*] And I want to thank him for being here, and all of you.

Harry Truman also said that anyone who pays too much to personal popularity or who makes decisions that affect the well-being of our Nation on the basis of public opinion polls is not worthy to be President of this country. It's nice to have both—[*laughter*]—to do what's right, to do what's correct, just, and also to be popular. He couldn't do it, and I've not found it possible either.

In April of 1977, when I went to you on television and to the Congress in a Joint Session, I pointed out in my evening television address that to present a comprehensive energy policy to the Congress for adoption would undoubtedly cost me 15 percentage points in the public opinion polls. It was one of the few mistakes I've made. [*Laughter*] I grossly underestimated how unpopular that would prove to be.

But in the long run it has been the right thing to do, and the Congress, with your help, is now moving in a courageous way toward evolving for us, in law, a substantive and permanent and adequate national energy policy. It's long overdue. It'll give us a framework around which we can build our lives, around which State and local governments can cooperate with one another and with the Federal Government, and around which private citizens can make decisions that will be right for themselves, for their families, for their communities, and also for our Nation.

I'm very grateful that I had a chance this morning to come and speak to and meet with the Coalition of Northeastern Governors. They have, along with you, been in the forefront of exploring for new ways to accommodate rapid change. And we live in a country where rapid change is now and will be part of our lives, but we have got a country that is resilient. We're tough; we're strong; we still have a pioneer spirit. The American people respond when they have a clear guidance and an understanding and are told the truth about the problems that we face and the challenges that confront our Nation.

We have never failed in history to unite in a time of crisis when the well-being of our Nation was at stake. In the past we've had an advantage, however, in some ways. In the First World War we knew what the challenge was; we united. During the Great Depression, we knew what the challenge was. It was not quite so well defined, but we drew ourselves together in a common purpose and with a common spirit. We worked together, and we prevailed. In the Second World War the challenge was evident. The American people united in a common purpose, with a common commitment, with courage, and we prevailed.

And now there's a rapidly developing understanding that our Nation is challenged or threatened even again, and we are uniting finally. And when we do unite and work together toward a common purpose of having energy security, we will prevail. This is inherent in the character of American people.

We're different. One of the strengths of our country is our extreme diversity. We're a nation comprised of people from every nation on Earth. Hundreds of different languages are known by Americans. Wide-ranging ethnic heritages, customs, religious beliefs are preserved, because they are precious to us. Blood ties to other countries are precious to us. But at the same time, we put our differences apart or aside when our country is threatened, and we unite toward a common purpose.

We're a nation of immigrants, yes, we're even a nation of refugees, but that gives us strength, not weakness. And I'm very proud of what this has done in the last few weeks in our country. People are aroused to meet this challenge successfully.

One of the most important characteristics of American governmental system is our system of federalism—federalism, the coalition prescribed under our Constitution and laws for cooperation between a county official, a mayor, a Governor, a President, a Member of the Congress, because every mayor in this room, every county official in this room represents exactly the same people that I do. There's no difference of approach; there's no difference of responsibility.

And one of the most debilitating things in a time like this is for there to be an attempt made politically to benefit because our Nation is being challenged. It's not a time to grasp for selfish advantage. It's a time for us to put aside differences, except in an open debate that's part of democracy, and work toward the future. We've done it in many ways.

Your Governor has been a superb example of what can be done. I remember when I was inaugurated President, the State in this country that had the highest unemployment rate was Rhode Island. The unemployment rate in Providence, Rhode Island, was more than 10 percent. Now it's less than 6 percent. The unemployment rate in the entire State of Rhode Island was 9½ percent. Now it's less than 6 percent.

There was a transformation taking place in your State and in your local communities that was very difficult. But because of good cooperation and the analysis of a common problem and the sharing of information, the tough arguments at times about how best to reach a goal, we have been successful jointly.

We've tried to organize the Federal Government to meet your needs more efficiently, when there was cooperation. I remember the devastating snowfall and ice storm that occurred in your State. It was one of the biggest burdens placed on their communities in years. But there was a good sharing, without recrimination, without blame, without casting stones, and we shared the responsibility along with the private citizens here and prevailed.

One great opportunity that we have as well now is to bring prosperity to our downtown urban areas in large cities and also middle- and small-sized cities. There is a sharing of responsibility here. The Department of Transportation has been working with your Governor and local officials to bring about a relocation of the Providence, Rhode Island, station complex and move it closer to your State Capitol. This will be a successful project that will give your downtown area a stimulus that will give you a better life for all people in this region in the years to come.

These are the kinds of cooperative efforts that pay rich dividends for us all.

I'd like just to mention two other things that extend far beyond Cranston or Providence or Rhode Island, even Washington. Ours is a strong nation. We are a nation at peace. I'm the first President in 56 years that has served so far without a single American being killed in combat overseas. This is not a personal triumph for me, but it's an indication that our Nation is a peace-loving nation. But we are a peace-loving nation that understands that peace can only be ours if we are strong, and we will stay strong.

There's not only a requirement for military strength, which we will maintain second to none, but there's also a requirement that the American people be strong, that we again have that word I used before—unity—and confidence in one another and a common purpose, because the best way that we can have peace is for any potential adversary to know that America is militarily strong, economically strong, politically strong, that we have the will and resolve to protect ourselves, but also that we are a nation which is morally strong, that our ethical standards are high, that the principles on which our Nation was founded still prevail.

I think we've had a remarkable demonstration of that just recently. When the Holy Father came here, Pope John Paul II, the reception that he received in our country was unanticipated and startling in its significance. I had a few minutes with him privately in the Oval Office, after we greeted the Members of the House and Senate, the Cabinet, the Supreme Court Justices, and others, and I asked if he was surprised. He said yes. And I said I was, too. "I knew that you'd be received with open arms and with friendship and hospitality in our country, but I never dreamed that you would have 1½ million people assembled in Grant Park in Chicago," the biggest group of people ever assembled in the United States for any purpose, and the overwhelming response from people of all faiths to him and kind of an outpouring, a demonstration of the hunger for the characteristics of life which never change.

Things do change that cause us concern, but there are some things that never change—the strength of families, basic commitments to love, to understanding, to compassion, to unselfishness. Those never change.

And I'm very grateful that we live in a country of that kind that is strong, that can accommodate change, that can bear inconvenience, that can marshal our forces together when our Nation is tested, that can put aside personal differences of background and commitment and interest and unite for a common purpose, that has a system of government that can meld us together to serve the same people, and where our standards of morality and ethics are the underlying, girding strength that provides the basis for everything else which we hope to achieve. It makes me proud to be President of a country like that—my country and your country.

Thank you very much.

NOTE: The President spoke at 10:22 a.m. in the Narragansett Ballroom at the Cranston Hilton Hotel.

Mission in Addis Ababa from 1977 until earlier this year.

He was born April 13, 1927, in Oxnard, Calif. He received a B.A. from the University of California at Berkeley in 1948.

Matheron began his career with the State Department in 1949 and was posted in Paris, Saigon, and Rome. From 1959 to 1960, he was an intelligence research specialist at the State Department. In 1960–61 he took African studies at the University of California at Los Angeles.

From 1961 to 1964, Matheron was a political officer, stationed in Lagos, Yaounde, and Kinshasa. From 1964 to 1965, he was principal officer in Bukavu. In 1965–66 he attended the Armed Forces Staff College.

From 1966 to 1967, Matheron was Executive Secretary of the Agency for International Development in Saigon. He was at the State Department from 1967 to 1972 as an international relations officer, then a political-military officer. From 1970 to 1972, he was counselor for political affairs, then Deputy Chief of Mission in Ouagadougou.

From 1972 to 1974, he was Deputy Chief of Mission in Tananarive. He attended the National War College in 1974–75. From 1975 to 1977, he was a foreign service inspector.

United States Ambassador to Swaziland

*Nomination of Richard C. Matheron.
October 29, 1979*

The President today announced that he will nominate Richard C. Matheron, of Bakersfield, Calif., to be Ambassador Extraordinary and Plenipotentiary of the United States to the Kingdom of Swaziland. He would replace Donald R. Norland, who has been transferred to another position. Matheron was Deputy Chief of

President's Commission on the Accident at Three Mile Island

*Remarks on Receiving the Commission's
Final Report.   October 30, 1979*

I've just met with Dr. Kemeny, the Chairman, and with the members and the staff of the Commission to investigate the accident at Three Mile Island. And I've received the Commission's final report, which has just been delivered to me this morning.

As I indicated when the Commission was formed, its task was one of the most important which has ever been assigned to a Presidential commission. Its findings and its recommendations will be studied very carefully by me, by the members of my administration, the Congress, the American public at large, members of the industry, and, I think, indeed, many leaders in foreign countries, who've been waiting to see what the Commission's analysis and recommendations would comprise.

They have fulfilled this extremely challenging task with the greatest degree of care and dispatch. Over a 6-month period they have met frequently. They've investigated thoroughly. The attendance at the meetings has been almost perfect, and each member, highly diverse among themselves, has been a great contribution to the overall recommendations.

The staff and the Commission members deserve the gratitude of the American people, and on behalf of our Nation, Chairman Kemeny, I want to thank you personally and, for all of us, for the great work you've done.

This accident at Three Mile Island brought home the need to assure that nuclear power is as safe as possible. This report will guide us all in learning about the accident itself and in assuring the higher degree of safety for our citizens.

Throughout my own Presidency, I've given a high priority to furthering the safety of nuclear energy. It has been and will continue to be one of the most critical tasks of our generation. The Commission has made many far-reaching recommendations to improve nuclear safety—I think, specifically, 44 different recommendations—and these far-reaching recommendations deserve our immediate and careful attention and study.

This is a complicated report. It's highly technical in nature in some respects and will require very careful assessment. Some of its recommendations can be carried out by the industry, some by me through Executive order, some will require legislative recommendations and decisions by the Congress.

Our own assessment and our decisions on what to do cannot be made immediately, and we'll have to be very careful and very methodical in our recommendations to the public. After my advisers and I complete our analysis, then I will report to the Congress and to the Nation on further steps which are needed to improve and protect the public health and safety as it relates to nuclear power.

The Commission will now be disbanded, but I've asked the Commission members and, particularly, Chairman Kemeny to make themselves available to me in case there are followup questions that we need to have answered or additional consultations with them on specific recommendations included in the report.

This afternoon at 1:30, Dr. Kemeny and the members of the Commission and staff will have a definitive briefing for the press, but I wanted to express my thanks to him and to the Commission at this point. And he will be available to you and others during the afternoon to answer more specific questions.

Dr. Kemeny, thank you very much, on behalf of our country.

NOTE: The President spoke at 11:37 a.m. to reporters assembled in the Briefing Room at the White House.

Department of Education

Statement on the Nomination of Shirley Hufstedler To Be Secretary.   *October 30, 1979*

Judge Shirley Hufstedler has one of the best minds in the country. To fill the position of first Secretary of the new Department of Education, I wanted a strong, creative thinker who could take a new, fresh look at the way we educate our children. In Judge Shirley Hufstedler, we have found that person.

She is deeply committed to the quality of education and enjoys my full confidence and support. I am certain she will be an outstanding Secretary.

NOTE: Deputy Press Secretary Rex Granum read the President's statement at approximately 11:45 a.m. to reporters assembled in the Briefing Room at the White House, after announcing that the President will nominate Judge Hufstedler to be Secretary of Education.

Also included in the press release is a question-and-answer session with reporters.

Research Apprenticeships Program

Announcement of the Program.
October 30, 1979

The President today announced a program of apprenticeships in research laboratories for minority high school students, beginning in the summer of 1980. The program was developed by Jim McIntyre, Director of the Office of Management and Budget, and Frank Press, Director of the Office of Science and Technology Policy, together with Special Assistants to the President Louis Martin and Esteban Torres.

The objectives of this research apprenticeships program are to stimulate broader interest in minority communities in careers in science and engineering and to establish individual working relationships between students and active researchers. The program is designed to strengthen the Nation's and the Government's efforts to recruit and sustain minority students in science and engineering fields. The numerical goal for 1980 is to employ at least 1,000 students in summer jobs through this program. The goal for subsequent years is 2,000.

Participating agencies are the Department of Defense, the Department of Energy, the National Institutes of Health, the National Science Foundation, the Department of Agriculture, the National Aeronautics and Space Administration, and the Environmental Protection Agency.

Individual researchers who wish to participate in the program will submit a supplemental request to existing or pending research grants and contracts. The request will state the kinds of work experience which can be offered, the routes through which interested students will be sought in local or other high schools, and the special activities that will be organized to provide educational enrichment beyond the work itself.

The student and the researchers will be expected to submit a brief evaluation of the experience, to guide assessment and expansion of the program.

Department of Energy

Nomination of George W. Cunningham To Be an Assistant Secretary.   October 30, 1979

The President today announced his intention to nominate George W. Cunningham, of Newbern, Tenn., to be Assistant Secretary of Energy for Nuclear Energy. Cunningham has been Deputy Chief of the U.S. Mission to the International Atomic Energy Agency in Vienna, Austria, since 1978.

He was born December 3, 1930, in Union City, Tenn. He received a B.S. in chemical engineering and an M.S. in metallurgy from the University of Tennessee and a Ph. D. in metallurgical engineering from Ohio State University.

From 1955 to 1966, Cunningham was with the Batelle Memorial Institute. From 1966 to 1978, he was with the Atomic

Energy Commission and its successor agencies, beginning as a metallurgical engineer and finally serving as Program Director of Nuclear Energy with the Energy Department.

Department of Energy

Nomination of Thomas E. Stelson To Be an Assistant Secretary.   October 30, 1979

The President today announced his intention to nominate Thomas E. Stelson, of Atlanta, Ga., to be Assistant Secretary of Energy for Conservation and Solar Applications. He would replace Omi Walden, who is assuming the position of Adviser to the Secretary for Conservation and Solar Marketing. Stelson has been vice president for research of Georgia Institute of Technology's College of Engineering since 1974.

He was born August 24, 1928, in Iowa City, Iowa. He received bachelor's (1949), master's (1950), and doctoral (1952) degrees from Carnegie Institute of Technology.

From 1952 to 1971, Stelson was on the faculty at Carnegie-Mellon University, where he served as head of the department of civil engineering from 1959 to 1971 and Alcoa Professor from 1961 to 1971. From 1971 to 1974, he was dean and professor of civil engineering at Georgia Tech.

District of Columbia Law Revision Commission

Reappointment of Stephen I. Danzansky as a Member.   October 30, 1979

The President today announced that he has reappointed Stephen I. Danzansky as a member of the District of Columbia Law Revision Commission for a 4-year term.

Danzansky, 40, is a Washington attorney who has served on the board of directors of Self Determination for D.C. Metropolitan Commission and serves as special counsel to the Citizen Coalition for Planning and Zoning Reform of the District of Columbia.

Office of the Special Representative for Trade Negotiations

Nomination of Robert Hormats To Be a Deputy Special Representative. October 30, 1979

The President today announced that he will nominate Robert Hormats, of Chevy Chase, Md., to be Deputy Special Representative for Trade Negotiations. He would replace Alonzo McDonald. Hormats has been Senior Deputy Assistant Secretary of State for Economic and Business Affairs since 1977.

He was born April 13, 1943, in Baltimore, Md. He received an M.A. (1966), an M.A.L.D. (1967), and a Ph. D. (1969) from Fletcher School of Law and Diplomacy.

Hormats was a staff member, then senior staff member, on the National Security Council from 1969 to 1973. He was a guest scholar at the Brookings Institution and an international affairs fellow of the Council on Foreign Relations from 1973 to 1974. He also served as a senior consultant to the Commission on Critical Choices for Americans in 1973.

From 1974 to 1977, Hormats was senior staff member for international economic affairs at the National Security Council.

Office of the Special Representative for Trade Negotiations

Nomination of Michael B. Smith To Be a Deputy Special Representative.
October 30, 1979

The President today announced that he will nominate Michael B. Smith, of Potomac, Md., to be Deputy Special Representative for Trade Negotiations. He would replace Alan Wolff, resigned. Smith has been chief negotiator for textile matters of the United States since 1975.

He was born June 16, 1936, in Marblehead, Mass. He graduated from Harvard College in 1958.

Smith joined the Foreign Service in 1958 and was stationed in Tehran and N'Djamena, Chad. He was Staff Assistant to the Under Secretary for Economic Affairs from 1965 to 1966. From 1967 to 1968, Smith was deputy principal officer in Strasbourg, and from 1969 to 1970, he was principal officer in Lyon.

Smith was assigned to the White House in 1970 as Chief of Presidential Correspondence. In 1973 he was reassigned to the State Department as Deputy Chief of the Fibers and Textiles Division, and in 1974 he became Chief of the Division.

United States Ambassador to Burma

Nomination of Patricia M. Byrne.
October 30, 1979

The President today announced that he will nominate Patricia M. Byrne, of South Euclid, Ohio, to be Ambassador Extraordinary and Plenipotentiary of the United States to the Socialist Republic of the Union of Burma. She would replace Maurice Bean, resigned. Byrne has been Ambassador to the Republic of Mali since 1976.

She was born June 1, 1925, in Cleveland, Ohio. She received an A.B. from Vassar College in 1946 and an M.A. from the Johns Hopkins University School of Advanced International Studies in 1947.

Byrne joined the Foreign Service in 1949 and was posted in Athens, Saigon, Izmir, Ankara, and at the State Department. She was a member of the U.S. Delegation to the 1961–62 Geneva Conference on Laos, and was political officer in Vientiane from 1962 to 1963.

She was at the State Department from 1964 to 1968 in positions including Chief for East Asia Personnel and Special Assistant to the Deputy Under Secretary for Administration. In 1968–69 she attended the National War College.

From 1969 to 1972, Byrne was political officer in Paris for Asian affairs, and from 1972 to 1975, she was Deputy Chief of Mission in Colombo. In 1975–76 she took the senior seminar in foreign policy at the Foreign Service Institute.

United States Coordinator for Refugee Affairs

Exchange of Letters on the Resignation of Ambassador at Large Dick Clark.
October 30, 1979

To Dick Clark

Fritz [1] had reported to me your pledge to remain neutral in the political campaign and to devote your efforts to assisting refugees and other suffering people. I consider this work to be of transcendant importance.

Therefore, I accept your resignation with regret, and appreciation.

JIMMY CARTER

[1] EDITOR'S NOTE: Vice President Mondale.

October 29, 1979

Dear Mr. President:

I am writing to advise you of my decision to resign from the Administration.

I do so with reluctance because of my respect for you personally, because of what you stand for, and what you have tried to accomplish. This decision is made all the more difficult because of my admiration for and friendship with Vice President Walter Mondale.

My original intention was to remain neutral in the Presidential Primary contest. Careful thought and further reflection have convinced me that such a position is untenable and unwise. I think you would agree with me that to remain uninvolved in a matter of such importance to the country is irresponsible. Consequently, I have made my choice. I will be joining Senator Edward Kennedy's Campaign Committee following my resignation.

It is with regret that I leave my present position as Coordinator of Refugee Affairs. It has been a rewarding job. Working with Secretary Vance has been a particular pleasure and a rare opportunity. In January, when the Secretary asked me to take this position, I was reluctant to do so, but he urged me to accept even if only for a few months in order to reorganize scattered jurisdiction and the hodgepodge of existing programs. That objective has now been completed:

—A new Office of Refugee Programs has been established in the Department of State with a Director at the Assistant Secretary level. Previous jurisdictions in the Bureau of International Organization Affairs, the Bureau of Human Rights and Humanitarian Affairs, and the Agency for International Development are now under that single authority.

—An Interagency Committee on Refugee Affairs has been established and is working effectively to coordinate all existing refugee programs in the Government, both foreign and domestic.

—The Refugee Act of 1979 has passed the Senate (85–0) and will be voted on in the House in the next few days. It is the first comprehensive refugee legislation in the nation's history and will end existing inequities and inconsistencies in our refugee program.

—With your support, we have increased our refugee resettlement program to over 200,000 annually, and the appropriation for implementation has now passed both Houses. The authorization has passed the House and is to be taken up in the Senate in the next day or two.

—Much has been accomplished in achieving a greater burden sharing by the international community in dealing with Indochinese refugee problems.

In summary, those tasks assigned to me in January have now been accomplished with the support of others in the Administration and in the Congress. An effective Coordinator will be needed to give direction to these on-going programs, but I am confident that such a person can be found.

Therefore, I am resigning effective November 1, but will, of course, be available to assist in any way I can.

Again, thank you for your many kindnesses. It has been a privilege to work with you.

Sincerely,

DICK CLARK
Dick Clark

[The President, The White House, Washington, D.C.]

Alaska Public Lands Legislation

Statement on Approval by the Senate Energy and Natural Resources Committee.
October 30, 1979

I am pleased to note that the Senate Energy and Natural Resources Committee voted to report the Alaska lands bill earlier this afternoon. While the protections afforded by the committee's bill are not as substantial as those which I originally proposed and which I continue to support, the committee's action today is an important step.

I would like to commend Senator Jackson and the other members of his committee who have devoted their time and energy to this legislation. In particular, I would like to express my thanks to Senator Tsongas, who has led the effort in committee to strengthen the bill.

The passage of legislation protecting Alaska's priceless natural heritage is the highest environmental priority of my administration. The legislation I proposed to the Congress not only protects Alaska's cultural and natural heritage but also accommodates the need for balanced development of Alaska's natural resources. Earlier this year the House passed such a bill. I am hopeful that the Senate will as well.

Industrial Innovation Initiatives

Remarks Announcing a Program To Encourage Innovation.   October 31, 1979

One of the most important responsibilities that I have as President is to make sure that in the 1980's, and also now, we have a strong and vital economy with adequate job opportunities and with the competitive position of our country maintained in world markets and also in giving our own people a better quality of life. We have additional problems in controlling inflation, solving our energy problem, dealing with housing needs, improving our agricultural communities, and many others in a list of important considerations for every American.

Since I've been in office, we've tried to

form a very close partnership with the different elements of American society, particularly in the private sector, and, in addition to that, to restore what we had begun to lose in a very serious fashion, and that is the innovative nature of the American free enterprise system and our initiatives that, in the past, have been one of our most precious resources of our country.

Today I'm announcing a program and sending a message to Congress which will significantly enhance our Nation's industrial innovative capacity and thereby help to revitalize America's industrial base. This program is the result of a thorough, 18-month analysis, and it's been conducted by the Domestic Policy Staff, by representatives from the private sector of our economy, and also, in particular, by the Department of Commerce. It represents the most wideranging initiative ever made to spur initiative and innovation and to unleash America's creative genius.

Industrial innovation, or the development and commercialization of new products and new processes, is an essential, but increasingly overlooked factor in a strong and growing American economy. This will help to ensure economic vitality, improve productivity, international competitiveness, the creation of jobs, and a better quality of life for every American.

Further industrial innovation is necessary if we are to solve some of our Nation's most pressing problems—restraining the cost of products and thereby reducing inflation, providing new energy supplies and better conserving existing supplies of energy, ensuring adequate food production for ourselves and for the world's population, protecting our environment and our natural resources, and improving health care for every American.

Our Nation's history, as you know, is filled with a rich tradition of industrial innovation. For over a century, America has been the world's leader in developing new products, new processes, new technologies, and also new ways of assuring wide distribution of new products and their beneficial use by humanity.

We are still the world's leader, but our products are meeting with growing competition from abroad. Many of the world's leading industrial countries are now attempting to develop competitive advantages through their own innovative capability and an increasing concentration of their efforts in this realm of economic life. This is a challenge which we can no longer afford to ignore. To respond to this challenge, we must initiate our own policies to foster the Nation's competitive capability and entrepreneurial spirit in the decades ahead.

The actions that I'm announcing today meet this goal. First of all, they will loosen some of the stifling restraints that have been placed upon innovation by government. Secondly, they represent a first major step toward forging a public and private partnership which will rally cooperative efforts to spur industrial growth. Third, they will enhance our economic position, in enabling America's industry to develop and to market new processes and products, both here in our own country and also abroad.

These actions will be detailed to you shortly, and they include the development, for the first time in our history, of a uniform Government patent policy. This will foster the widest possible use of the results of Government-supported research and, at the same time, will protect the interests of the Government and, therefore, the population of our country at large.

We'll also include the widest possible dissemination in this country of technical information which is developed in Government laboratories, in universities and private industry through Government-sponsored research, in other industrialized nations, and also buried in our own patent files. The derivation and promulgation of this available information throughout the American economic system will be enhanced greatly by this new proposal.

Programs to encourage the cooperative development of vitally needed resources and technologies are now largely ignored. We will establish two corporations for industrial development, specifically to assist small businesses. A lot of the innovation and initiative comes from small business. This will be a major target of our innovative processes and efforts, because small businesses do, quite often, have startup problems.

These actions, along with others that will be outlined as part of this program, will make a major difference in our Nation's ability to develop and to pursue industrial innovation.

I'd like to point out, however, that this will not solve the problem alone. This problem has arisen over a long period of years. It's recognized as being a serious problem by labor, by industry, and by government at all levels. There's no doubt about it. And it will take years to overcome the problem in its entirety. It will also require a sound economic climate. But the two are mutually supportive. More innovation will help the economic climate; a better economic climate will also help to encourage innovation.

Today's announcement does represent an important first step in dealing specifically with this problem of industrial innovation and more generally with similar types of economic problems that will be facing our country in the 1980's. With the cooperation of the private sector and the Congress, these problems of today, which are different in many ways and in major ways from those we've experienced before, can be solved. I'm committed to work toward their resolution.

Secretary Juanita Kreps will now provide some additional words about the program and answer questions from you.

Unfortunately for me and for our Nation, this is one of her last days in office. And I want to take this opportunity to commend her on her fine work on this program, typical of a superb performance that she has exhibited for us in this country as Secretary of Commerce, and I am particularly grateful to her for the great work that she's done in the last 34 months. She's already promised to make her advice and counsel and services available to us when she retires from this public job. But there's no way I can adequately express my personal thanks to her and the thanks on behalf of a grateful nation.

Secretary Juanita Kreps.

NOTE: The President spoke at 9:37 a.m. to reporters assembled in the Briefing Room at the White House.

Following the President's remarks, Secretary of Commerce Juanita M. Kreps, Frank Press, Director of the Office of Science and Technology Policy, Stuart E. Eizenstat, Assistant to the President for Domestic Affairs and Policy, and Jordan Baruch, Assistant Secretary of Commerce for Science and Technology, held a news conference on the program.

Industrial Innovation Initiatives

Message to the Congress on Administration Actions and Proposals.   October 31, 1979

To the Congress of the United States:

Industrial innovation—the development and commercialization of new products and processes—is an essential element of a strong and growing American economy. It helps ensure economic vitality, improved productivity, international competitiveness, job creation, and an improved quality of life for every American. Further, industrial innovation is necessary if we are to solve some of the Nation's most pressing problems—reducing inflation, providing new energy supplies and better conserving existing supplies, ensuring adequate food for the world's population, protecting the environment and our natural resources, and improving health care.

Our Nation's history is filled with a rich tradition of industrial innovation. America has been the world leader in developing new products, new processes, and new technologies, and in ensuring their wide dissemination and use. We are still the world's leader. But our products are meeting growing competition from abroad. Many of the world's leading industrial countries are now attempting to develop a competitive advantage through the use of industrial innovation. This is a challenge we cannot afford to ignore any longer. To respond to this challenge, we must develop our own policies for fostering the Nation's competitive capability and entrepreneurial spirit in the decades ahead. This Message represents an important first step in that direction.

I am today announcing measures which will help ensure our country's continued role as the world's leader in industrial innovation. These initiatives address nine critical areas:

- Enhancing the Transfer of Information
- Increasing Technical Knowledge
- Strengthening the Patent System
- Clarifying Anti-trust Policy
- Fostering the Development of Small Innovative Firms
- Opening Federal Procurement to Innovations
- Improving Our Regulatory System
- Facilitating Labor/Management Adjustment to Technical Change
- Maintaining a Supportive Climate for Innovation.

INITIATIVES

1. *Enhancing the Transfer of Information.* Often, the information that underlies a technological advance is not known to companies capable of commercially developing that advance. I am therefore taking several actions to ease and encourage the flow of technical knowledge and information. These actions include establishing the Center for the Utilization of Federal Technology at the National Technical Information Service to improve the transfer of knowledge from Federal laboratories; and, through the State and Commerce Departments, increasing the availability of technical information developed in foreign countries.

2. *Increasing Technical Knowledge.* We have already made significant efforts to assure an adequate investment in the basic research that will underlie future technical advances. This commitment is reflected in a 25 percent growth in funding during the first two years of my Administration. I am taking some additional steps that will increase Federal support for research and development:

First, I will establish a program to cooperate with industry in the advancement of generic technologies that underlie the operations of several industrial sectors. This activity will broaden the $50 million initiative I announced in May to further research in automotive research. Second, in order to help harness the scientific and technological strength of American universities, I have directed a significant enhancement in support of joint industry-university research proposals. This program will be modeled on a successful program at the National Science Foundation, and I have set a target of $150 million in Federal support for it.

3. *Strengthening the Patent System.* Patents can provide a vital incentive for innovation, but the patent process has become expensive, time-consuming, and unreliable. Each year, fewer patents are issued to Americans. At my direction, the Patent and Trademark Office will undertake a major effort to upgrade and modernize its processes, in order to restore the incentive to patent—and ultimately develop—inventions. I will also seek legislation to provide the Patent and Trademark Office with greater authority to re-examine patents already issued, thereby reducing the need for expensive, time-consuming litigation over the validity of a patent.

For over thirty years the Federal agencies supporting research and development in industry and universities have had conflicting policies governing the disposition of pertinent rights resulting from that work. This confusion has seriously inhibited the use of those patents in industry. To remove that confusion and encourage the use of those patents I will support uniform government patent legislation. That legislation will provide exclusive licenses to contractors in specific fields of use that they agree to commercialize and will permit the government to license firms in other fields. If the license fails to commercialize the inventories, the government will retain the right to recapture those rights. I will also support the retention of patent ownership by small businesses and universities, the prime thrust of legislation now in Congress, in recognition of their special place in our society.

4. *Clarifying Anti-trust Policy.* By spurring competition, anti-trust policies can provide a stimulant to the development of innovations. In some cases, however, such as in research, industrial cooperation may have clear social and economic benefits for the country. Unfortunately, our anti-trust laws are often mistakenly viewed as preventing all cooperative activity.

The Department of Justice, at my direction, will issue a guide clearly explaining its position on collaboration among firms

2071

in research, as part of a broader program of improved communication with industry by the Justice Department and the Federal Trade Commission. This statement will provide the first uniform anti-trust guidance to industrial firms in the area of cooperation in research.

5. *Fostering the Development of Small Innovative Firms.* Small innovative firms have historically played an important role in bringing new technologies into the marketplace. They are also an important source of new jobs. Although many of the initiatives in this Message will encourage such companies, I will also implement several initiatives focused particularly on small firms.

First, I propose the enhancement by $10 million of the Small Business Innovation Research Program of the National Science Foundation. This program supports creative, high-risk, potentially high-reward research performed by small business. Further, the National Science Foundation will assist other agencies in implementing similar programs, with total Federal support eventually reaching $150 million per year.

Second, in order to experiment with ways to ease the ability of small firms to obtain start-up capital, I will help establish two Corporations For Innovation Development to provide equity funding for firms that will develop and market promising high-risk innovations. These not-for-profit firms will be established with State or regional capital and the Federal government will provide each with matching loan funds up to $4 million.

6. *Opening Federal Procurement to Innovations.* The Federal government is the Nation's largest single purchaser of goods and services. Through its purchases, the Federal government can influence the rate at which innovative products enter the market.

For that reason, I am directing the Office of Federal Procurement Policy to introduce procurement policies and regulations that will remove barriers now inhibiting the government from purchasing innovative products. Special attention will be given to substituting performance for design specifications and, wherever feasible, selection will be on the basis of costs over the life of the item, rather than merely the initial purchase price.

7. *Improving our Regulatory System.* During my Administration, I have already taken a number of actions to help assure that regulation does not adversely affect innovation. Working with the Congress, I have moved successfully toward deregulation of airlines and other industries, and I expect the pressure of competition to trigger innovative new ways to cut costs and improve service. In environmental, health and safety regulation, I have emphasized the use of cost-impact analysis, where appropriate, to take account of the burdens on industry in the regulatory process. To provide better coordination between the regulatory agencies, I have created the Regulatory Council, composed of the heads of 35 regulatory agencies. This Council is working to reduce inconsistencies and duplications among regulations, to eliminate needless rule-making delays, to reduce paperwork, and to minimize the cost of compliance.

I am today proposing additional steps to improve our regulatory system. First, the Administrator of EPA will intensify his efforts, wherever possible, to use performance standards in regulations, specifying only the required goal, rather than the means of achieving it. Second, all Executive Branch environmental, health and safety regulatory agencies will prepare a five-year forecast of their priorities and concerns. This information will give industry the time to develop compliance technology. Third, all administrators of Federal executive agencies responsible for clearance of new products will be directed to develop and implement an expedited process for projects having a strong innovative impact or exceptional social benefit, and to do so without jeopardizing the quality of the review process.

8. *Facilitating Labor and Management Adjustments to Technical Change.* Although innovation can increase the number of workers employed within an industry over the long term, or even create an entire new industry, individual innovations may occasionally cause workers to be displaced.

In order to assure adequate time for workers and management to adjust to changes caused by innovations, I am directing the Secretaries of Labor and Commerce to work jointly with labor and management to develop a Labor/Technology Forecasting System. The System would develop advance warning of industrial changes and permit timely adjustments.

9. *Maintaining a Supportive Federal Climate.* The initiatives announced in this Message are only the first steps in our efforts to ensure American technological strength. We must also develop and maintain a climate conducive to industrial innovation. The Federal government must take the lead in creating that climate. And the Federal government's efforts must be continuing ones. I am committed to these goals.

I am charging the National Productivity Council with the continuing tasks of monitoring innovation, developing policies to encourage innovation and assisting the Departments and agencies in implementing the policies announced today. I am also establishing a Presidential award for technological innovation to make clear to this Nation's inventors and entrepreneurs that we place the highest national value on their contributions.

Each of the initiatives I have just proposed supports an important component in the innovation process. In combina-

tion, these initiatives should make a major difference in our Nation's ability to develop and pursue industrial innovation. However, these incentives will not by themselves solve our current difficulties in encouraging needed innovation. In our economic system, industrial innovation is primarily the responsibility of the private sector. The manager of the firm must decide whether to develop and market innovative new products or whether to find and employ new ways of making existing products. Although the Federal government can establish a climate that encourages innovative activity, it is the private sector that finally determines whether innovation will take place.

In addition, the steps outlined in this Message must be viewed in the context of our current severe inflation problem. With costs rising at an abnormally high rate, managers naturally have a disincentive to spend the sums needed for adequate industrial innovation. I understand and fully appreciate that changing certain of our tax laws could provide additional incentives for investment in innovation. Indeed, my approval of adjustments in the capital gains tax in the Revenue Act of 1978 has alleviated some shortages of venture capital. Many of the suggested alterations of our tax system are intertwined with other economic challenges—such as fighting inflation. While it might be possible to make changes in the tax code that would promote innovation, these changes should not be viewed in isolation from other aspects of our economy. I will therefore evaluate tax laws affecting industrial innovation at the time that I consider my fiscal policies for Fiscal Year 1981.

CONCLUSION

Innovation is a subtle and intricate process, covering that range of events from the inspiration of the inventor to the marketing strategy of the eventual producer. Although there are many places in the chain from invention to sale where we have found modification of Federal policy to be appropriate, there is no one place where the Federal government can take action and thereby ensure that industrial innovation will be increased. We have therefore chosen a range of initiatives, each of which we believe to be helpful. In aggregate, we expect them to have a significant impact. Nonetheless, they represent only an early skirmish in what must be a continuing battle to maintain the technological strength of the American economy. I pledge myself to this task and ask the Congress to join me in meeting our common challenge.

JIMMY CARTER

The White House,
October 31, 1979.

Small Business Administration

Memorandum From the President.
October 31, 1979

Memorandum for A. Vernon Weaver
Subject: The Small Business Administration's (SBA) Membership on the Regulatory Council

When I established the Regulatory Council last year I directed that it be the focal point of efforts to assess the cumulative impact of regulation and to coordinate Federal regulatory activity. I hope that many of the improvements in government regulations that the Council is instituting will be of direct benefit to our nation's small businesses.

Government regulation sometimes poses special problems for small business. The Small Business Administration has done a great deal to make us aware of these problems and has worked closely with regulatory agencies to resolve them. This is an appropriate time to acknowledge formally the importance of the Small Business Administration's role in the Administration's regulatory reform effort by including SBA as a Council member.

I am pleased to grant your request for membership and I look forward to SBA's participation in the work of the Regulatory Council.

JIMMY CARTER

NOTE: The text of the memorandum was released on November 1.

Panama Canal Commission

Appointment of Fernando Manfredo as Deputy Administrator. November 1, 1979

The President today announced the appointment of Fernando Manfredo as Deputy Administrator of the Panama Canal Commission. Mr. Manfredo, formerly the Panamanian Minister of Presidencia, has been engaged in Panama Canal treaty implementation activities for Panama during the past year.

Mr. Manfredo has been active in local Panamanian civic and business organizations and served as adviser to many private and government organizations in the Republic of Panama.

Death of Mamie Eisenhower

Statement by the President.
November 1, 1979

Rosalynn and I share the sadness of a loving nation at the death of Mamie Eisenhower and send our deepest sympathy to her family.

A warm and gracious First Lady, she carried out her public and private duties, despite a lifetime of fragile health, in a way that won her a special place in the heart of Americans and of people all over the world. To generations of Americans, in war and peace, she embodied sincerity and traditional values.

As we have missed the General-President whose triumphant life she shared, we will miss this gentle lady.

President's Environmental Youth Awards

Remarks on Presenting the Awards.
November 1, 1979

THE PRESIDENT. Hello, everybody. Doug Costle [1] is testifying and is on the way over here, but Barbara Blum and others are present who can represent the Environmental Protection Agency very well.

As President I want to say how grateful I am to all of you for coming, and particularly for the young people who will win the awards. One of the gratifying things about this program is that over 200,000 young Americans have been given awards for outstanding work in protecting the quality of life of American people.

Their projects pay rich dividends as they are conducted and concluded, but they also lay a groundwork for advanced scientists, for Members of Congress, my own administration, and Presidents to see how we can, through these processes, have a better way of preserving our precious heritage and environmental quality.

There's another aspect, I think, that's equally important for now and the future. When a 3-year-old American or an 18-year-old American or anyone in between takes on a project, sometimes they can add a sense of innovation and a freshness of thought that a more senior American would never contribute. And they lay the

---

[1] Administrator, Environmental Protection Agency.

groundwork for themselves, in their own lives, to continue this work in years ahead.

I've read down the list of awards and seen the diversity of projects that have been concluded. Some of them are quite exciting and quite productive already.

And at this time Barbara Blum will read the citations, the awards will be given out, and I'd like to congratulate each one of the recipients of the awards personally.

Barbara?

Ms. BLUM. Thank you, Mr. President. I'd just like to echo what Jimmy Carter has said. It's been a great pleasure to work with the youth of this country in his Environmental Youth program and to bring people into the environmental movement and into caring that have never been there before to care and are just beginning to be our future.

Mr. President, today we have four young men who represent the Cub Scout Pack 981 in Annapolis, Maryland. For several weeks they studied aquatic life in marshes in the Chesapeake Bay area— one of the most important areas of our country—and they culminated their studies by doing something pretty creative: They floated popcorn on the water and then followed the popcorn as if it were an oil spill to see the movement of the waters. I think that was very creative.

[At this point, Ms. Blum, Deputy Administrator of the Environmental Protection Agency, introduced Scott M. Laurie, Christopher R. Petchler, Kevin E. Kovelant, and John Woerner to the President, who presented each with an award.]

Next we have something else pretty special—everybody's really pretty special today—but we have three young men from Cincinnati, Ohio, who, as part of the Civil Air Patrol—and they represent a group of children who, with their own money, took courses in radiation monitoring. There is a nuclear facility that's about to open in their area, and now they're going to be prepared in case of an emergency to do monitoring, both air and water.

[*Ms. Blum introduced Robert H. Green and Lizbeth A. and Anthony J. Etienne to the President, who presented each with an award.*]

Mr. President, this next young woman that we have here today was selected by her very own classmates at Rosemead High School. She is representing them today. Their class made four movies. They made movies on energy, on the environment, on pollution problems. They were the actors, they were the scriptwriters, they were the producers, and they were the distributors of this. They showed the films to civic groups and other schools, and they have made quite a contribution there in educating other people their age and older.

[*Ms. Blum introduced Mary Jane Roddy to the President, who presented her with an award.*]

Mr. President, next we have some high school students from Lakeland, Florida. They've done something pretty special too. They tested the water quality in the lakes around Lakeland—and we who are from the South know how many there are there—in order to determine, for the area development commission, the quality of the water and the wildlife that was present in the area. And as such, they've done as much for clean drinking water for Florida as any adults ever have in the history of the State.

[*Ms. Blum introduced James F. Skinner, Cindi Parker, and Randolph L. Barber to the President, who presented each with an award.*]

Mr. President, next we have two campers, summer campers, from the National Wildlife Federation Camp. They spent the whole summer session studying the open areas, studying the woodlands, mapping, compassing, and they also studied the interdependence of animals in the meadows and the forest habitats. And doing this, and through their camping experiences, they have been provided a real

understanding, that they're sharing with their classmates now, on how the natural environment affects the social and historical environments, too.

[*Ms. Blum introduced Kimberly Shafer and Nathan Liepold to the President, who presented each with an award.*]

And next, as you can well see, we have a Cub Scout, an Explorer Scout, and a Boy Scout. They're representing a coming together of your youth program, Mr. President, and the Boy Scouts of America. There will be 500 young men and women who are going to be participating in promoting energy conservation, at your request and call for energy conservation—5 million within the next year. And these young people are representative of those 5 million people.

[*Ms. Blum introduced Michael Birlew, Kevin Ward, and Tana Landgraf to the President, who presented each with an award.*]

THE PRESIDENT. I think the entire audience and the news media can see the contributions that these young people have already made and the wide difference among their projects. They've taken this as an initiative on their own, some acting as individuals, some acting as part of very fine organizations, some at summer camps, some within their own home community, some in the ocean, some in the woods, some in the South, some in the North. And they are representative of literally tens of thousands of young people who participated in this youth environment project to make sure that Americans at their age and of all ages know how important it is to preserve the quality of life for our people.

And on behalf of our Nation, I'd like to again express my deep thanks to them, individually and collectively, and also to express my thanks for all those tens of thousands that they represent by coming here to the White House to receive these awards. Thank you very much for being here. I'm very proud of what these young people have done and what they mean to us now and in the future.

Thank you again, everybody. Now go home and go back to work.

NOTE: The President spoke at 12:10 p.m. in the Rose Garden at the White House.

Council on Environmental Quality

Nomination of Robert H. Harris To Be a Member.   November 1, 1979

The President today announced that he will nominate Robert H. Harris, of Fairview, W. Va., to be a member of the Council on Environmental Quality. He would replace Charles Warren, resigned. Harris has been associate director of the toxic chemicals program at the Environmental Defense Fund since 1973.

He was born October 16, 1941, in Fairmont, W. Va. He received a B.S. in civil engineering from West Virginia University in 1963, an M.S. in environmental health engineering from California Institute of Technology in 1965, and a Ph. D. in environmental sciences and engineering from Harvard University in 1971.

From 1971 to 1973, Harris was an assistant professor of civil engineering at the University of Maryland, teaching courses in microbiology, ecology of polluted waters, and introduction to environmental engineering. He was also an associate with Ralph Nader's Corporate Accountability Research Group from 1972 to 1973.

Harris was a visiting associate research biochemist at the University of California at Berkeley from 1978 until earlier this year, on leave from EDF, doing research on environmental carcinogens. He is the author of numerous publications and has served as a consultant on environmental matters.

United States Ambassador to Morocco

Nomination of Angier Biddle Duke.
November 1, 1979

The President today announced that he will nominate Angier Biddle Duke, of New York City, to be Ambassador Extraordinary and Plenipotentiary of the United States to the Kingdom of Morocco. He would replace Richard B. Parker, who has resigned. Duke has been president of the National Committee on American Foreign Policy since 1976.

He was born November 30, 1915, in New York City. He attended Yale University. He served in the U.S. Army, then the U.S. Air Force from 1941 to 1945.

Duke joined the Foreign Service in 1949 and served as second secretary and consul in Buenos Aires until 1951. He was special assistant to the Ambassador in Madrid from 1951 to 1952 and served as Ambassador to El Salvador from 1952 to 1953.

From 1955 to 1960, Duke was president of the International Rescue Committee, and from 1956 to 1958, he also served as vice president of CARE.

He returned to Government service in 1961 as Chief of Protocol for the White House, with the rank of Ambassador, serving in that position until 1965 and again in 1968. From 1965 to 1968, he was Ambassador to Spain. From 1968 to 1969, Duke was Ambassador to Denmark.

From 1974 to 1976, he was commissioner of civic affairs and public events of the city of New York. He has served as chairman of the New York State Council on Ethnic Affairs since earlier this year.

2077

Department of Housing and Urban Development

Nomination of Victor Marrero To Be Under Secretary.   November 1, 1979

The President today announced his intention to nominate Victor Marrero, of the Bronx, New York, to be Under Secretary of Housing and Urban Development. He would replace Jay Janis, who has been appointed Chairman of the Federal Home Loan Bank Board. Marrero has been a commissioner of the New York State Division of Housing and Community Renewal and vice chairman of the New York State Housing Finance Agency since 1978.

He was born September 1, 1941, in Santurce, P.R. He received a B.A. from New York University in 1964 and a J.D. from Yale Law School in 1968.

From 1968 to 1969, Marrero was assistant to New York Mayor John V. Lindsay. From 1970 to 1973, he was assistant administrator and neighborhood director with the South Bronx Model Cities Office, and from 1972 to 1973, he was district manager of the South Bronx Office of the Mayor's Office for Neighborhood Government.

In 1973 Marrero was executive director of the New York City Department of Planning. From 1974 to 1975, he was special counsel to Comptroller Harrison J. Goldin. In 1975 he was first assistant counsel to Gov. Hugh L. Carey. From 1976 to 1977, he was chairman of the New York City Planning Commission.

Marrero is a founder and first chairman of the Puerto Rican Legal Defense and Education Fund and of the South Bronx Community Housing Corp. He is a public member of the Federal Home Loan Bank Board Savings and Loan Advisory Committee.

Financial Institutions Deregulation Legislation

White House Statement on Senate Approval of the Legislation. November 2, 1979

The President applauds the Thursday night Senate action which would give an important break to small savers. The bill approved by the Senate contains major recommendations that the President submitted to Congress in May.

The President proposed and now, under the leadership of Banking Committee Chairman Senator William Proxmire, the Senate has agreed that major deregulatory reforms in the financial area are needed: the phaseout of federally imposed deposit interceilings that limit the interest that savers earn on their savings accounts, the reversal of an appellate court decision that would have prohibited the proconsumer automatic transfer system, and the validation nationwide of proconsumer NOW accounts and share draft accounts at credit unions.

"The Senate has taken a significant step," the President said, "to provide equity for savers in our country and to assist depository institutions in competing more effectively for funds." The President urged that the House-Senate conference committee members "act promptly to return to both Houses for final approval legislation that will provide this critically important relief to small savers."

Will Rogers Day, 1979

Proclamation 4698.   November 2, 1979

By the President of the United States of America

A Proclamation

November 4, 1979, is the one hundredth anniversary of the birth of America's leading philosopher-humorist, Will Rogers.

His commentary on people and events in public life amused us all—and made us a little wiser, too. He judged people with penetrating insight, but with kindness and affection.

He once said, "I never tell jokes. I just watch the government and report the facts." The wit and the wisdom exemplified by that comment made this Nation a better place in which to live.

In recognition of his contribution to the enrichment of our lives, the Ninety-Sixth Congress, by House Joint Resolution 3, has requested the President to designate November 4, 1979, as Will Rogers Day.

Now, THEREFORE, I, JIMMY CARTER, President of the United States of America, do hereby proclaim Sunday, November 4, 1979, as Will Rogers Day.

IN WITNESS WHEREOF, I have hereunto set my hand this second day of November, in the year of our Lord nineteen hundred seventy-nine, and of the Independence of the United States of America the two hundred and fourth.

JIMMY CARTER

[Filed with the Office of the Federal Register, 11:39 a.m., November 2, 1979]

Wright Brothers Day, 1979
Proclamation 4699.   November 2, 1979

By the President of the United States of America

A Proclamation

The age of aviation began on December 17, 1903, near Kitty Hawk, North Carolina, when two bicycle makers, Wilbur and Orville Wright, made the first successful flight in an airplane. This achievement brought little acclaim to the Wright Brothers at the time. Today, however, we know it as one of the most important events in our modern world.

The spirit of the Wright Brothers lives on. The same American ingenuity and persistence has recently been displayed again in the first successful man-powered flight across the English Channel. In June of this year, Bryan Allen pedaled for almost three hours to propel the Gossamer Albatross, a 60-pound polyester-bodied aircraft designed by Paul MacCready, a distance of 22 miles.

The same spirit has led to the phenomenal development of aviation since the Wright Brothers' first successful flight 76 years ago. Aviation is one of the most important industries in America today, both for jobs and services provided. United States aircraft manufacturers currently have orders for over 1,000 jet transports, and scheduled traffic for United States domestic and international flights this year will exceed 300 million passengers for the first time.

To commemorate the historic achievements of the Wright Brothers, the Congress, by a joint resolution of December 17, 1963 (77 Stat. 402, 36 U.S.C. 169), designated the seventeenth day of December of each year as Wright Brothers Day and requested the President to issue a proclamation annually inviting people of the United States to observe that day with appropriate ceremonies and activities.

Now, THEREFORE, I, JIMMY CARTER, President of the United States of America, do hereby call upon the people of this Nation, and their local and national governmental officials, to observe Wright Brothers Day, December 17, 1979, with appropriate ceremonies and activities, both to recall the accomplishments of the Wright Brothers and to provide a stimulus to aviation in this country and throughout the world.

IN WITNESS WHEREOF, I have hereunto set my hand this second day of November, in the year of our Lord nineteen hundred seventy-nine, and of the Independence of the United States of America the two hundred and fourth.

JIMMY CARTER

[Filed with the Office of the Federal Register, 11:40 a.m., November 2, 1979]

Aid for Kampucheans

Proclamation 4700. November 2, 1979

By the President of the United States of America

A Proclamation

Thirty-seven years ago, a holocaust began that was to take the lives of more than six million human beings. The world stood by silently, in a moral lapse whose enormity still numbs the human mind.

We now face, once again, the threat of avoidable death and suffering for literally millions of people, and this time we must act swiftly to save the men, women, and children who are our brothers and sisters in God's family.

The International Committee of the Red Cross and the United Nations' Children's Fund recently appealed jointly for $111 million in aid to help the millions of Kampucheans, formerly known as Cambodians, who are facing death from starvation during the next six months. We must respond to this appeal, and we must also respond to the related needs for food, medicine, and shelter for Kampuchean refugees who are fleeing to Thailand.

A major program has been launched by the American government to support this relief effort, but it is too important to be left to the government alone. I am certain that the American people, as individuals and families, through churches, schools, voluntary organizations, and businesses, will want to be a part of this emergency humanitarian response to a desperate and terrible need.

Now, THEREFORE, I, JIMMY CARTER, President of the United States of America, do hereby call upon all Americans to give generously to the voluntary relief agency of their choice to alleviate this terrible suffering, asking specifically that the donation be earmarked for Kampuchean relief. Further, I hereby designate each Saturday and Sunday in November until Thanksgiving as days for Americans in their synagogues, churches, and other places of worship to donate to this cause, and I call upon leaders of the religious community to take whatever measures are needed to publicize and facilitate these donations.

IN WITNESS WHEREOF, I have hereunto set my hand this second day of November, in the year of our Lord nineteen hundred seventy-nine, and of the Independence of the United States of America the two hundred and fourth.

JIMMY CARTER

[Filed with the Office of the Federal Register, 1:29 p.m., November 2, 1979]

Digest of Other White House Announcements

The following listing includes the President's public schedule and other items of general interest announced by the White House Press Office and not included elsewhere in this issue.

October 28

The President returned to the White House from Camp David, Md.

October 29

The President met at the White House with:

—Vice President Walter F. Mondale;

—Members of the House of Representatives to discuss hospital cost containment legislation.

The President participated in a briefing

by administration officials on energy given for community leaders in the East Room at the White House.

In the evening, the President attended a dinner meeting in the State Dining Room, to discuss energy legislation with a bipartisan group of Congressmen.

October 30

The President met at the White House with:

—Zbigniew Brzezinski, Assistant to the President for National Security Affairs;

—Nelson H. Cruikshank, Counselor to the President on Aging;

—members of the Ad Hoc Leadership Council of Organizations on Aging;

—singer Joan Baez, to discuss relief efforts for Indochina refugees.

The President participated in a briefing by administration officials on the strategic arms limitation treaty given for community leaders from Illinois and Mississippi in the East Room at the White House.

The President announced the appointment of Moon Landrieu, Secretary of Housing and Urban Development, as a member of the Advisory Commission on Intergovernmental Relations for a 2-year term.

October 31

The President met at the White House with:

—David L. Aaron, Deputy Assistant for National Security Affairs;

—Vice President Mondale, Secretary of Health, Education, and Welfare Patricia R. Harris, Secretary of Housing and Urban Development Moon Landrieu, Secretary of Labor Ray Marshall, Secretary of Transportation Neil Goldschmidt, James T. McIntyre, Jr., Director of the Office of Management and Budget, Stuart E. Eizenstat, Assistant to the President for Domestic Affairs and Policy, and Alonzo L. McDonald,

Jr., Assistant to the President, to discuss domestic policies;

—Frank B. Moore, Assistant to the President for Congressional Liaison;

—Stansfield Turner, Director of Central Intelligence, and Mr. Aaron;

—Mr. McIntyre.

November 1

The President met at the White House with:

—Mr. Aaron;

—Senator Thad Cochran of Mississippi;

—Mr. Moore;

—members of the National Commission for Employment Policy;

—Representative Dan Rostenkowski of Illinois.

The President participated in a briefing on the administration's programs and policies given for civic and community leaders from Maryland in the East Room at the White House.

November 2

The President met at the White House with:

—Mr. Aaron;

—Mr. Moore;

—Hedley W. Donovan, Senior Adviser to the President;

—Senator Donald W. Riegle, Jr., of Michigan.

The President left the White House for a weekend stay at Camp David.

NOMINATIONS SUBMITTED TO THE SENATE

The following list does not include promotions of members of the Uniformed Services, nominations to the Service Academies, or nominations of Foreign Service officers.

Submitted October 30, 1979

RICHARD CAVINS MATHERON, of California, a Foreign Service officer of Class one, to be Ambassador Extraordinary and Plenipotentiary of the United States of America to the Kingdom of Swaziland.

NOMINATIONS—Continued

Submitted October 31, 1979

PATRICIA M. BYRNE, of Ohio, a Foreign Service officer of Class one, to be Ambassador Extraordinary and Plenipotentiary of the United States of America to the Socialist Republic of the Union of Burma.

ROBERT D. HORMATS, of Maryland, to be a Deputy Special Representative for Trade Negotiations, with the rank of Ambassador, vice Alonzo Lowry McDonald, Jr., resigned.

MICHAEL BRACKETT SMITH, of Maryland, to be a Deputy Special Representative for Trade Negotiations, with the rank of Ambassador, vice Alan William Wolff, resigned.

Submitted November 1, 1979

EDWARD DEAN PRICE, of California, to be United States District Judge for the Eastern District of California, vice a new position created by P.L. 95–486, approved October 20, 1978.

HORACE T. WARD, of Georgia, to be United States District Judge for the Northern District of Georgia, vice a new position created by P.L. 95–486, approved October 20, 1978.

DAVID K. WINDER, of Utah, to be United States District Judge for the District of Utah, vice a new position created by P.L. 95–486, approved October 20, 1978.

SIDNEY A. DIAMOND, of Arizona, to be Commissioner of Patents and Trademarks, vice Donald W. Banner, resigned.

Submitted November 2, 1979

ANGIER BIDDLE DUKE, of New York, to be Ambassador Extraordinary and Plenipotentiary of the United States of America to the Kingdom of Morocco.

ROBERT H. HARRIS, of Maryland, to be a member of the Council on Environmental Quality, vice Charles Hugh Warren, resigned.

CHECKLIST OF WHITE HOUSE PRESS RELEASES

The following listing contains releases of the White House Press Office which are not included in this issue.

CHECKLIST—Continued

Released October 29, 1979

Statements: support for the proposed hospital cost containment legislation—by administration officials

Released October 30, 1979

Biographical data: Shirley Hufstedler, to be nominated to be Secretary of Education

Released October 31, 1979

News conference: on the President's industrial innovation initiatives—by Secretary of Commerce Juanita Kreps, Jordan Baruch, Assistant Secretary of Commerce for Science and Technology, Frank Press, Director, Office of Science and Technology Policy, and Stuart E. Eizenstat, Assistant to the President for Domestic Affairs and Policy

Fact sheet: President's industrial innovation initiatives

Announcement: nomination of Edward Dean Price to be United States District Judge for the Eastern District of California

Announcement: nomination of Horace T. Ward to be United States District Judge for the Northern District of Georgia

Announcement: nomination of David K. Winder to be United States District Judge for the District of Utah

Released November 2, 1979

Fact sheet: aid for Kampucheans

ACTS APPROVED BY THE PRESIDENT

Approved October 29, 1979

H.R. 3173_____ Public Law 96–92 International Security Assistance Act of 1979.

Approved October 30, 1979

H.R. 4580_____ Public Law 96–93 District of Columbia Appropriation Act, 1980.

Approved October 31, 1979

H.R. 5506_____ Public Law 96–94 An act to amend the Energy Policy and Conservation Act to extend for two months certain authorities relating to the international energy program.

ACTS APPROVED—Continued

Approved October 31—Continued

H.R. 1825_____ Public Law 96–95
Archaeological Resources Protection Act of 1979.

H.R. 5386_____ Public Law 96–96
An act to amend the Higher Education Act of 1965 to provide that any reduction in the amount appropriated for fiscal year 1980 pursuant to section 101(a) of such Act from the amount so appropriated for fiscal year 1979 shall be borne equally by all the States.

S. 436_____ Public Law 96–97
An act to amend section 15(d) of the Tennessee Valley Authority Act of 1933 to increase the amount of debt which may be incurred by the Tennessee Valley Authority.

ACTS APPROVED—Continued

Approved November 1, 1979

H.R. 3923_____ Public Law 96–98
An act to amend chapter 25 of title 44, United States Code, to extend for one year the authorization of appropriations for the National Historical Publications and Records Commission, and for other purposes.

Approved November 2, 1979

H.J. Res. 3_____ Public Law 96–99
A joint resolution designating November 4, 1979, as Will Rogers Day.

S. 975_____ Public Law 96–100
Intelligence and Intelligence-Related Activities Authorization Act for Fiscal Year 1980.

United Nations Pledging Conference on Refugee Relief

Appointment of the U.S. Delegation.
November 3, 1979

Following are the members of the U.S. Delegation to the United Nations Pledging Conference on Refugee Relief:

Representative

SECRETARY OF STATE CYRUS VANCE

Deputy Representative

AMBASSADOR DONALD McHENRY, U.S. Representative to the United Nations

Alternate Representatives

HON. MATTHEW NIMETZ, Counselor, Department of State

AMBASSADOR WILLIAM VANDEN HEUVEL, U.S. Deputy Representative to the United Nations

Congressional Advisers

SENATOR CLAIBORNE PELL
SENATOR MAX BAUCUS
SENATOR JOHN DANFORTH
SENATOR JACOB JAVITS
SENATOR JAMES SASSER
REPRESENTATIVE JOHN ANDERSON
REPRESENTATIVE ELIZABETH HOLTZMAN
REPRESENTATIVE CLARENCE LONG
REPRESENTATIVE LESTER WOLFF
REPRESENTATIVE C. W. "BILL" YOUNG
REPRESENTATIVE CLEMENT ZABLOCKI

Governors

GOV. RICHARD D. LAMM
GOV. WILLIAM G. MILLIKEN
GOV. ROBERT D. RAY
GOV. RICHARD A. SNELLING

Senior Advisers

HON. MARJORIE CRAIG BENTON, U.S. Representative to the Executive Board of the U.N. Children's Fund

HON. BEVERLY CARTER, Ambassador at Large and Coordinator for State and Local Governments

REV. THEODORE HESBURGH

HON. RICHARD HOLBROOKE, Assistant Secretary of State for East Asian and Pacific Affairs

HON. CHARLES WILLIAM MAYNES, Assistant Secretary of State for International Organization Affairs

HON. LEO PERLIS, AFL–CIO

AMBASSADOR RICHARD W. PETREE, U.S. Representative to the U.N. Security Council

Emergency Energy Conservation Act of 1979

Remarks on Signing S. 1030 Into Law.
November 5, 1979

THE PRESIDENT. This is a very good occasion in the evolution of an acceptable energy policy for our country. We face at all times the possibility of an emergency shortage, a very severe reduction in supplies of gasoline and diesel fuel for the transportation of the people of America. And I want to thank very much the key Members of the House and Senate—there's no way to name them all—who've been instrumental in passing this Emergency Energy Conservation Act of 1979, quite often referred to as the gas rationing bill.

This has been a difficult issue because of the necessity for evolving a fair allocation of gasoline and diesel fuel if our Nation does face a severe shortage. Majority Leader Byrd in the Senate and Majority Leader Jim Wright in the House, Senator Jackson, Senator Johnston, Senator Domenici, John Dingell in the House, and Tim Wirth, Bud Brown, Toby Moffett, and many others have helped to make this legislation possible.

I'm very grateful to have the opportunity as President now to evolve a gas and diesel fuel rationing proposal which will be presented to the Congress and to the public over the next few months. This is an important responsibility. Charlie Duncan, the Secretary of Energy, is here. It'll primarily be his Department which will build on the previous proposal, and to provide additions or corrections to it to accommodate the desires of the American people, as expressed by the Congress.

This has not been an easy piece of legislation to pass. [*Laughter*] I don't think anyone standing behind me would disagree with that fact. It's been a laborious and detailed negotiation, and if we do face a severe shortage, then I have adequate authority. If the shortage is prospective in nature, the prospect of a severe shortage, then with the concurrence of the Congress, the time for the implementation of the rationing plan can be abbreviated.

I'm very happy that this has been accomplished. We now face additional major decisions in the House and Senate. This week, for instance, the Senate will vote on the energy security corporation: legislation which will permit our Nation to strengthen our defenses, to avoid a direct threat to our Nation's security, with a heavy emphasis of conservation as a first step, on a short-term basis; and increasing emphasis in the middle term of gasohol and other more readily available energy measures; and then in the longer run, geo-thermal supplies, solar energy, and synthetic fuels.

Without the energy security corporation, it would be almost impossible to have synthetic fuels and other supplies developed on a competitive basis; we'll have an almost complete domination of energy supply opportunities in our country by just a few major oil companies. So, the passage of the energy security corporation this week by the Senate is crucial to provide competition, to let our Nation have adequate energy supplies, and also, of course, to implement a major additional conservation effort—all of these factors to contribute to our Nation's security.

I might say in closing that I'm very grateful to the men and the women of the House and Senate who have labored so long over this legislation. I'd like to sign the bill now, and then I'd like to call on a couple of people to say a word for their colleagues in the House and Senate.

[*At this point, the President signed the bill.*]

I will try to do a good job working with Charlie Duncan to justify your confidence in us and present to you a rationing program that will be acceptable, adequate, fair, and which would bring joy to the eyes of all of us.

I'd like to call on John Dingell to say a word.

REPRESENTATIVE DINGELL. Mr. President, thank you for the kind words you said about my colleagues and I in the House who did work very hard on this, as you know. It was a bipartisan undertaking at the end. [*Laughter*]

SENATOR DOMENICI. We just straightened it out for you.

THE PRESIDENT. And there were some bipartisan obstructions at the beginning. [*Laughter*]

REPRESENTATIVE DINGELL. As a matter of fact, you're correct. [*Laughter*]

But, Mr. President, the men you see standing behind you, and I won't mention their names, but people like Toby and Phil and Bill and Bud and Jim Broyhill and a number of my colleagues who are not here and our distinguished colleagues in the Senate, who are well known to you, worked very hard on this, and we think we gave you a good bill.

You are working hard on the energy program of the Nation, and I think you provided very real leadership. And this is just one more evidence of what you have accomplished. And although it is a major stride forward, many very large strides remain, and we all look forward to working with you, because the country needs it.

Thank you, Mr. President.

THE PRESIDENT. Thank you very much, John.

Mr. Domenici?

SENATOR DOMENICI. Thank you, Mr. President.

When I first came to the Senate 7 years ago, if you'd told me that gasoline rationing was as critically important to have as a standby program as this bill is, I would have said it's impossible. But indeed it is.

If you'd also have told me 7 months ago that it was possible to get unanimous action of the House and Senate, Republicans and Democrats, House and Senate, all together with one bill that pleases the White House, I would have said that's totally fanciful. [*Laughter*] But here it is. And it's a real indication of teamwork, Mr. President, not only with the White House but with the House and both parties and the recognition of the very serious situation we're in in the country. It's going to take this kind of teamwork to get out of the problem we're in, and I expect to be part of that team.

THE PRESIDENT. Well, you've proven that already, Senator.

Charlie Duncan, would you like to come forward and say a word? Charlie's the one that's got to do all the work. [*Laughter*]

SECRETARY DUNCAN. One part of the rationing bill that's very important, in my judgment, is the conservation portion of it and the State plans. It's a national problem that lends itself to local initiatives, and I think we've built that into this legislation, and that's a very appropriate thing to do.

THE PRESIDENT. I apologize for not mentioning that myself. I think the crux of this bill is that the first opportunity for conservation programs to be evolved, as wisely decided by the Congress, is at the State level. And the Federal program would only go into effect if it was considered necessary in the absence of an adequate authority or action on the part of the States. I thank you, Charlie, for pointing that out.

Well, my gratitude to all of you. I think we've done the Nation a great service.

Thank you very much.

NOTE: The President spoke at 9:35 a.m. at the ceremony in the Cabinet Room at the White House.

As enacted, S. 1030 is Public Law 96–102, approved November 5.

Indochinese Refugees in the United States

Announcement of Federal Emergency Assistance to Affected School Districts. November 6, 1979

The administration has asked the Congress to approve the reprograming of $6 million in FY 1980 funds for the Office of Education in order to provide emergency assistance to school districts which have been most affected by the influx of Indochinese refugee children.

In letters to the chairmen of the Senate and House Appropriations Committees' Subcommittees on Labor, Health, Education, and Welfare, HEW Secretary Patricia Harris requested the reprograming as an immediate and temporary measure to provide immediate help to these school districts.

The funds would be reprogramed from five areas in the Special Projects and Training appropriation of the Office of Education. Secretary Harris' letters explain that the supplemental appropriation request for refugee activities which will be submitted in January, with the President's 1981 budget, will include $6 million to restore the funds proposed for reprograming.

Since the President's decision in June to double the number of new Indochinese refugees entering the United States, an estimated 20,000 refugee children have arrived. An additional 45,000 are expected by the end of the current school year.

There is a critical need for educational assistance, because many of the new group of Indochinese refugees have no proficiency in English and lack other basic skills. Many of the refugee children require several types of special educational services.

Because many of the refugees are resettling in only a few States and localities, the impact on some school districts has been substantial. Because States and local agencies have already determined their budgets for the 1979–80 school year, they have limited flexibility to divert resources to serve the Indochinese refugee children.

The administration sent legislation to the Congress earlier this year that would provide aid on a comprehensive, on-going basis to refugees and to local governments and school districts that need assistance in dealing with refugee programs. The President urges passage of that bill to provide a sound foundation for future aid in this area.

Census 1980

Proclamation 4701. November 6, 1979

By the President of the United States of America

A Proclamation

Our Constitution requires that there be a census of the people in the United States once every ten years. The Twentieth Decennial Census will be taken beginning April 1, 1980.

It is vitally important to everyone that this census be a complete and accurate report of the Nation's population and resources. Its results determine the representation of the States in the House of Representatives, the redrawing of congressional boundaries, and State and local redistricting. They also provide the basis for distributing large amounts of funds under various Federal programs among the States and communities.

The census is also important for a broader purpose. Americans are a free and mobile people. Significant and rapid changes take place in our country. To better understand ourselves and make intelligent decisions for the future, we depend greatly on our census.

Now, THEREFORE, I, JIMMY CARTER, President of the United States of America, do hereby declare and make known that under the law it is the duty of every person to participate in the census by answering all questions in the census schedule applying to him or her and the family to which he or she belongs, and to the home being occupied.

Every person in the United States can be sure that there will be no improper use of the information given in the census. Answers cannot be released in any way which will harm the individual. By law individual information collected will not be used for purposes of taxation, investigation, or regulation, or in connection with military or jury service, the compulsion of school attendance, the regulation of immigration, or with the enforcement of any national, State, or local law or ordinance.

IN WITNESS WHEREOF, I have hereunto set my hand this sixth day of November, in the year of our Lord nineteen hundred seventy-nine, and of the Independence of the United States of America the two hundred and fourth.

JIMMY CARTER

[Filed with the Office of the Federal Register, 3:14 p.m., November 6, 1979]

Department of Transportation

Nomination of Susan J. Williams To Be an Assistant Secretary.　November 6, 1979

The President today announced that he will nominate Susan J. Williams, of McLean, Va., to be Assistant Secretary of Transportation for Governmental and Public Affairs. She would replace Terrence Bracy, resigned. Williams has been serving as Acting Assistant Secretary of Transportation since last July.

She was born July 31, 1940, in Philadelphia, Pa. She received a B.A. from Upsala College.

From 1962 to 1965, Williams was an editor at the Center for Applied Linguistics, and from 1965 to 1973, she was an education consultant to the Department of Health, Education, and Welfare.

From 1962 to 1965, Williams was an cial assistant to D.C. Delegate Walter Fauntroy. From 1977 to 1979, she was Director of Congressional Relations for the Transportation Department, and from March to July 1979, she was Deputy Assistant Secretary for Governmental and Public Affairs.

Williams was a founder and vice chairman of the Northern Virginia Democratic Women's Political Caucus. She is vice chairman of the Commission for Children of Fairfax County, Va.

National Council on the Handicapped

Nomination of Howard A. Rusk To Be a Member and Designation as Chairman. November 6, 1979

The President today announced his intention to nominate Howard A. Rusk as a member of the National Council on the Handicapped and to designate him as Chairman on confirmation.

Rusk, 78, has been a professor and chairman of the Department of Rehabilitation Medicine at New York University School of Medicine since 1946. He has served as a consultant on rehabilitation to the United Nations Secretariat and to the city of New York. He is the author of several books and has received numerous awards and honors.

The National Council on the Handicapped was established in November 1978 by Public Law 95–602 to establish general policies regarding Federal activities affecting the handicapped and review the activities of the Rehabilitation Services Administration and the National Institute of Handicapped Research.

National Institute of Handicapped Research

Nomination of Margaret Joan Giannini To Be Director.　November 6, 1979

The President today announced that he will nominate Margaret Joan Giannini, of Pelham Manor, N.Y., to be Director of the National Institute of Handicapped Research, a new position.

Giannini is a professor in the Department of Pediatrics and director of the Mental Retardation Institute at New York Medical College.

She was born May 27, 1921, in Camden, N.J. She graduated from Boston University and Temple University and received an M.D. from Hahnemann Medical College in 1945. She did her internship at New York Medical College in 1945–46 and was a resident in pathology in 1946–47 and in pediatrics in 1947–48.

From 1948 to 1950, Giannini was a practicing pediatrician. She has been a professor of pediatrics at New York Medical College since 1950 and director of the Mental Retardation Institute since 1956.

Giannini has also served as attending pediatrician at Metropolitan Hospital Medical Center and as a pediatric consultant for the city of New York's Bureau for Handicapped Children. She was interregional adviser in mental retardation to the United Nations Department of World Technical Cooperation in 1978. She has served as president of the American Association on Mental Deficiency.

The First Lady's Trip to Thailand

Remarks on Her Departure From the White House.   November 7, 1979

THE PRESIDENT. I would like to say to my wife, Rosalynn, and to Surgeon General Richmond, to Mrs. Young, who is our National Chairman for the Year of the Child, that I'm deeply grateful to them for their willingness to go to Thailand, to observe at first hand the consequences of the horrible tragedy that is occurring there.

It's imperative that our Nation exert its

moral leadership as an example to the entire world of the true feelings of Americans, as we have observed with deep concern and with horror the unprecedented loss of life, because of starvation and persecution, of the people of Cambodia, many of whom have now fled into Thailand. It's important that we maintain our commitment and our concern to all the starving people there, regardless of their political affiliation, regardless of the circumstances under which they suffer.

Secondly, I would like for the Surgeon General and my wife and others in the group to assess the bureaucratic obstacles that exist. This is an international effort, but our Nation plays a major role in shaping the means by which relief—food, medical care—can be delivered to the starving and suffering people who have crossed the border into Thailand. And I would hope that when they come back, they can report accurately what can be done to remove any such obstacles from the delivery of this care. We recognize that the warring parties in Kampuchea have provided an unwarranted obstacle to the delivery of food, and I would hope they would explore every possibility for the breaking down of these obstacles.

The third thing I've asked Rosalynn to do is to deliver to Prime Minister Kriangsak and the Royal Family of Thailand a personal message of appreciation and admiration for the courage and the generosity of the Thais in receiving literally hundreds of thousands of refugees into a country already somewhat impoverished, already having exhibited great generosity in the past.

This tragedy, where almost one-half the total population of Kampuchea has died, is of unbelievable proportions, and it's important that the world and the people of the United States maintain their intense interest and their intense commitment until the tragedy is relieved. Our country has already committed a major share of the total international effort. We are ready to do more. We have no political motives. We have one single commitment, and that is to stop the suffering and the starvation among these unfortunate people. This trip, we hope, will increase both the public and private commitment to alleviate suffering there.

Rosalynn and Jean and Dr. Richmond, our hearts and our prayers go with you. And we look forward to this weekend, when you return, for a means by which our Nation can be reinspired to assist in every possible way the people who are suffering so deeply.

Would you like to say just a word?

MRS. CARTER. This is a tragic situation, and our whole country is concerned. I want to go also to see what every American can do to help.

Thank you very much.

NOTE: The President spoke at 7:26 a.m. on the South Lawn of the White House.

Indochinese Refugees in the United States

Announcement of Improved Health Screening and Medical Care for U.S.-Bound Refugees. November 7, 1979

The Public Health Service (PHS) has assigned 11 public health professionals to Southeast Asia to improve health screening and medical care for U.S.-bound refugees.

The professionals, six of whom are physicians, are assisting the Intergovernmental Committee for European Migration with screening and the World Health Organization with providing medical care. They have been sent within the past month to locations in Thailand, Indonesia, Malaysia, Hong Kong, and Singapore.

Earlier this year, the President announced that the United States would double to 14,000 the number of Indochinese refugees allowed to enter the country each month. Assignment of the public health professionals will help assure continued success in avoiding any significant outbreak of communicable disease among resettled refugees in this country.

The Public Health Service, in cooperation with the Immigration and Naturalization Service, the Department of State, and voluntary refugee resettlement agency representatives abroad, is also taking steps to assure that adequate records are kept for all medical screening procedures, findings, and treatments, and establish a system for collecting and analyzing data to measure the incidence of disease and health and immunization status.

In addition, PHS has increased its staff at affected U.S. ports of entry and has instituted systems for forwarding medical records to the refugees' destinations. In this country PHS is assessing the health status of refugees and helping them find a continuing source of health care in their new communities.

Federal Emergency Management Agency

Nomination of Richard J. Green To Be an Associate Director. November 7, 1979

The President today announced that he will nominate Richard J. Green, of Bricktown, N.J., to be an Associate Director of the Federal Emergency Management Agency, a new position. Green has been Deputy Assistant Director of the National Science Foundation since 1972.

He was born April 15, 1928, in Newark, N.J. He received a B.S. in biology from Holy Cross College in 1949 and an M.S. in physics from Fordham University in 1955.

2091

From 1955 to 1957, Green was program manager for Pratt & Whitney Aircraft. From 1957 to 1961, he was supervisor of nuclear and aerospace lubricants development for Mobil Oil Company. From 1961 to 1962, he was chief of aircraft maintenance and armament for the U.S. Air Force.

From 1963 to 1966, Green was an executive assistant at the National Aeronautics and Space Administration, where he worked on joint NASA-Defense Department matters in the Office of the Administrator. From 1966 to 1970, he was manager of the Apollo Lunar Surface Experiments program for NASA.

From 1970 to 1972, Green was operations deputy at the National Science Foundation. Since 1972 he has been Deputy Assistant Director of NSF, where he has planned and directed the National Solar and Geothermal Energy Research and Development programs and managed the Research Applied to National Needs program.

Energy Security Corporation and Synthetic Fuels Program

White House Statement on Senate Action on Legislation.
November 7, 1979

The President this afternoon expressed his pleasure at the Senate's actions in approving the initiation of a strong synthetic fuels program and the establishment of an energy security corporation.

"While there is much more work to be done and further action in the House to be completed," the President said, "the Senate's actions ensure that there will be a strong synthetic fuels program and a significant institution to carry it out. I congratulate Chairman Jackson, Senator Johnston, and Senator Domenici for their able and dedicated work.

"The critical conservation and gasohol titles of the Senate Energy Committee bill remain to be passed, and the administration will continue its close cooperation with congressional leaders in support of this important legislation. The uncertain nature of our energy supplies does not need to be reemphasized; but today's action, together with the continued steady progress of the energy mobilization board and the windfall profits tax, is a step toward regaining control of our Nation's future."

Welfare Cash Assistance Reform Legislation

Statement on House of Representatives Approval of the Legislation.
November 7, 1979

I want to commend Speaker Tip O'Neill, Congressmen James Corman and Charles Rangel, and the other Members of the House of Representatives for the passage this evening of my cash assistance reform proposal.

This is a crucial step forward in the Nation's 10-year effort to provide vitally needed reform of the welfare system.

When enacted, this proposal will

—lift 2 million families above the poverty line,

—provide added income for 1.6 million elderly Americans by providing cash payments instead of food stamp eligibility,

—tighten and streamline administrative requirements resulting in savings of hundreds of millions of dollars, and,

—provide fiscal relief for States with the heaviest welfare costs.

I look forward to speedy House consideration of the companion jobs legislation, which is critically important to our reform program, and to Senate action on my entire welfare reform package.

Even in this period of necessary fiscal stringency, we must not fail to do what we can for those who are most in need.

Visit of Prime Minister John M. Lynch of Ireland

Remarks at the Welcoming Ceremony. November 8, 1979

THE PRESIDENT. *An Taoiseach* [Prime Minister], welcome to you.

This is a wonderful occasion for our Nation to welcome to our country the Prime Minister of the Republic of Ireland, the President of the European Community, and a great friend of the United States. In all three of these roles, Mr. Prime Minister, you're welcome to the United States of America.

You represent a nation which is the ancestral home of 20 million American citizens, so we are bound to you in many ways. We are bound to you because we share common goals, the goals of democracy and freedom, the goals of peace, the goals of mutual trade and common benefit and respect for basic human rights, not only in our own nations but throughout the world.

It's a great pleasure to have you here, because your friendship is continuing a longstanding relationship between our two countries. More than 200 years ago, before we had a country, as a matter of fact, the people of Ireland proved to be our friends. Benjamin Franklin visited Dublin as an emissary of the colonies to ask for the support and encouragement of the people of Ireland and for our own independence and our own freedom. Your people gave us that support and that encouragement. We're grateful to you. Since then we've shared a mutual understand-

ing and a mutual sympathy for the ideals and aspirations and hopes and dreams of the people of this Nation and the people of yours.

You come here representing not only a great nation but carrying a great and powerful international voice. The soldiers representing your country are now serving to preserve the peace in the Congo, in Cyprus, in Lebanon, in a benevolent action, and also actions requiring a great deal of personal courage, which has always been a characteristic of the Irish people.

You come here representing leadership in the councils of Europe, and we have benefited greatly from close personal consultations with you on matters that affect the entire European community because you occupy the Presidency of that great body of sovereign nations.

We share other things in common not quite so pleasant. We both have experienced the adverse consequences of terrorism, of a threat of violence, of murders perpetrated and murders threatened against innocent people. Those who advocate violence and terrorism violate the laws of God and the laws of man.

I look forward to our discussions this morning, again this evening, and tomorrow, because we have so many ways in which our two nations in harmony can promote the common aspirations of our people, a quest for a peaceful and a just society for the people of your nation, for the people of the United States, and the entire world.

Mr. Prime Minister, on behalf of all Americans, but particularly on behalf of all of those of us who bear Irish blood in our veins, we welcome you from a great country to a great country. Thank you for coming.

THE PRIME MINISTER. I would like to thank you, Mr. President, for your very kind words, for your gracious tribute to my country, for each contribution towards building this great United States of America and to its contribution towards keeping world peace by having our soldiers serve with U.N. forces in different parts of the world—in the Congo, in the Middle East, in Lebanon, in Cyprus—and indeed, such is our commitment, even though it does impose a strain on us, we are very glad and willing to give it.

My wife and I were very, very delighted to have received earlier this year your invitation, Mr. President, to come and visit you formally, and we certainly looked forward with much anticipation to this visit today, as we do to our visits to many of your other great American cities in the course of the next 7 or 8 days.

I am very proud to be here as the head of a government which has always had warm and friendly relations with the elected leaders of the United States. I trust that these relations and our political ties will be strengthened in some way as a result of this visit.

I'm deeply aware that I represent people, people that always have had special, close bonds, both material and spiritual, with the people of America. We in Ireland, as you know, are your closest friends in Europe and, may I add, certainly amongst your best friends anywhere. We look with pride and affection on the ties that bind our two countries together. Our history, both histories, have many common strands. Perhaps nowhere is this better illustrated than here in the White House, which has served no fewer than 12 U.S. Presidents of Irish descent.

The architect of the house was one James Hoban, who sailed to America from Ireland in 1785. He is said to have adapted his design for the White House from the house called Leinster House in Dublin, which is the seat of the Irish Parliament. Indeed, Hoban probably inspired the very name of the White House, because when, in 1814, it was demolished

by fire, he advised in the course of his restoration that all the exterior walls be painted white.

Another aspect of my visit to your country, as you have observed, Mr. President, is that I am currently a President of the European Council, that is, President of the Council of Heads of State or Government of the European Economic Communities. As you know, this Presidency changes every 6 months amongst the member countries, and now there are nine. Next year we will have 12 [10], with the accession of Greece, and perhaps in a few more years we will be 12, with the accession of Spain and Portugal.

The Community is already the largest trading bloc in the world. One of the Community's primary aims is the advance of economic equality throughout its member states. As the Community strengthens economically, its political influence increases. That influence is being and will be used to promote peace and stability throughout the whole world.

A recent example of this type of activity was the completion by the Irish Presidency, on behalf of the Community, of the second Lomé Convention, which provides for aid for 58 developing countries in Africa, in the Caribbean, and in the Pacific.

I recall that my last visit to the White House was in January 1973, just after Ireland had acceded to the European Economic Community. And I can say that our accession has brought prosperity to our farms, our industries, and our businesses, and has added a whole new dimension to Ireland's role in the world.

In 1979 in the Community we have passed two milestones along the road to a more united Europe. One was the introduction of the European monetary system, and the second was the holding of the world's first truly international elections, the free elections to the new European

Parliament.

The peoples of the United States and Europe possess a common heritage in the fields of culture, literature, and the arts. We also share a belief in fundamental rights and freedoms, the dignity of the individual, and the sanctity of human life.

I was very glad this morning to hear you, Mr. President, denounce again the taking of human life for no matter what purpose by terrorists, abhorring as we all do the activities of those terrorists and those who help them to carry out their vile and horrific deeds.

But apart from having these things in common, we have at the same time, in both America and Europe, a fascinating variety of people and lifestyles. I am sure you will join with me, Mr. President, in hoping that the political institutions which we have will take account of this diversity.

Finally, I want to take advantage of this occasion to express to you, Mr. President, my sincere thanks for your generous statement in August 1977 on the situation in Northern Ireland, in which you pledged the complete support of the United States for the people of Northern Ireland in their quest for a peaceful and just society. In the words of your own Declaration of Independence, written over two centuries ago, "Governments derive their powers from the consent of the governed." And that's of utmost importance. This principle is one to which we, in Ireland, are dedicated today and one on which we consider that progress in Northern Ireland must be based.

On behalf of the Government of Ireland, Mr. President, I wish to express our best wishes to you and to the continued prosperity and happiness of your great nation. To the people who came to witness this ceremonial this morning, I say thanks on behalf of the people of Ireland, and to all of you Americans, President

downwards, as we say in Ireland, *Bail ó Dhia ort féin agus ar do chuid oibre,* may God bless you and bless your work.

Thank you.

NOTE: The President spoke at 10:45 a.m. on the South Lawn of the White House.

Visit of Prime Minister Lynch of Ireland

Remarks to Reporters Following a Meeting. November 8, 1979

THE PRIME MINISTER. Ladies and gentlemen, the President has invited me to say a few words on the outcome of our talks this morning. And I think we can say they were very, very comprehensive, and there was a recognition of the problems that we and the United States have in common as well as the problems that we, as members of the EEC, have also with the United States. There was a high degree of accord.

We recognized the need to move forward towards solving world problems like inflation and oil supply and felt that action taken, so far as we can, in consort would be for the mutual advantage not only of our two countries, not only of U.S. and the EEC but of the world generally.

We mentioned, of course, the degree of investment that is now taking place, and has been for some years, by American industrialists in Ireland, the favorable climate in which they operate there, and naturally, I expressed that that degree of investment would continue. And may I say, the President didn't demur, because I was able to satisfy him—even though he didn't need being satisfied—that this was to the advantage of the United States as well as to us in Ireland, because by locating in Ireland, thereby gaining access to the Common Market communities of 260 million people, access to markets that otherwise mightn't be available to them.

2095

We spoke, of course, at some length on the problems in Northern Ireland, and we discussed, even though we haven't knowledge of the contents, the proposed initiative and the document to be published by the British in relation to finding a modus vivendi between the two communities in the north of Ireland and naturally expressed our interest in it and hoped that it would lead to a greater degree of cooperation and harmony and, ultimately, peace between those two communities in the north and to North Ireland as a whole.

We emphasized—reemphasized, shall I say, in the case of the President, on his part—that he endorsed again what he said in 1977—I referred to it publicly on the lawn earlier this morning—and emphasized also the need that terrorism should be put down no matter where it raises its head, especially in the north of Ireland, and those who support terrorists must certainly be deterred from doing so.

Perhaps I may jump the gun to some extent by saying that at the end of our talks, I suggested to the President that sometime he might find it possible to visit Ireland, and the President said he certainly would be interested. So, we're looking forward to that day, and I hope that we can give the President of the United States the kind of a warm welcome that I have received from the people of the United States and from the Chief Executive of the United States.

Thank you, Mr. President.

THE PRESIDENT. I think the Prime Minister has covered very well the attitude and the tone of our remarks and also the substantive nature of them. There are no bilateral differences between ourselves and Ireland. The discussions were exclusively devoted to the common purposes that we espouse and the harmony with which we work to resolve differences that exist between our two countries together, compared to the rest of the world.

I might say, especially, that we appreciate the extremely close working relationship with Prime Minister Jack Lynch in his role as President of the European Council, the community of nations in Europe. It's important to point out that we have no role to play in their deliberations. But our consultation with him on issues of mutual interest—the implementation of the Multilateral Trade Negotiations, the implementation of the agreement on energy conservation that was concluded in Tokyo, and other matters that are of common interest to all the people of Europe and our Nation—have been very productive.

It's important also to point out that a President of the United States represents more Irish people than the Prime Minister of Ireland, and I'm constantly aware of my duties to Ireland, Mr. Prime Minister. It would be almost impossible for a President to ignore those duties to your country and to the people who love your country.

We are very delighted, again, to have you here, and we will be discussing in great depth the problems in the Middle East, the need for a worldwide peace, for the control of nuclear weapons, for the control of terrorism, for the bringing of peace to Africa, and the honoring of human rights throughout the world.

And I would like to say again what I said this morning, that we will do everything we possibly can to prevent American citizens' assistance to the terrorists in Ireland, who do so much to obstruct the realization of the hopes and dreams of all the Irish people, no matter what their religious background or convictions might be, for a prosperous and a peaceful Ireland for all.

Thank you very much.

NOTE: The Prime Minister spoke at 12:20 p.m. on the South Grounds of the White House.

Visit of Prime Minister Lynch of Ireland

Press Statement.   November 8, 1979

The President met today with Prime Minister Jack Lynch of Ireland. Prime Minister Lynch, in addition to being the Head of Government of Ireland, is for the last half of 1979 also the President of the European Council of Heads of State or of Government of the Nine countries of the European Community.

The President and the Prime Minister reviewed the close relations between their two countries and discussed a number of key world issues which are of particular concern to the European Community, with which the United States enjoys close cooperation, based on common interests and values.

The President and the Prime Minister also discussed at length the tragic communal problems in Northern Ireland. They condemned support for organizations engaged directly or indirectly in campaigns of violence which only delays the day when peace and reconciliation can come to Northern Ireland. They noted with interest the proposal of the British Government to convene a Conference of the principal political parties in Northern Ireland and shared the hope that progress could be made towards a form of administration acceptable to both parts of the community there. The President reaffirmed his statement of August, 1977 looking to support for American investment in Northern Ireland when the violence is ended.

The official visit of Prime Minister and Mrs. Lynch to Washington and to several other American cities demonstrates the great friendship between the two nations, and also the great respect of the American Government and people for a country which in recent years has enjoyed rapid economic growth and taken its place among the industrialized nations of the world. The Prime Minister spoke of the contribution of American investment to this growth and reiterated his Government's continuing support for such investment.

The Prime Minister invited the President to visit Ireland at a mutually agreeable date and the President accepted the invitation with pleasure.

United States Ambassador to Sri Lanka and the Republic of Maldives

Nomination of Donald R. Toussaint. November 8, 1979

The President today announced that he will nominate Donald R. Toussaint, of McLean, Va., to be Ambassador Extraordinary and Plenipotentiary of the United States to the Democratic Socialist Republic of Sri Lanka and to serve concurrently as Ambassador to the Republic of Maldives. He would replace W. Howard Wriggins, who is retiring. Toussaint has been Deputy Chief of Mission in Manila since 1978.

He was born May 21, 1927, in Oakland, Calif. He received a B.A. (1947) and Ph. D. (1956) from Stanford University, an M.A. from Yenching University in Peking in 1949, and a graduate diploma from the Institut d'Études Politiques in Paris in 1952. He served in the U.S. Navy from 1945 to 1946.

From 1947 to 1949, Toussaint was a teacher at Yenching University, and in 1950–51 he was a teaching assistant at Stanford. From 1952 to 1953, he was director of the overseas development program of Stanford's Hoover Institute, and in 1953–54 he was an instructor with the University of Maryland overseas program. Toussaint joined the Foreign Service in

2097

1956 and served as a foreign affairs officer at the State Department. He took Indonesian language training in 1958–59 and was a political officer in Jakarta from 1959 to 1960. From 1960 to 1961, he was consular and administrative officer in Medan, and from 1961 to 1964, he was economic officer in Jakarta.

From 1964 to 1968, Toussaint was at the U.S. Mission to the United Nations, as adviser, then senior adviser for political and security affairs. He attended the Imperial Defense College in London in 1969–70 and was counselor for political affairs in Tehran from 1970 to 1972. From 1972 to 1975, he was Deputy Chief of Mission in Jakarta.

In 1975–76 Toussaint attended the senior seminar in foreign policy. He was Deputy Assistant Secretary of State for International Organization Affairs from 1976 to 1977 and deputy coordinator of the United Nations Conference on Science and Technology from 1977 to 1978.

Visit of Prime Minister Lynch of Ireland

Toasts at the State Dinner.   November 8, 1979

THE PRESIDENT. Prime Minister and Mrs. Lynch, Jack and Máirín, we're delighted to welcome you to the White House again, the first time in your role as the head of a great nation. I know that everyone here who is of Irish descent feels particularly at ease, because—as Jack pointed out to the group of enthusiastic welcomers this morning—the architect of the White House was a very famous Irishman, trained in Dublin, from Kilkenny, named James Hoban. And those of you who have visited Ireland know that this White House bears a very strange and not accidental resemblance to the home of the Irish Parliament. So, we're very delighted

to have you here in an Irish home where many Irish Presidents have served.

Jack Lynch is famous in Ireland for many things: first of all, as an athlete who was noted for his prowess on the playing fields. And he's also famous as a political leader, a man of quiet courage, a gentle man, a man who's a moderate leader, who's strong and courageous.

Our country has benefited greatly from many famous Irishmen as well—Daniel Boone, John Wayne, Bing Crosby, John L. Sullivan, and, in a more modern day, George Meany, Tip O'Neill, and many others that I don't have the time to name. Many assembled in this room are proud of their Irish blood. And I think that one of the most famous, George M. Cohan, expressed it very well when he said that he was "a real live nephew of my Uncle Sam," and later in the same song, "I'm proud of all the Irish blood that's in me." This could be kind of a theme song of many Americans.

Once, when an American visited Dublin, the former mayor, Mayor Briscoe said, "On behalf of 30 million Irishmen, I welcome you to Dublin." And he later said, "I'm talking about 5 million in Ireland and 25 million in the United States." [*Laughter*] Both figures were slight exaggerations, but we do have 20 million Americans here who are Irish or of Irish descent, and on St. Patrick's Day, Mr. Prime Minister, there are at least 200 million—[*laughter*]—Americans who are Irish.

Americans are particularly proud of Ireland and what you have done. Not many people, not enough people know that Ireland has the fastest growing economy in Europe—a nation which is now a better and better place to live for young and old; a nation playing a growing leadership role in the councils of Europe and indeed the entire world; a nation which has benefited, as have we, with rapidly increasing American investments; a nation who still sends missionaries and priests to the United States, to Georgia, and to many other parts of the world; a nation that is committed to peace enough to be a demonstrator of courage, whose soldiers now serve in a sacrificial way in the Congo, in Cyprus, in Lebanon; a nation that has indeed found its leadership role in Europe and throughout the world.

Those who know history understand that Ireland was the nurturer of the seed of Western civilization throughout the Dark Ages and has meant so much to our country—in the past, in the present, and will in the future—in our heritage, our belief in freedom, our culture, our love of arts. And we are all proud that Ireland has now been recognized in every nation as occupying a legitimate and well-deserved role of leadership in the political, cultural life of Europe and the world.

Ireland is also a nation which has suffered from bloodshed and division. Ireland is not alone in modern day suffering. I talked to my wife not too long ago, at 6 o'clock our time, which was 6 o'clock in the morning in Thailand. She's now, about 7:30, arrived at one of the refugee camps that she'll be visiting all during this day, our night, and she'll be exploring ways where our great and prosperous and blessed country can help those who suffer from starvation and persecution.

A little earlier this evening I had to cancel my planned, long-planned trip to Canada, because Americans are suffering from international terrorism in being held against their will, and my responsibility is to protect the lives of Americans in foreign countries and here at home.

Our guest, the Prime Minister of the great nation of Ireland, represents the kind of leadership necessary in a world that's still plagued with suffering and with threats, with violence to the laws of man and God, and with terrorism. He's a man of quiet strength. As I said earlier,

as on the playing fields, in his leadership role he's a man of gentleness. He has a firm voice of reason, and because of his quiet strength, Ireland and we and the other nations who look to him for leadership benefit greatly.

I would like for all of you to join me in a toast to Prime Minister and Mrs. Jack Lynch, our friends, to the Irish everywhere, and to the indomitable spirit of their lovely land, which is also our lovely land. To the Irish and to our notable guest of this evening.

THE PRIME MINISTER. *Mr. President, Miss Lillian—glad to see you here, delighted you have come—Ambassadors, ladies and gentlemen:*

When I see the President of the United States using as a script two sides of a small envelope—[*laughter*]—it ill-behooves me to take out my script here this evening. [*Laughter*] There are a few points in it that perhaps I would like to refer to it in order to get across to you. And I'd, first of all, like to thank you, Mr. President, for your gracious welcome, for your kind words about my country, about my wife, and about me.

I just want to recall an occasion, oh, some 30 years ago, when a very well-known American came to Ireland, and he had performed admirably in the Berlin Olympics of 1936, I think it was. His name was Jesse Owens. And he had won the 100, the 220, the relay, and the long jump; he had four Olympic gold medals. And I introduced Jesse Owens as a great athlete, as a gentleman, and a lot of other things. And when he got up to address the assembly—it was some kind of an athletic seminar—he said, "Thank you, Mr. Lynch, for saying exactly what I had written down for you." [*Laughter*] Your President has said things about me that I mightn't have written for him, but I know they were too profuse, but certainly about my country, he said nothing that I wouldn't have wanted him to say anyway.

But we have had a gracious welcome here. My wife, Máirín, and I have been especially touched by the warmth of that welcome, and I think the spirit of it emphasized the spirit of America through the ages. Just over 400 years ago, the population of the United States, that is, the area occupied by the United States, was less than the population of my country now. And into this territory people have flowed from all over the world, people of Europe, from Africa, and of Asia, and they have made their home here. And you in America have provided them with the hospitality which all the bounty of nature has made possible and, as well, the virtue of good and just government has secured.

In Europe today, we face the problems that the United States faced many, many years ago. Europe is now integrating, as the States once did. And although the times are not the same, the European Community now has a comity of nations, each acutely conscious of its own sovereignty, but each willing to compromise in the interests of the greater good, as the States once did in America and still do today. But we have our problems in the process of this evolution, problems in which you have given an example for the rest of us to overcome.

I think the United States can be truly said as the world's outstanding example of unity in diversity. And the words in your motto, "E Pluribus Unum," describe not just aspiration but attainment. And we outside the States, those of us in Ireland and in other countries in Europe, look on your achievement with pride and genuinely with pride, since so many of our forebears were part of that achievement. But to you Americans belong the real pride, because you must live every day with the burden and with the responsibility which America's power brings in the world today.

As the President has said, Ireland currently holds the Presidency of the European Community, and in that capacity we represent fellow Europeans at numerous international conferences, including the United Nations. We in Europe see ourselves as a community in an interdependent world, as a potent and growing force, building on our relations with both developing and developed countries in a friendly and a cooperative spirit.

In pursuing this policy, the EEC's relationship with the United Nations is particularly significant. You, Mr. President, have said—and we welcome what you'd said in this respect—that you see European strength and unity not as a threat, but as a boon. The plain truth is that Europe and the United States need each other. Interdependence is not just an empty phrase; it describes a fact.

I don't have to go into the problems that we face together in the world of today: the depletion of resources, the abuse of human rights, the increase in armaments and nuclear proliferation, starvation and global confrontation. We both—not just as a small nation, like Ireland is—but we both, in our capacity as a member of the European Community, with the United States, have to face up to these problems.

We have the problems of new technology, and we're moving into worlds where none of us has ever been: the shift in the balance of trade involving the developing countries—and we must look after them as well—and the demographic changes which can alter the whole structure of a society. And all these problems can be dealt only in a coordinated way, and certainly I can see much damage being done in a return to an old-fashioned protectionism or economic nationalism. You, Mr. President, have expressed time and time again the value to the West and the developing world of Multinational Trade Negotiations designed to avoid just such dangers.

We think that in Ireland we have a special role to play in symbolizing the common interests between the United States and Europe, as well as the great potential still to be tapped in an even closer cooperation between the two continents.

Our island is roughly 200 miles wide, 300 miles long. We're close to the European mainland. We're the closest European country to the United States of America. In fact, there are so many parishes on the west coast of Ireland that describe themselves as the nearest parish to the United States—[*laughter*]—that one outbids the other—I don't know yet which is. But I think in my part of the country, in the southwest of Cork, we can claim that we really are the closest parish to the United States. [*Laughter*]

Mr. President, your having spoken from the back of an envelope, as I said, I'd better not have any more recourse to my script, except to say that we are glad we have this opportunity of being here, of being your official guests, glad of the opportunity of representing the European Economic Community here in Washington on this occasion.

Back at home we have some progress to report; we have difficulties. We went into these difficulties today with the President, with the Secretary of State, with the Foreign Relations Committee of the House and of the Senate. I believe one is Foreign Relations and the other is Foreign Affairs; I forget which is which.

But I was glad to see my old friend Tip O'Neill there this afternoon, a man who has given a great lead as far as insight and understanding of the Irish situation is concerned. We welcome that. You, Mr. President, in August 1977, similarly showed the same interest and the same concern.

We're doing fairly well in Ireland. We are proceeding economically. Our population is increasing—which is unusual in Europe at the present time—perhaps not as much as we would like, as there's a story about a lady who, having had six children, people were wondering why she didn't have the seventh. Somebody said to her, "Well, you've produced six beautiful children, terrific assets, a compliment to the nation, and why don't you go ahead?" She said, "No, nothing doing as far as I'm concerned. I read the other day that every seventh child born into the world is a Chinese." [*Laughter*]

Notwithstanding that admonition, our population is, happily, growing. And more and more of our population are staying at home, with the result that there will be less Hobans, less O'Neills, perhaps even Carters. I think there are about 120 Carters in the Irish telephone directory. There are a few Lynchs. There was a Lynch who in some way contributed to the Declaration of Independence. But there will be less Lynchs coming to the United States in the future. We thank God for that. We thank our association with Europe, and as well, we thank American investment in our country.

Mr. President, I am delighted to be with you. I'm delighted to be your guest. I'm delighted that your mother has come along to join us, because she proved so popular in Ireland that people like me who—[*laughter*]—we were getting worried about our own particular position, vis-a-vis the electorate. In fact, your son told us today, Miss Lillian, that you want to go back there sometime soon and for a longer period. We hope you do. And the next time you come, will you please bring your son? We'd like to have him as well. [*Laughter*]

Mr. President, ladies and gentlemen, I'd like you to join me now in a toast, a toast to the President, Mrs. Carter, and the people of this great nation, the United States of America. As I said on the White House lawn today, *"Bail ó Dhia ort féin agus ar do chuid oibre,"* may God's blessing be with you and with your work. To the President of the United States, Mrs. Carter, and the people of the United States.

THE PRESIDENT. I wish I had time to recognize all the great Irish leaders who are here. I'm very delighted that Mr. George Meany is present and Tip O'Neill; Joe Garrahy, Governor; Brendan Byrne, Governor; Leonard Bernstein, right in front of me here; and my mother, who's a real honorary citizen of Ireland. And I've asked my mother, in the absence of my wife, to join us in the receiving line. We look forward to meeting every one of you.

Thank you very much.

NOTE: The President spoke at 7:50 p.m. in the East Room at the White House.

Energy Security Corporation and Synthetic Fuels and Conservation Programs

White House Statement on Senate Approval of Legislation. November 9, 1979

The President this morning expressed his pleasure with the Senate's actions in approving a strong synthetic fuels and conservation program and the establishment of an energy security corporation.

While refinements in the bill will have to be made, the most important elements of the President's program are intact and strong. The President said, "The Senate has ensured that there will be a strong synthetic fuels program and a significant institution to carry it out. The bill's conservation program is a strong, substantial initiative. I congratulate Chairman Jackson, Senator Johnston, and Senator Domenici for their able and dedicated work.

"My administration will continue its close cooperation with congressional lead-ers in support of this legislation. The uncertain nature of our energy supplies cannot be overemphasized; but this action, together with the continued steady progress of the energy mobilization board and the windfall profits tax, is a step toward regaining control of our Nation's future."

Strategic Arms Limitation Treaty

White House Statement on Approval of the Treaty by the Senate Foreign Relations Committee. November 9, 1979

The President is deeply gratified by the vote of the Senate Foreign Relations Committee to favorably report the SALT II treaty to the Senate floor. We are particularly grateful for the thoroughness with which the committee has explored all aspects of the treaty.

The President would like to express special appreciation to Senators Church and Javits for their leadership during the extended hearings and markup of SALT II.

It is the President's hope that all Senators will explore the SALT II treaty and related issues with the same intensity as the members of the Senate Foreign Relations Committee. We believe after such study Senators will reach the conclusion that SALT II is in the best interests of the United States and will vote to ratify the treaty.

American Hostages in Iran

White House Statement. November 9, 1979

The seizure of more than 60 Americans in our Embassy in Tehran has provoked strong feelings here at home. There is outrage. There is frustration. And there is deep anger.

There is also pride in the courage of those who are in danger and sympathy for them and for their families. But the most important concern for all Americans at this moment is safety of our fellow citizens held in Tehran.

The President shares these feelings. He is pursuing every possible avenue in a situation that is extremely volatile and difficult. His efforts involve many countries and individuals. Many of these efforts must of necessity be conducted without publicity, and all require the calmest possible atmosphere.

The President knows that no matter how deeply we may feel, none of us would want to do anything that would worsen the danger in which our fellow Americans have been placed.

He calls on all Americans, public officials and private citizens alike, to exercise restraint, and to keep the safety of their countrymen uppermost in their minds and hearts. Members of the families of the American hostages with whom the President met this morning have asked to join with him in this appeal. The President expects every American to refrain from any action that might increase the danger to the American hostages in Tehran.

NOTE: Press Secretary Jody Powell read the statement to reporters assembled in the Briefing Room at the White House.

The President had met with the members of the families at the State Department.

United States Assistance to Central America and the Caribbean

Message to the Congress Transmitting Proposed Legislation. November 9, 1979

To the Congress of the United States:

Many of our neighbors in Central America and the Caribbean are in crisis— crisis marked by economic problems, terrorism, and popular frustration. The resolution of these problems in ways that will preserve the independence and security of these countries, while expanding democracy and supporting human rights, is very much in the national interest of the United States.

Prompt and effective U.S. assistance is vital.

—Nicaragua's economy has been crushed by bitter and prolonged strife. We have been asked to help, and we are doing so. But more is needed to restore public confidence, private initiatives, and popular well-being.

—The Governments in El Salvador and Honduras have pledged democracy and moderation. These and other Central American countries are embarked on accelerated development efforts of direct benefit to the poor. Assistance in these efforts is essential in creating the conditions under which democratic institutions can grow and thrive.

—The countries of the Eastern Caribbean are young and struggling democracies. They need help now for nation-building and for economic development.

I am therefore today proposing action to expand our support for development and security in Central America and the Caribbean. This will augment our existing development and security assistance programs in these regions, which in turn complement the contributions of several other governments and international agencies.

I have directed that, subject to normal congressional notification procedures, funds be reprogrammed for use in Central America and the Caribbean. These include:

—$5 million from the fiscal year 1980 Economic Support Funds for development projects in Central American countries other than Nicaragua.

—$10 million from fiscal year 1979 and fiscal year 1980 development assistance funds for public works and high employment impact projects in the Caribbean. These projects are an important part of our fiscal year 1979–80 contributions of $66.9 million budgeted for the Caribbean Development Group, chaired by the World Bank.

We are also reprogramming Food for Peace funds to increase food assistance in the area, especially in Nicaragua. We will also likely be reprogramming $5 to $10 million in Foreign Military Sales credits and International Military Education and Training funds for the Caribbean, and similar amounts for such programs in Central America. We are still working out the final details of these proposed reprogrammings and will fully inform the appropriate congressional committees of our proposed actions.

Reprogramming, however, is not enough. The enclosed bill would provide $80 million in flexible Economic Support funding, $75 million to assist in the reconstruction of the Nicaraguan economy and $5 million for early-impact development projects in other Central American countries.

I strongly urge rapid congressional action on this bill.

Such action will demonstrate that the United States can be relied upon to support democratic aspirations, the rebuilding of broken economies, and the security of our friends in this nearby region. Our additional funds for Central American development should substantially augment existing programs. Furthermore, we hope that other nations and international institutions will increase their efforts to accelerate the social and economic development of Central America.

With your help we can make clear where we stand.

                        JIMMY CARTER

The White House,
    November 9, 1979.

Digest of Other White House Announcements

The following listing includes the President's public schedule and other items of general interest announced by the White House Press Office and not included elsewhere in this issue.

November 5

The President returned to the White House from Camp David, Md.

The President met at the White House with:

—Zbigniew Brzezinski, Assistant to the President for National Security Affairs;

—Senators J. Bennett Johnston of Louisiana, Mark O. Hatfield of Oregon, and Pete V. Domenici of New Mexico;

—Mr. and Mrs. William Fisher of Carnegie, Pa., and Mr. and Mrs. Marvin Porterfield of Martinsburg, W. Va., hosts of meetings the President had in their homes with private citizens on July 12 and 13;

—Joe Reed, president of the Alabama Democratic Black Caucus, and black civic and community leaders from Alabama;

—Senator Alan K. Simpson of Wyoming.

The White House announced that the President is and has been closely monitoring and receiving regular reports on efforts to obtain the release of the American Embassy staff in Tehran, who are being detained by Iranian students. A meeting of high-level officials was held this morning in the White House to review the situation and to consider further approaches which might be appropriate.

The White House announced that in reaction to the killing of 5 people and the wounding of 12 others during a demonstration of the Workers' Viewpoint Organization in Greensboro, N.C., on November 3, the President has spoken with Attorney General Benjamin Civiletti, and he has directed that he cooperate fully with local officials and that the Department of Justice pursue its own investigation under Federal law to do everything possible to bring the perpetrators to justice.

November 6

The White House announced that the President met with senior foreign policy advisers this morning to discuss the situation in Iran. The United States has been given assurances by the authorities in Iran that the safety and well-being of Americans will be protected. The United States expects that these assurances will be honored. The White House further announced that in the meantime, the administration is doing everything possible to secure the release of the Embassy staff. The administration does not consider public comment on these efforts to be appropriate or helpful while they are in progress.

The President met at the White House with:

—Dr. Brzezinski;

—Frank B. Moore, Assistant to the President for Congressional Liaison;

—U.S. Ambassador to Saudi Arabia John C. West;

—Vice President Walter F. Mondale;

—James T. McIntyre, Jr., Director of the Office of Management and Budget;

—Secretary of State Cyrus R. Vance, Ambassador Robert S. Strauss, Personal Representative of the President to the Middle East peace negotiations, and Sol M. Linowitz, whom the President has designated as Ambassador Strauss' successor in that position;

—the National Security Council;

—former Attorney General Ramsey Clark and William G. Miller, Senate Intelligence Committee staff member, who are acting as the President's emissaries in efforts to secure the release of the American Embassy staff.

The President transmitted to the Congress the 1978 annual report of the Director of the National Cancer Program, and the 1976, 1977, and 1978 annual reports of the Department of Health, Education, and Welfare on Occupational Safety and Health.

November 7

The President met at the White House with:

—Dr. Brzezinski;

—the Democratic congressional leadership;

—Mr. Moore;

—former Senator Muriel Humphrey of Minnesota;

—Secretary of the Interior Cecil D. Andrus, Stuart E. Eizenstat, Assistant to the President for Domestic Affairs and Policy, Anne Wexler, Assistant to the President, and representatives of national environmental groups;

—Mayor Carl Officer of East St. Louis, Ill.;

—Senator J. James Exon of Nebraska.

The President participated in the briefing by administration officials on the strategic arms limitation treaty given for civic and community leaders from Connecticut, New Jersey, Oregon, and Puerto Rico in the East Room at the White House.

November 8

The President met at the White House with:

—Dr. Brzezinski;

—Vice President Mondale, Secretary of the Treasury G. William Miller, Charles L. Schultze, Chairman of the Council of Economic Advisers, Alfred E. Kahn, Advisor to the President on Inflation, Mr. Eizenstat, and Mr. McIntyre;

—Members of the House of Representatives;

—Mr. Moore;

—Senator Howell Heflin of Alabama;

—Senator Daniel Patrick Moynihan of New York;

—Members of the House of Representatives.

The White House announced that the President will postpone his visit to Canada to remain at the White House and continue to closely monitor the situation in Iran and direct efforts to secure the release of the Americans there. The visit to Canada will be rescheduled to a mutually convenient date early next year. The President's decision to postpone this visit is not based on new developments or any expectation of an immediate change in the situation in Iran. Rather, it is based upon his desire to remain in Washington, where his foreign policy advisers are immediately available and so that he can continue to monitor closely and direct the situation there.

November 9

The President met at the White House with:

—Dr. Brzezinski;

—Vice President Mondale, Secretary Vance, Deputy Secretary of State Warren M. Christopher, Secretary of Defense Harold Brown, Hedley W. Donovan, Senior Adviser to the President, Hamilton Jordan, Assistant to the President, Lloyd N. Cutler, Counsel to the President, and Dr. Brzezinski;

—Mr. Moore.

The President transmitted to the Congress the 1978 annual report on the Administration of the National Sickle Cell Anemia, Cooley's Anemia, Tay-Sachs, and Genetic Diseases Act.

The President declared a major disaster for the Territory of American Samoa as a result of flooding, mudslides, and landslides, beginning on October 28, which caused extensive property damage.

NOMINATIONS SUBMITTED TO THE SENATE

The following list does not include promotions of members of the Uniformed Services, nominations to the Service Academies, or nominations of Foreign Service officers.

Submitted November 6, 1979

JOSE A. CABRANES, of Connecticut, to be United States District Judge for the District of Connecticut, vice John O. Newman, elevated.

ROBERT J. MCNICHOLS, of Washington, to be United States District Judge for the Eastern District of Washington, vice a new position created by P.L. 95–486, approved October 20, 1978.

MARGARET JOAN GIANNINI, of New York, to be Director of the National Institute of Handicapped Research (new position).

NOMINATIONS—Continued

Submitted November 6—Continued

SUSAN J. WILLIAMS, of Virginia, to be an Assistant Secretary of Transportation, vice Terrence L. Bracy, resigned.

Submitted November 7, 1979

RICHARD J. GREEN, of New Jersey, to be an Associate Director of the Federal Emergency Management Agency (new position).

GEORGE FUMICH, JR., of Virginia, to be an Assistant Secretary of Energy (Fossil Energy), vice Robert D. Thorne, resigned.

Submitted November 9, 1979

DONALD R. TOUSSAINT, of Virginia, a Foreign Service officer of Class one, to be Ambassador Extraordinary and Plenipotentiary of the United States of America to the Democratic Socialist Republic of Sri Lanka and to serve concurrently and without additional compensation as Ambassador Extraordinary and Plenipotentiary of the United States of America to the Republic of Maldives.

CHECKLIST OF WHITE HOUSE PRESS RELEASES

The following listing contains releases of the White House Press Office which are not included in this issue.

Released November 6, 1979

Announcement: nomination of Jose A. Cabranes to be United States District Judge for the District of Connecticut

Announcement: nomination of Robert J. McNichols to be United States District Judge for the Eastern District of Washington

Biographical data: Sol M. Linowitz, designated as the successor to Ambassador Robert S. Strauss, Personal Representative of the President to the Middle East peace negotiations

Released November 8, 1979

Transcript: announcement of the postponement of the President's trip to Canada—by Press Secretary Jody Powell

ACTS APPROVED BY THE PRESIDENT

Approved November 4, 1979

S. 1905_____ Public Law 96–101
Milwaukee Railroad Restructuring Act.

Approved November 5, 1979

S. 1030_____ Public Law 96–102
Emergency Energy Conservation Act of 1979.

H.R. 4394_____ Public Law 96–103
Department of Housing and Urban Development—Independent Agencies Appropriation Act, 1980.

H.R. 2515_____ Public Law 96–104
An act to authorize on a temporary basis certain business and agricultural loans, notwithstanding interest limitations in State constitutions or statutes, and for other purposes.

Approved November 8, 1979

S.J. Res. 117_____ Public Law 96–105
A joint resolution to provide for a temporary extension of certain Federal Housing Administration authorities, and for other purposes.

Approved November 9, 1979

H.R. 4249_____ Public Law 96–106
An act to amend title 23 of the United States Code, the Surface Transportation Assistance Act of 1978, and for other purposes.

S. 428_____ Public Law 96–107
Department of Defense Authorization Act, 1980.

H.R. 4387_____ Public Law 96–108
An act making appropriations for Agriculture, Rural Development, and Related Agencies programs for the fiscal year ending September 30, 1980, and for other purposes.

H.R. 5218_____ Public Law 96–109
An act to amend the Foreign Assistance Act of 1961 to authorize special Caribbean hurricane relief assistance.

PRESIDENTIAL DOCUMENTS

Iranian Students in the United States

Announcement on Actions To Be Taken by the Department of Justice. November 10, 1979

The President has directed the Attorney General to identify any Iranian students in the United States who are not in compliance with the terms of their entry visas, and to take the necessary steps to commence deportation proceedings against those who have violated applicable immigration laws and regulations.

As an initial measure, the Immigration and Naturalization Service of the Department of Justice will issue a notice requiring all Iranian students to report their present location and status immediately to the nearest INS office, and will take additional steps to locate and identify such students to determine legal status. For students found to be in illegal status, deportation proceedings will be conducted in accordance with constitutional due process requirements.

Oil Imports From Iran

Remarks Announcing Discontinuance of United States Imports. November 12, 1979

We continue to face a grave situation in Iran, where our Embassy has been seized and more than 60 American citizens continue to be held as hostages in an attempt to force unacceptable demands on our country. We're using every available channel to protect the safety of the hostages and to secure their release.

Along with the families of the hostages, I have welcomed and I appreciate the restraint that has been shown by Americans during this crisis. We must continue to exhibit such constraint, despite the intensity of our emotions. The lives of our people in Iran are at stake.

I must emphasize the gravity of the situation. It's vital to the United States and to every other nation that the lives of diplomatic personnel and other citizens abroad be protected and that we refuse to permit the use of terrorism and the seizure and the holding of hostages to impose political demands.

No one should underestimate the resolve of the American Government and the American people in this matter. It is necessary to eliminate any suggestion that economic pressures can weaken our stand on basic issues of principle. Our position must be clear. I am ordering that we discontinue purchasing of any oil from Iran for delivery to this country.

These events obviously demonstrate the extreme importance of reducing oil consumption here in the United States. I urge every American citizen and every American business to redouble efforts to curtail the use of petroleum products. This action will pose a real challenge to our country. It will be a test of our strength and of our determination.

I've directed Secretary Duncan to work with the Congress and with other Federal, State, and local officials, and with leaders of industry to develop additional measures to conserve oil and to cope with this new situation. We will strive to ensure equitable and fair distribution of petroleum products and to ensure a minimum of disruption of our Nation's economy.

These American measures must be part of an effective international effort, and we will consult with our allies and with other oil-consuming nations about further actions to reduce oil consumption and oil imports.

America does face a difficult task and a test. Our response will measure our character and our courage. I know that we Americans shall not fail.

Thank you very much.

NOTE: The President spoke at 2:01 p.m. to reporters assembled in the Briefing Room at the White House.

Oil Imports From Iran

Proclamation 4702.   November 12, 1979

IMPORTS OF PETROLEUM AND PETROLEUM PRODUCTS

By the President of the United States of America

A Proclamation

The Secretary of the Treasury in a memorandum dated November 12, 1979, and the Secretary of Energy in consultation with the Secretaries of State and Defense, have informed me that recent developments in Iran have exacerbated the threat to the national security posed by imports of petroleum and petroleum products. Those developments underscore the

threat to our national security which results from our reliance on Iran as a source of crude oil. The Secretaries have recommended that I take steps immediately to eliminate the dependence of the United States on Iran as a source of crude oil.

I agree with these recommendations and that the changes proposed are consistent with the purposes of Proclamation 3279, as amended.

Now, THEREFORE, I, JIMMY CARTER, President of the United States of America, by the authority vested in me by the Constitution and the laws of the United States, including Section 232 of the Trade Expansion Act of 1962, as amended, (19 U.S.C. 1862) do hereby proclaim that:

SECTION 1. Section 1 of Proclamation 3279, as amended, is further amended by the addition of a new paragraph (e) to read as follows:

Sec. 1(e). Notwithstanding any other provision of this Proclamation, no crude oil produced in Iran (except crude oil loaded aboard maritime vessels prior to November 13, 1979) or unfinished oil or finished products refined in possessions or free trade zones of the United States from such crude oil, may be entered into the customs territory of the United States.

SEC. 2. Section 11 of Proclamation No. 3279, as amended, is further amended in paragraph (1) to read as follows:

(1) The term "imports", when applied to crude oil other than that produced in Iran, includes both entry for consumption and withdrawal from warehouse for consumption, but excludes unfinished oil and finished products processed in the United States territories and foreign trade zones from crude oil produced in the United States.

IN WITNESS WHEREOF, I have hereunto set my hand this 12th day of November, in the year of our Lord nineteen hundred and seventy-nine and of the Independence of the United States of

America the two hundred and fourth.

JIMMY CARTER

[Filed with the Office of the Federal Register, 12:58 p.m., November 13, 1979]

Hospital Cost Containment Legislation

Letter to the Members of the House of Representatives.   November 13, 1979

You will have an opportunity this week to help our fight against inflation by passing Hospital Cost Containment legislation that can save Americans more than $40 billion over the next five years. I urge you to join in this effort.

For more than two years, the Congress has been considering cost containment legislation. Many legitimate concerns have been raised by Members as well as by the hospital industry. Recently, the Ways and Means and Commerce Committees have approved legislation which responds to those concerns in a fair, reasonable and balanced way. The legislation which you will be voting on is *not* the same legislation that was proposed in the last Congress. And, thus, it is not the same legislation against which so many of the objections to cost containment have been directed.

The modifications which have now been made to the original cost containment bill minimize the Federal government's involvement and place the highest priority on voluntary actions by the hospitals:

• The bill recognizes the request for a priority voluntary effort initiated by the nation's hospitals two years ago. Only if the hospitals fail to meet their own voluntary national goal would the stand-by Federal program go into effect.

• The bill exempts states with successful cost containment programs. States which do not yet have such programs are provided specific incentives to establish and implement them.

• All small hospitals—those with less than 4,000 admissions a year—would be exempt from the bill's coverage.

• The bill will not result in new regulatory burdens on hospitals. Hospitals will have to provide only one additional line of information (wages for non-supervisory personnel) on the Medicare cost forms which they currently submit to the Federal government.

• The bill permits a complete pass-through of the increases in the price of goods and services that hospitals purchase. Thus, hospitals are not penalized because of inflation in the general economy.

• The stand-by Federal program cannot be put into effect over the objection of either House of Congress.

• The bill contains a sunset provision to limit the program to a maximum of five years.

This modified cost containment legislation will have a significant impact in reducing the hospital industry's inflation rate, which over the past decade has increased twice as fast as the inflation rate in the overall economy. Hospital inflation has been at such high levels because of a lack of competition within the industry. Without the type of consumer marketplace which exists in other sectors of the economy, hospitals generally have no incentive to reduce waste or inefficiency and to curb costs. The Federal government itself now contributes 40% to all hospital costs and has an obligation to the American people to assure that Federal tax dollars are not wasted.

While ensuring continued high-quality care, the legislation before you can bring efficiency and businesslike practices to the hospital industry. And it can do so with a minimum of Federal involvement and red tape.

Of equal importance, no other bill before the Congress will have such a direct effect on reducing the cost of living for all Americans. A vote for this bill will clearly and properly be seen by the public as a vote to reduce inflation. It will also be seen as a measure of Congress's commitment in working to fight inflation.

We cannot now afford to turn our backs on the solution developed by two House Committees after several years of difficult work. The time for delay and additional study is past. The time for positive action against inflation is now. I urge you to take that action by voting for Hospital Cost Containment legislation.

Sincerely,

JIMMY CARTER

NOTE: This is the text of identical letters addressed to each Member of the House of Representatives.

Aid for Kampucheans

Remarks at a White House Meeting on Relief Efforts and the First Lady's Trip to Thailand. November 13, 1979

THE PRESIDENT. I'm very grateful that all of you have come to the White House to talk about one of the most important issues that faces humanity and will face it in our lifetime. It's a rare occasion in human memory when there has been a possibility of holocaust, threatening to destroy an entire race of people. It happened, perhaps, in the time of the Armenians, earlier in this century, and later, of course, among Jews and others in the time of Hitler, and now among the people of Cambodia, or Kampuchea, as it's presently known.

There also is a rare occasion when in the life of a great nation its government and its people can react in an unselfish, dynamic, and effective way to alleviate extraordinary human suffering, such as the case, again, with the refugees and the starving people of the Cambodian region.

I was very pleased that the three Senators, then my wife and Dr. Richmond, Mrs. Young and her group, and now a group of Congresswomen and others have been to that region to dramatize the need for action, and also to bring back tangible recommendations on how the suffering might be alleviated more effectively.

It's a difficult issue to resolve. There are major obstacles to overcome: obstacles of war, over which we have no control in that long-troubled part of the world; the issue of diplomatic bridges that are very hard to cross; and also, of course, are very serious problems in administration, in dealing with the bureaucratic needs, to derive help from those eager to give and actually to deliver it effectively to those who are most in need.

Rosalynn and Senators Danforth, Baucus, and Sasser, Dr. Richmond, and others have brought back very specific recommendations on what might be done. I'm not going to try to preempt their reports to you. They can make their reports much better than can I. I'm one of those who's listening, and, like you, I am eager to act in accordance with the best interests of those who are crying out for assistance.

There are three basic areas of response: One is the United States Government itself—and the Congress has reacted very well in approving almost $70 million worth of aid. And I will go to the Congress for additional aid if it's necessary. Second is an appeal to private organizations, volunteer organizations of all kinds, represented by many of you here. And that's a resource of assistance which is eager to be tapped and which has already done yeoman's work, even before governmental help could be effective. And the third recommendation is concerning international relationships.

And I would like to caution you about that: This is a judgment and a decision that we can't make in this room.

And one of the vivid reports that Rosalynn brought back to me was that quite often a United States initiative is counterproductive in the eventual carrying out of a recommendation. If the initiative comes from one of the less developed nations of the world or comes directly from the United Nations or, perhaps, comes from other countries than we, it's much more effective.

So, I would like to urge you to restrain your own inclinations to give public condemnation or public advice on what the Vietnamese ought to do, what the warring parties in Kampuchea ought to do, what the United Nations ought to do. Let that be handled through diplomatic channels. I can assure you that I will not permit these efforts to be abandoned or ignored. But I think that the public calling for action might be the very thing that would prevent that action being carried out. That's my only caution to you.

And I have a second one—I forgot. I think the more all of us forgo credit for action to be taken, the more effective the effort will be. There is a great yearning, I know, within the United States Government, within the Red Cross, within UNICEF, within Catholic charities, within the Protestant churches, within benevolent groups, to want to give aid and then have that assistance be publicly acknowledged and recognized. That is a human trait, but the more we can subjugate those natural, human desires for quiet giving and close cooperation with others, with a minimum of jealousy and a minimum of grasping for recognition, the more effective we'll all be.

I'm sure that's a cautionary word that you don't need, because there's an overwhelming unselfishness and benevolent attitude among this group. And you've taken the initiative, and there's been no evidence of a grasping for recognition. But in the future, this is going to be a long, slow, tedious process, and that needs to be recognized and avoided.

The last point I'd like to make is this: The Thai people and the Thai Government both deserve every possible recognition, expression of gratitude, and thanks. They are a poor country. Many of the Thai people suffer terribly from poverty, disease, and hunger. It's not a popular political thing to bring in enormous numbers of refugees from an alien and antagonistic country, who's been historical enemies on occasion, and still not arouse the condemnation of the Thais, who themselves suffer. And this has been a very great demonstration of both kindness and also courage, political courage.

I know that this is something that you'll want to help with. The Thais are not able to accept literally hundreds of thousands of refugees into their country and feed those refugees on their own. And we've got to be especially generous to the Thais in our thanks and in our direct help and the recognition of what they are contributing.

I look forward with great eagerness to the summary of your recommendations. I will be getting it through the National Security Council and through my wife, who always has easy access to me. And I think that her involvement is one that can be of help to you as well. She'll be working with the wives of Senators and other Members of Congress, and female Members of Congress. She will also be working with any of you who want her to help in providing an avenue to the public and also an avenue directly to me.

But I'm very grateful to all of you for being willing to come. I think this will be one of the most important meetings ever taking place in the White House. And I'm grateful that I am President of people like you.

Thank you very much.

REVEREND HESBURGH. *Mrs. Carter, Mrs. Vance, ladies and gentlemen:*

Just short of 3 weeks ago, on October 24, this same group of leaders from our various religious faiths and from the various private voluntary organizations met in Washington to discuss what we might do together and in concert to meet the tragedy in Cambodia. The purpose was to consult how the American people, how the American Government, and how the United Nations might best respond to avoid what appeared to be a growing holocaust, already half accomplished, if you will.

We called on the voluntary agencies, first of all, to increase their efforts and to work together to help the Cambodians. We urged Americans to provide them all with financial support. And in a special letter to the President, we urged greater United States Government efforts in order to assist, as quickly and as effectively as possible, this people in great need.

We met that same day at the White House with the President, and never was a letter answered more quickly. Hardly before the letter was in his hands, he granted us all of the various requests we had for increased aid and said he was willing to do whatever else might be necessary to do to avert this holocaust.

I think today, in the light of the appeal made by United Nations Children's Fund, UNICEF, the International Committee of the Red Cross, the appeals by all of our various voluntary agencies for more than $300 million for Cambodian relief, and after the generous and immediate response of the President of the United States voiced by our Secretary of State, Mr. Vance, at the Pledging Conference of the United States on Monday, November 5— when many of you were present, and I too—it seemed to us that the time was now appropriate to update our October 24 meeting in an effort to relieve the growing misery of the Cambodians.

It was again against this same background as our last meeting that I, as chairman of the Overseas Development Council, and cochaired by the Reverend Paul McLeary, who is chairman of the American Council on Voluntary Agencies, that we invited this group again, on very short notice, to this second consultation to exchange information on the situation in Thailand and Cambodia after other relief is taking place there.

In this second consultation we have four things we would like to do: first, to find out what the various agencies are now doing; second, what they are planning to do for the near-term future; third, what fundraising efforts have been undertaken to date; and fourth, what are the various bottlenecks and needs that we have to move forward quickly and efficiently. There is, of course, a fifth topic which I'm sure will emerge from our discussion with Mrs. Carter, and that is how can we improve and institutionalize exchange of information among ourselves and coordination of the various activities—governmental and nongovernmental and intergovernmental—here and overseas.

It seems to me that the vigor of the pluralistic American response to this Cambodian tragedy is most welcome, but it does raise for all of us a great challenge to work together and, as the President just said, to work together without seeking praise in so doing.

I would like to say that the visit to Cambodia and Thailand in October by Senators Danforth, Sasser, and Baucus, who are here with us this morning, on my left, your right, and also the various Governors and the Congresswomen and, most particularly, of our First Lady, Mrs. Carter—all of this has heightened and increased the consciousness of Americans for the need of all of the generous action we might put forward to alleviate this growing tragedy.

May I say, Mrs. Carter, in introducing

you, that we are looking forward to hearing the report from you and your colleagues on the situation with respect to Cambodian refugees in Thailand, and any other recommendations or questions you may have of this group, which represents, I think, the cream of the private voluntary effort. After your comments we will be hearing from all of these various agencies active in Cambodia on the questions posed earlier, and we are looking forward later in the day to discussing our conclusions further with you.

Mrs. Carter, it's with real pride and great satisfaction that I'd like to present you.

Mrs. Carter. Thank you very much. I'm very pleased to have you all here today. I welcome you.

And I did go to Cambodia. And I'm very happy to have this opportunity to report to you about my trip, and also to thank you for what you have done already and for what you continue to do, and to work with you on ways that we can better help those who are suffering in this area of the world.

As the President has said, I went to Thailand on his behalf to express the profound concern of the people of our country for the tragedy that is unfolding in Indochina. My visit was very brief, but I think I can say positively that it was one of the most significant events of my life. I came away filled with admiration for the representatives of your organizations who are there struggling with this massive problem of relief for thousands and thousands of human beings who are starving and homeless and ill and bereaved. And I came away also, as Jimmy said, filled with gratitude for the efforts of the people of Thailand and for the Government of Thailand.

And I'm sure that every person in this room knows what faces us in the coming weeks. The problem is one that is not going away anytime soon. We will be faced

with it for a long time. While our international efforts have brought vast improvements—and I saw in the refugee camp at Sakeo some beginnings of hope for those few who have been brought back from the very edge of death. The camp, since the time that the Senators was there, has really made progress; in fact, some people told us that a miracle had happened in the last few weeks. The camp is only about 3 weeks old, but people are being fed and are being taken care of in that camp now. And you will have a further report on that from some of those who went with me.

But the picture in the near future looks very bleak, because a wave of new refugees are expected to come across the border into Thailand from Kampuchea—a number estimated anywhere from 100,000 to 250,000, maybe 300,000—that are now right at the border, that are expected to come now that the dry season is here and the fighting has begun again. They will be pushed over into Thailand.

And for those of us who have seen with our own eyes the dimension of the problem and the terrible suffering and starvation, the thought of so many more people in the same situation who will be coming into Thailand is almost more than you can bear, when you are there and look at it.

I'd like to tell you briefly about my trip. I was accompanied by some of those here that are here at that head table, who will be reporting to you also. Some of us worked together; some of us dispersed so that we could gather more information, because we were only there for a few hours, a day, 2 days.

We went to the refugee camps in Thailand, Kampuchea, that I have already talked about, Sakeo. We witnessed the disease, the dislocation of persons, suffering, starvation. We saw many, young and old. We saw children separated from their parents, afflicted with malaria and malnutrition.

In the camp at Ubon, for refugees from

Laos, conditions were substantially better. There are approximately 37,000 persons there. That camp is 4 or 5 years old. They eat well, but they don't go out of the camp. They have been there, some for 3 or 4 years, waiting to resettle abroad. And although the living conditions are so much better than Sakeo, they are still not anything that you would call good.

It is sad to see them with no purpose. They at first thought they might go back into Laos. Now they know they won't, or don't want to. And they're waiting to be resettled, some of them with feeling that they've been forgotten by the world, because the focus has been on the Kampucheans, the focus has been on the boat people. And these people really feel forgotten. I was touched by them. And one of the girls that worked with me said that one of the main problems they have with these people is mental depression, just existing day to day for 4 or 5 years, waiting to see what happens to them.

At the transit center, the refugee transit center in Bangkok, we saw overcrowded and humiliating conditions where refugees awaiting final processing for immigration must endure. These were things that I don't think I'll ever forget. These were people who have already been chosen to go to other countries and have to wait in an unbelievable place, some for a month and a half or 2 months. We try to process ours, the ones that are coming to the United States, much earlier, but still the conditions are unbearable.

While we were there in Bangkok, we had candid discussions with representatives of the international volunteer organizations to discuss their goals, their frustrations, and the need for better coordination. We did have a very good meeting, and everybody, I think, vented their frustrations, and everybody decided that there was a great need for coordination.

We met with the King and Queen of Thailand to discuss the whole spectrum of the refugee problem and the need for further sites, because we must have further sites for this 200,000 to 300,000 that are expected to come into Thailand from Cambodia—and they're expected to come in in the next 3 or 4 weeks. The situation is urgent.

We had a long discussion with Prime Minister Kriangsak, a fruitful discussion, about the political and foreign policy risks that are facing the Thai Government because of their policies. It is important that the international community provide visible and demonstrable political, economic, and security support to the Thais.

As we flew back to Washington, we got together on the airplane and worked on our report for the President, which stresses the urgency of the situation, and we did lay out some specific recommendations. We will give you that report this morning. In fact, you have in your brochure a folder with our recommendations in it.

We need your careful consideration of our recommendations. We need your creative ideas for how to implement them, your support, and your consensus. I do not know when I have ever felt a sense of urgency more about cutting redtape and unblocking logjams and moving ahead.

I think I can say with some assurance that the American people are ready to help. They are already mobilizing help, as you here indicate and as I have seen and heard through my mail and telephone calls and with people in the whole country concerned about this problem. But they need to know how to help, and they need to know now. They need to know where to turn; they need to know that now. They need to know what is needed, and it's our responsibility to give the people of our country specific information about ways they can reach out to their fellow man. We cannot lose time. Time is—the situation is urgent.

I understand that most of you who are here have prepared briefing papers about your programs and your problems. I know that you will be addressing yourselves to this issue throughout the day, and I look forward to being with you again at the end of the afternoon so that I can have a report for the things that you talk about during the day.

But now I want to call on the members of my traveling party, who've brought back new information which might be helpful to you. And then I would like to share—after we get through with the reports we will look at the recommendations, and I can tell you then some of the steps that we are already taking to implement some of these recommendations.

First I want to call on Dr. Richmond for his report. Dr. Richmond is the Surgeon General, and he traveled with me to Thailand.

NOTE: The President spoke at 10:07 a.m. in the State Dining Room at the White House. Attending the meeting were representatives and officials of Federal and international agencies and various humanitarian organizations.

Aid for Kampucheans

Memorandum From the President.
November 13, 1979

Presidential Determination No. 80–5

Memorandum for the Secretary of State
Subject: Determination pursuant to Section 2(c)(1) of Migration and Refugee Assistance Act of 1962, as amended, (The "Act"), authorizing the use of $2,000,000 of funds made available from the United States Emergency Refugee and Migration Assistance Fund

In response to the urgent financial needs of the Relief Program within Kampuchea, I hereby determine that it is important to the national interest that up to $2,000,000 from the United States Emergency Refugee and Migration Assistance Fund be made available through the Department of State for transfer to the United Nations Children's Fund for this purpose.

The Secretary of State is requested to inform the appropriate committees of Congress of this Determination and the obligation of funds under this authority.

This Determination shall be published in the FEDERAL REGISTER.

JIMMY CARTER

[Filed with the Office of the Federal Register, 4:24 p.m., November 20, 1979]

Superior Court of the District of Columbia

Nomination of Iraline Barnes To Be an Associate Judge.   November 13, 1979

The President today announced that he will nominate Iraline Barnes as an Associate Judge of the Superior Court of the District of Columbia. Ms. Barnes, 32, is a graduate of Howard University and the University of Michigan Law School. She would replace Judge W. Byron Sorrell, who retired in August.

Following law school, Ms. Barnes served as a law clerk for Superior Court Judge Eugene Hamilton. She then worked as a trial attorney for the Civil Division of the Justice Department and as an assistant United States attorney for the District of Columbia. Since June 1978 she has served as an Administrative Judge for the Board of Surface Mining and Reclamation Appeals at the Department of the Interior.

National Advisory Committee on Oceans and Atmosphere

Appointment of Five Members.
November 13, 1979

The President today announced the appointment of five persons as members of the National Advisory Committee on Oceans and Atmosphere. They are:

MICHAEL R. NAESS, of Houston, Tex., senior executive vice president and director and chief operating officer of the Services Group, Zapata Corp., Houston, Tex.;

JACK R. VAN LOPIK, dean of Louisiana State University's Center for Wetland Resources and a professor in the Department of Marine Sciences;

JAMES M. WADDELL, JR., of Beaufort, S.C., a South Carolina State senator and chairman of the South Carolina Coastal Council;

DON WALSH, director of the Institute for Marine and Coastal Studies at the University of Southern California and a professor of ocean engineering;

ROBERT M. WHITE, administrator of the National Research Council, formerly chairman of the National Academy of Sciences' Climate Research Board, and president of the Joint Oceanographic Institutions.

Marine Mammal Commission

Appointment of Two Members.
November 13, 1979

The President today announced the appointment of two persons as members of the Marine Mammal Commission. They are:

MURRAY L. JOHNSON, a Tacoma, Wash., surgeon and research biologist who is curator of mammals for the Puget Sound Museum of Natural History and collaborator in mammalogy with the U.S. National Park System;

ROGER S. PAYNE, of Lincoln, Mass., a research zoologist with the New York Zoological Society's Center for Field Biology and Conservation, whose principal research interest is the behavior of whales.

Woodrow Wilson International Center for Scholars

Appointment of Four Members of the
Board of Trustees. November 13, 1979

The President has appointed four persons as members of the Board of Trustees of the Woodrow Wilson International Center for Scholars in the Smithsonian Institution. They are:

THEODORE C. BARREAUX, of Alexandria, Va., vice president in charge of the Washington office of the American Institute of Certified Public Accountants;

MAX M. KAMPELMAN, a partner in the Washington, D.C., law firm of Fried, Frank, Harris, Shriver, and Kampelman;

JESSE H. OPPENHEIMER, a partner in the San Antonio, Tex., law firm of Oppenheimer, Rosenberg, Kelleher & Wheatley, active in civic affairs in San Antonio;

ANNE FIROR SCOTT, an assistant professor of history at Duke University and author of several books on women in American life.

Blocking Iranian Government Property

Executive Order 12170. November 14, 1979

Pursuant to the authority vested in me as President by the Constitution and the laws of the United States including the International Emergency Economic Powers Act, 50 U.S.C.A. sec. 1701 *et seq.,* the National Emergencies Act, 50 U.S.C. sec. 1601 *et seq.,* and 3 U.S.C. sec. 301,

I, JIMMY CARTER, President of the United States, find that the situation in Iran constitutes an unusual and extraordinary threat to the national security, foreign policy and economy of the United States and hereby declare a national emergency to deal with that threat.

I hereby order blocked all property and interests in property of the Government of Iran, its instrumentalities and controlled entities and the Central Bank of

Iran which are or become subject to the jurisdiction of the United States or which are in or come within the possession or control of persons subject to the jurisdiction of the United States.

The Secretary of the Treasury is authorized to employ all powers granted to me by the International Emergency Economic Powers Act to carry out the provisions of this order.

This order is effective immediately and shall be transmitted to the Congress and published in the FEDERAL REGISTER.

JIMMY CARTER

The White House,
   November 14, 1979.

[Filed with the Office of the Federal Register,
   9:16 a.m., November 14, 1979]

Blocking Iranian Government Property

*Announcement on the President's Action.
November 14, 1979*

The President has today acted to block all official Iranian assets in the United States, including deposits in United States banks and their foreign branches and subsidiaries. This order is in response to reports that the Government of Iran is about to withdraw its funds. The purpose of this order is to ensure that claims on Iran by the United States and its citizens are provided for in an orderly manner.

The order does not affect accounts of persons other than the Government of Iran, the Central Bank of Iran, and other controlled entities. The precise amounts involved cannot be ascertained at this time, but there is no reason for disturbance in the foreign exchange or other markets.

The President is taking this action pursuant to the International Emergency Economic Powers Act, which grants the President authority "to deal with any unusual and extraordinary threat to the national security, foreign policy, or economy of the United States."

Blocking Iranian Government Property

*Message to the Congress Reporting on the
U.S. Action. November 14, 1979*

To the Congress of the United States:

Pursuant to Section 204(b) of the International Emergency Economic Powers Act, 50 U.S.C.A. § 1703, I hereby report to the Congress that I have today exercised the authority granted by this Act to block certain property or interests in property of the Government of Iran, its instrumentalities and controlled entities and the Central Bank of Iran.

1. The circumstances necessitating the exercise of this authority are the recent events in Iran and the recent actions of the Government of Iran.

2. These events and actions put at grave risk the personal safety of United States citizens and the lawful claims of United States citizens and entities against the Government of Iran and constitute an extraordinary threat to the national security and foreign policy of the United States.

3. Consequently, I have ordered blocked all property and interests in property of the Government of Iran, its instrumentalities and controlled entities and the Central Bank of Iran which are or become subject to the jurisdiction of the United States or which are or come within the possession of persons subject to the jurisdiction of the United States. I have authorized the Secretary of the Treasury to employ all powers granted to me by the International Emergency Economic Powers Act to carry out the blocking.

4. Blocking property and property interests of the Government of Iran, its instrumentalities and controlled entities and the Central Bank of Iran will enable the United States to assure that these resources will be available to satisfy lawful claims of citizens and entities of the United States against the Government of Iran.

5. This action is taken with respect to Iran for the reasons described in this report.

JIMMY CARTER

The White House,
    November 14, 1979.

Convention on the Inter-American Institute for Cooperation on Agriculture

Message to the Senate Transmitting the Convention.   November 14, 1979

To the Senate of the United States:

I transmit herewith, for Senate advice and consent to ratification, the Convention on the Inter-American Institute for Cooperation on Agriculture (the Convention) which was signed at Washington on March 6, 1979. For the information of the Senate, I also transmit the report of the Department of State with respect to the Convention.

The Convention is a revision of the 1944 Convention on the Inter-American Institute of Agricultural Sciences. It clarifies the 1944 Convention and strengthens and broadens the mandate of the Inter-American Institute of Agricultural Sciences (the Institute).

Membership in the Institute under the Convention is open to states which are members of the OAS and the existing Institute, or other American states whose admission is accepted by the Inter-American Board of Agriculture.

Under the Convention, the Institute will consist of three principal organs—the Inter-American Board of Agriculture, the Executive Committee, and the General Directorate. The Inter-American Board of Agriculture will be the highest organ of the Institute and will consist of one representative from each Member State. The new Convention stipulates that such representatives should preferably be persons connected with agriculture or rural development. This Board will be responsible for setting policy and budgetary priorities of the Institute.

To reflect the changed responsibilities of the Institute, its name has been changed to the Inter-American Institute for Cooperation on Agriculture.

The Convention will enter into force when two-thirds of the states parties to the 1944 Convention have deposited instruments of ratification. Correspondingly, the 1944 Convention will cease to be in force for those states for which the new Convention is in force.

I recommend that the Senate give early and favorable consideration to the Convention and advice and consent to ratification.

JIMMY CARTER

The White House,
    November 14, 1979.

Trade Sanctions Against Zimbabwe-Rhodesia

*Memorandum From the President.
November 14, 1979*

Presidential Determination No. 80–6

*Memorandum for the Secretary of State
Subject:* Maintenance of Sanctions Against Zimbabwe-Rhodesia Under Section 408(b) of the Department of State Authorization Act, Fiscal Years 1980 and 1981

Pursuant to Section 408(b) of the Department of State Authorization Act, Fiscal Years 1980 and 1981 (93 Stat. 405), I hereby determine that it is in the national interest of the United States to continue sanctions against Zimbabwe-Rhodesia at this time.

You are requested, on my behalf, to report this determination promptly to the Speaker of the House of Representatives and the Chairman of the Committee on Foreign Relations of the Senate.

You are further requested to report to me immediately upon the conclusion of the present Constitutional Conference on Zimbabwe-Rhodesia being held in London, describing the conclusions of that conference and your recommendations for action by the United States with respect to the termination of sanctions.

This determination shall be published in the FEDERAL REGISTER.

JIMMY CARTER

[Filed with the Office of the Federal Register, 4:25 p.m., November 20, 1979]

JUSTIFICATION FOR PRESIDENTIAL DETERMINATION UNDER SECTION 408(b) OF THE DEPARTMENT OF STATE AUTHORIZATION ACT, FISCAL YEARS 1980 AND 1981 CONCERNING SANCTIONS AGAINST ZIMBABWE-RHODESIA

PROBLEM

Section 408(b) of the Department of State Authorization Act, Fiscal Years 1980 and 1981, requires that sanctions against Zimbabwe-Rhodesia be terminated by November 15, 1979, unless the President determines that it would not be in the national interest of the United States and so reports to the Congress.

JUSTIFICATION

Encouraging progress has been made in recent months toward a peaceful resolution of the conflict in Zimbabwe-Rhodesia; however, the negotiations presently being conducted by the United Kingdom with the parties have not yet been concluded, and differences still remain. A termination of sanctions at this stage could lead all the parties to harden their positions and would jeopardize the chances for a successful settlement for Zimbabwe-Rhodesia.

The British Government has not yet concluded negotiations that would end the rebellion in Rhodesia. They have stated that this will occur when the British Governor arrives in Salisbury and assumes authority. At the present time, the great bulk of British sanctions remain in force and none of our major allies has taken action to terminate sanctions.

The negotiations are now at a critical stage. We hope they will be rapidly and successfully concluded. While the talks continue, it would be premature for the United States to alter its position on sanctions. We would, however, be prepared to lift sanctions when a British Governor assumes authority in Salisbury and a process leading to impartial elections has begun. Our policy will continue to be that no party should have a veto over fair settlement proposals.

This issue will be kept under continuous review and the President will promptly notify the Congress when conditions warrant the lifting of sanctions.

Budget Deferrals

Message to the Congress. November 15, 1979

To the Congress of the United States:

In accordance with the Impoundment Control Act of 1974, I herewith report six new deferrals totalling $511.1 million and two revisions to previously transmitted deferrals increasing the amount deferred by

$14.9 million. These items affect programs in the Departments of Commerce, Justice, State and Transportation; the International Communication Agency; the Railroad Retirement Board; and the President's Commission on Pension Policy.

The details of the deferrals are contained in the attached reports.

JIMMY CARTER

The White House,
    November 15, 1979.

NOTE: The attachments detailing the deferrals are printed in the FEDERAL REGISTER of November 20, 1979.

American Federation of Labor and Congress of Industrial Organizations

Remarks at the 13th Constitutional Convention.   November 15, 1979

THE PRESIDENT. *President Meany, Secretary-Treasurer Lane Kirkland, men and women of the greatest labor movement in the world:*

It's always good to be among old friends and, today especially, to be among such strong and sure American patriots. I might say that the strength and the accomplishments of your great organization teach us a lesson which I am sure that our Nation will remember in the months ahead. Over the years, you have certainly learned the advantages of reelecting your president, and I hope you'll remember this. [*Laughter*]

MR. MEANY. I'll buy that.

THE PRESIDENT. President Meany said, "I'll buy that." [*Laughter*]

I think it's accurate to say that President Meany, your president, and Presidents who live in the White House have not always agreed completely. Mr. Meany, you cannot deny that statement. [*Laughter*] And all of us presidents, labor

and government, must realize and we must confess that we are not perfect and sometimes we make mistakes. But together we work for our country and sometimes, most of the time, with notable success.

I've reflected for several weeks about what I would say to you this afternoon about our mutual goals, our legislative successes together, our national accord, and our solid working relationship. With great pride I had intended to point out our accomplishments during the last 34 months: increasing the strength of our Nation, a nation that has stayed at peace; rebuilding our urban centers; continuing our fight against inflation; our progress in expressing our deep compassion for the downtrodden and the weak throughout our society and throughout the world; a dramatic breakthrough in minimum wage law legislation; putting America back to work so that we now have the greatest number of our citizens employed and the greatest percentage of our labor force employed than ever before in the history of the United States, and we can be proud of that achievement together.

It's a great record. It's a record that we have made together. It's one which we can improve in the months ahead. For instance, this country still needs and we are determined to get strong labor law reform. But I must leave these subjects for Ray Marshall to discuss with you, and I am sure that he will carry out this assignment magnificently. He has the approach and the attitude of a working man, and in my judgment he's one of the truly great Secretaries of Labor who have ever served. I am certainly proud that he is a member of the Carter Cabinet.

But today we have other important matters to consider. For a brief time this afternoon I want to speak with you and all Americans about some fundamental principles upon which our Nation was founded and which we must never forget. To some, these ideals may seem at times to be old-fashioned or outmoded. But we've been clearly reminded in recent days that these principles mean just as much to us now as they have ever meant during any time of critical decision in the history of our Nation.

These fundamentals have old names to which we must continually give new meaning—names like "strength," "courage," "patriotism," "independence," "the love of freedom," "human rights," "justice," "concern for the common good."

This is the 12th day that more than a hundred innocent human beings, some 60 of whom are members of the United States diplomatic mission, have been held hostage in our Embassy in Iran. For a rare time in human history, a host government has condoned and even encouraged this kind of illegal action against a sovereign territory and official diplomatic relations of another nation. This is an act of terrorism—totally outside the bounds of international law and diplomatic tradition.

In this time of trial, our deep concern is for the lives of these brave hostages, our Nation's loyal citizens and faithful representatives. Every American feels anger and outrage at what is happening to them, just as every American feels concern for their safety and pride in their great courage. This crisis calls for firmness, and it calls for restraint. And I'm proud that this situation has brought forth calm leadership by officials and private citizens throughout this country.

Firmness does require patience, and it requires perseverance. Firmness also means measured action, deliberate actions that clarify the real issues, reduce the likelihood of violence, protect our interests, and ensure justice.

The United States has done nothing and will do nothing that could be used to justify violent or imprudent action by anyone. While we are pursuing all avenues of diplomatic resolution, we're also acting unilaterally as appropriate—with restraint, yes, but without hesitation.

First, in order to discourage violence and possible bloodshed here, which when televised and transmitted back to Iran might threaten the safety of the hostages, I've discouraged the issuing of permits for demonstrations on Federal properties here in Washington. Consistent with our laws and pursuant to my own powers and responsibilities, I have also encouraged local and State officials to take similar legal action.

Second, I've directed our immigration authorities to review the visas of some 50,-000 Iranian students, who are guests here in our country. Our Nation is fully committed to the enhancement of human rights, the protection of legal rights, and the enhancement of civil justice. All provisions of the United States Constitution will be honored. All foreign nationals who are here lawfully may continue here with their work or their studies. But those who are here illegally will be processed promptly and lawfully for deportation back to their own country.

Third, I want to remove any question that our principles might be compromised by our supposed need for Iranian oil. Early this week, therefore, I ordered an immediate halt to any purchases or shipments of Iranian oil to the United States of America.

I'm determined to make clear that we will never allow any foreign country to dictate any American policy.

Fourth, in order to protect our economic interests and to ensure that claims on Iran by the United States or by United States citizens are settled in an orderly manner, we've legally frozen official Iranian property and financial assets. The order does not affect any accounts other than those of the Government of Iran, the Central Bank of Iran, or other government-controlled entities.

Yesterday I further instructed Secretary of State Vance and Ambassador McHenry to oppose any discussion of Iran's problems in the United Nations Security Council as long as American hostages are being held. Only after the hostages are released will we be willing to address Iran's concerns and, then, under the provisions of international law and under the charter of the United Nations. The members of the United Nations Security Council, I am pleased to announce to you, have agreed unanimously with our own proposal.

It's important for all of us to remember that we will not compromise our fundamental principles of justice no matter how grave the provocation nor how righteous our indignation. At the same time, we will continue to use our influence around the world to obtain the same kinds of human rights for people everywhere.

In this instance, we are upholding an important principle on behalf of the entire world community. It's a clear tenet of international law and diplomatic tradition that the host government is fully responsible for the safety and well-being of the property and the legal representatives of another country. Less than a year ago— and this is a fact not generally known or recognized—less than a year ago, 70,000 American citizens were in Iran. As you know, thousands of people were killed during the upheavals there, but almost miraculously and because of the good work of Cyrus Vance and others, our people were brought home safely. I thank God for it. Despite the turmoil, each succeeding Iranian Government—and they were being changed, as you know, quite rapidly—protected the citizens of other countries.

Foreign visitors are often vulnerable to abuse. An embassy is not a fortress. There are no embassies anywhere in the world that can long withstand the attack of a mob if the mob has the support of the host government itself. We had received repeated assurances of protection from the highest officials in the Iranian Government, even a day or two before the mob was incited to attack and before that protection was withdrawn at the last minute. The principle of inviolability of embassies is understood and accepted by nations everywhere, and it's particularly important to smaller nations which have no recourse to economic or military power. This is why the United Nations Security Council has also unanimously supported our demand for the release of the American hostages.

In accordance with this principle, as recognized and observed by all civilized countries, the Iranian Government and its leaders are fully responsible for the safety and well-being of our representatives in Iran, in Tehran, and they will be held accountable for that responsibility. It is unthinkable that any responsible government in today's modern world could regard the seizure and the holding of the diplomatic officials of another nation as a realistic means to advance any cause whatsoever. Terrorism is not an acceptable means to resolve disputes between individuals or between nations.

No act has so galvanized the American public toward unity in the last decade as has the holding of our people as hostages in Tehran. We stand today as one people. We are dedicated to the principles and the honor of our Nation. We've taken no action which would justify concern among the people or among the Government of Iran. We have done nothing for which any American need apologize. The actions of Iranian leaders and the radicals who invaded our Embassy were completely unjustified. They and all others must know that the United States of America will not yield to international terrorism or to blackmail.

These difficult days have reminded us of basic facts and principles which are fundamental to the existence of us as a people. We will honor all constitutional protections and international law and custom, and we will not let our freedom and our security be jeopardized.

The developments in Iran have made it starkly clear to all of us that our excessive dependence on foreign oil is a direct, physical threat to our freedom and security as Americans. That's why we must all join together in the battle for an energy-secure America. This struggle demands the deliberate and the conscientious participation of every single citizen. Unfortunately, our dependence on foreign oil has been growing for the last 5 or 6 years, especially, when it should have been diminishing. As a nation we have become dependent on the undependable and addicted to the unaffordable.

At Camp David this summer, one man summed up the significance of our energy problems better than any other person there. It was Lane Kirkland. He said to me, "Mr. President, the issue is freedom."

That is exactly the issue today. That's why I've been calling on the Congress and encouraging the American people for the last 2½ years to recognize the danger of excessive dependence on foreign oil. That's why I've ordered phased decontrol of oil prices to make conservation pay and to stimulate domestic energy sources.

This is an extremely important, a vital issue. Do not be misled by political demagoguery. I and every other public official in this country have an obligation to speak the truth and to deal responsibly with the hard facts, and they are hard facts. We cannot close down all nuclear powerplants, burn less coal, refuse to build oil refineries, refuse to explore for new oil sources, oppose the production of synthetic fuels, and at the same time encourage the waste of energy by artificially holding down its price in order to encourage more consumption. This is a ridiculous combination of proposals, which could only be put forward in an election campaign. America knows better.

I am very pleased that our national energy program is now moving steadily through the Congress, after enormous difficulty there and sharp debate. Now more than ever before, it's essential that we have an energy security corporation and a windfall profits tax in order to take care of the poor, encourage production, build a better transportation system. Armed with these new programs, our technology, our creativity, our abundance, our vision, our firm will, America can finally control its own resources, and we can continue to control our own destiny.

Our love of freedom will not be auctioned off for foreign oil. Hundreds of thousands of our forebears gave their very lives for our freedom. Our freedom is not for sale—now or ever in the future.

Every important victory that this Nation has ever won—with Americans struggling together—has made us stronger as a nation. So will it be with the energy problem. There's a clear choice for Americans to make: We can either keep pouring out billions and billions and billions of dollars to foreign countries to import oil—which also buys us inflation, unemployment, and national dependency and insecurity—or we can take some of that money and invest it in America to hire American workers, to unleash American ingenuity, to develop American resources, to promote American energy that Americans own and control. That's the way to approach the energy problem, and that's what we must do together.

There are millions and millions of people who can help directly with this challenge, and there are hundreds of thousands of jobs involved. Next year we anticipate that we will send overseas $70 billion to pay for foreign oil. Just think how many fine things we could do in America with that much money.

So, in the last few days we have been reminded once again of our essential need of energy security so that we can continue to protect the basic principles of our country, and together that's what we must achieve, both for ourselves and, even more importantly, for our children and grandchildren. America must always be militarily strong and economically strong, and that America will always be.

One final comment I'd like to make: America must also maintain its moral and its ethical strength. We are not a selfish people. History has recorded many times America's great generosity, as it does today in Thailand and Kampuchea, formerly known as Cambodia. Even as we face problems of great economic concern here in our own country, we are sparing no effort to help those who are suffering and starving in every way we can.

Compassion enhances American strength. It's one of our deepest values, one to which we will always cling and remain true. Concern for human life and justice is as vital as military power to our special place in the family of nations. Human rights is a compelling idea of our lifetime. Our hearts and our aid will continue to go to those who are suffering, who are starving, or who are deprived of freedom. In this time of tension and turmoil I'm proud that our commitment to American strength and to American principles is unshakable.

And now, in closing, I want to turn aside from our national and international preoccupations for just a moment.

A few weeks ago, with the White House sparkling in the sunlight behind him, Pope John Paul II asked God to bless America's quest for freedom, social justice, and peace. When his moving speech was done, he turned with a great insight to a man seated in front of him, on the front row. While millions around the world watched, the Holy Father clasped the hands of a great American, and he said, and I quote, because I was right there listening, "I know about you, and I know that you have done much good in your life for the working people of the United States and the people of other nations." That man was George Meany.

It was a moving moment, and as President I was especially proud to be an American. No American has fought harder for economic justice for union members and also for millions who've never carried a union card than your leader has, George Meany. No American has believed more deeply in human dignity, not only for workers but for all the helpless and the dispossessed people, the poor and sometimes forgotten people still beyond the reach of the benefits of our own great national bounty. And no American has loved his country more, not only for the democracy at home but for the beacon of freedom and basic human rights which we will continue to keep shining throughout the world.

Mr. Meany, on behalf of the American people, thank you. May God bless all of you.

Mr. Meany. Thank you.

NOTE: The President spoke at 2:25 p.m. in the Sheraton Washington Hotel ballroom.

Later in the day, the President attended a reception for international guests of the AFL–CIO constitutional convention, which was held on the State Floor at the White House.

Department of Transportation

Nomination of William B. Johnston To Be an Assistant Secretary.   November 15, 1979

The President today announced that he will nominate William B. Johnston, of Clifton, Va., to be an Assistant Secretary of Transportation. He would replace Chester Davenport, who has resigned.

Johnston has been Associate Director of the White House Domestic Policy Staff since 1977.

He was born August 25, 1945, in Washington, D.C. He received a B.A. from Yale University in 1967.

From 1973 to 1975, Johnston was a consultant to the Ford Foundation, and from 1975 to 1976, he was a consultant to the Labor Department.

From 1972 to 1976, Johnston was a research associate at the Center for Social Policy Studies. In 1976 he was on the national issues staff of the Carter Presidential campaign and worked on the Carter transition team.

Federal Emergency Management Agency

Nomination of William H. Wilcox To Be an Associate Director.   November 15, 1979

The President today announced that he will nominate William H. Wilcox, of Harrisburg, Pa., to be an Associate Director of the Federal Emergency Management Agency, a new position. His area of responsibility would be response and recovery.

Wilcox has been Administrator of the Federal Disaster Assistance Administration since 1978.

He was born June 9, 1919, in Philadelphia, Pa. He received a B.A. from the University of Connecticut and an M.P.A. from Wayne University. He served in the Armed Forces from 1942 to 1945.

From 1954 to 1971, Wilcox was executive director of the Greater Philadelphia Movement. He also served as chairman of the Philadelphia Committee on City Policy and as a member of the Executive Board of Gaudenzia House.

From 1971 to 1978, Wilcox was secretary of community affairs of the Common-

wealth of Pennsylvania. While in State government, he coordinated various State disaster recovery activities, including activities related to the Johnstown Flood of 1977. He also served as the State fuel allocation officer and directed a statewide home weatherization program for the elderly and low-income families.

United States-Japan Economic Relations Group

Joint Announcement.   November 15, 1979

President Carter and Prime Minister Ohira announced today that the following persons had agreed to serve on the U.S.-Japan Economic Relations Group: Ambassador Robert S. Ingersoll (U.S. chairman), A. W. Clausen, Hugh T. Patrick, Edson W. Spencer, Ambassador Nobuhiko Ushiba (Japanese chairman), Akio Morita, Shuzo Muramoto and Kiichi Saeki.

This Group was established by President Carter and Prime Minister Ohira at their bilateral May 2 meeting in Washington, when they agreed that a small group of distinguished persons drawn from private life would submit recommendations to the President and the Prime Minister concerning actions to maintain a healthy bilateral economic relationship between the United States and Japan.

On June 25, during President Carter's bilateral Summit meetings with Prime Minister Ohira in Tokyo, it was agreed that the co-chairmen of the Group would be former Ambassadors Robert Ingersoll and Nobuhiko Ushiba. Since their selection in late June, the co-chairmen have been considering potential nominees for the Group. The selections by the President and the Prime Minister reflect the recommendations of their respective co-chairmen.

The Group will hold its first meeting in mid-December, with the objective of submitting timely recommendations to the President and the Prime Minister.

Mr. Ingersoll was formerly Ambassador to Japan (1972–73), Assistant Secretary of State for East Asian and Pacific Affairs (1974), and Deputy Secretary of State (1974–1976). Chairman of the Japan Society since September 1978, Mr. Ingersoll has been a member of many international business committees and councils, including the Advisory Council on U.S.-Japan Relations and the Emergency Committee for American Trade. He is also Deputy Chairman of the Board of Trustees of the University of Chicago.

Mr. Ushiba, a graduate of the Faculty of Law of Tokyo Imperial University, entered the Japanese Foreign Service in 1932. He has served in various capacities abroad and in Tokyo, including Ambassador to Canada (1961–64), Vice Minister of Foreign Affairs (1967–70), and Ambassador to the United States (1970–73). Mr. Ushiba was named State Minister for External Economic Relations in November 1977 and served as Ambassador for the Multilateral Trade Negotiations from December 1978 until recently.

Mr. Spencer is chairman and chief executive officer of Honeywell, Inc. He was a Rhodes Scholar 1948–50 and has been with the Honeywell firm since 1954. From 1959–65 he was their Far East regional manager in Tokyo. He is a director of Northwest Bancorporation and International Harvester.

Professor Patrick is a professor of Economics at Yale University. He holds the Ph. D. degree in economics from the University of Michigan and has several times in his career been granted fellowships for study in Japan. On the faculty of Yale since 1960 and a member of the interuniversity Japan Economic Seminar, he is the author of numerous scholarly publications and co-editor of "Asia's New Giant," a definitive study of the Japanese economy published in 1976.

Mr. Clausen is president and chief executive officer of BankAmerica Corporation and its wholly-owned subsidiary, Bank of America N.T. & S.A. He has been associated with Bank of America since 1949 before his election to his present position in 1969. A graduate of Carthage College, he received his LL.B. from the University of Minnesota and is a graduate of the Harvard Advanced Management Program. He is a member of the Policy Committee of The Business Roundtable, a member of the Business Council, director of the U.S.-U.S.S.R. Trade and Economic Council and of the National Council for United States-China Trade and co-chairman of the Japan-California Association, as well as a member of the Japan-U.S. Advisory Council.

Mr. Muramoto is president of Dai-Ichi Kangyo Bank Ltd. He graduated from the economic department of Tokyo University and entered Dai-Ichi Bank where he has served as Senior Managing Director and Deputy President. From 1971–76 he has been Deputy President of Dai-Ichi Kangyo Bank Ltd.

Mr. Morita is chairman and chief executive officer of Sony Corporation. After graduating from the science department of Osaka University, he established Tokyo Tsush in Kogyo Ltd. (to become Sony Co. in 1958) and became its executive manager. He has been Deputy President, and President and Chief Operating Officer of Sony Corporation.

Mr. Saeki has been president of Nomura Research Institute from 1965 to the present. A graduate of Tokyo University, he has served as staff member of the Economic Stabilization Board, director of a division of the Agency for Economic Research and Planning, and president of the National Defense College, Defense Agency.

Hospital Cost Containment Legislation

Statement by the White House Press Secretary on House of Representatives Disapproval of the Legislation.   November 15, 1979

Let me say a word about hospital cost containment.

The President asked specifically that I say that the action of the House of Representatives is a blow to the fight against inflation. He asked me to say in addition that the action in the House was a victory for a highly financed, special-interest lobby, and a defeat for the common good. He asked that I point out that the action of the House today will add literally tens of billions of dollars to the Federal deficit in the coming years, and tens of billions of dollars to the cost of living for Americans who are already having difficulty making ends meet.

However, he also asked that I say that the ballgame is not yet over and that we intend to continue to fight to contain hospital costs, which have increased 1,000 percent since 1960, and that we expect that hospital cost containment legislation will yet be passed either as a separate bill or as part of a national health insurance plan, one of which is now being considered by the Senate Finance Committee.

NOTE: Press Secretary Jody Powell read the statement at 5:25 p.m. to reporters assembled in the Briefing Room at the White House.

The press release also includes a transcript of the question-and-answer session which followed the statement.

White House Conference on Libraries and Information Services

Remarks at a Meeting of the Conference. November 16, 1979

*Chairman Charles Benton, Library Director Juanita Brightwell, other distin-*guished *leaders who represent one of the finest aspects of American life:*

I really appreciate the book concerning the duties of a trustee for libraries. In the future I may be looking for my old job back. [*Laughter*] So, Juanita, if you can keep it open for me for 5 years I'll really appreciate it. [*Laughter*]

I'm delighted to be here with you this morning. It's been one of the developments in my own administration to which I've looked forward with great anticipation. I don't have a text. I don't feel that I need one to talk to you.

I had a quick introduction to Washington, to Washington society life, and to newspaper coverage of the First Family. The first stories that came out, as a matter of fact, were about Amy's reading habits at the table of an official banquet when the President of Mexico came to see us. She read a book throughout the banquet dinner. When I defended Amy I had several of my Cabinet members ask for permission to do the same at the next banquet. [*Laughter*] As a matter of fact, we have had to put a restraint on that—but since I was a little boy, my own family has had the habit of reading at the table. We have a lively conversation and read simultaneously, and Amy is just carrying on one of the Carter family traditions. I hate to admit this, being an outdoor type and an athletic type, but my family never had to ask me what I wanted for Christmas, because they always knew that I would reply "books."

And when I first went home from the Navy, as Charles pointed out, my first public position was as the trustee of the Sumter County Library Board. I still have my library card. It's Number 5, and I use it whenever I'm home.

This morning I would like to talk to you about some of the elements of libraries that are important to a young boy growing up in an isolated community. Students in our public schools, business leaders and employees of business who are fairly narrowly restricted in their ability to get a continuing formal education, and those who occupy positions of leadership with rapidly varying and challenging responsibilities from day to day—in all those elements of life libraries and access to books and other information play an important role.

Times change very fast. Information available to the world is exploding more rapidly than it can be accommodated, and the function of libraries is to collect information, to collate information, to assess information, to store information, and to let information be available to those who need it.

There are many people in our modern society who are isolated in some form or another—the deaf, the blind, the immobile, the afflicted, those who live in isolated communities are obvious examples, but there are others. Those who have a particular life's career in a fairly narrowly defined area, but who desire constantly to stretch their minds and to stretch their hearts and to know more about the world around them, other people, opportunities for a more gratifying existence, are in the same category as those who are physically isolated. Libraries can play this role to make available to people, in a special occasion for an unexpected event, an opportunity for study.

Science, business, politics, government is an area where rapid information is crucial in dealing with challenges of the day, where long-time study to prepare for an event is impossible, because events that are important cannot be predicted. And there, the instant access to information and the calm and reasoned guidance of a qualified librarian can make the difference between the success or failure, even, of a life.

A President in particular is faced with varied responsibilities. And my access to the Library of Congress and my access to books is one of the most important elements of my life. Amy reads, sometimes two or three books a day. She and I have both had rapid reading lessons since I've been President. I read two or three books a week, sometimes more, and in addition to that have instant access to the broad-ranging information which is available here in Washington and, obviously, in many other communities in our country.

The Library of Congress was started, as you know, when the Government decided to buy the book collection of President Thomas Jefferson. He withdrew from formal schooling when his life was in the formative stage and began private study—with a tutor, yes, but heavily dependent not on classroom instructions, but on his access to a varied gamut of books. And I would guess that one of the most well educated Presidents who has ever served had limited formal schooling, and that was President Harry Truman. His education came primarily from books, history books and others from his local library.

I'm not at all criticizing or playing down the importance of formal education, but no matter how broad an educational experience has been in a person's life, sometimes determined by the state of a person's birth or the wealth of a family or opportunities that all can't share—no matter how broad a formal education might be, libraries are still important if that person desires to continue in education throughout one's life. This need for knowledge about history or current events is particularly important in a democracy, where the strength of a nation depends to a major degree on a well-informed public.

One of the most important responsibilities that I have had on my own shoulders is to make sure that in controversial events that the public has a maximum access to knowledge about that event. In the past our country has made some serious mistakes in war, in morality, in the functioning of government. In the few years before I became President this was especially true. And in almost every instance, if those circumstances are analyzed, the errors or mistakes were made because the public was excluded from the process of making decisions of our own government.

An enlightened public, openly debating a controversial issue, sometimes creates confusion. It's much easier to negotiate in utmost secrecy than to let the Congress and the public know the terms of the negotiation and the progress being made. But when the controversial issues can be examined from a broad range of points of view, a nation or a government or a President is much more likely, ultimately, to avoid mistakes and to make the right decision that can preserve our own Nation's security, our well-being, and also peace throughout the world.

I'd like to add just one more comment. We've made good progress in the last number of years in promoting the science of libraries, of information, of communication. Each generation is inclined to think we've gone as far as we can with television, instantaneous transmission of messages and photographs, satellite relay stations, but I would guess that the progress we make in the future, in the next 10 years, the next hundred years, will be just as rapid and just as startling as that we've made in the past.

There must be a flexibility built into a government's structure and also in the minds and hearts of American people outside the government, where most of the responsibility must lie. I'm convinced that the new Department of Education will have a greatly expanded and much more effective role in emphasizing the importance of books, of learning, and particularly of libraries. I'm determined that this will be the case.

But I believe that this White House Conference and those who attend it and those who will listen to your voice or whom you can influence when you get home will have a much more broad-reaching effect than anything a President can do or a Cabinet Secretary can do or the Federal Government can do.

In a local Lions Club, a local church, a local Rotary Club, a League of Women Voters, Jaycees, in any organization, in a local radio station, television station, newspaper, there are avenues for you to reach a broad range of Americans who don't presently know the advantages of libraries. Many people, because of ignorance or because they've forgotten the joy of learning, don't have access to the opportunities that you can offer.

And I hope if you don't do anything else at this conference, that you will learn from one another how best to present the opportunities of library use and then take that message home and distribute it with the greatest degree of enthusiasm and commitment. When people are reminded, they'll respond. And the joys of books and the joys of visual presentations, the joys of movies, slides, paintings, lectures, debates, instruction, music, drama are all parts of a library program. And I hope that you will broaden your own concept of what libraries can do as a result of this conference.

I'm very grateful that you would come to Washington, in sometimes a sacrificial way, to participate in learning more about how your own career and your own interests can be made more effective. As we spread the word about libraries and learning and democracy and understanding and communication and progress and harmony and peace through your own work, through your work you can remember that you've got a friend in the White House.

Thank you very much.

NOTE: The President spoke at 9:40 a.m. in the International Ballroom at the Washington Hilton Hotel.

In his opening remarks, the President referred to Charles Benton, Chairman of the National Commission on Libraries and Information Science.

Iranian Situation and United States Energy Conservation

Remarks at a White House Briefing for State Governors. November 16, 1979

First of all, let me welcome you here to the White House and express my appreciation for your willingness to join in with me in perhaps one of the most difficult and complicated challenges which our Nation has ever faced in peacetime.

I deeply appreciate the letter I got from Governor Bowen and Governor Lamm expressing your support for what we are trying to do, and also suggesting on your own behalf that the Governors would espouse and pursue a fast-track conservation program, that you are dedicated to the sharing of information and new ideas among yourselves and with other agencies of government, both local and Federal, that you will work with the private sector as much as possible to encourage long-range conservation measures. And I understand as well that you intend to have a major conservation conference sometime before too long.

This kind of support from you is very important to me. Governor Brown in California and others immediately expressed your approval and your willingness to help in putting into effect the pro-

hibition against the acceptance of Iranian oil to our country, and the overwhelming sense that I have is that we have a nation which is united, eager to do the best we can under difficult circumstances, and highly supportive of what we are attempting to accomplish in Iran.

I've just gotten a report that there are maybe 80,000 Iranians demonstrating outside our Embassy in a highly emotional state, and we are trying as best we can to protect the honor of our country and to protect the lives of the hostages, who are courageous, dedicated, and who deserve every protection that we can give them.

I would like to add one word of caution, if you don't mind, and I hope that you'll relay it to the people back home who listen to your voice. I've had a large number of expressions of support for us, sympathy for our hostages, and the expression of strong condemnation for what is going on in Iran by Iranians, particularly those who live in our country, who have lived here for years as responsible citizens. And it would be a serious mistake for us to deprive them of their rights or deprive them of their citizenship or deprive them of our friendship.

There is an inclination in a time of crisis to condemn every person who has connections with Iran, but I hope that you will caution all Americans, as I'm trying to do now, not to abuse the fine tens of thousands of Iranians who live in our country and who have a voice to speak out, as they have to me directly; and also to recognize that in Iran it's the radicals and the militants and the irresponsible elements there who are responsible for the tragedy which we are trying to prevent.

We are trying to act with circumspection, but also with firmness. Ours is not a country that responds or ever will respond to intimidation or blackmail; we will not honor in any possible way the threats or actions of terrorists. I've tried to act moderately, but without deviation from the principles on which our Nation was founded, and which make us justifiably proud. A few of the things that we have done I'm sure you understand, and on some you've had to join in with me.

I have discouraged the issuing of permits for demonstrations on any Federal property, where the demonstrations might result in violence or abusive acts or perhaps bloodshed or loss of life, because I think the transmission of television or other photographs or reports of those instances might very well result in a danger to the lives of Americans who are being held hostage.

In addition, as you know, I have issued instructions that we will not accept the shipment of any Iranian oil to our country. I did that to make it vividly clear that our country is not subject to the threat of an embargo or a threat of any other kind.

I don't know the ultimate results of that decision in international oil markets. The high likelihood is that supplies to our country will be reduced. That's something that I am perfectly willing to face, particularly since I have leaders like you marching shoulder to shoulder with me to face that eventuality. The American people cannot underestimate the importance of the strictest possible conservation matters and actions at this moment.

There is no reason to panic, fortunately. Because of actions that you and I and others have taken in the past few months, we have a fairly good supply of crude oil, gasoline, home heating oil on hand, and we'll be able to see the trends in the weeks ahead. But an early and a permanent commitment to the sharpest possible reduction in waste of energy of all kinds will be helpful. And a preparation for con-

tingency plans within your own States, and working in harmony with us, will be a very important element.

I've asked the Immigration and Naturalization Service to examine the visas of Iranian students and others who are here. If they are here legally, they'll be encouraged to stay, or permitted to stay if they choose to pursue their studies or to pursue their work. If they are here illegally, their papers will be processed completely in accordance with our Constitution and laws and the proprieties that we must observe, and they will be deported if they aren't complying with those laws or constitutional provisions.

In order to protect our own economy and the rights and privileges of American business leaders and others, our banks, American citizens, I have frozen the assets of Iran which are directly or indirectly related to the government ownership or control. This is so that debts owed by Iran to us will be paid, and so that we will not have an adverse effect on our economy because of the forfeiture of those debts, because of impoundment in Iran of our assets or properties.

And the last action that I've taken that I'll mention, in order to save time, is that I have discouraged any meeting of or debate in the United Nations Security Council of the Iranian problem. This was requested by Iran, but my own decision has been that this would not be appropriate as long as they are holding hostages in our Embassy there. And I'm proud to say that the United Nations Security Council unanimously has condemned the Iranian Government for what it has condoned or permitted. And they have also unanimously rejected any proposal by Iran for debate or discussion of this issue while the hostages are being held.

This is a serious matter, as you know. It's not a reason for panic. It's not reason to abandon the principles or laws or proprieties in our own country. We do not want to be guilty of the same sort of improper action which we are condemning in Iran. And it's, to repeat myself, not a cause for us to abuse any Iranian citizen who's in our country. If there are those here who act improperly, the laws are adequate to care for them. If they are here illegally, our deportation processes will be carried out in a completely proper and predictable way.

I'm grateful that less than 2 weeks ago the Congress passed and I signed an energy emergency act which gives us the ability, working together, to care for the needs of our country if we have a serious shortage or threatened shortage of energy. State conservation measures have been assessed, and with your help, I think the law is adequate in that respect. The gas rationing authority given to me is a step in the right direction, but still not adequate, and we hope to have it improved in the future.

We are now preparing a gasoline rationing plan. As soon as this very complicated procedure is completed, it will be revealed to the public and to the Congress. And we would welcome, Dick,[1] your committee working with Charlie Duncan in the preparation of the gasoline rationing proposal. It cannot be implemented, except with congressional action, unless we have a 20-percent shortage. And this, as you know, would wreak havoc in our national economy, if we had to wait that long.

So, we do have problems with it, but we have a fairly adequate means by which Governors can take the initiative, in each one of your own States, to implement very

strict conservation measures. I don't know what the future will bring, but whether it's a slight shortage, a permanent shortage, a serious shortage, or further disruption in supplies, there is no doubt in anyone's mind in this room, I'm sure, that we versa, a permanent consultative intermation coming from you to us, and vice versa, a permanent consultative interrelationship between Governors and other officials and the Federal Government, and the closest possible partnership in dealing with an unpredictable and potentially serious situation.

We've been working on this matter for 2½ years. I first made the proposals for an energy policy for our Nation in April of 1977. After 18 months of work, the Congress passed a partial energy package about a year ago, in November of 1978. And we are on the verge, I believe, of taking additional substantive steps.

There is no way that all of you could approve of every element of the energy plan. No one does. It's the result of an enormous effort to compromise and to work together, because, in effect, I lead two energy nations. One is the greatest consuming nation on Earth, by far, and the other one is one of the greatest energy producing nations on Earth. And the inherent conflicts that exist under those circumstances certainly has now been very carefully assessed and, I think, will be successfully addressed.

Hard feelings have erupted and, in most cases, have been assuaged. And I think the Congress is well on the way now toward completing their work for a comprehensive energy proposal. We are determined not to violate any laws. We're determined not to encroach on the prerogatives and responsibilities of the State and local governments. We're determined to enhance and not to reduce the effectiveness and the independence of the free enterprise

---

[1] Governor Lamm.

system of our country. We would like to have the Federal Government role minimized, and to the extent that individual citizens, families, businesses, local and State governments can act responsibly and aggressively with the maximum degree of innovation in conserving energy and producing new energy sources, then to that degree the Federal role can be minimized.

Again, I'm grateful that you would come here. This afternoon you'll have a fairly complete description and an elaboration on some of the items that I've covered with you. Charlie Duncan, John Sawhill, Secretary Vance, William Miller, the Secretary of Treasury, will all be here to discuss these matters with you and to answer your questions.

But I think for just a few minutes before I leave, you might want to comment or ask a question yourselves.

NOTE: The President spoke at 1:04 p.m. in the East Room at the White House.

Department of Commerce

Nominations of Philip M. Klutznick To Be Secretary and Luther H. Hodges, Jr., To Be Deputy Secretary.   November 16, 1979

I have two announcements.

First of all, as I suspect you already know, the President will nominate Philip M. Klutznick, a Chicago attorney and businessman, former U.S. Representative, with the rank of Ambassador, to the U.N. Economic and Social Council, as Secretary of Commerce. Mr. Klutznick has had a great deal of experience in the two most important areas of concern to the Commerce Department—trade, particularly in its international aspects, and economic development. If you don't already have his biography, you will by the time this briefing is over. And I think it outlines very

clearly his long-term and broad experience in both of those areas.

In addition, the President will nominate Luther Hodges, Jr., to serve in the new position of Deputy Secretary in the Department of Commerce. That position will be created when, as we expect shortly, the reorganization bill goes into effect, creating a new Department of Commerce and Trade.

NOTE: Press Secretary Jody Powell read the announcements at the regular news briefing for reporters, which began at approximately 4:45 p.m. in the Briefing Room at the White House.

National Family Week, 1979

Proclamation 4703.   November 16, 1979

By the President of the United States of America

A Proclamation

We are a nation of families. This country was settled and built by families of all kinds. A source of strength in our past, families are America's hope for the future. All families are important, but the extended family, the foster family and the adoptive family play a special role by relieving the isolation of those who lack the comfort of a loving nuclear family.

Families are the most universal and enduring element in human existence. A family is a reservoir of shared experiences, shared joys and sorrows and, most of all, shared love that spans generations and distances.

As we come together at this Thanksgiving season, we gather with our families to express our gratitude. Our family circles expand to welcome and include others in the warmth of the holiday season. It is a time for all of us to cherish those we love and to celebrate family life.

We must continue this attention to families all year round, however. Through the coming White House Conference on Families, our new Office on Families, and through new approaches that would encourage more adoptive and foster parents, governments and citizens together can learn to become better family advocates of the American family. We must nurture the family as it has nurtured us.

Now, THEREFORE, I, JIMMY CARTER, President of the United States of America, in accordance with a joint resolution of Congress, do hereby proclaim the week of November 18, 1979, as National Family Week and call upon all the American people to observe this week with appropriate activities in their homes and communities.

IN WITNESS WHEREOF, I have hereunto set my hand this sixteenth day of November, in the year of our Lord nineteen hundred seventy-nine, and of the Independence of the United States of America the two hundred and fourth.

JIMMY CARTER

[Filed with the Office of the Federal Register, 2:57 p.m., November 16, 1979]

National Council of Negro Women

Remarks at a White House Reception.
November 16, 1979

I'm sure none of you have husbands whose wives come in late. [*Laughter*]

It's a wonderful opportunity for me and Rosalynn to have you here in the White House. This is an exciting time for us. I know from experience that you have been part of the tremendous improvements that have been made in American life.

All the Presidents have lived in this house except George Washington, who was the first one.

And nothing could be accomplished in our Nation, through government, if it weren't for dedicated and courageous people who know how to work together for the improvement of the lives of those who are not quite so fortunate as the leaders, like yourselves.

One of my favorite women has said that without volunteers, America would not have a soul. And when Rosalynn said that, I listened very carefully. [*Laughter*] And I would say that without the 27 organizations represented here this afternoon, America would not have a major part of its soul.

Your president and I have a lot in common. Dorothy's from the South; so am I. She left the South; so did I. I'm intending to go back; I don't know about her. Her mother and my mother were nurses. She and I spent a lot of time, have been a lot of times to Baptist churches. [*Laughter*] She and I both have had a long day. Right, Dorothy? And we have one more thing in common. She's been your president, and she's been reelected, and I'm looking forward to next year to—[*laughter*]——

The most important thing about all of you in the National Council of Negro Women is that where your hearts are and where your hands are are where the people live who need help and a better life. Your founder, Mary McCloud Bethune, had two things in mind—jobs and education. And that's been the root of the changes that have benefited the lives of those in our country who have felt the burden of discrimination.

You have felt discrimination because of two things—one, because you're women; one, because you're black. We've made great progress in both areas, but we've got a long way to go. And I hope that all of you will help not only with the racial discrimination that still exists in some areas of our life but also will help to get the equal rights amendment passed for this country.

The thing that I appreciate about you is that you're not just confining your influence to a few things. You look around you, close by, to make families stronger. You look down at the little ones around you and say, "I want these children to have a better education than I had a chance to have." You look up and remember that our inspiration comes from God and that there are some things in this world that never change, and they're the most precious things of all. And you look outside of your own homes to make better communities and a better nation. And you help with things like the elderly, things like jobs, better transportation, better housing. Whenever there's a need, your minds and your hearts and your hands have been dedicated to meeting that need. And you're also dedicated to peace.

We've got to have a SALT agreement completed this year, because as you well know, if a nation goes to war, the poor and the black have always been the first ones to go. And I believe that one of the most important things that all of you could do is to induce the Members of the Senate of the United States to ratify the SALT agreement, because we do not want to have a hundred million American citizens killed by nuclear weapons. And that's an important task for us all.

I appreciate your going to the Hill today. When you speak, the Congress listens. And you have talked to them today about a very important consideration for matters overseas.

Before I came in this house as President, we had very little interest or involvement in the affairs of Africa. We have changed that.

I pointed out earlier that you're not afraid to speak out, and as you know, I chose an Ambassador to the United Nations that was not afraid to speak out. Andrew Young spelled out the policy not only for our country, but his voice was heard, and his advice was followed, and his policies were adopted by many other nations on Earth.

And now we have a growing commitment to Africa to guarantee that racial discrimination is wiped out, that majority rule exists, and that we never again in the future have to face the burdens of apartheid, which is a disgrace for the human race. We are now making progress in Namibia. Meetings are going on this week that give us some hope for the independence and the autonomy of that country. And in Zimbabwe-Rhodesia, as you know, we are also seeing good progress.

When I came into office, we had the so-called Byrd amendment, which forced us to trade with an unacceptable government in what was then known as Rhodesia. The Congress eliminated the Byrd amendment, and sanctions were imposed by us, by Great Britain, and by other countries. We've seen the benefits of it, because the pressure of those sanctions have caused the reluctant parties to come by now and negotiate what we hope will be a time of freedom for the new nation of Zimbabwe-Rhodesia.

Some of the Members of the Congress want the sanctions to be lifted, but I think we ought not to lift those sanctions until we have a British Governor-General in Zimbabwe-Rhodesia and we have the electoral process well underway. And if you'll help me, we're going to hold those sanctions off until we get those two things done.

The last thing I want to say is this.

We've had some accomplishments in our country in the last 34 months and in the last 34 years, but there are many areas where black voices and black women's voices are not yet heard adequately. Eleanor Holmes Norton is doing a good job in the equal employment area, and government is trying to eliminate the legal bases for discrimination. But still the judiciary, the Federal judiciary, has a lot to say about it.

I've tried to seek your advice, and others like you all over the country, and start appointing black judges, because they don't serve for 4 years, they don't serve for 8 years, they serve for a lifetime. And again, we've got a long way to go. But I'm very proud to say that I have already appointed more black judges in this country than all other Presidents who've lived in this house put together—because Dorothy would never let me forget about it. [*Laughter*]

And so, I'm very grateful to you, as President, for being my partner. This is the greatest nation on Earth. And if we have disappointments and if we have differences sometimes, if we have debates and divisions and if we have times when we have temporary inconveniences and delays in realizing the full desires of our lives, we ought to recognize that, underneath, our country is the strongest and the best and the freest country on Earth.

We've got a lot to be thankful for. God's blessed us. And if we work together, as you have done so well, then we'll make the greatest nation on Earth even greater in the future.

Thank you very much. God bless you for all being here.

NOTE: The President spoke at 6:07 p.m. in the East Room at the White House.

In his remarks, the President referred to Dorothy Height, president of the council.

Digest of Other White House Announcements

The following listing includes the President's public schedule and other items of general interest announced by the White House Press Office and not included elsewhere in this issue.

November 10

The President met at the White House with Zbigniew Brzezinski, Assistant to the President for National Security Affairs.

November 13

The President met at the White House with:

—Dr. Brzezinski;

—Frank B. Moore, Assistant to the President for Congressional Liaison.

The White House announced that the President has canceled his trip to Pennsylvania to continue to closely monitor the situation in Iran. While he regretted that the situation in Iran required the cancellation, his decision was not based on any expectation of an immediate change in the situation there.

November 14

The President met at the White House with:

—Secretary of State Cyrus R. Vance and Dr. Brzezinski;

—the Republican congressional leadership;

—Mr. Moore;

—James T. McIntyre, Jr., Director of the Office of Management and Budget, and Robert A. Frosch, Administrator of the National Aeronautics and Space Administration, to discuss the fiscal year 1981 budget;

—Vice President Walter F. Mondale;

—Mr. McIntyre.

The President participated in a briefing on the administration's programs and policies given for civic and community leaders from Minnesota in the East Room at the White House.

November 15

The President met at the White House with:

—Dr. Brzezinski;

—Mr. Moore.

The President attended an interfaith service at the National Cathedral in Washington, D.C., for the hostages in the American Embassy in Iran.

November 16

The President met at the White House with:

—Dr. Brzezinski;

—Vice President Mondale, Secretary Vance, Secretary of Defense Harold Brown, Hamilton Jordan, Assistant to the President, Hedley W. Donovan, Senior Adviser to the President, Lloyd N. Cutler, Counsel to the President, and Dr. Brzezinski;

—Mr. Moore;

—Mr. Donovan;

—Mr. McIntyre.

The White House announced that the President has canceled both his trip to Florida and vacation on Sapelo Island, Ga., in order to continue to closely monitor the situation in Iran. The President regrets that the continuing situation in Iran requires the cancellation of his trip to Florida.

NOMINATIONS SUBMITTED TO THE SENATE

The following list does not include promotions of members of the Uniformed Services, nominations to the Service Academies, or nominations of Foreign Service officers.

NOMINATIONS—Continued

Submitted November 13, 1979

THEODORE COMPTON LUTZ, of Virginia, to be Urban Mass Transportation Administrator, vice Richard Stephen Page, resigned.

IRALINE GREEN BARNES, of the District of Columbia, to be an Associate Judge of the Superior Court of the District of Columbia for a term of 15 years, vice W. Byron Sorrell, retired.

Submitted November 14, 1979

SHIRLEY MOUNT HUFSTEDLER, of California, to be Secretary of Education (new position).

Submitted November 16, 1979

WILLIAM B. JOHNSTON, of Virginia, to be an Assistant Secretary of Transportation, vice Chester Davenport, resigned.

WILLIAM H. WILCOX, of Pennsylvania, to be an Associate Director of the Federal Emergency Management Agency (new position).

CHECKLIST OF WHITE HOUSE PRESS RELEASES

The following listing contains releases of the White House Press Office which are not included in this issue.

Released November 13, 1979

Transcript: remarks and a question-and-answer session at a briefing on hospital cost containment legislation—by Vice President Walter F. Mondale and Alfred E. Kahn, Advisor to the President on Inflation

News conference: on relief efforts for Kampucheans—by Rev. Theodore M. Hesburgh, Chairman of the Select Commission on Immigration and Refugee Policy and chairman of the board of the Overseas Development Council, James P. Grant, president, Overseas Development Council, and Matthew Nimetz, Acting Coordinator for Refugee Affairs, Department of State

Released November 14, 1979

News conference: on blocking Iranian Government property—by Secretary of the Treasury G. William Miller

News conference: on the approval of H.R. 4955, authorizing supplemental appropriations for migration and refugee assistance for fiscal year 1980 and 1981—by Ambassador

CHECKLIST—Continued

Released November 14—Continued

Henry D. Owen, Special Representative of the President for International Economic Summits

Released November 16, 1979

News conference: on the White House briefing for State Governors to discuss the Iranian situation and U.S. energy conservation—by Charles W. Duncan, Jr., Secretary, and John C. Sawhill, Under Secretary, Department of Energy

Biographical data: Philip M. Klutznick, nominated to be Secretary of Commerce

Announcement: nomination of Luther H. Hodges, Jr., to be Deputy Secretary of Commerce

---

ACTS APPROVED BY THE PRESIDENT

Approved November 13, 1979

H.R. 4955_____ Public Law 96–110
An act to authorize additional appropriations for migration and refugee assistance for the fiscal years 1980 and 1981 and to authorize humanitarian assistance for the victims of the famine in Cambodia.

Approved November 15, 1979

S. 1281_____ Public Law 96–111
An act to revitalize the pleasure cruise industry by clarifying and waiving certain restrictions in the Merchant Marine Act, 1936, and the Merchant Marine Act, 1920, to permit the entry of the steamship vessel United States, steamship vessel Oceanic Independence, steamship vessel Santa Rosa, and the steamship vessels Mariposa and Monterey into the trade.

Approved November 16, 1979

S. 640_____ Public Law 96–112
Maritime Appropriation Authorization Act for Fiscal Year 1980.

ACTS APPROVED—Continued

Approved November 16—Continued

H.R. 998_____ Public Law 96–113
An act to amend the Agricultural Adjustment Act of 1938, as amended, to exempt State prison farms from paying of marketing quota penalties.

H.R. 2196_____ Public Law 96–114
Congressional Award Act.

H.J. Res. 68_____ Public Law 96–115
A joint resolution to authorize the President to issue a proclamation designating the week beginning on November 18, 1979, as "National Family Week".

H.R. 5279_____ Public Law 96–116
An act to provide for the distribution within the United States of the International Communication Agency film entitled "Reflections: George Meany".

H.J. Res. 199_____ Public Law 96–117
A joint resolution to amend the Act of October 21, 1978 (92 Stat. 1675; Public Law 95–498).

S. 838_____ Public Law 96–118
An act to authorize appropriations for fiscal years 1980, 1981, and 1982 to carry out cooperative programs with the States for the conservation of anadromous fish, and for other purposes.

H.J. Res. 428_____ Public Law 96–110
A joint resolution designating December 1979 as "National Child Abuse Prevention Month".

S. 1728_____ Public Law 96–120
An act to designate the United States Federal Courthouse Building located at 655 East Durango, San Antonio, Texas, as the "John H. Wood, Jr., Federal Courthouse".

S. 1160_____ Public Law 96–121
An act to authorize appropriations for the Federal Fire Prevention and Control Act of 1974, and for other purposes.

H.R. 3319_____ Private Law 96–18
An act for the relief of Jose Quintana Dominguez Sendejas.

American Hostages in Iran

White House Statement.   November 17, 1979

We welcome this announcement that some of the Americans held in the Embassy in Tehran will be released. We are thankful the ordeal may be over for them and that they may be soon reunited with their families.

We strongly urge that the authorities in Iran now move to secure the safe release of all those still being held. Their ordeal is not over. The United States Government will continue to work in every channel open to it to achieve that end.

American Hostages in Iran

Statement Requesting Special Prayers for the Hostages During the Thanksgiving Holiday Weekend.   November 17, 1979

As we approach our traditional day of national thanksgiving, the hearts of all Americans are heavy with concern for the safety of those held hostage in Iran.

We join with people of all faiths throughout the world who adhere to fundamental principles of human rights and international law. We are united with them in seeking an end to acts of terrorism against innocent people.

On Thanksgiving Day and during the holiday weekend, I ask all Americans to make a special prayer at churches and synagogues and places of public meeting.

Let us seek God's guidance in our search for peace and human brotherhood and pray for the safe return of those whose lives are threatened. May we come with gratitude for our abundant blessings and humility before the heavy burden of world responsibility that our blessings and power have brought.

American Hostages in Iran

White House Statement.   November 19, 1979

Three of our hostages in Tehran have been released and have left Iran. After a brief period of rest and care, they will be reunited with their families here in the United States.

The remaining hostages must also be released. Their detention is without justification. The Government of Iran is responsible for achieving their immediate and safe release, and the United States has the right to expect that Iran will do so.

The specter has been raised of other American diplomatic hostages being placed on trial. Such a step would be a further flagrant violation of elementary human rights, religious precepts, and international law and practice. Worldwide outrage at the detention of the hostages would be greatly heightened by any attempt to put these diplomatic personnel on trial.

NOTE: On November 18, three persons were released from the American Embassy and flown to the U.S. Air Force hospital in Wiesbaden, Federal Republic of Germany. On the following day, the Iranian captors released 10 more persons, who joined their colleagues in Wiesbaden before they all were returned to the United States.

Regulation of Small Businesses and Organizations

Memorandum From the President.
November 16, 1979

Memorandum for the Heads of Executive Departments and Agencies

The Administration has made a firm commitment to strengthen the small business sector of our economy. In furtherance of that commitment, I want you to make sure that Federal regulations will not place unnecessary burdens on small businesses and organizations. Regulatory programs are important to the safety and health of the Nation; their goals, however, can sometimes be achieved in ways that minimize the burden on small businesses and organizations.

I want you to take the following steps:

• Ensure that any new rules and regulations issued by your agency will be applied whenever possible in a flexible manner, taking into account the size and nature of the regulated businesses and orga-

nizations while fulfilling the social and economic goals of the underlying statutes.

• As you review existing regulatory and reporting requirements, take particular care to determine where, within statutory limits, it is possible to tailor those requirements to fit the size and nature of the businesses and organizations subject to them.

• Identify those rules and regulations in the semiannual agenda required by Executive Order 12044, and in the Regulatory Council's *Calendar of Federal Regulations,* for which flexible alternatives and plans for implementation are being considered.

• Assign responsibility for overseeing the examination and implementation process to the agency official you designated in accordance with my June 14, 1978 memorandum on the White House Conference on Small Business, and ensure that that official works closely with your agency's representative to the Regulatory Council.

• Report the results of the above examination and plans for implementation by December 15 to the Office of Advocacy of the Small Business Administration. The Small Business Administration will work closely with the Regulatory Council and the Office of Management and Budget to ensure that agency-specific actions are consistent with and supportive of the government-wide regulatory reform program.

These measures will continue our progress toward achieving important regulatory goals without unnecessarily burdening the small businesses and organizations that are such a vital force in our Nation's life.

JIMMY CARTER

NOTE: The text of the memorandum was released on November 19.

Regulation of Small Businesses and Organizations

Letter to the Heads of the Independent Regulatory Agencies.   November 16, 1979

Dear Mr. Chairman:

This Administration has made a firm commitment to strengthen the small business sector of our economy. Today I have directed the Heads of Executive Departments and Agencies to take a series of steps to ensure that federal regulatory programs do not place unnecessary burdens on small businesses and organizations. I believe it is essential that we minimize the regulatory burden on small businesses and organizations where it is possible to do so without undermining the goals of our social and economic programs.

With the cooperation of the independent regulatory commissions in this effort to bring relief to small businesses, we can effectively respond to public concerns by showing flexibility in our regulatory policy where it is warranted and possible. I, therefore, am asking you, as Chairman of your agency, to consider taking actions similar to those contained in my memorandum of November 16 on this subject to the Heads of Executive Departments and Agencies.

Sincerely,

JIMMY CARTER

NOTE: The text of the letter was released on November 19.

Regulation of Small Businesses and Organizations

Announcement on the President's Directive to Executive Departments and Agencies. November 19, 1979

The President has directed executive departments and agencies to ensure that their regulatory programs, while achiev-ing their goals, do not place unnecessary burdens on small businesses and organizations. This action followed his decision on October 31 to add the Small Business Administration to the Regulatory Council in order to strengthen that Council's capacity to meet the concerns of small business.

The President expressed his appreciation to Senators John Culver and Gaylord Nelson and Congressmen Andy Ireland, Marty Russo, and Neal Smith, sponsors of specific small business legislation now before Congress, for their leadership in helping America's small business men and women.

The President's memorandum to department and agency heads today directs them to take the following steps:

—Ensure that new regulations take into account the size and nature of the regulated businesses while achieving intended social and economic goals of regulations.

—Determine where existing regulatory and reporting requirements can be tailored to fit the size and nature of the businesses and organizations subject to them.

—Identify those rules and regulations in the semiannual agenda required by Executive Order 12044 and in the Regulatory Council's Calendar of Federal Regulations for which flexible alternatives are being considered.

—Report the results of this process to the Office of Advocacy of the Small Business Administration by December 15.

The review of existing rules and development of implementation plans will be undertaken with the assistance of the Regulatory Council and the Office of Management and Budget. All actions under the directive must be consistent with the laws under which the agencies operate.

The President also sent a letter to the heads of independent agencies today requesting that they consider a similar review of existing and new regulations within their agencies.

2143

District of Columbia Retirement Reform Act

Statement on Signing S. 1037 Into Law. November 19, 1979

I have approved S. 1037, a bill which will provide a sound financial basis and important benefit reforms in the retirement systems for police, firefighters, teachers, and judges of the District of Columbia.

We have long recognized that these retirement systems face an ever-growing unfunded liability and need to be actuarially based to meet future commitments to District employees. Unlike previous administrations, mine has accepted the Federal share of the responsibility and costs for solving the District's current pension problems.

Last year, however, Congress enacted legislation that, in my view, overstated Federal responsibility. Accordingly, I withheld my approval of that legislation. At the same time, I expressed my desire to work with the Congress and the District of Columbia to develop acceptable retirement funding and reform legislation. I believe that S. 1037 reflects a laudable compromise among all the interested groups and achieves that objective.

Last year's legislation identified the Federal financial responsibility to the D.C. police, firefighters, teachers, and judges retirement systems as the entire unfunded liability attributable to employees who retired before home rule took effect on January 2, 1975. That was excessive. In contrast, S. 1037 defines the Federal share as 80 percent of the funded liability for those employees who retired on the basis of years of service and 33⅓ percent for disability retirees before home rule. Under this, the Federal Government will make annual payments of up to $52 million to the District retirement systems over the next 25 years.

S. 1037 also provides many desirable reforms in service and disability benefits. They should do much to curb past abuses and provide more reasonable benefit levels. While I continue to believe that these reforms should apply to current as well as future employees, they represent a major improvement over the present statutory provisions. Coupled with the strengthened fiscal, managerial, and reporting requirements in the bill, they will contribute significantly to a sound future for the District's retirement system.

NOTE: As enacted, S. 1037 is Public Law 96–122, approved November 17.

Exclusions From the Federal Labor-Management Relations Program

Executive Order 12171.   November 19, 1979

By the authority vested in me as President by the Constitution and statutes of the United States of America, including Secion 7103(b) of Title 5 of the United States Code, and in order to exempt certain agencies or subdivisions thereof from coverage of the Federal Labor-Management Relations Program, it is hereby ordered as follows:

1–1.   *Determinations.*

1–101. The agencies or subdivisions thereof set forth in Section 1–2 of this Order are hereby determined to have as a primary function intelligence, counterintelligence, investigative, or national security work. It is also hereby determined that Chapter 71 of Title 5 of the United States Code cannot be applied to those agencies or subdivisions in a manner consistent with national security requirements and considerations. The agencies or subdivisions thereof set forth in Section 1–2 of this Order are hereby excluded from coverage under Chapter 71 of Title 5 of the United States Code.

1–102. Having determined that it is necessary in the interest of national security, the provisions of Chapter 71 of Title 5 of the United States Code are suspended with respect to any agency, installation, or activity listed in Section 1–3 of this Order. However, such suspension shall be applicable only to that portion of the agency, installation, or activity which is located outside the 50 States and the District of Columbia.

1–2. *Exclusions.*

1–201. The Information Security Oversight Office, General Services Administration.

1–202. The Federal Research Division, Research Services, the Library of Congress.

1–203. Agencies or subdivisions of the Department of the Treasury:

(a) The U.S. Secret Service.

(b) The U.S. Secret Service Uniformed Division.

(c) The Office of Special Assistant to the Secretary (National Security).

(d) The Office of Intelligence Support (OIS).

(e) The Office of the Assistant Secretary (Enforcement and Operations) (OEO).

(f) The Office of Criminal Enforcement, Bureau of Alcohol, Tobacco, and Firearms.

(g) The Office of Investigations, U.S. Customs Service.

(h) The Criminal Investigation Division, Internal Revenue Service.

1–204. Agencies or subdivisions of the Department of the Army, Department of Defense:

(a) Office of Assistant Chief of Staff for Intelligence.

(b) U.S. Army Intelligence and Security Command.

(c) U.S. Army Foreign Science and Technology Center.

(d) U.S. Army Intelligence Center and School.

(e) U.S. Army Missile Intelligence Agency.

(f) Foreign Intelligence Office, U.S. Army Missile Research and Development Command.

1–205. Agencies or subdivisions of the Department of the Navy, Department of Defense:

(a) Office of Naval Intelligence.

(b) Naval Intelligence Command Headquarters and Subordinate Commands.

(c) Headquarters, Naval Security Group Command.

(d) Naval Security Group Activities and Detachments.

(e) Fleet Intelligence Center, Europe and Atlantic (FICEURLANT).

(f) Fleet Intelligence Center, Pacific (FICPAC).

(g) Units composed primarily of employees engaged in the operation, repair, and/or maintenance of "off line" or "on line" cryptographic equipment.

(h) Units composed primarily of employees of Naval telecommunications activities in positions which require a cryptographic authorization.

1–206. Agencies or subdivisions of the Department of the Air Force, Department of Defense:

(a) Office of Space Systems, Office of the Secretary of the Air Force.

(b) Office of Special Projects, Office of the Secretary of the Air Force.

(c) Engineering Office, Space and Missile Systems Organization (Air Force Systems Command).

(d) Program Control Office, Space and Missile Systems Organization (Air Force Systems Command).

(e) Detachment 3, Space and Missile Systems Organization (Air Force Systems Command).

(f) Defense Dissemination Systems Program Office, Space and Missile Systems Organization (Air Force Systems Command).

(g) Satellite Data System Program Office, Space and Missile Systems Organization (Air Force Systems Command).

(h) Project Office at El Segundo, California, Office of the Secretary of the Air Force.

(i) Project Office at Patrick Air Force Base, Florida, Office of the Secretary of the Air Force.

(j) Project Office at Fort Myer, Virginia, Office of the Secretary of the Air Force.

(k) Air Force Office of Special Investigations.

(l) U.S. Air Force Security Service.

(m) Foreign Technology Division, Air Force Systems Command, Wright-Patterson Air Force Base.

(n) 1035 Technical Operations Group (Air Force Technical Applications Center), Air Force Systems Command, and subordinate units.

(o) 3480 Technical Training Wing, Air Training Command, Goodfellow Air Force Base, Texas.

1–207. The Defense Intelligence Agency, Department of Defense.

1–208. The Defense Investigative Service, Department of Defense.

1–209. The Office of Enforcement and the Office of Intelligence, including all domestic field offices and intelligence units, of the Drug Enforcement Administration, Department of Justice.

1–210. Offices of the Assistant Secretary for Defense Programs, Department of Energy.

1–211. Offices within the Agency for International Development:

(a) The Immediate Office of the Auditor General.

(b) The Office of Inspections and Investigations.

(c) The Office of Security.

(d) The Office of the Area Auditor General/Washington.

1–3. *Units outside the 50 States and the District of Columbia.*

1–301. The Drug Enforcement Administration, Department of Justice.

JIMMY CARTER

The White House,
November 19, 1979.

[Filed with the Office of the Federal Register, 1:52 p.m., November 19, 1979]

National Science Board

Message to the Congress Transmitting a Report. November 19, 1979

To the Congress of the United States:

I am pleased to submit to the Congress the Eleventh Annual Report of the National Science Board, *Science Indicators—1978*. This report is the fourth in a series examining important aspects of the state of American science and technology.

Science and technology play a vital role in maintaining our Nation's economic well-being and make fundamental contributions toward the solution of many of our social problems. As this report illustrates, the United States continues to rank high internationally in most areas of science.

Science Indicators—1978 also addresses the balance between fundamental or long-term research and shorter-term applied research and development. Proper investment in basic research is crucial to using and maintaining the Nation's scientific and technical talent. My 1980 budget reflects this Administration's desire to increase support of scientific research and development as an investment in the Nation's future.

This report should be of interest to all those concerned with the Nation's scientific effort. I commend *Science Indicators—1978* to the attention of the Congress and those in the scientific endeavor.

JIMMY CARTER

The White House,
November 19, 1979.

NOTE: The report is entitled "Science Indicators 1978—Report of the National Science Board, 1979" (Government Printing Office, 263 pages).

United States Ambassador to Equatorial Guinea

Nomination of Mabel Murphy Smythe.
November 20, 1979

The President today announced that he will nominate Mabel Murphy Smythe, of Newtown, Conn., to be Ambassador Extraordinary and Plenipotentiary of the United States to the Republic of Equatorial Guinea. Smythe is currently Ambassador to the United Republic of Cameroon and would serve concurrently as Ambassador to Equatorial Guinea. Smythe has been Ambassador to Cameroon since 1977.

She was born April 3, 1918, in Montgomery, Ala. She received a B.A. from Mount Holyoke College in 1937, an M.A. from Northwestern University in 1940, and a Ph. D. from the University of Wisconsin in 1942.

Smythe was an assistant professor at Lincoln University from 1942 to 1945, a professor at Tennessee Agricultural and Industrial State University in 1945–46, and a professor at Brooklyn College in 1946–47. From 1951 to 1953, she was an instructor at Shiga University in Japan.

In 1953 she was deputy director of research for the NAACP Legal Defense and Education Fund. She was an instructor at New Lincoln (High) School from 1954 to 1959 and principal of that school from 1959 to 1969. From 1970 to 1977, she was director of research and publications from the Phelps-Stokes Fund, and from 1972 to 1977, she also served as vice president of the fund.

Smythe has served as a member of the Advisory Commission on International Educational and Cultural Affairs and the Advisory Council on African Affairs at the State Department. She is a consultant and the author of numerous articles and several books.

European Office of the United Nations

Nomination of Gerald B. Helman To Be the
U.S. Representative. November 20, 1979

The President today announced that he will nominate Gerald B. Helman, of Ann Arbor, Mich., to be Representative of the United States to the European Office of the United Nations, with the rank of Ambassador. He would replace William vanden Heuvel, who has been transferred to another position. Helman has been Deputy Assistant Secretary of State for International Organization Affairs since 1977.

He was born November 4, 1932, in Detroit, Mich. He received an A.B. (1953) and LL.B. (1956) from the University of Michigan. He practiced law in Michigan in 1956.

In 1956 Helman joined the Foreign Service, and he was posted at the State Department and in Milan, Vienna, and Barbados. From 1968 to 1973, he was counselor for political-military affairs at USNATO in Brussels. In 1973–74 he was a Woodrow Wilson Fellow at Princeton University.

From 1974 to 1976, Helman was Deputy Director of the Office of NATO and Atlantic Political-Military Affairs at the State Department. From 1976 to 1977, he was Director of the Office of United Nations Political Affairs in the Bureau of International Organization Affairs at State.

International Atomic Energy Agency

Nomination of the U.S. Representative and Alternate Representatives to the 23d Session of the General Conference.
November 20, 1979

The President today announced that he will nominate Under Secretary of Energy John M. Deutch to be United States Representative to the 23d session of the General Conference of the International Atomic Energy Agency, to be held in New Delhi, India, from December 4 to 11.

The President also announced that he will nominate Gerard C. Smith and Roger Kirk as Alternate Representatives on this delegation. Smith is U.S. Representative to the International Atomic Energy Agency, Ambassador at Large, and U.S. Special Representative for Non-

Proliferation Matters. Kirk is Deputy Representative of the United States to the International Atomic Energy Agency.

American Hostages in Iran

White House Statement. November 20, 1979

There are reports that the American citizens being illegally held as hostages in Tehran with the support of the Iranian Government might soon be put through some sort of "trial." This would be a flagrant violation of international law and basic religious principles, and the Government of Iran would bear full responsibility for any ensuing consequences. The United States is seeking a peaceful solution to this problem through the U.N. and every other available channel. This is far preferable to the other remedies available to the United States. Such remedies are explicitly recognized in the Charter of the United Nations. The Government of Iran must recognize the gravity of the situation it has created.

Department of Justice

Nomination of Charles B. Renfrew To Be Deputy Attorney General.
November 20, 1979

The President today announced that he will nominate Charles B. Renfrew, of San Francisco, Calif., to be Deputy Attorney General. He would replace Benjamin Civiletti, who has been appointed Attorney General. Renfrew has been a U.S. district judge for the Northern District of California since 1972.

He was born October 31, 1928, in Detroit, Mich. He received an A.B. from Princeton University in 1952 and a J.D.

from the University of Michigan Law School in 1956.

From 1956 to 1972, Renfrew was with the San Francisco firm of Pillsbury, Madison & Sutro, as an associate from 1956 to 1965 and a member from 1965 to 1972.

United States Space Policy

Announcement of the President's Decisions Concerning Land Remote-Sensing Activities. November 20, 1979

The President today announced the designation of the Commerce Department's National Oceanic and Atmospheric Administration (NOAA) to manage all operational civilian remote-sensing activities from space. This designation is one of several policy decisions announced today after a review of civilian space policy mandated by a Presidential directive in October 1978.

Early in his administration the President directed a comprehensive review of space policy. The review, completed in May 1978, resulted in a Presidential directive that established a national space policy framework. It created a Policy Review Committee on Space, chaired by the Director of the Office of Science and Technology Policy, Frank Press. One of the tasks of the Policy Review Committee has been to assess the Nation's future civil space remote-sensing requirements. That review was the basis for the policy decisions announced today.

Designation of a single agency, NOAA, to manage all civil operational satellite activities will lend itself to further integration and potential cost saving in the future. NOAA's experience in successfully operating and managing three generations of weather satellites prepares it to assume the responsibility for land re-

mote-sensing in addition to its ongoing atmospheric and oceanic activities. NOAA's first action will be to develop a transition plan, in coordination with other appropriate agencies, for moving to a fully integrated satellite-based land remote-sensing program.

Initially, our operational land remote-sensing efforts will rely on experience derived from the LANDSAT program. LANDSAT was begun in 1972 by the National Aeronautics and Space Administration (NASA) as a satellite effort specifically designed to observe surface features of the Earth.

The President's decision establishes a three-part framework to serve remote-sensing activities:

—Integration of civilian operational activities under NOAA;

—Joint or coordinated civil/military activities where both parties' objectives can be best met through this approach;

—Separate defense activities which have no civilian counterpart.

Other space policy decisions developed by this review and announced today are:

—The Commerce Department will seek ways to further private sector opportunities in civil land remote-sensing activities, through joint ventures with industry, a quasi-government corporation, leasing, etc., with the goal of eventual operation of these activities by the private sector.

—We will continue the policy of providing LANDSAT data to foreign users and promoting development of complementary and cooperative nationally operated satellite systems so as to increase benefits for all nations.

—The Department of Commerce will establish and chair a Program Board for continuing Federal coordination and regulation of civil remote-sensing activities. The involved Federal organizations will be represented (i.e., the Departments of Defense, Interior, Agriculture, State, Transportation, and Energy, and NASA, the Central Intelligence Agency, the Agency for International Development, and the Environmental Protection Agency). The National Governors' Association and the National Conference of State Legislatures will be invited to participate.

—Separate weather programs for the military and civil sectors will be maintained under the Departments of Defense and Commerce, because of their differing needs. We will continue procurement of current spacecraft until development of a new system design is justified. Future polar-orbiting satellite development and procurement will be jointly undertaken by Defense, Commerce, and NASA to maximize technology-sharing and minimize cost.

—Ocean observations from space can meet common civil and military data requirements. Accordingly, if we decide to develop ocean satellites, joint Defense/Commerce/NASA management of the program will be pursued.

Death of Steven J. Crowley

Statement by the President.
November 21, 1979

Marine Corporal Steven J. Crowley's death is a tragic loss and a stark reminder of the dangers the men and women of our Armed Forces face in the service of their Nation.

On behalf of all Americans, I extend my heartfelt sympathy to Steven Crowley's family and to the U.S. Marine Corps.

NOTE: Corporal Crowley, of Port Jefferson, N.Y., was killed during a mob attack on the American Embassy in Islamabad, Pakistan.

Aid for Ugandan Refugees

Memorandum From the President.
November 19, 1979

Memorandum for the Secretary of State
Subject: Determination pursuant to Section 2(c)(1) of the Migration and Refugee Assistance Act of 1962, as amended, (the "Act") authorizing the use of $1 million of funds made available from the United States Emergency Refugee and Migration Assistance Fund

In order to respond to a special appeal by the United Nations High Commissioner for Refugees on behalf of refugees and displaced persons in Uganda, I hereby determine, pursuant to Section 2 (c)(1) of the Act; that it is important to the national interest that up to $1 million from the United States Emergency Refugee and Migration Assistance Fund be made available through the Department of State for transfer to the United Nations High Commissioner for Refugees.

The Secretary of State is requested to inform the appropriate committee of the Congress of this Determination and the obligation of funds under this authority.

This Determination shall be published in the FEDERAL REGISTER.

JIMMY CARTER

NOTE: The memorandum was announced on November 21.

Digest of Other White House Announcements

The following listing includes the President's public schedule and other items of general interest announced by the White House Press Office and not included elsewhere in this issue.

November 17

The President met at the White House with Zbigniew Brzezinski, Assistant to the President for National Security Affairs.

The President left the White House to spend the Thanksgiving holiday at Camp David, Md.

November 19

The President transmitted to the Congress the 1978 annual report of the National Cancer Advisory Board.

November 20

In the afternoon, the President returned to the White House from Camp David to discuss with his advisers the situation concerning the American hostages in Iran. Following the meeting, the President returned to Camp David.

November 21

The White House announced that the President telephoned Gen. Mohammad Zia-ul-Haq, President of Pakistan, to express his concern for ensuring the continued safety of Americans in Islamabad. The President also expressed the appreciation of the American Government for the action on the part of the Pakistani military to rescue the American Embassy staff besieged during a mob attack on the Embassy in Islamabad.

November 23

The President met with his foreign policy advisers at Camp David.

NOMINATIONS SUBMITTED TO THE SENATE

The following list does not include promotions of members of the Uniformed Services, nominations to the Service Academies, or nominations of Foreign Service officers.

Submitted November 20, 1979

WILLIAM GARTON BOWDLER, of Florida, a Foreign Service officer of the Class of Career Minister, to be an Assistant Secretary of State.

GERALD BERNARD HELMAN, of Michigan, a Foreign Service officer of Class one, to be the Representative of the United States of America to the European Office of the United Nations, with the rank of Ambassador.

MABEL MURPHY SMYTHE, of Connecticut, now Ambassador Extraordinary and Plenipotentiary of the United States of America to the United Republic of Cameroon, to serve concurrently and without additional compensation as Ambassador Extraordinary and Plenipotentiary of the United States of America to the Republic of Equatorial Guinea.

The following-named persons to be the Representative and Alternate Representatives of the United States of America to the Twenty-third Session of the General Conference of the International Atomic Energy Agency:

Representative:

JOHN M. DEUTCH, of Massachusetts

Alternate Representatives:

GERARD C. SMITH, of the District of Columbia

ROGER KIRK, of the District of Columbia

CHECKLIST OF WHITE HOUSE PRESS RELEASES

All releases of the White House Press Office have been included in this issue.

**ACTS APPROVED BY
THE PRESIDENT**

Approved November 17, 1979

S. 1037_____ Public Law 96–122
District of Columbia Retirement Reform
Act.

Approved November 20, 1979

H.J. Res. 440_____ Public Law 96–123
A joint resolution making further continuing
appropriations for the fiscal year 1980, and
for other purposes.

H.R. 5811_____Public Law 96–124
An act to allow the Interest Rate Modification Act of 1979, passed by the Council of the
District of Columbia, to take effect immediately.

National Child Abuse Prevention Month, 1979

Proclamation 4704. November 26, 1979

By the President of the United States of America

A Proclamation

America's children are our most precious resource, and in this final month of the International Year of the Child I urge all Americans to consider what they can do to prevent child abuse and neglect.

The needs of children are best met in families where provisions can be made for the special needs and limitations of all family members. Even loving parents sometimes fail to provide adequate supervision, or find themselves in situations where needs are not met or emotions are difficult to control.

I urge communities and helping organizations to work with families to alleviate conditions that result in the abuse and neglect of children. I especially urge all those who feel unable to cope with problems to seek out help.

Our Nation's children are our Nation's future. We all share in the responsibility for making sure they grow up in a healthful environment. I appeal to public agencies, private organizations and the business community to support needed social, educational and health services in their communities to strengthen families during the critical child-rearing years.

Working together, with sensitivity and concern, we can reduce the incidence and lifelong damage of child abuse.

Now, THEREFORE, I, JIMMY CARTER, President of the United States of America, do hereby proclaim the month of December, 1979, as National Child Abuse Prevention Month.

IN WITNESS WHEREOF, I have hereunto set my hand this twenty-sixth day of November, in the year of our Lord nineteen hundred seventy-nine, and of the Independence of the United States of America the two hundred and fourth.

JIMMY CARTER

[Filed with the Office of the Federal Register, 3:04 p.m., November 26, 1979]

Office of Personnel Management

Nomination of J. Jackson Walter To Be Director of the Office of Government Ethics. November 26, 1979

The President today announced that he will nominate J. Jackson Walter, of Tallahassee, Fla., to be Director of the Office of Government Ethics, a new position.

Walter is currently at the Office of Government Ethics and was previously assistant secretary of the Florida Department of Labor and Employment Security.

He was born November 6, 1940, in Abington, Pa. He received an A.B. from Amherst College in 1962 and an LL.B. from Yale Law School in 1966.

From 1970 to 1976, Walter practiced law, concentrating on land development and regulatory matters. From 1976 to 1978, he was executive director of the Florida Department of Business Regulation. From 1978 to 1979, he was secretary of that department.

President's Management Improvement Council

Appointment of Richard C. Leone as a Member. November 26, 1979

The President today announced the appointment of Richard C. Leone, of Princeton, N.J., to be a member of the President's Management Improvement Council.

Leone, 39, is a consultant and writer on financial and economic affairs and public policy. He is author of a forthcoming book, "Financing Government in the United States," and serves as an adviser on financial management and economic development to the U.S. Conference of Mayors.

Iranian Aliens

Executive Order 12172. November 26, 1979

DELEGATION OF AUTHORITY WITH RESPECT TO ENTRY OF CERTAIN ALIENS INTO THE UNITED STATES

By virtue of the authority vested in me as President by the Constitution and laws of the United States, including the Immigration and Nationality Act, as amended, 8 USC 1185 and 3 USC 301, it is hereby ordered as follows:

SECTION 1–101. Delegation of Authority. The Secretary of State and the Attorney General are hereby designated and empowered to exercise in respect of Iranians holding nonimmigrant visas, the authority conferred upon the President by section 215(a)(1) of the Act of June 27, 1952 (8 USC 1185), to prescribe limitations and exceptions on the rules and regulations governing the entry of aliens into the United States.

SEC. 1–102. Effective Date. This order is effective immediately.

JIMMY CARTER

The White House,
November 26, 1979.

[Filed with the Office of the Federal Register, 10:45 a.m., November 27, 1979]

Department of the Interior and Related Agencies Appropriations Bill

Remarks on Signing H.R. 4930 Into Law. November 27, 1979

THE PRESIDENT. This morning we are gathered here to sign into law the Interior appropriations bill, which has a special significance above and beyond its meeting the needs of the Interior Department. It does provide the first budgetary commitment to the long-range evolution of synthetic fuels, but I think of even more personal importance, this bill, for the first time, will provide real help for the poor and the elderly people of our Nation in meeting the rapidly increasing costs of energy.

We have already distributed to the States $250 million to help the poor and the elderly meet their increasingly high energy bills—$250 million. This bill will provide an additional $1,350 million, a total of $1.6 billion this winter. We will expedite the distribution of these funds, and I want to congratulate the Congress on taking this action in a rapid and effective way.

I've asked the Congress, from the windfall profits tax, to provide, on a permanent basis for the next 10 years, $2.4 billion each year to help the poor and the elderly to meet their rising energy bills.

The last 3 weeks have been a trying time in the history of our country. It has been made vividly obvious to everyone in the United States that our Nation is overly dependent on the import of foreign oil. In 1980 it's estimated that we will purchase from foreign countries 3 billion barrels of oil. In order to pay for this, we'll send overseas $70 billion of American money. Along with oil that we import, we also import inflation and unemployment.

In July, after the Iranian revolution had interrupted for a few months our own supply of imported oil, I went to the American people for the sixth time since my inauguration as President and called on the Congress to take rapid action on five different elements of meeting our energy needs: First was an appeal to the Congress to give me full authority to implement a gasoline rationing plan when and if it's needed; second was an appeal to provide low-income assistance for energy cost increases for the poor and the elderly, which I will sign into law in just a few minutes; third was to pass a windfall profits tax, to provide for the well-being of the American public, and to derive this income, which is needed, from the unearned profits of the oil companies of this country.

The House has passed an adequate windfall profits tax bill. The Senate is now in the process of debating this bill on the floor and will be voting on a series of amendments. I hope the strongest possible windfall profits tax will be forthcoming from the Congress.

The House and the Senate have acted on the energy mobilization board, legislation which will permit us to expedite decisions on projects that will provide better energy production in our country. The differences between the two Houses must now be resolved in conference.

And the fifth request that I made to the Congress was to implement for us an ability to proceed rapidly with the development of synthetic fuels, solar energy, including gasohol, and strong conservation matters. This legislation has now been passed in its entirety by the Senate. It's been passed partially by the House, and my hope is that this action can now be completed by both Houses and signed into law.

Any delay in implementing this complete package of energy proposals will be a deep disappointment to the American people. Time is of the essence, and I can say from the bottom of my heart as President that it involves the security of our Nation. Failure to pass adequate energy legislation to reduce our dependence on foreign oil is a clear and present danger to the security of the United States.

We stand here as a sober and determined group, the President and the key Members of Congress. We are working as hard as we can to meet the energy needs of our country. There are only two actions which we can take to resolve this difficulty: One is to enhance conservation, the saving of energy, the elimination of waste of energy; and on the other hand, the increased production of energy in our own country.

This is a complicated and difficult matter, but I want to congratulate again the Members of the House and Senate for the action that they've already taken and to encourage them to join in with me in an expeditious action on the remaining three items that are so crucial to our Nation.

I'd like now to call on Senator Robert Byrd to say a word representing the Senate, if he will, and then I'll call on the representative of the House and then one of our fine Governors, who will help to administer this program for the poor and the elderly. And then I'll sign the legislation.

Senator Byrd?

SENATOR BYRD. Mr. President, the legislation that you are about to sign represents a commitment on the part of the Congress with respect to a comprehensive synfuels program. It also represents a commitment on the part of the Congress to aid the elderly and the poor in the face of rising energy costs.

I would only want to pay special tribute, Mr. President, to Senator Javits, who is the author of the amendment in the Senate to add $1.2 billion in aid to the elderly and to the poor. I also want to express my deep appreciation to Ted Stevens, who is the ranking minority member on the Senate appropriations subcommittee for the Department of the Interior. And also, I want to thank Dee Huddleston, who acted as chairman of the subcommittee. And certainly I would want to express my heartfelt gratitude to Sid Yates, Congressman Yates, who is chairman of the House conferees, because without the cooperation and the understanding that marked the conference, we would not have been able to send to your desk a bill for you to sign.

You're very right in saying that in the face of world developments, we have to do something and do it expeditiously, to deal with our reliance on unreliable sources of foreign oil. The Senate has passed an energy mobilization board bill. It has passed an omnibus energy bill, establishing an energy security corporation. And in that legislation, of course, is included conservation provisions; a synthetic fuels program provision is in that bill. And we now are in the process of getting conferees appointed so that these Senate and House conferees, once they're named, can meet in conference to iron out the areas of differences.

So, we're working. And I assure you that we're going to do all that we can to get those conference reports back to each House as soon as possible—and that won't be easy, as we have seen in the past. I've never seen anything so contentious as the subject of energy when it reaches the Senate floor.

THE PRESIDENT. I've noticed that. [*Laughter*]

SENATOR BYRD. And if I were to take off my jacket and my shirt, I could show you some scars—[*laughter*]—that you may remember were inflicted upon me when I helped to break the spirit of a filibuster a couple of years ago.

But in any event, we applaud you for your leadership in this vital area, and we're going to do the best we can in the Senate to do our part.

Thank you very much for inviting us.

THE PRESIDENT. Thank you very much, Bob.

I met earlier this morning with the Speaker of the House, who had to go back to the Hill to get the House work underway today. And of course, Jamie Whitten, who's the chairman of the appropriations committee, has worked in a yeoman's way to get this legislation to my desk. Many others have been involved. I'd like to call on Congressman Natcher, however, to speak for the House at this time.

REPRESENTATIVE NATCHER. Thank you very much, Mr. President.

As you will recall, on the House side we started with a House joint resolution. This is important legislation, and legislation which, of course, will be a milestone in programs where we have people in need and people that are suffering. We passed this bill, Mr. President, in the House by 185 majority, and as you know, that's quite a feat. Ordinarily in the House, legislation like this will pass with a vote 20 or 30 majority, but we passed it on a vote of 185 majority.

We succeeded through the efforts of Sid Yates, my chairman, Jamie Whitten of Mississippi, and the appropriations committee, permitting this legislation to go through on the Senate Interior appropriation bill. This is the way it should have happened; it expedited the legislation. And, Mr. President, we are now down to the point where you are signing. And I want to commend you and to say thank you for presenting to the Congress this legislation.

Thank you very much.

THE PRESIDENT. Thank you very much, Congressman Natcher.

Perhaps more than—certainly more than most payments that will go out to people who are urgently in need, the Governors of this country are deeply involved. They've helped to draft the legislation; they've helped to administer the programs that are already in existence; they've already received the $250 million that has been disbursed; and they will be playing a major role in the rapid disbursement of these funds to the poor and the elderly. And I've asked Governor Ella Grasso of Connecticut to say a word for the Governors.

GOVERNOR GRASSO. Thank you, Mr. President.

I think that you have shown us one more time that a majority is one who truly believes. And I want to thank you for your insistence and your determination and your leadership in making the fulfillment of this very real need of crisis intervention moneys a reality. And I congratulate the Members of Congress, as well, for

moving with such dispatch to be of help: help to needy families, help to the working poor, and help to the elderly.

The enactment of this legislation, in a very real sense, changes a season of concern into a winter of new hope, and for that, Mr. President, we are most grateful. And we join with you in a continuing pledge of conservation, so that our resources may be fully and properly utilized and we may reach that day, under your leadership, of true energy independence.

Thank you.

THE PRESIDENT. Thank you very much.

If anyone has the uncontrollable urge to speak—*[laughter]*—otherwise, I will proceed to sign the bill.

[At this point, the President signed the bill.]

Thank you very much, everyone.

NOTE: The President spoke at 9:30 a.m. at the ceremony in the Cabinet Room at the White House.

As enacted, H.R. 4930 is Public Law 96–126, approved November 27.

Jobs for the Hardcore Unemployed

Announcement of Administration Programs. November 27, 1979

The White House announced today that, for the first time, five Federal agencies and departments have agreed to fill a specific percentage of the jobs created by their economic development programs with the hardcore unemployed. Under these agreements reached through the White House Interagency Coordinating Council, headed by Presidential Assistant Jack Watson, approximately 80,000 permanent, private sector jobs will be made available to the unemployed through economic development projects funded in FY 1980.

The five agencies entering into this agreement with the Department of Labor (DOL) are: the Economic Development Administration (EDA), the Community Services Administration (CSA), the Department of Transportation (DOT), the Department of Housing and Urban Development (HUD), and the Farmers Home Administration (FmHA). Their efforts to direct a greater number of jobs created by Federal economic development programs to the hardcore unemployed are central to the employment initiatives announced by the White House last April. These initiatives are among the President's administrative actions aimed at the persistent problem of high unemployment in both rural and urban areas.

Programs covered by the agreements include HUD's $675 million Urban Development Action Grant program, for which a 10-percent employment goal has been established; EDA's proposed $3 billion (including $1.8 billion in loan guarantees) public works and business development activities, with a 10- to 15-percent goal; the Urban Mass Transportation Administration's new $200 million ($80 million appropriated by Congress) Urban Initiatives program, with a 10- to 15-percent goal; CSA's $35 million title VII program, with a 25-percent goal; and FmHA's $1.2 billion Business and Industrial Loan program, with a 20-percent goal.

In addition to the 80,000 private sector jobs that will result from this agreement, approximately 100,000 private sector jobs will be made available to the hardcore unemployed under the new Private Sector Initiatives program of the recently reenacted Comprehensive Employment and Training Act. This effort is also consistent with the President's goals of targeting Federal resources to those with the greatest need and utilizing existing programs and resources more effectively.

The White House also announced that 14 local jurisdictions will receive 2-year grants, under the Targeted Jobs Demonstration program, to link already funded economic development projects with Federal employment and training efforts. The demonstration program is another component of the President's Employment Initiatives. Funded at $3 million, the demonstration program is an interagency effort involving DOL, HUD, EDA, CSA, DOT, and the Small Business Administration.

Fund recipients under the program are Portland, Oreg., Buffalo, N.Y., New York City, Seattle, Wash., Browning, Mont., San Antonio, Tex., Metcalfe, Miss., Portland, Maine, Wilmington, Del., Milwaukee, Wis., Paterson, N.J., Lynn, Mass., Genesee County, Mich., and Philadelphia, Pa. Each recipient is to develop practical and effective strategies for placing the hardcore unemployed in the greatest feasible number of jobs created by Federal economic development and transit-related activities. Techniques will be explored to ensure that a maximum number of the business opportunities which result from economic development and transit projects go to small, minority, and community businesses. An interagency work group will monitor the demonstration effort, and HUD has lead administrative responsibility.

Interagency Committee on Emergency Medical Services

Appointment of Two Members.
November 27, 1979

The President today announced the appointment of two persons as members of the Interagency Committee on Emergency Medical Services. They are:

ALLEN JOSEPH HERBERT, a Ruston, La., physician in family practice and clinical assistant professor of family medicine and pediatrics at Louisiana State University School of Medicine;

MARVIN J. MOORE, of Fort Worth, Tex., community relations director for Trinity Emergency Medical Services, a system serving eight counties. He is a freelance broadcaster and producer and is active in community affairs.

President's Advisory Committee for Women

Appointment of Freddie Lang Groomes as a Member. November 27, 1979

The President today announced the appointment of Freddie Lang Groomes as a member of the President's Advisory Committee for Women.

Groomes is assistant to the president, director of university human affairs, and assistant professor of counseling and human systems at Florida State University. She was a member of the Florida Governor's Commission on the Status of Women from 1973 to 1978 and chaired the commission from 1977 to 1978. She is national president of the American Association for Affirmative Action.

Personal Representative of the President

Nomination of Sol M. Linowitz for the Rank of Ambassador While Serving in the Position. November 27, 1979

The President today nominated Sol M. Linowitz for the rank of Ambassador while he serves as Personal Representative of the President.

Linowitz replaces Robert S. Strauss, who has resigned as Personal Representa-

tive of the President, effective November 29, 1979.

Miami Conference on the Caribbean

Remarks by Videotape to the Conference in Miami, Florida. November 26, 1979

Good evening.

Even though I cannot be with you in person this evening, I want to use this conference to reaffirm my commitment and that of the United States to economic development and democracy in the Caribbean. We ourselves are part of the Caribbean community, and we know that development and democracy are key to realizing the strength of the region and meeting its challenges.

The Caribbean today is passing through a time of rapid change, and our mutual challenge is to steer a course economically, socially, and politically that will lead to a better life for all our people.

Twenty years ago only three island nations in the Caribbean were independent. Today there are 13 such sovereign nations, and that number is likely to increase by as many as 5 in the next few years. Behind these numbers is a stirring history. Its beginning was an unpleasant story, marked by lonely struggles against slavery, colonialism, and, too often, indifference by the outside world. But the drive of the Caribbean peoples toward freedom and modern development is primarily a proud story, one of courage, imagination, and determination in the face of hardship.

Today, however, with independence largely won, the Caribbean still faces many problems. Perhaps the most serious problems are economic. Spiraling oil prices, unstable commodity markets, uneven growth, inflation, and unemployment are certainly not unique to the Caribbean. But these global trends have struck the small countries of the Caribbean with special severity. They add a major burden to the always imposing challenge of the building and development of independent nations. And economic deprivation creates vulnerabilities to extremism and to foreign intervention.

In facing these problems, the Caribbean has some significant advantages. In addition to its beauty and climate, vigorous political institutions and talented human resources provide special opportunities. From the resurgent social democracy of the Dominican Republic to the established parliamentary traditions of some English-speaking peoples, free institutions have fostered development within a stable framework.

The awarding of this year's Nobel Prize to the distinguished development economist, W. Arthur Lewis from Trinidad,[1] exemplifies the achievements and contributions of the island's peoples.

Citizens of the United States and the Caribbean stand together with a common pride in our achievement. We stand for the rights of people to be free of oppression, free from arbitrary abuse, and free to participate in a nation's political life.

These rights of freedom are precious. Whatever the claimed justification, we will not be silent when these rights are abused. We stand with those who are genuinely committed to economic development. We stand with those who espouse social justice and human rights and who work to translate them from abstract goals into real programs. We stand with those who are genuinely committed to international relations based on mutual respect.

As President, I've sought consistently to implement these principles and to

---

[1] Sir Arthur is a native of Saint Lucia.

strengthen relations in the nation and in the region. We negotiated canal treaties with Panama, in keeping with our determination to forge new and better relationships with developing countries. We've worked with 30 countries and 15 international institutions to establish a Caribbean group which has expanded and coordinated the flow of aid to the region and will support efforts in the future to design, fund, and implement regionally integrated development activities.

My administration has increased direct economic assistance to the Caribbean, nearly doubling bilateral aid obligations over the past 2 years. As actual disbursements reflect these increases, we will be contributing more than ever before to generate employment and to help basic human needs. This is particularly true for the newly independent countries of the eastern Caribbean.

We've come rapidly to the assistance of countries like the Dominican Republic and Dominica, friends in need of emergency aid to rebound from natural disasters. We've repeatedly shown our eagerness to support political freedom and democratic processes. But such governmental action, no matter how important, is still not enough. And that's why your meeting is so important.

The United States has vast untapped resources of technology, skills, and good will. I will use my office and my influence to help mobilize the people of the United States to work with the people of the Caribbean for common goals, social and economic development, and democracy.

In the United States, our universities, our agricultural and labor organizations, business and industry, churches and other benevolent institutions, State and local governments, and individual private citizens can all play a vital role in establishing mutually advantageous relationships with our friends in the Caribbean. We can all benefit from improvements in education, agriculture, tourism, industry, trade, health, transportation, employment opportunities, and personal friendships among our people.

The answers for the future are in the Caribbean's own talents and traditions, not in the false promises of foreign models. Solutions will not emerge by blaming our problems on our own friends. To seek freedom, justice, independence, and a better life, one needs to work closely with those who genuinely share the goals of development and democracy. I hope that all the other basin States of Venezuela and Colombia, Mexico and Central America, will play a vigorous role in this effort.

The Caribbean group is an excellent example of the benefits of a multilateral effort. Closer cooperation between the Caribbean community and the Central American Common Market and, perhaps also, the Andean Pact could be another step toward greater progress. Like the Caribbean, Central America is experiencing a period of profound change. Unlike the Caribbean, where nations are struggling to defend democratic institutions while they modernize, many of the nations of Central America are seeking to develop democratic institutions which had not previously existed. Nevertheless, both regions have much in common and also much to learn from each other.

Few societies can more genuinely speak of a common destiny than ours, for the United States and the Caribbean, the ties of history and geography are continuously renewed by what can only be described as one of the most intense people-to-people relationships in the world today. It's a relationship filled with exciting possibilities that are waiting to be explored. As leaders and molders of opinion, we have a special responsibility to build understanding, to defend the region's democratic institutions, and to promote development of social and economic justice.

On behalf of the United States, I pledge our continuing respect and support for all these efforts.

Thank you very much.

NOTE: The President spoke at 2:15 p.m. in the Cabinet Room at the White House. His remarks were videotaped for use at the conference on November 28.

The transcript of the remarks was released on November 28.

Diplomatic Relations

Remarks on Receiving Diplomatic Credentials From Foreign Ambassadors.
November 28, 1979

This morning I have received the credentials of the Ambassadors of several nations. This is a very important and a very solemn occasion for me whenever I have this opportunity. There is a vivid reminder in this ceremony of the importance of diplomatic relationships.

In looking down this row of representatives, who are quite distinguished in their own right, the differences among us are apparent. We represent countries with different backgrounds, different political systems, different customs, heritage, commitments, goals, opportunities, different levels of income, different alliances with widely varying countries. The only way to bridge the inherent gaps between countries and to maintain peace and proper relationships is through the honoring of the integrity of diplomatic immunity.

It's extremely important that mob violence be controlled and that international terrorism not be permitted to reign. All countries are afflicted at times with mob violence and terrorism. The tragedy of the occurrences in Iran is that in a departure from accepted custom and tradition down through the centuries, in this instance the Government itself has both condoned and encouraged the seizure of an American Embassy and our personnel through mob violence and through terrorism.

The inviolability of embassies is absolutely indispensable in easing tensions and resolving problems that exist among nations and in searching for a common ground of peace and communication among people. This is vital to every country. It's particularly vital to those countries who are small and who are weak and who do not have military power or economic power to exert in defending one's own institutions and one's own rights.

In this principle, the attitude of our own country, our efforts to have our hostages released and to restore the integrity of our diplomatic institutions, is an effort not only for the rights and benefits of the United States but for the rights and benefits of all nations.

Some of the countries represented here, almost all of them, have strongly supported the condemnation of the Iranian Government's actions in seizing our Embassy and holding our hostages captive. We need the help of all countries. The rule of law is only as strong as the efforts of those who are committed to defend it. We are very grateful for the help of those nations who have joined us in this effort.

The harming of innocent people is condemned by every law of mankind and by every law of God, no matter what religious principles or economic or political principles prevail in a country. We are determined to work as peacefully as possible to achieve the release of our hostages as early as we possibly can and, of course, commensurate with that, to defend and to protect the unchanging principles on which our Nation and other nations are founded.

My hope is that all countries represented here and those others who have representatives in our Capital City will join with us in bringing a quick and peaceful resolution to the problem which afflicts not only the United States but all countries.

Again, all of the diplomats here are welcome. I'm very grateful that you've brought your families with you, and we are also honored to have your presence here in Washington. Good luck to all of you.

Thank you very much.

NOTE: The President spoke at 11:58 a.m. in the Oval Office, where he received diplomatic credentials from Ambassadors Rafael Solis Cerda of Nicaragua, Redha Malek of Algeria, Nicholas F. Parkinson of Australia, Ricardo Midence Soto of Honduras, Budimir Loncar of Yugoslavia, and Peter Hermes of the Federal Republic of Germany.

The Cyprus Conflict

Letter to the Speaker of the House and the Chairman of the Senate Foreign Relations Committee. November 28, 1979

Dear Mr. Speaker: (Dear Mr. Chairman:)

In accordance with the provisions of Public Law 95–384, I am submitting the following report on progress made during the past 60 days toward the conclusion of a negotiated solution of the Cyprus problem.

In my last Cyprus report to the Congress, dated September 25, I noted that the recess in the intercommunal talks continues despite persistent and intensive efforts by UN Secretary General Wald-heim and his staff to bring the two par-ties back to the conference table. I regret to report that in the intervening 60 days these efforts have still not borne fruit.

The United States shares the view that only sustained intercommunal talks can lead to a just and lasting settlement of the Cyprus problem. We believe that the continuing good-offices efforts of the Sec-retary General are the most promising way to achieve a serious negotiation. I am pleased that our November 1978 propos-als provided impetus for the current UN initiative. We have strongly supported that initiative since it began, and we shall continue to do so. In part due to our sup-port, the Secretary General and his staff are making progress toward finding a formula on the basis of which the talks might resume.

The current session of the UN General Assembly is creating opportunities to ex-plore avenues of progress on the Cyprus question. Secretary Vance had meetings with President Kyprianou in New York on September 26 and October 4. Other U.S. officials are in contact with princi-pals in the Cyprus dispute, and with in-terested third parties, to prepare for the General Assembly debate on Cyprus. We hope that after the General Assembly com-pletes its discussion of Cyprus, both sides will find it possible to resume the inter-communal negotiations. It is essential that they not allow the quest for short-term advantage to erode their mutual objec-tive of finding a settlement which meets the basic needs of all people on the island.

The long and tortuous history of the Cyprus problem demonstrates that peace-ful progress has never been easy. The ob-stacles, while formidable, are not insur-mountable. We continue to believe that progress is achievable, and we are vigor-ously seeking it. Toward that end, we remain in close touch with all parties to the Cyprus dispute, the United Nations, our European allies, and other states which have a legitimate role to play and which desire to contribute to the achieve-ment of our common goal.

Sincerely,

JIMMY CARTER

NOTE: This is the text of identical letters ad-dressed to Thomas P. O'Neill, Jr., Speaker of the House of Representatives, and Frank Church, chairman of the Senate Foreign Re-lations Committee.

Milk Price Support Bill
Statement on Signing H.R. 4167 Into Law. November 28, 1979

I have today signed H.R. 4167, which will support milk prices at between 80 and 90 percent of parity for the next 2 years. This is the latest in a series of im-portant steps my administration has taken to ensure that dairy farmers have the eco-nomic incentive they need to produce ample supplies of milk and thereby re-duce inflationary pressure.

For most of the last 2 years, supplies of dairy products have been tight and prices high, at least partly as a result of deci-sions made before this administration came into office that held returns to dairy farmers to very low levels. The re-sult was a cutback in dairy herds, which made it impossible for the industry to respond to strengthened economic incen-tives in 1977 and 1978. The industry has now overcome the effects of these low re-turns, and we can expect good produc-tion this year and next.

There is currently some concern that milk production could exceed demand sometime during the next 2 years. It may become necessary to give the Secretary of

Agriculture authority to adjust the future rate of increase in support levels should supplies become excessive.

I recognize that the dairy outlook is unusually uncertain this year. Secretary Bergland has been in constant touch with key Members of Congress and with leaders of the dairy industry throughout the development of this legislation. They have assured the Secretary that they will work with the Department of Agriculture to monitor dairy developments and to seek legislative action if it appears government stocks will reach excessive levels.

I am pleased with this administration's record of support for sound dairy programs. Our dairy programs work and work well, because they serve both producers and consumers. With this law, we will be continuing this important effort for another 2 years.

NOTE: As enacted, H.R. 4167 is Public Law 96–127, approved November 28.

United States-United Kingdom Agreement on Atomic Energy for Mutual Defense Purposes

Message to the Congress Transmitting an Amendment to the Agreement.
November 28, 1979

To the Congress of the United States:

I am pleased to transmit to the Congress, pursuant to Section 123d of the Atomic Energy Act of 1954, as amended (42 U.S.C. 2153), the text of an amendment to the Agreement Between the Government of the United States of America and the Government of the United Kingdom of Great Britain and Northern Ireland for Cooperation on the Uses of Atomic Energy for Mutual Defense Purposes of July 3, 1958, as amended, and my written approval, authorization and determination concerning the agreement. The joint classified and unclassified memoranda submitted to me by the Secretaries of Energy and Defense which provide a summary analysis of the amendment are also enclosed.

The amendment extends for five years (until December 31, 1984) those provisions which permit the transfer of non-nuclear parts, source, by-product special nuclear material and other material for nuclear weapons and special nuclear material for fueling military propulsion reactors.

In my judgement, the proposed amendment meets all statutory requirements. The United Kingdom intends to continue to maintain viable nuclear forces. In light of our previous close cooperation and the fact that the United Kingdom has committed its nuclear forces to NATO, I have concluded that it is in our security interest to continue to assist them in maintaining a credible nuclear force.

I have approved the amendment and authorized its execution and urge the Congress give it favorable consideration.

JIMMY CARTER

The White House,
November 28, 1979.

United States-United Kingdom Agreement on Atomic Energy for Mutual Defense Purposes

Memorandum From the President.
November 28, 1979

Memorandum for the Secretary of Defense, the Secretary of Energy

Subject: Proposed Amendment to the US–UK Agreement for Cooperation on the Uses of Atomic Energy for Mutual Defense Purposes

I have reviewed your joint letter to me of November 2, 1979, recommending approval of a proposed Amendment to the Agreement Between the Government of the United States of America and the Government of the United Kingdom for Cooperation on the Uses of Atomic Energy for Mutual Defense Purposes. I note from your joint recommendation that the United Kingdom is participating with the United States pursuant to an international agreement by substantial and material contributions to the mutual defense and security. The proposed Amendment will permit cooperation which will further improve our mutual defense posture and be in support of NATO.

I hereby:

• approve the program outlined in the proposed Amendment to the 1958 Agreement;

• determine that cooperation under the proposed Amendment will promote and will not constitute an unreasonable risk to the common defense and security; and

• authorize the execution of the proposed Amendment for the Government of the United States in a manner specified by the Secretary of State.

JIMMY CARTER

Veterans' Disability Compensation and Survivors' Benefits Amendments of 1979

Statement on Signing H.R. 2282 Into Law. November 28, 1979

It is a great pleasure to sign into law H.R. 2282, the Veterans' Disability Compensation and Survivors' Benefits Amendments of 1979. This bill increases by 9.9 percent the rates of compensation for service-disabled veterans and their survivors.

Benefits to disabled veterans and their survivors are a reflection of our deep gratitude to those men and women injured or killed in the service of their country. My administration has consistently supported periodic increases in benefits for them as the cost of living rises. In keeping with that policy I have recommended and the Congress has enacted increased compensation each year since I took office.

My budget last January proposed an increase in compensation benefits, effective this fiscal year. I am pleased that H.R. 2282 accomplishes this by substantially increasing benefits for about 2½ million service-disabled veterans and their survivors, retroactive to October 1, 1979.

NOTE: As enacted, H.R. 2282 is Public Law 96–128, approved November 28.

Department of Defense

Nomination of Togo D. West, Jr., To Be General Counsel. November 28, 1979

The President today announced that he will nominate Togo D. West, Jr., of Washington, D.C., to be General Counsel of the Department of Defense. He would replace Deanne Siemer, who has resigned. West has been Special Assistant to the Secretary of Defense since earlier this year.

He was born June 21, 1942, in Winston-Salem, N.C. He received a B.S.E.E. (1965) and a J.D. (1968) from Howard University.

West was a law clerk with the firm of Covington & Burling in 1967 and 1968 and was law clerk to Judge Harold R. Tyler of the U.S. District Court for the

Southern District of New York in 1968 and 1969. He was a judge advocate in the Military Justice Division of the U.S. Army in 1969 and 1970.

From 1970 to 1973, West was attorney-adviser to the Assistant Secretary of the Army for Manpower and Reserve Affairs. He was an associate with Covington & Burling from 1973 to 1975 and in 1976 and 1977. From 1975 to 1976, he was Associate Deputy Attorney General. From 1977 to 1979, he was General Counsel to the Department of the Navy.

National Labor Relations Board

Nomination of William A. Lubbers To Be General Counsel.   November 28, 1979

The President today announced that he will nominate William A. Lubbers, of Bethesda, Md., to be General Counsel of the National Labor Relations Board (NLRB). He would replace John Irving, who has resigned. Lubbers has been with the NLRB since 1952 and has served as Executive Secretary since 1978.

He was born September 21, 1924, in Cedar Grove, Wis. He received a B.A. from the University of Wisconsin in 1948 and an LL.B. from the University of Wisconsin Law School in 1950. He served in the U.S. Army from 1943 to 1945.

In 1950 Lubbers was an organizer with the American Federation of State, County & Municipal Employees, and from 1951 to 1952, he was with the Wage Stabilization Board, in the Office of Case Analysis, then the Office of the General Counsel.

Lubbers joined the NLRB in 1951 as staff counsel on the staff of member Abe Murdock. From 1957 to 1977, he was on the staff of member John H. Fanning, as staff counsel, supervisory staff counsel,

and Deputy Chief Counsel. From 1977 to 1978, he was Solicitor of the NLRB.

United States International Trade Commission

Nomination of Michael J. Calhoun To Be a Member.   November 28, 1979

The President today announced that he will nominate Michael J. Calhoun, of Washington, D.C., to be a member of the United States International Trade Commission for a term expiring December 16, 1988. He would replace Joseph Parker, whose term is expiring. Calhoun has been assistant minority counsel for international trade of the House Ways and Means Committee since 1976.

He was born November 11, 1947, in Columbia, S.C. He received a B.A. from Princeton University in 1970 and a J.D. from Harvard Law School in 1974. He took a postgraduate law program in international economics at the London School of Economics in 1975.

From 1974 to 1976, Calhoun was an associate with the Washington law firm of Covington & Burling.

United States International Trade Commission

Nomination of Robert E. Baldwin To Be a Member.   November 28, 1979

The President today announced that he will nominate Robert E. Baldwin, of Madison, Wis., to be a member of the United States International Trade Commission for a term expiring June 16, 1981. He would replace Italo Ablondi, who has resigned. Baldwin has been a consultant to the World Bank in Washington, D.C., since 1978 and is a former chairman of the economic department at the University of Wisconsin.

He was born July 12, 1924, in Niagara Falls, N.Y. He received an A.B. from the University of Buffalo in 1945 and a Ph. D. in economics from Harvard University in 1950.

Baldwin was on the faculty of the University of Buffalo from 1945 to 1946, Harvard University from 1950 to 1957, and the University of California from 1957 to 1964. He was Chief Economist in the Office of the Special Trade Representative from 1963 to 1964 and a professor of economics at the University of Wisconsin from 1964 to 1967.

From 1967 to 1968, Baldwin was a research professor with the Brookings Institution, and in 1969–70 he had a Ford Faculty Research Fellowship. He returned to the faculty of the University of Wisconsin in 1970 and served as F. W. Taussig research professor there in 1974 and chairman of the economics department from 1975 to 1978. In 1974–75 he was on a research contract for the Labor Department's Bureau of International Labor.

Baldwin has served as a consultant to the U.N. Conference on Trade and Development and is on the board of editors of several economic journals.

THE PRESIDENT'S NEWS CONFERENCE OF NOVEMBER 28, 1979

SITUATION IN IRAN

THE PRESIDENT. For the last 24 days our Nation's concern has been focused on our fellow Americans being held hostage in Iran. We have welcomed some of them home to their families and their friends.

But we will not rest nor deviate from our efforts until all have been freed from their imprisonment and their abuse. We hold the Government of Iran fully responsible for the well-being and the safe return of every single person.

I want the American people to understand the situation as much as possible, but there may be some questions tonight which I cannot answer fully, because of my concern for the well-being of the hostages.

First of all, I would like to say that I am proud of this great Nation, and I want to thank all Americans for their prayers, their courage, their persistence, their strong support and patience. During these past days our national will, our courage, and our maturity have all been severely tested, and history will show that the people of the United States have met every test.

In the days to come, our determination may be even more sorely tried, but we will continue to defend the security, the honor, and the freedom of Americans everywhere. This Nation will never yield to blackmail. For all Americans, our constant concern is the well-being and the safety of our fellow citizens who are being held illegally and irresponsibly hostage in Iran.

The actions of Iran have shocked the civilized world. For a government to applaud mob violence and terrorism, for a government actually to support and, in effect, participate in the taking and the holding of hostages is unprecedented in human history. This violates not only the most fundamental precepts of international law but the common ethical and religious heritage of humanity. There is no recognized religious faith on Earth which condones kidnaping. There is no recognized religious faith on Earth which condones blackmail. There is certainly no religious faith on Earth which condones the sustained abuse of innocent people.

We are deeply concerned about the inhuman and degrading conditions imposed on the hostages. From every corner of the world, nations and people have voiced their strong revulsion and condemnation of Iran and have joined us in calling for the release of the hostages.

Last night, a statement of support was released and was issued by the President of the United Nations General Assembly, the Security Council, on behalf of all of its members. We expect a further Security Council meeting on Saturday night, at which more firm and official action may be taken to help in obtaining the release of the American hostages. Any claims raised by government officials of Iran will ring hollow while they keep innocent people bound and abused and threatened.

We hope that this exercise of diplomacy and international law will bring a peaceful solution, because a peaceful solution is preferable to the other remedies available to the United States. At the same time, we pursue such a solution with grim determination. The Government of Iran must recognize the gravity of the situation, which it has itself created, and the grave consequences which will result if harm comes to any of the hostages.

I want the American people to know and I want the world to know that we will persist in our efforts, through every means available, until every single American has been freed. We must also recognize now, as we never have before, that it is our entire Nation which is vulnerable, because of our overwhelming and excessive dependence on oil from foreign countries. We have got to accept the fact that this dependence is a direct physical threat to our national security, and we must join together to fight for our Nation's energy freedom.

We know the ways to win this war: more American energy and the more efficient use of what we have. The United States Congress is now struggling with this extremely important decision. The way to victory is long and difficult, but we have the will, and we have the human and the natural resources of our great Nation.

However hard it might be to see into the future, one thing tonight is clear: We stand together. We stand as a nation unified, a people determined to protect the life and the honor of every American. And we are determined to make America an energy-secure nation once again. It is unthinkable that we will allow ourselves to be dominated by any form of overdependence at home or any brand of terrorism abroad. We are determined that the freest nation on Earth shall protect and enhance its freedom.

I'd be glad to answer questions.

QUESTIONS

WORLD REACTION TO IRANIAN SITUATION

Q. Mr. President, the Ayatollah Khomeini said the other day—and I'm using his words—he doesn't believe you have the guts to use military force. He puts no credibility in our military deterrent. I'm wondering, how do we get out of this mess in Iran and still retain credibility with our allies and with our adversaries overseas?

THE PRESIDENT. We have the full support of our allies, and in this particular instance, we have no adversaries overseas. There is no civilized country on Earth which has not condemned the seizure and the holding of the hostages by Iran.

It would not be advisable for me to explore publicly all of the options open to our country. As I said earlier, I'm determined to do the best I can through diplomatic means and through peaceful means to ensure the safety of our hostages and their release. Other actions which I might decide to take would come in the future, after those peaceful means have been exhausted.

But I believe that the growing condemnation of the world community on Iran will have a beneficial effect.

SHAH OF IRAN

Q. Mr. President, why did you reverse your policy and permit the Shah to come into this country when, one, medical treatment was available elsewhere; two, you had been warned by our chargé that the Americans might be endangered in Tehran; and three, the Bazargan government was so shaky that it was questionable whether he could deliver on the promise to protect our Embassy? And last of all, in view of the consequences, do you regret the decision?

THE PRESIDENT. No. The decision that I made, personally and without pressure from anyone, to carry out the principles of our country, to provide for the means of giving the Shah necessary medical assistance to save his life, was proper. At the same time, we notified the Government of Iran. We were assured by the Prime Minister and the Foreign Minister that our Embassy would be protected, and it was protected for several days, in spite of threats from outside.

Then peremptorily, after Khomeini made an aggravating speech to the crowds in the street and withdrew protection from the Embassy, it was attacked successfully. The Embassy was protected by our people for the length of time possible without help from the host government. No embassy on Earth is a fortress that can withstand constant attacks by a mob, unless a host government comes to the rescue of the people within the embassy.

But I took the right decision. I have no regrets about it nor apologies to make, because it did help to save a man's life, and it was compatible with the principles of our country.

EFFECT ON U.S. POLITICAL ACTIVITIES

Q. Mr. President, we appear to be in a rather dangerous period of international tension and volatility, especially in the Islamic world, and it comes at a time when we're about to embark on our quadrennial election campaign, with all that that will bring. Have you given any thought to whether, following examples of other national emergencies, it may be wise to try to mute the political fallout of this by trying to bring opponents in and outside of your party into some kind of emergency coalition for this purpose?

THE PRESIDENT. We have attempted to keep the political leaders in our Nation informed, both publicly and through other channels. We have given frequent briefings, for instance, on the Hill, both to the Members of the Senate and to the House. We have encouraged all of those who have become announced candidates for President to restrain their comments, which might be misconstrued overseas, and to have a maximum degree of harmony among those who might be spokesmen for our country.

I myself, in order to stay close to the scene here, where constantly changing events could be handled by me as President, have eliminated the major portion of political-oriented activities.

I don't think the identity of the Islamic world is a factor. We have the deepest respect and reverence for Islam and for all those who share the Moslem faith. I might say that, so far as I know, all the Islamic nations have joined us in condemning the activities and the actions of the Government of Iran. So, I don't think religious divisions are a factor here at all.

But I will have to continue to restrict my own political activities and call on those who might be opposing me in the future for President to support my position as President and to provide unity for our country and for our Nation in the eyes of those who might be looking for some sign of weakness or division in order to perpetuate their abuse of our hostages.

SECURITY FOR EMBASSIES

Q. What can the U.S. do now, what can it do to prevent future incidents of the nature of Iran? How can you satisfy the public demand to end such embarrassment?

THE PRESIDENT. Well, this is an unprecedented and unique occurrence. Down through history, we have had times when some of our people were captured by terrorists or who were abused, and there have obviously been instances of international kidnaping which occurred for the discomforture of a people or a government. So far as I know, this is the first time that such an activity has been encouraged by and supported by the government itself, and I don't anticipate this kind of thing recurring.

We have taken steps already, in view of the disturbances in the Middle East and the Persian Gulf region, to guard our people more closely, to provide them with higher degree of security, and to make arrangements with the host governments to provide assistance, if it's needed, in the fastest possible way.

Many other nations have reduced severely the number of persons overseas. I think one of the points that should be made is that a year ago, we had 70,000 Americans in Iran—70,000. There were literally thousands of people who were killed in the Iranian revolution, from all nations. We were able to extract Americans from Iran safely. It was a superb demonstration of cooperation and good conduct on the part of the State Department and other American officials.

So, there will be disturbances in the future, but I think we are well protected as we possibly can be, without withdrawing into a shell, from protecting American interests in nations overseas.

My own experience, so far, has been that the leaders of nations have recommitted themselves to provide security for embassies of all countries. I think we've learned a lesson from this instance. But, because it is so unique, in the high degree of irresponsibility of the Iranian Government leaders, I don't believe that we'll see another reoccurrence of it any time soon.

HENRY KISSINGER

Q. Mr. President, former Secretary of State Kissinger has criticized your administration's handling of the situation in Iran. He has suggested that it came about because, partly because of the perceived weakness in American foreign policy, and that it has further damaged America's image as a result.

How do you respond?

THE PRESIDENT. I would rather not respond. There's no reason for me to get into a public debate at this time with former Secretary Kissinger about who is or who is not responsible for the events that took place in Iran.

Obviously, what has occurred could not have been predicted. And for 30 years, our country has had a relationship with a fairly stable government there. The changes took place very rapidly. So far as I know, no one on Earth predicted them.

And I think it's not becoming at this moment and not conducive to better American understanding to get involved in answering allegations that I or someone else may have been culpable and may have caused a further aggravation of a very difficult situation.

Q. Mr. President, just one followup. What role did the former Secretary play in your decision to permit the Shah into the country?

THE PRESIDENT. None. I did not hear at all from the Secretary, former Secretary Kissinger, nor did he contact Secretary Vance at any time during the days when we were deciding that the Shah should come into the United States for medical care to save his life. In previous weeks and months since the Shah was deposed, Secretary Kissinger and many others let it be known that they thought that we should provide a haven for the Shah. But Secretary Kissinger played no role in my decision to permit the Shah to come in for medical treatment.

SHAH OF IRAN

Q. Mr. President, speaking of the Shah, if he is well enough to travel, would you like him to leave the country?

THE PRESIDENT. That's a decision to be made by the Shah and by his medical advisers. When he decided to come to our country, with my permission, I was informed then, and I have been informed since, that as soon as his medical treatment was successfully completed, that his intention was to leave. And I have not encouraged him to leave. He was free to come here for medical treatment, and he will leave on his own volition.

U.S. RELATIONS WITH ISLAMIC NATIONS

Q. Mr. President, yes, I would like to follow up Mr. Schorr's [Daniel Schorr, Des Moines Register] question. The consequences of the crisis in Iran is drifting the United States into almost a cold war with the Islamic countries. Watching TV news for 25 days, Americans soon will believe the whole Moslem world is hating them. Moreover, they are not told that the Shiites are a very minor minority among the population of the Islamic world, because the most majority is Sunni. Don't you think you get any help from any Islamic country, and what will your policy be towards the Islamic countries under these circumstances?

THE PRESIDENT. Well, the premise of your question is completely wrong. We're not approaching any sort of cold war with the Islamic countries. So far as I know, every Islamic country has condemned Iran for its capture of our hostages, and has been very supportive. This includes Moslem nations which, in the past, have not been close friends of ours—Iraq, Libya, and others. So, I don't see this as confrontation at all between our Nation and the Islamic world.

It's certainly not part of the Islamic faith to condone, as I said earlier, blackmail or the persecution or harm of innocent people or kidnaping or terrororism.

So, I think that we have a very good relationship with the people and the governments of the Islamic world, and I don't think it's deteriorated in this instance. In some ways, we've been drawn closer to these people, because they see what has occurred in Iran as something of a disgrace for their own religious faith, and they don't see this as typical of what Moslems believe.

I might add, also, that this is not typical of the Shiite faith, either. It's the misguided actions of a few people in Iran who are burning with hatred and a desire for revenge, completely contrary to the teachings of the Moslem faith.

U.S. REACTION TO IRANIAN SITUATION

Q. Mr. President, there's a feeling of hostility throughout the country toward Iran, because of the hostages. Senator Long said that the taking of our Embassy in Iran, in his words, is an act of war. There are rumors, since denied, that our Navy has been called up for service. I ask you, as our Commander in Chief, is war possible, is war thinkable?

THE PRESIDENT. It would be a mistake for the people of our country to have aroused within them hatred toward anyone; not against the people of Iran, and certainly not against Iranians who may be in our country as our guests. We certainly do not want to be guilty of the same violation of human decency and basic human principles that have proven so embarrassing to many of the Iranian citizens themselves.

We obviously prefer to see our hostages protected and released completely through peaceful means. And that's my deepest commitment, and that will be my goal. The United States has other options available to it, which will be considered, depending upon the circumstances. But I think it would not be well-advised for me to speak of those specifically tonight.

IRANIAN STUDENTS IN THE UNITED STATES

Q. Mr. President, we have had 55,000 Iranian students in this country. We've been very good to them, very hospitable. Even the new Finance Minister of Saudi Arabia was a student who once demonstrated in Washington against law and order. Shouldn't we be very careful in letting any of these students come in here? Shouldn't we screen them in the future and make them agree that they will not demonstrate?

THE PRESIDENT. Well, it's very difficult for an Iranian citizen or a student to get a visa at the American Embassy in Iran at this time [*Laughter*] And I think the influx of Iranians to our country now would be minimal.

I'm determined to enforce the law about Iranian students. Some of them have violated the law. They are now being screened; they are being assessed in their commitment and the legality of their presence here. We have already finished this procedure with more than 22,000. About 17,000 have proven to be here completely legally and are indeed full-time students. Among the other 5,000, about several hundred have already departed; others are now having to prove that, contrary to the earliest evidence, they do indeed have a right to be in our country. If they are here illegally, they will be expelled.

There is one exception to that rule: If a citizen of Iran can prove that if he or she returned to Iran that they would be executed or abused because of their political beliefs, they can seek asylum here. And if that asylum, in our judgment, is justified, we will provide it for them.

But this procedure is going forward in accordance with American law, in accordance with American fairness, in accordance with the full principles of the United States Constitution.

DEADLINE FOR RELEASING AMERICAN
HOSTAGES

Q. Mr. President, can this crisis go on indefinitely, or ought the Ayatollah Khomeini understand that at some point the American people may demand and other nations may expect that you move forward to resolve it by whatever means you find necessary?

THE PRESIDENT. It would not be possible or even advisable for me to set a deadline about when or if I would take certain action in the future. This is an ever-present consideration on my mind. I'm carrying out all of the duties that normally fall on a President's shoulder, which are adequate, but I never forget one moment that I'm awake about the hostages whose lives and whose safety depend on me. And I am pursuing every possible avenue to have the hostages released.

Any excessive threats or any excessive belief among the Iranians that they will be severely damaged by military action, as long as these negotiations are proceeding and as long as legalities can be followed, might cause the death of the hostages, which we are committed to avoid. So, that's one of the questions that I cannot answer: to set down a certain deadline beyond which we would take extra action, that might result in the harm or the death of the hostages.

We are proceeding, I guarantee you, in every possible way, every possible moment, to get the hostages freed and, at the same time, protect the honor and the integrity and the basic principles of our country. That's all I can do, but I am doing it to the best of my ability, and I believe we will be successful.

U.S. STRENGTH ABROAD

Q. Mr. President, many Americans view the Iranian situation as one in a succession of events that proves that this country's power is declining. How can you assure Americans tonight that our power is not declining abroad, and how are you reassessing priorities for the eighties in terms of foreign policy?

THE PRESIDENT. The United States has neither the ability nor the will to dominate the world, to interfere in the internal affairs of other nations, to impose our will on other people whom we desire to be free, to make their own decisions. This is not part of the commitment of the United States.

Our country is the strongest on Earth. We're the strongest militarily, politically, economically, and I think we're the strongest morally and ethically. Our country has made great strides, even since I've been in office. I've tried to correct some of the defects that did exist. We have strengthened the military alliances of our country, for instance. NATO now has a new spirit, a new confidence, a new cohesion, improving its military capabilities, much more able to withstand any threat from the east, from the Soviet Union or the Warsaw Pact, than it was before.

We've espoused again the principles that unite Americans and make us admired throughout the world, raising the banner of human rights. We're going to keep it high. We have opened up avenues of communication, understanding, trade, with people that formerly were our enemies or excluded us—several nations in Africa, the vast people and the vast country of the People's Republic of China. In doing so, we've not alienated any of our previous friends.

I think our country is strong within itself. There is not an embarrassment now about our Government, which did exist in a few instances in years gone by. So, I don't see at all that our country has become weak. We are strong, and we are getting stronger, not weaker. But if anybody thinks that we can dominate other people with our strength, military or political strength or economic strength, they are wrong. That's not the purpose of our country.

Our inner strength, our confidence in ourselves, I think, is completely adequate. And I believe the unity that the American people have shown in this instance, their patience, is not at all a sign of weakness. It is a sign of sure strength.

INVESTIGATION OF THE SHAH

Q. Mr. President, serious charges have been placed against the Shah concerning the repression of his own people and the misappropriation of his nation's funds. Is there an appropriate vehicle to investigate those charges, and do you foresee a time when you would direct your administration to assist in that investigation?

THE PRESIDENT. I don't know of any international forum within which charges have ever been brought against a deposed leader who has left his country. There have been instances of changing governments down through the centuries in history, and I don't know of any instance where such a leader, who left his country after his government fell, has been tried in an international court or in an international forum.

This is a matter that can be pursued. It should be pursued under international law, and if there is a claim against the Shah's financial holdings, there is nothing to prevent other parties from going into the courts, in accordance with the law of a nation or internationally, and seeking a redress of grievances which they claim.

But as I said earlier, I don't think there's any forum that will listen to the Iranians make any sort of claim, justified or not, as long as they hold against their will and abuse the hostages, in complete contravention to every international law and every precept or every commitment or principle of humankind.

BROOKS JACKSON [Associated Press]. Thank you, Mr. President.

THE PRESIDENT. Thank you very much.

NOTE: President Carter's fifty-third news conference began at 9 p.m. in the East Room at the White House. It was broadcast live on radio and television.

Crude Oil Transportation System

Letter to the Speaker of the House and the President of the Senate. November 29, 1979

Dear Mr. Speaker: (Dear Mr. President:)

I am writing you concerning my decision on a west-to-east crude oil transportation system under Title V of the Public Utility Regulatory Policies Act of 1978 (Public Law 95–617).

Title V of PURPA provided for the submission of proposals for the construction of a west-to-east crude oil transportation system. It directed the Secretary of the Interior, after consultation with heads of appropriate Federal agencies, to establish an expedited schedule for conducting reviews and making recommendations concerning the submitted proposals. It required that the Interior Secretary secure recommendations from other Federal agencies and comments from State and local governments and the general public. He was then directed to prepare a report containing those recommendations and comments, together with his own recommendations, and submit it to the President. On October 15, 1979, Secretary Andrus submitted his report and recommendations to me.

Section 507(a) of Title V directs the President to issue his decision concerning the proposals within 45 days after receipt of the report, or within 60 days thereafter if he determines, and so notifies the Congress, that additional time is necessary. Pursuant to that section, by this letter I am notifying you of my determination that additional time will be required to permit thorough consideration of the Secretary's recommendation, and of additional information on unresolved issues.

I will reach a decision expeditiously thereafter.

Sincerely,

JIMMY CARTER

NOTE: This is the text of identical letters addressed to Thomas P. O'Neill, Jr., Speaker of the House of Representatives, and Walter F. Mondale, President of the Senate.

Panama Canal

Executive Order 12173.   November 29, 1979

CONTINUING APPLICABILITY OF PANAMA CANAL REGULATIONS

By the authority vested in me as President of the United States of America by Section 301 of Title 3 of the United States Code, by the Panama Canal Code (76A Stat. 1), as amended, and by Public Law 96–70 (93 Stat. 452), and in accordance with the rights granted to the United States of America by the Panama Canal Treaty of 1977 "to manage, operate, and maintain the Panama Canal, its complementary works, installations and equipment and to provide for the orderly transit of vessels through the Panama Canal," it is hereby ordered as follows:

1–101. All regulations that were adopted by the President or his delegates pursuant to former Title 2 of the Canal Zone Code (76A Stat. 6–50), repealed by Section 303(a)(1) of Public Law 96–70, or actions taken pursuant thereto, that were in effect on September 30, 1979, and that address matters which the President is authorized to regulate pursuant to Public Law 96–70, shall remain in effect unless or until amended, superseded, or otherwise terminated by the President or the Panama Canal Commission. This extension shall not apply to the extent that any such regulation or action is inconsistent with the provisions of the Panama Canal Treaty of 1977, its implementing agreements, or Public Law 96–70.

1–102. The Secretary of Defense shall exercise the powers and carry out the responsibilities vested in the President of the United States by the Panama Canal Code (76A Stat. 1), as amended, and Public Law 96–70 (93 Stat. 452), except for those powers and responsibilities vested in the President by Sections 1102(b), 1103, 1104, 1105(a), 1106(b), 1108, 1109(a), 1112(d), 1243(a)(1), 1321(c), 1344(b), 1504(b), 1601(a), 2206(b) and 3301 of Public Law 96–70. This delegation shall be effective for 120 days after the date of this Order.

JIMMY CARTER

The White House,
    November 29, 1979.

[Filed with the Office of the Federal Register, 2:23 p.m., November 29, 1979]

Department of Justice

Nomination of Sanford M. Litvack To Be an Assistant Attorney General.
November 29, 1979

The President today announced that he will nominate Sanford M. Litvack, of Rockville Centre, N.Y., to be Assistant

Attorney General. He would replace John Shenefield, who has been appointed Associate Attorney General.

Litvack has practiced law with the New York City firm of Donovan, Leisure, Newton & Irvine since 1961 and has been a member of the firm since 1969.

He was born April 29, 1936, in Brooklyn, N.Y. He received a B.A. from the University of Connecticut in 1957 and an LL.B. from Georgetown Law Center in 1959.

From 1959 to 1961, Litvack was a trial attorney with the Justice Department's Antitrust Division.

Civil Aeronautics Board

Nomination of Marvin S. Cohen To Be a Member, and Redesignation as Chairman. November 29, 1979

The President today announced that he will nominate Marvin S. Cohen for reappointment as a member of the Civil Aeronautics Board, for a term expiring December 31, 1985.

The President intends to redesignate Cohen as Chairman of the CAB when his term as Chairman expires on December 31, 1979.

Federal Paperwork Reduction

Remarks on Signing Executive Order 12174. November 30, 1979

THE PRESIDENT. Ever since I've been involved in public life, in the minds of many Americans, government—particularly the Federal Government—and redtape have been synonymous phrases.

In my first Cabinet meeting here after I was inaugurated President, the first item of business that I brought up was my determination to eliminate redtape and paperwork from the Federal Government. I've been in office now almost 3 years, and with the help of these Members of Congress behind me and executive agencies, we've had a substantial degree of success.

We have been able to reduce the total number of hours devoted to Federal paperwork by 15 percent, which is a substantial achievement. This amounts to 130 million hours of filling out paperwork each year. That's as though every person in Dubuque, Iowa, to take a typical State—[*laughter*]—was working 40 hours a week the whole year. That's how much paperwork we've already eliminated. That's 15 percent, but we've still got a long way to go.

And I'm very deeply grateful to the men standing behind me, particularly Senator Chiles, who's in the forefront this year, Congressman Brooks, and Congressman Frank Horton. Obviously, others have done a great deal of work, including Senator Nelson and others.

A while back Frank Horton delivered to me the result of a long study of paperwork elimination. It consisted of several hundred recommendations. We have already implemented, Frank, more than half those recommendations, and we're working on the implementation of the others.

Today, I'm going to sign an Executive order that will go as far as I can legally go in reducing paperwork further. This sets a definite limit, or paperwork budget, that cannot be exceeded by any one of the Federal agencies without my direct approval; further, to reduce the amount of paperwork that they require either within Government or outside of the Federal Government.

Secondly, I'm eliminating every degree of interagency duplication. Quite often the same data from an American citizen are required by more than one Federal agency, and their sharing of information when it comes in can greatly eliminate or reduce the amount of paperwork involved. If forms and reports are necessary—and many of them are—we're trying to reduce the number of forms required, to cut down on the length of those particular forms, and also to reduce the frequency with which reports and other data have to be submitted to the Federal Government.

In addition, we're implementing sunset provisions so that after a certain period of time, the paperwork required is automatically eliminated, unless it's reassessed by the Federal agencies and determined still to be of urgent need for the carrying out of the Government's business. Quite often, once a form or report or request is initiated into a requirement, it perpetuates itself long past the time when it's no longer needed.

Under the sponsorship of these men behind me, there has already been introduced the paperwork and redtape reduction act of 1979. I strongly support that legislation and will be working with these leaders to get it implemented. It will put real legal teeth into additional steps that I cannot legally do now because I don't have the authority. But under their sponsorship, I'll have a new law with which I can work closely with the congressional leaders to reduce paperwork throughout the Federal Government.

And the last thing that I'd like to mention is that we are sending to the Congress today an administration proposal to reduce congressional reports that are required by the executive branch. This will either completely eliminate or substantially reduce 224 different reports that have been required by the executive branch of Government, by Congress, in

days gone by, years gone by, decades gone by. And these have now been assessed, and we believe that this number can be eliminated or drastically reduced or consolidated and eliminate a great deal of burden on the executive branch of Government and also the Congress.

As everybody knows, many of these reports are never looked at. Nobody ever sees them after they are evolved with tremendous input by the private sector of American economy, by local and State governments, and particularly by small business, where they are a very serious and onerous burden.

And we are doing everything we can to cut down redtape and paperwork, and I'm deeply grateful for the leadership that's been shown by the congressional representatives here this morning.

I'd like to ask Senator Chiles if he has a comment to make, and then following that, Chairman Brooks and, also, Chairman Frank Horton. Lawton, would you speak to——

SENATOR CHILES. Well, Mr. President, I think you're indicating your support of and your attack on paperwork as you did when you first came to this office, as you said, in your first Cabinet meeting. I think the ball is now in our court with the bill that we now have. And I think with your sponsorship and with the bipartisan group that we've put together in both the House and the Senate, we're going to be able to move that bill quickly.

I find the great problem is that I know we've made some progress, but as I go around my State, I can't find anybody that's felt that progress yet. They all are waiting to see when we're going to reduce it. And so, I think that it's something that we have to take additional steps. But I think that we've got the ball moving there, and with your help, we'll continue to move.

THE PRESIDENT. One of the things that I've done is to have in this same room all of the State school superintendents, for instance, and in a different meeting, I've had 18 or 20 representatives of the university system, and also mayors and Governors' representatives, to come in here and give me specific examples of what paperwork or reports or applications could be eliminated. And when they've done it, they've immediately gone to OMB, and we've cut them out. And we've made good progress so far.

Chairman Jack Brooks.

REPRESENTATIVE BROOKS. Thank you, Mr. President.

I would just like to commend you, Mr. President, for the results that you have already made in cutting down on the paperwork burdens and the results you've already achieved. And this is not a subject that's going to attract a lot of attention, and it won't help in the polls very much, but it's of tremendous importance to all the people, particularly the business community, because they're going to realize substantial benefits from what you're initiating today.

Now, I'm very pleased to say that the legislation that we're working on—that has been promoted substantially by Senator Chiles and others, and Frank Horton and myself, and your people; we're working on that legislation—I anticipate that it will be introduced this session, and we'll be ready to act on it the first of next year, very shortly after the beginning of the year.

With the legislation, with the Executive order in place, with the Government reorganizations and reforms that you have already put through, you will have clearly carried out your pledge to the American people to improve the efficiency of the Government, and I want to congratulate you on that achievement.

THE PRESIDENT. Thank you very much.

I might say that we've had remarkable success with our reorganization efforts under the leadership of these men here. I had the authority given to me early in my term to submit to the Congress reorganization plans, and so far, under the able leadership of Jack Brooks and Senator Ribicoff and Senator Nelson and others, we're batting a thousand, right? Haven't lost one yet.

Frank, would you like to say a word?

REPRESENTATIVE HORTON. Mr. President, speaking as the past Chairman of the Paperwork Commission, I'd just like to also add my congratulations to the administration for its determination and dedication to doing away with paperwork.

That was quite an interesting work that we did on the Paperwork Commission. I might say parenthetically, its life was 2 years. It self-destructed at the end of 2 years. And in October of 1977, I furnished to you the final report, which was right on time. In addition to finishing our work on time and not asking for an extension, we also turned back $1.4 million, which is also unheard of.

But as a result of what we suggested, some 60 percent of those recommendations have been carried out by the administration, and I'm sure, as a result of this Executive order, many more are going to be followed up on. The legislation that you referred to, that is sponsored in the House by Jack and myself and Tom Steed—who is also a member of the Commission and who's here with us today—that legislation will go a long way to carry out the legislative mandates that would have to be done in order to carry out the work of the Commission.

The other thing I'd like to say is that it's my feeling, in dealing with the people in my district, that they feel that there's what I call strangulation by regulation. And the manifestation of that strangulation is paperwork. And if we can do away with some of that paperwork, then they're going to be then aware of the fact that something is being done to eliminate that regulation.

Another thing is that Tom Steed, at our very first meeting, made the point that paperwork is like weeds: You can cut it down; it'll grow back. So, you've got to get to the root cause, and that's what this does and also what this legislation will do.

So, thanks a lot for your dedication, your personal interest in it, and making certain that this administration is carrying out the mandate. And I'll say that as a Republican, because I'm the one that gives it the bipartisan—[*laughter*]—like Tip O'Neill said when I gave him the report—he said, "How'd a Republican get to be Chairman of this Commission?" [*Laughter*]

THE PRESIDENT. Because of your good work.

I might say that it's a great pleasure for me to sign the Executive order now. Frank, this Executive order was originally five pages long. [*Laughter*] And it's now 2¼ pages long. So, we've already started on the good work.

[*At this point, the President signed the Executive order.*]

Well, that's a major step forward to getting redtape and paperwork burden off the shoulders of the American people, and I'm very grateful to all of you. Good luck to you.

One other point is—as a very important postscript—John Culver just said that our legislation that would provide for reduction in regulations, our deregulation legislation, is moving forward and they'll take a major stride, I think, next week.

John, thank you very much.

Thank you all.

NOTE: The President spoke at 10:53 a.m. in the Cabinet Room at the White House.

Federal Paperwork Reduction

Executive Order 12174.   November 30, 1979

PAPERWORK

By the authority vested in me as President by the Constitution and statutes of the United States of America, and in order to establish procedures that eliminate all paperwork burdens on the public above the minimum necessary to determine and implement public policy and ensure compliance with Federal laws, it is hereby ordered as follows:

1–101. Agencies shall minimize the paperwork burden—i.e., the time and costs entailed in complying with requests for information and recordkeeping requirements—imposed on persons outside the Federal government. Forms should be used only to the extent necessary to gather the basic information required to fulfill an agency's mission. When forms must be used, they should be as short as possible and should elicit information in a simple, straightforward fashion.

1–102. Each agency shall designate an existing official to be responsible for minimizing both the agency's use of forms and the paperwork burden resulting from proposed legislation and regulations.

1–103. Agencies shall pay particular attention to the special burdens faced by individuals and small organizations in responding to requests for information. To minimize these burdens agencies should, whenever possible, forego uniform or universal reporting requirements and rely instead on sampling, reduced frequency of reporting, differing compliance standards, or exemptions.

1–104. Each agency shall prepare an annual paperwork budget, i.e., an estimate of the total number of hours required to comply with requests for information. The budget should itemize each form used, describe its purpose and identify those affected by it. The Director of the Office of Management and Budget shall review and may modify each agency's proposed budget. After the Director has approved an agency's paperwork budget, it may be increased only by the Director upon request of the head of the agency.

1–105. Forms or similar requests for information shall be reviewed within two years after their initial issuance and then at least once every five years. Following review, they should be revised or abandoned to the extent they are not required to meet an agency's basic information needs. These reviews will be conducted by the agencies, and reports of the reviews will be submitted to the Director.

1–106. The Director shall audit compliance with this Order and may issue rules and regulations necessary to implement it. The Director may issue exemptions for agencies whose use of forms is limited. The Director also shall:

(a) Seek to eliminate duplication in requests for information by establishing a Federal information locator system, which will list all the types of information collected by Federal agencies and will be available for use by all agencies. This or similar systems will not contain any information obtained from the public. The Director shall take any other steps needed to prevent duplication, including the assignment to a particular agency of lead responsibility for the collection of certain types of information.

(b) Seek to inform the public and broaden public and agency comment by preparing and publishing in the FEDERAL REGISTER an annual paperwork calendar of significant requests for information. This calendar will be based on the information contained in the agencies' paperwork budgets.

(c) Report annually to the President on implementation of this Order and control of the paperwork burden generally.

1–107. The authority vested in the Director under this Order shall not affect any authority vested in him by any other Order. This Order shall be implemented in a manner consistent with all applicable Federal statutes.

1–108. For purposes of this Order, agency means those agencies covered by Executive Order 12044.

1–109. This Order will expire on September 30, 1983.

JIMMY CARTER

The White House,
   November 30, 1979.

[Filed with the Office of the Federal Register, 3:03 p.m., November 30, 1979]

Federal Paperwork Reduction

Message to the Congress.
November 30, 1979

To the Congress of the United States:

In the past two and one half years, my Administration has achieved real progress in cutting the paperwork burden government imposes on the public. Today I am announcing steps to expand and accelerate that effort.

I have today signed an Executive Order on paperwork reduction. I am also calling on the Congress to enact two bills which will help eliminate needless forms, cut duplication, streamline those forms which are necessary and strengthen central oversight of Federal paperwork.

Government efficiency is a central theme of my Administration. If we are to restore confidence in government, we must eliminate needless burdens on the public. We have pursued this goal through regulatory reform, civil service reform, reorganization, and other initiatives. Paperwork reduction is an important part of this program.

Some Federal paperwork is needed. The government must collect information to enforce the civil rights laws, compile economic statistics, design sound regulations, and for many other purposes. In recent years, however, government forms, surveys and interviews have mushroomed. Much of this paperwork is unnecessary or duplicates information being collected elsewhere.

My Administration has stopped the paperwork surge and started cutting this burden down to size. We have reduced the amount of time Americans spend filling out Federal forms by almost 15%— 127 million hours. That is the equivalent of 75,000 people working full-time for a year. We have evaluated the 520 recommendations of the Paperwork Commission and have already implemented more than half of them.

The Internal Revenue Service made it possible, for example, for five million taxpayers to switch from the long tax form to the short one. The Occupational Safety and Health Administration exempted 40,000 small businesses from reporting requirements. The Interstate Commerce Commission sliced a 70-page report required from 13,000 carriers down to 8 pages. The Labor and Treasury Departments slashed the paperwork burden that was crushing the small pension plans. I am today announcing that we are con-

solidating three reports required from the States on welfare and food stamp programs; this will eventually save 500,000 hours and $10 million per year.

The progress in cutting Federal paperwork has been substantial, but we must do more. Congress is enacting new requirements in energy, environmental protection, and other programs that will add to the paperwork burden. To continue our success in eliminating Federal paperwork, we need the broad management program I am announcing today.

The Executive Order I have signed establishes strong management tools for the Executive agencies. First of all, it creates a "paperwork budget." Each agency will submit an annual estimate of the numbers of hours required to fill out all its forms. The Office of Management and Budget will then hold agencies to that total or order it cut. The process will be similar to the spending budget; it will give agencies incentives to set priorities and to eliminate or streamline burdensome forms.

The Order creates a Federal Information Locator System, which will list all the types of information collected by Federal agencies. Before an agency collects information, it will check in this System to see if another agency already has the data.

The Order also requires agencies to consider the special paperwork problems of small organizations and small businesses. Data gathering that may be easy for a corporation with computerized records may be very costly for a small business person who keeps records by hand. Some reports must necessarily be universal and uniform, but in many cases agencies can meet their information needs while providing exemptions or less burdensome reports for small businesses. Some agencies already have started doing so. The Executive Order requires all agencies to review each form to identify those cases where small organizations can be exempted or given simpler forms. Senator John Culver deserves credit for leading the development of this concept of special consideration for small organizations.

Finally, the Order mandates a "sunset" process. This process will be similar to the legislation I am supporting to mandate sunset reviews for regulations, spending programs, and tax expenditures. The Paperwork Order requires that each form terminate every five years unless a new decision is made to continue it.

We also need legislation to build a complete paperwork control program and extend it to all agencies. Representatives Jack Brooks, Frank Horton, and Tom Steed and Senator Lawton Chiles have taken the lead in developing a Paperwork Reduction Act which will strengthen and unify existing paperwork oversight. The Federal Reports Act is insufficient in this regard. It gives OMB power to disapprove many agencies' forms, but the independent regulatory commissions are reviewed by the General Accounting Office and tax, education, and health manpower programs have no central review at all. These loopholes represent 81% of the total paperwork burden, of which tax forms are 73%.

This legislation will close these loopholes, providing central oversight for all forms. It also strengthens the paperwork clearance process by allowing members of the public to refuse to fill out forms that have not been properly cleared.

The legislation will provide additional tools to cut duplication in paperwork requirements. When several agencies want to collect overlapping data, the bill will empower the OMB to assign one agency to do the job. The bill will also deal with the special problems of statistical systems. One cause of duplication is that agencies collect statistical data under pledges of confidentiality, and these pledges hamper sharing the data. The bill will authorize such sharing while strengthening safeguards to ensure the data is used only for statistical purposes and never to abuse personal privacy. These provisions will also strengthen our Federal statistical systems, which are crucial to economic and other policymaking.

While controlling the paperwork imposed on the public, we must also hold down paperwork within the Government itself. I am therefore submitting to the Congress the Reports Elimination Act of 1979. This bill, together with administrative action we are taking now, will eliminate or simplify 278 annual agency reports, saving at least $5.5 million per year.

This overall paperwork reduction program has been developed in a cooperative effort with the leaders of the Senate Governmental Affairs and House Government Operations Committees. Working together, we will continue the progress on cutting away red tape.

I urge the Congress to act promptly on the two bills I have discussed.

JIMMY CARTER

The White House,
November 30, 1979.

Ambassador at Large and United States Coordinator for Refugee Affairs

Nomination of Victor Palmieri.
November 30, 1979

The President has asked me to say on his behalf that he intends to nominate

Victor Palmieri as Ambassador at Large, with special responsibilities for coordinating refugee affairs. Mr. Palmieri is one of the best managers in this country. He has made his reputation by solving large-scale, complicated problems in major organizational situations.

The President has selected him for this very important post, because the job of saving literally hundreds of thousands, perhaps millions of people, requires the best managerial skills that this Nation has to offer. Mr. Palmieri will have the President's full support in mobilizing every available resource of the Government and the private sector. Mr. Palmieri will be working closely with the First Lady, the Secretary of State, and the Secretary of Defense in carrying out the duties and responsibilities of this office.

NOTE: Press Secretary Jody Powell made the announcement at 11:32 a.m. to reporters assembled in the Briefing Room at the White House.

Following the announcement, the First Lady and Mr. Palmieri made brief remarks. Matthew Nimetz, Acting Coordinator for Refugee Affairs, Department of State, Ambassador Henry D. Owen, Special Representative of the President for International Economic Summits, and Lincoln Bloomfield, of the National Security Council staff, then answered reporters' questions. The press release also includes a transcript of those remarks and the question-and-answer session.

Law Enforcement Assistance Administration

Nomination of Ira M. Schwartz To Be Associate Administrator.   November 30, 1979

The President today announced that he will nominate Ira M. Schwartz, of Bellevue, Wash., to be Associate Administrator of Law Enforcement Assistance. He would replace John M. Rector, resigned.

Schwartz has been executive director of the Washington Council on Crime and Delinquency since 1977.

He was born November 1, 1944, in Minneapolis, Minn. He received a B.S. from the University of Minnesota in 1966 and an M.S.W. from the University of Washington in 1968.

From 1968 to 1969, Schwartz was senior planner in social services for the Minneapolis Department of Planning & Development. From 1969 to 1972, he was director of community services for the Hennepin County (Minnesota) Department of Court Services, and from 1969 to 1973, he was an instructor in the law enforcement program at North Hennepin State Junior College.

From 1972 to 1973, Schwartz was director of purchase services for the Hennepin County Welfare Department. From 1973 to 1977, he was executive director of the John Howard Association.

Department of Energy

Nomination of Leslie J. Goldman To Be an Assistant Secretary.   November 30, 1979

The President today announced that he will nominate Leslie J. Goldman, of Des Plaines, Ill., to be an Assistant Secretary of Energy. He would replace Harry Bergold, resigned, and his area of responsibility would be international affairs.

Goldman has been principal Deputy Assistant Secretary of Energy for International Affairs since earlier this year.

He was born April 22, 1945, in Chicago, Ill. He received a B.A. from the University of Michigan in 1967 and an LL.B. from the University of Michigan Law School in 1970.

From 1970 to 1977, Goldman was special counsel to Senator Adlai E. Stevenson. In 1977 he served as counsel to Special Assistant to the President James R. Schlesinger, then as Assistant Administrator for Energy Resource Development at the Federal Energy Administration. From October 1977 to September 1979, he was principal Deputy Assistant Secretary of Energy for Policy and Evaluation.

Department of Health, Education, and Welfare

Nomination of John A. Calhoun III To Be Chief of the Children's Bureau.
November 30, 1979

The President today announced that he will nominate John A. Calhoun III, of Belmont, Mass., to be Chief of the Children's Bureau at the Department of Health, Education, and Welfare. He would replace Blandina Cardenas Ramirez, who has resigned.

Calhoun is former commissioner of the Massachusetts Department of Youth Services, currently serving as an instructor at Harvard Graduate School of Education on a part-time basis.

He was born December 1, 1939, in Philadelphia, Pa. He received an A.B. from Brown University in 1962 and a Masters of Divinity from Episcopal Theological School in 1965.

From 1965 to 1966, Calhoun was an elementary schoolteacher in Philadelphia. From 1966 to 1970, he was with Action for Boston Community Development, where he served as director of the Job Corps, director of the New Careers program, director of the Summer Work and Cultural Enrichment programs, and director of the Manpower Program Development Department.

From 1970 to 1973, he was vice president of Technical Development Corp.,

where he worked on program development and administration in the field of corrections and technical assistance to various private and government agencies whose functions related to criminal justice. From 1971 to 1973, he was also director of the Court Resource Project.

From 1973 to 1976, Calhoun was executive director of the Justice Resource Institute, a nonprofit criminal justice reform agency which he helped found. He was commissioner of the Massachusetts Department of Youth Services from 1976 to 1979. He has been a part-time instructor at Harvard Graduate School of Education, teaching a course on "Delinquents, Schools and Families," since last August.

Calhoun has served as a consultant to numerous government and private agencies and is the author of a number of articles.

Conference on Security and Cooperation in Europe

Statement on a Report on United States Compliance With the Final Act.
November 30, 1979

My administration is deeply committed to the cause of human rights both here and abroad. As a means to promote respect for fundamental freedoms and the development of a more peaceful, stable world, the United States attaches great significance to the Final Act of the Conference on Security and Cooperation in Europe. This document, signed in 1975 at Helsinki by the leaders of 33 European nations, Canada, and the United States, pledges its signers to work toward lowering barriers and improving cooperation between East and West. Each nation made solemn promises to take steps to improve the lives of its citizens. These obligations required some adjustments in the foreign and domestic policies of all 35 nations.

I am extremely pleased that the U.S. Commission on Security and Cooperation in Europe has taken the lead in assessing U.S. implementation and identifying areas where American performance can be improved. The Commission's report, "Fulfilling Our Promises: The United States and the Helsinki Final Act"—released on November 8—is the first comprehensive review by any CSCE signatory which takes into account criticism from other Helsinki states as well as domestic observers.

CSCE signatory states which suppress human rights cannot in good conscience justify their record of compliance. But I believe our record of implementation has been second to none, even among the other democracies among the 35 participating states. American political history is testimony to the firm foundation of civil liberties enshrined in our own Constitution with its Bill of Rights, long before Helsinki.

As this report points out, our work is never complete. Our own traditions, reinforced by the Helsinki Final Act, pledge us to strive constantly for improvement in both domestic, civil, and economic rights, and in the expanded cooperation with other participating states. This report should go far to persuade other CSCE governments that the United States is serious about its obligations under the Helsinki accords.

I also hope that it will stimulate other Helsinki countries to undertake similar public assessments of their performance. Implementation of the Final Act is critical to peace and security in Europe and for our own Nation. We cannot permit the Helsinki agreement to become meaningless words on parchment. We must bring it to life, and I believe the CSCE

Commission has made a major contribution to that end.

Department of Transportation and Related Agencies Appropriation Act, 1980

Statement on Signing H.R. 4440 Into Law. November 30, 1979

This bill, H.R. 4440, includes funding for the Interstate Commerce Commission. The ICC's regulation of trucking and railroads is a top item on the regulatory reform agenda for 1980. I have submitted far-reaching bills to Congress to cut away the regulations that overburden these industries. The Commission itself has launched administrative reform actions.

Chairman Howard Cannon of the Senate Commerce, Science and Transportation Committee and Harold Johnson and Jim Howard of the House Public Works and Transportation Committee recently announced that they intend to seek passage of trucking reform legislation by June 1, 1980. Therefore, they and their colleagues who wrote this appropriation bill have asked the ICC to continue building a record of reforms but not to implement any major policy changes before that date. The regulatory reform we need should best come through legislation, and I applaud the chairmen's determination to press forward. If, of course, appropriate legislation is not enacted, I would expect the Commission to proceed with all powers to implement reform initiatives.

As to rail reform, I congratulate Chairmen Cannon and Russell Long of the Senate Commerce Committee and Harley Staggers and James Florio of the House Interstate and Foreign Commerce Committee for moving legislation this session. I hope that the Congress will resist pressure to weaken this measure by exempting specific commodities from the reforms. We cannot afford to accept only cosmetic change in rail regulation.

The existing trucking and railroad regulatory structures restrict competition, reduce efficiency, and increase costs. It is time for action, and I urge the Congress to pass meaningful trucking and railroad deregulation legislation.

NOTE: As enacted, H.R. 4440 is Public Law 96–131, approved November 30.

Digest of Other White House Announcements

The following listing includes the President's public schedule and other items of general interest announced by the White House Press Office and not included elsewhere in this issue.

November 25

The President returned to the White House from Camp David, Md.

November 26

The President met at the White House with:
—Zbigniew Brzezinski, Assistant to the President for National Security Affairs;
—Frank B. Moore, Assistant to the President for Congressional Liaison;
—Vice President Walter F. Mondale.

November 27

The President met at the White House with:
—Dr. Brzezinski;
—the Democratic congressional leadership;
—Mr. Moore;
—Stansfield Turner, Director of Central Intelligence, and Dr. Brzezinski;
—Mrs. Carter, for lunch.

In a ceremony in the Oval Office, the President was presented with an award by representatives of Outdoor Life magazine for his activities on behalf of conservation.

The President participated in a briefing on the administration's programs and policies given for civic and community leaders from Vermont, Maine, and New Hampshire in the East Room at the White House.

The White House announced that the President has canceled his trip to Seattle, Wash., and Portland, Oreg. The President regrets that the continuing situation in Iran requires the cancellation of the trip.

November 28

The President met at the White House with:
—Dr. Brzezinski;
—Representatives Jack Brooks of Texas and L. H. Fountain of North Carolina;
—Mr. Moore;
—James T. McIntyre, Jr., Director of the Office of Management and Budget.

The President transmitted to the Congress and to the Comptroller General copies of the reports issued by the United Nations Joint Inspection Unit during the first half of 1979.

The White House announced that Army Aide to the President, Maj. Jose A. Muratti, Jr., will represent the President at memorial services for Marine Corporal Steven J. Crowley, in Port Jefferson, New York. Corporal Crowley was killed during an attack on the American Embassy in Pakistan.

November 29

The President met at the White House with:
—Dr. Brzezinski;
—Vice President Mondale, Secretary of Health, Education, and Welfare

Patricia R. Harris, Secretary of Housing and Urban Development Moon Landrieu, Secretary of Labor Ray Marshall, Secretary of Transportation Neil Goldschmidt, Charles L. Schultze, Chairman of the Council of Economic Advisers, Jack H. Watson, Jr., Assistant to the President for Intergovernmental Affairs, Stuart E. Eizenstat, Assistant to the President for Domestic Affairs and Policy, Alonzo L. McDonald, Jr., Assistant to the President, and Mr. McIntyre, to discuss domestic policies;

—Mr. Moore;

—Mr. McIntyre and other administration officials to review the fiscal year 1981 budget;

—Mayor-elect Bill Green of Philadelphia, Pa.

The President participated in a briefing by administration officials on the strategic arms limitation treaty given for community leaders from Iowa, Indiana, and Michigan in the East Room at the White House.

The President has designated John A. Knauss as Vice Chairman of the National Advisory Committee on Oceans and Atmosphere (NACOA). Knauss has been a member of NACOA since 1978. He is dean of the Graduate School of Oceanography at the University of Rhode Island.

The President has accorded John W. McDonald, Jr., the personal rank of Ambassador while he serves as United States Representative to the Third General Conference of the United Nations Industrial Development Organization (UNIDO). The conference is to be held in New Delhi, India, from January 20 to February 8, 1980.

November 30

The President met at the White House with:

—Dr. Brzezinski;

—Vice President Mondale, Secretary of State Cyrus R. Vance, Secretary of Defense Harold Brown, Hamilton Jordan, Assistant to the President, Hedley W. Donovan, Senior Adviser to the President, and Dr. Brzezinski;

—a group of mayors and county officials to discuss the fiscal year 1981 budget;

—Mr. Moore;

—Representative Charles B. Rangel of New York and a delegation from his congressional district.

The President attended the funeral mass at Arlington National Cemetery for Cpl. Steven J. Crowley.

The President transmitted to the Congress the Aggregate Report on Personnel for fiscal year 1979.

The President left the White House for a weekend stay at Camp David.

NOMINATIONS SUBMITTED TO THE SENATE

The following list does not include promotions of members of the Uniformed Services, nominations to the Service Academies, or nominations of Foreign Service officers.

Submitted November 26, 1979

CHARLES B. RENFREW, of California, to be Deputy Attorney General, vice Benjamin R. Civiletti.

Submitted November 27, 1979

J. JACKSON WALTER, of Florida, to be Director of the Office of Government Ethics (new position).

GEORGE W. CUNNINGHAM, of Tennessee, to be an Assistant Secretary of Energy (Nuclear Energy), vice Phillip Samuel Hughes, resigned.

SOL M. LINOWITZ, of the District of Columbia, for the rank of Ambassador during the tenure of his service as Personal Representative of the President of the United States of America.

NOMINATIONS—Continued

Submitted November 28, 1979

Togo D. West, Jr., of the District of Columbia, to be General Counsel to the Department of Defense, vice Deanne C. Siemer, resigned.

William A. Lubbers, of Maryland, to be General Counsel of the National Labor Relations Board for a term of 4 years, vice John Stiles Irving, Jr., resigned.

The following-named persons to be members of the United States International Trade Commission for the terms indicated:

For the remainder of the term expiring June 16, 1980

Robert E. Baldwin, of Wisconsin, vice Italo H. Ablondi, resigned.

For the term expiring December 16, 1988

Michael J. Calhoun, of the District of Columbia, vice Joseph O. Parker, term expiring.

Withdrawn November 30, 1979

Robert E. Baldwin, of Wisconsin, to be a member of the United States International Trade Commission for the remainder of the term expiring June 16, 1980, vice Italo H. Ablondi, resigned, which was sent to the Senate on November 28, 1979.

Submitted November 30, 1979

Sanford M. Litvack, of New York, to be an Assistant Attorney General, vice John H. Shenefield, resigning.

Richard Alan Enslen, of Michigan, to be United States District Judge for the Western District of Michigan, vice Noel P. Fox, retired.

Diana E. Murphy, of Minnesota, to be United States District Judge for the District of Minnesota, vice a new position created by P.L. 95–486, approved October 20, 1978.

Robert G. Renner, of Minnesota, to be United States District Judge for the District of Minnesota, vice a new position created by P.L. 95–486, approved October 20, 1978.

Gilberto Gierbolini-Ortiz, of Puerto Rico, to be United States District Judge for the District of Puerto Rico, vice a new position created by P.L. 95–486, approved October 20, 1978.

William Matthew Kidd, of West Virginia, to be United States District Judge for the

NOMINATIONS—Continued

Submitted November 30—Continued

Southern District of West Virginia, vice a new position created by P.L. 95–486, approved October 20, 1978.

Marvin S. Cohen, of Arizona, to be a member of the Civil Aeronautics Board for the term of 6 years expiring December 31, 1985 (reappointment).

Robert E. Baldwin, of Wisconsin, to be a member of the United States International Trade Commission for the remainder of the term expiring June 16, 1981, vice Italo H. Ablondi, resigned.

Stephen R. Reinhardt, of California, to be United States Circuit Judge for the Ninth Circuit, vice a new position created by P.L. 95–486, approved October 20, 1978.

CHECKLIST OF WHITE HOUSE PRESS RELEASES

The following listing contains releases of the White House Press Office which are not included in this issue.

Released November 27, 1979

News conference: on the low-income energy assistance programs provided for in the Department of the Interior appropriations bill (P.L. 96–126)—by Secretary of Health, Education, and Welfare Patricia R. Harris and Stuart E. Eizenstat, Assistant to the President for Domestic Affairs and Policy

Released November 28, 1979

Advance text: opening statement at the President's news conference

Released November 29, 1979

Announcement: nomination of Richard Alan Enslen to be United States District Judge for the Western District of Michigan

Announcement: nomination of William M. Kidd to be United States District Judge for the Southern District of West Virginia

Announcement: nomination of Diana E. Murphy to be United States District Judge for the District of Minnesota

CHECKLIST—Continued

Released November 29—Continued

Announcement: nomination of Gilberto Gier-bolini-Ortiz to be United States District Judge for the District of Puerto Rico

Announcement: nomination of Stephen R. Reinhardt to be United States Circuit Judge for the Ninth Circuit

Announcement: nomination of Robert G. Renner to be United States District Judge for the District of Minnesota

Released November 30, 1979

Fact sheet: Federal paperwork reduction

News conference: on Federal paperwork reduction—by Wayne E. Granquist, Associate Director of the Office of Management and Budget for Management and Regulatory Policy

Biographical data: Victor Palmieri, nominated to be Ambassador at Large and United States Coordinator for Refugee Affairs

---

ACTS APPROVED BY THE PRESIDENT

Approved November 26, 1979

S. 1319_____ Public Law 96–125
Military Construction Authorization Act, 1980.

ACTS APPROVED—Continued

Approved November 27, 1979

H.R. 4930_____ Public Law 96–126
An act making appropriations for the Department of the Interior and related agencies for the fiscal year ending September 30, 1980, and for other purposes.

Approved November 28, 1979

H.R. 4167_____ Public Law 96–127
An act to amend section 201 of the Agricultural Act of 1949, as amended, to extend until September 30, 1981, the requirement that the price of milk be supported at not less than 80 per centum of the parity price therefor.

H.R. 2282_____ Public Law 96–128
Veterans' Disability Compensation and Survivors' Benefits Amendments of 1979.

Approved November 30, 1979

S. 411_____ Public Law 96–129
Pipeline Safety Act of 1979.

H.R. 4391_____ Public Law 96–130
Military Construction Appropriation Act, 1980.

H.R. 4440_____ Public Law 96–131
Department of Transportation and Related Agencies Appropriation Act, 1980.

S. 1157_____ Public Law 96–132
Department of Justice Appropriation Authorization Act, Fiscal Year 1980.

S. 1871_____ Public Law 96–133
An act to amend the Energy Policy and Conservation Act to extend certain authorities relating to the international energy program, and for other purposes.

PRESIDENTIAL DOCUMENTS

Week Ending Friday, December 7, 1979

Shah of Iran

White House Statement. December 2, 1979

The doctors at Cornell medical facility have told the Shah that he is able to leave the hospital in New York. They have indicated the Shah should not undertake a prolonged trip and that he needs a period of recuperation under medical supervision.

The United States Government has agreed for humanitarian reasons to provide a secure convalescent facility where he can recuperate pending further travel plans. The Shah is en route to Wilford Hall Air Force Hospital near San Antonio, Tex. At the Shah's request, the United States is continuing to assist in making arrangements for a permanent place of residence.

Architectural and Transportation Barriers Compliance Board

Appointment of 11 Members and Designation of Chairman. December 4, 1979

The President today announced the appointment of 11 persons as members of the Architectural and Transportation Barriers Compliance Board. They are:

PATRICK C. CASEY, of Taylor, Mich., a self-employed attorney;

DAVID F. CRUZ VELEZ, of Santurce, P.R., director of the Office of the Advisor of the Governor on the Comprehensive Development of the Handicapped;

CAROL A. GRANT, a rehabilitation counselor with the North Carolina Division of Vocational Rehabilitation and a former member of the North Carolina Governor's Study Committee on Architectural Barriers;

PAUL MULDAWER, of Atlanta, Ga., an award-winning architect and urban designer and member of HEW's National Advisory Committee on an Accessible Environment of the Architectural and Transportation Barriers Compliance Board;

KAY E. NEIL, of Omaha, Nebr., a retired businesswoman, former chairman of the Omaha Mayor's Advisory Committee on the Handicapped and the Nebraska Governor's Committee on the Employment of the Handicapped, now a member of the statewide Health Coordinating Council and honorary chairman of the Employment Advisory Council for the Handicapped;

WILLIAM A. PASSMORE, of Chicago, Ill., a job developer with the East Chicago Federal Programs Office, who was named Handicapped American of the Year in 1968 and is active in community affairs;

WILLIAM R. RALLS, of Okemos, Mich., an attorney and former chairman of the Michigan Rail Action Association;

WALTER H. RICHTER, director of government relations for Texas Electric Cooperatives, a former Texas State senator, and active in civic affairs;

MASON H. ROSE V, a city councilman and attorney in Rolling Hills, Calif., Chairman of the National Advisory Committee of the Architectural and Transportation Barriers Compliance Board;

ROBERT G. SAMPSON, of Arlington Heights, Ill., vice president and special assistant to the president of United Airlines, Inc., a member of People to People International Committee for the Handicapped and its affiliate, Disabled Professionals;

HALE J. ZUKAS, coordinator for community affairs and cofounder of the Center for Independent Living in Berkeley, Calif., an organization working with the disabled community there.

The President also announced the designation of Veterans Affairs Administrator Max Cleland as Chairman of this Board.

1980 Democratic Presidential Nomination

Remarks Announcing Candidacy. December 4, 1979

I speak to you this afternoon at a somber time. Fifty Americans continue to be held captive in Iran, hostages of a mob and a government that have become one and the same. This crisis, precipitated by this unlawful and unprecedented act, has demanded my closest attention since the first moment that it began.

But the process of democratic self-government is the heart of our liberties and our strength, and it must go forward. Every 4 years, in good times and in bad, in times of peace and in times of war, in times of crisis and in times of calm, the American people elect a President. So it has been since 1789, and so it will be in 1980.

For the last month, I have curtailed my political activities, and I would have preferred to postpone this announcement until a later time. However, election laws in certain States require formal declarations of candidacy within the next few days.

Therefore, I formally declare that I am a candidate for reelection as President of the United States of America.

I intend to be renominated by the Democratic Party, and I intend to ask the Democratic Convention to renominate the most effective Vice President in the history of the United States—Walter Mondale. We intend to lead the Democratic Party to victory next year, and we also intend to lead the Nation in continuing the good work which all of us have begun together.

As President, I have had to make some very difficult decisions, and I expect to make some more. I've made some mistakes, and I have learned from them. I've fought some bitter fights against selfish special interests, and I expect to go on leading the fight for the common good of the American people. I carry some scars, and I carry them with pride.

I also carry the knowledge, strengthened by my own experience in this office, that the greatness of our Nation and the goodness of the American people will prevail. We've set a firm and constructive course for the history of our people. It is a difficult course, but it's a right one and we must not turn aside.

The course of a great nation is not changed overnight. The problems we face are very difficult. There are no easy solutions, and I promise none. But there are solutions.

In the past 3 years, the United States has begun to move in a new and better direction. We are a strong nation. We are a nation at peace. We are enhancing our nation's security. We are improving social and economic justice, and we are leading the struggle for human rights throughout the world.

Our superb system of government and our great natural and human resources give us the strength and the flexibility to meet rapidly changing times. The world of the 1980's will be as different from the world of 1960 as 1960 was from the world of the 1930's. As we enter the next decade, the work that we've begun together will let us meet even the most serious challenges. What we do now will bring us safely and at an even better time of peace and security, if we have the determination to see it through and if we have the courage to continue making the hard decisions.

In these difficult times, our greatest single ally is the truth. As President and as a candidate, I will continue to ask you to join me in looking squarely at the truth. I will continue to talk sense to the American people. Only by facing up to the world as it is can we lift ourselves toward a better future. There is no such thing as cheap energy, and never will be; that is the truth. We cannot wish our way out of inflation; that is the truth. We cannot spend our way out of every problem; that is the truth. We cannot toss aside a generation's work, patient work in the control of nuclear power, nuclear explosives, nuclear bombs; and that is the truth. We cannot have peace without a strong defense; that is also the truth.

If we act together in the unifying spirit of our deep and unchanging values, we can triumph together, and that is the most important truth of all.

With the support of the American people, I propose to carry on the struggle

for a secure nation, for a just society, and for a peaceful world—and I intend to carry on this struggle as President of the United States.

Thank you very much.

NOTE: The President spoke at 2:32 p.m. in the East Room at the White House to members of the President's family, the Cabinet, the White House and Carter/Mondale Presidential Committee staffs, and campaign volunteers.

1980 Democratic Presidential Nomination

Remarks Concerning Candidacy and Campaign Plans.   December 2, 1979

Good evening.

Today I announced my candidacy for reelection, and so I speak to you tonight as President of the United States of America and also as a candidate. This is a paid political statement, but it is not a campaign speech.

Our American political system—one of the great miracles in the history of civilized human activity—runs on a schedule. My announcement could not be postponed. In just a few days, those who would enter early State primary contests must file as candidates, and then those of us who run for President must stand before the people for election.

During the campaign, we will take our record to you—what we have done in the past and what we propose for our Nation's future. We will be talking about a nation strong and at peace, about our demonstrated willingness to face tough problems with courage, about jobs provided for our people, and about restoring a sense of trust and confidence in our own Government.

With calm, strong, and effective leadership, with a prosperous and expanding economy, with inflation and energy shortages behind us, with people believing again, we can set our course for the kind of future about which we have all dreamed. I will discuss these themes with you, and I will do it effectively, but I will not do it tonight.

I was scheduled tomorrow to begin a week-long political tour to set the tone of the reelection campaign for 1980. It was also, to be frank about it, a money-raising trip. While there are certain clear advantages to campaigning as President, they are symbolic and historic rather than financial. The President, like all other candidates, needs campaign contributions.

My campaign travels must be, for a time, postponed. I must remain here, near the White House, because of the situation in Iran. While the crisis continues, I must be present to define and to lead our response to an ever-changing situation of the greatest sensitivity and importance.

I am proud—but not surprised—at the quiet unity of the American people over the past 4 weeks as we have faced this outrageous situation together. Not since Pearl Harbor, some 40 years ago, have we felt such a nationwide surge of determination and mutual purpose. But I must warn you that this crisis may not be resolved easily or quickly. It is possible that in the days ahead, our patience and sense of unity may waver as frustration builds up among us. I am determined to do everything I can to have the hostages released as soon as possible.

At the height of the Civil War, President Abraham Lincoln said, "I have but one task, and that is to save the Union."

Now I must devote my concerted efforts to resolving the Iranian crisis. The overriding fact is that 50 of our fellow Americans have been unjustifiably thrust into agony and danger, and I have a personal responsibility to get them out of that danger as fast as possible.

During this crisis I will, of course, continue to perform the many other tasks that are part of my job as President. And though I cannot yet campaign, myself, we will carry out our campaign duties as best we can under the circumstances. Vice President Mondale, my wife, Rosalynn, and members of my family, and other friends and supporters across the Nation will have to replace me until I can be on the campaign trail myself. Until then, I need your understanding, your help, and your support.

Thank you, and good night.

NOTE: The President's remarks were videotaped on December 2 in the Map Room at the White House for broadcast on December 4 on the CBS television network. Time for the broadcast was purchased by the Carter/Mondale Presidential Committee.

As printed above, the item follows the transcript of the remarks, which was released on December 4.

American Hostages in Iran

Remarks by the Vice President on the Treatment of the Hostages. December 5, 1979

Over the past several weeks, we have been hearing a drumfire of propaganda out of Tehran, some of it from people calling themselves students, some of it from the government-controlled radio and television in Iran, and some of it from various officials or people in authority. The message is very clear. It says over and over that the world and the American people should ignore the hostages, forget about the innocent people bound hand and foot, overlook the continued outrage to law and standards of human behavior. We are told to forget all that and focus on the hatred of one man. We are not going to forget, and the American people are not going to get their priorities confused.

How are our hostages being treated? The facts are there for all to see, and the simple fact is that 50 human beings are being held at inhuman conditions, contrary to all civilized standards, in order to prove a political point. They are not permitted regular visitors. They are isolated and not allowed to speak, except to their captors. As far as we know, the hostages have not been allowed to receive mail or messages. There has never been a systematic accounting of the numbers and welfare of the hostages.

The so-called students have not permitted any outside observers even to see these people for 10 days. They are refusing to let international organizations, such as the Red Cross, into the compound. They refuse visits by religious organizations. They refuse representatives of neutral states. Even prisoners of war are guaranteed certain standards of human treatment. But these standards are being dragged in the dirt every day by a group of kidnapers, with the acquiescence of the government.

We are hearing daily propaganda about the alleged crimes of our people in Tehran, most of whom volunteered to serve their country at a difficult and dangerous time. We are not and will not respond to that propaganda.

I would note that one of those being held as a so-called spy in Tehran is, in fact, a private American citizen who simply happened to be visiting the Embassy on business at the time of the attack on November 4. It was many days before we even learned, indirectly, that he was being held. That man, like the rest, has now been held for 31 days—tied up, denied contact with his family, denied exercise, denied access even to the comfort of religion.

We hear a great deal about the crimes of the Shah, but that is not the issue. The issue which disturbs the American people is that 50 of our fellow citizens are being abused, in violation of international law. These are our brothers and sisters.

Yesterday, the United Nations Security Council passed a resolution which called—as the first most important priority, as it should—for the release of the American hostages. That is the issue. It is the only issue, and we're not going to forget they must be set free.

NOTE: The Vice President spoke at 12:01 p.m. to reporters assembled in the Briefing Room at the White House.

Commission on Proposals for the National Academy of Peace and Conflict Resolution

Appointment of Three Members. December 5, 1979

The President has appointed three persons as members of the Commission on Proposals for the National Academy of Peace and Conflict Resolution. They are:

ARTHUR H. BARNES, president of the New York Urban Coalition and vice president of the Institute for Mediation and Conflict Resolution, a private, nonprofit organization that mediates community disputes and teaches the techniques of mediation, negotiation, and arbitration;

ELISE BOULDING, a professor of sociology at the Institute of Behavioral Science at the University of Colorado, an expert, lecturer, and writer in the field of peace research;

JAMES HOWARD LAUE, director of the Center for Metropolitan Studies at the University of Missouri—St. Louis, an expert in the field of conflict resolution, especially as it applies to community conflict of all types.

This Commission was created by Public Law 95–561 on November 1, 1978, to determine the feasibility of establishing a National Academy of Peace and Conflict Resolution to assist the Federal Government in accomplishing the goal of promoting international peace.

President's Cancer Panel

*Appointment of Two Members and
Designation of Chairman.   December 5, 1979*

The President today announced the appointment of two persons as members of the President's Cancer Panel. They are:

Bernard Fisher, director of oncology and professor of surgery at the University of Pittsburgh and a specialist in breast cancer. Fisher serves on several committees of the National Cancer Institute and is on the editorial boards of a number of journals on cancer.

Joshua Lederberg, president of the Rockefeller University in New York City, an expert in genetics, and winner of the 1958 Nobel Prize in medicine for studies on the organization of the genetic material in bacteria. Lederberg has also been designated Chairman of the President's Cancer Panel.

Fiscal Assistance to State and Local Governments

*White House Statement on the House
Government Operations Committee's
Approval of Legislation.
December 5, 1979*

The House Government Operations Committee today reported, by a vote of 27 to 12, legislation that would provide countercyclical aid to State and local governments and targeted fiscal assistance to the most distressed cities and counties. The bill was introduced by the leadership of the House Government Operations Committee and is supported by the administration.

The legislation would provide up to $1 billion to State and local governments if the economy goes into a recession. It also would provide $250 million to cities and counties that experience high unemployment. The legislation would provide essential aid to most needy cities, counties, and rural towns, and help them maintain essential police, fire, and sanitation services, and prevent layoffs of essential employees.

The President expressed his appreciation to Chairman Jack Brooks and Chairman L. H. Fountain for their cooperation and fine work on this legislation and his hope that the legislation will move quickly through the House Rules Committee and the House floor, so that the Congress can complete action on this legislation by the end of this year.

United Nations

*Nomination of H. Carl McCall To Be
Alternate U.S. Representative for Special
Political Affairs.   December 6, 1979*

The President today announced that he will nominate H. Carl McCall, of New York City, to be the Alternate Representative of the United States for Special Political Affairs in the United Nations, with the rank of Ambassador. He would replace Richard Petree, who has been appointed Deputy U.S. Representative in the Security Council.

McCall is a New York State senator. He was born October 17, 1935, in Boston, Mass. He received an A.B. from Dartmouth College in 1958 and an M. Div. from Andover Newton Theological School in 1963. He served in the U.S. Army in 1959.

From 1965 to 1972, McCall was project director for the Taconic Foundation. From 1967 to 1968, he was deputy administrator of the New York City Human Resources Administration. From 1971 to 1975, he was executive director of the Florence and John Schumann Foundation. He has been a New York State senator since 1974.

McCall is an ordained minister of the United Church of Christ and a preaching minister at Metropolitan Community United Methodist Church in Harlem. He is secretary for the Urban Church of the United Church of Christ and serves as a consultant to the Ministerial Interfaith Association of Harlem.

McCall is chairman of the New York City Council Against Poverty, the Citizen's Voter Education Committee of New York State, the editorial board of the New York Amsterdam News, and the National Association of Minority Broadcasters. He is president of Inner City Broadcasting Corp. and serves on the advisory board of the African American Institute.

Aid for Kampucheans

White House Statement.   December 6, 1979

Starvation still threatens millions of Cambodian lives, despite a massive international relief effort. This sad reality is due to no failure of global concern. The international community has offered the means and has the will to allay the suffering of the Cambodian people.

Growing quantities of food and medical supplies are now reaching that country, but too often the relief cannot get through to those in need. Instead, the flow of aid is deliberately blocked and obstructed by the Vietnamese and Heng Samrin authorities. Their Soviet allies have not brought any discernible influence to bear to alleviate the situation, while supporting Vietnam heavily.

—Relief supplies are piling up in Phnom Penh and other points of initial delivery, because local and Vietnamese authorities continually change or delay agreed arrangements for distribution.

—Taxes and tariffs are collected on the delivery of relief supplies—in effect, imposing a surcharge on human survival.

—We continue to receive reports that relief supplies are diverted or stockpiled for the use of military forces and that what distribution does take place is skewed to favor officials and supporters of the Heng Samrin regime.

—There is even interference with the attempts of the Kampuchean people to feed themselves. For example, refugees have reported the mining of rice fields to prevent a harvest.

In the face of widespread human anguish, this delay and diversion of humanitarian efforts is unconscionable.

As many as 2 million Cambodians may have died under the brutal Pol Pot regime. Now, in the wake of a Vietnamese invasion and occupation of Cambodia, the long-suffering people of that country face a new wave of oppression, hunger, and disease.

To counter this mounting tragedy, we call upon responsible leaders in both Hanoi and Moscow to recognize and act upon the compelling humanitarian requirements of the Cambodian people—which they thus far have not done. We call on them to cooperate fully with the international community in opening all routes for supplies to enter Cambodia—which they thus far have not done. We call on them to take the steps necessary to speed the distribution of humanitarian aid to starving people throughout all parts of that country—which they thus far have not done. We call on them not to feed the flames of war, but use aircraft and airfields to ferry food to feed the people of Kampuchea.

Bill of Rights Day, Human Rights Day and Week, 1979

Proclamation 4705.   December 6, 1979

By the President of the United States of America

A Proclamation

On December 15, 1791, the Bill of Rights became part of the Constitution of the United States. On December 10, 1948, the United Nations General Assembly adopted the Universal Declaration of Human Rights. In marking these anniversaries, we renew our dedication both to our own liberties and to the promotion of human rights everywhere on earth.

In our open society, a freely elected government, an independent judiciary, a free and vigorous press, and the vigilance of our citizens combine to protect our rights and liberties—civil, political, economic and social.

We can be proud of what we have achieved so far. Yet we cannot rest satisfied until the Bill of Rights is a living reality for every person in the United States. The Equal Rights Amendment would help do that by explicitly guaranteeing the basic rights of American women. I urge every state that has not yet done so to ratify this wise and necessary measure in the coming year.

The Universal Declaration of Human Rights sets global standards that reflect the same vision that inspired our own Bill of Rights. Almost every country has endorsed the Declaration. Yet in too much of the world its promise is mocked.

Arbitrary arrest and imprisonment, summary executions and torture, disappearances and acts of genocide still shatter the lives of millions. Fundamental human liberties are continually threatened by the silencing of political dissenters, by discrimination based on race, religion, ethnic origin and sex, by violations of the freedoms of assembly, association, expression and movement, and by the suppression of trade unions. And as the kidnapping and abuse of American Embassy employees in Iran have reminded us, the internationally protected rights of diplomatic envoys are a basic condition of civilized relations among nations.

Those who cause others anguish—whether they are the secret police of dictators, the faceless bureaucrats of totalitarian states or the chanting mobs of revolutionary zealots—must know that we will not defend them, but their victims.

Bill of Rights Day and Human Rights Day and Week should be marked by redoubled support for international efforts on behalf of the full range of human rights.

I renew my request to the Senate to give its advice and consent to the Genocide Convention, the Convention on the Elimination of all Forms of Racial Discrimination, the Covenant on Civil and Political Rights, the Covenant on Economic, Social and Cultural Rights, and the American Convention on Human Rights. I commend the Senate Foreign Relations Committee for holding hearings on these treaties, and I urge all Americans to support their ratification.

Now, THEREFORE, I, JIMMY CARTER, President of the United States of America, do hereby proclaim December 10, 1979, as Human Rights Day and December 15, 1979, as Bill of Rights Day, and call on all Americans to observe Human Rights Week beginning December 10, 1979. Let us rededicate ourselves to promoting the ideals embodied in the Bill of Rights and the Universal Declaration so that, one day, they will be enjoyed by all peoples of the world.

IN WITNESS WHEREOF, I have hereunto set my hand this sixth day of December, in the year of our Lord nineteen hundred seventy-nine, and of the Independence of the United States of America the two hundred and fourth.

JIMMY CARTER

[Filed with the Office of the Federal Register, 10:45 a.m., December 7, 1979]

Department of Education

Remarks at the Swearing In of Shirley Hufstedler as Secretary.   December 6, 1979

THE PRESIDENT. This is a good day for our Nation. Many people look around us in this great country, and we see the notable achievements that have benefited our own lives in so many varied ways that we tend to give credit to diverse reasons for the great achievements of America: that we've started out in a land that was unexplored, without knowing what our natural resources were, with the most heterogeneous population, I guess, of any nation on Earth—widely diverse motivations and interests and backgrounds, religions, beliefs, languages, great challenges, all too frequent wars, racial problems. And still, in spite of all those obstacles, our Nation has been the greatest of all.

We've overcome obstacles, and we've answered questions, and we've solved problems, and we've made progress, because our people have always believed in good education. It's let us transcend potential language barriers and the barriers of communication. It's let us explore the frontiers of knowledge to learn about the world around us, to stretch our hearts and minds to people throughout the world, and to bind ourselves together in a spirit of unity of purpose and understanding.

We still have a long way to go in providing a quality education for all American people. I promised you in my own campaign more than 3 years ago, that if I was elected President that one of my goals would be to establish a separate Department of Education, to give it a high profile in Government, to let it have a single purpose which would focus the attention of the Nation on unmet needs and potential ways to resolve and to meet those needs.

At the same time, a department must encompass a wide gamut of opportunities for learning. And as I've sought around the last 3 or 4 months for a person to be the first Secretary of Education in our Nation, I was very grateful to be able to induce Judge Shirley Hufstedler to take over this job. She's a person who has a wide range of interests herself. She's a person of character. She is strong. She has a breadth of experience and background in education and scholarship that will stand her in good stead in this difficult achievement.

She has demonstrated a feeling of compassion for those who need help in our society, and she has sound and good judgment. She's interested in colonial Williamsburg. She's interested in jet propulsion. She's interested in good symphony orchestras. She's interested in teaching ethics to young people. She's interested in a fine quality of justice in the court system of our country. She believes in excellence, and she believes in the value of individual human beings, and she sees education as a means of binding all these varied interests, purposes, and opportunities together.

I've talked to Shirley about this opportunity and the fact that the classroom is just one place among many where Americans can constantly expand their educational opportunities—also, of course, in the museums, in the concert halls, through the public media, in the workplace, in libraries, and in the encounters among Americans themselves.

We have tried to improve education in our Nation from the Federal level, recognizing that the encroachment in the decisionmaking process for the management of schools, the establishment of curriculum, the choosing of persons to teach and to administer ought to be entirely a local and a State responsibility. But the Federal Government has a role to play. We've had a greater increase in Federal aid to the educational system than any other administration ever, in the period of 3 years that I've been in office. That's just part of the problem and the opportunity.

I'm very glad now to introduce to you Judge Shirley Hufstedler, who will be the first Secretary of Education. She started out herself in the career as a secretary. She then taught part-time, typing. She taught shorthand. She taught English. She taught music. And now, she is becoming a secretary once again. [*Laughter*] Having completed that full circle, I know she'll be eager to address you now.

Judge Shirley Hufstedler.

JUDGE HUFSTEDLER. *Mr. President,*

Mr. Chief Justice, Mrs. Carter, members of my dear beloved extended family, colleagues, friends of education:

It is, of course, for me, a glorious day. It is for education an event of great visibility in the creation of the Department of Education. But the beginnings of today involve many people and many things, but most of all it began with an idea, an idea by which the values of the United States and the meaning of education for every person could be demonstrated to the country and to the world through the creation of an equal partnership at the Cabinet level for the Department.

Ideas, like children, can never reach their full potential without faith, without love, without determination, and without nurturing. This Department could not have happened and that idea could not be well begun unless the administration created a climate in which that nourishment could occur.

But even with the nurturing strength of the administration for education, the idea could not have grown this far but for the thoughtful cooperation of myriads of people in this country—on the Hill, in the communities, among scholars, among leaders—to make it happen. This Department can never nourish the idea of education unless those who were against the idea and those who were for it will come together in a spirit of cooperation to make all these ideas come true.

I would hope, Mr. President, that we can see new coalitions, new hope, new faith, new charity, and new dedication to the concept of education. In the words of George Washington, "Let us raise a standard." And the standard, if you please, that I would like each of you— and all the people who cannot be here, but who are represented by each of you—

to raise the standard to say, "Let this not simply be a country with freedom and justice; let us be a country of freedom, justice, and quality education for all."

NOTE: The President spoke at 3 p.m. in the East Room at the White House. Chief Justice of the United States Warren E. Burger administered the oath of office to Judge Hufstedler following her remarks.

International Trade Functions

Executive Order 12175.   December 7, 1979

REORGANIZATION OF FUNCTIONS RELATING TO INTERNATIONAL TRADE

By the authority vested in me as President of the United States of America by Section 9 of Reorganization Plan No. 3 of 1979 (transmitted to the Congress on September 25, 1979), the time period prescribed by Section 906 of Title 5 of the United States Code having elapsed without the adoption of a resolution of disapproval by either House of Congress, it is hereby ordered that Section 2(b)(1) of that Plan, establishing the Office of Deputy Secretary of Commerce, is effective immediately.

JIMMY CARTER

The White House,
    December 7, 1979.

[Filed with the Office of the Federal Register, 11:47 a.m., December 7, 1979]

President's Commission on the Coal Industry

Executive Order 12176.   December 7, 1979

By the authority vested in me as President by the Constitution of the United

States of America, and in order to extend the time for the President's Commission on the Coal Industry to complete its report, Sections 1–401 and 1–402 of Executive Order No. 12103 of December 14, 1978 are hereby revised to read as follows:

"1–401. The final report required by section 1–202 of this Order shall be transmitted no later than March 15, 1980.

"1–402. The Commission shall terminate on March 15, 1980."

JIMMY CARTER

The White House,
    December 7, 1979.

[Filed with the Office of the Federal Register, 11:48 a.m., December 7, 1979]

Meetings With Prime Minister Odvar Nordli of Norway and Prime Minister Andreas van Agt of the Netherlands

White House Statement.   December 7, 1979

In separate meetings this morning, the President met with the Prime Minister of Norway, Odvar Nordli, and the Prime Minister of the Netherlands, Andreas van Agt. These meetings were undertaken at the request of the two Prime Ministers; the requests were separate, and the Prime Ministers met with the President separately.

The President discussed with both leaders the forthcoming NATO Alliance decisions on TNF modernization and arms control. Both leaders conveyed their Governments' views, and the President made clear the importance he attaches to the forthcoming decisions and to an Alliance consensus.

President's Commission on the Accident at Three Mile Island

Remarks Announcing Actions in Response to the Commission's Report.   December 7, 1979

The purpose of this brief statement this afternoon is to outline to you and to the public, both in this country and in other nations of the world, my own assessment of the Kemeny report recommendations on the Three Mile Island accident. And I would like to add, of course, in the presentation some thoughts and actions of my own.

I have reviewed the report of the Commission, which I established to investigate the accident at the Three Mile Island nuclear powerplant. The Commission, headed by Dr. John Kemeny, found very serious shortcomings in the way that both the Government and the utility industry regulate and manage nuclear power.

The steps that I am taking today will help to assure that nuclear powerplants are operated safely. Safety, as it always has been and will remain, is my top priority.

As I've said before, in this country nuclear power is an energy source of last resort. By this I meant that as we reach our goals on conservation, on the direct use of coal, on development of solar power and synthetic fuels, and enhanced production of American oil and natural gas—as we reach those goals, then we can minimize our reliance on nuclear power.

Many of our foreign allies must place much greater reliance than we do on nuclear power, because they do not have the vast natural resources that give us so many alternatives. We must get on with the job of developing alternative energy resources, and we must also pass, in order to do this, the legislation that I have proposed to the Congress in making an effort, at every level of society, to conserve energy. To conserve energy and to develop energy resources in our country are the two basic answers for which we are seeking. But we cannot shut the door on nuclear power for the United States.

The recent events in Iran have shown us the clear, stark dangers that excessive dependence on imported oil holds for our Nation. We must make every effort to lead this country to energy security. Every domestic energy source, including nuclear power, is critical if we are to be free as a country from our present overdependence on unstable and uncertain sources of high-priced foreign oil.

We do not have the luxury of abandoning nuclear power or imposing a lengthy moratorium on its further use. A nuclear powerplant can displace 35,000 barrels of oil per day, or roughly 13 million barrels of oil per year. We must take every possible step to increase the safety of nuclear power production. I agree fully with the letter and the spirit and the intent of the Kemeny commission's recommendations, some of which are within my own power to implement, others of which rely on the Nuclear Regulatory Commission, or the NRC, or the utility industry itself.

To get the Government's own house in order, I will take several steps. First, I will send to the Congress a reorganization plan to strengthen the role of the Chairman of the NRC, to clarify assignment of authority and responsibility, and provide this person with the power to act on a daily basis as a chief executive officer with authority to put needed safety requirements in place and to implement better procedures. The Chairman must be able to select key personnel and to act on behalf of the Commission during any emergency.

Second, I intend to appoint a new Chairman of the Nuclear Regulatory Commission, someone from outside that agency, in the spirit of the Kemeny commission's recommendation. In the meantime, I've asked Commissioner Ahearne, now on the NRC, to serve as the Chairman. Mr. Ahearne will stress safety and the prompt implementation of the needed reforms.

In addition, I will establish an independent advisory committee to help keep me and the public of the United States informed of the progress of the NRC and the industry in achieving and in making clear the recommendations that nuclear power will be safer.

Third, I'm transferring responsibility to the Federal Emergency Management Agency, the FEMA, to head up all offsite emergency activities and to complete a thorough review of emergency plans in all the States of our country with operating nuclear reactors by June 1980.

Fourth, I have directed the Nuclear Regulatory Commission and the other agencies of the Government to accelerate our program to place a resident Federal inspector at every reactor site.

Fifth, I'm asking all relevant Government agencies to implement virtually all of the other recommendations of the Kemeny commission—I believe there were 44 in all. A detailed fact sheet is being issued to the public, and a more extended briefing will be given to the press this afternoon.

With clear leadership and improved organization, the executive branch of Government and the NRC will be better able to act quickly on the crucial issues of improved training and standards, safety procedures, and the other Kemeny commission recommendations. But responsibility to make nuclear power safer does not stop with the Federal Government. In fact, the primary, day-by-day responsibility for safety rests with utility company management and with suppliers

of nuclear equipment. There is no substitute for technically qualified and committed people working on the construction, the operation, and the inspection of nuclear powerplants.

Personal responsibility must be stressed. Some one person must always be designated as in charge, both at the corporate level and also at the powerplant site. The industry owes it to the American people to strengthen its commitment to safety.

I call on the utilities to implement the following changes. First, building on the steps already taken, the industry must organize itself to develop enhanced standards for safe design, operation, and construction of plants. Second, the nuclear industry must work together to develop and to maintain in operation a comprehensive training, examination, and evaluation program for operators and for supervisors. This training program must pass muster with the NRC through accreditation of the training programs to be established. Third, control rooms in nuclear powerplants must be modernized, standardized, and simplified as much as possible to permit better informed decisionmaking among regular operating hours and, of course, during emergencies.

I challenge our utility companies to bend every effort to improve the safety of nuclear power.

Finally, I would like to discuss how we manage this transition period during which the Kemeny recommendations are being implemented. There are a number of new nuclear plants now awaiting operating licenses or construction permits. Under law, the Nuclear Regulatory Commission is an independent agency. Licensing decisions rest with the Nuclear Regulatory Commission, and, as the Kemeny commission noted, it has the authority to proceed with licensing these plants on a case-by-case basis, which may be used as circumstances surrounding a plant or its application dictate.

The NRC has indicated, however, that it will pause in issuing any new licenses and construction permits in order to devote its full attention to putting its own house in order and tightening up safety requirements. I endorse this approach which the NRC has adopted, but I urge the NRC to complete its work as quickly as possible and in no event later than 6 months from today. Once we've instituted the necessary reforms to assure safety, we must resume the licensing process promptly so that the new plants we need to reduce our dependence on foreign oil can be built and operated.

The steps I'm announcing today will help to ensure that our safety has the safety of nuclear plants. Nuclear power does have a future in the United States. It's an option that we must keep open. I will join with the utilities and their suppliers, the Nuclear Regulatory Commission, the executive departments and agencies of the Federal Government, and also the State and local governments to assure that the future is a safe one.

And now Dr. Frank Press, Stu Eizenstat, and John Deutch will be glad to answer your questions about these decisions and about nuclear power and the future of it in our country. Frank?

NOTE: The President spoke at 2:45 p.m. in Room 450 of the Old Executive Office Building.

Following the President's remarks, Frank Press, Director of the Office of Science and Technology Policy, Stuart E. Eizenstat, Assistant to the President for Domestic Affairs and Policy, and Under Secretary of Energy John M. Deutch held a news conference on the announcements.

Department of State

Nomination of Deane R. Hinton To Be an Assistant Secretary.   December 7, 1979

The President today announced that he will nominate Deane R. Hinton, of Chicago, Ill., to be an Assistant Secretary of State. He would replace Julius L. Katz, resigned, and his area of responsibility would be economic and business affairs.

Hinton has been United States Representative to the European Communities, with the rank of Ambassador Extraordinary and Plenipotentiary, since 1975.

He was born March 12, 1923, in Missoula, Mont. He received an A.B. from the University of Chicago in 1943. He served in the U.S. Army from 1943 to 1945.

Hinton joined the Foreign Service in 1946 and was posted in Damascus, Mombasa, Paris, and at the State Department. He was Chief of Overseas Development and the Finance Section at USEC in Brussels from 1958 to 1961. He attended the National War College in 1961–62.

From 1962 to 1963, Hinton was Chief of the Commodity Programming Division at the Bureau of Economic Affairs. From 1963 to 1967, he was Director of the Office of Atlantic Political-Economic Affairs in the Bureau of European Affairs. From 1967 to 1971, he was Director of the USAID mission and counselor for economic affairs in Guatemala, then in Santiago.

From 1971 to 1973, Hinton was detailed to the White House as Deputy Executive Director of the Council on International Economic Policy. He was Ambassador to the Republic of Zaire from 1974 to 1975. In 1975 he served as senior adviser to the Under Secretary of State for Economic Affairs.

American Hostages in Iran

Remarks to State Department Employees.
December 7, 1979

. . . in the last 30 days has been not only the support and understanding and patience of the American people and the strength of the hostages' families but also the superb work of the State Department and all of you, who I know have put in many extra hours, prayers, and extra commitments to help protect the lives and the safety of our hostages.

The most important single message that I can give to you is this: As far as I am concerned, as far as the State Department is concerned, as far as our Nation is concerned, there is one issue, and that is the early and the safe release of the American hostages from their captors in Tehran. And it's important for us to realize that from the very first hour of the captivity of our hostages by a mob, who is indistinguishable from the Government itself, that has been our purpose. And we have tried to restrain every other nation and the United Nations and the people in our own country from confusing the issues.

At this time, I am not interested in trying to resolve whether or not the Shah was a good or bad leader or the history of Iran. I'm not trying to interfere in the Government of Iran or the inclination of the people there, and we do not want to confuse the issue by injecting these extraneous questions or debates into the present situation. When that does happen, in my opinion, it delays the day when we will see the American hostages come home.

I am not going to take any military action that would cause bloodshed or arouse the unstable captors of our hostages to attack them or to punish them. I'm going to be very moderate, very cautious, guided and supported and ad-vised by Secretary Vance. Our purpose is to get the hostages home and get them safe. That's my total commitment, and I know you join with me as full partners in this effort.

Just one other comment: I'm not trying to be presumptuous in speaking for them, but there's no doubt in my mind that every hostage and every person who loves those hostages, not just the families but 220 million American people, thank you—working with Secretary Vance and all those in this Department—for the superb work that you have done in ensuring, so far, the safety in which I am confident and which I pray every moment of my life will be successful in getting our hostages home where they belong.

Thank you very much.

NOTE: The President spoke at 4:20 p.m. in the lobby at the State Department. Prior to his remarks, the President and Secretary of State Cyrus R. Vance met with members of the families of the hostages in the Benjamin Franklin Room.

The press release does not include the President's opening remarks.

Digest of Other
White House Announcements

The following listing includes the President's public schedule and other items of general interest announced by the White House Press Office and not included elsewhere in this issue.

December 1

The President declared a major disaster for the Marshall Islands of the Trust Territory of the Pacific Islands as a result of sea wave action and flooding, beginning on or about November 26, which caused extensive public and private property damage.

December 2

The President returned to the White House from Camp David, Md.

December 3

The President met at the White House with:

—Zbigniew Brzezinski, Assistant to the President for National Security Affairs;

—Frank B. Moore, Assistant to the President for Congressional Liaison;

—Vice President Walter F. Mondale;

—Mayor Tom Bradley of Los Angeles to discuss the 1984 summer Olympics to be held in Los Angeles, Calif.;

—Charles L. Schultze, Chairman of the Council of Economic Advisers;

—James T. McIntyre, Jr., Director of the Office of Management and Budget, and other administration officials to review the fiscal year 1981 budget.

In reaction to the terrorist attack on a Navy schoolbus near San Juan, P.R., which resulted in the death of two U.S. sailors and the injury of several others, the White House announced, on behalf of the President, that this was a despicable act of murder; that the full resources of the Federal Bureau of Investigation and the Department of Justice will be available as needed to help identify and bring to justice those responsible for a senseless act of terrorism; and that such actions are not consistent with the beliefs of the vast majority of Puerto Ricans, whatever their political views.

December 4

The President met at the White House with:

—Dr. Brzezinski;

—the National Security Council.

December 5

The President met at the White House with:

—Dr. Brzezinski;

—Ambassador Sol M. Linowitz, Personal Representative of the President to the Middle East peace negotiations;

—a group of leaders of the American Islamic community to assure the group, and through them to assure American Muslims, that the United States is not hostile towards Islam as a religion; to emphasize the need for Americans of all faiths to stand behind efforts to gain the release of the hostages; and to give the President an opportunity to listen to the group's advice and opinions on the situation in Iran;

—Members of the House of Representatives.

December 6

The President met at the White House with:

—David L. Aaron, Deputy Assistant for National Security Affairs;

—Secretary of Energy Charles W. Duncan, Jr., Secretary of the Treasury G. William Miller, Alfred E. Kahn, Advisor to the President on Inflation, Stuart E. Eizenstat, Assistant to the President for Domestic Affairs and Policy, Alonzo L. McDonald, Jr., Assistant to the President, Mr. Schultze, and Mr. McIntyre;

—Mr. Moore;

—the board of directors of the National Farmers Organization;

—Hedley W. Donovan, Senior Adviser to the President.

December 7

The President met at the White House with:

—Dr. Brzezinski;

—Vice President Mondale, Secretary of State Cyrus R. Vance, Secretary of Defense Harold Brown, Lloyd N. Cutler, Counsel to the President, Dr. Brzezinski, and Mr. Donovan;

—Mr. Moore;

—Members of the House of Representatives to discuss the energy security corporation legislation;

—a group of Governors and State legislators to discuss the fiscal year 1981 budget.

The President participated in a briefing on the administration's programs and policies given for civic and community leaders from Virginia in the East Room at the White House.

NOMINATIONS SUBMITTED TO THE SENATE

The following list does not include promotions of members of the Uniformed Services, nominations to the Service Academies, or nominations of Foreign Service officers.

Submitted December 3, 1979

LESLIE J. GOLDMAN, of Illinois, to be an Assistant Secretary of Energy (International Affairs), vice Harry E. Bergold, Jr., resigned.

IRA M. SCHWARTZ, of Washington, to be Associate Administrator of Law Enforcement Assistance, vice John M. Rector, resigned.

JOHN A. CALHOUN III, of Massachusetts, to be Chief of the Children's Bureau, Department of Health, Education, and Welfare, vice Blandina Cardenas, resigned.

HELEN JACKSON FRYE, of Oregon, to be United States District Judge for the District of Oregon, vice a new position created by P.L. 95–486, approved October 20, 1978.

JAMES ANTHONY REDDEN, JR., of Oregon, to be United States District Judge for the District of Oregon, vice a new position created by P.L. 95–486, approved October 20, 1978.

NOMINATIONS—Continued

Submitted December 3—Continued

OWEN M. PANNER, of Oregon, to be United States District Judge for the District of Oregon, vice Otto R. Skopil, Jr., elevated.

BARBARA J. ROTHSTEIN, of Washington, to be United States District Judge for the Western District of Washington, vice a new position created by P.L. 95–486, approved October 20, 1978.

Submitted December 6, 1979

H. CARL MCCALL, of New York, to be the Alternate Representative of the United States of America for Special Political Affairs in the United Nations, with the rank of Ambassador.

THOMAS EUGENE STELSON, of Georgia, to be an Assistant Secretary of Energy (Conservation and Solar Applications), vice Omi Gail Walden, resigned.

HARRY T. EDWARDS, of Michigan, to be United States Circuit Judge for the District of Columbia Circuit, vice David L. Bazelon, retired.

Submitted December 7, 1979

DEANE R. HINTON, of Illinois, a Foreign Service Officer of the class of Career Minister, to be an Assistant Secretary of State.

EARL BEN GILLIAM, of California, to be United States District Judge for the Southern District of California, vice a new position created by Public Law 95–486, approved October 20, 1978.

CHECKLIST OF WHITE HOUSE PRESS RELEASES

The following listing contains releases of the White House Press Office which are not included in this issue.

Released December 1, 1979

Announcement: nomination of Helen Jackson Frye to be United States District Judge for the District of Oregon

Announcement: nomination of James Anthony Redden, Jr., to be United States District Judge for the District of Oregon

Announcement: nomination of Owen M. Panner to be United States District Judge for the District of Oregon

CHECKLIST—Continued

Released December 1—Continued

Announcement: nomination of Barbara J. Rothstein to be United States District Judge for the Western District of Washington

Released December 4, 1979

Advance text: remarks announcing candidacy for the 1980 Democratic Presidential nomination

Released December 5, 1979

Announcement: nomination of Harry T. Edwards to be United States Circuit Judge for the District of Columbia Circuit

Released December 6, 1979

Announcement: nomination of Earl Ben Gilliam to be United States District Judge for the District of Columbia Circuit

Released December 7, 1979

Statement: actions in response to the report of the President's Commission on the Accident at Three Mile Island (as announced in the President's remarks in Room 450 of the Old Executive Office Building)

Fact sheet: the President's response to the recommendations of the President's Commission on the Accident at Three Mile Island

ACTS APPROVED BY THE PRESIDENT

Approved December 5, 1979

S. 1686_____ Public Law 96–134
An act to designate the building known as the Federal Building in Wilmington, Delaware, as the "J. Caleb Boggs Building".

H.R. 1885_____ Public Law 96–135
An act to amend Civil Service retirement provisions as they apply to certain employees of the Bureau of Indian Affairs and of the Indian Health Service who are not entitled to Indian employment preference and to modify the application of the Indian employment preference laws as it applies to those agencies.

S. 132_____ Private Law 96–19
An act for the relief of Dirk Vierkant.

S.151_____ Private Law 96–20
An act for the relief of Jerry W. Manandic and Ceferino W. Manandic.

S. 170_____ Private Law 96–21
An act for the relief of Janet Abraham, also known as Janet Susan Abraham.

H.R. 4483_____ Private Law 96–22
An act for the relief of Jung-Sook Mun.

Approved December 7, 1979

H.J. Res. 448_____ Public Law 96–136
A joint resolution proclaiming the week of December 3 through December 9, 1979 as "Scouting Recognition Week".

Scouting Recognition Week, 1979

Proclamation 4706.   December 7, 1979

By the President of the United States of America

A Proclamation

Scouting teaches boys and girls self-reliance, physical fitness and good citizenship. It fosters character development and nurtures a love and understanding of nature and of other people.

Scouting has a long and proud tradition of service and leadership training. Many of our Nation's most accomplished men and women in every field of endeavor are former Scouts, and cite Scouting as one of their most important early experiences.

Through the years Scouts have broadened their activities to meet the changing needs of young Americans and help them prepare for useful and rewarding lives.

In recent years Scouts have been particularly active in promoting energy awareness and conservation, and are continuing this important effort. They are also planning activities designed to aid in taking an accurate census next year.

By House Joint Resolution 448, the Congress has designated the week of December 3 through December 9, 1979 as "Scouting Recognition Week."

Now, THEREFORE, I, JIMMY CARTER, President of the United States of America, call upon all Americans to recognize the contributions of Scouting and to support Scouting programs in their communities.

IN WITNESS WHEREOF, I have hereunto set my hand this seventh day of December, in the year of our Lord nineteen hundred seventy-nine, and of the Independence of the United States of America the two hundred and fourth.

JIMMY CARTER

[Filed with the Office of the Federal Register, 10:33 a.m., December 10, 1979]

NOTE: The text of the proclamation was released on December 8.

American Hostages in Iran

Announcement of Attorney General Civiletti's Appearance Before the International Court of Justice.   December 9, 1979

The President has asked Attorney General Benjamin Civiletti to travel to the Netherlands tonight to appear personally before the International Court of Justice in the United States case against Iran.

The Court is holding hearings at The Hague Monday on the request of the United States for an interim order that

Iran should immediately release and ensure the safety of the Americans held hostage in Tehran. In the view of the United States, the continued detention of the hostages is a gross violation of the basic rules of international law and human rights.

In light of the importance and urgency of this case, the President has asked the Attorney General personally to present the position of the United States to the Court. Roberts B. Owen, Legal Adviser to the Department of State, will also be appearing before the Court for the United States.

Dinner Honoring Thomas P. O'Neill, Jr.

Remarks at the Fundraising Dinner for the O'Neill Chair at Boston College.
December 9, 1979

Mr. Speaker, Millie O'Neill, sons and daughters, who've brought grandchildren and who have blessed this marriage of 38 years, and friends of Tip O'Neill from all over this Nation:

Thank you, Father Monan, president of Boston College, for your kind introduction.

Many people have asked why I'm here tonight in the midst of some very important business in Iran. When I was presented with my schedule for this month, my immediate and firm Presidential response was, "I am not going to any fundraising events for the time being." And Frank Moore, my congressional liaison chief, said, "Mr. President, the Speaker thinks you ought to be there." [*Laughter*] So, it is a real pleasure for me to be— [*laughter*]—it's a real pleasure for me to be here with a thousand other close friends—[*laughter*]—of Tip O'Neill's to honor Boston College and its most distinguished graduate.

Tip is a man of great achievement. Tip is a man of great caution. He roomed with [Representative] Eddie Boland here for more than 23 years before he decided that his seat was safe enough to bring Millie down from Boston—[*laughter*]—and I guarantee you it was a great boon to our Nation when he finally decided to do so. Tip, you don't need to worry. The voters of the Eighth District of Massachusetts know the value, which I cherish along with you, of reelecting the incumbent. [*Laughter*]

Tip O'Neill is a wonderful political analyst, philosopher, and adviser. He told me that the key to his own success in politics—and I've made the same point recently—is to wait your turn. [*Laughter*]

We have a very serious purpose tonight. It's to honor a man who, for 27 years, has served his entire country with distinction and greatness, which is good training for an even greater career, Tip, in the future. We are also here to support and to honor Boston College, whose contributions to our entire Nation have become more evident with each passing year. I understand that this dinner has raised a record figure of $1.2 million, and I hope that this is only the beginning of generous, ever more generous support for Boston College of those who love it and who honor it and who recognize its great contribution.

By naming an endowed chair for him, the college is indeed honoring a rare man. I could take up the entire evening listing for you his qualities and his accomplishments. But just let me say that in this last 3 years he's become for me a great personal friend—and a President needs all the friends he can get. [*Laughter*] I turn to him constantly for advice, as he knows;

for his knowledge, most of which comes from Millie, which I appreciate— [*laughter*]—for his instincts in politics, in times of trial and tribulation, of hopes and dreams and frustrations and desires; and for his support, which has been unwavering.

When I took office and this country faced more than 8-percent unemployment, Tip made sure that the Congress of the United States passed the most ambitious jobs programs since the New Deal, the Great Depression. He's often said that work and wages are what the Democratic Party is all about.

I remember those depression years, Tip, when you were in college and I was a farmboy. The day's wages for a grown, able man was a dollar; for a woman working alongside of him, 50 cents; for a child less than 16 years old, 25 cents a day. And the Democratic Party was struggling with a minimum wage law, opposed by some who called it the verge of socialism, to guarantee factory workers 25 cents an hour.

Today, after 3 years, there are 8 million more Americans on the job with work and wages, earning their own way, living in dignity because of that belief. This past month we added hundreds of thousands of new jobs and brought the unemployment rate down again. Now, that's Tip O'Neill, Democratic Party government, and I am proud to be part of it.

He's long believed in giving our young people the best education that this country can offer. This affair tonight is a vivid demonstration of that commitment. In the last 3 years since Tip O'Neill has been Speaker, Federal aid to education has increased by 60 percent, and now we have a new Department of Education to focus ever more attention on this integral part of America's present and its future. And Tip O'Neill deserves much of the credit.

That's Tip O'Neill, Democratic Party government, and I'm proud to be part of it.

When it became imperative to act with our national security at stake, he led the House to enact without delay the most far-reaching energy program our country has ever seen. Victory is now in sight for both Houses of the Congress if we work together. That's Tip O'Neill, Democratic Party government, and I'm proud to be a part of it.

Tip has never been afraid to stand up and to speak up for what he believes and to work for what he knows is right. At a time when people have hungered for leaders who tell the truth, the unvarnished truth, he has spoken the truth, unafraid of the consequences.

Most of all, however, I admire Tip O'Neill's undiluted patriotism. It's a patriotism that seeks to build on the greatness of America. It's a patriotism that never changes. It's a patriotism deep within his heart. It's a patriotism he's not embarrassed to express. It's a patriotism that preserves the enduring values that founded our country: a commitment to peace, the freedom, and the opportunity of our land, the compassion and the generosity of our people that seeks to harness change, never afraid of it, and to build an even greater future for our children and our grandchildren. That's the patriotism of Tip O'Neill, and that is the root of the strength of America.

The events in Iran remind us that our basic values mean as much today as at any time in our Nation's history. Now those qualities are being severely tested, not just by a mob in Iran, who hold hostage innocent Americans, but by the changing nature of the entire world. I have no doubt that we in America will prevail, because we are right, because we are strong, because we are united.

Our form of government has endured every test. Americans have never found a question that we could not answer if we were united. Americans have never found an obstacle that we could not overcome if we were united. Americans have never found a challenge we could not meet if we were united. Our form of government has endured, and it has grown. It has improved itself in quality for two centuries. And long after the mobs have gone home in Iran, long after there have been many changes of government and constitutions and ideologies elsewhere in the world, American democracy and the ideal of America will stand as they do today—the brightest and the best hope of mankind, a clear, undimmed beacon of fundamental human rights and human values.

Tonight America stands as the greatest nation on Earth. Boston College stands as a great and a fortunate institution. Tip O'Neill has enhanced the greatness of both, and we are all grateful to him.

Ladies and gentlemen, let me introduce the Speaker of the House of the United States of America, Thomas P. O'Neill, Jr.

NOTE: The President spoke at 10:11 p.m. in the Regency Ballroom at the Hyatt Regency Hotel.

Federal Council on the Aging

Remarks at the Swearing-In Ceremony for Five Members. December 10, 1979

THE PRESIDENT. This is a very good day for our country and a very exciting time for me, and I know it is for all those assembled around behind me. We have an opportunity with the White House Conference on the Aging, scheduled for 1981, to have another exhilarating and challenging presentation to make to our Nation for one of the most important issues of our time.

In the last 20 years, there have been two previous White House Conferences on the Aging, and both of them have, in effect, transformed the thinking of Americans about those among us who have reached an age, potentially, of retirement, but who have so much to offer to our country in a rapidly increasing fashion. We have this afternoon, also, an opportunity to address the Federal Council on the Aging by swearing in five new members to that very important body.

In the last 3 years, we have made a good bit of progress in issues dealing with the aging. We've passed legislation, finally, to prohibit discrimination among Americans because of age. We've had a chance to strengthen the Older Americans Act. We've had an opportunity to expand the SSI, primarily for elderly people. And, in addition, we have strengthened and made much more secure social security, which is the basis for our social programs for those who've reached the retirement age.

It's very important that we recognize the need for elderly people to have a maximum opportunity for self-determination. Their lives have become ever more valuable with the passing years, because they've accumulated experience. After retirement, or at the age of retirement, they have, sometimes, time to contribute to their country. They have vivid insight into the problems and challenges of our time. They have a broad perspective, in having seen crises come and go. They are completely conversant with the elements that comprise American society. They have confidence in our country, because they've seen us meet similar challenges in the past.

Many elements of American societal life can be harnessed to provide a partnership with the aging people of our country. In academic circles, in business and labor, local, State, and Federal agencies of government, in community programs, in churches and other benevolent institutions, there is an opportunity for free interchange of advice and counsel, communication and common work, to realize the hopes and dreams of many Americans, regardless of age.

I would like at this time to recognize those who will be leading the White House Conference on the Aging, to be conducted next year. The Chairman is Sadie Alexander, immediately behind me, who will be saying a few words in a moment. She's a famous person on her own. She's been part of the progress made in our country in the finest possible way. She happens to be the first black woman ever awarded an earned Ph. D. in this country, in economics, and she later achieved her doctor of laws degree from the University of Pennsylvania.

Their Executive Director will be a very well known person in Washington, former Congressman from California, Jerry Waldie. Our Deputy Chairman is a man who conducted the last White House Conference on the Aging, who's been in the forefront of eliminating discrimination of all kinds in our country and been a constant prod for the conscience of America, Dr. Arthur Flemming. The Cochairmen and Chairwomen of this group will be Dr. Neugarten, Miss Morales, and Miss Winston.

And this is a wonderful group who will lead the planning and help to conduct the White House Conference on the Aging. My wife and I and other members of my immediate family and my entire administration will be supportive of this very fine effort.

And now I would like to call on our new Chairperson, Dr. Alexander, to say a few words.

DR. ALEXANDER. *Mr. President, Mrs. Carter, Madame Secretary, members of the commission, and distinguished guests:*

As a child I lived some years in Washington, and I remember that my mother used to frequently take us to chapel at Howard University, 4 o'clock on Sunday afternoon. On one of these occasions, Booker T. Washington was to speak. And I heard my mother and her lady friends discussing what they would wear to the reception for Mr. Carter—Mr. Washington. [*Laughter*] Yes, that's on my mind; we're going to give him a great one, too.

When we got to the chapel and Mr. Washington was introduced, he of course thanked the persons who were responsible for his invitation, and then he stated how he regretted that he couldn't possibly remain for the reception. He was to meet with some very important people, upon whose decision would rest whether or not Tuskegee would continue. He said, "You know, perhaps it's fortunate I cannot spend the night in Washington. I find that people who come here for appointments— seem impossible for them to leave. They never seem to realize that they were appointed by one administration." [*Laughter*] But he said, "I'm afraid that if I inhale the air of Washington for a whole evening, I, too, might not be able to leave." Well, I want to assure you that I will be able to leave. [*Laughter*]

I have not come back too often, because I was too busy in Philadelphia. Last June, I told the members of my firm that I was going to leave by December 31 of this year. Nobody believed me. But then I went ahead quietly to get my work out of the way. I only have two important cases left, and I intend to get them off the docket. But I thought to myself that the French expression, that important ventures cast their shadows, was certainly true in my case.

2213

I wondered, after I had made the decision to leave the practice of law, which I'd been in for 52 years, that I might not be as happy as I thought I would be. And along came this unexpected call from Madame Secretary. And what did she tell me? She had an appointment with the President, and she was going to present to him my name to chair this very important commission.

I am grateful to the President. I am grateful to Madame Secretary. I am grateful to the committee and to all of you who I know. The commission will receive your support. I thank you.

THE PRESIDENT. Pat Harris told me I was getting a senior citizen to head up our Conference. I didn't know I was getting somebody so young. [*Laughter*] Dr. Alexander is the same age as my mother. They were both born in 1898. And I think the vivacious attitude that she has, and the full life that she lives, and the tremendous contribution that she will undoubtedly make in the future, is indicative of the need for all of us in this country never to consider any person, regardless of age, other than a tremendous potential asset for our country.

I know that my mother is as young as I am, or as she was 35 or 40 years ago or 50 years ago. And many people who are not as well known as Lillian Carter or Dr. Alexander have the same ability to contribute on a continuing basis to a better life for all Americans. There is no doubt in my mind that under her leadership, the White House Conference on the Aging will be not only successful and beneficial to others, but it will be exciting and enjoyable and stimulating and inspirational as well. And I'm deeply grateful to Dr. Alexander for being willing to serve in this capacity.

We have with us also, in addition to those who will run the White House Conference, the members who will serve with Nelson Cruikshank, the Chairman, who's also my Presidential Counselor on the Aging. And these members are Dr. Jean Perdue, of Florida, Miss Mary Mulvey, of Rhode Island—right? I think I've got the States right, I'm not sure. Mr. Cy Carpenter, of Minnesota. Everytime I swear in a group, I always have at least one person from Minnesota—[*laughter*]—a lot more than from Georgia. I never have figured that out. [*Laughter*] And Dr. Aaron Henry, who's almost from Georgia; he's from Mississippi and an old friend of mine. And John Martin, who will be reappointed.

I might say that this group will now be sworn in by Secretary Pat Harris. I would like to say a word before I depart this meeting, though, and that is that Nelson Cruikshank not only serves as the Chairman of the Federal Council on the Aging, but he serves as my personal Counselor on the Aging. This is a group that not only gives advice to the President but also to the Nation at large, to all the agencies of the Federal and other governments, and, in addition, to the Congress. It's a constant stimulation to us all, and it's the only advisory council in the Government that's predominantly made up of the aging, who have a particular knowledge and insight and ability to deal with this exciting possibility for us to improve life in the future.

As you know, over a period of years ahead, a larger and larger portion of American citizens will have reached the retirement age. They not only provide a great responsibility for us to ensure that they have an adequate life, those particularly who are poor and who need the direct and daily help in their lives from the Government, but they also provide a tremendous resource, a reservoir of talent and ability and inspiration and dedication that can help the rest of us enjoy a better life, even before the retirement age.

So, I'm very grateful to Nelson Cruikshank and this group, who will now be sworn in. And I'd like to thank all of those who are present here for their willingness to serve along with me in making us have a better nation for the aging. And I'd like now to call on the Secretary, Pat Harris, who will administer the oath of office. All of you have my congratulations and my thanks.

And now, Secretary Harris.

SECRETARY HARRIS. Thank you, sir.

THE PRESIDENT. Good luck to you, Pat. Thank you very much. Thank you, everybody.

[*At this point, the President left the Cabinet Room, and Secretary of Health, Education, and Welfare Patricia R. Harris administered the oath of office to the five members of the Council.*]

SECRETARY HARRIS. Congratulations to you. The five people I've just sworn in are taking up their responsibilities at a critical time in the development of Federal policy for the aging. That point was reemphasized for me in a recent book entitled "The View in Winter." A key element in this book is the recognition that for the first time in our history old age has come to be the expected, not the exceptional, condition.

Happily, all of us in this room can reasonably expect to live what used to be called a ripe old age; some of us, of course, sooner than later. That fact is a triumph of our health and social service systems, but it also has fundamental implications for future policy. Today, 11 percent of our population is age 65 or older; by the year 2020, which isn't very far away, older people will make up almost 16 percent of our population. That's about one in every seven people.

We cannot continue a public policy that views old age as the exception rather than the rule. Public policy toward older Americans must focus on helping them maintain their economic, physical, and social independence. That will not be an easy task, but it is one that we must accomplish.

What is needed is a national policy that emphasizes the strengths, rather than the weakness or problems of older Americans. As members of the Federal Council on Aging, the five people I have just sworn in will play an important part in shaping that policy. Each brings a special expertise to the deliberations of the Council.

Mary Mulvey has broad experience in education and research. Jean Perdue has spent years providing health care to the elderly. Cy Carpenter has firsthand experience with the employment problems of older Americans. Aaron Henry understands the problems of aging blacks, particularly those in rural areas. And John Martin, who is back for a second term on the Council, brings with him the practical experience of administering Federal programs for the aging.

But perhaps the most difficult task has been left to the leadership of the 1981 White House Conference on Aging—difficult because they have such a short time within which to reach their objectives.

Let me briefly outline the concerns of older Americans that this conference must address: the need for improved economic well-being, the need for suitable housing at a reasonable price, the need for comprehensive quality health care that is readily accessible to the aging, the need for a more comprehensive system for delivering social services, the need for a Federal policy on long-term care, the need for greater employment opportunities for those who want or need to work, the need for a national policy on retirement, the need for a national policy encouraging biomedical research into the aging process, and the need for a national policy to overcome stereotypes on aging.

Were I not so well acquainted with the leadership of this conference, I would wonder if the job could be done. But, I know it will be. I know of no one who is more qualified by experience, training, and character to undertake this massive task than Dr. Sadie Tanner Mossell Alexander.

The President has already told you the highlights of Sadie Alexander's career. She has made a career of breaking down stereotypes. Now, I see that one of the conference's specific responsibilities is with the destruction of the stereotype of aging. With Sadie Alexander at the helm of this conference, that particular stereotype doesn't have a chance.

I want to say something. The President was noting that Sadie and his mother were born in the same year. I know a little something about that generation, and I'm beginning to think that those were the truly liberated, movement vanguard women. They had no models, as I had with Sadie Alexander. And there's a member of my family, my mother, who now tells me—Sadie, 'cause she doesn't tell her age—tells me I am now older than she will ever admit to being. [*Laughter*] But that was the generation that really began the liberation of women. But you will be pleased this time, Sadie— you won't have to do it all by yourself.

You will have the help of some very able people: your chairperson emeritus, your deputy chairpersons, and your staff, headed by Jerry Waldie. Jerry has the special advantage of knowing the workings of government from at least three angles. He served 13 years in the California Assembly, five of them as majority leader. He served 8 years as a Member of Congress from California. And most recently, he has come to know the workings of the Federal bureaucracy through his activities as Chairperson of the Federal Mine Safety and Health Review Commission. He is uniquely qualified to reshape government policies at all levels, in order to serve the needs of older Americans better. We're very lucky to have him in this role.

This Nation has no precedents for dealing with the situation that now confronts it. The aging of America is a new phenomenon, and we are only beginning to understand what it really means to be old, the problems and the rewards, the difficulties and the satisfactions. Ronald Blythe summarized it well in his book "The View in Winter." "Old age," he says, "is full of death and full of life; it is a tolerable achievement and it is a disaster; it transcends desire and taunts it; it is long enough and it is far from being long enough."

Our challenge is to develop policies that will enhance the meaning of all our lives, young and old alike. With the leadership announced today, I am confident we will achieve the goal. And for every one of us in this room, that goal is important, because if we are lucky, we will live long enough to benefit from what they do. And certainly, all of us hope that we do, and we wish them well.

NOTE: The President spoke at 2:30 p.m. in the Cabinet Room at the White House.

Federal Home Loan Bank Board

Nomination of John H. Dalton To Be a Member.   December 10, 1979

The President today announced his intention to nominate John H. Dalton as a member of the Federal Home Loan Bank Board. He would replace Anita Miller, who has resigned.

Dalton is former President of the Government National Mortgage Association and was national treasurer of the Carter/Mondale Presidential Committee from March to November 1979.

He was born December 13, 1941, in New Orleans, La. He received a B.S. from the U.S. Naval Academy in 1964 and an M.B.A. from Wharton School of Finance and Commerce at the University of Pennsylvania.

Dalton served in the U.S. Navy from 1964 to 1969 in the nuclear submarine program. From 1971 to 1977, he was an account executive with the Dallas, Tex., firm of Goldman, Sachs & Co., working with institutions and individuals in the management of their equity and fixed income investments. He was President of the Government National Mortgage Association from 1977 until last March.

United States Ambassador to Norway

Nomination of Sidney Anders Rand. December 10, 1979

The President today announced that he will nominate Sidney Anders Rand, of Northfield, Minn., to be Ambassador Extraordinary and Plenipotentiary of the United States to Norway. He would replace Louis A. Lerner, who is resigning. Rand has been president of St. Olaf College since 1963.

He was born May 9, 1916, in Eldren, Minn. He received a B.A. from Concordia College in 1938 and a C.T. from Luther Theological Seminary in 1943.

From 1943 to 1945, Rand was a Luth-

eran pastor in Nashwauk, Minn. He was a faculty member at Concordia College, Moorhead, Minn., from 1945 to 1951 and president of Waldorf College, Forest City, Iowa, from 1951 to 1956.

From 1956 to 1960, Rand was executive director of the Board of Christian Education of the Evangelical Lutheran Church. From 1960 to 1963, he was executive director of the Board of College Education of the American Lutheran Church. From 1962 to 1963, he was a tutor with the Ecumenical Institute of the World Council of Churches in Celigny, Switzerland.

Rand is a member of the Norwegian American Historical Association, and in 1974 he was made a knight first class of the Order of St. Olaf by the Government of Norway.

United Nations Commission on Human Rights

Appointment of Jerome J. Shestack as U.S. Representative.   December 10, 1979

The President today announced that he will appoint Jerome J. Shestack, of Philadelphia, Pa., to be U.S. Representative to the United Nations Commission on Human Rights. He replaces Edward Mezvinsky, resigning. Shestack is an attorney in Philadelphia and president of the International League for Human Rights.

He was born February 11, 1923, in Atlantic City, N.J. He received a B.A. from the University of Pennsylvania in 1943 and an LL.B. from Harvard Law School in 1949. He served in the U.S. Navy from 1943 to 1946.

From 1949 to 1950, Shestack was an instructor at Northwestern Law School, and from 1950 to 1952, he was an instructor at Louisiana State University Law School. In 1952 he served as deputy city solicitor of Philadelphia.

From 1953 to 1955, Shestack was first deputy city solicitor. In 1953 he was also an instructor at the University of Pennsylvania Law School. Since 1955 he has been with the firm of Schnader, Harrison, Segal and Lewis; he has been a partner since 1956.

Shestack is president of the International League for Human Rights, a nongovernmental international human rights organization with consultative status at the United Nations and with affiliates in some 35 nations. He is founder and cochairman of the Lawyers Committee for International Human Rights, a public interest law association which deals with international human rights problems. He has chaired a number of international human rights conferences.

Shestack was a founding member of the Lawyers Committee for Civil Rights Under Law and has served on the board of directors of the Mexican-American Legal Defense Fund. He was a founder of the section of individual rights and responsibilities of the American Bar Association and served as chairman of the section in 1969–70.

In 1973 he became the first chairman of the Commission on Mentally Disabled of the American Bar Association, where he established projects to help provide legal services and promote rights for the mentally disabled. He served on the first steering committee to organize the legal services program of the Office of Economic Opportunity and then became a member of the OEO National Advisory Committee to the Legal Services Program.

Shestack is chairman of the ABA Standing Committee on Legal Aid and Indigent Defendants and is on the board of directors of the American Jewish Committee.

Price Advisory Committee

Appointment of Six Members.
December 10, 1979

The President today announced the selection of six prominent public sector representatives to serve as members of the anti-inflation program's Price Advisory Committee.

The President announced on September 28 that an advisory panel would be named in order to broaden public participation in the design and implementation of the voluntary price standard. Panel membership was enlarged from five to six to ensure greater public input.

A Pay Advisory Committee, with six representatives each from the business, labor, and public sectors, was named on October 16. That panel, which is chaired by Harvard University economist John T. Dunlop, has been meeting regularly to discuss possible changes in the voluntary pay standard.

The Price Committee will advise the Council on Wage and Price Stability on the development of policies to encourage anti-inflationary price behavior. The policies are intended to slow the rate of inflation and assure equitable distribution of the burden of restraint. The Committee may recommend modifications of the price standard, new or revised interpretations of the standard, or make any other recommendations on the standards that it considers necessary to assure fairness and equity.

The Committee's first meeting is scheduled for Thursday, December 13,

1979, at 10 a.m. in Room 2008, New Executive Office Building. The Chairman will be announced at the first meeting.

The following persons will serve as members of the Price Advisory Committee:

ROBERT ATWOOD, a partner in the international accounting firm of Deloitte Haskins & Sells. He is currently director of the firm's national affairs office in Washington.

BARBARA BERGMANN, professor of economics at the University of Maryland.

CAROL SCHWARTZ GREENWALD, visiting associate professor of business administration at Harvard Business School and former commissioner of banks of the Commonwealth of Massachusetts.

STANLEY RUTTENBERG, president of the consulting firm of Ruttenberg, Friedman, Kilgallon, Gutchess & Associates and former Assistant Secretary of Labor.

JOHN SHEAHAN, professor of economics at Williams College and author of "Wage-Price Guidepost."

ALBERT T. SOMMERS, chairman, senior vice president and chief economist of the Conference Board.

Federal Government Pension Plans
Executive Order 12177.   December 10, 1979

By the authority vested in me as President of the United States of America by Section 121(a)(1) of the Budget and Accounting Procedures Act of 1950, as amended (92 Stat. 2541, Public Law 95–595, 31 U.S.C. 68a), and Section 301 of Title 3 of the United States Code, and in order to provide consistency among the financial and actuarial statements of Federal Government pension plans, it is hereby ordered as follows:

1–101. All the functions vested in the President by Section 121(a) of the Budget and Accounting Procedures Act of 1950, as amended (31 U.S.C. 68a), are delegated to the Director of the Office of Management and Budget. The Director may, from time to time, designate other officers or agencies of the Federal Government to perform any or all of the functions hereby delegated to the Director, subject to such instructions, limitations, and directions as the Director deems appropriate.

1–102. The head of an Executive agency responsible for the administration of any Federal Government pension plan within the meaning of Section 123(a) of the Budget and Accounting Procedures Act of 1950, as amended (31 U.S.C. 68c), except subsection (a)(9) and (b), shall ensure that the administrators of those plans comply with the form, manner, and time of filing as required by the Director of the Office of Management and Budget.

1–103. Subject to the provisions of Section 1–101 of this Order, and in the absence of any contrary delegation or direction by the Director, the Secretary of the Treasury, with respect to the development of the form and content of the annual reports, shall perform the functions set forth in Section 121(a) of the Budget and Accounting Procedures Act of 1950, as amended (31 U.S.C. 68a). In performing this function, the Secretary shall also be responsible for consulting with the Comptroller General.

JIMMY CARTER

The White House,
    December 10, 1979.

[Filed with the Office of the Federal Register, 11:05 a.m., December 11, 1979]

Foreign Assistance Functions

Executive Order 12178.   December 10, 1979

FUNCTIONS UNDER THE FOREIGN ASSIST-
ANCE ACT OF 1961, AS AMENDED

By the authority vested in me as President of the United States of America by Section 633 of the Foreign Assistance Act of 1961, as amended (22 U.S.C. 2393), Executive Order No. 11223 of May 12, 1965, is hereby amended by adding at the end thereof the following Section:

"Sec. 6. I determine it to be in furtherance of the purposes of the Foreign Assistance Act of 1961, as amended, and in the national security interest of the United States that the functions authorized by chapter 7 of Part II of that Act, relating to air base construction in Israel, be performed without regard to the following additional specified provisions of law:

(1) Title IX of the Federal Property and Administrative Services Act of 1949, as amended (40 U.S.C. 541–544);

(2) Section 612 of the Military Construction Authorization Act, 1967, as amended (31 U.S.C. 723a);

(3) Section 719 of the Defense Production Act of 1950, as amended (50 U.S.C. App. 2168); and

(4) Section 111 of the Federal Property and Administrative Services Act of 1949, as amended (40 U.S.C. 759).".

JIMMY CARTER

The White House,
    December 10, 1979.

[Filed with the Office of the Federal Register, 11:15 a.m., December 11, 1979]

Nationwide Outdoor Recreation Plan

Message to the Congress Transmitting the Plan.   December 11, 1979

To the Congress of the United States:

It is with pleasure that I transmit the third Nationwide Outdoor Recreation Plan to the Congress of the United States, as required by P.L. 88–29 (16 U.S.C. 460*l*–1(c)). This Plan has been prepared by the Department of the Interior to address a number of current recreation issues, and assess the existing supply, demand, and opportunities associated with outdoor recreation in America.

The Plan was derived from a new planning process which maximizes public involvement and leads to specific actions. The rivers and trails directives issued in my 1979 Environmental Message are among the major decisions which originated with this Plan. Also included in the Plan are specific actions related to Federal land acquisition policy, environmental education, recreation access for the handicapped, and energy conservation. The Urban Parks and Recreation Recovery Program, which I proposed as one of my urban initiatives, is already helping to enhance close-to-home recreation opportunities, conserving energy while meeting basic recreation needs.

The challenge of enhancing recreation opportunity cannot be met by government action alone. New partnerships among all levels of government and the private sector will be required. New ways of combining resources from a variety of existing programs must be tested to meet our Nation's recreation needs.

JIMMY CARTER

The White House,
    December 11, 1979.

American Anhydrous Ammonia Industry

Letter to the Speaker of the House and the President of the Senate Transmitting a Report. December 11, 1979

Dear Mr. Speaker: (Dear Mr. President:)

In accordance with section 203(b)(2) of the Trade Act of 1974, enclosed is a report to the Congress setting forth my determination that import relief for the U.S. anhydrous ammonia industry is not in the national economic interest, and explaining the reasons for my decision.

Sincerely,

JIMMY CARTER

IMPORT RELIEF ACTION

ANHYDROUS AMMONIA

As required under section 203(b)(2) of the Trade Act of 1974, I am transmitting this report to Congress setting forth the action I will take with respect to anhydrous ammonia covered by the affirmative finding on October 12, 1979 of the U.S. International Trade Commission (USITC) under section 406 of the Trade Act. As my action differs from that recommended by the USITC, I have included the reasons for my decision:

After considering all relevant aspects of the case, including those considerations set forth in section 202(c) of the Trade Act of 1974, I have determined that provision of import relief is not in the national economic interest for the following reasons:

(1) Anticipated conditions in the U.S. and overseas markets for anhydrous ammonia do not warrant import relief at this time. The industry is currently operating at 86 percent of capacity and should continue to operate at comparable levels,

prices are sharply higher and expected to continue rising, and strong market conditions are projected for the current and next marketing years. Given anticipated growth in demand for grains and other crops, it is critical that farmers have access to sufficient fertilizer supplies at reasonable prices.

(2) Relief would not limit the growth in U.S. imports of anhydrous ammonia but will merely shift the source of foreign supplies from the Soviets to other low-cost producers. Thus, the domestic industry would realize little benefit from relief and relief would be unlikely to promote industry adjustment.

I have directed the U.S. Trade Representative to request the U.S. International Trade Commission to follow closely overall market conditions for ammonia until further notice and to issue annual reports beginning in November 1980. I would plan to have these reports discussed with appropriate Soviet officials through existing channels.

NOTE: This is the text of identical letters addressed to Thomas P. O'Neill, Jr., Speaker of the House of Representatives, and Walter F. Mondale, President of the Senate.

American Anhydrous Ammonia Industry

Memorandum From the President. December 11, 1979

Memorandum for the Special Representative for Trade Negotiations

Subject: Determination under Section 406 and 202 of the Trade Act of 1974; Anhydrous Ammonia from the Union of Soviet Socialist Republics

Pursuant to section 406(b) and 202 of the Trade Act of 1974 (P.L. 93–618, 88 Stat. 1978), I have determined the action I will take with respect to the report of the United States International Trade Commission (USITC), transmitted to me on October 12, 1979, concerning the results of its investigation of a petition for import injury filed on behalf of 12 U.S. producers and one U.S. distributor of anhydrous ammonia provided for under items 417.22 and 480.65 of the Tariff Schedules of the United States (TSUS).

After considering all relevant aspects of the case, including those considerations set forth in section 202(c) of the Trade Act of 1974, I have determined that provision of import relief is not in the national economic interest for the following reasons:

1. Anticipated conditions in the U.S. and overseas markets for anhydrous ammonia do not warrant import relief at this time. The industry is currently operating at 86 percent of capacity and should continue to operate at comparable levels, prices are sharply higher and expected to continue rising, and strong market conditions are projected for the current and next marketing years. Given anticipated growth in demand for grains and other crops, it is critical that farmers have access to sufficient fertilizer supplies at reasonable prices.

2. Relief would not limit the growth in U.S. imports of anhydrous ammonia but will merely shift the source of foreign supplies from the Soviets to other low-cost producers. Thus, the domestic industry would realize little benefit from relief and relief would be unlikely to promote industry adjustment.

You should request the U.S. International Trade Commission to issue a factual report on overall market conditions for ammonia as prescribed under section 332 of the Tariff Act of 1930. This report should be prepared on an annual basis, beginning in November 1980, until further notice. I would plan to have these reports discussed with appropriate Soviet officials through existing channels.

This determination is to be published in the FEDERAL REGISTER.

JIMMY CARTER

[Filed with the Office of the Federal Register, 12:10 p.m., December 11, 1979]

Holiday for Federal Employees
Executive Order 12179.   December 11, 1979

PROVIDING FOR THE CLOSING OF GOVERNMENT DEPARTMENTS AND AGENCIES ON MONDAY, DECEMBER 24, 1979

By virtue of the authority vested in me as President of the United States, it is hereby ordered as follows:

SECTION 1–1. *General Provisions.*

1–101. All Executive departments and agencies shall be closed and their employees excused from duty on Monday, December 24, 1979, the day before Christmas Day, except as provided by Section 1–102 below.

1–102. The heads of Executive departments and agencies may determine that certain offices and installations of their organizations, or parts thereof, must remain open and that certain employees must report for duty on December 24, 1979, for reasons of national security or defense or for other public reasons.

SECTION 1–2. *Pay and leave for Employees.*

1–201. Monday, December 24, 1979, shall be considered a holiday for the purposes of the pay and leave of employees of the United States.

JIMMY CARTER

The White House,
  December 11, 1979.

[Filed with the Office of the Federal Register,
    12:11 p.m., December 11, 1979]

Geneva Protocol to the General Agreement on Tariffs and Trade

Proclamation 4707.   December 11, 1979

PROCLAMATION TO CARRY OUT THE GENEVA (1979) PROTOCOL TO THE GENERAL AGREEMENT ON TARIFFS AND TRADE AND FOR OTHER PURPOSES

By the President of the United States of America

A Proclamation

1. Pursuant to Section 101(a) of the Trade Act of 1974 (19 U.S.C. 2111(a)), I determined that certain existing duties and other import restrictions of the United States and of foreign countries were unduly burdening and restricting the foreign trade of the United States and that one or more of the purposes stated in Section 2 of the Trade Act of 1974 (19 U.S.C. 2102) would be promoted by entering into the trade agreements identified in the third and fourth recitals of this proclamation.

2. Sections 131, 132, 133, 134, 135, and 161(b) of the Trade Act of 1974 (19 U.S.C. 2151, 2152, 2153, 2154, 2155, and 2211(b)) and Section 4(c) of Executive Order No. 11846 of March 27, 1975, (3 CFR 1971–1975 Comp. 974), have been complied with.

3. Pursuant to Section 101(a)(1) of the Trade Act of 1974 (19 U.S.C. 2111

(a)(1)), I, through my duly empowered representative, (1) on July 11, 1979, entered into a trade agreement with other contracting parties to the General Agreement on Tariffs and Trade (61 Stat. (pts. 5 and 6)), as amended (the General Agreement), with countries seeking to accede to the General Agreement, and the European Economic Community, which agreement consists of the Geneva (1979) Protocol to the General Agreement, including a schedule of United States concessions annexed thereto (hereinafter referred to as "Schedule XX (Geneva-1979)"), a copy of which Geneva (1979) Protocol (including Schedule XX (Geneva–1979) annexed thereto) is annexed to this proclamation as Part 1 of Annex I, (2) on November 18, 1978, entered into a trade agreement with the Hungarian People's Republic, including a schedule of United States concessions annexed thereto, a copy of which agreement, and schedule, is annexed to this proclamation as Part 2 of Annex I, (3) on October 31, 1979, entered into a trade agreement with the United Mexican States, which agreement consists of an exchange of letters, one enclosing a schedule of United States concessions, a copy of which exchange of letters, including such enclosed schedule, is annexed to this proclamation as Part 3 of Annex I, and (4) on March 2, 1979, entered into a trade agreement with the Socialist Republic of Romania, which agreement consists of an exchange of letters, one enclosing a schedule of United States concessions, a copy of which exchange of letters, including such enclosed schedule, is annexed to this proclamation as Part 4 of Annex I; and on October 24, 1979, the American Institute in Taiwan entered into a trade agreement with the Coordination Council for North American Affairs (see the Taiwan Relations Act, Sections 4(b)(1), 6(a)(1), and 10 (a), 93 Stat. 15, 17, and 18, E.O. 12143, sections 1–203 and 1–204, 44 Fed. Reg. 37191), which agreement consists of an exchange of letters, one enclosing a schedule of the United States concessions, a copy of which exchange of letters, including such enclosed schedule, is annexed to this proclamation as Part 5 of Annex I.

4. Pursuant to Section 102 of the Trade Act of 1974 (19 U.S.C. 2112), I have determined that barriers to (and other distortions of) international trade were unduly burdening and restricting the foreign trade of the United States, and, through the Special Representative for Trade Negotiations (the Special Representative), I have consulted with the appropriate Committees of the Congress, notified the House of Representatives and the Senate of my intention to enter into the agreements identified in Section 2(c) of the Trade Agreements Act of 1979 (93 Stat. 148), transmitted to the Congress copies of such agreements (a copy of one of which agreements, with the Hungarian People's Republic, is annexed to this proclamation as Part 6 of Annex I), together with a draft of an implementing bill and a statement of administrative action, and such implementing bill, approving the agreements and the proposed administrative action, has been enacted into law (Section 2(a) of the Trade Agreements Act of 1979 (93 Stat. 147)).

5. (a) Pursuant to Section 502 of the Trade Agreements Act of 1979 (93 Stat. 251), I have determined that appropriate concessions have been received from foreign countries under trade agreements entered into under Title I of the Trade Act of 1974 (19 U.S.C. 2111 *et seq.*);

(b) Pursuant to Section 601(a) of the Trade Agreements Act of 1979 (93 Stat. 267), I have determined that duty-free treatment for certain articles now classified in the items of the Tariff Schedules of the United States (19 U.S.C. 1202) (TSUS) listed in, and certified pursuant to, Section 601(a)(2) of that Act (93 Stat. 267), will provide treatment comparable to that provided by foreign countries under the Agreement on Trade in Civil Aircraft;

(c) Pursuant to Section 503(a)(2) (A) of the Trade Agreements Act of 1979 (93 Stat. 251), I have determined, after providing interested parties an opportunity to comment, that each article identified in Annex IV to this proclamation is not import sensitive;

(d) Pursuant to Section 855(a) of the Trade Agreements Act of 1979 (93 Stat. 295), I have determined that adequate reciprocal concessions have been received, under trade agreements entered into under the Trade Act of 1974, for the application of the rate of duty appearing in rate column numbered 1 on January 1, 1979, for the comparable item on a proof gallon basis in the case of alcoholic beverages classified in all items in subpart D of part 12 of schedule 1 of the TSUS, except items 168.09; 168.12, 168.43, 168.77, 168.81, 168.87, and 168.95;

(e) Pursuant to Section 2(b)(2)(A) of the Trade Agreements Act of 1979 (93 Stat. 147), I have determined that obligations substantially the same as those applicable to developing countries set forth in the agreements listed in Section 2(c)(1), (2), (3), (4), and (5) of that Act (93 Stat. 148) will be observed in Taiwan.

6. Each modification of existing duty proclaimed herein which provides with respect to an article for a decrease in duty below the limitation specified in Sections 101(b)(1) or 109(a) of the Trade Act of 1974 (19 U.S.C. 2111(b)(1) or 2119 (a)), and each modification of any other import restriction or tariff provision so proclaimed is authorized by one or more

of the following provisions or statutes:

(a) Section 101(b)(2) of the Trade Act of 1974 (19 U.S.C. 2111(b)(2)), by virtue of the fact that the rate of duty existing on January 1, 1975, applicable to the article was not more than 5 percent ad valorem (or ad valorem equivalent);

(b) Section 109(b) of the Trade Act of 1974 (19 U.S.C. 2119(b)), by virtue of the fact that I have determined, pursuant to that section, that the decrease authorized by that section will simplify the computation of the amount of duty imposed with respect to the article;

(c) Sections 503(a)(2)(A) and 503 (a)(3) to (6) of the Trade Agreements Act of 1979 (93 Stat. 251 and 252) by virtue of the fact that they permit departures from the staging provisions of Section 109(a) of the Trade Act of 1974 (19 U.S.C. 2119(a));

(d) Sections 502(a), 855(a), and 601 (a) of the Trade Agreements Act of 1979 (93 Stat. 251, 295, and 267) by virtue of the authority in such sections for specified concessions based on reciprocity, but in the case of the last such section only after the conditions for acceptance of the Agreement on Trade in Civil Aircraft, identified in Section 2(c)(10) of that Act (93 Stat. 148), are fulfilled;

(e) Sections 505 through 513, inclusive, of the Trade Agreements Act of 1979 (93 Stat. 252–257) by virtue of the fact that they permit exceeding the limitations specified in Sections 101 or 109 of the Trade Act of 1974 (19 U.S.C. 2111 or 2119);

(f) Section 255 of the Trade Expansion Act of 1962 (19 U.S.C. 1885) by virtue of the fact that it permits termination of proclamations issued pursuant to authority contained in that act;

(g) Section 2(a) of the Trade Agreements Act of 1979 (93 Stat. 147) by virtue of its approval of the agreements identified in Section 2(c) of that Act (93 Stat. 148); and

(h) Section 304(a)(3)(J) of the Tariff Act of 1930 (19 U.S.C. 1304(a) (3)(J)) and Section 602(f) of the Trade Act of 1974 (19 U.S.C. 2101 note), by virtue of the fact that I have found that the effectiveness of the proviso to Section 304(a)(3)(J) with respect to the marking of articles provided for in headnote 2 of part 1 of schedule 2 of the TSUS is required or appropriate to carry out the first agreement identified in the third recital of this proclamation.

7. In the case of each decrease in duty, including those of the type specified in clause (a) or (b) of the sixth recital of this proclamation, which involves the determination of the ad valorem equivalent of a specific or compound rate of duty, and in the case of each modification in the form of an import duty, the United States International Trade Commission determined, pursuant to Section 601(4) of the Trade Act of 1974 (19 U.S.C. 2481 (4)) in accordance with Section 4(e) of Executive Order No. 11846 of March 27, 1975, (3 CFR 1971–1975 Comp. 973), and at my direction, the ad valorem equivalent of the specific or compound rate, on the basis of the value of imports of the article concerned during a period determined by it to be representative, utilizing, to the extent practicable, the standards of valuation contained in Sections 402 and 402a of the Tariff Act of 1930 (19 U.S.C. 1401a and 1402) applicable to the article during such representative period.

8. Pursuant to the Trade Act of 1974 and the Trade Agreements Act of 1979, I determined that the modification or continuance of existing duties or other import restrictions or the continuance of existing duty-free or excise treatment hereinafter proclaimed is required or ap-

propriate to carry out the trade agreements identified in the third recital of this proclamation or one or more of the trade agreements identified in Section 2(c) of the Trade Agreements Act of 1979 (93 Stat. 148).

9. Following unsatisfactory negotiations with the European Economic Community under Articles XXIV: 6 and XXVIII of the General Agreement regarding the maintenance by the European Economic Community of unreasonable import restrictions upon imports of poultry from the United States, the President, by Proclamation 3564 of December 4, 1963 (77 Stat. 1035), suspended certain United States tariff concessions; as a result of the reciprocal concessions contained in the Geneva (1979) Protocol to the General Agreement, I determine that the termination of such suspension of tariff concessions contained in Proclamation 3564 (except those applicable to automobile trucks valued at $1,000 or more (provided for in TSUS item 692.02)) is required to carry out the General Agreement.

Now, THEREFORE, I, JIMMY CARTER, President of the United States of America, acting under the authority vested in me by the Constitution and the statutes, including but not limited to Title I and Section 604 of the Trade Act of 1974, Section 2 and Titles V, VI, and VIII of the Trade Agreements Act of 1979, Section 255 of the Trade Expansion Act of 1962, and Section 301 of Title 3 of the United States Code, do proclaim that:

(1) At the close of December 31, 1979, the suspension of tariff concessions contained in Proclamation 3564 (except those applicable to automobile trucks valued at $1,000 or more (provided for in TSUS item 692.02)) shall terminate.

(2) The amendment to Section 466 of the Tariff Act of 1930 (19 U.S.C. 1466) provided for in Section 601(a)(3) of the Trade Agreements Act of 1979 (93 Stat. 268) shall be effective with respect to entries made under Section 466 on and after the date designated by the President under paragraph 5(b) of this proclamation.

(3) The rate of duty applicable to each item as to which the determination has been made in recital 5(d) is the rate of duty appearing in rate column numbered 1 on January 1, 1979, for the comparable item on a proof gallon basis or such rate as reduced under Section 101 of the Trade Act of 1974 (19 U.S.C. 2111).

(4) Subject to the provisions of the General Agreement, of the Geneva (1979) Protocol, of other agreements supplemental to the General Agreement, of the other agreements identified in recitals 3 and 4, and of United States law (including but not limited to provisions for more favorable treatment), the modification or continuance of existing duties or other import restrictions and the continuance of existing duty-free or excise treatment provided for in Schedule XX (Geneva–1979) (except those provided for in the items listed in Parts 1C, 1D, 2D, 2E, 2K, 3C, 3D, 4C, and 4D of Annex I to Schedule XX which are required to implement the Agreement on Implementation of Article VII of the General Agreement on Tariffs and Trade and those provided for in Section 1, Chapter 4, Unit C, note 2 (cheese quotas), and in Section 1, Chapter 10, Unit B, note 2 (chocolate quotas), all of which will be the subject of one or more separate proclamations), in the agreements identified in the third and fourth recitals of this proclamation, and in trade agreements legislation, shall become effective on or after January 1, 1980, as provided for herein.

(5) To this end—

(a) Except as provided for in subparagraph (b), the modifications to the TSUS made by Annex II, Section A of Annex III, and Sections B(1) through (4) of Annex IV of this proclamation shall be effective with respect to articles entered, or withdrawn from warehouse, for consumption on and after the effective dates specified in those annexes;

(b) The modifications provided for in Section A of Annex II to this proclamation which are authorized by Section 601 (a) of the Trade Agreements Act of 1979 (93 Stat. 267) shall apply to articles entered, or withdrawn from warehouse, for consumption on and after the date designated by the President when he determines that the requirements of Section 2 (b) of the Trade Agreements Act of 1979 (93 Stat. 147) have been met with respect to the Agreement on Trade in Civil Aircraft;

(c) The Special Representative shall make any determinations relevant to the designation of the effective dates of the modifications of the TSUS made by Sections B through G of Annex III, and Sections B(5) through (10) of Annex IV of this proclamation, and shall publish in the FEDERAL REGISTER the effective date with respect to each of the modifications made by these sections; such modifications shall apply to articles entered, or withdrawn from warehouse, for consumption on and after such effective date;

(d) The modifications to the TSUS made by Section C of Annex IV to this proclamation, relating to special treatment for the least developed developing countries (LDDC's), shall be effective with respect to articles entered, or withdrawn from warehouse, for consumption on and after the effective dates as provided for in Section B of Annex IV; whenever the rate of duty specified in the column numbered 1 for any TSUS item is reduced to the same level as the corresponding rate of duty specified in the

column entitled "LDDC" for such item, the rate of duty in the column entitled "LDDC" shall be deleted from the TSUS, and when the duty rates for all such items in Annex IV have been deleted, the modifications to the TSUS made by Section C of Annex IV to this proclamation shall be deleted;

(e) Section A of Annex IV shall become effective on January 1, 1980.

IN WITNESS WHEREOF, I have hereunto set my hand this eleventh day of December in the year of our Lord nineteen hundred and seventy-nine, and of the Independence of the United States of America the two hundred and fourth.

JIMMY CARTER

[Filed with the Office of the Federal Register, 9:50 a.m., December 12, 1979]

NOTE: The annexes are printed in the FEDERAL REGISTER of December 13, 1979.

Cheese and Chocolate Crumb Imports

Proclamation 4708.   December 11, 1979

IMPORT LIMITATIONS ON CERTAIN CHEESE AND CHOCOLATE CRUMB

By the President of the United States of America

A Proclamation

Import limitations have been imposed on certain dairy products, including certain cheese and chocolate crumb, pursuant to the provisions of Section 22 of the Agricultural Adjustment Act, as amended, 7 U.S.C. 624, (Section 22). Those limitations are set forth in Part 3 of the Appendix to the Tariff Schedules of the United States (TSUS).

Sections 701 and 703 of the Trade Agreements Act of 1979, P.L. 96–39 (The

Act), require that the President proclaim a) limitations on the quantity of types of cheese specified therein which may enter the United States in any calendar year after 1979 to an annual aggregate quantity of not more than 111,000 metric tons and b) increases in a specified manner, of the quantity of chocolate crumb now subject to certain import quotas which may be entered in any calendar year after 1979. Such limitations and increases are required to become effective on January 1, 1980.

It is provided in Sections 701 and 703 of the Act that such proclamation shall be considered a proclamation issued under Section 22 and which meets the requirements of such section.

The Act also approved bilateral agreements entered into during the Multilateral Trade Negotiations (MTN) by the United States and certain foreign countries with respect to the quantity of cheese and chocolate crumb subject to such limitations that may be imported from such countries. These agreements contained the provision that "the United States agrees to take all necessary measures to permit the maximum utilization of the quotas."

On the basis of the information submitted to me, I find and declare that the import limitations hereinafter proclaimed with respect to cheese and chocolate crumb are in accord with the requirements of Sections 701 and 703 of the Act and the bilateral agreements approved by such Act which were entered into by the United States and certain foreign countries with respect to the quantity of cheese and chocolate crumb subject to such limitations that may be imported from such countries.

Now, THEREFORE, I, JIMMY CARTER, President of the United States of America, acting under and by virtue of the authority vested in me as President, and in conformity with the provisions of Section 22 of the Agricultural Adjustment Act of 1933, as amended, the Tariff Classification Act of 1962, the Trade Act of 1974, the Trade Agreements Act of 1979, and the bilateral agreements relating to cheese and chocolate crumb approved by the Trade Agreements Act of 1979, do hereby proclaim that Part 3 of the Appendix to the Tariff Schedules of the United States is amended, effective January 1, 1980, as set forth in the Annex to this proclamation.

IN WITNESS WHEREOF, I have hereunto set my hand this eleventh day of December, in the year of our Lord nineteen hundred and seventy-nine, and of the Independence of the United States of America the two hundred and fourth.

JIMMY CARTER

[Filed with the Office of the Federal Register, 9:51 a.m., December 12, 1979]

NOTE: The annex is printed in the FEDERAL REGISTER of December 13, 1979.

Generalized System of Preferences for Developing Countries

Executive Order 12180.   December 11, 1979

AMENDING THE GENERALIZED SYSTEM OF PREFERENCES

By virtue of the authority vested in me by the Constitution and statutes of the United States of America, including Title V of the Trade Act of 1974 (88 Stat. 2066, 19 U.S.C. 2461 *et seq.*), as amended by Section 1111 of the Trade Agreements Act of 1979 (93 Stat. 315), and Section 604 of the Trade Act of 1974 (88 Stat. 2073, 19 U.S.C. 2483), and as President of the United States of America, in order to adapt the preferential treatment under the Generalized System of Preferences (GSP) for articles from countries designated as beneficiary developing countries which are currently eligible for such treatment, to the numerous changes of the law and of the Tariff Schedules of the United States (TSUS) (19 U.S.C. 1202) which have resulted from the enactment of the Trade Agreements Act of 1979 (93 Stat. 144 *et seq.*) and Proclamation 4707 to Carry Out the Geneva (1979) Protocol to the General Agreement on Tariffs and Trade and for Other Purposes; and to make conforming modifications to the TSUS, it is hereby ordered as follows:

SECTION 1. General Headnote 3(c)(ii) of the TSUS, is modified by substituting therefor the new General Headnote 3(c)(ii) as provided in Annex I, attached hereto and made a part hereof.

SEC. 2. Annex II of Executive Order No. 11888 of November 24, 1975, as amended, listing articles that are eligible for benefits of the GSP when imported from any designated beneficiary developing country, is further amended as provided in Annex II, attached hereto and made a part hereof.

SEC. 3. Annex III of Executive Order No. 11888, as amended, listing articles that are eligible for benefits of the GSP when imported from all designated beneficiary countries except those specified in General Headnote 3(c)(iii) of the TSUS, is further amended as provided in Annex III, attached hereto and made a part hereof.

SEC. 4. General Headnote 3(c)(iii) of the TSUS, listing articles that are eligible for benefits of the GSP except when imported from the beneficiary countries listed opposite these articles, is modified as provided in Annex IV, attached hereto and made a part hereof.

SEC. 5. General Headnote 3(c)(i) of the TSUS is modified by deleting from the list of independent designated beneficiary countries "Central African Empire" and "Yemen Arab Republic", and by substituting therefor, in alphabetical order, "Central African Republic," and "Yemen (Sana)", respectively.

SEC. 6. The amendments and modifications made by this Order shall be effective with respect to articles both: (1) imported on and after January 1, 1976, and (2) entered, or withdrawn from warehouse, for consumption on and after January 1, 1980.

JIMMY CARTER

The White House,
December 11, 1979.

[Filed with the Office of the Federal Register, 9:52 a.m., December 12, 1979]

NOTE: The annexes are printed in the FEDERAL REGISTER of December 13, 1979.

Generalized System of Preferences for Developing Countries

Executive Order 12181.   December 11, 1979

AMENDING THE GENERALIZED SYSTEM OF PREFERENCES

By virtue of the authority vested in me by the Constitution and statutes of the United States of America, including Title V and Section 604 of the Trade Act of 1974 (88 Stat. 2066, 19 U.S.C. 2461 et seq.; 88 Stat. 2073, 19 U.S.C. 2483), and as President of the United States of America, in order to modify, as provided by Section 504(c) of the Trade Act of 1974 (88 Stat. 2070, 19 U.S.C. 2464(c)), the limitations on preferential treatment for eligible articles from countries designated as beneficiary developing countries, and to adjust the original designation of eligible articles taking into account information and advice received in fulfillment of Sections 503(a) and 131–134 of the Trade Act of 1974 (88 Stat. 2069, 19 U.S.C. 2463(a); 88 Stat. 1994, 19 U.S.C. 2151–2154), it is hereby ordered as follows:

SECTION 1. The Tariff Schedules of the United States (TSUS) (19 U.S.C. 1202) are modified by striking out items 791.24 and 791.26, including the superior heading thereto, and inserting in lieu thereof the following:

"791.26 Other.... 5% ad val. 15% ad val."

SEC. 2. Annex II of Executive Order No. 11888, as amended, listing articles that are eligible for benefits of the GSP when imported from any designated beneficiary country is further amended by deleting item 652.99 and by adding items 145.08, 653.00, and 653.01 thereto.

SEC. 3. Annex III of Executive Order No. 11888, as amended, listing articles that are eligible for benefits of the GSP when imported from all designated beneficiary countries except those specified in General Headnote 3(c)(iii) of the TSUS, is further amended by deleting item 145.08 therefrom.

SEC. 4. General Headnote 3(c)(iii) of the TSUS, listing articles that are eligible for benefits of the GSP except when imported from the beneficiary countries listed opposite those articles, is amended by deleting therefrom the following:

"145.08......Philippine Republic
724.35.....Republic of Korea";

and by adding thereto, in numerical sequence, the following:

"724.35.....Mexico".

SEC. 5. The amendments made by Executive Order 12124 of February 28, 1979, with respect to TSUS items 680.55 and 680.56 shall be effective as to articles that are both (1) imported on or after January 1, 1976, and (2) entered, or withdrawn from warehouse, for consumption on or after October 21, 1978, and as to which the liquidations of the entries or withdrawals have not become final and conclusive under Section 514 of the Tariff Act of 1930 (19 U.S.C. 1514).

SEC. 6. The amendments made with respect to items 145.08 and 724.35 by Sections 2, 3, and 4 of this Order shall be effective as to articles that are both (1) imported on or after January 1, 1976, and (2) entered, or withdrawn from warehouse, for consumption on or after March 1, 1979, and as to which the liquidations of the entries or withdrawals have not become final and conclusive under Section 514 of the Tariff Act of 1930 (19 U.S.C. 1514).

SEC. 7. The amendments made with respect to items 652.99, 653.00, and 653.01 by Section 2 of this Order shall be effective as to articles that are both (1) imported on or after January 1, 1976, and (2) entered, or withdrawn from warehouse, for consumption on or after July 26, 1979, and as to which the liquidations of the entries or withdrawals have not become final and conclusive under Section 514 of the Tariff Act of 1930 (19 U.S.C. 1514).

SEC. 8. The amendments made by Section 1 of this Order shall be effective with respect to articles that are both (1) imported on or after January 1, 1976, and (2) entered, or withdrawn from warehouse, for consumption on or after the third day following the date of publication of this Order in the FEDERAL REGISTER.

JIMMY CARTER

The White House,
  December 11, 1979.

[Filed with the Office of the Federal Register,
  9:53 a.m., December 12, 1979]

Department of Commerce

Nomination of Homer E. Moyer, Jr., To Be General Counsel. December 11, 1979

The President today announced that he will nominate Homer E. Moyer, Jr., of Washington, D.C., to be General Counsel of the Commerce Department. He would replace C. L. Haslam, resigning. Moyer has been Counsellor to the Secretary of Commerce since earlier this year and was Deputy General Counsel from 1976 to 1979.

He was born November 20, 1942, in Atlanta, Ga. He graduated from Emory University in 1964 and from Yale Law School in 1967.

From 1968 to 1971, Moyer was an attorney in the Office of the Judge Advocate General of the Navy. From 1971 to 1973, he was a fellow with the Public Law Education Institute in Washington. From 1973 to 1976, he practiced law with the firm of Covington & Burling.

Appalachian Regional Commission

Nomination of Albert P. Smith To Be Federal Cochairman. December 12, 1979

The President today announced that he will nominate Albert P. Smith, of Russellville, Ky., to be Federal Cochairman of the Appalachian Regional Commission. He would replace Robert W. Scott, resigned.

Smith is editor and publisher of the Russellville, Ky., News-Democrat and Logan Leader and head of a publishing company, Al Smith Communications, Inc., which owns these and four other weekly newspapers in western Kentucky and Tennessee.

He was born January 9, 1927, in Sara-

sota, Fla. He served in the U.S. Army in 1945 and 1946 and attended Vanderbilt University in 1946–47.

Smith was with the New Orleans Times-Picayune from 1947 to 1954, as assistant State editor and day police and criminal courts reporter. From 1954 to 1957, he was assistant city editor of the New Orleans Item.

In 1957 he became editor and part owner of the Russellville News-Democrat. Over the next 20 years he bought the other newspapers, and in 1977 he consolidated all the companies into Al Smith Communications, Inc.

Smith has also been producer and moderator for the weekly Kentucky educational television program "Comment on Kentucky" since 1974. He served as president of the Kentucky Press Association in 1975. He is chairman of the Kentucky Arts Commission and chairman of the Kentucky Oral History Commission. He is on the advisory board of the Tennessee River Valley Association.

Soviet Mission to the United Nations

White House Statement on the Bombing of the Mission. December 12, 1979

The United States Government strongly and unequivocally condemns last night's criminal bombing of the Soviet Mission to the United Nations. There have been two cowardly bomb attacks against foreign diplomatic missions in New York in the last week, both allegedly perpetrated by the same group, which calls itself Omega 7. (The Cuban Mission to the U.N. was also attacked on December 7.) We want to emphasize that the United States is totally committed to the carrying out of its responsibilities for the protection of foreign diplomats in the United States.

Ambassador McHenry has expressed the official regrets of the U.S. Government to the Soviet Permanent Representative to the U.N., and the Department of State has made a parallel statement of regret to the Soviet Chargé d'Affaires. We shall do all in our power to see that such outrages are not repeated.

Department of the Navy

Nomination of Joseph A. Doyle To Be an Assistant Secretary. December 12, 1979

The President today announced that he will nominate Joseph A. Doyle, of New York City, to be Assistant Secretary of the Navy. He would replace Edward Hidalgo, who has been appointed Secretary of the Navy, and his responsibility would be manpower, reserve affairs, and logistics.

Doyle has been a partner in the New York law firm of Shearman and Sterling since 1956.

He was born June 13, 1920, in New York City. He received a B.S. from Georgetown University in 1941 and an LL.B. from Columbia University School of Law in 1947.

Doyle served in the U.S. Navy from 1941 to 1945. He was a naval aviator and served on board the U.S.S. *Enterprise* in the Pacific from 1943 to 1945. He was awarded the Navy Cross, the Distinguished Flying Cross, and the Air Medal.

Doyle joined the law firm of Shearman and Sterling in 1947 as an associate and became a partner in 1956.

United States Defense Policy

Remarks to Members of the Business Council. December 12, 1979

Chairman Reg Jones, members of the Business Council:

It's indeed a pleasure for me to be with you again. This afternoon I would like to make a very important statement to you, following which the chairman and I will walk down the hall, and I'd like to greet each one of you individually, as has been my custom in the past when we've been together. And then we'll have a chance for a few questions that you might want to put to me concerning energy or inflation or legislation before the Congress or Iran or other matters of interest to you.

But my first concern, and the first concern of every President who has ever lived in this house, is and must be the security of our Nation. This security rests on many kinds of strength, on arms and also on arms control, on military power and on economic vitality and the quality of life of our own people, on modern weapons, and also on reliable energy supplies. The well-being of our friends and our allies is also of great importance to us. Our security is tied to human rights and to social justice which prevails among the people who live on Earth and to the institutions of international force and peace and order which we ourselves have helped to build.

We all hope and work and pray that we will see a world in which the weapons of war are no longer necessary, but now we must deal with the hard facts, with the world as it is. In the dangerous and uncertain world of today, the keystone of our national security is still military strength, strength that is clearly recognized by

Americans, by our allies, and by any potential adversary.

Twice in this century, each time in the aftermath of a global war, we were tempted in this country by isolationism. The first time, we succumbed to that temptation, withdrawing from our global responsibilities, and you know what the result was. A generation later the world was again engulfed by war. But after the Second World War, we built a national consensus, based on our own moral and political values, around the concept of an active role for America in preserving peace and security for ourselves and for others.

Despite all the changes that have swept across this world in the last 30 years, that basic consensus has endured. We've learned the mistake of military intervention in the internal affairs of another country when our own American security was not directly involved. But we must understand that not every instance of the firm application of the power of the United States is a potential Vietnam. The consensus for national strength and international involvement, already shaken and threatened, survived that divisive and tragic war.

Recent events in Iran have been a vivid reminder of the need for a strong and united America, a nation which is supported by its allies and which need not bluff or posture in the quiet exercise of our strength and in our continued commitment to international law and the preservation of peace. Today, regardless of other disagreements among ourselves, we are united in the belief that we must have a strong defense and that military weakness would inevitably make war more likely.

So, the issue we face is not whether we should be strong; the issue is how we will be strong. What will be our defense responsibilities for the 1980's and beyond? What challenges must we confront in meeting those responsibilities? What defense programs do we need, and how much will we spend to meet them? How can we correlate most successfully our military readiness and our arms control efforts? To begin with, our defense program must be tailored to match our responsibilities.

In Europe our military forces have provided the foundation for one of the longest periods of peace and prosperity that continent has ever enjoyed. Our strength, both conventional and nuclear, helps to maintain peace while our allies work together and build together through the European Community and also nurture their historical ties to the countries of Eastern Europe. Our mutual commitments within the Atlantic Alliance are vital to us all, and those commitments are permanent and unshakable.

American military strength provides the framework within which our mature friendships with Japan, Korea, Australia, New Zealand, the Philippines, and Thailand all contribute to stability in the Pacific basin and throughout the world.

The prospects for peace in the Middle East have been enhanced by a strong America and by confidence in us among our friends in Egypt and in Israel. We are determined to continue the progress which has been made in the Middle East.

We must and we will continue to meet these and our other responsibilities. But there are reasons for concern about our ability to sustain our beneficial and our peaceful influence throughout the world—real reasons for concern.

For nearly 20 years now, the Soviet Union has been increasing its real defense spending by 3 or 4 percent each year, 3 or 4 percent compounded annually. In contrast, our own defense spending has declined in real terms every year from 1968 through 1976. This is creating a real challenge to American leadership and to our influence in the world.

We will almost certainly face other challenges, less direct, though no less serious. The 1980's are very likely to bring continued turbulence and upheaval, as we've experienced in the 1970's. Problems of energy price and energy supply will continue to strain the economy of the developed world and will put even more severe pressures on the developing nations. Political instability, which is already serious enough, may even intensify as the newer nations struggle to cope with these problems, which are serious enough for us.

As in the past, when the winds of change threaten to arouse storms of conflict, we must be prepared to join our friends and our allies in resisting threats to stability and to peace. The steady buildup by the Soviets and their growing inclination to rely on military power to exploit turbulent situations call for calm, deliberate, and sustained American response.

Through the mid-1970's, the United States relied on the defense strategy and also on force structures devised during the early 1960's, a time when we enjoyed strategic nuclear superiority and a tactical nuclear monopoly, when Soviet seapower was limited and the Soviet military presence outside Eastern Europe almost nonexistent. All that had changed by the time I took office as President.

Beginning in 1976 and continuing in my own administration, we've set out to counterbalance the growth in Soviet military power by launching new efforts that draw on our own considerable strengths. During each of the last 4 years, there has been a moderate increase in real defense spending. In Europe we've taken steps, as you know, to reverse a decade of relative decline in the military strength of the Atlantic Alliance.

When I first began to meet with Atlantic Alliance leaders almost 3 years ago, I found them very troubled by the state of our military strength in the Atlantic Alliance. I promised to raise our own level of defense spending, in real terms, by some 3 percent per year, and our NATO Allies responded by making the same pledge. With American leadership, NATO also took the crucial step of adopting a bold, long-term defense program, which will extend over 15 years. That program is helping us to increase our capacity to deter or to defeat any surprise attack that may be launched against our European allies and, therefore, against ourselves.

We are also taking steps to redress the balance in other theater nuclear forces. This action, as you know, we've been pursuing in the last few days.

In the early 1960's, the United States removed its medium-range missiles from Europe. We could do this then, because there was overwhelming United States strategic superiority. But the Soviet Union did not show similar restraint. The accelerating development of their relatively long-range, mobile, multiwarhead SS–20 missile is a major escalation in theater nuclear armaments. With the advent of rough strategic parity, this new missile creates a potentially dangerous weakness in NATO's ability to deter aggression. In the SALT II negotiations, we carefully protected our freedom to correct this weakness.

Just a few hours ago, I was informed that the NATO Alliance resolved to strengthen its theater nuclear weapons to offset actual Soviet deployments. The agreement reached this afternoon in Europe was a unanimous agreement very encouraging to all of us. Now, on the basis of strength, we can negotiate with the Warsaw Pact to reduce nuclear weapons and also to reduce, we hope, conventional weapons throughout the European theater.

In the area of intercontinental or strategic forces, we also face adverse trends that must be corrected. Improved Soviet air defenses now threaten to make our strategic bombers vulnerable. The cruise missile will be our solution to that problem. Production of the first generation of air-launched cruise missiles will begin next year.

In addition, our land-based Minuteman ICBM's are becoming increasingly vulnerable because of the improved accuracy of the Soviet Union's multiwarhead missiles. That's why we decided last spring to produce the MX missile. The relatively small number of MX missiles to be deployed will have mobility and a large number of shelters and will be far less vulnerable than our present fixed-shelter Minutemen. Further, in response to any first strike against us, the MX will have the capability to attack a wide variety of Soviet military targets.

The MX missile, deployed as I've just described, will not undermine stability, but it will deter attack and encourage negotiations on further nuclear arms limits. In addition, by increasing the difficulty of any contemplated Soviet strike, it will contribute to the survivability of our own strategic bombers and submarines. Even with SALT II, America needs the MX to maintain the strategic nuclear balance.

We are also modernizing our strategic submarine force. The first new Trident submarine has already been launched, and the first of our new Trident missiles, with a range of more than 4,000 miles, have already been put to sea.

Thus, each leg of our strategic triad is being modernized—cruise missiles for our bombers, the MX for our intercontinental missiles, and Trident for our undersea deterrent. Nor will we neglect our conventional forces, though here we must rely heavily on the parallel efforts of our allies, in Asia as well as in Europe. They must bear their proportional share of the increased costs of a common defense.

I'm determined to keep our naval forces more powerful than those of any other nation on Earth. Our shipbuilding program will sustain a 550-ship navy in the 1990's, and we will continue to build the most capable ships afloat. Seapower is indispensable to our global strategy, in peace and also in war.

And finally, we are moving rapidly to counterbalance the growing ability of the Soviet Union, directly or through surrogates, to use its military power in Third World regions, and we must be prepared to deal with hostile actions against our own citizens or our vital interests from others as well. For this purpose, we need not only stronger forces but better means for rapid deployment of the forces that we already have.

Our 1981 defense budget and our 5-year defense program will meet this need in two different ways. The first will be a new fleet of maritime prepositioning ships that will carry the heavy equipment and the supplies for three Marine brigades that can be stationed in forward areas where United States forces may be needed. With their supplies already near the scene of action, the troops themselves can then be moved in by air very rapidly. The second innovation will be a new fleet of large cargo aircraft to carry Army tanks and other equipment over intercontinental distances.

Having rapid deployment forces does not necessarily mean that we will use them. We intend for their existence to deter the very developments that would otherwise invoke their use.

We must always remember that no matter how capable or advanced our weapons systems, our military security depends on the abilities, the training, and the dedication of the people who serve in our Armed Forces. I'm determined to recruit and to retain, under any foreseeable circumstances, an ample level of such skilled and experienced military personnel.

To sum up, the United States is taking strong action: first, to improve all aspects of our strategic forces, thus assuring our deterrent to nuclear war; second, to upgrade our forces in NATO and in the Pacific, as part of a common effort with our allies; third, to modernize our naval forces and keep them the best in the world; fourth, to strengthen our rapid deployment capabilities to meet our responsibilities outside NATO; and fifth, to maintain an effective force of highly trained military personnel.

We must sustain these commitments in order to maintain peace and security in the 1980's. To ensure that we press forward vigorously, I will submit for fiscal year 1981 a budget to increase funding authority for defense to more than $157 billion, a real growth of more than 5 percent over my request for fiscal year 1980. Just as in 1979 and in 1980, requested outlays for defense during fiscal year 1981 will grow by more than 3 percent, in real terms, over the preceding year. We will sustain this effort.

My 5-year defense program provides a real funding increase that will average more than 4½ percent each year. I intend to carry out this program. With careful and efficient management, we should be able to do so within the budget increases I propose. If inflation increases or exceeds the projected rates that we now expect, I intend to adjust the defense budget as needed, just as has been done in 1980 fiscal year.

Much of this program which I've outlined to you will take 5 years or more to reach fruition. The imbalances it will correct have been caused by more than a decade of disparity. This cannot be remedied overnight, so we must be willing to see this program through. To ensure that we do so, I'm setting a growth rate for defense that will be tolerable for our country over the long haul.

The most wasteful and self-defeating thing that we could do would be to start this necessary program, then alter it or cut it back after a year or two when such an action might become politically attractive. The defense program that I'm proposing for the next 5 years will require some sacrifice—but sacrifice that we can well afford. It will not increase at all the percentage of our gross national product devoted to defense, which will remain steady at almost exactly 5 percent per year.

We must have a long-range, balanced approach to the allocation of Federal expenditures. We will continue to meet such crucial needs, of course, as jobs and housing and education and health, but we must realize that a prerequisite to the enjoyment of such progress is to assure peace for our Nation. So, in asking congressional support for our defense efforts, I'm asking for consistent support, steadfast support—not just for 1980 or 1981, but until these commitments have been fulfilled.

Sustained American strength is the only possible basis for the wider, truly reciprocal détente which we seek with the Soviet Union. Only through strength can we create global political conditions hospitable to worldwide economic and political progress and to controlling both conventional and nuclear weapons.

As the strongest, most advanced country on Earth, we have a special obligation to seek security through arms control as well as through military power. So, I welcome the debate by the Senate in its consideration of the SALT II treaty. It will enable us to build a clearer understanding that these efforts in both arms control and in defense are vital to our security and they are mutually compatible, one with another.

There are several reasons why SALT II will strengthen the military aspect of our national security:

First, we can better maintain strategic equivalence in nuclear weapons with SALT II. Without it, the Soviet Union can add more to the power of their own forces, widen any advantage that they may achieve in the early 1980's, and conceal from us what they are doing. For us, maintaining parity with these uncontrollable Soviet activities would add to our costs in time, money, and also uncertainty about our own safety.

Second, we can better maintain the combat efficiency and readiness of our nonnuclear forces with SALT II than we can without it. Whatever the level of the defense budget, more of it will have to go into strategic weapons, atomic weapons, if SALT II is not ratified.

Third, we can better strengthen the unity, resolve, and capability of the NATO Alliance with SALT II than we can without it. That's why the heads of other NATO countries have urged strongly its ratification.

Fourth, we can better continue the SALT process, which has now been going on for more than 30 years, the process of negotiating further reductions in the world's nuclear arsenals, with SALT II than without it. Without SALT II and

all its limits, its rules, and definitions in place, any agreement in SALT III would, at the very best, take many more years to achieve.

And finally, we can better control the proliferation of nuclear weapons among currently nonnuclear nations with SALT II than without it. This could be one of the most important factors involved in our pending decision on the SALT treaty.

All of these issues are extremely important, and they are intimately interrelated. A strong defense is a matter of simple common sense; so is SALT II.

I will do my utmost as President to keep America strong and to keep our Nation secure, but this cannot be done without sustained effort and without some sacrifice, which our Nation can certainly afford.

The best investment in defense is in weapons that will never have to be used and in soldiers who will never have to die. But the peace we enjoy is the fruit of our strength and our will to use this strength if we need to. As a great nation devoted to peace, we must and we will continue to build that American strength.

Thank you very much.

NOTE: The President spoke at 5 p.m. in the East Room at the White House.

Domestic Volunteer Service Act Amendments of 1979

Statement on Signing S. 239 Into Law.
December 13, 1979

I have today signed S. 239, which reauthorizes funding for the domestic volunteer service programs administered by the ACTION agency. The most notable of these is VISTA, a program through which volunteers donate their talents to help low-income people combat poverty and poverty-related problems.

I am especially pleased that this bill emphasizes use of existing authority for the new urban volunteer program, an important part of the comprehensive urban policy which I first presented in March 1978. Included in my urban initiatives and adopted in this act are the Urban Volunteer Corps, which will provide neighborhood groups with skilled volunteers, and a Good Neighbor Fund to make small grants to local urban organizations that undertake projects for community development. In addition, the act authorizes a fixed-income consumer counseling program to help low-income elderly people manage their money and Helping Hand programs through which volunteer, in-home services will be provided to reduce the number of the elderly and the handicapped requiring institutionalization.

In my urban policy I called for a partnership involving Federal, State, and local governments, the private sector, and neighborhood groups to revitalize the Nation's distressed urban communities. An important part of that policy was the desire to encourage citizens to take an active part in this revitalization activity. S. 239 will help to make such voluntary efforts a reality.

Some of the activities covered by the new urban volunteer program are currently being conducted on a demonstration basis in selected areas around the country, where, at minimal cost, volunteers have been successful in helping to solve problems and improve the quality of life in their communities.

With the passage of this legislation, 15 out of the 19 legislative proposals I originally submitted to Congress in my urban policy have been signed into law.

Finally, I want to recognize the diligent efforts and support of Senator Alan Cranston, and Representative Carl Perkins in getting this legislation enacted.

NOTE: As enacted, S. 239 is Public Law 96–143, approved December 13.

United States Ambassador to Turkey

Nomination of James W. Spain.
December 13, 1979

The President today announced that he will nominate James W. Spain, of California, to be Ambassador Extraordinary and Plenipotentiary of the United States to Turkey. He would replace Ronald I. Spiers, who is resigning. Spain was Ambassador to the United Republic of Tanzania from 1975 until earlier this year.

He was born July 22, 1926, in Chicago, Ill. He received an M.A. from the University of Chicago in 1949 and a Ph. D. from Columbia University in 1959. He served in the U.S. Army from 1946 to 1947.

Spain was a consultant to the Secretary of the Army in Tokyo from 1949 to 1950 and cultural officer in Karachi from 1951 to 1953. From 1953 to 1955, he was a research fellow with the Ford Foundation, and from 1955 to 1963, he was a research lecturer at Columbia University.

Spain was a member of the policy planning staff at the State Department in 1963 and 1964 and Director of the Office of Research and Analysis for Near East-South Asian Affairs from 1964 to 1966. From 1966 to 1969, he was country director for Pakistan and Afghanistan, and in 1969 he was Chargé d'Affaires in Islamabad.

From 1970 to 1972, Spain was consul general in Istanbul. From 1972 to 1974, he was Deputy Chief of Mission in Ankara. In 1974–75 he was diplomat in residence at Florida State University.

American Hostages in Iran

Statement by the White House Press Secretary.   December 13, 1979

We have read reports from Iran today that international observers will be allowed to see our people who are being held hostage.

I want to emphasize that for any such visit to the hostages to accomplish a humanitarian objective and to be responsive to international opinion and to acceptable standards of behavior, it is important that those who see the hostages be allowed to see all of them, to talk with them, and to report to the families of the hostages and to the world on the condition of each hostage. Any observers allowed on the Embassy compound should be qualified, internationally recognized, impartial, neutral observers and should include a qualified medical doctor. Visits by these observers should occur regularly and frequently until the hostages are released.

If this occurs, we would consider it a step forward.

NOTE: Press Secretary Jody Powell read the statement at approximately 11:45 a.m. during his regular briefing for reporters in the Briefing Room at the White House.

Gannett Newspaper and Broadcast Executives

Remarks and a Question-and-Answer Session at a White House Briefing. December 13, 1979

THE PRESIDENT. Good afternoon.

Well, it's a pleasure to be back with you. The last time I was joined with this group was in the same building in a different room, and now you see what Room 450 looks like. This is where your reporters put me through a grilling on the occasions when I come over for a press conference.

Some people ask me how I react to those press conferences, and it's hard for me to answer that question honestly and on the record. But I was thinking about one of the things that Hedley Donovan [1] said—one of your past associates. When he was at Fortune, he was working late at night, I understand, typing, bent over, sweating, worrying, and somebody came up and said, "Do you really enjoy writing?" And he said, "Well, let me put it this way: I enjoy having written." [*Laughter*] That's kind of the way with me. I enjoy having had press conferences, but I don't particularly enjoy it at the time.

I'm delighted to be with you. This is an important occasion, I know, in the history of Gannett. You have achieved a great level of performance and, also, business success. A very reliable source I have within Gannett has told me confidentially that you're now the largest news chain in the Nation, has more readers. The same reliable source told me when he was working for me that it was very important to have a better working relationship with the press. [*Laughter*] I understand that Vice President Walt Wurfel [2] has put that philosophy to work since he's been with you.

I thank you for coming. I would like to say a couple of things and then answer two or three questions if you don't mind.

ADMINISTRATION POLICIES

Our Nation is now embroiled in a circumstance in Iran that's not only difficult

[1] Senior Adviser to the President.
[2] Walter W. Wurfel, former Deputy Press Secretary to the President.

but also extremely sensitive and may have historic connotations for the future. I think it's demonstrated that Americans can be remarkably united, that Americans can be remarkably resolved, and that, contrary to our basic nature, Americans can also be very patient, when patience is the better part of valor.

I think we've learned, as I said yesterday in my speech to the Business Council, that it's a general consensus now in our country that military strength and also a strong nation is not contrary to the desires for peace. I think we've learned from the Vietnam war that to become unnecessarily involved in the internal affairs of another country when our own security is not directly threatened is a serious mistake. But we've also learned since then, particularly now, that a strong America, willing to exert its strength when necessary, is an integral part of the psyche of our country and also a legitimate role for America to play.

I don't know what the future will bring in the Iran situation. It's so far been handled with, I think, dispatch and also with wisdom. I've got good advisers, and we're very cautious about how we have approached this difficult circumstance.

We have emphasized over and over, not adequately yet, that there is no confrontation or schism between the world of Islam, the Moslem countries and our own country. This is not the point at all. And as far as the hostages are concerned, they are the only issue for us. It's not a proper time for us to discuss the wisdom or the role that the Shah played as a good or bad leader. It's not a proper time for us to get involved in a debate about whether he is or has been sick, or how sick, or where he goes, or to discuss the history of Iran.

It's important, and we have recognized the importance of maintaining one issue foremost in our mind and in our national consciousness in our dealing with other countries, in our dealing with Iran, in our dealing with the United Nations, and that is the early and the safe release of the American hostages. I'm very proud of the way our Nation has performed.

We do have adequate military presence in the Arabian Sea at the mouth of the Persian Gulf. We've not made idle threats; we've not had to. We've made a clear statement of our purpose and our resolve, which will be exercised if necessary. What we want is peace, and what we want is a good relationship, now and in the future, with the people of Iran. We're not trying to decide what form of government they should have. We're not trying to interfere in their own internal affairs. We think they've violated every international law imaginable—the Geneva agreements, the premises on which the United Nations Charter is based.

And we've had an additional responsibility, which has been difficult, but, I think, which has been successfully achieved so far, of keeping world opinion on our side. This even involves the less developed countries and other Moslem nations who would not ordinarily be inclined to do so. It has encompassed, as well, nations who in the past have not been our close friends. And in the United Nations Security Council vote, the three small nations, coincidentally, happen to have been and are Moslem countries.

Our presentation to the International Court of Justice by the Attorney General this week has been well received. We anticipate—I can't say for sure—that we'll have a ruling from that Court, perhaps even as early as tomorrow. I have no way to determine that accurately; that's what the Attorney General believes. And we hope it will be resolved in our favor. We're trying to keep legality, propriety, and world opinion and the right on our side.

I think we've seen in this incident a very serious additional piece of evidence that our Nation is vulnerable to our suppliers of oil. My guess is that the trend in OPEC oil production among the Arab and non-Arab countries in the coming months will be downward, not upward. And with a shorter and shorter supply in prospect, there's no doubt in my mind that prices will be going up. It would be a mistake for me to mislead the American people.

Some of the countries are producing more oil than they want to produce. Saudi Arabia is a typical example—a very good example, not typical. They would be adequately compensated, in money of all denominations and foreign holdings, with a much lower level of production. They are not the only country producing perhaps more than they would prefer to produce for their own, narrowly focused, parochial needs.

Other countries have an attenuation in their production, because their explorations have not been successful in revealing additional supplies of oil. And there are additional countries who would like to use a shortage of oil, or a reduction in their sales of oil, for political purposes. I don't know of any instance where there is an inclination among the Arab oil-producing countries to increase production.

So, we're going to see shortages, and it's a very serious problem for us in not having an adequate national energy policy. As you know, I proposed such a policy in April of 1977, after I'd been in office 90 days, and the Congress has still not acted. They've not passed any legislation, not one line of legislation relating to oil. And, as you know, there is a very difficult and sensitive problem on the Hill in passing legislation to take away the prerogatives, sometimes the exaggerated prerogatives, unwarranted prerogatives, of the oil companies.

I, in effect, represent two major and different kinds of nations. One is by far the largest oil-consuming nation on Earth, and at the same time, one of the largest oil-producing nations on Earth. And for the first time in the last 2 years, we have seen a rough equivalency between the influence on the Hill of oil consumers compared to oil producers. In the past the field was open to oil producers exclusively, and you could understand that when oil was $1.50 a barrel.

I'd like very much now to answer two or three questions of yours, if you have any, and, Al,[3] perhaps I could call on you for the first question, if the others don't object. [*Laughter*]

QUESTIONS

PUBLIC OPINION POLLS

Q. In light of what's happened in the polls recently and the general tone of editorials about your administration, are you reading newspapers any more and enjoying them any more? [*Laughter*]

THE PRESIDENT. A few months ago I doubted very seriously the authenticity and accuracy of the polls. [*Laughter*] Lately my opinion of them has increased substantially. [*Laughter*]

But I would guess, to be serious about it, that a lot of the poll response has been because of the Iranian question, a natural desire on the part of Americans to support their President in a time of crisis or challenge. That's part of it. The other part, to be equally frank, is that I believe that the expectations that were felt among many Democrats concerning Senator Kennedy's ability has been attenuated since he became an active candidate. That was almost inevitable, and I don't say that in derrogation of him. But those two factors are obviously at play.

---

[3] Allen H. Neuharth, president and chief executive officer, Gannett Co., Inc.

We have a long way to go. There's only one poll that counts, as my wife said on the "Today" show this morning, and that's the final vote. But we're prepared. I think it's obvious that in 1975, 1976, that we were constantly underestimated, maybe even by some of your editorial writers and reporters. But we've got a good ability to organize, and we have a longstanding, even a lifetime commitment, at least a political lifetime commitment, to stay close to the American people. We do this through my own interrelationships and those of my staff and those of my family. And I think that sensitivity of American needs and desires and hopes and aspirations and concerns pay rich dividends.

But we know how to organize, and we are successful and have been in the past in conducting a campaign. So, I would guess that we have a good chance next year. I look forward to it with anticipation and confidence.

AMERICAN HOSTAGES IN IRAN

Q. Mr. President, you mentioned the patience of the American people. There was an instance in the late sixties when some British diplomats were taken hostage in Peking and were held for—I think it was over a year. It got to the point where people stopped talking about it and the Government of Britain stopped talking about it. They were released. Is it possible or conceivable that this situation could drag on in Tehran until we get sort of the same situation?

THE PRESIDENT. I'm determined that that will not happen, Don.[4]

We had, as you know, one of our Ambassadors who was captured in Manchuria—maybe the incident to which you refer, maybe a different one—and he

[4] Don Campbell, White House correspondent, Gannett News Service.

stayed imprisoned for more than a year. It was during President Truman's administration. He was finally released, I think, in the fall or winter of 1949. I'm not sure about the exact date.

There, President Truman—I've reread the history on it and even the private memoranda that were exchanged within the White House—and President Truman did ask the Joint Chiefs of Staff and others to analyze how he might, through physical action if necessary, cause the release of our Ambassador and his staff. It was not done, and eventually the Ambassador was released.

I'm determined that in this particular incident we will not forget those hostages one day and that we will continue to keep the issue of their illegal incarceration in the forefront of the consciousness not only of America but of the entire world. There are a series of steps that we can take. There are also steps that the Iranians are taking, not for the same purpose, to keep this a vivid issue in the minds of the people throughout the world.

We will not let it become a dormant issue, or we will not let the status quo become acceptable. In my judgment there has been some change, substantial change, in the attitude even among the Iranians. And if you go back and look at the early comments or statements that were made and compare them to the more recent ones, you see that there has been some evolutionary change, not always in the right direction, but, I think, in general it has.

The promise that our hostages would be tried individually as war criminals and perhaps even executed was the earliest threats made. That has, to some degree, been changed. Their early expectation that the Shah would be returned to them through blackmail—I think those expectations have now been lowered, if not eliminated altogether, and so I think that, in itself, is good.

But I will not permit this incident to become acceptable and to be dragged out. I'll do my utmost to prevent that. I don't want that to be interpreted as threatening military action. I'll do everything I can to avoid any bloodshed, provided our hostages are not physically harmed.

Maybe one more question.

GASOLINE RATIONING

Q. Mr. President, in light of your comments about the oil shortage possibility, what is the likelihood of rationing?

THE PRESIDENT. In my opinion we must do something about the excessive consumption of oil products, particularly gasoline. We made an effort in the International Energy Agency this week, as you may know. The Secretary of Energy went over there, and we pointed out to the other members—I think it's almost all the democratic developed nations on Earth, except France is not a member; 24 nations, I believe—we pointed out to them that the prospects next year are for a reduction in oil exports from the OPEC countries of about a million and a half to 2 million, maybe as high as 2½ million barrels per day, and that we needed to form an alliance, in effect, or a commitment that instead of increasing our bids for spot market oil as the shortages did evolve, if they do, then we would have an arrangement ahead of time for us to lower our demand for imported oil collectively, so that we could share the shortages.

We are part of that process, and we will have another meeting in March to follow up on those tentative commitments made at that meeting this week.

Gasoline is obviously the easiest energy supply to curtail as far as waste is concerned, because Americans do waste so much. There are several ways that this can be done. One is voluntary action on the part of Governors and States—this involves a gamut of things; secondly, an in-crease in the price of gasoline through an imposed tax. We are considering that as one of the options. Rationing is another option that we are considering. Either one of those last two would require congressional action, and before long—I don't know exactly the time schedule yet—I'll be having some meetings on it this week—we will decide what approach to take.

An increase in the price of gasoline has shown, in the last few months, to be much closer related to conservation than we had previously anticipated. There was a guess earlier, a presumption earlier, that the elasticity factor was one-tenth, which means that if you increase the price of gasoline 10 percent, you would only have a 1-percent reduction in consumption. It's probably twice that much, which has been a fairly pleasant surprise, that we have had voluntary conservation among Americans.

This summer, for instance, we had an average, not only in gas consumption reduced, but we had an average increase in mileage derived from automobiles all over the country of 1 mile per gallon, which is a substantial amount of saving. This is because of smaller cars, more careful driving, and so forth. In addition to that, there are other factors—less use of automobiles and, of course, more sharing of automobiles as they make the trip. We have experienced lately a 7- or 8-percent reduction in gasoline consumption.

So, we are exploring opportunities. I've not yet made a decision on how to cut gasoline consumption more. We can do it without hurting our economy.

Al.

MR. NEUHARTH. Thank you very much.

THE PRESIDENT. Thank you very much. I've enjoyed being with you.

NOTE: The President spoke at 2:21 p.m. in Room 450 of the Old Executive Office Building.

Christmas Pageant of Peace

*Remarks on Lighting the National
Community Christmas Tree.
December 13, 1979*

Christmas means a lot of things. It means love. It means warmth. It means friendship. It means family. It means joy. It means light. But everyone this Christmas will not be experiencing those deep feelings. At this moment there are 50 Americans who don't have freedom, who don't have joy, and who don't have warmth, who don't have their families with them. And there are 50 American families in this Nation who also will not experience all the joys and the light and the happiness of Christmas.

I think it would be appropriate for all those in this audience and for all those listening to my voice or watching on television to pause just for a few seconds in a silent prayer that American hostages will come home safe and come home soon—if you'd please join me just for a moment.

[*Pause for silent prayer.*]

Thank you very much.

Nineteen seventy-nine has not been a bad year. Many good things have happened to us individually and have also happened to our Nation. Not far from here, on the north side of the White House, we saw a remarkable ceremony, headed by a Jew, the leader of Israel, a Moslem, the President of Egypt, and myself, a Christian, the President of our country, signing a treaty of peace. This peace treaty was a historic development, and it was compatible with the commitment that we feel so deeply in the religious season now upon us.

Our Nation also opened up its arms of understanding, diplomatic relationships, and friendship—our Nation, the strongest on Earth, and China, the most populous nation on Earth. The establishment of new friendships is part of the Christmas season.

I went to Vienna and met with President Brezhnev. And he and I signed the SALT II treaty, which will help to limit and to reduce the spread of nuclear weapons, to bring about a better understanding between our two great countries, and to search for the kind of reduction of armaments that will lead, I think, to the realization of the true spirit of Christmas.

This fall we had a visit from a great spiritual leader, Pope John Paul II, who traveled throughout our country and who spoke in a quiet voice of understanding, of compassion, of love, of commitment, of morality, of ethics, of the unchanging things that are part of the spirit of Christmas. And I remember one thing in particular that he said on the White House lawn. He said, "Do not be afraid. Do not be afraid." And as you know, that's the same message that the angels brought to the shepherds near Bethlehem the night that our Savior was born: "Fear not. Be not afraid." Many of the problems in our world derive from fear, from a lack of confidence in ourselves and, particularly, a lack of confidence in what we can do, with God.

We hope we'll soon see peace in Zimbabwe-Rhodesia, a nation that has suffered much in the last few years. But we've also seen some needs for additional effort.

This is the Year of the Child, but it's possibly true that in Cambodia, or Kampuchea, the children will have suffered more in 1979 than in any other year in our lifetime—children so weak, so starved, that they don't even have the strength to cry. We've seen Vietnam refugees put to sea with very little hope of ever reaching land again. And our country has reached out its arms to help those starving children and those refugees adrift.

We've seen divisions among people because of religious beliefs. The recent events in Iran are an unfortunate example of that misguided application of belief in God. But I know that all Americans feel very deeply that the relationships between ourselves and the Moslem believers in the world of Islam is one of respect and care and brotherhood and good will and love.

So, we do have disappointments; we do have suffering; we do have divisions; we often have war. But in the midst of pain, we can still remember what Christmas is—a time of joy, a time of light, a time of warmth, a time of families, and a time of peace.

In our great country we have an awful lot for which we can be thankful: the birth of our Savior, the initiation of religious holidays tomorrow night for the Jews of America, and a realization that in our Nation we do have freedom to worship or not worship as we please. So, let's remember our blessings, yes, but let's also remember the needs for us to be more fervent in our belief in God and especially in the sharing of our blessings with others.

Thank you very much. Merry Christmas to you all.

And now we'll go over—Amy and I and Rosalynn—and we'll light the lights that signify Christmas. Thank you very much.

Is everybody ready?

I'm going to ask Amy to throw the switch.

[*At this point, Amy Carter threw the switch that lit the star on top of the National Community Christmas Tree and the lights on the 50 smaller trees, which traditionally represent the 50 States.*]

I want to tell you what just happened. Around the periphery of this crowd, there are 50 small Christmas trees, one for each American hostage, and on the top of the great Christmas tree is a star of hope. We will turn on the other lights on the tree when the American hostages come home.

Merry Christmas, everybody.

NOTE: The President spoke at 5:50 p.m. on the Ellipse.

Cahaba River in Alabama

Message to the Congress Transmitting a Study. December 14, 1979

To the Congress of the United States:

Pursuant to the Wild and Scenic Rivers Act (Public Law 90–542, as amended), I am transmitting the attached study of the feasibility of adding the Cahaba River in Alabama to the national Wild and Scenic Rivers system. Although the study finds that the river does not possess the qualities to be eligible to be added to the national system, the State of Alabama has initiated efforts to manage the river to protect its attributes, including its recreational qualities.

JIMMY CARTER

The White House,
    December 14, 1979.

NOTE: The 196-page report, prepared by the Department of Agriculture's Forest Service and the Alabama Forestry Commission, is entitled "Cahaba River, Alabama—Wild and Scenic River Study."

Christmas 1979

Statement by the President. December 14, 1979

Rosalynn and I send our warmest Christmas greetings to those of our fellow citizens who celebrate this religious holiday.

At this time of traditional joy and family festivity, as we join in thanking God for His blessings to us as a nation and as individuals, we ask that you offer a special prayer for the Americans who are being held hostage in Iran and for their families. We remember also the plight of all people, whatever their nationality, who suffer from injustice, oppression, hunger, war, or terrorism.

May this Christmas season truly be the beginning of a time of peace among nations and good will among all peoples, and may the spirit of love and caring continue from this holy season through the coming year.

Emergency Board To Investigate a Railway Labor Dispute

Executive Order 12182.   December 14, 1979

CREATING AN EMERGENCY BOARD TO IN-
VESTIGATE A DISPUTE BETWEEN THE
LONG ISLAND RAIL ROAD AND CERTAIN
OF ITS EMPLOYEES

A dispute exists between The Long Island Rail Road and certain of its employees represented by Participating Labor Organizations designated in list attached hereto and made part hereof.

This dispute has not heretofore been adjusted under the provisions of the Railway Labor Act, as amended; and

This dispute, in the judgment of the National Mediation Board, threatens substantially to interrupt interstate commerce to a degree such as to deprive a section of the country of essential transportation service:

Now, THEREFORE, by the authority vested in me by Section 10 of the Railway Labor Act, as amended (45 U.S.C. 160), it is hereby ordered as follows:

1-101. *Establishment of Board.* There is established a board of three members to be appointed by the President to investigate this dispute. No member of the board shall be pecuniarily or otherwise interested in any organization of railroad employees or any carrier.

1-102. *Report.* The board shall report its finding to the President with respect to the dispute within 30 days from the date of this Order.

1-103. *Maintaining Conditions.* As provided by Section 10 of the Railway Labor Act, as amended, from this date and for 30 days after the board has made its report to the President, no change, except by agreement, shall be made by The Long Island Rail Road, or by its employees, in the conditions out of which the dispute arose.

JIMMY CARTER

The White House,
    December 14, 1979.

Participating Labor Organizations

International Brotherhood of Teamsters (IBT)
United Transportation Union (UTU)
Brotherhood of Locomotive Engineers (BLE)
Brotherhood of Railroad Carmen (BRC)
Brotherhood of Railroad Signalmen (BRS)
Railroad Yardmasters of America (RYA)
Police Benevolent Association (PBA)

[Filed with the Office of the Federal Register, 11:15 a.m., December 17, 1979]

Emergency Board To Investigate a Railway Labor Dispute

Appointment of the Membership.
December 14, 1979

The President today announced the three persons whom he will appoint as members of the Emergency Board to investigate the Long Island Rail Road dispute. They are:

James J. Reynolds, of Washington, D.C., a former Assistant Secretary of Labor and Under Secretary of Labor in the Kennedy and Johnson administrations. Reynolds was president of the American Institute of Merchant Shipping until his retirement in 1978. He will serve as Chairman of this Emergency Board.

Ida Klaus, of New York City, an arbitrator and mediator with more than 40 years' experience in the labor relations field. She has served as special arbitrator under the U.S. Steel agreement since 1975. She was executive director of the Office of Labor Relations and Collective Bargaining of the New York City Board of Education from 1962 to 1975.

Nicholas H. Zumas, of Washington, D.C., an attorney and arbitrator who has been in private practice since 1965. He is a member of the District of Columbia Board of Labor Relations and has served as assistant to the Under Secretary of Health, Education, and Welfare.

Digest of Other White House Announcements

The following listing includes the President's public schedule and other items of general interest announced by the White House Press Office and not included elsewhere in this issue.

December 8

The President met at the White House with:

—Zbigniew Brzezinski, Assistant to the President for National Security Affairs;

—Frank B. Moore, Assistant to the President for Congressional Liaison.

December 10

The President met at the White House with:

—Dr. Brzezinski;

—Mr. Moore;

—members of the Presidential Commission on World Hunger to receive the Commission's preliminary report;

—Vice President Walter F. Mondale.

December 11

The President met at the White House with:

—Dr. Brzezinski;

—the Democratic congressional leadership;

—Mayor Kenneth A. Gibson of Newark, N.J.;

—Mr. Moore;

—Kenneth T. Blaylock, president of the American Federation of Government Employees;

—Representative Harold E. Ford of Tennessee.

The President and Mrs. Carter hosted a Christmas reception in the evening for Members of Congress and their guests on the State Floor of the White House.

December 12

The President met at the White House with:

—Dr. Brzezinski;

—Mr. Moore;

—Stansfield Turner, Director of Central Intelligence;

—Vice President Mondale, Paul A. Volcker, Chairman of the Board of Governors of the Federal Reserve System, James T. McIntyre, Jr., Director of the Office of Management and Budget, Charles L. Schultze, Chairman of the Council of Economic Advisers, and Alfred E. Kahn, Advisor to the President on Inflation.

The White House announced that the President has designated Max M. Kampelman as Chairman of the Woodrow Wilson International Center for Scholars in the Smithsonian Institution. Kampelman was appointed a member of the board of trustees of the Center last month. He is a Washington, D.C., attorney.

December 13

The President met at the White House with:

—Dr. Brzezinski;

—Attorney General Benjamin R. Civiletti;

—Mr. Moore;

—members of the Price Advisory Committee;

—former President Gerald R. Ford;

—representatives of women's organizations.

The President and Mrs. Carter hosted a Christmas reception in the afternoon for members of the Residence staff and their families on the State Floor of the White House.

The President and Mrs. Carter hosted a Christmas reception in the evening for members of the White House press corps on the State Floor of the White House.

The President transmitted to the Congress the 1978 annual reports of the Great Lakes Basin Commission, Missouri River Basin Commission, New England River Basins Commission, Ohio River Basin Commission, Pacific Northwest River Basins Commission, and Upper Mississippi River Basin Commission.

December 14

The President met at the White House with:

—Dr. Brzezinski;

—Vice President Mondale, Secretary of Defense Harold Brown, Deputy Secretary of State Warren M. Christopher, Hedley W. Donovan, Senior Adviser to the President, Hamilton Jordan, Assistant to the President, and Dr. Brzezinski;

—Mr. Moore;

—Thomas R. Ehrlich, Director of the International Development Cooperation Agency;

—6-year-old Betsy Burch, of Stone Mountain, Ga., the 1980 March of Dimes Poster Child;

—Mrs. Carter, for lunch;

—members of the United States-Japan Economic Relations Group;

—Mr. McIntyre, and other administration officials to review the fiscal year 1981 budget;

—Secretary of State Cyrus R. Vance.

The President and Mrs. Carter hosted a Christmas reception in the evening for members of the White House staff on the State Floor of the White House.

The President transmitted to the Congress the fiscal year 1978 annual report of ACTION.

The President left the White House for a weekend stay at Camp David, Md.

NOMINATIONS SUBMITTED TO THE SENATE

The following list does not include promotions of members of the Uniformed Services, nominations to the Service Academies, or nominations of Foreign Service officers.

Submitted December 11, 1979

PHILIP M. KLUTZNICK, of Illinois, to be Secretary of Commerce.

VICTOR MARRERO, of New York, to be Under Secretary of Housing and Urban Development, vice Jay Janis.

SIDNEY ANDERS RAND, of Minnesota, to be Ambassador Extraordinary and Plenipotentiary of the United States of America to Norway.

Submitted December 12, 1979

HOMER E. MOYER, JR., of the District of Columbia, to be General Counsel of the Department of Commerce, vice Charles Linn Haslam, resigning.

JOSEPH A. DOYLE, of New York, to be an Assistant Secretary of the Navy, vice Edward Hidalgo, elevated.

REGINALD E. GILLIAM, JR., of Virginia, to be a member of the Interstate Commerce Commission for the term of 7 years from January 1, 1976, vice Kenneth H. Tuggle.

VICTOR H. PALMIERI, of California, to be Ambassador at Large and United States Coordinator for Refugee Affairs.

ALBERT P. SMITH, of Kentucky, to be Federal Cochairman of the Appalachian Regional Commission, vice Robert Walter Scott, resigned.

Submitted December 13, 1979

JOHN J. PARTINGTON, of Rhode Island, to be United States Marshal for the District of Rhode Island for the term of 4 years, vice Donald W. Wyatt, term expired.

Submitted December 14, 1979

JAMES W. SPAIN, of California, a Foreign Service officer of the Class of Career Minister, to be Ambassador Extraordinary and Plenipotentiary of the United States of America to Turkey.

LUTHER H. HODGES, JR., of North Carolina, to be Deputy Secretary of Commerce (new position).

NOMINATIONS—Continued

Submitted December 14—Continued

HENRY WOODS, of Arkansas, to be United States District Judge for the Eastern District of Arkansas, vice a new position created by P.L. 95–486, approved October 20, 1978.

RAUL A. RAMIREZ, of California, to be United States District Judge for the Eastern District of California, vice a new position created by P.L. 95–486, approved October 20, 1978.

RICHARD S. ARNOLD, of Arkansas, to be United States Circuit Judge for the Eighth Circuit, vice a new position created by P.L. 95–486, approved October 20, 1978.

CHECKLIST OF WHITE HOUSE PRESS RELEASES

The following listing contains releases of the White House Press Office which are not included in this issue.

Released December 10, 1979

News conference: on their preliminary report on world hunger—by members of the Presidential Commission on World Hunger

Announcement: appointment by Secretary of Health, Education, and Welfare Patricia R. Harris of persons to positions with the 1981 White House Conference on Aging

Released December 11, 1979

Announcement: establishment of an interagency work group to study the health effects of herbicides

Released December 12, 1979

Announcement: establishment of a Federal anti-arson program

Advance text: remarks to the Business Council on U.S. defense policy

Announcement: nomination of John J. Partington to be United States Marshal for the District of Rhode Island

Released December 13, 1979

Transcript: remarks on the establishment of a Federal anti-arson program—by Vice President Walter F. Mondale and Jack H. Watson, Jr., Assistant to the President for Intergovernmental Affairs

Announcement: nomination of Raul A. Ramirez to be United States District Judge for the Eastern District of California

CHECKLIST—Continued

Released December 14, 1979

Announcement: establishment of an Emergency Board to investigate the Long Island Rail Road labor dispute

Announcement: nomination of Richard S. Arnold to be United States Circuit Judge for the Eighth Circuit

Announcement: nomination of Henry Woods to be United States District Judge for the Eastern District of Arkansas

Transcript: remarks announcing administration support for the Chrysler Corp. aid legislation—by Vice President Mondale

ACTS APPROVED BY THE PRESIDENT

Approved December 12, 1979

H.R. 3354_____ Public Law 96–137
An act to authorize appropriations for fiscal year 1980 for conservation, exploration, development, and use of naval petroleum reserves and naval oil shale reserves, and for other purposes.

H.R. 4259_____ Public Law 96–138
An act authorizing the President of the United States to present a gold medal to the American Red Cross.

S. 1491_____ Public Law 96–139
An act to designate the building known as the Federal Building, at 211 Main Street, in Scott City, Kansas, as the "Henry D. Parkinson Federal Building".

S. 1535_____ Public Law 96–140
An act to designate the Federal Building in Rochester, New York, the "Kenneth B. Keating Federal Building".

ACTS APPROVED—Continued

Approved December 12—Continued

S. 1655_____ Public Law 96–141
An act to designate the building known as the Department of Labor Building in Washington, District of Columbia, as the "Frances Perkins Department of Labor Building".

S. 497_____ Public Law 96–142
An act to extend for three fiscal years the authorizations of appropriations under section 789 and title XII of the Public Health Service Act relating to emergency medical services to revise and improve the authorities for assistance under such title XII, to increase the authorizations of appropriations and revise and improve the authorities for assistance under part B of title XI of such Act for sudden infant death syndrome counseling and information projects, and for other purposes.

Approved December 13, 1979

S. 239_____ Public Law 96–143
Domestic Volunteer Service Act Amendments of 1979.

H.R. 5871_____ Public Law 96–144
An act to authorize the apportionment of funds for the Interstate System, to amend section 103(e)(4) of title 23, United States Code, and for other purposes.

Approved December 14, 1979

H.R. 3407_____ Public Law 96–145
An act to waive the time limitation on the award of certain military decorations to members of the Intelligence and Reconnaissance Platoon of the 394th Infantry Regiment, 99th Infantry Division, for acts of valor performed during the Battle of the Bulge.

H.R. 4732_____ Public Law 96–146
An act to fix the annual rates of pay for the Architect of the Capitol and the Assistant Architect of the Capitol.

PRESIDENTIAL DOCUMENTS

Week Ending Friday, December 21, 1979

Shah of Iran

Statement by the White House Press
Secretary on the Shah's Departure From the
United States. December 15, 1979

The former Shah of Iran departed Lackland Air Force Base this morning for Panama. He will establish residence there in response to a longstanding request [invitation] [1] from the Government of Panama. The Government of Panama has stated its hope that the provision of a place of residence for the Shah in Panama will help to bring about a peaceful resolution of the present crisis.

President Carter has expressed to President Royo the appreciation of the American people for the humanitarian and statesmanlike attitude of the Government of Panama.

The Shah entered the United States on October 22 for diagnosis and evaluation of his medical condition at Cornell Medical Facility in New York. On December 2, he entered Wilford Hall Air Force Hospital at Lackland Air Force Base. There he has continued his recuperation.

As the Shah stated when he entered the United States, he intended to leave the United States when his medical condition permitted. After an examination and consultation yesterday, his physicians, headed by Dr. Benjamin Keane, advised the

---

[1] Printed in the transcript.

Shah that his medical condition does not preclude his taking up residence in Panama.

NOTE: Press Secretary Jody Powell read the statement at 11:46 a.m. during his regular briefing for reporters in the Briefing Room at the White House.

Revoking Rhodesian Sanctions

Executive Order 12183. December 16, 1979

By the authority vested in me as President by the Constitution and statutes of the United States of America, including Section 5 of the United Nations Participation Act of 1945, as amended (22 U.S.C. 287c), and in order to terminate current limitations relating to trade and other transactions involving Zimbabwe-Rhodesia, it is hereby ordered as follows:

1-101. (a) Subject to the provisions of this order, the following are hereby revoked with respect to transactions occurring after the effective date of this order:

(1) Executive Order 11322 of January 5, 1967 (32 FR 119);

(2) Executive Order 11419 of July 29, 1968 (33 FR 10837); and

(3) Executive Order 11978 of March 18, 1977 (42 FR 15403).

(b) To the extent consistent with this order, all determinations, authorizations, regulations, rulings, certificates, orders, directives, licenses, contracts, agreements, and other actions made, issued, taken, or entered into under the provisions of such Executive orders and not previously revoked, superseded, or otherwise made inapplicable, shall continue in full force and effect until amended, modified, or terminated by appropriate authority.

1–102. (a) The Secretaries of State, the Treasury, Commerce, and Transportation, and the heads of other government agencies, shall retain the authority and responsibility for the enforcement of Executive Orders 11322, 11419, and 11978 with respect to transactions occurring prior to the effective date of this order.

(b) The revocation, in Section 1–101 of this order, of such prior Executive orders shall not affect:

(1) any act done or omitted to be done or any suit or proceeding finished or started in civil or criminal cases prior to the revocation, but all such liabilities, penalties, and forfeitures under the Executive orders shall continue and may be enforced in the same manner as if the revocation had not been made; or

(2) any violation of any rules, regulations, orders, licenses, or other forms of administrative action under those revoked orders during the periods those orders were in effect.

1–103. (a) The Secretaries of State, the Treasury, Commerce, and Transportation, and the heads of other government agencies, shall take the appropriate measures to implement this order.

(b) In carrying out their respective functions and responsibilities under this order, the Secretaries of the Treasury, Commerce, and Transportation, and the heads of other government agencies, shall, as appropriate, consult with the Secretary of State. Each such Secretary and agency head and the Secretary of State shall also consult with other government agencies and private persons, as appropriate.

JIMMY CARTER

The White House,
    December 16, 1979.

[Filed with the Office of the Federal Register,
    11:16 a.m., December 17, 1979]

National Unity Day, 1979
Proclamation 4709.   December 16, 1979

*By the President of the United States
of America*

A Proclamation

Fifty American citizens are being held hostage in Iran by a mob and a government that have become one and the same. The United States has made it clear to the leaders of Iran that we hold them personally and fully responsible for the well-being and safe return of every American in their hands.

The people of the United States are unanimous in their concern for their fellow citizens held in Iran. Americans have shown this concern in numerous ways that are consistent with our country's respect for law—the ringing of church bells, letters to the Iranian Mission at the United Nations, and messages to the hostages themselves.

A most fitting symbol of this concern is the American flag itself. We respect our flag because we know that it stands for freedom. It stands for justice. It stands for human dignity. It stands too for our united determination to uphold these great ideals.

To demonstrate support for the hostages in Iran, the Congress has, by joint resolution, designated December 18, 1979.

as "National Unity Day." It has requested the President of the United States to call upon all citizens and organizations to observe that day by prominently displaying the American flag.

Now, Therefore, I, Jimmy Carter, President of the United States of America, do hereby designate December 18, 1979, as National Unity Day. I direct the appropriate officials of the Government to display the flag on all Government buildings during that day. I urge all Americans to observe National Unity Day, December 18, 1979, by flying the Stars and Stripes from their homes and other suitable places.

In Witness Whereof, I have hereunto set my hand this sixteenth day of December, in the year of our Lord nineteen hundred seventy-nine, and of the independence of the United States of America the two hundred and fourth.

Jimmy Carter

[Filed with the Office of the Federal Register, 11:17 a.m., December 17, 1979]

Multilateral Trade Negotiations

Memorandum From the President. December 14, 1979

Memorandum for the Special Representative for Trade Negotiations

Subject: Determination Regarding the Multilateral Trade Negotiations

I have signed the enclosed document concerning certain international trade agreements pursuant to the authority vested in me under the Constitution and laws of the United States, including the Trade Agreements Act of 1979 (Public Law 96–39, 93 Stat. 144) and section 301 of title 3 of the United States Code.

On my behalf, please transmit copies of this document to the Speaker of the House of Representatives and the President of the Senate.

This document shall be published in the Federal Register.

Jimmy Carter

Presidential Determination Regarding the Acceptance and Application of Certain International Trade Agreements

1. Pursuant to section 102 of the Trade Act of 1974 (19 U.S.C. 2112(b)), I, through my duly empowered representative, on April 12, 1979, entered into the international agreements negotiated in the Tokyo Round of Multilateral Trade Negotiations. These agreements were:

(i) Agreement on Interpretation and Application of Articles VI, XVI and XXIII of the General Agreement on Tariffs and Trade;

(ii) Agreement on Implementation of Article VI of the General Agreement on Tariffs and Trade;

(iii) Agreement on Implementation of Article VII of the General Agreement on Tariffs and Trade;

(iv) Agreement on Government Procurement;

(v) Agreement on Technical Barriers to Trade;

(vi) Agreement on Import Licensing Procedures;

(vii) Agreement on Trade in Civil Aircraft;

(viii) International Dairy Arrangement, and

(ix) Arrangement Regarding Bovine Meat.

These agreements are collectively referred to herein as the "MTN agreements".

2. In accordance with sections 102 and 151 of the Trade Act of 1974 (19 U.S.C. 2112 and 2191), the MTN agreements were submitted to Congress for its approval. Section 2 of the Trade Agreements Act of 1979 (93 Stat. 147) approves the MTN Agreements and authorizes the President to accept each of the MTN agreements provided that the President determines that all, or all but one, of the major industrial countries (as defined in section 126(d) of the Trade Act of 1974 (19 U.S.C. 2136(d))) is also accepting the agreement. If the President determines that only one major industrial country is not accepting an agreement, the President may nevertheless accept such an agreement if he determines that the acceptance of that agreement by that country is not essential to the effective operation of the Agreement, and if:

(A) that country is not a major factor in trade in the products covered by that agreement;

(B) the President has authority to deny the benefits of the agreement to that country and has taken steps to deny the benefits of the agreement to that country; or

(C) a significant portion of United States trade would benefit from the agreement, notwithstanding such nonacceptance, and the President determines and reports to the Congress that it is in the national interest of the United States to accept the agreement.

3. Section 2 of the Trade Agreements Act of 1979 also provides that no agreement accepted by the President shall apply between the United States and any other country unless the President determines that such country:

(A) has accepted the obligations of the agreement with respect to the United States, and

(B) should not otherwise be denied the benefits of the agreement with respect to the United States because such country has not accorded adequate benefits, including substantially equal competitive opportunities for the commerce of the United States to the extent required under section 126(c) of the Trade Act of 1974 (19 U.S.C. 2136(c)), to the United States.

4. Section 701 of the Tariff Act of 1930, as amended effective January 1, 1980 (93 Stat. 151) provides that the President must determine that certain conditions must be met before a country can be considered a "country under the Agreement" and, therefore, entitled to the injury determination provided for in section 703(a) and 705(b) of the Tariff Act of 1930 (93 Stat. 152 and 159).

5. Section 601(a) of the Trade Agreements Act of 1979 (93 Stat. 267) authorizes the President to proclaim certain modifications in the Tariff Schedules of the United States if the President determines that the conditions under section 2(b) of the Trade Agreements Act of 1979 (93 Stat. 147) on acceptance of the Agreement on Trade in Civil Aircraft have been fulfilled.

Now, THEREFORE, I, JIMMY CARTER, President of the United States of America, acting under and by virtue of the authority vested in me as President, and in conformity with the provisions of sections 2 and 601(a) of the Trade Agreements Act of 1979 (93 Stat. 147 and 267), herein referred to as "the Act", section 701 of the Tariff Act of 1930, as amended effective January 1, 1980 (93 Stat. 151), and section 301 of title 3 of the United States Code do hereby

1. Determine that:

a. With respect to the Agreement on Interpretation and Application of Articles VI, XVI and XXIII of the General Agreement on Tariffs and Trade, the Agreement on Implementation of Article VI of the General Agreement on Tariffs and Trade, the Agreement on Technical Barriers to Trade, the Agreement on Import Licensing Procedures, and the Agreement on Trade in Civil Aircraft,

(i)   in accordance with sections 2(b) (1) and (3) of the Act (93 Stat. 147), each major industrial country (as defined in section 126(d) of the Trade Act of 1974 (19 U.S.C. 2136(d)) is also accepting the agreement with the exception of Japan;

(ii) in accordance with section 2(b) (3) of the Act (93 Stat. 147), the acceptance of these agreements by Japan is not essential to the effective operation of the agreements for that period of time during which Japan is completing its Constitutional procedures to accept the agreements and in light of the stated intention of the Government of Japan to act in the interim in line with the agreements within its existing powers; and

(iii) in accordance with section 2(b) (3)(C) of the Act (93 Stat. 148), a significant portion of United States trade will benefit from these agreements, notwithstanding the anticipated short delay in acceptance by Japan, and it is in the national interest of the United States to accept these agreements.

b. The conditions in sections 701(b) (3)(A), (B) and (C) of the Tariff Act of 1930, as amended effective January 1, 1980 (93 Stat. 151), will have been met with respect to Venezuela, Honduras, Nepal, North Yemen, El Salvador, Paraguay and Liberia.

c. With respect to the International Dairy Arrangement,

(i)   in accordance with sections 2(b) (1) and (3) of the Act (93 Stat. 147), each major industrial country (as defined in section 126(d)) is also accepting the agreement with the exception of Canada;

(ii) in accordance with section 2(b) (3) of the Act (93 Stat. 147), the acceptance of this agreement by Canada is not essential to the effective operation of the agreement; and

(iii) in accordance with section 2(b) (3)(A) of the Act, Canada is not a major factor in trade in the products covered by the agreement.

d. With respect to the Arrangement Regarding Bovine Meat, in accordance with sections 2(b)(1) and (3) of the Act (93 Stat. 147), each major industrial country (as defined in section 126(d) of the Trade Act of 1974 (19 U.S.C. 2136(d)) is also accepting the agreement.

e. In accordance with section 601(a) of the Trade Agreements Act of 1979 (93 Stat. 267),

(i)   the conditions under section 2(b) of that Act (93 Stat. 147) on acceptance of the Agreement on Trade in Civil Aircraft have been fulfilled;

(ii) the modifications provided for in section A of Annex II to Proclamation No. 4707 of December 11, 1979, which were authorized by section 601(a) of the Trade Agreements Act of 1979 (93 Stat. 267), shall be effective with respect to articles entered, or withdrawn from warehouse, for consumption on and after January 1, 1980; and

(iii) the amendment to section 466 of the Tariff Act of 1930 (19 U.S.C. 1466) provided for in section 601(a)(3) of the Trade Agreements Act of 1979 (93 Stat. 268) shall be effective with respect to entries made under section 466 on and after January 1, 1980.

2. Authorize the United States Special Representative, for Trade Negotiations, or his designee, on behalf of the United States of America,

(a) to sign and accept the Agreement on Interpretation and Application of Articles VI, XVI, and XXIII of the General Agreement on Tariffs and Trade, the Agreement on Implementation of Article VI of the General Agreement on Tariffs and Trade, the Agreement on Technical Barriers to Trade, the Agreement on Import Licensing Procedures, the Agreement on Trade in Civil Aircraft, the International Dairy Arrangement and the Arrangement Regarding Bovine Meat;

(b) to sign the Agreement on Government Procurement subject to satisfactory completion of negotiations on entity coverage under the Agreements; and

(c) to sign the Agreement on Implementation of Article VII of the General Agreement on Tariffs and Trade subject to acceptance.

3. Delegate the functions of the President under section 2(b) of the Trade Agreements Act of 1979 (the Act) and

section 701(b) of the Tariff Act of 1930, as amended by section 101 of the Act, to the Special Representative for Trade Negotiations who shall exercise such authority with the advice of the Trade Policy Committee and in accordance with the provisions of this determination.

JIMMY CARTER

The White House,
    December 14, 1979.

[Filed with the Office of the Federal Register, 4:10 p.m., December 14, 1979]

NOTE: The memorandum was announced on December 17.

Strategic Arms Limitation Treaty

Letter to 19 Members of the Senate. December 17, 1979

Thank you for your letter concerning the Senate's view of the SALT II agreement. I welcome your commendation of the statements Secretary Brown and I have made relating to the Five Year Defense Program.

I have also noted your comments about certain aspects of SALT II's terms and about the shift in the comparative military positions of the Soviet Union and the United States, and your views on a number of further considerations bearing on various aspects of the Soviet-American relationship.

The issues you raise have been probed in depth during the hearings before the Senate committees, and will be further examined in preparing for the floor debate and in the course of the debate itself. I therefore share your interest in discussing these matters in detail with me and members of my Administration.

I also share your desire to achieve a bipartisan consensus on these issues of long-range national security strategy and arms control, and to that end we should begin these meetings at an early date. I am confident we can find the common ground on which the prompt ratification of this treaty, so important to our own national security and the peace of the world, will be achieved.

Sincerely,

JIMMY CARTER

NOTE: This is the text of identical letters addressed to Senators Henry Bellmon of Oklahoma, Lloyd Bentsen of Texas, David L. Boren of Oklahoma, Rudolph E. Boschwitz of Minnesota, Lawton Chiles of Florida, John C. Danforth of Missouri, Dennis DeConcini of Arizona, Pete V. Domenici of New Mexico, David Durenberger of Minnesota, J. James Exon of Nebraska, S. I. Hayakawa of California, H. John Heinz III of Pennsylvania, Sam Nunn of Georgia, Larry Pressler of South Dakota, Harrison Schmitt of New Mexico, Alan K. Simpson of Wyoming, Richard Stone of Florida, John W. Warner of Virginia, and Edward Zorinsky of Nebraska.

Visit of Prime Minister Margaret Thatcher of the United Kingdom

Remarks at the Welcoming Ceremony. December 17, 1979

THE PRESIDENT. It's indeed an honor for me, on behalf of the people of our Nation, to welcome to the United States the Prime Minister of the United Kingdom, Margaret Thatcher.

Our country has in its ancestry people from almost every nation on Earth. We are, Madame Prime Minister, indeed a commonwealth of almost every nation, located within the boundaries of one country. But there is no doubt that from your own country has come the heritage and the political faith and the civilization of our country, as the preeminent and the prime source.

We share a lot in common. Although our cars, or our automobiles, may drive on opposite sides of the highway, our people generally move in the same direction. And we share, or at least we attempt to share, a common language. Sometimes we don't succeed. But in the most important things, we do see issues and ideas, challenges, hopes, and expectations in the same way.

We're bound together with a common belief that our national security is intertwined with yours. When we deal with important issues of the present and future years, like energy, our consultations are very close. We are bound together through trade and through culture, through tourism and through blood kin. Perhaps the most important things, however, which bind us together are a common belief in freedom and democracy, the right of people to speak their own minds without interference, and the belief in equal justice for all.

We believe in the dignity of individual human beings, in the importance of it, and the enhancement of human rights throughout the world. We also set a benchmark for other nations to study and perhaps to emulate on how great and sovereign nations can deal with one another in a constructive and harmonious way, even when at times there are differences between us.

As another strong Prime Minister of the United Kingdom has said—Winston Churchill—"The price of greatness is responsibility." It's obvious to all Americans that in the last 7 months, Madame Prime Minister, you've exhibited greatness in the form of assuming responsibility; not only to deal with important and difficult domestic issues, which we also have in our own country, but in searching for ways in which you can meet the challenges of the international world.

You've helped us in the evolution of our SALT treaty, and your strong support for it plays a major role in shaping opinion in our own country. The recent decision made in the European Community, Atlantic Alliance nations on theater nuclear forces have felt the benefit of your strong leadership. We joined together many months ago in strengthening this NATO Alliance. And, of course, we share as well a determination that in the future our efforts on controlling both conventional and nuclear weapons will be successful.

We had long discussions in Tokyo earlier this year about how to deal with the increasing price of energy and the prospective shortage of energy on a worldwide basis. And I'm very grateful that we do share that responsibility, because you add great strength to our own efforts and help to induce other countries to be responsible and forthright in meeting this challenge in a successful way.

Our people have been deeply grateful and filled with admiration at the successful efforts that you have brought to resolving the longstanding problems in Zimbabwe-Rhodesia. And we hope that soon that nation, because of your own efforts, will be blessed with a majority-rule government, and will be free of war and combat, and can indeed have peace and join the democratic nations of the world.

I want the American people to get to know you, Madame Prime Minister, as I have come to know you and admire you. And I particularly want to emphasize that our people in Great Britain, the United Kingdom, and the United States have always seen our finest achievements in times of crisis and in times of challenge. I particularly want to thank you personally, on behalf of all Americans, and remind all the citizens of this country that from the very first moment when American hos-

tages were captured and held illegally in Iran, your government has been in the forefront of those who have helped us in every way; both privately and through diplomatic means, and through public means, you've been staunch allies, staunch friends, staunch supporters of ours. And I deeply appreciate it.

I might say in closing, Madame Prime Minister, that this is typical of the interrelationship which our two nations have always enjoyed in the past. You are at home here. This is not your first visit. Many Americans already know you and admire you from a distance. And I'm very grateful that you've come at this time, not a time of dormancy or a time of self-satisfaction, but a time of crisis and a time of challenge, as a strong leader of one of the great nations on Earth.

Madame Prime Minister, we deeply appreciate your visit; the people of my government, the people of our Nation welcome you to the United States. Thank you very much. God bless you and the people whom you represent.

THE PRIME MINISTER. Mr. President, thank you very much for your warm welcome and for the very generous terms in which you expressed it. I'm delighted to be back in Washington and to have the opportunity of meeting you, Mr. President, and many other friends once again.

I don't need to dwell on the emotion which any British Prime Minister must feel on taking part in this ceremony on the White House lawn for the first time. The United States is the most powerful force for freedom and democracy the world over, and we salute and we honor you.

Our meeting, Mr. President, extends a long and historic series. The friendship between our two countries stretches far into the past. It rests on a natural affinity and affection which stand above the buffetings of fate and fortune. The relationship, as you've said, Mr. President, is indeed an exceptional one. It's exceptional in its ease; it's exceptional in its durability; it's exceptional in its consequences. And I look to see it deepened further in the talks that we are about to begin.

Mr. President, this isn't an easy time for the United States, and I want you to know that every British home has followed anxiously the events of the last 6 weeks in Tehran. The cruel ordeal inflicted on the hostages has aroused the indignation of the civilized world, and our hearts go out to the hostages and our thoughts are with them and their families here.

Our admiration goes to the American people for their patience and wisdom and self-control. You yourself, Mr. President, if I may say so, have won enormous respect in Britain for the statesmanship, calmness, and courage with which you've faced an agonizing problem. At times like this you're entitled to look to your friends for support. We are your friends. We do support you. And we shall support you. Let there be no doubt about that.

Mr. President, as well as the grievous events in Iran, there is much to discuss; for example, Rhodesia, which you have mentioned, where we're deeply grateful for your understanding and support throughout the negotiations, and not least in the last few days; on defense, where we applaud the program that you've just announced and where we take our full part in the modernization of the theater nuclear forces in NATO; on energy and economic problems, where we're both actively seeking to control inflation and to use our resources better; and on Europe, where I will tell you of my confidence that the Community will resolve its present difficulties and emerge a stronger partner for the United States. After this splendid welcoming cere-

mony, Mr. President, for which I do indeed thank you, I look forward to tackling our formidable agenda and on reaching a broad measure of agreement. We bring you affectionate greetings and good wishes to all the people of the United States of America.

NOTE: The President spoke at 10:09 a.m. on the South Lawn of the White House.

Following the ceremony, the President and the Prime Minister held meetings in the Oval Office and the Cabinet Room at the White House.

Visit of Prime Minister Thatcher of the United Kingdom

Remarks Following a Meeting.
December 17, 1979

THE PRESIDENT. Prime Minister Thatcher and I have had very extensive and very productive conversations, even negotiations on a few points. There are no differences between us that cause any concern among Americans or people who live in Great Britain. We've reached agreement on a few items which we have discussed.

We have had long discussions about Iran. I've expressed again my thanks to the Prime Minister about the strong and unequivocal support on that issue. We've expressed our admiration and appreciation for the progress that has been made by her and by Lord Carrington in negotiating for a peaceful and democratic settlement in Rhodesia and again pledged our full support in their efforts in that difficult issue.

We've discussed the appreciation that we feel for the British for their strong support for SALT II, the strong role that they played in developing the theater nuclear force agreement among the European nations, Atlantic Alliance, in the last few days. We discussed matters of trade and commerce and the future of our two countries in dealing with the problem of energy.

In every instance we have made good progress. There are very few, if any, differences between the people of Great Britain and the people of the United States. It's a delight for us to have her here, and she will be meeting with some of our congressional leaders and some of the Cabinet officers this afternoon. I will be with her again tonight.

We are very grateful that you've come, Madame Prime Minister, and we look forward to seeing you this afternoon, this evening, at the banquet. And in the meantime our officials will be discussing matters with one another.

Thank you again for being with me. Perhaps you'd like to make a statement for the press.

THE PRIME MINISTER. Thank you.

Mr. President, I would like really to confirm what you've said, how well and how easily the talks and discussions went. I don't find that surprising in any way. We, after all, share very similar views about the importance of defending freedom under the law and therefore the importance of giving defense a good deal of priority in our national programs. We notice what the President has done for defense over here, and we've felt that we in Great Britain have been able to respond, and we also put it in the forefront of our election program.

We are particularly grateful to the President for the great help we have had in trying to bring the Rhodesian problem to a successful settlement and a successful conclusion. At all stages we've kept in touch with the President and with Secretary Vance, and they've been most helpful.

Of course a large part of our discussions were taken up with Iran, for reasons which everyone in the whole world will understand. And we indicated very clearly to the President that when the United States wishes to go to the Security Council for further powers under chapter seven, Great Britain will be the first to support him in his endeavors. You'd expect nothing less, and you will receive nothing less but our full support.

Naturally, we're concerned about energy, the Middle East, the future of oil supplies, and we've talked too about that. You all look now just a little bit chilly, so perhaps I can conclude those—so am I—those few comments with everything went extremely well. We're very happy to be here, very grateful to the President for giving us so much of his time, and we felt that everything went just as you would expect it to go between America and Great Britain, and that couldn't be more satisfactory.

Thank you.

NOTE: The President spoke at 12:48 p.m. on the South Grounds of the White House.

President's Special Commission for the Study of Ethical Problems in Medicine and Biomedical and Behavioral Research

Executive Order 12184.   December 17, 1979

RELATING TO THE PRESIDENT'S COMMIS- SION FOR THE STUDY OF ETHICAL PROBLEMS IN MEDICINE AND BIOMEDI- CAL AND BEHAVIORAL RESEARCH

Public Law 95–622 established the President's Commission for the Study of Ethical Problems in Medicine and Biomedical and Behavioral Research. Appropriations to fund the work of the Commission, although authorized, have not been sought or received, but entities within the Department of Health, Education and Welfare have authority and funds which may be available to carry on activities identical to those to be undertaken by the Commission. Therefore, in order to permit these entities to support the conduct of those activities by the Commission, and under the authority vested in me as President by the Constitution of the United States, it is ordered:

1–101. There is established the President's Special Commission for the Study of Ethical Problems in Medicine and Biomedical and Behavioral Research. The Special Commission established by this Order shall be constituted in accordance with and subject to the provisions of Title III of Public Law 95–622, except that it shall receive financial support, to the extent permitted by law and subject to the availability of funds, from the Department of Health, Education and Welfare. The Administrator of General Services shall provide administrative support services to the Special Commission on a reimbursable basis.

1–102. The Special Commission established by this Order shall terminate upon enactment and availability of appropriations for the Commission established by Public Law 95–622, and in any event, unless extended, no later than two years from the date of this Order. No funds transferred by the Department of Health, Education and Welfare pursuant to this Order shall be expended by either Commission following termination of the Special Commission.

JIMMY CARTER

The White House,
  December 17, 1979.

[Filed with the Office of the Federal Register, 10:39 a.m., December 18, 1979]

Conservation of Petroleum and Natural Gas

Executive Order 12185. December 17, 1979

By the authority vested in me as President of the United States of America by Section 403(b) of the Powerplant and Industrial Fuel Use Act of 1978 (92 Stat. 3318; Public Law 95–620) and Section 301 of Title 3 of the United States Code, in order to encourage additional conservation of petroleum and natural gas by recipients of Federal financial assistance, it is hereby ordered as follows:

1–101. Each Federal agency, as that term is defined in Section 103(a)(25) of the Powerplant and Industrial Fuel Use Act of 1978 (92 Stat. 3297), shall effectuate through its financial assistance programs the purposes of that Act relating to the conservation of petroleum and natural gas.

1–102. Each Federal agency which extends financial assistance shall review those programs of financial assistance and identify those which are most likely to offer opportunities for significant conservation of petroleum and natural gas.

1–103. Within two months, and annually thereafter, each agency shall publish for comment a list of those programs which it has identified as likely to offer significant opportunity for conservation. The public shall be given 60 days to submit comments, including suggestions for rules which would effectuate the conservation purposes of the Act.

1–104. After receiving public comment and suggestions, and after consulting with the Director of the Office of Management and Budget, each agency shall publish proposed rules designed to achieve conservation of petroleum and natural gas in connection with the receipt of financial assistance.

Proposed rules should be published within 30 days of the close of the comment period under Section 1–103.

1–105. Final rules shall be adopted by each agency in accordance with the provisions of Sections 102(b), 403(b) and 701(a) of the Powerplant and Industrial Fuel Use Act of 1978, and the provisions of this Order, not later than 180 days from the date of this Order.

1–106. No one shall be awarded any financial assistance unless that award complies with the provisions of the conservation rules adopted by the agency pursuant to this Order.

1–107. To the extent permitted by law and where not inconsistent with the financial assistance program, final rules may provide for the reduction or suspension of financial assistance under any award. Such reduction or suspension shall not be ordered until there has been an opportunity for a hearing on the record, and shall last for such time as the recipient fails to comply with the terms of the conservation rule.

1–108. No conservation rule shall be adopted which is inconsistent with the statutory provisions establishing the financial assistance program.

1–109. No conservation rule shall be used to enforce compliance with any prohibition under the Act against any person or facility which has been specifically determined by the Secretary of Energy as subject to or exempt from a prohibition under the Act. The conservation rules shall be used to enforce other new ways of achieving the purposes of the Act related to the conservation of petroleum and natural gas.

1–110. In order to assess the effectiveness of this program, each agency shall annually prepare a report on its activities in accord with Section 403(b)(1)(B) of the Act. These reports shall be submitted to the President through the Secretary of Energy.

1–111. The Secretary of Energy shall prepare for the President's consideration and transmittal to the Congress the report required by Section 403(c) of the Act.

1–112. The Director of the Office of Management and Budget may issue any rules, regulations, or orders he deems necessary to ensure the implementation of this Order. The Director may exercise any of the authority vested in the President by Section 403(b) of the Act, and may redelegate such of that authority as he deems appropriate to the head of any other agency.

JIMMY CARTER

The White House,
    December 17, 1979.

[Filed with the Office of the Federal Register,
    10:40 a.m., December 18, 1979]

Settlement of Conflict in Zimbabwe-Rhodesia

White House Statement.   December 17, 1979

Today, final agreement was reached at Lancaster House on a Rhodesian settlement. The world can celebrate a triumph of reason and an extraordinary diplomatic success. A long, destructive, and tragic conflict is ending.

This settlement is a tribute to the parties concerned, who rose above bitterness and suspicion to agree upon a formula for peace. It is a tribute to the United Kingdom, whose leaders took the issue directly in hand and applied a remarkable combination of wisdom, courage, persistence, and skill. The concerned African states played a vital role.

Active American involvement in the search for a Rhodesian settlement began in the last administration. In cooperation with the British we intensified that effort, and, since last summer, have given our full support to the British negotiations.

The settlement which has been attained can lead to an enduring peace in Zimbabwe and promote tranquillity in the region. It is founded upon majority rule with protection of minority rights and reflects the interest of all of the parties.

As the process leading to an independent Zimbabwe unfolds, it will be incumbent upon the international community, and especially the surrounding states, to support and respect the electoral process and its outcome.

For its part, the United States looks forward to the day when an independent Zimbabwe can be welcomed to the family of nations.

Chanukah

Remarks at the Lighting of the National Menorah.　December 17, 1979

It's a real honor for me to come from the White House here to this ceremony celebrating the commencement of Chanukah, last night, the Feast of Lights.

As many of you know, the season of Chanukah commemorates the victory of religious freedom. At the commencement of the celebration of this annual event, this season of thanksgiving and closeness to God, there was a miracle within which the candle which was supposed to only burn a short time burned for 8 days and nights.

This miracle showed that God meets our needs. If we depend on Him, He will meet our needs. This also shows that there is a need to celebrate courage and to re-member that hope in one's breast need never die.

This season, religious season, commemorates the perpetuation of age-old dreams and the hunger of men and women down through the ages to maintain a spirit committed to life under the most difficult circumstances, the most difficult persecutions, the most difficult dangers, and under the most difficult suffering. It also commemorates humankind's commitment to be free.

These commitments to live and to be free are ever present these days in the minds and hearts of all Americans, because we know that 50 of our fellow human beings, our fellow citizens, are not free and they want to live. We pray that this will prevail, this desire to be free and to maintain life.

The first candle that I lit, the *shammes* candle, has given its light now in this glass cage to five other candles. It has not itself been diminished. It shows that when we give life and love to others, the life and love in our own hearts is not diminished. As a matter of fact it grows the more we share it. So, tonight we pray that our closeness to God, our memory of these fine commitments of human beings down through the ages will strengthen our desires to share our life and our love, not only with the 50 American hostages, for whom we pray constantly, but for men and women throughout the world who don't always have freedom and whose lives might be in danger.

I'm very grateful that this beautiful menorah has been dedicated for the commemoration of the season of Chanukah, and I'm very grateful as President to be partaking in this commemoration of a season when human beings are drawn closer to God and, in that spirit, have confidence that the future will bring us a better life with God and with one another.

Thank you very much.

NOTE: The President spoke at 6:58 p.m. at Lafayette Square.

The ceremony was sponsored by the American Friends of Lubavitch.

Visit of Prime Minister Thatcher of the United Kingdom

Toasts at the State Dinner.
December 17, 1979

THE PRESIDENT. As you all know, England is one of the first nations on Earth, perhaps the first, to have a woman as ruler of the country, and we are very honored tonight to have the Prime Minister of the United Kingdom, who's a distinguished guest. She's able to share the responsibilities for the United Kingdom with the Queen. Unfortunately, the President of the United States has to do both. [*Laughter*]

One of the ceremonial duties of every President when the Prime Minister of the United Kingdom, Great Britain, comes here, is to remind him or her that the British burned this house in 1812. [*Laughter*] Fortunately, we had a very lively woman who lived here then, Dolley Madison, who unrolled these portraits of George Washington and his wife, Martha, took them out beyond the Potomac River, and saved them. And George Washington returned to the White House, in his portrait, after the war was over. I hope that after the visit of this British entourage that the present President might be able to return to the White House after the next election year. [*Laughter*] But I can't make any predictions about that.

I've had a chance today to meet with Prime Minister Margaret Thatcher, and I met her earlier when she visited this country before she was Prime Minister. And I met with her in some very intense economic and energy discussions and talked about the interrelationship among the democratic developed nations of the Earth in Tokyo early this year. I've been very highly impressed with her. Charles Dickens said in "The Pickwick Papers," "She knows what's what, she does." [*Laughter*] And I think this very accurately describes the Prime Minister of Great Britain.

Today we talked about strategic arms limitation talks, the control of conventional weapons, the deployment of theater nuclear forces in Europe, the strengthening of the Atlantic Alliance, the European Community and how those nations interrelate one with another, the problems in Rhodesia. And I want officially to congratulate her and Lord Carrington for the tremendous achievement that was announced today when the Patriotic Front initialed the agreement on which you've worked so successfully, and I want to congratulate you both.

This shows what the yearning for peace and freedom can do, when given an opportunity by a distinguished and strong and courageous leader and a diplomat who knows the sensitivities of others and who honors those sensitivities in a strong and forceful way. It's indeed a triumph, and we are grateful to be part of the announcement today.

We talked about the future of Namibia, which I think will be greatly enhanced by the achievement of the recent days. We talked about the refugees, not only in Indochina but around the world, the unfortunate people, and the need for the developed democratic nations on Earth, who've been blessed so greatly, to give them a better life, some alleviation of their suffering, some hope for the future.

We talked about the intricate problems of energy, of nations who are great energy producers, and nations who are great, perhaps excessive, energy consumers. We talked about the domestic problems of inflation and providing jobs for our people. We talked about international trade and how this might draw nations closer together and to transcend international borders.

We talked about terrorism, the harming of innocent people to achieve political goals which quite often, most often, are indeed unworthy. She is dealing on a daily basis with terrorism in Northern Ireland. We stand staunchly beside her in condemning bloodshed and violence, death and murder, and I hope that our country will always be an assistant to her and to the leaders of Great Britain in dealing with this threat to peace and freedom and the proper interrelationship of human beings.

We talked about Iran and another exhibition of international terrorism, where innocent people are being persecuted, held prisoner, threatened with their very lives for the achievement of unworthy political goals.

We talked about many other issues that are important to our people. But the overwhelming sense that I had was one that we constantly share responsibilities and opportunities, both now, in the future, and in the past. The ties that bind the people of Great Britain with those of the United States are so strong that nothing can sever them one from another.

We are a nation, as I said this morning, of diverse nationalities. Perhaps the most diverse constituency in the world is the one that I have. People from all over this Earth came here to live. But we have a special relationship with Great Britain,

our mother country. Walt Whitman, who perhaps more than any other American poet represented what Americans see and feel and believe, said, "I hear the running of the Thames River in my speech." Perhaps you can't hear the running of the Thames River in my speech since I'm a Georgian—[*laughter*]—but I don't think anyone can escape who lives here— whether we're from the South or the North, whether our ancestors came from England or Ireland or Poland or from China or from Japan or from the Philippines—we have part of England in us, because the principles on which our Nation was founded, our deep concepts of freedom and individuality, of democratic government originated in our mother country.

We are very honored to have Prime Minister Margaret Thatcher as our guest, and we would like to pay tribute now to her, to her nation, and to the United Kingdom. And I would like to propose a toast to Her Majesty the Queen.

To the Queen.

THE PRIME MINISTER. *Mr. President, Mrs. Carter, ladies and gentlemen:*

It has been my first visit to Washington as head of the British Government, and I should like, at the end of a memorable day, to say thank you. Thank you, to you, Mr. President, to you, Mrs. Carter, and through you to the American people for the wonderfully warm welcome I've been given everywhere.

I know, Mr. President, that as you pointed out at the beginning of your speech, the relationship between America and Britain started off with one or two errors of judgment on our side. [*Laughter*] Looking around me at the beauty here and at the wonderful nation you've created, I'm really rather glad that my predecessors weren't successful in all things they tried to carry out.

Now, I know that official visits to Washington recur almost with the regularity of the passing seasons, but as far as I'm concerned, this really has been an exceptional event in the year for me. Alas, I'll not be staying long, but it makes a great difference to me to have this chance of direct discussion and to sense at first hand what it is that quickens the pulse of the American people, their yearnings and preoccupations.

I'm very much aware, Mr. President, of the ordeal that the United States is going through at the moment. It's a double ordeal, for the fate of the 50 hostages in Tehran, from whom our thoughts are never far, and for the temper of the United States as a whole. You'll not want me to speak at length about this now, but I'd be giving you a false impression if I allowed the evening to proceed any further without letting you know how much we, in Britain, support you in your ordeal at this time.

The United States is our friend, our ally, and our time-honored partner in peace and war. The history and the destiny of our countries have been and always will be inextricably intertwined. Our friendship goes back a very long way. We are, after all, among the very few countries in the world whose constitutions and national identities have remained intact over two centuries. I hope you won't mind, Mr. President, my recalling that George Washington was a British subject until well after his 40th birthday. [*Laughter*] I've been told, to my surprise, that he does not have a place in the British Dictionary of National Biography. I suppose the editors must have regarded him as a late developer. [*Laughter*]

I confess to you that in some ways my visit got off to rather a shaky start, because I was told on arrival at Andrews Field that I had interrupted your Secretary of State, Mr. Vance, in one of his few moments of relaxation. He was watching the Redskins playing the Cowboys. [*Laughter*] He had to take his eye off the game to greet me. I'm very grateful, but I don't think the Redskins can have been very grateful to me, because it was no doubt as a result of this diversion of Mr. Vance's attention that the Redskins lost the game. I do apologize for having intervened in your internal affairs. [*Laughter*]

Mr. Vance's opposite number, Lord Carrington, who's with us this evening, has, as you know—and as you very kindly said, Mr. President—had something of a triumph in the Rhodesia negotiations at Lancaster House in London. If you think he looks a little pale, it's because he's been shut up in Lancaster House for many months, indeed has become known as the prisoner of Lancaster House. And he's so pleased to be free at last.

Lord Carrington would, I know, want me to repeat this evening how grateful the British Government are to the United States authorities for the stalwart support they've given us unfailingly over Rhodesia. And you, Mr. President, and you, Mr. Vance, we would like to give our warmest and most heartfelt thanks, because without your support the whole process would have been incomparably more difficult, and we may never have reached success.

May I say one more thing, Mr. President. The government which I lead has been in power now for just over half a year. We face great difficulties, some of them deep-seated and longstanding and some stemming from beyond our shores— and I don't pretend that anything is going to be remedied immediately. But we are determined upon a change. We're determined to return to the first principles which have traditionally governed our political and economic life, namely, the overall responsibility of the individual rather than the state for his own welfare, and the paramountcy of Parliament for the protection of fundamental rights.

The government I lead has a resounding mandate to restore the faith and the fortunes of the nation. We shall stick at the task whatever the difficulties and however great the endurance required. And we shall do so, Mr. President, in the conviction that our allies across the Atlantic have confidence in us, just as we have confidence in the strength and ingenuity of the United States to meet any challenge and triumph over any adversity that confronts them.

And it's in that spirit that I would like to ask all your other guests this evening to drink a toast to you, the President of the United States of America.

The President.

NOTE: The President spoke at 7:50 p.m. in the East Room at the White House.

Visit of Prime Minister Thatcher of the United Kingdom

White House Statement.   December 18, 1979

The President met December 17 with Prime Minister Margaret Thatcher of the United Kingdom. Prime Minister Thatcher is making an official visit to the United States, her first to this country as Prime Minister.

The President and the Prime Minister reviewed the exceptionally close relations between their two countries and discussed a number of key world issues which are of particular concern to both. These included the Iran crisis, the Rhodesia settlement, Middle East, Northern Ireland, theater nuclear force modernization and arms control, strategic cooperation,

SALT, the comprehensive test ban talks, international economic issues and energy, common approaches to the Caribbean and aid to developing countries, transatlantic defense trade, and bilateral economic and commercial issues.

The President expressed his appreciation and that of the entire American people for the United Kingdom's assistance and support in connection with the international effort to secure release of American hostages held by Iran in defiance of universally accepted standards of decency and law. The President and the Prime Minister agreed that the principle of civilized behavior and the rule of law, vital to the whole world community, is at stake in the present crisis. The Prime Minister made it clear that Britain shared the anguish of America and would do its utmost to convince the Iranian authorities to release all the hostages unharmed.

The President congratulated the Prime Minister on her government's vigorous role in the Lancaster House negotiations and the potential these have for contributing to peace and stability in southern Africa. The Prime Minister expressed warm appreciation for the full support of the United States for an all-party solution to outstanding issues and its readiness to promote further progress in Rhodesia towards a fully democratic, independent state, within the framework of the arrangements agreed upon by the parties directly concerned.

The Prime Minister explained the British Government's recent political initiative in proposing a conference of the principal political parties in Northern Ireland with the aim of finding an acceptable way of giving the people of Northern Ireland more responsibility for their own affairs. Both leaders condemned support for organizations and individuals engaged directly or indirectly in campaigns of violence and agreed that such campaigns only delay the day when peace and reconciliation can come to Northern Ireland. The President reaffirmed U.S. policy concerning the tragic problem of Northern Ireland as set forth in his statement of August 1977.

In security matters directly affecting their two countries, the President and the Prime Minister (1) applauded the decision taken last week by NATO governments to proceed with effective modernization and deployment of theater nuclear forces and with arms control proposals designed to reduce, on a basis of equality, nuclear weapons of both NATO and the Warsaw Pact; (2) agreed that the earliest possible ratification of the SALT II treaty would significantly contribute to a safer and more stable international security environment.

The President and Prime Minister agreed on the importance of maintaining a credible British strategic deterrent force and U.S./U.K. strategic cooperation. The leaders agreed that their governments should continue their discussions of the most appropriate means of achieving these objectives for the future. In this connection the President and Prime Minister discussed the importance of increased efforts to strengthen NATO's defenses, both nuclear and conventional. The President reviewed the new U.S. Five-Year Defense Plan, noting that in order to carry out that plan the United States will be increasing defense spending, in real terms, steadily over the next 5 years.

The President and Prime Minister reaffirmed their strong support for the NATO Long-Term Defense Program and for the NATO aim of 3-percent real growth in annual defense spending. The Prime Minister noted plans for further significant increases in the U.K. defense budget to improve the effectiveness of United Kingdom conventional forces, including provision of modernized equipment and reserves. The Prime Minister agreed that it was essential for America's European Allies to share equitably in any collective defense buildup to meet the needs of the common defense.

During her visit to the United States, the Prime Minister is also meeting with Secretary of Defense Brown, Chairman of the Joint Chiefs of Staff, General Jones, and other senior defense officials; Members of Congress; Chairman Volcker of the Federal Reserve Board; U.N. Secretary-General Waldheim, and the President of the U.N. General Assembly.

Prime Minister Thatcher invited the President to visit the United Kingdom at a mutually agreeable date, and the President accepted the invitation with pleasure.

American Hostages in Iran

White House Statement.   December 18, 1979

There continue to be confusing and sometimes conflicting reports that American citizens being illegally held as hostages might be placed before some type of public trial or tribunal. As we made clear on November 20, such an action would be a further provocation to the United States and to the world community. The gravity of the situation created by the illegal and irresponsible holding of the hostages would be compounded by any such public exploitation of American citizens. The authorities in Iran would bear full responsibility for any ensuing consequences.

As also stated on November 20, the United States is seeking a peaceful solution through every available channel.

This is far preferable to the other remedies available to the United States.

NOTE: Press Secretary Jody Powell read the statement at approximately 3:45 p.m. during his regular briefing for reporters in the Briefing Room at the White House.

International Bank for Reconstruction and Development

Nomination of Colbert I. King To Be U.S. Executive Director.   December 19, 1979

The President today announced that he will nominate Colbert I. King, of Rockville, Md., to be United States Executive Director of the International Bank for Reconstruction and Development. He would replace Edward R. Fried, resigned.

King has been Deputy Assistant Secretary of the Treasury for Legislative Affairs (International) since 1977.

He was born September 20, 1939, in Washington, D.C. He received a B.A. from Howard University in 1961. He served in the U.S. Army from 1961 to 1963.

From 1963 to 1964, King was with the U.S. Civil Service Commission. From 1964 to 1970, he was State Department Attaché in Bonn, West Germany. From 1970 to 1971, he was Special Assistant to the Under Secretary of Health, Education, and Welfare.

From 1971 to 1972, King was Chief of the Policy and Program Development Staff at VISTA. From 1972 to 1976, he was minority staff director for the Senate Committee on the District of Columbia and was on Senator Charles McC. Mathias, Jr.'s staff, as legislative assistant, then chief of the legislative department. From 1976 to 1977, King was director of government relations for Potomac Electric Power Co.

International Bank for Reconstruction and Development

Nomination of David S. King To Be U.S. Alternate Executive Director. December 19, 1979

The President today announced that he will nominate David S. King, of Kensington, Md., to be U.S. Alternate Executive Director of the International Bank for Reconstruction and Development. He would replace William Dixon, resigned.

King has been a partner in the Washington law firm of Williams and King since 1970, specializing in international trade, and is a former U.S. Representative from Utah.

He was born June 20, 1917, in Salt Lake City, Utah. He received a B.A. from the University of Utah in 1937 and a J.D. from Georgetown College of Law in 1942.

From 1942 to 1943, King was law clerk to Justice Harold M. Stephens of the U.S. Court of Appeals for the District of Columbia. From 1943 to 1944, he was Counsel to the Office of Price Administration, and from 1944 to 1947, he was counsel to the Utah State Tax Commission.

From 1947 to 1959, King was a partner in the Salt Lake City law firm of King & Anderson. He represented the Second District of Utah from 1959 to 1962 and from 1964 to 1966. In 1963 and 1964, he practiced law in Salt Lake City, specializing in the organization of national banks.

From 1967 to 1969, King was U.S. Ambassador to the Malagasy Republic and to Mauritius.

He is chairman of the Federal Bar Association Committee on International Resources.

2269

United States Arms Control and Disarmament Agency

Resignation of George M. Seignious II as Director and Nomination of Ralph Earle II. December 19, 1979

The President today accepted with regret the resignation, for reasons of health, of George M. Seignious as Director of the U.S. Arms Control and Disarmament Agency and announced his intention to nominate Ralph Earle II as Director.

Seignious was appointed Director of ACDA on the resignation of Paul C. Warnke in November 1978 and was sworn in on December 4, 1978. He was confirmed by the Senate on March 1, 1979.

Earle has been serving since November 1978 as Chairman of the U.S. Delegation to the Strategic Arms Limitation Talks and as Special Representative for Arms Control and Disarmament Negotiations, with the rank of Ambassador.

Seignious will continue as Director until Earle assumes office. On assumption of the office of Director, Earle intends to resign from his present positions.

The President also announced his intention to nominate Seignious as the at-large delegate on U.S. arms control delegations, such as the SALT and MBFR delegations, with the personal rank of Ambassador.

Earle was born September 26, 1928, in Bryn Mawr, Pa. He received an A.B. from Harvard College in 1950 and an LL.B. from Harvard Law School in 1955. He served in the U.S. Army from 1950 to 1952.

Earle practiced law with the firm of Morgan, Lewis and Bockius in Philadelphia from 1956 to 1968. In 1968 and 1969, he served as Principal Deputy Assistant Secretary of Defense, and subsequently as Acting Assistant Secretary of Defense and as Special Advisor for Europe and NATO in the Office of the Secretary of Defense.

From 1969 to 1972, Earle was defense adviser to the U.S. Mission to NATO. In 1972 and 1973, he was a consultant for SALT in the Office of the Secretary of Defense. He was the ACDA representative on the U.S. Delegation to SALT from 1973 until 1977, when he became Alternate Chairman of the Delegation.

Department of State

Nomination of Matthew Nimetz To Be Under Secretary for Security Assistance, Science and Technology. December 19, 1979

The President today announced his intention to nominate Matthew Nimetz as Under Secretary of State for Security Assistance, Science and Technology. He would replace Lucy Wilson Benson, who has resigned.

Nimetz has been Counselor of the Department of State since 1977.

He was born June 17, 1939, in New York City. He received a B.A. from Williams College in 1960, a B.A. (1962) and M.A. (1966) from Balliol College, Oxford University, and an LL.B. from Harvard Law School in 1965.

From 1965 to 1967, Nimetz was law clerk to Justice John M. Harland of the U.S. Supreme Court. From 1967 to 1969, he was a staff assistant to President Johnson. From 1969 to 1971 and 1972 to 1977, he was with the New York City firm of Simpson, Thacher & Bartlett. From 1975 to 1977, he also served as a commissioner of the Port Authority of New York and as a member of the New York State Health Advisory Council.

Department of State

*Nomination of Rozanne L. Ridgway To Be
Counselor of the Department.
December 19, 1979*

The President today announced his intention to nominate Rozanne L. Ridgway as Counselor to the Department of State. She would replace Matthew Nimetz, who will be nominated as an Under Secretary of State.

Ridgway has been U.S. Ambassador to Finland since 1977.

She was born August 22, 1935, in St. Paul, Minn. She received a B.A. from Hamline University in 1957.

Ridgway joined the Foreign Service in 1957 as an information specialist at the State Department and served in Manila and Palermo. From 1967 to 1970, she was political officer in Oslo, and from 1970 to 1972, she was an international relations officer at the State Department.

From 1972 to 1973, Ridgway was Deputy Director of Policy Planning and Coordination in the Bureau of Inter-American Affairs. From 1973 to 1975, she was Deputy Chief of Mission in Nassau. She served as Deputy Assistant Secretary of State for Oceans and Fisheries Affairs from 1975 to 1977.

Department of the Air Force

*Nomination of Joseph Charles Zengerle III To
Be an Assistant Secretary. December 19, 1979*

The President today announced that he will nominate Joseph Charles Zengerle III, of Washington, D.C., to be an Assistant Secretary of the Air Force. He would replace Antonia Handler Chayes, who has been appointed Under Secretary of the Air Force, and his area of responsi-

bility would be manpower, reserve affairs, and installations.

Zengerle has been with the Washington law firm of Shea & Gardner since 1974.

He was born August 16, 1942, in Jamaica, N.Y. He received a B.S. from the U.S. Military Academy in 1964 and a J.D. from the University of Michigan Law School in 1971.

In 1972 Zengerle was an associate with the Washington firm of Arnold & Porter. In 1972 and 1973, he was law clerk to Judge Carl McGowan of the U.S. Court of Appeals for the District of Columbia Circuit, and in 1973 and 1974, he was law clerk to Chief Justice Warren Burger of the U.S. Supreme Court.

Regulatory Reform Legislation

*White House Statement on Action by the
Senate Administrative Practices and
Procedures Subcommittee. December 19, 1979*

The Senate Administrative Practices and Procedures Subcommittee has drafted and today reported out S. 2147, the Regulatory Flexibility and Administrative Reform Act of 1979.

The President congratulated Senators John Culver and Paul Laxalt and their colleagues on the subcommittee on an impressive job of melding and refining regulatory reform proposals from the administration, other Senators, and many expert witnesses. He said that this issue urgently needs to be addressed by responsible and well-crafted legislation.

The President is gratified that major provisions of the bill carry forward the essentials of his regulatory reform program, established through Executive orders and other administrative initiatives. These include strengthening regulatory management and cost-effective decisionmaking, elimination of unnecessary regulatory burdens, enhanced opportunities for meaningful public participation, and reduction of redtape and unnecessary delay in the regulatory process. This is the type of balanced reform effort which will streamline the Government's efforts to protect the health, safety, and welfare of our citizens, without wasting public or private resources.

The President hopes for speedy and responsible action in the full Judiciary Committee and in the Senate Governmental Affairs Committee, where Senator Ribicoff has introduced and held hearings on similar legislation.

United States-Peru Treaty on Penal Sentences

Message to the Senate Transmitting the Treaty.   December 20, 1979

To the Senate of the United States:

With a view to receiving the advice and consent of the Senate to ratification, I transmit herewith the Treaty between the United States of America and Peru on the Execution of Penal Sentences, which was signed at Washington on July 6, 1979.

I transmit also, for the information of the Senate, the report of the Department of State with respect to the Treaty.

The Treaty would permit citizens of either nation who had been convicted in the courts of the other country to serve their sentence in their home country; in each case the consent of the offender as well as the approval of the authorities of the two Governments would be required.

This Treaty is significant because it represents an attempt to resolve a situation which has inflicted substantial hardships on a number of citizens of each

country and has caused concern to both Governments. The Treaty is similar to those currently in force with Bolivia, Canada and Mexico. I recommend that the Senate give favorable consideration to this Treaty at an early date.

JIMMY CARTER

The White House,
    December 20, 1979.

Council on Wage and Price Stability

Message to the Congress Transmitting a Report.   December 20, 1979

To the Congress of the United States:

In accordance with Section 5 of the Council on Wage and Price Stability Act, as amended, I hereby transmit to the Congress the nineteenth quarterly report of the Council on Wage and Price Stability. The report contains a description of the Council's activities during the second quarter of 1979 in monitoring both prices and wages in the private sector and various Federal Government activities that may lead to higher costs and prices without creating commensurate benefits. It discusses Council reports, analyses, and filings before Federal regulatory agencies. It also describes the Council's activities of monitoring wages and prices as part of the anti-inflation program.

The Council on Wage and Price Stability will continue to play an important role in supplementing fiscal and monetary policies by calling public attention to wage and price developments or actions by the Government that could be of concern to American consumers.

JIMMY CARTER

The White House,
    December 20, 1979.

Small Community and Rural Development Policy

Remarks Announcing the Policy.
December 20, 1979

Being here this afternoon to announce the administration's small community and rural development policy is a very special occasion for me. It's special, because I know how important this policy will be to rural America, and I know how important rural America is to our country.

As a life-long resident of Plains, Georgia, and as a farmer; as an organizer and the original manager of a seven-county rural area planning and development commission; as a State senator, representing a rural district; as a Governor, representing a predominantly rural State; and as a President: I feel that I know rural America.

I know its greatness; I know its beauty. I know its diversity and its resilience in time of trial and trouble and testing. I know its strength, and I know the character of the people who live in rural America. I know the critically important role that it plays in the production of food and fiber, of energy and of wood, minerals. I understand the ultimate, strategic value of the land, and what it will mean in the future, as a force for peace, and the beneficial influence of our Nation around the world. And I also know the problems of rural America: its pockets of poverty; its problems of isolation; the hardships and deprivation of some of its residents, which they still have to endure.

I grew up on a farm, within 7 or 8 miles of my town, of my present home. My wife's ancestors and mine are buried, who were born in the 1700's; we haven't moved very far. I remember my life on the farm during the Depression, when we didn't have electricity, we didn't have tractors. We did the work with our hands.

Wages for an able-bodied man were a dollar a day. And health problems and education problems and racial discrimination problems were very difficult to overcome.

We made a lot of progress. And I am convinced, as President, that we ought not to measure the quality of life of people according to how densely the area is populated. I don't care if a thousand years from now Plains still has 700 people; but I would like to make sure that those 700 have a good education, good homes to live in, good transportation opportunities, good health; that they know what's going on in the rest of the world; that they have a purposeful life; that they have jobs; and that the quality of their life will equal that of any other community in this country.

For the first 150 years or so of our Nation's existence we were primarily a rural nation. National policy and rural policy were often almost always the same. More lately, as our cities have grown and the suburbs have grown, we've become predominantly an urban nation. But now the demographic trends of the 1950's and 1960's, the migration of people from the rural areas into the cities has reversed. And since 1970 the population of the rural areas has increased 40 percent more than has the population in our urban centers.

The rural economy is also growing. It's becoming more diverse. In contrast to the rural America known by myself and by my parents and my grandparents and yours, a much larger proportion of the rural residents are now employed, not in agriculture as such, but in manufacturing and trade and the provision of services to other human beings. These changes create new demands, new challenges, new opportunities. They require us to take stock of who we are and what we want in life. They point to the need for wise use and continued productivity of the bountiful rural resources that God has given us. And they challenge us to renew our commitment to address basic, unmet needs, and to redress longstanding inequities.

There have been calls for a more conscious national policy for our rural areas for more than 50 years. It's become increasingly evident that rural areas are unique, that they are not well served by government programs designed for the majority of the population.

With the leadership of Senator Humphrey, Senator Talmadge, Tom Foley, other Members of Congress, including those on this platform this afternoon, this concern eventually has become translated into the Rural Development Act of 1972 and its evolutionary changes since that time. This provided the letter of the law, but it could not provide the spirit and a sense of common purpose that must come from those who execute the laws.

Thus, while programs have grown and prospered under this basic legislation, something important had been missing, as all of you well know. That is the dedicated and the wholehearted commitment of all of us to a better life in rural America: a mechanism by which we could join together, not complaining about one another and not complaining about the deprivations of rural life, but through an easy sense of common purpose and communication and cooperation, work together to overcome the problems, to meet the challenges, and to answer the difficult questions that face the people who don't live in the urban parts of our country.

The goals of our Nation's first comprehensive rural policy, which we'll describe this afternoon, are to create new jobs and provide a favorable climate for rural business and economic development; to promote the responsible use and the proper stewardship of rural America's natural resources; to address the special rural problems of distance and size; and to meet the basic human needs of rural Americans.

To accomplish these goals, the policy that I'm announcing today does three important things. First, in recognition of the need for a strong partnership between the public and private sectors of American life, and among all levels of government, we will recognize the primacy of local priorities and local decisionmaking. We will assure that Federal investments support and reinforce those State and local development initiatives. We will use Federal assistance to increase private sector cooperation and participation. We will target Federal assistance specifically toward individuals in rural communities which are most in need. We will make Federal programs more accessible and better adapted to rural circumstances. And we will help to strengthen local management and development capability.

Second, this policy presents an action agenda—nearly 100 specific actions that address pressing rural needs and translate the policy principles into tangible results. This agenda of things to be done expands on the White House rural development initiatives that have evolved in an uncoordinated way, perhaps, in the White House over the last 2½ years, and it's based on months of extensive consultations, as you know, with all of you here.

Beginning more than a year ago, we began to put together a program, and more than 6 months ago, we called you in to let you look over what we had done because of your initial recommendations and ideas. And then we have forged this, not in an isolated ivory tower here in Washington, but we've kind of put into practice, in putting this program together, what you wanted done, and other people around the country, including, obviously, Members of Congress, State and local officials, and rural leaders of all kinds of organizations. Just a few weeks ago I, myself, met with the leaders of 50 different rural organizations in the Cabinet Room. Many of you were there.

Third, our policy will provide us with the ability to develop programs to solve problems and to get things done without unnecessary delay. In order to implement this strategy, that is, to get things done without delay, I will seek authority for an under secretary of small community and rural development at the U.S. Department of Agriculture, to work for me and to assist the Secretary of Agriculture, working under him, in rural development activities throughout the entire administration.

I will form a working group of high-level Federal program managers in many different agencies, I think about 17 of them, to ensure implementation of the program being introduced today, and this working group will be cochaired by Jack Watson, and by the under secretary for rural development, working under the Secretary of Agriculture.

I will appoint a citizens advisory council to monitor the progress that we make and to advise me and the Secretary of Agriculture on needed Federal actions. I'll invite the Nation's Governors to establish in each State a rural development council to ensure effective coordination among the different levels of government. And I'll direct my Cabinet and all the heads of my agencies to review all relevant policies and programs in existence now, or to be proposed to the Congress in the future, in order to monitor implementation of the policy that will be described today. And I would like to ask them, and

will, to designate a senior official in each agency to serve as a rural advocate and to act as a point of contact for small community and rural leaders like you, who are seeking information and assistance.

I'm pleased with the achievements that we've realized in the last 2½ years or so since I've been President in addressing the problems of rural America and the small communities. It's a good record, and it provides experience and a firm foundation for the policy initiatives that we've announced today. But the more we have dealt with these problems, the more we've seen the need for a comprehensive national policy with a large group of people directly involved in it.

This policy is the first of its kind. It redeems my own pledge that the rural areas of our country will receive the attention that they've needed and which they have deserved for so long. It also represents a return to the principle that government should encourage but never dictate the decisions made by American people and by local initiative. With your cooperation some elements of this program have already been tested in action.

The comprehensive policy we announced today is not the end of our work. It's just the beginning. It'll give us the tools to do the job, to finish the job, something that I know from my experience, both as a farmer and as a President, that rural America knows how to do, to start a job, to do it well, and to finish it.

In closing let me say that I want to express my gratitude for the strong and continued support that we've had in preparing this policy, to all of you, the groups and individuals who've contributed, too numerous to mention specifically—but I would like to thank Senator Patrick Leahy, the chairman of the Senate Subcommittee on Rural Development, who will follow me at this podium; Congressman Wes Watkins, the chairman of the Congressional Rural Caucus; Governor Jim Hunt, my good friend and chairman of the Governors' subcommittee on small cities and rural development; Lynn Cutler, county commissioner from Iowa; David Humes, mayor of Hayti Heights, in Missouri; Charles Bannerman, the president of the Delta Foundation and cochairman of the Rural Coalition; the Rural Caucus; the National Governors' Association; the Rural Coalition; and many other individuals and groups that have given us so much encouragement.

Together, I'm convinced that you and I together and all those who work with us can bring a new and a better life to rural America. I'm dedicated to it. With your help we will not fail.

Thank you very much.

[*At this point, Senator Leahy and Governor Hunt spoke. The President then resumed speaking as follows.*]

We have an overflow crowd. Part of the group is in the Treaty Room down the hall. So, I'll be listening very carefully to Congressman Watkins, who's done such a good job on this program, from the other room, and this will give him a double audience. It's in honor of him that I'm going to stop in the other group and listen to his speech. Wes, good luck to you.

NOTE: The President spoke at approximately 2:30 p.m. to a group of community and civic leaders assembled in Room 450 of the Old Executive Office Building.

The transcript also includes the remarks of Jack H. Watson, Jr., Assistant to the President for Intergovernmental Affairs, Hal Wilson, cochairman of the Rural Coalition and director of the Housing Assistance Corporation, as well as those of Senator Leahy, Governor Hunt, Representative Watkins, Mayor Humes, and Supervisor Cutler.

Commissioner of Education

Nomination of William Lee Smith.
December 20, 1979

The President today announced that he will nominate William Lee Smith, of Maryland, to be Commissioner of Education. He would replace Ernest Boyer, resigned. This position will be abolished when the Department of Education is activated in 1980.

Smith has been Director of the Teacher Corps at the Department of Health, Education, and Welfare since 1973.

He was born January 3, 1929, in Boston, Mass. He received a B.A. from Wiley College in 1949, an M. Ed. from Massachusetts State Teachers College in 1955, and a Ph. D. from Case Western Reserve University in 1970.

Smith was a social groupworker from 1954 to 1956. He was with the Cleveland, Ohio, public schools from 1956 to 1968, as a high school teacher, guidance counselor, and principal. From 1968 to 1969, he was executive director of the Pace Association (Program of Action by Citizens in Education) in Cleveland.

Smith joined the U.S. Office of Education at HEW in 1969 as Chief of the Career Opportunity Program. He served subsequently as Director of the Division of School Programs, Acting Director of the Teacher Corps, Associate Commissioner for Educational Personnel Development and Director of the National Center for Improvement of Educational Systems, Acting Deputy Commissioner for Development, and Associate Commissioner for Career Education.

Smith has served as Chairman of the U.S. Delegation to the International Management Training on Educational Change Training Program of the Organization for Economic Cooperation and Development (OECD) in Oslo, Norway, and the U.S. Delegation to the OECD Conference on Teacher Policy in Paris, France. He has received numerous awards for his work in education.

National Commission on Libraries and Information Science

Nomination of Three Members.
December 20, 1979

The President today announced three persons whom he will nominate to be members of the National Commission on Libraries and Information Science for terms expiring July 19, 1984. They are:

Helmut A. Alpers, vice president of the General Bookbinding Co. of Chesterland, Ohio. Alpers spent 18 years with IBM, where he was extensively involved in information systems. He was a delegate to the White House Conference on Libraries and Information Services, held in November 1979.

Carlos A. Cuadra, of Los Angeles, president of Cuadra Associates, Inc., for reappointment. Cuadra is also an adjunct professor at UCLA's Graduate School of Library and Information Science, and has been a member of this Commission since 1971.

Margaret S. Warden, of Great Falls, Mont., chair of the Constitutional Convention Proceedings Printing Committee and a former Montana State senator. She served on the Advisory Committee for the White House Conference on Libraries and Information Services. She is a former librarian and a member of the Montana State Library Advisory Council.

International Economic Sanctions Against Iran

Remarks Announcing Intention To Seek
United Nations Action.   December 21, 1979

THE PRESIDENT. From the first day the American Embassy was invaded and our diplomatic staff was seized as hostages by Iran, we have pursued every legal channel available to us to secure their safe and prompt release. On at least four separate occasions the world community, through the United Nations Security Council and through the International Court of Justice, has expressed itself clearly and firmly in calling upon the Iranian Government to release the American hostages.

Yet Iran today still stands in arrogant defiance of the world community. It has shown contempt not only for international law but for the entire international structure for securing the peaceful resolution of differences among nations.

In an irresponsible attempt at blackmail, to which the United States will never yield, kidnapers and terrorists, supported by Iranian officials, continue to hold our people under inhumane conditions. With each day that passes, our concern grows for the health and for the well-being of the hostages. We have made clear from the very beginning that the United States prefers a peaceful solution, in preference to the other remedies which are available to us under international law. For a peaceful resolution to be achieved, it is now clear that concrete action must be taken by the international community.

Accordingly, I have decided to ask for an early meeting of the United Nations Security Council to impose international economic sanctions upon Iran, under title VII of the United Nations Charter. The Government of Iran must realize that it cannot flaunt with impunity the expressed will and law of the world community. The Security Council must act to enforce its demand that Iran release the hostages. The world community must support the legal machinery it has established, so that the United Nations and the International Court of Justice will continue to be relevant in settling serious disputes which threaten peace among nations.

I can think of no more clear and compelling challenge to the international community than the one we face today. The lives of over 50 innocent people are at stake; the foundation of civilized diplomacy is at stake; the integrity of international law is at stake; the credibility of the United Nations is at stake. And at stake, ultimately, is the maintenance of peace in the region. As we call on the Security Council to act, on behalf of international law and on behalf of peace, we again call on the Government of Iran to end this crisis by releasing the hostages without delay.

And now, because our holy days approach—a time to think of peace—I would like to add a few special words for the American people, indeed the people of good will in all countries, including Iran, who share concern for 50 innocent human beings who hope, themselves, for peace and for the salvation of their lives.

Henry Longfellow wrote a Christmas carol in a time of crisis, the War Between the States, in 1864. Two verses of that carol particularly express my thoughts and prayers and, I'm sure, those of our Nation in this time of challenge and of concern and of crisis. And I would like to quote from that poem:

"And in despair I bowed my head.
'There is no peace on earth,' I said.
'For hate is strong and mocks the song
Of peace on earth, good will to men.'

Then pealed the bells, more loud and deep,
'God is not dead, nor does he sleep.
The wrong shall fail, the right prevail,
With peace on earth, good will to men.'"

Thank you very much.

REPORTER. Mr. President, do you have any hope of observers getting to see the hostages on Christmas Day?

THE PRESIDENT. We don't know what the answer to that question is. We always hope, but we don't expect it to happen.

Q. Sir, do we have the votes in the Security Council?

THE PRESIDENT. We'll have to answer that question later.

NOTE: The President spoke at 4:01 p.m. to reporters assembled in the Briefing Room at the White House.

Price Controls on Heavy Crude Oil

Executive Order 12186. December 21, 1979

CHANGE IN DEFINITION OF HEAVY OIL

By the authority vested in me as President by the Constitution and statutes of the United States of America, including the Emergency Petroleum Allocation Act of 1973, as amended (15 U.S.C. 751 *et seq.*), Executive Order No. 12153 is hereby amended by deleting Section 1–102, renumbering Section 1–103 as 1–102, and deleting in Section 1–101 the figure "16.0° API" and inserting in lieu thereof "20.0° API.".

JIMMY CARTER

The White House,
December 21, 1979.

[Filed with the Office of the Federal Register,
10:50 a.m., December 26, 1979]

Price Controls on Heavy Crude Oil

White House Statement. December 21, 1979

The President today acted to lift price controls from expanded volumes of heavy crude oil production. By signing an amendment to Executive Order 12153, the President decontrolled, effective immediately, heavy crude oil with an average specific gravity up to 20.0° API. In taking this action today, the President expressed his deep appreciation to Senator Cranston and the California delegation for their assistance in this effort.

This action follows a Presidential directive to the Department of Energy at the time Executive Order 12153 was signed (August 17, 1979). That order decontrolled heavy crude oil production below 16.0° API. The President asked DOE to review and hold public hearings on the advisability of expanding the definition of heavy crude oil above the 16.0° level. The action taken today responds to the findings and recommendations made by DOE as a result of the hearing and review process.

Both Executive Order 12153 and the amendment signed today apply only to current production of heavy crude oil or production from known reservoirs. Newly discovered supplies of heavy crude are covered under the President's April 5, 1979, decision to decontrol this category of oil effective June 1, 1979.

It is expected that decontrol of oil in the 16.0°–20.0° range will significantly accelerate production of this resource and will yield approximately 140 million barrels of additional supplies between now and 1986. Daily production should increase by about 65,000 barrels per day in 1981, and peak at an added 130,000 barrels per day in 1983.

The President does not recommend that oil in the 16.0°–20.0° range be exempt from the windfall profits tax, as he did for heavy crude oil below 16.0° API. The extra incentives provided by the decontrol action itself are sufficient to generate added production as well as to prevent heavy oil wells in this range from being shut in, because they are only marginally economic or uneconomic under price controls.

Digest of Other White House Announcements

The following listing includes the President's public schedule and other items of general interest announced by the White House Press Office and not included elsewhere in this issue.

December 15

The President spoke by telephone with the Shah of Iran prior to his departure from Lackland A.F.B., Texas, for Panama.

December 16

The President returned to the White House from Camp David, Md.

December 17

The President met at the White House with:

—Zbigniew Brzezinski, Assistant to the President for National Security Affairs;

—Frank B. Moore, Assistant to the President for Congressional Liaison;

—a group of Chassidic rabbis from New York;

—James T. McIntyre, Jr., Director of the Office of Management and Budget, and other administration officials to review the fiscal year 1981 budget.

2279

December 18

The President met at the White House with:
—Dr. Brzezinski;
—the Democratic congressional leadership;
—Mr. Moore;
—a group of Democratic Party State chairmen and vice chairmen;
—Mayor George Athanson of Hartford, Conn.

The President and Mrs. Carter hosted a Christmas reception in the afternoon for members of the U.S. Secret Service and their guests on the State Floor of the White House.

December 19

The President met at the White House with:
—Dr. Brzezinski;
—Ambassador Donald F. McHenry, U.S. Representative to the United Nations;
—Mr. Moore;
—a group of VISTA volunteers, Stuart E. Eizenstat, Assistant to the President for Domestic Affairs and Policy, and Jack H. Watson, Jr., Assistant to the President for Intergovernmental Affairs, to mark the 15th anniversary of the Federal volunteer service program;
—Vice President Walter F. Mondale;
—Mr. McIntyre and other administration officials to review the fiscal year 1981 budget.

The President and Mrs. Carter hosted a Christmas reception for members of the Cabinet and their guests in the Residence.

December 20

The President met at the White House with:
—Dr. Brzezinski;
—Representative Stephen J. Solarz of New York and constituents from his congressional district;

—Mr. Moore;
—Charles L. Schultze, Chairman of the Council of Economic Advisers;
—Senator Patrick J. Leahy of Vermont;
—members of the Congressional Coal Caucus.

The President participated in a briefing by administration officials on administration policies and programs given for community and civic leaders from Illinois in the East Room at the White House.

The President transmitted to the Congress the 1977 annual report of the National Endowment for the Arts and the National Council on the Arts.

December 21

The President met at the White House with:
—Dr. Brzezinski;
—Vice President Mondale, Secretary of State Cyrus R. Vance, Secretary of Defense Harold Brown, Hamilton Jordan, Assistant to the President, Hedley W. Donovan, Senior Adviser to the President, and Dr. Brzezinski;
—Mr. Moore;
—Mr. McIntyre and other administration officials to review the fiscal year 1981 budget;
—former professional football player Roosevelt Grier;
—Mr. McIntyre and other administration officials to review the fiscal year 1981 budget.

The President left the White House for a stay at Camp David.

NOMINATIONS SUBMITTED TO THE SENATE

The following list does not include promotions of members of the Uniformed Services, nominations to the Service Academies, or nominations of Foreign Service officers.

NOMINATIONS—Continued

Submitted December 19, 1979

COLBERT I. KING, of Maryland, to be United States Executive Director of the International Bank for Reconstruction and Development for a term of 2 years, vice Edward R. Fried, resigned.

DAVID S. KING, of Maryland, to be United States Alternate Executive Director of the International Bank for Reconstruction and Development for a term of 2 years, vice William P. Dixon, resigned.

G. WIX UNTHANK, of Kentucky, to be United States District Judge for the Eastern District of Kentucky, vice a new position created by P.L. 95–486, approved October 20, 1978.

HIPOLITO FRANK GARCIA, of Texas, to be United States District Judge for the Western District of Texas, vice a new position created by P.L. 95–486, approved October 20, 1978.

CLYDE FREDERICK SHANNON, JR., of Texas, to be United States District Judge for the Western District of Texas, vice Dorwin W. Suttle, retired.

Submitted December 20, 1979

JOSEPH CHARLES ZENGERLE III, of the District of Columbia, to be an Assistant Secretary of the Air Force, vice Antonia Handler Chayes, elevated.

THOMAS K. BERG, of Minnesota, to be United States Attorney for the District of Minnesota for the term of 4 years, vice Andrew W. Danielson, resigned.

WILLIAM LEE SMITH, of Maryland, to be Commissioner of Education, vice Ernest LeRoy Boyer, resigned.

The following-named persons to be members of the National Commission on Libraries and Information Science for terms expiring July 19, 1984:

HELMUT A. ALPERS, of Connecticut, vice Joseph Becker, term expired.

CARLOS A. CUADRA, of California (reappointment).

MARGARET S. WARDEN, of Montana, vice John E. Velde, Jr., term expired.

CHECKLIST OF WHITE HOUSE PRESS RELEASES

The following listing contains releases of the White House Press Office which are not included in this issue.

CHECKLIST—Continued

Released December 15, 1979

News conference: on the International Court of Justice decision regarding the holding of the American hostages in Iran—by Attorney General Benjamin R. Civiletti

Released December 18, 1979

Announcement: nomination of G. Wix Unthank to be United States District Judge for the Eastern District of Kentucky

Announcement: nomination of Hipolito Frank Garcia to be United States District Judge for the Western District of Texas

Announcement: nomination of Clyde Frederick Shannon, Jr., to be United States District Judge for the Western District of Texas

Released December 19, 1979

Announcement: nomination of Thomas K. Berg to be United States Attorney for the District of Minnesota

Released December 20, 1979

Fact sheet: small community and rural development policy

Policy statement and action agenda: small community and rural development policy

Transcript: remarks and a question-and-answer session on action by the congressional Conference Committee on the windfall profits tax legislation—by Press Secretary Jody Powell

Released December 21, 1979

Announcement: transmittal to Congress of proposed legislation on financing of small businesses

ACTS APPROVED BY THE PRESIDENT

Approved December 16, 1979

H.J. Res. 458_____ Public Law 96–147 A joint resolution to authorize and request the President to issue a proclamation designating December 18, 1979, "National Unity Day".

S. 901_____ Public Law 96–148 An act to amend the Clean Water Act of 1977 to extend the moratorium on industrial cost recovery.

S. 1788_____ Public Law 96–149 An act to amend the National Consumer Cooperative Bank Act to provide for a small business representative on the Bank's Board.

ACTS APPROVED—Continued

Approved December 20, 1979

H.R. 5163_____ Public Law 96–150
An act to authorize the sale to certain foreign nations of certain excess naval vessels.

H.R. 3892_____ Public Law 96–151
Veterans Health Programs Extension and Improvement Act of 1979.

H.R. 5651_____ Public Law 96–152
An act to establish by law the position of Chief of the Capitol Police, and for other purposes.

H.R. 1888_____ Private Law 96–23
An act for the relief of Kenneth and Jacqueline Traylar.

H.R. 2594_____ Private Law 96–24
An act for the relief of Lunette Joyce Clarke.

S. 2145_____ Private Law 96–25
An act to authorize the burial of Elizabeth Myers McNeil in the Veals Chapels Cemetery, Fort Jackson, South Carolina.

ACTS APPROVED—Continued

Approved December 21, 1979

H.R. 3875_____ Public Law 96–153
Housing and Community Development Amendments of 1979.

H.R. 5359_____ Public Law 96–154
Department of Defense Appropriation Act, 1980.

S. 1874_____ Public Law 96–155
An act to amend the Act incorporating the American Legion so as to redefine eligibility for membership therein.

H.R. 1616_____ Private Law 96–26
An act for the relief of Caroline M. Babcock.

H.R. 1889_____ Private Law 96–27
An act for the relief of Naomi Chen.

H.R. 2477_____ Private Law 96–28
An act for the relief of Jesus Reveles y Rivera.

H.R. 2532_____ Private Law 96–29
An act for the relief of Gail Williamson.

PRESIDENTIAL DOCUMENTS

Windfall Profits Tax Legislation

Statement by the President.
December 22, 1979

The House and Senate conferees have taken important steps toward reconciling their differences on the windfall profits tax. The basic agreement reached on revenue levels brings us closer to enactment of a windfall tax which will pay for vital investments in *American* alternatives to imported oil.

Progress on the tax has been painfully slow. First we were promised action by October, then by Thanksgiving, and then by Christmas. Although the Congress made progress before it adjourned, we still do not have a windfall profits tax in law.

When I announced my decision to phase out controls on domestic crude oil last April, I made clear that the windfall profits tax was an essential companion to decontrol. The schedule was carefully set to encourage American energy production and to give the Congress plenty of time to act on the tax. It is my present intention to continue the necessary general decontrol schedule, but I will postpone further increases in the price allowed for marginal wells until a windfall profits tax satisfactory to me is on my desk.

It must be clear that the costs of delay are high. I am determined that the American public will be protected with a windfall profits tax which is fair and which provides the funds we need to invest in our energy future.

The conference committee and their staff will continue work on the tax between now and the start of the new congressional session to ensure that precious time is not lost. It is also critical that the conferees on the energy mobilization board and the energy security corporation complete their work without further delay. We must not dissipate our opportunity for actions during this time of crisis. The eyes of the world are focused on us to see if we meet our energy challenges. What Congress does over the next few weeks will determine whether this country will meet its challenge.

We can and must send a strong and accurate signal that we, the American people, are determined to cut our dependence on imported oil. The windfall profits tax, the energy mobilization board, and the energy security corporation are critical to this effort, and we will not shirk our duty.

Pan American World Airways-National Airlines Merger

Letter to the Chairman of the Civil Aeronautics Board.   December 22, 1979

To Chairman Marvin Cohen

I have reviewed the following orders proposed by the Civil Aeronautics Board:

Pan American Acquisition of, Control of, and Merger with National
Docket 33283

and

Texas International-National Acquisition Case
Docket 33112

I do not intend to disapprove the Board's orders within the 60 days allowed by statute.

In these orders, the Board approved the acquisition of National Airlines by Pan American World Airways. However, the Board deleted from the authority granted the merged airline the right now held by National, to provide service between Miami and London. Instead, the Board has initiated a separate proceeding to select a successor to National to operate the Miami-London route.

Under the Airline Deregulation Act of 1978, the President is given 60 days following a CAB decision such as this affecting international routes to review the decision. The President may disapprove a Board decision "solely upon the basis of foreign relations or national defense considerations . . . but not upon the basis of economic or carrier selection considerations."

Questions have been raised about that portion of the Board's decision deleting the Miami-London route from the transferred authority. I do not find sufficiently compelling foreign relations or national defense considerations to disturb the Board's decision on this issue or any other issue. I note that Pan American is one of several applicants for the Miami-London route in a proceeding now under consideration by the Board. I also note that the Board's opinion here underscores the right of the United States to assure any American carrier serving Miami-London complete competitive equality with any Brit-

ish carrier providing similar service, a right which must be assured in the final disposition of this matter.

To assure the opportunity for judicial review of the Board's action, I note that no foreign relations or national defense consideration underlies my action here.

Sincerely,

JIMMY CARTER

[The Honorable Marvin S. Cohen, Chairman, Civil Aeronautics Board, Washington, D.C. 20428]

United States Savings Bonds Program

Memorandum From the President.
December 26, 1979

Memorandum for the Heads of Executive Departments and Agencies

The U.S. Savings Bonds Program has played an important role in sound debt management and in our continuing efforts to help control inflation. Over $80 billion in Savings Bonds are currently held by Americans.

In 1980, the Savings Bonds Program will assume an additional purpose. The new Series EE Savings Bonds, which will be introduced to payroll sales during the first six months of 1980, will be designated U.S. Energy Savings Bonds, Series EE.

While helping to finance the large Federal energy expenditure required in the coming years, U.S. Energy Savings Bonds will also help to focus the country's attention on the national goals of reducing energy consumption and increasing domestic supplies.

Series EE Savings Bonds not only offer increased benefits to the country as a whole but to each individual saver as well. The interest rate on these securities will be increased from 6.5 percent to 7 percent for Bonds held for the full 11 years to maturity.

I believe it is appropriate for employees of the Federal Government to take the leadership responsibility in furthering the sale of U.S. Energy Savings Bonds. We must set the example for all Americans to follow.

Consequently, I have appointed Secretary of Defense Harold Brown to serve as Chairman of the Interagency Savings Bonds Committee.

The introduction this year of the U.S. Energy Savings Bonds, Series EE not only presents new challenges, but also new opportunities for close cooperation at all levels of government.

Secretary Brown and the members of the Committee have a special duty to ensure that all Departments and Agencies complete the transition to U.S. Energy Savings Bonds, Series EE smoothly and effectively, maintaining a high record of employee participation in the Savings Bonds Program.

Secretary Brown has my full support in undertaking this new responsibility. In turn, I want him to be able to count on your full support through your active personal involvement in this year's payroll savings campaign in your agency.

JIMMY CARTER

Budget Deferrals

Message to the Congress. December 26, 1979

To the Congress of the United States:

In accordance with the Impoundment Control Act of 1974, I herewith report three new deferrals totalling $28.7 million and three revisions to previously transmitted deferrals increasing the amount deferred by $34.5 million. These items affect programs in the Departments of Defense and Treasury, the National Consumer Cooperative Bank, the National Commission on Social Security, and the District of Columbia.

The details of the deferrals are contained in the attached reports.

JIMMY CARTER

The White House,
December 26, 1979.

NOTE: The attachments detailing the deferrals are printed in the FEDERAL REGISTER of December 31, 1979.

United States International Trade Commission

Designation of Catherine May Bedell as Chairman. December 26, 1979

The President today announced that he has designated Catherine May Bedell as Chairman of the United States International Trade Commission (USITC).

Bedell has been a member of USITC and its predecessor agency, the United States Tariff Commission, since 1971. She has previously served as Chairman. She is a former U.S. Representative from the State of Washington.

Iranians in the United States

White House Statement on a Court Decision Upholding the President's Authority To Investigate Student Visas. December 27, 1979

The decision by the Court of Appeals confirms the view that the administration has held all along—that the action taken in surveying Iranian students was both constitutional and lawful. The President is, of course, gratified by the decision. The

Attorney General has assured the President the program will continue to be carried out expeditiously in strict compliance with due process standards.

As of December 20, more than 45,000 of the nearly 55,000 students interviewed under the program were found to be in the country legally. Some 6,500 were found to be out of status, with the balance requiring a further check of documents.

Energy Emergency in Oregon

Memorandum From the President.
December 27, 1979

Memorandum for the Administrator of the Environmental Protection Agency

Subject: Determination Under Section 110(f) of the Clean Air Act

Governor Atiyeh of the State of Oregon petitioned me on December 22, 1979, for a determination under Section 110(f) of the Clean Air Act that a regional energy emergency exists in Oregon of such severity that a temporary suspension of the federally promulgated new source construction and permitting prohibition under Section 110 and Part D of the Clean Air Act and appropriate provisions of Oregon's State Implementation Plan is necessary to help alleviate potentially high levels of unemployment caused by possible curtailments of electricity supply to the region. After considering the information and views provided to me by Governor Atiyeh, the Secretary of the Department of Energy, and the Administrator of EPA, I am hereby making the requested determination, subject to the conditions listed below:

(1) This determination applies only to the Harborton facility discussed in the Governor's petition.

(2) This determination expires on February 7, 1980. I will rescind this determination before that date if the potential energy shortage is substantially eased in the interim.

(3) Oregon's Department of Environmental Quality will monitor the air quality impact of operating the Harborton facility and will require the termination of its operation if air quality levels approach the primary ambient air quality standards. In no case would this declaration permit excesses of the health related primary ambient air quality standards.

(4) The Governor calls for a statewide electricity conservation effort. The State will submit to EPA and DOE biweekly reports on electricity consumption levels in the State, including the effects of its electricity conservation program. This determination is made in full recognition of Oregon's excellent record in the area of energy conservation.

(5) The operation of the Harborton facility will not result in a reduction in the electric energy output of other fossil fuel fired generating facilities in the State of Oregon.

(6) PGE will make maximum practicable effort to purchase available electric power from other regional utilities. State regulatory authorities will seek to remove regulatory impediments to power purchase by PRE and allow timely recovery of prudently incurred purchased power costs.

This determination shall be published in the FEDERAL REGISTER.

JIMMY CARTER

[Filed with the Office of the Federal Register, 8:56 a.m., December 31, 1979]

NOTE: The text of the memorandum was released on December 28.

American Hostages in Iran and Soviet Intervention in Afghanistan

Remarks to Reporters.   December 28, 1979

Secretary of State Vance will proceed to the United Nations tomorrow to press the world's case against Iran in order to obtain the speediest possible release of American hostages, in accordance with the demands which have already been made earlier by the United Nations Security Council and the International Court of Justice.

The United States reserves the right to protect our citizens and our vital interests in whatever way we consider appropriate in keeping with principles of international law and the Charter of the United Nations. But our clear preference is now, and has been from the beginning of this crisis, for a quick and a peaceful solution of this problem through concerted international action.

We must never lose sight of our basic goals in this crisis—the safety of our fellow citizens and the protection of the long-term interests of the United States. A thoughtful and determined policy, which makes clear that Iran will continue to pay an increasingly higher price for the illegal detention of our people, is the best policy to achieve those goals, and it is the policy that I will continue to pursue.

Another serious development which has caused increased concern about peace and stability in the same region of the world is the recent Soviet military intervention in Afghanistan, which has now resulted in the overthrow of the established government and the execution of the President of that country. Such gross interference in the internal affairs of Afghanistan is in blatant violation of accepted international rules of behavior.

This is the third occasion since World War II that the Soviet Union has moved militarily to assert control over one of its neighbors, and this is the first such venture into a Muslim country by the Soviet Union since the Soviet occupation of Iranian Azerbaijan in the 1940's.

The Soviet action is a major matter of concern to the entire international community. Soviet efforts to justify this action on the basis of the United Nations Charter are a perversion of the United Nations that should be rejected immediately by all its members.

I have discussed this serious matter personally today with several other heads of government, all of whom agree that the Soviet action is a grave threat to peace. I will be sending the Deputy Secretary of State to Europe this weekend to meet with representatives of several other nations to discuss how the world community might respond to this unwarranted Soviet behavior. Soviet military action beyond its own borders gives rise to the most fundamental questions pertaining to international stability, and such close and extensive consultation between ourselves and with our allies are urgently needed.

Thank you very much.

REPORTER. Mr. President, do we have the votes in the U.N. Security Council, and do we have the Russians' promise they won't veto our resolution?

THE PRESIDENT. I expect we will see adequate support in the United Nations Security Council for our position.

Q. Have you gotten in touch with Brezhnev?

THE PRESIDENT. I have sent him a message.

NOTE: The President spoke at 4:30 p.m. in the Briefing Room at the White House.

Endangered Species Act Amendments

Statement on Signing S. 1143 Into Law. December 28, 1979

I am very pleased today to sign into law S. 1143, a 3-year reauthorization of the Endangered Species Act. This act is one of the most far-reaching and progressive laws ever enacted by any nation to protect wildlife and plant resources. Reauthorization of the act has been one of my high legislative priorities.

In addition to reauthorization, the bill I am signing strengthens our endangered species protection program by including plant, as well as animal, species in the emergency listing and international cooperation provisions. The act also authorizes funds to the Department of Agriculture to enforce provisions related to plants.

The bill revises the procedures for implementing the Convention on International Trade in Endangered Species of Wild Fauna and Flora. The Congress has established a strong and independent International Convention Advisory Commission to advise the Secretary of the Interior on scientific authority responsibilities related to the convention. The scientific integrity of the convention will be preserved by the Commission's advice on the effects of trade, the listing of species on the convention appendices, and the interpretation and implementation of the convention.

I look forward to and will continue to support the implementation of a vigorous endangered species program.

NOTE: As enacted, S. 1143 is Public Law 96–159, approved December 28.

Financial Institutions Deregulation Bill

Statement on Signing H.R. 4998 Into Law. December 28, 1979

I am deeply gratified by the passage of this legislation, which will help many Americans to obtain residential mortgage loans that would otherwise have been unavailable in many States. The administration has strongly supported a limited Federal preemption of State usury ceilings on mortgage loans, and the Congress approval of this provision will alleviate serious mortgage availability problems in the coming months in States with binding usury ceilings.

I am also pleased that the Congress has deferred the effective date of a court decision which would have prohibited depository institutions from offering share drafts, remote service, and automatic transfer accounts. These services have benefited millions of Americans, and we will work with the Congress to give institutions permanent legislative authority to offer these accounts.

Finally, I am pleased to note the extension of NOW account authority to federally chartered savings and loan institutions in New Jersey. Senator Williams and the New Jersey congressional delegation deserve credit for this provision, which will remove a serious competitive inequity. We will continue to seek nationwide NOW account authority.

I am hopeful that the bill I am signing today is only an interim step toward the passage of historic financial reform legislation early next year, legislation that would assure small savers a fair rate of return on their deposits, give our Nation's central bank the necessary tools to implement an effective noninflationary monetary policy, provide broader powers for thrift institutions to compete in a modern financial environment, and remove obsolete regulatory constraints.

The administration will work actively to assure the phaseout of Regulation Q deposit rate ceilings and the passage of legislation to stem the decline in Federal Reserve membership. During a period of high inflation, it is simply unacceptable for the Federal Government to force small savers to accept a submarket rate of return on their deposits. Similarly, as Chairman Volcker and Secretary Miller have noted, the decline in Federal Reserve membership ultimately threatens the ability of our central bank to conduct monetary policy, and it is critically important to stem membership attrition on a fair and equitable basis.

The banking committees are to be commended for their progress toward this landmark legislation, which was outlined in my 1979 State of the Union message. We will work closely with the Congress to assure the enactment of comprehensive financial reform legislation.

NOTE: As enacted, H.R. 4998 is Public Law 96–161, approved December 28.

National Medal of Science

Announcement of Award to 20 Recipients. December 28, 1979

The President today announced the award of the National Medal of Science to 20 recipients. The Medal is the highest honor the Federal Government accords the Nation's scientists and engineers.

The recipients are:

ROBERT H. BURRIS, W. H. Peterson professor of biochemistry, University of Wisconsin, Madison, Wis.;

ELIZABETH C. BROSBY, professor of anatomy, University of Michigan, Ann Arbor, Mich.;

JOSEPH LEO DOOB, professor of mathematics, University of Illinois, Urbana, Ill.;

RICHARD PHILLIPS FEYNMAN, Richard Chase Tolman professor of physics, California Institute of Technology, Pasadena, Calif.;

DONALD E. KNUTH, professor of computer science, Stanford University, Stanford, Calif.;

ARTHUR KORNBERG, professor of biochemistry, Stanford University, Stanford, Calif.;

EMMETT NORMAN LEITH, professor of electrical engineering, University of Michigan, Ann Arbor, Mich.;

HERMAN F. MARK, professor of chemistry, Polytechnic Institute of New York, Brooklyn, N.Y.;

RAYMOND D. MINDLIN, James Kip Finch professor of applied science, Columbia University, New York, N.Y.;

ROBERT N. NOYCE, chairman, Intel Corp., Santa Clara, Calif.;

SEVERO OCHOA, Roche Institute of Molecular Biology, Nutley, N.J.;

EARL R. PARKER, professor of metallurgy, University of California, Berkeley, Calif.;

EDWARD MILLS PURCELL, professor of physics, Harvard University, Cambridge, Mass.;

SIMON RAMO, vice chairman of the board, TRW, Inc., Redondo Beach, Calif.;

JOHN H. SINFELT, scientific adviser, EXXON Corporate Research Laboratories, Linden, N.J.;

LYMAN SPITZER, JR., Charles A. Young professor of astronomy, Princeton University, Princeton, N.J.;

EARL REECE STADTMAN, chief, Laboratory of Biochemistry, National Health, Lung, and Blood Institute, National Institute of Health, Bethesda, Md.;

GEORGE LEDYARD STEBBINS, JR., professor of genetics, University of California, Davis, Calif.;

PAUL A. WEISS, Rockefeller University, New York, N.Y.;

VICTOR F. WEISSKOPF, Institute professor of physics, Massachusetts Institute of Technology, Cambridge, Mass.

The National Medal of Science was established in 1959 by the 86th Congress. It is presented to individuals who, in the judgment of the President, "are deserving of special recognition by reason of their outstanding contributions to knowledge in the physical, biological, mathematical, or engineering sciences." To date, 133 Medals have been awarded, beginning in 1962. Each President beginning with Kennedy has awarded Medals. President Carter presented the most recent awards on November 22, 1977.

The presentation of the award to the 1979 recipients will occur in the near future.

Decontrol of Marginal Oil Wells

Executive Order 12187. December 29, 1979

BASE PRODUCTION CONTROL LEVEL FOR MARGINAL PROPERTIES

By the authority vested in me as President by the Constitution and statutes of the United States of America, including the Emergency Petroleum Allocation Act of 1973, as amended (15 U.S.C. 751 *et seq.*), and notwithstanding the delegations to the Secretary of Energy in Executive Order No. 11790, as amended by Executive Order No. 12038, and in order to delay the decontrol of marginal oil wells, it is hereby ordered as follows:

1–101. For purposes of the pricing regulations adopted pursuant to the Emergency Petroleum Allocation Act of 1973, with respect to months commencing after December 31, 1979, the base production control level for marginal properties shall equal 20 percent of the total number of barrels of old crude oil produced and sold from the property concerned during calendar year 1978, divided by 365, multiplied by the number of days during the month in 1978 which corresponds to the month concerned.

1–102. For purposes of this Order, the term "marginal properties" has the same meaning as that term under the crude oil pricing regulations adopted pursuant to the Emergency Petroleum Allocation Act of 1973, as amended.

1–103. The Secretary of Energy may, pursuant to Executive Order No. 11790, as amended by Executive Order No. 12038, adopt such regulations as he deems necessary or appropriate to conform the crude oil pricing regulations to this Order.

JIMMY CARTER

The White House,
    December 29, 1979.

[Filed with the Office of the Federal Register, 12:43 p.m., December 31, 1979]

NOTE: The text of the Executive order was released on December 31.

Export Controls for Foreign Policy Purposes

Letter to the Speaker of the House and the President of the Senate. December 29, 1979

Dear Mr. Speaker: (Dear Mr. President:)

In accordance with the authority contained in section 6 of the Export Administration Act of 1979 (Public Law 96–72 of September 29, 1979; hereinafter "the Act"), I hereby extend export controls maintained for foreign policy purposes as specified in Enclosure 1. In accordance with section 6(e) of the Act I hereby notify Congress of this extension.

I am also submitting, as Enclosure 2, my conclusions with respect to: the criteria set forth in section 6(b) of the Act; the nature and result of alternative means attempted to achieve the purposes of these controls or the reasons for extending them without attempting any such alternative means; and the ways in which such controls will further significantly the foreign policy of the United States or will further its declared international obligations.

Pursuant to section 6(k) of the Act, the countries and the goods and technologies listed in Enclosure 1 will be clearly identified in Export Administration Regulations published in the FEDERAL REGISTER as being subject to export controls for foreign policy purposes.

With reference to section 4(c) of the Act, adequate evidence has been presented demonstrating that, notwithstanding foreign availability, the absence of these controls would prove detrimental to the foreign policy of the United States.

Revisions of the regulations are being issued with an effective date of January 1, 1980, to comply with section 6(a)(2). They will be reissued in final form later in 1980, in order to take into consideration public comments received pursuant to section 13(b) of the Act.

Sincerely,

JIMMY CARTER

[Enclosure 1]

EXPORT CONTROLS FOR FOREIGN POLICY PURPOSES EXTENDED FOR THE PERIOD JANUARY 1 THROUGH DECEMBER 31, 1980

I. All countries except members of the North Atlantic Treaty Organization, Japan, Australia, and New Zealand:

A. A validated license is required for the export of crime control and detection instruments, equipment, and related technical data.

B. Applications for validated export licenses will generally be considered favorably on a case-by-case basis unless there is evidence that the government of the importing country may have violated internationally recognized human rights and that the judicious use of export controls would be helpful in deterring the development of a consistent pattern of such violations or in distancing the United States from such violations.

II. South Africa and Namibia only:

A. A validated license is required for the export of:

1. All U.S.-origin commodities and technical data for military and police entities;

2. Aircraft and helicopters and items controlled pursuant to the South African arms embargo for all consignees; and

3. Computers for government consignees exceeding performance levels permitted for shipment at national discretion under multilaterally agreed security export controls.

B. Applications for validated export licenses will:

1. Be denied for military or policy entities except, on a case-by-case basis, for medicines, medical supplies, and medical equipment not primarily destined to military or police entities or for their use; and

2. Generally be considered favorably on a case-by-case basis for:

a. Aircraft and helicopters for which adequate written assurances have been obtained against military, paramilitary, or police use; and

b. Computers which would not be used to support the South African policy of apartheid.

III. Libya, Iraq, People's Democratic Republic of Yemen, and Syria only:

A. A validated license is required for the export of aircraft valued at $3 million or more and helicopters over 10,000 pounds empty weight.

B. Applications for validated export licenses will generally be considered favorably on a case-by-case basis for such aircraft and helicopters for civil use if issuance of the licenses would be consistent with the policies set forth in subsections 3(4), 3(8), and 3(10) of the Act and subject to the requirement in subsection 6(i) of the Act to notify Congressional committees.

IV. Libya only:

A. A validated license is required for off-highway wheel tractors of carriage capacity of 10 tons or more.

B. Applications for validated export licenses will generally be considered favorably on a case-by-case basis for such tractors in reasonable quantities if for civil use, such as transportation of oil field equipment.

V. North Korea, Vietnam, Kampuchea, and Cuba only:

A. A validated license is required for all commodities and technical data except:

1. Technical data generally available to the public and educational materials;
2. Personal baggage, crew baggage, vessels and aircraft on temporary sojourn, ship stores, and plane stores;
3. Foreign-origin items in transit through the United States;
4. Shipments for U.S. Government personnel and agencies; and
5. Gift parcels not exceeding $200 of commodities such as food, clothing (non-military), and medicines.

B. Applications for validated licenses will generally be denied. Exports on a non-commercial basis to meet emergency needs will be considered on a case-by-case basis.

VI. USSR only:

A validated license is required for the export of petroleum equipment.

VII. All countries:

A. A validated license is required for the export of the following commodities and related technical data:

1. Commodities which could be of significance for nuclear explosive purposes; and

2. Any commodities which the exporter knows or has reason to know will be used directly or indirectly for:

a. Designing, developing, or fabricating nuclear weapons or nuclear explosive devices;

b. Devising, carrying out, or evaluating nuclear weapons tests or nuclear explosions;

c. Designing, constructing, fabricating, or operating the following facilities or components for such facilities:

    i. Facilities for the chemical processing of irradiated special nuclear or source material;

    ii. Facilities for the production of heavy water;

    iii. Facilities for the separation of isotopes of source and special nuclear material; or

    iv. Facilities for the fabrication of nuclear reactor fuel containing plutonium.

B. In reviewing applications for validated licenses pursuant to sub-paragraph VII A above, the following considerations are among those which will be taken into account:

1. The stated end-use of the component;
2. The sensitivity of the particular component and its availability elsewhere;
3. The types of assurances or guarantees given in the particular case; and
4. The non-proliferation credentials of the recipient country.

[Enclosure 2]

CONCLUSIONS WITH RESPECT TO CRITERIA, ALTERNATIVE MEANS, AND FURTHERANCE OF FOREIGN POLICY OR INTERNATIONAL OBLIGATIONS

I. *Crime Control and Detection Instruments and Equipment*

These controls continue in effect pursuant to section 6(j) of the Act.

No country has been formally determined to have a government engaging in a consistent pattern of gross violations of internationally recognized human rights. Therefore, except for the embargoes on North Korea, Vietnam, Kampuchea, Cuba, and the South African police and military, the validated license requirement for these items does not constitute a presumption that an application for such a license would be denied. However, where a consistent pattern of such violations appears to be developing, either positive or negative use of export controls might help to deter such development.

II. *South Africa and Namibia*

Prohibition of the export of virtually all items to military and police entities and controls on the export of aircraft and helicopters to all consignees and on the export of specified computers to government consignees are intended to distance the United States from the practice of apartheid, strengthen the effect of the United Nations arms embargo, and support racial justice throughout Africa.

There has been no movement toward fundamental social and political change in South Africa. Not extending controls would adversely affect the credibility of our South African policy in the minds of both the South African Government and black African nations.

The United States has attempted to influence the South African Government through public expressions of dissatisfaction with its social and political systems and reduction of diplomatic and other relationships. These other means have been insufficient to serve as an adequate alternative to export controls.

Regarding enforcement, it is recognized that it is extremely difficult, if not impossible, to prevent the South African military and police from acquiring U.S. goods indirectly. On the other hand, we believe that U.S. firms have been conscientious in complying with the controls. Foreign firms with no U.S. ties are probably less zealous in adhering to U.S. regulations, especially for items exported to them under general license and for U.S. components or technology incorporated in foreign manufactured products.

Most types of equipment and technology affected by the controls are available from foreign sources. However, Australia recently restricted sales of aircraft to South Africa.

The effects of the controls on U.S. exports can be only roughly estimated. Factors other than export controls affect the overall export picture.

In general terms, the U.S. share of the South African market dropped from 13 percent in 1977 to 11 percent in 1978. If the 13 percent share had been maintained, U.S. exports would have been $400 million higher in 1978. In 1977 the United States had the largest market share; in 1978 the United Kingdom and Germany had larger shares. Significant decreases in U.S. market shares occurred from 1977 to 1978 in pharmaceuticals, tires, chemicals, trucks, locomotives, motor vehicle components, and computers. For the first five months of 1979 the U.S. share of the market had recovered to 12.8 percent. There have been substantial U.S. sales since May.

Although it is difficult to determine whether losses are the result of the embargo or of other factors, examples reported by individual U.S. firms include the following:

—loss to a Japanese firm of a $45 million order for a commodity for which previous orders alternated between U.S. and German suppliers;

—inability of a U.S. company to provide technical data to its South African subsidiary, which resulted in the loss of $1 million in annual royalty payments and ultimately led to divestiture of the subsidiary;

—loss to a British firm which stresses U.S. export controls in its marketing efforts of three contracts for about $10 million and of estimated follow-on sales of about $26 million;

—placement with a non-U.S. firm of a $50 million order by a South African company which had previously purchased exclusively from U.S. companies;

—sourcing by a U.S. project manager of $500 million worth of contracts in 1979 without U.S. participation;

—damage to reputation as a reliable supplier because of inability to supply parts and servicing for previously sold equipment;

—loss of exports because of the difficulty of determining whether an insignificant portion might reach the military or police; and

—additional administrative expenditures in order to comply with U.S. regulations while attempting to meet existing contractual and servicing agreements.

III. *Terrorism*

The listing of Libya, Iraq, People's Democratic Republic of Yemen, and Syria in the heading of part III of Enclosure 1 of this notification constitutes the determination, pursuant to subsection 6 (i)(1) of the Act, as to which countries have repeatedly provided support for acts of international terrorism.

Exports to these countries of crime control and detection instruments and equipment (which include vehicles designed to military specifications), aircraft valued at $3 million or more, and helicopters over 10,000 pounds empty weight are controlled pursuant to section 6(i) of the Act.

Syria and Iraq have not made major purchases of U.S. aircraft since 1976. The People's Democratic Republic of Yemen trades largely with the USSR and exports of aircraft to that nation have been minimal. Libya, however, has the potential to continue to be a significant market for U.S. aircraft and helicopter manufacturers.

Controls on the export to these countries of U.S.-origin aircraft valued at $3 million or more and helicopters over 10,000 pounds can be effectively enforced.

Large transport aircraft are available from French, German, and British companies as well as from the Soviet Union. Helicopters are produced by the same countries, as well as by Israel and Japan.

Examples of consequences attributed to these controls by individual U.S. firms include the following:

—U.S. helicopter manufacturers report that they have not pursued inquiries from or marketing efforts in these four countries because of the uncertainties caused by the U.S. controls; and

—a major U.S. aircraft manufacturer may lose a $186 million sale of aircraft to Libya because of application of this control.

IV. *Libya*

Controls on the export to Libya of large tractors further the foreign policy objective of regional stability and are consistent with our policy on military sales to that country. Libyan troops have been directly involved in three countries in the past year (Chad, Uganda, and the Central African Republic) and are on a high state of alert along the border with Egypt, where a brief border war broke out in 1977.

Large tractors could be used to transport tanks and other outsized military vehicles, thereby enhancing the mobility of Libya's sizable armored force.

This type of vehicle is available from foreign suppliers in adequate quantities to serve the Libyan market. However, U.S. controls prevent an American contribution to Libyan military activity.

Controls of sales of off-highway tractors of carriage capacity of 10 tons or more can be effectively enforced.

Discontinuation of the controls would be seen by other friendly countries as a United States contribution to strengthening Libyan capability to mount hostile actions along its borders.

The controls supplement other means designed to influence Libyan behavior, including numerous demarches on issues such as Libyan activity in Uganda. There are very few alternative means available to the United States. For example, Libya has no need for U.S. economic or military assistance.

In 1977 the U.S. exported to Libya 330 vehicles of this type with a value of $7.1 million; these figures dropped in 1978 to 14 vehicles at $0.3 million. A sale of about $60 million was lost to a foreign firm in 1978. Industry representatives estimate a potential Libyan market of about $50 million. There is also some indirect adverse effect on exports to other markets.

V. *Embargoes of Communist Countries*

The embargoes on exports to North Korea, Vietnam, Kampuchea, and Cuba are administered not only under the Export Administration Act but also under the Trading With the Enemy Act. The latter authority continues by virtue of sections 101(b) and (c) and 207 of Public Law 95–223, and has been extended twice pursuant to national interest determinations, the most recent being from September 14, 1979, to September 14, 1980.

These embargoes were originally imposed for security reasons. During the Korean conflict we imposed an embargo against North Korea. During the Vietnam war we embargoed trade with communist controlled portions of that country and, when the communists took over complete control in 1975, this embargo was extended to all of Vietnam and to Kampuchea. The embargo against Cuba came at a time when Cuban actions presented a serious threat in the Western hemisphere.

The circumstances which prompted imposition of these embargoes have changed over the years. However, it would be irresponsible to discard them on that basis alone. Ending a virtually total embargo is a dramatic action with significant policy ramifications.

North Korea is still technically in a state of war with the United States, the Republic of Korea, and the United Nations. It is expanding its offensive military and subversive potential and suppressing human rights. It recently rejected U.S. overtures for tripartite discussions on ways to ease tensions on the Korean peninsula.

In the case of Vietnam, we announced our willingness some time ago to end the embargo at such time as normal diplomatic relations are established and Ambassadors are in place. Subsequent Vietnamese invasion and occupation of Kampuchea have blocked progress.

Controls on exports to Kampuchea should be similar to those affecting Vietnam, particularly in light of the present occupation. The United States is making a major exception to the embargo of Kampuchea in the form of humanitarian aid to the people.

Full normalization of trade and diplomatic relations with Cuba hinges upon Cuban willingness to address, among other issues, restraint in other countries and compensation for American citizens whose property was expropriated by the Cuban Government.

The controls on North Korea, Vietnam, Kampuchea and Cuba are understood and generally supported by the public, so there is little difficulty in enforcing them.

Other countries are not formally cooperating with the United States in these embargoes. However, third country exports to North Korea are minimal because that country is in default on its international trade payments, there is very little trade of any kind with Kampuchea, and Vietnam and Cuba now largely orient their former trade with the United States toward the USSR.

All of the OECD countries combined exported only $435 million to Vietnam in 1977. Even without the embargo, the Vietnamese would probably have turned elsewhere whenever possible, buying from the United States only when it was in their particular interest to do so. The most notable loss has been the replacement of U.S. firms by European firms in oil and gas exploration activities in and offshore Vietnam.

In 1959, U.S. firms supplied 64 percent of Cuba's total imports. If the embargo were lifted, the USSR would probably continue to be Cuba's major trade partner, but U.S. exporters, with the advantage of proximity, could be expected to replace some Japanese, Canadian, and European firms currently exporting to Cuba.

In aggregate value, U.S. exports to Cuba would likely not exceed $300 million annually over the medium term and would probably reach no more than $100–150 million in the first year if trade were resumed.

Because Cuba does not represent a substantial incremental market for any specific U.S. industries, the embargo has not retarded the ability of any U.S. economic sectors to compete in world trade. Exporting to Cuba would not, therefore, substantially raise production levels or efficiency in any industries.

VI. *Petroleum Equipment to the USSR*

The control on the export of petroleum equipment to the USSR provides a flexible foreign policy tool. When necessary and appropriate it can be used to sensitize the Soviets regarding actions which are damaging to United States foreign policy interests.

The United States supports the improvement of bilateral economic relations with the Soviet Union as an element in our effort to improve overall relations. At the same time it is recognized that improvement in one sector of the bilateral relationship cannot be long sustained if it is not accompanied by improvements in other areas. Discontinuation of this control would represent a change in policy not warranted by existing circumstances in our relationship with the USSR.

Among the various means of furthering U.S. objectives vis-a-vis the Soviet Union, this control continues to be useful.

While the United States Government can effectively control exports of U.S.-produced petroleum equipment, for most items adequate quantities of similar equipment are available from foreign sources. There is only limited foreign availability of some deep submersible pumps and seismic equipment.

The effect of the controls on U.S. exports can be only roughly estimated since other factors affect the data. Although no license applications have been denied since the control was imposed in August 1978, some exports have been lost.

U.S. exports of petroleum equipment to the USSR average about two percent of total U.S. petroleum equipment exports. The U.S. share of the Soviet market had been generally increasing until the third quarter of 1978. In 1974, U.S. suppliers received 13.6 percent of all Soviet oil and natural gas machinery orders placed with Western manufacturers. The 26.9 percent U.S. share of the 1977 Soviet market for petroleum equipment increased markedly to 55.5 percent in the first quarter of 1978 and to 51.1 percent for the third quarter. It dropped to 8.0 percent for the last quarter, bringing the figure for all of 1978 down to 44.6 percent. The U.S. shares for the first three quarters of 1979 were 23.5, 20.0, and 9.7 percent.

Although it is difficult to determine whether losses are the result of the controls or of other factors, reports by U.S. firms include the following:

—loss to foreign competition of contracts for gas lift equipment valued at about $70 million (plus larger anticipated follow-on sales) because of delays and uncertainty in the U.S. licensing process;

—expenditures in the range of hundreds of thousands of dollars attributable to late delivery penalties and other costs related to the licensing process;

—use of the U.S. license requirement by foreign companies as leverage to obtain sales, since U.S. companies must schedule delivery to allow time for a license review and U.S. firms are never certain that the license will be granted.

VII. *Nuclear Non-Proliferation Controls*

Section 17(d) of the Act and section 309(c) of the Nuclear Non-Proliferation Act of 1978 (Public Law 95–242 of March 10, 1978), are interpreted as intending that:

a) nuclear non-proliferation controls do not expire on December 31, 1979, and a determination to extend them is thus not required; and

b) the criteria and other factors set forth in sections 6 (b) and (e) of the Act are not applicable to these controls.

The Congress is therefore notified that these controls continue in force.

Nuclear non-proliferation controls further significantly the foreign policy of the United States and its declared international obligations.

NOTE: This is the text of identical letters addressed to Thomas P. O'Neill, Jr., Speaker of the House of Representatives, and Walter F. Mondale, President of the Senate.

Economic Compact Between New York and New Jersey

Statement on Signing H.R. 4943 Into Law. December 31, 1979

H.R. 4943 grants approval to the interstate compact between New York and New Jersey, providing for increased economic and industrial development in the New York City and northern New Jersey metropolitan region. While this bill is only a small part of the Port Authority's bold program, I take great personal pleasure in signing it.

Congressman Peter Rodino and the other Members of Congress from these two great States deserve considerable credit for expediting the passage of this legislation. I also extend my congratulations to Governors Carey and Byrne, Mayor Koch, and Alan Sagner and Peter Goldmark of the Port Authority of New York and New Jersey.

As I have emphasized throughout the past 3 years, the most effective remedy for the problems of our older urban centers— and of the Northeast in general—is to restore the private economic base of our inner cities. The steps taken in this direction by the Port Authority serve as a fine example of what government can do to retain existing businesses and jobs and to attract new private-sector development and employment.

NOTE: As enacted, H.R. 4943 is Public Law 96–163, approved December 28.

Department of Energy National Security and Military Applications of Nuclear Energy Authorization Act of 1980

*Statement on Signing S. 673 Into Law.
December 31, 1979*

I have signed S. 673, the Department of Energy National Security and Military Applications of Nuclear Energy Authorization Act of 1980.

In addition to authorizing appropriations in fiscal year 1980 for the Department of Energy's national security programs, S. 673 authorizes the creation of a facility to demonstrate the feasibility of storing certain nuclear wastes from defense activities. This project is known as the Waste Isolation Pilot Plant (WIPP), and its proposed location is in New Mexico. Specifically, the bill provides that:

"The Secretary of Energy shall proceed with the Waste Isolation Pilot Plant construction project. . . . Notwithstanding any other provision of law, the Waste Isolation Pilot Plant is authorized as a defense activity of the Department of Energy . . . for the express purpose of providing a research and development facility to demonstrate the safe disposal of radioactive wastes resulting from the defense activities and programs of the United States exempted from regulation by the Nuclear Regulatory Commission."

In signing S. 673, I am not endorsing this approach to the WIPP facility. As

evidenced by the efforts of the Interagency Review Group on Nuclear Waste Management, which I established in March 1978, my administration is committed to the safe management of nuclear wastes. I have reviewed a number of alternatives for managing both defense and commercial wastes, and I believe that the future of WIPP ought to be resolved only in the context of an overall nuclear waste management policy. I will be making a comprehensive statement on the management of nuclear wastes in the near future.

NOTE: As enacted, S. 673 is Public Law 96–164, approved December 29.

Knoxville International Energy Exposition of 1982

*Statement on Signing H.R. 5079 Into Law.
December 31, 1979*

I take great pleasure in signing H.R. 5079, which authorizes United States participation in Energy-Expo '82—the International Energy Exposition to be held in Knoxville, Tennessee, in 1982.

Energy-Expo '82 has the prospect of being critically important to the future of every nation and perhaps of every individual on Earth. With "Energy Turns the World" as its theme, the exposition will focus attention on one of the world's most pressing problems, and give participating nations an opportunity to demonstrate working prototypes of their newest energy-related inventions and developments as well as to discuss their energy policies in a variety of conferences.

The planning of this internationally significant event has been going on for several years. In April 1977, I granted it Federal recognition as being in the national interest; in December 1978, I invited all the nations with which the United States has diplomatic relations to take part; and in August of this year I transmitted to Congress the proposal for United States participation which I now have the satisfaction of signing into law.

Knoxville, known as the Energy Capital of the World, is an appropriate site for Energy-Expo '82. It is surrounded by energy production—the Appalachian coalfields, Oak Ridge, the Tennessee Valley Authority—and it is the home of the University of Tennessee, with its diverse energy research facilities.

I look forward expectantly to Energy-Expo '82 and to the benefits it can bring to the people of this Nation and the world.

NOTE: As enacted, H.R. 5079 is Public Law 96–169, approved December 29.

Beef and Veal Imports Bill

Statement on Signing H.R. 2727 Into Law. December 31, 1979

I am pleased to sign into law today H.R. 2727, the Meat Import Act of 1979, a measure that will change the procedure we use to regulate imports of beef and veal into the United States.

Under the Meat Import Act of 1964, the Secretary of Agriculture had the authority to limit beef and veal imports. However, because the level of U.S. imports was tied to the level of U.S. production, the limitations were most restrictive when U.S. consumers most needed beef, and least restrictive when our cattle producers were suffering the most from low prices.

The new law makes much more sense. It provides that at least 1.25 billion pounds of imported beef will be available each year. That level increases when domestic production is low and more imports are needed. It better protects consumers against short supplies, and it better protects cattlemen against low prices. I believe it is a balanced measure which will provide needed stability and certainty for both the domestic cattle industry and the American consumer.

This bill has been a long time in development, and it is the result of cooperation and hard work by cattlemen, the Congress, and the administration.

It retains sufficient Presidential discretion in instances where the countercyclical formula does not fully protect the public interest. The bill is considerably less restrictive than last year's unacceptable measure. I especially want to thank Senators Talmadge and Bentsen and Congressmen Ullman, Foley, and Bedell for their diligence in developing this measure with the administration. It is a good and fair bill, and I am pleased to sign it into law.

NOTE: As enacted, H.R. 2727 is Public Law 96–177, approved December 31.

Foreign Military Sales Credits for Israel

White House Statement.   December 31, 1979

The President met with Israeli Minister of Defense Ezer Weizman on December 28, 1979. Subsequently, the President has decided to request the Congress to increase by $200 million the foreign military sales (FMS) credits previously authorized for Israel in the special legislation in support of the peace treaty.

The decision was based on consideration of such factors as inflation and Israel's balance of payments deficit and takes into account the fact that the Israeli

Government has instituted since November extremely tough austerity measures designed to overcome these economic problems.

The decision, taken at a time when the President is determined to hold down Federal expenditures, reflects our sympathy and concern for Israel's security and well-being.

Presently, U.S. FMS credits for Israel total $2.2 billion, in addition to a grant of $800 million, to be disbursed over a period of approximately 3 years.

Digest of Other White House Announcements

The following listing includes the President's public schedule and other items of general interest announced by the White House Press Office and not included elsewhere in this issue.

December 27

The President announced the recess appointment of William A. Lubbers as General Counsel of the National Labor Relations Board. Lubbers was nominated for this position on November 28.

December 28

The President returned to the White House from Camp David, Md.

The President met at the White House with his foreign policy advisers to discuss the situation in Iran and other developments in that region.

The White House announced that due to the situation in Iran the President will not participate in the Democratic Presidential candidates debate in Des Moines, Iowa.

December 29

The President met at the White House with Dr. Brzezinski.

December 31

The President declared a major disaster for the State of Washington as a result of severe storms, high tides, mudslides, and flooding during the period December 13–23, which caused extensive property damage.

NOMINATIONS SUBMITTED TO THE SENATE

NOTE: The Senate having adjourned *sine die* on Friday, December 21, no nominations were submitted during the period covered by this issue. The second session of the 96th Congress will begin on Thursday, January 3, 1980.

CHECKLIST OF WHITE HOUSE PRESS RELEASES

NOTE: All releases of the White House Press Office have been included in this issue.

ACTS APPROVED BY THE PRESIDENT

Approved December 27, 1979

S. 716_____ Public Law 96–156
An act to amend the Retired Federal Employees Health Benefits Act, as amended, with respect to the Government contribution toward subscription charge.

S. 241_____ Public Law 96–157
Justice System Improvement Act of 1979.

H.R. 5645_____ Public Law 96–158
An act to grant to the Little Sisters of the Poor all right, title, and interest of the United States in the land comprising certain alleys in the District of Columbia.

H.R. 887_____ Private Law 96–30
An act for the relief of Elizabeth Berwick and Alexander Berwick, her husband.

H.R. 2531_____ Private Law 96–31
An act for the relief of Russell W. Allen.

Approved December 28, 1979

S. 1143_____ Public Law 96–159
An act to authorize appropriations to carry out the Endangered Species Act of 1973 during fiscal years 1980, 1981, and 1982, and for other purposes.

ACTS APPROVED—Continued

Approved December 28—Continued

H.R. 5537_____ Public Law 96–160
An act to amend the District of Columbia Self-Government and Governmental Reorganization Act with respect to the borrowing authority of the District of Columbia.

H.R. 4998_____ Public Law 96–161
An act to authorize automatic transfer accounts at commercial banks, remote service units at Federal savings and loan associations, and share draft accounts at Federal credit unions during the period beginning on December 31, 1979, and ending on April 1, 1980.

S. 585_____ Public Law 96–162
An act to authorize the Secretary of the Interior to engage in a feasibility study.

H.R. 4943_____ Public Law 96–163
An act granting the consent of Congress to the compact between the States of New York and New Jersey providing for the coordination, facilitation, promotion, preservation, and protection of trade and commerce in and through the Port of New York District through the financing and effectuation of industrial development projects.

H.R. 894_____ Private Law 96–32
An act for the relief of Gina Marie S. Hernandez.

H.R. 900_____ Private Law 96–33
An act for the relief of Grace Maria Salazar Santos.

H.R. 918_____ Private Law 96–34
An act for the relief of Maryrose and Rosemary Evangelista.

H.R. 1283_____ Private Law 96–35
An act for the relief of Pang Chong Ae.

H.R. 1489_____ Private Law 96–36
An act for the relief of In Sun Pineiro.

H.R. 1827_____ Private Law 96–37
An act for the relief of Emiko Okuma Colona.

H.R. 1887_____ Private Law 96–38
An act for the relief of Solomon Mani.

H.R. 3234_____ Private Law 96–39
An act for the relief of Rodolfo Jose Kozul.

H.R. 3320_____ Private Law 96–40
An act for the relief of Eileen Ferraren Fair.

Approved December 29, 1979

S. 673_____ Public Law 96–164
Department of Energy National Security and Military Applications of Nuclear Energy Authorization Act of 1980.

ACTS APPROVED—Continued

Approved December 29—Continued

H.R. 600_____ Public Law 96–165
An act to incorporate United Service Organizations, Incorporated.

H.R. 5015_____ Public Law 96–166
Federal Physicians Comparability Allowance Amendments of 1979.

H.R. 5224_____ Public Law 96–167
An act to continue through May 31, 1981, the existing prohibition on the issuance of fringe benefit regulations, and for other purposes.

H.J. Res. 462_____ Public Law 96–168
A joint resolution expressing the sense of Congress concerning the White House Preservation Fund.

H.R. 5079_____ Public Law 96–169
An act to provide for participation of the United States in the International Energy Exposition to be held in Knoxville, Tennessee, in 1982, and for other purposes.

H.R. 3343_____ Public Law 96–170
An act to permit civil suits under section 1979 of the Revised Statutes (42 U.S.C. 1983) against any person acting under color of any law or custom of the District of Columbia who subjects any person within the jurisdiction of the District of Columbia to the deprivation of any right, privilege, or immunity secured by the Constitution and laws.

H.R. 3948_____ Public Law 96–171
An act to require a study of the desirability of mandatory age retirement for certain pilots, and for other purposes.

H.R. 2771_____ Public Law 96–172
An act to change the name of the Palmetto Bend Reservoir on the Navidad River in Texas to Lake Texana.

H.R. 5025_____ Public Law 96–173
An act to amend title 10, United States Code, to provide that any person eligible for medical care under the Civilian Health and Medical Program of the Uniformed Services (CHAMPUS) who is a veteran with a service-connected disability may not be denied care and treatment for such disability under CHAMPUS solely because such person is eligible for care and treatment for such disability in Veterans' Administration facilities.

H.R. 5174_____ Public Law 96–174
An act to amend section 209 of title 18, United States Code.

H.R. 595_____ Public Law 96–175
Strategic and Critical Materials Transaction Authorization Act of 1979.

ACTS APPROVED—Continued

Approved December 29—Continued

H.R. 901_____ Private Law 96–41
An act for the relief of John A. Townsley.

H.R. 1619_____ Private Law 96–42
An act for the relief of Rolando R. Gaza, Teresita C. Gaza, and Rolynne Therese Gaza.

H.R. 2593_____ Private Law 96–43
An act for the relief of Mariana de Jesus Roca and Francisco Rubira Roca.

ACTS APPROVED—Continued

Approved December 31, 1979

H.R. 5523_____ Public Law 96–176
An act to establish an improved program for extra long staple cotton.

H.R. 2727_____ Public Law 96–177
An act to modify the method of establishing quotas on the importation of certain meat, to include within such quotas certain meat products, and for other purposes.

Index

U.S. GOVERNMENT PRINTING OFFICE : 1981 O - 52-880 : QL 2